Basic Financial Management

4th edition

Basic Financial Management

David F. Scott, Jr.
University of Central Florida

John D. Martin
University of Texas at Austin

J. William Petty
Abilene Christian University

Arthur J. Keown
Virginia Polytechnic Institute and State University

Prentice Hall, Englewood Cliffs, New Jersey 07632

Library of Congress Cataloging-in-Publication Data

Basic financial management/David F. Scott, Jr. . . . [et al.].
—4th ed.

p.   cm.
Bibliography.
Includes index.
ISBN 0-13-060716-9
1. Business enterprises—Finance.   2. Corporations—Finance.
I. Scott, David F.
HG4026.B318   1988
658.1'5—dc19   88-2524
                                                    CIP

Editorial/production supervision: Sonia Meyer
Interior design: Holly McLaughlin
Interior design supervision: Lorraine Mullaney
Cover design: Photo-Plus Art, Celine Brandes
Manufacturing buyer: Ed O'Dougherty

 © 1988, 1985, 1982, 1979 by Prentice Hall
A Division of Simon & Schuster
Englewood Cliffs, New Jersey 07632

Printed in the United States of America

10 9 8 7 6 5 4 3 2 1

ISBN 0-13-060716-9

Prentice-Hall International (UK) Limited, *London*
Prentice-Hall of Australia Pty. Limited, *Sydney*
Prentice-Hall Canada Inc., *Toronto*
Prentice-Hall Hispanoamericana, S.A., *Mexico*
Prentice-Hall of India Private Limited, *New Delhi*
Prentice-Hall of Japan, Inc., *Tokyo*
Simon & Schuster Asia Pte. Ltd., *Singapore*
Editora Prentice-Hall do Brasil, Ltda., *Rio de Janeiro*

To: Peggy, Sally, Donna, and Barbara

CONTENTS

PART TWO: Basic Tools of Financial Analysis, Planning, and Control

3

Financial Analysis   31

4

Financial Forecasting, Planning, and Budgeting   84

PART THREE: Working-Capital Management

5

Introduction to Working-Capital Management   120

6

Cash and Marketable Securities Management   143

7

Accounts Receivable and Inventory Management 210

8

Short-Term Financing 240

PART FOUR: Management of Long-Term Assets

9

Mathematics of Finance 263

10

Capital Budgeting 294

11

Capital Budgeting Under Uncertainty 348

PART FIVE: The Cost of Capital and Financial Structure

12

Valuation and Rates of Return   384

13

Cost of Capital   431

14

Analysis and Impact of Leverage 480

15

Planning the Firm's Financing Mix 518

16

Dividend Policy and Internal Financing 559

PART SIX: Long-Term Financing

17

Raising Funds in the Capital Market   590

18

Term Loans and Leases   620

19

Long–Term Debt, Preferred Stock, and Common Stock   642

20

Convertibles and Warrants   673

PART SEVEN: Special Topics in Financial Management

21

Corporate Restructuring: Combinations and Divestitures 709

22

Failure and Reorganization 728

23

International Business Finance 751

24

Small Business Finance 786

Appendices   807

PREFACE

From the latter part of the 1970s through the early 1980s, firms have been forced to make decisions in a highly volatile environment. For at least thirty years ending in the 1970s, relatively stable prices, cheap energy, and low cost for money represented the norm. In 1988, it would appear that we will not soon return to these economically stable conditions. In fact, all indications are that expensive energy and high money costs will continue indefinitely. Further complicating the external setting, the international scene has come closer to all of us. Executives can ill afford to disregard international developments as they affect their own company. Within this atmosphere, business decisions have become more difficult. Graduates of business colleges will have to be better prepared and more competitive. All in all, decisions will be more critical to the eventual success or failure of a firm.

A careful and thorough presentation of the financial consequences of management decisions is an underlying theme of *Basic Financial Management*. Also, the first three editions were based upon an extensive effort to determine if any general commonalities exist among financial management instructors in terms of their desires regarding the approach taken by a text. The results, derived from questionnaires and personal interviews of faculty members across the nation, suggested that a common thread exists in terms of the instructors' desires. The fourth edition of *Basic Financial Management* continues to be responsive to these needs and preferences.

Basic Financial Management provides the reader with an overview of financial management. The text is intended for use in an introductory course in financial management taught in a one-semester or one- or two-quarter course. The orientation continues to be managerial with an emphasis on the identification and solution of the financial problems confronting the business enterprise. Decision making within an enterprise valuation framework is stressed throughout the text and, thereby, provides a unifying theme across all discussions. In the preparation of the manuscript, three primary standards were used. First, we made a strong effort to offer *completeness* in treating each topic. Second, we have given *readability* a high priority. We have taken extra care to use a clear and concise writing style, especially in the treatment of concepts requiring the use of mathematics. Third, complete, *step-by-step examples* are frequently used to increase clarity and to crystallize the critical issues in the student's mind. In summary, the pedagogical approach taken, particularly for the more difficult topics, progresses from an intuitive presentation of the problem to the introduction and illustration of the appropriate decision-making framework.

The Fourth Edition

A number of changes and refinements have been made in the fourth edition of *Basic Financial Management*. We have added complete coverage of the Tax Reform Act of 1986 in Chapter 2. New problems and exercises throughout the text utilize the new tax rate structure in the computations.

Chapter 6 dealing with cash and marketable securities has been streamlined; the discussion on money market mutual funds has been expanded and related to both the 1981–1982 recession and the subsequent post-1982 recovery. The interest rate series found in this chapter has been updated.

Chapter 10 on capital budgeting has been altered to consider the aspects of the 1986 tax act and the material on capital budgeting practices has been increased. Care has been taken to relate corporate investment decision making to the theoretically correct evaluation models preferred by academics. This chapter is very teachable and highlights the logic and procedures for estimating relevant cash flows.

Chapter 12 on valuation and rates of return has been significantly revised and reworked. The material now relates better to the various cost of capital estimation models presented in Chapter 13. The importance of business valuation to both shareholders and managers is emphasized. Arbitrage pricing theory is presented and discussed in relation to other time-tested valuation schemes including the capital asset pricing model.

Chapter 15 dealing with the firm's financing mix and capital structure theory has been expanded. Agency theory, which is introduced early in the text in Chapter 1, is discussed here within the context of firm value and agency costs. The agency costs of debt are illustrated through the discussion of protective bond covenants. The dividend policy material in Chapter 16 has been revised and deals head-on with the impact of policy on stock prices. The dividend decision in practice is likewise presented.

Chapter 17 on the capital market has been thoroughly updated. The logic of financial intermediation is presented and the movement of funds through the economy is illustrated through discussions of the investment choices of pension funds and life insurance firms.

A totally new appendix has been added to Chapter 20 on convertibles and warrants. It focuses on futures and options within a financial management setting. In recognizing the importance of these special instruments and markets to the executive, we treat this new material in a decision-making framework. Students will find this appendix interesting and easy to master.

Chapter 21 on business combinations incorporates new material on restructuring and divestitures. Since the financial management process is now a global process, it was necessary to rework Chapter 23 on international business finance. Professor Raj Aggarwal of John Carroll University completely revised this chapter and added new material on international financing decisions.

Several changes to the text make using it more enjoyable to both students and instructors. Several chapters now include high interest inserts. These are labeled "Basic Financial Management in Practice." They emphasize slices of real world financial decision making, issues, and problems. Many chapters now contain a "case problem" in addition to the usual study problems. The instructor can assign the cases to stress more substantive issues and generate livelier class discussions. Most of these cases can be prepared within an hour. Additionally, the self-test problems within each chapter have been increased and the end-of-chapter problem set has been expanded by 25 percent.

Accompanying Materials

A complete and balanced instructional package has been developed to complement *Basic Financial Management.* Because a textbook in and of itself is incomplete in attaining the requisite educational goals for the student, additional materials are available. First, a case book has been developed. *Cases in Finance,* second edition, by David F. Scott, Jr., John D. Martin, J. William Petty, Arthur J. Keown, and John G. Thatcher provides a broad spectrum of short cases in terms of both complexity and topics, and is designed to parallel the topics covered in *Basic Financial Management,* providing the instructor with cases rather than problems that illustrate the use of financial tools and concepts in a real-world setting. Second, the *Study Guide* serves as an excellent supplement to the *Basic* text by providing a detailed sentence outline, self-test questions, and solved problem sets for each chapter. In addition, self-teaching supplements for mathematics of finance and capital budgeting are included. The *Study Guide* has been developed by the authors themselves. Third, approximately one hundred transparency masters that are useful in presenting the key issues of the text are available to adopters. Fourth, in addition to the *Instructor's Manual,* a *Supplemental Question-Problem Test File* has been prepared for adopters. This test bank has been increased in size by 20 percent from the third edition, and has also been revised. Personal computer software support is available for use with the text. Disks for both students and instructors have been prepared. Importantly, the instructor can access every end-of-chapter problem on disk. The test item file is also available from Prentice-Hall on disk.

Acknowledgments

We gratefully acknowledge the assistance, support, and encouragement of those individuals who have contributed to the successful completion and revision of *Basic Financial Management.* Specifically, we wish to recognize the very helpful insights provided by colleagues at our respective universities. For their careful review of the text, we are indebted to:

Hadi Alwan
Northern Illinois University

Dwight C. Anderson
Louisiana Tech University

Gary Benesh
Florida State University

Sam G. Berry
Virginia Commonwealth University

Russell P. Boisjoly
Simmons College

Virgil L. Brewer
Eastern Kentucky University

Jozelle Brister
Abilene Christian University

Don M. Chance
Virginia Polytechnic Institute and State University

Albert H. Clark
Georgia State University

David W. Cole
Ohio State University

Bernard C. Dill
Bloomsburg University

Mark Dorfman
University of Arkansas—Little Rock

Majorie Evert
Xavier University

Sidney R. Finkel
Canisius College

Lyn Fraser
Texas A&M University

John Gilster
University of Illinois

Dennis A. Gribenas
Data Systems International, Inc.

Samuel C. Hadaway
Financo, Inc.

Nancy Lee Halford
Madison Area Technical College

William R. Henry
Georgia State University

Jamie T. Holland
University of Central Florida

Keith Howe
Depaul University

Charles R. Idol
Idaho State University

Vahan Janjigian
University of Delaware

Djavad Kashefinejad
California State Polytechnic University

Howard C. Launstein
Marquette University

Leonard T. Long
American International College

Abbas Mamoozadeh
Slippery Rock University

Terry S. Maness
Baylor University

Barry Marks
North Texas State University

James A. Millar
University of Arkansas

Naval Modani
University of Central Florida

Shalini Perumpral
Radford University

John M. Pinkerton
Virginia Polytechnic Institute and State University

Peter A. Sharp
California State University at Sacramento

Suresh Srivastava
University of Maryland

Donald L. Stevens
University of Colorado—Denver

John G. Thatcher
Marquette University

Gary L. Trennepohl
Texas A&M University

Kenneth L. Westby
University of North Dakota

Finally, we thank the Prentice Hall staff who were a treat to work with, including Scott Barr, Sonia Meyer, Gary June, Joe O'Donnell, Anahid Tarpinian, Lorraine Mullaney, and Bruce Gregory. Their extraordinary patience and fine support throughout the writing, production, and marketing of the text was extremely valuable. Their guidance and help has had a significant and positive impact on the quality of the text.

Even with the very fine efforts of all involved in preparing the fourth edition of *Basic Financial Management*, some errors inevitably will exist. Unfortunately, for these we, the authors, must accept final responsibility.

1

The Role of Financial Management

Financial management during this century has undergone dramatic changes. Whereas financial managers were once limited to some bookkeeping, cash management, and the acquisition of funds, they now have a major voice in all aspects of raising and allocating financial capital. This book will introduce you to specific problems and areas that concern the financial manager. First we explain the environment surrounding the problem, then propose a solution methodology. We will also stress the interrelationships among the financial manager's various concerns and decisions. To develop a proper perspective on the role of the financial manager and the financial decision-making process, we will look first at the development of financial thought.

DEVELOPMENT OF FINANCIAL THOUGHT

At the turn of the century, financial thought focused on the legal environment within which the firm operated. The topics receiving most attention were mergers, formation of new companies, investment banking, public regulation, and the process of raising funds in the capital markets. The economic and business activity of the time determined what was of primary importance in the finance field. During the early 1900s, financial and economic news emphasized consolidations, mergers, and public regulation of the new business giants. This was the era when the great oil, auto, and steel firms were being formed and Teddy Roosevelt was making his name as a corporate trust buster.

In the 1920s the economy began to expand, and raising new funds in the capital markets became more important. As a result, the emphasis shifted from mergers and regulation to methods and procedures for acquiring funds. Arthur Stone Dewing devoted about a third of his landmark financial text, *The Financial Policy of Corporations* (1920), to the description of methods and procedures for acquiring funds. The remainder of the book dealt primarily with consolidations, mergers, and a legalistic look at corporate bankruptcy.

Business failures during the Great Depression of the 1930s helped change the focus of finance. While finance continued to be taught as a descriptive discipline, increased emphasis was placed on bankruptcy, liquidity management, and avoidance of financial problems. The political changes that dominated the thirties also influenced the field of finance, bringing increased government regulation and control of both business and the securities market, and increased requirements to disclose large volumes of corporate financial data. These data allowed analysts to more effectively assess potential corporate performance, stirring new interest in financial analysis.

During the 1940s and early 1950s financial theory continued to be taught as a descriptive discipline. The major financial texts of the day continued to emphasize methods and instruments for fund raising, corporate bankruptcy and reorganization, and mergers and consolidations. Increased emphasis was given, however, to liquidity management, financial planning, and cash budgeting.[1]

During the mid-1950s the field of finance underwent drastic changes. First, the point of view shifted from that of an outsider assessing the condition and performance of a firm to that of an insider charged with the management and control of the firm's financial operations. The work of Joel Dean promoted the area of capital budgeting as a major topic in finance. This led to an increased interest in related topics, most notably firm valuation. Interest in these topics grew and in turn spurred interest in security analysis, portfolio theory, and capital structure theory. In effect the field of finance evolved from a descriptive discipline dealing primarily with mergers, regulation, and the raising of capital funds to a more encompassing one dealing with all aspects of acquiring and efficiently utilizing those funds.

Development of the field of finance continues at a lively pace. Economic activity, financing innovations, and new theoretical developments in all areas are constantly reshaping financial thought.

Before discussing the financial decision-making process, we will examine the appropriate goal of the firm; we can then better understand the role and significance of financial decision making.

GOAL OF THE FIRM

In our work we will designate the goal of the firm to be *maximization of shareholder wealth*, by which we mean maximization of the total market value of the firm's common stock. As we will see, this is an extremely inclusive goal, in that it is affected by all financial decisions. To better understand it, we will first examine the frequently suggested goal of profit maximization, focusing on its deficiencies and drawbacks. Then

---

[1] Among the major financial texts of this period were Arthur S. Dewing's *Financial Policy of Corporations*, which went through five revisions between 1920 and 1953, and Charles W. Gerstenberg's *Financial Organization and Management of Business*, first published in 1939.

we will shift our attention to the goal of shareholder wealth maximization and see how it differs from profit maximization and why it is the appropriate goal for the firm.

Profit Maximization

While profit maximization is frequently used as the goal of the firm in microeconomics courses, it is not adequate for finance. The goal of profit maximization does stress the efficient use of capital resources. It assumes away, however, many of the complexities of the real world that we will try to address in our decisions. In being too simplistic, the goal of profit maximization is insufficient. Two of the major criticisms of this goal are that it does not deal adequately with uncertainty and with time.

Uncertainty of Returns

In beginning microeconomics courses uncertainty or risk is simply ignored. Projects and investment alternatives are compared by examining their expected values or weighted average profits. Whether or not one project is riskier than another does not enter these calculations. In reality, projects do differ with respect to risk characteristics, and to assume away these differences can result in incorrect decisions. To better understand the implications of ignoring risk, let us look at two mutually exclusive investment alternatives (that is, only one can be accepted). The first project involves the use of existing plant to produce plastic combs, a product with an extremely stable demand. The second project uses existing plant to produce electric vibrating combs. This latter product may catch on and do well, but it could also fail. The possible outcomes (optimistic prediction, pessimistic prediction, and expected outcome) are given in Table 1–1.

No variability is associated with the possible outcomes for the plastic comb project. If things go well, poorly, or as expected, the outcome will still be $10,000. With the electric comb, however, the range of possible outcomes goes from $20,000 if things go well, to $10,000 if they go as expected, to zero if they go poorly. If we look just at the expected outcomes, the two projects appear equivalent. They are not. The returns associated with the electric comb involve a much greater degree of uncertainty or risk.

Since the goal of profit maximization ignores uncertainty and considers these projects equivalent in terms of desirability, we must reject it. Later in this text we will examine the evaluation of risky projects. At the time we will find that investors are decidedly risk averse. To ignore this fact could lead to incorrect investment decisions.

Timing of Returns

The second major objection to the goal of profit maximization is that it ignores the timing of the project's returns. To illustrate, let us reexamine our plastic comb versus

TABLE 1–1. Possible Project Outcomes

	Profit	
	Plastic Comb	*Electric Comb*
Optimistic prediction	$10,000	$20,000
Expected outcome	10,000	10,000
Pessimistic prediction	10,000	0

TABLE 1–2. Timing of Profits

	Profit	
	Plastic Comb	*Electric Comb*
Year 1	$10,000	$ 0
Year 2	0	10,000

electric comb investment decision. This time let us ignore risk and say that each of these projects is going to return a profit of $10,000 for one year; however, it will be one year before the electric comb can go into production, while the plastic comb can begin production immediately. The timing of the profits from these projects is illustrated in Table 1–2.

In this case the total profits from each project are the same, but the timing of the returns differs. As we will see later, money has a definite time value. Thus, the plastic comb project is the better of the two. After one year the $10,000 profit from the plastic combs could be invested in a savings account earning 5 percent interest. At the end of the second year it would have grown to $10,500. Since investment opportunities are available for money in hand, we are not indifferent to the timing of the returns. Given equivalent flows, we want those flows sooner rather than later. Thus, ignoring the timing of the returns, as profit maximization does, can result in incorrect investment decisions.

Ignoring the timing and uncertainty associated with returns, then, makes the profit-maximization goal ineffective as a decision criterion. While it may be used in microeconomics courses, its inapplicability to real-world complexities makes it useless for our purposes. For this reason we will turn to a more robust goal for the firm: maximization of shareholder wealth.

Maximization of Shareholder Wealth

In formulating our goal of maximization of shareholder wealth we are doing nothing more than modifying the goal of profit maximization to deal with the complexities of the operating environment. We have chosen maximization of shareholder wealth—that is, maximization of the market value of the firm's common stock—because the effects of all financial decisions are thereby included. The shareholders react to poor investment or dividend decisions by causing the total value of the firm's stock to fall and react to good decisions by pushing the price of the stock up. In this way all financial decisions are evaluated, and all financial decisions affect shareholder wealth.

Obviously there are some serious practical problems in direct use of this goal and evaluating the reaction to various financial decisions by examining changes in the firm's stock value. Many things affect stock prices. To attempt to identify a reaction to a particular financial decision would simply be impossible. Fortunately, that is not necessary. In order to employ this goal, we need not consider every stock price change to be a market interpretation of the worth of our decisions. Other factors, such as economic expectations, also affect stock price movements. What we do focus on is the effect that our decision *should* have on the stock price if everything were held constant. The market price of the firm's stock reflects the value of the firm as seen by its owners. It takes into account uncertainty or risk, time, and any other factors that are important to the owners. Thus, the shareholder wealth maximization framework allows for a decision environment that includes the complexities and complications of the real world.

BASIC FINANCIAL MANAGEMENT IN PRACTICE
Creating Shareholder Wealth

Creating Shareholder Value. Because we are mindful of the heritage of excellence that has guided The Coca-Cola Company to the present, we cannot manage this Company only as a portfolio or a warehouse of valuable equities. We must regard ourselves as a factory that enhances the worth of these equities and produces value for our shareholders. We are approaching 1990 as a renaissance company made up of versatile, resilient and creative professionals. We are reinvigorating our business while it is producing record profits, and this will continue to be our collective wisdom.

Source: "Creating Shareholder Wealth." The Coca-Cola Company Annual Report, 1982, p. 7.

The Agency Problem

While our goal of the firm will be maximization of shareholder wealth, in reality the agency problem may interfere with the implementation of this goal. The *agency problem* is the result of a separation of management and the ownership of the firm. For example, a large firm may be run by professional managers who have little or no ownership position in the firm. As a result of this separation between the decision makers and owners, managers may make decisions that are not in line with the goal of maximization of shareholder wealth. They may approach work less arduously and attempt to benefit themselves in terms of salary and perquisites at the expense of shareholders. Exactly how significant a problem this is simply is not known at present. However, while this problem may interfere with the implementation of the goal of maximization of shareholder wealth in some firms, it does not affect the validity of this goal.

FINANCIAL DECISIONS AND RISK–RETURN RELATIONSHIPS

Much of our future discussion will center on evaluation of risk-return tradeoffs available to the financial manager. We will, in fact, find that almost all financial decisions involve some sort of risk-return tradeoff. The more risk the firm is willing to assume, the higher the expected return from the given course of action. For example, in the area of working-capital management, the less inventory held on hand, the higher the expected return (since less of the firm's assets are involved in non-income-producing functions), but also the greater the risk of running out of inventory. As we will see, similar examples will turn up in the areas of financial structure and management of long-term assets.

Allowing the financial manager to assess the various risk-return tradeoffs available and incorporating this into the maximization of shareholder wealth framework, we can show the financial decision-making process graphically as in Figure 1–1. Given the risk-return tradeoffs available to the financial manager, the various financial decisions are made assuming a firm goal of maximization of shareholder wealth. These decisions are then evaluated by the owners of the firm, and their correctness is reflected in changes in the firm's share price.

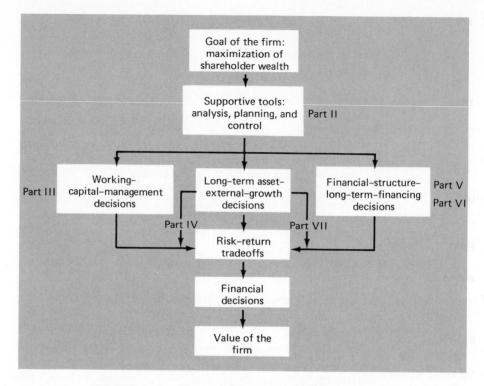

FIGURE 1–1. Financial Decision-Making Process

OVERVIEW OF THE TEXT ─────────────────────────────────

This text is divided into seven parts, each dealing with one major area of financial concern:

The Scope and Environment of Financial Management
Basic Tools of Financial Analysis, Planning, and Control
Working-Capital Management
Management of Long-Term Assets
The Cost of Capital and Financial Structure
Long-Term Financing
Special Topics in Financial Management

Figure 1–1 relates these selections to the financial decision-making process, indicating where each decision is discussed in the text. We describe these sections briefly below.

Part I: The Scope and Environment of Financial Management

Part I begins by discussing the history and role of financial management and develops the goal of the firm to be used in financial decision making. Chapter 2 develops the legal and tax environment in which these decisions are to be made. Since this environment sets the ground rules, it is necessary to understand it before decision principles can be formulated.

Part II: Basic Tools of Financial Analysis, Planning, and Control

Part II introduces the basic financial tools the financial manager uses in maintaining control over the firm and its operations. These tools enable the financial manager to locate potential problem areas, to move accurately, and to plan for the future. Also introduced are the preparation of financial statements and ratio analysis, which allow the financial manager to achieve greater control over ongoing operations. We introduce these financial tools at this early stage because they are used as input to all financial decisions.

Part III: Working-Capital Management

The third part of the book deals with working-capital management—that is, the management of current assets. Methods are discussed for determining the appropriate investment in cash, marketable securities, inventory, and accounts receivable. The risks associated with these investments, and the control of these risks, also are discussed.

Part IV: Management of Long-Term Assets

The capital-budgeting decision, involving the financial evaluation of investment proposals in fixed assets, is discussed in Part IV. First we examine the mathematics of finance and the concept of the time value of money. An understanding of this topic allows us to make benefits and costs that occur in different time periods comparable. We then look at methods for evaluating new projects under certainty. Finally the assumption of certainty is lifted, and methods are introduced to incorporate risk into the analysis.

Part V: Cost of Capital and Financial Structure

Part V discusses how a firm is valued and what costs are associated with alternative ways for raising new funds. The firm's capital structure is examined along with the impact of leverage on returns to the enterprise. This part closes with a discussion of the determination of the dividend–retained earnings decision.

Part VI: Long-Term Financing

Part VI describes and analyzes the various sources of long-term funding available to the firm, examining in detail the pros and cons of these sources in addition to their particular characteristics.

Part VII: Special Topics in Financial Management

The final part of the book begins with a discussion of mergers, business failures, and reorganizations, describing the legal environment in addition to the relevant financial decisions. International financial management is also discussed, focusing on how financial decisions are affected by the international environment. Finally, the last chapter examines financial management from the perspective of the owner-manager of a small firm.

Summary

This chapter outlines the framework for this book by first tracing the development of financial thought from the turn of the century to the present. During this period the field of finance reacted and changed with the prevailing economic environment. Business failures and the Depression of the thirties created concern and interest in working-capital management and bankruptcy. More recently, increased inflation and new theoretical developments have continued to reshape financial thought.

Given this historical framework, the goal of the firm was examined, and the commonly accepted goal of profit maximization was declared inappropriate because it does not deal adequately with uncertainty and time. The goal of maximization of shareholder wealth was accepted as the proper goal for the firm because it deals adequately with all the complexities of reality.

Finally the financial decision-making framework was examined and the format of the book related to this process. The seven parts of the book were analyzed and briefly previewed.

Study Questions

1–1. How has financial thought developed over the past century? What factors have affected it?

1–2. What are some of the problems involved in the use of profit maximization as the goal of the firm? How does the goal of shareholder wealth maximization deal with those problems?

1–3. Compare and contrast the goals of profit maximization and maximization of shareholder wealth.

1–4. Firms often involve themselves in projects that do not result directly in profits; for example, IBM and Mobil Oil frequently support public television broadcasts. Do these projects contradict the goal of maximization of shareholder wealth? Why or why not?

1–5. What is the relationship between financial decision making and risk and return? Would all financial managers view risk-return tradeoffs similarly?

Selected References

Anthony, Robert N. "The Trouble with Profit Maximization," *Harvard Business Review*, 38 (November–December 1960), 126–34.

Barnea, Amir, Robert A. Haugen, and Lemma W. Senbet. "Market Imperfections, Agency Problems, and Capital Structure: A Review," *Financial Management* 10 (Summer 1981), 7–22.

——— *Agency Problems and Financial Contracting.* Englewood Cliffs, NJ: Prentice-Hall, 1985.

Beranek, William. "Research Directions in Finance," *Quarterly Review of Economics and Business*, 21 (Spring 1981), 6–24.

Branch, Ben. "Corporate Objectives and Market Performance," *Financial Management*, 2 (Summer 1973), 24–29.

Cisel, David H., and Thomas M. Carroll. "The Determinants of Executive Salaries: An Econometric Survey," *Review of Economics and Statistics*, 62 (February 1980), 7–13.

Cooley, Phillip L. "Managerial Pay and Financial Performances of Small Business," *Journal of Business*, (September 1979), 267–76.

Donaldson, Gordon. "Financial Goals: Management vs. Stockholders," *Harvard Business Review*, 41 (May–June 1963), 116–29.

Findlay, M. Chapman, III, and G. A. Whitmore. "Beyond Shareholder Wealth Maximization," *Financial Management*, 3 (Winter 1974), 25–35.

Findlay, M. Chapman, III, and E. E. Williams. "A Positivist's Evaluation of the New Finance," *Financial Management*, 9 (Summer 1980), 7–17.

Hand, John H., William P. Lloyd, and Robert B. Rogow. "Agency Relationships in the Close Corporation," *Financial Management* 11 (Spring 1982), 25–30.

Jensen, Michael, and William H. Meckling. "Theory of the Firm: Managerial Behavior, Agency Costs, and Ownership Structure," *Journal of Financial Economics* 2 (October 1976), 305–360.

Lewellen, Wilbur G. "Management and Ownership in the Large Firm," *Journal of Finance*, 24 (May 1969), 299–322.

Simkowitz, Michael A., and Charles P. Jones. "A Note of the Simultaneous Nature of Finance Methodology," *Journal of Finance*, 27 (March 1972), 103.

Solomon, Ezra. *The Theory of Financial Management*, Chaps. 1 and 2. New York: Columbia University Press, 1963.

———. "What Should We Teach in a Course in Business Finance?" *Journal of Finance*, 21 (May 1966), 411–15.

Weston, J. Fred. "Developments in Finance Theory," *Financial Management*, 10 (1981), 5–22.

———. *The Scope and Methodology of Finance*, Englewood Cliffs, NJ: Prentice-Hall, 1966.

2

Legal Forms
of Organization
and the
Tax Environment

The financial manager must understand the **legal environment** in which the business functions. Otherwise, management decisions may be ineffective, if not entirely self-defeating. Two areas of primary concern are the alternative forms of business organization and the tax legislation affecting the firm's financial decisions. Accordingly, this chapter will (1) identify and evaluate the consequences of different legal forms of organization and (2) provide an overview of federal income taxes for corporations. Certainly the financial executive should not attempt to be entirely self-reliant in these matters; he should seek legal and tax counsel. However, an overview of the key issues should be helpful.

LEGAL FORMS OF BUSINESS ORGANIZATION

The legal forms of business organization are quite diverse and numerous. However, there are three basic categories: the sole proprietorship, the partnership, and the corporation. We will first examine the definition of and the procedures for establishing each of these forms, then identify the relevant factors for evaluating which form is best for a particular company.

Sole Proprietorship The **sole proprietorship** is a business owned by a single individual. The owner maintains title to the assets and is personally responsible, generally without limitation, for the liabilities incurred. The proprietor is entitled to the profits from the business but must also absorb any losses. This form of business is initiated by the mere act of beginning business operations. Typically, no legal requirement must be met in starting the operation, particularly if the proprietor is conducting the business in his own name. If a special name is used an assumed-name certificate should be filed, requiring a small registration fee. Some states require a periodic review of the certificate; otherwise the sole proprietorship has no time limit on its existence. Termination occurs upon the owner's death, or by the owner's choice. If the owner voluntarily terminates the business, he should cancel his assumed-name certificate. Briefly stated, the sole proprietorship is the absence of any *legal* business structure.

Partnership

The primary difference between a **partnership** and a sole proprietorship is that the partnership has more than one owner. Hence, a partnership is an association of two or more persons coming together as co-owners for the purpose of operating a business for a profit. Partnerships fall into two types: (1) general partnership and (2) limited partnership.

General Partnership

In a **general partnership** each partner is fully liable for the liabilities incurred by the partnership. Also, if a partner acts in a manner even having the appearance of conducting the firm's business, the remaining partners may be jointly liable for these actions. The relationship between partners is dictated entirely by the partnership agreement, which may be an oral commitment or a formal document. Generally the partners should draft a written agreement that explicitly sets forth the basic relationships within the firm. At a minimum, the agreement should include the nature and amount of capital to be invested by each partner, the authority of the individual partners, the means for determining how profits and losses are to be shared, the duration of the partnership, the procedures for admitting a new partner, and the method for reformulating the partnership in the event of a partner's death or withdrawal from the partnership. The inclusion of important terms in the agreement is essential to minimize later misunderstandings. In addition, if a dispute arises and court action becomes necessary to resolve the problem, the court may be required to act in a manner conflicting with the partners' original intent. For example, if no agreement is evident, the law stipulates that each partner is to share in the profits and losses equally.

Limited Partnership

In addition to the general partnership, in which all partners are jointly liable without limitation, many states provide for a **limited partnership.** The statutes within these states permit one or more of the partners to have limited liability, restricted to the amount of capital invested in the partnership. Several conditions must be met to qualify as a limited partner. First, at least one general partner must remain in the association, for whom the privilege of limited liability does not apply. Second, the names of the limited partners may not appear in the name of the firm. Third, the limited partners may not participate in the management of the business. If one of these restrictions is violated, all partners forfeit their right to limited liability. In essence, the intent of the statutes creating the limited partnership is to provide limited liability for a person whose interest in the partnership is purely as an investor. That individual may not assume a management function within the organization.

A somewhat unique limited partnership has developed within the decade of the

1980's, called a *Master Limited Partnership* (MLP). The partnership units of the MLP are frequently traded on the major stock exchanges. The MLP has usually resulted from a corporation "spinning off" a part of the firm, often times a productive asset, such as oil and gas production held by an oil company. By creating the MLP, the cash generated by the asset flows directly to the owners, which may reduce taxes and avoid possible conflicts of interest between shareholders and management.

Corporation

The **corporation** has been a significant factor in the economic development of the United States. As early as 1819, Chief Justice John Marshall set forth the legal definition of a corporation as "an artificial being, invisible, intangible, and existing only in the contemplation of law."[1] This entity *legally* functions separate and apart from its owners. As such, the corporation can individually sue, and be sued, purchase, sell, or own property, and is subject to criminal punishment for crimes. However, despite this legal separation, the corporation is comprised of owners who dictate its direction and policies. The owners elect a board of directors, who in turn select individuals to serve as the corporate officers, including the president, the vice-president, the secretary, and the treasurer. Ownership is reflected by common stock certificates, designating the number of shares owned by its holder. The number of shares owned relative to the total number of shares outstanding determines the stockholder's proportionate ownership in the business. Since the shares are transferable, ownership in a corporation may be changed by a shareholder simply remitting the shares to the new owner. The investor's liability is confined to the amount of the investment in the company, thereby preventing creditors from confiscating the stockholders' personal assets in settlement of unresolved claims. Finally, the life of a corporation is not dependent upon the status of the investors. The death or withdrawal of an investor does not affect the continuity of the corporation.

Comparison of Organization Forms

The foregoing presentation of the legal forms of operation is relatively straightforward. However, the actual choice among these legal entities when beginning a new business may be a difficult one. Not only must a number of different factors be considered, but the variables used in making the decision may be in conflict. One consideration might suggest that a partnership is the best route, while another might indicate that a corporation is needed. An overview of the important criteria is provided in Table 2–1. At the bottom of the table an indication is given, if appropriate, to the form of business that is generally favored.

Organization Requirements and Costs

In every instance, the sole proprietorship is the "cheapest" organization to organize. Generally, no legal requirement must be satisfied; the owner simply begins operating. (Exceptions do exist, depending upon the nature of the product or service.) The general partnership may possibly be as inexpensive to create as the proprietorship, in that no legal criterion must be met. However, if a partnership is to be functional in the long term, a written agreement is usually advisable. The importance of this contract cannot be overemphasized. This document, if properly prepared, may serve to avoid personal misunderstandings and may even minimize several disadvantages

---

[1] *The Trustees of Dartmouth College v. Woodward*, 4 Wheaton 636 (1819).

TABLE 2–1. Selection of Legal Form of Organization

Form of Organization	Organizational Requirements and Costs	Liability of the Owners	Continuity of the Business
Sole proprietorship	Minimum requirements: Generally no registration or filing fee.	Unlimited liability.	Dissolved upon proprietor's death.
General partnership	Minimum requirements: Generally no registration or filing fee. Partnership agreement not legally required but is strongly suggested.	Unlimited liability.	Unless partnership agreement specifies differently, dissolved upon withdrawal or death of partner.
Limited partnership	Moderate requirements: Written agreement often required, including identification of general and limited partners.	General partners: Unlimited liability.	General partners: Same as general partnership.
		Limited partners: Liability limited to investment in company.	Limited partners: Withdrawal or death does not affect continuity of business.
Corporation	Most expensive and greatest requirements: Filing fees; compliance with state regulations for corporations.	Liability limited to investment in company.	Continuity of business unaffected by shareholder withdrawal or death.
Form of organization normally favored	Proprietorship or general partnership	Limited partnership or corporation	Corporation

usually associated with the partnership form of organization. The limited partnership is more expensive, owing to statutory requirements. The partners must provide a certification of the general partners and the limited partners and indicate the rights and responsibilities of each. Also, a written agreement is compulsory. The corporation is typically the most expensive form of business. As indicated earlier, compliance with numerous statutory provisions is required. The legal costs and the time entailed in creating a corporation exceed those for the other legal types of organization. In short, the organizational requirements increase as the formality of the organization increases. However, this consideration is of minimum importance, and to forgo a choice because of its initial cost may prove to be expensive in the long run.

Liability of the Owners

The sole proprietorship and the general partnership have an inherent disadvantage: the feature of unlimited liability. For these organizations, no distinction is made between business assets and personal assets. The creditors lending money to the business can require the owners to sell personal assets if the firm is financially unable to repay its loans. The limited partnership alleviates this problem for the limited partner. However, care must be taken by a limited partner to retain this protection. Failure to give *due notice* or to refrain from actively participating in management may result in the loss of this privilege. The corporation has a definite advantage in terms of limited liability, with the creditors being able to look only to the corporate assets in resolving claims. However, this advantage for the corporation may not always be realized. If a firm is small, its president may be required to guarantee a loan personally. Also, if the corporate

Transferability of Ownership	Management Control and Regulations	Attractiveness for Raising Capital	Income Taxes
May transfer ownership in company name and assets.	Absolute management freedom, negligible formal requirements.	Limited to proprietor's personal capital.	Income from the business is taxed as personal income to the proprietor.
Requires the consent of all partners.	Majority vote of partners required for control; negligible formal requirements.	Limited to partners' ability and desire to contribute capital.	Income from the business is taxed as personal income to the partners.
General partners: Same as general partnership.	General partners: Same as general partnership.	General partners: Same as general partnership.	General partners: Same as general partnership.
Limited partners: May sell interest in the company.	Limited partners: Not permitted any involvement in management.	Limited partners: Limited liability provides a stronger inducement in raising capital.	Limited partners: Same as general partnership.
Easily transferred by transferring shares of stock.	Shareholders have final control, but usually board of directors controls company policies.	Usually the most attractive form for raising capital.	The corporation is taxed on its income and the stockholder is taxed when dividends are paid.
Depends upon the circumstances.	Control: Depends upon the circumstances. Regulation: Proprietorship and general partnership.	Corporation.	Depends upon circumstances.

form is being used to defraud creditors, the courts may "pierce the corporation veil" and hold the owners personally liable. Nevertheless, the limitation of liability is usually an important concern in the selection of the legal organization.

Continuity of Business

The continuity of the business is largely a function of the legal form of organization. The sole proprietorship is immediately dissolved upon the owner's death. Likewise, the general partnership is terminated upon the death or withdrawal of a partner. This weakness can be minimized in the partnership through the written agreement, by specifying what is to occur if a partner dies or desires to withdraw. Failure to incorporate such a provision into the agreement may result in a forced liquidation of the firm, possibly at an inopportune time. Finally, the corporation offers the greatest degree of continuity. The status of the investor simply does not affect the corporation's existence. Hence, the corporate form of conducting business has a distinct advantage in its perpetual nature.

Transferability of Ownership

Transferability of ownership is intrinsically neither good nor bad; its desirability depends largely upon the owners' preferences. In certain businesses the owners may want the option to evaluate any prospective new investors. In other circumstances, unrestricted transferability may be preferred. The sole proprietor has complete freedom to sell any interest in the business. At the other extreme, the members of a general partnership may not sell or assign their interest without the prior consent of the remaining partners. However, this limitation may be removed by providing otherwise in the partnership agreement. The limited partnership has a twofold nature: The assign-ment of interest by general partners requires the prior consent of the other partners, while the limited partners have unrestricted transferability. The corporation affords the investors complete flexibility in transferring their interest.

Management Control and Regulations

The sole proprietor has absolute control of the firm and is not restrained by government regulation. With the few exceptions relating to assumed or fictitious names and special licensing, the sole proprietorship may operate in any state without complying with registration and qualification requirements. The general partnership is likewise not impeded by any significant government regulations. However, since control within this legal form of business is normally based upon the majority vote, an increase in the number of partners reduces each partner's voice in management. The limited partnership is characterized by a restricted separation of ownership from control, which is nonexistent in the sole proprietorship and the general partnership. As to government regulation, the limited partnership requires detailed registration to inform the public of the authority of the individual partners. Within the corporation, the control factor has two dimensions: (a) the **formal control** vested in the stockholders having the majority of the voting common shares and (b) the **functional control** exercised by the corporate officers in conducting the daily operations. For the small corporation, these two controls usually rest in the same individuals. However, as the size of the corporation increases, the two facets become distinctly separate. Finally, the corporation is encumbered with substantial government regulation in terms of registrations as well as compliance with statutory requirements.

Attractiveness for Raising Capital

As a result of the limited liability, the ease of transferring ownership through the sale of common shares, and the flexibility in dividing the shares, the corporation is the supreme business entity in attracting new capital. In contrast, the unlimited liability of the sole proprietorship and the general partnership is a deterrent in raising equity capital. Between these extremes, the limited partnership does provide limited liability for the limited partners, which has a tendency to attract wealthy investors. However, the impracticality of having a large number of partners and the restricted marketability of an interest in a partnership prevent this form of organization from competing effectively with the corporation.

Income Taxes

Income taxation frequently has a major impact upon the owner's selection of the legal form of business. In the remainder of this chapter we will examine the basic tax implications for the financial manager. However, a brief comment at this point would appear appropriate.

   The sole proprietorship and the partnership organization are not taxed as separate entities; the owners report business profits on their personal tax returns. The earnings from the company are taxable to the owner, regardless of whether these profits have been distributed to the investors. This feature may place the owner in a cash squeeze if taxes are due but the income has been retained within the company. On the other hand, the corporation is taxed as a separate and distinct entity. This same income is taxed again when distributed to the shareholder in the form of dividends. Determination of the best form of legal entity with respect to taxes should be based upon the objective of maximizing the after-tax profits to the owners.[2] This decision depends partly upon the tax rates of the individual relative to those of the corporation. Also, whether or not the profits are to be retained in the business or paid as dividends to the common stockholders has a direct bearing on the issue.

FEDERAL INCOME TAXATION

Objectives of Income Taxation

Originally, the sole objective of the federal government in taxing income was to generate financing for government expenditures. Although this purpose continues to be important, *social* and *economic* objectives have been added. For instance, a company may receive possible reductions in taxes if (1) certain technological research is undertaken, or (2) if wages are paid to certain economically disadvantaged groups. Other socially oriented stipulations in the tax laws include exemptions for dependents, old age, and blindness, and a reduction in taxes if the income is associated with retirement. In addition, the government uses a number of procedures to stabilize the economy. In recessionary periods taxes may be reduced, giving the public more discretionary income in the hope that it will be spent to increase the demand for products and thereby generate new jobs.

In summary, three objectives may be given for the taxation of revenues: (1) the provision of revenues for government expenditures, (2) the achievement of socially desirable goals, and (3) economic stabilization.

Types of Taxpayers

In order to understand the tax system, we must first identify what constitutes a "taxpayer." Three basic types of taxable entities exist: individuals, corporations, and fiduciaries. Individuals are considered to include company employees, self-employed persons owning their own businesses, and members of a partnership. Income is reported by these individuals in their personal tax returns. Thus, a partnership does not pay income taxes as a separate entity. The corporation, as a separate legal entity, does report its income and remits a tax payment related to these profits. The owners (stockholders) of the corporation need not report these earnings in their personal tax returns, except when all or a part of the profits are distributed in the form of dividends. Finally, fiduciaries, such as estates and trusts, do file a tax return and pay taxes on the income generated by the estate or trust.

Although taxation of individual and fiduciary income is an important source of income to the government, neither is especially relevant to the financial manager. Since most firms of any size are corporations, we will restrict our interest to the basic procedures involved in computing income taxes for the corporation. In doing so, two caveats are necessary. First, tax legislation can be quite complex, with numerous exceptions to most general rules. We are providing only basic concepts, and we should hesitate to apply our limited understanding of taxes to a complex tax problem. We would be well advised to rely on a professional tax consultant. Second, tax legislation can change quickly, and certain details discussed here may cease to be applicable.

---

[2] The firm's objective is to maximize the shareholder wealth. However, since no risk is involved in selecting the form of business, maximizing profits will also maximize wealth.

TABLE 2–2.   R. E. Gibson Corporation Taxable Income

Sales		$500,000
Cost of goods sold		230,000
Gross profit		$270,000
Operating expenses		
Administrative expenses	$40,000	
Depreciation expenses	15,000	
Marketing expenses	45,000	
Total operating expenses		100,000
Operating income (earnings before		
interest and taxes)		$170,000
Other income		0
Interest expense		20,000
Taxable income		$150,000

Dividends paid to common stockholders ($10,000) are not tax-deductible expenses.

Income Taxes for Corporations

The taxable income for a corporation is based upon the gross income from all sources, except for allowable exclusions, less any tax-deductible expenses. Gross income equals the firm's dollar sales from its product less the cost of producing or acquiring the product. Tax-deductible expenses include any operating expenses, such as marketing expenses and administrative expenses. Also, *interest expense* paid on the firm's outstanding debt is a tax-deductible expense. However, dividends paid to the firm's stockholders, either preferred or common stockholders, are *not* deductible expenses. Other taxable income includes interest income and dividend income.

To demonstrate how to compute a corporation's taxable income, consider the R. E. Gibson Corporation, a manufacturer of home accessories. The firm originally established by Ruth Gibson, had sales of $500,000 for the year. The cost of producing the accessories totaled $230,000. Operating expenses were $100,000. The corporation has $125,000 in debt outstanding, with a 16 percent interest rate, which resulted in $20,000 interest expense ($125,000 × .16 = $20,000). Management paid $10,000 in dividends to the firm's common stockholders. No other income, such as interest or dividend income, was received. The taxable income for the Gibson Corporation would be $150,000, as shown in Table 2–2.

In continuing our study of corporate income tax we will examine the corporate tax-rate schedule, dividend exclusion for the corporation, depreciation, net operating losses, and capital gains and losses. Additional taxes may be imposed upon the corporation for the "excessive accumulation" of profits within the business. Finally, we will examine briefly the tax provision allowing a corporation to be taxed as a partnership, which became increasingly important with the Tax Reform Act of 1986.

TABLE 2–3.   Corporate Tax Rates

15%	$ 0–$50,000
25%	$50,001–$75,000
34%	over $75,000

An additional 5% tax is imposed on income between $100,000 and $335,000.

Corporate Rate Structure   The corporate tax rate structure is relatively simple. The specific rates effective for the corporation, as of 1987, are given in Table 2–3.

For example, the tax liability for the Gibson Corporation, which had $150,000 in taxable earnings, would be $41,750, calculated as follows:

Earnings	×	Marginal Tax Rate	=	Taxes
$ 50,000	×	15%		$ 7,500
25,000	×	25%		6,250
75,000	×	34%		25,500
$150,000				$39,250
Add 5% surtax for income exceeding $100,000 (5% × [$150,000 − $100,000])				2,500
Total tax liability				$41,750

The tax rates shown in Table 2–3 are defined as the *marginal* tax rates, which indicate the rate applicable for the next dollar of income. For instance, if a firm has earnings of $60,000 and is contemplating an investment that would yield $10,000 in additional profits, the tax rate to be used in calculating the taxes on this added income is 25 percent; that is, the marginal tax rate is 25 percent. However, if the corporation already expects $75,000 without the new investment, the extra $10,000 in earnings would be taxed at 34 percent, the marginal tax rate. In the example, where the Gibson company has taxable income of $150,000, its marginal tax rate is 39 percent. That is, any additional income from new investments will be taxed at a rate of 39 percent. However, after taxable income exceeds $335,000, the marginal tax rate declines to 34 percent when the 5 percent surtax no longer applies.

In addition to the marginal tax rate, we may also compute the *average* tax rate. For the firm earning $150,000 and owing $41,750 in taxes, the average tax rate is 27.8 percent, calculated as follows:

$$\text{average tax rate} = \text{total tax liability} \div \text{taxable income}$$
$$= \quad \$41,750 \quad \div \quad \$150,000$$
$$= \quad 27.8 \text{ percent}$$

Although it is of interest to know the average tax rate, the marginal tax rate is far more important in financial decisions. As will become increasingly clear throughout the text, we always want to consider the tax consequences of any financial decision. The appropriate rate to be used in the analysis is the marginal tax rate, the rate that will be applicable for any changes in earnings as a result of the action being taken. Thus, *when making financial decisions involving taxes, always use the marginal tax rate in your calculations.*[3]

---

[3] After the company's taxable income exceeds $335,000, both the marginal and average tax rates equal 34%, owing to the elimination of the 5% surtax that applies to taxable income between $100,000 and $335,000.

Dividend Exclusion

A corporation may normally exclude 80 percent of any dividends received from another corporation. For instance, if corporation A owns common stock in corporation B and receives dividends of $1000 in a given year, only $200 will be subject to tax, with the remaining $800 (80% of $1000) being tax exempt. If the corporation receiving the dividend income is in a 34 percent tax bracket, only $68 in taxes (34% of $200) will result.

Depreciation

If an asset is purchased that has a limited life beyond one year but its usefulness gradually declines over time, the taxpayer is not permitted to show the cost of the asset as a tax deduction in the year it is acquired. However, if the property is used in a business or profession or in the production of income, a part of the original cost may be written off as a tax deduction in each year of the asset's anticipated economic life. Examples of assets that may be depreciated include machinery and buildings.

Computing Depreciation Prior to 1987. Historically, there have been two commonly used methods for computing depreciation: **straight-line (SL)** and **double-declining balance (DDB).** Of the two, straight-line (SL) is the simplest to understand and to use. Consider the following example: A firm purchases a fixed asset for $12,000 that has a 5-year expected life and a $2000 anticipated salvage value at the end of that period. Straight-line depreciation on the asset would be $2400 per year. ($12,000 ÷ 5 years = $2400). While there is a $2000 salvage value, this value is disregarded in computing annual depreciation expense for tax purposes.

The double-declining balance method (DDB) is referred to as an accelerated depreciation method, since it provides for a more rapid rate of expensing the asset cost than the straight-line method. This method involves depreciating the *undepreciated* value of the asset at twice the rate of the straight-line method. This method is demonstrated in Table 2–4. In terms of the preceding example, the straight-line rate was $2400 ÷ $12,000, or .2. Thus, the double-declining rate is 2 × .2, or .4.

Under the DDB method the asset would never be fully depreciated. The Internal Revenue Code allows the firm to switch over from DDB to straight-line any time before the end of the asset's useful life. The optimal time to make the switch is in that year where straight-line depreciation exceeds that of the DDB method. Note in Table 2–4 that the switch occurs in year 4.

TABLE 2–4. Computation of Double-Declining Balance Depreciation Expense

Year	Book Value of Asset First of Year)	Depreciation Rate	Depreciation Expense	Accumulated Depreciation	Book Value (End of Year)
1	$12,000.00	.40	$4,800.00	$ 4,800.00	$7,200.00
2	7,200.00	.40	2,880.00	7,680.00	4,320.00
3	4,320.00	.40	1,728.00	9,408.00	2,592.00
4	2,592.00	—	1,296.00[a]	10,704.00	1,296.00
5	1.296.00	—	1,296.00	12,000.00	.00

[a] Switching to straight-line depreciation in year 4 produced a depreciation expense of $1296 ($2592/2) for each of the two remaining years in the useful life of the asset, which exceeds the depreciation expense in these years if the double-declining balance method had been used.

With regard to the two methods for computing depreciation, it should be noted that the double-declining method offers the very real advantage of deferring the payment of taxes. The larger amounts of depreciation in the earlier years decrease taxable income in these years; however, smaller amounts of depreciation in later years subsequently increase taxable income. Consequently, taxes are deferred until these later years.

Computing Depreciation after 1986. For assets acquired in 1987 or later, the **Accelerated Cost Recovery System** (ACRS) is to be used in computing annual depreciation. Initially established in 1981, the ACRS was modified by tax law, effective January 1, 1987, to include three key variables in computing depreciation: (1) the asset depreciation range (2) the method of depreciation, and (3) the *averaging convention*.

Prior to 1981, a depreciable asset was depreciated over its economic useful life. Now the depreciation period is based upon the **asset depreciation range (ADR)** system, which groups assets into classes by asset type and the industry. Given the type of asset, both the method of depreciation and the actual number of years to be used in depreciating the asset may then be determined. These methods and lives (classes) are presented in Table 2–5. The first column classifies depreciable property into eight groups. The second column designates whether the asset is to be depreciated using double declining balance (200 percent), 150 percent declining balance, or straight line. The last column indicates the depreciation life (class), which designates the number of years to be used in calculating depreciation.

The last consideration in computing depreciation is that tax legislation restricts the amount of depreciation that may be taken in the year an asset is acquired or

TABLE 2–5. Depreciation Methods and Lives

Type of Asset	Method	Lives (Class)
Property with ADR of 4 years or less, excluding automobiles and light trucks.	Double-declining balance.	3-year
Property with ADR of more than 4 years and less than 10 years. Automobiles, light trucks, and R&D property are to be included.	Double-declining balance.	5-year
Property with ADR of 10 years or more and less than 16 years, and property without an ADR that is not classified elsewhere are to be included.	Double-declining balance	7-year
Property with ADR of 16 years or more and less than 20 years.	Double-declining balance.	10-year
Property with ADR of 20 years or more and less than 25 years.	150% declining balance	15-year
Property with ADR of 25 years or more, other than real property, such as buildings.	Straight line	27.5-year
Real property (buildings) with ADR greater than 25 years.	Straight line	31.5-year

TABLE 2–6. Depreciation Percentages for Personal Property[a]

Recovery Year	3-Year (200% DDB)	5-Year (200% DDB)	7-Year (200% DDB)	10-Year (200% DDB)	15-Year (150% DB)	20-Year (150% DB)
1	33.0%	20.0%	14.3%	10.0%	5.0%	3.8%
2	45.0	32.0	24.5	18.0	9.5	7.2
3	15.0	19.2	17.5	14.4	8.6	6.7
4	7.0	11.5[b]	12.5	11.5	7.7	6.2
5		11.5	8.9[b]	9.2	6.9	5.7
6		5.8	8.9	7.4	6.2	5.3
7			8.9	6.6[b]	5.9[b]	4.9
8			4.5	6.6	5.9	4.5[b]
9				6.5	5.9	4.5
10				6.5	5.9	4.5
11				3.3	5.9	4.5
12					5.9	4.5
13					5.9	4.5
14					5.9	4.5
15					5.9	4.5
16					3.0	4.5
17						4.5
18						4.5
19						4.5
20						4.5
21						1.7
Total	100.0	100.0	100.0	100.0	100.0	100.0

[a] Assumes half-year convention applies.
[b] Switchover to straight-line depreciation over remaining useful life.

sold. These limitations have been called **averaging conventions.** The two primary conventions, or limitations, may be stated as follows:

1. **Half-Year Convention:** Personal property such as machinery is treated as having been placed in service or disposed of at the midpoint of the taxable year. Thus, a half-year of depreciation generally is allowed for the taxable year in which property is placed in service or disposed of.
2. **Mid-Month Convention:** Real property, such as buildings, is treated as being placed in service or disposed of in the middle of the month. Accordingly, a half-month of depreciation is allowed for the month disposed of or placed in service.

Using the ACRS to compute the depreciation for assets other than buildings results in a different percentage of the asset being depreciated each year. These percentages are shown in Table 2–6. For buildings, the straight-line depreciation method is used. In lieu of the declining-balance method, a firm may use straight-line depreciation for any asset, regardless of asset class. However, the number of years designated for the particular asset class must still be used.

To demonstrate the use of the ACRS, assume that a piece of equipment costs $12,000 and has been assigned to a 5-year class. Using the percentages in Table 2–6 for a 5-year class asset, the depreciation deductions would be calculated as shown in Table 2–7.

TABLE 2–7. ACRS Demonstrated

Year	Annual Depreciation	Depreciation Percentage
1	2,400	20.0%
2	3,840	32.0
3	2,304	19.2
4	1,380	11.5
5	1,380	11.5
6	696	5.8
	$12,000	100.0%

Note that the averaging convention which allows for the half-year of depreciation in the first year results in a half-year of depreciation beyond the fifth year, or in year 6.

Net Operating Loss Deduction

If a corporation has an operating loss (losses from operating a business) the loss may be applied against income in other years. The tax laws provide for a **net operating loss carryback and carryforward,** which permits the taxpayer first to apply the loss against the profits in the three prior years (carryback). If the loss has not been completely absorbed by the profits in these three years, the loss may be carried forward to each of the fifteen following years (carryforward). At that time, any loss still remaining may no longer be used as a tax deduction. To illustrate, a 1988 operating loss may be used to recover, in whole or in part, the taxes paid during 1985, 1986, and 1987. If any part of the loss still remains, this amount may be used to reduce taxable income, if any, during the fifteen-year period of 1989 through 2003. A complete example of net operating loss deduction is provided on page 22.

Capital Gains and Losses

An important tax consideration prior to 1987 was the preferential tax treatment for capital gains; i.e., gains from the sale of the assets not bought or sold in the ordinary course of business. The Tax Reform Act of 1986 repealed any special treatment of capital gains. Currently capital gains are treated as ordinary income in computing taxable income. However, if a corporation has capital losses that exceed capital gains in any year, these net capital losses may not be deducted from ordinary income. The net losses may, however, be carried back and applied against net capital gains in each of the three years before the current year. If the loss is not completely used in the three prior years, any remaining loss may be carried forward and applied against any net gains in each of the next five years. For example, if a corporation has an $80,000 net capital loss in 1987, it may apply this loss against any net gains in 1984, 1985, and 1986. If any loss remains, it may be carried forward and applied against any gains through 1992.

Accumulated Earnings Tax

The earnings generated by a corporation are potentially subject to "double taxation," first at the corporate level and then at the stockholder level as the firm's profits are distributed in the form of dividends. If the shareholders had no immediate need for dividend income, the corporation could retain its profits and perhaps even employ the funds for the personal benefit of the company's owners. For example, management could retain the corporate profits but make a personal loan to the stockholders. Also,

Example. As an example of the net operating loss carryback and carryforward, assume D. Francis, Inc., a trucking operation, has had the following profits and losses reported from 1981 through 1988:

1981	$ 52,000
1982	76,000
1983	100,000
1984	(152,000)
1985	100,000
1986	(194,000)
1987	12,000
1988	94,000

In 1984 and 1986 the corporation incurred operating losses, which may be applied to reduce taxable income and taxes in other years. The tax payments and tax refunds for each year are calculated in Table 2–8.

TABLE 2–8. D. Francis, Inc., Tax Payments and Refunds

Year	Taxable Income	Tax Consequence
1981	$ 52,000	TAX PAYMENT OF $8,000
		15% of $50,000 plus 25% of $2,000.
1982	76,000	TAX PAYMENT OF $14,090
		15% of $50,000 plus 25% of $25,000 plus 34% of $1000.
1983	100,000	TAX PAYMENT OF $22,250
		15% of $50,000 plus 25% of $25,000 plus 34% of $25,000.
1984	(152,000)	TAX REFUND OF $30,250
		$52,000 of the $152,000 loss is applied against 1981 income for a refund of $8,000; $76,000 of the loss is applied against 1982 income for a refund of $14,090, leaving $24,000 to be applied against 1983 income of $100,000 for a refund of $8,-160—34% of $24,000.
1985	100,000	TAX PAYMENT OF $22,250
		Same computation as 1983.
1986	(194,000)	TAX REFUND OF $36,340 AND $18,000 CARRYFORWARD
		$76,000 of the loss is applied against 1983 income ($24,000 had already been used in 1984) for a refund of $14,090; $100,000 of the loss is applied against 1985 income for a refund of $22,250. The remaining $18,000 loss ($194,000—$176,000) is to be carried to future years.
1987	12,000	NO TAX PAYMENT OR REFUND; $6000 CARRYFORWARD
		The $18,000 carryforward from 1986 is used to avoid having to pay any tax, leaving $6000 carryforward ($18,000–$12,000) for future years.
1988	94,000	TAX PAYMENT OF $18,170
		Tax is calculated on $88,000 income ($94,000 income less the $6000 carryforward originating in 1986): 15% of $50,000 plus 25% of $25,000 plus 34% of $13,000.

if the profits were accumulated within the firm, the price of the common stock should rise. Until the stock is sold, the investor would not be required to pay any tax.

To prevent such stratagems, a penalty surtax in addition to the regular income tax is assessed at the corporate level on any accumulation of earnings by a corporation for the purpose of avoiding taxes on its shareholders. The penalty is 17½ percent on the first $100,000 and 38½ percent for any greater amount. The tax does not apply to the retention of profits for *reasonable business needs*. Nor must the money be reinvested immediately as long as there is evidence that future needs require the current accumulation of earnings. Although it is difficult to state exactly when the accumulation of profits is thought to be *reasonable*, several examples would include (1) providing for the replacement of plant and equipment, (2) retiring debt created in connection with the corporation's business, (3) providing for working-capital requirements, and (4) financing the acquisition of a new business.

Subchapter S Corporation

The tax considerations in deciding between the sole proprietorship or partnership and the corporation are important. Owners attempt to select the form of business organization that maximizes their *after-tax* returns. To minimize the tax influence upon the decision, Congress established the **Subchapter S Corporation,** which enables a corporation to be taxed as a partnership. This provision eliminates the "double taxation" effect on the corporation. The Subchapter S Corporation files a tax return for information purposes only and pays no taxes. The taxes from the business are paid by the stockholder, whether or not the earnings are distributed. However, to qualify as a Subchapter S Corporation, the following requirements must be met:

1. The firm must be a domestic corporation.
2. There may be no more than 35 shareholders at the beginning of the corporation's life. These shareholders must be individuals, estates, or certain trusts.
3. The corporation cannot be a member of an affiliated group eligible to file a consolidated tax return with another corporation.
4. There may be only one class of stock.
5. A nonresident alien cannot be a stockholder.

Thus, only small to moderate-sized firms typically can satisfy the Subchapter S Corporation requirements. However, if the qualifications can be met, the company may potentially receive the benefits of being a corporation while being taxed as a partnership.

The Subchapter S Corporation became even more important in 1987, when the changes in tax rates placed the individual rates below the corporate rates. Thus, not only does the Subchapter S Corporation avoid the double taxation, it also allows the owners of the firm to be taxed at a lower rate.

Corporate Taxes: An Example

To illustrate certain portions of the tax laws for a corporation, assume that the Griggs Corporation had sales during the past year of $5 million; its cost of goods sold was $3 million; and operating expenses of $1 million were incurred. In addition, it received $185,000 in interest income and $100,000 in dividend income from another corporation. In turn, it paid $40,000 in interest and $75,000 in dividends. Also, old machinery which had originally cost $350,000, was sold for $200,000. The equipment was purchased 5 years ago and it was being depreciated (straight-line) over a 10-year life. Finally, the company sold a piece of land for $100,000 that had cost $50,000 six years ago.

TABLE 2–9. Griggs Corporation Tax Computations

Sales			$ 5,000,000
Cost of goods sold			(3,000,000)
Gross profit			$ 2,000,000
Operating expenses			(1,000,000)
Operating income			$ 1,000,000
Other taxable income and expenses:			
Interest income		$ 185,000	
Dividend income	$ 100,000		
Less 80% exclusion	(80,000)	20,000	
Interest expense		(40,000)	165,000
Gain on sale of equipment:			
Selling price		$ 200,000	
Book value		(175,000)	25,000
			$ 1,190,000
Gain on land sale:			
Selling price		$ 100,000	
Cost		(50,000)	$ 50,000
Total taxable income			$ 1,240,000

Tax computation:

15% × $	50,000	= $	7,500
25% ×	25,000	=	6,250
34% ×	1,165,000	=	396,100
	$1,240,000		

Add 5% surtax for income between $100,000 and $335,000	$ 11,750
Tax liability	$ 421,600

Based upon the tax rates from Table 2–3, Griggs's tax liability is $421,600, as shown in Table 2–9. Note that the $75,000 Griggs paid in dividends is not tax deductible. Also, since the firm's taxable income exceeds $335,000 where the 5-percent surtax is no longer applied, the marginal tax rate and the average tax rate both equal 34 percent. That is, we could have computed Griggs' tax liability as 34 percent of $1,240,000, or $421,600.

Implications of Taxes in Financial Decision Making

Taxes play an important role in financial decision making. Hardly a decision is made by the financial manager without considering the impact of taxes. Although a complete understanding of these tax consequences is not feasible until the underlying financial principles have been presented, a brief integration of taxes into the three primary decision areas of the financial manager should prove helpful.

Taxes and Capital Investment Decisions

As will be explained in more depth later, income taxes are a significant element in evaluating the firm's investment decisions. When the company is analyzing the possible acquisition of a plant or equipment, the returns from the investment should be measured on an after-tax basis. Otherwise the company will be omitting an important variable. For example, suppose management is considering the purchase of production equipment costing $1000. If the $1000 is spent, the financing of the expenditure must come from *after-tax dollars*. Stated differently, the firm may keep this $1000 without having to be concerned about any tax consequences. However, if the capital is expended on a capital project (plant or equipment), a portion of the cash inflows to be received from the investment will be taxed. Ignoring the time value of money, assume the project, if accepted, is expected to generate $1200 in *cash inflows before taxes*, which at first might appear to be satisfactory. However, this $1200 is *before-tax dollars*, which simply means that the firm has not paid the taxes that will be owed as a result of receiving these funds. If the company eventually has to pay $300 in taxes, only $900 will be received in *after-tax cash flows*, which is the amount directly comparable with the $1000 investment cost. Clearly the project is undesirable, but the taxes had to be included in the analysis before this fact could be determined.

In computing the taxes resulting from an investment decision, the method of depreciation affects the timing and the amount of cash flow after taxes. The depreciation method will have an impact upon the timing of taxes. Although the *total amount* of taxes is not altered, the use of accelerated depreciation, as opposed to straight-line depreciation, does result in lower taxable profits in the earlier years of the project's life and larger profits in later years. In this manner, less taxes are paid in the initial years without counterbalancing higher taxes in later years. If the time value of money is recognized, this shift in taxes to later time periods is beneficial.

Taxes and the Firm's Capital Structure

The second major policy variable for the financial manager is to determine the appropriate mix between debt and equity financing. Extensive controversy on this issue has continued for well over two decades. However, regardless of the different views maintained, the tax laws do give debt financing a definite cost advantage over preferred stock and common stock. As already noted, *interest payments are a tax-deductible expense, while dividend payments to preferred stockholders and to common stockholders may not be used as deductions in computing a corporation's taxable profits.*

Taxes and Corporate Dividend Policies

The importance of taxes with respect to the firm's dividend policy is recognized primarily at the common stockholder level rather than at the corporate level. However, since the financial manager's objective is to maximize the common stockholder's wealth, the impact of taxes upon the shareholder is important. Remember that corporate earnings are taxed, whether or not the earnings are paid out in dividends or retained to be reinvested. Yet if the dividends are paid, the investor will be required to report this income. On the other hand, if the profits are retained and reinvested, the price of the company's stock should increase. However, until the stock is actually sold at a gain, the shareholder is not required to recognize the income. Hence, the opportunity for the firm's common investors to delay the tax payment might influence their preference between gain and dividend income. In turn, this preference may affect the corporation's dividend policy.

Summary

Financial managers should be aware of the external influences affecting the company. An important part of this overall environment is the legal atmosphere for the firm. This chapter has examined two key elements: the legal forms of business organization and the tax structure.

Legal Forms of Organization

The sole proprietorship is a business operation owned and managed by a single individual. The initiation of this form of business is extremely simple and generally does not involve any substantial organizational costs. The proprietor has complete control of the firm but must be willing to assume full responsibility for the outcome.

The general partnership, which is simply a coming together of two or more individuals, is quite similar to the sole proprietorship. The limited partnership has been created by states to permit all but one of the partners to have limited liability if agreeable to all partners.

The corporation has served to increase the flow of capital from the investment public to the business community. Although larger organizational costs and regulations are imposed upon this legal entity, the corporation is more conducive to raising large amounts of capital. Limited liability, continuity of life, and ease of transfer in ownership, which increases the marketability of the investment, have contributed greatly in attracting large numbers of investors into the business. The formal control of the corporation is vested in the parties having the greatest number of shares. However, day-to-day operations are determined by the corporate officers, who theoretically serve on behalf of the common stockholders.

Taxes

Several forms of taxation exist; however, the primary tax concern in a business relates to income taxation. The objective of income taxes from a national perspective is three-fold: (1) to provide a revenue source for the government, (2) to achieve socially desirable goals, and (3) to facilitate economic stability. In implementing the tax structure three taxable entities exist: the individual, including partnerships, the corporation, and the fiduciary. Only information on the corporate entity has been given here.

For the most part, the taxable income for the corporation is equal to the firm's operating income plus capital gains less any interest expense. The corporation is allowed an income exclusion of 80 percent of the dividends received from another corporation. Also, if the Internal Revenue Service considers the corporation to be retaining unreasonable amounts of earnings within the business, an accumulated earnings tax may be imposed. To minimize the tax influence in selecting the form of legal organization, a corporation may choose to be a Subchapter S Corporation and be taxed as a partnership, provided certain qualifications can be satisfied.

Tax consequences have a direct bearing upon the decisions of the financial manager. The relationships result from the taxability of investment income and from the difference in tax treatment for interest expense and dividend payments. Also, shareholders' tax status may influence their preference between gains from stock sale and dividends, which may influence corporate dividend policy.

Study Questions

2–1. Define (a) sole proprietorship, (b) partnership, and (c) corporation.

2–2. Identify the primary characteristics of each form of legal organization.

2–3. Using the following criteria, specify the legal form of business that is favored: (a) organizational requirements and costs, (b) liability of the owners, (c) continuity of business, (d) transferability of ownership, (e) management control and regulations, (f) capability to raise capital, and (g) income taxes.

2–4. Does a partnership pay taxes on its income? Explain.

2–5. When a corporation receives a dividend from another corporation, how is it taxed?

2–6. What is the purpose of the net operating deduction?

2–7. What is the rationale for an accumulated earnings tax?

2–8. What is the purpose of the Subchapter S Corporation? In general, what type of firm would qualify as a Subchapter S Corporation?

Self-Test Problems

ST–1. (*Corporate Income Tax*) The Dana Flatt Corporation had sales of $2 million this past year. Its cost of goods sold was $1.2 million and the operating expenses were $400,000. Interest expenses on outstanding debts were $100,000, and the company paid $40,000 in preferred stock dividends. The corporation received $10,000 in preferred stock dividends and interest income of $12,000. The firm sold stock for $40,000 that had been owned for two years; the original cost of the stock was $30,000. Determine the corporation's taxable income and its tax liability.

ST–2. (*Carryback-Carryforward*) Stocking, Inc. has a chain of fast-food restaurants. The firm has been operating for eight years, during which time the profits have fluctuated significantly. The taxable income for the past 8 years is shown below. Compute the tax payments and refunds for each year.

1982	$ (50,000)	1986	$ 50,000
1983	25,000	1987	150,000
1984	150,000	1988	200,000
1985	(225,000)	1989	(50,000)

Study Problems

2–1. (*Depreciation*) Compute the annual depreciation for an asset that cost $250,000 and that has an ADR of 6 years. Use the ACRS in your calculations.

2–2. (*Depreciation*) You acquired a depreciable asset this year, costing $500,000. Your accountant tells you it has a 12-year ADR.
   a. Using the ACRS, compute the annual depreciation.
   b. What assumption is being made about when in the year you bought the asset?

2–3. (*Corporate Income Tax*) The William B. Waugh Corporation is a regional International Harvester dealer. The firm sells new and used trucks and is actively involved in the parts business. During the most recent year the company generated sales of $3 million. The combined cost of goods sold and the operating expenses were $2.1 million. Also, $400,000 in interest expense was paid during the year. The firm received $6000 during the year in dividend income from 1000 shares of common stock that had been purchased three years previously. However, the stock was sold toward the end of the year for $100 per share; its initial cost was $80 per share. The company also sold land that had been recently purchased and had been held for only four months. The selling price was $50,000; the cost was $45,000. Calculate the corporation's tax liability.

2–4. (*Corporate Income Tax*) Sales for L. B. Menielle, Inc. during the past year amounted to $5 million. The firm provides parts and supplies for oil field service companies. Gross profits for the year were $3 million. Operating expenses totaled $1 million. The interest and dividend income from securities owned were $20,000 and $25,000, respectively. The firm's interest expense was $100,000. The firm sold securities on two occasions during the year, receiving a gain of $40,000 on the first sale but losing $50,000 on the second. The stock sold first had been owned for four years; the stock sold second had been purchased three months prior to the sale. Compute the corporation's tax liability.

2–5. (*Carryback-Carryforward*) The taxable income for B. Davies, Inc., for the past seven years is given below. From the information provided, determine the firm's tax payments and tax refunds in each year.

1983	$ 25,000	1987	$(125,000)
1984	(75,000)	1988	(20,000)
1985	100,000	1989	80,000
1986	50,000		

2–6. (*Corporate Income Tax*) Sandersen, Inc., sells minicomputers. During the past year the company's sales were $3 million. The cost of its merchandise sold came to $2 million, and cash operating expenses were $400,000; depreciation expense was $100,000, and the firm paid $150,000 in interest on bank loans. Also, the corporation received $50,000 in dividend income but paid $25,000 in the form of dividends to its own common stockholders. Calculate the corporation's tax liability.

2–7. (*Carryback-Carryforward*) Given the income figures below for the A. O. Faubus Corporation, compute the tax payment or tax refund in each year.

1982	$ 40,000	1986	$ 60,000
1983	(60,000)	1987	(100,000)
1984	30,000	1988	50,000
1985	80,000	1989	(75,000)

2–8. (*Corporate Income Tax*) A. Don Drennan, Inc., had sales of $6 million during the past year. The company's cost of goods sold was 70 percent of sales; operating expenses, including depreciation, amounted to $800,000. The firm sold a capital asset (stock) for $75,000, which had been purchased five months earlier at a cost of $80,000. Determine the company's tax liability.

2–9. (*Corporate Income Tax*) The Robbins Corporation is an oil wholesaler. The company's sales last year were $1 million, with the cost of goods sold equal to $600,000. The firm paid interest of $200,000, and its cash operating expenses were $100,000. Also, the firm received $40,000 in dividend income while paying only $10,000 in dividends to its preferred stockholders. Depreciation expense was $150,000. Compute the firm's tax liability. Based on your answer, does management need to take any additional action?

2–10. (*Corporate Income Tax*) The Fair Corporation had sales of $5 million this past year. The cost of goods sold was $4.3 million and operating expenses were $100,000. Dividend income totaled $5000. The firm sold land for $150,000 that had cost $100,000 five months ago. The firm received $150 per share from the sale of 1000 shares of stock. The stock was purchased for $100 per share three years ago. Determine the firm's tax liability.

2–11. (*Carryback-Carryforward*) The taxable income for Farina's, Inc., during the past seven years is shown below. Compute the tax payments and tax refunds.

1982	$(100,000)	1986	$ (10,000)
1983	125,000	1987	275,000
1984	250,000	1988	(300,000)
1985	(100,000)		

2–12. (*Corporate Income Tax*) Sales for J. P. Hulett, Inc. during the past year amounted to $4 million. The firm supplies statistical information to engineering companies. Gross profits totaled $1 million while operating and depreciation expenses were $500,000 and $350,000, respectively. Dividend income for the year was $12,000. Compute the corporation's tax liability.

2–13. (*Corporate Income Tax*) Anderson & Dennis, Inc. sells computer software. The company's past year's sales were $5 million. The cost of its merchandise sold came to $3 million. Operating expenses were $175,000, plus depreciation expenses totaling $125,000. The firm paid $200,000 interest on loans. The firm sold stock during the year, receiving a $40,000 gain on a stock owned 6 years but losing $60,000 on stock held four months. Calculate the company's tax liability.

2–14. (*Carryback-Carryforward*) Mama-Cheatham's Bakery has been operating for 8 years. Fluctuating overhead has caused significant changes in profits. The taxable income for the business operations are given below. Compute the tax payments and refunds for each of the 8 years.

1981	$ 25,000	1985	$ 50,000
1982	25,000	1986	(10,000)
1983	(50,000)	1987	(25,000)
1984	(20,000)	1988	40,000

2–15. (*Corporate Income Tax*) G. R. Edwin, Inc., had sales of $6 million during the past year. The cost of goods sold amounted to $3 million. Operating expenses totaled $2.6 million and interest expense was $30,000. Determine the firm's tax liability.

Self-Test Solutions

SS–1.

Sales			$2,000,000
Cost of goods sold			1,200,000
Gross profit			$ 800,000
Tax-deductible expenses:			
Operating expense		$400,000	
Interest expense		100,000	500,000
			$ 300,000
Other income:			
Interest income			$ 12,000
Preferred dividend income		$ 10,000	
Less 80% exclusion		8,000	2,000
Taxable ordinary income			$ 314,000
Gain on sale:			
Selling price		$ 40,000	
Cost		30,000	10,000
Taxable income			$ 324,000

Tax liability:

.15 × $ 50,000 =	$	7,500
.25 × 25,000 =		6,250
.34 × 249,000 =		84,660
5% surtax		11,200
		$109,610

SS–2.

Year	Taxable Income	Tax Payments	Carryback	Carryforward	Tax Refunds
1982	$ (50,000)				
1983	25,000			$25,000 from 1982	
1984	150,000	$32,000[a]	$125,000 from 1985	25,000 from 1982	
1985	(225,000)				$32,000[b]
1986	50,000			50,000 from 1985	
1987	150,000	22,250[c]	50,000 from 1989	50,000 from 1985	
1988	200,000	61,250			
1989	(50,000)				14,750[d]

[a] Taxes are based upon $125,000 ($150,000 taxable income − $25,000 carryforward from 1982).
[b] The tax refund results from a $125,000 carryback to 1984 to recoup the taxes paid in 1984.
[c] Taxes are based upon $100,000 ($150,000 taxable income − $50,000 carryforward).
[d] The tax refund results from a $50,000 carryback to 1987. The taxes in 1987 were originally $22,250, based upon $100,000 income. With the $50,000 carryback from 1989, the taxes for 1987 are recomputed on $50,000, or $7,500. The difference between the amount originally paid in 1987, or $22,250, and the recalculated $7,500 in taxes is $14,750.

Selected References

Dyl, Edward A. "Capital Gains Taxation and Year-end Stock Market Behavior," *Journal of Finance*, 32 (March 1977), 165–75.

Explanation of Tax Equity and Fiscal Responsibility Act of 1982. Chicago: Commerce Clearing House, Inc., 1982.

1987 Federal Tax Course. New York: Commerce Clearing House, 1986.

1987 Federal Tax Course. Englewood Cliffs, NJ: Prentice-Hall, 1986.

3

Financial Analysis

Financial analysis involves the assessment of a firm's past, present, and anticipated future financial condition. The objective is to identify any weaknesses in the firm's financial health that could lead to future problems and to determine any strengths the firm might capitalize upon. For example, an internal financial analysis performed by a firm's staff might be aimed at assessing the firm's liquidity or measuring its past performance. Alternatively, financial analysis may come from outside the firm in an effort to determine the firm's creditworthiness or investment potential. Regardless of the origins of the analysis, the tools used are basically the same.

Financial ratios are the principal tool of financial analysis, since they can be used to answer a variety of questions regarding a firm's financial well-being. For example, a commercial bank loan officer considering an application for a six-month loan might want to know whether the applicant firm is solvent or liquid; a potential investor in the firm's common stock might want to know how profitable the firm has been; and an internal financial analyst might want to know whether the firm can reasonably afford to borrow all or part of the funds needed to finance a planned expansion. Answers to these and related questions can be obtained through the use of financial ratios.

We begin our discussion of financial analysis with an overview of the firm's basic financial statements. These include the balance sheet, income statement, and statement of changes in financial condition (source and use of funds statement). The next step is to survey a set of key financial ratios that can be used to assess the firm's financial condition.

BASIC FINANCIAL STATEMENTS

Three **financial statements** are generally used to depict the financial status of a firm. These statements provide the raw material for the financial analyst, and they must be fully understood before any meaningful analysis can be undertaken. For a

TABLE 3–1. Jimco, Inc. Balance Sheet December 31, 1987 ($000)

Assets

Current assets:		
Cash	$ 1,400	
Marketable securities—at cost (market		
value, $320)	300	
Accounts receivable	10,000	
Inventories	12,000	
Prepaid expenses	300	
Total current assets		$24,000
Fixed assets:		
Land	2,000	
Plant and equipment	$12,300	
Less: Accumulated depreciation	7,300	
Net plant and equipment	5,000	
Total fixed assets		7,000
Total assets		$31,000

Liabilities and Owners' Equity

Current liabilities:		
Accounts payable	$3,000	
Notes payable, 9%, due March 1, 1988	3,400	
Accrued salaries, wages, and other expenses	3,100	
Current portion of long-term debt	500	
Total current liabilities		$10,000
Long-term liabilities:		
Deferred income taxes	1,500	
First mortgage bonds, 7%, due January		
1, 1988	6,300	
Debentures, 8½%, due June 30, 1994	2,900	
Total long-term liabilities		10,700
Owners' equity:		
Common stock (par value $1.00)	100	
Additional paid-in capital	2,000	
Retained earnings	8,200	
Total owners' equity		10,300
Total liabilities and owners'		$31,000
equity		

helpful review of accounting principles and terms, see the two appendixes at the end of this chapter.[1]

Balance Sheet

The **balance sheet** represents a statement of the financial position of the firm on a given date, including its asset holdings, liabilities, and owner-supplied capital. Assets represent the resources owned by the firm, whereas liabilities and owner's equity indicate how those resources were financed. Table 3–1 gives an example balance sheet for Jimco, Inc. as of December 31, 1987. Jimco had $31 million in assets, which it financed with $10 million in current (short-term) liabilities that must be

---

[1] Appendix 3A is a review of the fundamental accounting practices underlying financial statement preparation, and Appendix 3B is a glossary of accounting terminology.

repaid within the current year, $10,700,000 in noncurrent (long-term) liabilities, and $10,300,000 in owner-supplied funds. (Each term used in the balance sheet is defined in Appendix 3B.)

BASIC FINANCIAL MANAGEMENT IN PRACTICE
Debt, where is thy sting?

"It's been around for a few years, but debt defeasance is still alive and well," reports John Deming, director of accounting for KMG Main Hurdman. Debt defeasance allows firms to retire debt at a discount from par. The firm does not actually retire the debt with a lump sum payment. Rather, it simply sets aside a fund to service the debt. Bondholders are unaffected. But the accountants consider the issue to have been retired the minute the servicing fund is created, and permit the company to take the discount into earnings immediately.

Defeasance tends to be most popular when interest rates are high and old debt trades at big discounts. But even with interest rates down, companies are still booking profits from retiring old issues. Last year U.S. Steel, to take but one example, extinguished $399 million worth of old 4⅝% and 7¾% debt. That resulted in an extraordinary gain of $51 million, some 13% of total profits. Borden used the same device to pick up $11.8 million, 6% of its profits.

Moral? When confronted by debt defeasance and all the other accounting curveballs, 1985's annual report readers must devote extra time and attention to entries above the bottom line, and to footnotes. But then, the most successful investors already know that.

Source: Greene, Richard, "Recommended Reading," Forbes Inc. *Forbes*, 137 (May 5, 1986), 82–83.

Limitations of the Balance Sheet

Although a firm's balance sheet might be prepared within guidelines of generally accepted accounting practice,[2] the analyst must be aware of certain limitations of the statement. Some of the more important ones to the financial analyst are listed below:

1. The balance sheet does not reflect current value, because accountants have adopted historical cost as the basis for valuing and reporting assets and liabilities.[3]
2. Estimates must be used to determine the level of several accounts. Examples

---

[2] The sources of accounting principles are many; however, the main contributors certainly have been the Opinions of the Accounting Principles Board (APB), which was created by the American Institute of Certified Public Accountants (AICPA), and since 1973 the Financial Accounting Standards of the Financial Accounting Standards Board (FASB).

[3] There has been some interest among those in the accounting profession to adjust the cost basis of the firm's assets through the use of an index of the general price level. One such index is the "Gross National Product Implicit Price Deflator" issued quarterly by the Office of Business Economics of the Department of Commerce. However, the general policy statement provided by "Opinion 6" of the Accounting Principles Board of the Institute of Certified Public Accountants recommends that accounting statements be prepared and maintained on a cost basis. On March 23, 1976, the Securities and Exchange Commission issued A.S.R. 190, which required the disclosure of replacement cost information for certain very large firms. This represents a first step away from strict adherence to the historical cost principle.

include accounts receivable estimated in terms of collectibility; inventories based on salability; and fixed (noncurrent) assets based on useful life.[4]

3. The depreciation of long-term assets is accepted practice; however, appreciation or enhancement in asset values is generally ignored.[5] This is particularly crucial to firms holding large investments in appreciable assets such as land, timberlands, and mining properties.

4. Many items that have financial value are omitted from the balance sheet because they involve extreme problems of objective evaluation. The most obvious example consists of the human resources of the firm.[6]

In most cases the analyst can do little to alleviate these shortcomings; however, he or she should at least be aware of their existence in order to temper the analysis accordingly.

Income Statement

The **income statement** represents an attempt to measure the net results of the firm's operations over a specified interval, such as one quarter or one year. The income statement (sometimes referred to as a **profit and loss statement**) is compiled on an *accrual* rather than a *cash basis*. This means that an attempt is made to match the firm's revenues from the period's operations with the expenses incurred in generating those revenues. Thus, the reported revenues and expenses need not represent actual cash flows for the period, so that the computed net earnings for the period do not equal the actual cash provided by the firm's operations. A condensed income statement for the year ended December 31, 1987, is provided in Table 3–2 for Jimco, Inc. (The terms used in the income statement are defined in Appendix 3B.)

Net Income and Cash Flow

There are two basic reasons why the firm's net income does not equal net cash flow for the period. First, revenues and expenses are included in the income statement even though no cash flow might have occurred. For example, sales revenues consist of credit as well as cash sales. Furthermore, cash collections from prior period credit sales are not reflected in the current period's sales revenues. In addition, the expenses for the period represent all those expenditures made in the process of generating the period's revenues. Thus, wages, salaries, utilities, and other expenses may not be paid during the period in which they are *recognized* in the income statement. Second, certain expenses included within the income statement are not cash expenses at all. For example, depreciation expense does not involve a cash outflow to the firm, yet

---

[4] In "Opinion 20" the Accounting Principles Board states that preparing financial statements requires estimating the effects of future events. Examples of items for which estimates are necessary include uncollectible receivables, inventory obsolescence, service lives and salvage values of depreciable assets, warranty costs, periods benefited by a defined cost, and recoverable mineral reserves. Since future events cannot be perceived with certainty, estimating requires the exercise of judgment. The implication here is that no reference guidelines can be constructed regarding these estimates; thus subjectivity enters in determining the affected accounts.

[5] The tax act of 1981 created the Accelerated Cost Recovery System (ACRS). This system greatly simplified the determination of asset useful life where accelerated depreciation (cost recovery) was elected. The ACRS was modified slightly by the TEFRA in 1982. See Chapter 2 for a description of ACRS.

[6] The subject of human resource accounting has received increased attention in recent years. For an overview of the subject, see Edwin H. Caplan and Stephen Landeckich, *Human Resource Accounting: Past, Present, and Future* (National Association of Accountants, 1974); and Eric Flamholtz, *Human Resource Accounting* (Encino, CA: Dickinson Publishing Company, 1974).

TABLE 3–2.   Jimco, Inc. Statement of Income for the Year Ended December 31, 1987 ($000 except per share data)

Net sales		$51,000
Cost of goods sold		(38,000)
Gross profit		$13,000
Operating expenses		
Selling expenses	$3,100	
Depreciation expense	500	
General and administrative expense	5,400	(9,000)
Net operating income (NOI)		$ 4,000
Interest expense		(1,000)
Earnings before taxes (EBT)		$ 3,000
Income taxes[a]		(1,200)
Net income (NI)		$ 1,800
Disposition of net income		
Common stock dividends		$ 300
Change in retained earnings		1,500
Per share data (dollars)		
Number of shares of common stock		100,000 shares
Earnings per common share ($1,800,000 ÷ 100,000 shares)		$ 18
Dividends per common share ($ 300,000 ÷ 100,000 shares)		$ 3

[a] A tax rate of 40% on all income is assumed here for simplicity.

it is deducted from revenues for the period in computing net income. Other examples of noncash expenses include the amortization of goodwill, patent rights, and bond discounts. We will elaborate on the difference between cash flow and net income when we discuss the cash budget in the next chapter.

BASIC FINANCIAL MANAGEMENT IN PRACTICE

Why doesn't the net income figure capture managerial success? Because it reflects not only operating decisions, like what style of jeans to sell or where to locate the transmission factory, but also purely financial decisions, like how much leverage to put in the balance sheet. Moreover, a buyer of a business will be much more concerned with its operating income than with the net income. After all, the acquiring company can control leverage, interest costs and taxes by the way it pays for the purchase, but it can't instantly transform a badly managed factory into a good one.

Source: Ozanian, Michael, "How's Business?" Forbes Inc. *Forbes*, 138 (August 11, 1986), 120+.

Statement of Changes in Financial Position

The **statement of changes in financial position** (often referred to as a **source and use of funds statement**) provides an accounting for the resources provided during a specific period and the uses to which they were put. Specifically, the source and use statement provides the basis for answering such questions as these:

1. Where did the profits go?
2. Why were the dividends not larger?

3. Why was money borrowed during the period?
4. How was the expansion in plant and equipment financed?
5. How was the retirement of debt accomplished?
6. What became of the proceeds of the bond issue?

Because of the very useful information found in the source and use statement it has become a standard tool of financial analysis, as well as one of the firm's three basic financial statements.[7]

No single format is universally adopted for the source and use of funds statement. The form used here is as follows:

Cash: Beginning balance
Plus: Sources of cash for the period
Minus: Uses of cash for the period
Cash: Ending balance

The source and use statement explains the changes that took place in the firm's cash balance over the period of interest. Note that *funds* are defined as *cash*, such that the two terms can be used interchangeably.

Sources of Funds

The firm can obtain funds (cash) from one of four principal sources:

1. From its operations (commonly referred to as funds provided by operations)
2. By borrowing (by means of a short-term note payable or long-term debt in the form of a bond issue)
3. By the sale of assets
4. By issuing common or preferred stock

The firm's sources of funds (with the exception of funds provided by operations) can be identified by observing changes in the balance sheet between the beginning and ending of the period for which the statement is being prepared. For example, a decrease in accounts receivable over the period would signal that the firm collected more dollars from its credit accounts than it created through new credit sales; hence this was a source of funds. In general, a decrease in an asset balance denotes a source of funds. Furthermore, an increase in a liability account signals that net additional borrowing took place during the period, thus providing a source of funds to the firm. An increase in the common and preferred stock accounts also indicates sources of funds to the firm. Finally, funds provided by operations are found by summing net income for the period and any noncash expenses (such as depreciation and amortizations of goodwill or bond discount). Note that noncash expenses are deducted from the firm's revenues, since they are tax deductible. However, since no cash changes hands for these noncash expenses, they must be added back to net income to measure the funds provided by the firm's operations. For example, if net income for the period were $40,000 and noncash expenses were $8000, then funds provided by operations would equal $48,000.

---

[7] Opinion 19 of the Accounting Principles Board indicates that the source and use statement should accompany the income statement and balance sheet as a basic financial statement. It also specifies that the statement be entitled the Statement of Changes in Financial Position.

Uses of Funds

A firm uses funds (cash) to purchase assets, repay loans, repurchase outstanding shares of its common and preferred stock, and pay cash dividends to preferred and common stockholders. Thus, uses of funds are just the opposite of the sources discussed earlier. That is, issuing or selling bonds is a source of funds, whereas repaying a loan is a use.

Preparing the Source and Use Statement for Jimco, Inc.

Jimco's comparative balance sheets for 1986 and 1987 are given in Table 3–3. These statements, along with Jimco's 1987 income statement (Table 3–2), provide all the information needed to prepare the firm's statement of sources and uses of funds for the year ended December 31, 1987.

The column entitled *changes* in Table 3–3 provides the basis for determining Jimco's sources and uses of funds. Note that cash decreased by $100,000 during the year. Since this change in cash is *explained* by the statement of sources and uses of funds, we will ignore it for the time being. Marketable securities did not change; thus no source or use of funds was provided. The accounts receivable balance increased by $1,500,000, indicating that more credit sales were made during the period than were collected. Hence, the firm *used* funds to invest in accounts receivable. Likewise, inventories and prepaid expenses increased by $700,000 and $100,000, respectively, indicating uses of funds. In addition, Jimco increased plant and equipment by $1,100,000, which constitutes still another use of funds.[8] Note that the increase in accumulated depreciation of $500,000 equals depreciation expense for the period. Since depreciation expense is included in the source and use statement in conjunction with our analysis of the firm's income statement, we will defer considering this item.

Looking at the changes in the firm's liabilities, we note first that accounts payable decreased by $200,000. This indicates that the firm paid off more accounts payable than it created during the year. This constitutes a use of funds. Notes payable increased by $2,500,000, signaling a source of funds from short-term borrowing. The accrued salaries, wages, and other expense accounts decreased by $700,000 during the period, which indicates a use of funds. Deferred income taxes increased by $100,000 (source). Both the first mortgage bonds and the debenture bonds decreased for the period by $300,000 and $100,000, respectively. Both decreases constitute uses of funds for the period.

The common stock accounts (common stock at par and paid-in capital) did not change for the period, indicating no new stock was issued and none was repurchased. Jimco's retained earnings increased by $1,500,000. This represents the net income for 1987 of $1,800,000 less common stock dividends of $300,000. Since net income is included as a source of funds (as a part of funds provided by operations) and

---

[8] The use of funds attributed to the purchase of plant and equipment can also be obtained from an analysis of the change in the net plant and equipment account. For Jimco, Inc., this can be accomplished as follows:

Net plant and equipment (1987)	$5000
Plus: Depreciation expense for the period	500
	5500
Less: Net plant and equipment (1986)	(4400)
Net purchase (sale) of plant and equipment	$1100

TABLE 3–3. Jimco, Inc. Comparative Balance Sheets December 31, 1986 and 1987 ($000)

Assets			
	1986	*1987*	*Changes*
Current assets:			
Cash	$ 1,500	$ 1,400	$ (100)
Marketable securities	300	300	—
Accounts receivable	8,500	10,000	1,500
Inventories	11,300	12,000	700
Prepaid expenses	200	300	100
Total current assets	$21,800	$24,000	$2,200
Fixed assets:			
Land	$ 2,000	$ 2,000	$ —
Plant and equipment	11,200	12,300	1,100
Less: Accumulated depreciation	(6,800)	(7,300)	(500)
Net plant and equipment	4,400	5,000	600
Total fixed assets	6,400	7,000	600
Total assets	$28,200	$31,000	$2,800

Liabilities and Owner's Equity			
	1986	*1987*	*Changes*
Current liabilities:			
Accounts payable	$ 3,200	$ 3,000	$ (200)
Notes payable	900	3,400	2,500
Accrued salaries, wages, and other expenses	3,800	3,100	(700)
Current portion of long-term debt	500	500	—
Total current liabilities	$ 8,400	$10,000	$1,600
Long-term liabilities:			
Deferred income taxes	$ 1,400	$ 1,500	$ 100
First mortgage bonds	6,600	6,300	(300)
Debenture bonds	3,000	2,900	(100)
Total long-term liabilities	$11,000	$10,700	$ (300)
Owners' equity:			
Common stock (par value $1.00)	$ 100	$ 100	—
Additional paid-in capital	2,000	$ 2,000	—
Retained earnings	6,700	8,200	$1,500
Total owners' equity	$ 8,800	$10,300	$1,500
Total liabilities and owners' equity	$28,200	$31,000	$2,800

dividends are accounted for as a use of funds, the change in the retained earnings account is not used directly in preparing the source and use of funds statement.

To summarize, sources and uses are determined by analyzing the changes in the balance sheet accounts between two points in time (for example, between December 31, 1986, and December 31, 1987). However, the change in accumulated depreciation in the balance sheet is disregarded. In place of this change, we show the depreciation expense for the year as a source of funds. Also, the change in retained earnings is not included directly in the statement. Since the change in retained earnings equals net income less dividends paid, we prefer to list these latter items separately in place of the change in retained earnings.

TABLE 3–4. Jimco, Inc. Statement of Sources and Uses of Funds for the Year Ended December 31, 1987 ($000)

Cash balance (December 31, 1986)		$1,500	
Sources of funds:			
Funds provided by operations:			
Net income	$1,800		
Depreciation	500	2,300	47%
Increase in deferred income taxes		100	2%
Increase in notes payable		2,500	51%
Total funds provided		$4,900	100%
Uses of funds:			
Common stock dividends		$ 300	6%
Purchase of plant and equipment		1,100	22%
Increase in accounts receivable		1,500	30%
Increase in inventories		700	14%
Increase in prepaid expenses		100	2%
Decrease in accounts payable		200	4%
Decrease in accrued salaries, wages, and other expenses		700	14%
Decrease in mortgage bonds		300	6%
Decrease in debenture bonds		100	2%
Total uses of funds		$5,000	100%
Cash balance (December 31, 1987)		$1,400	

Table 3–4 contains Jimco's statement of sources and uses of funds for the year ended December 31, 1987. Note that Jimco's sources of funds were from operations (47%), deferred taxes (2%), and notes payable (51%). The firm's principal uses of funds related to the purchase of plant and equipment (22%); increases in accounts receivable (30%) and inventories (14%); and reductions in accounts payable (4%) and accrued expenses (14%). Thus, the source and use of funds statement provides the analyst with a useful tool for determining *where the firm obtained cash* during a prior period and *how that cash was spent*.

FINANCIAL RATIOS

Financial ratios give the analyst a way of making meaningful comparisons of a firm's financial data at different points in time and with other firms. For example, the inventories for a firm with $10 million in annual sales would be expected to be larger than those for a comparable firm with sales of only $5 million. However, the ratio of sales to inventory might well be similar for the two firms. *Thus, financial ratios represent an attempt to standardize financial information to facilitate meaningful comparisons*.

Financial ratios provide the basis for answering some very important questions concerning the financial *well-being* of the firm. Examples include the following:

1. *How liquid is the firm?* Liquidity refers to the firm's ability to meet maturing obligations and to convert assets into cash. This factor is obviously very important to the firm's creditors.

2. *Is management generating sufficient profits from the firm's assets?* Since the primary purpose for purchasing an asset is to produce profits, the analyst often seeks an indication of the adequacy of the profits being realized. If the level of

profits appears insufficient in relation to the investment, an investigation into the reasons for the inferior returns is in order.

3. *How does the firm's management finance its investments?* These decisions have a direct impact upon the returns provided to the common stockholders.

4. *Are the common stockholders receiving sufficient returns on their investment?* The objective of the financial manager is to maximize the value of the firm's common stock, and the level of returns being received by the investors relative to their investment is a key factor in determining that value.

The mathematical skills required in ratio analysis are quite simple. However, using and interpreting financial ratios to answer questions such as those stated above requires a great deal of skill and a thorough understanding of the tools of financial analysis. The balance of this chapter will be devoted to a discussion of financial ratios and their use in financial analysis.

Using Financial Ratios

Financial ratios provide useful tools for analysis when compared against a standard or norm. Two such norms are commonly used. The first consists of similar ratios for the same firm from previous financial statements. An analysis based upon comparisons of this type is commonly referred to as a **trend analysis.** A second norm comes from the ratios of other firms that are considered comparable in their general characteristics to the subject firm—generally this involves the use of published industry average ratios.

There are two widely used sources of industry average ratios. Dun and Bradstreet publishes annually a set of 14 key ratios for each of the 125 lines of business. Robert Morris Associates, the national association of bank loan and credit officers, publishes a set of 16 key ratios for over 300 lines of business. Table 3–5 gives an example of Robert Morris standard ratios for the farm machinery and equipment manufacturing industry.

The ratio norms in Table 3–5 are classified by firm size to provide the basis for more meaningful comparisons. Thus, a firm with total assets of less than $1 million would not be compared with firms having a much larger asset base. Note also that **common size financial statements** are reported as well as the 16 key ratios. The common size balance sheet simply represents each asset, liability, and owner's equity account as a percent of total assets, whereas each entry in the income statement is stated as a percent of sales. Thus, ratios have been effectively related to each of the 17 entries in the balance sheet and 6 entries in the income statement. Furthermore, three levels are reported for each of the 16 key ratios. These refer to the first, second, and third quartiles. Thus, the analyst is given some idea as to how much variation exists within the industry in regard to each ratio.

Categories of Financial Ratios

For ease of presentation we shall discuss financial ratios in terms of four basic categories, each representing an important aspect of the firm's financial condition. The categories consist of liquidity, efficiency, leverage, and profitability ratios. Each category is discussed through the use of an example set of financial ratios computed using the 1987 financial statements of Jimco, Inc. Jimco's balance sheet and income statement were presented in Tables 3–1 and 3–2, respectively.

Jimco, Inc. is involved in the manufacture and sale of light-duty garden tractors and implements. The firm has been in business for more than 20 years and is considered by its competitors to be well managed.

Liquidity Ratios

Liquidity ratios provide the basis for answering the question, *Does the firm have sufficient cash and near cash assets to pay its bills on time?*

Current liabilities represent the firm's maturing financial obligations. The firm's ability to repay these obligations when due depends largely on whether it has sufficient cash together with other assets that can be converted into cash before the current liabilities mature. The firm's current assets are the primary sources of funds to repay current and maturing financial obligations. Thus, a logical measure of liquidity is found in the *current ratio*.

Current Ratio. The **current ratio** is computed as follows:

$$\text{current ratio} = \frac{\text{current assets}}{\text{current liabilities}}$$

$$= \frac{\$24,000,000}{\$10,000,000} \qquad (3\text{--}1)$$

$$= 2.40 \text{ times}$$

$$\text{industry average} = 1.7 \text{ times}$$

Thus, for 1987 Jimco's current assets were 2.40 times larger than its current liabilities. Although no firm plans to liquidate a major portion of its current assets to meet its matching current liabilities, this ratio does indicate the margin of safety (the liquidity) of the firm.

Using the industry norms provided in Table 3–5, Jimco's current ratio is higher than the median industry ratio of 1.7.[9] Note that Jimco has between $10 million and $50 million in total assets; thus the third-column figures are appropriate. In addition, Jimco's 2.40 current ratio falls well within range of the first and third quartile of 1.4 to 4.0 observed for its industry. Thus, Jimco's current ratio is not *out of line* with respect to many of the firms in its industry.

Acid Test or Quick Ratio. Since inventories are generally the least liquid of the firm's assets, it may be desirable to remove them from the numerator of the current ratio, thus obtaining a more refined liquidity measure. For Jimco, the **acid test ratio** is computed below:

$$\text{acid test ratio} = \frac{\text{current assets} - \text{inventories}}{\text{current liabilities}}$$

$$= \frac{\$12,000,000}{\$10,000,000} \qquad (3\text{--}2)$$

$$= 1.20 \text{ times}$$

$$\text{industry average} = .6$$

[9] Note that *1986* industry ratios are used in the analysis, since more recent information was not available at the time of writing. The analyst will find that published industry averages are generally a year behind, owing to the time required to collect and publish them.

TABLE 3–5. Robert Morris Associates Industry Average Ratios, 1986

Manufacturers Farm Machinery & Equipment	63(6/30–9/30/85)			59(10/1/85–3/31/86)		
Asset Size **Number of Statements**[b]	**0–1MM**[a] **29**	**1–10MM** **68**	**10–50MM** **19**	**50–100MM** **6**	**All** **122**	
Assets	%	%	%	%	%	
Cash and equivalents	3.7	7.9	5.9		6.5	
Accounts and notes receivable–trade (net)	21.3	20.4	21.0		20.7	
Inventory	40.7	41.5	45.4		42.0	
All other current	1.8	2.5	2.3		2.4	
Total current	67.4	72.4	74.6		71.6	
Fixed assets (net)	22.8	23.2	20.0		22.4	
Intangibles (net)	1.0	.2	.1		.4	
All other noncurrent	8.7	4.2	5.3		5.6	
Total assets	100.0	100.0	100.0		100.0	
Liabilities						
Notes payable—short term	16.8	15.8	16.1		16.1	
Current maturity—LTD	8.1	5.6	3.9		5.8	
Accounts and notes payable—trade	13.1	11.9	10.8		12.0	
Income taxes payable	.5	.3	.5		.5	
All other current	5.7	6.8	9.4		7.0	
Total current	44.2	40.4	40.6		41.4	
Long-term debt	20.1	19.3	17.2		18.8	
Deferred taxes	.2	.8	.6		.7	
All other noncurrent	3.7	1.4	.5		1.9	
Net worth	31.7	38.1	41.0		37.3	
Total liabilities and net worth	100.0	100.0	100.0		100.0	
Income data						
Net sales	100.0	100.0	100.0		100.0	
Gross profit	34.6	28.5	26.6		30.0	
Operating expenses	36.4	24.6	22.1		27.3	
Operating profit	−1.7	3.9	4.6		2.6	
All other expenses (net)	2.8	2.1	3.8		2.5	
Profit before taxes	−4.6	1.8	.8		.1	
Ratios[c]						
Current	2.6	2.6	4.0		2.5	
	1.5	1.8	1.7		1.7	
	1.1	1.4	1.4		1.3	
Quick	1.1	1.3	1.0		1.2	
	.6	.6	.6		.6	
	.2	.4	.4		.3	
Sales/receivables[d]	20 18.4	24 15.4	30 12.2		24 15.3	
	32 11.3	43 8.5	46 8.0		41 8.8	
	64 5.7	57 6.4	83 4.4		63 5.8	
Cost of sales/inventory[e]	73 5.0	94 3.9	89 4.1		87 4.2	
	126 2.9	122 3.0	159 2.3		130 2.8	
	192 1.9	166 2.2	243 1.5		183 2.0	
Cost of sales/payables	13 27.4	16 23.5	15 23.8		15 23.6	
	26 14.0	27 13.5	24 15.2		28 13.1	
	51 7.2	46 8.0	42 8.7		47 7.8	
Sales/working capital	3.9	3.5	2.7		3.4	
	8.0	5.1	4.4		5.1	
	21.5	9.1	9.2		9.9	

TABLE 3–5. *(continued)*

Manufacturers Farm Machinery & Equipment	63(6/30–9/30/85)		59(10/1/85–3/31/86)		
Asset Size **Number of Statements[b]**	**0–1MM[a]** **29**	**1–10MM** **68**	**10–50MM** **19**	**50–100MM** **6**	**All** **122**
ratios[c]					
EBIT/interest	(25) 3.3 1.4 −.8	(66) 3.2 1.5 .7	2.1 1.3 .3		(115) 3.1 1.4 .4
Cash flow/current maturity of long-term debt	(14) 1.3 .5 −2.7	(47) 4.7 2.1 .3	(15) 4.4 .8 −.1		(81) 3.5 1.4 .1
Fixed assets/tangible net worth	.3 .8 1.8	.3 .6 1.2	.3 .5 .7		.3 .6 1.2
Total debt/tangible net worth	.9 2.8 12.0	.8 1.7 3.9	1.0 1.7 2.3		.9 2.0 3.8
Profit before taxes/tangible net worth (%)	(25) 28.4 6.8 −50.0	(65) 22.2 7.2 −7.0	15.9 4.9 −8.8		(115) 22.6 7.2 −8.8
Profit before taxes/total assets (%)	10.5 1.6 −13.6	7.6 2.6 −2.3	6.7 1.5 −3.1		8.3 2.3 −3.6
Sales/net fixed assets	19.3 10.6 5.3	12.3 7.5 5.2	13.0 7.8 4.9		13.1 7.5 5.2
Sales/total assets	2.6 1.7 1.3	2.1 1.7 1.3	1.9 1.5 1.0		2.1 1.6 1.3
Depreciation, depletion, amortization/ sales (%)	(26) 1.7 3.1 4.1	(62) 1.4 2.3 3.8	(18) 1.4 2.2 2.9		(112) 1.4 2.4 3.8
Officers' compensation/sales (%)		(22) 1.3 2.0 4.1			(34) 1.7 3.3 7.0
Net sales ($) Total assets ($)	28398M[f] 15401M	399237M 247773M	592449M 388115M	532810M 383468M	1552894M 1034757M

[a] MM = $ million.

[b] When there are fewer than ten financial statements for a particular size category, the composite data are not shown in that category because such a small sample is usually not represented and could be misleading.

[c] Three ratio values are reported. The middle value is the median and represents the ratio falling halfway between the strongest ratio and the weakest ratio. The figure that falls halfway between the median and the strongest ratio is the upper quartile and the figure that falls halfway between the median and the weakest ratio is the lower quartile.

[d] The columns in bold type are "days' receivables" or average collection period.

[e] The column in bold type are "days' inventory" or the average number of days that a dollar is held in inventory.

[f] M = $ thousand.

Once again Jimco's acid test ratio is higher than the median ratio for its industry of .6. In this instance Jimco's acid test ratio is even higher than the third quartile (1.0), indicating a very strong liquidity position. Thus, on the basis of its current and acid test ratios, Jimco offers no visible evidence of a liquidity problem.

Efficiency Ratios

Efficiency ratios provide the basis for assessing how effectively the firm is using its resources to generate sales. For example, a firm that produces $8 million in sales using $4 million in assets is certainly using its resources more efficiently than a similar firm that had $6 million invested in assets.

Efficiency ratios could be defined for each asset category in which a firm invests. Our discussion will include a limited number of key efficiency ratios, related to accounts receivable, inventories, net fixed assets, and total assets.

Average Collection Period. The **average collection period ratio** served as the basis for determining how rapidly the firm's credit accounts are being collected. The lower this number is, other things being the same, the more efficient the firm is in managing its investment in accounts receivable. We can also think of this ratio in terms of the number of daily credit sales contained in accounts receivable. That is, the average collection period is equal to the accounts receivable balance divided by the firm's average daily credit sales. Computing the ratio for Jimco, we find

$$\text{average collection period} = \frac{\text{accounts receivable}}{\text{annual credit sales}/360}$$

$$= \frac{\$10,000,000}{\$(51,000,000/360)} = 70.6 \tag{3-3}$$

$$\text{industry average} = 45 \text{ days}$$

Therefore, on average, Jimco collects its credit sales every 70.6 days.

The **accounts receivable turnover ratio** is often used in the place of the average collection period ratio, since it contains the same information content as the average collection period. For Jimco this ratio would equal

$$\text{accounts receivable turnover} = \frac{\text{credit sales}}{\text{accounts receivable}}$$

$$= \frac{\$51,000,000}{\$10,000,000} = 5.10 \text{ times} \tag{3-4}$$

Thus, Jimco is turning its accounts receivable over at a rate of 5.10 times per year. This easily translates into an average collection period of 70.6 days. That is, if Jimco's receivables turnover is 5.10 times in a 360-day year, then its average collection period must be 360/5.10 = 70.6 days.

The industry norm for the receivables turnover ratio is 8.0 times, which translates into an average collection period of 360/8 = 45 days. In terms of both standards Jimco does not compare favorably with the industry norm. In fact, Jimco's average collection period is only slightly less than the highest quartile (lowest in terms of receivable turnover) in the industry. This *could* indicate the presence of some slow-paying accounts, which calls for analysis in greater depth.[10] Before performing such an analysis it is necessary to know whether Jimco's credit terms are longer than those of other firms in the industry. For example, if Jimco allows its customers terms calling for payment in 75 days when 45 days is the industry norm, then the longer average collection period is to be expected.

Inventory Turnover. The effectiveness or efficiency with which a firm is managing its investment in inventories is reflected in the number of times that its inventories are turned over (replaced) during the year. The **inventory turnover ratio** is defined as follows:

$$\text{inventory turnover} = \frac{\text{cost of goods sold}}{\text{inventories}}$$

$$= \frac{\$38{,}000{,}000}{\$12{,}000{,}000} \tag{3-5}$$

$$= 3.17 \text{ times}$$

$$\text{industry average} = 2.3 \text{ times}$$

Thus, Jimco turns over its inventories 3.17 times per year.[11] Where quarterly or monthly information is available, an average inventory figure should be used in order to eliminate the influence of any seasonality in inventory levels from the ratio.

Jimco's inventory turnover ratio of 3.17 compares very favorably with the industry norm of 2.3 times. Therefore, Jimco invests less in inventories per dollar of sales than does the average firm in its industry.

Fixed Asset Turnover. To measure the efficiency with which the firm utilizes its investment in fixed assets, we calculate the **fixed asset turnover ratio** as follows:

$$\text{fixed asset turnover} = \frac{\text{sales}}{\text{net fixed assets}}$$

$$= \frac{\$51{,}000{,}000}{\$7{,}000{,}000} \tag{3-6}$$

$$= 7.286 \text{ times}$$

$$\text{industry average} = 7.8 \text{ times}$$

---

[10] Although it will not be discussed here, one tool for further assessing the liquidity of a firm's receivables is an **aging of accounts receivable schedule.** Such a schedule identifies the number and dollar value of accounts outstanding for various periods. For example, accounts that are less than 10 days old, 11 to 20 days, and so forth might be examined. Still another way to construct the schedule would involve analyzing the length of time to eventual collection of accounts over a past period. For example, how many accounts were outstanding less than 10 days when collected, between 10 and 20 days, and so forth.

[11] Some analysts prefer the use of sales in the numerator of the inventory turnover ratio. However, cost of goods sold is used here, since inventories are stated at cost, and to use sales in the numerator would add a potential source of distortion to the ratio when comparisons are made across firms that have different "markups" on their cost of goods sold.

Thus, Jimco appears to have a slightly larger investment in fixed assets relative to its sales volume than is the case for the industry norm.

Total Asset Turnover. The **total asset turnover ratio** indicates how many dollars in sales the firm squeezes out of each dollar it has invested in assets. For Jimco, we calculate this ratio as follows:

$$\text{total asset turnover} = \frac{\text{sales}}{\text{total assets}}$$

$$= \frac{\$51{,}000{,}000}{\$31{,}000{,}000} \quad\quad (3\text{--}7)$$

$$= 1.645 \text{ times}$$

$$\text{industry average} = 1.5 \text{ times}$$

Jimco's total asset turnover ratio compares satisfactorily with the industry norm of 1.5. This ratio indicates that Jimco's management has efficiently utilized its resources in generating sales as compared with other firms in its industry.

Since total assets equals the sum of fixed and current assets, we can use our turnover ratios for both total and fixed assets to analyze the efficiency with which the firm manages its investment in current assets. For example, since Jimco's total asset turnover ratio was higher than the industry norm, the lower than average fixed asset turnover indicates that Jimco's investment in current assets must be smaller, in relation to sales, than the industry norm.

Leverage Ratios

Leverage ratios provide the basis for answering two questions: *How has the firm financed its assets?* and *Can the firm afford the level of fixed charges associated with its use of non-owner-supplied funds such as bond interest and principal repayments?* The first answer is sought through the use of *balance sheet leverage ratios*, the second by using income statement based on ratios, or simply *coverage ratios*.

It will be useful at this point to define **leverage.** As related to financial ratios the term will be used to mean financial leverage.[12] Financial leverage results when a firm obtains financing for its investments from sources other than the firm's owners. For a corporation, this means funds from any source other than the common stockholders. Thus, **financial leverage** will be defined here as resulting from the firm's use of debt financing, financial leases, and preferred stock. These sources of financing share a common characteristic: They all require a fixed cash payment or return for their use. That is, debt requires contractually set interest and principal payments, leases require fixed rental payments, and preferred stock usually requires a fixed cash dividend. This attribute provides the basis for the *leverage* in financial leverage. If the firm earns a return higher than that which is required by the suppliers of leverage funds, then the excess goes to the common stockholders. However, should the return earned fall below the required return, then the common stockholders must make up the

---

[12] The concept of leverage is discussed more fully in Chapter 14.

difference out of the returns on their invested funds. This, in a nutshell, is the concept of financial leverage.

Balance Sheet Leverage Ratios. These ratios provide the basis for answering the question, *Where did the firm obtain the financing for its investments?* The label **balance sheet leverage ratios** is used to indicate that these ratios are computed using information from the balance sheet alone.

Debt Ratio. The **debt ratio** measures the extent to which the total assets of the firm have been financed using borrowed funds. For Jimco, the ratio is computed as follows:

$$\text{debt ratio} = \frac{\text{total liabilities}}{\text{total assets}} \text{ or}$$

$$\frac{\text{current liabilities} + \text{noncurrent liabilities}}{\text{total assets}}$$

$$= \frac{\$(10{,}000{,}000 + 10{,}700{,}000)}{\$31{,}000{,}000} \tag{3-8}$$

$$= .668, \text{ or } 66.8\%$$

$$\text{industry average} = 58.9\%$$

Thus, Jimco has financed approximately 67 percent of its assets with borrowed funds. This compares with only 58.9 percent for the industry. Note that this ratio is found by using the common size balance sheet in Table 3–5. Simply sum the percent of total assets financed by current liabilities, long-term debt, and all other noncurrent liabilities. Jimco has relied on the use of nonowner financing to a far greater extent than the average firm in its industry. This, in turn, will mean that Jimco may have difficulty trying to borrow additional funds in the future.

Long-Term Debt to Total Capitalization. The **long-term debt** to **total capitalization ratio** indicates the extent to which the firm has used long-term debt in its permanent financing. **Total capitalization** represents the sum of all the permanent sources of financing used by the firm, including long-term debt, preferred stock, and common equity. For Jimco, the ratio is computed as follows:

$$\frac{\text{long-term debt}}{\text{to total capitalization}} = \frac{\text{long-term (noncurrent) liabilities}}{\text{long-term debt} + \text{preferred stock} + \text{common equity}}$$

$$= \frac{\$10{,}700{,}000}{(\$10{,}700{,}000 + 10{,}300{,}000)} \tag{3-9}$$

$$= .509, \text{ or } 50.9\%$$

$$\text{industry average} = 28.96\%$$

Therefore, Jimco has obtained a little more than half its permanent financing from debt sources.

Once again referring to the common size balance sheet in Table 3–5 for an industry norm, note that current liabilities account for 40.6 percent of total assets; thus permanent financing is equal to $(1 - .406)$, or 59.4 percent of total assets. Furthermore, long-term debt accounts for 17.2 percent of total assets; thus it accounts for $17.2/59.4 = 28.96$ percent of the firm's total capitalization. It is evident that Jimco utilizes far more long-term debt in its total capitalization than is characteristic of its industry.

One final point should be made concerning the balance sheet leverage ratios. This point concerns the importance of lease financing as a source of financial leverage. Since most firms must include the present value of long-term financial lease agreements in the assets and liabilities of the balance sheet, it is now possible to assess their impact on the firm's balance sheet leverage ratios.[13] Annual lease payments generally are contained in footnotes to the firm's financial statements; thus, their effect on the firm's coverage ratios, which are discussed next, can be assessed.

Coverage Ratios. These ratios are a second category of leverage ratios and they are used to measure the firm's ability to cover the finance charges associated with its use of financial leverage. Thus, they provide the basis for answering the question, Has the firm used too much financial leverage?

Times Interest Earned Ratio. The **times interest earned ratio** indicates the firm's ability to meet its interest payments out of its annual operating earnings. The ratio measures the number of times the firm is covering its interest. Jimco's ratio is computed as follows:[14]

$$\begin{array}{l} \text{times} \\ \text{interest} \\ \text{earned} \end{array} = \frac{\begin{array}{c}\text{net operating income (NOI) or}\\ \text{earnings before interest and taxes (EBIT)}\end{array}}{\text{annual interest expense}}$$

$$= \frac{\$4,000,000}{\$1,000,000} \qquad\qquad (3\text{--}10)$$

$$= 4.00 \text{ times}$$

$$\text{industry average} = 1.3 \text{ times}$$

This ratio is much higher than the industry norm of 1.3 times, which is somewhat surprising in light of Jimco's higher than average use of financial leverage. However,

---

[13] The Financial Accounting Standards Board in late 1976 issued Statement No. 13, which established that a lease that transfers substantially all of the benefits and risks incident to the ownership of property should be accounted for as an acquisition of an asset and the incurrence of an obligation by the lessee. As a result, many firms are now forced to include the value of their lease agreements directly in the balance sheet rather than treat them as operating leases which are reported in footnotes to the balance sheet. Chapter 18 discusses lease accounting further.

[14] The interchangeable use of EBIT and NOI presumes there was no "other" income earned by the firm. If the presence of other nonoperating income is thought to be transitory, then NOI should be used; if not, then EBIT is appropriate.

it appears that Jimco's earnings are such that it can reasonably *afford* the higher use of financial leverage.

The times interest earned ratio, although useful, has a number of potential weaknesses. First, net operating income (or EBIT) does not reflect the total amount of earnings available to meet interest and other finance-related charges. Specifically, net operating income understates the amount of income available to meet finance charges by an amount equal to the firm's depreciation expense for the period.[15] Also, when rental expense is considered to be one of the firm's fixed finance charges, it must be added to net operating income to determine the level of operating earnings available to cover finance charges. Note that rent expense is considered an operating expense in the preparation of the income statement. Therefore, it is subtracted from revenues in the process of computing net operating earnings or EBIT.

The second basic objection to the times interest earned ratio relates to the fact that the denominator of the ratio includes interest expense as the sole finance charge that must be covered. In practice, the firm must meet lease payments, principal payments, and preferred dividends to satisfy the claims resulting from its use of financial leverage. The next ratio described attempts to rectify each of these weaknesses.

Cash Flow Overall Coverage Ratio.   The purpose of this ratio is to compare the cash flow (from net operating income) available to meet fixed financial commitments against the cash flow requirements of these obligations. The financial commitments to be recognized include interest, lease payments, preferred dividends, and debt principal repayments. The cash available to pay these obligations equals net operating income plus depreciation. We also add lease payments to operating income plus depreciation, since lease payments have been deducted from revenues to calculate net operating income. We adjust debt principal repayment and preferred stock dividends which are not tax deductible to a before-tax basis, since we need to compute the amount of before-tax cash flows that are required to make these payments. For instance, we might assume that Jimco's current portion of long-term debt ($500,000) equals the principal repayment for the period. However, to pay $500,000 using after-tax income, we would have to earn $833,333 before taxes. That is, $833,333 income less taxes at a 40 percent rate ($333,333 = .40 times $833,333) leaves $500,000 after taxes to make the principal repayment. For preferred stock dividends and debt principal repayment, we have to make the following adjustments:

$$\text{before-tax cost of preferred stock dividends} = \frac{\text{preferred stock dividend}}{(1 - \text{marginal tax rate})}$$

$$\text{before-tax debt principal repayment requirement} = \frac{\text{principal repayment}}{(1 - \text{marginal tax rate})}$$

---

[15] Net operating income plus depreciation expense provides an estimate as to the cash flow available to cover the firm's finance charges from its operations. As stated earlier, a number of sources of cash are not related to the firm's operating earnings, such as the sale of assets or issuance of debt or equity. However, these sources are temporary in that they cannot be continually called upon to provide the basis for meeting the firm's annual finance charges. Thus operating earnings (EBIT) provides a more meaningful basis for computing a firm's coverage ratios.

We can now compute Jimco's cash flow coverage ratio, as follows:

$$\text{cash flow overall coverage ratio} = \frac{\text{net operating income + lease expense + depreciation}}{\text{interest + lease expense + preferred dividends}/(1 - \text{marginal tax rate}) + \text{principal payments}/(1 - \text{marginal tax rate})} \quad (3\text{--}11)$$

$$= \frac{\$(4,000,000 + 500,000)}{\$(1,000,000 + 500,000/(1 - .40))}$$

$$= \frac{\$4,500,000}{\$1,833,333} = 2.45 \text{ times}$$

Thus, Jimco's operating earnings were 4.00 times its interest expense, whereas the firm's operating cash flows were only 2.45 times its total finance charges.

One further refinement may be desirable in the cash flow overall coverage ratio. This relates to the coverage of any common dividends the firm wishes to pay. For example, should Jimco desire to pay dividends to the common stockholders totaling $300,000, then the firm must earn $300,000/(1 - .40) = $500,000 on a before-tax basis. Adding this figure for common dividends to the firm's existing finance charges reduces the coverage ratio to 1.93 times. This latter version of the coverage ratio will prove particularly useful when the firm is analyzing alternative sources of long-term financing and wishes to maintain a stable dividend payment to its common stockholders.

Summarizing the results of Jimco's leverage ratios, we have made two basic observations: First, Jimco has utilized more nonowner financing than is characteristic of its industry. Second, Jimco's earnings are such that it can apparently afford the higher use of financial leverage.

Profitability Ratios

The ratios discussed here help us answer some very important questions regarding the effectiveness of the firm's management in producing profits from the resources entrusted to them. Specifically, **profitability ratios** can be used to answer such questions as these: *How much of each sales dollar was management able to convert into profits? How much profit did the firm earn on each dollar of assets under its control?* For discussion purposes we will divide profitability ratios into two groups: profitability in relation to sales and profitability in relation to investment.

Profitability in Relation to Sales. These ratios can be used to assess the ability of the firm's management to control the various expenses involved in generating sales. The profit ratios discussed here are commonly referred to as **profit margins** and include the gross profit margin, operating profit margin, and net profit margin.

Gross Profit Margin. The **gross profit margin** is calculated as follows:

$$\text{gross profit margin} = \frac{\text{gross profit}}{\text{net sales}}$$

$$= \frac{\$13,000,000}{\$51,000,000} \qquad (3\text{–}12)$$

$$= .255, \text{ or } 25.5\%$$

$$\text{industry average} = 26.6\%$$

Thus Jimco's gross profit constitutes 25.5 percent of firm sales. This margin reflects the firm's markup on its cost of goods sold as well as the ability of management to minimize the firm's cost of goods sold in relation to sales (and the method for determining that cost).

The common size income statement found in Table 3–5 provides an industry norm of 26.6 percent. Thus, Jimco's gross profit margin does not appear to be out of line. Note that the gross profit margin reflects both the level of Jimco's cost of goods sold and the size of the firm's markup on those costs, or its pricing policy.

Operating Profit Margin. Moving down the income statement, the next profit figure encountered is net operating income (or earnings before interest and taxes— EBIT). This profit figure serves as the basis for computing the **operating profit margin.** For Jimco this profit margin is found as follows:

$$\text{operating profit margin} = \frac{\text{net operating income}}{\text{sales}}$$

$$= \frac{\$4,000,000}{\$51,000,000} \qquad (3\text{–}13)$$

$$= .0784, \text{ or } 7.84\%$$

$$\text{industry average} = 4.6\%$$

The operating profit margin reflects the firm's operating expenses as well as its cost of goods sold. Therefore, this ratio serves as an overall measure of operating effectiveness.

Again the industry norm is obtained from the common size income statement in Table 3–5. Jimco's operating profit margin is much greater than the industry norm of 4.6 percent. This is true in spite of the fact that the gross profit margin (25.5 percent) was less than its industry norm (26.6 percent). Thus, Jimco's operating expenses per dollar of sales were well below the industry norm.

Net Profit Margin. The final profit margin considered involves the net after-tax profits of the firm as a percent of sales. For Jimco the **net profit margin** is computed as follows:

$$\text{net profit margin} = \frac{\text{net income}}{\text{sales}} = \frac{\$1,800,000}{\$51,000,000} = .035, \text{ or } 3.5\% \qquad (3.14)$$

$$\text{industry average} = .5\%$$

Therefore, $.035 of each sales dollar is converted into profits after taxes. Note that this profit margin reflects the firm's cost of goods sold, operating expenses, finance charges (interest expense), and taxes. For the industry, profits before taxes are .8 percent of sales. Assuming that firms on the average pay approximately 40 percent of their taxable earnings in taxes, this produces a net profit margin of .008 (1 − .40) = .0048, or .5 percent. Hence, Jimco's net profit margin is far above par for its industry. In the next category of profitability ratios we investigate this above-average net profit margin to find out whether it results in an above-average return on the firm's total investment, and more important, to find out the return on the investment of the common stockholders.

Profitability in Relation to Investment. This category of profitability ratios attempts to measure firm profits in relation to the invested funds used to generate those profits. Thus, these ratios are very useful in assessing the overall effectiveness of the firm's management.

Operating Income Return on Investment. The **operating income return on investment** reflects the rate of return on the firm's total investment before interest and taxes. For Jimco, this return measure is computed as follows:

$$\text{operating income return on investment} = \frac{\text{net operating income}}{\text{total assets}}$$

$$= \frac{\$4,000,000}{\$31,000,000} \qquad (3\text{--}15)$$

$$= .129, \text{ or } 12.9\%$$

$$\text{industry average} = 6.9\%$$

Jimco's management produced a 12.9 percent return on its total assets before interest and taxes have been paid.[16] It is this 12.9 percent rate of return that should be compared with the cost of borrowed funds to determine whether leverage is *favorable* or *unfavorable*. If the firm is borrowing at a cost less than 12.9 percent, then leverage is favorable and will result in higher after-tax earnings to its stockholders.[17]

---

[16] Intangible assets are often subtracted from total assets in an effort to measure the firm's return on invested capital. The lack of physical qualities of intangible assets makes evidence of their existence elusive, their value often difficult to estimate, and their useful lives indeterminable. The Accounting Principles Board gives this subject attention in Opinion 17. However, since Jimco has no intangible assets, no adjustment is necessary.

[17] The concept of leverage is fully developed in Chapter 14. Very simply, when a firm borrows money that requires a fixed return, then the return to the common shareholders will be enhanced only if the return the firm earns on these borrowed funds exceeds their cost. For the firm as a whole the operating income rate of return measures the before-tax-and-interest rate of return on the firm's investment. This

This rate of return is particularly useful when assessing the operating effectiveness of the firm's management. The operating return on investment does not reflect the influence of the firm's use of financial leverage; thus it provides a measure of management's effectiveness in making operating decisions as opposed to financing decisions. The reason is that neither the numerator (operating income) nor the denominator (total assets) is affected by the way in which the firm has financed its assets.

An industry norm for this ratio is not readily available in Table 3–5. However, we can calculate one, using the information given there. Sales divided by total assets equals 1.5; and the operating profit margin is 4.6 percent of sales for the industry. Using the following relationship, we derive an industry norm of 6.9 percent. Thus, Jimco's operating rate of return compares favorably with the industry norm.

$$\frac{\text{operating income}}{\text{sales}} \times \frac{\text{sales}}{\text{total assets}} = \frac{\text{operating income}}{\text{total assets}} \qquad (3\text{--}16)$$
$$.046 \qquad \times \qquad 1.5 \qquad = \qquad .069, \text{ or } 6.9\%$$

In deriving the industry norm for the operating income return on investment ratio, we have identified a very useful relationship between operating profit margin and the ratio of sales divided by total assets (which we earlier referred to as total asset turnover). That is, *a firm's rate of return on investment is a function of (1) how much profit it squeezes out of each dollar of sales (as reflected in its operating profit margin), and (2) how much it has invested in assets to produce those sales (as reflected in the total asset turnover ratio).* Jimco's above-average operating profit margin, combined with its higher than average turnover of total investment in assets, produce an operating income return on investment well above its industry norm.

Return on Total Assets or Return on Investment. The **return on total assets** or **return on investment ratio** relates after-tax income to the firm's total investment in assets. For Jimco, this ratio is found as follows:

$$\text{return on total assets} = \frac{\text{net income}}{\text{total assets}}$$
$$= \frac{\$1,800,000}{\$31,000,000} \qquad (3\text{--}17)$$
$$= .058, \text{ or } 5.8\%$$
$$\text{industry average} = .75\%$$

Again total assets are used in an attempt to measure total investment. An industry norm can be obtained from Table 3–5 in a manner similar to that used with the operating rate of return. That is

---

rate must exceed the cost of borrowed funds for the firm as a whole to experience *favorable* financial leverage. The favorableness of financial leverage is determined by the effect of its use on earnings per share to the firm's common stockholders.

$$\text{return on total assets} = \frac{\text{net income}}{\text{sales}} \times \frac{\text{sales}}{\text{total assets}} \qquad (3\text{--}18)$$

Earlier the net income to sales ratio for the industry was estimated to be .5 percent. Using the industry's sales to total assets ratio of 1.5 produces an industry norm for return on total assets of .005 × 1.5 = .0075, or .75 percent. Thus, Jimco provides an excellent return on its total investment when compared to other firms in its industry.

Return on Common Equity. The **return on common equity ratio** measures the rate of return earned on the common stockholder's investment. Jimco earned the following rate of return for its common stockholders:

$$\text{return on common equity} = \frac{\text{net income available to common}}{\text{common equity}}$$

$$= \frac{\$1,800,000}{\$10,300,000} \qquad (3\text{--}19)$$

$$= .175, \text{ or } 17.5\%$$

$$\text{industry average} = .85\%$$

Net income available to common equity is simply net income less any preferred dividends the firm might have to pay. This earnings figure is sometimes referred to as **net common stock earnings (NCSE).**

Table 3–5 does not contain an industry norm for this ratio. However, the following relation can be used to derive an industry norm from the return on total assets ratio and the debt ratio:

$$\text{return on common equity} = \frac{\text{return on total assets}}{(1 - \text{debt ratio})} \qquad (3\text{--}20)$$

Recall that the debt ratio is simply total liabilities divided by total assets. The industry norm for the return on common equity ratio is found as follows:

$$\frac{.005}{(1 - .589)} = .0085, \text{ or } .85\%$$

Thus, Jimco's 17.5 percent return compares *very* favorably with that of the industry. This higher than average return reflects both the firm's efficient use of its investment in assets to generate sales (indicated by the turnover of total assets ratio) and its above-average use of financial leverage (as reflected in its debt ratio).

In summary, Jimco was observed to have slightly below-average profits in relation to its sales; however, the firm experienced above-average return on its total investment. This factor was a result of the firm's very efficient use of its assets to generate sales (as evidenced by the high total asset turnover ratio) and the fact that Jimco utilized more leverage than the norm for its industry.

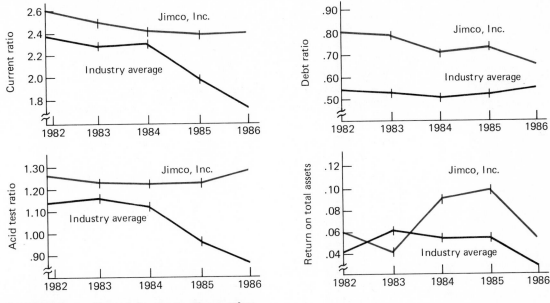

FIGURE 3–1.   Trend Analysis Illustration

Trend Analysis

We noted earlier that a firm's financial ratios can be compared with two types of standards. We have discussed industry norms as the basis for comparison; we now demonstrate the use of trend comparisons. Figure 3–1 displays graphs of Jimco's current ratio, acid test ratio, debt ratio, and return on total asset ratio for the past five years.

Surveying the trend in Jimco's liquidity ratios indicates that a gradual deterioration has been taking place. This deterioration in liquidity does not, at least for the present, represent a problem, as Jimco's current and acid test ratios compared very favorably with their respective industry norms. However, any continuation in the trend could pose a problem for Jimco and should be monitored closely.

Jimco's debt ratio appears to have declined slightly over the past 5 years, with moderate interim fluctuations. However, no material change in the ratio appears to have occurred over the period. In light of Jimco's current use of leverage, any further increases in this ratio may be unwarranted, however.

Finally, the return on total assets ratio for the past 5 years depicts the relatively volatile nature of Jimco's business, with returns ranging from 4 percent in 1983 to 10 percent in 1985. However, based upon Jimco's return on total assets ratio for 1987 and that of the industry, it would appear that Jimco has done as well or better than the median for its industry.

Summary of Jimco's Financial Ratios

Table 3–6 summarizes Jimco's financial ratios, as well as the corresponding industry norms. Each ratio is evaluated in relation to the appropriate norm. Briefly, the results of those comparisons are as follows:

1. Jimco's liquidity position is very closely in line with the industry.
2. Jimco has made extensive use of financial leverage. In fact, the firm has financed 67 percent of its assets with nonowner funds.

TABLE 3–6. Summary of Ratios for Jimco, Inc.

Ratio	Formula	Calculation	Industry Average	Evaluation
Liquidity ratios				
1. Current ratio	Current assets/current liabilities	$24,000,000/10,000,000 = 2.40 times	1.7 times	Satisfactory
2. Acid test ratio	(Current assets − inventories)/current liabilities	$12,000,000/10,000,000 = 1.20 times	0.6 times	Excellent
Efficiency ratios				
3. Average collection period	Average accounts receivable/(annual credit sales/360)	$10,000,000/($51,000,000/360) = 70.6 days	45 days	Poor
4. Inventory turnover	Cost of goods sold/ending inventory	$38,000,000/12,000,000 = 3.17 times	2.3 times	Good
5. Fixed asset turnover	Sales/fixed assets	$51,000,000/7,000,000 = 7.286 times	7.8 times	Satisfactory
6. Total asset turnover	Sales/total assets	$51,000,000/31,000,000 = 1.645 times	1.5 times	Satisfactory
Leverage ratios				
7. Debt ratio	Total liabilities/total assets	$20,700,000/31,000,000 = 66.8%	58.9%	Poor
8. Long-term debt to total capitalization	Long-term debt/total capitalization	$10,700,000/21,000,000 = 50.9%	28.96%	Poor
9. Times interest earned	Net operating income/annual interest expense	$4,000,000/1,000,000 = 4.00 times	1.3 times	Excellent
10. Cash flow overall coverage ratio	(NOI + lease expense + depreciation/interest + lease expense + principal payments/(1 − tax rate)	$4,500,000/1,833,333 = 2.45 times	N.A.[a]	—
Profitability ratios				
11. Gross profit margin	Gross profit/sales	$13,000,000/51,000,000 = 25.5%	26.6%	Satisfactory
12. Operating profit margin	Net operating income/sales	$4,000,000/51,000,000 = 7.84%	4.6%	Excellent
13. Net profit margin	Net income/sales	$1,800,000/51,000,000 = 3.5%	0.5%	Excellent
14. Operating income return on investment	Net operating income/total assets	$4,000,000/31,000,000 = 12.9%	6.9%	Excellent
15. Return on total assets	Net income/total assets	$1,800,000/31,000,000 = 5.8%	0.75%	Excellent
16. Return on common equity	Net income available to common/common equity	$1,800,000/10,300,000 = 17.5%	0.85%	Excellent

[a] Norm was not available.

3. The firm can apparently *afford* its higher use of financial leverage, as is indicated by the times interest earned ratio.

4. Jimco's profit margins are approximately equal to the respective norms; however, the firm has been able to convert these profit margins into better than average rates of return on investment. This resulted from the higher than average sales per dollar invested in assets as reflected in Jimco's efficiency ratios.

5. Finally, Jimco has benefited from the favorable use of financial leverage. The firm earned a very favorable 17.5 percent return on the investment of its common stockholders, compared with less than one percent for the industry.

AN INTEGRATED FORM OF FINANCIAL ANALYSIS BASED ON EARNING POWER

One format for performing an analysis of the firm using financial ratios is presented in Table 3–6. The basic procedure used there was to classify financial ratios into four categories that represent the important dimensions of the firm's financial well-being and then analyze each basic category. We will now discuss an alternative approach which focuses on the firm's earning power as measured by two of the firm's profitability ratios: the operating income return on investment and the return on common equity. This approach to financial analysis is particularly well suited to internal analyses carried out by the firm's management. The reason is that the analysis focuses directly on firm profitability, which reflects how well the firm is being managed. In addition, anyone outside the firm who is interested in evaluating how well the firm is being managed from the common shareholder's perspective would certainly find the analysis of earning power a valuable guide to carrying out that analysis.

The analysis of a firm's earning power involves a two-stage procedure designed to aid in answering two basic questions:

STAGE 1: *How effective has the firm's management been in generating sales using the total assets of the firm and converting those sales into operating profits?*

STAGE 2: *How effective has the firm's management been in designing a financial structure that increases the returns to the common shareholders? Here we analyze the effect of the firm's financing decisions (that is, the mixture of debt and owner financing used by the firm) on the rate of return earned on the common stockholder's investment.*

Figure 3–2 provides a template for carrying out the first stage of the analysis of Jimco's earning power. Note that the basis for this analysis is the operating income return on investment. This ratio measures the rate of return earned on the firm's assets before giving any consideration to how they have been financed. That is, the operating income rate of return is based upon net operating income, which in turn is measured before interest or dividends have been considered.

A total of seven ratios are calculated in the first stage of the analysis of Jimco's earning power. The first is the operating income return on investment (Step 1). Step 2 involves calculating the operating profit margin, which, along with the total asset turnover (Step 4), determines the operating income return on investment. Step 3 involves calculation of the gross profit margin, which provides the basis for assessing the impact of cost of goods sold on the operating profit margin calculated in Step 2.

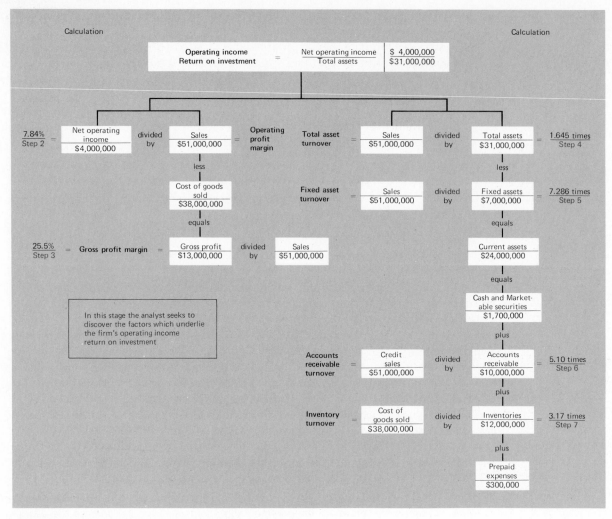

FIGURE 3–2.   Analyzing Earning Power: Stage 1
(Analyzing the Operating Income Return on Investment)

Steps 5, 6, and 7 involve the calculation of the fixed asset turnover, accounts receivable turnover, and inventory turnover ratios, which provide the basis for a detailed analysis of the determinants of the total asset turnover ratio (calculated in Step 4).

Note that by following the steps in Figure 3–2, the analyst is led through a detailed analysis of the determinants of the operating income return on investment. That is, each successive step provides the basis for understanding more about the determinants of the operating income return on investment. For example, the total asset turnover ratio is one of the two basic determinants of the operating income return on investment (the other is the operating profit margin). By analyzing the fixed asset turnover ratio in conjunction with the total asset turnover, the analyst can determine whether fixed or current assets caused the total asset turnover ratio

Step	Ratio	Formula	Calculation	Industry[a]	Evaluation
1	Operating income Return on investment	$\dfrac{\text{Net operating income}}{\text{Total assets}}$	$\dfrac{\$\ 4,000,000}{\$31,000,000} = 12.9\%$	9.7%	Satisfactory
2	Operating profit margin	$\dfrac{\text{Net operating income}}{\text{Sales}}$	$\dfrac{\$\ 4,000,000}{\$51,000,000} = 7.84\%$	6.9%	Satisfactory
3	Gross profit margin	$\dfrac{\text{Gross profit}}{\text{Sales}}$	$\dfrac{\$13,000,000}{\$51,000,000} = 25.5\%$	27.3%	Satisfactory
4	Total asset turnover	$\dfrac{\text{Sales}}{\text{Total assets}}$	$\dfrac{\$51,000,000}{\$31,000,000} = 1.645 \text{ times}$	1.4 times	Good
5	Fixed asset turnover	$\dfrac{\text{Sales}}{\text{Fixed assets}}$	$\dfrac{\$51,000,000}{\$\ 7,000,000} = 7.286 \text{ times}$	8.4 times	Poor
6	Accounts receivable turnover	$\dfrac{\text{Credit sales}}{\text{Accounts receivable}}$	$\dfrac{\$51,000,000}{\$10,000,000} = 5.10 \text{ times}$	6.9 times	Poor
7	Inventory turnover	$\dfrac{\text{Cost of goods sold}}{\text{Inventories}}$	$\dfrac{\$38,000,000}{\$12,000,000} = 3.17 \text{ times}$	2.7 times	Satisfactory

[a] Based upon Robert Morris Associates figures from Table 3–5.

FIGURE 3–2. (*continued*)

to deviate from the industry average. Furthermore, the accounts receivable turnover and inventory turnover ratios can be analyzed to determine the effect of the level of investment in these assets on total asset turnover, and, consequently, the observed operating income return on investment.

Figure 3–3 provides a template for use in analyzing the effect of the firm's financing decisions on the return earned on the common stockholder's investment. Note that we begin the analysis with the operating income return on investment ratio, which was the subject of the analysis in Figure 3–2. Next, Step 9 involves calculation of the return on total assets. This ratio is then adjusted for the influence of the firm's use of financial leverage in order to calculate the return on common equity. In Step 10 we measure the rate of return earned on the common stockholders' investment in the firm, which reflects both the firm's operating and financing decisions.

The ten-step procedure outlined in Figures 3–2 and 3–3 connects the return earned on common equity to the firm's use of financial leverage and the operating profitability. The operating rate of return ratio was shown to be determined by the firm's profit margins on sales (Steps 2 and 3) and the sales to asset relationship (Steps 4 through 7). The real value of this approach to financial analysis is its ability to demonstrate the interrelationships between the return earned on the owners' investment in the firm and a wide variety of financial attributes of the firm. The analyst is provided with a "roadmap" to follow in determining how successful the firm's management has been in managing its resources to maximize the return earned as the owners' investment. In addition, the analyst can determine why that particular return was earned.

Limitations of Ratio Analysis

The analyst who works with financial ratios must be aware of the limitations involved in their use. The following list includes some of the more important pitfalls that may be encountered in computing and interpreting financial ratios:

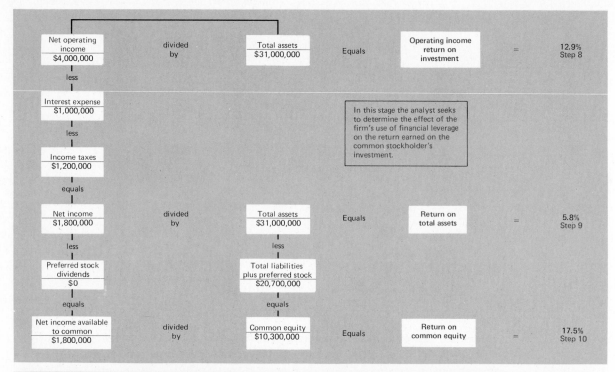

Step	Ratio	Formula	Calculation	Industry[a]	Evaluation
8	Operating income Return on investment	Net operating income / Total assets	$\frac{\$\ 4,000,000}{\$31,000,000} = 12.9\%$	9.7%	Satisfactory
9	Return on total assets	Net income / Total assets	$\frac{\$\ 1,800,000}{\$31,000,000} = 5.8\%$	3.5%	Good
10	Return on common equity	Net income available to common / Common equity	$\frac{\$\ 1,800,000}{\$10,300,000} = 17.5\%$	6.52%	Excellent

[a] Based upon Robert Morris Associates figures from Table 3–5.

**FIGURE 3–3.   Analyzing Earning Power: Stage 2
(The Return Earned on the Common Stockholder's Investment)**

1. **It is sometimes difficult to identify the industry category to which a firm belongs when the firm engages in multiple lines of business.**
2. **Published industry averages are only approximations and provide the user with *general guidelines* rather than scientifically determined averages of the ratios of all or even a representative sample of the firms within the industry.** Note, for example, the cautionary statement (Figure 3–4) prepared by Robert Morris Associates in conjunction with their published industry ratios (as contained in Table 3–5 on pages 42–43).
3. **Accounting practices differ widely among firms and can lead to differences in computed ratios.** For example, the use of last-in, first-out (LIFO) in inventory

FIGURE 3—4. Cautionary Statement on Use of Industry Norms.

Interpretation of Statement Studies Figures

RMA recommends that *Statement Studies* data be regarded only as general guidelines and not as absolute industry norms. There are several reasons why the data may not be fully representative of a given industry:

(1) The financial statements used in the *Statement Studies* are not selected by any random or statistically reliable method. RMA member banks voluntarily submit the raw data they have available each year, with these being the only constraints: (a) The fiscal year-ends of the companies reported may not be from April 1 through June 29, and (b) their total assets must be less than $100 million.

(2) Many companies have varied product lines; however, the *Statement Studies* categorize them by their primary product Standard Industrial Classification (SIC) number only.

(3) Some of our industry samples are rather small in relation to the total number of firms in a given industry. A relatively small sample can increase the chances that some of our composites do not fully represent an industry.

(4) There is the chance that an extreme statement can be present in a sample, causing a disproportionate influence on the industry composite. This is particularly true in a relatively small sample.

(5) Companies within the same industry may differ in their method of operations which in turn can directly influence their financial statements. Since they are included in our sample, too, these statements can significantly affect our composite calculations.

(6) Other considerations that can result in variations among different companies engaged in the same general line of business are different labor markets; geographical location; different accounting methods; quality of products handled; sources and methods of financing; and terms of sale.

For these reasons, RMA does not recommend the Statement Studies *figures be considered as absolute norms for a given industry. Rather the figures should be used only as general guidelines and in addition to the other methods of financial analysis. RMA makes no claim as to the representativeness of the figures printed in this book.*

valuation can, in a period of rising prices, lower the firm's inventory account and increase its inventory turnover ratio vis-à-vis that of a firm which utilizes first-in, first-out (FIFO). In addition, firms may choose different methods of depreciating their fixed assets.

4. **Financial ratios can be too high or too low.** For example, a current ratio that exceeds the industry norm may signal the presence of excess liquidity, which results in a lowering of overall profits in relation to the firm's investment in assets. On the other hand, a current ratio that falls below the norm indicates the possibility that the firm has inadequate liquidity and may at some future date be unable to pay its bills on time.

5. **An industry average may not provide a desirable target ratio or norm.** At best an industry average provides a guide to the financial position of the average firm in the industry. We might note here that the industry norms provided in Table 3–5 contain both the average ratio and the upper and lower quartiles for the firms used in preparing the average. Thus, the greater the difference in the upper and lower quartiles, the less meaningful is the industry average in terms of its ability to represent that ratio for the industry.

6. **Many firms experience seasonality in their operations.** Thus, balance sheets entries and their corresponding ratios will vary with the time of year when the statements are prepared. To avoid this problem, an average account balance should be used (for several months or quarters during the year) rather than the year-end total. For example, an average of month-end inventory balances might be used to compute a firm's inventory turnover ratio when the firm is subject to a significant seasonality in its sales (and correspondingly in its investment in inventories).

Given their limitations, financial ratios provide the analyst with a very useful tool for assessing a firm's financial condition. The analyst should, however, be aware of these potential weaknesses when performing a ratio analysis and temper his or her conclusions accordingly.

Summary

Basic Financial Statements

Three basic financial statements are commonly used to describe the financial condition and performance of the firm: the balance sheet, the income statement, and the statement of changes in financial condition (source and use of funds statement). The balance sheet provides a picture of the firm's assets, liabilities, and owners' equity on a particular date, whereas the income statement reflects the net revenues from the firm's operations over a given period. The statement of changes in financial condition combines information from both the balance sheet and income statement to describe sources and uses of funds for a given period in the firm's history.

Financial Ratios

Financial ratios are of four main kinds: (1) liquidity, (2) efficiency, (3) leverage, and (4) profitability ratios. The financial statements of Jimco, Inc., demonstrate the computation of a sample listing of ratios from each category. The set of possible ratio calculations is limited only by the analyst's imagination, and those discussed here represent only one possible listing that can be used in performing a financial analysis.

Use of Financial Ratios   Two methods were demonstrated for analyzing financial ratios. The first involved trend analysis for the firm over time; the second involved making ratio comparisons with industry norms. An example set of industry norms from Robert Morris Associates were presented and used in the analysis of Jimco, Inc. In addition, an integrated form of financial analysis based upon earning power was discussed. This approach to financial analysis was shown to focus the user's attention on the underlying determinants of a firm's profitability.

Study Questions

3–1.   The basic financial statements of an organization consist of the balance sheet, income statement, and statement of changes in financial position. Describe the nature of each and explain how their functions differ.

3–2.   Why is it that the preferred stockholders' equity section of the balance sheet changes only when new shares are sold, whereas the common equity section changes from year to year regardless of whether new shares are bought or sold?

3–3.   Why is it that net sales for a period do not necessarily represent cash inflow for the period?

3–4.   Discuss two reasons why net income for a particular period does not necessarily reflect a firm's cash flow during that period.

3–5.   The four basic groups of financial ratios are liquidity, efficiency, leverage, and profitability ratios. Discuss the nature of each group and list two example ratios that you would use to measure that aspect of a firm's financial condition.

3–6.   Discuss briefly the two sources of standards or norms that can be used in performing ratio analyses.

3–7.   Where can the analyst obtain industry norms? What limitations does the use of industry average ratios suffer from? Discuss briefly.

Self-Test Problems

ST–1.   (*Ratio Analysis and Short-term Liquidity*) Ray's Tool and Supply Company has been expanding its level of operations for the past two years. The firm's sales have grown rapidly as a result of the expansion in the Austin economy (Austin, Texas). However, Ray's is a privately held company, and the only source of available funds it has is a line of credit with the firm's bank. The company needs to expand its inventories to meet the needs of its growing customer base but also wishes to maintain a current ratio of at least 3 to 1. If Ray's current assets are $6,000,000, and its current ratio is now 4 to 1, how much can it expand its inventories (financing the expansion with its line of credit) before the target current ratio is violated?

ST–2.   (*Ratio Analysis of Loan Request*) On February 3, 1987, Mr. Jerry Simmons, chief financial officer for M & G Industries, contacted the firm's bank regarding a loan. The loan was to be used to repay notes payable and to finance current assets. Mr. Simmons wanted to repay the loan plus interest in one year. Upon receiving the loan request, the bank asked that the firm supply it with complete financial statements for the past two years. These statements are presented below:

M & G Industries Balance Sheets at the End of Calendar Year

	1986	1987
Cash	$ 9,000	$ 500
Accounts receivable	12,500	16,000
Inventories	29,000	45,500
Total current assets	$ 50,500	$ 62,000
Land	20,000	26,000
Buildings and equipment	70,000	100,000
Less: Allowance for depreciation	28,000	38,000
Total fixed assets	$ 62,000	$ 88,000
	$112,500	$150,000
Accounts payable	$ 10,500	$ 22,000
Bank notes	17,000	47,000
Total current liabilities	$ 27,500	$ 69,000
Long-term debt	28,750	22,950
Common stock	31,500	31,500
Retained earnings	24,750	26,550
	$112,500	$150,000

M & G Industries Income Statements for Years Ending December 31

	1986	1987
Sales	$125,000	$160,000
Cost of goods sold	75,000	96,000
Gross profit	$ 50,000	$ 64,000
Operating expense:		
Fixed cash operating expense	21,000	21,000
Variable operating expense	12,500	16,000
Depreciation	4,500	10,000
Total operating expense	38,000	47,000
Earnings before interest and taxes	$ 12,000	$ 17,000
Interest	3,000	6,100
Earnings before taxes	$ 9,000	$ 10,900
Taxes	4,500	5,450
Net income	$ 4,500	$ 5,450

a. Based upon the preceding statements, complete the following table.

M & G Industries Ratio Analysis

	Industry Averages	Actual 1986	Actual 1987
Current ratio	1.80		
Acid test ratio	.70		
Average collection period[a]	37 days		
Inventory turnover[a]	2.50 times		
Debt to total assets	58%		
Long-term debt to total capitalization	33%		
Times interest earned	3.8 times		
Gross profit margin	38%		
Operating profit margin	10%		
Net profit margin	3.5%		
Total asset turnover	1.14 times		
Fixed asset turnover	1.40 times		
Operating income return on investment	11.4%		
Return on total assets	4.0%		
Return on common equity	9.5%		

[a] Based on a 360-day year and on end-of-year figures.

b. Analyze Mr. Simmons's loan request. Would you grant the loan? Explain.

ST–3. (*Source and Use Statement*)

a. Prepare a statement of sources and uses of funds for M & G Industries for 1987, using information given in Self-Test Problem ST–1.

b. How does this fund statement supplement your ratio analysis from Self-Test Problem ST–1? Explain.

Study Problems

3–1. (*Ratio Analysis*) The Mitchem Marble Company has a target current ratio of 2 to 1 but has experienced some difficulties financing its expanding sales in the past few months. At present the current ratio of 2.5 to 1 is based upon current assets of $2.5 million. If Mitchem expands its receivables and inventories using its short-term line of credit, how much additional funding can it borrow before its current ratio standard is reached?

3–2. (*Ratio Analysis*) The balance sheet and income statement for the J. P. Robard Mfg. Company are as follows:

Balance Sheet ($000)

Cash	$ 500
Accounts receivable	2000
Inventories	1000
Current assets	$3500
Net fixed assets	$4500
Total assets	$8000
Accounts payable	$1100
Accrued expenses	600
Short-term notes payable	300
Current liabilities	$2000
Long-term debt	$2000
Owner's equity	$4000
	$8000

Income Statement ($000)

Net sales (all credit)	$8000
Cost of goods sold	(3300)
Gross profit	$4700
Operating expenses[a]	(3000)
Net operating income	$1700
Interest expense	(367)
Earnings before taxes	$1333
Income taxes (40%)	(533)
Net Income	$ 800

[a] Including depreciation expense of $500 for the year.

Calculate the following ratios:

Current ratio	Gross profit margin
Debt ratio	Operating profit margin
Times interest earned	Net profit margin
Average collection period	Operating return on investment
Inventory turnover	Return on total assets
Fixed asset turnover	Return on common equity
Total asset turnover	

3–3. (*Analyzing Profitability*) The R. M. Smithers Corporation earned a net profit margin of 5 percent based on sales of $10 million and total assets of $5 million last year.

    a. What was Smithers's rate of return on total assets?

    b. During the coming year the company president has set a goal of attaining a 12 percent return on total assets. How much must firm sales rise, other things being the same, for the goal to be achieved? (State your answer as an annual growth rate in sales.)

    c. If Smithers finances 30 percent of its assets by borrowing, what was its return on common equity for last year? What will it be next year if the return on total asset goal is achieved?

3–4. (*Using Financial Ratios*) The Brenmar Sales Company had a gross profit margin of 30 percent and sales of $9 million last year. Seventy-five percent of the firm's sales are on credit while the remainder are cash sales. Brenmar's current assets equal $1,500,000, its current liabilities $300,000, and it has $100,000 in cash plus marketable securities.

a. If Brenmar's accounts receivable are $562,500, what is its average collection period?

b. If Brenmar reduces its average collection period to 20 days, what will be its new level of accounts receivable?

c. Brenmar's inventory turnover ratio is 9 times. What is the level of Brenmar's inventories?

3–5. (*Ratio Analysis of Loan Request*) Pamplin, Inc. has recently applied for a loan from the Second National Bank to be used to expand the firm's inventory of soil pipe used in construction and agriculture. This expansion is predicated on expanded sales predicted for the coming year. Pamplin's financial statements for the two most recent years are as follows:

Pamplin, Inc. Balance Sheet at 12/31/86 and 12/31/87 (000's)

Assets		
	12/31/86	*12/31/87*
Cash	$ 200	$ 150
Accounts receivable	450	425
Inventory	550	625
Current assets	1200	1200
Plant and equipment	2200	2600
Less: Accumulated depreciation	1000	1200
Net plant and equipment	1200	1400
Total assets	$2400	$2600

Liabilities and Owners' Equity		
	1986	*1987*
Accounts payable	$ 200	$ 150
Notes payable—current (9%)	0	150
Current liabilities	200	300
Bonds	600	600
Owners' equity		
Common stock	300	300
Paid-in capital	600	600
Retained earnings	700	800
Total owners' equity	1600	1700
Total liabilities and owners' equity	$2400	$2600

Pamplin, Inc. Income Statement Year Ended 12/31/86 and 12/31/87

	1986	1987
Sales	$1200	$1450
Cost of goods sold	700	850
Gross profit	$ 500	$ 600
Operating expenses	30	40
Depreciation	220	200
Net operating income	$ 250	$ 360
Interest expense	50	60
Net income before taxes	$ 200	$ 300
Taxes (40%)	80	120
Net income	$ 120	$ 180

a. Compute the following ratios for Pamplin, Inc. from the financial statements provided above:

	1986	1987	Industry Norm
Current ratio			5.0 ×
Acid test (quick) ratio			3.0 ×
Inventory turnover			2.2 ×
Average collection period			90 days
Debt ratio			.33
Times interest earned			7.0 ×
Total asset turnover			.75 ×
Fixed asset turnover			1.0 ×
Operating profit margin			.20
Net profit margin			.12
Return on total assets			.09

b. Based on your answer in (a) above, what are Pamplin's financial strengths and weaknesses?

c. Would you make the loan? Why or why not?

3–6. (*Source and Use Statement*) Prepare a statement of changes in financial position for Pamplin, Inc. for the year ended December 31, 1987 (problem 3–4).

3–7. (*Source and Use Statement*) (a) Prepare a statement of sources and uses of funds for the Waterhouse Co. in the year 1987. (b) What were the firm's primary sources and uses of funds?

	1986	1987
Cash	$ 75,000	$ 82,500
Receivables	102,000	90,000
Inventory	168,000	165,000
Prepaid expenses	12,000	13,500
Fixed assets	325,500	468,000
Accumulated depreciation	94,500	129,000
Patents	61,500	52,500
	$649,500	$742,500

	1986	1987
Accounts payable	$124,500	$112,500
Taxes payable	97,500	105,000
Mortgage payable	150,000	—
Preferred stock	—	225,000
Additional paid-in capital—preferred	—	6,000
Common stock	225,000	225,000
Retained earnings	52,500	69,000
	$649,500	$742,500

Additional Information:

1. The only entry in the accumulated depreciation account is the depreciation expense for the period.

2. The only entries in the retained earnings account are for dividends paid in the amount of $18,000 and for the net income for the year.

3. The income statement for 1987 is as follows:

Sales	$187,500
Cost of sales	141,000
Gross profit	46,500
Operating expenses	12,000
Net income	$ 34,500

3–8. Prepare a balance sheet and income statement at December 31, 1987, for the Sharpe Mfg. Co. from the scrambled list of items below.

Accounts receivable	$120,000
Machinery and equipment	700,000
Accumulated depreciation	236,000
Notes payable—current	100,000
Net sales	800,000
Inventory	110,000
Accounts payable	90,000
Long-term debt	160,000
Cost of goods sold	500,000
Operating expenses	280,000
Common stock	320,000
Cash	96,000
Retained earnings—prior year	?
Retained earnings—current year	?

3–9. (*Financial Ratios—Investment Analysis*) The annual sales for Salco, Inc. were $4,500,000 last year. The firm's end-of-year balance sheet appeared as follows:

Current assets	$ 500,000	Liabilities	$1,000,000
Net fixed assets	$1,500,000	Owners' equity	$1,000,000
	$2,000,000		$2,000,000

The firm's income statement for the year was as follows:

Sales	$4,500,000
Less: Cost of goods sold	(3,500,000)
Gross profit	1,000,000
Less: Operating expenses	(500,000)
Net operating income	500,000
Less: Interest expense	(100,000)
Earnings before taxes	400,000
Less: Taxes	(200,000)
Net income	$ 200,000

a. Calculate Salco's total asset turnover, operating profit margin, and operating income return on investment.

b. Salco plans to renovate one of its plants, which will require an added investment in plant and equipment of $1 million. The firm will maintain its present debt ratio of .5 when financing the new investment and expects sales to remain constant, while the operating profit margin will rise to 13 percent. What will be the new operating income return on investment for Salco after the plant renovation?

c. Given that the plant renovation in part (b) occurs and Salco's interest expense rises by $50,000 per year, what will be the return earned on the common stockholders' investment? Compare this rate of return with that earned before the renovation.

3–10. (*Sources and Use Statement*) The consolidated balance sheets of the TMU Processing Company are presented below for June 1, 1986 and May 31, 1987 (millions of dollars). TMU earned $14 million after taxes during the year ended May 31, 1987, and paid common dividends of $10 million.

	June 1, 1986	May 31, 1987	Change Source	Change Use
Cash	$ 10	$ 8	_____	_____
Accounts receivable	12	22	_____	_____
Inventories	8	14	_____	_____
Current assets	$ 30	$ 44	_____	_____
Gross fixed assets	100	110	_____	_____
Less: Accumulated depreciation	(40)	(50)	_____	_____
Net fixed assets	$ 60	$ 60	_____	_____
Total assets	$ 90	$104	_____	_____
Accounts payable	$ 12	$ 9	_____	_____
Notes payable	7	7	_____	_____
Long-term debt	11	24	_____	_____
Common stock	20	20	_____	_____
Retained earnings	40	44	_____	_____
Total liabilities and owners' equity	$ 90	$104	_____	_____

a. Fill in the changes in TMU's balance sheet for 1987.
b. Prepare a source and use of funds statement for TMU Processing Company.
c. Summarize your findings.

3–11. (*Comprehensive Financial Analysis Problem*) The T. P. Jarmon Company manufactures and sells a line of exclusive sportswear. The firm's sales were $600,000 for the year just ended, and its total assets exceed $400,000. The company was started by Mr. Jarmon just 10 years ago and has been profitable every year since its inception. The chief financial officer for the firm, Brent Vehlim, has decided to seek a line of credit from the firm's bank totaling $80,000. In the past the company has relied on its suppliers to finance a large part of its needs for inventory. However, in recent months tight money conditions have led the firm's suppliers to offer sizable cash discounts to speed up payments for purchases. Mr. Vehlim wants to use the line of credit to supplant a large portion of the firm's payables during the summer months, which are the firm's peak seasonal sales period.

The firm's two most recent balance sheets were presented to the bank in support of its loan request. In addition, the firm's income statement for the year just ended was provided to support the loan request. These statements are found below:

T. P. Jarmon Company Balance Sheets for 12/31/86 and 12/31/87

Assets		
	1986	**1987**
Cash	$ 15,000	$ 14,000
Marketable securities	6,000	6,200
Accounts receivable	42,000	33,000
Inventory	51,000	84,000
Prepaid rent	1,200	1,100
Total current assets	$115,200	$138,300
Net plant and equipment	286,000	270,000
Total assets	$401,200	$408,300

Liabilities and Stockholders' Equity		
	1986	**1987**
Accounts payable	$ 48,000	$ 57,000
Notes payable	15,000	13,000
Accruals	6,000	5,000
Total current liabilities	$ 69,000	$ 75,000
Long-term debt	$160,000	$150,000
Common Stockholders' equity	$172,220	$183,300
Total liabilities and equity	$401,200	$408,300

T. P. Jarmon Company Income Statement
for the Year Ended 12/31/87

Sales		$600,000
Less: Cost of goods sold		460,000
Gross profits		$140,000
Less: Expenses		
General and administrative	$30,000	
Interest	10,000	
Depreciation	30,000	
Total		70,000
Profit before taxes		$70,000
Less: Taxes		27,100
Profits after taxes		$42,900
Less: Cash dividends		31,800
To retained earnings		$11,110

Jan Fama, associate credit analyst for the Merchants National Bank of Midland, Michigan, was assigned the task of analyzing Jarmon's loan request.

a. Calculate the financial ratios for 1987 corresponding to the industry norms provided below:

Ratio	Norm	Jarmon's Ratio	Evaluation
Current ratio	1.8 times		
Acid test ratio	.9 times		
Debt ratio	.5		
Long-term debt to total capitalization	.7		
Times interest earned	10 times		
Average collection period	20 days		
Inventory turnover (based on COGS)	7 times		
Return on total assets	8.4%		
Gross profit margin	25%		
Net profit margin	7%		
Operating return on investment	16.8%		
Operating profit margin	14%		
Total asset turnover	1.2 times		
Fixed asset turnover	1.8 times		

b. Which of the ratios reported above in the industry norms do you feel should be most crucial in determining whether the bank should extend the line of credit? What strengths and weaknesses are apparent from your analysis of Jarmon's financial ratios?

c. Based upon the ratio analysis you performed in part (b), would you recommend approval of the loan request? Discuss.

d. Prepare a statement of sources and uses of funds for Jarmon covering the year ended December 31, 1987. How does this statement directly support your ratio analysis of Jarmon?

e. Perform an analysis of Jarmon's earning power using the procedure laid out in Figures 3–2 and 3–3.

Case Problem

L. M. Myers, Inc.

Financial Analysis

L. M. Myers, Inc., is one of the three largest grain exporters in the United States. The firm also engages in soybean processing and several other related activities. During fiscal 1986–87 Myers derived 72.1 percent of its sales from its exporting activities, 14.8 percent from agriproducts, and the remainder from chemical and consumer products. Myers's nonexport sales are derived almost completely from soybean processing activities, including the production and sale of a number of food ingredients. One of the most promising soybean derivatives produced by the company is a newly developed meat substitute called "Prosoy." At present Prosoy is marketed almost strictly as a ground beef substitute; however, plans are under way to market the product in a number of other forms resembling familiar cuts of meat, such as bacon and even roasts. The success that the company has enjoyed with Prosoy in its initial three years of production promises to make soybean processing an even more important segment of the firm's overall sales. Other soybean-related products produced by the firm include a number of derivatives used in animal and poultry feeds. Myers's export business primarily involves corn, wheat, and some soybeans. The principal investment made by the firm related to its exporting operations involves a chain of grain elevators at strategic locations along the Mississippi River. These elevators are used to store grain and load it onto ships, which deliver it all over the world.

For the fiscal year just ended Myers experienced an overall sales growth of 10 percent. This increase represented a mere 5 percent increase in export-related activities and a whopping 20 percent increase in sales related to soybean processing. This and other factors have led the company to make a commitment to expand its processing capacity by $20 million during the next three years. The firm plans to finance the expansion through an $11 million bond issue and through the retention of earnings.

Owing to the seasonal nature of its export business, Myers has had to borrow heavily during the harvest months to finance seasonal inventory buildups and then repay the loans as sales are made throughout the year. In the past the company has arranged with a group of banks for a line of credit (discussed in Chapter 8) sufficient to meet its credit needs; however, in recent years this arrangement has become increasingly more cumbersome as the firm's total needs for funds have grown. This and cost considerations have led Myers's financial vice-president, Mr. James Graham, to consider the possibility of raising all or at least a part of the firm's credit needs through a commercial paper issue (discussed in Chapter 8). Mr. Graham is somewhat concerned about his firm's creditworthiness in light of the industry norms generally used by banks and other creditors. His concern relates to the fact that Myers has never issued commercial paper and the belief that only the most creditworthy of borrowers can successfully use the commercial paper market to raise funds.

a. Using the financial statements for Myers presented below, complete the calculation of the financial ratios contained in Exhibit 1.

b. Based upon your calculated ratios and the associated industry norms, what is your financial analysis of Myers?

L. M. Myers, Inc. Balance Sheets for Years Ended December 31 ($000)

Assets

	1986	1987
Cash	$ 11,451	$ 12,844
Accounts receivable	64,199	52,599
Marketable securities	—	33,995
Inventories	69,814	75,366
Deferred income taxes	2,948	2,750
Prepaid expenses	1,089	1,794
Total current assets	$149,501	$179,348
Investments and advances	11,681	12,012
Other assets	14,509	3,735
Net property and equipment	118,810	153,856
Total assets	$294,501	$348,951

Liabilities and Stockholders' Equity

	1986	1987
Accounts payable	$ 34,327	$ 35,099
Notes payable	14,544	20,907
Accrued income and other taxes	28,526	40,112
Other accrued expenses	19,854	22,299
Total current liabilities	$ 97,251	$118,417
Long-term debt	75,817	67,006
Cumulative preferred stock	582	565
Common stock	26,596	26,812
Capital surplus	2,030	2,606
Retained earnings	92,683	133,559
Less common stock held in treasury	(458)	(14)
Total stockholders' equity	121,433	163,528
Total liabilities and stockholders' equity	$294,501	$348,951

L. M. Myers, Inc. Income Statements for the Years Ended December 31 ($000)

	1986	1987
Sales (net)	$706,457	$777,104
Less: Cost of goods sold	637,224	662,093
Gross profit	$ 69,233	$115,011
Operating expenses:		
Selling and administrative expenses	17,612	17,804
Labor expense	9,418	15,263
Depreciation	6,976	7,428
Miscellaneous operating expenses	1,887	2,011
Total	$ 35,893	$ 42,506

L. M. Myers, Inc. Income Statements for the Years Ended December 31 ($000) (continued)

	1986	1987
Net operating income	$ 33,340	$ 72,505
Interest income	512	2,012
	33,852	74,517
Less: Interest expense	9,127	8,408
Earnings before taxes	$ 24,725	$ 66,109
Less: Taxes payable	5,440	25,232
Net income	$ 19,285	$ 40,877
Less: Preferred dividends	58	56
Net earnings available to common	$ 19,227	$ 40,821

EXHIBIT 1. Financial Ratios for L. M. Myers, Inc.

Ratio	1986	1987	Industry Norm[a]
Acid test ratio			1.00 ×
Current ratio			1.61 ×
Average collection period[b]			30.00 days
Inventory turnover[b]			10.1 ×
Debt ratio			49.1%
Long-term debt to total capitalization			31.0%
Times interest earned			5.87 ×
Cash flow overall coverage ratio			7.42 ×
Total asset turnover			2.1 ×
Gross profit margin			11.7%
Operating profit margin			7.6%
Operating income return on investment			14.75%
Return on total assets			8.45%
Return on common equity			21.39%

[a] These industry norms pertain to Myers's grain export operations, which comprised over 70 percent of the firm's sales for 1986. Also, the industry averages are applicable to both 1986 and 1987.

[b] Compute using end-of-year figures and assuming all sales are credit sales.

Self-Test Solutions

SS–1. Note that Ray's current ratio before the inventory expansion is as follows:

$$\text{current ratio} = \$6,000,000/\text{current liabilities} = 4$$

Thus, the firm's present level of current liabilities is $1,500,000. If the expansion in inventories is financed entirely with borrowed funds, then the change in inventories, ΔInv, is equal to the change in current liabilities and the firm's current ratio after the expansion can be defined as follows:

$$\text{current ratio} = (\$6,000,000 + \Delta\text{Inv})/(\$1,500,000 + \Delta\text{Inv}) = 3$$

Note that we set the new current ratio equal to the firm's target of 3 to 1. Solving for the value of ΔInv in the above equation, we determine that the firm can expand its inventories and finance the expansion with current liabilities by $750,000 and still maintain its target current ratio.

SS–2.   **M & G Industries Ratio Analysis**

		Industry Averages	1986	1987
a.	Current ratio	1.80	1.84	0.90
	Acid test ratio	0.70	0.78	0.24
	Average collection period	37 days	36 days	36 days
	Inventory turnover	2.50 ×	2.59 ×	2.11 ×
	Debt ratio	58%	50%	61.3%
	Long-term debt to total capitalization	33%	33.8%	28.3%
	Times interest earned	3.8 ×	4.0 ×	2.79 ×
	Gross profit margin	38%	40.0%	40.0%
	Operating profit margin	10%	9.6%	10.6%
	Net profit margin	3.5%	3.6%	3.4%
	Total asset turnover	1.14 ×	1.11 ×	1.07 ×
	Fixed asset turnover	1.40 ×	2.02 ×	1.82 ×
	Operating income return on investment	11.4%	10.6%	11.3%
	Return on total assets	4.0%	4.0%	3.6%
	Return on common equity	9.5%	8.0%	9.4%

b.   It appears that M & G is in a very weak position to request an additional loan. An examination of the ratios computed in part (a) shows that the liquidity of M & G has decreased considerably during the past year to a point well below the industry average. In addition, its debt ratio has risen to a point above the industry average, although the difference is not particularly large. However, an additional loan would increase this difference. The times interest earned ratio has decreased significantly over the previous year to a point well below the industry norm of 3.8 ×. The firm's profit margins are very near the respective norms. In sum, the return on the owners' investment is good, but the firm's low liquidity and extensive use of financial leverage do not warrant approval of the loan.

SS–3.   **M & G Industries Statement of Sources and Uses in Funds for the Year Ended December 31, 1987**

a. Cash balance, December 31, 1986	$ 9,000	%
Sources of Funds:		
Funds provided by operations:		
Net income	5,450	9.6
Depreciation	10,000	17.6
	$15,450	
Increase in accounts payable	11,500	20.2
Increase in bank notes	30,000	52.6
Total sources of funds	$56,950	100.0%
Uses of Funds:		
Increase in accounts receivable	$ 3,500	5.3
Increase in inventories	16,500	25.2
Purchase of land	6,000	9.2
Purchase of building and equipment	30,000	45.8
Retirement of long-term debt	5,800	8.9
Common stock dividends	3,650	5.6
Total uses of funds	$65,450	100.0%
Cash balance, December 31, 1987	$ 500	

b. The source and use of funds statement is an important supplement to ratio analysis. This statement directs the analysts' attention to where M & G Industries obtained financing during the period and how those funds were spent. For example, 52 percent of M & G's funds came from an increase in bank notes, while 20 percent came from an increase in accounts payable. In addition, the largest uses of funds were additions to buildings and equipment and increases in inventories. Thus, M & G did little in the most recent operating period to alleviate the financial problems we noted earlier in our ratio analysis. In fact, M & G aggravated matters by purchasing fixed assets using short-term sources of financing. It would appear that another short-term loan at this time is *not* warranted.

Selected References

Altman, Edward I. "Financial Ratios, Discriminant Analysis and the Prediction of Corporate Bankruptcy," *Journal of Finance*, 23 (September 1968), 598–609.

———, R. G. Haldeman, and P. Narayanan. "Zeta Analysis: A New Model to Identify Bankruptcy Risk of Corporations," *Journal of Banking and Finance*, 1 (June 1977), 29–54.

Beaver, William H. "Financial Ratios as Predictors of Failure," *Empirical Research in Accounting: Selected Studies in Journal of Accounting Research* (1966), 71–111.

Bedingfield, J. P., P. M. J. Reckers, and A. J. Stagliano. "Distributions of Financial Ratios in the Commercial Banking Industry, *Journal of Financial Research* (Spring 1985), 77–81.

Benishay, Haskell. "Economic Information in Financial Ratio Analysis," *Accounting and Business Research*, 2 (Spring 1971), 174–79.

Bowlin, Oswald D., John D. Martin, and David F. Scott, Jr. *Guide to Financial Analysis*, Chap. 2. New York: McGraw-Hill, 1979.

Chen, Kung H., and T. A. Shimerda. "An Empirical Analysis of Useful Financial Ratios," *Financial Management*, 10 (Spring 1981), 51–60.

Collins, R. A. "An Empirical Comparison of Bankruptcy Prediction Models," *Financial Management* (Summer 1980), 52–7.

Ford, J. K. *A Framework for Financial Analysis*. Englewood Cliffs, NJ: Prentice-Hall, 1981, Chap. 2, 3.

Foster, George. *Financial Statement Analysis*. Englewood Cliffs, NJ: Prentice-Hall, 1978.

Frecka, T., and C. F. Lee. "Generalized Ratio Generation Process and Its Implications," *Journal of Accounting Research* (Spring 1983), 308–16.

Helfert, Erich A. *Techniques of Financial Analysis* (4th ed.), Chap. 2. Homewood, IL: Richard D. Irwin, 1977.

Harrington, D. R., and B. D. Wilson. *Corporate Financial Analysis*. (Plano, TX: BPI, Inc., 1986, Chap. 1.

———. *Techniques of Financial Analysis*. Homewood, IL: Richard D. Irwin, 1987, Chap. 2.

Kieso, Donald E., and Jerry J. Weygandt. *Intermediate Accounting*. New York: Wiley, 1980.

Lev, Baruch. *Financial Statement Analysis: A New Approach*. Englewood Cliffs, NJ: Prentice-Hall, 1974.

Lewellen, W. G., and R. W. Johnson. "Better Way to Monitor Accounts Receivable," *Harvard Business Review*, 50 (May–June 1972), 101–9.

Murray, Roger F. "The Penn Central Debacle: Lessons for Financial Analysis," *Journal of Finance*, 26 (May 1971), 327–32.

O'Connor, Melvin C. "On the Usefulness of Financial Ratios to Investors in Common Stock," *Accounting Review*, 48 (April 1973), 339–52.

Pinches, G. E., J. C. Singleton, and A. Jahankhani. "Fixed Coverage as a Determinant of Electric Utility Bond Ratings," *Financial Management*, Summer 1978, pp. 45–85.

Robert Morris Associates. *Annual Statement Studies*. Philadelphia, Pa: Updated annually.

Seitz, N. *Financial Analysis: A Programmed Approach*. Reston, VA: Reston Publishing Co., 1979.

Sorter, George H., and George Benston. "Appraising the Defensive Position of a Firm: The Internal Measure," *Accounting Review*, 35 (October 1960), 633–40.

Stone, B. K. "The Payments-Pattern Approach to the Forecasting of Accounts Receivable," *Financial Management*, Autumn 1976, 65–82.

APPENDIX 3A
─Review of Selected Accounting Principles and Practices─

Successful financial analysis requires a thorough understanding of the basic principles that underlie the preparation of financial statements. Our objective in this appendix is to review the fundamental principles of financial accounting. A complete treatment is, of course, outside the purview of this text. In addition, we discuss the valuation of fixed assets and inventories, since both these account balances are materially affected by the underlying method used.

BASIC ACCOUNTING PRINCIPLES

Historical Cost Principle

The **historical cost principle** provides the basis for determining the book values of the firm's balance sheet accounts. The primary advantage of historical cost is its objectivity. Its primary disadvantage relates to the fact that the asset balances do not correspond to market values or replacement costs. Furthermore, since asset book values are not equal to market values, the book value of owners' equity does not equal its market value. In analyzing the firm's financial statements, the analyst must keep in mind that asset balances reflect historical costs of the related assets and not current market values.

Revenue Realization (Recognition) Principle

When a firm's income statement is prepared, the accountant must decide what revenues should be allocated to the period covered by the statement. As simple as this may sound, it can present some very serious difficulties. In principle, revenue is recognized during the period in which (1) the earning process is virtually complete and (2) an exchange transaction has occurred. In most cases these conditions are satisfied at the point of sale. However, in practice several methods other than determination of the amount of sales for the period can be used to measure revenue. These include

1. **Percentage of completion.** Here recognition of revenue is allowed in certain long-term contracts (construction) before the contract is completed. Revenue is recognized in each period equal to the product of the contract price and the ratio, period costs/total estimated project costs.
2. **End of production.** In some instances revenue is recognized before an actual sale (but after production has ended). This is the case where the price is certain as well as the amount, as in revenues involving agricultural commodities where governmental price floors are in effect.
3. **Receipt of cash.** The cash basis is used for revenue recognition when, as a result of the uncertainty of collection, it is impossible to establish the revenue figure at the time of sale. This is common where installment sales are made and payments cover long periods.

The diversity of methods used and the complexity of the problem of determining when revenues are realized can lead the analyst to erroneous conclusions. For example, during the 1960s a great number of franchising operations were established for a variety of businesses, such as McDonald's, Kentucky Fried Chicken, and Shakey's Pizza. In nearly all cases, as soon as the franchisor found an individual franchisee and received a down payment, the entire franchise price was treated as realized income. Consequently, to avoid any dip in income that would damage their growth in earnings, many franchisors signed up franchisees at an increasingly faster rate each year. This was necessary because the initial franchise fees were treated as revenue immediately—even though in many situations those fees were payable over a period of years and in some instances, as in the case of franchises that never got started, were refundable or uncollectible.

Matching Principle

To compute net income for a given year's operations accountants must identify all revenue and expense items that belong within the year. The **accrual basis of accounting** attempts to allocate revenue and expense properly among the years that an enterprise is in operation. This method utilizes the **revenue realization principle** such that revenue is recognized in the period in which it is earned, and uses the **matching principle** to determine the amount of expenses necessary during the period for the revenue to be generated. These expenses are thus *matched* against revenue for the period. The basic principle, therefore, involves matching expenses with the revenues, or "Let the expense follow the revenue." Thus, wage expense is not recognized when it is paid nor necessarily when work is performed, but when the work performed actually contributes to revenues.

An example of the potential difficulties posed for the analyst in implementation of the matching principle can be found in the depreciation policies followed by different firms for like assets. For example, one major U.S. airline, referred to here as airline A, depreciates its planes over 10 years. Another major U.S. airline, airline B, depreciates over as long as 16 years. Thus, other things being the same, airline A would report higher expenses and lower profits from its operations than would airline B. Depreciation methods are discussed later in this appendix.

Consistency Principle

The principle simply requires that accounting entities account for transactions according to the same methods from period to period. Companies can and do switch from one method of accounting to another; however, changes are restricted to situations in which it can be demonstrated that any newly adopted principle is preferable to the old. Furthermore, the nature and effect of the accounting change as well as the justification for it must be disclosed in the financial statements for the period in which the change is made. Such disclosures are made in footnotes to the financial statements, which offer supplemental and explanatory information.

Full Disclosure Principle

Since many events and circumstances that relate to the financial position of a firm may not be reflected in the body of the financial statement, this principle requires that there must be full disclosure in the financial statements of all relevant facts such that an informed reader can appropriately evaluate the statements. Common methods of disclosure include (1) parenthetical disclosure and (2) footnote disclosure. Particularly difficult problem areas include accounting for leases, investment credits, pension fund liabilities, franchising, options, and mergers. Furthermore, it may be necessary to report (in a footnote) events subsequent to the date of the financial statements in order to provide full disclosure.

Objectivity (Verifiability) Principle

The idea here is that data should be objectively determined and verifiable such that another accountant faced with the same situation would have arrived at the same conclusions. The purpose is to provide more credibility to financial statements.

This concludes our very brief overview of accounting principles. Perhaps most important to the analyst are the historical cost, revenue realization, and matching principles. We should also note that deviations from these general principles can and do occur. Notable exceptions arise where the item being analyzed is considered immaterial or insignificant, where accepted industry practice deviates from the guiding principle, or where governmental reporting requirements disagree in some way with the basic principle involved.

DEPRECIATION OF FIXED ASSETS

Depreciation expense represents an allocation of the cost of a fixed asset over its useful life. The objective is to match such costs with the revenues that result from their utilization in the enterprise. Furthermore, depreciation expense is used to reduce the balance sheet book value of the firm's fixed assets. Thus, the method used to determine depreciation expense also serves as the basis for determining the book value of fixed assets. Two methods commonly used for computing depreciation are straight line, and the accelerated cost recovery system. These depreciation methods were discussed in Chapter 2.

ACCOUNTING FOR INVENTORIES AND COST OF GOODS SOLD

Several methods can be used to determine a firm's cost of goods sold. Each relates to the basis used in valuing the firm's inventory, since the firm's purchases that are *not* passed through the income statement as cost of goods sold remain in the firm's inventory account. We will discuss two very common methods for determining the cost of goods sold and consequently the value of the inventory account. The first involves assigning to the period's cost of goods sold the prices paid for the oldest items of inventory held by the firm at the beginning of the period. This is commonly referred to as the **first-in, first-out** or **FIFO** method. The second assigns the cost of the most recently purchased inventory items to the period's cost of goods sold. This is called the **last-in, first-out** or **LIFO** method. The method selected can have a material effect on the firm's computed net earnings during a period where the prices of its purchases consistently rose or fell. For example, in a period when prices have been rising, the use of the FIFO method results in a lower cost of goods sold, a larger gross profit, a higher tax liability, a higher inventory amount, and a higher net earnings figure than LIFO; LIFO (which costs the firm's sale items using the most recent prices paid by the firm) will result in a lower inventory amount, a higher cost of goods sold figure, and, consequently, lower gross profits, lower taxes, and lower net earnings. The opposite result would follow should prices have fallen during the period.

What importance should be attached to the choice of methods for determining cost of goods sold? Under either method the cash flows that result from sales will be the same, for the actual cost of the items sold does not vary with the method chosen for computing cost of goods sold. However, a very real cash flow effect can result in terms of the amount of taxes that the firm must pay. During a period of rising prices LIFO results in lower taxes being paid than FIFO, while during a period of falling prices the opposite is true.[1] Furthermore, it should be noted that the reported inventory amounts may vary considerably with the application of one method as compared with the other—but the physical quantity and composition of the goods is not affected.

---

[1] The Internal Revenue Service does not allow frequent changes in inventory policy. Once a policy has been adopted, it may not be changed without the Commissioner's consent. Furthermore, changing the inventory costing method solely for the purpose of reducing taxes is not accepted by the Internal Revenue Service. Instead, the taxpayer must show that the new method more closely matches revenues with cost of goods sold. See Regulation 1.471–2 of the Internal Revenue Code for a more detailed discussion.

APPENDIX 3B
—Glossary of Accounting Terms—

accelerated depreciation. A term encompassing any method for computing depreciation expense wherein the charges decrease with time. Examples of accelerated methods include sum-of-the-years' digits and double-declining balance as contrasted with straight-line.

accounts payable. A current liability representing the total amount owed by a firm from its past (unpaid) credit purchases.

accounts receivable. A current asset including all monies owed to a firm from past (uncollected) credit sales.

accrual basis of accounting. The method of recognizing revenues when the earning process is virtually complete and when an exchange transaction has occurred, and recognizing expenses as they are incurred in generating those revenues. Thus, revenues and expenses recognized under the accrual basis of accounting are independent of the time when cash is received or expenditures are made. This contrasts with the cash basis of accounting.

accrued salaries and wages. Salary and wage expense the firm owes but has not yet paid (a current liability).

accumulated depreciation. The sum of depreciation charges on an asset since its acquisition. This total is deducted from gross fixed assets to compute net fixed assets. This balance sheet entry is sometimes referred to as the reserve for depreciation, accrued depreciation, or the allowance for depreciation.

ACRS. Accelerated Cost Recovery System. (See Chapter 2.)

administrative expense. An expense category used to report expenses incurred by the firm but not reflected in specific activities such as manufacturing or selling.

amortizing. The procedure followed in allocating the cost of long-lived assets to the periods in which their benefits are derived. For fixed assets the amortization is called depreciation expense, whereas for wasting assets (natural resources), it is called depletion expense.

asset. Anything owned by a firm or individual that has commercial value.

authorized capital stock. This indicates the total number of shares of stock the firm can issue and is specified in the articles of incorporation.

bad debt expense. An adjustment to income and accounts receivable reflecting the value of uncollectible accounts.

balance sheet. statement of financial position on a particular date. The balance sheet equation is as follows: total assets = total liabilities + owners' equity.

bond. Long-term debt instrument carried on the balance sheet at its face amount or par value (usually $1000 per bond), which is payable at maturity. The coupon rate on the bond is the percentage of the bond's face value payable in interest each year. Bonds usually pay interest semiannually.

book value. The net amount of an asset shown in the accounts of a firm. When referring to an entire firm, it relates the excess of total assets over total liabilities (also referred to as owners' equity and net worth).

capital. Sometimes, the total assets of a firm; at other times, the owners' equity alone.

capital stock. All shares of outstanding common and preferred stock.

capitalization. Stockholders' equity plus the par value of outstanding bonds.

cash flow. The excess (deficiency) of cash receipts over cash disbursements for a given period.

common stock. The stock interest of the residual owners of the firm. These owners have claim to earnings and asset values remaining after the claims of all creditors and preferred stockholders are satisfied.

cost of goods sold. The total cost allocated to the production of a completed product for the period.

current assets. Assets that are normally converted

into cash within the operating cycle of the firm (normally a period of one year or less). Such items as cash, accounts receivable, marketable securities, prepaid expenses, and inventories are frequently found among a firm's current assets.

current liabilities. Liabilities or debts of the firm that must be paid within the firm's normal operating cycle (usually one year or less), such as accounts and notes payable, income taxes payable, and wages and salaries payable.

debentures. Long-term debt (bonds) that are secured only by the integrity of the issuer (that is, no specific assets are pledged as collateral).

deferred income taxes. Income taxes that a firm recognizes as being owed based upon its earnings but that are not payable until a later date.

depreciable life. The period over which an asset is depreciated.

depreciation expense. Amortization of plant, property, and equipment cost during an accounting period.

dividend. A distribution of earnings to the owners of a corporation in the form of cash (cash dividend) or shares of stock (stock dividend).

double-declining balance depreciation. A method for computing declining balance depreciation expense in which the constant percentage is equal to 2/N, where N represents the depreciable life of the asset.

earnings. A synonym for net income or net profit after taxes. Owing to the ambiguity that arises in using the general term earnings, it is usually avoided in favor of more specific terms such as net operating earnings or earnings after tax.

earnings after taxes (EAT). Other terms often used synonymously are net income and net profit after taxes.

earnings before interest and taxes (EBIT). A commonly used synonym for net operating income. Note that where other income exists, EBIT equals net operating income plus other income.

earnings before taxes (EBT). Total net earnings after the deduction of all tax-deductible expenses.

earnings per share. Net income after taxes available to the common stockholders (after preferred divi-

dends) divided by the number of outstanding common shares.

equity financing. The raising of funds through the sale of common or preferred stock.

ERTA. Economic Recovery Tax Act of 1981.

A revenue or expense that is both unusual in nature and infrequent in occurrence. Such items and their tax effects are separated from ordinary income in the income statement.

FIFO. A method for determining the inventory cost assigned to cost of goods sold wherein the cost of the oldest items in inventory is charged to the period's cost of goods sold (first in, first out). Ending inventories therefore will reflect the prices paid for the most recent purchases. See also the discussion in Appendix 3A.

fixed assets. These assets share the characteristic that they are not converted into cash within a single operating cycle of the firm; they include buildings, equipment, and land.

general and administrative expense. Expenses associated with the managerial and policy-making aspects of a business.

goodwill. Included as an asset entry in the balance sheet to reflect the excess over fair market value paid for the assets of an acquired firm.

gross profit. The excess of net sales over cost of goods sold.

income statement. The statement of profit or loss for the period comprised of net revenues less expenses for the period. (See **accrual basis of accounting**.)

income tax. An annual expense incurred by the firm based upon income and paid to a governmental entity.

intangible asset. An asset that lacks physical substance, such as goodwill or patent.

interest expense. The price paid for borrowed money over some specified period of time.

inventory. The balance in an asset account such as raw materials, work in process, or finished goods. (See **LIFO** and **FIFO**.)

lease. A contract requiring payments by the user (lessee) to its owner (lessor) for the use of an asset. In accordance with FASB Statement 13 most financial lease agreements entered into after January 1, 1977, must be included in the assets and liabilities of the lessee's balance sheet. The right of the lessee to use the asset is represented by an asset called a lease-hold.

liability. An obligation to pay a specified amount to a creditor in return for some current benefit.

LIFO. A method for determining the inventory cost assigned to cost of goods sold whereby the cost of the most recent purchases of inventory is assigned to the period's cost of goods sold (last-in, first-out). Ending inventories thus contain the cost of the oldest items of inventory.

liquid assets. Those assets of the firm which can easily be converted into cash with little or no loss in value. Generally included are cash, marketable securities, and sometimes accounts receivable.

long-term debt. All liabilities of the firm that are not due and payable within one year. Examples include installment notes, equipment loans, and bonds payable.

marketable securities. The securities (bonds and stocks) of other firms and governments held by a firm.

net income. See **earnings after taxes (EAT).**

net operating income (NOI). Income earned by a firm in the course of its normal operations. Calculated as net sales less the sum of cost of goods sold and operating expenses.

net plant and equipment. Gross plant and equipment less accumulated depreciation.

net sales. Gross sales less returns, allowances, and cash discounts taken by customers.

notes payable. A liability (normally short-term) of the firm representing a monetary indebtedness.

operating expense. Any expense incurred in the normal operation of a firm.

owners' equity. Total assets minus total liabilities, sometimes referred to as net worth.

paid-in capital. The excess of total capital paid in over the stock's par or stated value. For example, if a share of stock with a $1 par value is sold by a firm for $10, the common stock account will be increased by $1 and paid-in capital will rise by $9.

par value. The face value of a security.

patent. The rights to the benefits of one's invention granted to the inventor by the government. These rights are extended for a maximum of 17 years.

preferred stock. The capital stock of the owners of the firm whose claim on assets and income is secondary to that of bondholders but preferred as to that of the common stockholders.

profit and loss statement. Another name for the income statement.

retained earnings. The sum of a firm's net income over its life less all dividends paid.

revenue. See **net sales.**

selling expense. An expense incurred in the selling of a firm's product. Examples would include salespeople's commissions and advertising expenditures.

sinking fund. Assets and their earnings set aside to retire long-term debt obligations of the firm. Payments into sinking funds are made after taxes and are usually described in the bond indenture (contract between the borrowing firm and the bondholders).

stock dividend. A dividend that results in a transfer of retained earnings to the capital stock and paid-in capital accounts. This contrasts with a cash dividend. (See **dividend.**)

TEFRA. Tax Equity and Fiscal Responsibility Act of 1982.

TBT leases. Tax Benefit Transfer leases created under the ERTA of 1981 and eliminated by TEFRA of 1982.

TRA. Tax Reform Act of 1986.

4

Financial Forecasting, Planning, and Budgeting

The impact of computers and financial software has had a dramatic impact on the practice of financial forecasting, planning, and budgeting. Financial spreadsheet programs allow the financial analyst to tabulate very large and cumbersome budgets which can, with the aid of a microcomputer, be easily modified to reflect any number of possible scenarios. This type of "trial and error" analysis can greatly enhance analysts' decision-making capability by allowing them quickly and easily to assess the importance of the projections and assumptions that go into any financial plan.

This chapter has two primary objectives: First, it will develop an appreciation for the role of forecasting in the firm's financial planning process. Basically, forecasts of future sales revenues and their associated expenses give the firm the information needed to project its future needs for financing. Second, the chapter will provide an overview of the firm's budgetary system, including the cash budget and the pro forma or planned income statement and balance sheet. Pro forma financial statements give the financial manager a useful tool for analyzing the effects of the firm's forecasts and planned activities on its financial performance, as well as its needs for financing. In addition, pro forma statements can be used as a benchmark or standard to compare against actual operating results. Used in this way, pro forma statements are an instrument for controlling or monitoring the firm's progress throughout the planning period.

FINANCIAL FORECASTING

The need for forecasting in financial management arises where the future financing needs of the firm are being estimated. The basic steps involved in predicting those financing needs include the following: Step 1: Project the firm's sales revenues and expenses over the planning period. Step 2: Estimate the levels of investment in current and fixed assets that are necessary to support the projected sales. Step 3: Determine the firm's financing needs throughout the planning period.

The Cash Flow Cycle

The entire firm's operations can be visualized through the use of a **cash flow cycle diagram.** The diagram, as shown in Figure 4–1 on page 87, depicts the firm's operations as a large pump that pushes cash through various reservoirs such as inventories and accounts receivable and dispenses cash for taxes, interest and principal payments on debt, and cash dividends to the shareholders. The problem in financial forecasting, then, is one of predicting cash inflows and outflows and the corresponding financial needs of the firm. These needs are related to the size of the various reservoirs that hold cash. These reservoirs represent the various assets in which the firm must make investments in order to produce the expected level of sales.

Tracing the Cash Flow Cycle

Since the firm's cash flow cycle is a continuous process, we will find it useful for illustrative purposes to consider the first cycle of a new firm. The process begins with the firm's cash reservoir, which consists initially of the owner's investment (funds raised through the issuance of stock) and funds borrowed from creditors. This cash is used to acquire plant and equipment, as well as supplies and materials. It is also used to pay wages and salaries, to pay for utilities such as heat and power, and to replace materials, plant, and equipment that are used or worn out in the process of making the firm's product. These expenditures make up the cost of goods sold for the firm's salable product. Sales are then made either for cash or on credit (with some leakage for bad debt losses). To this cash flow stream are added cash inflows resulting from the sale of assets such as equipment, land, or securities. In the final phase of the cycle, cash is dispersed to pay obligations to suppliers for materials purchased on credit, income taxes to the government, interest and principal to the firm's creditors, and cash dividends to the firm's owners. Finally, any cash not paid in dividends is reinvested in the firm and becomes a part of the owners' investment.

BASIC FINANCIAL MANAGEMENT IN PRACTICE

Cash flow is at least as important a measure of corporate health as reported earnings. But put a dozen investors in a room and you'll get almost as many different definitions of "cash flow" (FORBES, *Apr. 7, 1986*).

After grappling with the problem for more than six years, the Financial Accounting Standards Board has come up with the beginnings of a more precise definition. It would require all companies to use the same format to explain how cash and cash equivalents change from one reporting period to the next. The proposal still leaves companies with room for flexibility but will make investors' lives much easier. Why? Companies will have to show sources and uses of cash in three areas: operations, investing, financing.

Let's take a specific case: Lowe's Cos., the North Carolina-based retailer of building materials. Last year Lowe's said in its annual report that cash flow amounted to $2.31 per share in 1985 as compared with $2.20 the year before. An investor looking at these numbers might have assumed Lowe's had plenty of cash left over for dividends and other purposes.

Not necessarily so. Although Lowe's used a generally accepted definition of cash flow, it was not a strict definition. It failed to subtract the cash absorbed by higher inventories and receivables. Lowe's ended the year with hardly more cash than it started the year, and its long-term debt almost doubled from 1984 to 1985—despite the positive cash flow.

Does it really matter how you measure cash flow? Very much. While Lowe's is healthy—the increased inventory and receivables simply reflect growth in revenues— there are situations where a company can go broke while reporting positive cash flow. How can this be? Simple.

Suppose inventories and receivables rise faster than sales—reflecting slow pay by customers and unsold goods. Under the simpler method of reporting cash flow (which would not include working capital components), such a company could report a positive cash flow even while it was fast running out of cash.

When the smoke clears, investors will still need to do lots of homework. It's never enough to know just what the numbers are. You still have to figure out what the numbers mean. Again, Lowe's is an example. Even if it were forced to report a negative cash flow, it would still be a very healthy business; it would cease being one only if inventories and receivables increased faster than sales and the company's credit were deteriorating.

When it comes to some things, the more you try simplifying them, the more complicated they become.

Source: Pouschine, Tatiana, "Now You See It . . . ," Forbes Inc. *Forbes*, 139 (February 9, 1987, 70.)

Forecasting Cash Flows

The problem of financial forecasting, to summarize, consists of predicting future sales, which in turn provides the basis for predicting the level of investment in inventories, receivables, plant, and equipment required to support the firm's projected sales. Through the use of the cash budget the information from these projections is combined to provide an estimate of the firm's future financing needs.

Sales Forecast

The key ingredient in the firm's planning process is the **sales forecast.** This projection will generally be derived using information from a number of sources. At a minimum, the sales forecast for the coming year would reflect (1) any past trend in sales that is expected to carry through into the new year, and (2) the influence of any events that might materially affect that trend.[1] An example of the latter would be the initiation of a major advertising campaign or a change in the firm's pricing policy.

---

[1] A discussion of forecast methodology is outside the scope of this book. The interested reader is referred to John C. Chambers, Satinder K. Mullick, and Donald D. Smith, *An Executive's Guide to Forecasting* (New York: Wiley, 1974); Roger K. Chisholm and Gilbert R. Whitaker, Jr., *Forecasting Methods* (Homewood, IL.: Richard D. Irwin, 1971); Carl A. Dauten, *Business Cycles and Forecasting* (Cincinnati: Southwestern Publishing, 1974), and George G. C. Parker, "Financial Forecasting," in *Handbook of Corporate Finance*, E. I. Altman, editors, (New York: John Wiley and Sons: 1986).

In addition, the firm can obtain sales forecasts through the use of outside consulting firms that specialize in economic forecasting. These outside consultants can be used to provide the final sales forecast or to provide projections of general economic factors that the firm's analysts can use in preparing their own forecast sales.

FIGURE 4–1. Cash Flow Diagram

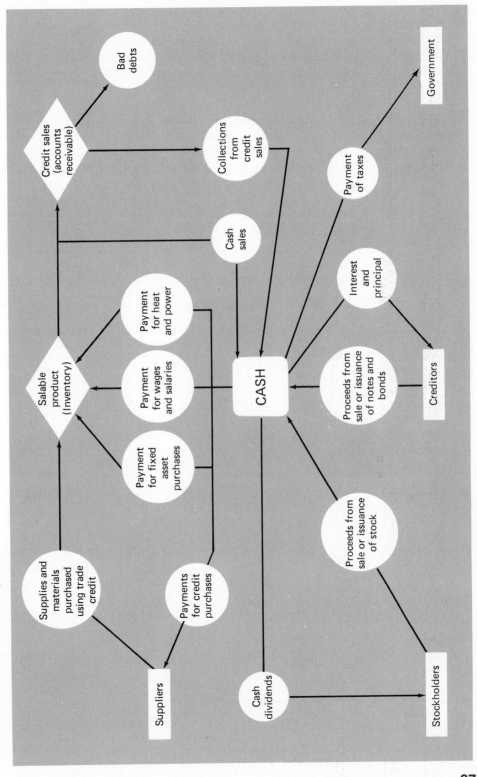

Forecasting Financial Variables

Traditional financial forecasting takes the sales forecast as a given and makes forecasts of its impact on the firm's various expenses, assets, and liabilities. There are two commonly used methods for making these projections: (1) the percent of sales method and (2) regression analysis. Only the former is discussed here. The regression method is discussed in the appendix to this chapter.

Percent of Sales Method of Financial Forecasting

The **percent of sales method** involves estimating the level of an expense, asset, or liability for a future period as a percent of the sales forecast. The percentage used can come from the most recent financial statement item as a percent of current sales, from an average computed over several years, from the judgment of the analyst, or from some combination of these sources.

Figure 4–2 presents a complete example of the use of the percent of sales method of financial forecasting. In that example each item in the firm's balance sheet that varies with sales is converted to a percent of 1987 sales. The forecast of the new balance for each item is then calculated by multiplying this percentage times the $12 million in projected sales for the 1988 planning period. This method of forecasting

FIGURE 4–2. Using the Percent of Sales Method to Forecast Future Financing Requirements

Assets	Present (1987)	Percent of Sales (1987 Sales = $10 M)	Projected (Based on 1988 Sales = $12 M)
Current assets	$2 M	$\frac{\$2\ M}{\$10\ M} = 20\%$	$.2 \times \$12\ M = \$2.4\ M$
Net fixed assets	4 M	$\frac{\$4\ M}{\$10\ M} = 40\%$	$.4 \times \$12\ M = \underline{4.8\ M}$
Total	$6 M		$7.2 M

Liabilities and Owners' Equity			
Accounts payable	$1.0 M	$\frac{\$1\ M}{\$10\ M} = 10\%$	$.10 \times \$12\ M = \$1.2\ M$
Accrued expenses	1.0 M	$\frac{\$1\ M}{\$10\ M} = 10\%$	$.10 \times \$12\ M = \$1.2\ M$
Notes payable	.5 M	NA[a]	no change	.5 M
Long-term debt	$2.0 M	NA[a]	no change	2.0 M
Total liabilities	$4.5 M			$4.9 M
Common stock	$ .1 M	NA[a]		$ .1 M
Paid-in capital	.2 M	NA[a]		.2 M
Retained earnings	1.2 M		$1.2\ M + [.05 \times \$12\ M \times (1 - .5)] =$	1.5 M[b]
Common equity	$1.5 M			$1.8 M
Total	$6.0 M		Total financing provided	$6.7 M
			Discretionary financing needed	.5 M[c]
			Total	$7.2 M

[a] Not applicable. These account balances are assumed not to vary with sales.

[b] Projected retained earnings equals the beginning level ($1.2 M) plus projected net income less any dividends paid. In this case net income is projected to equal 5 percent of sales and dividends are projected to equal half of net income: $.05 \times \$12\ M \times (1 - .5) = \$300,000$

[c] Discretionary financing needed equals projected total assets ($7.2 M) less projected total liabilities ($4.9 M) less projected common equity ($1.8 M) or $7.2\ M - 4.9\ M - 1.8\ M = \$500,000$.

future financing is not as precise or detailed as the cash budget based methodology presented later; however, it offers a relatively low-cost and easy-to-use first approximation of the firm's financing needs for a future period.

Note that in the example in Figure 4–2 both current and fixed assets are assumed to vary with the level of firm sales. This means that the firm does not have sufficient productive capacity to absorb a projected increase in sales. Thus, if sales were to rise by $1, fixed assets would rise by 40 cents, or 40 percent of the projected increase in sales. Note that if the fixed assets the firm presently owns had been sufficient to support the projected level of new sales, these assets should not be allowed to vary with sales. If this were the case, then fixed assets would not be converted to a precent of sales and would be projected to remain unchanged for the period being forecast.

Also, we note that accounts payable and accrued expenses are the only liabilities allowed to vary with sales. Both these accounts might reasonably be expected to rise and fall with the level of firm sales; hence the use of the percent of sales forecast. Since these two categories of current liabilities normally vary directly with the level of sales, they are often referred to as **spontaneous** sources of financing. We will have more to say about these forms of financing in Chapter 5 when we discuss working capital management. Notes payable, long-term debt, common stock, and paid-in capital are *not* assumed to vary directly with the level of firm sales. These sources of financing are termed **discretionary,** in that the firm's management must make a conscious decision to seek additional financing using any one of them. Finally, we note that the level of retained earnings *does* vary with estimated sales. The predicted change in the level of retained earnings equals the difference in estimated after-tax profits (projected net income) of $600,000 and common stock dividends of $300,000.

Thus, using the example from Figure 4–2, we estimate that firm sales will increase from $10 M to $12 M, which will cause the firm's needs for total assets to rise to $7.2 M. These assets will then be financed by $4.9 M in existing liabilities plus spontaneous liabilities, $1.8 M in owner funds including $300,000 in retained earnings from next year's sales, and, finally, $500,000 in discretionary financing, which can be raised by issuing notes payable, selling bonds, offering an issue of stock, or some combination of these sources.

In summary, we can estimate the firm's needs for discretionary financing, using the percent of sales method of financial forecasting, by following a four-step procedure:

STEP 1: *Convert each asset and liability account that varies directly with firm sales to a percent of current year's sales.*

$$\textbf{Example:} \quad \frac{\text{current assets}}{\text{sales}} = \frac{\$2 \text{ M}}{\$10 \text{ M}} = .2 \text{ or } 20\%$$

STEP 2: *Project the level of each asset and liability account in the balance sheet using its percent of sales multiplied by projected sales **or** by leaving the account balance unchanged where the account does not vary with the level of sales.*

Example: projected current assets =

$$\text{projected sales} \times \frac{\text{current assets}}{\text{sales}} = \$12\text{ M} \times .2 = \$2.4\text{ M}$$

STEP 3: *Project the level of new retained earnings available to help finance the firm's operations. This equals projected net income for the period less planned common stock dividends.*

Example: projected addition to retained earnings =

$$\text{projected sales} \times \frac{\text{net income}}{\text{sales}} \times \left(1 - \frac{\text{cash dividends}}{\text{net income}}\right)$$

$$= \$12\text{ M} \times .05 \times [1 - .5] = \$300,000$$

STEP 4: *Project the firm's need for discretionary financing as the projected level of total assets less projected liabilities and owners' equity.*

Example: discretionary financing needed =

projected total assets − projected total liabilities − projected owners' equity

$$= \$7.2\text{ M} - \$4.9\text{ M} - \$1.8\text{ M} = \$500,000$$

As we noted earlier, the principal virtue of the percent of sales method of financial forecasting is its simplicity. To obtain a more precise estimate of the amount and timing of the firm's future financing needs, we require a cash budget. The percent of sales method of financial forecasting does provide a very useful, low-cost forerunner to the development of the more detailed cash budget, which the firm will ultimately use to estimate its financing needs.

FINANCIAL PLANNING AND BUDGETING

Financial forecasts are put to use in constructing financial plans. These plans culminate in the preparation of a cash budget and a set of pro forma statements for a future period in the firm's operations.

Budget Functions

A **budget** is simply a forecast of future events. For example, students preparing for final exams make use of time budgets, which help them allocate their limited preparation time among their courses. Students also must budget their financial resources among competing uses, such as books, tuition, food, rent, clothes, and extracurricular activities.

Budgets perform three basic functions for the user. First, they indicate the amount and timing of the firm's needs for future financing. Second, they provide the basis for taking corrective action in the event that budgeted figures do not match actual or realized figures. Third, budgets provide the basis for performance evaluation. Plans are carried out by people, and budgets provide benchmarks that can be used to evaluate the performance of those responsible for carrying out those plans and, in turn, controlling their actions. Thus, budgets are valuable aids in both planning and control aspects of the firm's financial management.

In the pages that follow, we will develop an example budgetary system for a retailing firm. The primary emphasis will be on the cash budget and pro forma financial statements. These statements provide the information needed for a detailed estimate for the firm's future financing requirements.

The Budgetary System

Although our interest in financial planning focuses on the cash budget, a number of other budgets provide the basis for its preparation. This system of budgets allows planning for each source of cash flow, both inflow and outflow, that will affect the firm throughout the planning period. In general, a business will utilize four types of budgets: physical budgets, cost budgets, profit budgets, and cash budgets. Figure 4–3 presents an overview of the budgetary system.

Physical budgets include budgets for unit sales, personnel, unit production, inventories, and actual physical facilities. These budgets are used as the basis for generating cost and profit budgets. **Cost budgets** are prepared for every major expense category of the firm. For example, a manufacturing firm would prepare cost budgets for manufacturing or production cost, selling cost, administrative cost, financing cost, and research and development cost. These cost budgets along with the sales budget provide the basis for preparing a **profit budget.** Finally, converting all the budget information to a cash basis provides the information required to prepare the cash budget.

The Cash Budget

The **cash budget** represents a detailed plan of future cash flows and is composed of four elements: cash receipts, cash disbursements, net change in cash for the period, and new financing needed.

Example. To demonstrate the construction and use of the cash budget, consider Salco, Inc., a regional distributor of household furniture. Salco's sales are highly seasonal, peaking in the months of March through May. Roughly 30 percent of Salco's sales are collected one month after the sale, 50 percent two months after the sale, and the remainder during the third month following the sale.

Salco attempts to pace its purchases with its forecast of future sales. Purchases generally equal 75 percent of sales and are made two months in advance of anticipated sales. Payments are made in the month following purchases. For example, June sales are estimated at $100,000, thus April purchases are .75 × $100,000 = $75,000. Correspondingly, payments for purchases in May equal $75,000. Wages, salaries, rent, and other cash expenses are recorded in Table 4–1, which gives Salco's cash budget for the six-month period ended in June 1988. Additional expenditures are recorded in the cash budget related to the purchase of equipment in the amount of $14,000

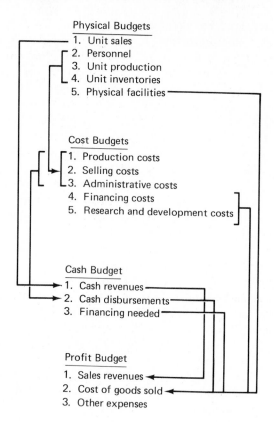

Physical Budgets
1. Unit sales
2. Personnel
3. Unit production
4. Unit inventories
5. Physical facilities

Cost Budgets
1. Production costs
2. Selling costs
3. Administrative costs
4. Financing costs
5. Research and development costs

Cash Budget
1. Cash revenues
2. Cash disbursements
3. Financing needed

Profit Budget
1. Sales revenues
2. Cost of goods sold
3. Other expenses

FIGURE 4—3. The Budget System

during February and the repayment of a $12,000 loan in May. In June Salco will pay $7500 interest on its $150,000 in long-term debt for the period of January–June 1988. Interest on the $12,000 short-term note repaid in May for the period January through May equals $600 and is paid in May.

Salco presently has a cash balance of $20,000 and wants to maintain a minimum balance of $10,000. Additional borrowing necessary to maintain that minimum balance is estimated in the final section of Table 4–1. Borrowing takes place at the beginning of the month in which the funds are needed. Interest on borrowed funds equals 12 percent per annum, or 1 percent per month, and is paid in the month following the one in which funds are borrowed. Thus, interest on funds borrowed in January will be paid in February equal to 1 percent of the loan amount outstanding during January.

The financing-needed line on Salco's cash budget indicates that the firm will need to borrow $36,350 in February, $65,874 in March, $86,633 in April, and $97,599 in May. Only in June will the firm be able to reduce its borrowing to $79,875. Note that the cash budget indicates not only the amount of financing needed during the period, but also when the funds will be needed.

Fixed versus Variable Budgets The cash budget given in Table 4–1 for Salco, Inc., is an example of a **fixed budget.** Cash flow estimates are made for a single set of monthly sales estimates. Thus, the estimates of expenses and new financing needed are meaningful only for the level of sales for which they were computed. To avoid this limitation, several budgets corresponding to different sets of sales estimates can be prepared. Such a flexible budget fulfills two basic needs: It gives information regarding the range of the firm's possible financing needs, and it provides a standard against which to measure the performance of subordinates who are responsible for the various cost and revenue items contained in the budget.[2]

This second function deserves some additional comment. The obvious problem that arises relates to the fact that costs vary with the actual level of sales experienced by the firm. Thus, if the budget is to be used as a standard for performance evaluation or control, it must be constructed to match realized sales and production figures. This can involve much more than simply "adjusting cost figures up or down in proportion to the deviation of actual from planned sales." That is, costs may not vary in strict proportion to sales, just as inventory levels may not vary as a constant percent of sales. Thus, preparation of a flexible budget involves reestimating all the cash expenses that would be incurred at each of several possible sales levels. This process might utilize a variant of the percent of sales method discussed earlier or the regression method discussed in the appendix.[3]

Budget Period

There are no strict rules for determining the length of the budget period. However, as a general rule it should be long enough to show the effect of management policies, yet short enough so that estimates can be made with reasonable accuracy. Applying this rule of thumb to the Salco example in Table 4–1 indicates that the six-month budget period is probably too short, in that it is not known whether the planned operations of the firm will be successful over the coming fiscal year. That is, for most of the first six-month period the firm is operating with a cash flow deficit. If this does not reverse in the latter six months of the year, then a reevaluation of the firm's plans and policies is clearly in order.

Longer-range budgets are also prepared in the form of the capital expenditure budget. This budget details the firm's plans for acquiring plant and equipment over a 5-year, 10-year, or even longer period. Furthermore, firms often develop comprehensive long-range plans extending up to 10 years into the future. These plans are generally not as detailed as the annual cash budget, but they do consider such major components as sales, capital expenditures, new product development, capital funds acquisition, and employment needs.

Pro Forma Financial Statements

The final stage in the budgeting process involves construction of a set of **pro forma financial statements** depicting the end result of the planning period's operations. Salco, Inc., is used to demonstrate the construction of the pro forma income statement and balance sheet. To do this, we need Salco's cash budget (found in Table 4–1)

---

[2] For a discussion of the development of flexible budgets the interested reader is referred to D. F. Scott, Jr., and L. J. Moore, "Simulating Cash Budgets," *Journal of Systems Management*, November 1973, pp. 28–33; and J. L. Pappas and G. P. Huber, "Probabilistic Short-Term Financial Planning," *Financial Management*, Summer 1975, pp. 13–20.

[3] A general overview of financial planning models is found in T. H. Naylor, "Elements of a Planning and Modeling System," *Conference Proceedings of the National Computer Conference*, 45 (Montvale, NJ: AFIPS Press, 1976), pp. 1017–26. An excellent discussion of the financial forecasting problem in general is found in George G. C. Parker, "Financial Forecasting," *Handbook of Corporate Finance*, ed. E. Altman (New York: Wiley, 1986), pp. 2.1–2.37.

TABLE 4–1. Salco Furniture Company, Inc. Cash Budget for the Six Months Ended June 30, 1988

Worksheet	Oct.	Nov.	Dec.
Sales	$55,000	62,000	50,000
Collections:			
First month (30%)			
Second month (50%)			
Third month (20%)			
Total			
Purchases			$56,250
Payments (one-month lag)			
Cash receipts:			
Collections			
Cash disbursements:			
Purchases			
Wages and salaries			
Rent			
Other expenses			
Interest expense on existing debt			
($12,000 note and $150,000 in long-term debt)			
Taxes			
Purchase of equipment			
Loan repayment ($12,000 note due in May)			
Total disbursements			
Net monthly change			
Plus: Beginning cash balance			
Less: Interest on short-term borrowing			
Equals: Ending cash balance—no borrowing			
Financing needed[a]			
Ending cash balance			
Cumulative borrowing			

[a] That amount of financing which is required to raise the firm's ending cash balance up to its $10,000 desired cash balance.

and its beginning balance sheet, which depicts the financial condition of the firm at the start of the planning period (see Table 4–2 on page 96).

The Pro Forma Income Statement

The **pro forma income statement** represents a statement of planned profit or loss for a future period. For Salco a six-month pro forma income statement is constructed from the information contained in the cash budget found in Table 4–1. The final statement is presented in Table 4–3 on page 97.

Net sales, found by summing the six monthly sales projections (January through June) from Table 4–1, total $533,000. Cost of goods sold is computed as 75 percent of sales, or $399,750. This figure could also have been found by summing purchases for November through April, which represent items sold from January through June. Recall that purchases are made two months in advance, so that items sold in January through June were purchased in November through April.

TABLE 4–1 (continued)

Jan.	Feb.	Mar.	Apr.	May	June	July	Aug.
60,000	75,000	88,000	100,000	110,000	100,000	80,000	75,000
15,000	18,000	22,500	26,400	30,000	33,000		
31,000	25,000	30,000	37,500	44,000	50,000		
11,000	12,400	10,000	12,000	15,000	17,600		
$57,000	55,400	62,500	75,900	89,000	100,600		
66,000	75,000	82,500	75,000	60,000	56,250		
56,250	66,000	75,000	82,500	75,000	60,000		
$57,000	55,400	62,500	75,900	89,000	100,600		
$56,250	66,000	75,000	82,500	75,000	60,000		
3,000	10,000	7,000	8,000	6,000	4,000		
4,000	4,000	4,000	4,000	4,000	4,000		
1,000	500	1,200	1,500	1,500	1,200		
				600	7,500		
		4,460			5,200		
	14,000						
				12,000			
$64,250	94,500	91,660	96,000	99,100	81,900		
$(7,250)	(39,100)	(29,160)	(20,100)	(10,100)	18,700		
20,000	12,750	10,000	10,000	10,000	10,000		
—	—	(364)	(659)	(866)	(976)		
12,750	(26,350)	(19,524)	(10,759)	(966)	27,724		
—	**36,350**	**29,524**	**20,759**	**10,966**	**(17,724)[b]**		
$12,750	10,000	10,000	10,000	10,000	10,000		
—	$36,350	65,874	86,633	97,599	79,875		

[b] Negative financing needed simply means the firm has excess cash that can be used to retire a part of its short-term borrowing from prior months.

Depreciation expense cannot be obtained from the cash budget, since it does not constitute a cash flow. Thus, this expense must be determined from the depreciation schedules of Salco's plant and equipment. On its existing fixed assets Salco has an annual depreciation expense of $17,200. In addition, the $14,000 piece of equipment purchased at the end of February will be depreciated over a 15-year life toward a $3650 salvage value. Using straight-line depreciation and depreciating the asset for four months of the budget period, we find this amounts to roughly $230. Thus, total depreciation expense for the period is $8830 [or ($17,200 ÷ 2) + $230].

Wages and salaries, rent, and other expenses are found by summing the relevant cash flow items from the cash budget for the months of January through June. This assumes, of course, that all these expenses are paid at the end of each month in which they are earned, rent is not paid in advance, and all other expenses are paid on a monthly basis except interest on short-term borrowing, which is paid in the

TABLE 4–2. Salco Furniture Co., Inc. Balance Sheet December 31, 1987

Assets		
Current assets		
Cash	$ 20,000	
Accounts receivable	104,400	
Inventories	101,250	
Total current assets		$225,650
Fixed assets		
Net plant and equipment		180,000
Total assets		$405,650

Liabilities and Owners' Equity		
Current liabilities		
Accounts payable	$ 56,250	
Notes payable (due in May 1985)	12,000	
Taxes payable	4,460	
Total current liabilities		$ 72,710
Noncurrent liabilities		
Long-term debt		150,000
Stockholders' equity		
Common stock ($1 per)	$ 20,000	
Paid-in capital	50,000	
Retained earnings	112,940	
Total owners' equity		182,940
Total liabilities and owners' equity		$405,650

month following its incurrence. Wages and salaries total $38,000, rent expense equals $24,000, and other expenses are expected to be $6900.

Subtracting the above operating expenses from gross profit leaves a net operating income of $55,520. Interest expense of $11,764 is then deducted from net operating income to obtain earnings before taxes of $43,756.[4] Federal income taxes payable are found using a 40 percent corporate income tax rate. For Salco this equals a tax expense for the period of $17,502. Finally, subtracting the estimated taxes from earnings before taxes indicates net income for the period of $26,254.

Net Cash Flow versus Net Income

The difference in the cash and accrual bases of accounting for corporate income is vividly demonstrated in the cash budget and pro forma income statements for the period. On a cash flow basis the firm has a substantial net negative cash flow, while on an accrual basis the firm earned $26,254. The difference, of course, relates to when revenues and expenses are accounted for or recognized in the two statements.

---

[4] Total interest expense *incurred* (but not necessarily paid) during the period equals $7500 on long-term debt plus $600 on the $12,000 note repaid in May, plus the sum of all interest incurred during the budget period on short-term borrowing. Note that we include $364 for February, $659 for March, and so forth, plus $799 for June, which was incurred but not paid until July.

TABLE 4–3. Salco Furniture Co., Inc. Pro Forma Income Statement for the Six-Month Period Ended June 30, 1988

Sales	(from cash budget—Table 4–1)		$533,000
Cost of goods sold	(75% of sales)		(399,750)
Gross profit	(calculation)		$133,250
Operating Expenses			
Depreciation	[($17,200 ÷ 2) + $230]	$ 8,830	
Wages and salaries	(from cash budget—Table 4–1)	38,000	
Rent	(from cash budget—Table 4–1)	24,000	
Other expenses	(from cash budget—Table 4–1)	6,900	(77,730)
Net operating income	(calculation)		$ 55,520
Interest expense	(calculation—see text footnote 4)		(11,764)
Earnings before taxes	(calculation)		$ 43,756
Income taxes payable	(40%)		(17,502)
Net income	(calculation)		$ 26,254

In the cash budget revenues and expenses are included in the months in which cash is actually received or disbursed. In the income statement revenues and expenses are included in the month in which the corresponding sale took place, which usually is not the same month in which cash is received. The income statement is therefore prepared on an accrual basis. See Appendix 3A for added discussion of the accrual basis of accounting.

The Pro Forma Balance Sheet

We can construct the pro forma balance sheet for Salco by using information from the cash budget (Table 4–1); the December 31, 1987, balance sheet (Table 4–2); and the pro forma income statement (Table 4–3). Salco's pro forma balance sheet for June 30, 1988, is presented in Table 4–4. Estimates of the individual statement entries are provided below.

Ending cash from the cash budget, $10,000, becomes the cash entry in Salco's pro forma balance sheet. The accounts receivable balance is found as follows:

Accounts receivable (12/31/87) (from Table 4–2)	$ 104,400
+ Credit sales (from Table 4–1)	533,000
− Collections (from Table 4–1)	(440,400)
Accounts receivable (6/30/88) (calculation)	$ 197,000

The beginning balance for accounts receivable is taken from the December 31, 1987, balance sheet (Table 4–2), and credit sales and collections are obtained by summing across the relevant cash budget monthly totals. Inventories are determined in a similar manner:

Inventories (12/31/87) (from Table 4–2)	$ 101,250
+ Purchases (from Table 4–1)	414,750
− Cost of goods sold (from Table 4–3)	(399,750)
Inventories (6/30/88) (calculation)	$ 116,250

TABLE 4–4.   Salco Furniture Co., Inc. Pro Forma Balance Sheet June 30, 1988

Assets		
Current assets		
Cash	$ 10,000	
Accounts receivable	197,000	
Inventories	116,250	
Total current assets		$323,250
Fixed assets		
Net plant and equipment		185,170
Total assets		$508,420

Liabilities and Owners' Equity		
Current liabilities		
Accounts payable	$ 56,250	
Notes payable[a]	79,875	
Accrued interest[b]	799	
Taxes payable	12,302	
Total current liabilities		$149,226
Noncurrent liabilities		
Long-term debt		150,000
Stockholders' equity		
Common stock	$ 20,000	
Paid-in capital	50,000	
Retained earnings	139,194	
Total owners' equity		$209,194
Total liabilities and owners' equity		$508,420

[a] Cumulative borrowing for the period was assumed to take the form of notes payable. This figure is taken from the cumulative borrowing row of cash budget contained in Table 4–1.

[b] This contains the $799 in interest incurred on June's total borrowing of $77,875, but which will not be paid until July.

Purchases were found by summing relevant monthly figures from the cash budget for all six months of the budget period; and cost of goods sold was taken from the pro forma income statement in Table 4–3. The net plant and equipment figure is found as follows:

Net plant and equipment (12/31/87) (from Table 4–2)	$180,000
+ Purchases of plant and equipment (from Table 4–1)	14,000
− Depreciation expense (from Table 4–3)	(8,830)
Net plant and equipment (6/30/88) (calculation)	$185,170

Purchases of plant and equipment are reflected in the cash budget, and depreciation expense is taken from the pro forma income statement. The only changes that took place during the period involved the $14,000 purchase and depreciation expense of

$8830, leaving a net balance of $185,170. Total assets for Salco are therefore expected to be $508,420.

The liability accounts are estimated using the same basic methodology used in finding asset balances. Accounts payable is found as follows:

Accounts payable (12/31/87) (from Table 4–2)	$ 56,250
+ Purchases (from Table 4–1)	414,750
– Payments (from Table 4–1)	(414,750)
Accounts payable (6/30/88) (calculation)	$ 56,250

Again purchases and payments were taken from the cash budget for each of the six months of the budget period. Notes payable are found as follows:

Notes payable (12/31/87) (from Table 4–2)	$ 12,000
+ Borrowing (6/30/86) (from Table 4–1)	79,875
– Repayments (from Table 4–1)	(12,000)
Notes payable (6/30/88) (calculation)	$ 79,875

Here it is assumed that the total new financing needed during the period ($79,875) would be raised through notes payable. Salco's use of short-term financing may or may not be desirable, as we shall see in Chapter 5 when we discuss working capital management. An accrued interest expense item of $799 is created as a result of interest expense in that amount that was incurred during June on short-term borrowing but will not be paid until July. Next, compute taxes payable as follows:

Taxes payable (12/31/87) (from Table 4–2)	$ 4,460
+ Tax liability for the period (from Table 4–3)	17,502
– Tax payments made during the period (from Table 4–1)	(9,660)
Taxes payable (6/30/88) (calculation)	$12,302

Long-term debt, common stock, and paid-in capital remain unchanged for the period, as no new stock or long-term debt was issued nor was any repurchased or retired. Finally, the retained earnings balance is found as follows:

Retained earnings (12/31/87) (from Table 4–2)	$112,940
+ Net income for the period (from Table 4–3)	26,254
– Cash dividends (from Table 4–1)	0
Retained earnings (6/30/88) (calculation)	$139,194

Since no common dividends were paid (none were considered in the cash budget—Table 4–1), the new retained earnings figure is $139,194.

Salco's mangement may now wish to perform a financial analysis using the newly prepared pro forma statements. Such an analysis would provide the basis for evaluating the firm's planned financial performance over the next six months. It would entail use of a set of ratios such as those discussed in Chapter 3, which could be compared with prior-year figures and industry averages. If this analysis identified any potential weakness, the firm could take steps to correct it before it became reality.

Financial Control

The pro forma statements just prepared can be used to *monitor* or control the firm's financial performance. One approach would involve preparing pro forma statements for each month during the planning period. Actual operating results for each month's operations could then be compared with the projected or pro forma figures. This type of analysis would provide an *early warning system* to detect financial problems as they develop. In particular, by comparing actual monthly (or even weekly) operating results with projected revenue and expense items (from pro forma income statements), the financial manager can maintain a very close watch on the firm's overall profitability and take an active role in determining the firm's overall performance for the planning period.

Financial Planning and Budgeting: Closing Comments

Two aspects of pro forma statements should be emphasized. First, these figures represent single point estimates of each of the items in the entire system of budgets and the resulting pro forma statements. Although these may be the *best estimates* as to what the future will hold for Salco, at least two additional sets of estimates may be desired, corresponding to the very worst set of circumstances that the firm might face, and the very best. These extremes provide the necessary input for formulating contingency financing plans, should a deviation from the expected figures occur. Second, notes payable was used as a *plug* figure for additional financing needed. The actual source of financing selected will depend on a number of factors, including (1) the length of the period for which the financing will be needed, (2) the cost of alternative sources of funds, and (3) the preferences of the firm's management regarding the use of debt versus equity. These factors will be further investigated in Chapter 8, when we discuss short-term financing, and in Chapter 15, which deals with the firm's financing mix.

COMPUTERIZED FINANCIAL PLANNING

In recent years a number of developments in both computer hardware (machines) and software (programs) have reduced the tedium of the planning and budgeting process immensely. Specifically, these developments include the introduction of "user friendly" or "easy to use" computer programs that are specialized for application to financial planning.

Financial planning software packages (sometimes referred to as electronic spreadsheets) were first made popular on large mainframe computers. These packages were designed to allow a computer novice to utilize computer technology to construct budgets and forecasts. The real advantage of the computer was realized in the use of these budgets where different scenarios could be evaluated quickly and at a low cost in man-hours. Thus, with the use of a computerized financial planning package, the financial analyst is able to utilize the computer to solve various planning and forecasting problems without becoming a computer expert or even having to consult with one.[5]

Another major development that has had a significant impact on the extent to which computers are used in the planning and budgeting process is the advent of the microcomputer. For mere hundreds of dollars the financial analyst's desk can contain the computing power it took hundreds of thousands of dollars to buy just a decade ago. The development of financial planning software has paralleled the development of microcomputer technology. The number of spreadsheet packages has mushroomed over the past five years. These packages generally sell for less than $500 and frequently include graphics programs as well as elementary database management software.[6] An extensive review of these programs is beyond the scope of this text. However, a visit to a local microcomputer shop (or your school's microcomputer lab) can provide you with an invaluable introduction to an indispensable tool for the financial analyst.

Summary

This chapter has developed the role of forecasting within the context of the firm's financial planning efforts. Forecasts of the firm's sales revenues and related expenses provide the basis for projecting future financing needs. Methods for forecasting financial variables include the percent of sales method and the regression method (discussed in the appendix).

Forecasts of firm sales and expenses were used to develop the cash budget for the planning period, which was then used to estimate the firm's future financing needs. In this chapter all **needed financing** was supplied through short-term notes. However, in Chapters 8 and 19 we will look more closely at sources of financing. Chapter 8 deals with the choice between current or short-term financing versus long-term financing, Chapter 19 with the choice among long-term sources (bonds, preferred stock, and common stock).

Pro forma financial statements provide the user with the basis for (1) evaluating the results of the firm's financial plans and (2) controlling the firm's operations during the planning period.

---

[5] One very popular financial planning package designed for mainframe computers is the IFPS (Interactive Financial Planning System) marketed by Execucom of Austin, Texas. For more information on this package (which can be viewed as an example of this type of software), the interested reader is referred to Paul Gray, *Student Guide to IFPS* (New York: McGraw-Hill, 1983).

[6] The number and variety of financial spreadsheet programs has expanded dramatically since the introduction of the original Visi-Calc program. Currently the most widely used program is Lotus 1.2.3.; however, integrated packages including spreadsheet, graphics, database, communication, and word processing programs are the direction of more recent developments in this type of software product. Examples of integrated products include Symphony, Framework, Jazz, and Excel. In addition to integrated software packages, there is a growing set of products referred to as "expert systems" which attempt to mimic the decisions of experts. To date these efforts have produced a limited number of financial applications software related to such things as the capital budgeting decision (discussed in Chapter 10), but they offer an opportunity to expand the capabilities of the financial manager of the future.

Study Questions

4–1. Discuss the shortcomings of the percent of sales method of financial forecasting.

4–2. Explain how a fixed cash budget differs from a variable or flexible cash budget.

4–3. What two basic needs does a flexible (variable) cash budget serve?

4–4. What would be the probable effect on a firm's cash position of the following events?
   a. Rapidly rising sales
   b. A delay in the payment of payables
   c. A more liberal credit policy on sales (to the firm's customers)
   d. Holding larger inventories

4–5. How long should the budget period be? Why would a firm not set a rule that all budgets be for a 12-month period?

4–6. A cash budget is usually thought of as a means of planning for future financing needs. Why would a cash budget also be important for a firm that had excess cash on hand?

4–7. Explain why a cash budget would be of particular importance to a firm that experiences seasonal fluctuations in its sales.

4–8. Is there a difference between estimated net profit after taxes for a period and the estimated net addition to the cash balance? Explain.

Self-Test Problems

ST–1. (*Financial Forecasting*) Use the percent of sales method to prepare a pro forma income statement for Calico Sales Co., inc. Projected sales for next year equal $4 million. Cost of goods sold equal 70 percent of sales, administrative expense equals $500,000, and depreciation expense is $300,000. Interest expense equals $50,000 and income is taxed at a rate of 40 percent. The firm plans to spend $200,000 during the period to renovate its office facility and will retire $150,000 in notes payable. Finally, selling expense equals 5 percent of sales.

ST–2. (*Pro Forma Statements and Liquidity Analysis*) The balance sheet for Odom Manufacturing Company on December 31, 1989, is found below:

Odom Manufacturing Co. Balance Sheet December 31, 1989

Cash	$ 250,000	Accounts payable	$ 850,000
Accounts receivable	760,000	Notes payable	550,000
Inventory	860,000	Current liabilities	$1,400,000
Current assets	$1,870,000	Long-term debt	800,000
Property, plant, and equipment	1,730,000	Common stock	600,000
		Retained earnings	800,000
		Total liabilities and	
Total assets	$3,600,000	stockholders' equity	$3,600,000

The Treasurer of the Odom Manufacturing wishes to borrow $500,000, the funds from which would be applied in the following manner:
1. $100,000 to reduce accounts payable
2. $ 75,000 to retire current notes payable
3. $175,000 to expand existing plant facilities

4. $ 80,000 to increase inventories

5. $ 70,000 to increase cash on hand

Repayment of the $500,000 will be in 20 years with interest paid annually.

   a. Assuming that the loan is obtained, prepare a pro forma balance sheet for Odom Manufacturing that reflects the use of the loan proceeds.

   b. Did the firm's liquidity improve after the loan was obtained and the proceeds were dispensed in the above manner? Why or why not?

ST–3. (*Cash Budget*) Stauffer, Inc. has estimated sales and purchase requirements for the last half of the coming year. Past experience indicates that it will collect 20 percent of its sales in the month of the sale, 50 percent of the remainder one month after the sale, and the balance in the second month following the sale. Stauffer prefers to pay for half its purchases in the month of the purchase and the other half the following month. Labor expense for each month is expected to equal 5 percent of that month's sales, with cash payment being made in the month in which the expense is incurred. Depreciation expense is $5000 per month; miscellaneous cash expenses are $4000 per month and are paid in the month incurred. General and administrative expenses of $50,000 are recognized and paid monthly. A $60,000 truck is to be purchased in August and is to be depreciated on a straight-line basis over 10 years with no expected salvage value. The company also plans to pay a $9000 cash dividend to stockholders in July. The company feels that a minimum cash balance of $30,000 should be maintained. Any borrowing will cost 12 percent annually, with interest paid in the month following the month in which the funds are borrowed. Borrowing takes place at the beginning of the month in which the need for funds arises. For example, if during the month of July the firm should need to borrow $24,000 to maintain its $30,000 desired minimum balance, then $24,000 will be taken out on July 1 with interest owed for the entire month of July. Interest for the month of July would then be paid on August 1. Sales and purchase estimates are shown below. Prepare a cash budget for the months of July and August (cash on hand 6/30 was $30,000, while sales for May and June were $100,000 and purchases were $60,000 for each of these months).

Month	Sales	Purchases
July	$120,000	$50,000
August	150,000	40,000
September	110,000	30,000

Study Problems

4–1. (*Financial Forecasting*) Sambonoza Enterprises projects its sales next year to be $4 million and expects to earn 5 percent of that amount after taxes. The firm is currently in the process of projecting its financing needs and has made the following assumptions (projections):

   1. Current assets will equal 20 percent of sales while fixed assets will remain at their current level of $1 million.

   2. Common equity is presently $0.8 million, and the firm pays out half its after-tax earnings in dividends.

   3. The firm has short-term payables and trade credit which normally equal 10 percent of sales and has no long-term debt outstanding.

   What are Sambonoza's financing needs for the coming year?

4–2. (*Financial Forecasting—Percent of Sales*) Tulley Appliances, Inc. projects next year's sales to be $20 million. Current sales are at $15 million based on current assets of $5 million and fixed assets of $5 million. The firm's net profit margin is 5 percent after taxes. Tulley forecasts that current assets will rise in direct proportion to the increase in sales but fixed assets will increase by only $100,000. At present Tulley has $1.5 million in accounts payable plus $2 million in long-term debt (due in 10 years) outstanding and common equity (including $4 million in retained earnings) totaling $6.5 million. Tulley plans to pay $500,000 in common stock dividends next year.

  a. What are Tulley's total financing needs (i.e., total assets) for the coming year?

  b. Given the firm's projections and dividend payment plans, what are its discretionary financing needs?

  c. Based upon the projections given and assuming the $100,000 expansion in fixed assets will occur, what is the largest increase in sales the firm can support without having to resort to the use of discretionary sources of financing?

4–3. (*Pro Forma Balance Sheet Construction*) Use the following industry average ratios to construct a pro forma balance sheet for the V. M. Willet Co.

Total asset turnover	2.0 times
Average collection period (assume a 360-day year)	9 days
Fixed asset turnover	5.0 times
Inventory turnover (based on cost of goods sold)	3.0 times
Current ratio	2.0 times
Sales (all on credit)	$4.0 million
Cost of goods sold	75% of sales
Debt ratio	50%

Cash		Current liabilities		
Accounts receivable		Long-term debt		
		Common stock plus		
Net fixed assets	$_____	retained earnings		_____
	$══════			$══════

4–4. (*Cash Budget*) The Sharpe Corporation's projected sales for the first eight months of 1988 are as follows:

January	$ 90,000	May	$300,000
February	120,000	June	270,000
March	135,000	July	225,000
April	240,000	August	150,000

Of Sharpe's sales, 10 percent is for cash, another 60 percent is collected in the month following sale, and 30 percent is collected in the second month following sale. November and December sales for 1987 were $220,000 and $175,000, respectively.

Sharpe purchases its raw materials two months in advance of its sales equal to 60 percent of their final sales price. The supplier is paid one month after it makes delivery. For example, purchases for April sales are made in February and payment is made in March.

In addition, Sharpe pays $10,000 per month for rent and $20,000 each month for other expenditures. Tax prepayments of $22,500 are made each quarter, beginning in March.

The company's cash balance at December 31, 1987, was $22,000; a minimum balance of $15,000 must be maintained at all times. Assume that any short-term financing needed to maintain cash balance would be paid off in the month following the month of financing if sufficient funds are available. Interest on short-term loans (12%) is paid monthly. Borrowing to meet estimated monthly cash needs takes place at the beginning of the month. Thus, if in the month of April the firm expects to have a need for an additional $60,500, these funds would be borrowed at the beginning of April with interest of $605 (.12 × 1/12 × $60,500) owed for April and paid at the beginning of May.

a. Prepare a cash budget for Sharpe covering the first seven months of 1988.

b. Sharpe has $200,000 in notes payable due in July that must be repaid or renegotiated for an extension. Will the firm have ample cash to repay the notes?

4–5. (*Financial Forecasting—Pro Forma Statements*) The Bell Retailing Company has been engaged in the process of forecasting its financing needs over the next quarter and has made the following forecasts of planned cash receipts and disbursements:

1. Historical and predicted sales:

Historical		Predicted	
April	$ 80,000	July	$130,000
May	100,000	August	130,000
June	120,000	September	120,000
		October	100,000

2. The firm incurs and pays a monthly rent expense of $3000.

3. Wages and salaries for the coming months are estimated as follows: with payments coinciding with the month in which the expense is incurred.

July	$18,000
August	18,000
September	16,000

4. Of the firm's sales, 40 percent is collected in the month of sale, 30 percent one month after sale, and the remaining 30 percent two months after sale.

5. Merchandise is purchased one month before the sales month and is paid for in the month it is sold. Purchases equal 80 percent of sales.

6. Tax prepayments are made on the calendar quarter, with a prepayment of $1000 in July based on earnings for the quarter ended June 30, 1985.

7. Utilities for the firm average 2 percent of sales and are paid in the month of their incurrence.

8. Depreciation expense is $12,000 annually.

9. Interest on a $40,000 bank note (due in November) is payable at an 8 percent annual rate in September for the three-month period just ended.

10. The firm follows a policy of paying no cash dividends.

Based on the above, supply the following items:

a. Prepare a monthly cash budget for the three-month period ended September 30, 1988.

b. If the firm's beginning cash balance for the budget period is $5000 and this is its minimum desired balance, determine when and how much the firm will need to borrow during the budget period. The firm has an $80,000 line of credit with its bank with interest (12 percent annual) paid monthly (for example, for a loan taken out at the end of December, interest would be paid at the end of January and every month thereafter so long as the loan was outstanding).

c. Prepare a pro forma income statement for Bell covering the three-month period ended September 30, 1988. Use a 40 percent tax rate.

d. Given the following balance sheet dated June 30, 1988, and your pro forma income statement from part (c), prepare a pro forma balance sheet for September 30, 1988.

Bell Manufacturing Co. Balance Sheet June 30, 1988

Cash	$ 5,000	Accounts payable	$104,000
Accounts receivable	102,000	Bank notes (8%)	40,000
Inventories	114,000	Accrued taxes	1,000
Current assets	221,000	Current liabilities	145,000
Net fixed assets	120,000	Common stock ($1 par)	100,000
		Paid-in capital	28,400
		Retained earnings	67,600
Total assets	$341,000	Total liabilities and capital	$341,000

4-6. (*Forecasting Accounts Receivable*) Sampkin Mfg. is evaluating the effects of extending trade credit to its out-of-state customers. In the past Sampkin has given credit to local customers but has insisted on cash upon delivery from customers in the bordering state of South Dakota. At present Sampkin's average collection period is 30 days based upon total sales; that is, including both its $900,000 in-state credit sales and its $300,000 out-of-state cash sales, the firm's accounts receivable balance is 30 days.

$$\text{average collection period} = \frac{\text{accounts receivable}}{\text{sales}/360}$$

$$= \frac{\$100,000}{\$1,200,000/360} = 30 \text{ days}$$

a. Calculate Sampkin's average collection period based upon credit sales alone.
b. If Sampkin extends credit to its out-of-state customers, it expects total credit sales to rise to $1,500,000. If the firm's average collection period remains the same, what will be the new level of accounts receivable?

4-7. (*Forecasting Accounts Receivable*) The Ace Traffic Company sells its merchandise on credit terms of 2/10, net 30 (2 percent discount if payment is made within 10 days or the net amount is due in 30 days). Only a part of the firm's customers take the trade discount, so that the firm's average collection period is 20 days.
a. Based upon estimated sales of $400,000, project Ace's accounts receivable balance for the coming year.
b. If Ace changes its cash discount terms to 1/10, net 30, it expects its average collection period will rise to 28 days. Estimate Ace's accounts receivable balance based on the new credit terms and expected sales of $400,000.

4-8. (*Percent of Sales Forecasting*) Which of the following accounts would most likely vary directly with the level of firm sales? Discuss each briefly.

	Yes	No
Cash	_____	_____
Marketable securities	_____	_____
Accounts payable	_____	_____
Notes payable	_____	_____
Plant and equipment	_____	_____
Inventories	_____	_____

4-9. (*Financial Forecasting—Percent of Sales*) The balance sheet of the Thompson Trucking Company (TTC) is found below:

Thompson Trucking Company Balance Sheet January 31, 1989 ($ millions)

Current assets	$10	Accounts payable	$ 5
Net fixed assets	15	Notes payable	0
Total	$25	Bonds payable	10
		Common equity	10
		Total	$25

TTC had sales for the year ended 1/31/89 of $50 million. The firm follows a policy of paying all net earnings out to its common stockholders in cash dividends. Thus, TTC generates no funds from its earnings that can be used to expand its operations (assume that depreciation expense is just equal to the cost of replacing worn-out assets.)

a. If TTC anticipates sales of $80 million during the coming year, develop a pro forma balance sheet for the firm for 1/31/90. Assume that current assets vary as a percent of sales, net fixed assets remain unchanged, accounts payable vary as a percent of sales, and use notes payable as a balancing entry.

b. How much "new" financing will TTC need next year?

c. What limitations does the percent of sales forecast method suffer from? Discuss briefly.

4-10. (*Financial Forecasting—Discretionary Financing Needed*) The most recent balance sheet for the Armadillo Dog Biscuit Co. is shown in the table below. The company is about to embark on an advertising campaign, which is expected to raise sales from the present level of $5 million to $7 million by the end of next year. The firm is presently operating at full capacity and will have to increase its investment in both current and fixed assets to support the projected level of new sales. In fact, the firm estimates that both categories of assets will rise in direct proportion to the projected increase in sales.

The firm's net profits were 6 percent of current year's sales but are expected to rise to 7 percent of next year's sales. To help support its anticipated growth in asset needs next year, the firm has suspended plans to pay cash dividends to its stockholders. In years past a $1.50 per share dividend has been paid annually.

Armadillo Dog Biscuit Co., Inc. ($ millions)

	Present Level	Percent of Sales	Projected Level
Current assets	$2.0		
Net fixed assets	$3.0		
Total	$5.0		
Accounts payable	$0.5		
Accrued expenses	$0.5		
Notes payable	—		
Current liabilities	$1.0		
Long-term debt	$2.0		
Common stock	$0.5		
Retained earnings	$1.5		
Common equity	$2.0		
Total	$5.0		

Armadillo's payables and accrued expenses are expected to vary directly with sales. In addition, notes payable will be used to supply the added funds needed to finance next year's operations that are not forthcoming from other sources.

a. Fill in the table and project the firm's needs for discretionary financing. Use notes payable as the balancing entry for future discretionary financing needed.

b. Compare Armadillo's current ratio and debt ratio (total liabilities/total assets) before the growth in sales and after. What was the effect of the expanded sales on these two dimensions of Armadillo's financial condition?

c. What difference, if any, would have resulted if Armadillo's sales had risen to $6 million in one year and $7 million only after two years? Discuss only; no calculations required.

4–11. (*Financial Forecasting—Changing Credit Policy*) Island Resorts, Inc., has $400,000 invested in receivables throughout much of the year. It has annual credit sales of $3,600,000 and a gross profit margin of 80 percent.

a. What is Island Resorts' average collection period? [**Hint:** Recall that average collection period = accounts receivable/(credit sales/360).]

b. By how much would Island Resorts be able to reduce its accounts receivable if it were to change its credit policies in a way that reduced its average collection period to 30 days without affecting annual credit sales?

4–12. (*Forecasting Discretionary Financing Needs*) Fishing Charter, Inc., estimates that it invests 30 cents in assets for each dollar of new sales. However, 5 cents in profits are produced by each dollar of additional sales, of which 1 cent can be reinvested in the firm. If sales rise from their present level of $5 million by $500,000 next year, and the ratio of spontaneous liabilities of sales is .15, what will be the firm's need for discretionary financing? (**Hint:** In this situation you do not know what the firm's existing level of assets is, nor do you know how they have been financed. Thus, you must estimate the change in financing needs and match this change with the expected changes in spontaneous liabilities, retained earnings, and other sources of discretionary financing.)

Case Problem

Lincoln Plywood Inc.

Financial Forecasting

Lincoln Plywood, Inc. (LPI), owns and operates a plywood fabricating in southern Georgia. LPI's primary product is 4 × 8 sheets of pine plywood used in the construction industry. The plywood is formed out of thin sheets of wood that are "peeled" from pine logs bought in the region. A number of varieties of thicknesses and grades of plywood can be made in LPI's plant, ranging from ¼ inch sheets used as paneling in new homes to ¾ inch sheets used in framing and heavy industrial applications. LPI's sales have grown rapidly over the past 10 years at an average of 10 percent per year. This growth has resulted from the housing boom that occurred during this period and in particular the very rapid rate of regional growth in the Atlanta area.

The firm's management has been pleased with the growth in sales; however, during the past 6 months it has begun to experience some cash flow problems that appear to have gotten out of control (LPI's current balance sheet is shown below). The firm's controller, James Christian, is aware of the decline in the firm's cash position and plans to correct the problem as soon as an appropriate course of action can be identified. One factor which he feels is surely making the problem worse is the firm's credit and collections policy. In particular, LPI recently "liberalized" its credit terms in an effort to stimulate demand in the face of stiffening competition. The full effect of the change is not known, but Christian plans to address that problem when he makes his projection of cash needs for the coming year.

Lincoln Plywood, Inc. Balance Sheet for December 31, 19x1

Assets

Cash		$ 125,000
Accounts Receivable	$ 517,500	
less: Allowance for Bad Debts	7,500	510,000
Inventories		725,000
Current Assets		$1,360,000
Plant and Equipment	$2,320,000	
less: Accumulated Depreciation	(1,280,000)	
Net Plant and Equipment		1,040,000
Total Assets		$2,400,000

Liabilities and Owner's Equity

Accounts Payable	$ 30,000
Accrued Taxes	50,000
Accrued Expenses	270,000
Current Liabilities	$ 350,000
Common Stock	$ 400,000
Retained Earnings	1,650,000
Common Equity	$2,050,000
Total Liabilities and Owner's Equity	$2,400,000

LPI's cash cycle is a relatively simple one. The firm purchases timber, processes that timber by turning it into various types of plywood products, sells the timber on credit, and collects its credit sales. The cash flow problem the firm currently faces is partly a result of its increasing the term over which credit sales can be repaid. In fact, following its recent liberalization of credit terms, the firm estimates that only 10 percent of its customers will pay within the month of the sale, 46% of the total will be collected in one month, and all but 2 percent of sales will be collected in the second month following the sale. Bad debt expense is estimated at 1 percent of sales in the income statement.

Christian plans to make a monthly cash budget for LPI spanning the next six months (January through June) and has already projected firm sales as follows:

Month	Projected Sales
January	$500,000
February	300,000
March	250,000
April	525,000
May	800,000
June	250,000

The monthly sales estimates reflect a long-established seasonality in the firm's sales. However, the firm's purchases of timber are not closely matched to its sales. The harvest of timber is heavily seasonal due to the problems associated with getting the timber out of the woods during the rainy winter months. Since LPI contracts up to eight months in advance for its timber purchases, it has a very good idea as to what its expenditures for timber will be over the six-month planning horizon. Specifically, LPI has contracted to make the following timber purchases:

Month	Purchase Contracts
January	$120,000
February	120,000
March	200,000
April	300,000
May	550,000
June	600,000

LPI's standard purchase contract calls for cash payment 30 days following the delivery, and its purchases during December were only $20,000. Timber purchases are added to the firm's inventories at cost plus a processing cost equal to half the cost of the timber. Thus, for the month of December LPI increased its inventories by a total of $30,000 and this is the outstanding balance of accounts payable for December. This balance will be paid in full in January.

In addition to its timber purchases, LPI plans to acquire a new chipping machine used to convert waste resulting from its processing of the timber to chips of wood that are then sold to paper mills, which convert the chips to paper stock. The new machine will cost $400,000 and will be purchased and paid for in June (payment will actually be made as late as possible in June). The firm also plans to acquire a new forklift truck in February which will cost $60,000. The purchase will be paid for in March. LPI's monthly depreciation expense for January is $15,000 but will increase by $1000 per month in February due to the purchase of the forklift, and it will increase again in July by $8000 per month due to the purchase of the chipper.

Christian estimates the firm's general and administrative expense to be $70,000 per month, with payment being made in the month of the expense's incurrence. The firm also has a category called miscellaneous cash expenses which is estimated to be at $20,000 per month and paid monthly. Although LPI has no formal policy with regard to its minimum cash balance, Christian feels that a $100,000 balance is the minimum he would like to have over the planning horizon. Finally, LPI plans to make a cash dividend payment to stockholders at the end of March and June equal to $100,000 and will also make quarterly tax payments of $50,000 in the months of January and April. (For planning purposes, a 30 percent tax rate is used in estimating LPI's tax liability.)

QUESTIONS

1. Prepare a month-by-month cash budget for LPI for the next six months. You may assume that any borrowing that must be undertaken will cost 1 percent interest per month, with interest paid the month following the month in which borrowing takes place. Assume borrowing is at the beginning of the month. November and December sales for the current year were $350,000 and $400,000, respectively.

2. Prepare pro forma income statements for the three-month periods ended with March and June. You may assume that inventories consist of materials and related labor expense.

Cost of goods sold equal 75 percent of sales and are comprised of materials and related labor.

3. Prepare a pro forma balance sheet for LPI for the end of March and June. You may assume that accrued expenses and common stock do not change over the six-month planning period.

4. Prepare a source and use of funds statement for the six-month period ended in June. Given LPI's financing requirements for the period, what suggestions do you have for James Christian for raising the necessary funds? Discuss your reasons for the stated plans.

Self-Test Solutions

SS–1. Calico Sales Co., Inc., Pro Forma Income Statement

Sales		$4,000,000
COGS (70%)		(2,800,000)
Gross profit		1,200,000
Operating expense		
Selling expense (5%)	$200,000	
Administrative expense	500,000	
Depreciation expense	300,000	(1,000,000)
Net operating income		200,000
Interest		(50,000)
Earnings before taxes		150,000
Taxes (40%)		(60,000)
Net income		$ 90,000

Although the office renovation expenditure and debt retirement are surely cash outflows, they do not enter the income statement directly. These expenditures affect expenses for the period's income statement, only through their effect on depreciation and interest expense. A cash budget would indicate the full cash impact of the renovation and debt retirement expenditures.

SS–2. Odom manufacturing Co. Pro Forma Balance Sheet

a.

Cash	$ 320,000		Accounts payable	$ 750,000
Accounts receivable	760,000		Notes payable	475,000
Inventory	940,000		Total current liabilities	$1,225,000
Total current assets	$2,020,000		Long-term debt	1,300,000
Property, plant, and			Common stock	600,000
equipment	$1,905,000		Retained earnings	800,000
			Total liabilities and	
Total assets	$3,925,000		shareholders' equity	$3,925,000

b. In order to assess whether or not the firm's liquidity position has improved with the securing of the $500,000 loan, its current financial position must be compared with its position before the loan was granted.

	Position before Loan	Position after Loan
Current ratio	1.34	1.65
Acid test ratio	0.72	0.88

These two ratios indicate that there has been an improvement in Odom's liquidity position and that the firm was justified in seeking the loan and in allocating the funds as previously described.

SS–3.

	May	June	July	Aug.
Sales	$100,000	$100,000	$120,000	$150,000
Purchases	60,000	60,000	50,000	40,000

Cash Receipts:

	May	June	July	Aug.
Collections from month of sale (20%)	20,000	20,000	24,000	30,000
1 month later (50% of uncollected amount)		40,000	40,000	48,000
2 months later (balance)			40,000	40,000
Total receipts			$104,000	$118,000

Cash Disbursements:

	May	June	July	Aug.
Payments for purchases—				
From 1 month earlier			$ 30,000	$ 25,000
From current month			$ 25,000	20,000
Total			$ 55,000	$ 45,000
Miscellaneous cash expenses			4,000	4,000
Labor expense (5% of sales)			6,000	7,500
General and administrative expense ($50,000 per month)			50,000	50,000
Truck purchase			0	60,000
Cash dividends			9,000	—
Total disbursements			(124,000)	(166,500)

	May	June	July	Aug.
			(20,000)	(48,500)
Plus: Beginning cash balance			30,000	30,000
Less: Interest on short-term borrowing (1% of prior month's borrowing)			0	(200)
Equals: Ending cash balance—without borrowing			10,000	(18,700)
Financing needed to reach target cash balance			20,000	48,700
Cumulative borrowing			20,000	68,700

Selected References

Carleton, W. T. "An Analytical Model for Long-Range Financial Planning," *Journal of Finance*, 25 (May 1970), 291–315.

———. C. L. Dick, and D. H. Downes. "Financial Policy Models: Theory and Practice," *Journal of Financial and Quantitative Analysis*, 8 (December 1973), 691–710.

Chambers, John C., Satinder K. Mullick, and Donald D. Smith. "How to Choose the Right Forecasting Technique," *Harvard Business Review*, 49 (July–August 1971), 45–74.

Francis, J. C., and D. R. Rowell. "A Simultaneous Equation Model of the Firm for Financial Analysis and Planning," *Financial Management* (Spring 1978), 29–44.

Pan, J., D. R. Nichols, and O. M. Joy. "Sales Forecasting Practices of Large U.S. Industrial Firms," *Financial Management*, 6 (Fall 1977), 72–77.

Pappas, J. L., and G. P. Huber. "Probabilistic Short-Term Financial Planning," *Financial Management*, 2 (Autumn 1973).

Parker, G. G. C., and E. L. Segura. "How to Get a Better Forecast," *Harvard Business Review*, 49 (March–April 1971), 99–109.

Seed, A. H., III. "Measuring Financial Performance in an Inflationary Environment," *Financial Executive* (January 1982), 40–50.

Weston, J. Fred. "Forecasting Financial Requirements," *Accounting Review*, 33 (July 1958), 427–40.

APPENDIX 4A
Alternative Forecast Methods

For illustrative purposes we will forecast 1988 inventories for the J. B. Chamblis Company (JBCC). Table 4A–1 gives JBCC's sales and inventories for 1986 and 1987, respectively. In 1986 inventories comprised 6.6 percent of sales and in 1987 they made up roughly 6.2 percent. Thus, for predictive purposes the analyst might use 6 to 7 percent of the 1988 forecasted sales to predict 1988 inventories.

TABLE 4A–1. Inventory and Sales Data for the J. B. Chamblis Company

Year	Inventory	Sales	Inventories as a Percent of Sales
1986	$1,414,102	$21,418,202	6.6%
1987	1,397,248	22,703,229	6.2

This rather simplistic (percent of sales) forecast method assumes that no other information is available that would indicate a change in the observed relationship between sales and inventories. For example, if the firm plans to restrict any buildup in inventories during the coming year (even though sales might be rising), then the historical percentages will overestimate the actual level of investment in inventories. Assuming that JBCC's inventory as a percentage of sales will be stable and that 1988 sales are predicted to be $23 million, then JBCC would predict inventories to be between 6 and 7 percent of that amount, or $1,380,000 to $1,610,000, respectively, using the percent of sales method.

Scatter Diagram and Simple Regression Methods

Historical sales and inventories for JBCC covering the past 10 years are given in Table 4A–2. Figure 4A–1 is a visual representation of the relationship between JBCC's inventories and sales.

Scatter Diagram Method

Figure 4A–1, called a **scatter diagram,** can be used to determine the relationship between sales and inventories. To estimate this relationship we simply fit a line through the scatter of points. The line is visually fitted such that the scatter of points about the line is minimized. To predict JBCC's inventories for 1988, first locate the estimate of 1988 sales on the horizontal axis. Next, draw a vertical line from the sales estimate up to the fitted line and then horizontally over to the inventory axis. Thus, for a sales estimate of $23 million we project an inventory level of $1,490,000 using the inventory-sales relationship in Figure 4A–1.

TABLE 4A–2. Historical Inventory and Sales Information for JBCC ($000)

Year	Inventory	Sales
1978	$1,155	$19,278
1979	1,277	19,751
1980	1,188	19,753
1981	1,097	19,948
1982	1,279	20,748
1983	1,275	21,250
1984	1,314	20,022
1985	1,225	20,761
1986	1,414	21,418
1987	1,397	22,703

Simple Regression Method

Least squares regression represents a procedure for mathematically fitting a line through a scatter diagram such as Figure 4A–1. The sum of the squared deviations of the observed sales-inventory points from the fitted line is minimized, thus the name **least squares.** These deviations are identified in Figure 4A–2 with dashed lines. If the regression line were to fit the observed sales-inventory data perfectly, then all data points would lie on the regression line, BB'.

The resulting regression equation for JBCC's inventory-sales relationship is

$$\text{estimated inventory}\,(t) = -\$210{,}224 + .0716\,\text{sales}\,(t) \qquad (4A\text{--}1)$$

where **sales (t)** is the level of sales for period t and **estimated inventory (t)** is the corresponding inventory forecast. Both $-\$210{,}244$ and .0716 are **coefficients** of the predictive equation and are determined in accordance with the least squares method.

To estimate 1988 inventories we simply substitute the 1988 sales estimates for sales into equation (4A–1). Using a sales projection of $23 million, we obtain an estimate of 1988 inventories as follows:

$$\text{estimated inventory}\,(1988) = -\$210{,}224 + .0716(\$23{,}000{,}000)$$

$$= \$1{,}436{,}576$$

Inventories for 1988 are estimated to be $1,436,576; however, estimated sales may not be the sole or even the most important determinant of JBCC's inventories. To include additional variables in the predicting equation a multiple regression equation can be used.

Multiple Regression Analysis

JBCC's inventory level could well be related to the lead time required to obtain shipments. In addition, other factors such as strikes, availability of raw materials, favorable buying opportunities, and simple errors in judgment could affect JBCC's investment in inventories. Thus, a predictive equation employing two or more predictor variables may prove more reliable than the simple regression equation. For example, consider the following two-variable regression equation:

$$\text{estimated inventories}\,(t) = a + b \cdot \text{sales}\,(t) + c \cdot \text{lead time}\,(t) \qquad (4A\text{--}2)$$

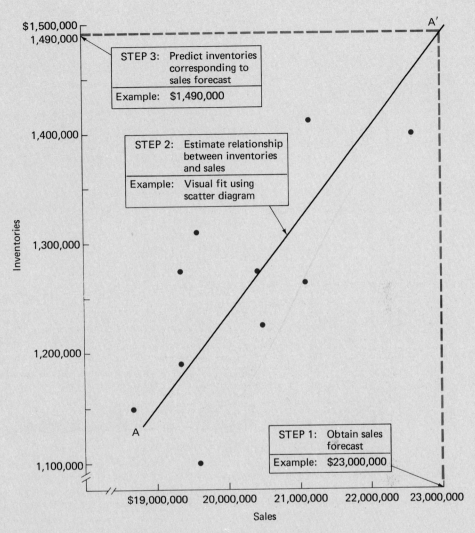

FIGURE 4A–1. Scatter Diagram for Predicting JBCC's Inventories (*Note*: Axes are discontinuous at the origin.)

where **sales** (*t*) is the level of sales for period *t* and **lead time** (*t*) represents the average lead time (in days) between the order date and actual receipt of materials for period *t*. The *a*, *b*, and *c* terms are the coefficients of the multiple regression equation, which are again estimated using the method of least squares.[1]

---

[1] An excellent reference for multiple regression analysis is found in Chapters 4 through 8 of N. R. Draper and H. Smith, *Applied Regression Analysis* (New York: Wiley, 1966).

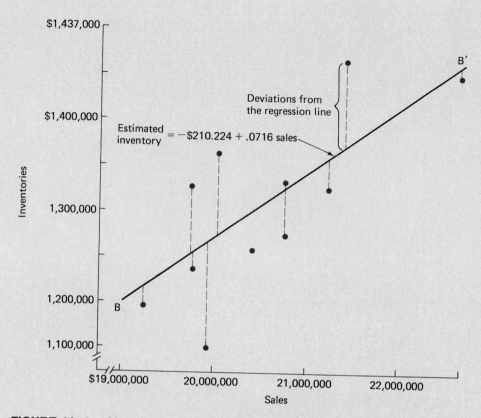

FIGURE 4A–2. Simple Regression Line for JBCC's Sales and Inventories

Table 4A–3 gives historical sales, lead time, and inventory data for JBCC spanning the last 10 years of its operations. These data serve as the basis for estimating the a, b, and c coefficients of equation (4A–2). The resulting multiple regression equation for JBCC's inventories is

$$\text{estimated inventories}\,(t) = -179{,}684 + .0574\,\text{sales}\,(t) \tag{4A–3}$$
$$+\ 9923.1\,\text{lead time}\,(t)$$

We can use equation 4A–3 to predict JBCC's 1988 inventory level by substituting for estimated 1988 sales ($23,000,000) and the estimated lead time (30 days). The resulting inventory estimate is

$$\text{estimated inventories}\,(1988) = -\$179{,}684 + .0574(\,\$23{,}000{,}000\,)$$
$$+\ 9923.1\,(\,30\,\text{days}\,)$$
$$=\ \$1{,}438{,}209$$

The resulting estimate of JBCC's 1988 inventories is $1,438,209. The multiple regression estimate offers the advantage of considering more information than the simple sales-inventory

TABLE 4A–3. Inventory, Sales, and Lead Time Data for JBCC, 1978–1987

Year	Inventory	Sales	Average Lead Time (Days)
1978	$1,155,000	$19,248,000	21
1979	1,277,000	19,751,000	32
1980	1,188,000	19,753,000	24
1981	1,097,000	19,948,000	17
1982	1,279,000	20,748,000	23
1983	1,275,000	21,250,000	24
1984	1,314,000	20,022,000	35
1985	1,225,000	20,761,000	22
1986	1,414,000	21,418,000	38
1987	1,397,000	22,703,000	27

regression equation. Whether it will prove more accurate depends upon how accurately average lead time can be projected for 1988 and upon the stability of the relationships between lead time, sales, and inventories.

Summary of Inventory Forecasts

Table 4A–4 gives the different forecasts for JBCC's 1988 inventories. Ultimately, one will prove to be the most accurate. Based upon all five estimates, the 1988 inventory level is projected to fall within the range of 6 to 7 percent of sales. Note that for a very small range of values for firm sales, the simplistic percent of sales method provides inventory projections very close to those of the more sophisticated regression methods. However, when the sales level used in computing the percent of sales differs substantially from the projected sales level, the percent of sales estimates can be grossly in error.

To understand the underlying reason for the errors resulting from the use of the percent of sales method, we have to define the method in equation form. That is, a percent of sales forecast for inventories can be defined as follows:

$$\text{estimated inventories}\,(t) = \frac{\text{inventories}}{\text{sales}} \times \text{estimated sales}\,(t)$$

Comparing this formulation with the simple regression model in equation (4A–1), we see that the percent of sales equation assumes an intercept of zero and a slope equal to the ratio of inventories to sales. This model is appropriate only where inventories vary as a constant proportion of sales for all levels of sales. Given that most firms maintain some

TABLE 4A–4. Inventory Forecasts for JBCC

Forecast Method	Predicted (1988)
Percent of sales:	
6%	$1,380,000
7%	1,610,000
Scatter diagram, Figure 4A–1	1,490,000
Simple regression, equation (4A–1)	1,436,576
Multiple regression, equation (4A–3)	1,438,209

safety stock of inventories that does not vary with sales and that inventories usually decrease as a percent of sales as sales rise, the percent of sales method provides only an approximation to the true model relating inventories and sales. However, where the level of sales used in calculating the percent of sales is very near the projected level of sales, the percent of sales forecast may provide reasonably accurate forecasts.

This concludes a very brief overview of techniques of financial forecasting. The subject is far too broad to cover here in its entirety. Rather, we have given a basic introduction to the use of several forecast models in financial planning, emphasizing the importance of the resulting forecasts to the ultimate success of the firm's planning efforts.

Study Problem

4A–1. The Jason Marshall Manufacturing Company (JMMC) is beginning its planning for next year. Jim Jamison, the firm's comptroller, is attempting to get a rough estimate of the firm's total needs for financing during the planning period. Jim has compiled income statement and balance sheet data for the last five years, which he hopes will enable him to project the firm's pro forma income statement and balance sheet. The historical financial statements for JMMC are found below:

JMMC Balance Sheets for 1985 through 1989

	1985	1986	1987	1988	1989
Current assets	$2,000	$3,000	$3,000	$4,000	$5,000
Net plant and equipment	2,000	2,000	3,000	4,000	4,000
Total assets	$4,000	$5,000	$6,000	$8,000	$9,000
Current liabilities	$1,000	$1,120	$1,270	$1,270	$1,400
Long-term debt	1,000	1,400	1,400	1,500	1,500
Common stock	1,000	1,000	1,000	2,000	2,000
Retained earnings	1,000	1,480	2,330	3,230	4,100
Total liabilities and owners' equity	$4,000	$5,000	$6,000	$8,000	$9,000

JMMC Income Statements for the Years Ended December 31, 1985 through 1989

	1985	1986	1987	1988	1989
Net sales	$4,000	$6,000	$8,000	$10,000	$12,000
Cost of goods sold	(2,000)	(3,000)	(4,000)	(5,000)	(6,000)
Gross profit	2,000	3,000	4,000	5,000	6,000
Selling expenses	(400)	(500)	(560)	(600)	(610)
General administrative expenses	(1,300)	(1,400)	(1,400)	(1,450)	(1,500)
Operating income	300	1,100	2,040	2,950	3,890
Interest expense	(100)	(140)	(140)	(150)	(150)
Net income before taxes	200	960	1,900	2,800	3,740
Taxes	(100)	(480)	(950)	(1,400)	(1,870)
Net income	$ 100	$ 480	$ 950	$ 1,400	$ 1,870
Cash dividends	$ 0	$ 0	$ 100	$ 500	$ 1,000

Sales for 1990 have been estimated at $16,000. Furthermore, the firm plans to replace worn-out equipment during 1990 such that net plant and equipment should not change materially. The firm plans to pay $1500 in cash dividends in 1990.

Jim believes that current assets and current liabilities are very responsive to the level of firm sales. In addition, cost of goods sold and both selling and administrative expenses tend to follow sales very closely. Net plant and equipment, long-term debt, and common stock are not expected to be very responsive to sales. Interest expenses varies closely with long-term debt, which is not expected to change in 1990.

a. Develop a pro forma balance sheet and income statement for 1990, using the percent of sales method and basing your percentages on the 1989 balance sheet and income statement figures. Use "additional financing needed" as a plug figure in the balance sheet.

b. Develop a pro forma balance sheet and income statement for JMMC, using scatter diagrams to predict current assets, current liabilities, cost of goods sold, and selling and administrative expenses. Note that sales (not time) is the appropriate independent variable in your analysis. Again use "additional financing needed" to balance the pro forma balance sheet.

c. Which of the above estimates of "additional financing needed" do you prefer? Why do they differ? Explain.

5

Introduction to Working Capital Management

Traditionally, **working capital** has been defined as the firm's investment in current assets. **Current assets** are comprised of all assets that the firm expects to convert into cash within the year, including cash, marketable securities, accounts receivable, and inventories. Managing the firm's working capital, however, has come to mean more than simply managing the firm's investment in current assets. In fact, a more descriptive title for this chapter might be *Net Working Capital Management*, where **net working capital** refers to the difference in the firm's current assets and its current liabilities:

$$\text{net working capital} = \text{current assets} - \text{current liabilities} \qquad (5\text{--}1)$$

Thus, in managing the firm's net working capital we are concerned with *managing the firm's liquidity*. This entails considering two related problems:

1. Managing the firm's investment in current assets
2. Managing the firm's use of short-term or current liabilities

This chapter provides the basic principles underlying the analysis of each of these problems. These principles are then applied in each of the remaining chapters in this section. Specifically, Chapter 6 discusses the management of the firm's investment in cash and marketable securities, while Chapter 7 addresses the problems associated with managing the firm's investments in accounts receivable and inventories. Finally, Chapter 8 presents a discussion of sources of short-term or current liabilities and their role in the sound financial management of the firm.

MANAGING CURRENT ASSETS

Chapters 6 and 7 investigate the decision-making process in managing the firm's investment in current assets, while Chapters 10 and 11 are devoted to the management of fixed-asset investments. At present we need only be aware that these investment decisions are undertaken in expectation of future benefits. That is, a firm invests in inventories because of the expected benefits derived from holding an inventory. Likewise, the firm acquires fixed assets because of the future cash flows those assets are expected to generate. In this chapter our interest in the firm's investment decisions relates to their effect on the firm's net working capital or liquidity. Other things remaining the same, the greater the firm's investment in current assets, the greater its liquidity.

As a means of increasing its liquidity, the firm may choose to invest additional funds in cash and/or marketable securities. Such action involves a tradeoff, however, since such assets earn little or no return. The firm thus finds that it can reduce its risk of illiquidity only by reducing its overall return on invested funds, and vice versa.

The Risk–Return Tradeoff from Investing in Current Assets

The **risk-return tradeoff** involved in managing the firm's liquidity via investing in marketable securities is illustrated in the following example. Firms A and B are identical in every respect but one: Firm B has invested $10,000 in marketable securities, which has been financed with common equity. That is, the firm sold shares of common stock and raised $10,000. The balance sheets and net incomes of the two firms are shown in Table 5–1. Note that Firm A has a current ratio of 2.5 (reflecting net working capital of $30,000) and earns a 10 percent return on its total assets. Firm B, with its larger investment in marketable securities, has a current ratio of 3 and has net working capital of $40,000. Since the marketable securities earn a return of only 6 percent before taxes (3 percent after taxes with a 50 percent tax rate), Firm B earns only 9.6 percent on its total investment. Thus, investing in current assets, and in particular in marketable securities, does have a favorable effect on liquidity, but it also has an unfavorable effect on the firm's rate of return earned on invested funds. The risk-return tradeoff involved in holding more cash and marketable securities, therefore, is one of added liquidity versus reduced profitability.

MANAGING THE FIRM'S USE OF CURRENT LIABILITIES

The second and final determinant of the firm's net working capital relates to its use of current versus long-term debt. Here, too, the firm faces a risk-return tradeoff. *Other things remaining the same, the greater its reliance upon short-term debt or current liabilities in financing its asset investments, the lower will be its liquidity*. On the other hand, the use of current liabilities offers some very real advantages to the user in that they can be less costly than long-term financing, and they provide the firm with a flexible means of financing its fluctuating needs for assets. We will discuss each of the advantages and disadvantages associated with the use of current liabilities as a source of financing. In addition, an example demonstrates the risk-return tradeoff associated with the use of current versus long-term liabilities.

TABLE 5–1. The Effects of Investing in Current Assets on Liquidity and Profitability

	Balance Sheets	
	Firm A	**Firm B**
Cash	$ 1,000	$ 1,000
Marketable securities		10,000
Accounts receivable	19,000	19,000
Inventories	30,000	30,000
Current assets	$ 50,000	$ 60,000
Net fixed assets	100,000	100,000
Total	$150,000	$160,000
Current liabilities	$ 20,000	$ 20,000
Long-term debt	30,000	30,000
Common equity	100,000	110,000
Total	$150,000	$160,000
Net income	$ 15,000	$ 15,300[a]

	Firm A		Firm B	
Current ratio [current assets/current liabilities]	$\dfrac{\$50,000}{\$20,000} =$	2.5 times	$\dfrac{\$60,000}{\$20,000} =$	3.0 times
Net working capital [current assets − current liabilities]		$ 30,000		$ 40,000
Return on total assets [net income/total assets]	$\dfrac{\$15,000}{\$150,000} =$	10%	$\dfrac{\$15,300}{\$160,000} =$	9.6%

[a] During the year Firm B held $10,000 in marketable securities, which earned a 6 percent return or $600 for the year. After paying taxes at a rate of 50 percent, the firm netted a $300 return on this investment.

Advantages of Current Liabilities

Flexibility

Current liabilities offer the firm a flexible source of financing. They can be used to match the timing of a firm's needs for short-term financing. If, for example, a firm needs funds for a three-month period during each year to finance a seasonal expansion in inventories, then a three-month loan can provide substantial cost savings over a long-term loan (even if the interest rate on short-term financing should be higher). This results from the fact that the use of long-term debt in this situation involves borrowing for the entire year rather than for the period when the funds are needed; this increases the level of interest the firm experiences. This brings us to the second advantage generally associated with the use of short-term financing.

Interest Cost

In general, interest rates on short-term debt are lower than on long-term debt for a given borrower. This relationship is usually referred to as the **term structure of interest rates.** For a given firm, the term structure might appear as follows:

Loan Maturity	Interest Rate
3 months	9.00%
6 months	9.25
1 year	9.80
3 years	10.20
5 years	10.90
10 years	11.40
30 years	12.80

Note that this term structure reflects the rates of interest applicable to a given borrower at a particular point in time; it would not describe the rates of interest available to another borrower or even those applicable to the same borrower at a different point in time.

Disadvantages of Current Liabilities

The use of current liabilities or short-term debt as opposed to long-term debt subjects the firm to a greater risk of illiquidity. That is, short-term debt due to its very nature must be repaid or *rolled over* more often, and so it enhances the possibility that the firm's financial condition might deteriorate to a point where the needed funds might not be available.[1]

A second disadvantage of short-term debt is the uncertainty of interest costs from year to year. For example, where a firm borrows during a six-month period each year to finance a seasonal expansion in current assets, it might incur a different rate of interest each year. This rate reflects the current rate of interest at the time of the loan, as well as the lender's perception of the firm's riskiness. If long-term debt were used, the interest cost would be known for the entire period of the loan agreement.

The Risk–Return Tradeoff from Using Current Liabilities

Consider the risk-return characteristics of Firm X and Firm Y, whose balance sheets and income statements are given in Table 5–2. Both firms had the same seasonal needs for financing throughout the past year. In December they each required $40,000 to finance a seasonal expansion in accounts receivable. In addition, during the four-month period beginning with August and extending through November both firms needed $20,000 to support a seasonal buildup in inventories. Firm X financed its seasonal financing requirements using $40,000 in long-term debt carrying an annual interest rate of 10 percent. Firm Y, on the other hand, satisfied its seasonal financing needs using short-term borrowing on which it paid 9 percent interest. Since Firm Y borrowed only when it needed the funds and did so at the lower rate of interest on short-term debt, its interest expense for the year was only $900, whereas Firm X incurred $4000 in annual interest expense.[2]

The end result of the two firms' financing policies is evidenced in their current ratio, net working capital, and return on total assets which appear at the bottom of Table 5–2. Firm X, using long-term rather than short-term debt, has a current ratio of 3 times and $40,000 in net working capital, whereas Firm Y's current ratio is only 1, which represents zero net working capital. However, owing to its lower interest expense, Firm Y was able to earn 10.8 percent on its invested funds, whereas Firm X produced a 10 percent return. Thus, a firm can reduce its risk of illiquidity through the use of long-term debt at the expense of a reduction in its return on invested funds. Once again we see that the risk-return tradeoff involves an increased risk of illiquidity versus increased profitability.

APPROPRIATE LEVEL OF WORKING CAPITAL

Managing the firm's net working capital position (that is, its liquidity) has been shown to involve simultaneous and interrelated decisions regarding investment in current

---

[1] The dangers of such a policy are readily apparent in the experiences of firms that have been forced into bankruptcy. Penn Central, for example, had $80 million in short-term debt that it was unable to refinance (roll over) when it became bankrupt.

[2] Interest expense calculations are found in the footnotes to Table 5–2.

TABLE 5–2. Effect of Current versus Long-term Debt on Firm Liquidity and Profitability

		Balance Sheets	
		Firm X	Firm Y
Current assets		$ 60,000	$ 60,000
Net fixed assets		140,000	140,000
	Total	$200,000	$200,000
Accounts payable		$ 20,000	$ 20,000
Notes payable		—	40,000
Current liabilities		$ 20,000	$ 60,000
Long-term debt		40,000	—
Common equity		140,000	140,000
	Total	$200,000	$200,000

		Income Statements	
Net operating income		$ 44,000	$ 44,000
Less: Interest expense		4,000[a]	900[b]
Earnings before taxes		40,000	43,100
Less: Taxes (50%)		20,000	21,550
Net income		$ 20,000	$ 21,550

Current ratio $\left[\dfrac{\text{current assets}}{\text{current liabilities}}\right]$ $\qquad \dfrac{\$60,000}{\$20,000} = 3 \text{ times} \qquad \dfrac{\$60,000}{\$60,000} = 1 \text{ time}$

Net working capital
[current assets − current liabilities] $\qquad\qquad$ $40,000 $\qquad\qquad$ $0

Return on total assets $\left[\dfrac{\text{net income}}{\text{total assets}}\right]$ $\qquad \dfrac{\$20,000}{\$200,000} = 10\% \qquad \dfrac{\$21,550}{\$200,000} = 10.8\%$

[a] Firm X paid interest during the entire year on $40,000 in long-term debt at a rate of 10 percent. Its interest expense for the year was .10 × $40,000 = $4,000.

[b] Firm Y paid interest on $40,000 for one month and on $20,000 for four months at 9 percent interest during the year. Thus, Firm Y's interest expense for the year equals $40,000 × .09 × 1/12 plus $20,000 × .09 × 4/12, or $300 + $600 = $900.

assets and use of current liabilities. Fortunately, a guiding principle exists that can be used as a benchmark for the firm's working capital policies: the **hedging principle, or principle of self-liquidating debt.** This principle provides a guide to the maintenance of a level of liquidity sufficient for the firm to meet its maturing obligations on time.[3]

---

[3] A value-maximizing approach to the management of the firm's liquidity would involve assessing the value of the benefits derived from increasing the firm's investment in liquid assets and weighing them against the added costs to the firm's owners resulting from investing in low-yielding current assets. Unfortunately, the benefits derived from increased liquidity relate to the expected costs of bankruptcy to the firm's owners, and these costs are "unmeasurable" by existing technology. Thus, a "valuation" approach to liquidity management exists only in the theoretical realm. For a discussion of bankruptcy costs and the associated measurement problems, see J. B. Warner, "Bankruptcy Costs: Some Evidence," *Journal of Finance*, May 1977, 337–49; and J. C. Van Horne, "Bankruptcy and Liquidity Costs," Research Paper No. 205, Stanford Graduate School of Business, 1976.

Hedging Principle

Very simply, the **hedging principle** involves *matching* the cash-flow-generating characteristics of an asset with the maturity of the source of financing used to finance its acquisition. For example, a seasonal expansion in inventories, according to the hedging principle, should be financed with a short-term loan or current liability. The rationale underlying the rule is straightforward. Funds are needed for a limited period of time, and when that time has passed, the cash needed to repay the loan will be generated by the sale of the extra inventory items. Obtaining the needed funds from a long-term source (longer than one year) would mean that the firm would still have the funds after the inventories they helped finance had been sold. In this case the firm would have "excess" liquidity, which it either holds in cash or invests in low-yield marketable securities until the seasonal increase in inventories occurs again and the funds are needed. This would result in an overall lowering of firm profits, as we saw earlier in the example presented in Table 5–2.

Consider a second example in which a firm purchases a new conveyor belt system, which is expected to produce cash savings to the firm by eliminating the need for two laborers and, consequently, their salaries. This amounts to an annual savings of $14,000, while the conveyor belt costs $150,000 to install and will last 20 years. If the firm chooses to finance this asset with a one-year note, then it will not be able to repay the loan from the cash flow generated by the asset. In accordance with the hedging principle, the firm should finance the asset with a source of financing that more nearly matches the expected life and cash flow generating characteristics of the asset. In this case, a 15- to 20-year loan would be more appropriate.

Permanent and Temporary Assets

The notion of *maturity matching* in the hedging principle can be most easily understood when we think in terms of the distinction between **permanent** and **temporary investments in assets** as opposed to the more traditional fixed and current asset categories. A permanent investment in an asset is one that the firm expects to hold for a period longer than one year. Note that we are referring to the period of time the firm plans to hold an investment, and not the useful life of the asset. For example, permanent investments are made in the firm's minimum level of current assets, as well as in its fixed assets. Temporary asset investments, on the other hand, are comprised of current assets that will be liquidated and *not* replaced within the current year. Thus, some part of the firm's current assets is permanent and the remainder is temporary. For example, a seasonal increase in level of inventories is a temporary investment; the buildup in inventories will be eliminated when it is no longer needed.

The hedging principle can now be stated very succinctly: *Asset needs of the firm not financed by spontaneous sources should be financed in accordance with the rule: Permanent asset investments are financed with permanent sources, and temporary investments are financed with temporary sources.*

Spontaneous, Temporary, and Permanent Sources of Financing

Since total assets must always equal the sum of spontaneous, temporary, and permanent sources of financing, the hedging approach provides the financial manager with the basis for determining the sources of financing to use at any point in time.

Now, what constitutes a temporary, permanent, and spontaneous source of financing? Temporary sources of financing consist of current liabilities. Short-term notes payable (discussed in Chapter 8) constitute the most common example of a temporary source of financing. Examples of notes payable include unsecured bank loans, commercial paper, and loans secured by accounts receivable and inventories. Permanent sources of financing include intermediate-term loans (discussed in Chapter 18), long-term debt, preferred stock, and common equity (discussed in Chapters 16 and 19).

Spontaneous sources of financing consist of trade credit and other accounts payable that arise *spontaneously* in the firm's day-to-day operations. For example, as the firm acquires materials for its inventories, trade credit is often made available spontaneously or on *demand* from the firm's suppliers. Trade credit appears on the firm's balance sheet as accounts payable, and the size of the accounts payable balance varies directly with the firm's purchases of inventory items. In turn, inventory purchases are related to anticipated sales. Thus, part of the financing needed by the firm is spontaneously provided in the form of trade credit.

In addition to trade credit, wages and salaries payable, accrued interest, and accrued taxes also provide valuable sources of spontaneous financing. These expenses accrue throughout the period until they are paid. For example, if a firm has a wage expense of $10,000 a week and pays its employees monthly, then its employees effectively provide financing equal to $10,000 by the end of the first week following a payday, $20,000 by the end of the second week, and so forth. Since these expenses generally arise in direct conjunction with the firm's ongoing operations, they too are referred to as *spontaneous*.

FIGURE 5–1. Hedging Financing Strategy

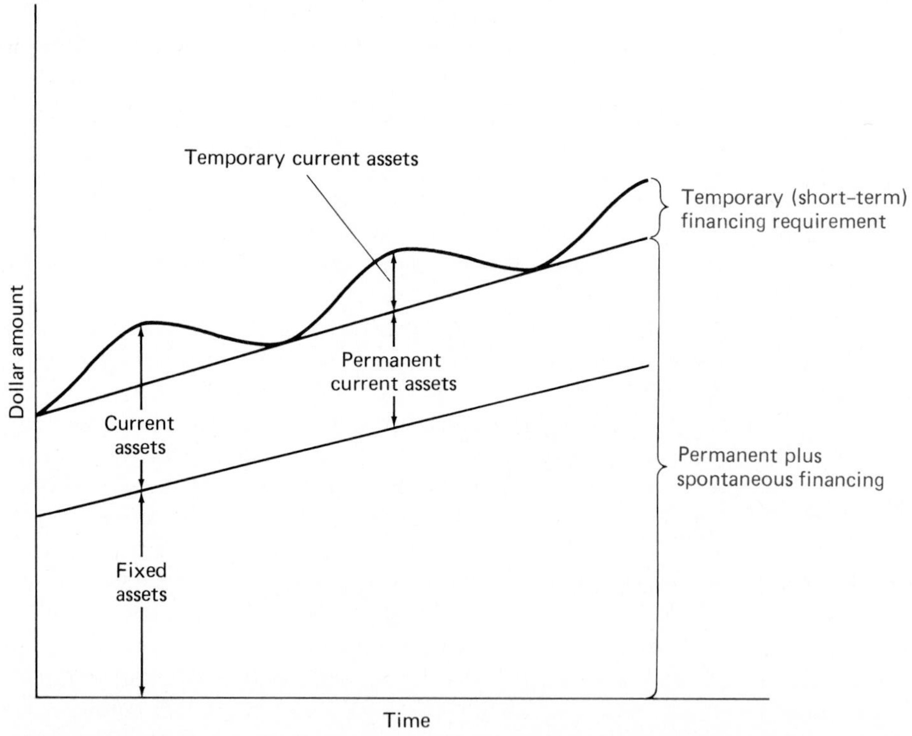

Note that permanent asset needs are matched exactly with spontaneous plus permanent sources of financing, while temporary current assets are financed with temporary (short-term) sources of financing.

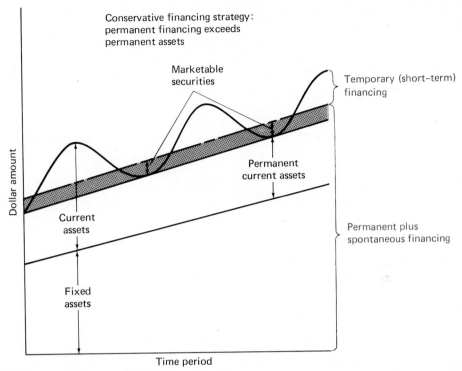

Shaded area represents the firm's use of permanent plus spontaneous financing *in excess* of the firm's permanent asset financing needs.

FIGURE 5–2. Conservative Financing Strategy: Spontaneous plus Permanent Sources of Financing Exceed Permanent Assets

Hedging Principle: Graphic Illustration

The hedging principle is depicted in Figure 5–1. Total assets are broken down into temporary and permanent asset investment categories. The firm's permanent investment in assets is financed by the use of permanent sources of financing (intermediate- and long-term debt, preferred stock, and common equity) or spontaneous sources (trade credit and other accounts payable).[4] Its temporary investment in assets is financed with temporary (short-term) debt.

Modifications to the Hedging Principle

Figures 5–2 and 5–3 depict two modifications of the strict hedging approach to working capital management. In Figure 5–2 the firm follows a more cautious plan, whereby permanent sources of financing exceed permanent assets in trough periods so that excess cash is available (which must be invested in marketable securities).[5] Note that the firm actually has excess liquidity during the low ebb of its asset cycle, and

---

[4] For illustration purposes spontaneous sources of financing are treated as if their amount were fixed. In practice, of course, spontaneous sources of financing fluctuate with the firm's purchases and its expenditures for wages, salaries, taxes, and other items that are paid on a delayed basis. In the appendix to this chapter we will discuss the more realistic case of fluctuating spontaneous sources of financing.

[5] Marketable securities and cash management are discussed in Chapter 6.

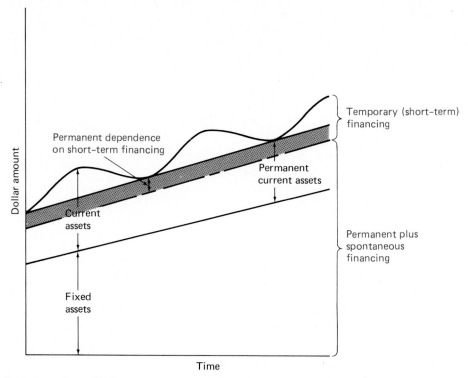

Shaded area reflects the firm's continuous use of short-term financing to support its permanent asset needs.

FIGURE 5–3. Aggressive Financing Strategy: Permanent Reliance on Short-Term Financing

thus faces a lower risk of being caught short of cash than a firm that follows the pure hedging approach. However, the firm also increases its investment in relatively low-yielding assets so that its return on investment is diminished (recall the example from Table 5–1).

In contrast, Figure 5–3 depicts a firm that continually finances a part of its permanent asset needs with temporary or short-term funds and thus follows a more aggressive stragegy in managing its working capital. Even when its investment in asset needs is lowest, the firm must still rely on short-term or temporary financing. Such a firm would be subject to increased risks of a cash shortfall in that it must depend on a continual *rollover* or replacement of its short-term debt with more short-term debt. The benefit derived from following such a policy relates to the possible savings resulting from the use of lower-cost short-term debt (as opposed to long-term debt—recall the example presented in Table 5–2).

Most firms will not exclusively follow any one of the three strategies outlined here in determining their reliance on short-term credit. Instead, a firm will at times find itself overly reliant on permanent financing and thus holding excess cash; at other times it may have to rely on short-term financing throughout an entire operating cycle. The hedging approach does, however, provide an important benchmark that can be used to guide decisions regarding the appropriate use of short-term credit.

Summary

There are problems involved in managing the firm's working capital, defined in terms of **net working capital,** which equals current assets less current liabilities. Working capital management involves managing the firm's liquidity, which, in turn, involves managing (1) the firm's investment in current assets and (2) its use of current liabilities. Each of these problems involves risk-return tradeoffs. Investing in current assets reduces the firm's risk of illiquidity at the expense of lowering its overall rate of return on its investment in assets. Furthermore, the use of long-term sources of financing enhances the firm's liquidity while reducing its rate of return on assets.

The **hedging principle,** or **principle of self-liquidating debt,** is a benchmark for working capital decisions. Basically, this principle involves matching the cash flow generating characteristics of an asset with the cash flow requirements of the source of funds used to finance its acquisition.

Chapters 6 and 7 discuss the problems involved in managing the firm's investment in current assets. This includes the management of cash, marketable securities, accounts receivable, and inventories. Chapter 8 discusses short-term financing. Two basic problems are encountered in attempting to manage the firm's use of short-term financing: (1) How much short-term financing should the firm use? (2) What specific sources should be selected? This chapter has addressed the first of these questions with the hedging or self-liquidating-debt principle. The answer to the second question involves analyzing the relative costs of the available sources of short-term credit, an issue addressed at length in Chapter 8.

Study Questions

5–1. Define and contrast the terms working capital and net working capital.

5–2. Discuss the risk-return relationship involved in the firm's asset investment decisions as it pertains to working-capital management.

5–3. What advantages and disadvantages are generally associated with the use of short-term debt? Discuss.

5–4. Explain what is meant by the statement "The use of current liabilities as opposed to long-term debt subjects the firm to a greater risk of illiquidity."

5–5. Define the hedging principle. How can this principle be used in the management of working capital?

5–6. Define the following terms:
   a. Permanent asset investments
   b. Temporary asset investments
   c. Permanent sources of financing
   d. Temporary sources of financing
   e. Spontaneous sources of financing

Self-Test Problems

ST–1. (*Investing in Current Assets and the Return on Common Equity*) Walker Enterprises is presently evaluating its investment in working capital for the coming year. Specifically, the firm is analyzing its level of investment in current assets. The firm projects that it will have sales of $4,000,000 next year, and its fixed assets are projected to total $1,500,000. The firm pays interest at a rate of 10 percent on its short- and long-term debt (which is managed by the firm so as to equal a target of 40 percent of assets). The firm projects its earnings before interest and taxes to be 15 percent of sales and faces a 30 percent tax rate.

a. If Walker decides to follow a working capital strategy calling for current assets equal to 40 percent of sales, what will be the firm's return on common equity?

b. Answer part (a) for a current asset to sales ratio of 60 percent.

c. Throughout our analysis we have assumed that the rate of return earned by the firm on sales is independent of its investment in current assets. Is this a valid assumption?

ST–2. (*Using Marketable Securities to Increase Liquidity*) The balance sheet for the Simplex Mfg. Co. is presented below for the year ended December 31, 19X5:

SIMPLEX MFG. CO. Balance Sheet December 31, 19X5

Cash	$10,000	
Accounts receivable	50,000	
Inventories	40,000	
Total current assets		$100,000
Net fixed assets		100,000
Total		$200,000
Current liabilities		$ 60,000
Long-term liabilities		40,000
Common equity		100,000
Total		$200,000

During 19X5 the firm earned net income after taxes of $20,000 based on net sales of $400,000.

a. Calculate Simplex's current ratio, net working capital position, and return on total assets ratio (net income/total assets) using the above information.

b. The vice-president for finance at Simplex is considering a plan for enhancing the firm's liquidity. The plan involves raising $20,000 in common equity and investing in marketable securities that will earn 8 percent before taxes and 4.8 percent after taxes. Calculate Simplex's current ratio, net working capital, and return on total asset ratio after the plan has been implemented, [**Hint:** Net income will now become $20,000, plus .048 times $20,000, or $20,960.]

c. Will the plan proposed in part (b) enhance firm liquidity? Explain.

d. What effect does the plan proposed in (b) have on firm profitability? Explain.

ST–3. (*Using Long-Term Debt to Increase Liquidity*) On April 30, 19X5, the Jamax Sales Company had the following balance sheet and income statement for the year just ended:

JAMAX SALES COMPANY Balance Sheet April 30, 19X5

Current assets		$100,000
Net fixed assets		200,000
Total		$300,000
Accounts payable	$30,000	
Notes payable (14%)[a]	40,000	
Total		$ 70,000
Long-term debt (10%)		100,000
Common equity		130,000
Total		$300,000

JAMAX SALES COMPANY Balance Sheet April 30, 19X5 (cont.)

Partial Income Statement for the year ended April 30, 19X5

Net operating income	$72,800
Less: Interest expense[b]	12,800
Earnings before taxes	$60,000
Less: Taxes (50%)	30,000
Net income	$30,000

[a] The short-term notes are outstanding during the latter half of the firm's fiscal year in response to the firm's seasonal need for funds.

[b] Total interest expense for the year consists of 14% interest on the firm's $40,000 note for a six-month period $(.14 \times \$40,000 \times 1/2)$, $2800, plus 10% of the firm's $100,000 long-term note for a full year $(.10 \times \$100,000)$, or $10,000. Thus, total interest expense for the year is $2800 plus $10,000 or $12,800.

a. Calculate JAMAX's current ratio, net working capital, and return on total assets.

b. The treasurer of JAMAX was recently advised by the firm's investment banker that its current ratio was considered below par. In fact, a current ratio of 2.00 was considered to be a sign of a healthy liquidity position. In response to this news the treasurer devised a plan wherein the firm would issue $40,000 in 13 percent long-term debt and pay off its short-term notes payable. This long-term note would be outstanding all year long, and when the funds were not needed to finance the firm's seasonal asset needs, they would be invested in marketable securities earning 8 percent before taxes. If the plan had been in effect last year, other things being the same, what would have been the firm's current ratio, net working capital, and return on total assets ratio? [**Hint:** The firm's net income with the change would have been $29,600.]

c. Did JAMAX's liquidity improve to the desired level (based on a desired current ratio of 2.0)?

d. How was the firm's profitability in relation to total investment affected by the change in financial policy?

Study Problems

5-1. (*Investing in Current Assets and the Return on Common Equity*) In June the MacMinn Company began planning for the coming year. A primary concern is its working capital management policy. In particular, the firm's management is considering the effects of its investment in current assets on the return earned on common shareholders' equity. The firm projects that it will have sales of $8,000,000 next year, and its fixed assets are projected to total $2,000,000. It pays interest at a rate of 12 percent on its short- and long-term debt (which is managed by the firm so as to equal a target of 30 percent of assets). Finally, the firm projects its earnings before interest and taxes to be 15 percent of sales and faces a 30 percent tax rate.

a. If Walker decides to follow a working capital strategy calling for current assets equal to 40 percent of sales, what will be the firm's return on common equity?

b. Answer part (a) for a current asset to sales ratio of 60 percent.

c. Throughout our analysis we have assumed that the rate of return earned by the firm on sales is independent of its investment in current assets. Is this a valid assumption?

5-2. (*Managing Firm Liquidity*) On September 30, 19X5, the balance sheet and income statement for Trecor Mfg. Company appeared as follows:

TRECOR MFG. COMPANY Balance Sheet
September 30, 19X5

Current assets	$ 500,000
Net fixed assets	500,000
Total	$1,000,000
Accounts payable	$ 100,000
Notes payable (17%)[a]	400,000
Total	$ 500,000
Long-term debt (12%)	100,000
Common equity	400,000
Total	$1,000,000

[a] Short-term notes are used to finance a three-month seasonal expansion in Trecor's asset needs. This period is the same for every year and extends from July through September with the note being due October 1.

TRECOR MFG. COMPANY Income Statement
for the Year Ended September 30, 19X5

Net operating income	$195,666
Less: Interest expense[a]	(29,000)
Earnings before taxes	166,666
Less: Taxes (40%)	(66,666)
Net income	$100,000

[b] Interest expense was calculated as follows:

Notes payable (.17 × $400,000 × 1/4 year) = $17,000
Long-term debt (.12 × $100,000 × 1 year) = 12,000
Total = $29,000

a. Calculate the current ratio, net working capital, return on total assets, and return on common equity ratio for Trecor.

b. Assume that you have just been hired as financial vice-president of Trecor. One of your first duties is to assess the firm's liquidity position. Based upon your analysis, you plan to issue $400,000 in common stock and use the proceeds to retire the firm's notes payable. Recalculate the ratios from part (a) above and assess the change in the firm's liquidity.

c. Given your actions in part (b) above, assume now that in the future you will finance your three-month seasonal need for $400,000 using a long-term bond issue which will carry an interest cost of 15 percent. (Note that during the time the funds are needed your current assets increase by $400,000 due to increased inventories and receivables.) In addition, you estimate that during the nine months you do not need the funds, they can be invested in marketable securities to earn a rate of 10 percent. Recalculate the financial ratios from part (a) for 19X6 where all revenues and nonfinance expenses are expected to be the same as in 19X5. Analyze the results of your plan.

5–3. (*Managing Firm Liquidity*) Reanalyze part (c) of problem 5–1 assuming that a three-month short-term note is used as opposed to the bonds. The note carries a rate of 15 percent per annum.

5–4. (*The Hedging Principle*) H. O. Hielregal, Inc., estimates that its current assets are about 25 percent of sales. The firm's current balance sheet is presented below:

H. O. HIELREGAL Balance Sheet December 31, 19X5 ($ millions)

Current assets	$2.0	Trade credit and	
Fixed assets	2.8	accounts payable	$ .8
		Long-term debt	1.0
Total	$4.8	Common equity	3.0
		Total	$4.8

Hielregal pays out all of its net income in cash dividends to its stockholders. Trade credit and accounts payable equal 10 percent of the firm's sales.

a. Based on the following five-year sales forecast, prepare five end-of-year pro forma balance sheets that incidate "additional financing needed" for each year as a balancing account. Fixed assets are expected to increase by $0.2 million each year.

Year	Predicted Sales ($ Millions)
19X6	10
19X7	11
19X8	13
19X9	14
19X0	15

a. Develop a financing policy for Hielregal using your answer to part (a) above that is consistent with the following goals:

1. A minimum current ratio of 2.0 and a maximum of 3.0.
2. A debt to total assets ratio of 35–45 percent. You may issue new common stock to raise equity funds.

Self-Test Solutions

SS–1. a. Walker's pro forma balance sheet for next year will appear as follows:

Current assets	$1,600,000	Debt (40% of assets)	$1,240,000
Fixed assets	1,500,000	Owner's equity	1,860,000
Total	$3,100,000	Total	$3,100,000

Projected earnings are calculated as follows:

Sales	$4,000,000
EBIT (15%)	$ 600,000
Interest	(124,000)
EBT	$ 476,000
Taxes	(142,800)
Net income	$ 333,200

Thus, the firm's return on common equity is

$$\$333,200/\$1,860,000 = 17.9\%$$

b. Under this scenario, Walker's pro forma balance sheet for next year will appear as follows:

Current assets	$2,400,000	Debt (40% of assets)	$1,560,000
Fixed assets	1,500,000	Owner's equity	2,340,000
Total	$3,900,000	Total	$3,900,000

Projected earnings are calculated as follows:

Sales	$4,000,000
EBIT (15%)	$ 600,000
Interest	(156,000)
EBT	$ 444,000
Taxes	(133,200)
Net income	$ 310,800

Thus, the firm's return on common equity is $310,800/3,900,000 = 13.3 percent.

c. One would expect that the firm would earn some positive return from investing in current assets. For example, the firm could hold some of its current assets in marketable securities earning some positive rate of return. Note, however, that so long as these current assets earn a rate of return less than the cost of financing the investment, the rate of return on the common shareholder's equity will decrease with increased investment in current assets.

SS–2. **a.**

$$\text{current ratio} = \frac{\text{current assets}}{\text{current liabilities}}$$

$$= \frac{\$100,000}{\$60,000} = \underline{1.67 \times}$$

$$\text{net working capital} = \text{current assets} - \text{current liabilities}$$

$$= \$100,000 - \$60,000 = \underline{\$40,000}$$

$$\text{return on total assets} = \frac{\text{net income}}{\text{total assets}}$$

$$= \frac{\$ 20,000}{\$200,000} = \underline{10\%}$$

b.

$$\text{current ratio} = \frac{\$120,000}{\$ 60,000} = \underline{2 \times}$$

$$\text{net working capital} = \$120,000 - \$60,000 = \underline{\$60,000}$$

$$\text{return on total assets} = \frac{\$ 20,960}{220,000} = \underline{9.52\%}$$

c. Yes, the firm's liquidity position as measured by the current ratio and the amount of net working capital has definitely improved. However, as we see in the answer to part (b), profitability has been adversely affected.

d. Simplex's return on total assets declined from 10 to 9.52 percent as a result of the new financing plan. This occurred because it was earning 10 percent after taxes on its $200,000 investment and it invested $20,000 in marketable securities earning only 4.8 percent after taxes. The result was a decline in firm profitability in relation to assets.

SS–3.   **a.** $\text{current ratio} = \dfrac{\text{current assets}}{\text{current liabilities}}$

$$= \frac{\$100,000}{\$\ 70,000} = \underline{1.43 \times}$$

$\text{net working capital} = \text{current assets} - \text{current liabilities}$

$$= \$100,000 - \$70,000$$

$$= \underline{\$\ 30,000}$$

$\text{return on total assets} = \dfrac{\text{net income}}{\text{total assets}}$

$$= \frac{\$\ 30,000}{\$300,000}$$

$$= \underline{10\%}$$

b. $\text{current ratio} = \dfrac{\$100,000}{\$\ 30,000} = \underline{3.33 \times}$

$\text{net working capital} = \$100,000 - \$30,000 = \underline{\$70,000}$

$\text{return on total assets} = \dfrac{\$\ 29,600}{\$300,000} = \underline{9.87\%}$

c.   Yes, the current ratio of 3.33 is now well above the 2.0 standard when the funds are needed. Furthermore, if we include the $40,000 in marketable securities in current assets, the current ratio rises to 4.67 ($100,000 + $40,000/$30,000 = 4.67) during those times when the funds are seasonally idle.

d.   Firm profitability declined slightly because the firm used a permanent source of financing to replace a more flexible short-term source. The firm actually saves interest expense through the plan during the six-month period when the funds are needed (13 percent on long-term funds versus 14 percent on short-term notes); however, during the six months when the funds are not needed, the firm can only earn a before-tax return of 8 percent, while the funds cost 13 percent.

   In this case, the added liquidity of the plan appears to overshadow the modest loss in expected profitability.

Selected References

Knight, W. D. "Working Capital Management—Satisficing versus Optimization," *Financial Management*, 1 (Spring 1972), 33–40.

Mehta, Dileep R. *Working Capital Management*. Englewood Cliffs, NJ: Prentice-Hall, 1974.

Merville, L. J., and L. A. Tavis. "Optimal Working Capital Policies: A Chance-Constrained Programming Approach," *Journal of Financial and Quantitative Analysis*, 8 (January 1973), 47–60.

_____. "A Total Real Asset Planning System," *Journal of Financial and Quantitative Analysis*, 9 (January 1974), 107–15.

Sartoris, W. L., and N. C. Hill. "A Generalized Cash Flow Approach to Short-Term Financial Decisions," *Journal of Finance*, 38 (May 1983), 349–60.

Smith, Keith V. *Management of Working Capital*. 2nd ed. New York: West Publishing, 1980.

Stancill, James McN. *The Management of Working Capital*. Scranton, PA: Intext, 1971.

Tinsley, P. A. "Capital Structure, Precautionary Balances, and Valuation of the Firm: The Problem of Financial Risk," *Journal of Financial and Quantitative Analysis*, 5 (March 1970), 33–62.

Van Horne, James C. "A Risk-Return Analysis of a Firm's

Working Capital Position," *Engineering Economist*, 14 (Winter 1969), 71–89.

Walker, Ernest W. "Toward a Theory of Working Capi-

tal," *Engineering Economist*, 9 (January–February 1964), 21–35.

APPENDIX 5A
—————A Numerical Illustration of the Hedging Principle—————

In the discussion of the hedging principle in Chapter 5 a graphic presentation was used. In this appendix an example problem is analyzed wherein all necessary computations are explained in detail. Two factors will become apparent in our analysis: First, the pattern of projected asset needs for a firm will not follow the smooth curves used in the Chapter 5 graphic presentation. This more erratic pattern of asset financing needs is more in keeping with realistic financial planning problems. Second, strict adherence to the hedging principle in every planning period will involve careful analysis and foresight.

The hedging principle can be applied to the financial planning problem using the five-step procedure otulined in Figure 5A–1. Note that each step in the procedure is stated both verbally and algebraically. The solution procedure or algorithm presented here is rather rudimentary. More sophisticated solutions to the problem of financial planning that use various forms of mathematical programming techniques are readily available.[1]

The financial planning problem faced by the Simplot Mfg. Co. and presented in Table 5A–1 is used to demonstrate the application of the hedging principle. Each step involved in applying the hedging strategy is discussed in detail below.

STEP 1: *Predicting the firm's needs for current, fixed, and total assets over the planning horizon.*

The forecast of these asset categories will involve use of the financial forecasting methodology set forth in Chapter 4. The percent of sales method of forecasting is widely used for this purpose. The results of the forecast of asset needs for the Simplot Mfg. Co. are found in columns (1), (2) and (3) of Table 5A–1. Note that Simplot's total asset needs contain a seasonal variation as well as an increase in permanent assets throughout the planning horizon. Total assets reach their lowest point for the year in the third quarter and peak in the first quarter. Comparing each year's total asset needs for the same quarters in each year (for example, quarter 1 of 19X5 and that same quarter in 19X6), we can easily see that Simplot's projected total assets are growing.

STEP 2: *Distinguish between the firm's permanent and temporary assets for each period in the planning horizon.*

To identify what part of the firm's total assets for a given period are permanent, the analyst must look forward over the planning horizon to determine that quarter in which

---

[1] For example, a linear programming model is developed for financial planning in G. A. Pogue and R. N. Bussard, "A Linear Programming Model for Short-Term Financial Planning under Uncertainty," *Sloan Managment Review*, 13 (Spring 1972), 69–99. Goal programming is used to address the financial planning problem in A. J. Keown and J. D. Martin, "A Two-Stage Chance-Constrained Goal Programming Model for Working Capital Management," *Engineering Economist*, (Spring 1977), 153–74.

FIGURE 5A–1. Applying the Heading Principle to Working Capital Management

Step	Description	Equation
1	Project the firm's asset needs for each quarter (month) of the planning horizon. The resulting forecast will be our estimates of the firm's total assets (TA), which can be further broken down into both current assets (CA) and fixed assets (FA).	$TA = CA + FA$
2	Distinguish between permanent asset (P) and temporary asset investment (T) for each quarter of the planning period.	$TA = P + T$
3	Project the level of spontaneous financing (SF) for each quarter.[a]	
4	Determine the level of permanent financing (PF) for each quarter of the planning horizon. This equals the difference in permanent assets (P^*) and spontaneous financing (SF^*) for the nearest calendar quarter where temporary assets (T) equals zero.[b]	$PF = P^* - SF^*$
5	Determine the level of short-term debt or temporary financing (TF). This equals the difference in total assets for the quarter and the sum of permanent (PF) plus spontaneous sources of financing (SF).	$TF = TA - (PF + SF)$

[a] In the example used in the text discussion, SF is estimated to rise steadily with the projected increase in total assets.

[b] The asterisk (*) on SF^* and P^* indicates those levels of SF and P corresponding to that particular calendar quarter where temporary financing equals zero. In this quarter, the sum of permanent financing sources plus spontaneous financing equals permanent assets.

the firm's total asset needs drop to their lowest level. This minimum level of total assets equals the firm's permanent assets. For Simplot this minimum level of total assets is observed during the third quarter of 19X5, where total assets equal $101 million. The analyst then looks forward into 19X6 to determine the next minimum level of total assets. Once again the third quarter of the year provides the lowest level of total assets, which for 19X6 equal $105 million. Thus, for quarter IV of 19X5 and all four quarters of 19X6 we estimate Simplot's permanent assets to be $105 million.[2]

STEP 3: Project spontaneous financing for each period within the planning horizon.

For illustrative purposes Simplot's spontaneous sources of financing are projected to increase $1 million each six-month period over the planning horizon. Therefore, for the first two quarters of 19X5 spontaneous financing will equal $5 million. In quarter III, it increases to $6 million, and so forth.

---

[2] Based upon the pattern of total assets projections we would expect Simplot's permanent assets to rise in quarter IV of 19X6; however, without projections of 19X7 assets we cannot determine the new level of permanent assets.

TABLE 5A–1. Using the Hedging Principle: Simplot Mfg. Co.

		Projected Assets						Projected Financing Plan		
Year	Quarter	(1) Fixed Assets	(2) Current Assets	(3) Total Assets	(4) Permanent Assets[b]	(5) Temporary Assets[c]	(6) Spontaneous Financing[d]	(7) Permanent Financing[e]	(8) Temporary or Short-term	(9) Total Financing
19X5	I	$60[a]	$60	$120	$101	$19	$5	$95	$20	$120
	II	60	45	105	101	4	5	95	5	105
	III	61	40	101	101	0	6	95	0	101
	IV	61	50	111	105	6	6	97	8	111
19X6	I	62	62	124	105	19	7	97	20	124
	II	62	48	110	105	5	7	97	6	110
	II	63	42	105	105	0	8	97	0	105
	IV	63	52	115	105	10	8	97	10	115

[a] All figures are in millions of dollars.

[b] Permanent assets are found by "looking ahead" in time to find the minimum level of total assets for any future period. In this example that minimum occurs in the third quarter of the year. For 19X5 permanent assets equal $101 million, and in 19X6 they equal $105 million.

[c] Temporary assets equal total assets less permanent assets. For example, temporary assets for quarter II of 1986 are $110 million − $105 million = $5 million.

[d] Spontaneous financing sources include trade credit and other payables such as accrued wages and accrued taxes that arise "spontaneously" with the firm's operations. In this example these financing sources are expected to rise in accordance with the overall "growth rate" in firm assets.

[e] The sum of spontaneous plus permanent financing sources is set equal to the firm's projected permanent asset needs in the quarter in which temporary assets equal zero. Thus, in quarter III of 19X5 where permanent assets are $101 million and spontaneous financing is $6 million, we determine permanent financing to be $95 million = $101 million − $6 million. Note that this relationship holds only where temporary assets are zero.

STEP 4:   *Estimate the firm's need for permanent financing.*

This step can be accomplished by using Table 5A–1 to locate those calendar quarters in which temporary asset investments are zero. In these quarters total assets equal permanent assets. Thus, for these quarters the firm's permanent plus spontaneous financing sources must equal total assets. Since we have already projected total assets in Step 1 and spontaneous financing in Step 3, we can easily solve for permanent sources of financing. Note that this procedure works only for those calendar quarters in which temporary assets and thus temporary sources of financing are zero. For the intervening quarters where temporary financing is nonzero, we simply set permanent financing equal to the level estimated for the most recent past quarter.

Beginning our analysis of the Simplot example in quarter I of 19X5, temporary assets are projected to equal zero in quarter III of that year. At this point, temporary financing should also equal zero in accordance with the hedging principle.[3] Thus, for quarter III of 19X5 total assets should be financed by spontaneous plus permanent sources of financing. Since spontaneous financing for this quarter has been estimated to equal $6 million, then permanent financing must equal $95 million. That is, permanent financing should equal total assets of $101 million less spontaneous financing of $6 million. This level of permanent financing should be used through quarter III of 19X5, when the

---

[3] The hedging principle states that emporary financing be used to finance temporary asset investments alone. Thus, where no temporary asset investments exist, the firm should be free of all temporary sources of financing.

level of permanent financing would again have to be estimated. The analyst next considers 19X6, where temporary assets are again observed to be zero in quarter III. This time permanent assets are $105 million and spontaneous financing is projected to equal $8 million. Thus, permanent financing for quarter IV of 19X5 and all of 19X6 rises to $97 million = $105 million − $8 million.

STEP 5: *Estimating the firm's temporary financing needs for each period in the planning horizon.*

Each period's estimate of temporary financing needs is found by subtracting the sum of permanent plus spontaneous financing from total assets (or simply total financing needed). Thus, for quarter I of 19X5 temporary financing is simply total assets of $120 million less the sum of permanent financing ($95 million) plus spontaneous financing ($5 million). Temporary financing for the quarter is therefore equal to $20 million.

This completes the development of Simplot's two-year financial plan. The plan indicates the appropriate use of spontaneous, short-term (temporary), and permanent financing in accordance with the hedging principle. As we have seen, following this principle involves dichotomizing the firm's projected needs for assets into permanent and temporary categories and then matching permanent assets with permanent plus spontaneous sources of financing and temporary assets with temporary financing sources.

A word of caution: The development of a financing plan that adheres strictly to the hedging principle may be more complicated than the Simplot example discussed here. In

FIGURE 5A–2. The Hedging Principle with Varying Spontaneous Financing

139

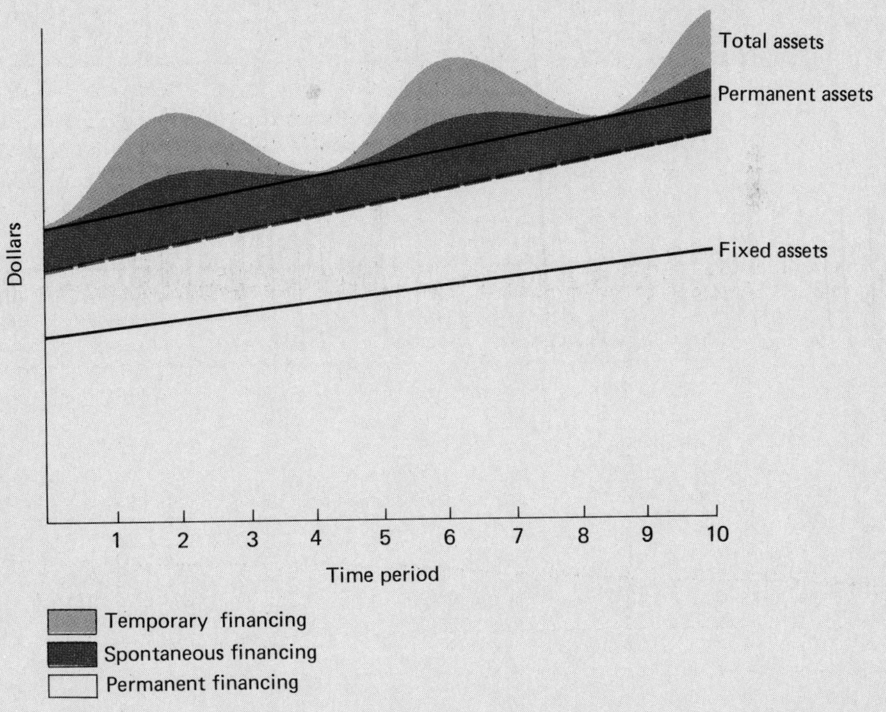

addition, as we noted in Chapter 5, the firm may not wish to follow the hedging principle exactly.

A key element in the application of the hedging principle that can greatly complicate the analysis is spontaneous sources of financing. Were it not for this type of financing, it would be a simple matter to match permanent asset and financing sources as well as temporary asset and temporary financing sources. However spontaneous financing sources, which are something of a hybrid in that they are used continuously by the firm but are short-term forms of financing, can end up financing both permanent and temporary asset needs. In the Simplot example the projected levels of spontaneous financing followed a simple growth trend that mirrored the firm's overall growth in assets. A somewhat more realistic pattern for spontaneous financing might follow the pattern of change in the level of current assets. For example, a principal source of spontaneous financing consists of trade accounts payable, which vary closely with the firm's inventories. Thus, as the firm's inventories expand temporarily with increased seasonal demand for its product, its accounts payable also expand. Similarly, when inventories contract, accounts payable are extinguished, and this important source of spontaneous financing disappears. Figure 5A–2 depicts this more realistic view of spontaneous financing in the application of the hedging principle. Note that spontaneous financing has been used partially to finance a seasonal and temporary need for funds. The Simplot example did not include consideration of this possibility, and its solution was simplified as a result.

Study Problems

5A–1. The projected asset needs for the Amorflex Print Company are tabulated below. The firm's projected levels of spontaneous financing also are included. Complete the financing plan for Amorflex, using the hedging principle. All figures are in millions of dollars.

Year	Quarter	(1) Fixed Assets	(2) Current Assets	(3) Total Assets	(4) Permanent Assets	(5) Temporary Assets
19X5	I	$100	$ 80	$180	$180	$ 0
	II	100	100	200	194	6
	III	102	110	212	194	18
	IV	102	105	207	194	13
19X6	I	104	90	194	194	0
	II	104	110	214	210	4
	III	106	115	221	210	11
	IV	106	112	218	210	8
19X7	I	108	102	210	210	0

Year	Quarter	(6) Spontaneous Financing	(7) Permanent Financing	(8) Temporary Financing	(9) Total Financing
19X5	I	$30			
	II	30			
	III	30			
	IV	30			
19X6	I	30			
	II	30			
	III	30			
	IV	30			
19X7	I	30			

5A–2. The current balance sheet for the J. S. Smith Manufacturing Company appears as follows:

J. S. SMITH MFG. CO. Balance Sheet March 31, 19X4 ($millions)

Current assets	$100	Accounts payable and	
Fixed assets	100	accrued expenses	$ 25
		Notes payable	25
Total	$200	Long-term debt	50
		Common equity	100
		Total	$200

Estimated current and fixed asset investments for the firm are presented for each quarter of the next three years, as follows:

Quarter Ended	Fixed Assets ($ Millions)	Current Assets ($ Millions)	Total Assets ($ Millions)	Permanent Assets ($ Millions)
6/30/X4	100	105	205	205
9/30/X4	100	106	206	205
12/31/X4	101	108	209	205
3/31/X5	101	104	205	205
6/30/X5	102	105	207	207
9/30/X5	102	107	209	209
12/31/X5	103	109	212	209
3/31/X6	103	106	209	209
6/30/X6	104	107	211	211
9/30/X6	104	109	213	212
12/31/X6	105	110	215	212
3/31/X7	105	107	212	212

The firm wants to develop a financial plan that will accommodate its total needs for funds. Furthermore, Smith believes that a minimum issue of $2 million is required to justify the issuance of long-term debt or common stock.

a. Develop a financing plan for Smith, using the hedging concept, where accounts payable and accrued expenses are expected to equal 25 percent of current assets and the firm expects quarterly earnings after taxes of $1 million. The firm also plans to pay cash dividends equal to the full $1 million each quarter.

b. Modify your plan in part (a) above to include compliance with the following objectives for each quarter in the planning period:

(1) A 40–60 percent debt ratio (total liabilities/total assets)

(2) A current ratio of 1.5 or higher

c. If short-term debt will cost Smith 6 percent and long-term debt 8 percent, what is the total cost of your plan in part (b) above to Smith over the three-year period? (**Hint:** Assume that short-term debt financing is retired at the end of each quarter and that any long-term debt issued during the planning period remains outstanding over the entire planning horizon.)

6

Cash and Marketable Securities Management

Chapter 5 introduced and overviewed the concept of working capital management. Now we will consider the various elements of the firm's working capital in some depth. This chapter and Appendix 6A center on the formulation of financial policies for management of cash and marketable securities. Taken together, they explore three major areas: (1) techniques available to management for favorably influencing cash receipts and disbursements patterns, (2) sensible investment possibilities that enable the company productively to employ excess cash balances, and (3) some straightforward models that can assist financial officers in deciding on how much cash to hold. Appendix 6A covers this latter area.

First it will be helpful to distinguish among some terms. **Cash** is the currency and coin the firm has on hand in petty cash drawers, in cash registers, or in checking accounts at the various commercial banks where its demand deposits are maintained. **Marketable securities** are those security investments the firm can quickly convert into cash balances. Those held by most firms in the United States tend to have very short maturity periods—less than one year. No law, of course, dictates that instruments with longer terms to maturity must be avoided. Rather, the decision to keep the average maturity quite short is based upon some sound business reasoning, which will be discussed later. Marketable securities are also referred to as **near cash** or **near-cash assets** because they can be turned into cash in a short period of time. Taken together, cash and near cash are known as **liquid assets.**

WHY A COMPANY HOLDS CASH

A thorough understanding of why and how a firm holds cash requires an accurate conception of how cash flows into and through the enterprise. Figure 6–1 depicts the process of cash generation and disposition in a typical manufacturing setting.

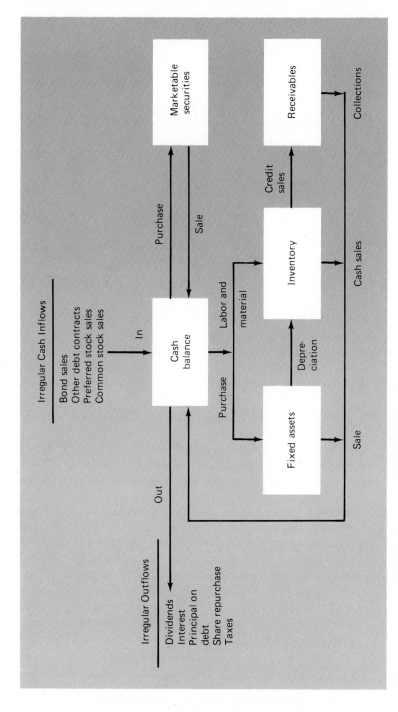

FIGURE 6-1. The Cash Generation and Disposition Process

The arrows designate the direction of the flow—that is, whether the cash balance is being increased or decreased.

Cash Flow Process   The firm experiences irregular increases in its cash holdings from several external sources. Funds can be obtained in the financial markets from the sale of securities, such as bonds, preferred stock, and common stock, or nonmarketable debt contracts can be entered into with lenders such as commercial banks. These irregular cash inflows do not occur on a daily basis. They tend to be episodic; the financing arrangements that give rise to them are effected at wide intervals. The reason is that external financing contracts usually involve huge sums of money stemming from a major need identified by the company's management, and these needs do not occur every day. For example, a new product might be in the process of being launched, or a plant expansion might be required to provide added productive capacity.

In most organizations the financial officer responsible for cash management also controls the transactions that affect the firm's investment in marketable securities. As excess cash becomes temporarily available, marketable securities will be purchased. When cash is in short supply, a portion of the marketable securities portfolio will be liquidated.

Whereas the irregular cash inflows are from external sources, the other main sources of cash to the firm arise from internal operations and occur on a more regular basis. Over long periods the largest receipts will come from accounts receivable collections and to a lesser extent from direct cash sales of finished goods. Many manufacturing concerns also generate cash on a regular basis through the liquidation of scrap or obsolete inventory. In the automobile industry large and costly machines called chip crushers grind waste metal into fine scrap that brings considerable revenue to the major producers. At various times fixed assets may also be sold, thereby generating some cash inflow. This is not a large source of funds except in unusual situations where, for instance, a complete plant renovation may be taking place.

Apart from the investment of excess cash in near-cash assets, the cash balance will experience reductions for three key reasons. First, on an irregular basis withdrawals will be made to (1) pay cash dividends on preferred and common stock shares, (2) meet interest requirements on debt contracts, (3) repay the principal borrowed from creditors, (4) buy the firm's own shares in the financial markets for use in executive compensation plans or as an alternative to paying a cash dividend, and (5) pay tax bills. Again, by an "irregular basis" we mean items *not* occurring on a daily or frequent schedule. Second, the company's capital expenditure program will designate that fixed assets be acquired at various intervals. Third, inventories will be purchased on a regular basis to ensure a steady flow of finished goods off the production line. Note that the arrow linking the investment in fixed assets with the inventory account is labeled *depreciation*. This indicates that a portion of the cost of fixed assets is charged against the products coming off the assembly line. This cost is subsequently recovered through the sale of the finished goods inventory, as the product selling price will be set by management to cover all the costs of production, including depreciation.

The variety of influences we have mentioned that constantly affect the cash balance held by the firm can be synthesized in terms of the classic motives for holding cash, as identified in the literature of economic theory.

Motives for Holding Cash

In a classic economic treatise John Maynard Keynes segmented the firm's, or any economic unit's, demand for cash into three categories: (1) the transactions motive, (2) the precautionary motive, and (3) the speculative motive.[1]

Transactions Motive

Balances held for transactions purposes allow the firm to dispense with cash needs that arise in the ordinary course of doing business. In Figure 6–1, transactions balances would be used to meet the irregular outflows as well as the planned acquisition of fixed assets and inventories.

The relative amount of transactions cash held will be significantly affected by the industry in which the firm operates. If revenues can be forecast to fall within a tight range of outcomes, then the ratio of cash and near cash to total assets will be less for the firm than if the prospective cash inflows might be expected to vary over a wide range. It is well known that utilities can forecast cash receipts quite accurately, because of stable demand for their services. This enables them to stagger their billings throughout the month and to time them to coincide with planned expenditures. Inflows and outflows of cash are thus synchronized. We would expect the cash holdings of utility firms relative to sales or assets to be less than those associated with a major retail chain that sells groceries. The grocery concern experiences a large number of transactions each day, almost all of which involve an exchange of cash.

Firms competing in the *same* industry may experience notably different strains on their cash balances. Transactions balances in the railroad industry are simultaneously influenced by a seasonal factor and a geographic factor. Consider the seasonal factor. During the summer months, all the railroads that crisscross the North American continent pay out large amounts of cash for materials and labor necessary to upgrade track beds. Old ties are replaced, new rail is laid, switches are adjusted, signal systems are overhauled. Now, consider the geographic factor. The railroad companies that serve the northern routes, including Canada, will also suffer sizable cash drains throughout the winter season. The harsh weather conditions are the cause. Snow must be swept out of switches, ice is actually burned off the rails, and derailments occur with far greater frequency than at any other time of the year. Cash balances for the railroads in the northern states and Canada will therefore be expected to be relatively higher during the winter season than for railroads operating in more southerly areas.

The Precautionary Motive

Precautionary balances are a buffer stock of liquid assets. This motive for holding cash relates to the maintenance of balances to be used to satisfy possible, but as yet indefinite, needs.

In our discussion of transactions balances we saw that cash flow predictability could affect a firm's cash holdings through synchronization of receipts and disbursements. Cash flow predictability also has a material influence on the firm's demand for cash through the precautionary motive. The airline industry provides a typical illustration. Air passenger carriers are plagued with a high degree of cash flow uncertainty. The weather, rising fuel costs, and continual strikes by operating personnel make cash forecasting difficult for any airline. The upshot of this problem is that

---

[1] John Maynard Keynes, *The General Theory of Employment, Interest, and Money* (New York: Harcourt Brace Jovanovich, 1936).

because of all the things that *might* happen, the minimum cash balances desired by the management of the air carriers tend to be large.

In addition to cash flow predictability, the precautionary motive for holding cash is affected by access to external funds. Especially important are cash sources that can be tapped on short notice. Good banking relationships and established lines of credit can reduce the need to keep cash on hand. This unused borrowing power will obviate somewhat the need to invest in precautionary balances.

In actual business practice, the precautionary motive is met to a large extent by the holding of a portfolio of *liquid assets*, not just cash. Notice in Figure 6–1 the two-way flow of funds between the company's holdings of cash and marketable securities. In large corporate organizations, funds may flow either into or out of the marketable securities portfolio on a daily basis. Because some actual rate of return can be earned on the near-cash assets, compared with a zero rate of return available on cash holdings, it is logical that the precautionary motive will be met in part by investment in marketable securities.

The Speculative Motive

Cash is held for speculative purposes in order to take advantage of hoped-for profit-making situations. Construction firms that build private dwellings will at times accumulate cash in anticipation of a significant drop in lumber costs. If the price of building supplies does drop, the companies that built up their cash balances stand to profit by purchasing materials in large quantities. This will reduce their cost of goods sold and increase their net profit margin. Generally, the speculative motive is the least important component of a firm's preference for liquidity. The transactions and precautionary motives account for most of the reasons why a company holds cash balances.

VARIATIONS IN LIQUID ASSET HOLDINGS

Decisions that concern the amounts of liquid assets to hold rest with the financial officer responsible for cash management. A number of factors that can be expected to influence the financial officer's investment in cash and near cash have just been reviewed. Not all these factors affect every firm. Moreover, factors that do affect many companies will do so in differing degrees. Since the executives responsible for the ultimate cash management choices will have different risk-bearing preferences, we might expect that liquid asset holdings among firms would exhibit considerable variation. Such is the case, as shown by Table 6–1.

TABLE 6–1. Liquid Asset Positions of Selected Firms for 1985 (%)

Ratios	Allegheny Power System, Inc.	American Electric Power	Chrysler Corporation	Ford Motor Company
Cash to total assets	0.4%	1.6%	1.2%	6.4%
Marketable securities to total assets	0.5	1.3	21.0	12.3
Total liquid assets to total assets	0.9	2.9	22.2	18.7

Source: Annual Reports, 1985, for the respective companies.

Allegheny Power and American Electric Power are both utilities and operate in an environment where cash flows are highly predictable relative to other industries. We see that Allegheny Power holds a very small proportion of its total assets in the form of liquid assets—only 0.9 percent. American Electric Power invests more heavily in liquidity, but to the extent of only 2.9 percent of total assets.

Even firms that operate in a regulated setting can experience sudden shifts in liquidity. At the end of 1978, Allegheny Power had a liquid asset to total asset ratio of 0.5 percent. At the end of 1981, however, it stood at a much higher 3.1 percent. By the end of 1982, this ratio had decreased to 0.3 percent, but as we see in Table 6–1, it rose to 0.9 percent by year-end 1985. Companies continually adjust their liquid asset positions to meet operating needs and to respond to the real investment requirements of strategic plans.

The Chrysler Corporation and the Ford Motor Company compete in a more risky global arena than do electric utilities like Allegheny Power and American Electric Power. We expect, then, that the overall cash management policies of firms in the automobile industry will be quite different from those of utilities. Chrysler is one of the great corporate rebuilding stories of recent decades. The firm required special relief in the form of the federal Chrysler Corporation Loan Guarantee Act of 1979. Without that act, it is unlikely that the firm would exist today. Then, the twin recessions of 1980 and 1981–82 spelled troubled times for the domestic automobile industry. Chrysler and Ford both bounced back strongly in the recovery that began in November 1982. For 1985, Chrysler posted a return on equity (as measured at book value) of 38.8 percent; this was fifth in the Fortune 500 rankings of the largest industrial firms in the United States. Ford achieved a return on equity of 20.5 percent in that same year.

Notice in Table 6–1 that Chrysler and Ford maintain stronger liquidity postures than either Allegheny or American Electric Power. At the end of 1985, Chrysler held a full 22.2 percent of its total assets in highly liquid form; Ford held 18.7 percent of its assets in liquid form. Unlike Ford, Chrysler held the great bulk of its liquid assets in the form of marketable securities rather than cash. There is an important advantage to the type of liquid asset mix displayed by Chrysler. Marketable securities earn a positive rate of return, while the mere holding of cash earns a zero return.

The examples of Chrysler and Ford suggest that it takes more than a knowledge of the industry class in which a firm operates to understand its cash management policies. The executives of these two companies perceive their liquidity needs quite differently. Different corporate strategies and different risk-bearing preferences with respect to the chances of running out of cash cause variations in levels of liquidity investment.

The examples given above of the liquid asset holdings of some specific firms are only snapshots at a fixed point in time. This tends to obscure the fact that assets are acquired, wasted, and sold every day. We must view the management of cash and near cash as a dynamic process. The flow of cash as depicted in Figure 6–1 never ceases. The cash inflows and outflows affecting the size of the firm's cash reservoir occur simultaneously. This ensures that the overall problem of cash and marketable securities management will be complex. In order to cut through this complexity it is imperative that the firm's cash management system be designed to operate with clearly defined objectives.

CASH MANAGEMENT OBJECTIVES AND DECISIONS

The Risk–Return Tradeoff

A companywide cash management program must be concerned with minimizing the firm's risk of insolvency. In the context of cash management, the term **insolvency** is used to describe the situation where the firm is unable to meet its maturing liabilities on time. In such a case the company is **technically insolvent** in that it lacks the necessary liquidity to make prompt payment on its current debt obligations. This problem could be met quite easily by carrying large cash balances to pay the bills that come due. Production, after all, would soon come to a halt should payments for raw material purchases be continually late or omitted entirely. The firm's suppliers would just cut off further shipments. In fact, fear of irritating a key supplier by being past due on the payment of a trade payable does cause some financial managers to invest in too much liquidity.

The management of the company's cash position, though, is one of those problem areas where you are criticized if you don't and criticized if you do. True, the production process will eventually be halted should too little cash be available to pay bills. If excessive cash balances are carried, however, the value of the enterprise in the financial marketplace will be suppressed because of the large cost of income forgone. The explicit return earned on idle cash balances is zero.

The financial manager must strike an acceptable balance between holding too much cash and too little cash. This is the focal point of the risk-return tradeoff. A large cash investment minimizes the chances of insolvency, but penalizes company profitability. A small cash investment frees excess balances for investment in both marketable securities and longer-lived assets; this enhances company profitability and the value of the firm's common shares, but increases the chances of running out of cash.

The Objectives

The risk-return tradeoff can be reduced to two prime objectives for the firm's cash management system:

1. Enough cash must be on hand to meet the disbursal needs that arise in the course of doing business.
2. Investment in idle cash balances must be reduced to a minimum.

Evaluation of these operational objectives, and a conscious attempt on the part of management to meet them, gives rise to the need for some typical cash management decisions.

The Decisions

Two conditions would allow the firm to operate for extended periods with cash balances near or at a level of zero: (1) a completely accurate forecast of net cash flows over the planning horizon, and (2) perfect synchronization of cash receipts and disbursements.

Cash flow forecasting is the initial step in any effective cash management program. This is usually accomplished by the finance function's evaluation of data supplied by the marketing and production functions in the company. The device used to forecast the cash flows over the planning period is the cash budget. Cash budgeting procedures were explained in Chapter 4, so there is no need to review them here. We emphasize, though, that the net cash flows pinpointed in the formal cash budget are mere estimates, subject to considerable variation. A totally accurate cash flow projection is only an ideal, not a reality.

Our discussion of the cash flow process depicted in Figure 6–1 showed that inflows and outflows are not synchronized. Some inflows and outflows are irregular; others are more continual. Some finished goods are sold directly for cash, but more likely the sales will be on account. The receivables, then, will have to be collected before a cash inflow is realized. Raw materials have to be purchased, but several suppliers are probably used, and each may have its own payment date. Further, no law of doing business fixes receivable collections to coincide with raw material payments dates. So the second criterion that would permit operation of the firm with extremely low cash balances is not met in actual practice either.

Given that the firm will, as a matter of necessity, invest in some cash balances, certain types of decisions related to the size of those balances dominate the cash management process. These include formulation of answers to the following questions:

1. What can be done to speed up cash collections and slow down or better control cash outflows?
2. What should be the composition of a marketable securities portfolio?
3. How should investment in liquid assets be split between actual cash holdings and marketable securities?

The remainder of this chapter dwells on the first two of these three questions. The third is explored in the appendix.

COLLECTION AND DISBURSEMENT PROCEDURES

The efficiency of the firm's cash management program can be enhanced by knowledge and use of various procedures aimed at (1) accelerating cash receipts and (2) improving the methods used to disburse cash. We will see that greater opportunity for corporate improvement lies with the cash receipts side of the funds flow process, although it would be unwise to ignore opportunities for favorably affecting cash disbursement practices.

Managing the Cash Inflow[2]

The reduction of float lies at the center of the many approaches employed to speed up cash receipts. **Float** (or total float) has four elements as follows:

1. **Mail float** is caused by the time lapse from the moment a customer mails a remittance check until the firm begins to process it.
2. **Processing float** is caused by the time required for the firm to process remittance checks before they can be deposited in the bank.
3. **Transit float** is caused by the time necessary for a deposited check to clear through the commercial banking system and become usable funds to the company. Credit is deferred for a maximum of two business days on checks that are cleared through the Federal Reserve System.[3]

---

[2] The discussions on cash receipt and disbursement procedures draw heavily on materials that were generously provided by the managements of the Chase Manhattan Bank, Continental Bank, and First National Bank of Chicago.

[3] One of the things that the Federal Reserve System does is provide check-clearing facilities for depository institutions. This is referred to as the "clearing system," or the "clearing mechanism." These terms will be

4. **Disbursing float** derives from the fact that funds are available in the company's bank account until its payment check has cleared through the banking system. Typically, funds available in the firm's banks *exceed* the balances indicated on its own books (ledgers).

We will use the term float to refer to the total of its four elements just described. Float reduction can yield considerable benefits in terms of usable funds that are released for company use and returns produced on such freed-up balances. As an example, for the year 1985 IBM reported total revenues of $50.1 billion. The amount of usable funds that would be released if IBM could achieve a one-day reduction in float can be approximated by dividing annual revenues (sales) by the number of days in a year.[4] In this case one day's freed-up balances would be

$$\frac{\text{annual revenues}}{\text{days in year}} = \frac{\$50,100,000,000}{365} = \$137,260,274$$

If these released funds, which represent one day's sales, of approximately $137.3 million could be invested to return 8 percent a year, then the annual value of the one-day float reduction would be

$$(\text{sales per day}) \times (\text{assumed yield}) = \$137,260,274 \times .08 = \$10,980,822$$

It is clear that effective cash management can yield impressive opportunities for profit improvement. Let us look now at specific techniques for reducing float.

The Lock-Box Arrangement

The lock-box system is the most widely used commercial banking service for expediting cash gathering. Banks have offered this service since 1946. Such a system speeds up the conversion of receipts into usable funds by reducing both mail and processing float. Additionally, it is possible to reduce transit float if lock boxes are located near Federal Reserve Banks and their branches. For large corporations that receive checks from all parts of the country, float reductions of two to four days are not unusual.

Figure 6–2 illustrates an elementary, but typical, cash collection system for a hypothetical firm. It also shows the origin of mail float, processing float and transit float. In this system the customer places his or her remittance check in the U.S. mail, which is then delivered to the firm's headquarters. This causes the mail float. Upon the checks' arrival at the firm's headquarters (or local collection center), general accounting personnel must go through the bookkeeping procedures needed to prepare them for local deposit. The checks are then deposited. This causes the processing float. The checks are then forwarded for payment through the commercial bank clearing mechanism. The checks will be charged against the customer's own bank account.

---

used several times in this chapter. Should the paying bank and collecting bank be located in the same Federal Reserve District, credit will be available to the collecting bank in one business day. Local clearinghouses exist apart from the Federal Reserve's clearing mechanism. These involve a consortium of local banks that meet each business day, through their representatives, in order to clear checks drawn on each other. Same-day funds availability is possible through the use of a local clearinghouse if published settlement times are met.

[4] Frederick W. Searby, "Use Your Hidden Cash Resources," *Harvard Business Review*, 46 (March–April 1968), 71–80.

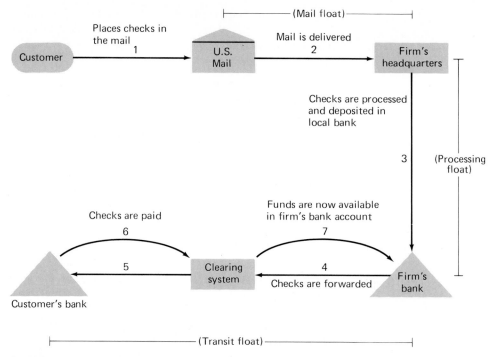

FIGURE 6–2. An Ordinary Cash-Gathering System

At this point the checks are said to be "paid" and become "good" funds available for use by the company that received them. This bank clearing procedure represents transit float and, as we said earlier, can amount to a delay of up to two business days.[5]

The lock-box arrangement shown in Figure 6–3 is based on a simple procedure. The firm's customers are instructed to mail their remittance checks not to company headquarters or regional offices, but to a numbered Post Office box. The bank that is providing the lock-box service is authorized to open the box, collect the mail, process the checks, and deposit the checks directly into the company's account.

Commercial banks have gone to great lengths in refining their lock-box procedures in an attempt to gain an edge over their competitors. Major banks have their own zip codes to accelerate postal handling. Even helicopters are sometimes used to speed documents from the Post Office to the bank or from the bank to a local clearinghouse.

Typically a large bank will collect payments from the lock box at one- to two-hour intervals, 365 days of the year. During peak business hours, the bank may pick up mail every 30 minutes.

Once the mail is received at the bank, the checks will be examined, totaled, photocopied, and microfilmed. A deposit form is then prepared by the bank, and each batch of processed checks is forwarded to the collection department for clearance.

---

[5] A clear description of the Federal Reserve check-clearing mechanism can be found in Thomas A. Gittings, "Sinking Float," *Economic Perspectives*, Federal Reserve Bank of Chicago, 4 (May–June 1980), 19–23.

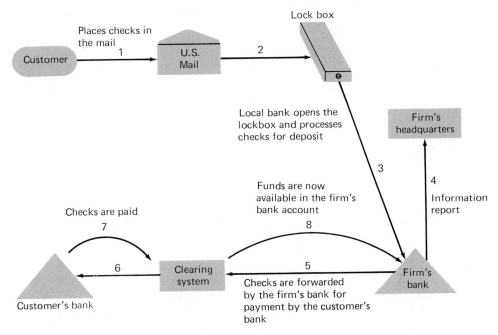

FIGURE 6–3.   A Simple Lock-Box System

Funds deposited in this manner are usually available for company use in one business day or less.

The bank can notify the firm via some type of telecommunications system the same day deposits are made as to their amount. At the conclusion of each day all check photocopies, invoices, deposit slips, and any other documents included with the remittances are mailed to the firm.

Note that the firm which receives checks from all over the country will have to utilize several lock boxes to take full advantage of a reduction in mail float. The firm's major bank should be able to offer as a service a detailed lock-box study, analyzing the company's receipt patterns to determine the proper number and location of lock-box receiving points.

The two systems described by Figures 6–2 and 6–3 are summarized in Table 6–2. There, the step numbers refer to those shown in Figure 6–2 (the ordinary system). Furthermore, Table 6–2 assumes that the customer and the firm's headquarters or its collection center are located in different cities. This causes the lag of two working days before the firm actually receives the remittance check. We notice at the bottom of Table 6–2 that the installation of the lock-box system can result in funds being credited to the firm's bank account a full *four* working days *faster* than is possible under the ordinary collection system.

Previously in this chapter we calculated the 1985 sales per day for IBM to be $137.3 million and assumed that firm could invest its excess cash in marketable securities to yield 8 percent annually. If IBM could speed up its cash collections by four days, as the hypothetical firm did in Table 6–2, the results would be startling. The

TABLE 6–2. Comparison of Ordinary Cash-Gathering System with Simple Lock-Box System

Step Numbers	Ordinary System and Time		Advantage of Lock Box
1	Customer writes check and places it in the mail	1 Day	
2	Mail is delivered to firm's headquarters	2 Days	Mail will not have to travel as far. Result: save 1 day
3	Accounting personnel process the checks and deposit them in the firm's local bank	2 Days	Bank personnel prepare checks for deposit. Result: save 2 days
4 and 5	Checks are forwarded for payment through the clearing mechanism	1 Day	As the lock boxes are located near Federal Reserve Banks or branches, transit float can be reduced.
6 and 7	The firm receives notice from its bank that the checks have cleared and the funds are now "good"	1 Day	Result: save 1 day
	Total working days	7	Overall result: Save 4 working days

gross annual savings to IBM (apart from operating the lock-box system) would amount to $43.9 million, as follows:

$$(\text{sales per day}) \times (\text{days of float reduction}) \times (\text{assumed yield})$$
$$= \$137,260,274 \times (4) \times .08 = \$43,923,288$$

As you might guess, the prospects for generating revenues of this magnitude are important not only to the firms involved, but also to commercial banks that offer lock-box services.

In summary, the benefits of a lock-box arrangement are these:

1. **Increased working cash.** The time required for converting receivables into available funds is reduced. This frees up cash for use elsewhere in the enterprise.
2. **Elimination of clerical functions.** The bank takes over the tasks of receiving, endorsing, totaling, and depositing checks. With less handling of receipts by

employees, better audit control is achieved and the chance of documents becoming lost is reduced.

3. **Early knowledge of dishonored checks.** Should a customer's check be uncollectible because of lack of funds, it is returned, usually by special handling, to the firm.

These benefits are not free. Usually the bank levies a charge for each check processed through the system. The benefits derived from the acceleration of receipts must exceed the incremental costs of the lock-box system, or the firm would be better off without it. Companies that find the average size of their remittances to be quite small, for instance, might avoid a lock-box plan. One major Chicago bank has pointed out that for companies with less than $500,000 in average monthly sales or with customer remittance checks averaging less than $1000, the lock-box approach would probably not yield a great enough benefit to offset its costs. Later in this chapter a straightforward method for assessing the desirability of a specific cash management service, such as the lock-box arrangement, will be illustrated.

Preauthorized Checks (PACs) Whereas the lock-box arrangement can often reduce total float by two to four days, for some firms the use of PACs can be an even more effective way of converting receipts into working cash. A PAC resembles the ordinary check, but it does not contain or require the signature of the person on whose account it is being drawn. A PAC is created only with the individual's legal authorization.

The PAC system is advantageous when the firm regularly receives a large volume of payments of a fixed amount from the same customers. This type of cash management service has proved useful to insurance companies, savings and loan associations, consumer credit firms, leasing enterprises, and charitable and religious organizations. The objective of this system is to reduce both mail and processing float. Notice, in relation to either the typical cash-gathering system (Figure 6–2) or the lock-box system (Figure 6–3), that the customer no longer (1) physically writes his or her own check or (2) deposits such check in the mail.

The operation of a PAC sytem is illustrated in Figure 6–4. It involves the following sequence of events:

1. The firm's customers authorize it to draw checks on their respective demand deposit accounts.
2. Indemnification agreements are signed by the customers and forwarded to the banks where they maintain their demand deposit accounts. These agreements authorize the banks to honor the PACs when they are presented for payment through the commercial bank clearing system.
3. The firm prepares a magnetic tape that contains all appropriate information about the regular payments.
4. At each processing cycle (monthly, weekly, semi-monthly) the corporation retains a hard copy listing of all tape data for control purposes. Usually the checks that are about to be printed will be deposited in the firm's demand deposit account, so a deposit ticket will also be forwarded to the bank.
5. Upon receipt of the tape the bank will produce the PACs, deposit them to the firm's account, forward them for clearing through the commercial banking system, and return a control report to the firm.

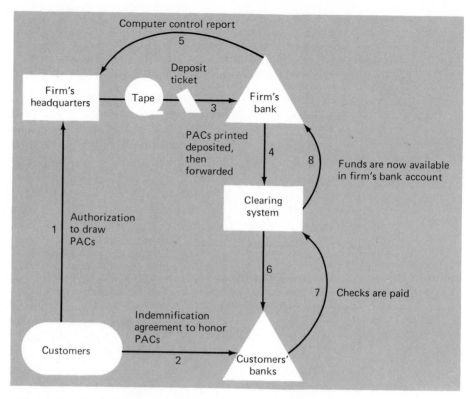

FIGURE 6—4. Preauthorized Check System (PAC)

For firms that can take advantage of a PAC system, the benefits include these:

1. **Highly predictable cash flows.**
2. **Reduced expenses.** Billing and postage costs are eliminated, and the clerical processing of customer payments is significantly reduced.
3. **Customer preference.** Many customers prefer not to be bothered with a regular billing. With a PAC system the check is actually written for the customer and the payment made even if he or she is on vacation or otherwise out of town.
4. **Increased working cash.** Mail float and processing float can be dramatically reduced in comparison with other payment processing systems.

Depository Transfer Checks   Both depository transfer checks and wire transfers are used in conjunction with what is known as **concentration banking.** A concentration bank is one where the firm maintains a major disbursing account.

In an effort to accelerate collections, many companies have established multiple collection centers. Regional lock-box networks are one type of approach to strategically located collection points. Even without lock boxes, firms may have numerous sales outlets throughout the country and collect cash over the counter. This requires many local bank accounts to handle daily deposits. Rather than have funds sitting in these multiple bank accounts in different geographic regions of the country, most firms will regularly transfer the surplus balances to one or more concentration banks. Centralizing the firm's pool of cash provides the following benefits:

1. **Lower levels of excess cash.** Desired cash balance target levels are set for each regional bank. These target levels consider both compensating balance requirements and necessary working levels of cash. Cash in excess of the target levels can be transferred regularly to concentration banks for deployment by the firm's top-level management.

2. **Better control.** With more cash held in fewer accounts, stricter control over available cash is achieved. Quite simply, there are fewer problems to keep track of. The concentration banks can prepare sophisticated reports that detail corporatewide movements of funds into and out of the central cash pool.

3. **More efficient investments in near-cash assets.** The coupling of information from the firm's cash forecast with data on available funds supplied by the concentration banks allows the firm quickly to transfer cash to the marketable securities portfolio.

Depository transfer checks provide a means for moving funds from local bank accounts to concentration accounts. The depository transfer check itself is an unsigned, nonnegotiable instrument. It is payable only to the bank of deposit (the concentration bank in our discussion) for credit to the firm's specific account. An authorization form is filed by the firm with each bank from which it might withdraw funds. This form instructs the bank to pay the depository transfer checks without any signature. The movement of cash through the use of depository transfer checks can operate with a conventional mail system or an automated system.

When the mail system is used, a company employee deposits the day's receipts in a local bank and fills out a preprinted depository transfer check for the exact amount of the deposit. The company then mails the depository transfer check to the firm's concentration bank. While this document is traveling in the mails, the checks just deposited at the local bank are being cleared. As soon as the concentration bank receives the depository transfer check, the firm's account is credited for the designated amount. The funds credited to the concentration account are not available for the firm's use, of course, until the document has been cleared with the local depository bank for payment.

If the firm's depository banks are geographically dispersed such that the mail will take several days in reaching the concentration bank, then *no* float reduction might be achieved through this system. In an attempt to reduce the mail float associated with conventional depository transfer check systems, some banks have initiated a type of special mail handling of these instruments. Continental Bank (Chicago), for example, cooperates with the U.S. Postal Service at O'Hare International Airport. Extra large, specially marked envelopes are used by firms to airmail their transfer checks to Chicago. These envelopes are intercepted at the airport, sorted into special Continental Bank pouches, and at frequent intervals are taken to the bank by special messenger for ultimate deposit of the contents. This procedure can cut as much as one full day off regular mail delivery schedules.

A recent innovation in speeding cash into concentration accounts is the **automated depository transfer check system.** In this system the mail float involved in moving the transfer document from the local bank to the concentration bank is *eliminated*. Here is how it works.

The local company employee makes the daily deposit as usual. This employee does *not*, however, manually fill out the preprinted depository transfer check; instead, he telephones the deposit information to a regional data collection center. Usually the center is operated for a fee by a firm, such as National Data Corporation. Various data collection centers will accumulate information throughout the day on the firm's regional deposits. Then, at specified cutoff times the deposit information from all local offices is transmitted to the concentration bank.

At this point the concentration bank prepares the depository transfer check and credits it to the company's account. A sample depository transfer check prepared at a concentration bank is shown in Figure 6–5. The transfer checks are placed into the commercial bank check-clearing process and presented to the firm's local bank for payment. When paid by the local bank, the funds become available in the concentration account for company use. Major banks claim that funds transferred by use of the automated depository transfer check system can become available for company use in one business day or less. This system is depicted in Figure 6–6.

Wire Transfers

The fastest way to move cash between banks is by use of **wire transfers,** which eliminate transit float. Funds moved in this manner, then, immediately become usable funds or "good funds" to the firm at the receiving bank. The following two major communication facilities are used to accommodate wire transfers:

1. **Bank Wire.** This is a private wire service used and supported by approximately 250 banks in the United States for transferring funds, exchanging credit information, or effecting securities transactions.

FIGURE 6–5. Sample Depository Transfer Check

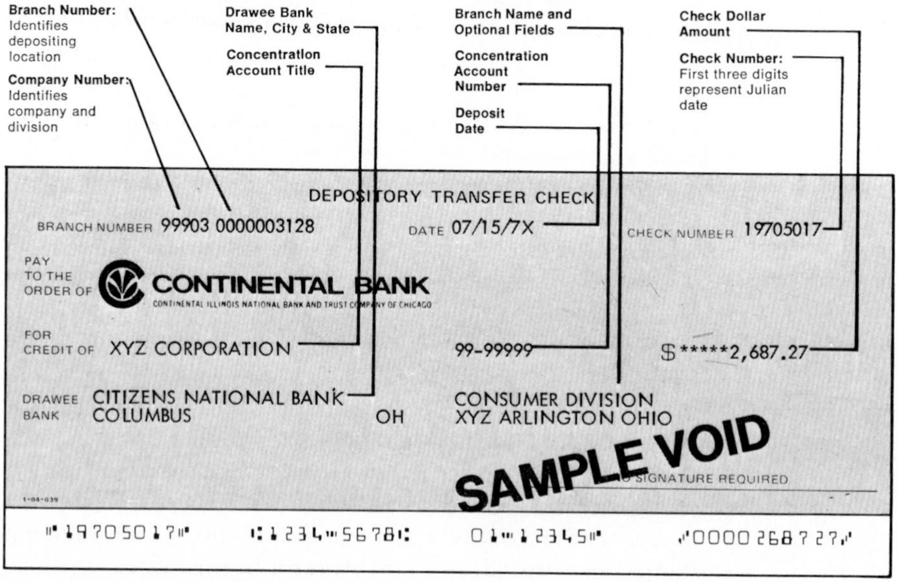

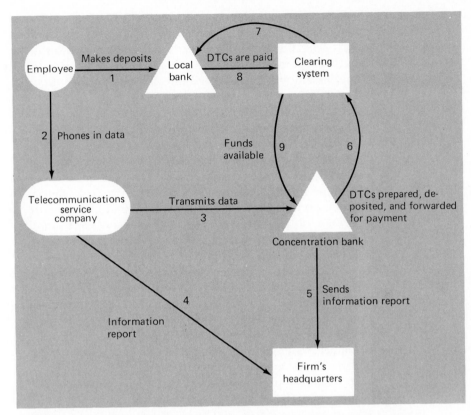

FIGURE 6–6. Automated Depository Transfer Check System (DTC)

2. **Federal Reserve Wire System.** The Fed Wire is directly accessible to commercial banks that are members of the Federal Reserve System. A commercial bank that is not on the Bank Wire or is not a member of the Federal Reserve System can use the wire transfer concept through its correspondent bank.

Wire transfers are often initiated on a standing-order basis. By means of a written authorization from company headquarters, a local depository bank might be instructed regularly to transfer funds to the firm's concentration bank. For example, available funds in excess of $100,000 might be transferred to the concentration bank every Tuesday and Thursday.

As might be expected, wire transfers are a relatively expensive method of marshaling funds through a firm's money management system. A single wire transfer costs about $4. This is about fifteen times as costly as a conventional depository transfer check. Generally, the movement of small amounts does not justify the use of wire transfers.

Managing the Cash Outflow

Significant techniques and systems for improving the firm's management of cash disbursements include (1) zero balance accounts, (2) payable-through drafts, and (3) remote disbursing. The first two offer markedly better control over companywide payments, and as a secondary benefit they *may* increase disbursement float. The last technique, remote disbursing, aims solely to increase disbursement float.

Zero Balance
Accounts
Large corporations that operate multiple branches, divisions, or subsidiaries often maintain numerous bank accounts (in different banks) for the purpose of making timely operating disbursements. It does make good business sense for payments for purchased parts that go into, say an automobile transmission to be made by the Transmission and Chassis Division of the auto manufacturer rather than its central office. The Transmission and Chassis Division originates such purchase orders, receives and inspects the shipment when it arrives at the plant, authorizes payment, and writes the appropriate check. To have the central office involved in these matters would be a total waste of company time.

What tends to happen, however, is that with several divisions utilizing their own disbursal accounts, excess cash balances build up in outlying banks and rob the firm of earning assets. Zero balance accounts are used to alleviate this problem. The objectives of a zero balance account system are (1) for the firm to achieve better control over its cash payments, (2) to reduce excess cash balances held in regional banks for disbursing purposes, and (3) to increase disbursing float.

Zero balance accounts permit centralized control (at the headquarters level) over cash outflows while maintaining divisional disbursing authority. Under this system the firm's authorized employees, representing their various divisions, continue to write checks on their individual accounts. Note that the numerous individual disbursing accounts are now *all* located in the same concentration bank. Actually, these separate accounts contain no funds at all, thus their appropriate label, "zero balance." These accounts have all the characteristics of regular demand deposit accounts including separate titles, numbers, and statements.

A schematic presentation of a zero balance account disbursing system is shown in Figure 6–7. The firm is assumed to have three operating divisions—each with its own zero balance account (ZBA). The system works as follows. The firm's authorized agents write their payment checks as usual against their specific accounts (Step 1). These checks clear through the banking system in the usual way. On a daily basis checks will be presented to the firm's concentration bank (the drawee bank) for payment. As the checks are paid by the bank, negative (debit) balances will build in the proper disbursing accounts (Step 2). At the end of each day the negative balances will be restored to a zero level by means of credits to the zero balance accounts (Step 3); a corresponding reduction in funds is made against the firm's concentration (master) demand deposit account (also Step 3). Each morning a report is electronically forwarded to corporate headquarters reflecting the balance in the master account as well as the previous day's activity in each zero balance account (Step 4). Using the report, the financial officer in charge of near-cash investments is ready to initiate appropriate transactions.

Managing the cash outflow through use of a zero balance account system offers the following benefits to the firm with many operating units:

1. Centralized control over disbursements is achieved, even though payment authority continues to rest with operating units.
2. Management time spent on superficial cash management activities is reduced. Exercises such as observing the balances held in numerous bank accounts, transferring funds to those accounts short of cash, and reconciling the accounts demand less attention.

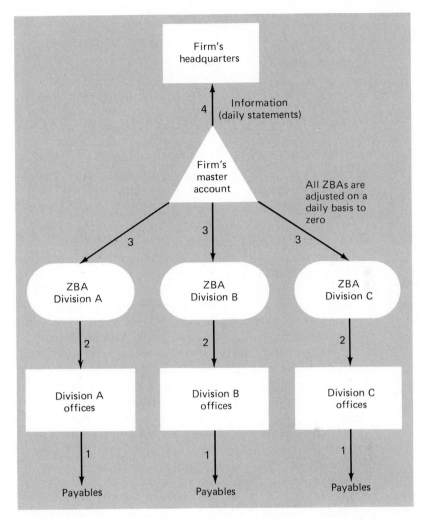

FIGURE 6–7. Zero Balance Account Cash Disbursement System (ZBA)

3. Excess balances held in outlying accounts can be reduced.
4. The costs of cash management can be reduced, as wire transfers to build up funds in outlying disbursement accounts are eliminated.
5. Funds may be made available for company use through an increase in disbursement float. When local bank accounts are used to pay nearby suppliers, the checks clear rapidly. The same checks, if drawn on a zero balance account located in a more distant concentration bank, will take more time to clear against the disbursing firm's account.

Payable-Through Drafts **Payable-through drafts** are legal instruments that have the physical appearance of ordinary checks (see Figure 6–8) but are *not* drawn on a bank. Instead, payable-through drafts are drawn on and payment is authorized by the issuing firm against

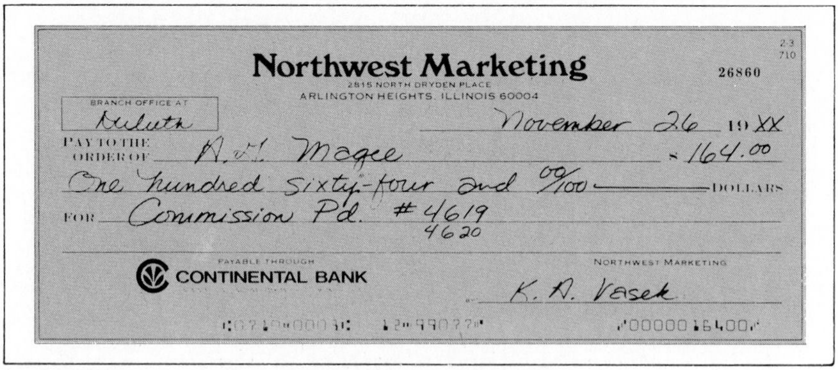

FIGURE 6–8. Sample Payable-Through Draft

its demand deposit account. Like checks, the drafts are cleared through the banking system and are presented to the issuing firm's bank. The bank serves as a collection point and passes the drafts on to the firm. The corporate issuer usually has to return by the following business day all drafts it does not wish to cover (pay). Those documents not returned to the bank are automatically paid. The firm inspects the drafts for validity by checking signatures, amounts, and dates. Stop payment orders can be initiated by the company on any drafts considered inappropriate.

The main purpose of using a payable-through draft system is *to provide for effective control over field payments*. Central office control over payments begun by regional units is provided as the drafts are reviewed in advance of final payment. Payable-through drafts, for example, are used extensively in the insurance industry. The claims agent does not typically have check-signing authority against a corporate disbursement account. This agent can issue a draft, however, for quick settlement of a claim.

In the not-so-distant past a firm could increase its disbursing float by use of payable-through drafts. In most cases this is no longer true. The Federal Reserve System requires transfer of available or "good" funds upon presentation of drafts to the payable-through bank. The payable-through bank will cover drafts but will be reluctant to absorb the float that would occur until the issuing firm authorized payment the next business day. Therefore, the drafts that are presented for payment will usually be charged *in total* against the corporate master demand deposit account. This is for purposes of measuring usable funds available to the firm on that day. Legal payment of the *individual drafts* will still take place after their review and approval by the firm. Figure 6–9 illustrates a payable-through draft system.

Remote Disbursing A few banks will provide the corporate customer with a cash management service specifically designed to extend disbursing float. The firm's concentration bank may have a correspondent relationship with a smaller bank located in a distant city. In that remote city the Federal Reserve System is unable to maintain frequent clearings of checks drawn on local banks. For example, a firm that is located in Dallas and maintains its master account there may open an account with a bank situated in, say, Amarillo, Texas. The firm will write the bulk of its payment checks against the account in the Amarillo bank. The checks will probably take at least one business day longer to clear, so the firm can "play the float" to its advantage.

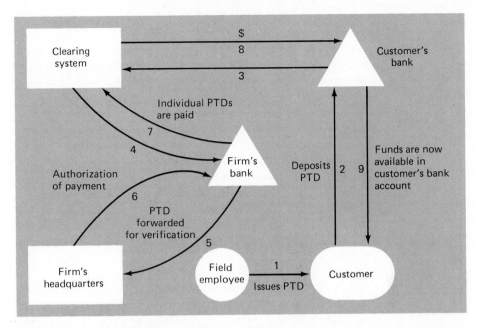

FIGURE 6–9. Payable-Through Draft Cash Disbursement System (PTD)

We emphasize that a firm must use this technique of remote disbursing with extreme care. If a key supplier of raw materials located in Dallas has to wait the extra day for funds drawn on the Amarillo account, the possibility of incurring ill-will might outweigh the apparent gain from an increase in the disbursing float. The impact on the firm's reputation of using remote disbursing should be explicitly evaluated.

As you might guess, the practice of remote disbursing has come under criticism by bank regulatory authorities. In early 1979 the Federal Reserve Bank of Dallas noted:

A policy discouraging remote disbursement—the use of remote banks by businesses, usually corporations, to delay payment of bills—has been adopted by the Board of Governors (of the Federal Reserve System). The Board believes the banking industry has a public responsibility not to design, offer, promote or otherwise encourage the use of a service expressly intended to delay final settlement. The Board is calling on the nation's banks to join in the effort to eliminate remote disbursement practices.[6]

ELECTRONIC FUNDS TRANSFER

In the purest economic sense, "total" float should equal zero days and therefore should be worth zero dollars to any business firm or other economic unit in the society. Float is really a measure of inefficiency of the financial system in an economy. It is a friction of the business environment that stems from the fact that all information

---

[6] "Remote Disbursement Policy Adopted," *Voice of the Federal Reserve Bank of Dallas*, February 1979, p. 10.

arising from business transactions cannot be instantaneously transferred among the parties involved.

Today the extensive use of electronic communication equipment is serving to reduce float. The central concept of electronic funds transfer (EFT) is simple. If Firm A owes money to Firm B, this situation ought to be immediately reflected on both the books and the bank accounts of these two companies. Instantaneous transfer of funds would eliminate float. Of course this ideal within the U.S. financial system has not been reached; the trend toward it, however, is readily observable.

Automated teller machines, like those imbedded in the wall of your supermarket or at the airline terminal, are familiar devices to most consumers. Businesses are now beginning to use even more advanced systems like terminal-based wire transfers to move funds within their cash management systems.[7]

The heart of EFT is the elimination of the check as a method of transferring funds. The elimination of the check may never occur, but certainly the move toward a financial system that uses fewer checks will. Transit, mail, and processing float become less important as EFT becomes more important. Simultaneously, this also implies that disbursing float becomes trivial.

The process of EFT should provide for a more efficient economy. Funds tied up in accounts receivable, for example, will be released for more productive alternative uses. This does not mean that financial institutions will have no cash management services to offer. It does mean that the nature of their cash management services will change.

EVALUATING COSTS OF CASH MANAGEMENT SERVICES

A form of breakeven analysis can help the financial officer decide whether a particular collection or disbursement service will provide an economic benefit to the firm. The evaluation process involves a very basic relationship in microeconomics:

$$\text{added costs} = \text{added benefits} \qquad (6\text{--}1)$$

If equation (6–1) holds exactly, then the firm is no better or worse off for having adopted the given service. We will illustrate this procedure in terms of the desirability of installing an additional lock box. Equation (6–1) can be restated on a per unit basis as follows:

$$P = (D)(S)(i) \qquad (6\text{--}2)$$

where P = increase in per-check processing cost if the new system is adopted

   D = days saved in the collection process (float reduction)

   S = average check size in dollars

   i = the daily, before-tax opportunity cost (rate of return) of carrying cash

[7] See Christopher Huppert and Nina Henry, "Risks and Rewards of Terminal-Based Wire Transfers," *Cashflow*, 4 (July–August 1983), 24–27.

Assume now that check processing cost, P, will rise by $.18 a check if the lock box is used. The firm has determined that the average check size, S, that will be mailed to the lock-box location will be $900. If funds are freed by use of the lock box, they will be invested in marketable securities to yield an *annual* before-tax return of 6 percent. It is possible with these data to determine the reduction in check collection time, D, that is required to justify use of the lock box. That level of D is found to be

$$\$.18 = (D)(\$900)\left(\frac{.06}{365}\right)$$

$$1.217 \text{ days} = D$$

Thus, the lock box is justified if the firm can speed up its collections by *more* than 1.217 days. This same style of analysis can be adapted to analyze the other tools of cash management.

Before moving on to a discussion of the firm's marketable securities portfolio, it will be helpful to draw together the preceding material. Table 6–3 on page 167 summarizes the salient features of the cash collection and disbursal techniques we have considered here.

BASIC FINANCIAL MANAGEMENT IN PRACTICE

Float and the Clearing System

We have seen that understanding the concept of *float* is central to understanding efficient cash management activities. The following discussion emphasizes the importance of float to the Federal Reserve System and also highlights the evolution of what we have called the "clearing system."

The Federal Reserve's check processing service began in 1916. It was free to member banks who would bundle up the checks they received each day and deposit them at the nearest Federal Reserve Bank or branch. The Fed would sort the checks according to the banks on which they were drawn and then send them right out to those banks for payment.

Member banks kept reserve accounts at the Fed which were used, among other things, to make and receive payments for checks. The Fed would credit the reserve accounts of banks that deposited checks for collection and charge the accounts of banks on which checks were drawn.

The Fed developed schedules of how long it normally took to process checks and present them in various locations around the country, and it gave credit to depositing banks according to those schedules rather than the actual collection time.

Thus banks that sent checks to a Federal Reserve Bank or branch for collection knew in advance exactly when they would receive credit in their reserve accounts, no matter what else happened.

The Fed's availability schedules went all the way up to eight days back in 1916, but now, thanks to computers and high-speed transportation, the maximum is two normal business days anywhere in the country.

Float and Monetary Policy

In addition to the expense and inefficiency, the Federal Reserve has other good reasons for being concerned about float. One is that it complicates the Fed's job of managing the money supply.

The Fed does this by trying to maintain appropriate levels of reserves in the banking system. As Federal Reserve credit, float is a part of bank reserves and is the most volatile and least predictable part.

Fluctuations in float mean that the banking system winds up with large variations in reserves for brief periods and the Fed must try to offset them. The less fluctuating float there is the more precise monetary policy can be.

For years the Federal Reserve has been taking steps to reduce float. In the 1970s, the Reserve Banks established dozens of new regional centers to process checks overnight, and made more effective use of air charter services.

Eliminate Float or Charge for It

In spite of these and other actions, Federal Reserve float reached a daily average of $6.7 billion in 1979, partly due to a tremendous increase in check volume. All this float was interfering with the Fed's efforts to stem inflation as well as costing billions to support.

In 1980, Congress passed the Monetary Control Act (MCA) which made sweeping changes in the Nation's financial system. The new law directed the Federal Reserve to begin charging for many of its services such as collecting checks, and to make them available to all depository institutions, not just banks which were members of the Federal Reserve System. The MCA also said the Federal Reserve must eliminate float or charge for it as a part of its check collection services. In effect, it was goodbye to loans without interest from the Fed.

Right off the Federal Reserve tried to reduce float with faster transportation and many other operational improvements. Success was dramatic and by 1982 total Federal Reserve float was at a daily average of $1.8 billion—down by almost $5 billion in three years. But even this was not good enough.

In early 1983, the Fed announced a major new program to squeeze Federal Reserve float out of the check stream. Among other things, the Fed pushed back the time of day when it could present checks to paying institutions. It offered institutions several new ways to get credit for deposits and it added the cost of all remaining holdover float to the price of its check services. By the end of the year when these new procedures were in full effect, Federal Reserve float was either eliminated or priced, just as the Monetary Control Act required.

Many depository institutions are not entirely happy about having to pay for something they used to get for free, but in the end the entire economy will be better off with float down and out. Check payments will be faster, monetary policy will be more precise, and much of the money the Federal Reserve formerly spent to support float will be available to the U.S. Treasury.

Source: L. C. Murdoch, Jr., "Float in the Check Stream," Federal Reserve Bank of Philadelphia (1984), 7–8, 10–12.

COMPOSITION OF MARKETABLE SECURITIES PORTFOLIO

Once the design of the firm's cash receipts and payments system has been determined, the financial manager faces the task of selecting appropriate financial assets for inclusion in the firm's marketable securities portfolio.

TABLE 6–3. Features of Selected Cash-Collection and Disbursal Techniques: A Summary

Technique	Objective	How Accomplished
Cash-Collection Techniques		
1. Lock-box system	Reduce (1) mail float, (2) processing float, and (3) transit float.	Strategic location of lock boxes to reduce mail float and transit float. Firm's commercial bank has access to lock box to reduce processing float.
2. Preauthorized checks	Reduce (1) mail float and (2) processing float.	The firm writes the checks (the PACs) *for* its customers to be charged against their demand deposit accounts.
3. (Ordinary) Depository transfer checks	Eliminate excess funds in regional banks.	Used in conjunction with concentration banking whereby the firm utilizes several collection centers. The transfer check authorizes movement of funds from a local bank to the concentration bank.
4. Automated depository transfer check	Eliminate the mail float associated with the ordinary transfer check.	Telecommunications company transmits deposit data to the firm's concentration bank.
5. Wire transfers	Move funds immediately between banks. This eliminates transit float in that only "good funds" are transferred.	Use of Bank Wire or the Federal Reserve Wire System.
Cash-Disbursal Techniques		
1. Zero balance accounts	(1) Achieve better control over cash payments, (2) reduce excess cash balances held in regional banks, and (3) possibly increase disbursing float.	Establish zero balance accounts for all of the firm's disbursing units. These accounts are all in the same concentration bank. Checks are drawn against these accounts, with the balance in each account never exceeding $0. Divisional disbursing authority is thereby maintained at the local level of management.
2. Payable-through drafts	Achieve effective central office control over field-authorized payments.	Field offices issue drafts rather than checks to settle up payables.
3. Remote disbursing	Extend disbursing float.	Write checks against demand deposit accounts held in distant banks.

General Selection Criteria

Certain criteria can provide the financial manager with a useful framework for selecting a proper marketable securities mix. These considerations include evaluation of the (1) financial risk, (2) interest rate risk, (3) liquidity, (4) taxability, and (5) yields among different financial assets. These criteria will be briefly delineated from the investor's point of view.

Financial Risk

Financial risk refers to the uncertainty of expected returns from a security attributable to possible changes in the financial capacity of the security issuer to make future payments to the security owner. If the chance of default on the terms of the instrument is high (low), then the financial risk is said to be high (low). It is clear that the financial risk associated with holding commercial paper, which we will see shortly is nothing more than a corporate IOU, exceeds that of holding securities issued by the United States Treasury.

In both financial practice and research, when estimates of risk-free returns are desired, the yields available on Treasury securities are consulted and the safety of other financial instruments is weighed against them. Because the marketable securities portfolio is designed to provide a return on funds that would otherwise be tied up in idle cash held for transactions or precautionary purposes, the financial officer will not usually be willing to assume much financial risk in the hope of greater return.

Interest Rate Risk[8]

The uncertainty that envelops the expected returns from a financial instrument attributable to changes in interest rates is known as **interest rate risk.** Of particular concern to the corporate treasurer is the price volatility associated with instruments that have long, as opposed to short, terms to maturity. An illustration can help clarify this point.

Suppose the financial officer is weighing the merits of investing temporarily available corporate cash in a new offering of U.S. Treasury obligations that will mature in either (1) 3 years or (2) 20 years from the date of issue. The purchase price of the 3-year notes or 20-year bonds is at their par value of $1000 per security. The maturity value of either class of security is equal to par, $1000, and the coupon rate (stated interest rate) is set at 7 percent, compounded annually.

If after one year from the date of purchase prevailing interest rates rise to 9 percent, the market prices of these currently outstanding Treasury securities will fall to bring their yields to maturity in line with what investors could obtain by buying a new issue of a given instrument. The market prices of *both* the 3-year and 20-year obligations will decline. The price of the 20-year instrument will decline by a greater dollar amount, however, than that of the three-year instrument.

One year from the date of issue the price obtainable in the marketplace for the original 20-year instrument, which now has 19 years to go to maturity, can be found by computing P as follows:

$$P = \sum_{T=1}^{19} \frac{\$70}{(1 + .09)^T} + \frac{\$1000}{(1 + .09)^{19}} = \$821.01$$

In the expression above (1) T is the year in which the particular return, either interest or principal amount, is received; (2) $70 is the annual interest payment; and (3) $1000 is the contractual maturity value of the bond. The rise in interest rates has forced the market price of the bond down to $821.01.

Now, what will happen to the price of the note that has two years remaining to maturity? In a similar manner, we can compute its price, P:

$$P = \sum_{T=1}^{2} \frac{\$70}{(1 + .09)^T} + \frac{\$1000}{(1 + .09)^2} = \$964.84$$

The market price of the shorter-term note will decline to $964.84. It is evident from Table 6–4 that the market value of the shorter-term security was penalized much less by the given rise in the general level of interest rates.

If we extended the illustration, we would see that, in terms of market price, a one-year security would be affected less than a two-year security, a 91-day security

---

[8] The computations in this discussion assume some knowledge of basic interest calculations. The concept can be grasped without the mathematical example, however. The "Mathematics of Finance" is covered in Chapter 9.

TABLE 6–4. Market Price Effect of a Rise in Interest Rates

Item	Three-year Instrument	Twenty-year Instrument
Original price	$1000.00	$1000.00
Price after one year	964.84	821.01
Decline in price	$ 35.16	$ 178.99

less than a 182-day security, and so on. Equity securities would exhibit the largest price changes because of their infinite maturity periods. To hedge against the price volatility caused by interest rate risk, the firm's marketable securities portfolio will tend to be composed of instruments that mature over short periods.

Liquidity In the present context of managing the marketable securities portfolio, **liquidity** refers to ability to transform a security into cash. Should an unforeseen event require that a significant amount of cash be immediately available, then a sizable portion of the portfolio might have to be sold. The financial manager will want the cash *quickly* and will not want to accept a large *price concession* in order to convert the securities. Thus, in the formulation of preferences for the inclusion of particular instruments in the portfolio, consideration will be given to (1) the time period needed to sell the security and (2) the likelihood that the security can be sold at or near its prevailing market price. The latter element, here, means that "thin" markets, where relatively few transactions take place or where trades are accomplished only with large price changes between transactions, will be avoided.

Taxability The tax treatment of the income a firm receives from its security investments does not affect the ultimate mix of the marketable securities portfolio as much as the criteria mentioned earlier. This is because the interest income from most instruments suitable for inclusion in the portfolio is taxable at the federal level. Still, the taxability of interest income and capital gains is seriously evaluated by some corporate treasurers.

The interest income from only one class of securities escapes the federal income tax. That class of securities is generally referred to as **municipal obligations,** or more simply as **municipals.** Owing to the tax-exempt feature of interest income from state and local government securities, they sell at lower yields to maturity in the market than do securities that pay interest which is taxable. The after-tax yield on a municipal obligation, however, could be higher than that obtainable from a non-tax-exempt security. This would depend mainly on the purchasing firm's tax situation.

Consider Table 6–5. A firm is assumed to be analyzing whether to invest in a one-year tax-free debt issue yielding 6 percent on a $1000 outlay, or a one-year taxable issue that yields 8 percent on a $1000 outlay. The firm pays federal taxes at the rate of 34 percent. The yields quoted in the financial press and in the prospectuses that describe debt issues are *before-tax* returns. The actual *after-tax* return enjoyed by the investor depends on his or her tax bracket. Notice that the actual after-tax yield received by the firm is only 5.28 percent on the taxable issue versus 6.00

TABLE 6–5. Comparison of After-Tax Yields

	Tax-exempt Debt Issue (6% Coupon)	Taxable Debt Issue (8% Coupon)
Interest income	$ 60.00	$ 80.00
Income tax (.34)	0.00	27.20
After-tax interest income	$ 60.00	$ 52.80
After-tax yield	$\frac{\$60.00}{\$1000.00} = 6\%$	$\frac{\$52.80}{\$1000.00} = 5.28\%$

Derivation of equivalent before-tax yield on a taxable debt issue:

$$r = \frac{r^*}{1-T} = \frac{.06}{1-.34} = 9.091\% \tag{6-3}$$

where r = equivalent before-tax yield,
 r^* = after-tax yield on tax-exempt security,
 T = firm's marginal income tax rate.

Proof:

Interest income [$1000 × .09091]	= $90.91
Income tax (.34)	30.91
After-tax interest income	$60.00

percent on the tax-exempt obligation. The lower portion of Table 6–5 shows that the fully taxed bond must yield 9.091 percent to make it comparable with the tax-exempt issue.

At times in the history of corporate income taxation, capital gains have been taxed at a lower rate than ordinary income (such as interest income). Under such circumstances, bonds selling at a discount from their face value may be attractive investments to tax-paying firms. Should a high level of interest rates currently exist, the market prices of debt issues that were issued in the past at low coupon rates will be depressed. This, as we said previously, brings their yield to maturity up to that obtainable on a new issue. Part of the yield to maturity on a bond selling at a discount is a capital gain, or the difference between the purchase price and the maturity value. Provided the firm held the fixed-income security for the requisite holding period, the return after tax that is earned could be higher than that derived from a comparable issue carrying a higher coupon but selling at par.[9] We say *could* be higher, as the marketplace is rather efficient and recognizes this feature of taxability; consequently, discount bonds will sell at lower yields than issues that have similar risk characteristics but larger coupons. For short periods, though, a firm *might* find a favorable yield advantage by purchasing discount bonds.

---

[9] Beginning in 1978 the holding period for long-term capital gain situations increased to 12 months. The Tax Reform Act of 1984 reduced the long-term capital-gain holding period for *individual investors* (not corporate investors) to six months. On October 22, 1986, the Tax Reform Act of 1986 became law. This sweeping revision of the tax code *eliminated* favorable tax rates for net capital gains effective January 1, 1987, for both corporations and individuals. As is obvious, tax laws change frequently. Congress and presidential administrations seem to have fun tinkering with the tax code. The important thing is to understand the basic method of analysis and then use the proper tax rate in effect at the specific point in time. Chapter 2 discusses the tax constraints on businesses in more detail.

Yields   The final selection criterion that we mention is a significant one—the yields that are available on the different financial assets suitable for inclusion in the near-cash portfolio. By now it is probably obvious that the factors of (1) financial risk, (2) interest rate risk, (3) liquidity, and (4) taxability all influence the available yields on financial instruments. Thus, the yield criterion involves a weighing of the risks and benefits inherent in these factors. If a given risk is assumed, such as lack of liquidity, a higher yield may be expected on the instrument lacking the liquidity characteristic.

Figure 6–10 summarizes our framework for designing the firm's marketable securities portfolio. The four basic considerations are shown to influence the yields available on securities. The financial manager must focus on the risk-return tradeoffs identified through analysis. Coming to grips with these tradeoffs will enable the financial manager to determine the proper marketable securities mix for the company. Let us look now at the marketable securities prominent in firms' near-cash portfolios.

Marketable Security Alternatives

U.S. Treasury Bills

U.S. Treasury bills are the best-known and most popular short-term investment outlet among firms. A Treasury bill is a direct obligation of the United States government sold on a regular basis by the U.S. Treasury. New Treasury bills are issued in denominations of $10,000, $15,000, $50,000, $100,000, $500,000, and $1,000,000. In effect, therefore, one can buy bills in multiples of $5000 above the smallest purchase price of $10,000 by combining $10,000 bills and $15,000 bills to reach the desired sum.

It is of interest to small firms and individuals to point out that prior to March 1970, bills could be obtained in denominations of $1000 and $5000. The Treasury did away with these small-sized securities in order to reduce processing costs associated with small orders and reduce the tendency of small savers to pull their funds out of commercial banks and savings and loan associations in order to invest in bills. This latter tendency was thought to strain the mortgage market to the extent that higher interest rates would result. So, while large corporations were purchasing bills yielding in excess of 15 percent during March 1980, smaller investors earning 5 to 5.5 percent on savings accounts and time deposits could find solace in the fact that they were holding down governmental processing costs and reducing pressure on the mortgage markets. Today, the existence of money-market mutual funds and bank money-market deposit accounts rectify this inequity.

At present bills are regularly offered with maturities of 91, 182, and 365 days. A nine-month bill has been sold from time to time, but due to its lack of popularity among investors it is not now being issued. The three-month and six-month bills are auctioned weekly by the Treasury, and the one-year bills are offered every four weeks. Bids (orders to purchase) are accepted by the various Federal Reserve Banks and their branches, which perform the role of agents for the Treasury. Each Monday,

FIGURE 6–10.   Designing the Marketable Securities Portfolio

Considerations	→	Influence	→	Focus Upon	→	Determine
Financial risk Interest rate risk Liquidity Taxability		Yields		Risk vs. return preferences		Marketable securities mix

bids are received until 1:30 P.M.; after that time they are opened, tabulated, and forwarded to the Treasury for allocation (filling the purchase orders).

Treasury bills are sold on a discount basis; for that reason the investor does not receive an actual interest payment. The return is the difference between the purchase price and the face (par) value of the bill.

The bills are marketed by the Treasury only in *bearer* form. They are purchased, therefore, without the investor's name on them. This attribute makes them easily transferable from one investor to the next. Of prime importance to the corporate treasurer is the fact that a very active secondary market exists for bills. After a bill has been acquired by the firm, should the need arise to turn it into cash, a group of securities dealers stand ready to purchase it. This highly developed secondary market for bills not only makes them extremely liquid, but also allows the firm to buy bills with maturities of a week or even less.

As bills have the full financial backing of the United States government, they are, for all practical purposes, risk-free. This negligible financial risk and high degree of liquidity makes the yields lower than those obtainable on other marketable securities. The income from Treasury bills is subject to federal income taxes, but *not* to state and local government income taxes. An often neglected taxability feature of Treasury bills relates to their capital gains status. In the eyes of the Internal Revenue Service, bills are *not* capital assets. This means any financial gain on their sale prior to maturity is taxed as an *ordinary* gain. This would not be the case with other government securities, such as Treasury notes (original maturities of one to seven years) or Treasury bonds (generally with original maturities of over five years). As Treasury notes and bonds approach maturity, they can become attractive alternatives to Treasury bills in the firm's near-cash portfolio.

Federal Agency **Federal agency securities** are debt obligations of corporations and agencies that
Securities have been created to effect the various lending programs of the United States government. Five such government-sponsored corporations account for the majority of outstanding agency debt. The "big five" agencies are

1. **The Federal National Mortgage Association (FNMA).** FNMA renders supplementary assistance to the secondary market for mortgages. During periods of tight credit FNMA provides liquidity by purchasing mortgages from private financial institutions, such as savings and loan associations. When credit is easier to obtain, FNMA sells mortgages.

2. **The Federal Home Loan Banks (FHLB).** The 12 regional banks in the FHLB system operate as a credit reserve system under the supervision of the Federal Home Loan Bank Board. The credit reserve system is provided for the benefit of the system's members, all of which engage in home mortgage lending.

3. **The Federal Land Banks.** The 12 regional banks are owned by almost 300 local Federal Land Bank Associations. Federal Land Bank loans are arranged by the local associations. Loans are made to persons who are (or become) members of the associations and who are engaged in agriculture, provide agricultural services, or own rural homes.

4. **The Federal Intermediate Credit Banks.** There are 12 of these banks which make loans to and purchase notes originating from loans made to farmers by other financial institutions involved in agricultural lending.

5. **The Banks for Cooperatives.** The 12 district Banks for Cooperatives make loans to cooperative associations, owned and controlled by farmers, that market farm products, purchase farm supplies, or provide general farm business services.

It is not true that the "big five" federally sponsored agencies are owned by the United States government and that the securities they issue are fully guaranteed by the government. The "big five" agencies are now entirely owned by their member associations or the general public. In addition, it is the issuing agency that stands behind its promises to pay, not the federal government.

These agencies sell their securities in a variety of denominations. The entry barrier caused by the absolute dollar size of the smallest available Treasury bill—$10,000—is not as severe in the market for agencies. A wide range of maturities is also available. Obligations can at times be purchased with maturities as short as 30 days or as long as 15 years. The vast majority of outstanding agency debt, in excess of 80 percent, will mature in 5 years or less.

Agency debt usually sells on a coupon basis and pays interest to the owner on a semi-annual schedule, although there are exceptions. Some issues have been sold on a discount basis, and some have paid interest only once a year.

If the likelihood is great that a marketable security will have to be liquidated before its contractual maturity date, then the financial officer must take care when making a selection of agency debt. The secondary market for the debt of the "big five" agencies is well developed in the shorter maturity categories—5 years or less. It is not as strong in the longer maturity categories. To move such an issue, then, the financial officer may have to sell it at a depressed price.

The income received by the investor in agency debt is subject to taxation at the federal level. Of the "big five" agencies, only the income from FNMA issues is taxed at the state and local level.

The yields available on agency obligations will always exceed those of Treasury securities of similar maturity. This yield differential is attributable to lesser marketability and greater default risk. The financial officer might keep in mind, however, that none of these agency issues has ever gone into default.

Bankers' Acceptances

Bankers' acceptances are one of the least understood instruments suitable for inclusion in the firm's marketable securities portfolio. Their part in United States commerce today is largely concentrated in the financing of foreign transactions. Generally, an acceptance is a draft (order to pay) drawn on a specific bank by an exporter in order to obtain payment for goods shipped to a customer, who maintains an account with that specific bank. An example of the sequence of events leading to the creation of a bankers' acceptance would go like this:

1. A retailer in San Francisco wants to import a shipment of stereo equipment from Tokyo. He goes to his commercial bank, which examines his credit standing and finds it satisfactory.
2. The importer's commercial bank sends the Tokyo exporter a letter of credit (a sophisticated reference letter) which authorizes the exporter to draw a draft on the San Francisco commercial bank. In the meantime, the importer has signed a contract with his bank agreeing to pay the bank the amount of the draft plus a commission in time for the bank to honor the draft at maturity.

3. Having received the letter of credit, the exporter draws a time draft on the San Francisco bank for the amount of the sale price and releases the stereo equipment for shipment. He retains possession of critical documents associated with the sale, such as the bill of lading, the transfer of title to the merchandise, and insurance papers.

4. The exporter will probably not want to wait several months for his funds, so he will obtain cash at once by selling (discounting) the draft with his bank in Tokyo at less than its face value. The shipping documents are turned over to the Tokyo bank.

5. The Tokyo bank will forward the draft and shipping documents to its correspondent bank in the United States. The correspondent bank will present the draft to the importer's San Francisco bank for acceptance.

6. The San Francisco bank (the drawee bank) will observe that the draft was authorized by its own letter of credit, will detach all shipping documents, and will stamp the draft "accepted." At this time, and not before, the bankers' acceptance is created. It is now a negotiable instrument, payable to the bearer.

7. The maturity period of the acceptance will be prearranged between the firm importing the stereo equipment and its San Francisco bank. When the draft is presented for acceptance, the maturity period begins, as most drafts are "sight drafts." This means, for instance, that if the maturity period is to be 90 days, the 90-day period begins *after* the drawee bank accepts the draft.

8. After accepting the draft, the San Francisco bank will notify its customer (the importer) that he can pick up the shipping documents, which will enable him to take possession of his stereo equipment. In exchange for the shipping documents, the drawee bank will obtain a signed document from the importer (a trust receipt) giving the bank a security interest in the goods. The importer can take title to the goods, sell them, and pay the San Francisco bank the face value of the acceptance (plus the stipulated service fee) shortly before its maturity.

9. The United States correspondent bank, which now holds the acceptance, will be instructed by the Tokyo bank to take either of two courses of action: (1) hold the acceptance until it matures as an investment or (2) immediately sell the acceptance in the market and credit its deposit account.

10. This latter course of action makes acceptances available to corporate treasurers for inclusion in near-cash portfolios.

Since acceptances are used to finance the acquisition of goods by one party, the document is not "issued" in specialized denominations; its dollar size is determined by the cost of the goods being purchased. Usual sizes, however, range from $25,000 to $1 million. The maturities on acceptances run from 30 to 180 days, although longer periods are available from time to time. The most common period is 90 days.

Acceptances, like Treasury bills, are sold on a discount basis and are payable to the bearer of the paper. A secondary market for the acceptances of large banks does exist. These transactions in acceptances are handled by only seven major dealers, all located in New York City. Included in this group are such well-known firms as the First Boston Corporation and Merrill Lynch, Pierce, Fenner & Smith, Inc.

The income generated from investing in acceptances is fully taxable at the federal, state, and local levels. Owing to their greater financial risk and lesser liquidity, acceptances provide investors a yield advantage over Treasury bills and agency obligations. In fact, the acceptances of major banks are a very safe investment, making the yield advantage over Treasuries worth looking at from the firm's vantage point.

Negotiable
Certificates of
Deposit

A **negotiable certificate of deposit, CD,** is a marketable receipt for funds that have been deposited in a bank for a fixed time period. The deposited funds earn a fixed rate of interest. These are not to be confused with ordinary passbook savings accounts or nonmarketable time deposits offered by all commercial banks. CDs are offered by major money-center banks.

CDs are offered by key banks in a variety of denominations running from $25,000 to $10,000,000. The popular sizes are $100,000, $500,000, and $1,000,000.

The original maturities on CDs can range from 1 to 18 months. Periodic reporting surveys of commercial banks that are members of the Federal Reserve System consistently indicate that from 70 to 87 percent of outstanding CDs have maturity periods of 4 months or less.

CDs are offered by banks on a basis differing from Treasury bills; that is, they are not sold at a discount. Rather, when the certificate matures, the owner receives the full amount deposited plus the earned interest.

A secondary market for CDs does exist, the heart of which is found in New York City. While CDs may be issued in registered or bearer form, the latter facilitates transactions in the secondary market and thus is the most common.

Even though the secondary market for CDs of large banks is well organized, it does not operate as smoothly as the aftermarket in Treasuries. CDs are more heterogeneous than Treasury bills. Treasury bills have similar rates, maturity periods, and denominations; more variety is found in CDs. This makes it harder to liquidate large blocks of CDs, because a more specialized investor must be found. The securities dealers who "make" the secondary market in CDs mainly trade in $1 million units. Smaller denominations can be traded but will bring a relatively lower price. The First Boston Corporation and Salomon Brothers are two of the major dealers in CDs.

The income received from an investment in CDs is subject to taxation at all government levels. In recent years CD yields have been above those available on bankers' acceptances.

Commercial
Paper

Commercial paper refers to short-term, unsecured promissory notes sold by large businesses to raise cash. These are sometimes described in the popular financial press as short-term corporate IOUs. Because they are unsecured, the issuing side of the market is dominated by large corporations, which typically maintain sound credit ratings. The issuing (borrowing) firm can sell the paper to a dealer who will in turn sell it to the investing public; if the firm's reputation is solid, the paper can be sold directly to the ultimate investor.

The denominations in which commercial paper can be bought vary over a wide range. At times paper can be obtained in sizes from $5000 to $5 million, or even more. Sometimes dealers will sell notes in multiples as small as $1000 or $5000 above the initial $5000 denomination. This depends on the dealer. The usual denominations are $25,000, $50,000, $100,000, $250,000, $500,000, and $1 million. Major dealers in the dealer-placed market include the First Boston Corporation; Goldman, Sachs & Co.; Merrill Lynch, Pierce, Fenner & Smith, Inc.; and Salomon Brothers.

Commercial paper can be purchased with maturities that range from three to 270 days. Notes with maturities exceeding 270 days are very rare, because they would have to be registered with the Securities and Exchange Commission—a task firms avoid, when possible, because of its time-consuming and costly nature.

These notes are *generally* sold on a discount basis in bearer form, although paper is available at times that is interest bearing and can be made payable to the order of the investor.

The next point is of considerable interest to the financial officer responsible for management of the firm's near-cash portfolio. For practical purposes, there is *no* active trading in a secondary market for commercial paper. This distinguishes commercial paper from all the previously discussed short-term investment vehicles. On occasion, a dealer or finance company (the borrower) will redeem a note prior to its contract maturity date, but this is not a regular procedure. Thus, when the corporation evaluates commercial paper for possible inclusion in its marketable securities portfolio, it should plan to hold it to maturity.

The return on commercial paper is fully taxable to the investor at all levels of government. Because of its lack of marketability, commercial paper in past years consistently provided a yield advantage over other near-cash assets of comparable maturity. The lifting of interest rate ceilings in 1973 by the Federal Reserve Board on certain large CDs, however, allowed commercial banks to make CD rates fully competitive in the attempt to attract funds. Over any time period, then, CD yields *may* be slightly above the rates available on commercial paper.

Repurchase Agreements

Repurchase agreements (repos) are legal contracts that involve the actual sale of securities by a *borrower* to the *lender*, with a commitment on the part of the borrower to *repurchase* the securities at the contract price plus a stated interest charge. The securities sold to the lender are U.S. government issues or other instruments of the money market such as those described above. The borrower is either a major financial institution—most important, a commercial bank—or a dealer in U.S. government securities.

Why might the corporation with excess cash prefer to buy repurchase agreements rather than a given marketable security? There are two major reasons. First, the original maturities of the instruments being sold can, in effect, be adjusted to suit the particular needs of the investing corporation. Funds available for very short time periods, such as one or two days, can be productively employed. The second reason is closely related to the first. The firm could, of course, buy a Treasury bill and then resell it in the market in a few days when cash was required. The drawback here would be the risk involved in liquidating the bill at a price equal to its earlier cost to the firm. The purchase of a repo removes this risk. The contract price of the securities that make up the arrangement is *fixed* for the duration of the transaction. The corporation that buys a repurchase agreement, then, is protected against market price fluctuations throughout the contract period. This makes it a sound alternative investment for funds that are freed up for only very short periods.

These agreements are usually executed in sizes of $1 million or more.[10] The maturities may be for a specified time period or may have no fixed maturity date. In the

[10] Occasionally, repurchase agreements smaller than $100,000 are transacted. See Norman N. Bowsher, "Repurchase Agreements," *Review,* Federal Reserve Bank of St. Louis, 61 (September 1979), 17–22.

TABLE 6–6. Money Market Funds Asset Composition, Year-End 1985

Type of Investment	Amount ($billions)	Percent of Total
U.S. Treasury bills	20.4	9.83%
Other Treasury securities	4.2	2.02
Other U.S. securities (agencies)	18.1	8.72
Repurchase agreements	26.1	12.58
Commercial bank and other domestic CDs	16.9	8.14
Eurodollar CDs	19.0	9.16
Commercial paper	87.5	42.18
Bankers acceptances	11.6	5.59
Cash reserves and other	3.7	1.78
Total net assets	207.5	100.00

Source: Investment Company Institute, *1986 Mutual Fund Fact Book* (Washington, D.C., 1986), p. 22.

latter case either lender or borrower may terminate the contract without advance notice.

The returns the lender receives on repurchase agreements are taxed at all governmental levels. Since the interest rates are set by direct negotiation between lender and borrower, no regular published series of yields is available for direct comparison with the other short-term investments. The rates available on repurchase agreements, however, are closely related to, but generally *less* than, Treasury bill rates of comparable maturities.

Money Market Mutual Funds

During the summer months of 1974, yields on three-month Treasury bills, three-month CDs, and four- to-six-month commercial paper reached 9.37, 12.48, and 11.85 percent, respectively.[11] Previous to 1974 the opportunity for small firms, and small savers in general, to take advantage of attractive rates of return on short-term securities was extremely limited. The smallest Treasury bill requires a $10,000 investment. While commercial paper can at times be obtained in $5000 denominations, it lacks the liquidity of Treasuries that is often preferable to financial managers.

The U.S. financial market system is an extraordinarily flexible vehicle of capitalism. This flexibility was again demonstrated in 1974 and 1975. During that time over 25 money market mutual funds, also called liquid-asset funds, began to sell their shares to the public.

Money market funds typically invest in a diversified portfolio of short-term, high-grade debt instruments such as those described above. Some such funds, however, will accept more interest rate risk in their portfolios and acquire some corporate bonds and notes. The portfolio composition of 348 money market funds at the end of 1985 is shown in Table 6–6. We see that commercial paper along with CDs represented slightly in excess of 50 percent of money market fund assets at this point in time. U.S. Treasury bills accounted for another 9.83 percent of the total. The average maturity period for these same 348 funds stood at 37 days at year-end 1985. The interest rate risk contained in this overall portfolio is, therefore, rather small.

The money market funds sell their shares to raise cash, and by pooling the funds of large numbers of small savers, they can build their liquid-asset portfolios. Many of

[11] Federal Reserve Bank of St. Louis, *U.S. Financial Data*, various issues, 1974.

TABLE 6–7. Investment Companies, Total Financial Assets Held, 1975–1985 (amounts in billions)

Type	Year										
	1975	1976	1977	1978	1979	1980	1981	1982	1983	1984	1985
Money market funds	3.7	3.7	3.9	10.8	45.2	74.4	181.9	206.6	162.5	209.7	207.5
Open-end investment companies	43.0	46.5	45.5	46.1	51.8	63.7	64.0	90.0	130.1	162.5	283.0

Source: Flow of Funds Section, *Flow of Funds Accounts, Assets and Liabilities Outstanding, 1962–85* (Washington, D.C.: Board of Governors of the Federal Reserve System, September 1986), p. 28.

these funds allow the investor to start an account with as little as $1000. This small initial investment, coupled with the fact that some liquid-asset funds permit subsequent investments in amounts as small as $100, makes this type of outlet for excess cash suited to the small firm. Furthermore, the management of a small enterprise may not be highly versed in the details of short-term investments. By purchasing shares in a liquid-asset fund, the investor is also buying managerial expertise.

Money market mutual funds offer the investing firm a high degree of liquidity. By redeeming (selling) shares, the investor can obtain cash quickly. Procedures for liquidation vary among the funds, but shares can usually be redeemed by means of (1) special redemption checks supplied by the fund, (2) telephone instructions, (3) wire instructions, or (4) a letter. When liquidation is ordered by telephone or wire, the mutual fund can remit to the investor by the next business day.

During the spring of 1980, yields on key money market instruments rose to near record levels. In March 1980, three-month Treasury bills, three-month CDs, and four-month commercial paper carried annual rates of return of 15.37, 16.87, and 16.17 percent, respectively. This made money market funds extraordinarily attractive to both corporations and individuals.

Actually, the flow of funds into the money market vehicles had already begun to accelerate by year-end 1979, as is substantiated by Table 6–7. Data for open-end investment companies are also presented for comparison purposes. Notice the fantastic jump in financial assets held by the money market funds from year-end 1978 to 1979. Then the U.S. economy suffered two recessions with little relief between them. The first began in January 1980 and ended 7 months later in July. The second began in July 1981 and ended in November 1982, or 17 months after it began. The Federal Reserve System was trying to wring a very high rate of inflation out of the economy. It did this by keeping interest rates high. This made short-term debt instruments popular with investors.

As a result, the financial assets of money market mutual funds swelled to $206.6 billion by the end of 1982. The national economic recovery that began in late 1982 was foreshadowed by an upswing in common equity prices as early as August of that same year.[12] Through early 1987 the economy avoided another recession and stock prices in general moved upward. Simultaneously, interest rates decreased over

---

[12] A fine article by A. L. Malabre Jr. discusses the concept of stock market prices as a leading economic indicator and also touches upon the relationship among stock price changes, interest rate movements, and money supply changes. See "The Stock Market and the Business Cycle," *The Wall Street Journal*, February 23, 1987, p. 1.

this 1982–87 time frame. Investors, then, reduced their holdings of money funds and moved into equities. The data for 1983 in Table 6–7 reflect these portfolio shifts. Notice that despite low nominal interest rates, money fund assets rebounded strongly in 1984 and 1985. Clearly, these funds have been totally accepted as an investment outlet by the investing public.

The returns earned from owning shares in a money market fund are taxable at all governmental levels. The yields will follow the returns the investor could receive by purchasing the marketable securities directly.

Money Market Deposit Accounts

The depressed economy of 1980–82 placed tremendous financial strain on the depository institutions in the United States. Both commercial banks and thrift institutions suffered. Congress reacted by passing the Depository Institutions Act in 1982. The objective of the act was to enable both banks and thrifts to compete with the fast-growing money market mutual funds. The result was that the Depository Institutions Deregulatory Committee authorized banks and thrifts to offer to investors a new type of account called the money market deposit account (MMDA).[13] The MMDAs became available to the public on December 14, 1982. These accounts differ from the money market fund accounts in significant ways:

1. They carry federal deposit insurance of up to $100,000 per account.
2. They require a minimum balance of $2,500. If the balance falls below the designated $2,500, it earns only the passbook savings rate.
3. Each account is limited to a maximum of six transactions per month, of which only three may be by check. In effect this means the other three transactions must be accomplished by use of preauthorized withdrawals.

The yield on the MMDAs is set individually by each offering bank or thrift institution. The maximum period for which the yield can be guaranteed by the financial institution is one month.

The third characteristic of the MMDAs renders them inappropriate for most businesses as a vehicle for the investment of excess cash. Firms do not want to be restricted on the number of times per month that they can tap their liquid asset reserves. On the other hand, the MMDAs have become very popular with *individual* investors. As was the intent of the Depository Institutions Act, a significant volume of funds has flowed from the money fund accounts to the MMDAs.

The Yield Structure of Marketable Securities

What type of return can the financial manager expect on a marketable securities portfolio? This is a reasonable question. Some insight can be obtained by looking at the past, although we must realize that future returns are not guided by past experience. It is also useful to have some understanding of how the returns on one type of

---

[13] The Depository Institutions Deregulatory Committee was established by the authority of the Depository Institutions Deregulation and Monetary Control Act of 1980. It includes representatives from the several federal agencies that oversee financial institutions. In January 1983 the Depository Institutions Deregulatory Committee permitted both banks and thrifts to offer what are called "super NOW accounts." These super NOW accounts differed from the MMDAs in that the number of transactions per month was *not* limited. The super NOW accounts, however, could be offered only to individuals and *not* to businesses. A good synopsis of the major banking acts that affect the U.S. economy (and other detailed information on the money market) can be found in Marcia Stigum, *The Money Market*, rev. ed. (Homewood, IL: Dow Jones–Irwin, 1983), pp. 124–27.

TABLE 6–8 Annual Yields (Percent) on Selected Three-Month Marketable Securities

Year	T-Bills	Agencies	Acceptances	Commercial Paper	CDs
1965	3.93	4.14	4.19	4.25	4.31
1966	4.81	5.22	5.37	5.51	5.43
1967	4.30	4.60	4.81	5.11	4.99
1968	5.27	5.54	5.72	5.92	5.79
1969	6.54	7.12	7.51	7.76	7.66
1970	6.58	6.94	7.50	7.89	7.68
1971	4.39	4.56	4.94	5.12	5.07
1972	4.02	4.22	4.52	4.63	4.61
1973	6.87	7.40	8.03	8.11	8.21
1974	7.78	8.73	9.85	10.06	10.28
1975	5.85	6.03	6.28	6.41	6.61
1976	5.03	5.15	5.18	5.28	5.31
1977	5.17	5.38	5.45	5.45	5.55
1978	7.12	7.68	7.91	7.73	8.05
1979	9.84	10.53	10.76	10.72	11.02
1980	11.51	12.09	12.72	12.66	13.07
1981	14.03	15.28	15.32	15.32	15.91
1982	10.69	11.68	11.89	11.89	12.27
1983	8.61	8.95	8.90	8.88	9.07
1984	9.52	10.13	10.14	10.10	10.37
1985	7.48	8.00	7.92	7.95	8.05
1986	5.98	6.49	6.39	6.49	6.52

Source: Salomon Brothers, "An Analytical Record of Yields and Yield Spreads," March 1980; and *Federal Reserve Bulletin*, 69 (November 1983), A 26, 70 (August 1984), A 24, 73 (February 1987), A 24.

instrument stack up against another. The behavior of yields on short-term debt instruments over the 1965–86 period is shown in Table 6–8. An examination of the data in that table permits the following generalizations:

1. The returns from the various instruments are highly correlated in the positive direction over time. That is, the yields tend to rise and fall together.
2. The yields are quite volatile over time. For example, notice the large increases in returns from 1968 to 1969, 1972 to 1973, 1978 to 1979, and 1980 to 1981. The financial manager, then, cannot plan on any given level of returns prevailing over a long time period. Also, observe the relatively high yields during 1974 that led to the formation of a large number of money market mutual funds. High yields prevailed again in 1979 and 1981 and aided their growth.
3. A basic change has occurred in the underlying structure of yields. Between 1966 and 1972, if we ranked the instruments in Table 6–8 from low to high yield, we would have

Treasury bills   (low yield)

Federal agency securities

Bankers' acceptances

Certificates of deposit

Commercial paper   (high yield)

From 1973 to 1982, however, the annual yields available on negotiable certificates of deposit exceeded those of commercial paper. This phenomenon is the direct result of Federal Reserve Board action that removed interest rate limits on large certificates of deposit.

The discussion in this chapter on designing the firm's marketable securities portfolio touched upon the essential elements of several near-cash assets. At times it is difficult to sort out the distinguishing features among these short-term investments. To alleviate that problem, Table 6–9 draws together their principal characteristics.

A GLANCE AT ACTUAL CASH MANAGEMENT PRACTICES ——————————

We have dealt at length in this chapter with (1) the collection and disbursement procedures the firm can use to manage its cash balances more effectively and (2) the composition of the firm's marketable securities portfolio. It is of interest to relate our discussion to the findings of some studies that focus on corporate cash management practices.

Surveys conducted by (1) Gitman, Moses, and White and (2) Mathur and Loy centered on both the cash management services offered by commercial banks and the investment of excess cash in the marketable securities portfolio.[14] Gitman, Moses, and White surveyed 300 of the 1000 largest industrial firms in the United States ranked by total sales dollars for 1975 (the *Fortune 1000* list). They received 98 responses to their questionnaire, for a response rate of 32.7 percent. With regard to speeding up the firm's cash receipts, it was found that 80 percent of the respondents used lock-box systems and 61 percent used selected disbursing points (remote disbursing) to slow down or better control cash payments.

The Mathur and Loy study centered on the 200 largest industrial firms from the *Fortune 500* list for 1979. Of these 200 firms, 160 were sampled. A response rate of 46 percent was achieved. This study showed that almost all of the respondents used lock-box services (96 percent). Additionally, concentration banking was employed by 80 percent of the survey participants.

These same two studies touched upon the management of the marketable securities portfolio. Gitman, Moses, and White found that the most favored security for the investment of excess cash was commercial paper. It was followed in popularity by repurchase agreements, Treasury securities, and CDs. Mathur and Loy also found that commercial paper was the most-favored marketable security investment. Furthermore, repurchase agreements and CDs ranked high on respondents' most favored lists. Mathur and Loy also reported that, on average, the firms invest in 3.6 different types of marketable securities.

We all know that commercial paper, CDs, and repurchase agreements are more risky investments than Treasury securities. It seems that those who are responsible for making marketable security investment decisions in large firms do not consider the risk differences among the traditional money market instruments to be very signifi-

---

[14] Lawrence J. Gitman, Edward A. Moses, and I. Thomas White, "An Assessment of Corporate Cash Management Practices," *Financial Management*, 8 (Spring 1979), 32–41; and Ike Mathur and David Loy, "Corporate-Banking Cash Management Relationships: Survey Results," *Journal of Cash Management*, 3 (October–November 1983), 35–46.

TABLE 6–9. Features of Selected Money Market Instruments

Instrument	Denominations	Maturities	Basis	Form	Liquidity	Taxability
U.S. Treasury bills—direct obligations of the U.S. government	$ 10,000 15,000 50,000 100,000 500,000 1,000,000	91 days 182 days 365 days 9-month not presently issued	Discount	Bearer	Excellent secondary market	Exempt from state and local income
Federal agency securities—obligations of corporations and agencies created to effect the federal government's lending programs	Wide variation; from $1000 to $1 million	5 days (Farm Credit consolidated systemwide discount notes) to more than 10 years	Discount or coupon; usually on coupon	Bearer or registered	Good for issues of "big five" agencies	Generally exempt at local level; FNMA issues are *not*
Bankers' acceptances—drafts accepted for future payment by commercial banks	No set size; typically range from $25,000 to $1 million	Predominantly from 30 to 180 days	Discount	Bearer	Good for acceptances of large "money market" banks	Taxed at all levels of government
Negotiable certificates of deposit—marketable receipts for funds deposited in a bank for a fixed time period	$25,000 to $10 million	1 to 18 months	Accrued interest	Bearer or registered; bearer is preferable from liquidity standpoint	Fair to good	Taxed at all levels of government
Commercial paper—short-term unsecured promissory notes	$5000 to $5 million; $1000 and $5000 multiples above the initial offering size are sometimes available	3 to 270 days	Discount	Bearer	Poor; no active secondary market in usual sense	Taxed at all levels of government
Repurchase agreements—legal contracts between a borrower (security seller) and lender (security buyer). The borrower will repurchase at the contract price plus an interest charge.	Typical sizes are $500,000 or more	According to terms of contract	Not applicable	Not applicable	Fixed by the agreement; that is, borrower will repurchase	Taxed at all levels of government
Money market mutual funds—holders of diversified portfolios of short-term, high-grade debt instruments	Some require an initial investment as small as $1000	Your shares can be sold at any time	Net asset value	Registered	Good; provided by the fund itself	Taxed at all levels of government

cant. They are willing to trade the greater riskiness inherent in the "non-Treasury" instruments for their higher expected yield.

Summary

Firms hold cash in order to satisfy transactions, precautionary, and speculative needs for liquidity. Because cash balances provide no direct return, the precautionary motive for investing in cash is met in part by holdings of marketable securities.

Cash Management Objectives and Decisions

The financial manager must (1) make sure that enough cash is on hand to meet the payment needs that arise in the course of doing business and (2) attempt to reduce the firm's idle cash balances to a minimum.

Collection and Disbursement Procedures

By use of (1) lock-box arrangements, (2) preauthorized checks, (3) special forms of depository transfer checks, and (4) wire transfers, the firm can achieve considerable benefits in terms of float reduction. Lock-box systems and preauthorized checks serve to reduce mail and processing float. Depository transfer checks and wire transfers move funds between banks; they are often used in conjunction with concentration banking. Both the lock-box and preauthorized check systems can be employed as part of the firm's concentration banking setup to speed receipts to regional collection centers.

The firm can delay and favorably affect the control of its cash disbursements through the use of (1) zero balance accounts, (2) payable-through drafts, and (3) remote disbursing. Zero balance accounts allow the company to maintain central-office control over payments while permitting the disbursing authority to rest with the firm's several divisions. Because key disbursing accounts are located in one major concentration bank, rather than in multiple banks across the country, excess cash balances that tend to build up in the outlying banks are avoided. Payable-through drafts are legal instruments that look like checks but are drawn on and paid by the issuing firm rather than its bank. The bank serves as a collection point for the drafts. The main reason for use of such a system is to provide for effective central-office control over field-authorized payments; it is not used as a major vehicle for extending disbursing float. Remote disbursing, however, is used to increase disbursing float. Remote disbursing refers to the process of writing payment checks on banks located in cities distant from the one where the check is originated.

Before any of these collection and disbursement procedures is initiated by the firm, a careful analysis should be undertaken to see if the expected benefits outweigh the expected costs.

Marketable Securities Portfolio

The factors of (1) financial risk, (2) interest rate risk, (3) liquidity, and (4) taxability affect the yields available on marketable securities. By considering these four factors simultaneously with returns desired from the portfolio, the financial manager can design the mix of near-cash assets most suitable for a firm.

The features of several marketable securities were investigated. Treasury bills and federal agency securities are extremely safe investments. Higher yields are obtainable on bankers' acceptances, CDs, and commercial paper in exchange for greater risk assumption. Unlike the instruments just mentioned, commercial paper enjoys no developed secondary market. The firm can hedge against price fluctuations through the use of repurchase agreements. Money market mutual funds, a recent phenomenon of our financial market system, are particularly well suited for the short-term investing needs of small firms.

Study Questions

6–1. What is meant by the cash flow process?

6–2. Identify the principal (classical) motives for holding cash and near-cash assets. Explain the purpose of each motive.

6–3. What is concentration banking and how may it be of value to the firm?

6–4. Distinguish between depository transfer checks and automated depository transfer checks (ADTC).

6–5. In general what type of firm would benefit from the use of a preauthorized check system? What specific types of companies have successfully used this device to accelerate cash receipts?

6–6. What are the two major objectives of the firm's cash management system?

6–7. What three decisions dominate the cash management process?

6–8. Within the context of cash management, what are the key elements of (total) float? Briefly define each element.

6–9. Distinguish between financial risk and interest rate risk as these terms are commonly used in discussions of cash management.

6–10. What is meant when we say, "A money market instrument is highly liquid"?

6–11. Which money market instrument is generally conceded to have no secondary market?

6–12. Your firm invests in only three different classes of marketable securities: commercial paper, Treasury bills, and federal agency securities. Recently, yields on these money market instruments of three months' maturity were quoted at 6.10, 6.25, and 5.90 percent. Match the available yields with the types of instruments your firm purchases.

6–13. What two major factors led to the inception of a large number of money market mutual funds during 1974 and 1975?

6–14. What two key factors might induce a firm to invest in repurchase agreements rather than a specific security of the money market?

Self-Test Problems

ST–1. (*Costs of Services*) Creative Fashion Designs is evaluating a lock-box system as a cash receipts acceleration device. In a typical year this firm receives remittances totaling $7 million by check. The firm will record and process 4000 checks over the same time period. Ocala National Bank has informed the management of Creative Fashion Designs that it will process checks and associated documents through the lock-box system for a unit cost of $.25 per check. Creative Fashion Designs' financial manager has projected that cash freed by adoption of the system can be invested in a portfolio of near-cash assets that will yield an annual before-tax return of 8 percent. Creative Fashion Designs' financial analysts use a 365-day year in their procedures.

a. What reduction in check collection time is necessary for Creative Fashion Designs to be neither better nor worse off for having adopted the proposed system?

b. How would your solution to part (a) be affected if Creative Fashion Designs could invest the freed balances only at an expected annual return of 5.5 percent?

c. What is the logical explanation for the differences in your answers to parts (a) and (b) above?

ST–2. (*Cash Receipts Acceleration System*) Artie Kay's Komputer Shops is a large, national distributor and retailer of microcomputers, personal computers, and related software. The company has its central offices in Dearborn, Michigan, not far from the Ford Motor Company executive offices and headquarters. Only recently has Artie Kay's begun to pay serious attention to its cash management procedures. Last week the firm received a proposal from the Detroit National Bank. The objective of the proposal is to speed up the firm's cash collections.

Artie Kay's now uses a centralized billing procedure. All checks are mailed to the Dearborn headquarters office for processing and eventual deposit. Remittance checks now take an average of five business days to reach the Dearborn office. The in-house processing at Artie Kay's is quite slow. Once in Dearborn, another three days are needed to process the checks for deposit at Detroit National.

The daily cash remittances of Artie Kay's average $200,000. The average check size is $800. The firm currently earns 10.6 percent on its marketable securities portfolio and expects this rate to continue to be available.

The cash acceleration plan suggested by officers of Detroit National involves both a lock-box system and concentration banking. Detroit National would be the firm's only concentration bank. Lock boxes would be established in (1) Seattle, (2) San Antonio, (3) Chicago, and (4) Detroit. This would reduce mail float by 2.0 days. Processing float would be reduced to a level of 0.5 days. Funds would then be transferred twice each business day by means of automated depository transfer checks from local banks in Seattle, San Antonio, and Chicago to the Detroit National Bank. Each depository transfer check (ADTC) costs $20. These transfers will occur all 270 business days of the year. Each check processed through the lock-box system will cost Artie Kay's $0.25.

a. What amount of cash balances will be freed if Artie Kay's adopts the system proposed by Detroit National?

b. What is the opportunity cost of maintaining the current banking arrangement?

c. What is the projected annual cost of operating the proposed system?

d. Should Artie Kay's adopt the new system? Compute the net annual gain or loss associated with adopting the system.

ST–3. (*Buying and Selling Marketable Securities*) Mountaineer Outfitters has $2 million in excess cash that it might invest in marketable securities. In order to buy and sell the securities, however, the firm must pay a transactions fee of $45,000.

a. Would you recommend purchasing the securities if they yield 12 percent annually and are held for

1. One month?
2. Two months?
3. Three months?
4. Six months?
5. One year?

b. What minimum required yield would the securities have to return for the firm to hold them for three months (what is the breakeven yield for a three-month holding period)?

Study Problems

6-1. (*Buying and Selling Marketable Securities*) Miami Dice & Card Company has generated $800,000 in excess cash that it could invest in marketable securities. In order to buy and sell the securities, the firm will pay total transactions fees of $20,000.

    a. Would you recommend purchasing the securities if they yield 10.5 percent annually and are held for:

        1. One month?

        2. Two months?

        3. Three months?

        4. Six months?

        5. One year?

    b. What minimum required yield would the securities have to return for the firm to hold them for two months (what is the breakeven yield for a two-month holding period)?

6-2. (*Cash Receipts Acceleration System*) James Waller Nail Corp. is a buyer and distributor of nails used in the home building industry. The firm has grown very quickly since it was established eight years ago. Waller Nail has managed to increase sales and profits at a rate of about 18 percent annually, despite moderate economic growth at the national level. Until recently, the company paid little attention to cash management procedures. James Waller, the firm's president, said: "With our growth—who cares?" Bending to the suggestions of several analysts in the firm's finance group, Waller did agree to have a proposal prepared by the Second National Bank in Tampa, Florida. The objective of the proposal is to accelerate the firm's cash collections.

    At present, Waller Nail uses a centralized billing procedure. All checks are mailed to the Tampa office headquarters for processing and eventual deposit. Under this arrangement, all customers' remittance checks take an average of five business days to reach the Tampa office. Once in Tampa, another two days are needed to process the checks for deposit at the Second National Bank.

    Daily cash remittances at Waller Nail average $750,000. The average check size is $3,750. The firm currently earns 9.2 percent annually on its marketable securities portfolio.

    The cash acceleration plan presented by the officers of Second National Bank involves both a lock-box system and concentration banking. Second National would be the firm's only concentration bank. Lock boxes would be established in (1) Los Angeles, (2) Dallas, (3) Chicago, and (4) Tampa. This would reduce funds tied up in mail float to 3.5 days. Processing float would be totally eliminated. Funds would then be transferred twice each business day by means of automated depository transfer checks from local banks in Los Angeles, Dallas, and Chicago to the Second National Bank. Each depository transfer check (ADTC) costs $27. These transfers will occur all 270 business days of the year. Each check processed through the lock box will cost Waller Nail $.35.

    a. What amount of cash balances will be freed if Waller Nail adopts the system proposed by Second National Bank?

    b. What is the opportunity cost of maintaining the current banking arrangement?

    c. What is the projected annual cost of operating the proposed system?

    d. Should Waller Nail Corp. adopt the system? Compute the net annual gain or loss associated with adopting the system.

6-3. (*Concentration Banking*) Walkin Chemicals operates in New Orleans. The firm produces and distributes industrial cleaning products on a nationwide basis. The firm presently uses a centralized billing system. Walkin Chemicals has annual credit sales of $438 million. Creole National Bank has presented an offer to operate a concentration banking system for the company. Walkin already has an established line of credit with Creole. Creole says it will operate the system on a flat fee basis of $250,000 per year. The analysis done by the bank's cash management services division suggests that two days in mail float and one day in processing float can be eliminated.

Since Walkin borrows almost continuously from Creole National, the value of the float reduction would be applied against the line of credit. The borrowing rate on the line of credit is set at an annual rate of 11 percent. Further, because of a reduction in clerical help, the new system will save the firm $65,000 in processing costs. Walkin uses a 365-day year in analyses of this sort. Should Walkin accept the bank's offer to install the new system?

6–4. (*Lock-Box System*) Advanced Electronics is located in Nashville, Tennessee. The firm manufactures components used in a variety of electrical devices. All the firm's finished goods are shipped to five regional warehouses across the United States.

First Volunteer Bank of Nashville is Advanced Electronics' lead bank. First Volunteer recently completed a study of Advanced Electronics' cash collection system. First Volunteer estimates that it can reduce Advanced Electronics' total float by 2.5 days with the installation of a lock-box arrangement in each of the firm's five regions.

The lock-box arrangement would cost each region $500 per month. Any funds freed up would be added to the firm's marketable securities portfolio and would yield 11.75 percent on an annual basis. Annual sales average $10,950,000 for each regional office. The firm and the bank use a 365-day year in their analyses. Should Advance Electronics' management approve the use of the proposed system?

6–5. (*Costs of Services*) The Mountain Furniture Company of Scranton, Pennsylvania, may install a lock-box system in order to speed up its cash receipts. On an annual basis, Mountain Furniture receives $40 million in remittances by check. The firm will record and process 15,000 checks over the year. The Third Bank of Scranton will administer the system at a cost of $.35 per check. Cash that is freed up by use of the system can be invested to yield 9 percent on an annual before-tax basis. A 365-day year is used for analysis purposes. What reduction in check collection time is necessary for Mountain Furniture to be neither better nor worse off for having adopted the proposed system?

6–6. (*Cash Receipts Acceleration System*) Ronda Ball Kitchens Corp. is a medium-sized manufacturer, buyer, and installer of quality kitchen equipment and apparatus. The firm, which was established five years ago, has grown very quickly. Despite some rough economic times that included two recessions in three years. Ball Kitchens has managed to increase sales and profits at an approximate rate of 20 percent annually. Until recently, the firm paid no attention to its cash management procedures. Ronda Ball, the company's president, just said, "We are too busy growing to worry about those trivial things." Bending to the pleas of several analysts in the firm's finance group, Ball did agree to have a proposal prepared by the Pan-Atlantic Bank in Orlando, Florida. The objective of the proposal is to speed up the firm's cash collections.

At present, Ball Kitchens uses a centralized billing procedure. All checks are mailed to the Orlando headquarters office for processing and eventual deposit. Under this arrangement all of the customers' remittance checks take an average of four business days to reach the Orlando office. Once in Orlando, another two days are needed to process the checks for deposit at the Pan-Atlantic Bank.

The daily cash remittances of Ball Kitchens average $500,000. The average check size is $2000. The firm currently earns 8.8 percent annually on its marketable securities portfolio.

The cash acceleration plan presented by the officers of Pan-Atlantic involves both a lock-box system and concentration banking. Pan-Atlantic would be the firm's only concentration bank. Lock boxes would be established in (1) Los Angeles, (2) Houston, (3) Chicago, and (4) Orlando. This would reduce funds tied up by mail float to 2.5 days. Processing float would be eliminated. Funds would then be transferred twice each business day by means of automated depository transfer checks from local banks in Los Angeles, Houston, and Chicago to the Pan-Atlantic Bank. Each depository transfer check (ADTC) costs $22. These transfers will occur all 270 business days of the year. Each check processed through the lock-box system will cost Ball Kitchens $.20.

a. What amount of cash balances will be freed if Ball Kitchens adopts the system proposed by Pan-Atlantic?

b. What is the opportunity cost of maintaining the current banking arrangement?

c. What is the projected annual cost of operating the proposed system?

d. Should Ball Kitchens adopt the new system? Compute the net annual gain or loss associated with adopting the system.

6–7. (*Buying and Selling Marketable Securities*) Saturday Knights Live Products, Inc., has $1 million in excess cash that it might invest in marketable securities. In order to buy and sell the securities, however, the firm must pay a transactions fee of $30,000.

a. Would you recommend purchasing the securities if they yield 11 percent annually and are held for

    1. One month?

    2. Two months?

    3. Three months?

    4. Six months?

    5. One year?

b. What minimum required yield would the securities have to return for the firm to hold them for three months (what is the breakeven yield for a three-month holding period)?

6–8. (*Concentration Banking*) Columbia Textiles, located in South Carolina, manufactures and distributes textile products on a nationwide basis. The firm has always used a centralized billing system. Columbia Textiles has annual credit sales of $365 million. South Carolina National Bank has approached Columbia Textiles with an offer to establish and operate a concentration banking system for the company. Columbia already has an established line of credit with this same bank. South Carolina National says it will operate the system on a flat fee basis of $200,000 per year. A detailed analysis done by the bank's cash management services division shows conclusively that two days in mail float and one day in processing float can be eliminated. Since Columbia borrows almost continuously from South Carolina National, the value of the float reduction would be applied against the line of credit. The borrowing rate on the line of credit is set at an annual rate of 15 percent. Additionally, because of a reduction in clerical help, the new system will save the firm $50,000 per year in processing costs. Columbia uses a 365-day year in analyses of this sort. Should Columbia accept the bank's offer to install the new system?

6–9. (*Lock-Box System*) Penn Foundry is located on the outskirts of State College, Pennsylvania. The firm specializes in the manufacture of aluminum and steel castings, which are used for numerous automobile parts. All of the firm's output is shipped to 10 warehouses near major auto assembly plants across the United States. First Quaker Bank of Philadelphia is Penn Foundry's lead bank. First Quaker has just completed a study of Penn's cash collection system. Overall, First Quaker estimates that it can reduce Penn's total float by 2.5 days with the installation of a lock-box arrangement in each of the firm's 10 regions. The lock-box arrangement would cost each region $300 per month. Any funds freed up would be added to the firm's marketable securities portfolio and would yield 10.5 percent on an annual basis. Annual sales average $5,475,000 for each regional office. The firm and the bank use a 365-day year in their analyses. Should Penn Foundry's management approve the use of the proposed system?

6–10. (*Valuing Float Reduction*) Griffey Manufacturing Company is forecasting that next year's gross revenues from sales will be $890 million. The senior treasury analyst for the firm expects the marketable securities portfolio to earn 9.60 percent over this same time period. A 365-day year is used in all the firm's financial procedures. What is the value to the company of one day's float reduction?

6–11. (*Costs of Services*) The Idaho Lumber Company may install a lock-box system in order to speed up its cash receipts. On an annual basis, Idaho receives $60 million of remittances by check. The firm will record and process 18,000 checks over the year. The Pocatello Fourth National Bank will administer the system for a unit cost of $.30 per check. Cash that is freed by the use of this system can be invested to yield 8 percent on an annual before-tax basis. A 365-day year is used for analysis purposes. What reduction in check collection time is necessary for Idaho Lumber to be neither better nor worse off for having adopted the proposed system?

6–12. (*Costs of Services*) Mustang Ski-Wear, Inc., is investigating the possibility of adopting a lock-box system as a cash receipts acceleration device. In a typical year this firm receives remittances totaling $12 million by check. The firm will record and process 6000 checks over this same time period. The Colorado Springs Second National Bank has informed the management of Mustang that it will expedite checks and associated documents through the lock-box system for a unit cost of $.20 per check. Mustang's financial manager has projected that cash freed by adoption of the system can be invested in a portfolio of near-cash assets that will yield an annual before-tax return of 7 percent. Mustang financial analysts use a 365-day year in their procedures.

    a. What reduction in check collection time is necessary for Mustang to be neither better nor worse off for having adopted the proposed system?

    b. How would your solution to part (a) above be affected if Mustang could invest the freed balances only at an expected annual return of 4.5 percent?

    c. What is the logical explanation for the difference in your answers to parts (a) and (b) above?

6–13. (*Valuing Float Reduction*) The Columbus Tool and Die Works will generate $18 million in credit sales next year. Collections occur at an even rate, and employees work a 270-day year. At the moment, the firm's general accounting department ties up five days' worth of remittance checks. An analysis undertaken by the firm's treasurer indicates that new internal procedures can reduce processing float by two days. If Columbus Tool invests the released funds to earn 8 percent, what will be the annual savings?

6–14. (*Lock-Box System*) Penn Steelworks is a distributor of cold-rolled steel products to the automobile industry. All its sales are on a credit basis, net 30 days. Sales are evenly distributed over its 10 sales regions throughout the United States. Delinquent accounts are no problem. The company has recently undertaken an analysis aimed at improving its cash management procedures. Penn determined that it takes an average of 3.2 days for customers' payments to reach the head office in Pittsburgh from the time they are mailed. It takes another full day in processing time prior to depositing the checks with a local bank. Annual sales average $4,800,000 for each regional office. Reasonable investment opportunities can be found yielding 7 percent per year. To alleviate the float problem confronting the firm, the use of a lock-box system in each of the 10 regions is being considered. This would reduce mail float by 1.2 days. One day in processing float would also be eliminated, plus a full day in transit float. The lock-box arrangement would cost each region $250 per month.

    a. What is the opportunity cost to Penn Steelworks of the funds tied up in mailing and processing? Use a 365-day year.

    b. What would the net cost or savings be from use of the proposed cash acceleration technique? Should Penn adopt the system?

6–15. (*Valuing Float Reduction*) Next year P. F. Anderson Motors expects its gross revenues from sales to be $80 million. The firm's treasurer has projected that its marketable securities portfolio will earn 6.50 percent over the coming budget year. What is the value of one day's float reduction to the company? Anderson Motors uses a 365-day year in all of its financial analysis procedures.

6–16. (*Cash Receipts Acceleration System*) Peggy Pierce Designs, Inc., is a vertically integrated, national manufacturer and retailer of women's clothing. Currently, the firm has no coordinated cash management system. A proposal, however, from the First Pennsylvania Bank aimed at speeding up cash collections is being examined by several of Pierce's corporate executives.

The firm currently uses a centralized billing procedure, which requires that all checks be mailed to the Philadelphia head office for processing and eventual deposit. Under this arrangement all the customers' remittance checks take an average of five business days to reach the head office. Once in Philadelphia another two days are required to process the checks for ultimate deposit at the First Pennsylvania Bank.

The firm's daily remittances average $1 million. The average check size is $2000. Pierce Designs currently earns 6 percent annually on its marketable securities portfolio.

The cash acceleration plan proposed by officers of First Pennsylvania involves both a lock-box system and concentration banking. First Pennsylvania would be the firm's only concentration bank. Lock boxes would be established in (1) San Francisco, (2) Dallas, (3) Chicago, and (4) Philadelphia. This would reduce funds tied up by mail float to three days, and processing float will be eliminated. Funds would then be transferred twice each business day by means of automated depository transfer checks from local banks in San Francisco, Dallas, and Chicago to the First Pennsylvania Bank. Each depository transfer check (ADTC) costs $15. These transfers will occur all 270 business days of the year. Each check processed through the lock-box system will cost $.18.

a. What amount of cash balances will be freed if Pierce Designs, Inc. adopts the system suggested by First Pennsylvania?
b. What is the opportunity of maintaining the current banking setup?
c. What is the projected annual cost of operating the proposed system?
d. Should Pierce adopt the new system? Compute the net annual gain or loss associated with adopting the system.

6–17. (*Marketable Securities Portfolio*) The Alex Daniel Shoe Manufacturing Company currently pays its employees on a weekly basis. The weekly wage bill is $500,000. This means that on the average the firm has accrued wages payable of ($500,000 + $0)/2 = $250,000.

Alex Daniel, Jr., works as the firm's senior financial analyst and reports directly to his father, who owns all of the firm's common stock. Alex Daniel, Jr., wants to move to a monthly wage payment system. Employees would be paid at the end of every fourth week. The younger Daniel is fully aware that the labor union representing the company's workers will not permit the monthly payments system to take effect unless the workers are given some type of fringe benefit compensation.

A plan has been worked out whereby the firm will make a contribution to the cost of life insurance coverage for each employee. This will cost the firm $35,000 annually. Alex Daniel, Jr., expects the firm to earn 7 percent annually on its marketable securities portfolio.

a. Based on the projected information, should Daniel Shoe Manufacturing move to the monthly wage payment system?
b. What annual rate of return on the marketable securities portfolio would enable the firm to just break even on this proposal?

6–18. (*Valuing Float Reduction*) The Cowboy Bottling Company will generate $12 million in credit sales next year. Collections of these credit sales will occur evenly over this period. The firm's employees work 270 days a year. Currently, the firm's processing system ties up four days' worth of remittance checks. A recent report from a financial consultant indicated procedures that will enable Cowboy Bottling to reduce processing float by two full days. If Cowboy invests the released funds to earn 6 percent, what will be the annual savings?

6–19. (*Valuing Float Reduction*) Montgomery Woodcraft is a large distributor of woodworking tools and accessories to hardware stores, lumber yards, and tradesmen. All its sales are on a credit basis, net 30 days. Sales are evenly distributed over its 12 sales regions throughout the United States. There is no problem with delinquent accounts. The firm is attempting to improve its cash management procedures. Montgomery recently determined that it took an average of 3.0 days for customers' payments to reach their office from the time they were mailed, and another day for processing before payments could be deposited. Annual sales average $5,200,000 for each region, and investment opportunities can be found to return 9 percent per year. What is the opportunity cost to the firm of the funds tied up in mailing and processing? In your calculations use a 365-day year.

6–20. (*Lock-Box System*) To mitigate the float problem discussed above, Montgomery Woodcraft is considering the use of a lock-box system in each of its regions. By so doing, it can reduce the mail float by 1.5 days and receive the *other* benefits of a lock-box system. It also estimates that transit float could be reduced to half its present duration of two days. Use of the lock-box arrangement in each of its regions will cost $300 per month. Should Montgomery Woodcraft adopt the system? What would the net cost or savings be?

6–21. (*Accounts Payable Policy and Cash Management*) Bradford Construction Supply Company is suffering from a prolonged decline in new construction in its sales area. In an attempt to improve its cash position, the firm is considering changes in its accounts payable policy. After careful study it has determined that the only alternative available is to slow disbursements. Purchases for the coming year are expected to be $37.5 million. Sales will be $65 million, which represents about a 20 percent drop from the current year. Currently, Bradford discounts approximately 25 percent of its payments at 3 percent 10 days, net 30, and the balance of accounts are paid in 30 days. If Bradford adopts a policy of payment in 45 days or 60 days, how much can the firm gain if the annual opportunity cost of investment is 12 percent? What will be the result if this action causes Bradford Construction suppliers to increase their prices to the company by 0.5 percent to compensate for the 60-day extended term of payment? In your calculations use a 365-day year and ignore any compounding effects related to expected returns.

6–22. (*Interest Rate Risk*) Two years ago your corporate treasurer purchased for the firm a 20-year bond at its par value of $1000. The coupon rate on this security is 8 percent. Interest payments are made to bondholders once a year. Currently, bonds of this particular risk class are yielding investors 9 percent. A cash shortage has forced you to instruct your treasurer to liquidate his bond.
  a. At what price will your bond be sold? Assume annual compounding.
  b. What will be the amount of your gain or loss over the original purchase price?
  c. What would be the amount of your gain or loss had the treasurer originally purchased a bond with a four-year rather than a 20-year maturity? (Assume all characteristics of the bonds are identical except their maturity periods.)
  d. What do we call this type of risk assumed by your corporate treasurer?

6–23. (*Marketable Securities Portfolio*) Red Raider Feedlots has $4 million in excess cash to invest in a marketable securities portfolio. Its broker will charge $10,000 to invest the entire $4 million. The president of Red Raider wants at least half of the $4 million invested at a maturity period of three months or less; the remainder can be invested in securities with maturities not to exceed six months. The relevant term structure of short-term yields follows:

Maturity Period	Available Yield (Annual)
One month	6.2%
Two months	6.4%
Three months	6.5%
Four months	6.7%
Five months	6.9%
Six months	7.0%

a. What should be the maturity periods of the securities purchased with the excess $4 million in order to maximize the before-tax income from the added investment? What will be the amount of the income from such an investment?

b. Suppose that the president of Red Raider relaxes his constraint on the maturity structure of the added investment. What would be your profit-maximizing investment recommendation?

c. If one-sixth of the excess cash is invested in each of the maturity categories shown above, what would be the before-tax income generated from such an action?

6–24. (*Comparison of After-Tax Yields*) The corporate treasurer of Aggieland Fireworks is considering the purchase of a BBB-rated bond that carries a 9 percent coupon. The BBB-rated security is taxable, and the firm is in the 46 percent marginal tax bracket. The face value of this bond is $1000. A financial analyst who reports to the corporate treasurer has alerted him to the fact that a municipal obligation is coming to the market with a 5½ percent coupon. The par value of this security is also $1000.

a. Which one of the two securities do you recommend the firm purchase? Why?

b. What must the fully taxed bond yield before tax to make it comparable with the municipal offering?

6–25. (*Comparison of Yields*) A large proportion of the marketable securities portfolio of Edwards Manufacturing is invested in Treasury bills yielding 6.52 percent before consideration of income taxes. Hoosierville Utilities is bringing a new issue of preferred stock to the marketplace. The new preferred issue will yield 9.30 percent before taxes. The corporate treasurer for Edwards wants to evaluate the possibility of shifting a portion of the funds tied up in Treasury bills to the preferred stock issue.

a. Calculate the ultimate yields available to Edwards from investing in each type of security. Edwards is in the 46 percent tax bracket.

b. What factors apart from the available yields should be analyzed in this situation?

6–26. (*Forecasting Excess Cash*) The C.K.S. Stove Company manufactures wood-burning stoves in the Pacific Northwest. Despite the recent popularity of this product, the firm has experienced a very erratic sales pattern. Owing to volatile weather conditions and abrupt changes in new housing starts, it has been extremely difficult for the firm to forecast its cash balances. Still, the company president is disturbed by the fact that the firm has never invested in any marketable securities. Instead, the liquid asset portfolio has consisted entirely of cash. As a start toward reducing the firm's investment in cash and releasing some of it to near-cash assets, a historical record and projection of corporate cash holdings is needed. Over the past five years sales have been $10 million, $12 million, $11 million, $14 million, and $19 million, respectively. Sales forecasts for the next two years are $23 and $21 million. Total assets for the firm are 60 percent of sales. Fixed assets are the higher of 50 percent of total assets or $4 million. Inventory and receivables amount to 70 percent of current assets and are held in equal proportions.

a. Prepare a worksheet that details the firm's balance sheets for each of the past five years and for the forecast periods.

b. What amount of cash will the firm have on hand during each year for short-term investment purposes?

Case Problem

California Transistor

(*Cash Management*)

Michael Broski is the assistant treasurer for California Transistor (CalTrans). He has been with the firm for nine years. The first six were spent within the technology ranks of the company as an electronics engineer. Broski, in fact, took his bachelor's degree in electronics engineering from a famous California-located university noted for its excellent faculty in all phases of engineering. After two years as a senior engineer for the organization, Broski indicated an interest in the administrative management of the firm. He spent one year as an analyst in the treasury department and has just completed his second as the assistant treasurer. During the latter three years, he has steeped himself in literature that focuses on the finance function of the corporate enterprise. In addition, he attended short courses and seminars by national management and accounting associations that dealt with most phases of the financial conduct of the firm. Within CalTrans, other cost accountants, cost analysts, financial analysts, and treasury analysts viewed Broski's rapid grasp of finance concepts as nothing short of phenomenal.

CalTrans is located on the outskirts of San Diego, California. The firm began in the middle 1950s as a small manufacturer of radio and television components. By the late 1950s, they had expanded into the actual installation and service of complete communications systems on navigable vessels. Ships from the U.S. Navy and from the tuna industry use the San Diego port facilities as a major repair yard. During the early years of the firm's activity, defense contracts typically accounted for 80 to 90 percent of annual revenues. CalTrans' management felt, however, that excessive reliance on defense contracts could lead to some very lean years with regard to business receipts. The company expanded during the 1960s into several related fields. Today CalTrans is active in the home entertainment market as well as the defense market. Transistors and integrated circuits are produced for a wide range of final products including radios, televisions, pocket calculators, citizens band receivers, stereo equipment, and ship communications systems. Defense-related business now accounts for 25 to 30 percent of the company's annual sales. This transition to a more diversified enterprise has tended to reduce the inherent "lumpiness" of cash receipts that plagues many small firms relying on defense contracts. In the early years of CalTrans' existence, progress payments on major contracts would often be months apart as the jobs moved toward completion. Currently, the firm enjoys a reasonably stable sales pattern over its fiscal year.

Broski has been studying the behavior of the company's daily and monthly net cash balances. Over the most recent 24 months, he observed that CalTrans' ending cash balance (by month) ranged between $144,000 and $205,000. Only twice during the period that he investigated had the daily closing cash balance even been as low as $100,000. Broski also noted that the firm had no outstanding short-term borrowings throughout these two years. This lead him to believe that CalTrans was carrying excessive cash balances; this was probably a tendency that had its roots in the period when defense contracts were the key revenue item for the company. This "first pass" analysis gained the attention of Donald Crawford, who is Broski's boss and CalTrans' treasurer. Crawford is 65 years old and due to retire on July 1 of this year. He has been CalTrans' only treasurer. Broski would like to move into Crawford's job upon his retirement and feels that the treasurer's recommendation might sew it up for him. He also knows that statements relating to excess cash balances being carried by the company will have to be made very tactfully and with Crawford's agreement. That bit of financial policymaking has always rested with the company treasurer. Broski decided that the best plan would be to present Crawford with a solid analysis of the problem and convince him that a reduction in balances held for transactions purposes would be in the best interests of the firm. As all key officers own considerable stock options, potential increases in corporate profitability usually are well received by management.

Earlier this year Broski attended a cash management seminar in Los Angeles, sponsored by the commercial bank with which CalTrans holds most of its deposits. The instructor spoke of the firm's cash balance as being "just another inventory." It was offered that the same principles that applied to the determination of an optimal stock of some raw material item also might be applied to the selection of an optimal average amount of transaction cash. Broski really liked that presentation. He walked away from it feeling that he could

EXHIBIT 1. **California Transistor: Fixed Costs Associated with Securities Liquidation**

Activity	Details
1. Long-distance phone calls.	Cost: $2.75
2. Assistant treasurer's time: 22 minutes	Annual salary for this position is $27,000
3. Typing of authorization letter, with three carbon copies, and careful proof-reading: 17 minutes.	Annual salary for this position is $8,000
4. Carrying original authorization letter to treasurer, who reads and signs it; 2 minutes by same secretary as above, and 2 minutes by the treasurer.	Annual salary for the treasurer is $38,000
5. Movement of authorization letter just signed by the treasurer to the controller's office, followed by the opening of a new account, recording of the transaction, and proofing of the transaction; 2 minutes by same secretary as above, 10 minutes for account opening by general accountant, and 8 minutes for recording and proofing by the same general accountant.	Annual salary for the general accountant is $12,000
6. Fringe benefits incurred on above times.	Cost: $4.42
7. Brokerage fee on each transaction.	Cost: $7.74

put it to work. He decided to adapt the basic economic order quantity model to his cash balance problem.

To make the model "workable," it is necessary to build an estimate of the fixed costs associated with adding to or subtracting from the company's inventory of cash. As CalTrans experienced no short-term borrowings within the past two years, Broski considered this element of the problem to be the fixed costs of liquidating a portion of the firm's portfolio of marketable securities.

In Exhibit 1, Broski has summarized the essential activities that occur whenever a liquidation of a part of the securities' portfolio takes place. In all of the firm's cost analysis procedures, it is assumed that a year consists of 264 working days. An eight-hour working day is also utilized in making wage and salary cost projections. Also, minutes of labor are converted into thousandths of an hour. The assistant treasurer felt that from the information in Exhibit 1, he could make a decent estimate of the fixed cost of a security transaction (addition to the firm's cash account).

CalTrans' marketable securities portfolio is usually concentrated in three major money market instruments: (1) treasury bills, (2) bankers' acceptances, and (3) prime commercial paper. A young analyst who works directly for Michael Broski supplied him with some recent rates of return on these types of securities (Exhibit 2). Broski expressed his concern to the analyst about the possibilities of high rates, such as those experienced during 1973 and 1974, continuing. His intuition or feel for the market led him to believe that short-term interest rates would be closer to 1975 levels during this next year than any other

EXHIBIT 2. **California Transistor: Selected Money Market Rates (*Annual Yields*)**

Year	Prime Commercial Paper: 90–119 Days	Bankers' Acceptances 90 Days	Three-Month Treasury Bills
1972	4.66%	4.47%	4.07%
1973	8.20	8.08	7.04
1974	10.05	9.92	7.89
1975	6.26	6.30	5.84
Simple Average	7.29	7.19	6.21

Source: *Federal Reserve Bulletin*, Board of Governors of the Federal Reserve System (January 1976), p. A 27.

levels identified in Exhibit 2. Thus, Broski decided to use a 6 percent annual yield in this study as a reasonable return to expect from his firm's marketable securities portfolio. Then a review of cash flow patterns over the last five years, including the detailed examination of the most recent 24 months, led to a projection of a typical monthly cash outflow (or demand for cash for transactions purposes) of $800,000.

QUESTIONS

1. Determine the optimal cash withdrawal size from the CalTrans marketable securities portfolio during a typical month.

2. What is the total cost (in dollars) for the use of cash held for transactions purposes during the period of analysis?

3. What will be the firm's average cash balance during a typical month?

4. Assuming that fractional cash withdrawals or orders can be made, how often will an order be placed? The firm operates continually for 30 days each month.

5. If the company's cash balance at the start of a given month is $800,000, how much of that amount would initially be invested in securities?

6. Graph the behavior pattern of the $800,000 balance (mentioned above) over a 30-day month. In constructing your graph, round off the frequency of orders to the nearest whole day, and disregard separation of the balance between cash and securities.

7. To understand the logic of the model further, provide a graph that identifies in general: (1) the total cost function of holding the cash, (2) the fixed costs associated with cash transfers, and (3) the opportunity cost of earnings forgone by holding cash balances. Use dollar amounts to label the key points on the axes as they were previously computed in questions 1 and 2. Also, identify the major assumptions of this model in a cash management setting.

Self-Test Solutions

SS–1. a. Initially, it is necessary to calculate Creative Fashions' average remittance check amount and the daily opportunity cost of carrying cash. The average check size is:

$$\frac{\$7,000,000}{4,000} = \$1,750 \text{ per check}$$

The daily opportunity cost of carrying cash is:

$$\frac{0.08}{365} = 0.0002192 \text{ per day}$$

Next, the days saved in the collection process can be evaluated according to the general format (see equation 6–1 in the text of this chapter) of:

$$\text{added costs} = \text{added benefits}$$

or

$$P = (D)(S)(i) \text{ [see equation 6–2]}$$

$$\$0.25 = (D)(\$1,750)(.0002192)$$

$$0.6517 \text{ days} = D$$

Creative Fashion Designs therefore will experience a financial gain if it implements the lock-box system and by doing so will speed up its collections by more than 0.6517 days.

b. Here the daily opportunity cost of carrying cash is:

$$\frac{0.055}{365} = 0.0001507 \text{ per day}$$

For Creative Fashion Designs to break even, should it choose to install the lock-box system, cash collections must be accelerated by 0.9480 days, as follows:

$$\$0.25 = (D)(\$1,750)(.0001507)$$

$$0.9480 \text{ days} = D$$

c. The breakeven cash acceleration period of 0.9480 days is greater than the 0.6517 days found in part (a). This is due to the lower yield available on near-cash assets of 5.5 percent annually, versus 8.0 percent. Since the alternative rate of return on the freed-up balances is lower in the second situation, more funds must be invested to cover the costs of operating the lock-box system. The greater cash acceleration period generates this increased level of required funds.

SS–2. **a.** Reduction in mail float:

$$(2.0 \text{ days})(\$200,000) = \$400.000$$

+ reduction in processing float:

$$(2.5 \text{ days})(\$200,000) = \underline{500,000}$$

$$= \text{total float reduction} = \underline{\underline{\$900,000}}$$

b. The opportunity cost of maintaining the present banking arrangement is:

$$\left(\begin{array}{l}\text{forecast yield on marketable} \\ \text{securities portfolio}\end{array}\right) \cdot \left(\begin{array}{l}\text{total float} \\ \text{reduction}\end{array}\right)$$

$$(.106)(\$900,000) = \underline{\underline{\$95,400}}$$

c. The average number of checks to be processed each day through the lock-box arrangement is:

$$\frac{\text{daily remittances}}{\text{average check size}} = \frac{\$200,000}{\$800} = 250 \text{ checks per day}$$

The resulting cost of the lock-box system on an annual basis is:

$$(250 \text{ checks})(\$0.25)(270 \text{ days}) = \$16,875$$

Next, we must calculate the estimated cost of the automated depository transfer check (ADTC) system. Detroit National Bank will *not* contribute to the cost of the ADTC arrangement because it is the lead concentration bank and thereby receives the transferred data. This means that Artie Kay's Komputer Shops will be charged for six ADTCs (three locations @ 2 checks each) each business day. Therefore, the ADTC system costs:

$$(6 \text{ daily transfers})(\$20 \text{ per transfer})(270 \text{ days}) = \$32,400$$

We now have the total cost of the proposed system:

Lock-box cost	$16,875
ADTC cost	32,400
Total cost	$49,275

d. Our analysis suggests that Artie Kay's Komputer Shops should adopt the proposed cash receipts acceleration system. The projected net annual gain is $46,125 as follows:

Projected return on freed balances	$95,400
Less: Total cost of new system	49,275
Net annual gain	$46,125

SS-3. **a.** Here we must calculate the dollar value of the estimated return for each holding period and compare it with the transactions fee to determine if a gain can be made by investing in the securities. Those calculations and the resultant recommendations follow:

		Recommendation
1.	$2,000,000 (.12) (1/12) = $20,000 < $45,000	No
2.	$2,000,000 (.12) (2/12) = $40,000 < $45,000	No
3.	$2,000,000 (.12) (3/12) = $60,000 > $45,000	Yes
4.	$2,000,000 (.12) (6/12) = $120,000 > $45,000	Yes
5.	$2,000,000 (.12) (12/12) = $240,000 > $45,000	Yes

b. Let (%) be the required yield. With $2 million to invest for three months we have:

$$\$200{,}000\,(\%)\,(3/12) \;=\; \$\ 45{,}000$$
$$\$200{,}000\,(\%) \qquad\quad =\; \$180{,}000$$
$$\$200{,}000\,(\%) \qquad\quad =\; \$180{,}000/2{,}000{,}000 = 9\%$$

The breakeven yield, therefore, is 9%.

Selected References

An Analytical Record of Yields and Yield Spreads. New York: Salomon Brothers, 1977.

Anderson, Paul F., and R. D. Boyd Harman. "The Management of Excess Corporate Cash," *Financial Executive*, 32 (October 1964), 26–30, 51.

Andrews, Horace, and Devdatt Shah. "Managing Short-Term Assets for Long-Term Growth," *FE*, 53 (March 1985), 54–56. (Note: *FE* was formerly titled *Financial Executive*)

Archer, Stephen H. "A Model for the Determination of Firm Cash Balances," *Journal of Financial and Quantitative Analysis*, 1 (March 1966), 1–11.

Arnold, Jasper H. "Banker's Acceptance: A Low-Cost Financing Choice," *Financial Executive*, 48 (July 1980), 14–19.

Arthur, William J. "Cash Flow Yardstick: Here's One Way To Make the Cash Flow Statement More Useful," *FE*, 54 (October 1986), 35–40.

Bacon, Peter W., and Richard E. Williams. "Interest Rate Futures: New Tool for the Financial Manager," *Financial Management*, 5 (Spring 1976), 32–38.

Barter, Brit J., and Richard J. Rendelman, Jr. "Fee-Based Pricing of Fixed Rate Bank Loan Commitments," *Financial Management*, 8 (Spring 1979), 13–20.

Batlin, C. A., and Susan Hinko. "Lockbox Management and Value Maximization," *Financial Management*, 10 (Winter 1981), 39–44.

Baumol, William J. "The Transactions Demand for Cash: An Inventory Theoretic Approach," *Quarterly Journal of Economics*, 65 (November 1952), 545–56.

Bennett, Barbara. "Standby Letters of Credit," Federal Reserve Bank of San Francisco, *Weekly Letter* (May 23, 1986), 1–3.

Bonocore, Joseph J. "Getting a Picture of Cash Management," *Financial Executive*, 48 (May 1980), 30–33.

Budin, Morris, and Robert J. Van Handel. "A Rule-of-

Thumb Theory of Cash Holdings by Firms," *Journal of Financial and Quantitative Analysis*, 10 (March 1975), 85–108.

Carraro, Kenneth C., and Daniel L. Thornton. "The Cost of Checkable Deposits in the United States," Federal Reserve Bank of St. Louis, *Review*, 68 (April 1986), 19–27.

Campbell, Tim, and Leland Brendsel. "The Impact of Compensating Balance Requirements on the Cash Balances of Manufacturing Corporations: An Empirical Study," *Journal of Finance*, 32 (March 1977), 31–40.

"Cash Management: The New Art of Wringing More Profit from Corporate Funds," *Business Week*, March 13, 1978, pp. 62–68.

Collins, J. Markham, and Alan W. Frankle. "International Cash Practices of Large U.S. Firms," *Journal of Cash Management*, 5 (July–August 1985), 42–48.

Cook, Timothy Q., and T. D. Rowe, eds. *Instruments of the Money Market* (6th ed.). Richmond, VA: Federal Reserve Bank of Richmond, 1986.

Daellenbach, Hans G. "Are Cash Management Optimization Models Worthwhile?" *Journal of Financial and Quantitative Analysis*, 9 (September 1974), 607–26.

Desalvo, Alfred. "Cash Management Converts Dollars into Working Assets," *Harvard Business Review*, 50 (May–June 1972), 92–100.

Emery, Gary W. "Some Empirical Evidence on the Properties of Daily Cash Flow," *Financial Management*, 10 (Spring 1981), 21–28.

Ferguson, Daniel M. "Optimize Your Firm's Lockbox Selection System," *Financial Executive*, 51 (April 1983), 8–12, 14–15, 18–19.

Ferri, Michael G., and H. Dennis Oberhelman. "A Study of the Management of Money Market Mutual Funds, 1975–1980," *Financial Management*, 10 (Autumn 1981), 24–29.

Gitman, Lawrence J., D. Keith Forrester, and John R. Forrester, Jr. "Maximizing Cash Disbursement Float," *Financial Management*, 5 (Summer 1976), 15–24.

Gitman, Lawrence J., and Mark D. Goodwin. "An Assessment of Marketable Securities Management Practices," *Journal of Financial Research*, 2 (Fall 1979), 161–69.

Gootar, Selvin. "The Electronic State of Cash Management," *FE*, 54 (November 1986), 10–15.

Joehnk, Michael D., Oswald D. Bowlin, and J. William Petty II. "Preferred Dividend Rolls: A Viable Strategy For Corporate Money Managers?" *Financial Management*, 9 (Summer 1980), 78–87.

Johnson, James M., David R. Campbell, and Leonard M. Savoie. "Corporate Liquidity: A Comparison of Two Recessions," *Financial Executive*, 51 (October 1983), 18–22.

Jones, Reginald H. "Face to Face with Cash Management: How One Company Does it," *Financial Executive*, 37 (September 1969), 37–39.

Kaplan, Steve. "Cash Management Coordination of Purchasing," *Journal of Cash Management*, 6 (January–February 1986), 25–28.

"Lock Box Banking—Key to Faster Collections," *Credit and Financial Management*, 69 (June 1967), 16–21.

Lordan, James F. "A Profile of Corporate Cash Management," *Magazine of Bank Administration*, 48 (April 1972), 15–19.

Maier, Steven F., and Larry A. Meeks. "Applications and Models: When Is the Right Time to Do a Lockbox Study?" *Journal of Cash Management*, 6 (March–April 1986), 32–34.

Maier, Steven F., David W. Robinson, and James H. Vander Weide. "A Short-Term Disbursement Forecasting Model," *Financial Management*, 10 (Spring 1981), 9–20.

Maier, Steven F., and James H. Vander Weide. "A Practical Approach to Short-Run Financial Planning," *Financial Management*, 7 (Winter 1978), 10–16.

————. "What Lockbox and Disbursement Models Really Do," *Journal of Finance*, 38 (May 1983), 361–71.

McConoughey, Deborah J. "Breakeven Analysis for Maturity Decisions in Cash Management," *Journal of Cash Management*, 5 (January–February 1985), 18–21.

Meltzer, Yale L. *Putting Money to Work: An Investment Primer*. Englewood Cliffs, NJ: Prentice-Hall, 1976.

Miller, Merton H., and Daniel Orr. "A Model of the Demand for Money by Firms," *Quarterly Journal of Economics*, 80 (August 1966), 413–35.

————. "The Demand for Money by Firms: Extension of Analytic Results," *Journal of Finance*, 23 (December 1968), 735–59.

Miller, Tom W., and Bernell K. Stone. "Daily Cash Forecasting and Seasonal Resolution: Alternative Models and Techniques for Using the Distribution Approach," *Journal of Financial and Quantitative Analysis*, 20 (September 1985), 335–51.

Myers, Stewart C., *Modern Developments in Financial Management*, Part 4. New York: Praeger, 1976.

Nauss, Robert M., and Robert E. Markland. "Solving Lock Box Location Problems," *Financial Management*, 8 (Spring 1979), 21–27.

Orgler, Yair E. *Cash Management*. Belmont, Calif.: Wadsworth, 1970.

Perkins, Daniel M. "Borrowing Strategies in Foreign Currencies," *Journal of Cash Management*, 6 (March–April 1986), 26–30.

Richards, Verlyn D., and Eugene J. Laughlin. "A Cash Conversion Cycle Approach to Liquidity Analysis," *Financial Management*, 9 (Spring 1980), 32–38.

Rinne, Heikki, Robert A. Wood, and Ned C. Hill. "Reducing Cash Concentration Costs by Anticipatory Forecasting," *Journal of Cash Management*, 6 (March–April 1986), 44–50.

Sartoris, William L., and Ned C. Hill. "A Generalized Cash Flow Approach to Short-Term Financial Decisions," *Journal of Finance*, 38 (May 1983), 349–60.

Scott, David F., Jr., Laurence J. Moore, Andre Saint-Denis, Edouard Archer, and Bernard W. Taylor III. "Implementation of a Cash Budget Simulator at Air Canada," *Financial Management*, 8 (Summer 1979), 46–52.

Searby, Frederick W. "Use Your Hidden Cash Resources," *Harvard Business Review*, 46 (March–April 1968), 71–80.

Senchack, Andrew J., and Don M. Heep. "Auction Profits in the Treasury Bill Market," *Financial Management*, 4 (Summer 1975), 45–52.

Shim, Jae K. "Estimating Cash Collection Rates from Credit Sales: A Lagged Regression Approach," *Financial Management*, 10 (Winter 1981), 28–30.

Smith, Keith V. *Management of Working Capital: A Reader*, Sec. 2. St. Paul, Minn.: West Publishing, 1974.

Stone, Bernell K. "Cash Planning and Credit-Line Determination with a Financial Statement Simulator: A Case Report on Short-Term Financial Planning," *Journal of Financial and Quantitative Analysis*, 8 (November 1973), 711–30.

———, and Ned C. Hill. "Cash Transfer Scheduling for Efficient Cash Concentration," *Financial Management*, 9 (Autumn 1980), 35–43.

———, and Robert A. Wood. "Daily Cash Forecasting: A Simple Method for Implementing the Distribution Approach," *Financial Management*, 6 (Fall 1977), 40–50.

Stone, Bernell K. "Corporate Trade Payments: Hard Lessons in Product Design," Federal Reserve Bank of Atlanta, *Economic Review*, 71 (April 1986), 9–21.

Syron, Richard, and Sheila L. Tschinkel. "The Government Securities Market: Playing Field for Repos," Federal Reserve Bank of Atlanta, *Economic Review*, 70 (September 1985), 10–19.

Vickson, R. G. "Simple Optimal Policy for Cash Management: The Average Balanced Requirement Case," *Journal of Financial and Quantitative Analysis*, 20 (September 1985), 353–369.

Weisse, Peter D. "Interest-Free Capital: A Quick Way To Increase Capital Is Through Your Accounts Receivable," *FE*, 54 (October 1986), 41–42.

APPENDIX 6A
Cash Management Models:
The Split between Cash and Near Cash

In this appendix we continue our discussion of the management of the firm's cash position. We have dwelled upon the overall objectives of company cash management, described some actual liquid asset holdings of selected industries and firms, and overviewed a wide array of cash collection and disbursement procedures.

We now consider the problem of properly dividing the firm's liquid asset holdings between cash and near cash.

LIQUID ASSETS: CASH VERSUS MARKETABLE SECURITIES

Through use of the cash-budgeting procedures outlined in Chapter 4, the financial manager can pinpoint time periods when funds will be in either short or excess supply. If a shortage of funds is expected, then alternative avenues of financing must be explored. On the other hand, the cash budget projections might indicate that large, positive net cash balances in excess of immediate transactions needs will be forthcoming. In this more pleasant situation the financial manager ought to decide on the proper split of the expected cash balances between actual cash holdings and marketable securities. To hold all of the expected cash balances as actual balances would needlessly penalize the firm's profitability.

The ensuing discussion centers on various methods by which the financial manager can develop useful cash balance level benchmarks.

Benchmark 1: When Cash Need Is Certain

A basic method for indicating the proper **average** amount of cash to have on hand involves use of the economic order quantity concept so familiar in discussions of inventory management (Chapter 7).[1] The objective of this analysis is to balance the lost income that the firm suffers from holding cash rather than marketable securities against the transactions costs involved in converting securities into cash. The rudiments of this decision model can easily be introduced by the use of an illustration.

Suppose that the firm knows with certainty that it will need $250,000 in cash for transactions purposes over the next two months and that this much cash is currently available. This transactions demand for cash will be represented by the variable T. Let us assume, for purposes of this illustration, that when the firm requires cash for its transactions needs it will sell marketable securities in any one of five lot sizes, ranging from $30,000 to $70,000. These cash conversion (order) sizes, C, are identified in line 1 of Table 6A–1.

Line 2 shows the number of times marketable securities will be turned into cash over the next two months if a particular order size is utilized. For example, should it be decided to liquidate securities in amounts of $40,000, then the number of cash conversions needed to meet transactions over the next two months is $250,000/\$40,000 = 6.25$. In general, the number of cash withdrawals from the near-cash portfolio can be represented as T/C.

Next, we assume that the firm's cash payments are of constant amounts and are made

---

[1] The roots of a quantitative treatment of the firm's cash balance as just another type of inventory are found in William J. Baumol, "The Transactions Demand for Cash: An Inventory Theoretic Approach," *Quarterly Journal of Economics*, 66 (November 1952), 545–56.

TABLE 6A–1. Determination of the Optimal Cash Order Size

1. Cash conversion size (the dollar amount of marketable securities that will be sold to replenish the cash balance)	$30,000	$40,000	$50,000	$60,000	$70,000
2. Number of cash orders per time period (the time period is two months in this example) ($250,000 ÷ line 1)	8.33	6.25	5.00	4.17	3.57
3. Average cash balance (line 1 ÷ 2)	$15,000	$20,000	$25,000	$30,000	$35,000
4. Interest income forgone (line 3 × .01)	$150.00	$200.00	$250.00	$300.00	$350.00
5. Cash conversion cost ($50 × line 2)	$416.50	$312.50	$250.00	$208.50	$178.50
6. Total cost of ordering and holding cash (line 4 + line 5)	$566.50	$512.50	$500.00	$508.50	$528.50

continually over the two-month planning period. This implies that the firm's cash balance behaves in the sawtooth manner shown in Figure 6A–1. The assertion of regularity and constancy of payments allows the firm's average cash balance over the planning period to be measured as $C/2$ (see Figure 6A–1). When marketable securities are sold and cash flows into the demand deposit account, the cash balance is equal to C. As payments are made on a regular and constant basis, the cash balance is reduced to a level of zero. The average cash balance over the period is then

$$\frac{C+0}{2} = \frac{C}{2}$$

The average cash balances corresponding to the different cash conversion sizes in our example are noted in line 3 of Table 6A–1.

Line 4 measures the opportunity cost of earnings forgone based upon holding the average cash balance recorded on line 3. If the *annual* yield available on marketable securities is 6 percent, then over the *two-month period* we are analyzing, the forfeited interest rate is

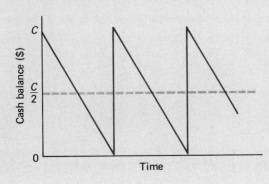

FIGURE 6A–1. Cash Balances According to the Inventory Model

$.06/6 = .01.$[2] Multiplying each average cash balance, $C/2$, by the .01 interest rate, i, available over the two-month period produces the opportunity costs entered on line 4.

The very act of liquidating securities, unfortunately, is not costless. Transacting conversions of marketable securities into cash can involve any of the following activities, which require the time of company employees as well as direct payment by the firm for various services:

1. Assistant treasurer's time to order the trade
2. Long-distance phone calls to effect the trade
3. Secretarial time to type authorization letters, make copies of the letters, and forward the letters to the company treasurer
4. Treasurer's time to read, approve, and sign the documents that authorize the trade
5. General accountant's time to record and audit the transaction
6. The value of fringe benefits incurred on the above times
7. The brokerage fee on each transaction

Suppose that the firm has properly studied the transaction costs, similar to those enumerated above, and finds they are of a fixed amount, b, per trade equal to $50. The transaction cost variable, b, is taken to be independent of the size of a particular securities order. Multiplying the transaction cost of $50 per trade by the number of cash orders that will take place during the planning period produces line 5. In general, the cash conversion cost (transaction cost) is equal to $b(T/C)$.

We are now down to the last line in Table 6A–1. This is the sum total of the income lost by holding cash rather than marketable securities and the cash-ordering costs. Line 6, then, is the total of lines 4 and 5. The inventory model seeks to *minimize* these *total costs* associated with holding cash balances. Table 6A–1 tells us, if cash is ordered on five occasions in $50,000 sizes over the two-month period, the total costs of holding an average cash balance of $25,000 will be $500. This is less than the total costs associated with any other cash conversion size.

At the beginning of the two-month planning horizon, all of the $250,000 available for transactions purposes need not be held in the firm's demand deposit account. To minimize the total costs of holding cash, only $50,000 should immediately be retained to transact business. The remaining $200,000 should be invested in income-yielding securities and then turned into cash as the firm's disbursal needs dictate.

It is useful to put our discussion of the inventory model for cash management into a more general form. Summarizing the definitions developed in the illustration, we have

C = The amount per order of marketable securities to be converted into cash,

i = the interest rate per period available on investments in marketable securities,

b = the fixed cost per order of converting marketable securities into cash,

T = the total cash requirements over the planning period,

TC = the total costs associated with maintenance of a particular average cash balance.

As just pointed out, the total costs (TC) of having cash on hand can be expressed as

---

[2] If we were studying a *one-month* planning period, rather than the two-month period being discussed, the annual yield would have to be stated on a monthly basis or $.06/12 = .005$.

$$TC = i\left(\frac{C}{2}\right) + b\left(\frac{T}{C}\right) \qquad (6A\text{--}1)$$

$$\underset{\substack{\text{total} \\ \text{interest} \\ \text{income} \\ \text{forgone}}}{} \qquad \underset{\substack{\text{total} \\ \text{ordering} \\ \text{costs}}}{}$$

If equation (6A–1) is applied to the \$50,000 cash conversion size column in Table 6A–1, the total costs can be computed in a direct fashion as follows:

$$TC = .01\left(\frac{\$50,000}{2}\right) + 50\left(\frac{\$250,000}{\$50,000}\right)$$

$$= \$250 + \$250 = \$500$$

You can see that the \$500 total cost is the same as was found deductively in Table 6A–1. The optimal cash conversion size, C^*, can be found by use of equation (6A–2):

$$C^* = \sqrt{\frac{2bT}{i}} \qquad (6A\text{--}2)$$

When the data in our example are applied to equation (6A–2), the optimal cash order size is found to be

$$C^* = \sqrt{\frac{2(50)(250,000)}{.01}} = \$50,000$$

This solution to our example problem is displayed graphically in Figure 6A–2. Notice that the optimal cash order size of \$50,000 occurs at the minimum point of the total cost curve associated with keeping cash on hand.

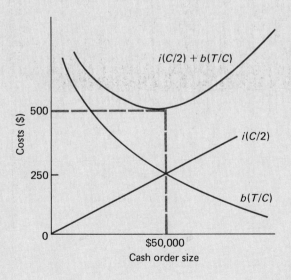

FIGURE 6A–2. Solution to the Inventory Model for Cash Management

The solution to equation (6A–2) tells the financial manager that the optimal cash order size, C^*, varies directly with the square root of the order costs, bT, and inversely with the yield, i, available on marketable securities. Notice that as transactions requirements, T, increase, owing perhaps to an augmented sales demand, the optimal cash order size does *not* rise proportionately.

The model also indicates that as interest rates rise on near-cash investments, the optimal cash order size decreases, with the effect dampened by the square-root sign as equation (6A–2) suggests. With higher yields to be earned on the marketable securities portfolio the financial manager will be more reluctant to make large withdrawals because of the interest income that will be lost.

Some final perspectives on the use of the economic order quantity model in cash management can be obtained by reviewing the assumptions upon which it is derived. Among the more important of these assumptions are the following:

1. Cash payments over the planning period are (a) of a regular amount, (b) continuous, and (c) certain.
2. No unanticipated cash receipts will be received during the analysis period.
3. The interest rate to be earned on investments remains constant over the analysis period.
4. Transfers between cash and the securities portfolio may take place at any time at a cost that is fixed, regardless of the amount to be transferred.

Clearly, the strict assumptions of the inventory model will not be completely realized in actual business practice. For instance, the amount and timing of cash payments will not be known with certainty; nor are cash receipts likely to be as discontinuous or lumpy as is implied. If relaxation of the critical assumptions is not so prohibitive as to render the model useless, than a benchmark for possible managerial action is provided. The model's output is not intended to be a precise and inviolable rule. On the other hand, if the assumptions of the model cannot be reasonably approximated, the financial manager must look elsewhere for possible guides that indicate a proper split between cash and marketable securities.

**Benchmark 2:
When Cash
Balances
Fluctuate
Randomly**

It is entirely possible that the firm's cash balance pattern does *not* at all resemble that indicated in Figure 6A–1. The assumptions of certain regularity and constancy of cash payments may be unduly restrictive when applied to some organizations.[3] Rather, the cash balance might behave more like the jagged line shown in Figure 6A–3. In this figure it is assumed that the firm's cash balance changes in an irregular fashion from day to day. The changes are unpredictable; that is, they are *random*. Further, let us suppose the chances that a cash balance change will be either (1) positive or (2) negative are equal at .5 each.

As cash receipts exceed expenditures, the cash balance will move upward until it hits an upper control limit, *UL*, expressed in dollars. This occurs at point *A* in Figure 6A–3. At such time, the financial officer will initiate an investment in marketable securities equal to *UL* − *RP* dollars, where *RP* is the cash return point.

If cash payments exceed receipts, the cash balance will move downward until it hits a lower control limit, *LL*. This situation is noted by point *B* in Figure 6A–3. When this occurs, the financial officer will sell marketable securities equal to *RP* − *LL* dollars. This will restore the cash balance to the return point, *RP*.

---

[3] This discussion is based upon Merton H. Miller and Daniel Orr, "A Model of the Demand for Money by Firms," *Quarterly Journal of Economics*, 80 (August 1966), 413–35.

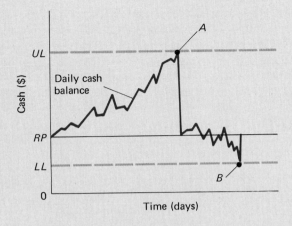

FIGURE 6A–3. Randomly
Fluctuating Cash Balances

To make this application of control theory to cash management operational, we must determine the upper control limit, *UL*, the lower control limit, *LL*, and the cash return point, *RP*. For the present case where a net cash increase is as likely to occur as a net cash decrease, use of the following variables will allow computation of the cash return point, *RP*.[4]

b = the fixed cost per order of converting marketable securities into cash

i = the daily interest rate available on investments in marketable securities

σ^2 = the variance of daily changes in the firm's expected cash balances (this is a measure of volatility of cash flow changes over time)

The optimal cash return point, *RP*, can be calculated as follows:

$$RP = \sqrt[3]{\frac{3b\sigma^2}{4i}} + LL \qquad (6A-3)$$

The upper control limit, *UL*, can be computed quite simply:

$$UL = 3RP - 2LL \qquad (6A-4)$$

The actual value for the lower limit, *LL*, is set by management. In business practice a minimum is typically established below which the cash balance is not permitted to fall. Among other things, it will be affected by (1) the firm's banking arrangements, which may require compensating balances, and (2) management's risk-bearing tendencies.

To illustrate use of the model, suppose that the annual yield available on marketable securities is 9 percent. Over a 360-day year, i becomes .09/360 = .00025 per day. Assume that the fixed cost, b, of transacting a marketable securities trade is $50. Moreover, the firm has studied its past cash balance levels and has observed that the standard deviation,

---

[4] Situations where the probabilities of cash increases and decreases are not equal are extremely difficult to evaluate within the framework of the Miller-Orr decision model. See Miller and Orr, "A Model of the Demand for Money by Firms," 427–29, 433–35.

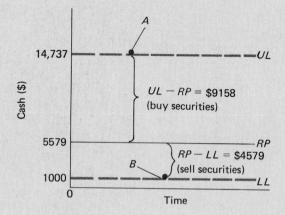

FIGURE 6A–4. Control Limit Model

σ, in daily cash balance changes is equal to $800. The firm sees no reason why this variability should change in the future. It is the firm's policy to maintain $1000 in its demand deposit account (*LL*) at all times. Finally, the firm has established that each day's actual cash balance is random. The equations that comprise this control limit system can be applied to provide guidelines for cash management policy.

The optimal cash return point for transactions purposes becomes

$$RP = \sqrt[3]{\frac{3(50)(800)^2}{4(.00025)}} + 1000 = (4579 + 1000) = \$5579$$

The upper cash balance limit that will trigger a transfer of cash to marketable securities is

$$UL = 3(5579) - 2(1000) = \$14,737$$

The cash balance control limits derived from this example are graphed in Figure 6A–4. Should the cash balance bump against the upper limit of $14,737 (point *A*), then the financial officer is instructed to buy $9158 of marketable securities. At the other extreme, if the cash balance should drop to the lower limit of $1000 (point *B*), then the financial officer is instructed to sell $4579 of marketable securities to restore the cash balance level to $5579. As long as the cash balance wanders within the *UL* to *LL* range, no securities transactions take place. By acting in this manner, the financial officer will *minimize* the sum of interest income forgone and the costs of purchasing and selling securities.[5]

Control Limit Model Implications

Use of equation (6A–3) results in determination of the optimal cash return point within the framework of the control limit model. Inspection of this equation indicates to the financial officer that the optimal cash return level, *RP*, will vary directly with the cube root of both the transfer cost variable, *b*, and the volatility of daily cash balance changes, σ^2. Greater transfer costs or cash balance volatility result in a greater *absolute* dollar spread between the upper control limit and the cash return point. This larger spread between *UL* and *RP*

---

[5] As with the Baumol inventory model, the Miller-Orr control limit model seeks to minimize the total cost of managing the firm's cash balance over a finite planning horizon.

means that securities purchases will be effected in larger lot sizes. It is further evident that the optimal cash return point varies inversely with the cube root of the lost interest rate.

Similar to the basic inventory model reviewed in the previous section, the control limit model implies that economies of scale are possible in cash management. In addition, the optimal cash return point always lies well below the midpoint of the range, UL to LL, over which the cash balance is permitted to "walk." This means that the liquidation of marketable securities will occur (1) more frequently and (2) in smaller lot sizes than purchases of securities. This suggests that firms with highly volatile cash balances must be acutely concerned with the liquidity of their marketable securities portfolio.

Benchmark 3: Compensating Balances

An important element of the commercial banking environment that affects corporate cash management deserves special mention. This is the practice of the bank's requiring, either formally or informally, that the firm maintain deposits of a given amount in its demand deposit account. Such balances are referred to as **compensating balances.**

The compensating balance requirement became typical banking practice after federal action forbade the payment of interest on demand deposits in the early 1930s.[6] In the face of prospective withdrawals the procedure allowed banks to maintain favorable levels of their basic raw material—deposits. Such balances are normally required of corporate customers in three situations: (1) where the firm has an established line of credit (loan commitment) at the bank, but it is not entirely used; (2) where the firm has a loan outstanding at the bank; and, or (3) in exchange for various other services provided by the bank to its customer.

As you would expect, compensating balance policies vary among commercial banks and, furthermore, are influenced by general conditions in the financial markets. Still, some tendencies can be identified. In the case of the unused portion of a loan commitment, the bank might require that the firm's demand deposits average anywhere from 5 to 10 percent of the commitment. If a loan is currently outstanding with the bank, the requirement will probably be 10 to 20 percent of the unpaid balance. During periods when monetary policy is restrictive, so-called tight money periods, the ranges just mentioned rise by about 5 percent across the board.[7]

Instead of charging directly for certain banking services, the bank may ask the firm to "pay" for them by the compensating balance approach. These services include check clearing, the availability of credit information, and any of the array of receipts acceleration or payment control techniques that we discussed in Chapter 6.

If the bank asks for compensation in the form of balances left on deposit rather than charging unit prices for services rendered, the requirement may be expressed as (1) an absolute amount or (2) an average amount. The latter is preferable to most firms, as it provides for some flexibility in use of the deposits. With the average balance requirement being calculated over a month, and in some instances as long as a year, the balance can be low on occasion as long as it is offset with heavy balances in other time periods.

---

[6] Paul S. Nadler, "Compensating Balances and the Prime at Twilight," *Harvard Business Review*, 50 (January–February 1972), 112.

[7] See Howard D. Crosse and George H. Hempel, *Management Policies for Commercial Banks*, 2nd ed. (Englewood Cliffs, NJ: Prentice-Hall, 1973), pp. 200–202; and E. E. Reed, R. V. Cotter, E. K. Gill, and R. Smith, *Commercial Banking*, 2nd ed. (Englewood Cliffs, NJ: Prentice-Hall, 1980), 246–47.

In the analysis that the financial officer undertakes to determine the split between cash and near cash, explicit consideration must be given to compensating balance requirements. This information can be used in conjunction with the basic inventory model (benchmark 1) or the control limit model (benchmark 2).

One approach is to use either of the models, and in the calculations ignore the compensating balance requirement. This is logical in many instances. Generally, the compensating balance required by the bank is beyond the firm's control.

In using the models, then, the focus is on the discretionary cash holdings above the required levels. Once the solution to the particular model is found, the firm's optimal average cash balance will be the *higher* of that suggested by the model or the balance requirement set by the bank.

A second approach is to introduce the size of the compensating balance into the format of the cash management model and carry out the requisite calculations. We noted previously that in the control limit model, the lower control limit (*LL*) could be the compensating balance requirement faced by the firm as opposed to a value of zero for *LL*. In the basic inventory model the compensating balance can be treated as a safety stock. In Figure 6A–1, then, the cash balance would not touch the zero level and trigger a marketable securities purchase; rather, it would fall to the level of the compensating balance (some amount greater than zero) and initiate the securities purchase. Under ordinary circumstances, in neither model is the calculated optimal order size of marketable securities altered by consideration of compensating balances, so useful information on the proper split between near cash and discretionary cash (cash held in excess of compensating balances) is still provided by these two benchmarks.

Recent trends indicate that compensating balances are slowly giving way to unit pricing of bank services. Under unit pricing, the bank quotes a stated price for the service. The firm pays that rate only for the services actually used. Such a trend means that the importance of this third benchmark may diminish in the foreseeable future. At the same time, the policies suggested by application of cash management models, similar to those just presented, may well attract attention.

Study Problems

6A–1. (*The Inventory Model*) The Richard Price Metal Working Company will experience $800,000 in cash payments next month. The annual yield available on marketable securities is 6.5 percent. The company has analyzed the cost of obtaining or investing cash and found it to be equal to $85 per transaction. Since cash outlays for Price Metal Working occur at a constant rate over any given month, the company has decided to apply the principles of the inventory model for cash management to provide answers to several questions.

    a. What is the optimal cash conversion size for the Price Metal Working Company?

    b. What is the total cost of having cash on hand during the coming month?

    c. How often (in days) will the firm have to make a cash conversion? Assume a 30-day month.

    d. What will be Price Metal Working's average cash balance?

6A–2. (*The Control Limit Model*) The Edinboro Fabric Company manufactures 18 different final products, which are woven, cut, and dyed for use primarily in the clothing industry. Owing to the whimsical nature of the underlying demand for certain clothing styles, Edinboro Fabric has a most difficult time forecasting its cash balance levels. The company maintains $2000 in its demand deposit account at all times. A detailed study of past cash balance levels has revealed that the standard deviation, σ, in daily cash balance changes has been equal to $600. The nature of the firm is not expected to undergo any structural changes in the foreseeable future, and for this reason the past volatility in cash balance levels is expected to continue in the future. Edinboro has determined that the cost of transacting a marketable securities trade is $85. Marketable securities are yielding 6 percent per annum. The firm always uses a 360-day year in its analysis procedures. Robert Cambridge, Edinboro's treasurer, has just returned from a three-day cash management seminar in New York City. He has decided to apply the control limit model for cash management to his firm's situation.

a. What is the optimal cash return point for Edinboro?
b. What is the upper control limit?
c. In what lot sizes will marketable securities be purchased? Sold?
d. Graph your results.

7

Accounts Receivable and Inventory Management

In the two previous chapters we developed a general overview of working capital management and took an in-depth look at the management of cash and marketable securities. In this chapter we will focus on the management of two more working capital items, accounts receivable and inventory. Much of our concern with accounts receivable and inventory is derived from the fact that they make up a large portion of the firm's assets; they actually compose 26.25 and 5.88 percent, respectively, of a typical firm's assets. Thus, because of their sheer magnitude any changes in their levels will affect profitability. For example, an increase in accounts receivable—that is, additional extension of trade credit—not only results in higher sales, but also requires additional financing to support the increased investment in accounts receivable. The costs of credit investigation and collection efforts and the chance of bad debts also are increased. With respect to inventory management, a larger investment in inventory leads to more efficient production and speedier delivery, hence increased sales. However, additional financing is required to support the increase in inventory and in handling and carrying costs.

In studying the management of these current assets, we will first examine accounts receivable management, focusing on its importance, what determines the investment in it, and what the decision variables are and how we determine them. After examining accounts receivable management, we will turn to inventory management and examine its importance and the order quantity and order point problems, which in combination determine the level of investment in inventory.

ACCOUNTS RECEIVABLE MANAGEMENT

All firms by their very nature are involved in selling either goods or services. While some of these sales will be for cash, a large portion will involve credit. Whenever a sale is made on credit, it increases the firm's accounts receivable. Thus, the importance of accounts receivable management depends upon the degree to which the firm sells on credit. Table 7–1 lists, for selected industries, the percentage of total assets made up by accounts receivable.

From Table 7–1 we can see that accounts receivable typically comprise over 25 percent of a firm's assets. In effect, when we discuss management of accounts receivable, we are discussing the management of one-quarter of the firm's assets. Moreover, since cash flows from a sale cannot be invested until the account is collected, control of receivables takes on added importance; efficient collection determines both profitability and liquidity of the firm.

Size of Investment in Accounts Receivable

The size of the investment in accounts receivable is determined by a number of factors. First, the percentage of credit sales to total sales affects the level of accounts receivable held. Although this factor certainly plays a major role in determining the investment in accounts receivable, it generally is not within the control of the financial manager. In essence, the nature of the business tends to determine the blend between credit sales and cash sales. For a large grocery store, sales tend to be made exclusively on a cash basis, while for most construction-lumber supply firms, sales are primarily credit. Thus, the nature of the business, and not the decisions of the financial manager, tends to determine the proportion of credit sales.

The level of sales is also a factor in determining the size of the investment in accounts receivable. Very simply, the more sales, the greater will be accounts receivable. As the firm experiences seasonal and permanent growth in sales, the level of investment in accounts receivable will naturally increase. Thus, while the level of sales affects

TABLE 7–1. Accounts Receivable as a Percentage of Total Assets for Major Industries

Industry	Accounts Receivable Relative to Total Assets
All industries	26.25%
Motor vehicles and equipment— manufacturing	52.32
General merchandising stores—retail	35.16
Total construction	24.90
Building materials, garden supplies, and mobile home dealers—retail	21.46
Automotive dealers and service stations—retail	14.45
Transportation	13.95
Apparel and accessory stores—retail	13.81
Food stores	8.89
Agricultural, forestry, and fishing	8.82
Hotels and other lodging places	7.44

Source: Internal Revenue Service, U.S. Treasury Department, *Statistics of Income, 1983, Corporate Income Tax Returns* (Washington, D.C.: Govenrment Printing Office, 1986), pp. 1–294.

the size of the investment in accounts receivable, it is not a decision variable for the financial manager.

The final determinants of the level of investment in accounts receivable are the credit and collection policies—more specifically, the terms of sale, the quality of customer, and collection efforts. The terms of sale specify both the time period during which the customer must pay and the terms; that is, is there a discount for paying early, and if so, how much? The type of customer or credit policy also affects the level of investment in accounts receivable. For example, the acceptance of poorer risks and their subsequent delinquent payments may lead to an increase in accounts receivable. The strength and timing of the collection efforts can affect the period for which past-due accounts remain delinquent, which in turn affects the level of accounts receivable. Collection and credit policy decisions may further affect the level of investment in accounts receivable by causing changes in the sales level and the ratio of credit sales to total sales. However, the three credit and collection policy variables are the only true decision variables under the control of the financial manager. Graphically, this situation is shown in Figure 7–1.

*Terms of Sale—
Decision
Variable*

The **terms of sale** identify the possible discount for early payment, the discount period, and the total credit period. They are generally stated in the form *a/b* net *c*, indicating that the customer can deduct *a* percent if the account is paid within *b* days; otherwise, the account must be paid within *c* days. Thus, for example, trade credit terms of 2/10, net 30 indicate that a 2 percent discount can be taken if the account is paid within 10 days; otherwise it must be paid within 30 days. What if the customer decides to forgo the discount and not pay until the final payment date? If such a decision is made, the customer has the use of the money for the time period between the discount date and the final payment date. However, failure to take the discount represents a cost to the customer. For instance, if the terms are 2/10, net 30, the annualized opportunity cost of passing up this 2 percent discount in

FIGURE 7–1. Determinants of Investment in Accounts Receivable

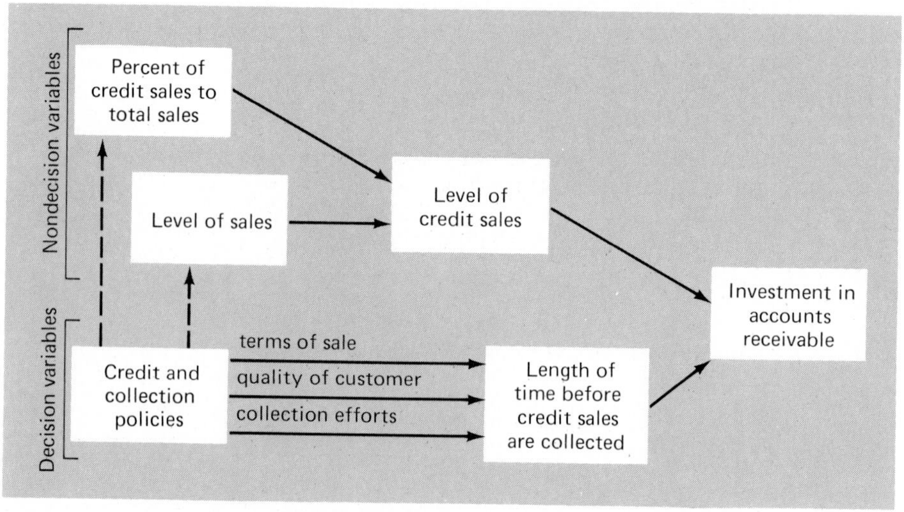

order to withhold payment for an additional 20 days is 36.73 percent. This is determined as follows:

$$\left(\begin{matrix}\text{annualized opportunity cost} \\ \text{of forgoing the discount}\end{matrix}\right) = \frac{a}{1-a} \times \frac{360}{c-b} \tag{7-1}$$

Substituting the values from the example, we get

$$36.73\% = \frac{.02}{1-.02} \times \frac{360}{30-10} \tag{7-2}$$

In industry the typical discount ranges anywhere from one-half percent to 10 percent, while the discount period is generally 10 days and the total credit period varies from 30 to 90 days. Although the terms of credit vary radically from industry to industry, they tend to remain relatively uniform within any particular industry.[1] Moreover, the terms tend to remain relatively constant over time, and they do not appear to be a frequently used decision variable.

Type of Customer— Decision Variable

A second decision variable involves determining the **type of customer** who is to qualify for trade credit. Quite obviously, several costs are associated with extending credit to lower-quality customers. First, as the probability of default increases with the extension of credit to lower-quality customers, it becomes more important to identify which of the possible new customers would be a poor risk. Thus, more time is spent investigating the lower-quality customer, and the costs of credit investigation increase.

Default costs also vary directly with the quality of the customer. As the customer's credit rating declines, the chance that the account will not be paid on time increases. In the extreme case, payment does not occur at all and the account must be written off. Thus, taking on lower-quality customers results in increases in default costs.

Collection costs also increase as the quality of the customer declines. The increase in delinquent accounts will force the firm to spend more time and money in collecting them. In summary, the decline in customer quality results in increased costs of credit investigation, collection, and default.

In determining whether or not credit should be granted to an individual customer, we are primarily interested in the customer's short-run welfare. Thus, liquidity ratios, other obligations, and the overall profitability of the firm become the focal point in this analysis. Credit-rating services, in particular Dun and Bradstreet, provide information on the financial status, operations, and payment history for most firms. Other possible sources of information would include credit bureaus, trade associations, chambers of commerce, competitors, bank references, public financial statements, and, of course, the firm's past relationships with the customer.

One way in which both individuals and firms are often evaluated as credit risks is through the use of credit scoring. **Credit scoring** involves the numerical evaluation of each applicant. An applicant receives a score based upon his or her answers to a

---

[1] Theodore N. Beckman and Ronald S. Foster, *Credits and Collections* (New York: McGraw-Hill, 1969), pp. 697–704.

simple set of questions. This score is then evaluated relative to a predetermined standard, its level relative to the standard determining whether or not credit should be extended. The major advantage of credit scoring is that it is inexpensive and easy to perform. For example, once the standards are set, a computer or clerical worker without any specialized training could easily evaluate any applicant.

The techniques used for constructing credit-scoring indexes range from the naive, simple approach of adding up default rates associated with the answers given to each question, to sophisticated evaluations using multiple discriminate analysis (MDA). MDA is a statistical technique for calculating the appropriate importance to be given to each question used in evaluating the applicant. Figure 7–2 shows a credit "scorecard" used by a large automobile dealer. The weights or scores attached to each answer are based upon the auto dealer's past experience with credit sales. For example, the scorecard indicates that individuals with no telephone in their home have a much higher probability of default than those with a telephone. One caveat should be mentioned: Whenever this type of questionnaire is used to evaluate credit applicants, it should be examined carefully to be sure that it does not contain any illegal discriminatory questions.

Another model that could be used for credit scoring has been provided by Edward Altman, who used multiple discriminant analysis to identify businesses that might go bankrupt. In his landmark study Altman used financial ratios to predict which firms would go bankrupt over the period 1946 to 1965. Using multiple discriminant analysis, Altman came up with the following index:

$$Z = 3.3\,\frac{\text{EBIT}}{\text{total assets}} + 1.0\,\frac{\text{sales}}{\text{total assets}} + 0.6\,\frac{\text{market value of equity}}{\text{book value of debt}} \quad (7\text{–}3)$$

$$+ 1.4\,\frac{\text{retained earnings}}{\text{total assets}} + 1.2\,\frac{\text{working capital}}{\text{total assets}}$$

Altman found that of the firms that went bankrupt over this time period, 94 percent had Z scores of less than 2.7 one year prior to bankruptcy and only 6 percent had scores above 2.7 percent. On the other hand, of those firms that did not go bankrupt, only 3 percent had Z scores below 2.7 and 97 percent had scores above 2.7.

Again, the advantages of credit-scoring techniques are low cost and ease of implementation. The credit scorer needs little or no training and with simple calculations can easily spot those credit risks that need more in the way of screening before credit should be extended to them.

Collection Efforts— Decision Variable

The key to maintaining control over the collection of accounts receivable is that the probability of default increases with the age of the account. Thus, control of accounts receivable focuses on the control and elimination of past-due receivables. One common way of evaluating the current situation is **ratio analysis.** By examining the average collection period, the ratio of receivables to assets, the ratio of credit sales to receivables (called the accounts receivable turnover ratio), and the amount of bad debts relative to sales over time, the financial manager can determine whether or not receivables are drifting out of control. In addition, an aging of accounts receivable provides a

FIGURE 7–2. Credit "Scorecard"

Telephone

Home	Relative	None				
5	1	0				

Living quarters

Own home no mortgage	Own home mortgage	Rent a house	Live with someone	Rent an apartment	Rent a room	
6	3	2	1	0	0	

Bank accounts

None	1	More than 1				
0	4	6				

Years at present address

Under 1/2	1/2–2	3–7	8 or more			
0	1	3	4			

Size of family including customer

1	2	3–6	7 or more			
2	4	3	0			

Monthly income

Under $400	$401–$600	$601–$900	$901–$1200	More than $1200		
0	1	2	6	8		

Length of present employment

Under 1/2 year	1/2–2 years	3–7 years	8 years or more			
0	1	2	4			

Percent of selling price on credit

Under 50	50–69	70–84	85–99			
5	3	1	0			

Interview discretionary points (+5 to −5)

Total

Score

Credit scorecard

_____
(Customer's name)

_____
(Street address)

_____
(City, State, Zip)

_____
(Home/Office telephone)

_____
(Credit scorer)

Credit scorecard evaluation

Dollar amount: $0–$2000

0–18	19–21	22 or more
Reject	Refer to main credit	Accept

Dollar amount: $2001–$5000

0–21	22–24	25 or more
Reject	Refer to main credit	Accept

Dollar amount: more than $5000

0–23	26–27	27 or more
Reject	Refer to main credit	Accept

If a previous loan customer, were payments received promptly?   Yes ☐   No* ☐

Are you willing to take responsibility for authorizing this loan?   Yes ☐   No* ☐

* Refer to main credit if answer to either question is _No_.

TABLE 7–2. Aging Account

Age of Accounts Receivable (Days)		Dollar Value (00)	Percent of Total
0–30		$2340	39%
31–60		1500	25
61–90		1020	17
91–120		720	12
Over 120		420	7
	Total	$6000	100%

breakdown both in dollars and in percentage terms of the proportion of receivables that are past due. Comparing the current aging of receivables with past data offers further insight into the degree of control that is being maintained over receivables. An example of an **aging account** or **schedule** appears in Table 7–2.

A ranking of measures used in monitoring accounts receivable compiled in a survey of 668 firms is provided in Table 7–3. This survey indicates that the aging account or schedule along with the accounts receivable turnover ratio and average collection period, which are actually variations of each other, serve as the primary tools used in monitoring the payment behavior of customers.

If changes are found in either the ratios or the aging of accounts, the manager should look for any possible changes in the overall credit policy or laxness in the collection procedures that might have brought on this situation. If changes are found, they should then be reevaluated.

Once the delinquent accounts have been identified, an effort should be made to collect them. For example, past-due letters, called **dunning letters,** should be sent if payment is not received on time, followed by an additional dunning letter in a more serious tone if the account becomes 3 weeks past due, followed after 6 weeks by a telephone call. Finally, if the account becomes 12 weeks past due, it might be turned over to a collection agency. Again, a direct tradeoff exists between collection expenses and lost goodwill on one hand and noncollection of accounts on the other. As before, this tradeoff should be evaluated in making the decision.

Thus far, we have discussed the importance and role of accounts receivable in the firm and then examined the determinants of the size of the investment in accounts

TABLE 7–3. Ranking of Measures Used in Monitoring Payment Behavior of Customers

Measure	Number of Responses	Percentage Assigning Rank			
		1	2	3	4
Accounts receivable turnover	123	17.1%	22.8%	56.9%	3.3%
Collection period	156	28.2	53.8	17.9	0.0
Aging schedule	181	68.5	25.4	6.1	0.0
Other	10	80.0	0.0	20.0	0.0

Source: K. B. Smith and S. B. Sell, "Working Capital Management in Practice," In *Readings on the Management of Working Capital*, 2nd ed., ed. K. B. Smith (St. Paul, MN.: West Publishing, 1980), pp. 78.

receivable. Since the credit and collection policies are the only discretionary variables for management, the primary focus has been placed on these determinants. In examining these decision variables, we have merely described their traits. In the appendix to this chapter these variables are analyzed in a decision-making context, which is termed marginal or incremental analysis.

INVENTORY MANAGEMENT

Inventory management involves the control of assets being produced to be sold in the normal course of the firm's operations. The general categories of inventory include raw materials inventory, work in process inventory, and finished goods inventory. The importance of inventory management to the firm depends upon the extent of the inventory investment. For an average firm, approximately 5.88 percent of all assets are in the form of inventory. However, the percentage varies widely from industry to industry, as can be seen in Table 7–4, and thus the importance of inventory management and control varies from industry to industry also. For example, it is much more important in the automotive dealer and service station trade, where inventories make up 49.29 percent of total assets, than in the hotel business, where the average investment in inventory is only 1.80 percent of total assets.

Purposes and Types of Inventory

The purpose of carrying inventories is to uncouple the operations of the firm—that is, to make each function of the business independent of each other function—so that delays or shutdowns in one area no longer affect the production and sale of the final product. Since production shutdowns result in increased costs, and since delays in delivery can lose customers, the management and control of inventory is an important duty of the financial manager.

Actually, the decision-making process with respect to investment in inventory involves a basic tradeoff between risk and return. The risk is that if the level of inventory is too low, the various functions of business are not effectively uncoupled and delays in production and customer delivery can result. The return results because reduced inventory investment saves money. As the size of the inventory increases, the storage

TABLE 7–4. Inventory as a Percentage of Total Assets for Major Industries

Industry	Inventory Relative to Total Assets
All industries	5.88%
Automotive dealers and service stations—retail	49.29
Building materials, garden supplies, and mobile home dealers—retail	39.53
Apparel and accessory stores	38.53
Food stores	28.24
Electrical and electronic equipment	15.05
Total construction	14.94
Agriculture, forestry, and fishing	9.46
Eating and drinking places	4.95
Petroleum and coal products	3.70
Hotels and other lodging places	1.80

Source: Internal Revenue Service, U.S. Treasury Department, *Statistics of Income, 1983, Corporate Income Tax Returns* (Washington, D.C.: Government Printing Office, 1986), pp. 1–294.

and handling costs in addition to the required return on capital invested in inventory will rise. Therefore, as the inventory a firm holds is increased, the risk of running out of inventory is lessened, but inventory expenses rise. To better illustrate the uncoupling function that inventories perform, we will look at several general types of inventories.

Raw Materials Inventory

Raw materials inventory consists of basic materials purchased from other firms to be used in the firm's production operations. These goods may include steel, lumber, petroleum, or manufactured items such as wire, ball bearings, or tires that the firm does not produce itself. Regardless of the specific form the raw materials inventory takes on, all manufacturing firms by definition maintain a raw materials inventory. Its purpose is to uncouple the production function from the purchasing function—that is, to make these two functions independent of each other, so that delays in shipment of raw materials do not cause production delays. In the event of a delay in shipment, the firm can satisfy its need for raw materials by liquidating its inventory. During the oil embargo of 1973 and the subsequent delays in oil shipments, for example, firms that used petroleum as an input in production and had an adequate supply in their raw materials inventory did not experience the production shutdowns that plagued similar firms with inadequate petroleum inventories.

Work in Process Inventory

Work in process inventory consists of partially finished goods requiring additional work before they become finished goods. The more complex and lengthy the production process, the larger will be the investment in work in process inventory. The purpose of work in process inventory is to uncouple the various operations in the production process so that machine failures and work stoppages in one operation will not affect the other operations. Assume, for example, there are ten different production operations, each one involving the piece of work produced in the previous operation. If the machine performing the first production operation breaks down, a firm with no work in process inventory will have to shut down all ten production operations. Yet if a firm has such inventory, the remaining nine operations can continue by drawing the input for the second operation from inventory rather than directly from the output of the first operation.

Finished Goods Inventory

The **finished goods inventory** consists of goods on which the production has been completed but that are not yet sold. The purpose of a finished goods inventory is to uncouple the production and sales functions so that it no longer is necessary to produce the good before a sale can occur—sales can be made directly out of inventory. In the auto industry, for example, where periodic strikes are common, if auto dealers did not carry an inventory of cars, sales would virtually cease during a strike period.

Stock of Cash

Although we have already discussed cash management at some length in Chapter 6, it is worthwhile to mention cash again in the light of inventory management. This is because the **stock of cash** carried by a firm is simply a special type of inventory. In terms of uncoupling the various operations of the firm, the purpose of holding a stock of cash is to make the payment of bills independent of the collection of accounts due. When cash is kept on hand, bills can be paid without prior collection of accounts.

The reason we have included cash as a type of inventory is that as we examine and develop inventory economic ordering quantity (EOQ) models, we will see a striking resemblance between the EOQ inventory and EOQ cash model; in fact, except for a minor redefinition of terms, they will be exactly the same.

Inventory Management Techniques

The importance of effective inventory management is directly related to the size of the investment in inventory. Since, on average, approximately 5.88 percent of a firm's assets are tied up in inventory, effective management of these assets is essential to the goal of shareholder wealth maximization. To control the investment in inventory, management must solve two problems: the order quantity problem and the order point problem.

The Order Quantity Problem

The **order quantity problem** involves determining the optimal order size for an inventory item given its expected usage, carrying costs, and ordering costs. Aside from a change in some of the variable names, it is exactly the same as the inventroy model for cash management (EOQ model) presented in Chapter 6.

The EOQ model attempts to determine the order size that will minimize total inventory costs. It assumes that

$$\text{total inventory costs} = \text{total carrying costs} + \text{total ordering costs} \qquad (7\text{--}4)$$

Assuming that inventory is allowed to fall to zero and then is immediately replenished (this assumption will be lifted when we discuss the order point problem), the average inventory becomes $Q/2$, where Q is inventory order size in units. This can be seen graphically in Figure 7–3.

If the average inventory is $Q/2$ and the carrying cost per unit is C, then carrying costs become:

$$\text{total carrying costs} = (\text{average inventory})(\text{carrying cost per unit}) \qquad (7\text{--}5)$$

$$= \left(\frac{Q}{2}\right) C \qquad (7\text{--}6)$$

FIGURE 7–3. Inventory Level and the Replenishment Cycle

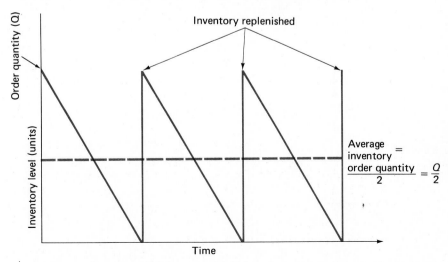

where Q = the inventory order size in units,

C = carrying costs per unit.

The carrying costs on inventory include the required rate of return on investment in inventory, in addition to warehouse or storage costs, wages for those who operate the warehouse, and costs associated with inventory shrinkage. Thus, ordering costs include both real cash flows and opportunity costs associated with having funds tied up in inventory.

The ordering costs incurred are equal to the ordering costs per order times the number of orders. If we assume total demand over the planning period is S and we order in lot sizes of Q, then S/Q represents the number of orders over the planning period. If the ordering cost per order is O, then

$$\text{total ordering costs} = (\text{number of orders})(\text{ordering cost per order}) \quad (7\text{--}7)$$

$$= \left(\frac{S}{Q}\right) O \quad (7\text{--}8)$$

where S = total demand in units over the planning period,

O = ordering cost per order.

Thus, total costs in equation (7--4) become

$$\text{total costs} = \left(\frac{Q}{2}\right) C + \left(\frac{S}{Q}\right) O \quad (7\text{--}9)$$

Graphically, this equation is illustrated in Figure 7--4.

FIGURE 7--4.   Total Cost and EOQ Determination

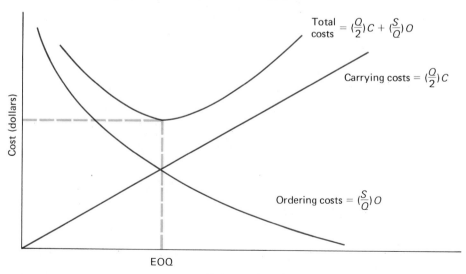

What we are looking for is the ordering size, Q^*, that provides the minimum total costs. By manipulating equation (7–9), we find that the optimal value of Q—that is, the economic ordering quantity (EOQ)—is[2]

$$Q^* = \sqrt{\frac{2SO}{C}} \qquad\qquad (7\text{--}10)$$

The use of the EOQ model can best be illustrated through the use of an example.

Example   Suppose a firm expects total demand (S) for its product over the planning period to be 5000 units, while the ordering cost per order (O) is $200, and the carrying cost per unit (C) is $2. Substituting these values into equation (7–10) yields

$$Q^* = \sqrt{\frac{2 \cdot 5000 \cdot 200}{2}} = \sqrt{1{,}000{,}000} = 1000 \text{ units}$$

Thus, if this firm orders in 1000-unit lot sizes, it will minimize its total inventory costs.

Examination of EOQ Assumptions

The major weaknesses of the EOQ model are associated with several of its assumptions, in spite of the fact that the model tends to yield quite good results. Where its assumptions have been dramatically violated, the EOQ model can generally be modified to accommodate the situation. The model's assumptions are as follows:

1. **Constant or uniform demand.** Although the EOQ model assumes constant demand, demand may vary from day to day. If demand is stochastic—that is, not known in advance—the model must be modified through the inclusion of a safety stock.

---

[2] This result can be obtained through calculus.

$$\text{total cost } (TC) = \left(\frac{Q}{2}\right) C + \left(\frac{S}{Q}\right) O$$

The first derivative with respect to Q defines the slope of the total cost curve. Setting this derivative equal to zero specifies the minimum point (zero slope) on the curve. Thus,

$$\frac{dTC}{dQ} = \frac{C}{2} - \frac{SO}{Q^2} = O$$

$$Q^2 = \frac{2SO}{C}$$

$$Q^* = \sqrt{\frac{2SO}{C}}$$

To verify that a minimum point is being found, rather than a maximum point where the slope would also equal zero, we check for a positive second derivative:

$$\frac{d^2TC}{dQ^2} = \frac{2SO}{Q^3} \geq 0$$

The second derivative must be positive, since SO and Q can only take on positive values; hence, this is a minimum point.

2. **Constant unit price.** The inclusion of variable prices resulting from quantity discounts can be handled quite easily through a modification of the original EOQ model, redefining total costs and solving for the optimum order quantity.
3. **Constant carrying costs.** Unit carrying costs may vary substantially as the size of the inventory rises, perhaps decreasing because of economies of scale or storage efficiency or increasing as storage space runs out and new warehouses have to be rented. This situation can be handled through a modification in the original model similar to the one used for variable unit price.
4. **Constant ordering costs.** While this assumption is generally valid, its violation can be accommodated by modifying the original EOQ model in a manner similar to the one used for variable unit price.
5. **Instantaneous delivery.** If delivery is not instantaneous, which is generally the case, the original EOQ model must be modified through the inclusion of a safety stock.
6. **Independent orders.** If multiple orders result in cost savings by reducing paperwork and transportation cost, the original EOQ model must be further modified. While this modification is somewhat complicated, special EOQ models have been developed to deal with it.[3]

These assumptions have been pointed out to illustrate the limitations of the basic EOQ model and the ways in which it can be modified to compensate for them. Moreover, an understanding of the limitations and assumptions of the EOQ model will provide the financial manager with a strong base for making inventory decisions.

The Order Point Problem

The two most limiting assumptions—those of constant or uniform demand and instantaneous delivery—are dealt with through the inclusion of safety stock. The decision on how much safety stock to hold is generally referred to as the **order point problem**; that is, how low should inventory be depleted before it is reordered?

Two factors go into the determination of the appropriate order point: (1) the procurement or delivery time stock and (2) the safety stock desired. The inclusion of these stocks is illustrated graphically in Figure 7–5. We observe that the order point problem can be decomposed into its two components, the **delivery time stock**—that is, the inventory needed between the order date and the receipt of the inventory ordered—and the **safety stock**—that is, the inventory held to accommodate any unusually large and unexpected usage during the delivery time. Thus, the order point is reached when inventory falls to a level equal to the delivery time stock plus the safety stock.

$$\begin{array}{c}\text{inventory order point} \\ \text{[order new inventory} \\ \text{when the level of} \\ \text{inventory falls to} \\ \text{this level]}\end{array} = \begin{pmatrix}\text{delivery time} \\ \text{stock}\end{pmatrix} + \begin{pmatrix}\text{safety} \\ \text{stock}\end{pmatrix} \qquad (7\text{–}11)$$

---

[3] For example, R. J. Tersire, *Material Management and Inventory Control* (New York: Elsevier—North Holland, 1976).

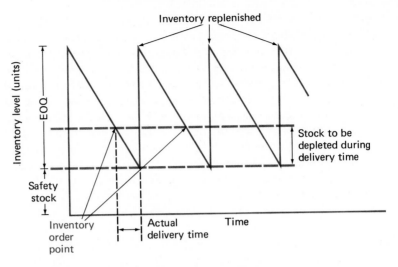

FIGURE 7–5. Order Point Determination

As a result of constantly carrying safety stock, the average level of inventory increases. Whereas before the inclusion of safety stock the average level of inventory was equal to EOQ/2, now it will be

$$\text{average inventory} = \frac{\text{EOQ}}{2} + \text{safety stock} \qquad (7\text{--}12)$$

In general, several factors simultaneously determine how much delivery time stock and safety stock should be held. First, the efficiency of the replenishment system affects how much delivery time stock is needed. Since the delivery time stock is the expected inventory usage between ordering and receiving inventory, efficient replenishment of inventory would reduce the need for delivery time stock.

The uncertainty surrounding both the delivery time and the demand for the product affects the level of safety stock needed. The more certain the patterns of these inflows and outflows from the inventory, the less safety stock required. In effect, if these inflows and outflows are highly predictable, then there is little chance of any stockout occurring. However, if they are unpredictable, it becomes necessary to carry additional safety stock to prevent unexpected stockouts.

The safety margin desired also affects the level of safety stock held. If it is a costly experience to run out of inventory, the safety stock held will be larger than it would be otherwise. If running out of inventory and the subsequent delay in supplying customers results in strong customer dissatisfaction and the possibility of lost future sales from that customer, then additional safety stock will be carried. A final determinant is the cost of carrying additional inventory, in terms of both the handling and storage costs and the opportunity cost associated with the investment in additional inventory. Very simply, the greater the costs, the smaller the safety stock.

The determination of the level of safety stock involves a basic tradeoff between the risk of stockout, resulting in possible customer dissatisfaction and lost sales, and the increased costs associated with carrying additional inventory.

Inflation and EOQ

Inflation affects the EOQ model in two major ways. First, while the EOQ model can be modified to assume constant price increases, often major price increases occur only once or twice a year and are announced ahead of time. If this is the case, the EOQ model may lose its applicability and may be replaced with **anticipatory buying**—that is, buying in anticipation of a price increase in order to secure the goods at a lower cost. Of course, as with most decisions, there are tradeoffs. The costs are the added carrying costs associated with the inventory that the firm would not normally be holding. The benefits, of course, come from buying at a lower price. The second way inflation affects the EOQ model is through increased carrying costs. As inflation pushes interest rates up, the cost of carrying inventory increases. In our EOQ model this means that C increases, which results in a decline in Q^*, the optimal economic order quantity:

$$\downarrow Q^* = \sqrt{\frac{2SO}{C \uparrow}} \tag{7–13}$$

This reluctance to stock large inventories because of high carrying costs became particularly prevalent during the late 1970s and early 1980s when inflation and interest rates were at high levels.

JUST-IN-TIME INVENTORY CONTROL

The **just-in-time inventory control system** is more than just an inventory control system, it is a production and management system. Not only is inventory cut down to a minimum, but the time and physical distance between the various production operations is also reduced. In addition management is willing to sacrifice costs to develop close relationships with suppliers to ensure speedy replenishment of inventory in the event of stockouts in return for being able to carry less safety stock.

The just-in-time inventory control system was originally developed in Japan by Taiichi Okno, a vice-president of Toyota. Originally the system was called the *kanban* system after the cards placed in the parts bins which were used to call for a new supply. The idea behind the system is that the firm should keep a minimum level of inventory on hand, relying on suppliers to furnish parts "just in time" for them to be assembled. This is in direct contrast to the traditional inventory philosophy of U.S. firms which is sometimes referred to as a "just in case" system which keeps healthy levels of safety stocks to ensure that production will not be interrupted. While large inventories may not be a bad idea when interest rates are low, when interest rates are high, as they have been in recent years, they become very costly.

While the just-in-time inventory system is intuitively appealing, it has not proved easy to implement. Long distance from suppliers and plants that were constructed with too much space to store inventory and not enough doors and loading docks to get inventory into the plant quickly have limited successful implementation. In addition, the firm's relationship with its suppliers has also been forced to change. Since the firm relies on suppliers to deliver high quality parts and materials immediately, it must have a close long-term relationship with them. But in spite of the difficulties of implementation, many U.S. firms are committed to moving toward a just-in-time system. General Motors, for example, cut its inventory by 17 percent between 1981 and

1984, saving the company hundreds of millions of dollars a year. In fact, between 1977 and 1983 the average level of inventory relative to total assets for all American corporations fell by 21.07 percent.

While the just-in-time system does not at first appear to bear much of a relationship to the EOQ model, it merely alters some of the assumptions of the model with respect to delivery time and ordering costs and draws out the implications. Actually it is just a new approach to the EOQ model which tries to produce the lowest average level of inventory possible. If we look at the average level of inventory as defined by the EOQ model, we find it to be:

$$\text{average inventory} = \frac{\sqrt{\frac{2SO\downarrow}{C}}}{2} + \text{safety stock}\downarrow$$

The just-in-time system attacks this equation in two places. First, by locating inventory supplies in convenient locations, laying out plants in such a way that it is inexpensive and easy to unload new inventory shipments, and computerizing the inventory order system, the cost of ordering new inventory, O, is reduced. Second, by developing a strong relationship with suppliers located in the same geographical area and setting up restocking strategies that cut time, the safety stock is also reduced. The philosophy behind the just-in-time inventory system is that the benefits associated with reducing inventory and delivery time to a bare minimum through adjustment in the EOQ model will more than offset the costs associated with the increased possibility of stockouts.

Summary

The size of the investment in accounts receivable depends upon three factors: the percentage of credit sales to total sales, the level of sales, and the credit and collection policies. However, only the credit and collection policies are decision variables open to the financial manager. The policies that the financial manager has control over include the terms of sale, the quality of customer, and the collection efforts.

While the typical firm has less assets tied up in inventory (5.88%) than it does in accounts receivable (26.25%), inventory management and control is still an important function of the financial manager. The purpose of holding inventory is to make each function of the business independent of the other functions—that is, to uncouple the firm's operations. The primary inventory management techniques involve questions of how much inventory should be ordered and when the order should be placed. The answers directly determine the average level of investment in inventory. The EOQ model was employed in answering the first of these questions. This model attempts to calculate the order size that minimizes the sum of the inventory carrying and ordering costs. Then we examined the order point problem, attempting to determine how low inventory should be allowed to drop before it is reordered. The order point was concluded to be reached when the inventory had fallen to a level equal to the delivery time stock plus the safety stock. The determinants of the level of safety stock involve a direct tradeoff between the risk of running out of inventory, thereby engendering customer dissatisfaction, and the increased costs associated with carrying additional inventory.

Recently a new approach to inventory control, the just-in-time inventory control method, has been used by many firms. The just-in-time inventory control system lowers inventory by reducing the time and distance between the various production functions. The idea behind the system is that the firm should keep a minimum level of inventory on hand, relying upon suppliers to furnish parts "just-in-time" for them to be assembled.

Study Questions

7–1. What factors determine the size of the investment a firm makes in accounts receivable? Which of these factors are under the control of the financial manager?

7–2. What do the following trade credit terms mean?
  a. 1/20, net 50
  b. 2/30, net 60
  c. net 30
  d. 2/10, 1/30, net 60

7–3. What is the purpose of the use of an aging account in the control of accounts receivable? Can this same function be performed through ratio analysis? Why or why not?

7–4. If a credit manager experienced no bad debt losses over the past year, would this be an indication of proper credit management? Why or why not?

7–5. What is the purpose of credit scoring?

7–6. What is the purpose of holding inventory? Name several types of inventory and describe their purpose.

7–7. Can cash be considered a special type of inventory? If so, what functions does it attempt to uncouple?

7–8. In order to control investment in inventory effectively, what two questions must be answered?

7–9. What are the major assumptions made by the EOQ model?

7–10. What are the risk-return tradeoffs associated with inventory management?

7–11. How might inflation affect the EOQ model?

Self-Test Problems

ST–1. (*EOQ Calculations*) A local gift shop is attempting to determine how many sets of wine glasses to order. The store feels it will sell approximately 800 sets in the next year at a price of $18.00 per set. The wholesale price that the store pays per set is $12.00. Costs for carrying one set of wine glasses are estimated at $1.50 per year while ordering costs are estimated at $25.00.
  a. What is the economic order quantity for the sets of wine glasses?
  b. What are the annual inventory costs for the firm if it orders in this quantity? (Assume constant demand and instantaneous delivery and thus no safety stock is carried.)

ST–2. (*EOQ Calculations*) Given the following inventory information and relationships for the F. Beamer Corporation:
  1. Orders can only be placed in multiples of 100 units.
  2. Annual unit usage is 300,000. (Assume a 50-week year in your calculations.)

3. The carrying cost is 30 percent of the purchase price of the goods.
4. The purchase price is $10 per unit.
5. The ordering cost is $50 per order.
6. The desired safety stock is 1000 units. (This does not include delivery time stock.)
7. Delivery time is 2 weeks.

Given this information:
a. What is the optimal EOQ level?
b. How many orders will be placed annually?
c. At what inventory level should a reorder be made?

Study Problems

7–1. (*Trade Credit Discounts*) Determine the effective annualized cost of foregoing the trade credit discount on the following terms:
a. 1/10, net 20
b. 2/10, net 30
c. 3/10, net 30
d. 3/10, net 60
e. 3/10, net 90
f. 5/10, net 60

7–2. (*Altman Model*) The following ratios were supplied by six loan applicants. Given this information and the credit-scoring model developed by Altman [equation (7–3)], which loans have a high probability of defaulting next year and thus should be avoided?

	$\dfrac{EBIT}{Total\ Assets}$	$\dfrac{Sales}{Total\ Assets}$	$\dfrac{Market\ Value\ of\ Equity}{Book\ Value\ of\ Debt}$	$\dfrac{Earnings}{Total\ Assets}$	$\dfrac{Working\ Capital}{Total\ Assets}$
Applicant 1	.2	.2	1.2	.3	.5
Applicant 2	.2	.8	1.0	.3	.8
Applicant 3	.2	.7	.6	.3	.4
Applicant 4	.1	.4	1.2	.4	.4
Applicant 5	.3	.7	.5	.4	.7
Applicant 6	.2	.5	.5	.4	.4

7–3. (*Ratio Analysis*) Assuming a 360-day year, calculate what the average investment in inventory would be for a firm, given the following information in each case.
a. The firm has sales of $600,000, a gross profit margin of 10 percent, and an inventory turnover ratio of 6.
b. The firm has a cost of goods sold figure of $480,000 and an average age of inventory of 40 days.
c. The firm has a cost of goods sold figure of $1,150,000 and an inventory turnover ratio of 5.
d. The firm has a sales figure of $25 million, a gross profit margin of 14 percent, and an average age of inventory of 45 days.

7–4. (*EOQ Calculations*) A downtown bookstore is trying to determine the optimal order quantity for a popular novel just printed in paperback. The store feels that the book will sell at four times its hardback figures. It would therefore sell approximately 3000 copies in the next year at a price of $1.50. The store buys the book at a wholesale figure of $1. Costs for carrying the book are estimated at $.10 a copy per year, and it costs $10 to order more books.

a. Determine the economic order quantity.

b. What would be the total costs for ordering the books 1, 4, 5, 10, and 15 times a year?

c. What questionable assumptions are being made by the EOQ model?

7–5. (*EOQ Calculations*) The local hamburger fast-food restaurant purchases 20,000 boxes of hamburger rolls every month. Order costs are $50 an order, and it costs $.25 a box for storage.

a. What is the optimal order quantity of hamburger rolls for this restaurant?

b. What questionable assumptions are being made by the EOQ model?

7–6. (*EOQ Calculations*) A local car manufacturing plant has a $75 per-unit per-year carrying cost on a certain item in inventory. This item is used at a rate of 50,000 per year. Ordering costs are $500 per order.

a. What is the economic order quantity for this item?

b. What are the annual inventory costs for this firm if it orders in this quantity? (Assume constant demand and instantaneous delivery.)

7–7. (*EOQ Calculations*) Swank Products is involved in the production of camera parts and has the following inventory, carrying, and storage costs:

1. Orders must be placed in round lots of 200 units.
2. Annual unit usage is 500,000 (Assume a 50-week year in your calculations.)
3. The carrying cost is 20 percent of the purchase price.
4. The purchase price $2 per unit.
5. The ordering cost is $90 per order.
6. The desired safety stock is 15,000 units. (This does not include delivery time stock.)
7. The delivery time is one week.

Given the above information:

a. Determine the optimal EOQ level.

b. How many orders will be placed annually?

c. What is the inventory order point? (That is, at what level of inventory should a new order be placed?)

d. What is the average inventory level?

7–8. (*EOQ Calculations*) Toledo Distributors have determined the following inventory information and relationships:

1. Orders can be placed only in multiples of 200 units.
2. Annual unit usage is 500,000 units. (Assume a 50 week year in your calculations.)
3. The carrying cost is 10 percent of the purchase price of the goods.
4. The purchase price is $5 per unit.
5. The ordering cost is $100 per order.
6. The desired safety stock is 5000 units. (This does not include delivery time stock.)
7. Delivery time is 4 weeks.

Given this information:

a. What is the EOQ level?

b. How many orders will be placed annually?

c. At what inventory level should a reorder be made?

d. Now assume the carrying costs are 50 percent of the purchase price of the goods and recalculate parts (a), (b), and (c). Are these the results you anticipated?

7–9. (*Comprehensive EOQ Calculations*) Knutson Products, Inc., is involved in the production of airplane parts and has the following inventory, carrying, and storage costs:

1. Orders must be placed in round lots of 100 units.
2. Annual unit usage is 250,000. (Assume a 50-week year in your calculations.)
3. The carrying cost is 10 percent of the purchase price.

4. The purchase price is $10 per unit.
5. The ordering cost is $100 per order.
6. The desired safety stock is 5000 units. (This does not include delivery time stock.)
7. The delivery time is one week.

Given the above information:

a. Determine the optimal EOQ level.
b. How many orders will be placed annually?
c. What is the inventory order point? (That is, at what level of inventory should a new order be placed?)
d. What is the average inventory level?
e. What would happen to the EOQ if annual unit sales doubled (all other unit costs and safety stocks remaining constant)? What is the elasticity of EOQ with respect to sales? (That is, what is the percent change in EOQ divided by the percent change in sales?)
f. If carrying costs double, what would happen to the EOQ level? (Assume the original sales level of 250,000 units.) What is the elasticity of EOQ with respect to carrying costs?
g. If the ordering costs double, what would happen to the level of EOQ? (Again assume original levels of sales and carrying costs.) What is the elasticity of EOQ with respect to ordering costs?
h. If the selling price doubles, what would happen to EOQ? What is the elasticity of EOQ with respect to selling price?

Self-Test Solutions

SS–1. a. The economic order quantity is

$$Q^* = \sqrt{\frac{2SO}{C}}$$

where S = total demand in units over the planning period
O = ordering cost per order
C = carrying costs per unit

Substituting the values given in the self-test problem into the EOQ equation we get

$$Q^* = \sqrt{\frac{2 \cdot 800 \cdot 25}{1.50}}$$

$$= \sqrt{26,667}$$

$$= 163 \text{ units per order}$$

Thus, 163 units should be ordered each time an order is placed. Note that the EOQ calculations take place based upon several limiting assumptions such as constant demand, constant unit price, and constant carrying costs, which may influence the final decision.

b. Total costs = carrying costs + ordering costs

$$= \left(\frac{Q}{2}\right)C + \left(\frac{S}{Q}\right)O$$

$$= \left(\frac{163}{2}\right)\$1.50 + \left(\frac{800}{163}\right)\$25$$

$$= \$122.25 + \$122.70$$

$$= \$244.95$$

Note that carrying costs and ordering costs are the same (other than a slight difference caused by having to order in whole rather than fractional units). This is because the total costs curve is at its minimum when ordering costs equal carrying costs, as shown in Figure 7–4.

SS–2.   a. $EOQ = \sqrt{\dfrac{2SO}{C}}$

$$= \sqrt{\dfrac{2(300,000)(50)}{3}}$$

= 3,162 units, but since orders must be placed in 100 unit lots, the effective EOQ becomes 3,200 units

b. $\dfrac{\text{Total usage}}{\text{EOQ}} = \dfrac{300,000}{3,200} = 93.75$ orders per year

c.   Inventory order point = delivery time + safety stock

$$= \dfrac{2}{50} \times 300,000 + 1,000$$

$$= 12,000 + 1,000$$

$$= 13,000 \text{ units}$$

Selected References

Altman, Edward I. "Financial Ratios, Discriminate Analysis and the Prediction or Corporate Bankruptcy." *Journal of Finance*, 23 (September 1968), 589–609.

Ammer, Dean S. "Materials Management as a Profit Center," *Harvard Business Review*, 47 (January–February 1969), 72–89.

Atkins, Joseph C., and Yong H. Kim. "Comment and Correction: Opportunity Cost in the Evaluation of Investment in Accounts Receivable," *Financial Management*, 6 (Winter 1977), 71–74.

Beranek, William. "Financial Implications of Lot-Size Inventory Models," *Harvard Business Review*, 47 (January–February 1969), 72–90.

———. *Working Capital Management*. Belmont, CA.: Wadsworth, 1966.

Brick, Ivan E., and William K. H. Fung. "The Effect of Taxes on the Trade Credit Decision," *Financial Management* 13 (Summer 1984), 24–30.

Brooks, Leroy D. "Risk-Return Criteria and Optimal Inventory Stocks," *Engineering Economist*, 25 (Summer 1980), 275–99.

Brosky, John J. *The Implicit Cost of Trade Credit and Theory of Optimal Terms of Sale*. New York: Credit Research Foundation, 1969.

Buffa, Elwood S. *Modern Production Management*, (5th ed.), chap. 11. Santa Barbara: Wiley, 1977.

Carpenter, Michael D., and Jack E. Miller. "A Reliable Framework for Monitoring Accounts Receivable," *Financial Management*, 8 (Winter 1979), 37–40.

Celec, Stephen E., and Joe D. Icerman. "A Comprehensive Approach to Accounts Receivable Management," *Financial Review*, 15 (Spring 1980), 23–34.

Dyl, Edward A. "Another Look at the Evaluation of Investments in Accounts Receivable," *Financial Management*, 6 (Winter 1977), 67–70.

Emery, Gary W. "A Pure Financial Explanation for Trade Credit," *Journal of Financial and Quantitative Analysis* 19 (September 1984), 271–85.

Greer, Carl C. "The Optimal Credit Acceptance Policy," *Journal of Financial and Quantitative Analysis*, 2 (December 1967), 399–415.

Halloren, John A., and Howard P. Lanser. "The Credit Policy Decision in an Inflationary Environment," *Financial Management*, 10 (Winter 1981), 31–38.

Herbst, Anthony F. "Some Empirical Evidence on the Determinants of Trade Credit at the Industry Level of Aggregation," *Journal of Financial and Quantitative Analysis*, 9 (June 1974), 377–94.

Hill, Ned C., and Kenneth D. Riener. "Determining the

Cash Discount in the Firm's Credit Policy," *Financial Management*, 8 (Spring 1979), 68–73.

Hillier, Frederick S., and Gerald J. Lieberman. *Introduction to Operations Research*, chap. 11. San Francisco: Holden-Day, 1974.

Kim, Yong H., and Joseph C. Atkins. "Evaluating Investments in Accounts Receivable: A Wealth Maximization Framework," *Journal of Finance*, 33 (May 1978), 403–12.

Lane, Sylvia. "Submarginal Credit Risk Classification," *Journal of Financial and Quantitative Analysis*, 7 (January 1972), 1379–85.

Long, Michael S. "Credit Screening System Selection," *Journal of Financial and Quantitative Analysis*, 11 (June 1976), 313–28.

Mao, James, C. T. "Controlling Risk in Accounts Receivable Management," *Journal of Business Finance & Accounting*, 1 (Autumn 1974), 395–403.

Marrah, George G. "Managing Receivables," *Financial Executive*, 38 (July 1970), 40–44.

Mehta, Dileep. "The Formulation of Credit Policy Models," *Management Science*, 15 (October 1968), 30–50.

——. *Working Capital Management*. Englewood Cliffs, NJ: Prentice-Hall, 1974.

Oh, John S. "Opportunity Cost in the Evaluation of Investment in Accounts Receivable," *Financial Management*, 6 (Summer 1976), 32–36.

Sachdeva, Kanwal S. "Accounts Receivable Decisions in a Capital Budgeting Framework," *Financial Management*, 10 (Winter 1981), 45–49.

Schiff, Michael. "Credit and Inventory Management," *Financial Executive*, 40 (November 1972), 28–33.

Smith, David E. *Quantitative Business Analysis*, chaps. 14 and 15. Santa Barbara: Wiley, 1977.

Smith, Keith V. *Management of Working Capital* (2nd ed.). New York: West Publishing, 1980.

Snyder, Arthur. "Principles of Inventory Management," *Financial Executive*, 32 (April 1964), 16–19.

Soldofsky, Robert M. "A Model for Accounts Receivable Management," *N.A.A. Bulletin*, January 1966, 55–58.

Vander Weide, J., and S. F. Maier. *Managing Corporate Liquidity*. New York: Wiley, 1985.

Walia, Tirlochan S. "Explicit and Implicit Cost of Changes in the Level of Accounts Receivable and the Credit Policy Decision of the Firm," *Financial Management*, 6 (Winter 1977), 75–78.

Welshans, Merle T. "Using Credit for Profit Making," *Harvard Business Review*, 45 (January–February 1967), 141–56.

Weston, J. Fred, and Pham D. Tuan. "Comment on Analysis of Credit Policy Changes," *Financial Management*, 9 (Winter 1980), 59–63.

Wrightsman, Dwayne. "Optimal Credit Terms for Accounts Receivable," *Quarterly Review of Economics and Business*, 9 (Summer 1969), 59–66.

APPENDIX 7A
—Marginal or Incremental Analysis of Credit Policies—

Marginal or incremental analysis will be discussed here in terms of a systematic comparison of the incremental returns and the incremental costs resulting from a change in the firm's credit policy. Three categories of changes in credit policy will be considered: a change in the discount period, the risk class of customers who receive credit, or the collection process. Whenever the incremental return from a proposed change in the management of accounts receivable is greater than the incremental costs of the additional investment, the change should be implemented. To illustrate, let us follow through an example.

Example   Assume that a firm currently has annual sales, all credit, of $8 million and an average collection period on non-bad-debt sales of 60 days. The current level of bad debts is $240,000 and the firm's opportunity cost or required rate of return is 20 percent. Further assume that the firm produces only one product, with variable costs equaling 75 percent of the selling price. The company is considering an increase in the credit period. As a result, new sales will be generated with an average collection period on non-bad-debt sales of 90 days, while old customers will change their payment habits to take advantage of the more generous credit period and increase their average collection period on non-bad-debt sales from 60 to 90 days. While these new customers will generate additional profits, they will also generate more bad debts (it is assumed the level of bad debts on the old customers will remain constant). In addition, in order to service new sales, it will be necessary to increase the level of average inventory from $1 million to $1,038,000.

As a result of this relaxation of the credit period, profits will increase, but so will the level of bad debts. In addition the investment in receivables will increase because of the additional credit sales *and* the slowdown in the cash collections from old customers as they take advantage of the more generous new credit terms. Finally, inventories will be increased. Marginal analysis quantifies and then compares the results of these changes to provide a decision on the desirability of the proposed credit policy change.

General Procedure   Marginal or incremental analysis involves a comparison of the incremental profit contribution (or benefits) from new sales with the incremental costs resulting from the change in credit policy. The decision concerning the change in credit policy is then made using the following rules (where the symbol Δ denotes *change in*):

If Δ profit contribution $- \Delta$ costs > 0, then accept the change in credit policy

If Δ profit contribution $- \Delta$ costs < 0, then reject the change in credit policy

If Δ profit contribution $- \Delta$ costs $= 0$, then be indifferent to the change in credit policy

A four-step procedure for performing marginal or incremental analysis on a change in credit policy will be followed:

STEP 1: *Estimate incremental profit contribution.*

STEP 2: *Estimate incremental costs (that is, the opportunity cost) associated with the delay in collection of accounts receivable caused by original customers paying later.*

STEP 3: *Estimate incremental costs (that is, the dollar-level required return) associated with the increase in investment in receivables and inventory due to new sales.*

STEP 4: *Compare the incremental revenues with the incremental costs.*

To help simplify the analysis, Table 7A–1 defines a set of terms and symbols used, while Table 7A–2 provides a step-by-step analysis.

Analysis:

Step 1: Estimate the incremental profit contribution (ΔP) resulting from the proposed change in credit policy.

> *Discussion*: This is equal to the portion of incremental (new) sales that goes toward profits [$\Delta S (1 - V)$] less the increased loss to bad debts (ΔB).

TABLE 7A–1. Marginal Analysis Definitions

S_{orig} = The original level of annual sales ($8,000,000)

ΔS = The incremental sales revenues resulting from the proposed change in credit policy ($9,000,000 - $8,000,000 = $1,000,000)

B_{orig} = The level of bad debt losses on original sales ($240,000)

ΔB = The incremental bad debts resulting from the proposed change in credit policy ($60,000)

ΔACP = The change in the average collection period on original collectible (non-bad-debt) sales (30 days)

ACP_{new} = The average collection period on new collectible (non-bad-debt) sales (90 days)

ΔI = The change in average inventory carried due to the increased sales level resulting from the proposed change in credit policy ($38,000) valued at cost

V = Variable costs as a percent of sales (assumed the same on both new and old sales = 75%)

R = The required return on the incremental investment in receivables and inventory due to increased sales resulting from the proposed change in credit policy (20%)[a]

ΔP = The incremental profit contribution (marginal benefits) resulting from the proposed change in credit policy = $(\Delta S)(1 - V) - \Delta B$

OC = The opportunity cost associated with original customers' changing their payment patterns = $(R)(\Delta ACP) \cdot [(S_{orig} - B_{orig})/360 \text{ days}]$

DRR = The dollar-level required return on the incremental investment in receivables and inventory resulting from the proposed change in credit policy = $\{(ACP_{new}) [(\Delta S - \Delta B)/360] (V) + \Delta I\} \cdot R$

---

[a] The required rate of return should reflect the risk of noncollection of accounts, and as such may not be the same rate that should be applied to the increased investment in inventory, accounts receivable from original customers, or accounts receivable from new customers. However, for our purposes a single rate will be used here.

TABLE 7A–2. Incremental Analysis of a Change in Credit Policy

Example:	Present Credit Policy	Proposed Credit Policy
Annual sales (all credit)	$8,000,000	$9,000,000
Average collection period on collectible sales		
Original sales	60 days	90 days
New sales		90 days
Bad debt losses		
Original sales	$ 240,000	$ 240,000
New Sales		$ 60,000
Variable costs[a]	75%	75%
Average inventory (at cost)	$1,000,000	$1,038,000
Required return on incremental investment in receivables and inventory (R)	20%	20%

[a] Note that a change in credit policy may well result in a change in credit costs due to increased or decreased clerical or collection costs. These costs could be accounted for by adjusting variable costs appropriately or by including them as an increased fixed cost.

Formula: ΔP = (new sales) (percent of sales going toward fixed costs and profits) $-$ (increased bad debts)

$$= (\Delta S)(1 - V) - \Delta B$$

$$= \$1,000,000(.25) - \$60,000$$

$$= \$250,000 - \$60,000$$

$$= \$190,000$$

Step 2: Determine the opportunity cost associated with the delay in collection of accounts receivable caused by original customers changing their payment patterns.

Discussion: This involves multiplying the required rate of return on investment in receivables (R) times the incremental increase in collectible receivables due to original customers taking longer to pay $[(\Delta ACP)(S_{orig} - B_{orig})/360]$.

Formula:

$$OC = \text{(required return)} \begin{pmatrix} \text{change in the average} \\ \text{collection period on} \\ \text{original collectible sales} \end{pmatrix} \begin{pmatrix} \text{daily level of} \\ \text{collectible sales} \\ \text{from original} \\ \text{customers} \end{pmatrix}$$

$$= (R)(\Delta ACP)[(S_{orig} - B_{orig})/360]$$
$$= (.20)(30 [(\$8,000,000 - \$240,000)/360]$$
$$= \$129,333$$

Step 3: Determine dollar-level required return on the marginal increase in investment in receivables and inventory due to new sales.

Discussion: The marginal increase in investment in collectible receivables due to new sales (ACP_{new}) $[(\Delta S - \Delta B)/360](V)$ is added to the increased investment in inventory (ΔI) and multipled times the required return on investment in inventory and receivables (R).

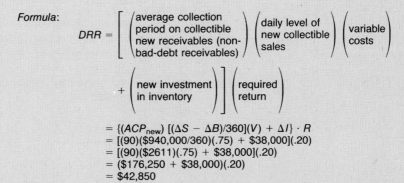

Formula:

$$DRR = \left[\left(\begin{array}{l} \text{average collection} \\ \text{period on collectible} \\ \text{new receivables (non-} \\ \text{bad-debt receivables)} \end{array} \right) \left(\begin{array}{l} \text{daily level of} \\ \text{new collectible} \\ \text{sales} \end{array} \right) \left(\begin{array}{l} \text{variable} \\ \text{costs} \end{array} \right) \right.$$

$$\left. + \left(\begin{array}{l} \text{new investment} \\ \text{in inventory} \end{array} \right) \right] \left(\begin{array}{l} \text{required} \\ \text{return} \end{array} \right)$$

$$= \{(ACP_{new}) \ [(\Delta S - \Delta B)/360](V) + \Delta I\} \cdot R$$
$$= [(90)(\$940,000/360)(.75) + \$38,000](.20)$$
$$= [(90)(\$2611)(.75) + \$38,000](.20)$$
$$= (\$176,250 + \$38,000)(.20)$$
$$= \$42,850$$

Step 4: Compare the incremental revenues with the incremental costs.

Formula:

$$\left(\begin{array}{l} \text{profit contribution} \\ \text{—from step 1} \end{array} \right) - \left(\begin{array}{l} \text{opportunity cost} \\ \text{associated with} \\ \text{original sales—} \\ \text{from step 2} \end{array} \right) - \left(\begin{array}{l} \text{required return associated} \\ \text{with the investment in} \\ \text{receivables associated with} \\ \text{new sales—from step 3} \end{array} \right)$$

$$= (\Delta P) - (OC) - (DRR)$$
$$= \$190,000 - \$129,333 - \$42,850$$
$$= \$17,817$$

Decision: Since the benefits outweigh the costs by $17,817 the proposed change in credit policy should be made.

The major area of confusion in this analysis lies in the calculation of the incremental "investment" in accounts receivable which takes place in steps 2 and 3 and results in an opportunity cost to the firm in the form of lost income on funds that are now invested in accounts receivable. As mentioned earlier, the "investment" in accounts receivable increases in two ways: (1) An opportunity cost occurs as original customers take advantage of the more generous credit period and pay later, causing a delay in the collection of accounts receivable, and (2) new customers are attracted to the firm as a result of the more lenient credit policy thus further increasing accounts receivable. The increased investment represents funds that the firm can no longer invest elsewhere to earn a positive return. Thus the increased level of accounts receivable is a source of an opportunity cost. *The opportunity cost arising from original customers' taking advantage of the new credit period is based upon the full collectible sales value* (the sales value less bad debts on those sales) *of the receivables*. What has happened is that the receipt of the collectible sales value of these receivables has been delayed, creating an **opportunity cost.** In the absence of the change in credit policy the full collectible sales value would have been received 30 days earlier; thus, if we multiply 30 days times the full daily collectible sales level, we get the increased investment caused by the delay in collection of original sales, which in turn creates the opportunity cost:

increased investment due to delay in collections because *original customers* take advantage of the new longer credit period $=$ increase in the length of time (in days) that original customers' collectible receivables are outstanding $\times$ daily level of original collectible sales

$= (\Delta ACP) \times (S_{orig} - B_{orig})/360 \text{ days}$

$= (30 \text{ days}) \times (\$8,000,000 - \$240,000)/360 \text{ days}$

$= \$646,667$

This calculation is actually part of step 2 in Table 7A–2 and this is repeated in that table. Note that the level of bad debts for the firm's original customers is assumed not to change in the analysis presented here.

Although the opportunity cost of carying new receivables caused by original customers' taking advantage of the new credit period is based upon the full collectible sales value, *the cost of carrying new receivables due to new customers' being attracted to the firm is based upon its variable cost*; that is, the incremental investment in accounts receivable from new customers should be assessed at its cost to the selling firm. Since, at the margin, production and selling costs are the variable cost portion of the incremental or marginal receivables, and these are the only investment the firm makes in accounts receivable due to new sales, the incremental investment in accounts receivable is equal to the variable cost portion of these receivables. In effect, the variable costs are the only cash outflows associated with the new investment in receivables for new customers. Thus

Marginal increase in investment due to attraction of *new customers* to the firm $=$ Marginal increase in receivables due to new sales $\times$ Percent variable costs of the new sales

$= (ACP_{new}) \times (\Delta S - \Delta B)/(360) \times (V)$

$= (90 \text{ days}) \times (\$940,000/360 \text{ days}) \times (.75)$

$= \$176,250$

This calculation is actually part of step 3 in Table 7A–2 and thus is repeated in that table.

To summarize, the full collectible value of the original accounts receivable is the appropriate measure with which to calculate the opportunity cost resulting from a delay in the collection of receivables caused by original customers changing their payment patterns, while only the variable cost portion of the cost of added accounts receivable is appropriate for the change in investment in receivables resulting from the bringing of new credit sales

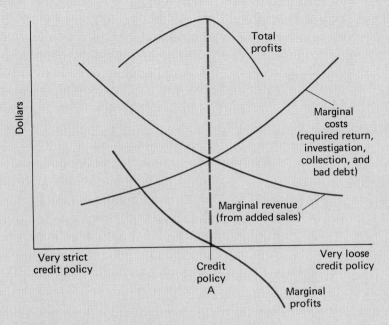

FIGURE 7A–1. Credit Policy and Profits

to the firm by the change in credit policy.[1] Table 7A–2 summarizes the calculations associated with this problem.

Examining Table 7A–2, we find that the total marginal benefits are $17,817 greater than the marginal costs. Thus, a change to the proposed credit policy is warranted. In summary, the logic behind this approach to credit policy is to examine the incremental or marginal benefits, the opportunity cost, and the required return associated with the change in credit policy. If the change promises more benefits than costs, the change should be made. If, however, the incremental costs are greater than the benefits, the proposed change should be avoided. Graphically, this logic is shown in Figure 7A–1. Under this philosophy, investment should continue until marginal costs are equal to marginal revenues, which occurs at credit policy A in Figure 7A–1.

In practice this analysis is by no means easy. The inputs, such as sales and cost changes resulting from a given change in receivables policy, are extremely difficult to estimate. Moreover, in general the accuracy of these estimates usually leave something to be desired. As a result, it is generally a good idea to change credit policies in a slow, controlled manner, making a minor change in one decision variable at a time, evaluating the results of this change, and then perhaps adjusting this variable further or changing another decision variable. In this way major errors are avoided, while the firm's credit policies move smoothly toward an optimum level.

---

[1] Stephen E. Celec and Joe D. Icerman, "A Comprehensive Approach to Accounts Receivable Management," *Financial Review*, 15 (Spring 1980), 23–34, provides an excellent discussion of the state of the art of accounts receivable management.

7A–1. What are the risk-return tradeoffs associated with adopting a more liberal trade credit policy?

7A–2. Explain the purpose of marginal analysis.

7A–1. (*Marginal Analysis*) The J. Flowers Corporation is considering relaxing its current credit policy. Currently the firm has annual sales (all credit) of $5 million and an average collection period of 90 days (assume a 360-day year). The current percent of bad debt losses is 4 percent and the firm's required rate of return on investment in receivables and inventory is 25 percent. Flowers produces sports equipment on which the variable costs are 70 percent of the selling price. Given the following information, should it adopt the new policy?

	Present Policy	Proposed Policy
Annual sales (all credit)	$5,000,000	$6,000,000
Average collection period on collectible sales		
Original sales	90 days	120 days
New sales		120 days
Average inventory	$800,000	$875,000
Bad debt losses in percent	4%	4% on original sales
		8% on new sales

7A–2. (*Marginal Analysis*) The S. Carlson Corporation is considering a major change in credit policy. Carlson is a major manufacturer of sportswear on which 80 percent of the selling price is variable costs. For any new investment in receivables and inventory, the firm would require a return of 30 percent. Given the following information, should Carlson adopt the proposed policy?

	Present Policy	Proposed Policy
Annual sales (all credit)	$11,000,000	$12,500,000
Average collection period on collectible sales		
Original sales	45 days	55 days
New sales		55 days
Average inventory	$900,000	$975,000
Bad debt losses in percent	5%	5% on original sales
		8% on new sales

7A–3. (*Marginal Analysis*) The D. Southard Company has annual sales of $5 million. All sales are credit and the credit terms are net 30 days, which is also the average collection period. The company is studying the possibility of relaxing credit terms for one year in hopes of securing new sales. The variable costs are 75 percent and the required rate of return on investment in receivables and inventory is 25 percent. Given the following information, which policy or policies should Southard adopt?

	Present Policy	Policy X	Policy Y
Annual sales (all credit)	$5,000,000	$5,600,000	$6,000,000
Average collection period on collectible sales			
Original sales	30 days	45 days	60 days
New collectible sales from policy X		45 days	60 days
New collectible sales from policy Y			60 days
Average inventory	$800,000	$840,000	$860,000
Bad debt losses in percent	5%	5% on original sales	5% on original sales
		7% on new sales	7% on new sales brought in by policy X
			9% on new sales brought in by policy Y

8

Short-term Financing

This chapter is one of four that discuss sources of financing. By convention all sources of financing that must be repaid within one year are considered to be short term, those that must be repaid in one to five years are intermediate term, and all sources with maturities longer than five years are classified as long term. Intermediate-term sources are discussed in Chapter 18 in conjunction with financial leases, while long-term sources are presented in Chapters 19 and 20.

Two major issues are involved in managing the firm's use of short-term financing: (1) How much short-term financing should the firm use? and (2) What specific sources of short-term financing should be selected? Chapter 5 used the *hedging principle* of working-capital management to answer the first of these two questions. Basically, that involved an attempt to match temporary needs for funds with short-term sources of financing and permanent needs with long-term sources.[1] The objective of this chapter will be to answer the second of the questions above: How should the financial manager select a source of short-term credit?

In general, three basic factors should be considered in selecting a source of short-term credit: (1) the effective cost of credit, (2) the availability of credit in the amount needed and for the period of time when financing is required, and (3) the influence of the use of a particular credit source on the cost and availability of other sources. We discuss the problem of estimating the cost of short-term credit before introducing the various sources of credit, as the procedure used is the same for all. The second and third factors listed above are discussed as they pertain to the individual sources of short-term credit.

---

[1] Temporary needs for funds arise in response to a temporary need for current assets. These include current assets that the firm does not plan to hold throughout the indefinite future. Permanent needs for funds arise in conjunction with a permanent need for certain assets. These assets consist of fixed assets plus the firm's minimum level of investment in current assets. Thus, when discussing working-capital management we abandoned the current-fixed asset classification in favor of the more useful concept of temporary and permanent assets.

ESTIMATING THE COST OF SHORT-TERM CREDIT

Approximate Cost-of-Credit Formula

The procedure used in estimating the cost of short-term credit is a very simple one and relies on the basic interest equation:

$$\text{interest} = \text{principal} \times \text{rate} \times \text{time} \tag{8-1}$$

where *interest* is the dollar amount of interest on a *principal* that is borrowed at some annual *rate* for a fraction of a year (represented by *time*). For example, a six-month loan for $1000 at 8 percent interest would require interest payments of $40:

$$\text{interest} = \$1000 \times .08 \times \frac{1}{2} = \$40$$

The problem faced in assessing the cost of a source of short-term financing, however, generally involves estimating the annual effective rate (RATE) where the interest amount, the principal sum, and the time for which financing will be needed are known. Thus, solving the basic interest equation for RATE produces[2]

$$\text{RATE} = \frac{\text{interest}}{\text{principal} \times \text{time}}$$

or

$$\text{RATE} = \frac{\text{interest}}{\text{principal}} \times \frac{1}{\text{time}} \tag{8-2}$$

Example The SKC Corporation plans to borrow $1000 for a 90-day period. At maturity the firm will repay the $1000 principal amount plus $30 interest. The effective annual rate of interest for the loan can be estimated using the RATE equation, as follows:

$$\text{RATE} = \frac{\$30}{\$1000} \times \frac{1}{90/360}$$

$$= .03 \times \frac{360}{90} = .12, \text{ or } 12 \text{ percent}$$

The effective annual cost of funds provided by the loan is therefore 12 percent.

The Annual Percentage Rate Formula

Compound interest was not considered in the simple RATE calculation. To consider the influence of compounding, we can use the following equation:

$$\text{APR} = \left(1 + \frac{r}{m}\right)^m - 1 \tag{8-3}$$

---

[2] A similar expression was used in Chapter 7 to estimate the effective cost of passing up discounts on trade credit.

where APR is the annual percentage rate, r is the nominal rate of interest per year (12 percent in the above example) and m is the number of compounding periods within a year [$m = 1/\text{TIME} = 1/(90/360) = 4$ in the example above]. Thus, the effective rate of interest on the example problem, considering compounding, is

$$\text{APR} = \left(1 + \frac{.12}{4}\right)^4 - 1 = .126, \text{ or } 12.6 \text{ percent}$$

The effect of compounding is to raise the effective cost of short-term credit. Since the differences between the two methods for periods less than one year are usually small, the simple interest version of RATE discussed above will be used.

SOURCES OF SHORT-TERM CREDIT

Short-term credit sources can be classified into two basic groups: unsecured and secured. **Unsecured** loans include all those sources that have as their security only the lender's faith in the ability of the borrower to repay the funds when due. There are three major sources of unsecured short-term credit: trade credit, unsecured bank loans, and commercial paper. **Secured** loans involve the pledge of specific assets as collateral in the event the borrower defaults in payment of principal or interest. The principal suppliers of secured credit include commercial banks, finance companies, and factors. The primary sources of collateral include accounts receivable and inventories.

Unsecured Sources: Trade Credit

Trade credit provides one of the most flexible sources of financing available to the firm.[3] To arrange for credit the firm need only place an order with one of its suppliers. The supplier checks the firm's credit and, if it is good, sends the merchandise. The purchasing firm then pays for the goods in accordance with the supplier's credit terms.

Credit Terms and Cash Discounts

Very often the credit terms offered with trade credit involve a cash discount for early payment. For example, a supplier might offer terms of 2/10, net 30, which means that a 2 percent discount is offered for payment within 10 days or the full amount is due in 30 days. Thus, a 2 percent penalty is involved for not paying within 10 days or for delaying payment from the tenth to the thirtieth day (that is, for 20 days). The effective annual cost of not taking the cash discount can be quite severe. Using a $1 invoice amount, the effective cost of passing up the discount period using the above credit terms and our RATE equation can be estimated:

$$\text{RATE} = \frac{\$.02}{\$.98} \times \frac{1}{20/360} = .3673, \text{ or } 36.73 \text{ percent}$$

Note that the 2 percent cash discount is the *interest* cost of extending the payment period an *additional* 20 days. Note also that the principal amount of the credit is

[3] In Chapter 5 we noted that trade credit is a primary source of spontaneous financing. That is, trade credit arises spontaneously with the firm's purchases.

$.98. This amount constitutes the full principal amount as of the tenth day of the credit period, after which time the cash discount is lost. The effective cost of passing up the 2 percent discount for 2 days is quite expensive, 36.73 percent. Furthermore, once the discount period has passed, there is no reason to pay before the final due date (the thirtieth day). Table 8–1 lists the effective annual cost of a number of alternative credit terms. Note that the cost of trade credit varies directly with the size of the cash discount and inversely with the length of time between the end of the discount period and the final due date.

Stretching on Trade Credit

Firms utilizing trade credit sometimes engage in *stretching* of trade accounts. This practice involves not paying within the prescribed credit period. For example, a firm might purchase materials under credit terms of 3/10, net 60; however, when faced with a shortage of cash, the firm might extend payment to the eightieth day. Continued violation of trade terms could eventually lead to a loss of credit. However, for short periods, and at infrequent intervals, stretching offers the firm a potentially useful source of short-term credit.

Advantages of Trade Credit

As a source of short-term financing, trade credit has a number of advantages. First, trade credit is easily and conveniently obtained as a normal part of the firm's operations. Second, no formal agreements are generally involved in extending credit. Furthermore, the amount of credit extended expands and contracts with the needs of the firm; this is the reason for its earlier classification as a spontaneous source of financing (Chapter 5).

Unsecured Sources: Bank Credit

Commercial banks provide unsecured short-term credit in two basic forms: lines of credit and transaction loans (notes payable). Maturities of both types of loans are usually one year or less, with rates of interest depending on the creditworthiness of the borrower and the level of interest rates in the economy as a whole.

Line of Credit

A **line of credit** is generally an informal agreement or understanding between the borrower and the bank as to the maximum amount of credit that the bank will provide the borrower at any one time. Under this type of agreement there is no *legal* commitment on the part of the bank to provide the stated credit. In a **revolving credit agreement,** which is a variant of this form of financing, a legal obligation is involved. The line of credit agreement generally covers a period of one year corresponding to

TABLE 8–1. Effective Rates of Interest on Selected Trade Credit Terms

Credit Terms	Effective Rate
2/10, net 60	14.69%
2/10, net 90	9.18
3/20, net 60	27.84
6/10, net 90	28.72

```
                           City National Bank
                             Snook, Texas


                                              July 14, 19XX



          Ms. Rebecca Swank
          Vice President and Treasurer
          Nuland Manufacturing Company
          Bryan, Texas

          Dear Ms. Swank:

          Following an analysis of your request, we have decided to extend
          to you a line of credit for working capital purposes in the amount
          of $300,000.  The credit is extended for your current fiscal year
          ending July 31, 19XX.  Borrowings under this line will be at our
          prime rate prevailing at the time.

          This credit is subject only to maintaining the firm's financial
          position.

                                              Sincerely,



                                              Francis L. Prince
                                              Executive Vice President
```

FIGURE 8–1. Letter of Agreement to Extend a Line of Credit

the borrower's *fiscal* year. Thus, if the borrower is on a July 31 fiscal year, its lines of credit will be based on the same annual period.

Credit Terms. Lines of credit generally do not involve fixed rates of interest, but state that credit will be extended *at ½ percent over prime* or some other spread over the bank's prime rate.[4] Furthermore, the agreement usually does not spell out the specific use that will be made of the funds beyond some general statement, such as *for working-capital purposes*. Figure 8–1 shows an example letter of agreement to extend a line of credit.

Lines of credit usually require that the borrower maintain a minimum balance in the bank throughout the loan period. This **compensating balance** (which can be stated as a percent of the line of credit or the loan amount) increases the effective

---

[4] The "prime rate of interest" represents the rate that a bank charges its most creditworthy borrowers.

cost of the loan to the borrower unless a deposit balance equal to or greater than the required compensating balance is ordinarily maintained in the bank.

The effective cost of short-term bank credit can be estimated using the RATE equation. Consider the following example:

Example   M&M Beverage Company has a $300,000 line of credit which requires a compensating balance equal to 10 percent of the loan amount. The rate paid on the loan is 12 percent per annum, $200,000 is borrowed for a six-month period, and the firm does not, at present, have a deposit with the lending bank. The dollar cost of the loan includes the interest expense and, in addition, the opportunity cost of maintaining an idle cash balance equal to the 10 percent compensating balance. To accommodate the cost of the compensating balance requirement, assume that the added funds will have to be borrowed and simply left idle in the firm's checking account. Thus, the amount actually borrowed (B) will be larger than the needed $200,000. In fact, the needed $200,000 will comprise 90 percent of the total borrowed funds due to the 10 percent compensating balance requirement, hence $.90B = \$200,000$, such that $B = \$222,222$. Thus, interest is paid on a $222,222 loan ($\$222,222 \times .12 \times \frac{1}{2} = \$13,333.32$), of which only $200,000 is available for use by the firm.[5] The effective annual cost of credit therefore is

$$\text{RATE} = \frac{\$13,333.32}{\$200,000} \times \frac{1}{180/360} = 13.33 \text{ percent}$$

If the firm normally maintains at least $20,000 (or 10 percent of the needed funds) in a demand deposit with the lending bank, then the cost of the credit is

$$\text{RATE} = \frac{\$12,000}{\$200,000} \times \frac{1}{180/360} = 12 \text{ percent}$$

In the M&M Beverage Company example the loan required the payment of principal ($222,222) plus interest ($13,333.32) at the end of the six-month loan period. Frequently, bank loans will be made on a discount basis. That is, the loan interest will be deducted from the loan amount before the funds are transferred to the borrower. Extending the M&M Beverage Company example to consider discounted interest involves reducing the loan proceeds ($200,000) in the previous example by the amount of interest for the full six months ($13,333.32). The effective rate of interest on the loan is now:

---

[5] Although technically incorrect, the same answer would have been obtained by assuming a total loan of $200,000, of which only 90 percent of $180,000 was available for use by the firm; that is,

$$\text{RATE} = \frac{\$12,000}{\$180,000} \times \frac{1}{180/360} = 13.33 \text{ percent}$$

Interest is now calculated on the $200,000 loan amount ($12,000 = \$200,000 \times .12 \times \frac{1}{2}$).

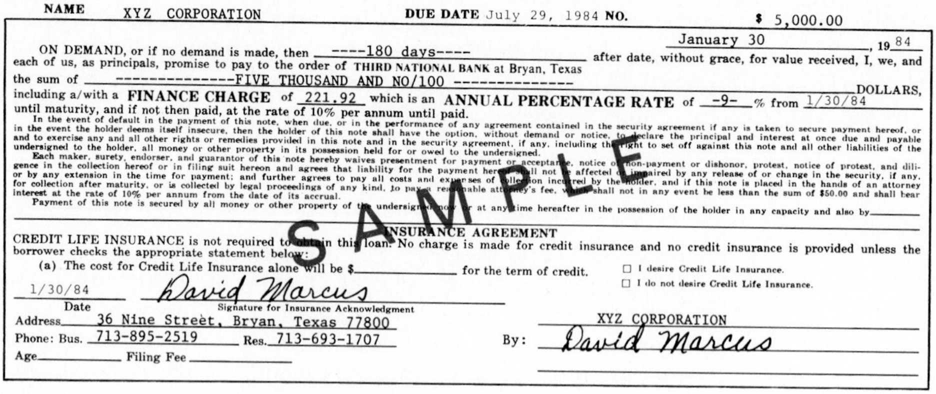

| NAME   XYZ CORPORATION | DUE DATE July 29, 1984 NO. | $ 5,000.00 |

ON DEMAND, or if no demand is made, then _____ ----180 days---- _____ after date, without grace, for value received, I, we, and each of us, as principals, promise to pay to the order of **THIRD NATIONAL BANK** at Bryan, Texas the sum of _____ --------------FIVE THOUSAND AND NO/100 -------------- _____ DOLLARS, including a/with a **FINANCE CHARGE** of _221.92_ which is an **ANNUAL PERCENTAGE RATE** of _-9-_ % from _1/30/84_ until maturity, and if not then paid, at the rate of 10% per annum until paid.

In the event of default in the payment of this note, when due, or in the performance of any agreement contained in the security agreement if any is taken to secure payment hereof, or in the event the holder deems itself insecure, then the holder of this note shall have the option, without demand or notice, to declare the principal and interest at once due and payable and to exercise any and all other rights or remedies provided in this note and in the security agreement, if any, including the right to set off against this note and all other liabilities of the undersigned to the holder, all money or other property in its possession held for or owed to the undersigned.

Each maker, surety, endorser, and guarantor of this note hereby waives presentment for payment or acceptance, notice of non-payment or dishonor, protest, notice of protest, and diligence in the collection hereof or in filing suit hereon and agrees that liability for the payment hereof shall not be affected or impaired by any release of or change in the security, if any, or by any extension in the time for payment; and further agrees to pay all costs and expenses of collection incurred by the holder, and if this note is placed in the hands of an attorney for collection after maturity, or is collected by legal proceedings of any kind, to pay a reasonable attorney's fee, which shall not in any event be less than the sum of $50.00 and shall bear interest at the rate of 10% per annum from the date of its accrual.

Payment of this note is secured by all money or other property of the undersigned _____ at any time hereafter in the possession of the holder in any capacity and also by _____

INSURANCE AGREEMENT

CREDIT LIFE INSURANCE is not required to obtain this loan. No charge is made for credit insurance and no credit insurance is provided unless the borrower checks the appropriate statement below:

(a) The cost for Credit Life Insurance alone will be $_____ for the term of credit. ☐ I desire Credit Life Insurance.
  ☐ I do not desire Credit Life Insurance.

_1/30/84_   _David Marcus_
Date   Signature for Insurance Acknowledgment
Address ___36 Nine Street, Bryan, Texas 77800___   XYZ CORPORATION
Phone: Bus. _713-895-2519_   Res. _713-693-1707_   By: _David Marcus_
Age_____   Filing Fee_____

FIGURE 8–2.   Example Short-term Bank Note

$$\text{RATE} = \frac{\$13,333.32}{\$200,000 - \$13,333.32} \times \frac{1}{180/360}$$

$$= .1429, \text{ or } 14.29 \text{ percent}$$

The effect of discounting interest was to raise the cost of the loan from 13.33 to 14.29 percent. This results from the fact that the firm pays interest on the same amount of funds as before ($222,222); however, this time it gets the use of $13,333.32 less, or $200,000 − $13,333.32 = $186,666.68.[6]

Transaction Loans   Still another form of unsecured short-term bank credit can be obtained in the form of **transaction loans.** Here the loan is made for a specific purpose. This is the type of loan that most individuals associate with bank credit. The loan is obtained by signing a promissory note similar to the one shown in Figure 8–2.

Unsecured transaction loans are very similar to a line of credit with regard to cost, term to maturity, and compensating balance requirements. In both instances commercial banks often require that the borrower *clean up* its short-term loans for a 30- to 45-day period during the year. This means, very simply, that the borrower must be free of any bank debt for the stated period. The purpose of such a requirement is to ensure that the borrower is not using short-term bank credit to finance a part of its permanent needs for funds.

---

[6] If M&M needs the use of a full $200,000, then they will have to borrow more than $222,222 to cover both the compensating balance requirement *and* the discounted interest. In fact, the firm will have to borrow some amount B such that

$$B - .10B - (.12 \times \tfrac{1}{2})B = \$200,000$$
$$.84B = \$200,000$$
$$B = \frac{\$200,000}{.84} = \$238,095$$

The cost of credit remains the same at 14.29 percent, as we see below:

$$\text{RATE} = \frac{\$14,285.70}{\$238,095 - \$23,810 - \$14,285.70} \times \frac{1}{180/360}$$
$$= .1429, \text{ or } 14.29\%$$

Unsecured Sources: Commercial Paper

Only the largest and most creditworthy companies are able to use **commercial paper,** which is simply a short-term *promise to pay* that is sold in the market for short-term debt securities.[7]

Credit Terms

The maturity of this credit source is generally six months or less, although some issues carry 270-day maturities. The interest rate on commercial paper is generally slightly lower (one-half to one percent) than the prime rate on commercial bank loans. Also, interest is usually discounted, although commercial paper is available at times that is interest bearing.

New issues of commercial paper are either placed directly (sold by the issuing firm directly to the investing public) or dealer placed. Dealer placement involves the use of a commercial paper dealer, who sells the issue for the issuing firm. Many major finance companies, such as General Motors Acceptance Corporation, place their commercial paper directly. The volume of direct versus dealer placements is roughly 4 to 1 in favor of direct placements. Dealers are used primarily by industrial firms that make only infrequent use of the commercial paper market or that, owing to their small size, would have difficulty placing the issue without the help of a dealer.

Commercial Paper as a Source of Short-Term Credit

A number of advantages accrue to the user of commercial paper:

1. **Interest rate.** Commercial paper rates are generally lower than rates on bank loans and comparable sources of short-term financing. Figure 8–3 displays historical rates of interest on short-term bank credit and commercial paper spanning the 15-month period ending April 1987.
2. **Compensating balance requirement.** No minimum balance requirements are associated with commercial paper. However, issuing firms usually find it desirable to maintain lines of credit agreements sufficient to back up their short-term financing needs in the event that a new issue of commercial paper cannot be sold or an outstanding issue cannot be repaid when due.
3. **Amount of credit.** Commercial paper offers the firm with very large credit needs a single source for all its short-term financing. To obtain the necessary funds from a commercial bank might require dealing with a number of banks, owing to the loan restrictions placed on the banks by the regulatory authorities.[8]
4. **Prestige.** Since it is widely recognized that only the most creditworthy borrowers have access to the commercial paper market, its use signifies a firm's credit status.

Using commercial paper for short-term financing, however, involves a very important *risk*. That is, the commercial paper market is highly impersonal and denies even the most creditworthy borrower any flexibility in terms of repayment. When bank credit is used, the borrower has someone with whom he can work out any temporary

---

[7] A limited discussion of commercial paper is presented here; the topic is discussed in detail in Chapter 6.

[8] Member banks of the Federal Reserve System are limited to 10% of their total capital, surplus, and undivided profits when making loans to a single borrower. Thus, where a corporate borrower's needs for financing are very large it may have to deal with a group of participating banks to raise the needed funds.

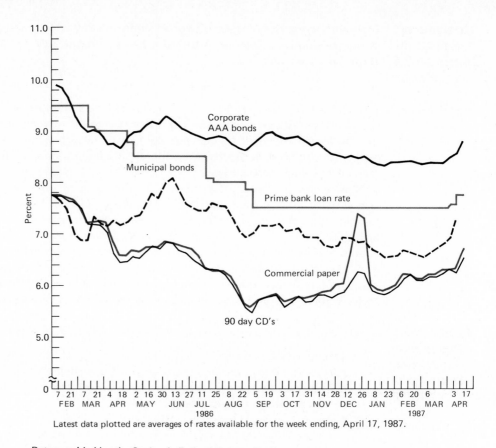

FIGURE 8–3. Historical Rates of Interest on Short-term Bank Credit and Commercial Paper

Latest data plotted are averages of rates available for the week ending, April 17, 1987.

Data provided by the St. Louis Federal Reserve Bank.

Legend:

Corporate Aaa Bonds: Long-term debt of the most credit worthy firms. (Discussed in Chapter 19.)

Prime Bank Loan Rate: Rate of interest charged to the most creditworthy borrowers on short-term loans.

90-Day CD s: Certificates of deposit carrying a 90-day maturity. (Discussed earlier in Chapter 6.)

difficulties he might encounter in meeting a loan deadline. This flexibility simply does not exist for the user of commercial paper.

Estimating the Cost of Commercial Paper

The cost of commercial paper can be estimated using the simple effective cost of credit equation (RATE). The key points to remember are that commercial paper interest is usually discounted and that if a dealer is used to place the issue, a fee must be paid. Even if a dealer is not used, the issuing firm will incur costs associated with preparing and placing the issue, which also must be considered in estimating the cost of credit.

Example   The EPG Mfg. Company uses commercial paper regularly to support its needs for short-term financing. The firm plans to sell $100 million in 270-day-maturity paper on which it expects to have to pay discounted interest at an annual rate of 12 percent per annum. In addition, EPG expects to incur a cost of approximately $100,000 in dealer placement fees and other expenses of issuing the paper. The effective cost of credit to EPG can be calculated as follows:

$$\text{RATE} = \frac{\$9 \text{ million} + \$100,000}{\$100 \text{ million} - \$100,000 - \$9 \text{ million}} \times \frac{1}{270/360}$$

$$= .1335, \text{ or } 1335 \text{ percent}$$

where the interest cost is calculated as $100 million $\times$ .12 $\times$ $270/360$ = $9 million. Thus, the effective cost of credit to EPG is 13.35 percent.

Secured Sources: Accounts Receivable Loans

Secured sources of short-term credit have certain assets of the firm pledged as collateral to secure the loan. Upon default of the loan agreement, the lender has first claim to the pledged assets in addition to its claim as a general creditor of the firm. Hence the secured credit agreement offers an added margin of safety to the lender.

Generally a firm's receivables are among its most liquid assets. For this reason they are considered by many lenders to be prime collateral for a secured loan. Two basic procedures can be used in arranging for financing based on receivables: pledging and factoring.

Pledging Accounts Receivable

Under the **pledging** arrangement the borrower simply pledges accounts receivable as collateral for a loan obtained from either a commercial bank or a finance company. The amount of the loan is stated as a percent of the face value of the receivables pledged. If the firm provides the lender with a **general line** on its receivables, then all of the borrower's accounts are pledged as security for the loan. This method of pledging is simple and inexpensive. However, since the lender has no control over the quality of the receivables being pledged, it will set the maximum loan at a relatively low percent of the total face value of the accounts, generally ranging downward from a maximum of around 75 percent.

Still another approach to pledging involves the borrower's presenting specific invoices to the lender as collateral for a loan. This method is somewhat more expensive in that the lender must assess the creditworthiness of each individual account pledged; however, given this added knowledge he will be willing to increase the loan as a percent of the face value of the invoices. In this case the loan might reach as high as 85 or 90 percent of the face value of the pledged receivables.

Credit Terms.   Accounts receivable loans generally carry an interest rate 2 to 5 percent higher than the bank's prime lending rate. Finance companies charge an even higher rate. In addition, the lender will usually charge a handling fee stated as a percent of the face value of the receivables processed which may be as much as 1 to 2 percent of the face value.

Example   The A. B. Good Company sells electrical supplies to building contractors on terms of net 60. The firm's average monthly sales are $100,000; thus, given the firm's two-month credit terms, its average receivables balance is $200,000. The firm pledges all its receivables to a local bank, which in turn advances up to 70 percent of the face value of the receivables at 3 percent over prime and with a 1 percent processing charge on *all* receivables pledged. A. B. Good follows a practice of borrowing the maximum amount possible, and the current prime rate is 10 percent.

The effective cost of using this source of financing for a full year is computed as follows:

$$\text{RATE} = \frac{\$18{,}200 + \$12{,}000}{\$140{,}000} \times \frac{1}{360/360} = 21.57 \text{ percent}$$

where the total dollar cost of the loan consists of both the annual interest expense (.13 × .70 × $200,000 = $18,200) and the annual processing fee (.01 × $100,000 × 12 months = $12,000). The amount of credit extended is .70 × $200,000 = $140,000. Note that the processing charge applies to *all* receivables pledged. Thus, the A. B. Good Company pledges $100,000 each month, or $1,200,000 during the year, on which a 1 percent fee must be paid, for a total annual charge of $12,000.[9]

One added point should be made about the cost of loans secured by the pledge of accounts receivable. The lender, in addition to making advances or loans, may be providing certain credit services for the borrower. For example, the lender may provide billing and collection services. The value of these services should *not* be considered a part of the cost of credit. In the preceding example A. G. Good Company may *save* credit department expenses of $10,000 per year by pledging all its accounts and letting the lender provide those services. In this case, the cost of short-term credit is only

$$\text{RATE} = \frac{\$18{,}200 + \$12{,}000 - \$10{,}000}{\$140{,}000} \times \frac{1}{360/360} = 14.43 \text{ percent}$$

Advantages and Disadvantages of Pledging.   The primary advantage of pledging as a source of short-term credit relates to the flexibility it provides the borrower. Financing is available on a continuous basis. As new accounts are created through credit sales, they provide the collateral for the financing of new production. Further-

---

[9] If only one month's accounts are factored and those accounts are collected in 60 days, then the cost of credit can be calculated as follows:

$$\text{RATE} = \frac{\$1{,}516.67 + \$1000}{\$70{,}000} \times \frac{1}{(60/360)} = .2157, \text{ or } 21.57 \text{ percent}$$

where interest equals $100,000 × .70 × .13 × ⅙ = $1,516.67 and the pledging fee equals .01 × $100,000 = $1000.

more, the lender may provide credit services that eliminate or at least reduce the need for similar services within the firm. The primary disadvantage associated with this method of financing is its cost, which can be relatively high compared with other sources of short-term credit, owing to the level of the interest rate charged on loans and the processing fee on pledged accounts.

BASIC FINANCIAL MANAGEMENT IN PRACTICE
The Ins and Outs of Factoring

Getting in

Factors are necessarily selective in the companies they agree to take on as clients. Detailed negotiations take place with prospective clients and their financial advisers; two key items of information that the factor will require are:

- Audited accounts for the past year and the current management accounts.
- A list of the customers and a monthly turnover projection for each.

Commencement date. Once agreement has been reached a date will be arranged for the factor to assume responsibility for the sales ledger.

Introducing the service. At the start of the factoring arrangement, it is usual for the client to send a letter to customers explaining the introduction of the factor. Where appropriate, the factor may speak personally to some customers.

Invoices. Once factoring starts, clients will be encouraged to invoice their customers immediately a valid debt has been created, passing copies of invoices to the factor or, in some cases, passing the invoices to the factor for mailing. Clients must ensure that their invoicing procedure is efficient, with the terms and conditions clearly stated so that they will be understood by customers.

Factoring. With recourse and non-recourse factoring, clients may only draw a financial facility within the credit limits agreed for each customer. These credit limits must be monitored constantly to ensure they are realistic.

Credit cover. In the case of non-recourse factoring, clients must ensure they have credit approval from the factor before delivering the goods or providing the service. They must seek credit cover for new customers before delivery, and should monitor the level of credit cover on existing customers to ensure that it is adequate.

Management accounts. During the course of the year, a factor will ask to see its client's management accounts, usually at about quarterly intervals, in order to monitor the progress of the business.

Day-to-day operation. A number of routine procedures and associated documentation will be employed in the operation of the factoring arrangement, depending on the precise system of the factor concerned. Factors will usually supply a concise set of operating instructions to guide the client.

Getting out

Companies should not be inhibited from entering into factoring arrangements for fear that they may find it difficult to discontinue the service. Indeed they may wish to discontinue for a variety of reasons. For instance:

- Acquisition by a larger parent who does not wish to factor.
- Change in the pattern of business, resulting for example in a significant reduction in customers.
- Replacement from another source of funding at present being taken from the factor.

• Generation of increased profits rendering factoring unnecessary.

A factoring agreement will almost certainly contain a clause relating to the notice requirement—usually about three months on either side. On deciding to withdraw from factoring, clients will need to address themselves to just three principal matters:

• The availability of funds to finance the buying back of the outstanding debts from the factor.

• The setting up of a sales ledger system and the acquisition of necessary sales ledger administration, credit control and collection staff, to be effective from the agreed handing-over date.

• Credit insurance arrangements to replace the credit cover at present provided by the factor in the case of a non-recourse agreement.

Factors have no wish to hold clients to agreements if their services are no longer needed. Indeed they will provide every assistance to effect a smooth change over when client wishes to terminate the arrangement.

Source: Maberly, Michael, "Factoring: A Catalyst For Growth and Profits," *Accountancy*, Institute of Chartered Accountants 97 (April 1986), 122–124.

Factoring Accounts Receivable

Factoring receivables involves the outright sale of a firm's accounts to a factor. A **factor** is a financial institution that acquires the receivables of other firms. The factor may be a commercial finance company that engages solely in the factoring of receivables (known as an **old line factor**) or it may be a commercial bank. The factor, in turn, bears the risk of collection and, for a fee, services the accounts. The fee is stated as a percent of the face value of all receivables factored (usually from 1 to 3 percent).

The factor typically does *not* make payment for factored accounts until the accounts have been collected or the credit terms have been met. Should the firm wish to receive immediate payment for its factored accounts, it can borrow from the factor, using the factored accounts as collateral. The maximum loan the firm can obtain is equal to the face value of its factored accounts less the factor's fee (1 to 3 percent) less a reserve (6 to 10 percent) less the interest on the loan. For example, if $100,000 in receivables is factored which carry 60-day credit terms, a 2 percent factor's fee, a 6 percent reserve, and interest at 1 percent per month on advances, then the maximum loan or advance the firm can receive is computed as follows:

Face amount of receivables factored	$100,000
Less: Fee (.02 × $100,000)	(2,000)
Reserve (.06 × $100,000)	(6,000)
Interest (.01 × $92,000 × 2 months)	(1,840)
Maximum advance	$ 90,160

Note that interest is discounted and calculated based upon a maximum amount of funds available for advance ($92,000 = $100,000 − $2000 − $6000). Thus, the effective cost of credit can be calculated as follows:

$$\text{RATE} = \frac{\$1840 + \$2000}{\$90,160} \times \frac{1}{60/360}$$
$$= 25.55 \text{ percent}$$

BASIC FINANCIAL MANAGEMENT IN PRACTICE

Comparison of a Manufacturer Who Does Not Factor With One Who Does

Both companies have salesmen or selling agents who take orders. In the case of the manufacturer who is not factored, the sales orders must be submitted to its own credit department for approval before merchandise may be shipped. Under a factoring arrangement, the order is reported to the factor for its credit approval. This may be granted in advance by the factor for all or certain customers of the manufacturer. There is considerable savings to the manufacturer who factors because it is not necessary for it to maintain its own credit department, to subscribe to credit agency services, or to maintain credit files on each customer. Of course, offsetting these cost savings is the commission charged by the factor for performing these services and for covering the related credit risk and bookkeeping services.

After credit approval has been secured in either case, the next step is to bill and ship the merchandise to the customer in accordance with the terms of the order. There is no difference in this procedure whether the manufacturer is factored or not, except that in the case of a factored account, it is necessary to provide additional copies of the invoices for use by the factor, and the invoice to the customer must bear the appropriate inscription if the account is on a "notification" basis. The factored client also must either send proof of shipment to the factor along with the invoices (not usual in recent years because of the volume of paper required) or keep shipping documentation available for the factor's inspection.

At this point, the manufacturer who is factored has done all that is required as far as the customer is concerned. It need not maintain an accounts receivable ledger with its customer because its account with the factor takes the place of individual accounts. It must still concern itself with the settlement of claims arising out of alleged unsatisfactory merchandise, late delivery, etc. as the factor's responsibility is a financial one, and not one which involves merchandising problems or customer remittance shortages and deductions.

Source: Walters, William H., "Factoring," *The CPA Journal*, 56 (June 1986), 66–72.

Secured Sources: Inventory Loans

Inventory loans provide a second source of security for short-term secured credit. The amount of the loan that can be obtained depends on both the marketability and perishability of the inventory. Some items, such as raw materials (grains, oil, lumber, and chemicals), are excellent sources of collateral, since they can easily be liquidated. Other items, such as work in process inventories, provide very poor collateral because of their lack of marketability.

There are several methods by which inventory can be used to secure short-term financing. These include a *floating* or *blanket lien, chattel mortgage, field warehouse receipt*, and *terminal warehouse receipt*.

Floating Lien Agreement

Under a **floating lien** agreement the borrower gives the lender a lien against all its inventories. This provides the simplest but least secure form of inventory collateral. The borrowing firm maintains full control of the inventories and continues to sell and replace them as it sees fit. Obviously, this lack of control over the collateral greatly dilutes the value of this type of security to the lender. Correspondingly, loans made with floating liens on inventory as collateral are generally limited to a relatively modest fraction of the value of the inventories covered by the lien. In addition, floating liens usually include future as well as existing inventories.

Chattel Mortgage Agreements

The lender can increase its security interest by having specific items of inventory identified (by serial number or otherwise) in the security agreement. Such an arrangement is provided by a **chattel mortgage.** The borrower retains title to the inventory but cannot sell the items without the lender's consent. This type of agreement is costly to implement, because specific items of inventory must be identified. It is used only for major items of inventory such as machine tools or other capital assets.

Field Warehouse Financing Agreements

Increased lender control over inventories used as loan collateral can be obtained through the use of a **field warehouse agreement.** Here the inventories used as collateral are physically separated from the firm's other inventories and placed under the control of a third-party field warehousing firm. Note that the inventories are not removed from the borrower's premises, but are placed under the control of a third party who is responsible for protecting the security interests of the lender. This arrangement is particularly useful where large, bulky items are used as collateral. For example, a refinery might use a part of its inventory of fuel oil to secure a short-term bank loan. Under a field warehousing agreement the oil reserves would be set aside in specific tanks or storage vessels, which would be controlled (monitored) by a field warehousing concern.

The warehousing concern, upon receipt of the inventory, takes full control of the collateral. This means that the borrower is no longer allowed to use or sell the inventory items without the consent of the lender. The warehousing firm issues a **warehouse receipt** for the merchandise, which carries title to the goods represented therein. The receipt may be negotiable, in which case title can be transferred through sale of the receipt, or nonnegotiable, whereby title remains with the lender. With a negotiable receipt arrangement the warehouse concern will release the goods to whoever holds the receipt, whereas with a nonnegotiable receipt the goods may be released only on the written consent of the lender.

The cost of such a loan can be quite high, since the services of the field warehouse company must be paid for by the borrower.

Example The M. M. Richards Company follows a practice of obtaining short-term credit based on its seasonal finished goods inventory. The firm builds up its inventories of outdoor furniture throughout the winter months for sale in spring and summer. Thus, for the two-month period ended March 31, it uses its fall and winter production of furniture as collateral for a short-term bank loan. The bank lends the company up to 70 percent of the value of the inventory at 14 percent interest plus a fixed fee of $2000 to cover the costs of a field warehousing arrangement. During this period the firm usually has about $200,000 in inventories, which it borrows against. The annual effective cost of the short-term credit is therefore

$$\text{RATE} = \frac{\$3267 + \$2000}{\$140,000} \times \frac{1}{60/360} = 22.57 \text{ percent}$$

where the financing cost consists of two month's interest ($140,000 $\times$ .14 $\times$ $^{60}/_{360}$ = $3267) plus the field warehousing fee of $2000.

Terminal Warehouse Agreements

The **terminal warehouse agreement** differs from the field warehouse agreement just discussed in only one respect. Here the inventories pledged as collateral are transported to a public warehouse that is physically removed from the borrower's premises. The lender has an added degree of safety or security because the inventory is totally removed from the borrower's control. Once again the cost of this type of arrangement is increased by the necessity for paying the warehouse concern; in addition, the inventory must be transported to and eventually from the public warehouse.

The same warehouse receipt procedure described earlier for field warehouse loans is used. Again, the cost of this type of financing can be quite high.

Summary

There are two basic problems encountered in managing the firm's use of short-term financing. The first of these involves determining the level of short-term financing the firm should use. This question was addressed in Chapter 5 through the use of the **hedging principle** of working-capital management. Basically, this principle suggests the use of short-term financing to finance temporary or short-term investments in assets. In this chapter we have sought to answer the second of the questions. That is: How should the financial manager select a source of short-term financing?

Three basic factors provide the key considerations in selecting a source of short-term financing: (1) the effective cost of credit, (2) the availability of financing in the amount and for the time needed, and (3) the effect of the use of credit from a particular source on the cost and availability of other sources of credit.

The various sources of short-term credit can be categorized into two groups: unsecured and secured. Unsecured credit, as opposed to secured credit, offers no specific assets as security for the loan agreement. The sources of unsecured short-term credit are many, however. The primary sources include trade credit, lines of credit and unsecured transaction loans from commercial banks, and commercial paper. Secured credit is generally provided to business firms by commercial banks, finance companies, and factors. The most popular sources of security involve the use of accounts receivable and inventories. Loans secured by accounts receivable include pledging agreements wherein a firm merely pledges its receivables as security for a loan, and factoring whereby the firm sells the receivables to a factor. A primary difference in these two arrangements relates to the ability of the lender to seek payment from the borrower in the event that the accounts used as collateral become uncollectible. In a pledging arrangement the lender retains the right of recourse in the event of default, whereas factoring generally is without recourse.

Loans secured by inventories can be made using one of several types of security arrangements. Among the most widely used are the floating lien, chattel mortgage, field warehouse agreement, and terminal warehouse agreement. The form of agreement used will depend upon the nature of the inventories being pledged as collateral and the degree of control the lender wishes to exercise over the loan collateral.

Study Questions

8–1. What distinguishes short-term, intermediate-term, and long-term debt?

8–2. What factors should be considered in selecting a source of short-term credit? Discuss each.

8–3. How can the formula "interest = principal × rate × time" be used to estimate the effective cost of short-term credit?

8–4. How can we accommodate the effects of compounding in our calculation of the effective cost of short-term credit?

8–5. There are three major sources of unsecured short-term credit. List and discuss the distinguishing characteristics of each.

8–6. What is meant by the following trade credit terms: 2/10, net 30? 4/20, net 60? 3/15, net 45?

8–7. Define the following:
   a. Line of credit
   b. Commercial paper
   c. Compensating balance
   d. Prime rate

8–8. List and discuss four advantages of the use of commercial paper.

8–9. What "risk" is involved in the firm's use of commercial paper as a source of short-term credit? Discuss.

8–10. List and discuss the distinguishing features of the principal sources of secured credit based upon accounts receivable.

8–11. List and discuss the distinguishing features of the primary sources of secured credit based upon inventories.

Self-Test Problems

ST–1. (*Analyzing the Cost of a Commercial Paper Offering*) The Marilyn Sales Company is a wholesale machine tool broker which has gone through a recent expansion of its activities resulting in a doubling of its sales. The company has determined that it needs an additional $200 million in short-term funds to finance peak season sales during roughly six months of the year. Marilyn's treasurer has recommended that the firm utilize a commercial paper offering to raise the needed funds. Specifically, he has determined that a $200 million offering would require 10 percent interest (paid in advance or discounted) plus a $125,000 placement fee. The paper would carry a six-month (180-day) maturity. What is the effective cost of credit?

ST–2. (*Analyzing the Cost of Short-Term Credit*) The Samples Mfg. Co. provides specialty steel products to the oil industry. Although the firm's business is highly correlated with the cyclical swings in oil exploration activity, it also experiences some significant seasonality. It is this seasonality in its need for funds that the firm is currently concerned about. The firm needs $500,000 for the two-month period July–August each year, and as a result the company's vice-president of finance is currently considering the following three sources of financing:
   a. Establish a line of credit with the First State Bank of Austin, Texas. The bank has agreed to provide Samples with the needed $500,000, carrying an interest rate of 14 percent

with interest discounted and a compensating balance of 20 percent of the loan balance. Samples does not have a bank account with First State and would have to establish one to satisfy the compensating balance requirement.

b. Samples can forgo its trade discounts over the two months of July and August when the funding will be needed. The firm's discount terms are 3/15, net 30 and the firm averages $500,000 in trade credit purchases during July and August.

c. Finally, samples could enter into a pledging arrangement with a local finance company. The finance company has agreed to extend Samples the needed $500,000 if it pledges $750,000 in receivables. The finance company has offered to advance the $500,000, with 12 percent annual interest payable at the end of the two-month loan term. In addition, the finance company will charge a one-half of one percent fee based on pledged receivables to cover the cost of processing the company's accounts (this fee is paid at the end of the loan period).

Analyze the cost of each of the alternative sources of credit and select the best one. Note that a total of $500,000 will be needed for a two-month period (July–August) each year.

ST–3. (*Analyzing the Cost of Short-Term Credit*) The treasurer of the Lights-a-Lot Mfg. Company is faced with three alternative bank loans. The firm wishes to select the one that minimizes its cost of credit on a $200,000 note which it plans to issue in the next ten days. Relevant information for the three loan configurations is found below:

a. An 18 percent rate of interest with interest paid at year-end and no compensating balance requirement.

b. A 16 percent rate of interest but carrying a 20 percent compensating balance requirement. This loan also calls for interest to be paid at year-end.

c. A 14 percent rate of interest which is discounted plus a 20 percent compensating balance requirement.

Analyze the cost of each of these alternatives. You may assume that the firm would not normally maintain any bank balance that might be used to meet the 20 percent compensating balance requirements of alternatives (b) and (c).

Study Problems

8–1. (*Estimating the Cost of Bank Credit*) Paymaster Enterprises has arranged to finance its seasonal working capital needs with a short-term bank loan. The loan will carry a rate of 12 percent per annum with interest paid in advance (discounted). In addition, Paymaster must maintain a minimum demand deposit with the bank of 10 percent of the loan balance throughout the term of the loan. If Paymaster plans to borrow $100,000 for a period of three months, what is the effective cost of the bank loan?

8–2. (*Estimating the Cost of Commercial Paper*) On February 3, 198X, the Burlington Western Company plans a commercial paper issue of $20 million. The firm has never used commercial paper before, but has been assured by the firm placing the issue that it will have no difficulty raising the funds. The commercial paper will carry a 270-day maturity and will require interest based upon a rate of 11 percent per annum. In addition, the firm will have to pay fees totaling $200,000 in order to bring the issue to market and place it. What is the effective cost of the commercial paper issue to Burlington Western?

8–3. (*Cost of Trade Credit*) Calculate the effective cost of the following trade credit terms where payment is made on the net due date.

a. 2/10, net 300
b. 3/15, net 30
c. 3/15, net 45
d. 2/15, net 60

8–4. (*Annual Percentage Rate*) Compute the cost of the trade credit terms in problem 8–3 using the compounding formula, or annual percentage rate.

8–5. (*Cost of Short-Term Financing*) The R. Morin Construction Company needs to borrow $100,000 to help finance the cost of a new $150,000 hydraulic crane used in the firm's commercial construction business. The crane will pay for itself in one year and the firm is considering the following alternatives for financing its purchase:

Alternative A—The firm's bank has agreed to lend the $100,000 at a rate of 14 percent. Interest would be discounted, and a 15 percent compensating balance would be required. However, the compensating balance requirement would not be binding on R. Morin, since the firm normally maintains a minimum demand deposit (checking account) balance of $25,000 in the bank.

Alternative B—The equipment dealer has agreed to finance the equipment with a one-year loan. The $100,000 loan would require payment of principal and interest totaling $116,300.

a. Which alternative should R. Morin select?

b. If the bank's compensating balance requirement were to necessitate idle demand deposits equal to 20 percent of the loan, what effect would this have on the cost of the bank loan alternative?

8–6. (*Cost of Short-Term Bank Loan*) On July 1, 198X, the Southwest Forging Corporation arranged for a line of credit with the First National Bank of Dallas. The terms of the agreement called for a $100,000 maximum loan with interest set at 1 percent over prime. In addition, the firm has to maintain a 20 percent compensating balance in its demand deposit throughout the year. The prime rate is currently 12 percent.

a. If Southwest normally maintains a $20,000 to $30,000 balance in its checking account with FNB of Dallas, what is the effective cost of credit through the line-of-credit agreement where the maximum loan amount is used for a full year?

b. Recompute the effective cost of credit to Southwest if Southwest will have to borrow the compensating balance and they borrow the maximum possible under the loan agreement. Again, assume the full amount of the loan is outstanding for a whole year.

8–7. (*Cost of Commercial Paper*) Tri-State Enterprises plans to issue commercial paper for the first time in the firm's 35-year history. The firm plans to issue $500,000 in 180-day maturity notes. The paper will carry a 10¼ percent rate with discounted interest and will cost Tri-State $12,000 (paid in advance) to issue.

a. What is the effective cost of credit to Tri-State?

b. What other factors should the company consider in analyzing whether to issue the commercial paper?

8–8. (*Cost of Accounts Receivable*) Johnson Enterprises, Inc., is involved in the manufacture and sale of electronic components used in small AM–FM radios. The firm needs $300,000 to finance an anticipated expansion in receivables due to increased sales. Johnson's credit terms are net 60, and its average monthly credit sales are $200,000. In general, the firm's customers pay within the credit period; thus the firm's average accounts receivable balance is $400,000.

Chuck Idol, Johnson's comptroller, approached the firm's bank with a request for a loan for the $300,000 using the firm's accounts receivable as collateral. The bank offered to make the loan at a rate of 2 percent over prime plus a 1 percent processing charge on all receivables pledged ($200,000 per month). Furthermore, the bank agreed to lend up to 75 percent of the face value of the receivables pledged.

a. Estimate the cost of the receivables loan to Johnson where the firm borrows the $300,000. The prime rate is currently 11 percent.

b. Idol also requested a line of credit for $300,000 from the bank. The bank agreed to grant the necessary line of credit at a rate of 3 percent over prime and required a 15 percent compensating balance. Johnson currently maintains an average demand deposit of $80,000. Estimate the cost of the line of credit to Johnson.

c. Which source of credit should Johnson select? Why?

8–9. (*Cost of Factoring*) MDM, Inc., is considering the factoring of its receivables. The firm has credit sales of $400,000 per month and has an average receivables balance of $800,000 with 60-day credit terms. The factor has offered to extend credit equal to 90 percent of the receivables factored less interest on the loan at a rate of 1½ percent per month. The 10 percent difference in the advance and the face value of all receivables factored consists of a 1 percent factoring fee plus a 9 percent reserve, which the factor maintains. In addition, if MDM, Inc., decides to factor its receivables, it will sell them all, so that it can reduce its credit department costs by $1500 a month.

a. What is the cost of borrowing the maximum amount of credit available to MDM, Inc., through the factoring agreement?

b. What considerations other than cost should be accounted for by MDM, Inc., in determining whether or not to enter the factoring agreement?

8–10. (*Inventory Financing*) In June of each year the Arlyle Publishing Company builds up its inventories for fall sales. The company has explored the possibility of a field warehouse security agreement as collateral for an inventory loan from its bank during the three summer months. During these months inventories average $400,000. The field warehouse arrangement will cost Arlyle a flat fee of $2000 a month on all its inventory regardless of the amount the firm borrows. The bank has agreed to lend up to 70 percent of the value of the inventory at a rate of 14 percent.

a. If Arlyle borrows $200,000 usign the inventory loan for June through August, what is the effective cost of credit?

b. What is the effective cost of borrowing $280,000 for the June through August period?

8–11. (*Cost of Secured Short-Term Credit*) The Sean-Janeow Import Co. needs $500,000 for the three-month period ending September 30, 198X. The firm has explored two possible sources of credit.

1. S–J has arranged with its bank for a $500,000 loan secured by accounts receivable. The bank has agreed to advance S–J 80 percent of the value of its pledged receivables at a rate of 11 percent plus a 1 percent fee based on all receivables pledged. S–J's receivables average a total of $1 million year-round.

2. An insurance company has agreed to lend the $500,000 at a rate of 9 percent per annum, using a loan secured by S–J's inventory of salad oil. A field warehouse agreement would be used, which would cost S–J $2000 a month.

Which source of credit should S–J select? Explain.

8–12. (*Cost of Short-Term Financing*) You plan to borrow $20,000 from the bank to pay for inventories for a gift shop you have just opened. The bank offers to lend you the money at 10 percent annual interest for the six months the funds will be needed.

a. Calculate the effective rate of interest on the loan.

b. In addition, the bank requires you to maintain a 15 percent compensating balance in the bank. Since you are just opening your business, you do not have a demand deposit at the bank that can be used to meet the compensating balance requirement. This means that you will have to put 15 percent of the loan amount from your own personal money (which you had planned to use to help finance the business) in a checking account. What is the cost of the loan now?

c. In addition to the compensating balance requirement in (b) above, you are told that interest will be discounted. What is the effective rate of interest on the loan now?

8–13. (*Cost of Factoring*) A factor has agreed to lend the JVC Corporation working capital on the following terms. JVC's receivables average $100,000 per month and have a 90-day average collection period (note that accounts receivable average $300,000 due to the 90 day average collection period). The factor will charge 12 percent interest on any advance (1 percent per month paid in advance), will charge a 2 percent processing fee on all receivables factored, and will maintain a 20 percent reserve. If JVC undertakes the loan it will reduce its own credit department expenses by $2000 per month. What is the annual effective rate of interest to JVC on the factoring arrangement? Assume that the maximum advance is taken.

8–14. (*Opportunity Cost of Decreasing Wages Payable*) In June of this year the AMB Manufacturing Company negotiated a new union contract with its employees. One of the provisions of the new contract involved increasing the frequency of its wage payments from once a month to once every two weeks. AMB's biweekly payroll averages $250,000 and the firm's opportunity cost of funds is 12 percent per annum.

    a. What is the annual dollar cost of this new wage payment scheme to AMB?

    b. What is the maximum percentage increase in wages that AMB would have been willing to accept in lieu of the increased frequency of wage payments?

Self-Test Solutions

SS–1. The discounted interest cost of the commercial paper issue is calculated as follows:

$$\text{Interest expense} = .10 \times \$200 \text{ million} \times 180/360 = \$10 \text{ million}$$

The effective cost of credit can now be calculated as follows:

$$\text{RATE} = \frac{\$10 \text{ million} + \$125,000}{\$200 \text{ million} - \$125,000 - \$10 \text{ million}} \times \frac{1}{180/360}$$

$$.46\%$$

SS–2.   **a.**

$$\frac{\text{Interest for}}{\text{two months}} = .14 \times - \times \$500,000$$

$$= \$11,667$$

$$\frac{\text{Loan proceeds}}{\text{(for \$500,000 loan)}} = \$500,000 - (.2 \times \$500,000 + \$11,667)$$

$$= \$388,333$$

$$\text{RATE} = \frac{\$11,667}{\$388,333} \times \frac{12}{2}$$

$$= .030043 \times 6 = .18026, \text{ or } 18.026\%$$

Note that Samples would actually have to borrow more than the needed $500,000 in order to cover the compensating balance requirement. However, as we demonstrated earlier, the effective cost of credit will not be affected by adjusting the loan amount for interest expense changes accordingly.

  b. The estimation of the cost of foregoing trade discounts is generally quite straightforward; however, in this case the firm actually stretches its trade credit for purchases made during July beyond the due date by an additional 30 days. If it is able to do this *without penalty*, then the firm effectively foregoes a 3 percent discount for not paying within 15 days and does not pay for an additional 45 days (60 days less the discount period of 15 days). Thus, for the July trade credit, Sample's cost is calculated as follows:

$$\text{RATE} = (.03/.97) \times (360/45) = 24.74\%$$

However, for the August trade credit the firm actually pays at the end of the credit period (the 30th day), so that the cost of trade credit becomes

$$\text{RATE} = (.03/.97) \times (360/15) = 74.22\%$$

c.

$$\frac{\text{Interest for}}{\text{two months}} = .12 \times \frac{2}{12} \times \$500,000$$

$$= \$10,000$$

$$\text{Pledging fee} = .005 \times \$750,000$$

$$= \$3750$$

$$\text{RATE} = \frac{\$10,000 + \$3,750}{\$500,000} \times \frac{12}{2}$$

$$= .0275 \times 6 = .165, \text{ or } 16.5\%$$

SS–3. a.

$$\text{RATE} = \frac{.18 \times \$200,000}{\$200,000} \times \frac{1}{1}$$

$$= .18, \text{ or } 18\%$$

b.

$$\text{RATE} = \frac{.16 \times \$200,000}{\$200,000 - .20 \times \$200.000} \times \frac{1}{1}$$

$$= .20, \text{ or } 20\%$$

c.

$$\text{RATE} = \frac{.14 \times \$200,000}{\$200,000 - .14 \times \$200,000 - .2 \times \$200,000} \times \frac{1}{1}$$

$$= .21212, \text{ or } 21.212\%$$

Alternative (a) offers the lower cost service of financing, although it carries the highest stated rate of interest. The reason for this, of course, is that there is no compensating balance requirement nor is interest discounted for this alternative.

Selected References

Abraham, A. B. "Factoring—The New Frontier for Commercial Banks," *Journal of Commercial Bank Lending*, 53 (April 1971), 32–43.

Addison, E. "Factoring: A Case History," *Financial Executive*, November 1963, pp. 32–33.

Baxter, Nevins D. *The Commercial Paper Market*, Princeton, N.J.: Princeton University Press, 1964.

———, and Harold T. Shapiro. "Compensating Balance Requirements: The Results of a Survey." *Journal of Finance*, 19 (September 1964), 483–96.

Brosky, John J. *The Implicit Cost of Trade Credit and Theory of Optimal Terms of Sale*. New York: Credit Research Foundation, 1969.

D'Agostino, R. S. "Accounts Receivable Loans—Worthless Collateral?" *Journal of Commercial Bank Lending*, 52 (July 1970), 34–42.

Daniels, F., S. Legg, and E. C. Yuelle. "Accounts Receivable and Related Inventory Financing," *Journal of Commercial Bank Lending*, 52 (July 1970), 38–53.

Denonn, Lester E. "The Security Agreement," *Journal of Commercial Bank Lending*, 50 (February 1968), 32–40.

Emery, G. W. "A Pure Financial Explanation for Trade Credit," *Journal of Financial and Quantitative Analysis*, 19 (September 1984), 271–86.

Hayes, D. A. *Bank Lending Policies: Domestic and International*, Ann Arbor: University of Michigan, 1971.

Kim, Y. H., and J. C. Atkins. "Evaluating Investment in Accounts Receivable: A Wealth Maximizing Framework." *Journal of Finance* (May 1978), 403–12.

Nadler, Paul S. "Compensating Balances and the Prime at Twilight," *Harvard Business Review*, 50 (January–February 1972), 112–20.

Pizzo, T. V. "Factoring as a Management Tool," *Credit and Financial Management* (December 1979), pp. 16–18.

Quarles, J. C. "The Floating Lien," *Journal of Commercial Bank Lending*, 52 (November 1970), 51–58.

Rogers, R. W. "Warehouse Receipts and Their Use in Financing," *Bulletin of the Robert Morris Associates*, 46 (April 1964), 317–27.

Schadrack, Frederick C., Jr. "Demand and Supply in the Commercial Paper Market," *Journal of Finance*, 25 (September 1970), 837–52.

Stone, Bernell K. "The Cost of Bank Loans," *Journal of Financial and Quantitative Analysis*, 7 (December 1972), 2077–86.

Wort, D. H. "The Trade Discount Decision: A Markov Chain Approach," *Decision Sciences*, Winter 1985, pp. 43–56.

9

Mathematics of Finance

In coming chapters we will concern ourselves with evaluating the desirability of investment proposals. In doing this we will recognize that there is a time value associated with money; that is, a dollar today is worth more than a dollar received a year from now. Intuitively this idea is easy to understand. We are all familiar with the concept of interest, and this concept illustrates what economists call an *opportunity cost* of passing up the earning potential of a dollar today. This opportunity cost is the time value of money.

In evaluating and comparing investment proposals, we will want to examine the dollar values accruing from accepting these proposals. To do this we must first make all dollar values comparable, and since a dollar received today is worth more than a dollar received in the future, we must move all dollar flows back to the present or out to a common future date. For this reason, an understanding of the mathematics of interest is essential to an understanding of advanced financial management.

COMPOUND INTEREST

Most of us encounter the concept of compound interest at an early age. Anyone who has ever had a savings account at a commercial bank or savings and loan association or purchased a U.S. government savings bond has received compound interest. **Compound interest** occurs when interest paid on the investment during the first period is added to the principal and, during the second period, interest is earned on this new sum.

As an example, suppose we place $100 in a savings account that pays 6 percent interest, compounded annually. How will our savings grow? At the end of the first year we have earned 6 percent, or $6 on our initial deposit of $100, giving us a total of $106 in our savings account. The mathematical formula illustrating this phenomenon is

$$FV_1 = P(1 + i) \tag{9-1}$$

where FV_1 = the future value of the investment at the end of one year

$\quad\quad i$ = the annual compound interest rate

$\quad\quad P$ = the principal or original amount invested at the beginning of the first year

In our example

$$
\begin{aligned}
FV_1 &= P(1 + i) \\
&= \$100(1 + .06) \\
&= \$100(1.06) \\
&= \$106
\end{aligned}
\tag{9-1}
$$

Carrying these calculations one period further, we find that we now earn the 6 percent interest on a principal of $106, which means we earn $6.36 in interest during the second year. Why do we earn more interest during the second year than we did during the first? Simply because we now earn interest on the sum of the original principal and the interest we earned in the first year. In effect we are now earning interest on interest; this is the concept of compound interest. Examining the mathematical formula illustrating the earning of interest in the second year, we find:

$$FV_2 = FV_1(1 + i) \tag{9-2}$$

which, for our example, gives

$$
\begin{aligned}
FV_2 &= \$106(1.06) \\
&= \$112.36
\end{aligned}
$$

Looking back at equation (9–1), we can see that FV_1, or $106, is actually equal to $P(1 + i)$, or $100 (1 + .06). If we substitute these values into equation (9–2), we get

$$
\begin{aligned}
FV_2 &= P(1 + i)(1 + i) \\
&= P(1 + i)^2
\end{aligned}
\tag{9-3}
$$

Carrying this forward into the third year, we find that we enter the year with $112.36 and we earn 6 percent, or $6.74 in interest, giving us a total of $119.10 in our savings account. Expressing this mathematically:

$$
\begin{aligned}
FV_3 &= FV_2(1 + i) \\
&= \$112.36(1.06) \\
&= \$119.10
\end{aligned}
\tag{9-4}
$$

If we substitute the value in equation (9–3) for FV_2 into equation (9–4), we find:

$$FV_3 = P(1 + i)(1 + i)(1 + i)$$
$$= P(1 + i)^3 \qquad\qquad (9\text{–}5)$$

By now a pattern is beginning to be evident. We can generalize this formula to illustrate the value of our investment if it is compounded annually at a rate of i for n years to be

$$FV_n = P(1 + i)^n \qquad\qquad (9\text{–}6)$$

where FV_n = the future value of the investment at the end of n years

n = the number of years during which the compounding occurs

i = the annual compound interest rate

P = the principal or original amount invested at the beginning of the first year

Table 9–1 illustrates how this investment of $100 would continue to grow for the first 10 years at a compound interest rate of 6 percent. It is easy to see that the amount of interest earned annually increases each year. Again, the reason is that each year interest is received on the sum of the original investment plus any interest earned in the past.

When we examine the relationship between the number of years an initial investment is compounded for and its future value graphically, as shown in Figure 9–1, we see that we can increase the future value of an investment by increasing the number of years we let it compound or compounding it at a higher interest rate. We can also see this by examining equation (9–6), since an increase in either i or n while P is held constant will result in an increase in FV_n.

Example   If we place $1000 in a savings account paying 5 percent interest compounded annually, how much will our account accrue to in 10 years? Substituting P = $1000, i = 5 percent, and n = 10 years into equation (9–6), we get

$$FV_n = P(1 + i)^n$$
$$= \$1000(1 + .05)^{10} \qquad\qquad (9\text{–}6)$$
$$= \$1000(1.62889)$$
$$= \$1628.89$$

Thus at the end of 10 years we will have $1628.89 in our savings account.

As the determination of future value can be quite time-consuming when an investment is held for a number of years, tables have been compiled for values of $(1 + i)^n$. An abbreviated compound interest table appears in Table 9–2. (A more

TABLE 9–1. Illustration of Compound Interest Calculations

Year	Beginning Value	Interest Earned	Ending Value
1	$100.00	$ 6.00	$106.00
2	106.00	6.36	112.36
3	112.36	6.74	119.10
4	119.10	7.15	126.25
5	126.25	7.57	133.82
6	133.82	8.03	141.85
7	141.85	8.51	150.36
8	150.36	9.02	159.38
9	159.38	9.57	168.95
10	168.95	10.13	179.08

comprehensive version of this table appears in Appendix A in the back of this book.) Note that the compounding factors given in these tables represent the value of $1 compounded at rate *i* at the *end* of the *n*th year. Thus, to calculate the future value of an initial investment we need only determine the table value and multiply this times the initial investment.

FIGURE 9–1. Future Value of $100 Initially Deposited and Compounded at 0, 5, and 10 Percent

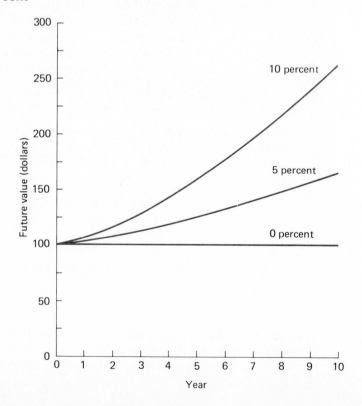

Example If we invest $500 in the bank where it will earn 8 percent compounded annually, how much will it be worth at the end of seven years? Looking in Table 9–2 in the row $n = 7$ and column $i = 8\%$, we find a value of 1.714. Substituting this in equation (9–6), we find

$$FV_n = P(1 + i)^n$$

$$= \$500(1.714) \qquad (9\text{–}6)$$

$$= \$857$$

Thus, we will have $857 at the end of seven years.

TABLE 9–2. **Compound Sum of $1**

n	1%	2%	3%	4%	5%	6%	7%	8%	9%	10%
1	1.010	1.020	1.030	1.040	1.050	1.060	1.070	1.080	1.090	1.100
2	1.020	1.040	1.061	1.082	1.102	1.124	1.145	1.166	1.188	1.210
3	1.030	1.061	1.093	1.125	1.158	1.191	1.225	1.260	1.295	1.331
4	1.041	1.082	1.126	1.170	1.216	1.262	1.311	1.360	1.412	1.464
5	1.051	1.104	1.159	1.217	1.276	1.338	1.403	1.469	1.539	1.611
6	1.062	1.126	1.194	1.265	1.340	1.419	1.501	1.587	1.677	1.772
7	1.072	1.149	1.230	1.316	1.407	1.504	1.606	1.714	1.828	1.949
8	1.083	1.172	1.267	1.369	1.477	1.594	1.718	1.851	1.993	1.144
9	1.094	1.195	1.305	1.423	1.551	1.689	1.838	1.999	2.172	2.358
10	1.105	1.219	1.344	1.480	1.629	1.791	1.967	2.159	2.367	2.594
11	1.116	1.243	1.384	1.539	1.710	1.898	2.105	2.332	2.580	2.853
12	1.127	1.268	1.426	1.601	1.796	2.012	2.252	2.518	2.813	3.138
13	1.138	1.294	1.469	1.665	1.886	2.133	2.410	2.720	3.066	3.452
14	1.149	1.319	1.513	1.732	1.980	2.261	2.579	2.937	3.342	3.797
15	1.161	1.346	1.558	1.801	2.079	2.397	2.759	3.172	3.642	4.177

In the future we will find several uses for equation (9–6); not only will we find the future value of an investment, but we can also solve for *P*, *i*, or *n*. In any case, we will be given three of the four variables and will have to solve for the fourth.

Example How many years will it take for an initial investment of $300 to grow to $774 if it is invested at 9 percent compounded annually? In this problem we know the initial investment, $p = \$300$, the future value, $FV_n = \$774$, the compound growth rate, $i = 9$ percent, and we are solving for the number of years it must compound for, $n = ?$ Substituting the known values in equation (9–6), we find

$$FV_n = P(1 + i)^n$$

$$\$774 = \$300(1 + .09)^n \qquad (9\text{–}6)$$

$$2.58 = (1 + .09)^n$$

Thus we are looking for a table value of 2.58, and we know it must be in the 9% column. Looking down the 9% column for the value closest to 2.58, we find that it occurs in the $n = 11$ row. Thus, it will take 11 years for an initial investment of $300 to grow to $774 if it is invested at 9 percent compounded annually.

Example At what rate must $100 be compounded annually for it to grow to $179.10 in 10 years? In this case we know the initial investment, $p = \$100$, the future value of this investment at the end of n years $FV_n = \$179.10$, and the number of years that the initial investment will compound for; $n = 10$ years. Substituting into equation (9–6), we get

$$FV_n = P(1 + i)^n$$

$$\$179.10 = \$100(1 + i)^{10} \tag{9-6}$$

$$1.791 = (1 + i)^{10}$$

We know we are looking in the $n = 10$ row for a table value of 1.791, and we find this in the $i = 6\%$ column. Thus, if we want our initial investment of $100 to accrue to $179.10 in 10 years, we must invest it at 6 percent.

COMPOUND INTEREST WITH NONANNUAL PERIODS

Until now we have assumed the compounding period was always annual; however, it need not be, as we can see by examining savings and loan associations and commercial banks that compound on a quarterly, daily, and in some cases continuous basis. Fortunately, this adjustment of the compounding period poses no major problem. If we invest our money for 5 years at 8 percent interest compounded semi-annually, we are really investing our money for 10 six-month periods during which we receive 4 percent interest each period. If it is compounded quarterly, we receive 2 percent interest per period for 20 three-month periods. This process can easily be generalized, giving us the following formula for finding the future value of an investment where interest is compounded in nonannual periods:

$$FV_n = P\left(1 + \frac{i}{m}\right)^{mn} \tag{9-7}$$

where FV_n = future value of the investment at the end of n years

n = number of years during which the compounding occurs

i = annual compound interest rate

P = principal or original amount invested at the beginning of the first year

m = the number of times compounding occurs during the year

In the case of continuous compounding, the value of m in equation (9–7) is allowed to approach infinity. As this happens, the value of $[1 + (i/m)]^{mn}$ approaches e^{in}, with e being defined as follows and having a value of approximately 2.71828:

$$e = \lim_{m \to \infty} \left(1 + \frac{1}{m}\right)^m \tag{9-8}$$

where ∞ indicates infinity. Thus the future value of an investment compounded continuously for *n* years can be determined from the following formula:

$$FV_n = P \cdot e^{in} \tag{9-9}$$

where FV_n = the future value of the investment at the end of *n* years

e = 2.71828

n = the number of years during which the compounding occurs

i = the annual compound interest rate

P = the principal or original amount invested at the beginning of the first year

While continuous compounding appears quite complicated, it is used frequently and is a valuable theoretical concept. Continuous compounding takes on this importance because it allows interest to be earned on interest more frequently than any other compounding period. We can easily see the value of intrayear compounding by examining Table 9–3. Since interest is earned on interest more frequently as the length of the compounding period declines, there is an inverse relationship between the length of the compounding period and the effective annual interest rate.

Example   If we place $100 in a savings account that yields 12 percent compounded quarterly, what will our investment grow to at the end of five years? Substituting $n = 5$, $m = 4$, $i = 12$ percent, and $P = \$100$ into equation (9–7), we find

$$FV_5 = \$100 \left(1 + \frac{.12}{4}\right)^{5 \cdot 4}$$

$$= \$100(1 + .03)^{20}$$

$$= \$100(1.806)$$

$$= \$180.60$$

Thus, we will have $180.60 at the end of five years.

Example   How much money will we have at the end of 20 years if we deposit $1000 in a savings account yielding 10 percent interest continuously compounded? Substituting $n = 20$, $i = 10$ percent, and $P = \$1000$ into equation (9–9) yields

$$FV_{10} = \$1000(2.71828)^{.10 \cdot 20}$$

$$= \$1000(2.71828)^2$$

$$= \$1000(7.38905)$$

$$= \$7389.05$$

Thus, we will have $7389.05 at the end of 20 years.

TABLE 9–3. The Value of $100 Compounded at Various Intervals

For One Year at *i* Percent

i =	2%	5%	10%	15%
Compounded annually	$102.00	$105.00	$110.00	$115.00
Compounded semi-annually	102.01	105.06	110.25	115.56
Compounded quarterly	102.02	105.09	110.38	115.87
Compounded monthly	102.02	105.12	110.47	116.08
Compounded weekly (52)	102.02	105.12	110.51	116.16
Compounded daily (365)	102.02	105.13	110.52	116.18
Compounded continuously	102.02	105.13	110.52	116.18

For 10 years at *i* Percent

i =	2%	5%	10%	15%
Compounded annually	$121.90	$162.89	$259.37	$404.56
Compounded semi-annually	122.02	163.86	265.33	424.79
Compounded quarterly	122.08	164.36	268.51	436.04
Compounded monthly	122.12	164.70	270.70	444.02
Compounded weekly (52)	122.14	164.83	271.57	447.20
Compounded daily (365)	122.14	164.87	271.79	448.03
Compounded continuously	122.14	164.87	271.83	448.17

PRESENT VALUE

Up until this point we have been moving money forward in time—that is, knowing how much we have at one point in time and trying to determine how much it will grow to in a certain number of years when compounded at a specific rate. We are now going to look at the reverse question: What is the value in today's dollars of a sum of money to be received in the future? In this case we are moving money back in time, back to the present. We will be determining the **present value** of a lump sum, which in simple terms is the current value of a future payment. What we will be doing is, in fact, nothing other than inverse compounding. The differences in these techniques come about merely from the investor's point of view. In compounding we talked about the compound rate or interest rate and the initial investment; in determining the present value we will talk about the *opportunity cost* of money or the discount rate and present value. Other than that, the technique and the terminology remain the same, and the mathematics are simply reversed. In equation (9–6) we were attempting to determine the future value of an initial investment. We now want to determine the initial investment or present value. By dividing both sides of equation (9–6) by $(1 + i)^n$, we get

$$P = FV_n \left[\frac{1}{(1 + i)^n} \right] \qquad (9\text{–}10)$$

where FV_n = the future value of the investment at the end of n years

n = the number of years until the payment will be received

i = the opportunity rate or discount rate

P = the present value of the future sum of money

As the mathematical procedure for determining the present value is exactly the inverse of determining the future value, we also find that the relationships among n, i, and p are just opposite of those we observed with the future value. The present value of a future sum of money is inversely related to both the number of years until the payment will be received and the opportunity rate. Graphically, this relationship can be seen in Figure 9–2.

While equation (9–10), the present-value equation, will be used extensively in evaluating new investment proposals, it should be stressed that equation (9–10) is actually the same as equation (9–6), where it is solved for P.

Example   What is the present value of $500 to be received 10 years from today if our opportunity rate is 6 percent? Substituting $FV_{10} = \$500$, $n = 10$, and $i = 6$ percent into equation (9–10), we find

$$P = \$500 \left[\frac{1}{(1 + .06)^{10}} \right]$$

$$= \$500 \left(\frac{1}{1.791} \right)$$

$$= \$500(.558)$$

$$= \$279$$

Thus, the present value of the $500 to be received in 10 years is $279.

FIGURE 9–2.   Present Value of $100 to Be Received at a Future Date and Discounted Back to the Present at 0, 5, and 10 Percent

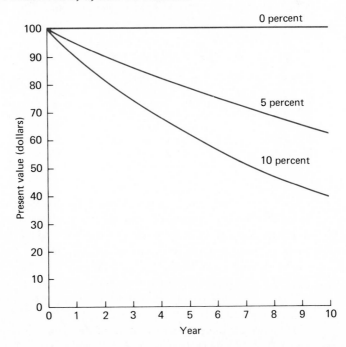

To aid in the computation of present values, tables have been compiled for values of $[1/(1 + i)^n]$; they appear in Appendix B in the back of this book. An abbreviated version of Appendix B appears in Table 9–4. A close examination shows that the values in Table 9–4 are merely the inverses of those in Appendix A. This, of course, is as it should be, as the values in Appendix A are $(1 + i)^n$ and those in Appendix B are $[1/(1 + i)^n]$. Now, to determine the present value of a sum of money to be received at some future date, we need only determine the appropriate table value and multiply it by the future value.

Example What is the present value of $1500 to be received at the end of 10 years if our opportunity cost is 8 percent? By looking in the $n = 10$ row and $i = 8\%$ column of Table 9–4, we find the value of $[1/(1 + .08)^{10}]$ is .463. Substituting this value into equation (9–10), we find

$$P = \$1500(.463)$$

$$= \$694.50$$

Thus, the present value of this $1500 payment is $694.50.

TABLE 9–4. Present Value of $1

n	1%	2%	3%	4%	5%	6%	7%	8%	9%	10%
1	.990	.980	.971	.962	.952	.943	.935	.926	.917	.909
2	.980	.961	.943	.925	.907	.890	.873	.857	.842	.826
3	.971	.942	.915	.889	.864	.840	.816	.794	.772	.751
4	.961	.924	.888	.855	.823	.792	.763	.735	.708	.683
5	.951	.906	.863	.822	.784	.747	.713	.681	.650	.621
6	.942	.888	.837	.790	.746	.705	.666	.630	.596	.564
7	.933	.871	.813	.760	.711	.665	.623	.583	.547	.513
8	.923	.853	.789	.731	.677	.627	.582	.540	.502	.467
9	.914	.837	.766	.703	.645	.592	.544	.500	.460	.424
10	.905	.820	.744	.676	.614	.558	.508	.463	.422	.386
11	.896	.804	.722	.650	.585	.527	.475	.429	.388	.350
12	.887	.789	.701	.625	.557	.497	.444	.397	.356	.319
13	.879	.773	.681	.601	.530	.469	.415	.368	.326	.290
14	.870	.758	.661	.577	.505	.442	.388	.340	.299	.263
15	.861	.743	.642	.555	.481	.417	.362	.315	.275	.239

Before moving on, it should again be stressed that we only have one present-value-future-value equation; that is, equations (9–6) and (9–10) are identical. We have introduced them as separate equations to simplify our calculations; in one case we are determining the value in future dollars and in the other case the value in today's dollars. In either case the reason is the same: In order to compare values on alternative investments and to recognize that the value of a dollar received today is not the same as that of a dollar received at some future date, we must measure the dollar values in dollars of the same time period. Since all present values are comparable, as they are all measured in dollars of the same time period, we can add and subtract the present value of inflows and outflows to determine the present value of an investment.

Example   What is the present value of an investment that yields $500 to be received in five years and $1000 to be received in 10 years if our opportunity rate is 4 percent? Substituting the values of $n = 5$, $i = 4$ percent, and $FV_5 = 500 and $n = 10$, $i = 4$ percent, and $FV_{10} = 1000 into equation (9–10) and adding these values together, we find

$$P = \$500 \left[\frac{1}{(1 + .04)^5} \right] + \$1000 \left[\frac{1}{(1 + .04)^{10}} \right]$$

$$= \$500(.822) + \$1000(.676)$$

$$= \$411 + \$676$$

$$= \$1087$$

Again, present values are comparable because they are measured in the same time period's dollars.

ANNUITIES

An **annuity** is a series of equal dollar payments for a specified number of years. Because annuities occur frequently in finance—for example, as bond interest payments—we will treat them specially. While the processes of compounding and determining the present value of an annuity can be dealt with using the methods we have just described, they can be time-consuming, especially for larger annuities. Thus, we have modified these formulas and developed tables to deal directly with annuities.

Compound Annuities

A **compound annuity** involves depositing or investing an equal sum of money at the end of each year for a certain number of years and allowing it to grow. Perhaps the money is being saved to provide for education, or for a new car, or a vacation home. In such cases we wish to know how much our savings will have grown to by some point in time.

Actually, we can find the answer by using equation (9–6), our compounding equation, and compounding each of the individual deposits to the future. For example, if to provide for a college education we are going to deposit $500 at the end of each year for the next five years in a bank where it will earn 6 percent interest, how much will we have at the end of five years? Compounding each of these values using equation (9–6), we find that we will have $2818.50 at the end of five years.

$$FV_5 = \$500(1 + .06)^4 + \$500(1 + .06)^3 + \$500(1 + .06)^2$$

$$+ \$500(1 + .06)^1 + \$500$$

$$= \$500(1.262) + \$500(1.191) + \$500(1.124) + \$500(1.060) + \$500$$

$$= \$631.00 + \$595.50 + \$562.00 + \$530.00 + \$500.00$$

$$= \$2818.50$$

TABLE 9–5. Illustration of a Five-Year $500 Annuity Compounded at 6%

Year	0	1	2	3	4	5
Dollar deposits at end of year		500	500	500	500	500
						$ 500.00
						530.00
						562.00
						595.50
						631.00
Future value of the annuity						$2818.50

From examining the mathematics involved and the graph of the movement of money through time in Table 9–5, we can see that this procedure can be generalized to

$$FV_n = A \left[\sum_{t=0}^{n-1} (1 + i)^t \right] \qquad (9–11)$$

where FV_n = the future value of the annuity at the end of the nth year

A = the annuity value deposited at the end of each year

i = the annual compound interest rate

n = the number of years for which the annuity will last

Because compounding an annuity is so time-consuming, tables are provided in Appendix C for $\left[\sum_{t=0}^{n-1} (1 + i)^t \right]$ for various combinations of n and i; an abbreviated version is shown in Table 9–6. Reexamining the previous example, in which we determined the value of $500 deposited at the end of each of the next 5 years in

TABLE 9–6. Sum of an Annuity of $1 for n Years

n	1%	2%	3%	4%	5%	6%	7%	8%	9%	10%
1	1.000	1.000	1.000	1.000	1.000	1.000	1.000	1.000	1.000	1.000
2	2.010	2.020	2.030	2.040	2.050	2.060	2.070	2.080	2.090	2.100
3	3.030	3.060	3.091	3.122	3.152	3.184	3.215	3.246	3.278	3.310
4	4.060	4.122	4.184	4.246	4.310	4.375	4.440	4.506	4.573	4.641
5	5.101	5.204	5.309	5.416	5.526	5.637	5.751	5.867	5.985	6.105
6	6.152	6.308	6.468	6.633	6.802	6.975	7.153	7.336	7.523	7.716
7	7.214	7.434	7.662	7.898	8.142	8.394	8.654	8.923	9.200	9.487
8	8.286	8.583	8.892	9.214	9.549	9.897	10.260	10.637	11.028	11.436
9	9.368	9.755	10.159	10.583	11.027	11.491	11.978	12.488	13.021	13.579
10	10.462	10.950	11.464	12.006	12.578	13.181	13.816	14.487	15.193	15.937
11	11.567	12.169	12.808	13.486	14.207	14.972	15.784	16.645	17.560	18.531
12	12.682	13.412	14.192	15.026	15.917	16.870	17.888	18.977	20.141	21.384
13	13.809	14.680	15.618	16.627	17.713	18.882	20.141	21.495	22.953	24.523
14	14.947	15.974	17.086	18.292	19.598	21.015	22.550	24.215	26.019	27.975
15	16.097	17.293	18.599	20.023	21.578	23.276	25.129	27.152	29.361	31.772

the bank at 6 percent after 5 years, we would look in the $n = 5$ year row and $i = 6\%$ column and find a table value at 5.637. Substituting this value into equation (9–11), we get

$$FV_5 = \$500(5.637)$$

$$= \$2818.50$$

This is the same answer we obtained earlier.

Rather than asking how much we will accumulate if we deposit an equal sum in a savings account each year, a more common question is how much we must deposit each year in order to accumulate a certain amount of savings. This problem frequently occurs with respect to saving for large expenditures and pension funding obligations.

For example, we may know that we need \$10,000 for our son's education in eight years; how much must we deposit at the end of each year in the bank at 6 percent interest in order to have the college money ready? In this case we know the values of n, i, and FV_n in equation (9–11); what we do not know is the value of A. Substituting these example values in equation (9–11), we find

$$\$10,000 = A \left[\sum_{t=0}^{8-1} (1 + .06)^t \right]$$

$$\$10,000 = A(9.897)$$

$$\frac{\$10,000}{9.897} = A$$

$$A = \$1010.41$$

Thus, we must deposit \$1010.41 in the bank at the end of each year for eight years at 6 percent interest in order to accumulate \$10,000 at the end of eight years.

Example How much must we deposit in an 8 percent savings account at the end of each year in order to accumulate \$5000 at the end of 10 years? Substituting the values $FV_{10} = \$5000$, $n = 10$, and $i = 8$ percent into equation (9–11), we find

$$\$5000 = A \left[\sum_{t=0}^{10-1} (1 + .08)^t \right]$$

$$\$5000 = A(14.487)$$

$$\frac{\$5000}{14.487} = A$$

$$A = \$345.14$$

Thus, we must deposit \$345.14 per year for 10 years at 8 percent in order to accumulate \$5000.

Present Value of an Annuity

Pension funds, insurance obligations, and interest received from bonds all involve annuities. To compare them, we would like to know the present value of each. While we can find this by using the present-value table in Appendix B, this can be time-consuming, particularly when the annuity lasts for several years. For example, if we wish to know what $500 received at the end of the next 5 years is worth to us given the appropriate discount rate or opportunity rate of 6 percent, we can simply substitute the appropriate values into equation (9–10), such that

$$P = \$500\left[\frac{1}{(1 + .06)}\right] + \$500\left[\frac{1}{(1 + .06)^2}\right] + \$500\left[\frac{1}{(1 + .06)^3}\right]$$

$$+ \$500\left[\frac{1}{(1 + .06)^4}\right] + \$500\left[\frac{1}{(1 + .06)^5}\right]$$

$$= \$500(.943) + \$500(.890) + \$500(.840) + \$500(.792)$$

$$+ \$500(.747)$$

$$= \$2106.00$$

Thus, the present value of this annuity is $2106.00. From examining the mathematics involved and the graph of the movement of these funds through time in Table 9–7, we see that this procedure can be generalized to

$$P = A\left[\sum_{t=1}^{n} \frac{1}{(1 + i)^t}\right] \tag{9–12}$$

where A = the annuity received at the end of each year

i = the annual interest or discount rate

P = the present value of the future annuity

n = the number of years for which the annuity will last

To simplify the process of determining the present value of an annuity, tables are provided in Appendix D for $\left[\sum_{t=1}^{n} 1/(1 + i)^t\right]$ for various combinations of n and i; an

TABLE 9–7. Illustration of a Five-Year $500 Annuity Discounted Back to the Present at 6 Percent

Year	0	1	2	3	4	5
Dollars received at the end of year		500	500	500	500	500
	$ 471.50 ←					
	445.00 ←					
	420.00 ←					
	396.00 ←					
	373.50 ←					
Present value of the annuity	$2106.00					

TABLE 9–8. Present Value of an Annuity of $1

n	1%	2%	3%	4%	5%	6%	7%	8%	9%	10%
1	0.990	0.980	0.971	0.962	0.952	0.943	0.935	0.926	0.917	0.909
2	1.970	1.942	1.913	1.886	1.859	1.833	1.808	1.783	1.759	1.736
3	2.941	2.884	2.829	2.775	2.723	2.673	2.624	2.577	2.531	2.487
4	3.902	3.808	3.717	3.630	3.546	3.465	3.387	3.312	3.240	3.170
5	4.853	4.713	4.580	4.452	4.329	4.212	4.100	3.993	3.890	3.791
6	5.795	5.601	5.417	5.242	5.076	4.917	4.767	4.623	4.486	4.355
7	6.728	6.472	6.230	6.002	5.786	5.582	5.389	5.206	5.033	4.868
8	7.652	7.326	7.020	6.733	6.463	6.210	5.971	5.747	5.535	5.335
9	8.566	8.162	7.786	7.435	7.108	6.802	6.515	6.247	5.995	5.759
10	9.471	8.983	8.530	8.111	7.722	7.360	7.024	6.710	6.418	6.145
11	10.368	9.787	9.253	8.760	8.306	7.887	7.499	7.139	6.805	6.495
12	11.255	10.575	9.954	9.385	8.863	8.384	7.943	7.536	7.161	6.814
13	12.134	11.348	10.635	9.986	9.394	8.853	8.358	7.904	7.487	7.103
14	13.004	12.106	11.296	10.563	9.899	9.295	8.746	8.244	7.786	7.367
15	13.865	12.849	11.938	11.118	10.380	9.712	9.108	8.560	8.061	7.606

abbreviated version is given in Table 9–8. Solving the previous example to find the present value of $500 received at the end of each of the next five years discounted back to the present at 6 percent, we look in the $n = 5$ year row and $i = 6\%$ column and find a table value for $\left[\sum_{t=1}^{5} 1/(1.06)^t\right]$, or 4.212. Substituting the appropriate values into equations (9–12), we find

$$P = \$500(4.212)$$

$$= \$2106$$

This, of course, is the same answer we calculated when we individually discounted each cash flow to the present. The reason is that we really only have *one* table; the Table 9–8 value for an n-year annuity for any discount rate i is merely the sum of the first n values in Table 9–4. We can see this by comparing the value in the present-value-of-an-annuity table (Table 9–8) for $i = 8\%$ and $n = 6$ years, which is 4.623, with the sum of the values in the $i = 8\%$ column and $n = 1, \ldots, 6$ rows of the present-value table (Table 9–4), which is equal to 4.623, as shown in Table 9–9.

TABLE 9–9. Present Value of a Six-Year Annuity Discounted at 8 Percent

One dollar received at the end of year	1	2	3	4	5	6
Present value						
.926 ←						
.857 ←						
.794 ←						
.735 ←						
.681 ←						
.630 ←						
4.623	Present value of the annuity					

Example What is the present value of a 10-year $1000 annuity discounted back to the present at 5 percent? Substituting n = 10 years, i = 5 percent, and A = $1000 into equation (9–12), we find

$$P = \$1000 \left[\sum_{t=1}^{10} \frac{1}{(1 + .05)^t} \right]$$

Determining the value for $\left[\sum_{t=1}^{10} 1/(1 + .05)^t \right]$ from Table 9–8, row n = 10, column i = 5%, and substituting it in, we get

$$P = \$1000(7.722)$$

$$= \$7722$$

Thus, the present value of this annuity is $7722.

As with our other compounding and present-value tables, given any three of the four unknowns in equation (9–12) we can solve for the fourth. In the case of the present-value-of-an-annuity table we may be interested in solving for A, if we know i, n, and P. The financial interpretation of this action would be: How much can be withdrawn, perhaps as a pension or to make loan payments, from an account that earns i percent compounded annually for each of the next n years if we wish to have nothing left at the end of n years? For an example, if we have $5000 in an account earning 8 percent interest, how large an annuity can we draw out each year if we want nothing left at the end of 5 years? In this case the present value, P, of the annuity is $5000, n = 5 years, i = 8 percent, and A is unknown. Substituting this into equation (9–12), we find

$$\$5000 = A(3.993)$$

$$\$1252.19 = A$$

Thus, this account will fall to zero at the end of 5 years if we withdraw $1252.19 at the end of each year.

This procedure of solving for A, the annuity value when i, n, and P are known, is also the procedure used to determine what payments are associated with paying off a loan in equal installments over time. Loans that are paid off this way, in equal periodic payments, are called *amortized loans*. For example, suppose a firm wants to purchase a piece of machinery. To do this, it borrows $6000 to be repaid in four equal payments at the end of each of the next four years, and the interest rate that is paid to the lender is 15 percent on the outstanding portion of the loan. To determine what the annual payments associated with the repayment of this debt will be, we simply use equation (9–12) and solve for the value of A, the annual annuity. Again we know three of the four values in that equation, P, i, and n. P, the present value of the future annuity, is $6000; i, the annual interest rate, is 15 percent; and n, the

TABLE 9–10. Loan Amortization Schedule Involving a $6000 Loan at 15 Percent to be Repaid in 4 Years

Year	Annuity	Interest Portion of the Annuity[a]	Repayment of the Principal Portion of the Annuity[b]	Outstanding Loan Balance after the Annuity Payment
1	$2101.58	$900.00	$1201.58	$4798.42
2	2101.58	719.76	1381.82	3416.60
3	2101.58	512.49	1589.09	1827.51
4	2101.58	274.07	1827.51	

[a] The interest portion of the annuity is calculated by multiplying the outstanding loan balance at the beginning of the year by the interest rate of 15 percent. Thus, for year 1 it was $6000.00 × .15 = $900.00, for year 2 it was $4798.42 × .15 = $719.76, and so on.

[b] Repayment of the principal portion of the annuity was calculated by subtracting the interest portion of the annuity (column 2) from the annuity (column 1).

number of years for which the annuity will last, is four years. A, the annuity received (by the lender and paid by the firm) at the end of each year, is unknown. Substituting these values into equation (9–12) we find

$$\$6000 = A \left[\sum_{t=1}^{4} \frac{1}{(1 + .15)^t} \right]$$

$$\$6000 = A(2.855)$$

$$\$2101.58 = A$$

In order to repay the principal and interest on the outstanding loan in four years the annual payments would be $2101.58. The breakdown of interest and principal payments is given in the *loan amortization schedule* in Table 9–10, with very minor rounding error. As you can see, the interest payment declines each year as the loan outstanding declines.

PRESENT VALUE OF AN UNEVEN STREAM

While some projects will involve single dollar flows and some annuities, many projects will involve uneven cash flows over several years. This situation will become quite common in Chapter 10, where we examine investments in fixed assets. There we will be comparing not only the present value of cash flows between projects, but also the cash inflows and outflows within a particular project, trying to determine that project's present value. However, this will not be difficult because the present value of any cash flow is measured in today's dollars and thus can be compared, through addition for inflows and subtraction for outflows, with the present value of any other cash flow that also is measured in today's dollars. For example, if we wished to find the present value of the following cash flows:

Year	Cash Flow
1	$500
2	200
3	−400
4	500
5	500
6	500
7	500
8	500
9	500
10	500

given a 6 percent discount rate, we would merely discount the flows back to the present and total them by adding in the positive flows and substracting the negative ones. However, this problem is complicated by the annuity of $500 that runs from years 4 through 10. To accommodate this factor, we can first discount the annuity back to the beginning of period 4 (or end of period 3) by using the present-value-of-an-annuity table and get its present value at that point in time. We then use the present-value-of-a-single-flow table (Table 9–4) and discount the present value of this annuity at the end of period 3 back to the present. In effect we discount twice, first back to the end of period 3 then back to the present. This is shown graphically in Table 9–11 and numerically in Table 9–12. Thus, the present value of this uneven stream of cash flows is $2657.94.

TABLE 9–11. Illustration of an Example of the Present Value of an Uneven Stream Involving One Annuity Discounted to Present at 6 Percent

Year	0		1	2	3	4	5	6	7	8	9	10
Dollars received at end of year			500	200	−400	500	500	500	500	500	500	500
	$ 471.50 ←											
	178.00 ←											
	−336.00 ←											
					$2791 ←							
	2344.44 ←											
Total present value	$2657.94											

TABLE 9–12. Determination of the Present Value of an Example with Uneven Stream Involving One Annuity Discounted to Present at 6 Percent

1.	Present value of $500 received at the end of one year = $500(.943) =	$ 471.50
2.	Present value of $200 received at the end of two years = $200(.890) =	178.00
3.	Present value of a $400 outflow at the end of three years = −$400(.840) =	−336.00
4.	(a) Value at the end of year 3 of a $500 annuity, years 4 through 10: $500(5.582) = $2791.00 (b) Present value of $2791.00 received at the end of year 3 = $2791.00(.840) =	2344.44
5.	Total present value =	$2657.94

Example What is the present value of an investment involving $200 received at the end of years 1 through 5, a $300 cash outflow at the end of year 6, and $500 received at the end of years 7 through 10 given a 5 percent discount rate? Here we have two annuities, one that can be discounted directly back to the present using the present-value-of-an-annuity table and one that must be discounted twice to bring it back to the present. This second annuity must first be discounted back to the beginning of period 7 or end of period 6, using the present-value-of-an-annuity table; then the present value of the annuity at the end of period 6 must be discounted back to the present, using the present-value-of-a-single-flow table. From the sum of the present value of these two annuities the present value of the $300 cash outflow at the end of year 6 is subtracted to give us the total present value of this investment. This is shown graphically in Table 9–13; the calculations are shown in Table 9–14. Thus, the present value of this series of cash flows is $1964.66.

TABLE 9–13. Illustration of an Example of Present Value of an Uneven Stream Involving Two Annuities Discounted at 5 Percent

Year	0	1	2	3	4	5	6	7	8	9	10
Dollars received at end of year		200	200	200	200	200	−300	500	500	500	500
	$ 865.80 ←										
	−223.80 ←										
							$1773 ←				
	1322.66 ←										
Total present value	$1964.66										

TABLE 9–14. Determination of Present Value of an Example with Uneven Stream Involving Two Annuities Discounted at 5 Percent

1.	Present value of first annuity, years 1 through 5 = $200(4.329) =	$ 865.80
2.	Present value of $300 cash outflow = −$300(.746) =	−223.80
3.	(a) Value at end of year 6 of second annuity, years 7 through 10 = $500(3.546) = $1773.00	
	(b) Present value of $1773.00 received at the end of year 6 = $1773.00(.746) =	1322.66
4.	Total present value =	$1964.66

PERPETUITIES

A **perpetuity** is an annuity that continues forever; that is, every year from now on this investment pays the same dollar amount. An example of a perpetuity is preferred stock that yields a constant dollar dividend infinitely. Determining the present value of a perpetuity is delightfully simple; we merely need to divide the constant flow by the discount rate.[1] For example, the present value of a $100 perpetuity discounted

---

[1] See Chapter 12 for a mathematical derivation.

back to the present at 5 percent is $100/.05 = $2000. Thus, the equation representing the present value of a perpetuity is

$$P = \frac{PP}{i} \tag{9–13}$$

where P = the present value of perpetuity

PP = the constant dollar amount provided by the perpetuity

i = the annual interest or discount rate

Example   What is the present value of a $500 perpetuity discounted back to the present at 8 percent? Substituting PP = $500 and i = .08 into equation (9–13), we find

$$P = \frac{\$500}{.08} = \$6250$$

Thus, the present value of this perpetuity is $6250.

BOND VALUATION: AN ILLUSTRATION OF THE TIME VALUE OF MONEY[2]

Bond valuation illustrates a combination of several discounting techniques and procedures including an annuity, a single cash flow, and semi-annual periods. When a bond is purchased, the owner receives two things: (1) interest payments, which are generally made semi-annually, and (2) at maturity, repayment of the full principal, regardless of how much the bond was purchased for. For example, let us look at a bond that pays $45 semi-annually and comes due in 20 years; that is, at the end of 20 years the bondholder will receive $1000, the return of the principal, and the bond will terminate. What is this bond worth? It is worth the present value of the cash flows it provides. Thus, as the appropriate market discount or interest rate changes, the value of the bond changes. Let us examine the value of this bond, assuming medium, low, and high market discount rates—say, 10, 6, and 14 percent, respectively.

Bond Value at 10 Percent   The bond value is the sum of the present value of the interest payment annuity that the bondholder receives and the present value of the return of bond principal at maturity computed at the market discount rate of 10 percent paid semi-annually; that is,

$$\begin{pmatrix} \text{Bond value} \\ \text{at 10\%} \\ \text{compounded} \\ \text{semi-annually} \end{pmatrix} = \begin{pmatrix} \text{present value} \\ \text{of interest} \\ \text{payments} \end{pmatrix} + \begin{pmatrix} \text{present value of} \\ \text{the return of} \\ \text{the principal} \end{pmatrix}$$

---

[2] This section is also covered in Chapter 12 and can be omitted without loss of continuity.

$$= A \left[\sum_{t=1}^{n \cdot m} \frac{1}{(1 + i/m)^t} \right] + FV_{n \cdot m} \left[\frac{1}{(1 + i/m)^{n \cdot m}} \right]$$

$$= \$45 \left[\sum_{t=1}^{40} \frac{1}{(1 + .05)^t} \right] + \$1000 \left[\frac{1}{(1 + .05)^{40}} \right] \qquad (9\text{--}14)$$

$$= \$45(17.159) + \$1000(.142)$$

$$= \$772.16 + \$142$$

$$= \$914.16$$

Thus, the value of this bond that pays $45 semi-annually, given a market discount rate of 10 percent, is $914.16.

Bond Value at 6 Percent   If the market discount rate drops to 6 percent paid semi-annually, the procedure for determining the bond value remains the same, the only change being that i now equals 6 percent. Logically, since the value of i appears only in the denominators of the present value of interest payments and the return of principal, the bond value should increase as i drops. Intuitively this makes sense, the cash flows to the bondholder all occur in the future, and they are now discounted back to the present at a lower discount rate, so their present value should increase. The value of this bond at a 6 percent market discount rate becomes

$$\begin{matrix} \text{Bond value} \\ \text{at 6\% compounded} \\ \text{semi-annually} \end{matrix} = \$45 \left[\sum_{t=1}^{40} \frac{1}{(1 + .03)^t} \right] + \$1000 \left[\frac{1}{(1 + .03)^{40}} \right]$$

$$= \$45(23.115) + \$1000(.307)$$

$$= \$1040.18 + \$307$$

$$= \$1347.18$$

Thus, if the market discount rate drops from 10 percent to 6 percent, the value of this bond will climb from $914.16 to $1374.18.

Bond value at 14 Percent   If the market discount rate climbs to 14 percent paid semi-annually, the bond value will drop, as the future cash flows to the bondholder are now discounted back to the present at a higher discount rate

$$\begin{matrix} \text{Bond value} \\ \text{at 14\% compounded} \\ \text{semi-annually} \end{matrix} = \$45 \left[\sum_{t=1}^{40} \frac{1}{(1 + .07)^t} \right] + \$1000 \left[\frac{1}{(1 + .07)^{40}} \right]$$

$$= \$45(13.332) + \$1000(.067)$$

$$= \$599.94 + \$67$$

$$= \$666.94$$

Thus, if the market discount rate climbs from 10 percent to 14 percent, the value of this bond will drop from $914.16 to $666.94. This illustrates the inverse relationship between interest rates or the market discount rate and bond prices. When the market discount rate goes up, bond values go down, and vice versa.

Summary

The existence of profitable investment alternatives and interest rates creates the time value of money. In future chapters we will find that in order to make logical financial decisions we must incorporate the time value of money into our calculations. The reason is that we will be comparing the costs and benefits of financial decisions that do not all occur during the same time period. To do this we must first make all dollar values comparable, and since money has a time value, we must move all dollar flows either back to the present or out to a common future date. All formulas presented in this chapter to move money back and forth in time actually stem from the simple compounding formula,

$$FV_n = P(1 + i)^n$$

and have been formulated to deal more simply with common financial situations— for example, discounting single flows, compounding annuities, and discounting annuities.

Compound Interest

The future or compound value (FV_n) at the end of n years of an original amount (P) invested at the beginning of the first year that is compounded at an annual interest rate of i can be determined using the following formula:

$$FV_n = P(1 + i)^n$$

As the determination of the future value of an investment can be quite time-consuming when the investment is held for a number of years, tables have been compiled for values of $(1 + i)^n$; these compilations appear in Table 9–2 and more completely in Appendix A to this book. Substituting the table value into the above equation, we find

$$FV_n = P \begin{bmatrix} \text{table value,} \\ \text{Appendix A,} \\ \\ n \text{ years,} \\ i \text{ percent} \end{bmatrix}$$

In the case in which nonannual compounding periods are used, the compounding equation is adjusted such that

$$FV_n = P\left(1 + \frac{i}{m}\right)^{mn}$$

where m is the number of times compounding occurs during the year.

Present Value

The present value of a future sum of money can be determined from the following equation:

$$P = FV_n\left[\frac{1}{(1 + i)^n}\right]$$

where FV_n = the future value of the investment at the end of n years

n = the number of years until payment will be received

i = the opportunity or discount rate

P = the present value of the future sum of money

This is exactly the same formula we used to find the compound value of money, except here we are solving for P instead of FV_n. To aid in the computation of present values, tables have been compiled for values of $[1/(1 + i)^n]$; they appear in Appendix B in the back of this book. Thus, to find the present value of a future sum of money we need only consult Table 9–4 or Appendix B and plug the appropriate value into the following equation:

$$P = FV_n\begin{bmatrix} \text{table value,} \\ \text{Appendix B,} \\ \\ n \text{ years,} \\ i \text{ percent} \end{bmatrix}$$

Compound Annuities

An annuity is a series of equal dollar payments for a specified number of years. A compound annuity involves depositing or investing an equal sum of money at the end of each year for a specified number of years and allowing it to grow. Mathematically, this process can be generalized to

$$FV_n = A\left[\sum_{t=0}^{n-1}(1 + i)^t\right]$$

where FV_n = the future value of the annuity at the end of the nth year

A = the annuity value deposited at the end of each year

i = the annual compound interest rate

n = the number of years for which the annuity will last

To simplify the process of compounding an annuity, an expanded version of Table 9–6 is provided in Appendix C for $\left[\sum_{t=0}^{n-1} (1 + i)^t\right]$ for various combinations of n and i. When we use this table, the calculation of a compound annuity reduces to determining the appropriate table value and plugging it into the following equation:

$$FV_n = A \begin{bmatrix} \text{table value,} \\ \text{Appendix C,} \\ \\ n \text{ years,} \\ i \text{ percent} \end{bmatrix}$$

Present Value of an Annuity

The present value of an annuity can be determined by using the formula:

$$P = A \left[\sum_{t=1}^{n} \frac{1}{(1 + i)^t}\right]$$

where A = the annuity received at the end of each year

i = the annual interest or discount rate

P = the present value of the future annuity

n = the number of years for which the annuity will last

To simplify this process an expanded version of Table 9–8 is provided in Appendix D for $\left[\sum_{t=1}^{n} \frac{1}{(1 + i)^t}\right]$. Using the table, we can determine the present value of an annuity as follows:

$$P = A \begin{bmatrix} \text{table value,} \\ \text{Appendix D,} \\ \\ n \text{ years,} \\ i \text{ percent} \end{bmatrix}$$

Perpetuities

A perpetuity is an annuity that continues forever. To determine the present value of a perpetuity we merely need to divide the constant flow by the discount rate. Thus,

$$P = \frac{PP}{i}$$

where P = the present value of the perpetuity

PP = the constant dollar amount provided by the perpetuity

i = the annual interest or discount rate

Study Questions

9–1. What is the time value of money? Why does it exist?

9–2. The processes of discounting and compounding are obviously related. Explain this relationship.

9–3. How would an increase in the interest rate (i) or a decrease in the holding period (n) affect the future value (FV_n) of a sum of money? Explain why.

9–4. Suppose you were considering depositing your savings in three banks, all of which paid 5 percent interest; bank A compounded annually, bank B compounded semi-annually, and bank C compounded continuously. Which bank would you choose? Why?

9–5. What is the relationship between the present-value table (Table 9–4) and the present-value-of-an-annuity table (Table 9–8)? What is the table factor from Table 9–8 for the present value of a 10-year annuity discounted back to present at 10 percent? Add up the table factors from Table 9–8 in the $i = 10\%$ column and rows $n = 1, \ldots, 10$. What is this value? Why do these values have the relationship they do?

9–6. What is an annuity? Give some examples of annuities. Distinguish between an annuity and a perpetuity.

9–7. What does continuous compounding mean?

Self-Test Problems

ST–1. You place $25,000 in a savings account paying annual compound interest of 8 percent for 3 years and then move it into a savings account that pays 10 percent interest compounded annually. How much will your money have grown at the end of 6 years?

ST–2. You purchase a boat for $35,000 and pay $5,000 down and agree to pay the rest over the next 10 years in 10 equal annual payments which include principal payments plus 13 percent compound interest on the unpaid balance. What will these payments be equal to?

ST–3. In order for an investment to grow eightfold in 9 years, at what rate would it have to grow?

ST–4. You have the opportunity to buy a bond for $1000 that will pay no interest during its 10-year life and have a value of $3,106 at maturity. What rate of return or yield does this bond pay?

Study Problems

9–1. (*Compound Interest*) What will the following investments accumulate to?
   a. $5000 invested for 10 years at 10 percent compounded annually
   b. $8000 invested for 7 years at 8 percent compounded annually
   c. $775 invested for 12 years at 12 percent compounded annually
   d. $21,000 invested for 5 years at 5 percent compounded annually

9–2. (*Compound Value Solving for n*) How many years will it take for the following?
   a. $500 to grow to $1039.50 if invested at 5 percent compounded annually
   b. $35 to grow to $53.87 if invested at 9 percent compounded annually
   c. $100 to grow to $298.60 if invested at 20 percent compounded annually
   d. $53 to grow to $78.76 if invested at 2 percent compounded annually

9-3. (*Compound Value Solving for i*) At what annual rate would the following have to be invested?
  a. $500 in order to grow to $1948.00 in 12 years
  b. $300 in order to grow to $422.10 in 7 years
  c. $50 in order to grow to $280.20 in 20 years
  d. $200 in order to grow to $497.60 in 5 years

9-4. (*Present Value*) What is the present value of the following future amounts?
  a. $800 to be received 10 years from now discounted back to present at 10 percent
  b. $300 to be received 5 years from now discounted back to present at 5 percent
  c. $1000 to be received 8 years from now discounted back to present at 3 percent
  d. $1000 to be received 8 years from now discounted back to present at 20 percent

9-5. (*Compound Annuity*) What is the accumulated sum of each of the following streams of payments?
  a. $500 a year for 10 years compounded annually at 5 percent
  b. $100 a year for 5 years compounded annually at 10 percent
  c. $35 a year for 7 years compounded annually at 7 percent
  d. $25 a year for 3 years compounded annually at 2 percent

9-6. (*Present Value of an Annuity*) What is the present value of the following annuities?
  a. $2500 a year for 10 years discounted back to the present at 7 percent
  b. $70 a year for 3 years discounted back to the present at 3 percent
  c. $280 a year for 7 years discounted back to the present at 6 percent
  d. $500 a year for 10 years discounted back to the present at 10 percent

9-7. (*Compound Value*) Mark Cox, who recently sold his Porsche, placed $10,000 in a savings account paying annual compound interest of 6 percent.
  a. Calculate the amount of money that will have accrued if he leaves the money in the bank for 1, 5, and 15 years.
  b. If he moves his money into an account that pays 8 percent or one that pays 10 percent, rework part (a) using these new interest rates.
  c. What conclusions can you draw from the relationship between interest rates, time, and future sums from the calculations you have done above?

9-8. (*Compound Interest with Nonannual Periods*) Calculate the amount of money that will be in each of the following accounts at the end of the given deposit period:

Account	Amount Deposited	Annual Interest Rate	Compounding Period (Compounded Every ___Months)	Deposit Period (Years)
Roy Brow	$ 1,000	10%	12	10
Bimbo Coles	95,000	12	1	1
Frankie Allen	8,000	12	2	2
Wayne Robinson	120,000	8	3	2
John Dixon	30,000	10	6	4
Del Curry	15,000	12	4	3

9-9. (*Compound Interest with Nonannual Periods*)
  a. Calculate the future sum of $5000, given that it will be held in the bank 5 years at an annual interest rate of 6 percent.
  b. Recalculate part (a) given that the compounding period is semi-annual; and bimonthly.
  c. Recalculate parts (a) and (b) for a 12 percent annual interest rate.
  d. Recalculate part (a) given that the time horizon used changes to 12 years (annual interest rate is still 6 percent).

e. With respect to the effect of changes in the stated interest rate and holding periods on future sums in parts (c) and (d), what conclusions do you draw when you compare these figures with answers found in parts (a) and (b)?

9–10. (*Solving for i in Annuities*) Nicki Johnson, a sophomore mechanical engineering student, receives a call from an insurance agent, who believes that Nicki is an older woman ready to retire from teaching. He talks to her about several annuities that she could buy that would guarantee her an annual fixed income. The annuities are as follows:

Annuity	Initial Payment into Annuity (at $t = 0$)	Amount of Money Received per Year	Duration of Annuity (Years)
A	$50,000	$8500	12
B	$60,000	$7000	25
C	$70,000	$8000	20

If Nicki could earn 11 percent on her money by placing it in a savings account, should she place it instead in any of the annuities? Which ones, if any? Why?

9–11. (*Future Value*) Sales of a new finance book were 15,000 copies this year and were expected to increase by 20 percent per year. What are expected sales during each of the next three years? Graph this sales trend and explain.

9–12. (*Future Value*) Reggie Jackson, formerly of the New York Yankees, hit 41 home runs in 1980. If his home run output grew at a rate of 10 percent per year, what would it have been over the following five years?

9–13. (*Loan Amortization*) Todd Dodge purchased a new house for $80,000. He paid $20,000 down and agreed to pay the rest over the next 25 years in 25 equal annual payments, which include principal payments plus 9 percent compound interest on the unpaid balance. What will these equal payments be equal to?

9–14. (*Solving for A in an Annuity*) To pay for your child's education you wish to have accumulated $15,000 at the end of 15 years. To do this you plan on depositing an equal amount into the bank at the end of each year. If the bank is willing to pay 6 percent compounded annually, how much must you deposit each year in order to obtain your goal?

9–15. (*Solving for i in Compound Interest*) If you were offered $1079.50 ten years from now in return for an investment of $500 currently, what annual rate of interest would you earn if you took the offer?

9–16. (*Present Value and Future Value of an Annuity*) In 10 years you are planning on retiring and buying a house in Ovida, Florida. The house you are looking at currently costs $100,000 and is expected to increase in value each year at a rate of 5 percent. Assuming you can earn 10 percent annually on your investments, how much must you invest at the end of each of the next 10 years in order to be able to buy your dream home when you retire?

9–17. (*Compound Value*) The Aggarwal Corporation established a sinking fund to retire a $10 million mortgage that matures on December 31, 1997. To retire this mortgage, the company plans to put a fixed amount into the fund at the end of each year for 10 years, with the first payment occurring on December 31, 1988. The Aggarwal Company expects to earn 9 percent annually on the money in the sinking fund. What equal annual contribution must they make to the sinking fund in order to accumulate the $10 million by December 31, 1997?

9–18. (*Compound Interest with Nonannual Periods*) After examining the various personal loan rates available to you, you find that you can borrow funds from a finance company at 12 percent compounded monthly, or from a bank at 13 percent compounded annually. Which alternative is the most attractive?

9–19. (*Present Value of an Uneven Stream of Payments*) You are given three investment alternatives to analyze. The cash flows from these three investments are as follows:

End of Year	Investment		
	A	B	C
1	$10,000		$10,000
2	10,000		
3	10,000		
4	10,000		
5	10,000	$10,000	
6		10,000	50,000
7		10,000	
8		10,000	
9		10,000	
10		10,000	10,000

Assuming a 20 percent discount rate, find the present value of each investment.

9–20. (*Present Value*) The Kumar Corporation is planning on issuing bonds that pay no interest, but can be converted into $1000 at maturity, seven years from their purchase. In order to price these bonds competitively with other bonds of equal risk, it is determined that they should yield 10 percent, compounded annually. At what price should the Kumar Corporation sell these bonds?

9–21. (*Perpetuities*) What is the present value of the following?
a. A $300 perpetuity discounted back to the present at 8 percent
b. A $1000 perpetuity discounted back to the present at 12 percent
c. A $100 perpetuity discounted back to the present at 9 percent
d. A $95 perpetuity discounted back to the present at 5 percent

9–22. (*Continuous Compounding*) What is the value of $500 after five years if it is invested at 10 percent compounded continuously? (If you don't have a calculator capable of solving this problem, simply set it up.)

9–23. (*Solving for n with Nonannual Periods*) About how many years would it take for your investment to grow fourfold if it were invested at 16 percent compounded semi-annually?

9–24. (*Bond Values*) You are examining three bonds with par value of $1000 (you receive $1000 at maturity) and are concerned with what would happen to their market value if interest rates (or the market discount rate) changed. The three bonds are:

Bond A—A bond with 3 years left to maturity that pays 10 percent per year compounded semi-annually

Bond B—A bond with 7 years left to maturity that pays 10 percent per year compounded semi-annually

Bond C—A bond with 20 years left to maturity that pays 10 percent per year compounded semi-annually

What would be the value of these bonds if the market discount rate was
a. 10 percent per year compounded semi-annually?
b. 4 percent per year compounded semi-annually?

    c. 16 percent per year compounded semi-annually?

    d. What observations can you make about these results?

9–25. (*Complex Present Value*) How much do you have to deposit today so that beginning 11 years from now you can withdraw $10,000 a year for the next 5 years (periods 11 through 15) plus an *additional* amount of $20,000 in that last year (period 15)? Assume an interest rate of 6 percent.

9–26. (*Loan Amortization*) On December 31, Beth Klemkosky bought a yacht for $50,000, paying $10,000 down and agreeing to pay the balance in 10 equal annual installments, which include both the principal and 10 percent interest on the declining balance. How big would the annual payments be?

9–27. (*Solving for i in an Annuity*) You lend a friend $30,000 which your friend will repay in five equal annual payments of $10,000, with the first payment to be received one year from now. What rate of return does your loan receive?

9–28. (*Solving for i in Compound Interest*) You lend a friend $10,000, for which your friend will repay you $27,027 at the end of 5 years. What interest rate are you charging your "friend"?

9–29. (*Loan Amortization*) A firm borrows $25,000 from the bank at 12 percent compounded annually to purchase some new machinery. This loan is to be repaid in equal annual installments at the end of each year over the next 5 years. How much will each annual payment be?

9–30. (*Present Value Comparison*) You are offered $1000 today, $10,000 in 12 years, or $25,000 in 25 years. Assuming that you can earn 11 percent on your money, which should you choose?

9–31. (*Compound Annuity*) You plan on buying some property in Florida 5 years from today. To do this you estimate that you will need $20,000 at that time for the purchase. You would like to accumulate these funds by making equal annual deposits in your savings account, which pays 12 percent annually. If you make your first deposit at the end of this year and you would like your account to reach $20,000 when the final deposit is made, what will be the amount of your deposits?

9–32. (*Complex Present Value*) You would like to have $50,000 in 15 years. To accumulate this amount you plan to deposit each year an equal sum in the bank, which will earn 7 percent interest compounded annually. Your first payment will be made at the end of the year.

    a. How much must you deposit annually to accumulate this amount?

    b. If you decide to make a large lump-sum deposit today instead of the annual deposits, how large should this lump-sum deposit be? (Assume you can earn 7 percnt on this deposit.)

    c. At the end of 5 years you will receive $10,000 and deposit this in the bank toward your goal of $50,000 at the end of 15 years. In addition to this deposit, how much must you deposit in equal annual deposits in order to reach your goal? (Again assume you can earn 7 percent on this deposit.)

9–33. (*Comprehensive Present Value*) You are trying to plan for retirement in 10 years, and currently you have $100,000 in a savings account and $300,000 in stocks. In addition you plan on adding to your savings by depositing $10,000 per year in your *savings account* at the end of each of the next 5 years and then $20,000 per year at the end of each year for the final 5 years until retirement.

    a. Assuming your savings account returns 7 percent compounded annually while your investment in stocks will return 12 percent compounded annually, how much will you have at the end of 10 years? (Ignore taxes.)

    b. If you expect to live for 20 years after you retire, and at retirement you deposit all of your savings in a bank account paying 10 percent, how much can you withdraw each year after retirement (20 equal withdrawals beginning one year after you retire) in order to end up with a zero balance at death?

9–34. (*Comprehensive Present Value*) You have just inherited a large sum of money and you are trying to determine how much you should save for retirement and how much you can spend now. For retirement you will deposit today (January 1, 1988) a lump sum in a bank account paying 10 percent compounded annually. You don't plan on touching this deposit until you retire in 5 years (January 1, 1993), and you plan on living for 20 additional years and then dropping dead on December 31, 2012. During your retirement you would like to receive income of $50,000 per year to be received the first day of each year, with the first payment on January 1, 1993, and the last payment on January 1, 2012. Complicating this objective is your desire to have one final three-year fling during which time you'd like to track down all the original members of "Leave It to Beaver" and "The Brady Bunch" and get their autographs. To finance this you want to receive $250,000 on January 1, 2008, and *nothing* on January 1, 2009, and January 1, 2010, as you will be on the road. In addition, after you pass on (January 1, 2013), you would like to have a total of $100,000 to leave to your children.

a. How much must you deposit in the bank at 10 percent on January 1, 1988, in order to achieve your goal? (Use a time line in order to answer this question.)

b. What kinds of problems are associated with this analysis and its assumptions?

Self-Test Solutions

SS–1. This is a compound interest problem in which you must first find the future value of $25,000 growing at 8 percent compounded annually for 3 years and then allow that future value to grow for an additional 3 years at 10 percent. First, the value of the $25,000 after 3 years growing at 8 percent is

$$FV_3 = P(1 + i)^n$$

$$FV_3 = \$25,000(1 + .08)^3$$

$$FV_3 = \$25,000(1.260)$$

$$FV_3 = \$31,500$$

Thus, after 3 years you have $31,500 and now this amount is allowed to grow for 3 years at 10 percent. Plugging this into equation (9–6), $P = \$31,500$, $i = 10\%$, $n = 3$ years, and we solve for FV_3:

$$FV_3 = \$31,500(1 + .10)^3$$

$$FV_3 = \$31,500(1.331)$$

$$FV_3 = \$41,926.50$$

Thus, after 6 years the $25,000 will have grown to $41,926.50.

SS–2. This loan amortization problem is actually just a present-value-of-an-annuity problem in which we know the values of i, n, and P and are solving for A. In this case the value of i is 13 percent, n is 10 years, and P is $30,000. Substituting these values into equation (9–12) we find

$$\$30,000 = A\left[\sum_{t=1}^{10} \frac{1}{(1 + .13)^t}\right]$$

$$\$30,000 = A(5.426)$$

$$\$5528.93 = A$$

SS–3. This is a simple compound interest problem in which FV_9 is eight times larger than P. Here again three of the four variables are known: $n = 9$ years, $FV_9 = 8$, and $P = 1$ and we are solving for i. Substituting these values into equation (9–6) we find

$$FV_9 = P(1 + i)^n$$

$$8 = 1(1 + i)^9$$

$$8.00 = (1 + i)^9$$

Thus we are looking for a table value of 8 in the Future Value Table in Appendix A which occurs in the 9-year row. If we look in the 9-year row for a value of 8.00, we find it in the 26% column (8.004). Thus, the answer is 26 percent.

SS–4.

$$FV_n = P(1 + i)^n$$

$$\$3,106 = \$1,000(1 + i)^{10}$$

$$3,106 = (1 + i)^{10}$$

$$3,106 = \begin{bmatrix} \text{TABLE VALUE} \\ \text{APPENDIX A} \\ n = 7 \\ ? = \% \end{bmatrix}$$

Looking in the $n = 10$ row of Appendix A, we find a value of 3.106 in the 12% column. Therefore, 12% $= i$.

Selected References

Draper, Jean E., and Jane S. Klingman. *Mathematical Analysis*, New York: Harper & Row, 1967.

Greynolds, Elbert B., Jr., Julius S. Aronofsky, and Robert J. Frame. *Financial Analysis Using Calculators: Time Value of Money*. New York: McGraw-Hill, 1980.

Hart, William L. *Mathematics of Investment* (5th ed.). Lexington, MA: D. C. Heath, 1975.

Howell, James E., and Daniel Teichroew. *Mathematical Analysis for Business Decisions*, Chap. 10. Homewood, IL: Richard D. Irwin, 1963.

Shao, Stephen P. *Mathematics for Management and Finance* (3rd ed.). Cincinnati: South-Western Publishing, 1974.

10

Capital Budgeting

In Chapter 9 we developed tools for making cash flows that occur in different time periods comparable. In this chapter these techniques are used in conjunction with additional decision rules to determine when to invest money in long-term assets, which has come to be called **capital budgeting.** In evaluating capital investment proposals we will compare the costs and benefits of each in a number of ways. Some of these methods take account of the time value of money, others do not; but each of these methods is used frequently in the real world.

We will look first at the purpose and importance of capital budgeting. Next, since capital budgeting techniques rely on cash flows as inputs, we will study the determination of these cash flows. Five capital budgeting criteria will then be provided for evaluating capital investments, followed by a look at capital budgeting in practice. Several advanced topics in capital budgeting will also be examined.

INTRODUCTION TO CAPITAL BUDGETING

Capital budgeting involves the decision-making process with respect to investment in fixed assets; specifically, it involves measuring the incremental cash flows associated with investment proposals and evaluating the attractiveness of these cash flows relative to the project's cost. Typically these investments involve rather large cash outlays at the outset and commit the firm to a particular course of action over a relatively long time horizon. Thus, if a capital budgeting decision is incorrect, reversing it tends to be costly.

For example, about 30 years ago the Ford Motor Company's decision to produce the Edsel entailed an outlay of $250 million to bring the car to market and losses of approximately $200 million during the 2½ years it was produced—in all, a $450 million mistake.[1] This type of decision is costly to reverse. Fortunately for Ford, it

---

[1] "The Edsel Dies, and Ford Regroups Survivors," *Business Week,* November 28, 1959, p. 27.

was able to convert Edsel production facilities to produce the Mustang, thereby avoiding an even larger loss. Today, it is General Motors making a major capital budgeting decision, investing $3.5 billion to construct its Saturn automobile plant. Only time will tell if this decision proves to be profitable.

In order to evaluate investment proposals, we must first set guidelines by which to measure the value of each proposal. In so doing we will focus our attention on cash flows rather than accounting profits. This choice rests on the fact that cash flows, and not accounting profits, are actually received and reinvested by the firm. By examining cash flows we are able correctly to analyze the timing of the benefits. In addition, we will examine cash flows on an after-tax basis, as only those flows are available for reinvesting in the firm or for paying shareholders. Moreover, we may find that not all the flows resulting from an investment proposal are incremental in nature. In other words, the total cash flows that result from a project may not be relevant in the analysis. It is only the incremental cash flows that interest us.

For example, assume that we are considering a new product line that will compete with one of our current products and reduce its sales. If so, in determining the cash flows associated with the proposed project, we would consider only the incremental sales brought to the company as a whole. New product sales achieved at the cost of losing sales of other products in our line would not be considered a benefit of adopting the new product.

In evaluating projects and determining cash flows, we will separate the investment decision from the financing decision. If accepting this project means we will have to raise new funds by issuing bonds, we will not consider the interest charges associated with raising funds as a relevant cash outflow. When we discount the incremental cash flows back to the present at the required rate of return, we are implicitly accounting for the cost of raising funds to finance the new project. In essence, the required rate of return reflects the cost of funds needed to support the project. In effect, we will first determine the desirability of the project and then determine how best to finance it.

MEASURING CASH FLOWS

In measuring cash flows, we will be interested only in the **incremental,** or differential, **after-tax cash flows** that can be attributed to the proposal being evaluated. Obviously, the worth of our decision depends upon the accuracy of our cash flow estimates. In general, a project's cash flows will fall into one of three categories: (1) the initial outlay, (2) the differential flows over the project's life, (3) the terminal cash flow. In introducing these cash flow categories, we look first at the actual calculation. This section will be followed by several capital budgeting criteria that will use these cash flows as inputs.

Initial Outlay

The **initial outlay** involves the immediate cash outflow necessary to purchase the asset and put it in operating order. This amount includes the cost of installing the asset (the asset's purchase price plus any expenses associated with shipping or installation), and any nonexpense cash outlays, such as increased working capital requirements. If we are considering a new sales outlet, there might be additional cash flows associated with investment in working capital in the form of increased inventory and cash necessary

TABLE 10–1. Summary of Calculation of Initial Outlay Incremental After-Tax Cash Flow

1. Installed cost of asset
2. Additional nonexpense outlays incurred (for example, working capital investments)
3. Additional expenses on an after-tax basis (for example, training expenses)
4. In a replacement decision, the *after-tax* cash flow associated with the sale of the old machine

to operate the sales outlet. While these cash flows are not included in the cost of the asset or even expensed on the books, they must be included in our analysis. The after-tax cost of expense items incurred as a result of new investment must also be included as cash outflows—for example, any training expenses or special engineering expenses that would not have been incurred otherwise. Finally, if the investment decision is a replacement decision, the cash inflow associated with the selling price of the old asset, in addition to any tax effects resulting from its sale, must be accounted for.

Obviously, determining the initial outlay is a complex calculation. Table 10–1 summarizes some of the more common calculations involved in determining the initial outlay. This list is by no means exhaustive, but it should help simplify the calculations involved in the example that follows.

Tax Effects—Sale of Old Machine

Perhaps the most confusing calculation occurs in determining the initial outlay of a replacement project and involves the incremental tax payment associated with the sale of the old machine. Although these calculations were examined in Chapter 2, a review is appropriate here. There are three possible tax situations dealing with the sale of an old asset:

1. **The old asset is sold for a price above the depreciated value.** Here the difference between the old machine's selling price and its depreciated value is considered recapture of depreciation and taxed at the marginal corporate tax rate. If, for example, the old machine was originally purchased for $15,000, had a book value of $10,000, and was sold for $17,000, the taxes due from recapture of depreciation would be ($17,000 − 10,000)(.34), or $2380.
2. The old asset is sold for its depreciated value. In this case no taxes result, as there is neither a gain nor a loss in the asset's sale.
3. The old asset is sold for less than its depreciated value. In this case the difference between the depreciated book value and the salvage value of the asset is used to offset ordinary income and thus results in tax savings. For example, if the depreciated book value of the asset is $10,000 and it is sold for $7000, assuming the firm's marginal corporate tax rate is 34 percent, the cash inflow from tax savings is ($10,000 − $7000)(.34), or $1020.

Example In order to clarify the calculation of the initial outlay, consider an example of a company in the 34 percent marginal tax bracket. This company is considering the purchase of a new machine to be used in oil and gas drilling for $30,000. It is in the five-year class and will be depreciated using the simplified straight-line method (this depreciation method will be explained later). The useful life of this new machine is also 5 years. The new machine will replace an existing machine originally purchased for $30,000 10 years ago which currently has 5 more years of expected useful life. The existing machine will generate $2000 of depreciation expenses for each of the next 5 years, at which time the book value will be equal to zero. To put the new machine in running order, it is necessary to pay shipping charges of $2000 and installation charges of $3000. Because the new machine will work faster than the old one, it will require an increase in goods-in-process inventory of $5000. Finally, the old machine can be sold to a scrap dealer for $15,000.

The installed cost of the new machine would be the $30,000 cost plus $2000 shipping and $3000 installation fees, for a total of $35,000. Additional outflows are associated with taxes incurred on the sale of the old machine and with increased investment in inventory. Although the old machine has a book value of $10,000, it could be sold for $15,000. The increased taxes from recapture of depreciation will be equal to the selling price of the old machine less its depreciated book value times the firm's marginal tax rate, or ($15,000 − $10,000)(.34), or $1700. The increase in goods-in-process inventory of $5000 must also be considered part of the initial outlay, with an offsetting inflow of $5000 corresponding to the recapture of this inventory occurring at the termination of the project. In effect, the firm invests $5000 in inventory now, resulting in an initial cash outlay, and liquidates this inventory in five years, resulting in a cash inflow at the end of the project. The total outlays associated with the new machine are $35,000 for its installed cost, $1700 in increased taxes, and $5000 in investment in inventory, for a total of $41,700. This is somewhat offset by the sale of the old machine for $15,000. Thus, the net initial outlay associated with this project is $26,700. These calculations are summarized in Table 10–2.

TABLE 10–2. Calculation of Initial Outlay for Example Problem

Outflows:		
Purchase Price	$30,000	
Shipping fee	2,000	
Installation fee	3,000	
Installed cost of machine		$35,000
Increased taxes from sale of old machine ($15,000 − 10,000)(.34)		1,700
Increased investment in inventory		5,000
Total outflows		$41,700
Inflows:		
Salvage value of old machine		15,000
Net initial outlay		$26,700

Differential Flows over the Project's Life

The differential cash flows over the project's life involve the incremental after-tax cash flows resulting from increased revenues, plus labor or material savings, and reductions in selling expenses. Overhead items, such as utilities, heat, light, and executive salaries, are generally not affected. However, any resultant change in any of these categories must be included. Any increase in interest payments incurred as a result of issuing bonds to finance the project should *not* be included, as the costs of funds needed to support the project are implicitly accounted for by discounting the project back to the present using the **required rate of return**—the rate of return a project must earn to justify raising funds to finance it. Finally, an adjustment for the incremental

TABLE 10–3.   Summary of Calculation of Differential Cash Flows on an After-Tax Basis

1. Added revenue offset by increased expenses
2. Labor and material savings
3. Increases in overhead incurred
4. Depreciation tax shield on an incremental basis in a replacement decision
5. Do *not* include interest expenses if the project is financed by issuing debt, as this is accounted for in the required rate of return

change in taxes should be made, including any increase in taxes that might result from increased profits or any tax savings from an increase in depreciation expenses. Increased depreciation expenses affect tax-related cash flows by reducing taxable income and thus lowering taxes. Table 10–3 lists some of the factors that might be involved in determining a project's differential cash flows. Before looking at an example, we will briefly examine the calculation of depreciation.

Depreciation and the Tax Reform Act of 1986

The Tax Reform Act of 1986 not only changed the tax rates corporations pay on their income, but also affected the calculation of their income. Not only was the investment tax credit that allowed for a tax credit up to 10 percent of qualified investments gone, but a modified version of the old Accelerated Cost Recovery System (ACRS) was introduced to be used for most tangible depreciable property placed in service beginning in 1987. Under this method, the life of the asset is determined according to the asset's class life; for example, most computer equipment has a 5-year asset life. The asset is then depreciated using the 200 percent declining balance method or on an optional straight-line method. With respect to its treatment of depreciation, the Tax Reform Act of 1986 had both good and bad news for businesses. The bad news was that in general the depreciable lives of most assets increased, while the good news was that most depreciable business assets may now be written off using the 200 percent declining balance method rather than the 150 percent declining balance method.

Depreciation Calculation— A Simplified Straight-Line Depreciation Method

For pedagogical purposes depreciation is calculated using a simplified straight-line method. It is simplified in the sense that it will ignore the half-year convention that only allows a half-year's deduction in the year the project is placed in service and a half-year's deduction in the first year after the recovery period. By ignoring the half-year convention we are able to calculate annual depreciation by taking the project's initial depreciable value and dividing by its class or depreciable life as follows:

$$\frac{\text{annual depreciation using}}{\text{the simplified straight-line method}} = \frac{\text{initial depreciable value}}{\text{depreciable life}}$$

The initial depreciable value is equal to the cost of the asset plus any expenses necessary to get the new asset into operating order.

This is not how depreciation would actually be calculated. The reason we have simplified the calculation is to allow you to focus directly on what should and should not be included in the cash flow calculations rather than being bogged down in tedious depreciation calculations. Moreover, since the tax laws change rather frequently, we are more interested in recognizing the tax implications of depreciation rather than understanding the specific depreciation provisions of the current tax laws.

Our concern with depreciation is to highlight its importance in generating cash flow estimates and to indicate that the financial manager must be aware of the current tax provisions when evaluating capital budgeting proposals.

Extending the earlier example, which illustrated the calculations of the initial outlay, suppose that purchasing the machine is expected to reduce salaries by $10,000 per year and fringe benefits by $1000 annually, because it will take only one man to operate, whereas the old machine requires two operators. In addition, the cost of defects will fall from $8000 per year to $3000. However, maintenance expenses will increase by $4000 annually. The annual depreciation on this new machine is $7000 per year, while the depreciation expense lost with the sale of the old machine is $2000 for each of the next 5 years. Annual depreciation on the new machine is calculated using the simplified straight-line method just described—that is, taking the cost of the new machine plus any expenses necessary to put it in operating order and dividing by its depreciable life. For the new machine these calculations are reflected in Table 10–4.

Since the depreciation on the old machine is $2000 per year, the increased depreciation will be from $2000 per year to $7000 per year, or an increase of $5000 per year. Although this increase in depreciation expenses is not a cash flow item, it does affect cash flows by reducing book profits, which in turn reduces taxes.

To determine the annual net cash flows resulting from the acceptance of this project, the net savings *before* taxes using both book profit and cash flows must be found. The additional taxes are then calculated based upon the before-tax book profit. For this example, Table 10–5 shows the determination of the differential cash flows on an after-tax basis. Thus, the differential cash flows over the project's life are $9620.

Terminal Cash Flow

The calculation of the terminal cash flow is in general quite a bit simpler than the previous two calculations. Flows associated with the project's termination generally include the salvage value of the project plus or minus any taxable gains or losses associated with its sales.

Under the current tax laws, in most cases there will be a forecasted taxable gain (resulting in a negative cash flow) associated with the salvage value at termination. This is because the current laws allow all projects to be depreciated to zero, and if a project has a book value of zero at termination and a positive salvage value, then that salvage value will be taxed. The tax effects associated with the salvage value of

TABLE 10–4. Calculation of Depreciation for the New Machine Using the Simplified Straight-Line Method

New machine purchase price	$30,000
Shipping fee	2,000
Installation fee	3,000
Total depreciable value	$35,000
Divided by depreciable life	$35,000/5
Equals: Annual depreciation	$ 7,000

TABLE 10–5. Calculation of Differential Cash Flows for the Example Problem

	Book Profit	Cash Flow
Savings: Reduced salary	$10,000	$10,000
Reduced fringe benefits	1,000	1,000
Reduced defects ($8000 − $3000)	5,000	5,000
Costs: Increased maintenance expense	−4,000	−4,000
Increased depreciation expense ($7000 − $2000)	−5,000	
Net savings before taxes	$ 7,000	$12,000
Taxes (@ 34%)	−2,380 ⟶	−2,380
Net cash flow after taxes		$ 9,620

the project at termination are determined exactly like the tax effects on the sale of the old machine associated with the initial outlay. The salvage value proceeds are compared with the depreciated value, in this case zero, to determine the tax.

In addition to the salvage value, there may be a cash outlay associated with the project termination. For example, at the close of a strip-mining operation, the mine must be refilled in an ecologically acceptable manner. Finally, any working capital outlay required at the initiation of the project—for example, increased inventory needed for the operation of a new plant—will be recaptured at the termination of the project. In effect the increased inventory required by the project can be liquidated when the project expires. Table 10–6 provides a sample list of some of the factors that might affect a project's terminal cash flow.

Extending the example to termination, the depreciated book value and salvage value of the machine at the termination date will be equal to zero. However, there will be a cash flow associated with the recapture of the initial outlay of work in process inventory of $5000. This flow is generated from the liquidation of the $5000 investment in work in process inventory. Therefore, the expected total terminal cash flow equals $5000.

If we were to construct a cash flow diagram from this example (Figure 10–1), it would have an initial outlay of $26,700, differential cash flows during years 1 through 5 of $9620, and an additional terminal cash flow at the end of year 5 of $5000. The cash flow occurring in year 5 is $14,620, the sum of the differential cash flow in year 5 of $9620 and the terminal cash flow of $5000.

Cash flow diagrams similar to Figure 10–1 will be used through the remainder of this chapter with arrows above the time line indicating cash inflows and arrows below the time line denoting outflows.

While the calculations above for determining the incremental, after-tax, net cash flows do not cover all possible cash flows, they do set up a framework in which al-

TABLE 10–6. Summary of Calculation of Terminal Cash Flow on an After-Tax Basis

1. The after-tax salvage value of the project
2. Cash outlays associated with the project's termination.
3. Recapture of nonexpense outlays that occurred at the project's initiation (for example, working capital investments)

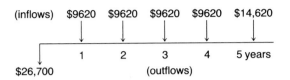

FIGURE 10–1. Example Cash Flow Diagram

most any situation can be handled. To simplify this framework, and to provide an overview of the calculations, Table 10–7 summarizes the rules in Tables 10–1, 10–3, and 10–6.

NONDISCOUNTED CASH FLOW CRITERIA FOR CAPITAL BUDGETING DECISIONS

We are now ready to consider the interpretation of cash flows. Cash flows represent the benefits generated from accepting a capital-budgeting proposal. In the remainder of this chapter this cash flow information is assumed to be given, and we will examine whether or not the project should be accepted.

We will consider five commonly used criteria for determining acceptability of investment proposals. The first two are the least sophisticated, in that they do not incorporate the time value of money into their calculations; the final three do take account of it.

Nondiscounted Cash Flow Criterion 1: Payback Period

The **payback period** is the number of years needed to recover the initial cash outlay. As this criterion measures how quickly the project will return its original investment, it deals with cash flows rather than accounting profits. The accept-reject criterion involves whether or not the project's payback period is less than or equal to the firm's maximum desired payback period. For example, if a firm's maximum desired payback period is 3 years and an investment proposal requires an initial cash outlay of $10,000 and yields the following set of annual cash flows, what is its payback period? Should the project be accepted?

TABLE 10–7. Summary of Calculation of Incremental After-Tax Cash Flows

A. Initial Outlay
  1. Installed cost of asset
  2. Additional nonexpense outlays incurred (for example, working-capital investments)
  3. Additional expenses, on an after-tax basis (for example, training expenses)
  4. In a replacement decision, the *after-tax* flow associated with the sale of the old machine
B. Differential Cash Flows over the Project's Life
  1. Added revenue offset by increased expenses
  2. Labor and material savings
  3. Increases in overhead incurred
  4. Depreciation tax shield on an incremental basis in a replacement decision
  5. Do *not* include interest expenses if the project is financed by issuing debt, as this is accounted for in the required rate of return
C. Terminal Cash Flow
  1. The after-tax salvage value of the project
  2. Cash outlays associated with the project's termination
  3. Recapture of nonexpense outlays that occurred at the project's initiation (for example, working capital investments)

Year	After-Tax Cash Flow
1	$2000
2	4000
3	3000
4	3000
5	1000

In this case, after 3 years the firm will have recaptured $9000 on an initial investment of $10,000, leaving $1000 of the initial investment to be recouped. During the fourth year a total of $3000 will be returned from this investment, and, assuming it will flow into the firm at a constant rate over the year, it will take one-third of the year ($1000/$3000) to recapture the remaining $1000. Thus, the payback period on this project is 3⅓ years, which is more than the desired payback period. Using the payback period criterion, the firm would reject this project.

Although the payback period is used frequently, it does have some rather obvious drawbacks, which can best be demonstrated through the use of an example. Consider two investment projects, A and B, which involve an initial cash outlay of $10,000 each and produce the annual cash flows shown in Table 10–8. Both projects have a payback period of 2 years; therefore, in terms of the payback period criterion both are equally acceptable. However, if we had our choice, it is clear we would select A over B—for at least two reasons. First, regardless of what happens after the payback period, project A returns our initial investment to us earlier within the payback period. Thus, if there is a time value of money, the cash flows occurring within the payback period should not be weighted equally, as they are. In addition, all cash flows that occur after the payback period are ignored. This violates the principle that investors desire more in the way of benefits rather than less—a principle that is hard to deny, especially when we are talking about money.

Although these deficiencies limit the value of the payback period as a tool for investment evaluation, it does have several positive features. First, it deals with cash flows, as opposed to accounting profits, and therefore focuses on the true timing of the project's benefits and costs, although these cash flows are not adjusted for the time value of money. Second, it is easy to visualize, quickly understood, and easy to calculate. Finally, while the payback period method does have serious deficiencies, it is often used as a rough screening device to eliminate projects whose returns do not materialize until later years. This approach emphasizes the earliest returns which

TABLE 10–8. Payback Period Example Projects

	A	B
Initial cash outlay	−$10,000	−$10,000
Annual net cash inflows:		
Year 1	6,000	5,000
2	4,000	5,000
3	3,000	0
4	2,000	0
5	1,000	0

in all likelihood are less uncertain and provides for the liquidity needs of the firm. Although these advantages of the payback period are certainly significant, its disadvantages severely limit its value as a discriminating capital budgeting criterion.

Nondiscounted Cash Flow Criterion 2: Accounting Rate of Return

The **accounting rate of return (AROR)** compares the average after-tax profits with the average dollar size of the investment. The average profits figure is determined by adding up the after-tax profits generated by the investment over its life and dividing by the number of years. The average investment is determined by adding the initial outlay and the project's actual expected salvage value and dividing by two. This computation attempts to calculate the average value of an investment by simply averaging the initial and liquidation values. Thus, the accounting rate of return for an investment with an expected life of n years can be calculated as follows:

$$AROR = \frac{\sum_{t=1}^{n} (\text{accounting profit after tax}_t)/n}{(\text{initial outlay} + \text{expected salvage value})/2} \qquad (10\text{--}1)$$

The accept-reject criterion associated with the accounting rate of return compares the calculated return with a minimum acceptable AROR level. If the AROR is greater than this minimum acceptable level, the project is accepted; otherwise it is rejected.

Consider an investment in new machinery that requires an initial outlay of $20,000 and has an expected salvage value of zero after 5 years. Assume that this machine, if acquired, will result in an increase in after-tax profits of $800 each year for 5 years. In this case the average accounting profit is $800, while the average investment is ($20,000 + 0)/2, or $10,000. For this example, the AROR would be $800/$10,000, or 8 percent.

While this technique seems straightforward enough, its limitations detract significantly from its value as a discriminating capital budgeting criterion. To examine these limitations, let us first determine the AROR of three proposals, each with an expected life of 5 years. Assume that the initial outlay associated with each project is $10,000 and it will have an expected salvage value of zero in 5 years. The minimum acceptable AROR for this firm is 8 percent, and the annual accounting profits from the three proposals are given in Table 10–9. In each case, the average annual accounting profit is $500 and the average investment is $5000—that is, ($10,000 + 0)/2. Therefore, the AROR is 10 percent for each project, which indicates that the AROR method does not do an adequate job of discriminating among these projects.

TABLE 10–9. Annual Accounting Profits after Tax

Year	A	B	C
1	$ 0	$500	$ 0
2	1000	500	0
3	500	500	0
4	500	500	0
5	500	500	2500

A casual examination leads us to the conclusion that project B is the best, as it yields its returns earlier than either project A or C. However, the AROR technique gives equal weight to all returns within the project's life without any regard for the time value of money. The second major disadvantage associated with the AROR method is that it deals with accounting profit figures rather than cash flows. For this reason it does not truly reflect the proper timing of the benefits.

In spite of the criticisms, the accounting rate of return has been a relatively popular tool for capital budgeting analysis, primarily because it involves familiar terms that are easily accessible. Also it is easily understood. The AROR provides a measure of accounting profits per average dollar invested, and the intuitive appeal of this measurement has kept the method alive over the years. For our purposes, the AROR is inadequate, as it does not treat cash flows and does not take account of the time value of money.

DISCOUNTED CASH FLOW CRITERIA FOR CAPITAL BUDGETING DECISIONS

The final three capital budgeting criteria to be examined base decisions on the investment's cash flows after adjusting for the time value of money. For the time being, the problem of incorporating risk into the capital budgeting decision is ignored. This issue will be examined in Chapter 11. In addition, we will assume that the appropriate discount rate, required rate of return, or cost of capital is given. The determination of this rate is the topic of Chapters 12 and 13.

We will examine three discounted cash flow capital budgeting techniques—net present value, profitability index, and internal rate of return.

1: Net Present Value

The **net present value (NPV)** of an investment proposal is equal to the present value of its annual net cash flows after tax less the investment's initial outlay. The net present value can be expressed as follows:

$$NPV = \sum_{t=1}^{n} \frac{ACF_t}{(1 + k)^t} - IO \qquad (10\text{--}2)$$

where ACF_t = the annual after-tax cash flow in time period t (this can take on either positive or negative values)

k = the appropriate discount rate, that is, the required rate of return or the cost of capital[2]

IO = the initial cash outlay

n = the project's expected life

The project's net present value gives a measurement of the *absolute* value of an investment proposal in terms of today's dollars. Since all cash flows are discounted back to the present, comparing the difference between the present value of the annual cash flows and the investment outlay does not violate the time value of money assump-

---

[2] The required rate of return or cost of capital is the rate of return necessary to justify raising funds to finance the project or, alternatively, the rate of return necessary to maintain the firm's current market price per share. These terms will be defined in greater detail in Chapter 13.

tion. The difference between the present value of the annual cash flows and the initial outlay determines the net value of accepting the investment proposal in terms of today's dollars. Whenever there is a positive value associated with the acceptance of a project, we will accept the project; and whenever there is a negative value associated with the acceptance of a project, we will reject the project. If the project's net present value is zero, then we are indifferent as to its acceptance or rejection. This accept-reject criterion is illustrated below:

$$NPV > 0.0 \quad \text{Accept}$$

$$NPV < 0.0 \quad \text{Reject}$$

The following example illustrates the use of the net present value capital-budgeting criterion.

Example A firm is considering new machinery, for which the after-tax cash flows are shown in Table 10–10. If the firm has a 12 percent required rate of return, the present value of the after-tax cash flows is $47,678, as calculated in Table 10–11. Furthermore, the net present value of the new machinery is $7678. Since this value is greater than zero, the net present value criterion indicates that the project should be accepted.

TABLE 10–10. NPV Illustration of Investment in New Machinery

	After-Tax Cash Flow
Initial outlay	−$40,000
Inflow year 1	15,000
Inflow year 2	14,000
Inflow year 3	13,000
Inflow year 4	12,000
Inflow year 5	11,000

TABLE 10–11. Calculation for NPV Illustration of Investment in New Machinery

	After-Tax Cash Flow	Present Value Factor at 12 Percent	Present Value
Inflow year 1	$15,000	.893	$13,395
Inflow year 2	14,000	.797	11,158
Inflow year 3	13,000	.712	9,256
Inflow year 4	12,000	.636	7,632
Inflow year 5	11,000	.567	6,237
Present value of cash flows			$47,678
Investment initial outlay			40,000
Net present value			$ 7,678

Note that the worth of the net present value calculation is a function of the accuracy of cash flow predictions. Before the NPV criterion can be reasonably applied, incremental costs and benefits must first be estimated, including the initial outlay, the differential flows over the project's life, and the terminal cash flow.

In comparing the NPV criterion with those that we have already examined, we find it far superior. First of all, it deals with cash flows rather than accounting profits. In this regard it is sensitive to the true timing of the benefits resulting from the project. Moreover, recognizing the time value of money allows comparison of the benefits and costs in a logical manner. Finally, since projects are accepted only if a positive net present value is associated with them, the acceptance of a project using this criterion will increase the value of the firm, which is consistent with the goal of maximizing the shareholders' wealth.

The disadvantage of the NPV method stems from the need for detailed, long-term forecasts of the incremental cash flows accruing from the project's acceptance. In spite of this drawback, the net present value is the most theoretically correct criterion that we will examine. The following example provides an additional illustration of its application.

Example A firm is considering the purchase of a new computer system which will cost $30,000 initially to aid in credit billing and inventory management. The incremental after-tax cash flows resulting from this project are provided in Table 10–12. The required rate of return demanded by the firm is 10 percent. In order to determine the system's net present value, the three-year $15,000 cash flow annuity is first discounted back to present at 10 percent. From the present-value-of-an-annuity table in Appendix D in the back of this book, we find that the appropriate present-value factor is 2.487. Thus, the present value of this $15,000 annuity is $37,305.

TABLE 10–12. NPV Example Problem of a Computer System

	After-Tax Cash Flow
Initial outlay	−$30,000
Year 1	15,000
Year 2	15,000
Year 3	15,000

Since the cash inflows have been discounted back to the present, they can now be compared with the initial outlay, since both of the flows are now stated in terms of today's dollars. Subtracting the initial outlay ($30,000) from the present value of the cash inflows ($37,305), we find that the system's net present value is $7305. Since the NPV on this project is positive, the project should be accepted.

2: Profitability Index (Benefit/ Cost Ratio)

The **profitability index,** or **benefit/cost ratio,** is the ratio of the present value of the future net cash flows to the initial outlay. While the net present value investment criterion gives a measure of the absolute dollar desirability of a project, the profitability index provides a relative measure of an investment proposal's desirability—that is, the ratio of the present value of its future net benefits to its initial cost. The profitability index can be expressed as follows:

$$PI = \frac{\sum_{t=1}^{n} \frac{ACF_t}{(1 + k)^t}}{IO} \qquad (10\text{--}3)$$

where ACF_t = the annual after-tax cash flow in time period t (this can take on either positive or negative values)

k = the appropriate discount rate; that is, the required rate of return or the cost of capital

IO = the initial cash outlay

n = the project's expected life

The decision criterion with respect to the profitability index is to accept the project if the PI is greater than 1.00, and to reject the project if the PI is less than 1.00. However, if the profitability index exactly equals 1.00, we are indifferent between acceptance and rejection of the project. This accept-reject criterion is illustrated below:

$$PI > 1.0 \quad \text{Accept}$$

$$PI < 1.0 \quad \text{Reject}$$

Looking closely at this criterion, we see that it will always yield the same accept-reject decision as does the net present value criterion. Whenever the present value of the project's net cash flow is greater than its initial cash outlay, the project's net present value will be positive, signaling an accept decision. When this is true, then the project's profitability index will also be greater than 1, as the present value of the net cash flows (the PI's numerator) is greater than its initial outlay (the PI's denominator). While these two decision criteria will always yield the same decision, they will not necessarily rank acceptable projects in the same order. This problem of conflicting ranking will be dealt with at a later point.

Since the net present value and profitability index criteria are essentially the same, they have the same advantages over the other criteria examined. Both employ cash flows, recognize the timing of the cash flows, and are consistent with the goal of maximization of shareholders' wealth. The major disadvantage of this criterion, as of the net present value criterion, is that it requires long, detailed cash flow forecasts.

Example A firm with a 10 percent required rate of return is considering investing in a new machine with an expected life of six years. The after-tax cash flows resulting from this investment are given in Table 10–13. Discounting the project's future net cash flows back to the present yields a present value of $53,667; dividing this value by the initial outlay of $50,000 gives a profitability index of 1.0733, as shown in Table 10–14. This tells us that the present value of the future benefits accruing from this project is 1.0733 times the level of the initial outlay. Since the profitability index is greater than 1.0, the project should be accepted.

TABLE 10–13. Profitability Index (PI) Illustration of Investment in New Machinery

	After-Tax Cash Flow
Initial outlay	−$50,000
Inflow year 1	15,000
Inflow year 2	8,000
Inflow year 3	10,000
Inflow year 4	12,000
Inflow year 5	14,000
Inflow year 6	16,000

TABLE 10–14. Calculation for PI Illustration of Investment in New Machinery

	After-Tax Cash Flow	Present Value Factor at 10 Percent	Present Value
Initial outlay	−$50,000	1.0	−$50,000
Inflow year 1	15,000	0.909	13,635
Inflow year 2	8,000	0.826	6,608
Inflow year 3	10,000	0.751	7,510
Inflow year 4	12,000	0.683	8,196
Inflow year 5	14,000	0.621	8,694
Inflow year 6	16,000	0.564	9,024

$$PI = \frac{\sum_{t=1}^{n} \frac{ACF_t}{(1 + k)^t}}{IO}$$

$$= \frac{\$13,635 + \$6,608 + \$7,510 + \$8,196 + \$8,694 + \$9,024}{\$50,000}$$

$$= \frac{\$53,667}{\$50,000}$$

$$= 1.0733$$

3: Internal Rate of Return

The **internal rate of return (IRR)** attempts to answer this question: What rate of return does this project earn? For computational purposes, the internal rate of return is defined as the discount rate that equates the present value of the project's future net cash flows with the project's initial cash outlay. Mathematically, the internal rate of return is defined as the value *IRR* in the following equation:

$$IO = \sum_{t=1}^{n} \frac{ACF_t}{(1 + IRR)^t} \tag{10-4}$$

where ACF_t = the annual after-tax cash flow in time period t (this can take on either a positive or negative value)

IO = the initial cash outlay

n = the project's expected life

IRR = the project's internal rate of return

Intuitively, the internal rate of return is a hard concept to grasp. As another way of viewing it, assume that a project requires an initial outlay of IO and results in annual net cash flows after tax of $ACF_1, ACF_2, \ldots, ACF_n$. If we alternatively took our initial outlay of IO and placed it in a bank where it earned a rate of return equal to the internal rate of return, we could withdraw an amount equal to ACF_1 at the end of the first year, ACF_2 the second year, and so forth; finally, when ACF_n was withdrawn at the end of the nth year, we would have exhausted our funds. In other words, a project's internal rate of return is simply the rate of return that the project earns.

The decision criterion associated with the internal rate of return is to accept the project if the internal rate of return is greater than the required rate of return, sometimes called the **hurdle rate** by investors. We reject the project if its internal rate of return is less than this required rate of return. This accept-reject criterion is illustrated below:

IRR > required rate of return   Accept

IRR < required rate of return   Reject

If the internal rate of return on a project is equal to the shareholders' required rate of return, accepting the project should not result in any change in the firm's stock price. This is because the firm is earning exactly the rate that its shareholders are requiring. On the other hand, if the project yields an internal rate of return greater than the investor's required rate of return, its acceptance should increase the firm's stock price. Similarly, the acceptance of a project with an internal rate of return below the investors' required rate of return will decrease the firm's stock price.

In general, the internal rate of return criterion provides the same accept-reject decision for an investment proposal as the net present value and profitability index criteria. If discounting the future cash flows back to the present at the required rate of return, k, yields a zero net present value, then the profitability index must equal 1.0. In this instance, the internal rate of return will be equal to k, the required rate of return. This happens because the future cash inflows discounted back to present at k must be equal to the initial outlay for the net present value to be zero. Thus, k is the internal rate of return because it is the discount rate that equates the initial outlay with the present value of the future cash inflows. Consequently, when one of the discounted cash flow criteria is at its indifference point, they all are.

Furthermore, if the net present value is positive, the profitability index must exceed 1.0, and the internal rate of return will be greater than the cost of capital or required rate of return. For this reason, when one of these criteria indicates the project is acceptable, they all suggest that the investment should be made. Finally, if one criterion indicates that a project should be rejected, all three standards will signal rejection. In essence, if the net present value is negative, the profitability index must be less than 1.0. Also, in this situation, a discount rate less than the required rate of return is required to make the present value of the future flows equal to the initial outlay, which indicates that the internal rate of return is less than the required rate of return.

In general, all the discounted cash flow criteria are consistent and will give similar accept-reject decisions. In addition, since the internal rate of return is another discounted cash flow criterion, it exhibits the same general advantages and disadvantages as both the net present value and profitability index, and occasionally has an additional disadvantage of being tedious to calculate.

Computing the IRR for Even Cash Flows

With today's calculators, the determination of internal rates of return is merely a matter of memorizing a few key strokes. In this section, however, we are going to put our calculators aside and examine the mathematical process of calculating internal rates of return. The reason for this is to allow you to develop a better understanding of what internal rates of return really are.

The calculation of a project's internal rate of return can be either very simple or relatively complicated. As an example of straightforward solution, assume that a firm with a required rate of return of 10 percent is considering a project that involves an initial outlay of $45,555. If the investment is taken, the after-tax cash flows are expected to be $15,000 per annum over the project's 4-year life. In this case, the internal rate of return is equal to IRR in the following equation:

$$\$45,555 = \frac{\$15,000}{(1 + IRR)^1} + \frac{\$15,000}{(1 + IRR)^2} + \frac{\$15,000}{(1 + IRR)^3} + \frac{\$15,000}{(1 + IRR)^4}$$

From our discussion of the present value of an annuity in Chapter 9, we know that this equation can be reduced to

$$\$45,555 = \$15,000 \left[\sum_{t=1}^{4} \frac{1}{(1 + IRR)^t} \right]$$

Appendix D gives table values for $\left[\sum_{t=1}^{4} 1/(1 + i)^t \right]$ for various combinations of i and n, which further reduces this equation to

$$\$45,555 = \$15,000 \begin{bmatrix} \text{table value,} \\ \text{Appendix D,} \\ \text{4 years,} \\ \text{IRR percent} \end{bmatrix}$$

Dividing both sides by $15,000, this becomes:

$$3.037 = \begin{bmatrix} \text{table value,} \\ \text{Appendix D,} \\ \text{4 years,} \\ \text{IRR percent} \end{bmatrix}$$

Hence, we are looking for a table value of 3.037 in the four-year row of Appendix D. This value occurs when i equals 12 percent, which means that 12 percent is the internal rate of return for the investment. Therefore, since 12 percent is greater than the 10 percent required return, the project should be accepted.

Computing the IRR for Uneven Cash Flows

Unfortunately, the internal rate of return can be solved directly in the tables only when the future after-tax net cash flows are in the form of an annuity or a single payment. When these flows are in the form of an uneven series of flows, a trial and error approach is necessary. To do this, we first determine the present value of the future after-tax net cash flows using an arbitrary discount rate. If the present value of the future cash flows at this discount rate is larger than the initial outlay, the rate is increased; if it is smaller than the initial outlay, the discount rate is lowered; and the process begins again. This search routine is continued until the present value of the future after-tax cash flows is equal to the initial outlay. The interest rate that creates this situation is the internal rate of return.

To illustrate the procedure, consider an investment proposal that requires an initial outlay of $3817 and returns $1000 at the end of year 1, $2000 at the end of year 2, and $3000 at the end of year 3. In this case, the internal rate of return must be determined using trial and error. This process is shown in Table 10–15, in which an arbitrarily selected discount rate of 15 percent was chosen to begin the process. The trial and error technique slowly centers in on the project's internal rate of return of 22 percent. The project's internal rate of return is then compared with the firm's required rate of return, and if the IRR is the larger, the project is accepted.

TABLE 10–15. Computing the IRR for Uneven Cash Flows

Initial outlay	−$3817
Flow year 1	1000
Flow year 2	2000
Flow year 3	3000

Solution: Pick an arbitrary discount rate and use it to determine the present value of the inflows. Compare the present value of the inflows with the initial outlay; if they are equal, you have determined the IRR. Otherwise raise the discount rate if the present value of the inflows is larger than the initial outlay or lower the discount rate if the present value of the inflows is less than the initial outlay. Repeat this process until the IRR is found.

1. Try i = 15 percent:

	Net Cash Flows	Present Value Factor at 15 Percent	Present Value
Inflow year 1	$1000	.870	$ 870
Inflow year 2	2000	.756	1512
Inflow year 3	3000	.658	1974
Present value of inflows			$4356
Initial outlay			−$3817

TABLE 10–15. *(continued)*

1. Try *i* = 20 percent:

	Net Cash Flows	Present Value Factor at 20 Percent	Present Value
Inflow year 1	$1000	.833	$ 833
Inflow year 2	2000	.694	1388
Inflow year 3	3000	.579	1737
Present value of inflows			$3958
Initial outlay			−$3817

1. Try *i* = 15 percent:

	Net Cash Flows	Present Value Factor at 22 Percent	Present Value
Inflow year 1	$1000	.820	$ 820
Inflow year 2	2000	.672	1344
Inflow year 3	3000	.551	1653
Present value of inflows			$3817
Initial outlay			−$3817

Example A firm with a required rate of return of 10 percent is considering three investment proposals. Given the information in Table 10–16, management plans to calculate the internal rate of return for each project and determine which projects should be accepted.

Because project A is an annuity, we can easily calculate its internal rate of return by determining the table value necessary to equate the present value of the future cash flows with the initial outlay. This computation is done as follows:

$$IO = ACF_t \left[\sum_{t=1}^{n} \frac{1}{(1 + IRR)^t} \right]$$

$$\$10,000 = \$3362 \left[\sum_{t=1}^{4} \frac{1}{(1 + IRR)^t} \right]$$

$$\$10,000 = \$3362 \begin{bmatrix} \text{table value,} \\ \text{Appendix D,} \\ \text{4 years,} \\ \text{IRR percent} \end{bmatrix}$$

$$2.974 = \begin{bmatrix} \text{table value,} \\ \text{Appendix D,} \\ \text{4 years,} \\ \text{IRR percent} \end{bmatrix}$$

TABLE 10–16. Three IRR Investment Proposal Examples

	A	B	C
Initial outlay	$10,000	$10,000	$10,000
Inflow year 1	3,362	0	1,000
Inflow year 2	3,362	0	3,000
Inflow year 3	3,362	0	6,000
Inflow year 4	3,362	13,605	7,000

We are looking for a table value of 2.974, in the four-year row of Appendix D, which occurs in the i = 13 percent column. Thus, 13 percent is the internal rate of return. Since this rate is greater than the firm's required rate of return of 10 percent, the project should be accepted.

Project B involves a single future cash flow of $13,605, resulting from an initial outlay of $10,000; thus, its internal rate of return can be determined directly from the present-value table in Appendix B as follows:

$$IO = ACF_t \left[\frac{1}{(1 + IRR)^t} \right]$$

$$\$10,000 = \$13,605 \left[\frac{1}{(1 + IRR)^4} \right]$$

$$\$10,000 = \$13,605 \begin{bmatrix} \text{table value,} \\ \text{Appendix B,} \\ \text{4 years,} \\ \text{IRR percent} \end{bmatrix}$$

$$.735 = \begin{bmatrix} \text{table value,} \\ \text{Appendix B,} \\ \text{4 years,} \\ \text{IRR percent} \end{bmatrix}$$

This tells us that we should look for a table value of .735 in the four-year row of Appendix B, which occurs in the i = 8 percent column. We may therefore conclude that 8 percent is the internal rate of return. Since this rate is less than the firm's required rate of return of 10 percent, project B should be rejected.

The uneven nature of the future cash flows associated with project C necessitates the use of the trial and error method. The internal rate of return for project C is equal to the value of IRR in the following equation:

$$\$10,000 = \frac{\$1000}{(1 + IRR)^1} + \frac{\$3000}{(1 + IRR)^2} + \frac{\$6000}{(1 + IRR)^3} + \frac{\$7000}{(1 + IRR)^4} \qquad (10\text{--}5)$$

Arbitrarily selecting a discount rate of 15 percent and substituting it into equation (10–5) for IRR reduces the right-hand side of the equation to $11,090, as shown in Table 10–17. Therefore, since the present value of the future cash flows is larger than the initial outlay, we must raise the discount rate in order to find the project's internal rate of return. Substituting 20 percent for the discount rate, the right-hand side of equation (10–5) now becomes $9763. As this is less than the initial outlay of $10,000, we must now decrease the discount rate. In other words, we know that the internal rate of return for this project is between 15 and 20 percent. Since the present value of the future flows discounted back to present at 20 percent was only $237 too low, a discount

TABLE 10–17. Computing the IRR for Project C

1. Try *i* = 15 percent:

	Net Cash Flows	Present Value Factor at 15 Percent	Present Value
Inflow year 1	$1,000	.870	$ 870
Inflow year 2	3,000	.756	2,268
Inflow year 3	6,000	.658	3,948
Inflow year 4	7,000	.572	4,004
Present value of inflows			$11,090
Initial outlay			$10,000

2. Try *i* = 20 percent:

	Net Cash Flows	Present Value Factor at 20 Percent	Present Value
Inflow year 1	$1,000	.833	$ 833
Inflow year 2	3,000	.694	2,082
Inflow year 3	6,000	.579	3,474
Inflow year 4	7,000	.482	3,374
Present value of inflows			$ 9,763
Initial outlay			$10,000

3. Try *i* = 19 percent:

	Net Cash Flows	Present Value Factor at 19 Percent	Present Value
Inflow year 1	$1,000	.840	$ 840
Inflow year 2	3,000	.706	2,118
Inflow year 3	6,000	.593	3,558
Inflow year 4	7,000	.499	3,493
Present value of inflows			$10,009
Initial outlay			$10,000

rate of 19 percent is selected. As shown in Table 10–17, a discount rate of 19 percent reduces the present value of the future inflows down to $10,009, which is approximately the same as the initial outlay. Consequently, project C's internal rate of return is approximately 19 percent.[3] Since the internal rate of return is greater than the firm's required rate of return of 10 percent, this investment should be accepted.

---

[3] If desired, the actual rate can be more precisely approximated through interpolation as follows:

		Discount Rate	Present Value
		19%	$10,009
		20	9,763
	Difference	1%	$ 246

Proportion $9 is of $246 $= \dfrac{\$9}{\$246} = .0366\%$

$19\% + .0366\% = 19.0366\%$

Complications with the IRR: Multiple Rates of Return

While any project can have only one NPV and one PI, a single project under certain circumstances can have more than one IRR. The reason for this can be traced to the calculations involved in determining the IRR. Equation (10–4) states that the IRR is the discount rate that equates the present value of the project's future net cash flows with the project's initial outlay:

$$IO = \sum_{t=1}^{n} \frac{ACF_t}{(1 + IRR)^t} \qquad (10\text{–}4)$$

However, since equation (10–4) is a polynomial of a degree n, it has n solutions. Now if the initial outlay (IO) is the only negative cash flow and all the annual after-tax cash flows (ACF_t) are positive, then all but one of these n solutions is either a negative or imaginary number and there is no problem. But problems occur when there are sign reversals in the cash flow stream; in fact there can be as many solutions as there are sign reversals. Thus, a normal pattern with a negative initial outlay and positive annual after-tax cash flows $(-, +, +, +, \ldots, +)$ after that has only one sign reversal, hence only one positive IRR. However, a pattern with more than one sign reversal can have more than one IRR. Consider, for example, the following pattern of cash flows.[4]

	After-Tax Cash Flow
Initial outlay	−$ 1,600
Year 1	+$10,000
Year 2	−$10,000

In this pattern of cash flows there are two sign reversals, from − $1,600 to + $10,000 and then from + $10,000 to − $10,000, so there can be as many as two positive IRRs that will make the present value of the future cash flows equal to the initial outlay. In fact two internal rates of return solve this problem, 25 and 400 percent. Graphically what we are solving for is the discount rate that makes the project's NPV equal to zero; as Figure 10–2 illustrates, this occurs twice.

Which solution is correct? The answer is that neither solution is valid. While each fits the definition of IRR, neither provides any insight into the true project returns. What has happened is that the firm has borrowed or received $10,000 from the project at the end of year 1 and must return this sum at the end of year 2. The real question is this: What is the use of this $10,000 worth for one year? The answer depends upon what the investment opportunities are like to the firm. If they are 30 percent, then the value of receiving $10,000 at the end of year 1 and returning it at the end of year 2 is $3000 received at the end of year 2, since this is what the firm would be left with. The internal rate of return on this (an initial outlay of $1600 and a positive inflow of $3000 at the end of year 2) is 37 percent. Thus, neither of the internal rates of return, 25 or 400 percent, was valid. In summary, when there is

[4] This example is taken from James H. Lorie and Leonard J. Savage, "Three Problems in Rationing Capital," *Journal of Business*, 28 (October 1955), 229–39.

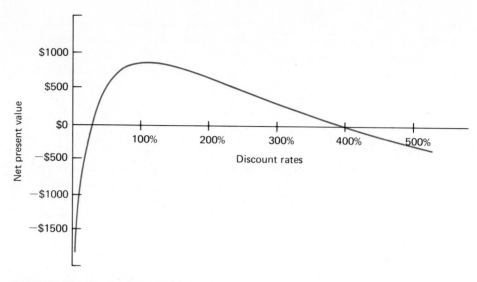

FIGURE 10–2.   Multiple IRRs

more than one sign reversal in the cash flow stream, the possibility of multiple IRRs exists, and the normal interpretation of the IRR loses its meaning.

Discounted Cash Flow Criteria: Comprehensive Example

To demonstrate further the computations for the discounted cash flow techniques, assume that a manufacturing firm in the electronic components field is in the 34 percent marginal tax bracket with a 15 percent required rate of return or cost of capital. Management is considering replacing a hand-operated assembly machine with a fully automated assembly operation. Given the information in Table 10–18, we

TABLE 10–18.   Comprehensive Capital Budgeting Example

Existing situation:	One full-time operator—salary $12,000
	Variable overtime—$1000 per year
	Fringe benefits—$1000 per year
	Cost of defects—$6000 per year
	Current book value—$10,000
	Expected life—15 years
	Expected salvage value—$0
	Age—10 years
	Annual Depreciation—$2000 per year
	Current salvage value of old machine—$12,000
	Annual maintenance—$0
	Marginal tax rate—34 percent
	Required rate of return—15 percent
Proposed situation:	Fully automated operation—no operator necessary
	Cost of machine—$50,000
	Shipping fee—$1000
	Installation costs—$5000
	Expected economic life—5 years
	Depreciation method—simplified straight line over 5 years
	Salvage value after 5 years—$0
	Annual maintenance—$1000
	Cost of defects—$1000

TABLE 10–19. Calculation of Initial Outlay for the Comprehensive Example

Outflows:	
Cost of new machine	$50,000
Shipping fee	1,000
Installation cost	5,000
Increased taxes on sale of old machine	680
($12,000 − $10,000) (.34)	
Inflows:	
Salvage value—old machine	−12,000
Net initial outlay	$44,680

want to determine the cash flows associated with this proposal, the project's net present value, profitability index, and internal rate of return, and then to apply the appropriate decision criteria.

First, the initial outlay is determined to be $44,680, as reflected in Table 10–19. Next, the differential cash flows over the project's life are calculated as shown in Table 10–20, yielding an estimated $15,008 cash flow per annum. In making these computations, the incremental change in depreciation was determined by first calculating the original depreciable value which is equal to the cost of the new machine ($50,000) plus any expense charges necessary to get the new machine in operating order (shipping fee of $1000 plus the installation fee of $5000). This depreciable amount was then divided by 5 years. The annual depreciation lost with the sale of the old machine was then subtracted out ($10,000/5 years = $2000 per year for the old machine's remaining 5 years of life). Once the change in taxes is determined from the incremental change in book profit, it is subtracted from the net cash flow savings before taxes, yielding the $15,008 net cash flow after taxes.

Finally, the terminal cash flow associated with the project has to be determined. In this case, since the new machine is expected to have a zero salvage value, there will be no terminal cash flow. The cash flow diagram associated with this project is shown in Figure 10–3.

TABLE 10–20. Calculation of Differential Cash Flows for the Comprehensive Example

	Book Profit	Cash Flow
Savings: Reduced salary	$12,000	$12,000
Reduced variable overtime	1,000	1,000
Reduced fringe benefits	1,000	1,000
Reduced defects ($6,000 − $1,000)	5,000	5,000
Costs: Increased maintenance expense	−1,000	−1,000
Increased depreciation expense	−9,200	
($11,200 − $2,000)		
Net savings before taxes	$ 8,800	$18,000
Taxes (34%)	−2,992 ⟶	−2,992
Net cash flow after taxes		$15,008

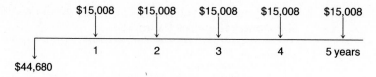

FIGURE 10–3. Cash Flow Diagram

The net present value for this project is calculated below:

$$NPV = \sum_{t=1}^{n} \frac{ACF_t}{(1 + k)^t} - IO$$

$$= \sum_{t=1}^{5} \frac{\$15{,}008}{(1 + .15)^t} - \$44{,}680$$

$$= \$15{,}008 \begin{bmatrix} \text{table value,} \\ \text{Appendix D,} \\ \text{5 years,} \\ \text{15 percent} \end{bmatrix} - \$44{,}680 \qquad (10\text{–}2)$$

$$= \$15{,}008(3.352) - \$44{,}680$$

$$= \$50{,}307 - \$44{,}680$$

$$= \$5{,}627$$

Since its net present value is greater than zero, the project should be accepted. The profitability index, which gives a measure of relative desirability of a project, is calculated as follows:

$$PI = \frac{\displaystyle\sum_{t=1}^{n} \frac{ACF_t}{(1 + k)^t}}{IO}$$

$$= \frac{\$50{,}307}{\$44{,}680} \qquad (10\text{–}3)$$

$$= 1.13$$

Since the project's PI is greater than 1, the project should be accepted.

The internal rate of return can be determined directly from the present-value-of-an-annuity table, as follows:

$$IO = \sum_{t=1}^{n} \frac{ACF_t}{(1 + IRR)^t}$$

$$\$44{,}680 = \$15{,}008 \begin{bmatrix} \text{table value,} \\ \text{Appendix D,} \\ \text{5 years,} \\ \text{IRR percent} \end{bmatrix} \qquad (10\text{–}4)$$

$$2.977 = \begin{bmatrix} \text{table value,} \\ \text{Appendix D,} \\ \text{5 years,} \\ \text{IRR percent} \end{bmatrix}$$

Looking in the 5-year row of the present-value-of-an-annuity table in Appendix D, we find that the value of 2.977 occurs between the 20 percent column (2.991) and the 21 percent column (2.926). As a result, the project's internal rate of return is between 20 and 21 percent, and the project should be accepted.

Applying the decision criteria to this example, we find that each of them indicates the project should be accepted, as the net present value is positive, the profitability index is greater than 1.0, and the internal rate of return is greater than the firm's required rate of return of 15 percent.

A GLANCE AT ACTUAL CAPITAL BUDGETING PRACTICES

The methods used in practice for capital budgeting are precisely those that we have described in this chapter. However, over the past 30 years the popularity of these methods has shifted rather dramatically. In the 1950s the payback period and AROR methods dominated capital budgeting, but through the 1960s and 1970s the discounted cash flow decision techniques slowly displaced the nondiscounted techniques. This movement from the payback period and AROR to net present value and the internal rate of return is shown in Table 10–21, which indicates the growth in popularity of these techniques as reflected in surveys of practices over the years. Interestingly, while a large majority of firms use the NPV and IRR as their primary techniques, a large majority of firms also use the payback period as a secondary decision method for capital budgeting. In a sense they are using the payback period to control for risk. The logic behind this is that since the payback period dramatically emphasizes early cash flows, which are presumably more certain—that is, have less risk—than cash flows that occur later in a project's life, its use will lead to projects with more certain cash flows.

TABLE 10–21. Past Surveys of Capital Budgeting Practices—Percent of Respondents Using Each Technique

Capital Budgeting Technique	Klammer, 1959	Klammer, 1964	Klammer, 1970	Petty et al., 1972	Kim and Farragher, 1975	Gitman and Forrester, 1977	Kim and Farragher, 1979	Kim, Crick, and Kim, 1986
Primary method:								
NPV	5%	15%	27%	15%	26%	13%	19%	21%
IRR	8	17	30	41	37	53	49	49
Payback	34	24	12	11	15	9	12	19
AROR	34	30	26	31	10	25	8	8
Secondary method:								
NPV	2%	3%	7%	14%	7%	28%	8%	24%
IRR	1	2	6	19	7	14	8	15
Payback	18	21	32	37	33	44	39	35
AROR	4	9	11	24	3	14	3	19

Sources:
Thomas Klammer, "Empirical Evidence of the Adoption of Sophisticated Capital Budgeting Techniques," *Journal of Business*, July 1972, pp. 387–97; J. William Petty, David F. Scott, Jr., and Monroe M. Bird, "The Capital Expenditure Decision-Making Process of Large Corporations," *Engineering Economist*, Spring 1975, pp. 159–72; S. H. Kim and E. J. Farragher, "Capital Budgeting Practices in Large Industrial Firms," *Baylor Business Studies*, November 1976, pp. 19–25; Lawrence J. Gitman and John R. Forrester, Jr., "A Survey of Capital Budgeting Techniques Used by Major U.S. Firms," *Financial Management*, Fall 1977, pp. 66–71; S. H. Kim and E. J. Farragher, "Current Capital Budgeting Practices," *Management Accounting*, June 1981, pp. 26–30; Suks H. Kim, T. Crick, and Sesungs H. Kim, "Do Executives Practice What Academics Preach?" *Management Accounting*, November 1986, pp. 49–52.

TABLE 10–22. Project Size and Decision-making Authority

Project Size	Typical Boundaries	Primary Decision Site
Very small	Up to $100,000	Plant
Small	$100,000 to $1,000,000	Division
Medium	$1 million to $10 million	Corporate investment committee
Large	Over $10 million	CEO & board

A reliance on the payback period came out even more dramatically in a recent study of the capial budgeting practices of 12 large manufacturing firms.[5] Information for this study was gathered from interviews over one to three days in addition to an examination of the records of about 400 projects. This study revealed a number of things of interest. First, firms were typically found to categorize capital investments as mandatory (regulations and contracts, capitalized maintenance, replacement of anti-quated equipment, product quality) or discretionary (expanded markets, new busi-nesses, cost cutting), with the decision-making process being different for mandatory and discretionary projects. Second, it was found that the decision-making process was different for projects of differing size. In fact, approval authority tended to rest in different locations, depending upon the size of the project. Table 10–22 provides the typical levels of approval authority.

The study also showed that while the discounted cash flow methods are used at most firms, the simple payback criterion was the measure relied upon primarily in one-third of the firms examined. The use of the payback period seemed to be even more common for smaller projects, with firms severely simplifying the discounted cash flow analysis and/or relying primarily on the payback period. Thus, while dis-counted cash flow decision techniques have become more widely accepted, their use depends to an extent upon the size of the project and where within the firm the decision is being made.

ADVANCED TOPICS IN CAPITAL BUDGETING

Up to this point we have focused solely on the accept-reject output of the capital budgeting decision for a single project. Sometimes, however, we must choose among a number of acceptable projects. At other times the number of projects that can be accepted or the total budget is actually limited; that is, capital rationing is imposed. In these cases different rankings may result, depending upon the discounted cash flow criterion being used. Before examining the reasons for these differences, we will explore the rationale behind capital rationing and project ranking and the ways in which they affect capital budgeting decisions.

---

[5] Marc Ross, "Capital Budgeting Practices of Twelve Large Manufacturers," *Financial Management*, 15 (Winter 1986), 15–22.

Capital Rationing

The use of our capital budgeting decision rules implies that the size of the capital budget is determined by the availability of acceptable investment proposals. However, a firm may place a limit on the dollar size of the capital budget. This situation is called **capital rationing.**

Using the internal rate of return as our decision rule, we have accepted all projects with an internal rate of return greater than the firm's required rate of return. This rule is illustrated in Figure 10–4, where projects A through E would be chosen. However, when capital rationing is imposed, the dollar size of the total investment is limited by the budget constraint. In Figure 10–4 the budget constraint of $X precludes the acceptance of an attractive investment, project E. This situation obviously contradicts prior decision rules. Moreover, the solution of choosing the projects with the highest internal rate of return is complicated by the fact that some projects may be indivisible; for example, it is meaningless to recommend that half a computer be acquired.

Rationale for Capital Rationing

We will first ask why capital rationing exists and whether or not it is rational. In general, three principal reasons are given for imposing a capital rationing constraint. First, the management may feel that market conditions are temporarily adverse. In the seventies this reason was frequently given. At that time interest rates were at an all-time high, and stock prices were depressed. Second, there may be a shortage of qualified managers to direct new projects. This circumstance can occur when projects are of such a technical nature that qualified managers are simply not available. Third, there may be intangible considerations. For example, the management may simply fear debt, wishing to avoid interest payments at any cost. Or perhaps the common stock issuance may be limited in order to preserve the current owners' strict voting control over the company or to maintain a stable dividend policy.

Despite strong evidence that capital rationing exists in practice, the question remains as to its effect on the firm. In brief, the effect is negative in direction, and its degree depends upon the severity of the rationing. If the rationing is minor and noncontinuing, then the firm's share price will not suffer to any great extent. In this case capital rationing can probably be excused, although it should be noted that capital rationing entailing rejection of projects with positive net present values is contrary to the

FIGURE 10–4. Projects Ranked by IRR

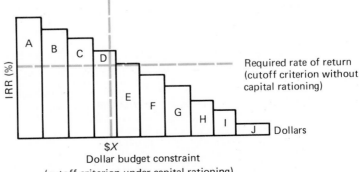

firm's goal of maximization of shareholders' wealth. If, on the other hand, the capital rationing is a result of the firm's decision to limit dramatically the number of new projects or to limit total investment to internally generated funds, then this policy will eventually have a significantly negative effect on the firm's share price. For example, a lower share price will eventually result from lost competitive advantage if, owing to a decision to limit arbitrarily its capital budget, a firm fails to upgrade its products and manufacturing process.

Capital Rationing and Project Selection

If the firm decides to impose a capital constraint on investment projects, the appropriate decision criterion is to select the set of projects that has the highest net present value subject to the capital constraint. This guideline may preclude merely taking the highest-ranked projects in terms of the profitability index or the internal rate of return. If some or all of the projects are indivisible, as shown in Figure 10–4, the last project accepted may be only partially accepted. Although partial acceptances may be possible in some cases, the indivisibility of most capital investments prevents it. If a project is a sales outlet or a truck, it may be meaningless to purchase half a sales outlet or half a truck.

To illustrate this procedure, consider a firm with a budget constraint of $1 million and five indivisible projects available to it, as given in Table 10–23. If the highest-ranked projects were taken, projects A and B would be taken first. At that point there would not be enough funds available to take project C; hence, projects D and E would be taken. However, a higher total net present value is provided by the combination of projects A and C. Thus projects A and C should be selected from the set of projects available. This illustrates our guideline: to select the set of projects that maximizes the firm's net present value.

Project Ranking

In the past, we have proposed that all projects with a positive net present value, a profitability index greater than 1.0, or an internal rate of return greater than the required rate of return be accepted, assuming there is no capital rationing. However, this acceptance is not always possible. In some cases, where two projects are judged acceptable by the discounted cash flow criteria, it may be necessary to select only one of them, as they are mutually exclusive. **Mutually exclusive** projects occur when a set of investment proposals perform essentially the same task; thus, acceptance of one will necessarily mean rejection of the others. For example, a company considering the installation of a computer system may evaluate three or four systems, all of which may have positive net present values; but the acceptance of one system will automatically mean rejection of the others. In general, to deal with mutually exclusive projects, we will merely rank them by means of the discounted cash flow criteria and select

TABLE 10–23. Capital-Rationing Example of Five Indivisible Projects

Project	Initial Outlay	Profitability Index	Net Present Value
A	$200,000	2.4	$280,000
B	200,000	2.3	260,000
C	800,000	1.7	560,000
D	300,000	1.3	90,000
E	300,000	1.2	60,000

the project with the highest ranking. On occasion, unfortunately, problems of conflicting ranking may arise.

Problems in Project Ranking

There are three general types of ranking problems—the size disparity problem, the time disparity problem, and the unequal lives problem. Each involves the possibility of conflict in the ranks yielded by the various discounted cash flow capital-budgeting criteria. As noted earlier, when one discounted cash flow criterion gives an accept signal, they will all give an accept signal, but they will not necessarily rank all projects in the same order. In most cases this disparity is not critical; however, for mutually exclusive projects the ranking order is important.

Size Disparity

The **size disparity problem** occurs when mutually exclusive projects of unequal size are examined. This problem is most easily illustrated with the use of an example.

Example Suppose that a firm with a cost of capital of 10 percent is considering two mutually exclusive projects, A and B. Project A involves a $200 initial outlay and cash inflow of $300 at the end of one year, while project B involves an initial outlay of $1500 and a cash inflow of $1900 at the end of one year. The net present value, profitability index, and internal rate of return for these projects are given in Figure 10–5.

FIGURE 10–5. Size Disparity Ranking Problem

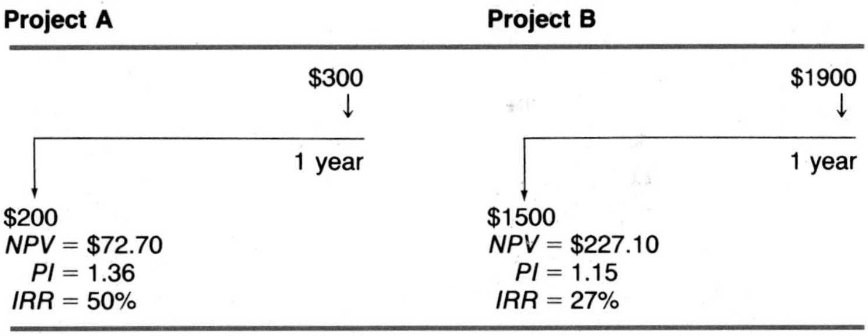

Project A	Project B
$300 ↓	$1900 ↓
1 year	1 year
$200	$1500
NPV = $72.70	NPV = $227.10
PI = 1.36	PI = 1.15
IRR = 50%	IRR = 27%

In this case, if the net present value criterion is used, project B should be accepted, while if the profitability index or the internal rate of return criterion is used, project A should be chosen. The question now becomes, Which project is better? The answer depends on whether or not capital rationing exists. Without capital rationing, project B is better because it provides the largest increase in shareholders' wealth; that is, it has a larger net present value. If there is a capital constraint, the problem then focuses on what can be done with the additional $1300 that is freed if project A is chosen (costing $200, as opposed to $1500). If the firm can earn more on project A plus the project financed with the additional $1300 than it can on project B, then project A and the marginal project should be accepted. In effect, we are attempting to select the set of projects that maximize the firm's NPV. Thus, if the marginal project has a net present value greater than $154.40, selecting it plus project A with a net present value of $72.70 will provide a net present value greater than $227.10, the net present value for project B.

In summary, whenever the size disparity problem results in conflicting rankings, between mutually exclusive projects, the project with the largest net present value will be selected, provided there is no capital rationing. When capital rationing exists, the firm should select the set of projects with the largest net present value.

Time Disparity

The **time disparity problem** and the conflicting rankings that accompany it result from the differing reinvestment assumptions made by the net present value and internal rate of return decision criteria. The NPV criterion assumes that cash flows over the life of the project can be reinvested at the required rate of return or cost of capital, while the IRR criterion implicitly assumes that the cash flows over the life of the project can be reinvested at the internal rate of return. Again, this problem may be illustrated through the use of an example.

Example   Suppose a firm with a required rate of return or cost of capital of 10 percent and with no capital constraints is considering the two mutually exclusive projects illustrated in Figure 10–6. The net present value and profitability index indicate that project A is the better of the two, while the internal rate of return indicates that project B is the better. Project B receives its cash flows earlier than project A, and the different assumptions made as to how these flows can be reinvested results in the difference in rankings. Which criterion should be followed depends upon which reinvestment assumption is used. The net present value criterion is preferred in this case because it makes the most acceptable assumption for the wealth-maximizing firm. It is certainly the most conservative assumption that can be made, since the required rate of return can be looked on as the lowest possible reinvestment rate. Moreover, as we have already noted, the net present value method maximizes the value of the firm and the shareholders' wealth.

FIGURE 10–6.   Time Disparity Ranking Problem

Project A				Project B		
$100	$200	$2000		$650	$650	$650
↓	↓	↓		↓	↓	↓
1	2	3 years		1	2	3 years
$1000				$1000		

$NPV = \$758.10$	$NPV = \$616.55$
$PI = 1.758$	$PI = 1.617$
$IRR = 35\%$	$IRR = 42 \text{ to } 43\%$

Like the size disparity problem, the time disparity problem becomes more complicated under capital rationing. As already stated, when a capital constraint is not imposed, net present value is the appropriate decision-making criterion. But when there is a capital constraint, the cutoff rate or actual required rate of return is no longer equal to the firm's normal required rate of return or cost of capital. That is, the firm no longer invests in all projects with returns greater than its required rate of return. Instead, the lowest return on a project accepted is above the normal required rate of return or cost of capital. Hence, owing to the capital rationing constraint, the lowest rate of return accepted is actually the firm's true required rate of return. In other words, under capital rationing the normal required rate of return or cost of capital loses its meaning, and the true required rate of return becomes the lowest rate of return on any project selected. Of course, if a capital constraint is not imposed, these two values will be identical. However, under capital rationing, the reinvestment rate assumptions produce conflicting rankings that can be resolved only through a redetermination of each project's net present value using the actual required rate of return. If capital rationing makes the lowest rate of return earned on any project 20 percent rather than the 10 percent cost of capital, then 20 percent is the firm's true required rate of return under capital rationing. Redetermining the net present value for projects A and B in the example above, using a 20 percent required rate of return, produces a net present value of $380.10 for project A and of $368.90 for project B. Thus, project A should be taken.

Unequal Lives   The final ranking problem to be examined centers on the question of whether or not it is appropriate to compare mutually exclusive projects with different life spans.

Example   Suppose a firm with a 10 percent required rate of return is faced with the problem of replacing an aging machine and is considering two replacement machines, one with a 3-year life and one with a 6-year life. The relevant cash flow information for these projects is given in Figure 10–7.

FIGURE 10–7. Unequal Lives Ranking Problem

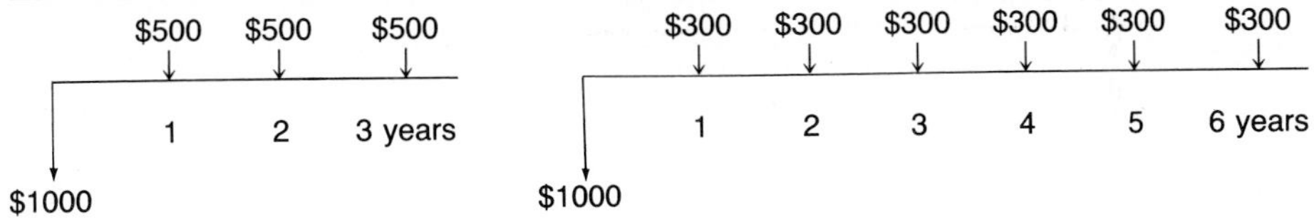

Project A	Project B

$NPV = \$234.50$
$PI = 1.2435$
$IRR = 23 \text{ to } 24\%$

$NPV = \$306.50$
$PI = 1.3065$
$IRR = 20\%$

Examining the discounted cash flow criteria, we find the net present value and profitability index criteria indicating that project B is the better project, while the internal rate of return favors project A. This ranking inconsistency is caused by the different life spans of the projects being compared. In this case the decision is a difficult one because the projects are not comparable.

The problem of incomparability of projects with different lives is not merely a result of the different lives; rather, it arises because future profitable investment proposals may be rejected without being included in the analysis. This can easily be seen in a replacement problem such as the present example, where two mutually exclusive machines with different lives are being considered. In this case a comparison of the net present values alone on each of these projects would be misleading. If the project with the shorter life were taken, at its termination the firm could replace the machine and receive additional benefits, while acceptance of the project with the longer life would exclude this possibility, a possibility that is not included in the analysis. The key question thus becomes, Does the investment decision being made today include all future profitable investment proposals in its analysis? If not, the projects are not comparable. In this case, if project B is taken, then the project that could have been taken after 3 years when project A terminates is automatically rejected without being included in the analysis. Thus, acceptance of project B not only forces rejection of project A, but also forces rejection of any replacement machine that might have been considered for years 4 through 6 without including this replacement machine in the analysis.

There are several methods to deal with this situation. The first option is merely to assume that the cash inflows from the shorter-lived investment will be reinvested at the cost of capital until the termination of the longer-lived asset. While this approach is the simplest, merely calculating the net present value, it actually ignores the problem at hand—that of allowing for participation in another replacement opportunity with a positive net present value. The proper solution thus becomes the projection of reinvestment opportunities into the future—that is, making assumptions as to possible future investment opportunities. Unfortunately, while the first method is too simplistic to be of any value, the second is extremely difficult, requiring extensive cash flow forecasts. The final technique for confronting the problem is to assume that reinvestment opportunities in the future will be similar to the current ones. The most common way of doing this is by creating a replacement chain to equalize life spans. The present example would call for the creation of a two-chain cycle for project A—that is, we assume that project A can be replaced with a similar investment at the end of three years. Thus, project A would be viewed as two A projects occurring back to back, as illustrated in Figure 10–8. The net present value on this replacement chain is $426.50, which is comparable with project B's net present value. Thus, project A should be accepted because the net present value of its replacement chain is greater than the net present value of project B.

INFLATION AND CAPITAL BUDGETING DECISIONS

In recent years it has become important to consider the effect of inflation in capital budgeting decisions. While every project is affected a little differently by inflation, there are four general ways in which inflation can affect capital budgeting decisions:

1. Increased inflation will cause the required rate of return on the project to rise. As cash flows received in the future will buy less with increased inflation, investors

FIGURE 10–8. Replacement Chain Illustration: Two A Projects

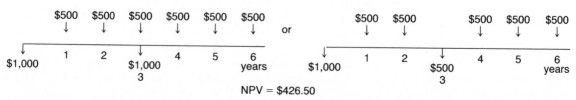

NPV = $426.50

will demand a higher required rate of return on funds invested. This is called the Fisher Effect. It states that the required rate of return on a project is

$$R_j = R_j^* + \rho$$

where R_j is the required rate of return in nominal terms, R_j^* is the required rate of return in real terms, and ρ is the weighted average anticipated inflation rate over the life of the project.[6]

2. Both anticipated cash inflows and outflows could be affected by inflation. Inflation may well affect materials, wages, sales, and administrative expenses while also affecting the selling price of the item being produced. It is obviously impossible to generalize on exactly how it will affect these items for all projects, but it is safe to assume it could have a significant impact on both cash inflows and outflows.

3. The salvage value of the project could also be affected by inflation. Again it is impossible to generalize on exactly what the relationship will be on all capital-budgeting projects.

4. The fact that depreciation charges do not change with inflation also distorts capital-budgeting decisions. Since depreciation charges are based upon original costs rather than replacement costs, they are not affected by inflation. As such, if inflation increases while depreciation remains constant, a smaller percentage of the cash inflows is sheltered by depreciation and thus a larger percentage is taxed. The end result of this is that the real after-tax cash flows decline over time as taxes increase faster than inflation because everything but depreciation is free to rise with inflation.

What is the answer as to how to adjust capital budgeting decisions for inflation? It is to anticipate and include any effects of expected inflation in the cash flow estimates and to also include it in the estimate of the required rate of return. Since it does affect the magnitude of the cash flows, it must be allowed for in order to produce an appropriate capital budgeting decision.

Summary

The process of capital budgeting involves decision making with respect to investment in fixed assets. Specifically, we examined the measurement of incremental cash flows associated with such investment proposals and the evaluation of those proposals. In measuring cash flows we focused on the **incremental** or differential **after-tax cash flows** attributed to the investment proposal. In general, a project's cash flows will fall into one of three categories: (1) the initial outlay, (2) the differential flows over the project's life, (3) the terminal cash flow. A summary of the typical entries in each of these categories appeared in Table 10–7.

We examined five commonly used criteria for determining the acceptance or rejection of capital-budgeting proposals. The first two methods, the payback period and

---

[6] Actually $(1 + R_j) = (1 + R_j^*)(1 + \rho)$; thus, $R_j = R_j^* + \rho + R_j^*\rho$. However, since $R_j^*\rho$ is assumed to be extremely small and inconsequential, it is generally dropped from consideration.

accounting rate of return, do not incorporate the time value of money into their calculations, while the net present value, profitability index, and internal rate of return do. These methods are summarized in Table 10–24. Finally, the problems of capital rationing were introduced. In particular we examined conflicting rankings caused by the size disparity, the time disparity, and unequal lives problems.

TABLE 10–24. Capital Budgeting Criteria

Nondiscounted Cash Flow Methods

1.   Payback period = number of years required to recapture the initial investment.

Accept if payback < maximum acceptable payback period
Reject if payback > maximum acceptable payback period

Advantages:
1. Uses cash flows.
2. Is easy to calculate and understand.
3. May be used as rough screening device.

Disadvantages:
1. Ignores the time value of money.
2. Ignores cash flows occurring after the payback period.

2. $\text{Accounting rate of return} = \dfrac{\sum\limits_{t=1}^{n} (\text{accounting profit after tax}_t)/n}{(\text{initial investment} + \text{expected salvage value})/2}$

where n = project's expected life.

Accept if $AROR$ > minimum acceptable rate of return
Reject if $AROR$ < minimum acceptable rate of return

Advantages:
1. Involves familiar, easily accessible terms.
2. Is easy to calculate and understand.

Disadvantages:
1. Ignores the time value of money.
2. Uses accounting profits rather than cash flows.

Discounted Cash Flow Methods

3. Net present value = present value of the annual cash flows after tax less the investment's initial outlay.

$$NPV = \sum_{t=1}^{n} \frac{ACF_t}{(1+k)^t} - IO$$

where ACF_t = the annual after-tax cash flow in time period t (this can take on either positive or negative values),
k = the appropriate discount rate, that is, the required rate of return or the cost of capital,[a]
IO = the initial cash outlay,
n = the project's expected life.

Accept if NPV > 0.0
Reject if NPV < 0.0

Advantages:
1. Uses cash flows.
2. Recognizes the time value of money.
3. Is consistent with the firm goal of shareholder wealth maximization.

Disadvantages:
1. Requires detailed long-term forecasts of the incremental benefits and costs.

TABLE 10–24. (*continued*)

4. Profitability index = the ratio of the present value of the future net cash flows to the initial outlay.

$$PI = \frac{\sum_{t=1}^{n} \frac{ACF_t}{(1 + k)^t}}{IO}$$

Accept if $PI > 1.0$
Reject if $PI < 1.0$

Advantages:
1. Uses cash flows.
2. Recognizes the time value of money.
3. Is consistent with the firm goal of shareholder wealth maximization.

Disadvantages:
1. Requires detailed long-term forecasts of the incremental benefits and costs.

5. Internal rate of return = the discount rate that equates the present value of the project's future net cash flows with the project's initial outlay.

$$IO = \sum_{t=1}^{n} \frac{ACF_t}{(1 + IRR)^t}$$

where IRR = the project's internal rate of return.

Accept if $IRR >$ required rate of return
Reject if $IRR <$ required rate of return

Advantages:
1. Uses cash flows.
2. Recognizes the time value of money.

Disadvantages:
1. Requires detailed long-term forecasts of the incremental benefits and costs.
2. Can involve tedious calculations.
3. Possibility of multiple IRRs.

[a] The cost of capital is discussed in Chapter 13.

Study Questions

10–1. Why is the capital budgeting decision such an important process? Why are capital budgeting errors so costly?

10–2. Why do we focus on cash flows rather than accounting profits in making our capital budgeting decisions? Why are we interested only in incremental cash flows rather than total cash flows?

10–3. If depreciation is not a cash flow expense, does it affect the level of cash flows from a project in any way?

10–4. If a project requires additional investment in working capital, how should this be treated in calculating cash flows?

10–5. How do sunk costs affect the determination of cash flows associated with an investment proposal?

10–6. What are the criticisms of the use of the payback period as a capital budgeting technique? What are its advantages? Why is it so frequently used?

10–7. In some countries, expropriation of foreign investments is a common practice. If you were considering an investment in one of those countries, would the use of the payback period criterion seem more reasonable than it otherwise might? Why?

10–8. What are the criticisms of the use of the accounting rate of return as a capital budgeting technique? What are its advantages?

10–9. Briefly compare and contrast the three discounted cash flow criteria. What are the advantages and disadvantages of the use of each of these methods?

10–10. What are mutually exclusive projects? Why might the existence of mutually exclusive projects cause problems in the implementation of the discounted cash flow capital budgeting criteria?

10–11. What reasons are commonly given for capital rationing? Is capital rationing rational?

10–12. How should the comparision of two mutually exclusive projects of unequal size be dealt with? Would your approach change if capital rationing existed?

10–13. What causes the time disparity ranking problem? What reinvestment rate assumptions are associated with the net present value and internal rate of return capital budgeting criteria?

10–14. When might two mutually exclusive projects having unequal lives be incomparable? How should this problem be dealt with?

10–15. Often government action to push or slow down the economy is implemented by altering the capital budgeting decision-making process of the firm. How might the following changes affect capital budgeting decisions?

a. A movement by the Federal Reserve to reduce interest rates

b. An increase in the investment tax credit

c. A change in the tax laws allowing an increase in the rate of accelerated depreciation

Self-Test Problems

ST–1. The Scotty Gator Corporation of Meadville, Pennsylvania, maker of Scotty's electronic components, is considering replacing one of its current hand-operated assembly machines with a new fully automated machine. This replacement would mean the elimination of one employee, generating salary and benefit savings. Given the following information, determine the cash

Existing situation:	One full-time machine operator—salary and benefits, $25,000 per year
	Cost of maintenance—$2000 per year
	Cost of defects—$6000
	Original depreciable value of old machine—$50,000
	Annual Depreciation—$5000 per year
	Expected life—10 years
	Age—five years old
	Expected salvage value in 5 years—$0
	Current salvage value—$5000
	Marginal tax rate—34 percent
Proposed situation:	Fully automated machine
	Cost of machine—$60,000
	Installation fee—$3000
	Shipping fee—$3000
	Cost of maintenance—$3000 per year
	Cost of defects—$3000 per year
	Expected life—five years
	Salvage value—$20,000
	Depreciation method—simplified straight-line method over 5 years

ST–2.

a.

    b.   Net present value
    c.   Profitability index
    d.   Internal rate of return
    Should this project be accepted?

ST–3.   The B. Pari Corporation is considering signing a one-year contract with one of two computer-based marketing firms. While one is more expensive, it offers a more extensive program and thus will provide higher after-tax net cash flows. Assume these two options are mutually exclusive and that the required rate of return is 12 percent. Given the following after-tax net cash flows:

Year	Option A	Option B
0	−$50,000	−$100,000
1	70,000	130,000

    a.   Calculate the net present value
    b.   Calculate the profitability index
    c.   Calculate the internal rate of return
    d.   If there is no capital rationing constraint, which project should be selected? If there is a capital returning constraint, how should the decision be made?

Study Problems

10–1.   (*Capital Gains Tax*) The J. Harris Corporation is considering selling one of its old assembly machines. The machine, purchased for $30,000 five years ago, had an expected life of 10 years and an expected salvage value of zero. Assume Harris uses simplfed straight-line depreciation, creating depreciation of $3000 per year, and could sell this old machine for $35,000. Also assume a 34 percent marginal tax rate.
    a.   What would be the taxes associated with this sale?
    b.   If the old machine were sold for $25,000, what would be the taxes associated with this sale?
    c.   If the old machine were sold for $15,000, what would be the taxes associated with this sale?
    d.   If the old machine were sold for $12,000, what would be the taxes associated with this sale?

10–2.   (*Cash Flow Calculations*) The Winky Corporation, maker of electronic components, is considering replacing a hand-operated machine used in the manufacture of electronic components with a new fully automated machine. Given the following information, determine the cash flows associated with this replacement.

Existing situation:	Two full-time machine operators—salaries $10,000 each per year
	Cost of maintenance—$5000 per year
	Cost of defects—$5000 per year
	Original cost of old machine—$30,000
	Expected life—10 years
	Age—five years old
	Expected salvage—$0
	Depreciation method—simplified straight-line over 10 years, $3,000 per year
	Current salvage value—$10,000
	Marginal tax rate—34 percent

Proposed Situation: Fully automated machine
Cost of machine—$55,000
Installation fee—$5000
Cost of maintenance—$6000 per year
Cost of defects—$2000 per year
Expected life—five years
Salvage value—$0
Depreciation method—simplified straight-line over 5 years

10–3. (*Capital Budgeting Calculation*) Given the cash flow information in problem 10–2 and a required rate of return of 15 percent, compute the following for the automated mixing machine:
a. Payback period
b. Net present value
c. Profitability index
d. Internal rate of return
Should this project be accepted?

10–4. (*AROR Calculation*) Two mutually exclusive projects are being evaluated using the accounting rate of return. Each project has an initial cost of $20,000 and a salvage value of $4000 after 6 years. Given the following information:

	Annual Accounting Profits after Tax	
Year	Project A	Project B
1	$ 2,000	$10,000
2	2,000	10,000
3	2,000	10,000
4	13,000	5,000
5	13,000	5,000
6	14,000	5,000

a. Determine each project's AROR.
b. Which project should be selected, using this criterion? Would you support that recommendation? Why or why not?

10–5. (*IRR Calculation*) Determine the internal rate of return on the following projects:
a. An initial outlay of $10,000 resulting in a single cash flow of $17,182 after 8 years
b. An initial outlay of $10,000 resulting in a single cash flow of $48,077 after 10 years
c. An initial outlay of $10,000 resulting in a single cash flow of $114,943 after 20 years
d. An initial outlay of $10,000 resulting in a single cash flow of $13,680 after 3 years

10–6. (*IRR Calculation*) Determine the internal rate of return on the following projects:
a. An initial outlay of $10,000 resulting in a cash flow of $1993 at the end of each year for the next 10 years
b. An initial outlay of $10,000 resulting in a cash flow of $2054 at the end of each year for the next 20 years
c. An initial outlay of $10,000 resulting in a cash flow of $1193 at the end of each year for the next 12 years
d. An initial outlay of $10,000 resulting in a cash flow of $2843 at the end of each year for the next 5 years

10–7. (*IRR Calculation*) Determine the internal rate of return to the nearest percent on the following projects:

    a. An initial outlay of $10,000 resulting in a cash flow of $2000 at the end of year 1, $5000 at the end of year 2, and $8000 at the end of year 3

    b. An initial outlay of $10,000 resulting in a cash flow of $8000 at the end of year 1, $5000 at the end of year 2, and $2000 at the end of year 3

    c. An initial outlay of $10,000 resulting in a cash flow of $2000 at the end of years 1 through 5 and $5000 at the end of year 6

10-8. (*Cash Flow—Capital Budgeting Calculation*) The C. Duncan Chemical Corporation is considering replacing one of its machines with a new, more efficient machine. The old machine presently has a book value of $100,000 and could be sold for $60,000. The old machine is being depreciated on a simplified straight-line basis down to a salvage value of zero over the next 5 years, generating depreciation of $20,000 per year. The replacement machine would cost $300,000, and have an expected life of 5 years, after which it could be sold for $50,000. Because of reductions in defects and material savings, the new machine would produce cash benefits of $90,000 per year before depreciation and taxes. Assuming simplified straight-line depreciation, a 34 percent marginal tax rate, and a required rate of return of 15 percent, find:

    a. The payback period
    b. The net present value
    c. The profitability index
    d. The internal rate of return

10-9. (*Cash Flow—Capital-Budgeting Calculation*) The R. Boisjoly Chemical Corporation is considering replacing a 5-year-old machine that originally cost $50,000, presently has a book value of $25,000, and could be sold for $60,000. This machine is currently being depreciated using the simplified straight-line method down to a terminal value of zero over the next 5 years, generating depreciation of $5000 per year. The replacement machine would cost $125,000, and have a 5 year expected life over which it would be depreciated down using the simplified straight-line method and have no salvage value at the end of 5 years. The new machine would produce savings before depreciation and taxes of $45,000 per year. Assuming a 34 percent marginal tax rate and a required rate of return of 10 percent, calculate:

    a. The payback period
    b. The net present value
    c. The profitability index
    d. The internal rate of return

10-10. (*Cash Flow—Capital Budgeting Calculation*) The Mad Dog Hansen Electronic Components Corporation is considering replacing a 10-year-old machine that originally cost $30,000, has a current book value of $10,000 with 5 years of expected life left, and is being depreciated using the simplified straight-line method over its 15-year expected life down to a terminal value of zero in 5 years, generating depreciation of $2000 per year. The replacement machine being considered would cost $80,000 and have a 5-year expected life over which it would be depreciated using the simplified straight-line method down to zero. At termination in 5 years the new machine would have a salvage value of $40,000. Material efficiencies resulting from the replacement would result in savings of $30,000 per year before depreciation and taxes. Currently, the old machine could be sold for $15,000. Assuming simplified straight-line depreciation, a 34 percent marginal tax rate, and a required rate of return of 20 percent, calculate:

    a. The payback period
    b. The net present value
    c. The profitability index
    d. The internal rate of return

10-11. (*NPV PI and IRR Calculations*) Brownsville Girl, Inc., is considering a major expansion of its product line and has estimated the following cash flows associated with such an expansion. The initial outlay associated with the expansion would be $1,950,000 and the project would generate incremental after-tax cash flows of $450,000 per year for six years. The appropriate required rate of return is 9 percent.

a. Calculate the net present value.

b. Calculate the profitability index.

c. Calculate the internal rate of return.

d. Should this project be accepted?

10-12. (*Internal Rate of Return Calculations*) Given the following cash flows, determine the internal rate of return for projects A, B, and C.

	Project A	Project B	Project C
Initial investment:	$50,000	$100,000	$450,000
Cash Inflows:			
Year 1	$10,000	25,000	200,000
Year 2	15,000	25,000	200,000
Year 3	20,000	25,000	200,000
Year 4	25,000	25,000	—
Year 5	30,000	25,000	—

10-13. (*NPV with Varying Required Rates of Return*) Big Steve's, makers of swizzle sticks, is considering the purchase of a new plastic stamping machine. This investment requires an initial outlay of $100,000 and will generate after-tax cash inflows of $18,000 per year for 10 years. For each of the listed required rates of return, determine the project's net present value.

a. The required rate of return is 10 percent.

b. The required rate of return is 15 percent.

c. Would the project be accepted under part (a) or (b)?

d. What is this project's internal rate of return?

10-14. (*Comprehensive Cash Flow—Capital Budgeting Calculation*) The L. Knutson Company, a manufacturer of electronic components in the 34 percent marginal tax bracket, is considering the purchase of a new fully automated machine to replace an older, manually operated one. The machine being replaced, now 5 years old, originally had an expected life of 10 years, was being depreciated using the simplified straight-line method from $20,000 down to zero, thus generating $2000 in depreciation per year, and could be sold for $25,000. It took one man to operate the old machine, and he earned $15,000 per year in salary and $2000 per year in fringe benefits. The annual costs of maintenance and defects associated with the old machine were $7000 and $3000, respectively. The replacement machine being considered had a purchase price of $50,000, a salvage value after 5 years of $10,000, and would be depreciated over 5 years using the simplified straight-line depreciation method down to zero. In order to get the automated machine in running order, there would be a $3000 shipping fee and a $2000 installation charge. In addition, because the new machine would work faster than the old one, investment in raw materials and goods-in-process inventories would need to be increased by a total of $5000. The annual costs of maintenance and defects on the new machine would be $2000 and $4000, respectively. The new machine also requires maintenance workers to be specially trained; fortunately, a similar machine was purchased 3 months ago, and at that time the mainte-nance workers went through the $5000 training program needed to familiarize themselves with the new equipment. The firm's management is uncertain whether or not to charge half of this $5000 training fee toward the new project. Finally, in order to purchase the new machine, it appears the firm would have to borrow an additional $20,000 at 10 percent interest from its local bank, resulting in additional interest payments of $2000 per year. The required rate of return on projects of this kind is 20 percent.

a. What is the project's initial outlay?
b. What are the differential cash flows over the project's life?
c. What is the terminal cash flow?
d. Draw a cash flow diagram for this project.
e. If the firm requires a minimum payback period on projects of this type of 3 years, should this project be accepted?
f. Calculate the project's AROR.
g. What is its net present value?
h. What is its profitability index?
i. What is its internal rate of return?
j. Should the project be accepted? Why or why not?

10–15. (*Size Disparity Ranking Problem*) The D. Dorner Farms Corporation is considering purchasing one of two fertilizer-herbicides for the upcoming year. The more expensive of the two is the better and will produce a higher yield. Assume these projects are mutually exclusive and that the required rate of return is 10 percent. Given the following after-tax net cash flows:

Year	Project A	Project B
0	−$500	−$5000
1	700	6000

a. Calculate the net present value.
b. Calculate the profitability index.
c. Calculate the internal rate of return.
d. If there is no capital rationing constraint, which project should be selected? If there is a capital rationing constraint, how should the decision be made?

10–16. (*Time Disparity Ranking Problem*) The R. Rogers Corporation is considering two mutually exclusive projects. The cash flows associated with those projects are as follows:

Year	Project A	Project B
0	−$50,000	−$ 50,000
1	15,625	0
2	15,625	0
3	15,625	0
4	15,625	0
5	15,625	$100,000

The required rate of return on these projects is 10 percent.
a. What is each project's payback period?
b. What is each project's net present value?
c. What is each project's internal rate of return?
d. What has caused the ranking conflict?
e. Which project should be accepted? Why?

10–17. (*Unequal Lives Ranking Problem*) The B. T. Knight Corporation is considering two mutually exclusive pieces of machinery that perform the same task. The two alternatives available provide the following set of after-tax net cash flows:

Year	Equipment A	Equipment B
0	−$20,000	−$20,000
1	12,590	6,625
2	12,590	6,625
3	12,590	6,625
4		6,625
5		6,625
6		6,625
7		6,625
8		6,625
9		6,625

Equipment A has an expected life of 3 years, while equipment B has an expected life of 9 years. Assume a required rate of return of 15 percent.

a. Calculate each project's payback period.

b. Calculate each project's net present value.

c. Calculate each project's internal rate of return.

d. Are these projects comparable?

e. Compare these projects using replacement chains. Which project should be selected? Support your recommendation.

10–18. (*Capital Rationing*) The Cowboy Hat Company of Stillwater, Oklahoma, is considering seven capital investment proposals, for which the funds available are limited to a maximum of $12 million. The projects are independent and have the following costs and profitability indexes associated with them:

Project	Cost	Profitability Index
A	$4,000,000	1.18
B	3,000,000	1.08
C	5,000,000	1.33
D	6,000,000	1.31
E	4,000,000	1.19
F	6,000,000	1.20
G	4,000,000	1.18

a. Under strict capital rationing, which projects should be selected?

b. Is this an optimal strategy?

10–19. (*Cash Flow—Capital Budgeting Calculation*) The Beamer Corp. is considering expanding its highly technical construction facilities. The construction will take a total of four years until it is completed and ready for operation. The following data and assumptions describe the proposed expansion:

1. In order to make this expansion feasible, R&D expenditures of $200,000 must be made immediately to ensure that the construction facilities are competitively efficient ($t = 0$).

2. At the end of the first year the land will be purchased and construction on stage 1 of the facilities will begin, involving a cash outflow of $150,000 for the land and $300,000 for the construction facilities.

3. Stage 2 of the construction will involve a $300,000 cash outflow at the end of year 2.

4. At the end of year 3, when production begins, inventory will be increased by $50,000.

5. The first sales from operation of the new plant will occur at the end of year 4 and be $800,000 and continue at that level for 10 years (with the final flow from sales occurring at the end of year 13).

6. Operating costs on these sales are composed of $100,000 fixed operating costs per year and variable operating costs equal to 40 percent of sales.

7. The construction facilities will be depreciated using the simplified straight-line method over their 10-year life down to zero. When the plant is closed it will be sold for $50,000. (*Note*: Assume the investment in plant is depreciated using the simplified straight-line method from $600,000 down to zero over its 10-year life during years $t = 4$–13.) Do not depreciate the land.

8. When the plant is closed, the land will be sold for $200,000 ($t = 13$).

9. The company is in the 34 percent marginal tax bracket.

Given a 12 percent required rate of return, what is the NPV of this project? Should it be accepted?

10–20. (*Cash Flow—Capital Budgeting Calculation*) The Steel Mill Corporation of Asbury Park, New Jersey, must replace its executive jet and is considering two mutually exclusive planes as replacements. As far as it is concerned, both planes are identical and each will provide annual benefits, before maintenance, taxes, and depreciation, of $40,000 per year for the life of the plane; however, the costs on each are decidedly different. The first is a Lays Jet and costs $94,000. It has an expected life of 7 years, will be depreciated using the simplified straight-line method down to zero, and will require major maintenance at the end of year 4. The annual maintenance costs are $8000 for the first three years, $25,000 in year 4, and $10,000 for years 5 through 7. Its salvage value at the end of year 7 is $24,000.

The other plane is a Honeybilt Jet costing $100,000 and also having an expected life of 7 years, over which it will be depreciated using the simplified straight-line method down to zero. Its maintenance expenses are expected to be $9000 the first four years, rising to $18,000 annually for years 5 through 7. In years 3 and 5 the jet engine must be overhauled at an expense of $15,000 each time; this overhaul expense is in excess of the maintenance expenses. Finally, at the end of year 7 this jet will have a salvage value of $30,000. Given a 34 percent marginal tax rate and a 10 percent required rate of return, what is the NPV on each jet? Which should be taken?

Case Problems

Danforth & Donnalley Laundry Products Company

Capital Budgeting: Relevant Cash Flows

On April 14, 1988, at 3:00 P.M., James Danforth, president of Danforth & Donnalley (D&D) Laundry Products Company, called to order a meeting of the financial directors. The purpose of the meeting was to make a capital budgeting decision with respect to the introduction and production of a new product, a liquid detergent called Blast.

D&D was formed in 1965 with the merger of Danforth Chemical Company, headquartered in Seattle, Washington, producers of Lift-Off detergent, the leading laundry detergent on the West Coast, and Donnalley Home Products Company, headquartered in Detroit, Michigan, makers of Wave detergent, a major midwestern laundry product. As a result of the merger, D&D was producing and marketing two major product lines. Although these products were in direct competition, they were not without product differentiation: Lift-Off was a low-suds, concentrated powder, and Wave was a more traditional powder detergent. Each line brought with it considerable brand loyalty, and by 1988, sales from the two detergent lines had increased tenfold from 1965 levels, with both products now being sold nationally.

In the face of increased competition and technological innovation, D&D spent large amounts of time and money over the past four years researching and developing a new, highly concentrated liquid laundry detergent. D&D's new detergent, which they called Blast, had many obvious advantages over the conventional powdered products. It was felt that with Blast the consumer would benefit in three major areas. Blast was so highly concentrated that only 2 ounces was needed to do an average load of laundry as compared with 8 to 12 ounces of powdered detergent. Moreover, being a liquid, it was possible to pour Blast directly on stains and hard-to-wash spots, eliminating the need for a pre-soak and giving it cleaning abilities that powders could not possibly match. And, finally, it would be packaged in a lightweight, unbreakable plastic bottle with a sure-grip handle, making it much easier to use and more convenient to store than the bulky boxes of powdered detergents with which it would compete.

The meeting was attended by James Danforth, president of D&D; Jim Donnalley, director of the board; Guy Rainey, vice president in charge of new products; Urban McDonald, controller; and Steve Gasper, a newcomer to D&D's financial staff, who was invited by McDonald to sit in on the meeting. Danforth called the meeting to order, gave a brief statement of its purpose, and immediately gave the floor to Guy Rainey.

Rainey opened with a presentation of the cost and cash flow analysis for the new product. To keep things clear, he passed out copies of the projected cash flows to those present (see Exhibits 1 and 2). In support of this information, he provided some insight as to how these calculations were determined. Rainey proposed that the initial cost for Blast included $500,000 for the test marketing, which was conducted in the Detroit area and completed in the previous June, and $2 million for new specialized equipment and packaging facilities. The estimated life for the facilities was 15 years, after which they would have no salvage value. This 15-year estimated life assumption coincides with company policy set by Donnalley not to consider cash flows occurring more than 15 years into the future, as estimates that far ahead "tend to become little more than blind guesses."

Rainey cautioned against taking the annual cash flows (as shown in Exhibit 1) at face value since portions of these cash flows actually are a result of sales that had been diverted from Lift-Off and Wave. For this reason, Rainey also produced the annual cash flows that had been adjusted to include only those cash flows incremental to the company as a whole (as shown in Exhibit 2).

At this point, discussion opened between Donnalley and McDonald, and it was concluded that the opportunity cost on funds is 10 percent. Gasper then questioned the fact that no

EXHIBIT 1. D&D Laundry Products Company	Year	Cash Flows	EXHIBIT 2. D&D Laundry Products Company	Year	Cash Flows
	1	$280,000		1	$250,000
Annual Cash Flows from the Acceptance of Blast (Including flows resulting from sales diverted from the existing product lines)	2	280,000	*Annual Cash Flows from the Acceptance of Blast (Not including those flows resulting from sales diverted from the existing product lines)*	2	250,000
	3	280,000		3	250,000
	4	280,000		4	250,000
	5	280,000		5	250,000
	6	350,000		6	315,000
	7	350,000		7	315,000
	8	350,000		8	315,000
	9	350,000		9	315,000
	10	350,000		10	315,000
	11	250,000		11	225,000
	12	250,000		12	225,000
	13	250,000		13	225,000
	14	250,000		14	225,000
	15	250,000		15	225,000

costs were included in the proposed cash budget for plant facilities, which would be needed to produce the new product.

Rainey replied that, at the present time, Lift-Off's production facilities were being utilized at only 55 percent of capacity, and since these facilities were suitable for use in the production of Blast, no new plant facilities other than the specialized equipment and packaging facilities previously mentioned need be acquired for the production of the new product line. It was estimated that full production of Blast would only require 10 percent of the plant capacity.

McDonald then asked if there had been any consideration of increased working capital needs to operate the investment project. Rainey answered that there had and that this project would require $200,000 of additional working capital; however, as this money would never leave the firm and always would be in liquid form it was not considered an outflow and hence was not included in the calculations.

Donnalley argued that this project should be charged something for its use of the current excess plant facilities. His reasoning was that, if an outside firm tried to rent this space from D&D, it would be charged somewhere in the neighborhood of $2 million, and since this project would compete with the current projects, it should be treated as an outside project and charged as such; however he went on to acknowledge that D&D has a strict policy that forbids the renting or leasing out of any of its production facilities. If they didn't charge for facilities, he concluded, the firm might end up accepting projects that under normal circumstances would be rejected.

From here, the discussion continued, centering on the questions of what to do about the "lost contribution from other projects," the test marketing costs, and the working capital.

QUESTIONS

1. If you were put in the place of Steve Gasper, would you argue for the cost from market testing to be included as a cash outflow?

2. What would your opinion be as to how to deal with the question of working capital?

3. Would you suggest that the product be charged for the use of excess production facilities and building?

4. Would you suggest that the cash flows resulting from erosion of sales from current laundry detergent products be included as a cash inflow? If there were a chance of competition introducing a similar product if you do not introduce Blast, would this affect your answer?

5. If debt is used to finance this project, should the interest payments associated with this new debt be considered cash flows?

6. What are the NPV, IRR, and PI of this project, including cash flows resulting from lost sales from existing product lines? What are the NPV, IRR, and PI of this project excluding these flows? Under the assumption that there is a good chance that competition will introduce a similar product if you don't, would you accept or reject this project?

Harding Plastic Molding Company

Capital Budgeting: Ranking Problems

On January 11, 1988, the finance committee of Harding Plastic Molding Company (HPMC) met to consider eight capital budgeting projects. Present at the meeting were Robert L. Harding, president and founder, Susan Jorgensen, comptroller, and Chris Woelk, head of research and development. Over the past five years, this committee has met every month to consider and make final judgment on all proposed capital outlays brought up for review during the period.

Harding Plastic Molding Company was founded in 1962 by Robert L. Harding to produce plastic parts and molding for the Detroit automakers. For the first 10 years of operations, HPMC worked solely as a subcontractor for the automakers, but since then has made strong efforts to diversify in an attempt to avoid the cyclical problems faced by the auto industry. By 1978, this diversification attempt had led HPMC into the production of over 1,000 different items, including kitchen utensils, camera housings, and phonographic and recording equipment. It also led to an increase in sales of 800 percent during the 1972–1987 period. As this dramatic increase in sales was paralleled by a corresponding increase in production volume, HPMC was forced, in late 1986, to expand production facilities. This plant and equipment expansion involved capital expenditures of approximately $10.5 million and resulted in an increase of production capacity of about 40 percent. Because of this increased production capacity, HPMC has made a concerted effort to attract new business and consequently has recently entered into contracts with a large toy firm and a major discount department store chain. While non-auto-related business has grown significantly, it still only represents 32 percent of HPMC's overall business. Thus, HPMC has continued to solicit nonautomotive business, and as a result of this effort and its internal research and development, the firm has four sets of mutually exclusive projects to consider at this month's finance committee meeting.

Over the past 10 years, HPMC's capital budgeting approach has evolved into a somewhat elaborate procedure in which new proposals are categorized into three areas: profit, research and development, and safety. Projects falling into the profit or research and development areas are evaluated using present value techniques, assuming a 10 percent opportunity rate; those falling into the safety classification are evaluated in a more subjective framework. Although research and development projects have to receive favorable results from the present value criteria, there is also a total dollar limit assigned to projects of this category, typically running about $750,000 per year. This limitation was imposed by Harding primarily because of the limited availability of quality researchers in the plastics industry. Harding felt that if more funds than this were allocated, "we simply couldn't find the manpower to administer them properly." The benefits derived from safety projects, on the other hand, are not in terms of cash flows; hence, present value methods are not used at all in their evaluation. The subjective approach used to evaluate safety projects is a result of the pragmatically difficult task of quantifying the benefits from these projects into dollar terms. Thus, these projects are subjectively evaluated by a management-worker committee with a limited budget. All eight projects to be evaluated in January are classified as profit projects.

The first set of projects listed on the meeting's agenda for examination involve the utilization of HPMC's precision equipment. Project A calls for the production of vacuum containers for thermos bottles produced for a large discount hardware chain. The containers would be manufactured in five different size and color combinations. This project would be carried out over a three-year period, for which HPMC would be guaranteed a minimum return plus a percentage of the sales. Project B involves the manufacture of inexpensive photographic equipment for a national photography outlet. Although HPMC currently has excess plant capacity, each of these projects would utilize precision equipment of which the excess capacity is limited. Thus, adopting either project would tie up all precision facilities. In addition, the purchase of new equipment would be both prohibitively expensive and involve a time delay of approximately two years, thus making these projects mutually exclusive. (The cash flows associated with these two projects are given in Exhibit 1.)

The second set of projects involves the renting of computer facilities over a one-year period to aid in customer billing and perhaps inventory control. Project C entails the evaluation of a customer billing system proposed by Advanced Computer Corporation. Under this

EXHIBIT 1. **Harding Plastic Molding Company**

	Cash Flows	
Year	Project A	Project B
0	$-75,000	$-75,000
1	10,000	43,000
2	30,000	43,000
3	100,000	43,000

system all the bookkeeping and billing presently being done by HPMC's accounting department would be done by Advanced. In addition to saving costs involved in bookkeeping, Advanced would provide a more efficient billing system and do a credit analysis of delinquent customers, which could be used in the future for in-depth credit analysis. Project D is proposed by International Computer Corporation and includes a billing system similar to that offered by Advanced and, in addition, an inventory control system that will keep track of all raw materials and parts in stock and reorder when necessary, thereby reducing the likelihood of material stockouts, which has become more and more frequent over the past three years. (The cash flows for these projects are given in Exhibit 2.)

The third decision that faces the financial directors of HPMC involves a newly developed and patented process for molding hard plastics. HPMC can either manufacture and market the equipment necessary to mold such plastics or it can sell the patent rights to Polyplastics Incorporated, the world's largest producer of plastics products. (The cash flows for projects E and F are shown in Exhibit 3.) At present, the process has not been fully tested, and if HPMC is going to market it itself, it will be necessary to complete this testing and begin production of plant facilities immediately. On the other hand, the selling of these patent rights to Polyplastics would involve only minor testing and refinements, which could be completed within the year. Thus, a decision as to the proper course of action is necessary immediately.

The final set of projects up for consideration revolve around the replacement of some of the machinery. HPMC can go in one of two directions. Project G suggests the purchase and installation of moderately priced, extremely efficient equipment with an expected life

EXHIBIT 2. **Harding Plastic Molding Company**

	Cash Flows	
Year	Project C	Project D
0	$-8,000	$-20,000
1	11,000	25,000

EXHIBIT 3. **Harding Plastic Molding Company**

	Cash Flows	
Year	Project E	Project F
0	$-30,000	$-271,500
1	210,000	100,000
2		100,000
3		100,000
4		100,000
5		100,000
6		100,000
7		100,000
8		100,000
9		100,000
10		100,000

EXHIBIT 4.   Harding Plastic Molding Company

	Cash Flows	
Year	Project G	Project H
0	$-500,000	$-500,000
1	225,000	150,000
2	225,000	150,000
3	225,000	150,000
4	225,000	150,000
5	225,000	150,000
6		150,000
7		150,000
8		150,000
9		150,000
10		150,000

of five years; project H advocates the purchase of a similarly priced, although less efficient, machine with life expectancy of 10 years. (The cash flows for these alternatives are shown in Exhibit 4.)

As the meeting opened, debate immediately centered on the most appropriate method for evaluating all the projects. Harding suggested that as the projects to be considered were mutually exclusive, perhaps their usual capital budgeting criteria of net present value was inappropriate. He felt that, in examining these projects, perhaps they should be more concerned with relative profitability or some measure of yield. Both Jorgensen and Woelk agreed with Harding's point of view, with Jorgensen advocating a profitability index approach and Woelk preferring the use of the internal rate of return. Jorgensen argued that the use of the profitability index would provide a benefit-cost ratio, directly implying relative profitability. Thus, they merely need to rank these projects and select those with the highest profitability index. Woelk agreed with Jorgensen's point of view, but suggested that the calculation of an internal rate of return would also give a measure of profitability and perhaps be somewhat easier to interpret. To settle the issue, Harding suggested that they calculate all three measures, as they would undoubtedly yield the same ranking.

From here the discussion turned to an appropriate approach to the problem of differing lives among mutually exclusive projects E and F, and G and H. Woelk argued that there really was not a problem here at all, that as all the cash flows from these projects can be determined, any of the discounted cash flow methods of capital budgeting will work well. Jorgensen argued that although this was true, some compensation should be made for the fact that the projects being considered did not have equal lives.

QUESTIONS

1. Was Harding correct in stating that the NPV, PI, and IRR necessarily will yield the same ranking order? Under what situations might the NPV, PI, and IRR methods provide different rankings? Why is it possible?

2. What are the NPV, PI, and IRR for projects A and B? What has caused the ranking conflicts? Should project A or B be chosen? Might your answer change if project B is a typical project in the plastic molding industry? For example, if projects for HPMC generally yield approximately 12 percent, is it logical to assume that the IRR for project

B of approximately 33 percent is a correct calculation for ranking purposes? (*Hint*: Examine the reinvestment rate assumption.)

3. What are the NPV, PI, and IRR for projects C and D? Should project C or D be chosen? Does your answer change if these projects are considered under a capital constraint? What return on the marginal $12,000 not employed in project C is necessary to make one indifferent to choosing one project over the other under a capital rationing situation?

4. What are the NPV, PI, and IRR for projects E and F? Are these projects comparable even though they have unequal lives? Why? Which project should be chosen? Assume that these projects are not considered under a capital constraint.

5. What are the NPV, PI, and IRR for projects G and H? Are these projects comparable even though they have unequal lives? Why? Which project should be chosen? Assume that these projects are not considered under a capital constraint.

Self-Test Solutions

SS–1. STEP 1: First calculate the initial outlay

Initial outlay	
Outflows:	
Cost of machine	$60,000
Installation fee	3,000
Shipping fee	3,000
Inflows:	
Salvage value—old machine	− 5,000
Tax savings on sale of old machine ($25,000 − $5,000) (.34)	− 6,800
	$54,200

STEP 2: Calculate the differential cash flows over the project's life

	Book Profit	Cash Flow
Savings: Reduced salary	$25,000	$25,000
Reduced defects	3,000	3,000
Costs: Increased maintenance	− 1,000	− 1,000
Increased depreciation ($13,200 − $5000)[a]	− 8,200	
Net savings before taxes	$18,800	$27,000
Taxes (.34)	− 6,392	− 6,392
Annual net cash flow after taxes		$20,608

[a] Annual depreciation on the new machine is equal to the cost of the new machine ($60,000) plus any expenses necessary to get it in operating order (the shipping fee of $3000 plus the installation fee of $3000) divided by the depreciable life (five years).

STEP 3: Calculate the terminal cash flow

Salvage value—new machine	$20,000
Less: Taxes—recapture of depreciation ($20,000 × .34)	6,800
	$13,200

Thus, the cash flow in the final year will be equal to the annual net cash flow in that year of $20,608 plus the terminal cash flow of $13,200 for a total of $33,808.

SS–2. **a.** Payback period $= \dfrac{\$54,200}{\$20,608} = 2.630$ years

b. $NPV = \displaystyle\sum_{t=1}^{n} \frac{ACF_t}{(1+k)^t} - IO$

$= \displaystyle\sum_{t=1}^{4} \frac{\$20,608}{(1+.15)^t} + \frac{\$33,808}{(1+.15)^5} - \$54,200$

$= \$20,608(2.855) + \$33,808(.497) - \$54,200$

$= \$58,836 + \$16,803 - \$54,200$

$= \$21,439$

c. $PI = \dfrac{\displaystyle\sum_{t=1}^{n} \dfrac{ACF_t}{(1+k)^t}}{IO}$

$= \dfrac{\$75,639}{\$54,200}$

$= 1.396$

d. $IO = \displaystyle\sum_{t=1}^{n} \frac{ACF_t}{(1+IRR)^t}$

$\$54,200 = \$20,608 \begin{bmatrix} \text{table value,} \\ \text{Appendix D,} \\ \text{4 years,} \\ \text{IRR percent} \end{bmatrix} + \$33,808 \begin{bmatrix} \text{table value,} \\ \text{Appendix B,} \\ \text{5 years,} \\ \text{IRR percent} \end{bmatrix}$

Try 29%:
$\$54,200 = \$20,608(2.203) + \$33,808(.280)$

$= \$45,399 + 9,466$

$= \$54,865$

Try 30%:
$\$45,200 = \$20,608(2.166) + \$33,808(.269)$

$= \$44,637 + 9,094$

$= \$53,731$

Thus, the IRR is just below 30 percent and the project should be accepted since the NPV is positive, the PI is greater than 1.0, and the IRR is greater than the required rate of return of 15 percent.

SS–3. **a.** $NPV_A = \$70,000 \left[\dfrac{1}{(1+.12)^1} \right] - \$50,000$

$= \$70,000(.893) - \$50,000$

$= \$62,510 - \$50,000$

$= \$12,510$

$$NPV_B = \$130,000 \left[\frac{1}{(1 + .12)^1} \right] - \$100,000$$

$$= \$130,000(.893) - \$100,000$$

$$= \$116,090 - \$100,000$$

$$= \$16,090$$

b. $PI_A = \dfrac{\$62,510}{\$50,000}$

$$= 1.2502$$

$PI_B = \dfrac{\$116,090}{\$100,000}$

$$= 1.1609$$

c.

$$\$50,000 = \$70,000 \begin{bmatrix} \text{TABLE VALUE} \\ \text{APPENDIX B} \\ \text{1 YEAR} \\ IRR_A \text{ PERCENT} \end{bmatrix}$$

$$.7143 = \begin{bmatrix} \text{TABLE VALUE} \\ \text{APPENDIX B} \\ \text{1 YEAR} \\ IRR_A \text{ PERCENT} \end{bmatrix}$$

Looking in the one year row of Appendix B a value of .714 is found in the 40 percent column. Thus, the IRR is 40 percent.

$$\$100,000 = \$130,000 \begin{bmatrix} \text{TABLE VALUE} \\ \text{APPENDIX B} \\ \text{1 YEAR} \\ IRR_B \text{ PERCENT} \end{bmatrix}$$

$$.7692 = \begin{bmatrix} \text{TABLE VALUE} \\ \text{APPENDIX B} \\ \text{1 YEAR} \\ IRR_B \text{ PERCENT} \end{bmatrix}$$

Looking in the one-year row of Appendix B a value of .769 is found in the 30 percent column. Thus, the IRR is 30 percent.

d. If there is no capital rationing, project B should be accepted because it has a larger net present value. If there is a capital constraint, the problem focuses on what can be done with the additional $50,000 (the additional money that could be invested if project A with an initial outlay of $50,000 were selected over project B with an initial outlay of $100,000). In the capital constraint case, if Pari can earn more on project A plus the marginal project financed with the additional $50,000 than it can on project B, then project A and the marginal project should be accepted.

Selected References

Alpin, Richard D., and George L. Casler. *Capital Investment Analysis*. Columbus, Ohio: Grid, 1973.

Bacon, Peter W. "The Evaluation of Mutually Exclusive Investments," *Financial Management*, 6 (Summer 1977), 55–64.

Bernhard, Richard H. "Mathematical Programming Models for Capital Budgeting—A Survey, Generalization and Critique," *Journal of Financial and Quantitative Analysis*, 4 (June 1969), 111–58.

Bierman, Harold, Jr. "A Reconciliation of Present Value Capital Budgeting and Accounting," *Financial Management*, 6 (Summer 1977), 52–54.

———, and Seymour Smidt. *The Capital Budgeting Decision* (6th ed.). New York: Macmillan, 1984.

Bodie, Zvi. "Compound Interest Depreciation in Capital Investment," *Harvard Business Review*, 60 (May–June 1982), 58–60.

Dorfman, Robert. "The Meaning of Internal Rates of Return," *Journal of Finance,* 36 (December 1981), 1011–1021.

Dudley, Carlton L., Jr. "A Note on Reinvestment Assumptions in Choosing Between Net Present Value and Internal Rate of Return," *Journal of Finance*, 27 (September 1972), 907–15.

Folger, H. Russell. "Ranking Techniques and Capital Rationing," *Accounting Review*, 47 (January 1972), 134–43.

Gitman, Lawrence J., and John R. Forrester, Jr. "Forecasting and Evaluation Practices and Performance: A Survey of Capital Budgeting," *Financial Management*, 6 (Fall 1977), 66–71.

Haka, Susan F., Lawrence A. Gordan, and George F. Pinches. "Sophisticated Capital Budgeting Selection Techniques and Firm Performance," *Accounting Review*, 60 (October 1985), 651–69.

Herbst, Anthony. "The Unique, Real Internal Rate of Return: Caveat Emptor!" *Journal of Financial and Quantitative Analysis*, 13 (June 1978), 363–70.

Hoskins, Colin G., and Glen A. Mumey. "Payback: A Maligned Method of Asset Ranking?" *Engineering Economist*, 25 (Fall 1979), 53–65.

Jean, William H. *Capital Budgeting: The Economic Evaluation of Investment Projects*. Scranton, Pa.: International Textbook, 1969.

Keane, Simon M. "The Internal Rate of Return and the Reinvestment Fallacy," *Journal of Accounting and Business Studies*, 15 (June 1979), 48–55.

Kim, Suk H. "Capital Budgeting Practices in Large Corporations and Their Impact on Over-all Profitability," *Baylor Business Studies*, November–December 1978, January 1979, pp. 48–66.

———, "Current Capital Budgeting Practices," *Management Accounting*, 28 (June 1981), 26–30.

———, and E. J. Farragher. "Capital Budgeting Practices in Large Industrial Firms," *Baylor Business Studies*, November 1976, pp. 19–25.

———, and Larry Guin. "A Summary of Empirical Studies on Capital Budgeting Practices," *Business and Public Affairs*, 13 (Fall 1986), 21–25.

———, Trevor Crick, and Sesung H. Kim. "Do Executives Practice What Academics Teach?" *Management Accounting*, 33 (November 1986), 49–52.

Klammer, Thomas. "The Association of Capital Budgeting Techniques with Firm Performance," *Accounting Review*, April 1973, pp. 535–64.

———. "Empirical Evidence of the Adoption of Sophisticated Capital Budgeting Techniques," *Journal of Business*, July 1972, pp. 387–97.

Logue, Dennis E., and T. Craig Tapley. "Performance Monitoring and the Timing of Cash Flows," *Financial Management*, 14 (Autumn 1985), 34–39.

Lorie, James H., and Leonard J. Savage. "Three Problems in Rationing Capital," *Journal of Business*, 28 (October 1955), 229–39.

Mao, James C. T. "The Internal Rate of Return as a Ranking Criterion," *Engineering Economist*, 11 (Winter 1966), 1–13.

McConnell, John J., and Chris J. Muscarella. "Corporate Capital Expenditure Decisions and the Market Value of the Firm," *Journal of Financial Economics*, 14 (September 1985), 399–422.

Mehta, Dileep R., Michael D. Curley, and Hung-Gay Fung. "Inflation Cost of Capital and Capital Budgeting Procedures," *Financial Management*, 13 (Winter 1984), 48–54.

Merrett, A. J., and Allen Sykes. *Capital Budgeting and Company Finance*, London: Longmans, 1966.

Narayanan, M. P. "Observability and the Payback Criterion," *Journal of Business*, 58 (July 1985), 309–23.

Osteryoung, Jerome. *Capital Budgeting: Long-Term Asset Selection* (2nd ed.). Columbus, OH: Grid, 1979.

———. "A Survey into the Goals Used by Fortune's 500 Companies in Capital Budgeting Decisions," *Akron Business and Economic Review*, October 1975, pp. 57–65.

Petty, J. William, and Oswald D. Bowlin. "The Financial Manager and Quantitative Decision Models," *Financial Management*, 4 (Winter 1976), 32–41.

Petty, J. William, David F. Scott, Jr., and Monroe M. Bird. "The Capital Expenditure Decision-Making Process of Large Corporations," *Engineering Economist*, 20 (Spring 1975), 159–72.

Quirin, G. David, and John C. Wiginton, *Analyzing Capital Expenditures*. Homewood, IL: Richard D. Irwin, 1981.

Rappaport, Alfred, and Robert A. Taggart, Jr. "Evaluation of Capital Expenditure Proposals Under Inflation," *Financial Management*, 11 (Spring 1982), 5–13.

Rosenblatt, Meir J. "A Survey and Analysis of Capital Budgeting Decision Process in Multi-Division Firms," *Engineering Economist*, 25 (Summer 1980), 259–73.

Ross, Marc. "Capital Budgeting Practices of Twelve Large Manufacturers," *Financial Management*, 15 (Winter 1986), 15–22.

Sarnat, Marshall, and Haim Levy. "The Relationship of Rules of Thumb to the Internal Rate of Return: A Restatement and Generalization," *Journal of Finance*, 24 (June 1969), 479–90.

Schall, Laurence D., Gary L. Sundem, and William R. Geljsbeek, Jr. "Survey and Analysis of Capital Budgeting Methods," *Journal of Finance*, 33 (March 1978), 281–87.

Schnell, James S., and Roy S. Nicholosi. "Capital Expenditure Feedback: Project Reappraisal," *Engineering Economist*, 19 (Summer 1974), 253–61.

Schwab, Bernhard, and Peter Lusztig. "A Comparative Analysis of the Net Present Value and the Benefit-Cost Ratios as Measures of the Economic Desirability of Investments," *Journal of Finance*, 24 (June 1969), 507–16.

Solomon, Ezra. "The Arithmetic of Capital-Budgeting Decisions," *Journal of Business*, 29 (April 1956), 124–29.

Statman, Meir, and Tyzoon T. Tyebjee. "Optimistic Capital Budgeting Forecasts," *Financial Management*, 14 (Autumn 1985), 27–33.

Teichroew, Daniel, Alexander A. Robichek, and Michael Montalbano. "An Analysis of Criteria for Investment and Financing Decisions under Certainty," *Management Science*, 12 (November 1965), 151–79.

Viscione, Jerry, and John Neuhauser. "Capital Expenditure Decisions in Moderately Sized Firms," *Financial Review* (1974), pp. 16–23.

Weaver, James B. "Organizing and Maintaining a Capital Expenditure Program," *Engineering Economist*, 20 (Fall 1974), 1–36.

Weingartner, H. Martin. *Mathematical Programming and the Analysis of Capital Budgeting Problems*. Copyright H. Martin Weingartner, 1963.

———. "Capital Rationing: n Authors in Search of a Plot," *Journal of Finance*, 32 (December 1977), 1403–31.

11

Capital Budgeting Under Uncertainty

In discussing capital budgeting techniques in the previous chapter, we implicity assumed the level of risk associated with each investment proposal was the same. In this chapter we will lift that assumption and examine various ways in which risk can be incorporated into the capital budgeting decision. To do this we will first discuss the concept of risk and then move on to its measurement, followed by a discussion of various methods for incorporating it into the decision-making process. We conclude with a discussion of portfolio risk.

RISK AND THE INVESTMENT DECISION

Up to this point we have ignored risk; that is, we have treated the expected cash flows resulting from an investment proposal as being known with perfect certainty. In reality the future cash flows associated with the introduction of a new sales outlet or a new product are merely estimates of what is expected to happen in the future, not necessarily what will happen in the future. For example, when the Ford Motor Company made its decision to introduce the Edsel, you can bet that the expected cash flows it based its decision on were nothing like the cash flows it realized. In effect, the cash flows we have assumed known with perfect certainty have in actuality merely been our best estimate of the expected future cash flows. A cash flow diagram based on the possible outcomes of an investment proposal rather than the expected values of these outcomes appears in Figure 11–1.

In this chapter we will assume that under risk we do not know beforehand what cash flows will actually result from a new project. However, we do have expectations concerning the possible outcomes and are able to assign probabilities to these outcomes. Stated another way, although we do not know what the cash flows resulting from

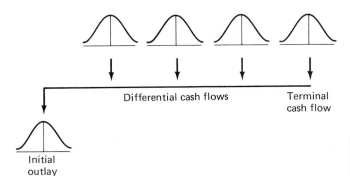

FIGURE 11–1. Cash Flow Diagram Based on Possible Outcomes

the acceptance of a new project will be, we can formulate the probability distributions from which the flows will be drawn.

Thus far, we have talked about risk only in a general manner, indicating that risk occurs when there is some question as to what the future outcome of an event will be. Now we will define risk in such a way that statistical measures of risk become possible. We will then proceed with an examination of the logic behind this definition. **Risk** can be defined as a relative measure of the degree of variability of possible outcomes over time. Thus, when risk is applied to the capital-budgeting area, we are concerned with the variability or range of possible outcomes for the project's net present value.

The fact that the degree of variability causes the risk can easily be shown by examining a coin toss game. Consider the possibility of flipping a coin—heads you win, tails you lose—for 25 cents with your finance professor. Most likely you would be willing to take on this game, indicating that the utility gained from winning 25 cents is about equal to the utility lost if you lose 25 cents. On the other hand, if the flip is for $1000 you may be willing to play only if you are offered more than $1000 if you win, say $1500 if it comes out heads. That is to say, you will only accept the game if you win $1500 if it turns out heads and lose $1000 if it turns out tails. In each case the probability of winning and losing is the same; that is, there is an equal chance of the coin's landing heads or tails; but the width of the dispersion changes, and that is why the second coin toss is more risky and why it will not be taken unless the payoffs are altered. The key here is the fact that only the dispersion changes; the probability of winning or losing is the same in each case. Thus, the dispersion causes the risk.

The final question to be addressed is whether or not individuals are in fact risk-averse, given their behavior in state lotteries, at racetracks, and at Las Vegas. While we do see people gambling where the odds of winning are against them, it should be stressed that the monetary return from this action is not the only return they receive. They also receive a nonmonetary, psychic reward when gambling, allowing them to fantasize that they will break the bank, never have to work again, and retire to some offshore island. Actually, the heart of the question is how wealth is measured. While these people appear to be acting as risk-seekers, they actually attach an additional nonmonetary return to gambling, and if this is considered, their actions seem totally rational. It should also be noted that while these people appear to be pursuing risk on one hand, on the other hand they are also eliminating risk by purchasing insurance and diversifying their investments.

Thus far we have made several points. First, in the previous chapter we made the implicit assumption that the cash flows being evaluated were known with complete certainty, which is not true. In the remainder of this chapter it will be assumed that while future cash flows are not known with certainty, the probability distribution from which they come is known. Second, we have illustrated the fact that it is the dispersion of the probability distribution that causes the risk. Thus, later when we quantify risk, a measure of dispersion will be used. Finally, some behavior, for example, gambling, seems to indicate that not all individuals are risk-averse. Yet when the intangible rewards are considered, the behavior of these individuals becomes congruent with that of other, risk-averse individuals.

QUANTITATIVE RISK MEASURES

When risk is considered in the capital-budgeting decision, each project must be evaluated with respect to both return and risk. Before describing two risk measures, we will explore probability distributions and the concept of the expected return, which will serve as our measure of return in this chapter.

Probability Distributions

Probability distributions illustrate the complete set of probabilities over all possible outcomes for that particular event. There are two general types of probability distributions—discrete and continuous. A **discrete probability distribution** is one in which a probability is assigned to each possible outcome in the set of all possible outcomes. For example, if we are considering a coin toss, there would be two possible outcomes, each with a .50 probability of occurring; if we were considering a horse race with 10 horses, there would be 10 possible outcomes, with the probability of each outcome depending on the speed of each horse. An investment opportunity with five possible outcomes, as shown in Table 11–1, is another example of a discrete distribution.

This distribution is illustrated graphically in Figure 11–2, giving us a picture of all the possible outcomes and the probabilities associated with them.

Note that the sum of all probabilities attached to all possible outcomes must add up to 1.0. This is because one of these outcomes must occur; otherwise all possible outcomes have not been identified.

Whereas in a discrete probability distribution probabilities are assigned to specific outcomes, in a **continuous probability distribution** there are an infinite number

TABLE 11–1. A Discrete Probability Distribution

Possible Outcome (X_i)	Probability of Occurrence $P(X_i)$
$ 5,000	.10
$ 7,000	.25
$ 8,000	.30
$ 9,000	.25
$11,000	.10

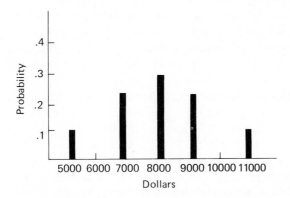

FIGURE 11–2. A Discrete Probability Distribution

of possible outcomes, in which the probability of an event is related to a range of possible outcomes. The easiest way to illustrate a continuous distribution is graphically, as in Figure 11–3. Probability in this case is measured by the area under the curve.

Thus, when provided with a continuous distribution, we can answer the question, What is the probability that an outcome will fall within a certain range of values? A discrete distribution, on the other hand, lets us answer the question, What is the probability that a specific outcome will occur? The key to understanding the difference between these questions—and the underlying differences between these classifications of distributions—is that for discrete distributions the number of possible outcomes is finite, while for continuous distributions it is infinite.

While continuous distributions are quite common and valuable, in general they require a degree of calculus that might be confusing. Thus, in the remainder of the book we will be concerned primarily with discrete probability distributions.

Expected Value

The expected value of a distribution is the arithmetic mean or average of all possible outcomes, where those outcomes are weighted by the probability that each outcome will occur. Thus, the expected value, $\bar{X}$, can be calculated as follows:

$$\bar{X} = \sum_{i=1}^{N} X_i P(X_i) \qquad (11\text{–}1)$$

where N = the number of possible outcomes

X_i = the value of the ith possible outcome

$P(X_i)$ = the probability that the ith outcome will occur

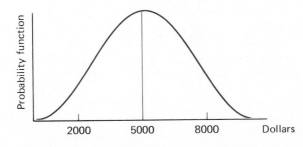

FIGURE 11–3. A Continuous Probability Distribution

To illustrate the computation of the expected value, consider the investment opportunity given in Table 11–1. To determine the expected value of this distribution, we need only multiply each possible outcome by its probability of occurrence and sum as follows:

$$\text{expected value} = \$5000(.10) + \$7000(.25) + \$8000(.30) + \$9000(.25)$$
$$+ \$11,000(.10)$$
$$= \$8000$$

In the previous chapter we ignored risk and took the expected value to be the only possible outcome. Reflecting back on this, it is easy to see that when we are estimating cash flows that are to occur in the future, we cannot estimate them with certainty. Therefore, the expected value only provides us with the mean of the probability distribution from which that future cash flow will come. While the expected value provides us with a measure of central tendency, it tells us nothing about the amount of dispersion contained in the probability distribution. To measure dispersion, we will examine the standard deviation and coefficient of variation.

Standard Deviation

The **standard deviation** provides a measure of the spread of the probability distribution. The larger the standard deviation, the greater the dispersion of the distribution. It is calculated by squaring the difference between each outcome and its expected value, weighting each value by its probability, summing over all possible outcomes, and taking the square root of this sum. Thus, the standard deviation becomes

$$\sigma = \sqrt{\sum_{i=1}^{N} (X_i - \bar{X})^2 P(X_i)} \qquad (11\text{–}2)$$

where
N = the number of possible outcomes

X_i = the value of the ith possible outcome

$\bar{X}$ = the expected value

$P(X_i)$ = the probability that the ith outcome will occur

The calculations for the standard deviation for the distribution given in Table 11–1 are provided in Table 11–2.

In the case of a normal distribution,[1] The standard deviation gives us even more than a measure of the absolute dispersion of that distribution. In this case we can, by consulting a table of areas under the normal curve, determine the probability that the outcome will be above or below a specific value. For example, in a normal distribution there is a 68.3 percent probability that the outcome will be within one standard deviation plus or minus of the expected value and a 95.0 percent probability that it will be within two standard deviations. Thus, if we are looking at two normal

---

[1] A **normal distribution** is a special class of bell-shaped distributions with symmetrically decreasing density where the curve approaches but never reaches the X axis.

TABLE 11–2.   Calculation of the Standard Deviation for the Distribution in Table 11–1

Step 1: Calculate Differences $(X_i - \bar{X})$	Step 2: Square Differences $(X_i - \bar{X})^2$	Step 2: Squared Differences Times Probabilities $(X_i - \bar{X})^2 P(X_i)$
$ 5,000 - \$8,000 = - \$3,000$	$9,000,000$	$9,000,000(.10) = \$900,000$
$7,000 - 8,000 = - 1,000$	$1,000,000$	$1,000,000(.25) = 250,000$
$8,000 - 8,000 = 0$	0	$0(.30) = 0$
$9,000 - 8,000 = 1,000$	$1,000,000$	$1,000,000(.25) = 250,000$
$11,000 - 8,000 = 3,000$	$9,000,000$	$9,000,000(.10) = \underline{900,000}$

	Step 5: Take the Square Root
Step 4: Sum	

$$\sum_{i=1}^{N} (X_i - \bar{X})^2 P(X_i) = \$2,300,000 \qquad\qquad \sigma = \sqrt{\sum_{i=1}^{N} (X_i - \bar{X})^2 P(X_i)} = \underline{\underline{\$1,517}}$$

distributions, one with an expected value of $1000 and a standard deviation of $200, the other with an expected value of $2000 and a standard deviation of $300, we can conclude that the second distribution has more dispersion, and hence more absolute risk associated with it. This does not mean that the second distribution is less desirable, just that it has more absolute risk. While the standard deviation gives us a good measure of a distribution's absolute dispersion, it is also desirable to measure dispersion or risk relative to return to provide the manager with a relative measure of risk. This is the purpose of the coefficient of variation.

Coefficient of Variation

The **coefficient of variation** provides us with a measure of the relative dispersion of a probability distribution—that is, the risk per unit of return. Mathematically, it is defined as the standard deviation divided by the expected value, or

$$\gamma = \frac{\sigma}{\bar{X}} \qquad\qquad (11\text{–}3)$$

This measure derives its value from the fact that using the standard deviation to compare the riskiness of two projects can be misleading when the projects are of unequal size.

For example, let us look at two normal distributions given in Table 11–3. In this

TABLE 11–3.   Coefficient of Variation

		Project A	Project B
Expected value	$\bar{X}$	$1,000	$2000
Standard deviation	σ	$ 200	$ 300
Coefficient of variation	$\sigma/\bar{X}$	0.20	0.15

case distribution B has more absolute risk, as indicated by its standard deviation; however, distribution A has more risk associated with it relative to its expected value. The value of examining the relative risk can easily be seen when examining distributions containing the same level of absolute risk or standard deviation but dramatically different levels of expected value. For example, consider two projects, both with standard deviations of $1000, one having an expected value of $1000 while the other has an expected value of $1,000,000. In each case the absolute risk is the same, as measured by the standard deviation, but the relative risk is not. Thus, the use of the coefficient of variation along with the standard deviation is especially important when two projects of unequal size are being compared. To ignore the coefficient of variation in this case could lead to misconceptions as to the relative level of uncertainty contained in each project.

METHODS FOR INCORPORATING RISK INTO CAPITAL BUDGETING

In the previous chapter we ignored any risk differences between projects. Unfortunately, this assumption was not valid; different investment projects do in fact contain different levels of risk. We will now look at several methods for incorporating risk into the analysis. The first technique, the certainty equivalent approach, attempts to incorporate the manager's utility function into the analysis. The second technique, the risk-adjusted discount rate, is based on the notion that investors require higher rates of return on more risky projects.

Certainty Equivalent Approach

The **certainty equivalent approach** involves a direct attempt to allow the decision maker to incorporate his utility function into the analysis. The financial manager is allowed to substitute the certain dollar amount that he or she feels is equivalent to the expected but risky cash flow offered by the investment for that risky cash flow in the capital budgeting analysis. In effect, a set of riskless cash flows is substituted for the original risky cash flows, between both of which the financial manager is indifferent. To a certain extent this process is like the old television program "Let's Make a Deal." On that show Monty Hall asked contestants to trade certain outcomes for uncertain outcomes. In some cases contestants were willing to make a trade, and in some cases they were not; it all depended upon how risk-averse they were. The main difference between what we are doing and what was done on "Let's Make a Deal" is that on the TV show contestants were in general not indifferent between the certain outcome and the risky outcome, while in the certainty equivalent approach they are indifferent between the two outcomes.

To illustrate the concept of a certainty equivalent, let us look at a simple coin toss. Assume you can only play the game once and if it comes out heads, you win $10,000, and if it comes out tails you win nothing. Obviously, you have a 50 percent chance of winning $10,000 and a 50 percent chance of winning nothing, with an expected value of $5000. Thus, $5000 is your uncertain expected value outcome. The certainty equivalent then becomes the amount you would demand to make you indifferent between playing and not playing the game. If you are indifferent between receiving $3000 for certain and not playing the game, then $3000 is the certainty equivalent. Relating this back to the "Let's Make a Deal" example, often Monty Hall would offer contestants their choice of money or what was behind door number 2.

In doing this he would offer the contestant more and more money until the contestant did not know what to do. At that point, when the contestant was jumping up and down, indifferent between his two choices, Monty had found the "door" or uncertain outcome's certainty equivalent. The dollar value that made the contestant indifferent between the money and what was behind the "door" is the certainty equivalent of the "door."

In order to simplify future calculations and problems, let us define certainty equivalent coefficients (α_t) that represent the ratio of the certain outcome to the risky outcome, between which the financial manager is indifferent. In equation form, α_t can be represented as follows:

$$\alpha_t = \frac{\text{certain cash flow}_t}{\text{risky cash flow}_t} \tag{11--4}$$

Thus, the αs can vary between 0, in the case of extreme risk, and 1, in the case of certainty. To obtain the value of the equivalent certain cash flow, we need only multiply the risky cash flow and the α_t. When this is done, we are indifferent between this certain cash flow and the risky cash flow. In the previous example of the simple coin toss, the certain cash flow was $3000, while the risky cash flow was $5000, the expected value of the coin toss; thus, the certainty equivalent coefficient is 3000/5000 = .6. Thus, in summary, by multiplying the certainty equivalent coefficient (α_t) times the expected but risky cash flow, we can determine an equivalent certain cash flow.

Once this risk is taken out of the project's cash flows, those cash flows are discounted back to present at the risk-free rate of interest, and the project's net present value or profitability index is determined. If the internal rate of return is calculated, it is then compared with the risk-free rate of interest rather than the firm's required rate of return in determining whether or not it should be accepted or rejected. The certainty equivalent method can be summarized as follows:

$$NPV = \sum_{t=1}^{n} \frac{\alpha_t ACF_t}{(1 + i_F)^t} - IO \tag{11--5}$$

where α_t = the certainty equivalent coefficient in time period t

ACF_t = the annual after-tax expected cash flow in time period t

IO = the initial cash outlay

n = the project's expected life

i_F = the risk-free interest rate

Let us examine a graphic presentation of the concept of certainty equivalents to illustrate its meaning. Assume that we can plot annual cash flows in risk-return space and that ACF_1 and ACF_2 in Figure 11--4 represent the location of the annual after-tax net cash flows during years 1 and 2. If I_1 and I_2 represent indifference curves of the decision maker, then $\alpha_1 ACF_1$ and $\alpha_2 ACF_2$ represent riskless equivalents of ACF_1 and ACF_2. As is evident from Figure 11--4, ACF_2 is riskier than ACF_1, and thus is scaled

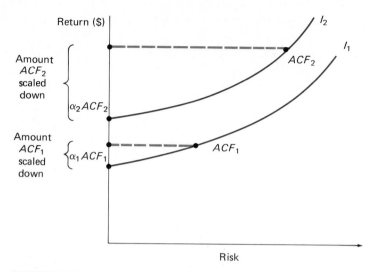

FIGURE 11–4. Certainty Equivalents

down more. The degree to which the risky cash flows are scaled down—that is, how small the α_t is—will depend upon (a) the amount of risk or dispersion associated with the subjective probability distribution assigned to the expected annual cash flow: the more risk, the lower the α_t value; (b) the decision maker's feelings about the attractiveness of the distribution's form: the more attractive the distribution, the higher the α_t values; and (c) to what extent the random variations in the annual cash flows from this project are expected to cancel out with variations in flows from other projects: the more variations that are canceled out, the higher the α_t values.[2]

The certainty equivalent approach can be summarized as follows:

STEP 1: *Risk is removed from the cash flows through substituting equivalent certain cash flows for the risky cash flows. If the certainty equivalent coefficient (α_t) is given, this is done by multiplying each risky cash flow by the appropriate α_t value.*

STEP 2: *These riskless cash flows are then discounted back to the present at the riskless rate of interest.*

STEP 3: *The normal capital-budgeting criteria are then applied, except in the case of the internal rate of return criterion, where the project's internal rate of return is compared with the risk-free rate of interest rather than the firm's required rate of return.*

Example A firm with a 10 percent required rate of return is considering building new research facilities with an expected life of 5 years. The initial outlay associated with this project involves a certain cash outflow of $120,000. The expected cash inflows and certainty equivalent coefficients, α_t, are as follows:

---

[2] These last two types of risk—risk associated with nonnormal distributions and risk in a portfolio concept— will be dealt with more fully later in the chapter.

Year	Expected Cash Flow	Certainty Equivalent Coefficient, α_t
1	$10,000	.95
2	20,000	.90
3	40,000	.85
4	80,000	.75
5	80,000	.65

The risk-free rate of interest is 6 percent. What is the project's net present value?

To determine the net present value of this project using the certainty equivalent approach, we must first remove the risk from the future cash flows. We do so by multiplying each expected cash flow by the corresponding certainty equivalent coefficient, α_t.

Expected Cash Flow	Certainty Equivalent Coefficient, α_t	$\alpha_t \times$ (Expected Cash Flow) = Equivalent Riskless Cash Flow
$10,000	.95	$ 9,500
20,000	.90	18,000
40,000	.85	34,000
80,000	.75	60,000
80,000	.65	52,000

The equivalent riskless cash flows are then discounted back to the present at the riskless interest rate, not the firm's required rate of return. The required rate of return would be used if this project had the same level of risk as a typical project for this firm. However, these equivalent cash flows have no risk at all; hence, the appropriate discount rate is the riskless rate of interest. The equivalent riskless cash flows can be discounted back to present at the riskless rate of interest, 6 percent, as follows:

Year	Equivalent Riskless Cash Flow	Present Value Factor at 6 Percent	Present Value
1	$ 9,500	.943	$ 8,958.50
2	18,000	.890	16,020.00
3	34,000	.840	28,560.00
4	60,000	.792	47,520.00
5	52,000	.747	38,844.00

$$NPV = -\$120,000 + \$8958.50 + \$16,020 + \$28,560 + \$47,520$$
$$+ \$38,844$$
$$= \$19,902.50$$

Applying the normal capital budgeting decision criteria, we find that the project should be accepted, as its net present value is greater than zero.

Risk-Adjusted Discount Rates

The use of risk-adjusted discount rates is based on the concept that investors demand higher returns for more risky projects. This relationship between risk and return is illustrated graphically in Figure 11–5.

The required rate of return on any investment should include compensation for delaying consumption equal to the risk-free rate of return, plus compensation for any risk taken on. If the risk associated with the investment is greater than the risk involved in a typical endeavor, the discount rate is adjusted upward to compensate for this added risk. Once the firm determines the appropriate required rate of return for a project with a given level of risk, the cash flows are discounted back to present at the risk-adjusted discount rate. Then the normal capital budgeting criteria are applied, except in the case of the internal rate of return, in which case the hurdle rate with which the project's internal rate of return is compared now becomes the risk-adjusted discount rate. Expressed mathematically, the net present value using the risk-adjusted discount rate becomes

$$NPV = \sum_{t=1}^{n} \frac{ACF_t}{(1 + i^*)^t} - IO \qquad (11\text{–}6)$$

where ACF_t = the annual after-tax expected cash flow in time period t

IO = the initial cash outlay

i^* = the risk-adjusted discount rate

n = the project's expected life

The logic behind the risk-adjusted discount rate stems from the idea that if the level of risk in a project is different from that in the typical firm project, then the management must incorporate the shareholders' probable reaction to this new endeavor into the decision-making process. If the project has more risk than a typical project, then a higher required rate of return should apply. Otherwise, marginal projects will lower the firm's share price—that is, reduce shareholders' wealth. This will occur as the market raises its required rate of return on the firm to reflect the addition of a more risky project, while the incremental cash flows resulting from the acceptance of the new project are not large enough to fully offset this change. By the same logic, if the project has less than normal risk, a reduction in the required rate of return is appropriate. Thus, the risk-adjusted discount method attempts to apply more

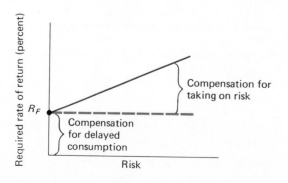

FIGURE 11–5. Risk-Return Relationship

stringent standards—that is, require a higher rate of return—to projects that will increase the firm's risk level. This is because these projects will lead shareholders to demand a higher required rate of return to compensate them for the higher risk level of the firm. If this adjustment is not made, the marginal projects containing above-average risk could actually lower the firm's share price.

Example A toy manufacturer is considering the introduction of a line of fishing equipment with an expected life of 5 years. In the past, this firm has been quite conservative in its investment in new products, sticking primarily to standard toys. In this context, the introduction of a line of fishing equipment is considered an abnormally risky project. Management feels that the normal required rate of return for the firm of 10 percent is not sufficient. Instead, the minimally acceptable rate of return on this project should be 15 percent. The initial outlay would be $110,000, and the expected cash flows from this project are as given below:

Year	Expected Cash Flow
1	$30,000
2	30,000
3	30,000
4	30,000
5	30,000

Discounting this annuity back to the present at 15 percent yields a present value of the future cash flows of $100,560. Since the initial outlay on this project is $110,000, the net present value becomes −$9440, and the project should be rejected. If the normal required rate of return of 10 percent had been used as the discount rate, the project would have been accepted with a net present value of $3730.

In practice, when the risk-adjusted discount rate is used, projects are generally grouped according to purpose, or risk class; then the discount rate preassigned to that purpose or risk class is used. For example, a firm with a required rate of return of 12 percent might use the following rate-of-return categorization:

Project	Required Rate of Return
Replacement decision	12%
Modification or expansion of existing product line	15
Project unrelated to current operations	18
Research and development operations	25

The purpose of this categorization of projects is to make their evaluation easier, but it also introduces an arbitrariness into the calculations that makes the evaluation less meaningful. The tradeoffs involved in the classification above are obvious; time and effort are minimized, but only at the cost of precision.

TABLE 11–4. Computational Steps in the Certainty Equivalent and Risk-Adjusted Discount Rate Methods

Certainty Equivalent	Risk-Adjusted Discount Rate
STEP 1: Adjust the expected cash flows, ACF_t, downward for risk by multiplying them by the corresponding certainty equivalent coefficient, α_t.	STEP 1: Adjust the discount rate upward for risk.
STEP 2: Discount the certainty equivalent, risk-less, cash flows back to the present using the *risk-free rate of interest*.	STEP 2: Discount the expected cash flows back to present using the risk-adjusted discount rate.
STEP 3: Apply the normal decision criteria, except in the case of the internal rate of return, where the risk-free rate of interest replaces the required rate of return as the hurdle rate.	STEP 3: Apply the normal decision criteria, except in the case of the internal rate of return, where the risk-adjusted discount rate replaces the required rate of return as the hurdle rate.

Certainty Equivalent versus Risk-Adjusted Discount Rate Methods

The primary difference between the certainty equivalent approach and the risk-adjusted discount rate approach involves the point at which the adjustment for risk is incorporated into the calculations. The certainty equivalent penalizes or adjusts downward the value of the expected annual after-tax cash flows, ACF_t, which results in a lower net present value for a risky project. The risk-adjusted discount rate, on the other hand, leaves the cash flows at their expected value and adjusts the required rate of return, i, upward to compensate for added risk. In either case the project's net present value is being adjusted downward to compensate for additional risk. The computational differences are illustrated in Table 11–4.

In addition to the difference in point of adjustment for risk, the risk-adjusted discount rate makes the implicit assumption that risk becomes greater as we move further out in time. While this is not necessarily a good or bad assumption, we should be aware of it and understand it. In this regard, it should be helpful to look at an example in which the risk-adjusted discount rate is used and then determine what certainty equivalent coefficients, α_t, would be necessary to arrive at the same solution.

Example   Assume that a firm with a required rate of return of 10 percent is considering introducing a new product. This product has an initial outlay of $800,000, an expected life of 15 years, and after-tax cash flows of $100,000 each year during its life. Because of the increased risk associated with this project, management is requiring a 15 percent rate of return. Let us also assume that the risk-free rate of return is 6 percent.

If the firm chose to use the certainty equivalent method, the certainty equivalent cash flows would be discounted back to the present at 6 percent, the risk-free rate of interest. The present value of the $100,000 cash flow occurring at the end of the first year discounted back to present at 15 percent is $87,000. The present value of this $100,000 flow discounted back to present at the risk-free rate of 6 percent is $94,300. Thus, if the certainty equivalent approach were used, a certainty equivalent coefficient, α_1, of .9226 would be necessary to produce a present value of $87,000. In other words, the same results can be obtained in the first year by using the risk-adjusted discount rate and adjusting the discount rate up to 15 percent or by using the certainty equivalent approach and adjusting the expected cash flows by a certainty equivalent coefficient of .9226.

Under the risk-adjusted discount rate, the present value of the $100,000 cash flow occurring at the end of the second year becomes $75,600, and to produce an identical present value under the certainty equivalent approach, a certainty equivalent coefficient of .8494 would be needed. Following this through for the life of the project yields the certainty equivalent coefficients given in Table 11–5.

What does this analysis suggest? It indicates that if the risk-adjusted discount rate method is used, we are adjusting downward the value of future cash flows that occur further in the future more severely than earlier cash flows. We can easily see this by comparing equations (11–5) and (11–6). The net present value using the risk-adjusted discount rate is expressed as

$$NPV = \sum_{t=1}^{n} \frac{ACF_t}{(1 + i^*)^t} - IO \tag{11-6}$$

and the certainty equivalent net present value is measured by

$$NPV = \sum_{t=1}^{n} \frac{\alpha_t ACF_t}{(1 + i_F)^t} - IO \tag{11-5}$$

Thus, for the net present values under each approach to be equivalent, the following must be true:

$$\frac{ACF_t}{(1 + i^*)^t} = \frac{\alpha_t ACF_t}{(1 + i_F)^t} \tag{11-7}$$

TABLE 11–5. Certainty Equivalent Coefficients Yielding the Same Results as the Risk-Adjusted Discount Rate of 15 Percent in the Illustrative Example

Year:	1	2	3	4	5	6	7	8	9	10
α_t:	.9226	.8494	.7833	.7222	.6653	.6128	.5654	.5215	.4797	.4427

Solving for α_t yields

$$\alpha_t = \frac{(1 + i_F)^t}{(1 + i^*)^t} = \left(\frac{1 + i_F}{1 + i^*}\right)^t \tag{11-8}$$

Thus, since i_F and i^* are constants and i^* is greater than i_F, the value of α_t, or $[(1 + i_F)/(1 + i^*)]^t$, must decrease as t increases for the present values under each approach to be equivalent. This is exactly what we concluded from Table 11–5.

In summary, the use of the risk-adjusted discount rate assumes that risk increases over time and that cash flows occurring further in the future should be more severely penalized.

OTHER APPROACHES TO RISK IN CAPITAL BUDGETING ————————

Simulation   Another method for incorporating risk into the investment decision is through the use of **simulation.** Whereas the certainty equivalent and risk-adjusted discount rate approaches provided us with a single value for the risk-adjusted net present value, a simulation approach gives us a probability distribution for the investment's net present value or internal rate of return. The idea behind simulation is to imitate the performance of the project being evaluated. This is done by randomly selecting observations from each of the distributions that affect the outcome of the project, combining those observations to determine the final output of the project, and continuing with this process until a representative record of the project's probable outcome is assembled.

The easiest way to develop an understanding of the computer simulation process is to follow through an example simulation for an investment project evaluation. Suppose a chemical producer is considering an extension to its processing plant. The simulation process is portrayed in Figure 11–6. First the probability distributions are determined for all the factors that affect the project's returns; in this case, let us assume there are nine such variables:

1. Market size
2. Selling price
3. Market growth rate
4. Share of market (which results in physical sales volume)
5. Investment required
6. Residual value of investment
7. Operating costs
8. Fixed costs
9. Useful life of facilities

Then the computer randomly selects one observation from each of the probability distributions, according to its chance of actually occuring in the future. These nine observations are combined, and a net present value or internal rate of return figure is calculated. This process is repeated as many times as desired, until a representative distribution of possible future outcomes is assembled. Thus, the inputs to a simulation include all the principal factors affecting the project's profitability, and the simulation output is a probability distribution of net present values or internal rates of return for the project. The decision maker bases the decision on the full range of possible outcomes. The project is accepted if the decision maker feels that enough of the distribution lies above the normal cutoff criteria ($NPV > 0$, $IRR >$ required rate of return).

Suppose that the output from the simulation of the chemical producer's project is as given in Figure 11–7. The firm's managers will examine the probability distribution, and if they consider enough of the distribution of possible net present values to be greater than zero, they will accept the project.

Use of a simulation approach to analyze investment proposals offers two major advantages. First, the financial managers are able to examine and base their decisions on the whole range of possible outcomes rather than just point estimates. Second, they can undertake subsequent sensitivity analysis of the project. That is, by modifying

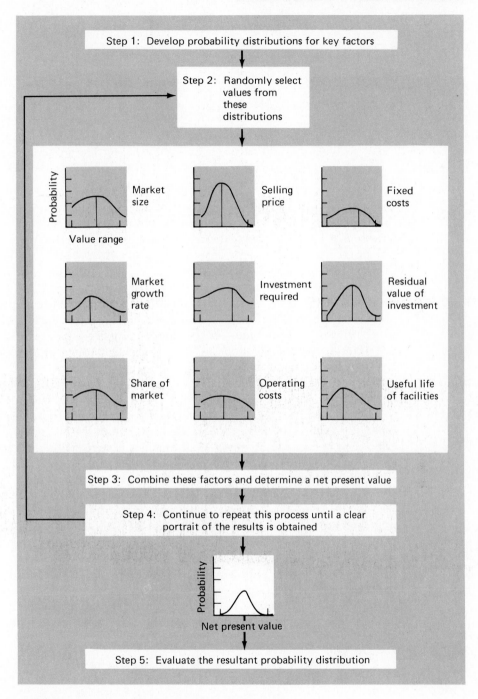

FIGURE 11–6.   Capital Budgeting Simulation

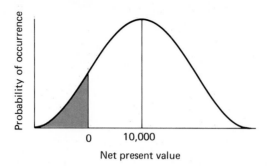

FIGURE 11–7. Output from Simulation

assumptions made about the values and ranges of the input factors and rerunning the simulation, the management can determine how sensitive the outcome of the project is to these changes. If the output appears to be highly sensitive to one or two of the input factors, the management may then wish to spend additional time refining those input estimates.

Probability Trees

A **probability tree** is a graphic exposition of the sequence of possible outcomes, presenting the decision maker with a schematic representation of the problem in which all possible outcomes are graphically displayed. Moreover, the computations and results of the computations are shown directly on the tree, so that the information can be easily understood.

To illustrate the use of a probability tree, suppose a firm is considering an investment proposal that requires an initial outlay of $1 million and will yield resultant cash flows for the next two years and that the risk-free rate is 10 percent. During the first year let us assume there are three possible outcomes, as shown in Table 11–6. Graphically, each of these three possible alternatives is represented on the probability tree in Figure 11–8 as one of the three possible branches.

The second step in the probability tree is to continue drawing branches in a similar manner so that each of the possible outcomes during the second year is represented by a new branch. For example, if outcome 1 occurs in year 1, a 20 percent chance of a $300,000 cash flow and an 80 percent chance of a $600,000 cash flow in year 2 have been projected. Two branches would be sent out from the outcome 1 node, reflecting these two possible outcomes. The cash flows that occur if outcome 1 takes place and the probabilities associated with them are called **conditional outcomes** and **conditional probabilities** because they can only occur if outcome 1 occurs during the first year. Finally, to determine the probability of the sequence of a $600,000 flow in year 1 and a $300,000 outcome in year 2, the probability of the $600,000

TABLE 11–6. Possible Outcomes in Year 1

	Probability		
	.5 Outcome 1	.3 Outcome 2	.2 Outcome 3
Cash flow	$600,000	$700,000	$800,000

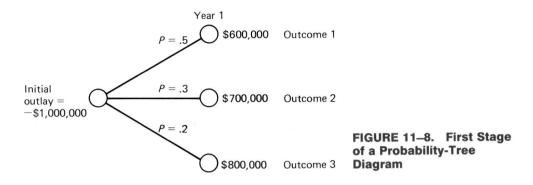

Year 1

$P = .5$ $600,000 Outcome 1

Initial
outlay =
−$1,000,000

$P = .3$ $700,000 Outcome 2

$P = .2$

$800,000 Outcome 3

**FIGURE 11–8. First Stage
of a Probability-Tree
Diagram**

flow (.5) is multiplied by the conditional probability of the second flow (.2), telling
us that this sequence has a 10 percent chance of occurring, which is called its **joint
probability.** Letting the values in Table 11–7 represent the conditional outcomes
and their respective conditional probabilities, we can complete the probability tree,
as shown in Figure 11–9.

The financial manager, by examining the probability tree, is provided with the
expected value for the investment, the range of possible outcomes, and a listing of
each possible outcome with the probability associated with it. In this case the expected
value is $66,634, and there is a 10 percent chance of incurring the worst possible
outcome with a net present value of −$206,800. There is also a 2 percent probability
of achieving the most favorable outcome, a net present value of $388,000.

In using a probability tree we are trying to separate the analysis of the timing of
the cash flows from a project (the discounting) and the analysis of risk. First the
flows will be discounted back to present, and then the distribution of possible net
present values unadjusted for risk will be analyzed. Thus, the discount rate used to
discount the future cash flows back to present when evaluating a probability tree is
the risk-free rate of return rather than the firm's normal required rate of return. The
logic is that in using a probability tree we are not trying to compensate for risk or
extract it from the distribution, but merely to adjust the flows for the time value of
money. The decision maker can then examine the entire distribution of possible
outcomes and subjectively decide if it is too risky or not.

The firm's required rate of return already has a premium for risk included in a
typical project of that firm; thus, if we did use the firm's normal required rate of
return, we would be double-counting for risk—once when we discount the flows

TABLE 11–7. Conditional Outcomes and Probabilities for Year 2

Year 1	If Outcome 1 $ACF_1 = \$600,000$		If Outcome 2 $ACF_1 = \$700,000$		If Outcome 3 $ACF_1 = \$800,000$	
Year 2	ACF_2	Then Probability	ACF_2	Then Probability	ACF_2	Then Probability
	$300,000	.2	$300,000	.2	$400,000	.2
	600,000	.8	500,000	.3	600,000	.7
			700,000	.5	800,000	.1

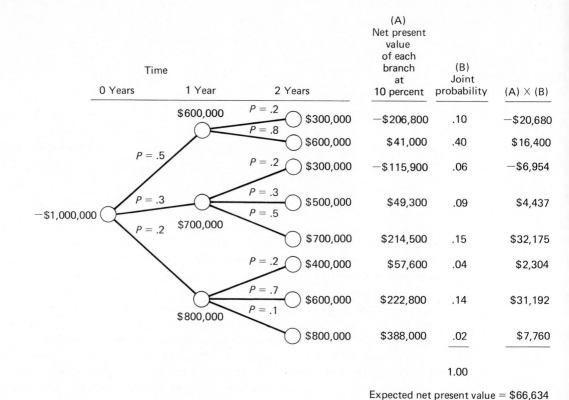

FIGURE 11–9. Probability Tree

back to present at the firm's normal discount rate (which includes an adjustment for risk), and again when the distribution of possible net present values is analyzed. To avoid this double-counting for risk, the risk-free rate of return will be used.

Decision making with probability trees does not mean the acceptance of any project with a positive expected net present value, because in calculating the expected net present value we have not yet allowed for risk. As a result, the decision maker must examine the entire distribution of possible net present values and from that decide, given his or her aversion to risk, if enough of this distribution is positive enough to warrant acceptance of the project. The probability tree allows the manager quickly to visualize the possible future events, their probabilities, and their outcomes. In addition, the calculation of the expected net present value and enumeration of the distribution should aid the financial manager in making decisions.

OTHER SOURCES AND MEASURES OF RISK ─────────────────

Time Dependence of Cash Flows

Up to this point, in all approaches other than the probability tree we have assumed the cash flow in one period is independent of the cash flow in the previous period. While this assumption is appealing because of its simplifying nature, in many cases it is invalid. For example, if a new product is introduced and the initial public reaction is poor, resulting in low initial cash flows, then cash flows in future periods are likely to be low. An extreme example of this is Ford's experience with the Edsel. Poor consumer acceptance and sales in the first year were followed by even poorer results in the second year. If the Edsel had been received favorably during its first year, it quite likely would have done well in the second year. The end effect of time dependence of cash flows is to increase the risk of the project over time. That is, since large cash flows in the first period lead to large cash flows in the second period, and low cash flows in the first period lead to low cash flows in the second period, the probability distribution of possible net present values tends to be wider than if the cash flows were not dependent over time. The greater the degree of correlation between flows over time, the greater will be the dispersion of the probability distribution.

Skewness   In all previous approaches other than simulation and probability trees, we have assumed that the distributions of net present values for projects being evaluated are normally distributed. Unfortunately, this assumption is not always valid. When it is true, the standard deviation provides an adequate measure of the distribution's dispersion; however, when the distribution is not normally distributed, reliance on the standard deviation can be misleading.

   A distribution that is not symmetric is said to be **skewed.** In this case, the distribution has either a longer "tail" to the right or to the left. For example, if a distribution is skewed to the right, most values will be clustered around the left end, and the distribution will appear to have a long tail on the right end of the range of values. Graphic illustrations of skewed distributions are presented in Figure 11–10.

   The difficulty associated with skewed distributions arises from the fact that the use of the expected value and standard deviation alone may not be enough to differentiate properly between two distributions. For example, the two distributions shown in Figure 11–11 have the same expected value and the same standard deviation; however, distribution A is skewed to the left while B is skewed to the right. If a financial manager were given a choice between these two distributions, assuming they are mutually exclusive, he or she would most likely choose distribution B, because it involves less chance of a negative net present value. Thus, skewness can affect the level of risk and the desirability of a distribution.

Portfolio Risk   Thus far in our analysis we have focused on the risk associated with each individual project under consideration. However, firms do not just invest in a single project but are generally involved in a number of projects at any one time. Therefore, we will now introduce the topic of the risk of projects in a portfolio context; that is, we will examine how the addition of a particular project will affect the overall riskiness of the firm. We will find that the addition of some projects, because of their particular

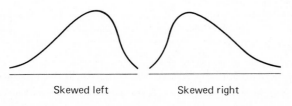

FIGURE 11–10. Examples of Skewed Distributions

Skewed left   Skewed right

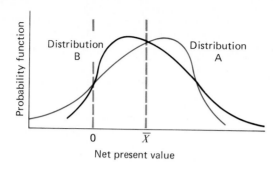

FIGURE 11–11. Two Distributions with Identical Expected Values and Standard Deviations But Different Skewness

cyclical patterns, is able to lower the overall riskiness of the firm better than the addition of other projects.

In the previous sections we have assumed that the mean and standard deviation were adequate measures of return and risk by which to judge a project. Now we are saying they may not be, provided the firm is involved in other projects. Why? First, some projects are complementary or involve economies of scale with other projects held by the firm. This condition might result when two projects share the same production facilities or the same marketing channels, or when the introduction of the new product may aid sales of a current product. As mentioned in Chapter 10, this complementary effect should be included in the relevant cash flows as incremental after-tax cash flows to the company as a whole. In other words, if there are any incremental cash flows to the company as a whole from the addition of the new project, even if they show up flowing into a previously existing project, they should be included in the capital-budgeting analysis. Thus, although the existence of complementary and economies-of-scale effects may be somewhat difficult to determine, they have already been allowed for in our capital-budgeting framework.

A second consideration is the potential diversification effect. If a project's cash flow patterns are cyclically divergent from those of the company, the overall risk of the company may be significantly reduced. In other words, when this project is added to the firm, the resultant risk level of the combination, as measured by the firm's standard deviation, may be less than the sum of the risk levels of the project and the firm held individually.

Before developing the implications of portfolio risk for capital budgeting, we will examine exactly how and why this diversification effect takes place.

Portfolio Risk: A Graphic Illustration The degree to which the diversification type portfolio effect takes place is a function of the relationship between the pattern of cash flows from the new project and the existing company. For example, let us look at a company that doubles its size by

TABLE 11–8. Cash Flows

	Normal	Recession	Expansion
Original firm	$1,000,000	$ 500,000	$1,500,000
New division	1,000,000	500,000	1,500,000
Combination	$2,000,000	$1,000,000	$3,000,000

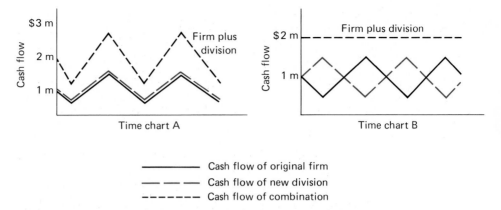

FIGURE 11–12. Diversification Effects on Cash Flow

adding a new division. First, assume that the cash flows from both the original company and the new division move directly with the business cycle. If we attach the dollar values given in Table 11–8 to this movement, the situation graphically depicted in chart A of Figure 11–12 is created. Examining the resultant variability of the combined cash flows, we see that when the cash flows move together, as in this case, their percentage variability remains the same. In this case there is no diversification portfolio effect. If, on the other hand, the new division produced cash flows that were countercyclical, the two series of cash flows would move in opposite directions, and a diversification portfolio effect would take place. If we attach the dollar values in Table 11–9 to this cash flow movement, the situation is as represented in chart B of Figure 11–12. In this case, because the variabilities of the cash flows of the original firm and the new division move in opposite directions, the variability of their combination is totally eliminated.

Obviously, the degree to which the total risk is reduced becomes a function of how the two sets of cash flows or returns move together. In order to measure this relationship, we use the concept of correlation. **Correlation** measures the linear relationship between any two sets of values. The **correlation coefficient,** a statistical measure, tells us two things about this relationship. First, it can take on either a positive or a negative sign. A positive sign indicates that the variables tend to move in the same direction; a negative sign, that they move in opposite directions. Also, the value that the correlation coefficient takes on, ranging from +1.0 down to −1.0, provides us with information about the degree or strength of this relationship. If its value is near zero, the linear relationship is weak; however, if the relationship is close to either +1.0 or −1.0, there is a strong linear relationship between the two

TABLE 11–9. Cash Flows

	Normal	Recession	Expansion
Original firm	$1,000,000	$ 500,000	$1,500,000
New division	1,000,000	1,500,000	500,000
Combination	$2,000,000	$2,000,000	$2,000,000

variables. Letting ρ denote the correlation coefficient, R_p the return on the new project, and R_{Firm} the return on the firm, Figure 11–13 graphically illustrates several possible situations.

The degree of correlation between projects takes on importance because it determines the extent to which the diversification portfolio effect will reduce the risk level of the combination. Negatively correlated combinations will provide the greatest level of risk reduction, while perfectly positively correlated projects, those with correla-

FIGURE 11–13.   Illustrations of Various Degrees of Correlation

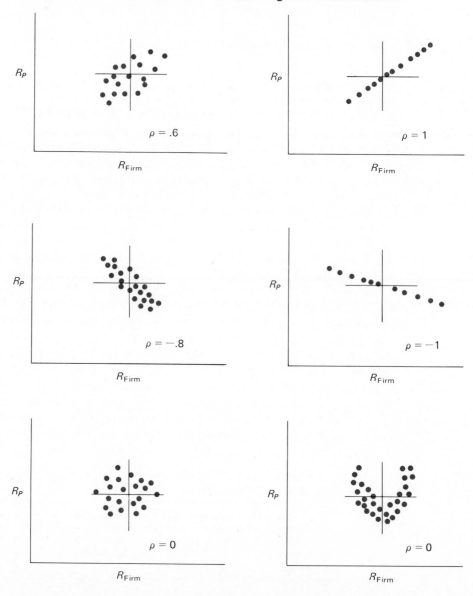

tion coefficients of $+1.0$, will not provide any diversification effect. If one thinks about it, it makes sense. Any impact from diversification results from combining projects with divergent return or cash flow patterns. If the correlation coefficient is 1.0, these patterns are identical; hence, there is no diversification value present. If, on the other hand, the correlation coefficient is -1.0, then the patterns move in opposite directions; hence, the diversification value is maximum.

Portfolio Risk:
A Mathematical
Illustration

To illustrate mathematically, suppose we are considering combining two assets, putting two-thirds of our money in investment A and the remaining third in investment B, and we want to determine the risk or standard deviation of this combination. The mathematical formula for the standard deviation of this two-asset combination is given in equations (11–9) and (11–10).

$$\sigma_{A+B} = \sqrt{\text{Variance } (A + B)} \qquad (11\text{–}9)$$

$$\sigma_{A+B} = \sqrt{W_A^2\sigma_A^2 + W_B^2\sigma_B^2 + 2W_AW_B\rho_{AB}\sigma_A\sigma_B} \qquad (11\text{–}10)$$

where σ_{A+B} = the standard deviation of the combination of asset A and asset B

W_A = the weight or fraction of total funds invested in asset A

W_B = the weight or fraction of total funds invested in asset B

σ_A = the standard deviation of asset A

σ_B = the standard deviation of asset B

ρ_{AB} = the correlation coefficient between assets A and B

Now let us assume that Table 11–10 provides the relevant information about each of these projects. If there is no diversification effect at all—that is, $\rho_{AB} = 1.0$—the standard deviation of this combination should be equal to its weighted average, 26.66 percent. That is to say that 26.66 percent is the weighted average standard deviation of this portfolio. If we had not discussed portfolio risk, we would expect the risk or standard deviation of this combination to be equal to its weighted average. However, there is a diversification portfolio effect, and its degree depends upon the correlation between the assets being combined. This can be shown mathematically by substituting the values provided in Table 11–10 into equation (11–10). This results in the following reduction in equation (11–10):

$$\sigma_{A+B} = \sqrt{(2/3)^2(.2)^2 + (1/3)^2(.4)^2 + 2\rho_{AB}(2/3)(1/3)(.2)(.4)}$$

$$\sigma_{A+B} = \sqrt{.0356 + .0356\rho_{AB}}$$

TABLE 11–10. Two-Asset Example of Diversification

Asset	σ	Weights (W)	$\sigma \times$ Weights
A	20%	2/3	13.33%
B	40	1/3	13.33%
		Weighted average $\sigma_{A+B} =$	26.66%

The only variable we now need in order to determine the standard deviation for the combination of assets is their correlation coefficient. Letting the correlation coefficient between assets A and B (ρ_{AB}) vary between $+1.0$ and -1.0 results in the following standard deviation for the combination:

	if $\rho_{AB} = 1.0$	if $\rho_{AB} = 0.0$	if $\rho_{AB} = -1.0$
$\sigma_{A+B} =$	$\sqrt{.0712} = 26.68\%$	$\sqrt{.0356} = 18.9\%$	$\sqrt{0} = 0\%$

Thus, the degree of correlation between projects determines to what extent risk can be eliminated when they are combined. It should be noted that the difference between the weighted average standard deviation (26.66%) and the one calculated using equation (11–10) and assuming ρ_{AB} equals 1.0 (26.68%) is merely the result of rounding error.

Unfortunately, in the real world perfectly negatively correlated projects are almost never found. In fact, most projects tend to be positively correlated with each other. Still, as long as positive correlations are not perfect, there will be a reduction in overall risk from these combinations. Historically, this desire to reduce the overall risk of the firm through diversification has led to much of the merger activity of the past.

The Value of Diversification

How exactly to view the value of a project's risk-reducing activity through diversification within the firm has been a subject of considerable controversy. The central question boils down to this: "Is there any value in diversifying among projects for the firm's shareholders when the shareholder may be able to accomplish the same risk reduction by diversifying his personal stockholdings?" Stated another way, "Will the shareholder pay for something (diversification) that he may be able to accomplish at no cost?" This brings us to the question of whether firm diversification achieves some value that stockholder diversification does not.

Firm diversification can reduce the chance of bankruptcy. If there is value in reducing this probability, then there is value to firm diversification. Quite obviously, in the real world there is a cost associated with bankruptcy. First, if a firm fails, its assets in general cannot be sold for their true economic value. Moreover, the amount of money actually available for distribution to stockholders is further reduced by selling costs and legal fees that must be paid. Finally, the opportunity cost associated with the delays related to the legal process further reduces the funds available to the shareholder. Therefore, since costs are associated with bankruptcy, reduction of the chance of bankruptcy has a very real value associated with it.

The risk of bankruptcy also entails indirect costs associated with changes in the firm's debt capacity and the cost of debt. As the firm's cash flow patterns stabilize, the risk of default will decline, giving the firm an increased debt capacity and possibly reducing the cost of this debt. Because interest payments are tax deductible, while dividends are not, debt financing is less expensive than equity financing. Thus, monetary benefits are associated with an increased debt capacity.[3] Since this reduction in default

---

[3] The benefits associated with debt financing and the relative costs of the various financing alternatives will be dealt with in more detail in Chapter 13.

risk cannot be duplicated by stockholder diversification of personal investments, there is a real value associated with it. The question now becomes how to include the benefits from the reduction of bankruptcy risk in our capital budgeting decision.

The most logical way of incorporating these benefits into our capital budgeting framework is to estimate a dollar value associated with them and treat this value as a cash inflow. The guiding logic behind our capital budgeting criteria was to consider the incremental after-tax cash flows to the company as a whole resulting from the acceptance of a project. This being the case, we must estimate the expected value of the reduction in bankruptcy costs, most likely a very small figure, and the expected value associated with expanded debt capacity and debt cost reductions. Quite frankly, there are problems associated with estimating these benefits; however, the benefits should be recognized and incorporated into the process. While their estimation will be deferred to more-advanced finance courses, the process of diversification and its value are important concepts and must be understood.

The subject of risk and capital budgeting is complicated and controversial, but we need to be familiar with the common measures of risk and means of treating it. In addition, we should recognize the limitations of these measures and techniques if we are to use them. In this section we have introduced these limitations and complications in such a manner as to lay a foundation for reexamining them in much greater detail in subsequent finance courses.

Summary

In this chapter we removed our assumption of certainty and dealt with the situation in which the firm is not sure exactly what the outcome of any investment will be. We first examined some terminology used to describe probability distributions, their central tendencies, and their level of dispersion. These statistical terms included discrete distribution, continuous distribution, expected value, standard deviation, and coefficient of variation. A discrete distribution is one in which a probability is assigned to each possible outcome in the set of all possible outcomes. A continuous distribution involves the case in which the number of possible outcomes is infinite and the probability of an event is related to a range of possible outcomes. Figure 11–14 depicts examples of each of these distributions. Both distributions are valuable; however, because of potential mathematical complications, we dropped continuous distributions and used discrete distributions in the remainder of the chapter. The expected value of a distribution is the arithmetic mean or weighted average of all possible outcomes. Mathematically, it is defined as

$$\overline{X} = \sum_{i=1}^{N} X_i P(X_i)$$

The standard deviation provides a measure of absolute risk or dispersion of the distribution. It can be defined as

$$\sigma = \sqrt{\sum_{i=1}^{N} (X_i - \overline{X})^2 P(X_i)}$$

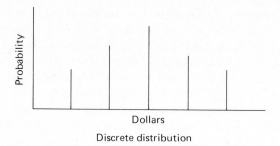

Discrete distribution

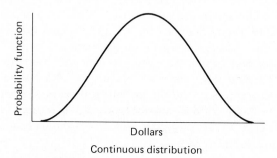

Continuous distribution

FIGURE 11–14. Distributions

The coefficient of variation provides a relative measure of risk or dispersion. It can be defined as

$$\gamma = \frac{\sigma}{\overline{X}}$$

Four methods can be used to incorporate risk into the capital budgeting decision: (1) the certainty equivalent method, (2) risk-adjusted discount rates, (3) simulation, and (4) probability trees. The certainty equivalent approach involves a direct attempt to incorporate the decision maker's utility function into the analysis. Under this method, cash flows are adjusted downward by multiplying them by certainty equivalent coefficients, α_t, which transform the risky cash flows into equivalent certain cash flows in terms of desirability. A project's net present value using the certainty equivalent method for adjusting for risk becomes

$$NPV = \sum_{t=1}^{n} \frac{\alpha_t ACF_t}{(1 + i_F)^t} - IO$$

The risk-adjusted discount rate involves an upward adjustment of the discount rate to compensate for risk. This method is based on the concept that investors demand higher returns for more risky projects.

The simulation and probability-tree methods are used to provide information as to the location and shape of the distribution of possible outcomes. Decisions could be based directly upon these methods, or they could be used to determine input into either certainty equivalent or risk-adjusted discount method approaches.

There is controversy over diversification and its value to the shareholder. We concluded that if there are bankruptcy costs and if reduction of the possibility of bankruptcy can increase debt capacity, then there is value in firm diversification. In the capital budgeting framework, the value from reduced bankruptcy costs and expanded debt capacity associated with a project's acceptance must be recognized and should be included as cash inflows associated with the acceptance of the project.

Study Questions

11–1. Differentiate between discrete and continuous probability distributions. What information can be gained from each type of distribution?

11–2. Is it possible for the expected value of a probability distribution to differ from the most likely outcome? Why or why not?

11–3. What is the relationship between the standard deviation and the coefficient of variation? Why do we need two measures of risk?

11–4. In the previous chapter we examined the payback period capital budgeting criterion. Often this capital budgeting criterion is used as a risk-screening device. Explain the rationale behind its use.

11–5. The use of the risk-adjusted discount rate assumes that risk increases over time. Justify this assumption.

11–6. What are the similarities and differences between the risk-adjusted discount rate and certainty equivalent methods for incorporating risk into the capital budgeting decision?

11–7. What is the value of using the probability-tree technique for evaluating capital budgeting projects?

11–8. Explain how simulation works. What is the value in using a simulation approach?

11–9. What does time dependence of cash flows mean? Why might cash flows be time dependent? Give some examples.

11–10. What does skewness mean? If a distribution is skewed, how does this affect the significance of its standard deviation and mean?

11–11. Through the diversification effect, the total risk of a portfolio can be reduced. How does this happen? How does the correlation between returns on the various projects affect this process?

Self-Test Problems

ST–1. The Cajun Lamy Corp. is considering two mutually exclusive projects. Both require an initial outlay of $25,000 and will operate for five years. The probability distributions associated with each project for years 1 through 5 are given below:

Cash Flow Years 1–5

Project A		Project B	
Probability	Cash Flow	Probability	Cash Flow
.20	$10,000	.20	$ 6,000
.60	15,000	.60	18,000
.20	20,000	.20	30,000

Since project B is the riskier of the two projects, the management of Cajun Lamy has decided to apply a required rate of return of 18 percent to its evaluation, but only a 12 percent required rate of return to project A.

a. Determine the expected value of each project's cash flows.

b. Determine each project's risk-adjusted net present value.

ST–2. Gator Thompson and Co. is considering two mutually exclusive projects. The expected values for each project's cash flows are given below.

Year	Project A	Project B
0	-$300,000	-$300,000
1	100,000	200,000
2	200,000	200,000
3	200,000	200,000
4	300,000	300,000
5	300,000	400,000

The company has decided to evaluate these projects using the certainty equivalent method. The certainty equivalent coefficients for each project's cash flows are given below.

Year	Project A	Project B
0	1.00	1.00
1	.95	.90
2	.90	.80
3	.85	.70
4	.80	.60
5	.75	.50

Given that this company's normal required rate of return is 15 percent and the after-tax risk-free rate is 8 percent, which project should be selected?

Study Problems

11–1. (*Risk Statistics*) Given the information below on projects A and B:

a. Calculate their expected values.

b. Calculate their standard deviations.

c. Calculate their coefficients of variation.

d. What do these statistics tell us?

Project A		Project B	
Probability	Outcome	Probability	Outcome
.10	$15,000	.15	$ 30,000
.20	25,000	.35	60,000
.40	30,000	.35	80,000
.20	35,000	.15	110,000
.10	45,000		

11–2. (*Probability Distributions*) The A. Fields Corp. of Lexington, Ky., is considering three projects with the following expected outcomes and distributions:

Project A		Project B	
Probability	Outcome	Probability	Outcome
.05	$ 1,000	.10	$ 1,000
.20	6,000	.40	7,000
.50	8,000	.40	9,000
.20	10,000	.10	15,000
.05	15,000		

Project C	
Probability	Outcome
.10	$ 4,000
.40	5,000
.30	10,000
.15	15,000
.05	22,000

Given this information:

a. Calculate their expected values.
b. Calculate their standard deviations.
c. Is the standard deviation a meaningful statistic for the distribution associated with project C? Why or why not?

11–3. (*Risk-Adjusted NPV*) The Beatosu Corporation is considering two mutually exclusive projects. Both require an initial outlay of $10,000 and will operate for 5 years. The probability distributions associated with each project for years 1 through 5 are given as follows:

Cash Flow Years 1–5

Project A		Project B	
Probability	Cash Flow	Probability	Cash Flow
.15	$4000	.15	$ 2,000
.70	5000	.70	6,000
.15	6000	.15	10,000

Since project B is the riskier of the two projects, the management of Beatosu Corporation has decided to apply a required rate of return of 15 percent to its evaluation but only a 12 percent required rate of return to project A.

a. Determine the expected value of each project's cash flows.
b. Determine each project's risk-adjusted net present value.
c. What other factors might be considered in deciding between these two projects?

11–4. (*Risk-Adjusted NVP*) The Goblu Corporation is evaluating two mutually exclusive projects, both of which require an initial outlay of $100,000. Each project has an expected life of five years. The probability distributions associated with the annual cash flows from each project are given below:

Cash Flow Years 1–5

Project A		Project B	
Probability	*Cash Flow*	*Probability*	*Cash Flow*
.10	$35,000	.10	$10,000
.40	40,000	.20	30,000
.40	45,000	.40	45,000
.10	50,000	.20	60,000
		.10	80,000

The normal required rate of return for Goblu is 10 percent, but since these projects are riskier than most, they are requiring a higher-than-normal rate of return on them. On project A they are requiring a 12 percent and on project B a 13 percent rate of return.
a. Determine the expected value for each project's cash flows.
b. Determine each project's risk-adjusted net present value.
c. What other factors might be considered in deciding between these projects?

11–5. (*Certainty Equivalents*) The J. Master Corp. is considering two mutually exclusive projects. The expected values for each project's cash flows are given below.

Year	Project A	Project B
0	−$1,000,000	−$1,000,000
1	500,000	500,000
2	700,000	600,000
3	600,000	700,000
4	500,000	800,000

They have decided to evaluate these projects using the certainty equivalent method. The certainty equivalent coefficients for each project's cash flows are given below.

Year	Project A	Project B
0	1.00	1.00
1	.95	.90
2	.90	.70
3	.80	.60
4	.70	.50

Given that this company's normal required rate of return is 15 percent and the after-tax risk-free rate is 5 percent, which project should be selected?

11–6. (*Certainty Equivalents*) Neustal, Inc., has decided to use the certainty equivalent method in determining whether or not a new investment should be made. The expected cash flows associated with this investment and the estimated certainty equivalent coefficients are as follows:

Year	Expected Values for Cash Flows	Certainty Equivalent Coefficients
0	−$90,000	1.00
1	25,000	0.95
2	30,000	0.90
3	30,000	0.83
4	25,000	0.75
5	20,000	0.65

Given that Neustal's normal required rate of return is 18 percent and that the after-tax risk free rate is 7 percent, should this project be accepted?

11-7. (*Risk-Adjusted Discount Rates and Risk Classes*) The G. Wolfe Corporation is examining two capital budgeting projects with 5-year lives. The first, project A, is a replacement project; the second, project B, is a project unrelated to current operations. The G. Wolfe Corporation uses the risk-adjusted discount rate method and groups projects according to purpose and then uses a required rate of return or discount rate which has been preassigned to that purpose or risk class. The expected cash flows for these projects are given below:

	Project A	Project B
Initial Investment:	$250,000	$400,000
Cash Inflows:		
Year 1	$ 30,000	$135,000
Year 2	40,000	135,000
Year 3	50,000	135,000
Year 4	90,000	135,000
Year 5	130,000	135,000

The purpose/risk classes and preassigned required rates of return are as follows:

Purpose	Required Rate of Return
Replacement decision	12%
Modification or expansion of existing product line	15
Project unrelated to current operations	18
Research and development operations	20

Determine the project's risk-adjusted net present value.

11-8. (*Certainty Equivalents*) "Nacho" Nachtmann Company uses the certainty equivalent approach when it evaluates risky investments. The company presently has two mutually exclusive investment proposals, with an expected life of four years each, to choose from with money it received from the sale of part of its toy division to another company. The expected net cash flows are given below.

Year	Project A	Project B
0	−$50,000	−$50,000
1	15,000	20,000
2	15,000	25,000
3	15,000	25,000
4	45,000	30,000

The certainty equivalent coefficients for the net cash flows are as follows:

Year	Project A	Project B
0	1.00	1.00
1	.95	.90
2	.85	.85
3	.80	.80
4	.70	.75

Which of the two investment proposals should be chosen, given that the after-tax risk-free rate of return is 6 percent?

11–9. (*Probability Trees*) The R. Robinson Corporation is evaluating an investment proposal with an expected life of two years. This project will require an initial outlay of $1,200,000. The risk-free rate of return is 15 percent. The resultant possible cash flows are given below.

Possible Outcomes in Year 1

	Probability		
	.6 Outcome 1	.3 Outcome 2	.1 Outcome 3
Cash flow =	$700,000	$850,000	$1,000,000

Conditional Outcomes and Probabilities for Year 2

If $ACF_1 = \$700,000$		If $ACF_1 = \$850,000$		If $ACF_1 = \$1,000,000$	
ACF_2	Probability	ACF_2	Probability	ACF_2	Probability
$ 300,000	.3	$ 400,000	.2	$ 600,000	.1
700,000	.6	700,000	.5	900,000	.5
1,100,000	.1	1,000,000	.2	1,100,000	.4
		1,300,000	.1		

a. Construct a probability tree representing the possible outcomes.
b. Determine the joint probability of each possible sequence of events taking place.
c. What is the expected NPV of this project?
d. What is the range of possible NPVs for this project?

11–10. (*Probability Trees*) The E. Swank Corporation is considering an investment project with an expected life of two years. The risk-free rate of return is 12 percent. The initial outlay on this project would be $600,000, and the resultant possible cash flows are given below.

Possible Outcomes in Year 1

	Probability		
	.4 Outcome 1	.4 Outcome 2	.2 Outcome 3
Cash flow =	$300,000	$350,000	$450,000

Conditional Outcomes and Probabilities for Year 2

If ACF$_1$ = $300,000		If ACF$_1$ = $350,000		If ACF$_1$ = $450,000	
ACF$_2$	**Probability**	**ACF$_2$**	**Probability**	**ACF$_2$**	**Probability**
$200,000	.3	$250,000	.2	$ 300,000	.2
300,000	.7	450,000	.5	500,000	.5
		650,000	.3	700,000	.2
				1,000,000	.1

a. Construct a probability tree representing the possible outcomes.
b. Determine the joint probability of each possible sequence of events taking place.
c. What is the expected NPV of this project?
d. What is the range of possible NPVs for this project?

11–11. (*Probability Trees*) M. Brooks, Inc., is considering expanding its operations into computer-based basketball games. Brooks feels that there is a 3-year life associated with this project, and it will initially involve an investment of $100,000. They also feel there is a 60 percent chance of success and a cash flow of $100,000 in year 1 and a 40 percent chance of "failure" and a zero cash flow in year 1. If the project "fails" in year 1, there is a 60 percent chance that it will merely break even in years 2 and 3, producing zero cash flows in those years. There is also a 40 percent chance that it will really fail and *cost* Brooks $40,000 in year 2 to get out of this line of business, with the project terminating and no cash flow occurring in year 3. If, on the other hand, this project succeeds in the first year, then cash flows in the second year are expected to be $200,000, $175,000, or $150,000 with probabilities of .30, .50, and .20, respectively. Finally, if the project succeeds in the third and final year of operation, the cash flows are expected to be either $30,000 more or $20,000 less than they were in year 2, with an equal chance of occurrence.
a. Construct a probability tree representing the possible outcomes.
b. Determine the joint probability of each possible sequence of events.
c. Given a 10 percent risk-free rate of return, what is the expected NPV?
d. What is the range of possible NPVs for this project?

Self-Test Solutions

SS–1. a.
$$\overline{X} = \sum_{i=1}^{N} X_i P(X_i)$$

$\overline{X}_A = 0.20(\$10,000) + 0.60(\$15,000) + 0.20(\$20,000)$
$\quad = \$2,000 + \$9,000 + \$4,000$
$\quad = \$15,000$

$\overline{X}_B = 0.20(\$6,000) + 0.60(\$18,000) + 0.20(\$30,000)$
$\quad = \$1,200 + \$10,800 + \$6,000$
$\quad = \$18,000$

b.
$$NPV = \sum_{t=1}^{n} \frac{ACF_t}{(1 + i^*)^t} - IO$$

$NPV_A = \$15,000(3.605) - \$25,000$
$\quad = \$54,075 - \$25,000$
$\quad = \$29,075$

$NPV_B = \$18,000(3.127) - \$25,000$
$\quad = \$56,286 - \$25,000$
$\quad = \$31,286$

SS–2.   Project A:

Year	(A) Expected Cash Flow	(B) α_t	(A·B) (Expected Cash Flow) × (α_t)	Present Value Factor at 8%	Present Value
0	−$300,000	1.00	−$300,000	1.000	−$300,000
1	100,000	.95	95,000	0.926	87,970
2	200,000	.90	180,000	0.857	154,260
3	200,000	.85	170,000	0.794	134,980
4	300,000	.80	240,000	0.735	176,400
5	300,000	.75	225,000	0.681	153,225
				$NPV_A =$	$406,835

Project B:

Year	(A) Expected Cash Flow	(B) α_t	(A·B) (Expected Cash Flow) × (α_t)	Present Value Factor at 8%	Present Value
0	−$300,000	1.00	−$300,000	1.000	−$300,000
1	200,000	.90	180,000	0.926	166,680
2	200,000	.80	160,000	0.857	137,120
3	200,000	.70	140,000	0.794	111,160
4	300,000	.60	180,000	0.735	132,300
5	400,000	.50	200,000	0.681	136,200
				$NPV_B =$	$383,460

Thus, project A should be selected since it has the higher NPV.

Selected References

Balachandran, Bala V., Nandu J. Nagarajan, and Alfred Rappaport. "Threshold Margins for Creating Economic Value," *Financial Management*, 15 (Spring 1986), 68–77.

Bierman, Harold, Jr., and Vithala R. Rao. "Investment Decisions with Sampling," *Financial Management*, 7 (Autumn 1978), 19–24.

Bonini, Charles P. "Capital Investment under Uncertainty with Abandonment Options," *Journal of Financial and Quantitative Analysis*, 12 (March 1977), 39–54.

Breen, William J., and Eugene M. Lerner. "Corporate Financial Strategies and Market Measures of Risk and Return," *Journal of Finance*, 28 (May 1973), 339–51.

Carter, E. Eugene. *Portfolio Aspects of Corporate Capital Budgeting*. Lexington, MA: D. C. Heath, 1974.

Cozzolina, John M. "A New Method of Risk Analysis," *Sloan Management Review*, 20 (Spring 1979), 53–65.

Galai, Dan, and Ronald W. Masulis. "The Option Pricing Model and the Risk Factor of Stock," *Journal of Financial Economics*, 3 (January–March 1976), 66–69.

Grayson, C. Jackson, Jr. *Decisions under Uncertainty: Drilling Decisions by Oil and Gas Operators*. Boston: Division of Research, Harvard Business School, 1960.

Greer, Willis R., Jr. "Capital Budgeting Analysis with the Timing of Events Uncertain," *Accounting Review*, 45 (January 1970), 103–14.

————. "Theory versus Practice in Risk Analysis: An Empirical Study," *Accounting Review*, 49 (July 1974), 496–505.

Hayes, Robert H. "Incorporating Risk Aversion into Risk Analysis," *Engineering Economist*, 20 (Winter 1975), 99–121.

Hertz, David B. "Investment Policies That Pay Off," *Harvard Business Review*, 46 (January–February 1968), 96–108.

————. "Risk Analysis in Capital Investment," *Harvard Business Review*, 42 (January–February 1964), 95–106.

Hillier, Frederick S. "A Basic Model for Capital Budgeting of Risky Interrelated Projects," *Engineering Economist*, 17 (Fall 1971), 1–30.

————. "The Derivation of Probabilistic Information for the Evaluation of Risky Investments," *Management Science*, 9 (April 1963), 443–57.

Hodder, James E., and Henry E. Riggs. "Pitfalls in Evaluating Risky Projects," *Business Review*, 63 (January–February 1985), 128–35.

Jarrett, Jeffrey E. "An Abandonment Decision Model," *Engineering Economist*, 19 (Fall 1973), 35–46.

Keeley, Robert, and Randolph Westerfield. "A Problem in Probability Distribution Techniques for Capital Budgeting," *Journal of Finance*, 27 (June 1972), 703–709.

Lessard, Donald R., and Richard S. Bower. "Risk-Screening in Capital Budgeting," *Journal of Finance*, 28 (May 1973).

Levy, Haim, and Marshall Sarnat. *Capital Investment and Financial Decisions*. Englewood Cliffs, NJ: Prentice-Hall, 1976.

————. "The Portfolio Analysis of Multiperiod Capital Investment under Conditions of Risk," *Engineering Economist*, 16 (Fall 1970), 1–19.

Lewellen, Wilbur G., and Michael S. Long. "Simulation versus Single-Value Estimates in Capital Expenditure Analysis," *Decision Sciences*, 3 (1972), 19–33.

Magee, J. F. "How to Use Decision Trees in Capital Investment," *Harvard Business Review*, 42 (September–October 1964), 79–96.

Marshuetz, Richard J. "How American Can Allocates Capital," *Harvard Business Review*, 63 (January–February 1985), 82–91.

Osteryoung, Jerome S., Elton Scott, and Gordon S. Roberts. "Selecting Projects with the Coefficient of Variation," *Financial Management* 6 (Summer 1977), 65–70.

Petty, J. William, David F. Scott, Jr., and Monroe M. Bird. "The Capital Expenditure Decision-Making Process of Large Corporations," *Engineering Economist*, 20 (Spring 1975), 159–72.

Robichek, Alexander A. "Interpreting the Results of Risk Analysis," *Journal of Finance*, 30 (December 1975), 1384–86.

Salazar, Rudolfo C., and Subrata K. Sen. "A Simulation Model of Capital Budgeting under Uncertainty," *Management Science*, 15 (December 1968), 161–79.

Schall, Lawrence D., and Gary L. Sundem. "Capital Budgeting Methods and Risk: A Further Analysis," *Financial Management*, 9 (Spring 1980), 7–11.

Spahr, Ronald W., and Stanley A. Martin. "Project Pricing in Limited Diversification Portfolios," *Engineering Economist*, 26 (Spring 1981), 207–22.

12

Valuation
and Rates of Return

What determines the real or intrinsic value of an asset? Why does the value of an asset change so radically at times? Why did IBM common stock sell for about $121 at the end of 1986, when earlier in the year it sold for $161? General Electric common stock, on the other hand, sold for $66 in early 1986, but by December had risen to $90. Why the change? Was IBM priced too high and GE too low at the beginning of the year?

An even more extreme situation existed in Dallas, Texas, between 1982 and 1984. A speculator could purchase land for $1 million and resell it within a matter of months for $2 million. The new purchaser could frequently "flip" the land again for $3 million or even $4 million within less than another year. By 1985, however, the financial institutions, which had been providing the credit to the speculators, became concerned about the dizzying rates of increase in land values. Government regulators of these institutions also began discouraging further financing of commerical land. Without the support of the financial markets, prospective buyers left the marketplace, setting in motion a sharp decline in values. The end result for many was foreclosure and financial insolvency, if not bankruptcy.

These examples simply highlight the difficulty, as well as the importance, of the need to value assets, and particularly to predict future values, both in business and personally. The *Maxims* of the French writer La Rouchefoucauld, written over three centuries ago, still speak to us: "The greatest of all gifts is the power to estimate things at their true worth."

In this chapter we examine the concepts and procedures for valuing assets, especially **financial assets** (securities), such as bonds, preferred stock, and common stock.[1]

---

[1] We describe the functioning of the capital markets and the attributes of bonds, preferred stock, and common stock in Chapter 19.

Since the financial manager's objective is to maximize the value of the firm's common stock, we need to understand the factors that underlie value. The cost of capital used in capital budgeting in Chapters 10 and 11 is based on the rates of return used to value the firm's financial securities; hence the value of a corporation's securities is dependent upon the value of its real assets, such as plant and equipment.

So there are at least two reasons for studying the valuation of financial assets:

1. In making financial decisions, our objective is to maximize common stock value. Understanding how to value financial securities is essential if we are to implement this objective.
2. The cost of capital used in making capital budgeting decisions is computed from the required rates of return used by investors in valuing the firm's securities. Thus, our discussion of security valuation lays the groundwork for estimating the firm's cost of capital in Chapter 13.

Briefly, this chapter is organized as follows: First, we offer definitions of value, including book value, liquidation value, market value, and intrinisic value. Next, we explain the important concepts of valuing an asset, especially in terms of the impact of risk and required rates of return on value. Third, we give specific attention to the valuation of bonds, preferred stock, and common stock. We next develop the concept of the investor's expected rate of return for a particular security. To add a bit of historical perspective, we will look at the experience of investors at generating returns over the past six decades. The chapter concludes with an appendix that provides a deeper understanding of bond valuation, including the concept of duration.

DEFINITIONS OF VALUE

The term *value* is often used in different contexts, depending on the application being made. Examples of different uses of this term include book value, liquidation value, market value, and intrinsic value.

Book value is the value of an asset as shown on a firm's balance sheet. It represents a historical value rather than a current worth. For example, the book value for common stock is the sum of the stock's par value, the paid-in capital, and the retained earnings. The par value and the paid-in capital equal the amount the company received when the securities were originally issued. Retained earnings is the amount of net income retained within the firm rather than being paid out as dividends to common shareholders. Thus, the retention of earnings is an indirect way for the stockholders to invest more money in the firm. If we want to know the book value *per common share*, we simply divide the total book value of the stock by the number of shares outstanding. For example, the book value for Ford Motor Company's common stock on December 31, 1985, was $53.25, computed as follows:

Par value ($000)	$ 558,453
Paid-in capital ($000)	12,228,724
Retained earnings ($000)	2,081,634
Total book value of common ($000)	$ 14,868,811
Number of shares outstanding	279,226,500
Book value per share	
($14,868,811,000 ÷ 279,226,500 shares)	$ 53.25

Liquidation value is the dollar sum that could be realized if an asset were sold individually and not as a part of a going concern. For example, if a product line is discontinued, the machinery used in its production might be sold. The sale price would be its liquidation value and would be determined independently of the firm's value. Similarly, if the firm's operations were discontinued and its assets were sold as a separate collection, the sales price would represent the firm's liquidation value.

The **market value** of an asset is the observed value for the asset in the marketplace. This value is determined by demand and supply forces working together in the marketplace, where buyers and sellers negotiate a mutually acceptable price for the asset. For instance, the market price for Ford common stock on Janaury 9, 1987, was $62.75. This price was reached by a large number of buyers and sellers working through the New York Stock Exchange. In theory, a market price exists for all assets. However, many assets have no readily observable market price because trading seldom occurs. For instance, the market price for the common stock of Blanks Engraving, a Dallas-based family-owned firm, would be more difficult to establish than the market value of J. C. Penny's common stock.

The **intrinsic value** of an asset can be defined as the present value of the asset's expected future cash flows. This value is also called the **fair value,** as perceived by the investor, given the amount, timing, and riskiness of future cash flows. In essence, intrinsic value is like the "value in the eyes of the investor." Given the risk, the investor determines the appropriate discount rate, sometimes called the *capitalization rate*, to use in computing the present or intrinsic value of the asset. Once the investor has estimated the intrinsic value of a security, this value can be compared with its market value. If the intrinsic value is greater than the market value, then the security is undervalued in the eyes of the investor. Should the market value exceed the investor's intrinsic value, then the security is overvalued.

We hasten to add that if the securities market is working efficiently, the market value and the intrinsic value of a security will be equal. That is, whenever a security's intrinsic value differs from its current market price, the competition among investors seeking opportunities to make a profit will quickly drive the market price back into equilibrium with intrinsic value. Thus, we may define an **efficient market** as one in which the values of all securities at any instant in time fully reflect all available information, which results in the market value and the intrinsic value being the same. If the markets are truly efficient, it is extremely difficult for an investor to make extra profits from an ability to predict prices.

The idea of market efficiency has been the backdrop for an intense battle between professional investors and university professors. The academic community has contended that a blindfolded monkey throwing darts at the list of securities in the *Wall Street Journal* could do as well as a professional money manager. Market professionals, on the other hand, retort that academicians are so immersed in research they could not recognize potential profits even if they were delivered to their offices. The war has been intense, but one that the student of finance should find intriguing.

THE BASICS OF VALUATION

For our purposes, we will refer to the value of an asset as its intrinsic value, which is the present value of its expected future cash flows, where these cash flows are

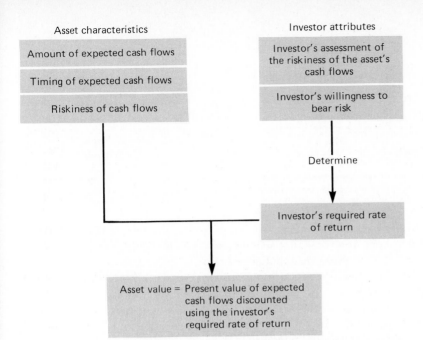

Asset characteristics

- Amount of expected cash flows
- Timing of expected cash flows
- Riskiness of cash flows

Investor attributes

- Investor's assessment of the riskiness of the asset's cash flows
- Investor's willingness to bear risk

Determine

↓

Investor's required rate of return

↓

Asset value = Present value of expected cash flows discounted using the investor's required rate of return

FIGURE 12–1. Basic Factors Determining an Asset's Value

discounted back to the present using the investor's required rate of return. Value is affected by three elements:

1. The amount and timing of the asset's expected cash flows
2. The riskiness of these cash flows
3. The investor's required rate of return for undertaking the investment

The first two factors are characteristics of the asset, while the required rate of return is the minimum rate necessary to attract an investor to purchase or hold a security. This rate must be high enough to compensate the investor for the risk perceived in the asset's future cash flows. These factors are depicted in Figure 12–1. As the figure shows, finding the value of an asset involves (1) assessing the asset's characteristics, which include the amount and timing of the expected cash flows and the riskiness of these cash flows; (2) determining the investor's required rate of return, which embodies the investor's attitude about assuming risk and perception of the riskiness of the asset; and (3) discounting the expected cash flows back to the present, using the investor's required rate of return. We will look at each of these considerations.

Expected Cash Flows

The *expected* benefits received from an investment take the form of the cash flows it will generate. Therefore, cash flows (not accounting profits) are the relevant variable to be analyzed in measuring returns. This principle holds true regardless of the type of security being valued: Whether we are analyzing a debt instrument, preferred stock, common stock, or any mixture of these securities (e.g., convertible bonds), the amount of expected future cash flows must be estimated in order to evaluate the benefits resulting from owning the investment.

Determining the amount of expected cash flows is almost never easy. In a world where the future is uncertain, the exact amount of cash flows to be produced from a security investment is seldom known. To illustrate: Assume you are considering an investment costing $10,000, where the future cash flows from owning the security depend upon the state of the economy and have been estimated as follows:

State of the Economy	Probability of the States[a]	Cash Flows from the Investment	Percentage Returns (Cash Flow ÷ Investment Cost)
Economic recession	20%	$1000	10% ($1000 ÷ $10,000)
Moderate economic growth	30%	1200	12% ($1200 ÷ $10,000)
Strong economic growth	50%	1400	14% ($1400 ÷ $10,000)

[a] The probabilities assigned to the three possible economic conditions have to be determined subjectively, which requires management to have a thorough understanding of both the investment cash flows and the general economy.

Thus, in any given year, the investment could produce any one of three possible cash flows depending upon the particular state of the economy. With this information, how should we select the most meaningful cash flow estimate for computing the security's value? One approach is to calculate an *expected* cash flow. The expected cash flow is simply the weighted average of the *possible* cash flow outcomes where the weights are the probabilities of the occurrence of the various states of the economy. (The same approach was used in Chapter 11 to measure expected cash flows for analyzing capital investments under uncertainty.) Let X_i designate the ith possible cash flow; N reflects the number of possible states of the economy, and $P(X_i)$ indicates the probability that the ith cash flow or state of economy will occur. The expected cash flow, $\bar{X}$, may then be calculated as follows:

$$\bar{X} = X_1 P(X_1) + X_2 P(X_2) + \cdots + X_N P(X_N) \qquad (12\text{--}1)$$

or

$$\bar{X} = \sum_{i=1}^{N} X_i P(X_i)$$

For the present illustration

$$\bar{X} = (.5)(\$1400) + (.3)(\$1200) + (.2)(\$1000) = \$1260$$

In addition to computing an expected dollar return from an investment, we can also calculate an expected percentage rate of return earned on the $10,000 investment on the security. The $1400 cash inflow, assuming strong economic growth, represents a 14 percent return ($1400 ÷ $10,000). Similarly, the $1200 and $1000 cash flows result in 12 percent and 10 percent returns, respectively. Using these percentage returns in place of the dollar amounts, the expected rate of return, $\bar{R}$, is

$$\bar{R} = (.5)(14\%) + (.3)(12\%) + (.2)(10\%) = 12.6 \text{ percent}$$

With our measure of expected returns, let us now consider how we can identify the riskiness of an investment.

Risk and Valuation

At this point, three questions are important. First, what is risk? Second, how do we measure it? Third, how does diversification affect the riskiness of all the securities individual investors own (their portfolio)?[2]

---

[2] The logic in this section is the same as that used in Chapter 11 for capital budgeting under uncertainty.

What is Risk? To help us understand the fundamental meaning of risk, we will consider two prospective investments:

1. The first investment is a U.S. Treasury bill, a government security, that matures in 90 days and promises to pay an annualized return of 5.5 percent. If we purchase and hold this security for 90 days, we are virtually assured of receiving no more and no less than 5.5 percent. For all practical purposes, the risk of loss is nonexistent.
2. The second investment involves the purchase of the stock of a local publishing company. Looking at the past returns of the firm's stock, we have made the following estimate of the annual returns from the investment:

Chance of Occurrence	Rate of Return on Investment
1 chance in 10 (10%)	0%
2 chances in 10 (20%)	5%
4 chances in 10 (40%)	15%
2 chances in 10 (20%)	25%
1 chance in 10 (10%)	30%

Investing in the publishing company could conceivably provide a return as high as 30 percent if all goes well or no return (zero percent) if everything goes against the firm. However, in future years, both good and bad, we could expect a 15 percent return on average:[3]

$$R = (.10)(0\%) + (.20)(5\%) + (.40)(15\%) + (.20)(25\%) + (.10)(30\%)$$

$$= 15 \text{ percent}$$

Comparing the Treasury Bill investment with the publishing company investment, we see that the Treasury bills offer an expected 5.5 percent rate of return, while the publishing company has an expected rate of return of 15 percent. However, our investment in the publishing firm is clearly more "risky"—that is, it has greater uncertainty as to the final outcome. Stated somewhat differently there is a greater variation or dispersion of possible returns, which in turn implies greater risk.[4]

Although the return from investing in the publishing firm is clearly less certain than for Treasury bills, a measure of risk is useful when the difference between two investments is not so evident. Such a measure was suggested in Chapter 11: the standard deviation (σ). The standard deviation is simply the square root of the "average squared deviation of each possible return from the expected return."

---

[3] We assume that the particular outcome or return earned in one year does *not* affect the return earned in the subsequent year. Technically speaking, the distribution of returns in any year is assumed to be independent of the outcome in any prior year.

[4] How can we possibly view variations above the expected return as risk? Should we not be concerned only with the negative deviations? Some would agree and view risk as only the negative variability in returns from a predetermined minimum acceptable rate of return. However, as long as the distribution of returns is symmetrical, the same conclusions will be reached.

That is

$$\sigma = \sqrt{\sum_{i=1}^{N} (R_i - \overline{R})^2 P(R_j)} \qquad (12\text{--}2)$$

where $N =$ the number of possible outcomes or different rates of return on the investment

$R_i =$ the value of the ith possible rate of return

$\overline{R} =$ the expected value of the rates of return

$P(R_i) =$ the chance or probability that the ith outcome or return will occur.

For the publishing company, the standard deviation would be 9.22 percent, determined as follows:

$$\sigma = \left[\begin{array}{l} (\ 0\% - 15\%)^2(.10) + (\ 5\% - 15\%)^2(.20) \\ + (15\% - 15\%)^2(.40) + (25\% - 15\%)^2(.20) \\ + (30\% - 15\%)^2(.10) \end{array} \right]^{1/2}$$

$$= \sqrt{85\%} = 9.22 \text{ percent}$$

Although the standard deviation of returns provides a measure of an asset's riskiness, how should we interpret the results? What does it mean? Is the 9.22 percent standard deviation for the publishing company investment good or bad? We can answer this question only by comparing the investment in the publishing firm against other investments. That is, the attractiveness of a security with respect to its return and risk cannot be determined in isolation. Only by examining other available alternatives can we reach a conclusion about a particular investment's risk. For example, if another investment, say an investment in a firm that owns a local radio station, has the same expected return as the publishing company, but a standard deviation of 7 percent, we would consider the risk associated with the publishing firm, 9.22 percent, to be excessive. In the technical jargon of modern portfolio theory, the radio company investment is said to "dominant" the publishing firm investment. In common sense terms, this condition is due to the fact that the radio company investment has the same expected return as the publishing company investment, but is less risky.

The attractiveness of the radio company investment over the publishing company investment, which has the same expected return but greater risk, is readily apparent. The real difficulty in selecting the "better" investment comes when one investment has a higher expected return, but also exhibits greater risk.

For instance, which investment would you have selected, the Treasury bills or the publishing company? The Treasury bills have a lower expected return (5.5 percent) than the publishing company (15 percent), but also expose us to far less risk: zero versus a 9.22 standard deviation. In this situation the choice is determined by our attitude toward risk, and there is no single right answer. You may choose the Treasury bills, and I may select the publishing company, without either of us being wrong. We are simply expressing our tastes and preferences about risk and return.

Risk and Diversification

Having defined the riskiness of an investment in terms of the variability of its anticipated returns, as measured by the standard deviation, we need to consider how risk is affected if we diversify our investment by holding a variety of securities. You may recall the disaster at the Union Carbide plant in Bhopal, India that occurred in summer 1984. Thousands of individuals were killed or injured. While the financial considerations cannot compare to the loss of life, if you had invested your life saving of $400,000 in Union Carbide shortly before the Bhopal tragedy, the value of your savings would have declined by 40 percent to $240,000 almost overnight.[5] Another example of a unique event that had a tremendous impact on a firm occurred when Pennzoil received an $11 billion award from a Texas court against Texaco for alleged misconduct when Texaco "tortiously" outbid Pennzoil in its effort to acquire Getty Oil Company. Based upon this single event, Pennzoil stock almost doubled from $46 per share to $90 per share in a matter of days. Texaco stock, on the other hand, declined from $38 to $25.[6]

The events affecting Union Carbide, Texaco, and Pennzoil were unique to those firms; they had little, if any, impact on other companies. Other examples of events that are unique to a single company include labor strikes, the discovery of a new product or the sudden obsolescence of an old one, errors in judgment by a firm's management regarding a large capital investment, and the resignation or death of a key executive.

How do you feel about these unique events? Obviously, if you had been a stockholder in Pennzoil you would have felt great, but you might have decided to invest in Texaco (not a bad company), or even worse, Union Carbide. Most of us would like to avoid such fluctuations; that is, we are risk-averse. Wouldn't it be great if we could reduce the risk associated with our portfolio, without having to accept a lower expected return? Good news; it is possible!

If we diversify our investments across different securities, rather than investing in only one stock, the variability in the holding-period returns of our portfolio should decline.[7] The reduction in risk will occur if the stock returns within our portfolio do not move precisely together over time—that is, if they are not perfectly correlated. Figure 12–2 shows graphically what we might expect to happen to the variability of returns as we add additional stocks to the portfolio. The reduction occurs because some of the volatility in returns of a stock are unique to that security. The unique variability of a single stock tends to be countered by the uniqueness of another security.[8] However, we should not expect to eliminate all risk from our portfolio. In practice, it would be rather difficult to cancel all the variations in returns of a portfolio because stock prices have some tendency to move together. Thus, we can divide the total risk (total variability) of our portfolio into two types of risk: (1) *firm-specific or*

---

[5] See "Union Carbide Shares Acquired by Bass Group," *Wall Street Journal*, January 21, 1985, pp. 2–3. We must add that the price of the stock recovered in about six months.

[6] See "Pennzoil Rejects Texaco Offer, *Wall Street Journal*, January 8, 1986, p. 3.

[7] The holding-period return of a stock or portfolio, expressed as a percent, is the combined income from the dividend yield (dividend/price) and the percentage change in the price of the stock or portfolio. For instance, if a stock sold for $50 on March 1 and $51 on March 31, and paid a $.50 dividend in March, the March monthly holding-period return would be 3 percent (a 1% dividend yield, $.50/$50, plus a 2% percent price increase, $1/$50).

[8] This concept is also presented in Chapter 11 with respect to the risk of capital investments.

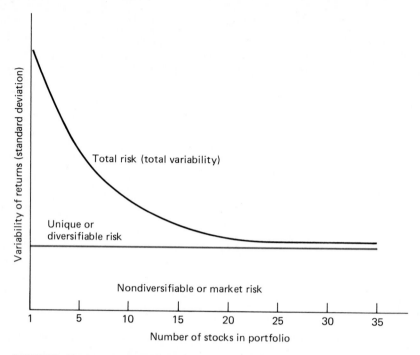

FIGURE 12–2. Variability of Returns Compared to Size of Portfolio

unique risk, and (2) *market-related risk*. Unique risk might also be called *diversifiable risk*, since it can be diversified away. Market risk in *nondiversifiable risk*; it cannot be eliminated, no matter how much we diversify. These two types of risk are shown graphically in Figure 12–2, where total risk declines until we have approximately 20 securities, after which the decline becomes very slight.[9] The remaining risk is the portfolio's market risk. At this point, our portfolio is highly correlated with all securities in the marketplace. Events that affect our portfolio now are not so much unique events, but changes in the general economy, major political events, and sociological changes. For example, when general interest rates rise, the price of stocks typically falls.

Since we can remove the unique, or unsystematic risk, there is no reason to believe that the market will reward us with additional returns for assuming risk that could be avoided by simply diversifying. Our new measure of risk should therefore measure how responsive a stock or portfolio is to changes in a "market portfolio," such as the New York Stock Exchange or the S&P 500 Index. This relationship could be determined by plotting past returns, say on a monthly basis, of a particular stock against the returns of the "market portfolio" for the same period. Such a plot for security A is presented in Figure 12–3. The returns for security A are seen to be 1.5 times as volatile on average as the market returns. That is, when the monthly returns

[9] A number of studies have noted that portfolios consisting of approximately 20 randomly selected common stocks have virtually no unique or diversifiable risk. See Robert C. Klemkosky and John D. Martin, "The Effect of Market Risk on Portfolio Diversification," *The Journal of Finance*, March 1975, pp. 147–154.

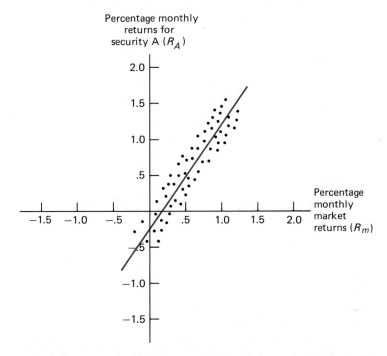

FIGURE 12–3. Security A Returns Compared to Market Returns

for the "market portfolio" increases 0.5 percentage points, the return for security A increases "on average" by 1.5 times that amount, or .75 percentage points. Likewise, when the market portfolio declines by .50 percentage points, the return for security A declines by .75 percentage points.

If we were to draw a line of "best fit" through the returns (a regression line), it would have a slope of 1.5, which suggests that security A's returns are 1.5 times as volatile as the general market. This means that security A has 1.5 times as much systematic risk as the general market. The slope of the line, which has come to be called *beta*, is a measure of a stock's systematic or market risk. In general, if a security's beta equals 1, its returns will vary in direct proportion with the market's returns. When a beta is larger (smaller) than 1, an individual security's returns are more (less) responsive to changes in the market, whether the returns are increasing or decreasing.[10]

---

[10] We will not calculate the beta for a security, since it is provided in investment services, such as the Merrill Lynch, Pierce, Fenner & Smith Investment Survey. For our purposes, we only seek to understand the concept. However, it could be computed as follows:

$$\beta_j = (r_{jm}\sigma_j\sigma_m/\sigma_m^2)$$

where β_j = the systematic or market risk of security j

r_{jm} = the correlation coefficient for measuring the relationship between security j returns and the market returns (See Chapter 11 for an explanation of the correlation coefficient.)

σ_j, σ_m = the standard deviation of security j returns and the standard deviation of the market returns, respectively

σ_m^2 = the variance (standard deviation squared) of the market returns

The concept of beta will serve us well as we measure the important element of a security's risk. It also proves useful when we try to estimate the investor's required rate of return, the third important variable in valuing an asset.

The Investor's Required Rate of Return

In this section we examine the concept of the investor's required rate of return, especially as it relates to the riskiness of the asset, and then we see how the required rate of return is measured.

The Required Rate of Return Concept

The **investor's required rate of return** may be defined as the minimum rate of return necessary to attract an investor to purchase or hold a security. This definition considers the investor's opportunity cost of making an investment; that is, if an investment is made, the investor must forego the return available from the next best investment. This "foregone return" is an opportunity cost of undertaking the investment and consequently is the investor's required rate of return. In other words, we invest with the intention of achieving a rate of return sufficient to warrant making the investment. The investment will be made only if the purchase price is low enough relative to the expected future cash flows to provide a rate of return greater than or equal to our required rate of return.

To help us better understand the nature of an investor's required rate of return, we may separate the return into its basic components: the risk-free rate of return plus a risk premium. Expressed as an equation:

$$R = R_f + RP \qquad (12\text{--}3)$$

where R = the investor's required rate of return

R_f = the risk-free return

RP = the risk premium

The risk-free rate of return rewards us for deferring consumption, and not for assuming risk. That is, the risk-free return reflects the basic fact that we invest today so that we can consume more later. By itself, the riskless or risk-free rate should be used only as the required rate of return, or discount rate, for *riskless* investments. Typically, our measure for the risk-free rate of return is the U.S. Treasury bill rate.

The risk premium, *RP*, is the additional return we must expect to receive for assuming risk. As the level of risk increases, we will demand additional expected returns. Even though we may or may not actually receive this incremental return, we must have reason to expect it; otherwise, why expose ourselves to the chance of losing all or part of our money?

Example   To demonstrate the required rate of return concept, consider Radio Corporation of America (RCA) bonds that mature in 1992. Based upon the market price of these bonds at the beginning of 1987, we can determine that investors are expecting a 9 percent return. The 90-day Treasury bill rate at that time was 5.5 percent, which means that RCA bondholders were requiring a risk premium of 3.5 percent.[11] Stated as an equation, we have

$$
\begin{array}{ccccc}
\text{required} & & \text{risk-free} & & \text{risk} \\
\text{rate} & = & \text{rate } (R_f) & + & \text{premium } (RP) \\
& = & 5.5\% & + & 3.5\% \\
& = & 9\% & &
\end{array}
$$

Measuring the Required Rate of Return

Having recognized that (1) systematic risk is the relevant source of risk, and (2) the required rate of return, R, equals the risk-free rate, R_f, plus, a risk premium, RP, we may now examine how we actually estimate investors' required rates of return. Since no one knows exactly how to estimate the risk premium we will use two popular approaches from the literature: (1) the capital asset pricing model (CAPM), and (2) the arbitrage pricing theory (APT).[12]

Measuring the Required Rate: The CAPM Approach. Equation 12–3 provides the natural starting point for measuring the investors' required rate of return. Rearranging this equation to solve for the risk premium (RP), we have

$$RP = R - R_f \tag{12–4}$$

which simply says that the risk premium for a security, RP, equals the security's expected return, R, less the risk-free rate existing in the market, R_f. For example, if the expected return for a security is 15 percent and the risk-free rate is 7 percent, the risk premium is 8 percent. Also, if the expected return for the market, R_m, is 12 percent, and the risk-free rate, RP, is 7 percent, the risk premium for the general market would be 5 percent. This 5 percent risk premium would apply to any security having systematic (nondiversifiable) risk equivalent to the general market, or a beta of 1.

In this same market, a security with a beta of 2 should provide a risk premium of 10 percent, or twice the 5 percent risk premium existing for the market as a whole. Hence, in general, the appropriate required rate of return for the jth security, R_j, should be determined by

$$R_j = R_f + \beta_j (R_m - R_f) \tag{12–5}$$

Equation (12–5) is the **capital asset pricing model (CAPM).** This equation designates the risk-return tradeoff existing in the market, where risk is defined in terms of

---

[11] The risk premium here can be thought of as a composite of a "default risk premium" (reflected in the difference in the bond's rate of return and the rate on a similar maturity government bond) and "term structure" premium (reflected in the difference in the 90 day Treasury bill rate and the long-term government bond rate).

[12] For more detailed treatment of these models, see B. Rosenberg, "The Capital Asset Pricing Model and the Market Model," *Journal of Portfolio Management*, Winter 1981, pp. 5–16; R. Roll and S. Ross, "The Arbitrage Pricing Theory Approach to Strategic Portfolio Planning," *Financial Analysts Journal*, May–June 1984, pp. 14–26; N. Chen, "Some Empirical Tests of the Theory of Arbitrage Pricing," *Journal of Finance*, December 1983, pp. 1393–1414; and Richard Roll, "A Critique of the Asset Pricing Theory's Tests," *Journal of Financial Economics*, March 1977, pp. 129–176.

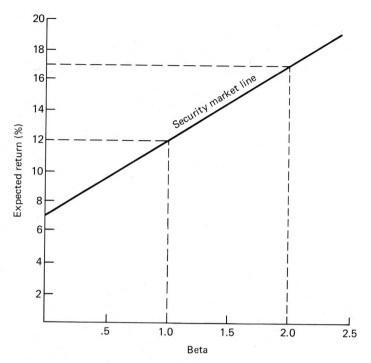

FIGURE 12–4. Security Market Line

beta. Figure 12–4 graphically illustrates the **CAPM** as the **security market line**.[13] As presented in this figure, securities with betas equal to 0, 1, and 2 should have required rates of return as follows:

If $\beta_j = 0.0$: $R_j = 7\% + 0.0(12\% - 7\%) = 7$ percent

If $\beta_j = 1.0$: $R_j = 7\% + 1.0(12\% - 7\%) = 12$ percent

If $\beta_j = 2.0$: $R_j = 7\% + 2.0(12\% - 7\%) = 17$ percent

where the risk-free rate, R_f, is 7 percent and the expected market return, R_m, is 12 percent.

---

[13] Two key assumptions are made in using the security market line. First, we assume that the marketplace where securities are bought and sold is highly efficient. Market efficiency indicates that the price of an asset responds quickly to new information, thereby suggesting that the price of a security reflects all available information. As a result, the current price of a security is considered to represent the best estimate of its future price. Second, the model assumes that a perfect market exits. A perfect market is one in which information is readily available to all investors at a nominal cost. Also, securities are assumed to be infinitely divisible, with any transaction costs incurred in purchasing or selling a security being negligible. Furthermore, investors are assumed to be single-period wealth maximizers who agree as to the meaning and the significance of the available information. Finally, within the perfect market, all investors are "price takers," which simply means that a single investor's actions cannot affect the price of a security. These assumptions are obviously not descriptive of reality. However, from the perspective of positive economics, the mark of a good theory is the accuracy of its predictions and not the validity of the simplifying assumptions that underlie its development.

Criticisms of CAPM.   For several years, CAPM was touted as the "new investment technology" and received the blessings of the vast majority of professional investors and finance professors. The attractiveness of the CAPM came largely from its ability to present important theoretical insights (which professors loved) in simple and practical terms that could be applied in practice (which professional investors loved). In more recent years, however, researchers have questioned whether the model really works; some have even asked: "Is beta dead?"[14]

The CAPM, like any abstract theory, has weaknesses. For example, we might well question whether the risk of an asset can be totally captured in the single dimension of sensitivity to the market, as proposed by the CAPM. There is some evidence that such things as the firm's size and even the time of year may affect risk-return relationships.[15] Also, we could well become discouraged in our efforts to measure a security's beta if we find that different computation methods and different periods of measurement (e.g., using three years of data versus five years) give noticeably different results. An even more basic issue is our ability to test the model empirically. Some would argue that we cannot verify the accuracy of the model because we cannot know with certainty that we are using the "true market portfolio" in comparing returns and systematic risk.[16]

While the critics of CAPM have been rather vocal in recent days, the model is not in total disrepute; it is still being used with reasonable confidence. However, a new theory must be used to displace the older one. One such candidate is the arbitrage pricing theory.

The Arbitrage Pricing Theory

The basic theme of the **arbitrage pricing theory (APT)** can be stated as follows:[17]

1. Actual security returns vary from their expected amounts because of *unanticipated* changes in a *number* of basic economic forces, such as unexpected changes in industrial production, inflation rates, the term structure of interest rates, and the difference in interest rates between high- and low-risk bonds.[18]

2. Just as the CAPM defined a portfolio's systematic risk to be its sensitivity to the general-market returns (i.e., its beta coefficient), APT suggests that the risk of a security is reflected in its sensitivity to the unexpected changes in the important economic forces.

3. Any two stocks or portfolios that have the same sensitivity to the important economic forces (that is, the same relevant or systematic risk) must have the same expected return. Otherwise, we could replace some of the stocks in our

---

[14] See Anise Wallace, "Is Beta Dead?" *Institutional Investor*, July 1980, pp. 23–30.

[15] See C. Barry and S. Brown, "Differential Information and the Small Firm Effect." *Journal of Financial Economics*, June 1984, pp. 283–294; N. Chen and D. Hsieh. "An Exploratory Investigation of the Firm Size Effect," *Journal of Financial Economics*, September 1985, pp. 451–471; and J. Jaffe and R. Westerfield, "The Week-End Effect in Common Stock Returns: The International Evidence," *Journal of Finance*, June 1985, pp. 433–454.

[16] See, for example, Richard Roll, "A Critique of the Asset Pricing Theory's Tests," *Journal of Financial Economics*, March 1977, pp. 129–176.

[17] The following description of the APT is taken in part from Dorothy H. Bower, Richard S. Bower, and Dennis E. Logue, "A Primer on Arbitrage Pricing Theory," *The Revolution in Corporate Finance*, (edited by Joel M. Stern and Donald H. Chew, Jr.), New York: Basil Blackwell, 1986, pp. 69–77.

[18] See R. Roll and S. Ross, "The Arbitrage Pricing Theory Approach to Strategic Portfolio Planning," *Financial Analysts Journal*, May–June 1984, pp. 14–26.

portfolio with other stocks having the same sensitivities, but higher expected returns and earn riskless profits.

4. We would expect portfolios that are highly sensitive to unexpected changes in the economy-wide forces to offer investors high expected returns. This relationship may be represented quantitatively as follows:

$$E(R_i) = R_f + (S_{i1})(RP_1) + (S_{i2})(RP_2) + \cdots + (S_{ij})(RP_j) + \cdots + (S_{in})(RP_n) \quad (12\text{--}6)$$

where $E(R)_i$ = the expected return for stock or portfolio i

R_f = the risk-free rate

S_{ij} = the sensitivity of stock i returns to unexpected changes in economic force j

RP_j = the market risk premium associated with an unexpected change in the jth economic force

n = the number of relevant economic forces

To help understand the APT model, we will draw from the actual research of Bower, Bower, and Logue, hereafter referred to as BBL for short.[19] After computing monthly returns for 815 stocks from 1970 through 1979, BBL used a technique called factor analysis to study the general movement of monthly returns for the 815 stocks. The technique identified four factors that helped to explain the movement of the returns, and also used equation 12–6 to represent the risk-return relationship in an APT format. The actual model appears as follows:

$$\text{Expected return for Stock } i = 6.2\% - 185.5\%(S_{i1}) + 144.5\%(S_{i2}) \\ + 12.4\%(S_{i3}) - 274.4\%(S_{i4})$$

The value of 6.2% in the equation is an estimate of the risk-free rate, as determined by the model; the remaining values, $-185.5, \ldots -274.4$, signify the market risk premiums for each of the four factors; and the $S_{i1}, \ldots, S_{i4}$ represent the sensitivities of stock i to the four factors.

The BBL factors are determined statistically from past return data and were not intuitively or economically identified. That is, the technique provides "factors" that tell us more about the movement in the returns than would any other factors. Each factor could conceivably relate to a single economic variable; however, it is more likely that each factor represents the influence of several economic variables.[20]

Having specified the APT risk-return relationship, BBL then used the model to estimate the expected (required) rates of return for 17 stocks. This estimation required

---

[19] Dorothy A. Bower, Richard S. Bower, and Dennis E. Logue, "Equity Screening Rates Using Arbitrage Pricing Theory," in C. F. Lee, ed., *Advances in Financial Planning* (Greenwich, CT: JAI Press, 1984).

[20] As noted earlier in the chapter, work is underway to determine the economic factors that most influence security returns. See R. Roll and S. Ross, "The Arbitrage Pricing Theory Approach to Strategic Portfolio Planning," *Financial Analysts Journal*, May–June 1984, pp. 14–26.

BBL to use regression analysis to study the relationships of the returns of the 17 stocks to the four factors. From this regression analysis, they were able to measure the sensitivity of each security's return to a particular factor. These "sensitivity coefficients" for a particular stock may then be combined with the APT model in equation (12–6) to estimate the investors' required rate of return.

Using 3 of the 17 stocks to demonstrate the calculation, the regression coefficients (sensitivity coefficients) for American Hospital Supply, CBS, and Western Union are shown below:

	Stock Sensitivity Coefficients (S)			
	Factor 1	*Factor 2*	*Factor 3*	*Factor 4*
American Hospital Supply	−0.050	0.010	0.040	0.020
CBS	−0.050	0.002	0.005	0.010
Western Union	−0.050	−0.020	−0.010	0.009

Using these stock sensitivity coefficients and the APT model, as developed by BBL, we can estimate the investors' expected (required) rate of return for each stock as follows:

$$\text{American Hospital Supply} = 6.2\% - 185.5\%(-0.050) + 144.5\%(0.010) + 12.4\%(0.040) - 274.4\%(.020)$$

$$= 11.93\%$$

$$\text{CBS} = 6.2\% - 185.5\%(-0.050) + 144.5\%(0.002) + 12.4\%(0.005) - 274.4\%(0.010)$$

$$= 13.08\%$$

$$\text{Western Union} = 6.2\% - 185.5\%(-0.050) + 144.5\%(-0.020) + 12.4\%(-0.010) - 274.4\%(0.009)$$

$$= 9.99\%$$

We have now used two approaches for measuring the required rate of return, or expected rate of return, of investors: the CAPM and the APT. The capital asset pricing model (CAPM) is a single-index model that considers the general market to be the only important factor in setting the values of individual stocks. The arbitrage pricing theory (APT), on the other hand, recognizes several economic factors in estimating returns (and values).

Whichever model is used, one key point remains: We cannot formulate a complete concept of valuation without understanding the nature of the investor's required rate of return. This rate, which serves as the discount rate in the valuation process, represents the minimal acceptable return to induce an investor to purchase or hold a security. In the discussions that follow, this link will be demonstrated clearly as we value different types of securities.

SUMMARY OF THE GENERAL VALUATION PROCESS

The valuation process involves calculating the present value of an asset's expected future cash flows using the investor's required rate of return. The investor's required rate of return, R, is determined by the level of the risk-free rate of interest, R_f, and the risk premium, RP, that the investor feels is necessary to compensate for the risks assumed in owning the asset. Therefore, the basic security valuation model can be defined mathematically as follows:

$$V = \frac{C_1}{(1+R)^1} + \frac{C_2}{(1+R)^2} + \cdots + \frac{C_N}{(1+R)^N}$$

or

$$V = \sum_{t=1}^{N} \frac{C_t}{(1+R)_t}$$

(12–7)

where V = the intrinsic value or present value of an asset producing expected future cash flows, C_t, in years 1 through N

R = the investor's required rate of return

Using equation (12–7), there are three basic steps in the valuation process:

STEP 1: *Estimate the C_t in equation (12–7), which is the amount and timing of the future cash flows the security is expected to provide.*

STEP 2: *Determine R, the investor's required rate of return, using equation (12–3), that is, (R = R$_f$ + RP). We do this by evaluating the riskiness of the security's future cash flows and determining an appropriate risk premium, RP. We then observe the risk-free rate (such as the rate of interest on 90-day Treasury bills) and add the two together for the required rate of return.*

STEP 3: *Calculate the intrinsic value, V, as the present value of expected future cash flows discounted at the investor's required rate of return.*

With these general principles of valuation as a foundation, we can investigate the procedures for valuing particular types of securities. Specifically, we will learn how to value a bond, preferred stock, and common stock.

BOND VALUATION

The process for valuing a bond requires first that we understand the terminology and institutional characteristics of a bond. More extensive coverage of the contractual provisions of a bond is provided in Chapter 19.

Nature of Bonds   When a company, or even a nonprofit institution, has a need for money, one source of financing is **bonds.** This type of financing instrument is simply a long-term promissory note issued by the borrower, promising to pay its holder a predetermined and fixed amount of interest each year. As a form of debt, a contract between the borrower and lender is executed, frequently called an **indenture.** Although the terms of the contract generally are extensive, incorporating detailed protective provisions for the creditor, only three items *directly* affect the cash flows from owning a bond: the bond's par value, maturity date, and the coupon rate of interest:

1. **Par value.** The amount the firm is to pay on the maturity date stated on the face of the bond. This amount, defined as the par value or face value, cannot be altered after the bond has been issued. Typically, the par value is set at $1000. Hence, the issuing company contractually agrees to pay the investor this amount when the debt matures. The *par value* is essentially independent of the *intrinsic value* of the bond. Thus, while the price of the bond fluctuates in response to changing economic and market conditions, the par value remains constant.

2. **Maturity date.** As already suggested, a bond normally has a maturity date, at which time the borrowing organization is committed to repay the loan. At this time the holder of the security, assuming the company does not default on the obligation, is to receive cash in the amount of the par value.

3. **Coupon interest rate.** Besides paying the owner of the bond the par value at the maturity date, the borrower promises to pay a specified amount of interest

FIGURE 12–5. Data Requirements for Bond Valuation

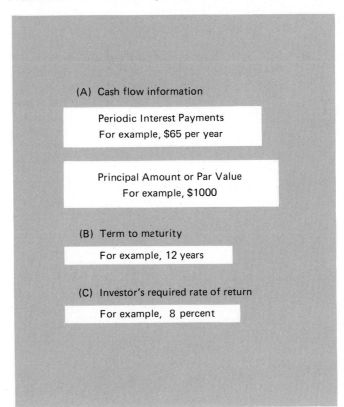

(A) Cash flow information

Periodic Interest Payments
For example, $65 per year

Principal Amount or Par Value
For example, $1000

(B) Term to maturity
For example, 12 years

(C) Investor's required rate of return
For example, 8 percent

each year. This annual amount is stated either in terms of dollars, such as $90, or as a percent of the par value. In either instance *the interest to be paid is inflexible.* When the contractural agreement specifies the interest as a percent of par value, this percentage is known as the **coupon interest rate** or the **contractual interest rate.** For instance, if the terms of a $1000 par value bond set the annual interest at $90, the coupon rate is 9 percent, that being $90 divided by $1000. Furthermore, this rate should not be confused with the required rate of return.

Valuation Procedure

The valuation process for a bond, as depicted in Figure 12–5, requires that we know three essential elements: (1) the amount of the cash flows to be received by the investor, (2) the maturity date of the loan, and (3) the investor's required rate of return. The amount of cash flows is dictated by the periodic interest to be received and by the par value to be paid at maturity. Given these elements, we can compute the value of the bond, or the present value.

Example Consider a bond issued by the Exxon Corporation, having a maturity date of 1998 and a stated coupon rate of 6½ percent.[21] The bonds were originally issued at a price of $1000. By 1986, however, since the investors' required rate of return had changed, the bond value was less than $1000. For instance, in late 1986, investors were requiring a return of approximately 8 percent for this type of security. At this time the value of the security was approximately $887, which can be calculated using the following three-step valuation procedure.

STEP 1: *Estimate the amount and timing of the expected future cash flows:*
Two types of cash flows are received by the bondholder:
1. *Annual interest payments equal to the coupon rate of interest times the face value of the bond. In this example the interest payments equal $65 = .065 × $1000. Assuming that 1986 interest payments have already been made, these cash flows will be received by the bondholder in each of the 12 years before the bond matures (1987–98 = 12 years).*
2. *The face value of the bond of $1000 to be received in 1998.*

To summarize, the cash flows received by the bondholder are as follows:

0	1	2	3	4		11	12
	$65	$65	$65	$65	. . .	$65	$65 +$1000 $1065

STEP 2: *Determine the investor's required rate of return by evaluating the riskiness of the bond's future cash flows. An 8 percent required rate of return for the Exxon bondholders is given.*

---

[21] In actuality, the company remits the interest to its bondholders on a semi-annual basis on January 15 and July 15. However, for the moment assume the interest is to be received annually. The effect of semi-annual payments will be examined later.

STEP 3: Calculate the intrinsic value of the bond as the present value of the expected future interest and principal payments discounted at the investor's required rate of return.

The present value of Exxon's bonds is found as follows:

$$\text{bond value} = V_b = \frac{\$\text{ interest in year 1}}{(1 + \text{required rate of return})^1}$$

$$+ \frac{\$\text{ interest in year 2}}{(1 + \text{required rate of return})^2}$$

$$+ \cdots + \frac{\$\text{ interest in year } N}{(1 + \text{required rate of return})^N}$$

$$+ \frac{\$\text{ par maturity value}}{(1 + \text{required rate of return})^N}$$

or, summing over the interest payments,

$$V_b = \underbrace{\sum_{t=1}^{N} \frac{\$\text{ interest in year } t}{(1 + \text{required rate of return})^t}}_{\text{present value of interest}} + \underbrace{\frac{\$\text{ par maturity value}}{(1 + \text{required rate of return})^N}}_{\substack{\text{present value of par value} \\ \text{at maturity}}}$$

Using I_t to represent the interest payment in year t, M to represent the bond's maturity value, and R_b to equal the bondholder's required rate of return, we get

$$V_b = \sum_{t=1}^{N} \frac{\$I_t}{(1 + R_b)^t} + \frac{\$M}{(1 + R_b)^N} \qquad (12\text{–}8a)$$

Since the interest payments I_t are an annuity for N years, and the maturity value is a one-time amount in year N, we can use the present-value factors in Appendixes B and D to solve for the present value of the bond as follows:

$$V_b = \$I_t \begin{pmatrix} \text{table value,} \\ \text{Appendix D,} \\ N \text{ years,} \\ R_b \text{ percent} \end{pmatrix} + \$M \begin{pmatrix} \text{table value,} \\ \text{Appendix B,} \\ N \text{ years,} \\ R_b \text{ percent} \end{pmatrix} \qquad (12\text{–}8b)$$

For Exxon,

$$V_b = \$65(7.536) + \$1000(.397)$$

$$= \$489.84 + \$397.00$$

$$= \$886.84$$

Thus, if investors consider 8 percent to be an appropriate required rate of return in view of the risk level associated with these Exxon bonds, paying a price of $886.84 would satisfy this return requirement.

Semi-annual Interest Payments

In the previous illustration, the interest payments were assumed to be paid annually. However, companies typically forward an interest check to bondholders semi-annually. For example, rather than disbursing $65 in interest at the conclusion of each year, Exxon Corporation pays $32.50 (half of $65) on January 15 and July 15.

In adapting equation (12–8a) to recognize semi-annual interest payments, several steps are involved.[22] First, thinking in terms of "periods" instead of years, a bond with a life of N years paying interest semi-annually should be thought to have a life of $2N$ periods. In other words, a 5-year bond ($N = 5$) that remits its interest on a semi-annual basis actually makes 10 payments. Yet while the number of periods has doubled, the *dollar* amount of interest being sent to the investors for each period and the bondholders' required rate of return are half of the equivalent annual figures. I_t becomes $I_t/2$ and R_b is changed to $R_b/2$; thus, for semi-annual compounding, equation (12–8a) becomes

$$V_b = \sum_{t=1}^{2N} \frac{\$I_t/2}{\left(1 + \dfrac{R_b}{2}\right)^t} + \frac{\$M}{\left(1 + \dfrac{R_b}{2}\right)^{2N}} \qquad (12\text{–}9a)$$

However, if the present-value tables are used, V_b is calculated as

$$V_b = \frac{\$I_t}{2}\begin{bmatrix} \text{table value,} \\ \text{Appendix D,} \\ 2N \text{ periods,} \\ R_b/2 \end{bmatrix} + \$M\begin{bmatrix} \text{table value,} \\ \text{Appendix B,} \\ 2N \text{ periods,} \\ R_b/2 \end{bmatrix} \qquad (12\text{–}9b)$$

Example   To see the effect of semi-annual interest payments upon the value of a bond, assume the Garrett Corporation has issued a 9 percent, $1000 bond. The debt is to mature in 6 years, and the investor's required rate of return is currently 8 percent. If interest is paid semi-annually, the number of periods is 12 (6 years × 2); the dollar interest to be received by the investor at the end of each 6-month period is $45 ($90 ÷ 2); and the required rate of return for 6 months is 4 percent (8 percent ÷ 2). Therefore, the equation is

$$V_b = \sum_{t=1}^{12} \frac{\$45}{(1 + .04)^t} + \frac{\$1000}{(1 + .04)^{12}} = \$1047.33$$

Equivalently,

$$V_b = \$45\begin{bmatrix} \text{table value,} \\ \text{Appendix D,} \\ 12 \text{ periods,} \\ 4 \text{ percent} \end{bmatrix} + \$1000\begin{bmatrix} \text{table value,} \\ \text{Appendix B,} \\ 12 \text{ periods,} \\ 4 \text{ percent} \end{bmatrix}$$

$$= \$45(9.385) + \$1000(.625)$$

$$= \$422.33 + \$625.00$$

$$= \$1047.33$$

---

[22] The logic for calculating the value of a bond that pays interest semi-annually is similar to the material presented in Chapter 9, where compound interest with nonannual periods was discussed.

Thus, the value (present value) of a bond paying $45 semi-annually, and $1000 at maturity (6 years), is $1047.33, provided the investor's required rate of return is 8 percent compounded semi-annually.[23]

PREFERRED STOCK VALUATION

Like a bondholder, the owner of preferred stock should receive a *constant income* from the investment in each period. However, the return from preferred stock comes in the form of *dividends* rather than *interest*. In addition, while bonds generally have a specific maturity date, most preferred stocks are perpetuities (nonmaturing). In this instance, finding the value (present value) of preferred stock, V_p, with a level cash flow stream continuing indefinitely, may best be explained by an example.

Example To illustrate the valuation of a preferred stock, consider American Telephone and Telegraph's preferred stock issue. Once again we use the three-step valuation procedure.

STEP 1: *Estimate the amount and timing of the receipt of the future cash flows the preferred stock is expected to provide.*

AT&T's preferred stock pays an annual dividend of $3.64. The shares do not have a maturity date; that is, they go to perpetuity.

STEP 2: *Evaluate the riskiness of the preferred stock's future dividends and determine the investor's required rate of return.*

The investor's required rate of return is assumed to equal 7.28 percent.

STEP 3: *Calculate the intrinsic value of the share of preferred stock, which is the present value of the expected dividends discounted at the investor's required rate of return.*

The valuation model for a share of preferred stock, V_p, is defined as follows:

$$
\begin{aligned}
V_p &= \frac{\text{dividend in year 1}}{(1 + \text{required rate of return})^1} \\
&+ \frac{\text{dividend in year 2}}{(1 + \text{required rate of return})^2} \\
&+ \cdots + \frac{\text{dividend in infinity}}{(1 + \text{required rate of return})^\infty} \\
&= \frac{D_1}{(1 + R_p)^1} \\
&+ \frac{D_2}{(1 + R_p)^2} \\
&+ \cdots + \frac{D_\infty}{(1 + R_p)^\infty} \\
&= \sum_{t=1}^{\infty} \frac{D_t}{(1 + R_p)^t}
\end{aligned}
\tag{12–10}
$$

---

[23] A slightly different answer may result from differences in rounding.

Since the dividends in each period are equal for preferred stock, equation (12–10) can be reduced to the following relationship.[24]

$$V_p = \frac{\text{annual dividend}}{\text{required rate of return}} = \frac{D}{R_p} \qquad (12\text{–}11)$$

Equation (12–11) represents the present value of an infinite stream of cash flows, where the cash flows are the same each year. We can determine the value of the AT&T preferred stock, using equation (12–11), as follows:

$$V_p = \frac{D}{R_p} = \frac{\$3.64}{.0728} = \$50$$

COMMON STOCK VALUATION

The third and last security we will learn to value is common stock. Like both bonds and preferred stock, a common stock's value is equal to the present value of all future cash flows expected to be received by the stockholder. However, in constrast to bonds, the owners of common shares are not promised interest income or a maturity payment at some specified time in the future. Nor does common stock entitle the holder to a predetermined constant dividend, as does preferred stock. For common stock, the dividend is based upon the profitability of the firm and upon management's decision to pay dividends or to retain the profits for reinvestment purposes. As a consequence, dividend streams tend to increase with the growth in corporate earnings. Thus, the uncertainty of future dividends is a prime distinguishing feature of common stock.

In addition to dividends, the common stockholder frequently relies upon stock price as a source of return. If the company is retaining a portion of its earnings to be reinvested, future profits and dividends should grow. This growth should be reflected in an increased market price of the common stock in future periods. Therefore, in

---

[24] To verify this result, consider the following equation

(i)
$$V_p = \frac{D_1}{(1 + R_p)} + \frac{D_2}{(1 + R_p)^2} + \cdots + \frac{D_n}{(1 + R_p)^n}$$

If we multiply both sides of this equation by $(1 + R_p)$, we have

(ii)
$$V_p(1 + R_p) = D_1 + \frac{D_2}{(1 + R_p)} + \cdots + \frac{D_n}{(1 + R_p)^{n-1}}$$

Subtracting (i) from (ii) yields

$$V_p(1 + R_p - 1) = D_1 - \frac{D_n}{(1 + R_p)^n}$$

As n approaches infinity, $D_n/(1 + R_p)^n$ approaches zero. Consequently,

$$V_p R_p = D_1 \qquad \text{and} \qquad V_p = \frac{D_1}{R_p}$$

Since $D_1 = D_2 = \cdots = D_n$, we need not designate the year. Therefore,

(iii)
$$V_p = \frac{D}{R_p}$$

developing a valuation model for common stock, both types of return (dividends and price appreciation) should be recognized.

To explain this process, let us begin by examining how an investor might value a common stock that is to be held for only one year.

Common Stock Valuation— Single Holding Period

For an investor holding a common stock for only one year, the value of the stock should equal the present value of both the expected dividend to be received in one year, D_1, and the anticipated market price of the share at year-end, P_1. If R_c represents a common stockholder's required rate of return, the value of the security, V_c, would be

$$V_c = \text{present value of dividend } (D_1)$$
$$+ \text{present value of market price } (P_1) \qquad (12\text{–}12)$$

$$= \frac{D_1}{(1 + R_c)} + \frac{P_1}{(1 + R_c)}$$

Example Suppose an investor is contemplating the purchase of Republic Bank of Texas common stock at the beginning of this year. The dividend at year-end is expected to be $1.64 and the market price by the end of the year is projected to be $22. If the investor's required rate of return is 18 percent, the value of the security would be

$$V_c = \frac{\$1.64}{1 + .18} + \frac{\$22}{1 + .18}$$

$$= \$1.39 + \$18.64$$

$$= \$20.03$$

Once again we see that valuation is the same three-step process. First we estimate the expected future cash flows from common stock ownership (a $1.64 dividend and a $22 end-of-year expected share price). Second, we estimate the investor's required rate of return after assessing the riskiness of the expected cash flows (assumed to be 18 percent). Finally, we discount the expected dividend and end-of-year share price back to the present at the investor's required rate of return.

Common Stock Valuation— Multiple Holding Period

Since common stock has no maturity date and is frequently held for many years, a multiple-holding-period valuation model is needed. The general common stock valuation model can be defined as follows:

$$V_c = \frac{D_1}{(1 + R_c)^1} + \frac{D_2}{(1 + R_c)^2} + \cdots + \frac{D_N}{(1 + R_c)^N} + \cdots + \frac{D_\infty}{(1 + R_c)^\infty} \qquad (12\text{–}13)$$

This equation simply indicates that we are discounting the dividend at the end of the first year, D_1, back one year, the dividend in the second year, D_2, back two years, . . . , the dividend in the Nth year back N years, . . . , and the dividend in infinity back an infinite number of years. The required rate of return is R_c. In using equation (12–13), we should note that the value of the stock is being established at the beginning of the year, say January 1, 1988. The most recent past dividend D_0 would have been paid the previous day on December 31, 1987. Thus, if we purchased the stock on January 1, the first dividend would be received in 12 months, on December 31, 1988, which is represented by D_1.

Fortunately, equation (12–13) can be reduced to a much more manageable form if dividends grow each year at a constant rate, g. The "constant growth" common stock valuation model is defined as follows:[25]

$$\text{common stock value} = \frac{\text{dividend in year 1}}{(\text{required rate of return}) - (\text{growth rate})}$$

$$V_c = \frac{D_1}{R_c - g} \quad (12\text{–}14)$$

Consequently, the value (present value) of a share of common stock whose dividends grow at a constant annual rate can be calculated using equation (12–14). Although the interpretation of this equation may not be intuitively obvious, we should remember that it solves for the present value of the future dividend stream growing at a rate, g, to infinity.

Example   Consider the valuation of a share of common stock that paid a $2 dividend at the end of the last year and is expected to pay a cash dividend every year from now to infinity. Each year the dividends are expected to grow at a rate of 10 percent. Based upon an assessment of the riskiness of the common stock, the investor's required

---

[25] Where common stock dividends grow at a constant rate of g every year, we can express the dividend in any year in terms of the dividend paid at the end of the previous year, D_0. For example, the expected dividend one year hence is simply $D_0(1 + g)$. Likewise, the dividend at the end of t years is $D_0(1 + g)^t$. Using this notation, the common stock valuation equation in (12–13) can be rewritten as follows:

$$V_c = \frac{D_0(1 + g)^1}{(1 + R_c)^1} + \frac{D_0(1 + g)^2}{(1 + R_c)^2} + \cdots + \frac{D_0(1 + g)^N}{(1 + R_c)^N} + \cdots + \frac{D_0(1 + g)^\infty}{(1 + R_c)^\infty} \quad (12\text{–}15)$$

If both sides of equation (12–15) are multiplied by $(1 + R_c)/(1 + g)$ and then equation (12–15) is subtracted from the product, the result is

$$\frac{V_c(1 + R_c)}{1 + g} - V_c = D_0 - \frac{D_0(1 + g)^\infty}{(1 + R_c)^\infty} \quad (12\text{–}16)$$

If $R_c > g$, which normally should hold, $[D_0(1 + g)^\infty/(1 + R_c)^\infty]$ approaches zero. As a result,

$$\frac{V_c(1 + R_c)}{1 + g} - V_c = D_0$$

$$V_c\left(\frac{1 + R_c}{1 + g}\right) - V_c\left(\frac{1 + g}{1 + g}\right) = D_0$$

$$V_c\left[\frac{(1 + R_c) - (1 + g)}{1 + g}\right] = D_0$$

$$V_c(R_c - g) = D_0(1 + g)$$

$$V_c = \frac{D_1}{R_c - g}$$

rate of return is 15 percent. Using this information, we would compute the value of the common stock as follows:

(i) Since the $2 dividend was paid last year (actually yesterday), we must compute the next dividend to be received, that is, D_1, where

$$D_1 = D_0(1 + g)$$
$$= \$2(1 + .10)$$
$$= \$2.20$$

(ii) Now using equation (12–14),

$$V_c = \frac{D_1}{R_c - g}$$
$$= \frac{\$2.20}{.15 - .10}$$
$$= \$44$$

EXPECTED RATES OF RETURN

Conceptually, each investor can have a different required rate of return for each individual security. However, the financial manager is interested in the required rate of return for the firm's securities that is implied by the market prices of those securities.

For example, the Alpha Co. has a bond with a current market price of $1000 that is maturing in one year; the bond's face value is $1000 and it pays $100 per year in interest. Using the bond valuation model in equation (12–8a),

$$V_b = \frac{\$I_1}{(1 + R_b)^1} + \frac{\$M}{(1 + R_b)^1} \qquad (12\text{–}8a)$$

we can solve for the investor's required rate of return implicit in the $1000 market price of the bond. That is:

$$\$1000 = \frac{\$100}{(1 + R_b)^1} + \frac{\$1000}{(1 + R_b)^1}$$

Solving for R_b, we find that the $1000 market price "implies" a required rate of return of 10 percent for investors at the margin—that is, investors who are just willing to purchase the bond for $1000 but will not pay a higher price for it. For these investors, the required rate of return equals the expected rate of return reflected in the bond's current market price. In this instance, both equal 10 percent.[26]

---

[26] This 10 percent required return for the investor at the margin is used in Chapter 13 to measure the cost of new debt capital to the firm. That is, if the firm sells a bond for $1000 and plans to repay the $1000 plus $100 interest one year later, then the cost of borrowing equals 10 percent. This 10 percent cost of borrowing is also the required rate of return of the investor at the margin.

Bondholder's Expected Rate of Return (Yield to Maturity)

The expected rate of return implicit in the current bond price is the discount rate that equates the present value of the future cash flows with the current market price of the bond.[27] The expected rate of return for a bond is also the rate of return the investor will earn if the bond is held to maturity, that being the **yield to maturity.** Thus, when referring to bonds, the terms *expected rate of return* and *yield to maturity* are often used interchangeably. For a more in-depth understanding of bond valuation, see the appendix at the end of the chapter.

Example   To illustrate, consider the bonds of the Brister Corporation, which are selling for $1140. The bonds carry a coupon interest rate of 9 percent and mature in 10 years.

In determining the **expected rate** of return implicit in the current market price, we need to find the rate that discounts the anticipated cash flows back to a present value of $1140, the existing market price for the bond. Trying 7 percent, we find the present value of future cash flows to be $1140.16, computed as follows:

Years	Cash Flow	Present Value Factors at 7 Percent	Present Value
1–10	$ 90 per year	7.024	$ 632.16
10	$1000 in year 10	0.508	508.00
		Present value at 7 percent:	$1140.16

Thus, the expected rate of return on the Brister Corporation's bonds for an investor who purchases the bonds for $1140 is approximately 7 percent.[28]

---

[27] When we speak of computing an expected rate of return, we are not describing the situation very accurately. Expected rates of return are ex ante (before the fact) and are based upon "expected and unobservable future cash flows" and therefore can only be "estimated."

[28] Finding the expected rate of return (yield to maturity) is a trial and error process. We try different rates until we find the rate that gets the present value of future cash flows (interest and maturity value) equal to the bond's current market price. Alternatively, many calculators with a finance option can solve for the rate. Also an approximate yield to maturity may be calculated by the following equation:

$$R_b = \frac{I + (M - V_b)/N}{(M + V_b)/2}$$

In our example where $I = \$90; M = \$1000, V_b = \$1140$, and $N = 10$ years:

$$R_b = \frac{\$90 + (\$1000 - \$1140)/10}{(\$1000 + \$1140)/2} = .0710 = 7.10\%$$

The slight difference between the 7.1 percent calculated above and the more accurate 7 percent determined above results because the approximation method does not discount the cash flows. The difference in results varies depending on the size of the difference between V_b and M and the number of years to maturity (N).

The Preferred Stockholder's Expected Rate of Return

In computing the preferred stockholder's expected rate we use the valuation equation for preferred stock. Earlier, equation (12–11) specified the value of a preferred stock, V_p, as

$$V_p = \frac{\text{annual dividend}}{\text{required rate of return}} = \frac{D}{R_p} \qquad (12\text{–}11)$$

Solving (12–11) for R_p,

$$R_p = \frac{\text{annual dividend}}{\text{value}} = \frac{D}{V_p} \qquad (12\text{–}17)$$

which simply indicates that the expected rate of return of a preferred security equals the dividend yield (dividend/price). For example, if the present market price of preferred stock is \$50 and it pays \$3.64 dividend, the expected rate of return implicit in the present market price is

$$R_p = \frac{D}{V_p} = \frac{\$3.64}{\$50} = 7.28 \text{ percent}$$

Therefore, investors at the margin (who pay \$50 per share for a preferred security that is paying \$3.64 in annual dividends) are expecting a 7.28 percent rate of return.

The Common Stockholder's Expected Rate of Return

The valuation equation for common stock was defined earlier as

$$\text{value} = \frac{\text{dividend in year 1}}{(1 + \text{required rate of return})^1} + \frac{\text{dividend in year 2}}{(1 + \text{required rate of return})^2}$$
$$+ \cdots + \frac{\text{dividend in year}\infty}{(1 + \text{required rate of return})^\infty} \qquad (12\text{–}13)$$

$$V_c = \frac{D_1}{(1 + R_c)^1} + \frac{D_2}{(1 + R_c)^2} + \cdots + \frac{D_\infty}{(1 + R_c)^\infty}$$

$$V_c = \sum_{t=1}^{\infty} \frac{D_t}{(1 + R_c)^t}$$

Owing to the difficulty of discounting to infinity, a key assumption was made that the dividends, D_t, increase at a constant annual compound growth rate of g. If this assumption is valid, equation (12–13) was shown to be equivalent to

$$\text{value} = \frac{\text{dividend in year 1}}{(\text{required rate of return} - \text{growth rate})} \qquad (12\text{–}14)$$

$$V_c = \frac{D_1}{(R_c - g)}$$

Thus, V_c represents the maximum value that an investor having a required rate of return of R_c would pay for a security having an anticipated dividend in year 1 of D_1 that is expected to grow in future years at rate g.[29] Solving equation (12–18) for R_c, we can compute the expected rate of return for common stock implicit in its current market price as follows:

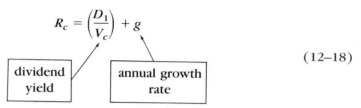

$$R_c = \left(\frac{D_1}{V_c}\right) + g$$

dividend yield

annual growth rate

(12–18)

From this equation, the common stockholder's expected rate of return is equal to the dividend yield plus a growth factor. Although the growth rate, g, applies to the growth in the company's dividends, the firm's earnings per share and the stock prices may also be expected to increase at the same rate. For this reason, g represents the annual percentage growth in the stock price. In other words, the investors' expected rate of return is satisfied by receiving dividends, expressed as a percentage of the price of the stock (dividend yield), and capital gains, as reflected by the percentage growth rate.

Example   As an example of computing the expected rate of return for a common stock, where dividends are anticipated to grow at a constant rate to infinity, assume that a firm's common stock A has a current market price of $44. If the expected dividend at the conclusion of this year is $2.20 and dividends and earnings are growing at a 10 percent annual rate (last year's dividend was $2.00), the expected rate of return implicit in the $44 stock price is as follows:

$$R_c = \frac{\$2.20}{\$44} + 10\% = 15 \text{ percent}$$

In summary, the expected rate of return implied by a given market price equals the required rate of return for investors at the margin. For these investors, the expected rate of return is just equal to their required rate of return, and therefore they are willing to pay the current market price for the security. These investors' required rate of return is of particular significance to the financial manager, since it represents the cost of new financing to the firm.

---

[29] At times the expected dividend at year-end (D_1) is not given. Instead we might only know the most recent dividend (paid yesterday), that is, D_0. If so, equation (12–14) must be restated as follows:

$$V_0 = \frac{D_1}{(R_c - g)} = \frac{D_0(1 + g)}{(R_c - g)}$$

Rates of Return: The Investor's Experience

In speaking of expected rates of return, we have used a number of hypothetical examples; however, it is also interesting to look at returns that have actually been received by investors. Such information is readily available. For example, Ibbotson and Sinquefield have provided annual rates of return as far back as 1926.[30] In their results, they summarize, among other things, the annual returns for four portfolios of securities:

1. A portfolio of U.S. Treasury bills (short-term government debt)
2. A portfolio of U.S. government bonds (long-term government debt)
3. A portfolio of corporate bonds (long-term debt issued by corporations)
4. A portfolio of common stock

Before comparing these returns, we should first think about what to expect. First, we would intuitively expect a Treasury bill to be the least risky of the four portfolios. Since a Treasury bill has a short-term maturity date, the price is less volatile (less risky) than the price of a long-term government security.[31] In turn, since there is a chance of default on a corporate bond which is essentially nonexistent for a long-term government bond, a long-term government bond is less risky than a long-term corporate bond. Finally, common stock is more risky than a corporate bond. The prices of common stocks are significantly more volatile than corporate bond prices. Common stocks also differ from bonds in that they are not obligated to provide a fixed amount of income.

With this in mind, we could reasonably expect different rates of return to the holders of these varied securities. If the market rewards an investor for assuming risk, the average annual rates of return should increase as risk increases.

A comparison of the annual rates of return for the four respective portfolios for the years 1926–81 is provided in Table 12–1. Four aspects of these returns are included in the table: (1) the average *nominal* annual rate of return; (2) the standard deviation of the returns, which measures the volatility or riskiness of the portfolios; (3) the average *real* annual rate of return, which is the nominal return less the inflation rate; and (4) the risk premium, which represents the additional return received beyond the risk-free rate (Treasury bill rate) for assuming risk. Looking first at the two columns of average annual returns and standard deviations, we gain a good overview of the risk-return relationships that have existed over the 56 years ending in 1981. For the most part, there has been a positive relationship between risk and return, with Treasury bills being least risky and common stocks being most risky. However, government bonds are the exception to the general pattern, where government bonds have offered no additional return beyond Treasury bills in spite of having more risk. Also, the government bonds have even been more risky than corporate bonds. This aberration has largely been the result of the five years 1977–81, during which time interest rates rose to all-time highs, which had a significantly negative impact on bond prices.

---

[30] Roger G. Ibbotson and Rex A. Sinquefield, *Stocks, Bonds, Bills, and Inflation: The Past and the Future*, Financial Analysts Research Foundation, Charlottesville, VA, 1982.

[31] For an explanation of the greater volatility for long-term bonds relative to short-term bonds, see Appendix 12A.

TABLE 12–1. Annual Rates of Return 1926–1981

Type of Security	Nominal Average Annual Returns	Standard Deviation of Returns	Real Average Annual Returns[a]	Risk Premium[b]
Treasury bills	3.1%	3.1%	0%	0%
Long-term government bonds	3.1	5.7	0	0
Corporate bonds	3.7	5.6	0.6	0.6
Common stocks	11.4	21.9	8.3	8.3

[a] Real return equals the nominal return less the average inflation rate from 1926 through 1981 of 3.1 percent.

[b] Risk premium equals the nominal security return less the average risk-free rate (Treasury bills) of 3.1 percent.

Source: Roger G. Ibbotson and Rex A. Sinquefield, *Stocks, Bonds, Bills, and Inflation: The Past and the Future*, Financial Analysts Research Foundation, Charlottesville, VA, 1982, p. 15.

The return information in Table 12–1 clearly demonstrates that only common stock has in the long run served as an inflation hedge and provided any substantial risk premium. However, it is equally apparent that the common stockholder is exposed to sizable risk, as demonstrated by a 21.9 percent standard deviation. In fact, in the 1926–81 time frame, common shareholders received negative returns in 19 of the 56 years, compared with only 1 in 56 for Treasury bills.

Summary

Valuation is an important factor in the financial manager's decision-making process. Failure to understand the concepts and computational procedures in valuing a security may often make sound decisions by the firm's executives unlikely. This fact is immediately evident in the financial officer's objective of maximizing the *value* of the firm's common stock.

For our purposes, *value is the present value of future cash flows expected to be received from an investment discounted at the investor's required rate of return*. In this context, the value of a security is a function of (1) the *expected cash inflows* from the asset, (2) the *riskiness* of the investment, and (3) the investor's *required rate of return*. In a world of uncertainty, the returns are measured in terms of the *expected cash flows* anticipated from the security, where the expected value recognizes the possible events and their probability of occurrence.

According to the capital asset pricing model (CAPM), risk should be defined in terms of the security's nondiversifiable or systematic risk. Such risk is measured by beta, which indicates the responsiveness of a security's return to changes in market returns. We can also think of systematic risk in terms of a security's sensitivity to various economic forces, as represented by the arbitrage pricing theory (APT). Whatever approach is taken in measuring risk, an investor must determine an appropriate required rate of return, depending upon the amount of risk inherent in the security. This minimum acceptable rate of return is equal to the risk-free rate plus a return premium for assuming the risk associated with the investment. In addition, the amount of the return premium, given a particular degree of risk, is dependent upon the investor's attitude toward the risk-return tradeoff. Simply stated, individual investors perceive risk differently and have different propensities for assuming risk.

Although valuing any security entails the same basic principles, the procedures used in each situation vary. For example, valuing a finite stream of cash flows involves computing the present value of the individual cash receipts for each period. An example of this type of valuation problem would be a bond that is scheduled to mature on a designated date. A second category of cash flow patterns involves an *infinite* cash flow stream, such as those from preferred stock and common stock. Although the underlying premise of valuation does not change—that is, value equals the present value of future cash flows—valuing such an asset requires a modification in the procedure. For securities with cash flows that are constant in each year, such as preferred stock, the present value equals the dollar amount of the annual dividend divided by the investor's required rate of return. Furthermore, for common stock where the future dividends are expected to increase at a constant growth rate, value may be given by the following equation:

$$\text{value} = \frac{\text{dividend in year one}}{(\text{required rate of return} - \text{growth rate})} \qquad (12\text{--}14)$$

The *expected rate of return* on a security is the required rate of return of investors who are willing to pay the present market price for the security, but no higher price. This rate of return is important to the financial manager because it equals the required rate of return of the firm's investors. This rate is the rate of return that makes the present value of future cash flows to be received by the investor just equal to the present market price of the security.

Study Questions

12–1. What are the basic differences between book value, liquidation value, market value, and intrinsic value?

12–2. Explain the three factors that determine the value of an asset.

12–3. a. What is meant by "the investor's required rate of return"?
   b. How have we measured the riskiness of an asset?
   c. How should the proposed measurement of risk be interpreted?

12–4. What is (a) unique risk, and (b) systematic risk (market or nondiversifiable risk)?

12–5. What is the meaning of beta? How is it used to calculate R, the investor's required rate of return?

12–6. Define the security market line. What does it represent?

12–7. a. Explain the logic behind the Arbitrage Pricing Theory (APT).
   b. How is the APT different from the CAPM?

12–8. Explain the relationship between an investor's required rate of return and the value of a security.

12–9. a. How does a bond's par value differ from its market value?
   b. Explain the difference between the coupon interest rate and a bondholder's required rate.

12–10. What is a general definition for the value of a security regardless of its type?

12–11. The common stockholders receive two types of return from their investment. What are they?

12–12. State how the investor's required rate of return is computed.

12–13. Define the investor's *expected* rate of return.

Self-Test Problems

ST–1. (*Expected Return and Risk*) Universal Corporation is planning to invest in a security that has several possible rates of return. Given the following probability distribution of returns, what is the expected rate of return on the investment? Also compute the standard deviation of the returns. What do the resulting numbers represent?

Probability	Return
.10	−10%
.20	5%
.30	10%
.40	25%

ST–2. Using the CAPM, estimate the appropriate required rate of return for the three stocks listed below, given that the risk-free rate is 5 percent, and the expected return for the market is 17 percent.

Stock	Beta
A	.75
B	.90
C	1.40

ST–3. Using the APT, along with the results of the Bower, Bower, and Logue research given in the chapter, estimate the appropriate required rates of return for the following three stocks:

Stock	Sensitivity Factor			
	Factor 1	Factor 2	Factor 3	Factor 4
A	−0.070	−0.020	0.010	0.003
B	−0.070	0.030	0.005	0.010
C	−0.070	−0.010	0.006	0.009

ST–4. (*Bond Valuation*) Trico bonds have a coupon rate of 8 percent, a par value of $1000, and will mature in 20 years. If you require a return of 7 percent, what price would you be willing to pay for the bond? What happens if you pay *more* for the bond? What happens if you pay *less* for the bond?

ST–5. (*Bond Valuation*) Sunn Co.'s bonds, maturing in 7 years, pay 8 percent interest on a $1000 face value. However, interest is paid semi-annually. If your required rate of return is 10 percent, what is the value of the bond? How would your answer change if the interest were paid annually?

ST–6. (*Bond Valuation*) Sharp Co. bonds are selling in the market for $1045. These 15-year bonds pay 7 percent interest on a $1000 par value. If they are purchased at the market price, what is the expected rate of return?

ST–7. (*Preferred Stock Valuation*) The preferred stock of Armlo pays a $2.75 dividend. What is the value of the stock if your required return is 9 percent?

ST–8. (*Common Stock Valuation*) Crosby Corporation's common stock paid $1.32 in dividends last year and is expected to grow indefinitely at an annual 7 percent rate. What is the value of the stock if you require an 11 percent return?

Study Problems

12–1. (*Expected Rate of Return and Risk*) Pritchard Press, Inc. is evaluating a security. One-year Treasury bills are currently paying 9.1 percent. Calculate the investment's expected return and its standard deviation. Should Pritchard invest in this security?

Probability	Return
.15	5%
.30	7%
.40	10%
.15	15%

12–2. (*Expected Rate of Return and Risk*) Syntex, Inc. is considering an investment in one of two common stocks. Given the information below, which investment is better, based upon risk and return?

Common Stock A		Common Stock B	
Probability	Return	Probability	Return
		.20	5%
.30	11%	.30	6%
.40	15%	.30	14%
.30	19%	.20	22%

12–3. (*Expected Rate of Return and Risk*) Friedman Manufacturing, Inc. has prepared the following information regarding two investments under consideration. Which investment should be accepted?

Security A		Security B	
Probability	Return	Probability	Return
.2	−2%	.10	4%
.5	18%	.30	6%
.3	27%	.40	10%
		.20	15%

12–4.   a. (*Required rate of return using CAPM*) Compute a "fair" rate of return for IBM common stock, which has a 1.2 beta. The risk-free rate is 6 percent and the market portfolio (New York Stock Exchange stocks) has an expected return of 16 percent.

   b. Why is the rate you have computed a "fair" rate?

12–5.   a. (*Required rate of return using APT*) If we use the arbitrage pricing theory to measure investors' required rate of return, what is our concept of risk?

   b. Using the results of the Bowers, Bowers, and Logue study of return variability, as captured in Equation (12–16), calculate the investors' required rate of return for the following stocks:

Stock	Sensitivity Factor			
	1	2	3	4
A	−0.070	0.030	0.005	0.010
B	−0.070	−0.010	0.006	0.009
C	−0.050	0.004	−0.010	−0.007
D	−0.060	−0.007	−0.006	0.006

   c. Assuming (i) a risk-free rate of 6.1 percent and (ii) an expected market return of 17.25 percent, estimate the investors' required rate of return for the four stocks in part (b), using the CAPM.

Stock	Beta
A	1.40
B	1.70
C	1.20
D	1.10

   d. What might explain the differences in your answers to parts (b) and (c)? After all, the same variable, required rate of return, is being "computed" in both cases.

12–6.   (*Bond Valuation*) Calculate the value of a bond that expects to mature in 12 years with a $1000 face value. The coupon interest rate is 8 percent and the investors' required rate of return is 12 percent.

12–7.   (*Preferred Stock Valuation*) What is the value of a preferred stock where the dividend rate is 14 percent on a $100 par value? The appropriate discount rate for a stock of this risk level is 12 percent.

12–8.   (*Bond Valuation*) Enterprise, Inc. bonds have a 9 percent coupon rate. The interest is paid semi-annually and the bonds mature in eight years. Their par value is $1000. If your required rate of return is 8 percent, what is the value of the bond? What is its value if the interest is paid annually?

12–9.   (*Bond Valuation*) You are willing to pay $900 for a 10-year bond ($1000 par value) that pays 8 percent interest (4 percent semi-annually). What is your expected rate of return?

12–10. (*Preferred Stock Valuation*) Solitron's preferred stock is selling for $42.16 and pays $1.95 in dividends. What is your expected rate of return if you purchase the security at the market price?

12–11. (*Preferred Stock Valuation*) You own 200 shares of Somner Resources' preferred stock, which currently sells for $40 per share and pays annual dividends of $3.40 per share. (a) What is your expected return? (b) If you require an 8 percent return and given the current price, should you sell or buy more stock?

12–12. (*Common Stock Valuation*) You intend to purchase Marigo common stock at $50 per share, hold it one year, and sell after a dividend of $6 is paid. How much will the stock price have to appreciate if your required rate of return is 15 percent?

12–13. (*Common Stock Valuation*) Made-It's common stock currently sells for $22.50 per share. The company's executives anticipate a constant growth rate of 10 percent and an end-of-year dividend of $2. (a) What is your expected rate of return? (b) If you require a 17 percent return, should you purchase the stock?

12–14. (*Common Stock Valuation*) Header Motor, Inc. paid a $3.50 dividend last year. At a growth rate of 5 percent, what is the value of the common stock if the investors require a 20 percent rate of return?

12–15. (*Capital Asset Pricing Model*) You are considering the purchase of 100 shares of Slick-Tex Inc.'s common stock. The historical beta on the security is 1.65 and the current market premium is 5.6 percent.

   a. If the riskless rate of interest is currently 12 percent, what will your required rate of return be?

   b. Given the rate of return computed in part (a), an expected dividend of $8.50 and a 5 percent growth rate, what value do you place on the stock?

12–16. (*Common Stock Valuation*) The common stock of Zaldi Co. is selling for $32.84. The stock recently paid dividends of $2.94 per share and has a projected growth rate of 9.5 percent. If you purchase the stock at the market price, what is your expected rate of return?.

12–17. (*Common Stock Valuation*) Honeywag common stock is expected to pay $1.85 in dividends next year, and the market price is projected to be $42.50 by year-end. If the investor's required rate of return is 11 percent, what is the current value of the stock?

12–18. (*Common Stock Valuation*) The market price for Hobart common stock is $43. The price at the end of one year is expected to be $48, and dividends for next year should be $2.84. What is the expected rate of return?

12–19. (*Bond Valuation*) Exxon 20-year bonds pay 9 percent interest annually on a $1000 par value. If you buy the bonds at $945, what is your expected rate of return?

12–20. (*Bond Valuation*) Zenith Co.'s bonds mature in 12 years and pay 7 percent interest annually. If you purchase the bonds for $1150, what is your expected rate of return?

12–21. (*Bond Valuation*) National Steel 15-year $1000 par value bonds pay 8 percent interest annually. The market price of the bonds is $1085, and your required rate of return is 10 percent.

   a. Compute the bond's expected rate of return.

   b. Determine the value of the bond to you, given your required rate of return.

   c. Should you purchase the bond?

12–22. (*Preferred Stock Valuation*) Pioneer's preferred stock is selling for $33 in the market and pays a $3.60 annual dividend.

   a. What is the expected rate of return on the stock?

   b. If an investor's required rate of return is 10 percent, what is the value of the stock for that investor?

   c. Should the investor acquire the stock?

12–23. (*Common Stock Valuation*) The common stock of NCP paid $1.32 in dividends last year. Dividends are expected to grow at an 8 percent annual rate for an indefinite number of years.
  a. If NCP's current market price is $23.50, what is the stock's expected rate of return?
  b. If your required rate of return is 10.5 percent, what is the value of the stock for you?
  c. Should you make the investment?

12–24. (*Capital Asset Pricing Model*) Johnson Manufacturing, Inc. is considering several investments. The rate on Treasury bills is currently 6.75 percent, and the expected return for the market is 12 percent. What should be the required rates of return for each investment (using the CAPM)?

Security	Beta
A	1.50
B	.82
C	.60
D	1.15

12–25. (*Capital Asset Pricing Model*) CSB, Inc. has a beta of .765. If the expected market return is 11.5 percent and the risk-free rate is 7.5 percent, what is the appropriate required return of CSB (using the CAPM)?

12–26. (*Capital Asset Pricing Model*) The expected return for the general market is 12.8 percent, and the risk premium in the market is 4.3 percent. Tasaco, LBM, and Exxos have betas of .864, .693, and .575, respectively. What are the appropriate required rates of return for the three securities?

Cumulative Review Problem

12–27. (*Valuing Securities*) You are considering three investments. The first is a bond that is selling in the market at $1100. The bond has a $1000 par value, pays interest at 13 percent, and is scheduled to mature in 15 years. For bonds of this risk class, you believe that a 14 percent rate of return should be required. The second investment that you are analyzing is a preferred stock ($100 par value) that sells for $90 and pays an annual dividend of $13. Your required rate of return for this stock is 15 percent. The last investment is a common stock ($25 par value) that recently paid a $2 dividend. The firm's earnings per share have increased from $3 to $6 in 10 years, which also reflects the expected growth in dividends per share for the indefinite future. The stock is selling for $20, and you think a reasonable required rate of return for the stock is 20 percent.
  a. Calculate the value of each security based on your required rate of return.
  b. Which investment(s) should be accepted? Why?
  c. 1. If your required rates of return changed to 12 percent for the bond, 14 percent for the preferred stock, and 18 percent for the common stock, how would your answers change to parts (a) and (b) above?
      2. Assuming again that your required rate of return for the common stock is 20 percent, but the anticipated growth rate changes to 12 percent, would your answers to (a) and (b) be different?

Self-Test Solutions

SS–1.

(A) Probability $P(X_i)$	(B) Return (X_i)	Expected Return $(\bar{X})$ (A) × (B)	Weighted Deviation $(X_i - \bar{X})^2\, p(X_k)$
.10	−10%	− 1%	52.9%
.20	5%	1%	12.8%
.30	10%	3%	2.7%
.40	25%	10%	57.6%
		$\bar{X} = 13\%$	$\sigma^2 = 126.0\%$
			$\sigma\ =\ 11.22\%$

From our studies in statistics, we know that if the distribution of returns was normal, then Universal could expect a return of 13 percent with a 67 percent possibility that this return would vary up or down by 11.22 percent between 1.78 percent (13% − 11.22%) and 24.22 percent (13% + 11.22%). However, the distribution is not normal, as is apparent from the probabilities.

SS–2.

Stock A	5% + .75(17% − 5%) = 14%
Stock B	5% + .90(17% − 5%) = 15.8%
Stock C	5% + 1.40(17% − 5%) = 21.8%

SS–3. Bower, Bower, and Logue results:
  a. Estimated risk-free rate: 6.2%
  b.

	Market Premiums for Factor		
1	**2**	**3**	**4**
−185.5%	144.5%	12.4%	−274.4%

Given the above information from Bower, Bower, and Logue, the required rates of return would be calculated as follows:

Stock A: 6.2% − 185.5%(−.070) + 144.5%(−0.020)
  + 12.4%(0.010) − 274.4%(0.003) = 15.60%

Stock B: 6.2% − 185.5%(−0.070) + 144.5%(0.030)
  + 12.4%(0.005) − 274.4%(0.010) = 20.84%

Stock C: 6.2% − 185.5%(−0.070) + 144.5%(−0.010)
  + 12.4%(0.006) − 274.4%(0.009) = 15.34%

SS–4.

$$\text{Price } (P_0) = \sum_{t=1}^{20} \frac{\$80}{(1.07)^t} + \frac{\$1000}{(1.07)^{20}}$$

Thus,

$80 (10.594) = \$ 847.52
$1000 (0.258) = \underline{\ \ 258.00}
price (P_0) = $1105.52

If you pay more for the bond, your required rate of return will not be satisfied. In other words, by paying an amount for the bond that exceeds $1105.52, the expected rate of return for the bond is less than the required rate of return. If you have the opportunity to pay less for the bond, the expected rate of return exceeds the 7 percent required rate of return.

SS–5. If interest is paid semi-annually:

$$\text{price } (P_0) = \sum_{t=1}^{14} \frac{\$40}{(1 + 0.05)^t} + \frac{\$1000}{(1 + 0.05)^{14}}$$

Thus,

$$
\begin{aligned}
\$ \quad 40 \, (9.899) &= \$395.96 \\
\$1000 \, (0.505) &= \underline{505.00} \\
\text{price } (P_0) \quad &= \underline{\underline{\$900.96}}
\end{aligned}
$$

If interest is paid annually:

$$\text{price } (P_0) = \sum_{t=1}^{7} \frac{\$80}{(1.10)^t} + \frac{\$1000}{(1.10)^7}$$

$$P_0 = \$80 \, (4.868) + \$1000 \, (0.513)$$

$$P_0 = \$902.44$$

SS–6. $\$1045 = \sum_{t=1}^{15} \dfrac{\$70}{(1 + R_b)^t} + \dfrac{\$1000}{(1 + R_b)^{15}}$

At 6% $\$70 \, (9.712) + \$1000 \, (0.417) = \$1096.84$

At 7%: $\$70 \, (9.108) + \$1000 \, (0.362) = \$1000.00$

Interpolation:

$$\text{Expected rate of return: } R_b = 6\% + \frac{\$51.84}{\$96.84} \, (1\%) = 6.54\%$$

SS–7. $\text{price } (P_0) = \left(\dfrac{\text{dividend}}{\text{required rate of return}} \right) = \dfrac{\$2.75}{0.09} = \$30.56$

SS–8. $\text{price } (P_0) = \left(\dfrac{\text{last year dividend} \, (1 + \text{growth rate})}{\text{required rate of return} - \text{growth rate}} \right)$

$$= \frac{\$1.32 \, (1.07)}{0.11 - 0.07}$$

$$= \$35.31$$

Selected References

Black F., and M. Scholes. "The Pricing of Options and Corporate Liabilities," *Journal of Political Economy*, 81 (1973), 637–657.

Bower, D., R. Bower, and D. Logue. "Arbitrage Pricing and Utility Stock Returns," *Journal of Finance*, September 1984, 1041–54.

—, —, and —. "Equity Screening Rates Using Arbitrage Pricing Theory," in C. F. Lee, ed., *Advances in Financial Planning*. Greenwich, CT: JAI Press, 1984.

Brennan, M., and E. Schwartz. "Evaluating Natural Resource Investments," *The Journal of Business*, 58 (April 1985), pp. 135–157.

Chen, N. "Some Empirical Tests of the Theory of Arbitrage Pricing," *Journal of Finance*, December 1983, 1393–1414.

Gordon, Myron. *The Investment, Financing and Valuation of the Corporation*. Homewood, IL: Richard D. Irwin, 1963.

Ibbotson, R. G., and R. A. Sinquefield. *Stocks, Bonds, Bills and Inflations: The Past and the Future*. Charlottesville, VA: Financial Analysts Research Foundation, 1982.

Keim, D. "Size-Related Anomalies and Stock Market Seasonality: Further Empirical Evidence," *Journal of Financial Economics*, June 1983, 13–32.

Lanstein, R. and W. Sharpe. "Duration and Security Risk," *Journal of Financial and Quantitative Analysis*, November 1978, 653–68.

Levy, H. "Tests of Capital Asset Pricing Hypotheses," *Research in Finance*, 1 (1979), 115–223.

Masulis, R. W. "The Effects of Capital Structure Change on Security Prices: A Study of Exchange Offers," *Journal of Financial Economics*, 8 (June 1980), 139–77.

Modigliani, F., and G. Pogue. "An Introduction to Risk and Return," *Financial Analysts Journal*, March–April and May–June 1974, 68–80, 69–86.

Roll, R. "A Critique of the Asset Pricing Theory's Tests," *Journal of Financial Economics*, March 1977, 126–76.

—. "Performance Evaluation and Benchmark Errors," *Journal of Portfolio Management*, 6 (Summer 1980), 5–12.

—, and S. Ross. "The Arbitrage Pricing Theory Approach to Strategic Portfolio Planning," *Financial Analysts Journal*, May–June 1984, 14–26.

—, and —. "An Empirical Investigation of the Arbitrage Pricing Theory," *Journal of Finance*, December 1980, 1073–1103.

Rosenberg, B. "The Capital Asset Pricing Model and the Market Model," *Journal of Portfolio Management*, Winter 1981, 5–16.

Williams, John B. *The Theory of Investment Value*. Cambridge, MA: Harvard University Press, 1938.

APPENDIX 12A
More on Bond Valuation: Understanding Key Relationships

In the text of Chapter 12, we have learned to find the value of a bond (V_b), given (1) the amount of interest payments (I_t), (2) the maturity value (M), (3) the length of time to maturity (N years), and (4) the investor's required rate of return, R_b. We have also learned how to compute the expected rate of return, which also happens to be the current interest rate on the bond, given (1) the current market value (V_b), (2) the amount of interest payments (I_t), (3) the maturity value (M), and (4) the length of time to maturity (N years). These computations represent the basics of bond valuation; however, a more complete understanding of bond valuation requires that we examine five additional key relationships:

FIRST RELATIONSHIP

The value of a bond is inversely related to changes in the investor's present required rate of return (the current interest rate). That is, as interest rates increase (decrease), the value of the bond decreases (increases).

To illustrate, assume that an investor's required rate of return for a given bond is 12 percent. The bond has a par value of $1000 and annual interest payments of $120, indicating a 12 percent coupon interest rate ($120 ÷ $1000 = 12%). Assuming a five-year maturity date, the bond would be worth $1000, computed as follows:

$$V_b = \frac{I_1}{(1 + R_b)^1} + \cdots + \frac{I_N}{(1 + R_b)^N} + \frac{M}{(1 + R)^N}$$

$$= \sum_{t=1}^{N} \frac{I_t}{(1 + R_b)^t} + \frac{M}{(1 + R_b)^N} \qquad (12\text{--}8a)$$

$$= \sum_{t=1}^{5} \frac{\$120}{(1 + .12)^t} + \frac{\$1000}{(1 + .12)^5}$$

$$V_b = \$120 \begin{pmatrix} \text{table value,} \\ \text{Appendix D,} \\ \text{5 years,} \\ \text{12 percent} \end{pmatrix} + \$1000 \begin{pmatrix} \text{table value,} \\ \text{Appendix B,} \\ \text{5 years,} \\ \text{12 percent} \end{pmatrix} \qquad (12\text{--}8b)$$

$$V_b = \$120(3.605) + \$1000(.567)$$

$$= \$432.60 + \$567.00$$

$$= \$999.60 \cong \$1000.00$$

If, however, the investor's required rate of return (going interest rate) increases from 12 to 15 percent, the value of the bond would decrease to $899.24:

$$V_b = \$120 \begin{pmatrix} \text{table value,} \\ \text{Appendix D,} \\ \text{5 years,} \\ \text{15 percent} \end{pmatrix} + \$1000 \begin{pmatrix} \text{table value,} \\ \text{Appendix B,} \\ \text{5 years,} \\ \text{15 percent} \end{pmatrix} \qquad (12\text{--}8b)$$

$$V_b = \$120(3.352) + \$1000(.497)$$

$$= \$402.24 + \$497.00$$

$$= \$899.24$$

On the other hand, if the investor's required rate of return decreases to 9 percent, the bond would increase in value to $1116.80:

$$V_b = \$120 \begin{pmatrix} \text{table value,} \\ \text{Appendix D,} \\ \text{5 years,} \\ \text{9 percent} \end{pmatrix} + \$1000 \begin{pmatrix} \text{table value,} \\ \text{Appendix B,} \\ \text{5 years,} \\ \text{9 percent} \end{pmatrix} \qquad (12\text{--}8b)$$

$$V_b = \$120(3.890) + \$1000(.650)$$

$$= \$466.80 + \$650.00$$

$$= \$1116.80$$

This inverse relationship between the investor's required rate of return and the value of a bond is presented in Figure 12A–1. Clearly, as an investor demands a higher rate of return, the value of the bond decreases. The higher rate of return desired by the investor can be achieved only by paying less for the bond. Conversely, a lower required rate of return yields a higher market value for the bond.

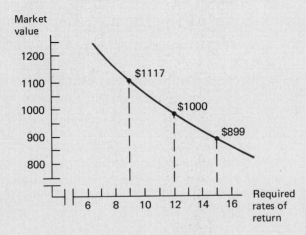

FIGURE 12A–1. Value and
Required Rates for a 5-Year
Bond at 12 Percent Coupon
Rate

Changes in bond prices represent an element of uncertainty for the bond investor. If the current interest rate (required rate of return) changes, the price of the bond also fluctuates. An increase in interest rates causes the bondholder to incur a loss in market value. Since future interest rates and the resulting bond value cannot be predicted with certainty, a bond investor is exposed to the risk of changing values as interest rates vary. This risk has come to be known as *interest rate risk*.

SECOND RELATIONSHIP

The market value of a bond will be less than the par value if the investor's required rate is above the coupon interest rate; but it will be valued above par value if the investor's required rate of return is below the coupon interest rate.

Using the previous example, we observed that:

a. The bond has a *market* value of $1000, equal to the par or maturity value, when the investor's required rate of return equals the 12 percent coupon interest rate. In other words,

required rate = *coupon rate*, then *market value* = *par value*
12%　　=　　12%　, then　　$1000　=　$1000

b. When the required rate is 15 percent, which exceeds the 12 percent coupon rate, the market value falls below par value to $899.24. That is

required rate > *coupon rate,* then *market value* < *par value*
15%　　>　　12%　, then　　$899.24　<　$1000

In this case the bond sells at a discount below par value; thus it is called a *discount bond*.

c. When the required rate is 9 percent, or less than the 12 percent coupon rate, the market value, $1116.80, exceeds the bond's par value. In this instance

required rate < *coupon rate*, then *market value* > *par value*
9%　　<　　12%　, then　　$1116.80　>　$1000

The bond is now selling at a premium above par value; thus, it is a *premium bond*.

THIRD RELATIONSHIP

As the maturity date approaches, the market value of a bond approaches its par value.

Continuing to draw from our prior example, the bond has 5 years remaining until the maturity date. At that time, the bond sells at a discount below par value ($899.24) when the required rate is 15 percent, and sells at a premium above par value ($1116.80) when the required rate is only 9 percent.

In addition to knowing value today, an investor would also be interested in knowing how these values would change over time, assuming no change in the current interest rates. For example, how will these values change when only 2 years remain until maturity rather than 5 years? Table 12A–1 shows the values with 5 years remaining to maturity, the values as recomputed with only 2 years left until the bonds mature, along with the changes in values between the 5-year bonds and the 2-year bonds. The following conclusions can be drawn from these results:

1. The premium bond sells for less as maturity approaches. The price decreases from $1116.80 to $1053.08 over the 3 years.
2. The discount bond sells for more as maturity approaches. The price increases from $899.24 to $951.12 over the 3 years.

TABLE 12A–1. Values Relative to Maturity Dates

Required Rate	Market Value if Maturity Is		Change in Value
	5 Years	2 Years	
9%	$1116.80	$1053.08	−$63.72
12	1000.00	1000.00	.00
15	899.24	951.12	51.88

The change in prices over the entire life of the bond is shown in Figure 12A–2 on page 427. The graph clearly demonstrates that the value of a bond, either a premium or a discount bond, approaches par value as the maturity date becomes closer in time.

FOURTH RELATIONSHIP

As already noted, a change in current interest rates (required rate of return) causes a change in the market value of a bond. However, the impact on value is greater for long-term bonds than it is for short-term bonds. Thus, long-term bonds have greater interest rate risk than do short-term bonds.

In Figure 12A–1 we observed the effect of interest rate changes on a five-year bond paying a 12 percent coupon interest rate. What if the bond did not mature until ten years from today instead of five years? Would the changes in market value be the same? Absolutely not. The changes in value would be more significant for the 10-year bond. For example, if we vary the current interest rates (the bondholder's required rate of return) from 9 percent

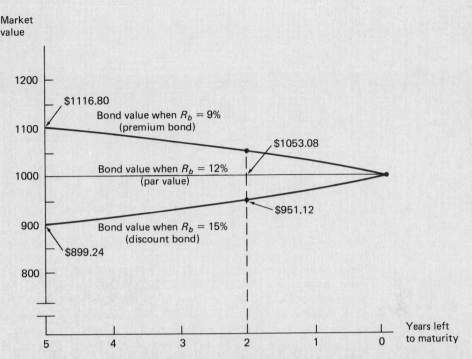

Market value

FIGURE 12A–2. Value of a 12 Percent Coupon Bond During The Life of the Bond

to 12 percent and then to 15 percent, as we did earlier with the 5-year bond, the values for both the 5-year and the 10-year bonds would be as follows:

Required Rate	Market Value for a 12% Coupon Rate Bond Maturing in:	
	5 Years	10 Years
9%	$1116.80	$1192.16
12	1000.00	1000.00
15	899.24	849.28

Using these values and the required rates, we can graph the changes in values for the two bonds relative to different interest rates. These comparisons are provided in Figure 12A–3. The figure clearly illustrates that the price of a long-term bond (say 10 years) is more responsive or sensitive to interest rate changes than the price of a short-term bond (say 5 years).

The reason long-term bond prices fluctuate more than short-term bond prices in response to interest rate changes is simple. Assume an investor bought a 10-year bond yielding a 12 percent interest rate. If the current interest rate for bonds of similar risk increased to 15 percent, the investor would be locked into the lower rate for 10 years. If, on the other

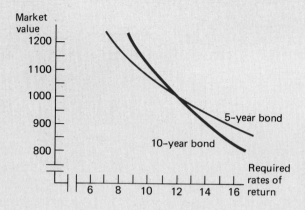

FIGURE 12A–3. Market
Values of a 5-Year and
10-Year Bond at Different
Required Rates

hand, a shorter-term bond had been purchased, say one maturing in 2 years, the investor would only have to accept the lower return for 2 years and not the full 10 years. At the end of year 2, the investor would receive the maturity value of $1000 and could buy a bond offering the higher 15 percent rate for the remaining 8 years. Thus, interest rate risk is determined, at least in part, by the length of time an investor is required to commit to an investment. However, the holder of a long-term bond may take some comfort from the fact that long-term interest rates are usually not as volatile as short-term rates. If the short-term rate changed one percentage point, for example, it would not be unusual for the long-term rate to change only .3 percentage points.

FIFTH RELATIONSHIP

The sensitivity of a bond's value to changing interest rates depends not only on the length of time to maturity, but also on the pattern of cash flows provided by the bond.

It is not at all unusual for two bonds with the same maturity to react differently to a change in interest rates. Consider two bonds, A and B, both with 10-year maturities and the same 10-percent interest rate. While the bonds are similar in terms of maturity date and the contractual interest rate, the structure of the interest payments is different for each bond. Bond A pays $100 interest annually, with the $1000 principal being repaid at the end of the tenth year. Bond B is called a zero-coupon bond; it pays no interest until the bond matures. At that time the bondholder receives $1593.70 in interest plus $1000 in principal. The value of both bonds, assuming a market interest rate (required rate of return) of 10 percent, is $1000. However, if interest rates fell to 6 percent, bond A's market value would be $1294, compared to $1447 for bond B. Why the difference? Both bonds have the same maturity, and each promises the same 10-percent rate of return. The answer lies in the differences in their cash flow patterns. Bond B's cash flows are received in the more distant future on average than are the cash flows for bond A. Since a change in interest rates always has a greater impact on the present value of later cash flows than on earlier cash flows (due to the effects of compounding), bonds with cash flows coming later on average will be more sensitive to interest rate changes than will bonds with earlier cash flows. This phenomenon was recognized in 1938 by Macaulay, who devised the concept of **duration.**

The **duration** of a bond is simply a measure of the responsiveness of its price to a change in interest rates. The greater the relative percentage change in a bond price in response to a given percentage change in the interest rate, the longer the duration. In computing duration, we consider not only the maturity or term over which cash flows are received but also the time pattern of interim cash flows. Specifically, duration is a weighted average time to maturity in which the weight attached to each year is the present value of the cash flow for that year. A measurement of duration may be represented as follows:

$$\text{duration} = \frac{-\sum_{t=1}^{N} \frac{tC_t}{(1+R_b)^t}}{P_0} \qquad (12A{-}1)$$

where t = the year the cash flow is to be received

   N = the number of years to maturity

   C_t = the cash flow to be received in year t

   R_b = the bondholder's required rate of return

   P_0 = the bond's present value

For our two bonds, A and B, duration would be calculated as follows:

$$\text{duration bond A} = \frac{-\left((1)\frac{\$100}{(1.1)^1} + (2)\frac{\$100}{(1.1)^2} + (3)\frac{\$100}{(1.1)^3}\right.}{\$1000}$$
$$= + \cdots + \cdots (9)\frac{\$100}{(1.1)^9} + (10)\frac{\$1100}{(1.1)^{10}}\right)$$

$$= -6.759$$

$$\text{duration bond B} = \frac{-\left((1)\frac{0}{(1.1)^1} + (2)\frac{0}{(1.1)^2} + (3)\frac{0}{(1.1)^3} + \cdots +\right.}{\$1000}$$
$$= + \cdots + (9)\frac{0}{(1.1)^9} + (10)\frac{\$2593.70}{(1.1)^{10}}\right)$$

$$= -10$$

Thus, while both bonds have the same maturity, 10 years, the zero coupon bond (bond B) is more sensitive to interest rate changes, as suggested by its higher duration which in this instance equals its maturity.[32] (The negative sign has been added to the equation to remind us that values move inversely with changing interest rates.) The lesson learned: In assessing a bond's sensitivity to changing interest rates, the bond's duration is the appropriate measure, not the term to maturity.

---

[32] Maturity and duration are the same only for zero coupon bonds or securities that pay only one cash flow and it occurs at maturity.

Summary

Certain key relationships exist in bond valuation. A brief summary of these factors would include the following:

1. A decrease in interest rates (required rates of return) will cause the value of a bond to increase; an interest rate increase will cause a decrease in value. The change in value caused by changing interest rates is called *interest rate risk*.
2. If the bondholder's required rate of return (current interest rate) equals the coupon interest rate, the bond will sell at par, or maturity value.
3. If the current interest rate exceeds the bond's coupon rate, the bond will sell below par value, or at a "discount."
4. If the current interest rate is less than the bond's coupon rate, the bond will sell above par value, or at a "premium."
5. Regardless of whether a bond is selling below or above par value, the value of the bond will gradually approach par value as the bond matures.
6. A bondholder owning a long-term bond is exposed to greater interest rate risk than when owning a short-term bond.
7. In understanding a bond's sensitivity to interest rate changes, we must consider not only the time to maturity, but also the time pattern of interim cash flows.

Study Problem

12A–1. (*Bond Valuation*) You own a bond that pays $100 in annual interest, with a $1000 par value. It matures in 15 years. Your required rate of return is 12 percent.
  a. Calculate the value of the bond.
  b. How does the value change if your required rate of return (i) increases to 15 percent or (ii) decreases to 8 percent?
  c. Explain the implications of your answers in part (b) as they relate to interest rate risk, premium bonds, and discount bonds.
  d. Assume that the bond matures in 5 years instead of 15 years. Recompute your answers in part (b).
  e. Explain the implications of your answers in part (d) as they relate to interest rate risk, premium bonds, and discount bonds.

12A–2. (*Duration*) Calculate the value and the duration for the following bonds:

Bond	Years to Maturity	Annual Interest	Maturity Value
P	5	$100	$1000
Q	5	70	1000
R	10	120	1000
S	10	80	1000
T	15	65	1000

Your required rate of return is 8 percent.

<p style="text-align:center">

13

Cost of Capital

Having studied both capital budgeting (Chapters 10 and 11) and the valuation of financial securities (Chapter 12), we are now ready to connect the firm's investment decisions with its financing decisions. At the fundamental level, the cost of capital provides this connecting link.[1] These interrelationships can be visualized as follows:

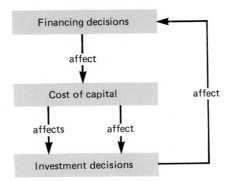

How a firm finances its assets affects its cost of capital, which in turn affects which investments will be accepted. Also, the investments that are selected, depending upon their riskiness, may affect the firm's cost of capital and determine in part what financing options are available.

In this chapter we will look in detail at the concepts behind the cost of capital, and we will learn the procedures for estimating the firm's cost of capital. For the time being, we will need to hold constant how the firm finances its investments; that is, we will assume a constant debt-equity mix. This assumption will be relaxed

---

[1] The term "cost of capital" may be used interchangably with the firm's required rate of return, the hurdle rate, the discount rate, and the opportunity cost.

in Chapter 15 when we study the relationship between the firm's cost of capital and its financing decisions. At that time we will consider the mix of debt and equity that may minimize the firm's capital costs, and thereby maximize its value.

In this chapter, we will look at the following issues:

1. The basic concepts underlying the estimation of the cost of capital for a firm
2. The key factors influencing a corporation's cost of capital
3. The assumptions generally required in measuring and using a firm's overall or company-wide cost of capital
4. The calculation of a corporation's overall cost of capital
5. The cost of capital of large firms
6. An approach to measuring a project-specific required rate of return as an alternative to the firm's weighted cost of capital (Appendix 13A).

THE CONCEPT OF THE COST OF CAPITAL

A firm's **cost of capital** is the rate that must be earned in order to satisfy the firm's investors, given the level of risk. If the firm earned exactly its cost of capital on an investment project, then we would expect the price of its common stock to remain unchanged following the acceptance of the project. However, if a rate different from the cost of capital was attained, we would expect the price of the stock to change. For example, in Figure 13–1 the internal rates of return for projects A, B, and C exceed the firm's cost of capital, so accepting these projects would increase the value of the firm's common stock. In contrast, investing in projects D and E would lower the stock value, which says that the best level of capital expenditures equals $17 million. *Therefore, the cost of capital is the rate of return on investments that leaves the price of the firm's common stock unchanged.* (Note that we assume that all the projects in Figure 13–1 are similar in terms of risk.)

FIGURE 13–1. Investment and Financing Schedules

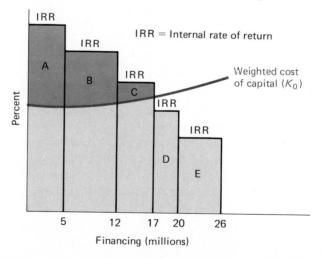

TABLE 13–1. Lynn Corporation Capital Structure

	Amount	Percentage of Capital Structure
Bonds (8% interest rate)	$ 600,000	30%
Preferred stock (10% dividend rate)	200,000	10%
Common stock	1,200,000	60%
Total liabilities and equity	$2,000,000	100%

While we are trying to find the rate of return on an investment that leaves the common stock price unchanged, we must also consider the other sources of capital, such as debt and preferred stock. To illustrate, the Lynn Corporation's capital structure is presented in Table 13–1. The company is using three sources of capital: debt, preferred stock, and common stock. Management is considering a $200,000 investment opportunity with an expected internal rate of return of 14 percent. The current cost of the firm's capital (minimum acceptable rate of return) for each source of financing has been determined to be:

Cost of debt capital	10%
Cost of preferred stock	12
Cost of common stock	16

Given this information, should the investment be made? The creditors and preferred stockholders would probably encourage us to undertake the project. However, since the 14 percent internal rate of return on the investment is less than the common stockholders' required rate of return, they might argue that the investment should be forgone. Who is right?

To answer this question, we must know what percentage of the $200,000 is to be provided by each type of investor. If we intend to maintain the same capital structure mix as reflected in Table 13–1 (30 percent debt, 10 percent preferred stock, and 60 percent common stock), we could compute a weighted cost of capital, where the weights equal the percentage of capital to be financed by each source. For our example, the weighted cost of the individual sources of capital is computed in Table 13–2 to be 13.8 percent. From this calculation we would conclude that an investment offering at least a 13.8 percent return would be acceptable to the company's

TABLE 13–2. Alfred Corporation Weighted Cost of Capital

	Weights (Percentage of Financing)	Cost of Individual Sources	Weighted Cost
Debt	30%	10%	3.0%
Preferred stock	10	12	1.2
Common stock	60	16	9.6
	100%	Weighted cost of capital:	13.8%

Debt   .3   x   AT TAX COST (TAX @ 40%)   WTD. AFTAX Cost
.10 (1 - t) = .06   =   .018

P.S.   .1   x   .12(1-t)   =   .012

C.S.   .6   x   .16   =   .096
+
12.6%

investors. In this illustration the investment should be undertaken, since the 14 percent rate of return more than satisfies all investors. *In summary, each type of capital (debt, preferred stock, and common stock) should be incorporated into the cost of capital, with the relative importance of particular source being based upon the percentage of the financing provided by each source.*

FACTORS DETERMINING THE COST OF CAPITAL

To gain further insight into the meaning of the firm's cost of capital, we should consider the elements in the business environment that cause a company's cost of capital to be high or low. Looking at Figure 13–2, we see four primary factors: general economic conditions, the marketability of the firm's securities (market conditions), operating

FIGURE 13–2. Primary Factors Influencing the Cost of a Particular Source of Capital

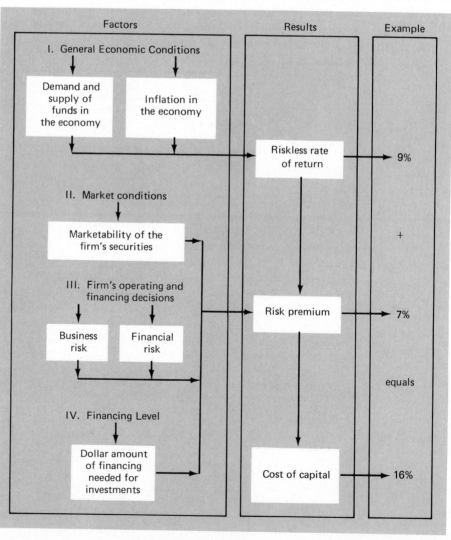

and financing conditions within the company and the amount of financing needed for new investments. These four variables also relate to our discussion in chapter 12, where we separated an investor's required rate of return into (a) the riskless or risk-free rate, and (b) the risk premium. These two segments also represent the key ingredients in the firm's cost of capital.

Factor 1: General Economic Conditions
The first factor, general economic conditions, determines the demand for and supply of capital within the economy, as well as the level of expected inflation. This economic variable is reflected in the riskless rate of return. This rate represents the rate of return on risk-free investments, such as the interest rate on short-term U.S. government securities. In principle, as the demand for money in the economy changes relative to the supply, investors alter their required rate of return. For example, if the demand for money increases without an equivalent increase in the supply, lenders will raise their required interest rate. At the same time, if inflation is expected to deteriorate the purchasing power of the dollar, investors require a higher rate of return to compensate for this anticipated loss.

Factor 2: Market Conditions
To this point, risk has had no impact upon the cost of capital. However, if an investor is purchasing a security where the risk of the investment is significant, the opportunity for additional returns is necessary to make the investment attractive. Essentially, as risk increases, the investor requries a higher rate of return. This increase is called a risk premium. If investors increase their required rate of return, this will simultaneously cause a higher cost of capital. Remember we defined risk in Chapter 12 as the potential variability of returns. If the security is not readily marketable when the investor wants to sell, or even if a continuous demand for the security exists but the price varies significantly, an investor will require a relatively high rate of return. On the other hand, if a security is readily marketable and its price is reasonably stable, the investor will have a lower required rate of return and the company's cost of capital will be lower.

Factor 3: Firm's Operating and Financing Decisions
Risk, or the variability of returns, also results from decisions made within the company. Risk resulting from these decisions is generally divided into two types, business risk and financial risk. **Business risk** is the variability in returns on assets and is affected by the company's investment decisions. **Financial risk** is the increased variability in returns to common stockholders as a result of using debt and preferred stock. As business risk and financial risk increase or decrease, the investor's required rate of return (and the cost of capital) will move in the same direction.

Factor 4: Amount of Financing
The last factor determining the corporation's cost of funds is the level of financing required. As the financing requirements of the firm become larger, the weighted cost of capital increases for several reasons. For instance, as more securities are issued, additional flotation costs (cost of selling securities) will affect the percentage cost of the funds to the firm. Also, as management approaches the market for large amounts of capital relative to the firm's size, the investors' required rate of return may rise. Suppliers of capital become hesitant to grant relatively large sums without evidence of management's capability to absorb this capital into the business. This concern is reflected in the proverbial "too much too soon." Also, as the size of the issue increases, there is greater difficulty in placing it in the market without reducing the price of the security, which also increases the firm's cost of capital.

A Summary Illustration To summarize, the important variables influencing a corporation's cost of capital include the following:

1. **General economic conditions.** This factor determines the risk-free rate or riskless rate of return.
2. **Marketability of a company's securities.** As the marketability of a security increases, investors' required rates of return decrease, lowering the corporation's cost of capital.
3. **Operating and financial decisions made by management.** If management accepts investments with high levels of risk or if it uses debt or preferred stock extensively, the firm's risk increases. Investors then require a higher rate of return, which causes a higher cost of capital to the company.
4. **Amount of financing being requested.** Requests for larger amounts of capital increase the firm's cost of capital.

An illustration of the cost of capital for a particular source is presented in the right-hand margin of Figure 13–2. The risk-free rate, determined by the general economic conditions, is 9 percent. However, owing to the additional risks associated with the security, the firm has to earn an additional 7 percent to satisfy the investors' required rate of return of 16 percent.

ASSUMPTIONS OF THE COST OF CAPITAL MODEL

In a complex business world, difficulties quickly arise in computing a corporation's cost of capital. For this reason, several simplifying assumptions are generally made.

Constant Business Risk Since business risk is defined as the potential variability of returns on an investment, the level of business risk within a firm is determined by management's investment policies. An investor's required rate of return for a company's securities and therefore the firm's cost of capital is a function of the firm's current business risk. If this risk level is altered, the corporation's investors will naturally change their required rates of return, which in turn modifies the cost of capital. However, the amount of change in the cost of capital resulting from a given increase or decrease in business risk is difficult to assess. For this reason, the cost of capital calculation assumes that any investment being considered will not significantly change the firm's business risk. In other words, *the cost of capital is an appropriate investment criterion only for an investment having a business risk level similar to that of existing assets.*

Constant Financial Risk Financial risk has been defined as the increased variability in returns on common stock resulting from the increased use of debt and preferred stock financing.[2] Also, financial risk relates to the threat of bankruptcy. As the percentage of debt in the capital structure increases, the possibility that the firm will be unable to pay interest and the principal balance is also increased. As a result, the level of financial risk in a company has an impact upon the investors' required rate of return. As the amount of debt rises, the common stockholders will increase their required rate of return. In other words, the costs of individual sources of capital are a function of the current financial structure. For this reason, the data used in computing the cost of capital

---

[2] This concept is further explained in Chapter 14.

are appropriate only if management continues to use the same financial mix. If the present capital structure consists of 40 percent debt, 10 percent preferred stock, and 50 percent common stock, this capital structure is assumed to be maintained in the financing of future investments.

Constant Dividend Policy

A third assumption required in estimating the cost of capital relates to the corporation's dividend policy. For ease of computation it is generally assumed that the firm's dividends are increasing at a constant annual growth rate. Also, this growth is assumed to be a function of the firm's earning capabilities and not merely the result of paying out a larger percentage of the company's earnings. Thus, it is implicitly assumed that the dividend payout ratio (dividends/net income) is constant. The rationale for this simplifying assumption is explained later.

The preceding assumptions are quite restrictive. Thus, management should be aware of the underlying assumptions of the cost of capital computation before using it in investment analyses. In a practical setting the financial executive may need a range of possible cost of capital values rather than a single-point estimate. For example, it may be more appropriate to talk in terms of a 10 to 12 percent range as an estimate of the firm's cost of capital, rather than assuming that a precise number can be determined. In this chapter, however, our principal concern will be with calculating a single cost of capital figure.

COMPUTING THE WEIGHTED COST OF CAPITAL

A firm's weighted cost of capital is a composite of the individual costs of financing, weighted by the percentage of financing provided by each source. Therefore, a firm's weighted cost of capital is a function of (1) the individual costs of capital and (2) the makeup of the capital structure—the percentage of funds provided by debt, preferred stock, and common stock. Also, as we noted earlier, the amount of funds raised affects the cost of capital. This last consideration, the level of financing, is not examined until later.

As we explain the procedures for computing a company's cost of capital, it is helpful to remember that three basic steps are involved:

1. Calculate the costs of capital for each individual source of financing used by the firm, which generally includes debt, preferred stock, and common stock.
2. Determine the percentage of debt, preferred stock, and common stock to be used in financing future investments.
3. Using the individual costs and the capital structure percentages in the first two steps, compute an overall or weighted cost of capital for the various amounts of financing that might be needed.

The computations are not difficult if we understand our purpose: We want to calculate the firm's overall cost of capital. A simple analogy would be calculating the average age of students in a course where 40 percent are 19 years old, 50 percent are 20 years old, and 10 percent are 21 years old. We can easily find the average age to be 19.7 years by weighting each age by the percentage in each age category [(40%)(19) + (50%)(20) + (10%)(21)]. In a similar way, the weighted cost of capital is estimated by weighting the cost of each individual source by the percentage of financing it provides. If we finance an investment by 40 percent debt at a 10 percent cost and 60 percent common equity at a cost of 18 percent, the weighted cost of capital is 14.8 percent (.40 × 10% + .60 × 18% = 14.8%). Thus, while the details become somewhat involved, the basic approach is relatively simple. As we move through the steps, try not to lose sight of this objective.

Determining Individual Costs of Capital

A large variety of financing instruments have been created by companies attempting to attract new investors. However, our interest will be restricted to the three basic types of securities: debt, preferred stock, and common stock. In calculating their respective costs, the objective is to determine *the rate of return the company must earn on its investments to satisfy investors' required rates of return after allowing for any flotation costs incurred in raising new funds.* Also, since the cash flows used in capital budgeting analysis (net present value, profitability index, and internal rate of return) are on an after-tax basis, the required rates of return should also be expressed on an after-tax basis.

Cost of Debt

The cost of debt may be defined as the rate that must be received from an investment *in order to achieve the required rate of return for the creditors.* In Chapter 12 the required rate of return for debt capital was found by a trial and error process, where we solved for R_d in the following equation:

$$P_0 = \frac{\$I_1}{(1 + R_d)^1} + \frac{\$I_2}{(1 + R_d)^2} + \cdots + \frac{\$I_N}{(1 + R_d)^N} + \frac{\$M}{(1 + R_d)^N} \qquad (13\text{--}1)$$

$$P_0 = \$I_t \left(\begin{array}{c} \text{table value,} \\ \text{Appendix D,} \\ N \text{ years,} \\ R_d \text{ percent} \end{array} \right) + \$M \left(\begin{array}{c} \text{table value,} \\ \text{Appendix B,} \\ N \text{ years,} \\ R_d \text{ percent} \end{array} \right)$$

where P_0 = the market price of the debt

$\$I_t$ = the annual dollar interest paid to the investor

$\$M$ = the maturity value of the debt

R_d = the required rate of return of the debt holder

N = the number of years to maturity

Example Assume that an investor is willing to pay $908.32 for a bond. The security has a $1000 par value, pays 8 percent in annual interest, and matures in 20 years. By trial and error, the investor's required rate of return is found to be 9 percent, which is the rate that sets the present value of the future interest payments and the maturity value equal to the price of the bond, or

$$\$908.32 = \sum_{t=1}^{20} \frac{\$80}{(1 + .09)^t} + \frac{\$1000}{(1 + .09)^{20}}$$

$$\$908.32 = \$908.32$$

However, if brokerage commissions and legal and accounting fees are incurred in issuing the security, the company will not receive the full $908.24 market price. As a result, the effective cost of these funds is larger than the investor's 9 percent required rate of return. To adjust for this difference, we would simply use the *net price* after flotation costs in place of the market price in equation (13–1). Thus, the equation becomes

$$NP_0 = \sum_{t=1}^{N} \frac{\$I_t}{(1 + k_d)^t} + \frac{\$M}{(1 + k_d)^N} \tag{13-2}$$

where NP_0 represents the net amount received by the company from issuing the debt, k_d equals the *before-tax* cost of debt, and the remaining variables retain their meaning from equation (13–1). If in the present example the company nets $850 after issuance costs, the equation should read

$$\$850 = \sum_{t=1}^{20} \frac{\$80}{(1 + k_d)^t} + \frac{\$1000}{(1 + k_d)^{20}}$$

$$= \$80 \begin{pmatrix} \text{table value,} \\ \text{Appendix D,} \\ \text{20 years,} \\ k_d \text{ percent} \end{pmatrix} + \$1000 \begin{pmatrix} \text{table value,} \\ \text{Appendix B,} \\ \text{20 years,} \\ k_d \text{ percent} \end{pmatrix}$$

Solving for k_d in equation (13–2) can be achieved only by trial and error. If *10 percent* is selected as a trial discount rate, a present value of $830.12 results. We know that the rate is above 9 percent because a 9 percent rate gave us a $908.32 value. We need the discount rate that gives us an $850.00 value. With this information, we may conclude that the before-tax cost of the debt capital is between 9 and 10 percent; therefore, we may approximate it by interpolating between these two rates. The computation may be shown as follows:

Rate	Value	Differences in Values	
9%	$908.32		
k_d	850.00 net proceeds }	$58.32 }	$78.20
10%	830.12		

Solving for k_d by interpolation,

$$k_d = .09 + \left(\frac{\$58.32}{\$78.20}\right)(.10 - .09) = .0975 = 9.75\%$$

Thus, the company's cost of debt, before recognizing the tax deductibility of interest, is 9.75 percent. However, the *after-tax* interest cost is found by multiplying the before-tax interest rate by [1 − (tax rate)]. If T is the company's marginal tax rate and k_d is the before-tax cost of debt, the after-tax cost of new debt financing, K_d, is found as follows:

$$K_d = k_d(1 - T) \tag{13-3}$$

If in the present example the corporation's tax rate is 34 percent, then the after-tax cost of debt is 6.44 percent:

$$K_d = 9.75\%(1 - .34) = 6.44\%$$

In summary, the firm must earn 6.44 percent on its borrowed capital *after the payment of taxes*. In doing so, it can achieve the investor's 9 percent required rate of return on his $908.32 investment.

Cost of Preferred Stock

Determining the cost of preferred stock follows the same logic as the cost of debt computations. *The objective is to find the rate of return that must be earned on the preferred stockholders' investment to satisfy their required rate of return.*

In Chapter 12 it was shown that the value of a preferred stock, P_0, that is nonmaturing and promising a constant dividend per year could be defined as follows:

$$P_0 = \frac{\text{dividend}}{\text{required rate of return for a preferred stockholder}} = \frac{D}{R_p} \qquad (13\text{--}4)$$

From this equation, the required rate of return, R_p, is defined as

$$R_p = \frac{\text{dividend}}{\text{market price}} = \frac{D}{P_0} \qquad (13\text{--}5)$$

If, for example, a preferred stock pays $1.50 in annual dividends and sells for $15, the investors' required rate of return is 10 percent:

$$R_p = \frac{\$1.50}{\$15} = 10\%$$

Yet even if these preferred stockholders have a 10 percent required rate of return, the effective cost of this capital will be greater owing to the flotation costs incurred in issuing the security. If a firm were to net $13.50 per share after issuance costs, rather than the full $15 market price, the cost of preferred stock, K_p, should be calculated using the net price received by the company. Therefore

$$K_p = \frac{\text{dividend}}{\text{net price}} = \frac{D}{NP_0} \qquad (13\text{--}6)$$

For the previous example, the cost would be

$$K_p = \frac{\$1.50}{\$13.50} = 11.11\%$$

No adjustment for taxes is required, since preferred stock dividends are not tax deductible. Thus, the firm must earn the cost of preferred capital after taxes have been paid, which for the preceding example was 11.1 percent.

Cost of Common Stock

While debt and preferred stock must be issued to receive any new money from these sources, common stockholders can provide additional capital in one of two ways. First, new common stock may be issued. Second, the earnings available to common stockholders can be retained, in whole or in part, within the company and used to finance future investments. This latter source of financing, which does not require a new common issue, represents the largest single source of capital for most U.S. corporations. As much as 70 percent of a company's financing in any year may come from the profits retained within the business. To distinguish between these two sources of common stock financing, we will use the term **internal common equity** to designate the profits retained within the business for investment purposes, and **external common equity** to represent a new issue of common stock.

Cost of Internal Common Equity

When managers are considering the retention of earnings as a means for financing an investment, they are serving in a *fiduciary* capacity. That is, the common stockholders have entrusted the company assets to management. If the company's objective is to maximize the wealth of its common stockholders, management should retain the profits *only if* the company's investments within the firm are at least as attractive as the stockholders' next best investment opportunity.[3] Otherwise the profits should be paid out in dividends, thereby permitting the investor to invest more profitably elsewhere.

How can management know the stockholders' alternative investment opportunities? Certainly identifying those specific investments is not feasible. However, the investors' required rate of return should be a function of competing investment opportunities. If the only other investment alternative of similar risk has a 12 percent return, one would expect a rational investor to set a minimum acceptable return on investment at 12 percent. In other words, *the investors' required rate of return should be equal to the expected rate of the best competing investment available.* Thus, if the common stockholder's required rate of return is used as a minimum return for investments financed by common stock investors, management may be assured that its investment policies are acceptable to the common stockholder.

In actually measuring the common stockholder's required rate of return, we will suggest three approaches: (1) the dividend-growth model, (2) the capital asset pricing model, and (3) the risk-premium approach.

The Dividend-Growth Model

In Chapter 12, the value of a common stock was defined as being equal to the present value of the expected future dividends, discounted at the common stockholders' *required rate of return*. Since the stock has no maturity date, these dividends extend to infinity. For an investor with a required rate of return of R_c, the value of a common stock, P_0, promising dividends of D_t in year t would be

$$P_0 = \frac{D_1}{(1 + R_c)^1} + \frac{D_2}{(1 + R_c)^2} + \cdots + \frac{D_n}{(1 + R_c)^n} + \cdots + \frac{D_\infty}{(1 + R_c)^\infty} \quad (13\text{--}7)$$

Since the market price of the security, P_0, is known, the required rate of return of an investor purchasing the security at this price can be determined by estimating future dividends, D_t, and solving for R_c using equation (13–7). Furthermore, if the dividends are increasing at a constant annual rate of growth, g, that is less than R_c, the required rate, R_c, may be measured as follows:[4]

$$R_c = \left(\frac{\text{dividend in year 1}}{\text{market price}}\right) + \left(\frac{\text{annual growth rate}}{\text{in dividends}}\right) = \frac{D_1}{P_0} + g \quad (13\text{--}8)$$

---

[3] Other factors may justify management's not adhering completely to this principle. These issues are examined when we discuss dividend policy in Chapter 16.

[4] For additional explanation, see Chapter 12.

To convert from the common investor's required rate of return in equation (13–8) to the cost of internal common funds, no adjustment is required for taxes. Dividends paid to the firm's common stockholders are *not* tax deductible; therefore, the cost is already on an after-tax basis. Also, flotation costs are not involved in computing the cost of internal common, since the funds are already within the business. Thus, the investor's required rate of return, R_c, is the same as the cost of internal common equity, K_c.

Example To demonstrate the computation, the Talbot Corporation's common stockholders recently received a $2 dividend per share, and they expect dividends to grow at an annual rate of 10 percent. If the market price of the security is $50, the investor's required rate of return is

$$R_c = K_c = \frac{D_1}{P_0} + g$$

$$= \frac{\$2(1 + .10)}{\$50} + .10 \qquad (13\text{–}8)$$

$$= \frac{\$2.20}{\$50} + .10 = .144$$

$$= 14.4\%$$

Note that the forthcoming dividend, D_1, is estimated by taking the past dividend, $2, and increasing it by 10 percent, the expected growth rate. That is, $D_1 = D_0 (1.10) = \$2(1.10) = \$2.20$.

The dividend-growth model has been a relatively popular approach for calculating the cost of equity. The primary difficulty, as you might expect is estimating the expected growth rate in future dividends. One possible source of such expectations are investment advisory services such as Merrill Lynch and Value Line. There are even services that collect and publish the forecasts of a large number of analysts. For instance, Institutional Broker's Estimate System (IBES) publishes earnings per share forecasts made by about 2000 analysts on a like number of stocks. While these forecasts are helpful in reducing the problems of the dividend-growth model, they are not a panacea. Growth estimates are generally available only for about 5 years, and not for the indefinite future, as required by the constant-growth model. Also, the analysts usually state their forecasts in terms of earnings rather than dividends, which does not meet the strict requirements of the dividend-growth model. Even so, the earnings information is helpful, since dividend growth in the long run is dependent on earnings. Even with these problems, the analysts' forecasts are helpful because they provide direct measures of the expectations that determine values in the market.

The use of analysts' forecasts in conjunction with the dividend-growth model to compute required rates of return for the Standard and Poor's 500 stocks has been studied by Harris.[5] Computing an average of the analysts' forecasts of 5-year growth

---

[5] Robert Harris, "Using Analysts' Forecasts to Estimate Shareholder Required Returns," *Financial Management*, Spring 1986, pp. 58–67.

rates in EPS, Harris used this average as a proxy for the growth rate in dividends. Then, using the dividend-growth model (Equation 13–8), he estimated an average cost of equity for the S&P 500 stocks. He next compared these required rates with the yields on U.S. Treasury bonds to see how much risk premium common stockholders were expecting. The analysis was conducted for each quarter from 1982 through 1984. Results of the Harris study are presented in Table 13–3. As the findings suggest, common stockholders have required a return of between 17.26 and 20.08 percent on average each year for 1982 through 1984. For the 3-year period, the average required rate of return was 18.41 percent. The average risk premiums of common stockholders each year, which are shown in the last column of Table 13–3, ranged from 4.28 percent to 7.16 percent, for an average of 6.16 percent. However, we should remember that these returns apply only for equity investments of average riskiness. As we well know, the risk of individual securities will differ from the average, as will the stockholders' required returns.

While the results in Table 13–3 look reasonable, the same computations for individual stocks may not be as plausible, largely due to measurement errors that occur when only one or a few stocks are analyzed. Moreover, the constant growth assumption of the model may be inconsistent with reality.

The CAPM Approach

Again drawing from Chapter 12, we can estimate the cost of equity using the capital asset pricing model (CAPM). Remember that investors should require a rate of return that at least equals the risk-free rate plus a risk premium appropriate for the level of

TABLE 13–3. Required Rates of Return and Risk Premiums

	Government Bond Yield	S&P 500	
		Required Return	Risk Premium
1982			
Quarter 1	14.27	20.81	6.54
Quarter 2	13.74	20.68	6.94
Quarter 3	12.94	20.23	7.29
Quarter 4	10.72	18.58	7.86
Average	12.92	20.08	7.16
1983			
Quarter 1	10.87	18.07	7.20
Quarter 2	10.80	17.76	6.96
Quarter 3	11.79	17.90	6.11
Quarter 4	11.90	17.81	5.91
Average	11.34	17.88	6.54
1984			
Quarter 1	12.09	17.22	5.13
Quarter 2	13.21	17.42	4.21
Quarter 3	12.83	17.34	4.51
Quarter 4	11.78	17.05	5.27
Average	12.48	17.26	4.78
Average 1982–1984	12.25	18.41	6.16

Source: Robert Harris, "Using Analysts' Forecasts to Estimate Shareholder Required Returns," *Financial Management*, Spring 1986, p. 62.

systematic risk associated with the particular security. Using the CAPM, we may represent the equity required rate of return (cost of internal equity) as follows:

$$R_c = K_c = R_f + \beta\ (R_m - R_f) \tag{13-9}$$

where $\quad R_c, K_c$ = the required rate of return of the equity shareholders, and also the cost of internal equity capital

$\qquad R_f$ = the risk-free rate

$\qquad \beta$ = beta, or the measure of a stock's systematic risk

$\qquad R_m$ = the expected rate of return for the market as a whole—that is, the expected return for the "average security"

For example, assume the risk-free rate to be 7 percent, the expected return in the market to be 16 percent, and the beta for Talbot Corporation's common stock to be .82. Then the cost of internal equity would be estimated as follows:

$$K_c = 7\% + .82(16\% - 7\%)$$

$$\underset{R_f}{} \quad \underset{\beta}{} \underset{R_m}{} \quad \underset{R_f}{}$$

$$= 14.4\%$$

While using the CAPM appears relatively easy, its appliction is not entirely straightforward, particularly in the corporate setting. In estimating the risk-free rate, the market rate, and the security's beta, the goal is to describe the expectations in the minds of the investors, since it is these expectations that determine how assets are valued. Such a task is difficult. However, as indicated earlier, financial service companies now help provide information about investor expectations.

The Risk-Premium Approach
Estimating the cost of equity is the most difficult step in determining a firm's cost of capital. In comparison, finding the cost of debt and the cost of preferred stock is relatively easy, given our decision to hold constant the firm's business risk and the financial risk. Since we know that common stockholders will demand a return premium above the bondholder's required rate of return, we may state the cost of equity as follows:

$$K_c = K_d + RP_c \tag{13-10}$$

where, as before, K_c and K_d represent the cost of common and debt, respectively. RP_c is the additional return premium common stockholders expect for assuming greater risk than bondholders. Since we can compute the cost of debt with some degree of confidence, the key to estimating the cost of equity is in knowing RP_c, the risk premium.

We again are in some difficulty, because we have no direct means of computing RP_c. We can only draw from our experience, which tells us that the risk premium of a firm's common stocks relative to its own bonds has for the most part been between 3 and 5 percent. In times when interest rates are historically high, the premium is usually low. In years when interest rates are at historical lows, the premium has been higher. Using an average premium of 4 percent, we would approximate the cost of equity capital as follows:

$$K_c = K_d + 4\%$$

For a firm with Aaa-rated bonds that have a cost of 9 percent, the cost of equity would be estimated to be 13 percent (9 percent cost of debt plus the 4 percent average premium); a more risky company, where its bonds are Baa with a 13 percent cost, could expect its cost of equity to approximate 17 percent (13 percent + 4 percent).

The risk-premium approach is somewhat similar in concept to CAPM in that both technique premium recognize that common stockholders require a risk premium. The differences between the two approaches come in using different beginning points (CAPM uses the risk-free rate and the risk-premium approach used the firm's cost of debt) and in how the risk premium is estimated. Both estimates of the risk premium involve subjectivity; however, CAPM has a more developed conceptual basis. Even so, the risk-premium approach is at times the best we can do, especially when the dividend-growth model and the CAPM give unreasonable estimates. Even if the dividend-growth and CAPM approaches are thought to fit the situation, the risk-premium technique gives us a good way to verify the reasonableness of our results.

Cost of New Common Stock

If internal common equity does not provide all the equity capital needed for new investments, the firm may need to issue new common stock. Again, this capital should not be acquired from the investors unless the expected returns on the prospective investments exceed a rate sufficient to satisfy the stockholders' required rate of return. Since the required rate of return of common stockholders was measured using equation (13–10), the only adjustment necessary is to consider the potential flotation costs incurred from issuing the stock. The flotation costs may be recognized by reducing the market price of the stock by the amount of these costs. Thus, the cost of new common stock, K_{nc}, is

$$K_{nc} = \frac{D_1}{NP_0} + g \qquad (13-11)$$

where NP_0 equals the net proceeds per share received by the company. If, in the previous example, flotation costs are 15 percent of the market price, the cost of capital for the new common stock, or external common, would be 15.18 percent, calculated as follows:

$$K_{nc} = \frac{\$2.20}{\$50 - .15(\$50)} + .10$$

$$= \frac{\$2.20}{\$42.50} + .10 = .1518$$

$$= 15.18\%$$

In this example, if management achieves a 15.18 percent return on the net capital received from common stockholders, they will satisfy the investors' required rate of return of 14.4 percent, as determined by equation (13–10).

Selection of Weights

The individual costs of capital will be different for each source of capital in the firm's capital structure. To use these costs of capital in our investment analyses, we must compute a composite or overall cost of capital. *The weights for computing this overall cost should reflect the corporation's financing mix.* For instance, if the creditors are expected to finance 30 percent of the new investments and the common stockholders are to provide the remaining 70 percent, the weighted cost should recognize this mix.

In selecting the financing weights for a composite cost of capital, several choices are available. Theoretically, the actual mix to be used in financing the proposed investments should be used as the weights. This approach, while attractive, presents a problem. The costs of capital for the individual sources depend upon the firm's financial risk, which is affected by its financial mix. If management alters the present financial structure, the individual costs will change, making it more difficult to compute the cost of capital. Thus, we will assume that the company's financial mix is relatively stable and that these weights will closely approximate future financing. Although this assumption may not be strictly met in any particular year, firms frequently have a **target capital structure** (desired debt-equity mix), which is maintained over the long term. The target financing mix provides the appropriate weights to be used in calculating the firm's weighted cost of capital.

Example The Ash Company's current financing mix is contained in Table 13–4. Management does not want to alter the firm's financial risk; it intends to maintain the same relative mix of capital in financing future investments. The individual costs of each source of capital have been determined as shown in Table 13–5. For the moment, we will restrict equity financing to the retained earnings available for reinvestment, or internally generated common equity. Table 13–6 combines the weights from Table 13–4 and the individual cost for each security into a single weighted cost of capital. Given that the assumptions of the weighted cost of capital concept are met and that common equity requirements can be satisfied internally, the company's weighted cost of capital is 12.7 percent. This rate is the firm's minimum acceptable rate of return for new investments.

TABLE 13–4. Ash, Inc. Capital Structure

Investor Group	Amount of Funds Raised ($)	Percentage of Total
Bonds	$1,750,000	35%
Preferred stock	250,000	5
Common stock	3,000,000	60
Total new financing	$5,000,000	100%

TABLE 13–5. Component Costs of Capital for Ash, Inc.

Investor Group	Component Costs
Bonds	7%
Preferred stock	13
Common stock	
Internally generated common	16
New common	18

TABLE 13–6. Weighted Cost of Capital for Ash, Inc., If Only Internal Common Is Used

(1) Investor Group	(2) Weight[a]	(3) Individual Costs[b]	(4) Weighted Costs (2 × 3)
Bonds	35%	7%	2.45%
Preferred stock	5	13	0.65
Common stock (internal only)	60	16	9.60
		Weighted cost of capital (K_0):	12.70%

[a] Taken from the desired financing mix presented in Table 13–4.
[b] Taken from Table 13–5.

LEVEL OF FINANCING AND THE WEIGHTED COST OF CAPITAL

Impact of a New Common Stock Issue

In the previous illustration, the weighted cost of capital was determined under the assumption that no new common stock was issued. If new common stock is issued, the firm's weighted cost of capital will increase, because external equity capital has a higher cost than internal equity due to the flotation costs.[6]

Generally the firm should use its cheapest sources of funds first while maintaining its desired debt-equity mix. In other words, since internally generated common costs less, it should be blended with debt until fully exhausted. Beyond this point, the weighted cost of capital increases, since the firm has to rely on new common stock for its equity financing. This basic concept is best explained through an example.

---

[6] For another approach to adjusting for flotation costs, see John R. Ezzell and R. Burr Porter, "Flotation Costs and the Weighted Average Cost of Capital," *Journal of Financial and Quantitative Analysis*, 11 (September 1975), 403–13.

Example The Crisp Corporation, an independent oil company, is contemplating three major capital investments in 1989. The first proposal is the acquisition of equipment used to examine geological formations. This new equipment should improve the success ratio in discovering productive oil and gas reserves. The second investment under consideration is water flooding equipment, which involves injecting large amounts of water into underground oil reserves. This process permits a more efficient recovery of the minerals. Third, new and advanced drilling equipment appears to offer significant cost savings in drilling for oil and gas. The costs and expected returns for these three investments are shown in Table 13–7. Management must decide which of these projects should be accepted.

TABLE 13–7. Crisp Corporation's Investment Opportunities

	Investment Cost	Expected Internal Rate of Return
Geological equipment	$1,500,000	14%
Water flooding equipment	2,000,000	18
Drilling eqiupment	2,500,000	11

If one or more of the proposed projects are accepted, the financing will consist of 50 percent debt and 50 percent common. Based upon the anticipated profits during 1989, the company should have $1,500,000 in profits available for reinvestment (internal common). The costs of capital for each source of financing have been computed and are presented in Table 13–8.

In this illustration the weighted cost of capital, K_0, is calculated as

$$K_0 = \left[\left(\begin{array}{c} \text{percentage of} \\ \text{debt financing} \end{array} \right) \times \left(\begin{array}{c} \text{cost of} \\ \text{debt} \end{array} \right) \right] + \left[\left(\begin{array}{c} \text{percentage of} \\ \text{common financing} \end{array} \right) \times \left(\begin{array}{c} \text{cost of} \\ \text{common} \end{array} \right) \right] \quad (13\text{--}12)$$

TABLE 13–8. Crisp Corporation's Individual Costs of Capital

Source	Cost
Debt (after-tax cost)	6%
Internally generated common ($1,500,000)	14
New common stock	18

If only internally generated common is utilized, the weighted cost of capital is 10 percent.

$$K_0 = [50\% \times 6\%] + [50\% \times 14\%] = 10 \text{ percent}$$

However, when new common stock is used rather than internally generated common, the weighted cost of capital is 12 percent:

$$K_0 = [50\% \times 6\%] + [50\% \times 18\%] = 12 \text{ percent}$$

Which weighted cost of capital should be used in evaluating the three investments?

To answer this question, two procedures should be used. First, we must rank the projects in descending order by their respective internal rates of return. Second, we must calculate the level of *total* financing at which point our internal equity is exhausted. In the Crisp Corporation illustration, $3 million in new investments may be financed with internal common and debt, without having to change the present financial mix of 50 percent debt and 50 percent common and without having to issue common stock. The $3 million is determined by solving the following equation:

$$\begin{array}{l}\text{internally generated}\\\text{common financing}\\\text{available}\end{array} = \left(\begin{array}{c}\text{percentage of}\\\text{common financing}\end{array}\right) \times \left(\begin{array}{c}\text{total financing}\\\text{from all sources}\end{array}\right) \quad (13\text{--}13)$$

For the Crisp Corporation,

$$\$1,500,000 = (50\%) \times (\text{total financing})$$

which indicates that if Crisp has $1,500,000 in internally generated common and management maintains a 50 percent debt ratio, it will be able to finance $3 million of total investments without issuing new common stock. Equation (13–13) may be restructured to solve directly for the amount of total financing; this is

$$\begin{array}{l}\text{total financing}\\\text{from all sources}\end{array} = \frac{\text{internally generated common}}{\text{percentage of common financing}}$$

$$= \frac{\$1,500,000}{.50} \quad (13\text{--}14)$$

$$= \$3,000,000$$

Therefore, for a total investment level of $3 million or less, the firm's weighted cost of capital is expected to be 10 percent. Beyond this level of total financing our internal common is totally exhausted, and the weighted cost of capital increases to 12 percent. This reflects the increased cost of new common beyond the $3 million in total financing from both debt and common.

The relationship between the weighted costs of capital and the amount of financing being sought is portrayed graphically in Figure 13–3. The graph depicts the firm's **weighted marginal cost of capital.** The term *marginal* is used because the computed cost of capital shows the weighted cost of each additional dollar of financing. This marginal cost of capital represents the appropriate criterion for making investment deci-

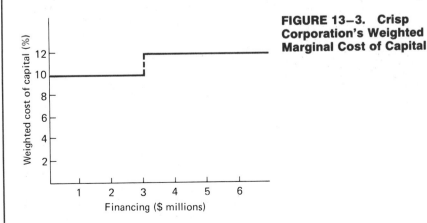

FIGURE 13–3. Crisp Corporation's Weighted Marginal Cost of Capital

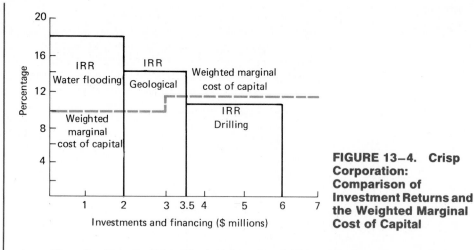

FIGURE 13–4. Crisp Corporation: Comparison of Investment Returns and the Weighted Marginal Cost of Capital

sions. Thus, the firm should continue to invest up to the point where the marginal rate of return earned on new investment (IRR) equals the marginal cost of new capital. This comparison is reflected in Figure 13–4, where the firm's optimal capital budget is found to be $3,500,000. The company should invest in water flooding machinery and the geological equipment. However, since the weighted marginal cost of capital is greater than the expected internal rate of return of the drilling equipment, this investment should be rejected.

General Effect of New Financing on Marginal Cost of Capital

Thus far, we have studied only the effect of increases in the cost of common stock on the firm's weighted marginal cost of capital. Similar effects will occur as the cost of any source of financing increases. If the 6 percent cost of debt capital for Crisp Corporation increased to 8 percent after the firm issued $2 million in bonds, an increase in the weighted marginal cost of capital would have occurred at the $4 million financing level from all sources. This **break** in the marginal cost of capital curve is determined as

$$\frac{\text{total financing}}{\text{from all sources}} = \frac{\text{maximum amount of lower-cost debt}}{\text{percentage of debt financing}}$$

$$= \frac{\$2,000,000}{.50} \tag{13–15}$$

$$= \$4,000,000$$

As a general rule, *changes in the weighted marginal cost of capital will take place when the cost of an individual source increases.* The break in the marginal cost of capital curve will occur at the dollar financing level where

$$\frac{\text{total financing}}{\text{from all sources}} = \frac{\begin{array}{c}\text{maximum amount of a}\\ \text{lower-cost source of capital}\end{array}}{\begin{array}{c}\text{percentage financing}\\ \text{provided by the source}\end{array}} \tag{13–16}$$

Summary of Computations The steps that have been described in calculating a firm's weighted *marginal* cost of capital may be summarized as follows:

1. Determine the percentage of financing to be used from each source of capital (debt, preferred stock, and common equity).
2. Compute the points on the marginal cost of capital curve where the weighted cost will increase.
3. Calculate the costs of each individual source of capital.
4. Compute the weighted cost of capital for the company, which will be different as the amount of financing increases.
5. Construct a graph that compares the internal rates of return with the weighted cost of capital, which will indicate which investments should be accepted.

MARGINAL COST OF CAPITAL: A CASE STUDY

An example will help bring together the principles for computing a firm's weighted cost of capital. J. M. Williams, Inc., is a manufacturer of medical and surgical instruments. The firm's desired financing mix is presented in Table 13–9. Management attempts to maintain a relatively constant capital structure mix from year to year.

The most recent earnings per share (1988) was $8, which was twice the earnings per share in 1982, and this represents a growth rate of 12 percent.[7] Dividends and the market price of the firm's common stock have grown at the same rate. The dividend payout ratio, which equals the ratio of common dividends to earnings available to common, has been 50 percent, and J. McDonald Williams, president, intends to hold to this dividend policy in the future.[8] Five potential investments are being examined by the company for 1989. The costs and the expected internal rates of return for these projects are provided in Table 13–10. To finance these investments, Williams expects to have $500,000 from 1989 retained earnings available for reinvestment, and new security issues can be sold. The firm's current financing mix will be maintained

TABLE 13–9. J. M. Williams, Inc. December 31, 1988

Total Liabilities and Equity	Capital Structure Mix (%)
Bonds	30.0%
Preferred stock	7.5
Common stock	62.5
Total liabilities and equity	100.00%

---

[7] This growth rate is computed by dividing the 1988 earnings per share by the 1982 earnings per share, $8/$4 = 2, which represents the compound interest factor for 6 years at 12 percent. That is, [EPS 1982 $(1 + g)^6$ = EPS 1988], or $4(1 + g)^6$ = $8; thus, $(1 + g)^6$ = $8/$4 = 2. Looking up a compound interest factor of two for six years in Appendix A, we find it corresponds to a growth rate of 12 percent. The same solution could be found by using the present value equation.

[8] Dividend policy is discussed in Chapter 16.

TABLE 13–10. J. M. Williams, Inc. 1989 Investment Opportunities

Investment	Estimated Cost	Projected Internal Rates of Return
A	$ 450,000	22%
B	500,000	19
C	300,000	17
D	250,000	14
E	500,000	12
Total proposed budget	$2,000,000	

and the firm's business risk should not change. The following information is available regarding the individual costs of capital:

1. **Bonds.** An amount not exceeding $240,000 could be issued in new bonds. The issue, after considering the effect of flotation costs, would have an effective before-tax cost of 13 percent. If additional debt is required, the effective yield would have to be increased to 16 percent.
2. **Preferred stock.** New preferred stock could be issued by Williams with a par value of $50, paying $6 in annual dividends. The market price of the security is $45, but $1.80 per share in flotation costs would be incurred for an issue size of $105,000 or less. Additional preferred stock could be sold at $45; however, the flotation costs would be $3.33 per share.
3. **Common stock.** Common stock can be sold at the existing $75 market price. If the issue size is not greater than $375,000, a 15 percent flotation cost would result. For any additional common stock, the flotation costs would increase to 20 percent of the market price.

With the foregoing information and by using the following five steps, we can construct a weighted marginal cost of capital curve.

*STEP 1: **Determine the Financial Mix***   *In Table 13–9, the desired financial mix for Williams was shown to be 30 percent in debt, 7.5 percent in preferred stocks, and 62.5 percent in common equity. For Step 1, we assume that future financing will be made in the same proportions.*

*STEP 2: **Compute When Costs Will Increase***   *With the above weights and knowing the amount of capital available at each cost, we can compute the points at which breaks in the marginal cost curve will occur. Remember that an increase in the weighted cost of capital occurs when one of the individual costs increases. For example, if the cost of debt rises, the weighted cost must also be higher. We need to know where these increases in the weighted cost will occur. For Williams, Inc., we know that the cost of the bonds increases if we issue more than $240,000 in new bonds. If debt represents 30 percent of all sources, how much in total financing will be possible before this increase in debt financing (bonds) affects the weighted marginal cost of capital? Using equation (13–16), we see that the weighted cost will increase when $800,000 in total capital has been raised, which is computed as follows:*

$$\begin{array}{l} \text{total financing available with} \\ \text{the lower-cost debt} \end{array} = \dfrac{\begin{array}{c}\text{total debt available at}\\ \text{lower cost}\end{array}}{\text{percentage of debt financing}}$$

$$= \dfrac{\$240,000}{.30}$$

$$= \$800,000$$

In other words, when we raise $800,000 in total financing and 30 percent is from debt, we will have used $240,000 in bonds (30 percent of $800,000). This same procedure must be followed for increases in the cost of preferred stock and for common equity, both for internally generated common and a new common stock. These calculations are shown in Table 13–11, and the results indicate two breaks in the curve. Increases in the marginal cost of capital occur as the amount of total financing reaches (1) $800,000 (cost of debt and common equity simultaneously increase), and (2) $1,400,000 (cost of preferred stock increases and cost of common equity increases). This result is presented in Figure 13–5.

STEP 3: Calculate the Cost of Individual Sources The next step in determining the weighted cost of capital requires computing the individual costs of capital from the various sources of financing. This procedure is presented in Table 13–12, where the

TABLE 13–11. J. M. Williams, Inc. Dollar Breaks in Marginal Cost of Capital Curve

I. Debt

$$\begin{array}{l} \text{total financing available with} \\ \text{the lower-cost debt} \end{array} = \dfrac{\text{total debt available at lower cost}}{\text{percentage of debt financing}}$$

$$= \dfrac{\$240,000}{.30}$$

$$= \$800,000$$

II. Preferred stock

$$\begin{array}{l} \text{total financing available with} \\ \text{cheaper preferred stock} \end{array} = \dfrac{\text{total preferred stock available at lower cost}}{\text{percentage of preferred stock financing}}$$

$$= \dfrac{\$105,000}{.075}$$

$$= \$1,400,000$$

III. Common stock

$$\begin{array}{l} \text{total financing available with} \\ \text{internal common} \end{array} = \dfrac{\text{total internal common available}}{\text{percentage of common financing}}$$

$$= \dfrac{\$500,000}{.625}$$

$$= \$800,000$$

$$\begin{array}{l} \text{total financing available with} \\ \text{both internal common and} \\ \text{with cheaper new common} \\ \text{stock} \end{array} = \dfrac{\begin{array}{c}\text{total internal common plus new}\\ \text{common stock at lower cost}\end{array}}{\text{percentage of common financing}}$$

$$= \dfrac{\$500,000 + \$375,000}{.625}$$

$$= \$1,400,000$$

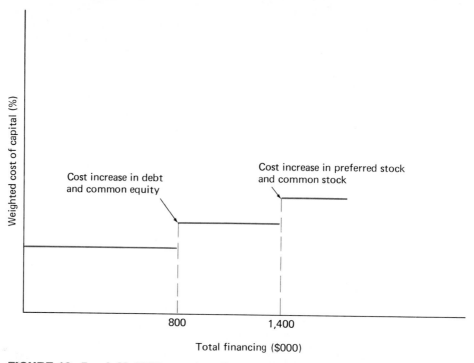

FIGURE 13–5.   J. M. Williams, Inc. Breaks in the Weighted Cost of Capital

amount of capital and the costs for these funds are provided. For debt the costs need only to be adjusted by William's marginal income tax rate. For a 34 percent income tax rate, the 13 percent and 16 percent costs of debt have an effective after-tax cost of 8.6 percent and 10.6 percent, respectively. The cost of preferred stock, which equals the dollar dividend relative to the net price per share received by the company, equals 13.9 percent for the first $105,000 and 14..4 percent for any greater amounts. The cost of internally generated common equals the dividend yield (the forthcoming dividend per share/price) plus the expected growth in dividends. An annual compound growth rate of 12 percent is estimated from the past growth in earnings per share. The dividend yield plus the 12 percent growth rate produces an 18 percent cost of internally generated common. The costs of new common stock are easily determined by adjusting the required rate of return of the common stockholders by the flotation costs in issuing the stock. These calculations yield a cost of new common up to $375,000 of 19 percent and 19.5 percent for an amount exceeding $375,000.

STEP 4:   *Solve for the Weighted Marginal Cost of Capital* *   With the preceding information, the weighted marginal costs of capital relative to the funds raised may be determined. Since the weighted cost of capital does not change for the first $800,000 in total financing, the weighted marginal cost of capital is determined by using the lowest costs of the individual sources. The weighted costs of financing up to $800,000 are calculated in Table 13–13. The percentage of capital that would be provided by each source is presented in column 2, and the cost of each individual source of capital appears in column 3 (taken from Table 13–12). Multiplying the weights (column 2) times the individual costs (column 3) and summing the results produces a weighted cost of 14.87 percent. This cost applies to any amount of financing (including debt, preferred stock, and common equity) up to but not exceeding $800,000.*

TABLE 13–12. J. M. Williams, Inc. Amount and Costs of Individual Sources, December 1988

Source	Amount Available	Cost Calculations
I. Debt		$\left(\dfrac{\text{after-tax}}{\text{cost of bonds}}\right) = \left(\dfrac{\text{before-tax}}{\text{cost}}\right)(1 - \text{tax rate})$
	(a) $0–240,000	$K_d = 13\%\,(1 - .34) = 8.6\%$
	(b) Over $240,000	$K_d = 16\%\,(1 - .34) = 10.6\%$
II. Preferred stock		$\left(\dfrac{\text{cost of}}{\text{preferred}}\right) = \left(\dfrac{\text{dividend per share}}{\text{market price less flotation costs}}\right)$
	(a) $0–105,000	$K_p = \dfrac{\$6}{\$45 - \$1.80} = 13.9\%$
	(b) Over $105,000	$K_p = \dfrac{\$6}{\$45 - \$3.33} = 14.4\%$
III. Common financing A. Internal common		$\left(\dfrac{\text{cost of}}{\text{internal common}}\right) = \left(\dfrac{\text{dividend in one year}}{\text{market price}}\right) + \text{growth}$
	$0–$500,000	$K_c = \dfrac{\$4(1 + .12)}{\$75} + .12 = 18.0\%$
B. New common stock		$\left(\dfrac{\text{cost of new common stock}}{}\right) = \left(\dfrac{\text{dividend in one year}}{\text{market price less flotation costs}}\right) + \text{growth}$
	(a) $0–$375,000	$K_c = \dfrac{\$4(1 + .12)}{\$75 - \$11.25} + .12 = 19.0\%$
	(b) Over $375,000	$K_{nc} = \dfrac{\$4(1 + .12)}{\$75 - \$15} + .12 = 19.5\%$

After the first $800,000 has been used to finance new investments, the costs of debt and common equity will increase. The costs increase because we will have exceeded $240,000 in debt and $500,000 in common equity. Taking the increased costs from Table 13–12 for these two sources (preferred stock cost has not changed), we calculate a weighted marginal cost of capital for an amount greater than $800,000

TABLE 13–13. J. M. Williams, Inc. Weighted Marginal Cost of Capital for $0–$800,000 Funds Raised

(1) Source	(2) Proportions	(3) Cost of Capital	(4) Weighted Cost of Capital (2 × 3)
Bonds	30.0%	8.6%	2.58%
Preferred stock	7.5	13.9	1.04
Common equity	62.5	18.0	11.25
	100.0%	Weighted cost of capital:	14.87%

TABLE 13–14.   J. M. Williams, Inc. Weighted Marginal Cost of Capital for $800,001—$1,400,000 Funds Raised

(1) Source	(2) Proportions	(3) Cost of Capital	(4) Weighted Cost of Capital (2 × 3)
Bonds	30%	10.6%	3.18%
Preferred stock	7.5	13.9	1.04
Common equity	62.5	19.0	11.88
	100.0%	Weighted cost of capital:	16.10%

but not exceeding $1,400,000. This weighted cost is now 16.10 percent and is given in Table 13–14, where the new costs for debt and common equity are shown in the boxes. Otherwise the calculation is no different from the weighted cost of capital for less than $800,000.

Should the firm finance over $1,400,000, the weighted marginal cost of capital will again rise. Since we now need over $105,000 in preferred stock and $875,000 in common equity in order to raise more than $1,400,000 in total financing, the costs of preferred stock and common equity will increase. These new costs are presented in Table 13–15. They result in a final weighted cost of capital of 16.45 percent.

TABLE 13–15.   J. M. Williams, Inc. Weighted Marginal Cost of Capital for More than $1,400,000 Funds Raised

(1) Source	(2) Proportions	(3) Cost of Capital	(4) Weighted Cost of Capital (2 × 3)
Bonds	30.0%	10.6%	3.18%
Preferred stock	7.5	14.4	1.08
Common equity	62.5	19.5	12.19
	100.0%	Weighted cost of capital:	16.45%

In summary, the weighted cost of capital for J. M. Williams, Inc., increases as the amount of money needed becomes larger, with the costs being as follows:

Total Financing	Weighted Cost
$0–$800,000	14.87%
$800,001–$1,400,000	16.10
Over $1,400,000	16.45

STEP 5:   *Compare Investment Returns with Weighted Costs* *The weighted marginal costs of capital are to be used in determining whether to accept any or all of the investment prospects being reviewed by Williams. A ranking of the projects, taken from Table 13–10, and a comparison of the returns against the weighted costs of capital*

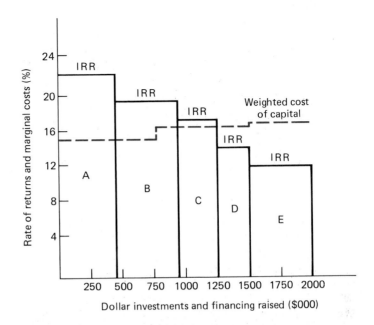

FIGURE 13–6. Investment Returns and Weighted Cost of Capital for J. M. Williams, Inc.

are given in Figure 13–6. As is evident from the figure, Williams' optimal capital budget for 1989 is $1,250,000. The particular investments that should be included in the budget are projects A, B, and C, with the returns for projects D and E falling short of the weighted cost of capital hurdle rate.

A FIRM'S COST OF CAPITAL: SOME RECENT EVIDENCE ———————

An interesting survey of the 100 largest corporations listed on the New York Stock Exchange was conducted by Blume, Friend, and Westerfield. Managers were asked to indicate various cost of capital figures.[9] The results are reported in Table 13–16.

Approximately 30 companies responded to the survey, of which 10 were public utilities and 20 were nonfinancial corporations from a variety of industries. From the results, we can see that higher costs of capital prevailed when public utilities were excluded, which implies that public utilities are less risky. Even more important, the results suggest that new common stock is slightly more expensive than internal common (retained earnings) and that internal common is four to five percentage points more costly than the *before-tax* cost of debt. We should also note that the weighted cost of capital, which falls around 12 to 13 percent, is at the bottom range of the cutoff or hurdle rate used to evaluate investments in plant and equipment. Thus, either new investments were considered more risky than existing investment, or management is imposing capital rationing.

---

[9] Marshall E. Blume, Irwin Friend, and Randolph Westerfield, "Impediments to Capital Formation: Summary Report of a Survey of Nonfinancial Corporations," Working Paper, Wharton School, University of Pennsylvania, 1980, p. 6.

TABLE 13–16. Average Costs of Capital and Investment: Cutoff Rates for Plant and Equipment

| Industries | Before-tax Cost-of-debt (%) | After-tax Cost (%) | | | | After-tax Cutoff Rate for Plant and Equipment Investments | |
		New Common Equity	Retained Earnings	Debt	Weighted Cost	Least Risky	Most Risky
All industries	12.5%	17.2%	16.6%	6.4%	12.4%	12.9%	19.6%
All industries except public utilities	12.5	17.8	17.0	6.3	13.1	13.1	20.3

Source: Marshall E. Blume, Irwin Friend, and Randolph Westerfield, "Impediments to Capital Formation: Summary Report of a Survey of Nonfinancial Corporations," Working Paper, Wharton School, University of Pennsylvania, 1980, p. 6.

In addition to the results summarized in Table 13–16, the authors found that:

1. The dividend-growth model is the most frequently used method for estimating the cost of equity. However, the CAPM is also coming to be used with the dividend-growth model.
2. If management perceives the cost of a particular source to be excessive, it will rely more heavily on other sources. That is, how a firm finances its investments is affected by management's perception of the relative costs of each source of capital.

Summary

Cost of capital is an important concept within financial management. For investment purposes, the cost of capital is the rate of return that must be achieved on the company's investments in order to satisfy the investor's required rate of return. If the rate of return from the corporation's investments equals the cost of capital, the price of the stock should remain unchanged. In other words, the firm's cost of capital may be defined as the rate of return from an investment that will leave the company's stock price unchanged. Therefore, the cost of capital, if certain assumptions are met, represents the minimum acceptable rate of return for new corporate investments.

The factors that affect a firm's cost of capital were shown to consist of four components. First, general economic conditions (as reflected in the demand and supply of funds in the economy), as well as inflationary pressures, affect the general level of interest rates. Second, the marketability of the firm's securities has an impact on the cost of capital. Any change in the marketability of a firm's stock will affect investors' required rate of return. These changes directly influence the firm's cost of capital. Third, the firm's operating and financial risks are reflected in its cost of capital. Finally, a relationship exists between a firm's cost of capital and the dollar amount of financing needed for future investments.

Cost of Individual Sources of Financing

The cost of debt is equal to the effective interest rate on new debt adjusted for the tax deductibility of the interest expense. The cost of preferred stock is equal to the effective dividend yield on new preferred stock. In making this computation, we should use the net price received by the company from the new issue. Thus,

$$\text{cost of preferred stock} = \frac{\text{annual dividend}}{\text{net price of preferred stock}} \qquad (13\text{--}6)$$

In calculating the cost of common equity, we distinguish between the costs of internally generated funds and the costs of new common stock. If historical data reasonably reflect the expectations of investors, the cost of internally generated capital is equal to the dividend yield on the common stock plus the anticipated percentage increase in dividends (and in the price of the stock) during the forthcoming year. If, however, the common equity is to be acquired by issuing new common stock, the cost of common should recognize the effect of flotation costs. This alteration results in the following equation for the cost of new common stock:

$$\left(\begin{array}{c}\text{cost of new} \\ \text{common}\end{array}\right) = \left(\frac{\text{dividend in year 1}}{\text{market price} - \text{flotation cost}}\right) + \left(\begin{array}{c}\text{annual growth rate} \\ \text{in dividends}\end{array}\right) \quad (13\text{--}11)$$

where (market price − flotation cost) is equivalent to the net market price.

We may also compute the cost of equity by using the Capital Asset Pricing Model or the Risk-Premium technique.

Weighted Cost of Capital

A firm's weighted cost of capital is a composite of the individual costs of financing weighted by the percentage of financing provided by each source. In this chapter we have assumed that the firm is to finance future investments in the same manner as past investments. The problem of defining the best set of weights is addressed in Chapter 15. Hence, the existing capital structure was used for developing the weighting scheme.

Marginal Cost of Capital

Since the amount of financing has an impact upon the firm's weighted cost of capital, the expected return from an investment must be compared with the marginal cost of financing the project. If the cost of capital rises as the level of financing increases, we should use the marginal cost of capital, and not the average cost of all funds raised. Following the basic economic principle of marginal analysis, investments should be made to the point where marginal revenue (internal rate of return) equals the marginal cost of capital.

Study Questions

13–1. Why do we calculate a firm's cost of capital?

13–2. Define the term cost of capital.

13–3. In computing the cost of capital, which sources of capital should be recognized?

13-4. In general, what factors determine a firm's cost of capital? In answering this question, identify the factors that are and those that are not within management's control.

13-5. What limitations exist in using the firm's cost of capital as an investment hurdle rate?

13-6. How does a firm's tax rate affect its cost of capital? What is the effect of the flotation costs associated with a new security issue?

13-7. **a.** Distinguish between internal common equity and new common stock.
  b. Why is a cost associated with internal common equity?

13-8. Define the expression *marginal cost of capital*. Why is the marginal cost of capital the appropriate investment criterion?

13-9. **a.** How might we adjust the required rate of return for an individual project where the risk level of the project is significantly different from the risk associated with the existing assets? (See Appendix 13A.)
  b. What limitations result from this method? (See Appendix 13A.)

Self-Test Problems

ST-1. (*Individual Costs of Capital*) Compute the cost for the following sources of financing:
  a. A $1000 par value bond with a market price of $970 and a coupon interest rate of 10 percent. Flotation costs for a new issue would be approximately 5 percent. The bonds mature in 10 years and the corporate tax rate is 34 percent.
  b. A preferred stock selling for $100 with an annual dividend payment of $8. If the company sells a new issue, the flotation cost will be $9 per share. The company's marginal tax rate is 30 percent.
  c. Internally generated common totaling $4.8 million. The price of the common stock is $75 per share, and the dividends per share were $9.80 last year. These dividends are not expected to increase.
  d. New common stock where the most recent dividend was $2.80. The company's dividends per share should continue to increase at an 8 percent growth rate into the indefinite future. The market price of the stock is currently $53; however, flotation costs of $6 per share are expected if the new stock is issued.

ST-2. (*Level of Financing*) The Argue Company has the following capital structure mix:

Debt	30%
Preferred stock	15
Common stock	55
	100%

Assuming that management intends to maintain the above financial structure, what amount of *total* investments may be financed if the firm uses (a) $100,000 of debt, (b) $150,000 of debt, (c) $40,000 of preferred stock, (d) $90,000 of preferred stock, (e) $200,000 of internally generated common equity, (f) $200,000 of internally generated common equity plus $300,000 in new common stock?

ST-3. (*Marginal Cost-of-Capital Curve*) The Zenor Corporation is considering three investments. The costs and expected returns of these projects are shown below:

Investment	Investment Cost	Internal Rate of Return
A	$165,000	16%
B	200,000	13
C	125,000	12

The firm would finance the projects by 40 percent debt and 60 percent common equity. The after-tax cost of debt is 7 percent for the first $120,000, after which the cost will be 11 percent. Internally generated common totaling $180,000 is available, and the common stockholders' required rate of return is 19 percent. If new stock is issued, the cost will be 22 percent.

a. Construct a weighted marginal cost of capital curve.

b. Which projects should be accepted?

ST–4. (*Weighted Cost of Capital*) Ed Timmerman is the new vice-president–finance for Jozell Brister, Inc. He is preparing his recommendations for the firm's capital budget. With the information provided below, prepare a graph comparing the company's weighted cost of capital and the prospective investment returns. Which investments should be made?

Investment	Investment Cost	Internal Rate of Return
A	$200,000	18%
B	125,000	16
C	150,000	12
D	275,000	10

The firm's capital structure consists of $2 million in debt, $500,000 in preferred stock, and $2.5 million in common equity. This capital mix is to be maintained for future investments.

The cost of debt (before-tax) is 12 percent for the first $120,000; thereafter, the cost will be 15 percent.

The company's preferred stock sells for $95 and pays a 14 percent dividend rate on a par value of $100. A new offering of this stock would entail underwriting costs and a price discount of 8 percent of the present market price. If the issue exceeded $50,000, the flotation costs would increase to 11 percent.

The common equity portion of the investments will be financed first by profits retained within the company of $150,000. If additional common financing is needed, new common stock can be issued at the $30 current price less flotation costs of $3 per share. Management expects to pay a dividend at the end of this year of $2.50, and dividends should increase at an annual rate of 9 percent thereafter. The firm's marginal tax rate is 34 percent.

Study Problems

13–1. (*Individual or Component Costs of Capital*) Compute the cost for the following sources of financing:

a. A bond that has a $1000 par value (face value) and a contract or coupon interest rate of 11 percent. A new issue would have a flotation cost of 5 percent of the $1125 market value. The bonds mature in 10 years. The firm's average tax rate is 30 percent and its marginal tax rate is 34 percent.

b. A new common stock issue that paid a $1.80 dividend last year. The par value of the stock is $15, and earnings per share have grown at a rate of 7 percent per year. This growth rate is expected to continue into the foreseeable future. The company maintains a constant dividend/earnings ratio of 30 percent. The price of this stock is now $27.50, but 5 percent flotation costs are anticipated.

c. Internal common equity where the current market price of the common stock is $43. The expected dividend this coming year should be $3.50, increasing thereafter at a 7 percent annual growth rate. The corporation's tax rate is 34 percent.

d. A preferred stock paying a 9 percent dividend on a $150 par value. If a new issue is offered, flotation costs will be 12 percent of the current price of $175.

e. A bond selling to yield 12 percent after flotation costs, but prior to adjusting for the marginal corporate tax rate of 34 percent. In other words, 12 percent is the rate that equates the net proceeds from the bond with the present value of the future cash flows (principal and interest).

13-2. (*Level of Financing*) The Mathews Company has the following capital structure mix:

Debt	$525,000
Preferred stock	225,000
Common stock	450,000

Using the same capital structure mix, what would the total investment amount be if the company uses:

a. $700,000 of debt

b. $67,500 of preferred stock

c. $300,000 of retained earnings

d. $100,000 of retained earnings plus $600,000 of new common stock

13-3. (*Individual or Component Costs of Capital*) Compute the cost for the following sources of financing:

a. A bond selling to yield 8 percent after flotation cost, but prior to adjusting for the marginal corporate tax rate of 34 percent. In other words, 8 percent is the rate that equates the net proceeds from the bond with the present value of the future cash flows (principal and interest).

b. A new common stock issue that paid a $1.05 dividend last year. The par value of the stock is $2, and the earnings per share have grown at a rate of 5 percent per year. This growth rate is expected to continue into the foreseeable future. The company maintains a constant dividend/earnings ratio of 40 percent. The price of this stock is now $25, but 9 percent flotation costs are anticipated.

c. A bond that has a $1000 par value (face value) and a contract or coupon interest rate of 12 percent. A new issue would net the company 90 percent of the $1150 market value. The bonds mature in 20 years, and the firm's average tax rate is 30 percent and its marginal tax rate is 34 percent.

d. A preferred stock paying a 7 percent dividend on a $100 par value. If a new issue is offered, the company can expect to net $85 per share.

e. Internal common equity where the current market price of the common stock is $38. The expected dividend this forthcoming year should be $3, increasing thereafter at a 4 percent annual growth rate. The corporation's tax rate is 34 percent.

13-4. (*Cost of Equity*) Salte Corporation is issuing new common stock at a market price of $27. Dividends last year were $1.45 and are expected to grow at an annual rate of 6 percent forever. Flotation costs will be 6 percent of market price. What is Salte's cost of equity?

13–5. (*Cost of Debt*) Belton is issuing a $1000 par value bond that pays 7 percent annual interest and matures in 15 years. Investors are willing to pay $958 for the bond. Flotation costs will be 11 percent of market value. The company is in an 18 percent tax bracket. What will be the firm's after-tax cost of debt on the bond?

13–6. (*Cost of Preferred Stock*) The preferred stock of Walter Industries sells for $36 and pays $2.50 in dividends. The net price of the security after issuance costs is $32.50. What is the cost of capital for the preferred stock?

13–7. (*Cost of Debt*) The Zephyr Corporation is contemplating a new investment to be financed 33 percent from debt. The firm could sell new $1000 par value bonds at a net price of $945. The coupon interest rate is 12 percent, and the bonds would mature in 15 years. If the company is in a 34 percent tax bracket, what is the after-tax cost of capital to Zephyr for bonds?

13–8. (*Cost of Preferred Stock*) Your firm is planning to issue preferred stock. The stock sells for $115; however, if new stock is issued, the company would receive only $98. The par value of the stock is $100 and the dividend rate is 14 percent. What is the cost of capital for the stock to your firm?

13–9. (*Cost of Internal Equity*) Pathos Co.'s common stock is currently selling for $21.50. Dividends paid last year were $.70. Flotation costs on issuing stock will be 10 percent of market price. The dividends and earnings per share are projected to have an annual growth rate of 15 percent. What is the cost of internal common equity for Pathos?

13–10. (*Cost of Equity*) The common stock for the Bestsold Corporation sells for $58. If a new issue is sold, the flotation cost is estimated to be 8 percent. The company pays 50 percent of its earnings in dividends, and a $4 dividend was recently paid. Earnings per share five years ago were $5. Earnings are expected to continue to grow at the same annual rate in the future as during the past five years. The firm's marginal tax rate is 34 percent. Calculate the cost of (a) internal common and (b) external common.

13–11. (*Cost of Debt*) Sincere Stationery Corporation needs to raise $500,000 to improve its manufacturing plant. It has decided to issue a $1000 par value bond with a 14 percent annual coupon rate, and a 10-year maturity. If the investors require a 9 percent rate of return:
   a. Compute the market value of the bonds.
   b. What will the net price be if flotation costs are 10.5 percent of the market price?
   c. How many bonds will the firm have to issue to receive the needed funds?
   d. What is the firm's after-tax cost of debt if its average tax rate is 25 percent and its marginal tax rate is 34 percent?

13–12. (*Cost of Debt*)
   a. Rework problem 13–11 assuming a 10 percent coupon rate. What effect does changing the coupon rate have on the firm's after-tax cost of capital?
   b. Why is there a change?

13–13. (*Weighted Cost of Capital*) The capital structure for the Carion Corporation is provided below. The company plans to maintain its debt structure in the future. If the firm has a 5.5 percent cost of debt, a 13.5 percent cost of preferred stock, and an 18 percent cost of common stock, what is the firm's weighted cost of capital?

Capital Structure ($000)	
Bonds	$1,083
Preferred stock	268
Common stock	3,681
	$5,032

13–14. (*Level of Financing*) Using the same capital structure mix as problem 13–13, what would the total investment amount be if the firm used the following?
  a. $200,000 of debt
  b. $40,000 of preferred stock
  c. $100,000 of retained earnings
  d. $100,000 of retained earnings plus $50,000 of new common stock

13–15. (*Weighted Cost of Capital*) Brenco, Inc.'s capital structure is provided below. Flotation costs would be (1) 15 percent of market value for a new bond issue, (2) $1.21 per share for common stock, and (3) $2.01 per share for preferred stock. The dividends for common stock were $2.50 last year and are projected to have an annual growth rate of 6 percent. The firm is in a 34 percent tax bracket. What is the weighted cost of capital if Brenco uses only internal common equity and the firm finances in the proportions shown below? Market prices are $1035 for bonds, $19 for preferred stock, and $35 for common stock.

Brenco, Inc. Balance Sheet

Type of Financing	Percentage of Future Financing
Bonds (8%, $1000 par, 16-year maturity)	38%
Preferred stock (5000 shares outstanding, $50 par, $1.50 dividend)	15
Common stock	47
Total	100%

13–16. (*Weighted Cost of Capital*) The Bach's Candy Corporation has determined the company's marginal costs of capital for debt, preferred stock, and common equity as follows:

Source	Amount of Capital	Cost
Debt	$0–$175,000	4.8%
	$175,001–$300,000	5.5
	over $300,000	6.0
Preferred stock	$0– $50,000	10.0
	$50,001– $75,000	12.0
	over $75,000	13.0
Common stock	$0–$400,000[a]	15.0
	$400,001–$750,000	18.0
	over $750,000	22.0

[a] $400,000 is available from internally generated common equity.

The firm maintains a capital mix of 45 percent debt, 5 percent preferred stock, and 50 percent common stock. Construct Bach's weighted marginal cost of capital curve.

13–17. (*Marginal Cost of Capital*) Mary Basett, Inc., a national advertising firm, is analyzing the following investment opportunities.

Investment	Investment Cost	Internal Rate of Return
A	$ 50,000	14.5%
B	200,000	17.9
C	325,000	15.6
D	125,000	12.4
E	400,000	10.9
F	75,000	13.8

The information needed to calculate the firm's weighted marginal cost of capital curve is presented below. Construct Basett's weighted marginal cost of capital curve and decide which investments should be accepted.

Source	Percentage	Amount of Capital	After-Tax Cost
Debt	40%	$0–$300,000	4.5%
		over $300,000	6.0
Preferred stock	8	$0–$ 50,000	9.5
		$50,001–$100,000	10.5
		over $100,000	11.0
Common stock	52	$0–$520,000	16.0
		over $520,000	18.0

13–18. (*Weighted Cost of Capital*) Stauffer Chemical Co. is considering five investments. The cost of each is shown below. Retained earnings of $650,000 will be available for investment purposes, and management can issue the following securities:

1. **Bonds.** $270,000 can be issued at an after-flotation, before-tax cost of 8.5 percent. Above $270,000 the cost will be 9.75 percent.
2. **Preferred stock.** The stock can be issued at the prevailing market price. Issuance will cost $1.55 per share up to an issue size of $90,000; thereafter costs will be $2.80 per share.
3. **Common stock.** The stock will be issued at the market price. For an issue of $250,000, flotation costs will be $1 per share. For any additional common, the flotation costs should then be $1.75 per share.

The tax rate for the firm is 34 percent. Common dividends last year were $1.80 and are expected to grow at an annual rate of 9 percent. Market prices are $975 for bonds, $39 for preferred stock, and $23 for common stock. Determine which projects should be accepted, based upon a comparison of the internal rates of return (IRR) of the investments and the weighted marginal cost of capital. The firm's capital structure is shown below, and the same mix is to be used for future investments.

Investment	Cost	IRR
A	$ 200,000	16%
B	650,000	12
C	115,000	9
D	875,000	10
E	180,000	15
Total	$2,020,000	

Capital Structure	Amount of Capital	Percentages of Financing
Bonds (9%, $1000 par, 18-year maturity)	$3,000,000	43%
Preferred stock (10%, $45 par, 30,000 shares outstanding)	1,350,000	20
Common stock	2,600,000	37
Total	$6,950,000	100%

13–19. (*Weighted Cost of Capital*) Heard Ski, Inc., is a regional manufacturer of ski equipment. The firm's target financing mix appears as follows:

	Percentage
Debt	30%
Preferred stock	10
Common stock	60
Total	100%

The corporation's management is currently involved in evaluating the capital budget. Six investments are under consideration. The costs and the expected internal rates of return for these projects are given as follows:

Investment	Cost	Internal Rate of Return
A	$175,000	16%
B	100,000	14
C	125,000	12
D	200,000	10
E	250,000	9
F	150,000	8

As the accept-reject criterion, Paul Heard, president of the firm, has compiled the necessary data for computing the firm's weighted marginal cost of capital. The cost information indicates the following:

1. Debt can be raised at the following before-tax costs:

Amount	Cost
$0–150,000	8.0%
$150,001–$225,000	9.0
over $225,000	10.5

2. Preferred stock can be issued paying an annual dividend of $8.50. The par value of the stock is $100. Also, the market price of the stock is $100. If new stock were issued, the company would receive a net price of $80 on the first $75,000. Thereafter, the net amount received would be reduced to $75.

3. Common equity is provided first by internally generated funds. Profits for the year that should be available for reinvestment purposes are projected at $150,000. Additional common

stock can be issued at the current $72 market price less 15 percent in flotation costs. However, if more than $225,000 in new common stock is required, a 20 percent flotation cost is expected. The dividend per share was $2.75 last year, and the long-term growth rate for dividends is 9 percent.

a. Given that the firm's marginal tax rate is 34 percent, compute the company's weighted marginal cost of capital at a financing level up to $1 million.

b. Construct a graph that presents the firm's weighted marginal cost of capital relative to the amount of financing.

c. What is the appropriate size of the capital budget, and which projects should be accepted?

Self-Test Solutions

The following notations are used in this group of problems:

k_d = the before-tax cost of debt

K_d = the after-tax cost of debt

K_p = the after-tax cost of preferred stock

K_c = the after-tax cost of internal common stock

K_{nc} = the after-tax cost of new common stock

T = the marginal tax rate

D_t = the dollar dividend per share, where D_0 is the most recently paid dividend and D_1 is the forthcoming dividend

P_0 = the value (present value) of a security

NP_0 = the value of a security less any flotation costs incurred in issuing the security

SS–1. a. $\$921.50 = \sum_{t=1}^{10} \dfrac{\$100}{(1 + k_d)^t} + \dfrac{\$1000}{(1 + k_d)^{10}}$

Rate	Value
11%	$940.90 ⎫
k_d%	$921.50 ⎬ $19.40 ⎫
12%	$887.00 ⎭ ⎬ $53.90

$k_d = 0.11 + \left(\dfrac{\$19.40}{\$53.90}\right) 0.01 = 11.36\%$

$K_d = 11.36\% \ (1 - 0.34) = 7.50\%$

b. $K_p = \dfrac{D}{NP_0}$

$K_p = \dfrac{\$8}{\$100 - \$9} = 8.79\%$

c. $K_c = \dfrac{D_1}{P_0} + g$

$K_c = \dfrac{\$9.80}{\$75} + 0\% = 13.07\%$

d. $K_{nc} = \dfrac{D_1}{NP_0} + g$

$K_{nc} = \dfrac{\$2.80(1 + 0.08)}{\$53 - \$6} + 0.08 = 14.43\%$

SS–2. dollar breaks $= \dfrac{\text{amount of financing at a given cost}}{\text{percentage of funds provided by the}}$
specific source

a. $\dfrac{\$100,000}{0.30} = \$333,333.33$

b. $\dfrac{\$150,000}{0.30} = \$500,000$

c. $\dfrac{\$ 40,000}{0.15} = \$266,666.67$

d. $\dfrac{\$ 90,000}{0.15} = \$600,000$

e. $\dfrac{\$200,000}{0.55} = \$363,636.36$

f. $\dfrac{\$500,000}{0.55} = \$909,090.91$

SS–3. a. Increases (breaks) in the weighted marginal cost of capital curve will occur as follows;
Increase from the cost of debt:

$$\dfrac{\$120,000}{.40} = \$300,000$$

Increase from the cost of common:

$$\dfrac{\$180,000}{.60} = \$300,000$$

Weighted cost of capital (K_0) for

$0–$300,000 Total Financing			
	Weights	**Costs**	**Weighted Costs**
Debt	40%	7%	2.80%
Common stock	60	19	11.40
			$K_0 = \underline{\underline{14.20\%}}$

Over $300,000 Total Financing			
	Weights	**Costs**	**Weighted Costs**
Debt	40%	11%	4.4%
Common stock	60	22	13.2
			$K_0 = \underline{\underline{17.6\%}}$

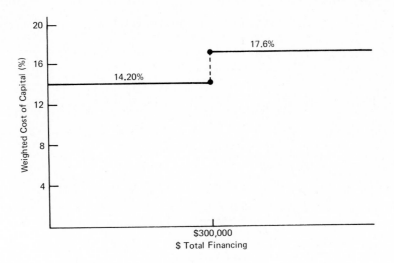

b. Only project A should be accepted.

SS–4. **(1)** Compute weights

	Capital Structure	Capital Mix (Weights)
Debt	$2,000,000	40%
Preferred stock	500,000	10
Common stock	2,500,000	50
	$5,000,000	100%

(2) Compute individual costs

Debt

$0–$120,000:   12% (1 − .34) = 7.92%
over $120,000: 15% (1 − .34) = 9.90%

Preferred Stock

$0–$50,000: $\dfrac{\$14}{\$95(1 - .08)} = \dfrac{\$14}{\$87.40} = 16.02\%$

over $50,000: $\dfrac{\$14}{\$95(1 - .11)} = \dfrac{4}{\$84.55} = 16.56\%$

Common Stock

$0–$150,000: $\left(\dfrac{\$2.50}{\$30}\right) + .09 = .1733 = 17.33\%$

over $150,000: $\left(\dfrac{\$2.50}{\$27}\right) + .09 = .1826 = 18.26\%$

(3) Calculate increases (breaks) in the weighted marginal cost of capital curve caused by increases in the cost of:

Debt

$$\frac{\$120,000}{.40} = \$300,000$$

Preferred Stock

$$\frac{\$50,000}{.10} = \$500,000$$

Common Stock

$$\frac{\$150,000}{.50} = \$300,000$$

(4) Construct the weighted cost of capital curve

0–$300,000 Total Financing

	Weights	Individual Costs	Weighted Costs
Debt	40%	7.92%	3.17
Preferred stock	10	16.02	1.60
Common stock	50	17.33	8.67
			$K_0 = 13.44\%$

At Least $300,001 But Not More Than $500,000

	Weights	Individual Costs	Weighted Costs
Debt	40%	9.90%	3.96%
Preferred stock	10	16.02	1.60
Common stock	50	18.26	9.13
			$K_0 = 14.69\%$

Over $500,000

	Weights	Individual Costs	Weighted Costs
Debt	40%	9.90%	3.96%
Preferred stock	10	16.56	1.66
Common stock	50	18.26	9.13
			$K_0 = 14.75\%$

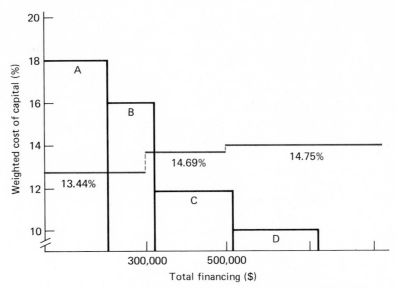

Accept investments A and B for a total of $325,000

Selected References

Aivazian, Varouj, and Jeffrey L. Callen. "Investment, Market Structure, and the Cost of Capital," *Journal of Finance*, 34 (March 1979), 85–92.

Ang, James S. "Weighted Average versus True Cost of Capital," *Financial Management*, 2 (Autumn 1973), 56–60.

Arditti, Fred D. "The Weighted Average Cost of Capital: Some Questions on Its Definition, Interpretation and Use," *Journal of Finance*, 28 (September 1973), 1001–8.

———, and Haim Levy. "The Weighted Average Cost of Capital as a Cutoff Rate: A Critical Analysis of the Classical Textbook Weighted Average," *Financial Management*, 6 (Fall 1977), 24–34.

———, and Milford S. Tysseland. "Three Ways to Present the Marginal Cost of Capital," *Financial Management*, 2 (Summer 1973), 63–67.

Beranek, William. "Some New Capital Budgeting Theorems." *Journal of Financial and Quantitative Analysis*, 13 (December 1978), 809–21.

Blume, Marshall E., Irwin Friend, and Randolph Westerfield. "Impediments to Capital Formation: Summary Report of a Survey of Nonfinancial Corporations."

Working Paper, Wharton School, University of Pennsylvania, 1980.

Boudreaux, Kenneth, and Hugh W. Long. "The Weighted Average Cost of Capital as a Cutoff Rate: A Further Analysis." *Financial Management*, 8 (Summer 1979), 7–14.

Brick, John R., and Howard E. Thompson. "The Economic Life of an Investment and the Appropriate Discount Rate," *Journal of Financial and Quantitative Analysis*, 13 (December 1978), 831–46.

Chambers, D. R., Robert S. Harris, and John J. Pringle. "Treatment of Financing Mix in Analyzing Investment Opportunities." *Financial Management*, 11 (Summer 1982), 24–41.

Elliott, J. Walter. "The Cost of Capital and U.S. Investment," *Journal of Finance*, 35 (September 1980), 981–1000.

Ezzell, John R., and R. Burr Porter. "Flotation Costs and the Weighted Average Cost of Capital," *Journal of Financial and Quantitative Analysis*, 11 (September 1976), 403–13.

Fuller, Russell J., and Halbert S. Kerr. "Estimating the Divisional Cost of Capital: An Analysis of the Pure-Play Technique." *Journal of Finance*, 36 (December 1981), 997–1009.

Gallinger, George W., and Glenn V. Henderson, Jr. "The SML and the Cost of Capital," Research Paper, Arizona State University, 1981.

Gehr, Adam K., Jr. "Risk-Adjusted Capital Budgeting Using Arbitrage," *Financial Management*, 10 (Winter 1981), 14–19.

Gitman, Lawrence J., and Vincent A. Mercurio. "Cost of Capital Techniques Used by Major U.S. Firms: Survey and Analysis of Fortune's 1000," *Financial Management*, 11 (Winter 1982), 21–29.

Gordon, Myron J., and L. I. Gould. "The Cost of Equity Capital: A Reconsideration," *Journal of Finance*, 33 (June 1978), 849–61.

Harris, Robert S., and John J. Pringle. "A Note on the Implications of Miller's Argument for Capital Budgeting," *Journal of Financial Research* (Spring 1983), 13–23.

Miles, James A., and John R. Ezzell. "The Weighted Average Cost of Capital, Perfect Capital Markets, and Project Life: A Clarification," *Journal of Financial and Quantitative Analysis*, 15 (September 1980), 719–30.

Modigliani, F., and M. Miller. "The Cost of Capital, Corporation Finance, and the Theory of Investment," *American Economic Review*, 48 (June 1958), 261–96.

Pettway, Richard H., and Bradford D. Jordon. "Diversification, Double Leverage, and the Cost of Capital," *Journal of Financial Research*, (Winter 1982), 289–301.

Scott, David F., Jr., and J. William Petty. "Determining the Cost of Common Equity Capital: The Direct Method," *Journal of Business Research*, 8 (March 1980), 89–103.

Van Horne, James C. "An Application of the Capital Asset Pricing Model to Divisional Required Returns," *Financial Management*, 9 (Spring 1980), 14–19.

APPENDIX 13A

Required Rate of Return for Individual Projects

Two basic assumptions are required in computing and using the firm's weighted cost of capital as a cutoff rate for new capital investments. First, the riskiness of the project being evaluated must be similar to the riskiness of the company's existing assets. In other words, acceptance of the investment will not alter the firm's overall business risk. In practice, however, many investment opportunities have their own unique level of risk. Second, future investments must be financed in the same proportions of debt, preferred stock, and common stock as past investments. However, in practice, different financing arrangements are frequently made for different projects, with the nature and the size of the investment dictating the financing strategy. Although the financial mix may influence the accept-reject decision for an individual project, this issue is addressed in Chapter 15. Consequently, in this appendix we will examine only the first issue, that of differing levels of project riskiness.[1] To simplify our discussion we will assume that only equity financing is used. Therefore, the cost of equity is the firm's cost of capital.

The limited usefulness of the weighted cost of capital is illustrated in Figure 13A–1, where the dashed line represents the firm's weighted marginal cost of capital, K_0. This cost

---

[1] For further explanation, see Ezra Solomon, "Measuring a Company's Cost of Capital," *Journal of Business* (October 1955), pp. 95–117; Steward C. Myers, "Interactions of Corporate Financing and Investment Decision—Implications for Capital Budgeting," *Journal of Finance* (March 1974), pp. 1–25; Richard S. Bower and Jeffery M. Jenks, "Divisional Screening Rates," *Financial Management* (Autumn 1975), pp. 42–49; Donald L. Tuttle and Robert H. Litzenberger, "Leverage Diversification and Capital Market Effects on a Risk-Adjusted Capital Budgeting Framework," *Journal of Finance* (June 1968), pp. 427–43; and John D. Martin and David F. Scott, Jr., "Debt Capacity and the Capital Budgeting Decision," *Financial Management* (Summer 1976), pp. 7–14.

of capital, as computed earlier in the chapter, does not allow for varying levels of project risk. In Figure 13A–1 this investment hurdle rate is appropriate only for projects whose risk equals σ_0. The **return-risk line** in the figure specifies the appropriate required rates of return for investments having different levels of risk. In addition, investments A and B in the figure may be used to illustrate incorrect decisions that would result from the use of the firm's cost of capital as the cutoff rate for project acceptance where the risk inherent in A is below the firm's risk level of σ_0 (which is reflected in K_0), and project B's risk exceeds σ_0. In this example, investment A would be rejected and investment B accepted if the required rate being used were the weighted marginal cost of capital. However, if the return-risk line accurately measures the market return-risk relationship, investment A should be accepted and investment B rejected. Although the expected return for investment A is below the firm's weighted marginal cost of capital, the reduction in company risk sufficiently justifies acceptance of the investment's lower expected return.

In identifying the relationship between the required rate of return and project risk, the **price of risk** in the market, or the **risk premium,** may be measured as

$$\begin{pmatrix} \text{risk} \\ \text{premium} \end{pmatrix} = \begin{pmatrix} \text{companywide marginal} \\ \text{cost of capital} \end{pmatrix} - \begin{pmatrix} \text{risk-free} \\ \text{rate} \end{pmatrix} \qquad (13\text{A}{-}1)$$

$$P = K_0 - R_f$$

This risk premium applies only to the firm's investments with an average level of risk. Only if this risk premium is standardized relative to the riskiness of the firm's average project is it relevant for other investments of different risk levels. The firm's excess return relative to the risk for a typical project would be

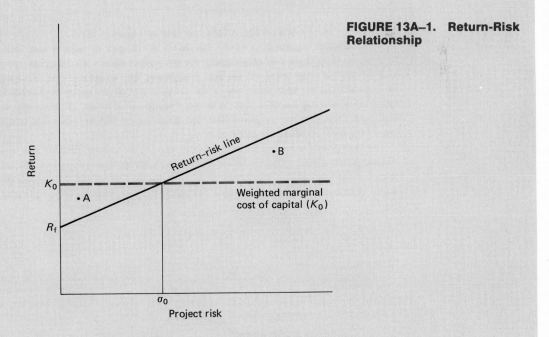

FIGURE 13A–1. Return-Risk Relationship

473

$$\left(\begin{array}{c}\text{excess return per}\\\text{unit of risk}\end{array}\right) = \frac{\left(\begin{array}{c}\text{companywide marginal}\\\text{cost of capital}\end{array}\right) - \left(\begin{array}{c}\text{risk-free}\\\text{rate}\end{array}\right)}{\text{risk for average project}} \qquad (13A\text{--}2)$$

$$EP = \frac{K_0 - R_t}{\sigma_0}$$

This excess return-risk relationship holds not only for the firm but for individual investments. Therefore, if K_j is the required rate of return for investment j, and σ_j is the risk for project j,

$$\frac{K_j - R_f}{\sigma_j} = \frac{K_0 - R_f}{\sigma_0} \qquad (13A\text{--}3)$$

Restructuring equation (13A--3), we have

$$K_j - R_f = (K_0 - R_t)\frac{\sigma_j}{\sigma_0} \qquad (13A\text{--}4)$$

Therefore

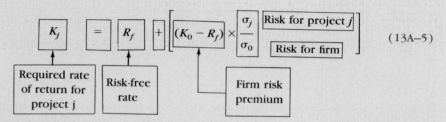

$$\qquad (13A\text{--}5)$$

Equation (13A--5) defines the return-risk line in Figure 13A--1.

Even though equation (13A--5) has been developed in such a way that it conceptually represents the return-risk relationship for the corporation's investments, several implementation problems arise. First, recall that computing the weighted cost of capital, K_0, is at best an approximation. Also, since use of the weighted cost of capital necessitates the assumption that the firm's capital structure will not change as a result of financing new investments, equation (13A--5) also requires that the financing of the jth asset not result in a change in the company's existing financial mix.[2]

To this point, no suggestion has been offered as to how project risk is to be measured. Although we would generally concur that the appropriate concept of risk involves an assessment of the variability of returns, how this dispersion should be measured is still open to some question. Earlier the standard deviation statistic was used to represent risk.[3]

---

[2] As previously mentioned, this limitation in theory may be avoided; however, in reality, the necessary adjustments are difficult and beyond the scope of this text. See references in footnote 1.

[3] The basis for this risk measurement is explained with respect to capital budgeting under uncertainty (Chapter 11) and valuation (Chapter 12).

Example To demonstrate the necessary calculations, assume that the cost of capital for Petroleum Exploration, Inc., is 14 percent, and the standard deviation of the returns for an average project is 6 percent.

The riskless interest rate on long-term U.S. government bonds, R_f, is 8 percent. In developing a return-risk relationship for investments, management has used the foregoing information for determining the minimum acceptable return for a project. Specifically, for project j the required rate of return is determined as follows:

$$K_j = R_f + (K_0 - R_f)\frac{\sigma_j}{\sigma_0}$$

$$(13A-5)$$

$$= .08 + (.14 - .08)\frac{\sigma_j}{.06}$$

Several investments, which are set forth in Table 13A–1, are currently being considered by the firm. Using equation (13A–5), we may determine the acceptability of the proposed investments. These computations, shown in Table 13A–2, indicate that investments B, D, and E should be accepted and investments A and C should be rejected. This analysis of whether to accept or reject these projects is also presented in Figure 13A–2. The decision rule should be to accept all projects that are on or above the return-risk line.

TABLE 13A–1. Petroleum Exploration, Inc. Investment Opportunities

Project	Expected Returns	Standard Deviation of Returns
A	10.0%	5.0%
B	12.0	2.0
C	14.0	7.5
D	16.0	8.0
E	17.0	7.0

TABLE 13A–2. Computation of Required Rates of Return

Project	Standard Deviation of Returns (Col. 3, Table 13A–1)	Computation of the Required Rate of Return [Equation (13A–5)]	Required Rate of Return	Expected Return (Col. 2, Table 13A–1)	Decision
A	.050	.08 + (.14 − .08)(.05/.06) =	.130 (13%)	.10 (10%)	Reject
B	.020	.08 + (.14 − .08)(.02/.06) =	.100 (10%)	.12 (12%)	Accept
C	.075	.08 + (.14 − .08)(.075/.06) =	.155 (15.5%)	.14 (14%)	Reject
D	.080	.08 + (.14 − .08)(.08/.06) =	.160 (16%)	.16 (16%)	Accept
E	.070	.08 + (.14 − .08)(.07/.06) =	.150 (15%)	.17 (17%)	Accept

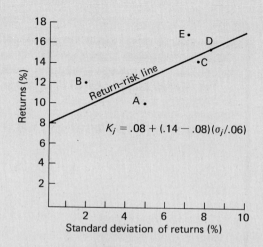

$$K_j = .08 + (.14 - .08)(\sigma_j/.06)$$

FIGURE 13A–2. Petroleum Exploration, Inc. Investment Opportunities

EFFECT OF DIVERSIFICATION

The previous explanation of the market return-risk relationship considered only one investment in isolation. However, if investors find risk distasteful—that is, if they are risk-averse—diversification can be used to reduce risk relative to the expected return of a portfolio of assets or to increase the expected return relative to the riskiness of the portfolio of investments. When a firm and/or investors make a variety of investments, we are concerned about the effect of a new project on the riskiness of the total portfolio of assets.

In examining the effect of diversification on the market risk-return relationship, we note that the ability to diversify occurs at two levels. First, the firm can diversify its holdings in capital investments, thereby reducing the variability of the cash flows within the company. Alternatively, the firm's investors can diversify their own investments. Considerable controversy has developed regarding the advantage of the firm's diversifying its investments when investors can diversify their own holdings. In essence, since investors can diversify, is there any benefit to be gained by the firm also diversifying? This issue is quite complex and extends beyond the purpose and scope of this text.[4] However, for simplicity, investors are assumed to hold diversified portfolios. Also, perfect markets are assumed to exist, where (1) information is readily available to all investors at no cost, (2) there are no transaction costs associated with buying/selling securities, (3) investment opportunities are readily accessible to all prospective investors, and (4) financial distress and bankruptcy costs are nonexistent. In this situation firm diversification is not a thing of value, and the capital-asset pricing model provides the appropriate criterion for accepting or rejecting the jth project. The required rate of return for the jth project, K_j, in this framework is defined as follows.[5]

---

[4] See Chapter 11 for a brief explanation of this issue.

[5] For an explanation of the correlation between the returns of two investments, r_{jm}, see Chapter 11.

$$\begin{pmatrix} \text{required rate} \\ \text{for project } j \end{pmatrix} = \begin{pmatrix} \text{risk-free} \\ \text{rate} \end{pmatrix} + \frac{\begin{matrix} \text{risk premium} \\ \text{for a widely} \\ \text{diversified} \\ \text{portfolio} \end{matrix}}{\begin{matrix} \text{standard} \\ \text{deviation} \\ \text{of the returns} \\ \text{for a widely} \\ \text{diversified} \\ \text{portfolio} \end{matrix}} \begin{pmatrix} \text{correlation} \\ \text{of project } j \\ \text{returns with} \\ \text{portfolio} \\ \text{returns} \end{pmatrix} \begin{pmatrix} \text{standard} \\ \text{deviation} \\ \text{of the } j\text{th} \\ \text{project} \end{pmatrix} \quad (13A-6)$$

$$K_j = R_f + \left(\frac{R_m - R_f}{\sigma_m}\right) r_{jm}\sigma_j$$

The capital-asset pricing model [equation (13A–6)] is similar to equation (13A–5). However, the excess return-risk relationship, $(R_m - R_f)/\sigma_m$, is for the market portfolio and not simply that of the firm. The expression $r_{jm}\sigma_j$ measures the portion of the standard deviation for project j that cannot be eliminated through investor diversification, or the undiversifiable risk for project j. Equation (13A–6) may be restated as:

$$K_j = R_t + (R_m - R_f)\left(\frac{r_{jm}\sigma_j}{\sigma_m}\right) \quad (13A-7)$$

Noting that

$$\beta_j = \frac{r_{jm}\sigma_j}{\sigma_m} \quad (13A-8)$$

we have

$$K_j = R_f + (R_m - R_f)\beta_j \quad (13A-9)$$

where b_j (beta) identifies the volatility of the jth project returns relative to the investor's widely diversified portfolio. Thus, β_j represents the effect of the jth project upon the riskiness of the investor's portfolio, which is also the relevant risk used in the market to value the asset.

Example To illustrate the use of the capital-asset pricing model for determining the required rate of return for a project, suppose that a capital investment is being considered with an expected return of 16 percent. Management believes that the riskiness of the project should be analyzed in terms of its contribution to the risk of a diversified investor's portfolio. The expected return for a diversified portfolio of assets, R_m, is 14 percent, and the risk-free rate, R_f, is 6 percent. The standard deviation of returns for the portfolio, σ_m, is 5 percent, while the standard deviation of the project returns, σ_j, is estimated to be 7 percent. The correlation coefficient between the two returns, r_{jm}, is anticipated to be .8. With this information, the beta for the investment is

$$\beta_j = \frac{r_{j,}\sigma_j}{\sigma_m}$$

$$= \frac{(.8)(.07)}{.05} \qquad (13A\text{--}8)$$

$$= 1.12$$

which indicates that a 1 percent change in the market portfolio's risk premium (that is, $R_m - R_f$) will produce an expected 1.12 percent change in the investment's risk premium ($K_j - R_f$). Thus, the project returns and the market portfolio returns encounter approximately the same amount of variability. As a result, the required rate of return for the project is roughly equal to the expected return for the market portfolio. To verify, equation (13A–9) may be used to compute the appropriate required rate of return for the project.

$$K_j = R_f + (R_m - R_f)\beta_j$$

$$= .06 + (.14 - .06)1.12 = .1496 \qquad (13A\text{--}9)$$

$$= 14.96\%$$

Since the 16 percent expected return for the investment exceeds the required rate of return of 14.96 percent, the investment should be made.

EVALUATION OF CAPM

While conceptually sound, the use of the capital-asset pricing model in calculating a project required rate of return is difficult, owing to measurement problems. The primary difficulty lies in the determination of r_{jm}, the relationship between the market returns and the project returns. Also, the model maintains that the relevant risk is limited to the portion of the risk that the *investor* cannot eliminate through diversification. For this premise to hold, bankruptcy costs are assumed to equal zero if the firm falls. In reality, bankruptcy costs are generally significant. Therefore, if a project increases significantly the probability of firm bankruptcy, total variability of project returns is the appropriate risk measure.

In summary, owing to the limiting assumptions associated with an overall cost of capital for the firm, this single hurdle rate is not generally appropriate for all the investments a firm will analyze. In particular if the risk associated with a specific investment is significantly different from the firm's existing assets, the weighted cost of capital should not be employed. In this context, a minimum acceptable rate of return that recognizes the different risk levels has to be used. To implement such an approach, financial management has to identify the relevant measure for risk. Several alternatives are available. First, the variability in returns for a single project, without any regard for the effect of diversification, could be used. Second, if management considers diversification to be a worthwhile activity, the riskiness of an individual project must be viewed in terms of its contribution to the risk of the firm's existing assets. Third, if the capital-asset pricing model is used, the appropriate risk measurement should recognize the portion of the risk that the investor cannot eliminate by diversifying among different securities.

Study Problems

13A–1. (*Required Return*) Hastings, Inc., is analyzing several investments. The expected returns and standard deviations of each project are tabulated below. The firm's cost of capital is 16.5 percent, and the standard deviation of the average project is 7 percent. The current rate on long-term U.S. government securities is 8.5 percent. Which investments should the firm accept?

Project	Investment's Expected Return	Standard Deviations of Returns
A	18.0%	7.0%
B	13.8	6.0
C	15.3	7.8
D	11.4	5.0

13A–2. (*Required Return*) Scudder Corporation is evaluating three investments that have the expected returns and standard deviations listed below. The management of the firm wants to determine the required rates of return of the projects using the capital-asset pricing model. The expected return of a diversified portfolio with a standard deviation of 6 percent is 15 percent. The rate on short-term U.S. government securities is 8 percent. Which investments should be made?

Investment	Expected Return	Standard Deviation	Correlation with the Market
A	18.8%	8.9%	.65
B	13.5	7.0	.80
C	15.0	6.5	.75

13A–3. (*Required Return*) Two capital investments are being examined by Wellton Corporation. Management wants to analyze the riskiness of the projects in terms of their effect on the riskiness of a diversified portfolio. The standard deviation of returns of project A is 9.82 percent and of B, 6.79 percent. The expected return for a diversified portfolio is 16 percent, and its standard deviation is 5 percent. The correlation coefficient between project A and the portfolio is estimated to be .536, and between project B and the portfolio, .742. The risk-free rate is 7 percent. Project A is expected to return 15.7 percent; project B, 17.5 percent. Which investment(s) should the company accept?

14

Analysis and Impact of Leverage

Our work in the previous two chapters allowed us to develop an understanding of how financial assets are valued in the marketplace. Drawing on the tenets of valuation theory, we presented various approaches to measuring the cost of funds to the business organization. The concepts to be covered in this chapter relate to the valuation process and the cost of capital, and also extend to the crucial problem of planning the firm's financing mix.

The cost of capital provides a direct link between the formulation of the firm's asset structure and its financial structure. This is illustrated in Figure 14–1. Recall that the cost of capital is a basic input to the time-adjusted capital budgeting models. It therefore affects the asset selection process that we have called capital budgeting. The cost of capital is affected, in turn, by the composition of the righthand side of the firm's balance sheet—that is, its financial structure.

The tools to be examined in this chapter can be useful aids to the financial manager in determining the firm's proper financial structure. Although these tools can certainly be applied in other settings, such as the product-pricing process, it is their application in designing a prudent financing mix that is stressed. First, the technique of breakeven analysis will be reviewed. This provides the foundation for the relationships to be highlighted in the remainder of the chapter. We will then examine the concept of operating leverage, some consequences of the firm's use of financial leverage, and the impact of the firm's earnings stream from combining operating and financial leverage in various degrees. Our immediate tasks are to distinguish two types of risk that confront the firm and to clarify some other teminology that will be used throughout this and the subsequent chapter.

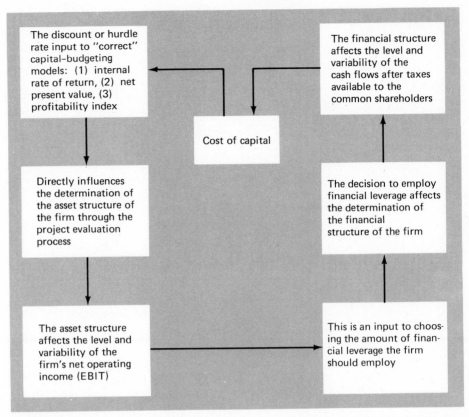

FIGURE 14–1. Cost of Capital as a Link between the Firm's Asset Structure and Financial Structure

BUSINESS RISK AND FINANCIAL RISK

In studying capital budgeting techniques we referred to **risk** as the likely variability associated with expected revenue streams. As our attention is now focused on the firm's financing decision rather than its investment decision, it is useful to separate the income stream variations attributable to (1) the company's exposure to business risk and (2) its decision to incur financial risk.

Business risk refers to the relative dispersion (variability) in the firm's expected earnings before interest and taxes (EBIT).[1] Figure 14–2 shows a subjectively estimated probability distribution of next year's EBIT for the Pierce Grain Company and the same type of projection for Pierce's larger competitor, the Blackburn Seed Company. The expected value of EBIT for Pierce is $100,000, with an associated standard deviation of $20,000. If next year's EBIT for Pierce fell one standard deviation short of the expected $100,000, the actual EBIT would equal $80,000. Blackburn's expected EBIT

---

[1] If what the accountants call "other income" and "other expenses" are equal to zero, then EBIT is equal to net operating income. These terms will be used interchangeably.

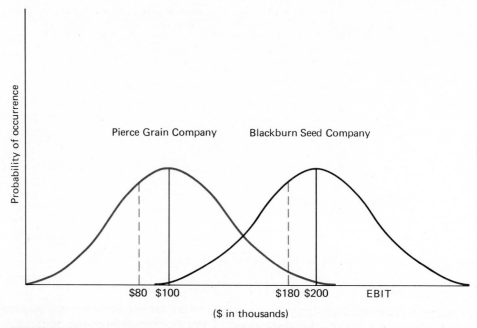

FIGURE 14–2. Subjective Probability Distribution of Next Year's EBIT

is $200,000, and the size of the associated standard deviation is $20,000. The standard deviation about the expected level of EBIT is the same for both firms. We would say that Pierce's degree of business risk exceeds Blackburn's owing to its larger coefficient of variation of expected EBIT, as follows:

$$\text{Pierce's coefficient of variation of expected EBIT} = \frac{\$20,000}{\$100,000} = .20$$

$$\text{Blackburn's coefficient of variation of expected EBIT} = \frac{\$20,000}{\$200,000} = .10$$

The relative dispersion in the firm's EBIT stream, measured here by its expected coefficient of variation, is the *residual* effect of several causal influences. Dispersion in operating income does not cause business risk; such dispersion, which we call business risk, is the result of several influences. Some of these are listed in Table 14–1, along with an example of each particular attribute. Notice that the company's cost structure, product demand characteristics, and intra-industry competitive position all affect its business risk posture. Such business risk is a direct result of the firm's investment decision. It is the firm's asset structure, after all, that gives rise to both the level and variability of its operating profits.

Financial risk, on the other hand, is a direct result of the firm's financing decision. In the context of selecting a proper financing mix, it refers to (1) the additional variability in earnings available to the firm's common shareholders and (2) the additional chance of insolvency borne by the common shareholder caused by the use of financial

TABLE 14–1. The Concept of Business Risk

Business Risk Attribute	Example[a]
1. Sensitivity of the firm's product demand to general economic conditions	If GNP declines, does the firm's sales level decline by a greater percent?
2. Degree of competition	Is the firm's market share small in comparison with other firms that produce and distribute the same product(s)?
3. Product diversification	Is a large proportion of the firm's sales revenue derived from a single major product or product line?
4. Operating leverage	Does the firm utilize a high level of operating leverage resulting in a high level of fixed costs?
5. Growth prospects	Are the firm's product markets expanding and (or) changing, making income estimates and prospects highly volatile?
6. Size	Does the firm suffer a competitive disadvantage due to lack of size in assets, sales, or profits that translates into (among other things) difficulty in tapping the capital market for funds?

[a] Affirmative responses indicate greater business risk exposure.

leverage.[2] **Financial leverage** means financing a portion of the firm's assets with securities bearing a fixed (limited) rate of return in hopes of increasing the ultimate return to the common stockholders. The decision to use debt or preferred stock in the financial structure of the corporation means that those who own the common shares of the firm are exposed to financial risk. Any given level of variability in EBIT will be magnified by the firm's use of financial leverage, and such additional variability will be embodied in the variability of earnings available to the residual owner and earnings per share. If these magnifications are negative, the common stockholder has a higher chance of insolvency than would have existed had the use of fixed charge securities (debt and preferred stock) been avoided.

The closely related concepts of business and financial risk are crucial to the problem of financial structure design. This follows from the impact of these types of risk on the variability of the earnings stream flowing to the company's residual owners. In the rest of this chapter we will study techniques that permit a precise assessment of the earnings stream variability caused by (1) operating leverage and (2) financial leverage. We have already defined financial leverage. Table 14–1 shows that the business risk of the enterprise is influenced by the use of what is called operating leverage. **Operating leverage** refers to the incurrence of fixed operating costs in the firm's income stream. To understand the nature and importance of operating leverage, we need to draw upon the basics of cost-volume-profit analysis (breakeven analysis).

BREAKEVEN ANALYSIS

The technique of breakeven analysis is familiar to legions of businesspeople. It is usefully applied in a wide array of business settings, including both small and large organizations. The fact that this tool is based on straightforward assumptions explains

---

[2] Note that the concept of financial risk used here differs from that used in our examination of cash and marketable securities management in Chapter 6.

a portion of its acceptance by the business community. But it is also true that companies have found the information gained from the breakeven model to be of positive benefit in decision-making situations.

Objective and Uses

The objective of breakeven analysis is to determine the breakeven quantity of output by studying the relationships among the firm's cost structure, volume of output, and profit. Alternatively, the breakeven level of sales dollars that corresponds to the breakeven quantity of output can be ascertained. We will develop the fundamental relationships by concentrating on units of output and then extend the procedure to permit direct calculation of the breakeven sales level.

What is meant by the breakeven quantity of output? It is that quantity of output, denominated in units, that results in an EBIT level equal to zero. Use of the breakeven model, therefore, enables the financial officer (1) to determine the quantity of output that must be sold to cover all operating costs, as distinct from financial costs, and (2) to calculate the EBIT that will be achieved at various output levels.

There are many actual and potential applications of the breakeven approach. Some of these include:

1. **Capital expenditure analysis.** As a *complementary* technique to discounted cash flow evaluation models, the breakeven model locates in a rough way the sales volume needed to make a project economically beneficial to the firm. It should *not* be used to replace the time-adjusted evaluation techniques.
2. **Pricing policy.** The sales price of a new product can be set to achieve a target EBIT level. Furthermore, should market penetration be a prime objective, the price could be set that would cover slightly more than the variable costs of production and provide only a partial contribution to the recovery of fixed costs. The negative EBIT at several possible sales prices can then be studied.
3. **Labor contract negotiations.** The effect of increased variable costs resulting from higher wages on the breakeven quantity of output can be analyzed.
4. **Cost structure.** The choice of reducing variable costs at the expense of incurring higher fixed costs can be evaluated. Management might decide to become more capital-intensive by performing tasks in the production process through use of equipment rather than laborers. Application of the breakeven model can indicate what the effects of this tradeoff will be on the breakeven point for the given product.
5. **Financing decisions.** Analysis of the firm's cost structure will reveal the proportion that fixed operating costs bear to sales. If this proportion is high, the firm might reasonably decide not to add any fixed financing costs on top of the high fixed operating costs.

Essential Elements of the Breakeven Model

To implement the breakeven model, we must separate the production costs of the company into two mutually exclusive categories: fixed costs and variable costs. You will recall from your study of basic economics that in the long run all costs are variable. Breakeven analysis, therefore, is a short-run concept.

Assumed Behavior of Costs

Fixed Costs. **Fixed costs,** also referred to as **indirect costs,** do not vary in total amount as sales volume or the quantity of output changes over some *relevant* range of output. Total fixed costs are independent of the quantity of product produced

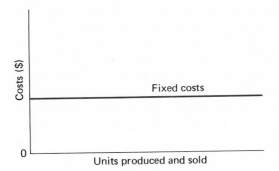

FIGURE 14–3. Fixed Cost Behavior over the Relevant Range of Output

and equal some constant dollar amount. Obviously, as production volume increases, fixed cost per unit of product falls. The reason is that total fixed costs are being spread over larger and larger quantities of output. The behavior of total fixed costs with respect to the company's relevant range of output is depicted in Figure 14–3. This total is shown to be unaffected by the quantity of product that is manufactured and sold. Over some other relevant output range, the amount of total fixed costs might be higher or lower for the same company.

In a manufacturing setting, some specific examples of fixed costs are these:

1. Administrative salaries
2. Depreciation
3. Insurance
4. Lump sums spent on intermittent advertising programs
5. Property taxes
6. Rent

Variable Costs. **Variable costs** are sometimes referred to as **direct costs.** Variable costs are fixed per unit of output but vary in total as output changes. Total variable costs are computed by taking the variable cost per unit and multiplying it by the quantity produced and sold. The breakeven model assumes proportionality between total variable costs and sales. Thus, if sales rise by 10 percent, it is assumed that variable costs will rise by 10 percent. The behavior of total variable costs with respect to the company's relevant range of output is depicted in Figure 14–4. Total variable costs are seen to depend on the quantity of product that is manufactured and sold.

FIGURE 14–4. Variable Cost Behavior over the Relevant Range of Output

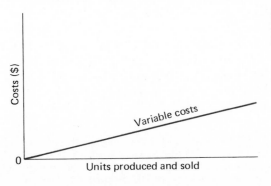

Notice that if zero units of the product are manufactured then variable costs are zero, but fixed costs are greater than zero. This implies that some contribution to the coverage of fixed costs occurs as long as the selling price per unit exceeds the variable cost per unit. This helps explain why some firms will operate a plant even when sales are *temporarily* depressed—that is, to provide some increment of revenue toward the coverage of fixed costs.

For a manufacturing operation, some examples of variable costs include these:

1. Direct labor
2. Direct materials
3. Energy costs (fuel, electricity, natural gas) associated with the production area
4. Freight costs for products leaving the plant
5. Packaging
6. Sales commissions

More on Behavior of Costs.   No one really believes that *all* costs behave as neatly as we have illustrated the fixed and variable costs in Figures 14–3 and 14–4. Nor does any law or accounting principle dictate that a certain element of the firm's total costs always be classified as fixed or variable. This will depend on the set of circumstances associated with the specific firm. In one firm utility costs may be predominantly fixed, whereas in another they may vary with output.[3]

Furthermore, some costs may be fixed for a while, then rise sharply to a higher level as a higher output is reached, remain fixed, and then rise again with further increases in production. Such costs may be termed either (1) **semi-variable** or (2) **semi-fixed.** The label is your choice, since both are used in industrial practice. An example might be the salaries paid production supervisors. Should output be cut back by 15 percent for a short period, the management of the organization is not likely to lay off 15 percent of the supervisors. Similarly, commissions paid to salespeople often follow a stepwise pattern over wide ranges of success. This sort of cost behavior is shown in Figure 14–5.

To implement the breakeven model and deal with such "difficult" costs, it is necessary that the financial manager (1) identify the most relevant output range for planning purposes and then (2) approximate the cost effect of semi-variable items over this range by segregating a portion of them to fixed costs and a portion to variable costs. In the actual business setting this procedure is not fun. It is not unusual for the analyst who deals with the figures to spend considerably more time on allocating costs to fixed and variable categories than to carrying out the actual breakeven calculations.

Total Revenue and Volume of Output

Besides fixed and variable costs, the essential elements of the breakeven model include total revenue from sales and volume of output. **Total revenue** means sales dollars and is equal to the selling price per unit multiplied by the quantity sold. The **volume of output** refers to the firm's level of operations and may be indicated as a unit quantity or sales dollars.

---

[3] In a greenhouse operation, where plants are grown (manufactured) under strictly controlled temperatures, heat costs will tend to be fixed whether the building is full or only half full of seedlings. In a metal stamping operation, where levers are being produced, there is no need to heat the plant to as high a temperature when the machines are stopped and the workers are not there. In this latter case, the heat costs will tend to be variable.

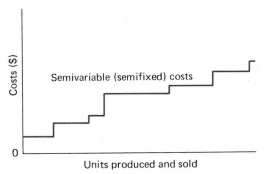

FIGURE 14–5. Semivariable Cost Behavior over the Relevant Range of Output

Finding the Breakeven Point

Finding the breakeven point in terms of units of production can be accomplished in several ways. All approaches require the essential elements of the breakeven model just described. The breakeven model is just a simple adaptation of the firm's income statement expressed in the following analytical format:

$$\text{sales} - (\text{total variable cost} + \text{total fixed cost}) = \text{profit} \qquad (14\text{–}1)$$

On a units of production basis, it is necessary to introduce (1) the price at which each unit is sold and (2) the variable cost per unit of output. Because the profit item studied in breakeven analysis is EBIT, we will use that acronym instead of the word "profit." In terms of units, the income statement shown in equation (14–1) becomes the breakeven model by setting EBIT equal to zero:

$$\left(\begin{array}{c}\text{sales price}\\\text{per unit}\end{array}\right)\left(\begin{array}{c}\text{units}\\\text{sold}\end{array}\right) - \left[\left(\begin{array}{c}\text{variable cost}\\\text{per unit}\end{array}\right)\left(\begin{array}{c}\text{units}\\\text{sold}\end{array}\right) + \left(\begin{array}{c}\text{total fixed}\\\text{cost}\end{array}\right)\right] = \text{EBIT} = \$0 \quad (14\text{–}2)$$

Our task now becomes that of finding the number of units that must be produced and sold in order to satisfy equation (14–2)—that is, to arrive at an EBIT = $0. This can be done by (1) trial and error analysis, (2) contribution margin analysis, or (3) algebraic analysis. Each approach will be illustrated using the same set of circumstances.

The Problem Situation

Even though the Pierce Grain Company manufactures several different products, it has observed over a lengthy period that the product mix is rather constant. This allows management to conduct its financial planning by use of a "normal" sales price per unit and "normal" variable cost per unit. The selling price is $10 and the variable cost is $6. Total fixed costs for the firm are $100,000 per year. What is the breakeven point in units produced and sold for the company during the coming year?

Trial and Error Analysis

The most cumbersome approach to determining the firm's breakeven point is to employ the trial and error technique illustrated in Table 14–2. The process simply involves the arbitrary selection of an output level and the calculation of a corresponding EBIT amount. When the level of output is found that results in an EBIT = $0, the breakeven point has been located. Notice that Table 14–2 is just equation (14–2) in worksheet form. For the Pierce Grain Company, total operating costs will be covered when 25,000 units are manufactured and sold. This tells us that if sales equal $250,000, the firm's EBIT will equal $0.

TABLE 14–2. The Pierce Grain Company Sales, Cost, and Profit Schedule

(1) Units Sold	(2) Unit Sales Price	(3) = (1) × (2) Sales	(4) Unit Variable Cost	(5) = (1) × (4) Total Variable Cost	(6) Total Fixed Cost	(7) = (5) + (6) Total Cost	(8) = (3) – (7) EBIT
1. 10,000	$10	$100,000	$6	$ 60,000	$100,000	$160,000	$−60,000 1.
2. 15,000	10	150,000	6	90,000	100,000	190,000	−40,000 2.
3. 20,000	10	200,000	6	120,000	100,000	220,000	−20,000 3.
4. 25,000	10	250,000	6	150,000	100,000	250,000	0 4.
5. 30,000	10	300,000	6	180,000	100,000	280,000	20,000 5.
6. 35,000	10	350,000	6	210,000	100,000	310,000	40,000 6.

Input Data
Unit sales price = $10
Unit variable cost = $6
Total fixed cost   = $100,000

Output Data
Breakeven point in units = 25,000 units produced and sold
Breakeven point in sales = $250,000

Contribution Margin Analysis   Unlike trial and error, use of the contribution margin technique permits direct computation of the breakeven quantity of output. The **contribution margin** is the difference between the unit selling price and unit variable costs, as follows:

$$
\begin{array}{l}
\text{Unit sales price} \\
-\ \underline{\text{Unit variable cost}} \\
=\ \underline{\underline{\text{Unit contribution margin}}}
\end{array}
$$

The use of the word "contribution" in the present context means contribution to the coverage of fixed operating costs. For the Pierce Grain Company, the unit contribution margin is:

$$
\begin{array}{lr}
\text{Unit sales price} & \$10 \\
\text{Unit variable cost} & \underline{-6} \\
\text{Unit contribution margin} & \underline{\underline{\$\ 4}}
\end{array}
$$

If the annual fixed costs of $100,000 are divided by the unit contribution margin of $4, we find the breakeven quantity of output for Pierce Grain is 25,000 units. With much less effort, we have arrived at the identical result found by trial and error. Figure 14–6 portrays the contribution margin technique for finding the breakeven point.

Algebraic Analysis   Explanation of the algebraic method for finding the breakeven output level can be facilitated by adoption of some notation. Let

$$Q = \text{the number of units sold}$$

$$Q_B = \text{the breakeven level of } Q$$

$$P = \text{the unit sales price}$$

$$F = \text{total fixed costs anticipated over the planning period}$$

$$V = \text{the unit variable cost}$$

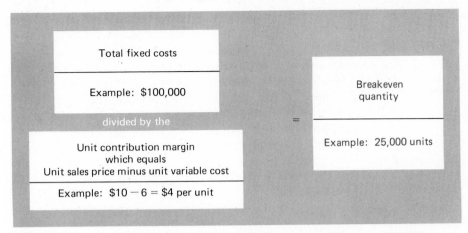

FIGURE 14–6.   Contribution Margin Approach to Breakeven Analysis

Equation (14–2), the breakeven model, is repeated below as equation (14–2a) with the model symbols used in place of words. The breakeven model is then solved for Q, the number of units that must be sold in order that EBIT will equal $0. We label the breakeven point quantity Q_B.

$$(P \cdot Q) - [(V \cdot Q) + (F)] = \text{EBIT} = \$0 \qquad (14\text{–}2a)$$

$$(P \cdot Q) - (V \cdot Q) - F = \$0$$

$$Q(P - V) = F$$

$$Q_B = \frac{F}{P - V} \qquad (14\text{–}3)$$

Observe that equation (14–3) says: divide total fixed operating costs, F, by the unit contribution margin, $P - V$, and the breakeven level of output, Q_B, will be obtained. The contribution margin analysis is nothing more than equation (14–3) in different garb.

Application of equation (14–3) permits direct calculation of Pierce Grain's breakeven point, as follows:

$$Q_B = \frac{F}{P - V} = \frac{\$100,000}{\$10 - \$6} = 25,000 \text{ units}$$

The Breakeven Point in Sales Dollars

In dealing with the firm that produces several products, it is convenient to compute the breakeven point in terms of sales dollars rather than units of output. Sales, in effect, become a common denominator associated with a particular product mix. Furthermore, an outside analyst may not have access to internal unit cost data. He or she may, however, be able to obtain annual reports for the firm. If the analyst can separate the firm's total costs as identified from its annual reports into their fixed and variable components, he or she can calculate a general breakeven point in sales dollars.

We will illustrate the procedure using the Pierce Grain Company's cost structure, contained in Table 14–2. Suppose that the information on line 5 of Table 14–2 is arranged in the format shown in Table 14–3. We will refer to this type of financial statement as an **analytical income statement.** This distinguishes it from audited income statements published, for example, in the annual reports of public corporations. If we are aware of the simple mathematical relationships on which cost-volume-profit analysis is based, Table 14–3 can be employed to find the breakeven point in sales dollars for the Pierce Grain Company.

First, let us explore the logic of the process. Recall from equation (14–1) that

$$\text{sales} - (\text{total variable cost} + \text{total fixed cost}) = \text{EBIT}$$

If we let total sales = S, total variable cost = VC, and total fixed cost = F, the above relationship becomes

$$S - (VC + F) = \text{EBIT}$$

Since variable cost per unit of output and selling price per unit are *assumed* constant over the relevant output range in breakeven analysis, the ratio of total sales to total variable cost, VC/S, is a constant for any level of sales. This permits us to rewrite the previous expression as

$$S - \left[\left(\frac{VC}{S} \right) S \right] - F = \text{EBIT}$$

and

$$S \left(1 - \frac{VC}{S} \right) - F = \text{EBIT}$$

At the breakeven point, however, EBIT = 0, and the corresponding breakeven level of sales can be represented as S^*. At the breakeven level of sales, we have

$$S^* \left(1 - \frac{VC}{S} \right) - F = 0$$

or

$$S^* \left(1 - \frac{VC}{S} \right) = F$$

Therefore

$$S^* = \frac{F}{1 - \dfrac{VC}{S}} \qquad (14\text{–}4)$$

TABLE 14–3. The Pierce Grain Company Analytical Income Statement

Sales	$300,000
Less: Total variable costs	180,000
Revenue before fixed costs	$120,000
Less: Total fixed costs	100,000
EBIT	$ 20,000

The application of equation (14–4) to Pierce Grain's analytical income statement in Table 14–3 permits the breakeven sales level for the firm to be directly computed, as follows:

$$S^* = \frac{\$100,000}{1 - \dfrac{\$180,000}{\$300,000}}$$

$$= \frac{\$100,000}{1 - .60} = \$250,000$$

Notice that this is indeed the same breakeven sales level for Pierce Grain that is indicated on line 4 of Table 14–2.

Graphic Representation, Analysis of Input Changes, and Cash Breakeven Point

In making a presentation to management, it is often more effective to display the firm's cost-volume-profit relationships in the form of a chart, rather than merely in figures and equations. Even those individuals who truly enjoy analyzing financial problems find figures and equations dry material at times. Furthermore, by quickly scanning the basic breakeven chart, the manager can approximate the EBIT amount that will prevail at different sales levels.

Such a chart has been prepared for the Pierce Grain Company. Figure 14–7 has been constructed for this firm using the input data contained in Table 14–2. Total fixed costs of $100,000 are added to the total variable costs associated with each production level to form the total costs line. When 25,000 units of product are manufactured and sold, the sales line and total costs line intersect. This means, of course, the EBIT that would exist at that volume of output is zero. Beyond 25,000 units of output, notice that sales revenues exceed the total costs line. This causes a positive EBIT. This positive EBIT or profits is labeled "original EBIT" in Figure 14–7.

The unencumbered nature of the breakeven model makes it possible to quickly incorporate changes in the requisite input data and generate the revised output. Suppose a favorable combination of events causes Pierce Grain's fixed costs to decrease by $25,000. This would put total fixed costs for the planning period at a level of $75,000 rather than the $100,000 originally forecast. Total costs, being the sum of fixed and variable costs, would be lower by $25,000 at all output levels. The revised total

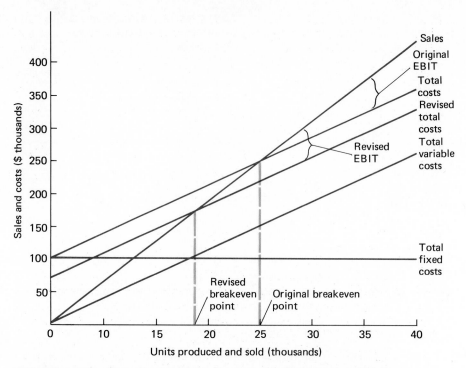

FIGURE 14–7. The Pierce Grain Company's Breakeven Chart

costs line in Figure 14–7 reflects Pierce Grain's reduction in fixed costs. Under these revised conditions, the new breakeven point in units would be as follows:

$$Q_B = \frac{\$75,000}{\$10 - \$6} = 18,750 \text{ units}$$

The revised breakeven point of 18,750 units is identified in Figure 14–7, along with the revised EBIT amounts that would prevail at differing output and sales amounts. The chart clearly indicates that at any specific production and sales level, the revised EBIT would exceed the original EBIT. This must be the case, as the revised total costs line lies below the original total costs line over the entire relevant output range. The effect on the breakeven point caused by other changes in (1) the cost structure or (2) the pricing policy can be analyzed in a similar fashion.

The data in Figure 14–7 can be used to demonstrate another version of basic cost-volume-profit analysis. This can be called **cash breakeven analysis.** If the company's fixed or variable cost estimates contain allowance for any noncash expenses, then the resultant breakeven point is higher on an accounting profit basis than on a cash basis. This means the firm's production and sales levels do not have to be as great to cover the cash costs of manufacturing the product.

What are these noncash expenses? The largest and most significant is depreciation expense. Another category is prepaid expenses. Insurance policies are at times paid to cover a three-year cycle. Thus, the time period for which the breakeven analysis is being performed might *not* involve an actual cash outlay for insurance coverage.

For purposes of illustration, assume that noncash expenses for Pierce Grain amount to $25,000 over the planning period, and that all these costs are fixed. We can compare the revised total costs line in Figure 14–7, which implicitly assumes a lower fixed *cash* cost line, with the sales revenue line to find the cash breakeven point. Provided Pierce Grain can produce and sell 18,750 units over the planning horizon, revenues from sales will be equal to cash operating costs.

Limitations of Breakeven Analysis

Earlier we identified some of the applications of breakeven analysis. This technique is a useful tool in many settings. It must be emphasized, however, that breakeven analysis provides a *beneficial guide* to managerial action, not the final answer. The use of cost-volume-profit analysis has drawbacks, which should be kept in mind. These include the following:

1. The cost-volume-profit relationship is assumed to be linear. This is realistic only over narrow ranges of output.
2. The total revenue curve (sales curve) is presumed to increase linearly with the volume of output. This implies *any* quantity can be sold over the relevant output range at that *single* price. To be more realistic, it is necessary in many situations to compute *several* sales curves and corresponding breakeven points at differing prices.
3. A constant production and sales mix is assumed. Should the company decide to produce more of one product and less of another, a new breakeven point would have to be found. Only if the variable cost to sales ratios were identical for products involved would the new calculation be unnecessary.
4. The breakeven chart and the breakeven computation are static forms of analysis. Any alteration in the firm's cost or price structure dictates that a new breakeven point be calculated. Breakeven analysis is more helpful, therefore, in stable industries than in dynamic ones.

OPERATING LEVERAGE

If fixed operating costs are present in the firm's cost structure, *operating leverage* results. Fixed operating costs do *not* include interest charges incurred from the firm's use of debt financing. Those costs will be incorporated into the analysis when financial leverage is discussed.

So operating leverage *arises* from the firm's use of fixed operating costs. But what is operating leverage? **Operating leverage** is the responsiveness of the firm's EBIT to fluctuations in sales. By continuing to draw upon our data for the Pierce Grain Company, we can illustrate the concept of operating leverage. Consider Table 14–4, where a possible fluctuation in the firm's sales level is being studied. It is assumed here that Pierce Grain is currently operating at an annual sales level of $300,000. This is referred to in the tabulation as the base sales level at t (time period zero). The question being asked: How will Pierce Grain's EBIT level respond to a positive 20 percent change in sales? A sales volume of $360,000, referred to as the forecast

TABLE 14–4. The Concept of Operating Leverage: An Increase in Pierce Grain Company Sales

Item	Base Sales Level, t	Forecast Sales Level, $t + 1$
Sales	$300,000	$360,000
Less: Total variable costs	180,000	216,000
Revenue before fixed costs	$120,000	$144,000
Less: Total fixed costs	100,000	100,000
EBIT	$ 20,000	$ 44,000

sales level at $t + 1$, reflects the 20 percent sales rise anticipated over the planning period. Assume that the planning period is one year.

Operating leverage relationships are derived within the mathematical assumptions of cost-volume-profit analysis. In the present example, this means that Pierce Grain's variable cost to sales ratio of .6 will continue to hold during time period $t + 1$, and the fixed costs will hold steady at $100,000.

Given the forecasted sales level for Pierce Grain and its cost structure, we can measure the responsiveness of EBIT to the upswing in volume. Notice in Table 14–4 that EBIT is expected to be $44,000 at the end of the planning period. The percentage change in EBIT from t to $t + 1$ can be measured as follows:

$$\text{percentage change in EBIT} = \frac{\$44,000_{t+1} - \$20,000_t}{\$20,000_t}$$

$$= \frac{\$24,000}{\$20,000}$$

$$= 120\%$$

We know that the projected fluctuation in sales amounts to 20 percent of the base period, t, sales level. This is verified below:

$$\text{percentage change in sales} = \frac{\$360,000_{t+1} - \$300,000_t}{\$300,000_t}$$

$$= \frac{\$60,000}{\$300,000}$$

$$= 20\%$$

By relating the percentage fluctuation in EBIT to the percentage fluctuation in sales, we can calculate a specific measure of operating leverage. Thus, we have

$$\begin{array}{l} \text{degree of operating leverage} \\ \text{from the base sales level(s)} \end{array} = \text{DOL}_s = \frac{\text{percentage change in EBIT}}{\text{percentage change in sales}} \quad (14\text{–}5)$$

TABLE 14–5. The Concept of Operating Leverage: A Decrease in Pierce Grain Company Sales

Item	Base Sales Level, t	Forecast Sales Level, $t + 1$
Sales	$300,000	$240,000
Less: Total variable costs	180,000	144,000
Revenue before fixed costs	$120,000	$ 96,000
Less: Total fixed costs	100,000	100,000
EBIT	$ 20,000	$ −4,000

Applying equation (14–5) to our Pierce Grain data gives

$$\text{DOL}_{\$300,000} = \frac{120\%}{20\%} = 6 \text{ times}$$

Unless we understand what the specific measure of operating leverage tells us, the fact that we may know it is equal to 6 times is nothing more than sterile information. For Pierce Grain, the inference is that for *any* percentage fluctuation in sales from the base level, the percentage fluctuation in EBIT will be six times as great. If Pierce Grain expected only a 5 percent rise in sales over the coming period, a 30 percent rise in EBIT would be anticipated as follows:

$$(\text{percentage change in sales}) = (\text{DOL}_s) = \text{percentage change in EBIT}$$

$$(5\%) \times (6) = 30\%$$

We will now return to the postulated 20 percent change in sales. What if the direction of the fluctuation is expected to be negative rather than positive? What is in store for Pierce Grain? Unfortunately for Pierce Grain, but fortunately for the analytical process, we will see that the operating leverage measure holds in the negative direction as well. This situation is displayed in Table 14–5.

At the $240,000 sales level, which represents the 20 percent decrease from the base period, Pierce Grain's EBIT is expected to be $−4000. How sensitive is EBIT to this sales change? The magnitude of the EBIT fluctuation is calculated as[4]

$$\text{percentage change in EBIT} = \frac{\$-4000_{t+1} - \$20,000_t}{\$20,000_t}$$

$$= \frac{\$-24,000}{\$20,000}$$

$$= -120\%$$

---

[4] Some students have conceptual difficulty in computing these percentage changes when negative amounts are involved. Notice by inspection in Table 14–5 that the *difference* between an EBIT amount of + $20,000 at t and − $4,000 at $t + 1$ is − $24,000.

Making use of our knowledge that the sales change was equal to -20 percent permits us to compute the specific measure of operating leverage as

$$\text{DOL}_{\$300,000} = \frac{-120\%}{-20\%} = 6 \text{ times}$$

What we have seen, then, is that the degree of operating leverage measure works in the positive or negative direction. A negative change in production volume and sales can be magnified severalfold when the effect on EBIT is calculated.

To this point our calculations of the degree of operating leverage have required two analytical income statements: one for the base period and a second for the subsequent period that incorporates the possible sales alteration. This cumbersome process can be simplified. If unit cost data are available to the financial manager, the relationship can be expressed directly in the following manner:

$$\text{DOL}_s = \frac{Q(P - V)}{Q(P - V) - F} \qquad (14\text{--}6)$$

Observe in equation $(14\text{--}6)$ that the variables were all previously defined in our algebraic analysis of the breakeven model. Recall that Pierce sells its product at $10 per unit, the unit variable cost is $6, and total fixed costs over the planning horizon are $100,000. Still assuming that Pierce is operating at a $300,000 sales volume, which means output (Q) is 30,000 units, we can find the degree of operating leverage by application of equation $(14\text{--}6)$:

$$\text{DOL}_{\$300,000} = \frac{30,000(\$10 - \$6)}{30,000(\$10 - \$6) - \$100,000} = \frac{\$120,000}{\$20,000} = 6 \text{ times}$$

Whereas equation $(14\text{--}6)$ requires us to know unit cost data to carry out the computations, the next formulation we examine does not. If we have an analytical income statement for the base period, then equation $(14\text{--}7)$ can be employed to find the firm's degree of operating leverage:

$$\text{DOL}_s = \frac{\text{revenue before fixed costs}}{\text{EBIT}} = \frac{S - VC}{S - VC - F} \qquad (14\text{--}7)$$

Use of equation $(14\text{--}7)$ in conjunction with the base period data for Pierce Grain shown in either Table 14–4 or 14–5 gives

$$\text{DOL}_{\$300,000} = \frac{\$120,000}{\$20,000} = 6 \text{ times}$$

The three versions of the operating leverage measure all produce the same result. Data availability will sometimes dictate which formulation can be applied. The crucial consideration, though, is that you grasp what the measurement tells you. For Pierce Grain, a 1 percent change in sales will produce a 6 percent change in EBIT.

Implications   As the firm's scale of operations moves in a favorable manner above the breakeven point, the degree of operating leverage at each subsequent (higher) sales base will decline. In short, the greater the sales level, the lower will be the degree of operating leverage. This is demonstrated in Table 14–6 for the Pierce Grain Company. At the breakeven sales level for Pierce Grain, the degree of operating leverage is *undefined*, since the denominator in any of the computational formulas is zero. Notice that beyond the breakeven point of 25,000 units, the degree of operating leverage declines. It will decline at a decreasing rate and asymptotically approach a value of 1.00. As long as some fixed operating costs are present in the firm's cost structure, however, operating leverage exists, and the degree of operating leverage (DOL_s) will exceed 1.00. Operating leverage is present, then, whenever the firm faces the following situation:

$$\frac{\text{percentage change in EBIT}}{\text{percentage change in sales}} > 1.00$$

The data in Table 14–6 are presented in graphic form in Figure 14–8.

The greater the firm's degree of operating leverage, the more its profits will vary with a given percentage change in sales. Thus, operating leverage is definitely an attribute of the business risk that confronts the company. From Table 14–6 and Figure 14–8 we have seen that the degree of operating leverage falls as sales increase past the firm's breakeven point. The sheer size and operating profitability of the firm, therefore, affects and can lessen its business risk exposure.

An understanding of the operating leverage concept can assist the manager who is contemplating an alteration in the firm's cost structure. It might be possible to replace part of the labor force with capital equipment (machinery). A possible result is an increase in fixed costs associated with the new machinery and a reduction in variable costs attributable to a lower labor bill. This conceivably could raise the firm's degree of operating leverage at a specific sales base. If the prospects for future sales increases are high, then increasing the degree of operating leverage might be a prudent decision. The opposite conclusion will be reached if sales prospects are unattractive.

TABLE 14–6.   The Pierce Grain Company Degree of Operating Leverage Relative to Different Sales Bases

Units Produced and Sold	Sales Dollars	DOL$_s$
25,000	$ 250,000	Undefined
30,000	300,000	6.00
35,000	350,000	3.50
40,000	400,000	2.67
45,000	450,000	2.25
50,000	500,000	2.00
75,000	750,000	1.50
100,000	1,000,000	1.33

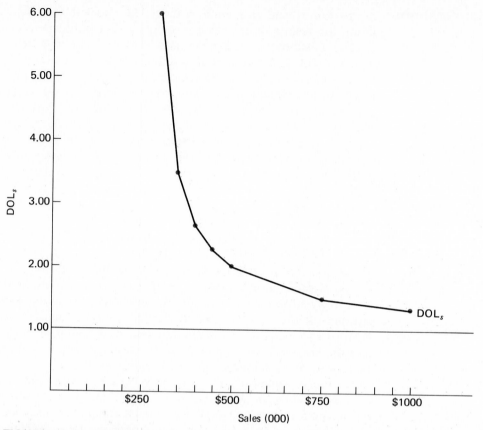

FIGURE 14–8. The Pierce Grain Company Degree of Operating Leverage Relative to Different Sales Bases

FINANCIAL LEVERAGE

We have defined **financial leverage** as the practice of financing a portion of the firm's assets with securities bearing a fixed rate of return in hope of increasing the ultimate return to the common stockholders. In the present discussion we focus on the responsiveness of the company's earnings per share to changes in its EBIT. For the time being, then, the return to the common stockholder being concentrated upon is earnings per share. We are *not* saying that earnings per share is the appropriate criterion for all financing decisions. In fact, the weakness of such a contention will be examined in the next chapter. Rather, a certain type of *effect* is caused by the use of financial leverage. This effect can be illustrated clearly by concentrating on an earnings per share criterion.

Let us assume that the Pierce Grain Company is in the process of getting started as a going concern. The firm's potential owners have calculated that $200,000 is needed to purchase the necessary assets to conduct the business. Three possible financing plans have been identified for raising the $200,000; they are presented in

TABLE 14–7. The Pierce Grain Company Possible Financial Structures

Plan A: 0% debt

		Total debt	$ 0
		Common equity	200,000[a]
Total assets	$200,000	Total liabilities and equity	$200,000

Plan B: 25% debt at 8% interest rate

		Total debt	$ 50,000
		Common equity	150,000[b]
Total assets	$200,000	Total liabilities and equity	$200,000

Plan C: 40% debt at 8% interest rate

		Total debt	$ 80,000
		Common equity	120,000[c]
Total assets	$200,000	Total liabilities and equity	$200,000

[a] 2000 common shares outstanding.
[b] 1500 common shares outstanding.
[c] 1200 common shares outstanding.

Table 14–7. In plan A no financial risk is assumed: the entire $200,000 is raised by selling 2000 common shares, each with a $100 par value. In plan B a moderate amount of financial risk is assumed: 25 percent of the assets are financed with a debt issue that carries an 8 percent annual interest rate. Plan C would use the most financial leverage: 40 percent of the assets would be financed with a debt issue costing 8 percent.[5]

Table 14–8 presents the impact of financial leverage on earnings per share associated with each fund-raising alternative. If EBIT should increase from $20,000 to $40,000, then earnings per share would rise by 100 percent under plan A. The same positive fluctuation in EBIT would occasion an earnings per share rise of 125 percent under plan B, and 147 percent under plan C. In plans B and C the 100 percent increase in EBIT (from $20,000 to $40,000) is magnified to a greater than 100 percent increase in earnings per share. The firm is employing financial leverage, and exposing its owners to financial risk, when the following situation exists:

$$\frac{\text{percentage change in earnings per share}}{\text{percentage change in EBIT}} > 1.00$$

By following the same general procedures that allowed us to analyze the firm's use of operating leverage, we can lay out a precise measure of financial leverage. Such a measure deals with the sensitivity of earnings per share to EBIT fluctuations. The relationship can be expressed as

$$\begin{array}{l}\text{degree of financial}\\\text{leverage from}\\\text{base EBIT level}\end{array} = \text{DFL}_{EBIT} = \frac{\text{percentage change in earnings per share}}{\text{percentage change in EBIT}} \quad (14\text{–}8)$$

---

[5] In actual practice moving from a 25 to a 40 percent debt ratio would probably result in a higher interest rate on the additional bonds. That effect is ignored here to let us concentrate on the ramifications of using different proportions of debt in the financial structure.

TABLE 14–8. The Pierce Grain Company Analysis of Financial Leverage at Different EBIT Levels

(1) EBIT	(2) Interest	(3) = (1) − (2) EBT	(4) = (3) × .5 Taxes	(5) = (3) − (4) Net Income to Common	(6) Earnings per Share	
Plan A: 0% debt; $200,000 common equity; 2000 shares						
$ 0	$ 0	$ 0	$ 0	$ 0	$ 0	
20,000	0	20,000	10,000	10,000	5.00	
40,000	0	40,000	20,000	20,000	5.00 ⎤	
60,000	0	60,000	30,000	30,000	10.00 ⎬	100%
80,000	0	80,000	40,000	40,000	15.00 ⎦	
					20.00	
Plan B: 25% debt; 8% interest rate; $150,000 common equity; 1500 shares						
$ 0	$4,000	$ (4,000)	$ (2,000)[a]	$ (2,000)	$ (1.33)	
20,000	4,000	16,000	8,000	8,000	5.33 ⎤	
40,000	4,000	36,000	18,000	18,000	12.00 ⎬	125%
60,000	4,000	56,000	28,000	28,000	18.67 ⎦	
80,000	4,000	76,000	38,000	38,000	25.33	
Plan C: 40% debt; 8% interest rate; $120,000 common equity; 1200 shares						
$ 0	6,400	$ (6,400)	$ (3,200)[a]	$ (3,200)	$ (2.67)	
20,000	6,400	13,600	6,800	6,800	5.67 ⎤	
40,000	6,400	33,600	16,800	16,800	14.00 ⎬	147%
60,000	6,400	53,600	26,800	26,800	22.33 ⎦	
80,000	6,400	73,600	36,800	36,800	30.67	

[a] The negative tax bill recognizes the credit arising from the carryback and carryforward provision of the tax code. See Chapter 2.

Use of equation (14–8) with each of the financing choices outlined for Pierce Grain is shown below. The base EBIT level is $20,000 in each case.

$$\text{Plan A:} \qquad \text{DFL}_{\$20,000} = \frac{100\%}{100\%} = 1.00 \text{ time}$$

$$\text{Plan B:} \qquad \text{DFL}_{\$20,000} = \frac{125\%}{100\%} = 1.25 \text{ times}$$

$$\text{Plan C:} \qquad \text{DFL}_{\$20,000} = \frac{147\%}{100\%} = 1.47 \text{ times}$$

Like operating leverage, the degree of financial leverage concept performs in the negative direction as well as the positive. Should EBIT fall by 10 percent, the Pierce Grain Company would suffer a 12.5 percent decline in earnings per share under plan B. If plan C were chosen to raise the necessary financial capital, the decline in earnings would be 14.7 percent. Observe that the greater the degree of financial leverage, the greater the fluctuations (positive or negative) in earnings per share. The common stockholder is required to endure greater variations in returns when the firm's management chooses to use more financial leverage rather than less. The degree of financial leverage measure allows the variation to be quantified.

Rather than taking the time to compute percentage changes in EBIT and earnings per share, the degree of financial leverage can be found directly, as follows:

$$DFL_{EBIT} = \frac{EBIT}{EBIT - I} \qquad (14-9)$$

In equation (14–9) the variable, I, represents the total interest expense incurred on *all* the firm's contractual debt obligations. If 6 bonds are outstanding, I is the sum of the interest expense on all 6 bonds. If the firm has preferred stock in its financial structure, the dividend on such issues must be inflated to a before-tax basis and included in the computation of I.[6] In this latter instance, I is in reality the sum of all fixed financing costs.

Equation (14–9) has been applied to each of Pierce Grain's financing plans (Table 14–8) at a base EBIT level of $20,000. The results are as follows:

Plan A: $DFL_{\$20,000} = \dfrac{\$20,000}{\$20,000 - 0} = 1.00$ time

Plan B: $DFL_{\$20,000} = \dfrac{\$20,000}{\$20,000 - \$4000} = 1.25$ times

Plan C: $DFL_{\$20,000} = \dfrac{\$20,000}{\$20,000 - \$6400} = 1.47$ times

As you probably suspected, the measures of financial leverage shown above are identical to those obtained by use of equation (14–8). This will always be the case.

COMBINING OPERATING AND FINANCIAL LEVERAGE

Changes in sales revenues cause greater changes in EBIT. Additionally, changes in EBIT translate into larger variations in both earnings per share (EPS) and total earnings available to the common shareholders (EAC), if the firm chooses to use financial leverage. It should be no surprise, then, to find out that combining operating and financial leverage causes rather large variations in earnings per share. This entire process is visually displayed in Figure 14–9.

Since the risk associated with possible earnings per share is affected by the use of combined or total leverage, it is useful to quantify the effect. For an illustration, we refer once more to the Pierce Grain Company. The cost structure identified for Pierce Grain in our discussion of breakeven analysis still holds. Furthermore, assume that plan B, which carried a 25 percent debt ratio, was chosen to finance the company's assets. Turn your attention to Table 14–9.

---

[6] Suppose (1) preferred dividends of $4000 are paid annually by the firm, and (2) it faces a 40 percent marginal tax rate. How much must the firm earn *before taxes* to make the $4000 payment out of after-tax earnings? Since preferred dividends are not tax deductible to the paying company, we have $4000/(1 − .40) = $6666.67. Recall from Chapter 2 that the Tax Reform Act of 1986 provided for the taxation of corporate incomes at a maximum rate of 34 percent for tax years beginning *after* June 30, 1987. This maximum rate applies to taxable incomes over $75,000. Under this new tax provision, the firm would only need to earn $6060.61 before taxes to make the $4000 preferred dividend payment. That is, $4000/ (1 − .34) = $6060.61. Note that from a financial policy viewpoint, the 1986 tax act reduced *somewhat* the tax shield advantages of corporate debt financing and simultaneously reduced the tax bias against preferred stock and common stock financing.

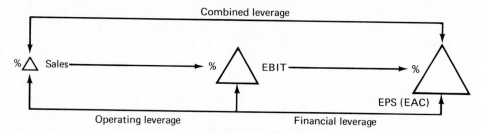

FIGURE 14–9. Leverage and Earnings Fluctuations

In Table 14–9 an increase in output for Pierce Grain from 30,000 to 36,000 units is analyzed. This represents a 20 percent rise in sales revenues. From our earlier discussion of operating leverage and the data in Table 14–9 we can see that this 20 percent increase in sales is magnified into a 120 percent rise in EBIT. From this base sales level of $300,000 the degree of operating leverage is 6 times.

The 120 percent rise in EBIT induces a change in earnings per share and earnings available to the common shareholders of 150 percent. The degree of financial leverage is therefore 1.25 times.

The upshot of the analysis is that the 20 percent rise in sales has been magnified to 150 percent, as reflected by the percentage change in earnings per share. The formal measure of combined leverage can be expressed as follows:

TABLE 14–9. The Pierce Grain Company Combined Leverage Analysis

Item	Base Sales Level, t	Forecast Sales Level, $t + 1$	Selected Percentage Changes
Sales	$300,000	$360,000	+20
Less: Total variable costs	180,000	216,000	
Revenue before fixed costs	$120,000	$144,000	
Less: Total fixed costs	100,000	100,000	
EBIT	$ 20,000	$ 44,000	+120
Less: Interest expense	4,000	4,000	
Earnings before taxes (EBT)	$ 16,000	$ 40,000	
Less: Taxes at 50%	8,000	20,000	
Net income	$ 8,000	$ 20,000	+150
Less: Preferred dividends	0	0	
Earnings available to common (EAC)	$ 8,000	$ 20,000	+150
Number of common shares	1,500	1,500	
Earnings per share (EPS)	$ 5.33	$ 13.33	+150

$$\text{Degree of operating leverage} = \text{DOL}_{\$300,000} = \frac{120\%}{20\%} = 6 \text{ times}$$

$$\text{Degree of financial leverage} = \text{DFL}_{\$20,000} = \frac{150\%}{120\%} = 1.25 \text{ times}$$

$$\text{Degree of combined leverage} = \text{DCL}_{\$300,000} = \frac{150\%}{20\%} = 7.50 \text{ times}$$

$$\left(\begin{array}{l}\text{degree of combined} \\ \text{leverage from the} \\ \text{base sales level}\end{array}\right) = \text{DCL}_s = \left(\frac{\begin{array}{c}\text{percentage change in} \\ \text{earnings per share}\end{array}}{\text{percentage change in sales}}\right) \quad (14\text{--}10)$$

This equation was used in the bottom portion of Table 14–9 to determine that the degree of combined leverage from the base sales level of $300,000 is 7.50 times. Pierce Grain's use of both operating and financial leverage will cause any percentage change in sales (from the specific base level) to be magnified by a factor of 7.50 when the effect on earnings per share is computed. A 1 percent change in sales, for example, will result in a 7.50 percent change in earnings per share.

Notice that the degree of combined leverage is actually the *product* (not the simple sum) of the two independent leverage measures. Thus, we have

$$(\text{DOL}_s) \times (\text{DFL}_{EBIT}) = \text{DCL}_s \quad (14\text{--}11)$$

$$\text{or} \qquad (6) \times (1.25) = 7.50 \text{ times}$$

It is possible to ascertain the degree of combined leverage in a direct fashion, without determining any percentage fluctuations or the separate leverage values. We need only substitute the appropriate values into equation (14–12):[7]

$$\text{DCL}_s = \frac{Q(P - V)}{Q(P - V) - F - I} \quad (14\text{--}12)$$

The variable definitions in equation (14–12) are the same ones that have been employed throughout this chapter. Use of equation (14–12) with the information in Table 14–9 gives

$$\text{DCL}_{\$300,000} = \frac{\$30,000(\$10 - \$6)}{\$30,000(\$10 - \$6) - \$100,000 - \$4000}$$

$$= \frac{\$120,000}{\$16,000}$$

$$= 7.5 \text{ times}$$

Implications   The total risk exposure the firm assumes can be managed by combining operating and financial leverage in different degrees. Knowledge of the various leverage measures we have examined aids the financial officer in determining the proper level of overall risk that should be accepted. If a high degree of business risk is inherent to the specific line of commercial activity, then a low posture with regard to financial risk would minimize *additional* earnings fluctuations stemming from sales changes. On the other hand, the firm that by its very nature incurs a low level of fixed operating costs might choose to use a high degree of financial leverage in the hope of increasing earnings per share and the rate of return on the common equity investment.

---

[7] As was the case with the degree of financial leverage metric, the variable, *I*, in the combined leverage measure must include the before-tax equivalent of any preferred dividend payments when preferred stock is in the financial structure.

Summary

In this chapter we began to study the process of arriving at an appropriate financial structure for the firm. Tools that can assist the financial manager in this task were examined. We were mainly concerned with assessing the variability in the firm's residual earnings stream (either earnings per share or earnings available to the common shareholders) induced by the use of operating and financial leverage. This assessment built upon the tenets of breakeven analysis.

Breakeven Analysis

Breakeven analysis permits the financial manager to determine the quantity of output or the level of sales that will result in an EBIT level of zero. The effect of price changes, cost structure changes, or volume changes upon profits (EBIT) can be studied. To make the technique operational, it is necessary that the firm's costs be classified as fixed or variable. Not all costs fit neatly into one of these two categories. Over short planning horizons, though, the preponderance of costs can be assigned to either the fixed or variable classification. Once the cost structure has been identified, the breakeven point can be found by use of (1) trial and error analysis, (2) contribution margin analysis, or (3) algebraic analysis.

Operating Leverage

Operating leverage is the responsiveness of the firm's EBIT to changes in sales revenues. It arises from the firm's use of fixed operating costs. When fixed operating costs are present in the company's cost structure, changes in sales are magnified into even greater changes in EBIT. The firm's degree of operating leverage from a base sales level is the percentage change in EBIT divided by the percentage change in sales. All types of leverage are two-edged swords. When sales decrease by some percentage, the negative impact upon EBIT will be even larger.

Financial Leverage

A firm employs financial leverage when it finances a portion of its assets with securities bearing a fixed rate of return. The presence of debt and/or preferred stock in the company's financial structure means that it is using financial leverage. When financial leverage is used, changes in EBIT translate into larger changes in earnings per share. The concept of the degree of financial leverage dwells on the sensitivity of earnings per share to changes in EBIT. The degree of financial leverage from a base EBIT level is defined as the percentage change in earnings per share divided by the percentage change in EBIT. All other things equal, the more fixed-charge securities the firm employs in its financial structure, the greater its degree of financial leverage. Clearly, EBIT can rise or fall. If it falls, and financial leverage is used, the firm's shareholders endure negative changes in earnings per share that are larger than the relative decline in EBIT. Again, leverage is a two-edged sword.

Combining Operating and Financial Leverage

Firms use operating and financial leverage in various degrees. The joint use of operating and financial leverage can be measured by computing the degree of combined leverage, defined as the percentage change in earnings per share divided by the percentage change in sales. This measure allows the financial manager to ascertain the effect on total leverage caused by adding financial leverage on top of operating leverage. Effects can be dramatic, because the degree of combined leverage is the product of the degrees of operating and financial leverage. In Table 14–10 we highlight the salient concepts and calculation formats discussed in this chapter.

TABLE 14–10. Summary of Leverage Concepts and Calculations

Technique	Description or Concept	Calculation	Text Reference
Breakeven Analysis 1. Breakeven point quantity	Total fixed costs divided by the unit contribution margin	$Q_B = \dfrac{F}{P - V}$	(14–3)
2. Breakeven sales level	Total fixed costs divided by 1 minus the ratio of total variable costs to the associated level of sales	$S^* = \dfrac{F}{1 - \dfrac{VC}{S}}$	(14–4)
Operating Leverage 3. Degree of operating leverage	Percentage change in EBIT divided by the percentage change in sales; or revenue before fixed costs divided by revenue after fixed costs	$DOL_S = \dfrac{Q(P - V)}{Q(P - V) - F}$	(14–6)
Financial Leverage 4. Degree of financial leverage	Percentage change in earnings per share divided by the percentage change in EBIT; or EBIT divided by EBT.[a]	$DFL_{EBIT} = \dfrac{EBIT}{EBIT - I}$	(14–9)
Combined Leverage 5. Degree of combined leverage	Percentage change in earnings per share divided by the percentage change in sales; or revenue before fixed costs divided by EBT.[a]	$DCL_S = \dfrac{Q(P - V)}{Q(P - V) - F - I}$	(14–12)

[a] The use of EBT here presumes no preferred dividend payments. In the presence of preferred dividend payments replace EBT with earnings available to common stock (EAC).

Study Questions

14–1. Distinguish between business risk and financial risk. What gives rise to, or causes, each type of risk?

14–2. Define the term *financial leverage*. Does the firm use financial leverage if preferred stock is present in the capital structure?

14–3. Define the term *operating leverage*. What type of effect occurs when the firm uses operating leverage?

14–4. What is the difference between the (ordinary) breakeven point and the cash breakeven point? Which will be the greater?

14–5. A manager in your firm decides to employ breakeven analysis. Of what shortcomings should this manager be aware?

14–6. What is meant by total risk exposure? How may a firm move to reduce its total risk exposure?

14–7. If a firm has a degree of combined leverage of 3.0 times, what does a negative sales fluctuation of 15 percent portend for the earnings available to the firm's common stock investors?

14–8. Breakeven analysis assumes linear revenue and cost functions. In reality these linear functions over large output and sales levels are highly improbable. Why?

Self-Test Problems

ST–1. (*Breakeven Point*) You are a hard-working analyst in the office of financial operations for a manufacturing firm that produces a single product. You have developed the following cost structure information for this company. All of it pertains to an output level of 10 million units. Using this information, find the breakeven point in units of output for the firm.

Return on operating assets	= 30%
Operating asset turnover	= 6 times
Operating assets	= $20 million
Degree of operating leverage	= 4.5 times

ST–2. (*Leverage Analysis*) You have developed the following analytical income statement for your corporation. It represents the most recent year's operations, which ended yesterday.

Sales	$20,000,000
Variable costs	12,000,000
Revenue before fixed costs	$ 8,000,000
Fixed costs	5,000,000
EBIT	$ 3,000,000
Interest expense	1,000,000
Earnings before taxes	$ 2,000,000
Taxes (0.50)	1,000,000
Net income	$ 1,000,000

Your supervisor in the financial studies office has just handed you a memorandum that asked for written responses to the following questions:

a. At this level of output, what is the degree of operating leverage?
b. What is the degree of financial leverage?
c. What is the degree of combined leverage?
d. What is the firm's breakeven point in sales dollars?
e. If sales should increase by 30 percent, by what percent would earnings before taxes (and net income) increase?
f. Prepare an analytical income statement that verifies the calculations from part (e) above.

ST–3. (*Fixed Costs and the Breakeven Point*) Bonaventure Manufacturing expects to earn $210,000 next year after taxes. Sales will be $4 million. The firm's single plant is located on the outskirts of Olean, N.Y. The firm manufactures a combined bookshelf and desk unit used extensively in college dormitories. These units sell for $200 each and have a variable cost per unit of $150. Bonaventure experiences a 30 percent tax rate.
a. What are the firm's fixed costs expected to be next year?
b. Calculate the firm's breakeven point in both units and dollars.

Study Problems

14–1. (*Breakeven Point and Operating Leverage*) Zeylog Corporation manufactures a line of computer memory expansion boards used in microcomputers. The average selling price of its finished product is $180 per unit. The variable cost for these same units is $110. Zeylog incurs fixed costs of $630,000 per year.
a. What is the breakeven point in units for the company?
b. What is the dollar sales volume the firm must achieve in order to reach the breakeven point?
c. What would be the firm's profit or loss at the following units of production sold: 12,000 units? 15,000 units? 20,000 units?
d. Find the degree of operating leverage for the production and sales levels given in part (c) above.

14–2. (*Breakeven Point and Operating Leverage*) Some financial data for each of three firms are shown below.

	Blacksburg Furniture	Lexington Cabinets	Williamsburg Colonials
Average selling price per unit	$15.00	$400.00	$40.00
Average variable cost per unit	$12.35	$220.00	$14.50
Units sold	75,000	4,000	13,000
Fixed costs	$35,000	$100,000	$70,000

a. What is the profit for each company at the indicated sales volume?
b. What is the breakeven point in units for each company?
c. What is the degree of operating leverage for each company at the indicated sales volume?
d. If sales were to decline, which firm would suffer the largest relative decline in profitability?

14–3. (*Fixed Costs and the Breakeven Point*) A & B Beverages expects to earn $50,000 next year after taxes. Sales will be $375,000. The store is located near the shopping district surrounding Blowing Rock University. Its average product sells for $27 a unit. The variable cost per unit is $14.85. The store experiences a 40 percent tax rate.

a. What are the store's fixed costs expected to be next year?

b. Calculate the store's breakeven point in both units and dollars.

14-4. (*Breakeven Point and Profit Margin*) A recent graduate of Clarion South University is planning to open a new wholesaling operation. Her target operating profit margin is 26 percent. Her unit contribution margin will be 50 percent of sales. Average annual sales are forecast to be $3,250,000.

a. How large can fixed costs be for the wholesaling operation and still allow the 26 percent operating profit margin to be achieved?

b. What is the breakeven point in dollars for the firm?

14-5. (*Leverage Analysis*) You have developed the following analytical income statement for your corporation. It represents the most recent year's operations, which ended yesterday.

Sales	$30,000,000
Variable costs	13,500,000
Revenue before fixed costs	$16,500,000
Fixed costs	8,000,000
EBIT	$ 8,500,000
Interest expense	1,000,000
Earnings before taxes	$ 7,500,000
Taxes (0.50)	3,750,000
Net income	$ 3,750,000

Your supervisor in the controller's office has just handed you a memorandum that asked for written responses to the following questions:

a. At this level of output, what is the degree of operating leverage?

b. What is the degree of financial leverage?

c. What is the degree of combined leverage?

d. What is the firm's breakeven point in sales dollars?

e. If sales should increase by 25 percent, by what percent would earnings before taxes (and net income) increase?

14-6. (*Breakeven Point*) You are a hard-working analyst in the office of financial operations for a manufacturing firm that produces a single product. You have developed the following cost structure information for this company. All of it pertains to an output level of 10 million units. Using this information, find the breakeven point in units of output for the firm.

Return on operating assets = 25%
Operating asset turnover = 5 times
Operating assets = $20 million
Degree of operating leverage = 4 times

14-7. (*Breakeven Point and Operating Leverage*) Allison Radios manufactures a complete line of radio and communication equipment for law enforcement agencies. The average selling price of its finished product is $180 per unit. The variable cost for these same units is $126. Allison Radios incurs fixed costs of $540,000 per year.

a. What is the breakeven point in units for the company?

b. What is the dollar sales volume the firm must achieve in order to reach the breakeven point?

c. What would be the firm's profit or loss at the following units of production sold: 12,000 units? 15,000 units? 20,000 units?

d. Find the degree of operating leverage for the production and sales levels given in part (c) above.

14–8. (*Breakeven Point and Operating Leverage*) Some financial data for each of three firms are shown below.

	Oviedo Seeds	Gainesville Sod	Athens Peaches
Average selling price per unit	$ 14.00	$200.00	$25.00
Average variable cost per unit	$ 11.20	$130.00	$17.50
Units sold	100,000	10,000	48,000
Fixed costs	$ 25,000	$100,000	$35,000

a. What is the profit for each company at the indicated sales volume?

b. What is the breakeven point in units for each company?

c. What is the degree of operating leverage for each company at the indicated sales volume?

d. If sales were to *decline*, which firm would suffer the largest relative decline in profitability?

14–9. (*Fixed Costs and the Breakeven Point*) Dot's Quik-Stop Party Store expects to earn $40,000 next year after taxes. Sales will be $400,000. The store is located near the fraternity-row district of Cambridge Springs State University and sells only kegs of beer for $20 a keg. The variable cost per keg is $8. The store experiences a 40 percent tax rate.

a. What are the Party Store's fixed costs expected to be next year?

b. Calculate the firm's breakeven point in both units and dollars.

14–10. (*Fixed Costs and the Breakeven Point*) Albert's Cooling Equipment hopes to earn $80,000 next year after taxes. Sales will be $2 million. The firm's single plant is located on the edge of Slippery Rock, PA, and manufactures only small refrigerators. These are used in many of the dormitories found on college campuses. The refrigerators sell for $80 per unit and have a variable cost of $56. Albert's experiences a 40 percent tax rate.

a. What are the firm's fixed costs expected to be next year?

b. Calculate the firm's breakeven point both in units and dollars.

14–11. (*Breakeven Point and Selling Price*) Gerry's Tool and Die Company will produce 200,000 units next year. All of this production will be sold as finished goods. Fixed costs will total $300,000. Variable costs for this firm are relatively predictable at 75 percent of sales.

a. If Gerry's Tool and Die wants to achieve an earnings before interest and taxes level of $240,000 next year, at what price per unit must it sell its product?

b. Based upon your answer to part (a), set up an analytical income statement that will verify your solution.

14–12. (*Breakeven Point and Selling Price*) Parks Castings, Inc., will manufacture and sell 200,000 units next year. Fixed costs will total $300,000, and variable costs will be 60 percent of sales.

a. The firm wants to achieve an earnings before interest and taxes level of $250,000. What selling price per unit is necessary to achieve this result?

b. Set up an analytical income statement to verify your solution to part (a).

14–13. (*Breakeven Point and Profit Margin*) A recent business graduate of Midwestern State University is planning to open a new wholesaling operation. His target operating profit margin is 28 percent. His unit contribution margin will be 50 percent of sales. Average annual sales are forecast to be $3,750,000.

   a. How large can fixed costs be for the wholesaling operation and still allow the 28 percent operating profit margin to be achieved?

   b. What is the breakeven point in dollars for the firm?

14–14.   (*Operating Leverage*) Rocky Mount Metals Company manufactures an assortment of woodburning stoves. The average selling price for the various units is $500. The associated variable cost is $350 per unit. Fixed costs for the firm average $180,000 annually.

   a. What is the breakeven point in units for the company?

   b. What is the dollar sales volume the firm must achieve in order to reach the breakeven point?

   c. What is the degree of operating leverage for a production and sales level of 5000 units for the firm? (Calculate to three decimal places.)

   d. What will be the projected effect upon earnings before interest and taxes if the firm's sales level should increase by 20 percent from the volume noted in part (c) above?

14–15.   (*Breakeven Point and Operating Leverage*) The Portland Recreation Company manufactures a full line of lawn furniture. The average selling price of a finished unit is $25. The associated variable cost is $15 per unit. Fixed costs for Portland average $50,000 per year.

   a. What is the breakeven point in units for the company?

   b. What is the dollar sales volume the firm must achieve in order to reach the breakeven point?

   c. What would be the company's profit or loss at the following units of production sold: 4000 units? 6000 units? 8000 units?

   d. Find the degree of operating leverage for the production and sales levels given in part (c) above.

   e. What is the effect on the degree of operating leverage as sales rise above the breakeven point?

14–16.   (*Fixed Costs*) Detroit Heat Treating projects that next year its fixed costs will total $120,000. Its only product sells for $12 per unit, of which $7 is a variable cost. The management of Detroit is considering the purchase of a new machine that will lower the variable cost per unit to $5. The new machine, however, will add to fixed costs through an increase in depreciation expense. How large can the *addition* to fixed costs be in order to keep the firm's breakeven point in units produced and sold unchanged?

14–17.   (*Operating Leverage*) The management of Detroit Heat Treating did not purchase the new piece of equipment (see problem 14–16 above). Using the existing cost structure, calculate the degree of operating leverage at 30,000 units of output. Comment on the meaning of your answer.

14–18.   (*Leverage Analysis*) An analytical income statement for Detroit Heat Treating is shown below. It is based upon an output (sales) level of 40,000 units. You may refer to the original cost structure data in problem (14–16).

Sales	$480,000
Variable costs	280,000
Revenue before fixed costs	$200,000
Fixed costs	120,000
EBIT	$ 80,000
Interest expense	30,000
Earnings before taxes	$ 50,000
Taxes	25,000
Net income	$ 25,000

a. Calculate the degree of operating leverage at this output level.
b. Calculate the degree of financial leverage at this level of EBIT.
c. Determine the combined leverage effect at this output level.

14–19. (*Breakeven Point*) You are employed as a financial analyst for a single-product manufacturing firm. Your supervisor has made the following cost structure information available to you, all of which pertains to an output level of 1,600,000 units.

> Return on operating assets = 15 percent
> Operating asset turnover = 5 times
> Operating assets = $3 million
> Degree of operating leverage = 8 times

Your task is to find the breakeven point in units of output for the firm.

14–20. (*Fixed Costs*) Des Moines Printing Services is forecasting fixed costs next year of $300,000. The firm's single product sells for $20 per unit and incurs a variable cost per unit of $14. The firm may acquire some new binding equipment that would lower variable cost per unit to $12. The new equipment, however, would add to fixed costs through the price of an annual maintenance agreement on the new equipment. How large can this increase in fixed costs be and still keep the firm's present breakeven point in units produced and sold unchanged?

14–21. (*Leverage Analysis*) Your firm's cost analysis supervisor supplies you with the following analytical income statement and requests answers to the four questions listed below the statement.

Sales	$12,000,000
Variable costs	9,000,000
Revenue before fixed costs	$ 3,000,000
Fixed costs	2,000,000
EBIT	$ 1,000,000
Interest expense	200,000
Earnings before taxes	$ 800,000
Taxes	400,000
Net income	$ 400,000

a. At this level of output, what is the degree of operating leverage?
b. What is the degree of financial leverage?
c. What is the degree of combined leverage?
d. What is the firm's breakeven point in sales dollars?

14–22. (*Leverage Analysis*) You are supplied with the following analytical income statement for your firm. It reflects last year's operations.

Sales	$16,000,000
Variable costs	8,000,000
Revenue before fixed costs	$ 8,000,000
Fixed costs	4,000,000
EBIT	$ 4,000,000
Interest expense	1,500,000
Earnings before taxes	$ 2,500,000
Taxes	1,250,000
Net income	$ 1,250,000

    a. At this level of output, what is the degree of operating leverage?
    b. What is the degree of financial leverage?
    c. What is the degree of combined leverage?
    d. If sales should increase by 20 percent, by what percent would earnings before taxes (and net income) increase?
    e. What is your firm's breakeven point in sales dollars?

14–23. (*Sales Mix and the Breakeven Point*) Toledo Components produces four lines of auto accessories for the major Detroit automobile manufacturers. The lines are known by the code letters A, B, C, and D. The current sales mix for Toledo and the contribution margin ratio (unit contribution margin divided by unit sales price) for these product lines are as follows:

Product Line	Percent of Total Sales	Contribution Margin Ratio
A	33⅓%	40%
B	41⅔	32
C	16⅔	20
D	8⅓	60

Total sales for next year are forecast to be $120,000. Total fixed costs will be $29,400.

    a. Prepare a table showing (1) sales, (2) total variable costs, and (3) the total contribution margin associated with each product line.
    b. What is the aggregate contribution margin ratio indicative of this sales mix?
    c. At this sales mix, what is the breakeven point in dollars?

14–24. (*Sales Mix and the Breakeven Point*) Because of production constraints, Toledo Components (see problem 14–23 above) may have to adhere to a different sales mix for next year. The alternative plan is outlined below.

Product Line	Percent of Total Sales
A	25%
B	36⅔
C	33⅓
D	5

    a. Assuming all other facts in problem 14–23 remain the same, what effect will this different sales mix have on Toledo's breakeven point in dollars?
    b. Which sales mix will Toledo's management prefer?

Case Problem

Erie General Producers

(Breakeven Analysis, Operating Leverage, Financial Leverage)

Erie General Producers (EGP) is a medium-sized public corporation that until recently consisted of two divisions. The Retail Furniture Group (RFG) has eight locations in the northeastern Ohio area, mostly concentrated around Cleveland. These retail outlets generate sales of contemporary, traditional, and early American furniture. Additionally, casual and leisure furniture lines are carried by the stores. The other (old) division of EGP is its Concrete Group (CG). The CG operates three plants in the North Tonawanda area of western New York. These plants produce precast concrete wall panels and concrete stave farm silos. The company headquarters of EGP is located in Erie, Pennsylvania. This community touches Lake Erie in northwestern Pennsylvania and is about 140 miles north of Pittsburgh. Since Erie is almost equidistant between Cleveland and North Tonawanda and is a connecting hub for several interstate highways, it makes a sensible spot for the firm's home offices.

EGP was started 10 years ago as Erie Producers by its current president and board chairman, Anthony Toscano. During the firm's existence it has enjoyed periods of both moderate and strong growth in sales, assets, and earnings. Key managerial decisions have always been dominated by Toscano, who openly boasts of the fact that his company has never suffered through a year of negative earnings despite the often cyclical nature of both the retail furniture (RFG) and concrete (CG) divisions.

Recently Mr. Toscano decided to acquire a third division for his firm. The division manufactures special machinery for the seafood processing industry and is appropriately called the Seafood Industry Group (SIG). The financial settlement for the acquisition took place yesterday. Currently, the SIG consists of one manufacturing plant in Erie. A single product is to be manufactured, assembled, and shipped from the facility. That product, however, represents a design breakthrough and carries with it a projected contribution margin ratio of .4000. This is greater than that enjoyed by either of EGP's other two divisions.

EGP's manufacturing operation in Erie will produce a new machine called "The Picker." The Picker was invented and successfully tested by Ben Pinkerton, the major stockholder and manager of a small seafood processing firm in Morattico, Virginia. Pinkerton plans and supervises all operations at Eastern Shore Processors. Eastern Shore specializes in freezing and pasteurizing crab meat. Freezing and pasteurizing procedures have been a boon to the seafood industry, for they permit the processor to retain a product without spoilage in hopes of higher prices at a later date. In comparing his industry to that of agriculture, Pinkerton aptly states: "The freezer is our grain elevator."

The seafood processing industry is characterized by a notable lack of capital equipment and a corresponding heavy use of human labor. Pinkerton will tell you that at Eastern Shore Processors a skilled crab meat picker will produce about 30 pounds of meat per day. No matter how skilled the human picker, however, he will leave about 10 pounds of meat per day in the top piece of the crab shell. This past year, after five years of trying, Pinkerton perfected a machine that would recover about 30 percent of this otherwise lost meat. In exchange for cash, Eastern Shore Processors sold all rights to The Picker to EGP. Thus, Toscano established the SIG and immediately made plans to manufacture The Picker.

Recent income statements for the older divisions of EGP are contained in Exhibits 1 and 2. Toscano has now decided to assess more fully the probable impact of the decision

EXHIBIT 1. Erie General Producers
Retail Furniture Group
Income Statement, December 31, Last Year

Sales	$12,000,000
Less: total variable costs	7,920,000
Revenue before fixed costs	$ 4,080,000
Less: total fixed costs	2,544,000
EBIT	$ 1,536,000
Less: interest expense	192,000
Earnings before taxes	$ 1,344,000
Less: taxes @ 50%	672,000
Net Profit	$ 672,000

EXHIBIT 2. Erie General Producers
Concrete Group
Income Statement, December 31, Last Year

Sales	$8,000,000
Less: total variable costs	5,920,000
Revenue before fixed costs	$2,080,000
Less: total fixed costs	640,000
EBIT	$1,440,000
Less: interest expense	80,000
Earnings before taxes	$1,360,000
Less: taxes @ 50%	680,000
Net Profit	$ 680,000

to establish the SIG on the financial condition of EGP. Toscano knew that such figures should have been generated prior to the decision to enter this special field, but his seasoned judgment led him to a quick choice. He has requested several pieces of information, detailed below, from his chief financial officer.

Questions and Problems

1. Using last year's results, determine the breakeven point in dollars for EGP (i.e., before investing in the new SIG). The breakeven point is defined here in the traditional manner where EBIT = $0. (*Hint*: Use an aggregate contribution margin ratio in your analysis).

2. Using last year's results, determine what volume of sales must be reached in order to cover *all* before-tax costs.

3. Next year's sales for the SIG are projected to be $4,000,000. Total fixed costs will be $640,000. This division will have no outstanding debt on its balance sheet. EGP uses a 50 percent tax rate in all its financial projections. Using the format of Exhibits 1 and 2, construct a pro forma income statement for the SIG.

4. After the SIG begins operations, what will be EGP's breakeven point in dollars (a) as traditionally defined and (b) reflecting the coverage of *all* before-tax costs? Base the new sales mix on last year's sales performance for the older divisions plus that anticipated next year for the SIG. Using your answer to part (b) of this question, construct an analytical income statement demonstrating that earnings before taxes = $0.

5. Using next year's anticipated sales volume for EGP (including the SIG), compute (a) the degree of operating leverage, (b) the degree of financial leverage, and (c) the degree of combined leverage. Comment on the meaning of each of these statistics.

6. Using projected figures, determine whether acquisition of the SIG will increase or decrease the vulnerability of EGP's earnings before interest and taxes (EBIT) to cyclical swings in sales. Show your work.

7. Review the key assumptions of cost-volume-profit analysis.

Self-Test Solutions

SS–1. **STEP 1.** *Compute the operating profit margin*:

$$(\text{margin}) \times (\text{turnover}) = \text{return on operating assets}$$

$$(M) \quad \times \quad (6) \quad = 0.30$$

$$M = 0.30/6 = 0.05$$

STEP 2. *Compute the sales level associated with the given output level*:

$$\frac{\text{sales}}{\$20,000,000} = 6$$

$$\text{sales} = \$120,000,000$$

STEP 3. *Compute EBIT*:

$$(.05)(\$120,000,000) = \$6,000,000 = \text{EBIT}$$

STEP 4. Compute revenue before fixed costs. Since the degree of operating leverage is 4.5 times, revenue before fixed costs (RBF) is 4.5 times EBIT, as follows:

$$RBF = (4.5)(\$6,000,000) = \$27,000,000$$

STEP 5. Compute total variable costs:

$$(\text{sales}) - (\text{total variable costs}) = \$27,000,000$$

$$\$120,000,000 - (\text{total variable costs}) = \$27,000,000$$

$$\text{total variable costs} = \$93,000,000$$

STEP 6. Compute total fixed costs:

$$RBF - \text{fixed costs} = EBIT$$

$$\$27,000,000 - \text{fixed costs} = \$6,000,000$$

$$\text{Fixed costs} = \$21,000,000$$

STEP 7. Find the selling price per unit (P), and the variable cost per unit (V):

$$P = \frac{\text{sales}}{\text{output in units}} = \frac{\$120,000,000}{10,000,000} = \$12.00$$

$$V = \frac{\text{total variable costs}}{\text{output in units}} = \frac{\$93,000,000}{10,000,000} = \$9.30$$

STEP 8. Compute the breakeven point:

$$Q_B = \frac{F}{P - V} = \frac{\$21,000,000}{\$12.00 - \$9.30}$$

$$= \frac{\$21,000,000}{\$2.70} = \underline{\underline{\$7,777,778 \text{ units}}}$$

The firm will break even when it produces and sells 7,777,778 units.

SS–2.   a. $\dfrac{\text{Revenue before fixed costs}}{\text{EBIT}} = \dfrac{\$8,000,000}{\$3,000,000} = \underline{\underline{2.67 \text{ times}}}$

b. $\dfrac{\text{EBIT}}{\text{EBIT} - I} = \dfrac{\$3,000,000}{\$2,000,000} = \underline{\underline{1.50 \text{ times}}}$

c. $DCL_{\$20,000,000} = (2.67)(1.50) = \underline{\underline{4.00 \text{ times}}}$

d. $S^* = \dfrac{F}{1 - \dfrac{VC}{S}} = \dfrac{\$5,000,000}{1 - \dfrac{\$12\,M}{\$20\,M}} = \dfrac{\$5,000,000}{1 - 0.60} = \dfrac{\$5,000,000}{0.40} = \underline{\underline{\$12,500,000}}$

e. $(30\%)(4.00) = \underline{\underline{120\%}}$

f.

Sales	$26,000,000
Variable costs	15,600,000
Revenue before fixed costs	$10,400,000
Fixed costs	5,000,000
EBIT	$ 5,400,000
Interest expense	1,000,000
Earnings before taxes	$ 4,400,000
Taxes (0.50)	2,200,000
Net income	$ 2,200,000

We know that sales have increased by 30 percent to $26 million from the base sales level of $20 million.

Let us focus now on the change in earnings before taxes. We can compute that change as follows:

$$\frac{\$4,400,000 - \$2,000,000}{\$2,000,000} = \frac{\$2,400,000}{\$2,000,000} = 120\%$$

Since the tax rate was held constant, the percentage change in net income will also equal 120 percent. The fluctuations implied by the degree of combined leverage measure are therefore accurately reflected in this analytical income statement.

SS–3. a.

$$\{(P \cdot Q) - [V \cdot Q + (F)]\} \quad (1 - T) = \$210,000$$

$$[(\$4,000,000) - (\$3,000,000) - F] \,(.7) = \$210,000$$

$$(\$1,000,000 - F) \,(.7) = \$210,000$$

$$\$700,000 - .7F = \$210,000$$

$$.7F = \$490,000$$

$$F = \underline{\$700,000}$$

Fixed costs next year, then, are expected to be $700,000.

b.

$$Q_B = \frac{F}{P - V} = \frac{\$700,000}{\$50} = \underline{14,000} \text{ units}$$

$$S^* = \frac{F}{1 - \dfrac{VC}{S}} = \frac{\$700,000}{1 - .75} = \frac{\$700,000}{.25} = \underline{\$2,800,000}$$

The firm will breakeven (EBIT = 0) when it sells 14,000 units. With a selling price of $200 per unit, the breakeven sales level is $2,800,000.

Selected References

Adar, Zvi, Amir Barnea, and Baruch Lev. "A Comprehensive Cost-Volume-Profit Analysis under Uncertainty," *Accounting Review*, 52 (January 1977), 137–49.

Bowlin, Oswald D., John D. Martin, and David F. Scott, Jr. *Guide to Financial Analysis*, Chap. 8. New York: McGraw-Hill, 1980.

Brigham, Eugene F., and T. Craig Tapley. "Financial Leverage and Use of the Net Present Value Investment Criterion: A Reexamination," *Financial Management*, 14 (Summer 1985), 48–52.

Clark, John J., Margaret T. Clark, and Andrew G. Verzilli. "Strategic Planning and Sustainable Growth," *Columbia Journal of World Business*, 20 (Fall 1985), 51.

Gahlon, James M., and James A. Gentry. "On the Relationship between Systematic Risk and the Degrees of Operating and Financial Leverage," *Financial Management*, 11 (Summer 1982), 15–23.

Ghandi, J. K. S. "On the Measurement of Leverage," *Journal of Finance*, 21 (December 1966), 715–26.

Golbe, Devra L., and Barry Schachater. "The Net Present Value Rule and An Algorithm for Maintaining a Constant Debt-Equity Ratio," *Financial Management*, 14 (Summer 1985), 53–58.

Gritta, Richard D. "The Effect of Financial Leverage on Air Carrier Earnings: A Break-Even Analysis," *Financial Management*, 8 (Summer 1979), 53–60.

Haslem, John A. "Leverage Effects on Corporate Earnings," *Arizona Business Review*, 19 (March 1970), 7–11.

Helfert, Erich A. *Techniques of Financial Analysis* (5th ed.), Chap. 6. Homewood, IL: Richard D. Irwin, 1982.

Higgins, Robert C. *Analysis for Financial Management*, Chap. 7. Homewood, IL: Richard D. Irwin, 1984.

Hunt, Pearson. "A Proposal for Precise Definitions of Trading on the Equity and Leverage," *Journal of Finance*, 16 (September 1961), 377–86.

Jaedicke, Robert K., and Alexander A. Robichek. "Cost-Volume-Profit Analysis under Conditions of Uncertainty," *Accounting Review*, 39 (October 1964), 917–26.

Lev, Baruch. "On the Association between Operating Leverage and Risk," *Journal of Financial and Quantitative Analysis*, 9 (September 1974), 627–42.

McConoughey, Deborah J. "Breakeven Analysis for Maturity Decisions in Cash Management," *Journal of Cash Management*, 5 (January–February 1985), 18–21.

Osteryoung, Jerome S., and Daniel E. McCarty. *Analytical Techniques for Financial Management*, Chap. 11. Columbus, OH: Grid, 1980.

Percival, John R. "Operating Leverage and Risk," *Journal of Business Research*, 2 (April 1974), 223–27.

Reinhardt, U. E. "Break Even Analysis for Lockheed's Tri Star: An Application of Financial Theory," *Journal of Finance*, 28 (September 1973), 821–38.

Shalit, Sol S. "On the Mathematics of Financial Leverage," *Financial Management*, 4 (Spring 1975), 57–66.

Shashua, Leon, and Yaaqov Goldschmidt. "Break-even Analysis Under Inflation," *Engineering Economist*, 32 (Winter 1987), 79–88.

Sullivan, Timothy G. "Market Power, Profitability and Financial Leverage," *Journal of Finance*, 29 (December 1974), 1407–14.

Thode, Stephen F., Ralph E. Drtina, and James A. Largay III. "Operating Cash Flows: A Growing Need for Separate Reporting," *Journal of Accounting, Auditing and Finance*, 1 (Winter 1986), 46–57.

Tsurumi, Yoshi, and Hiroki Tsurumi. "Value-Added Maximizing Behavior of Japanese Firms and Roles of Corporate Investment and Finance," *Columbia Journal of World Business*, 20 (Spring 1985), 29–35.

Viscione, Jerry A. *Financial Analysis: Principles and Procedures*, Chap. 4: Boston: Houghton Mifflin, 1977.

15

Planning the Firm's Financing Mix

In this chapter we direct our attention to the determination of an appropriate financing mix for the firm. It will facilitate the discussion to distinguish between financial structure and capital structure. **Financial structure** is the mix of all items that appear on the righthand side of the company's balance sheet. **Capital structure** is the mix of the *long-term* sources of funds used by the firm. In equation form, the relationship between financial and capital structure can be expressed as follows:

$$(\text{financial structure}) - (\text{current liabilities}) = \text{capital structure} \qquad (15\text{--}1)$$

Prudent **financial structure design** requires answers to the following two questions:

1. What should be the maturity composition of the firm's sources of funds?
2. In what proportions relative to the total should the various forms of *permanent* financing be utilized?

The first of these questions concerns the division of total funds sources into short-term and long-term components. The major influence on the maturity structure of the financing plan is the nature of the assets owned by the firm. A company heavily committed to real capital investment, represented primarily by fixed assets on its balance sheet, *should* finance those assets with permanent (long-term) types of financial capital. Furthermore, the permanent portion of the firm's investment in current assets should likewise be financed with permanent capital. Alternatively, assets held on a temporary basis are to be financed with temporary sources. The present discussion assumes that the bulk of the company's current liabilities are comprised of temporary capital.

If this elaboration seems familiar to you, it should. It is a review of what was called the *hedging concept* in both Chapters 5 and 8. Accordingly, our focus in this chapter is on the second of the two questions noted above—what is usually called capital structure management.

The *objective* of capital structure management is to mix the permanent sources of funds used by the firm in a manner that will maximize the company's common stock price. Alternatively, this objective may be viewed as a search for the funds mix that will minimize the firm's composite cost of capital. We can call this proper mix of funds sources the **optimal capital structure.**

Table 15–1 looks at equation (15–1) in terms of a simplified balance sheet format. It helps us visualize the overriding problem of capital structure management. The sources of funds that give rise to financing fixed costs (long-term debt and preferred equity) must be combined with common equity in the proportions most suitable to the investing marketplace. If that mix can be found, then holding all other factors constant, the firm's common stock price will be maximized.

While equation (15–1) quite accurately indicates that the corporate capital structure may be viewed as an absolute dollar *amount*, the *real* capital structure problem is one of balancing the array of funds sources in a proper manner. Our use of the term capital structure emphasizes this latter problem of relative magnitude, or proportions.

The rest of this chapter will cover three main areas. First, we discuss the theory of capital structure in order to provide a perspective. Second, we examine the basic tools of capital structure management. We conclude with comments on actual capital structure management and a summary.

BASIC FINANCIAL MANAGEMENT IN PRACTICE

Financing Mix and Corporate Strategy

It is important to understand the basics of capital structure theory because the choice of an appropriate *financing mix* is a central component of overall business strategy. The theory, then, affects strategy.

This is illustrated in the following excerpt from the 1985 annual report published by the Coca-Cola Company. Notice how the concepts of *financial leverage* and *debt capacity* are woven into the discussion.

In the financial arena, the Coca-Cola Company is pursuing a more aggressive policy. We are using greater financial leverage whenever strategic investment opportunities are available. We are reinvesting a larger portion of our earnings by increasing dividends at a lesser rate than earnings per share growth. We are maintaining our effective income tax rate at a level well below our historical rate. And, we are continuing to repurchase our common shares when excess cash or debt capacity exceed near-term investment requirements.

Another principle in our strategy requires us to consider divesting assets when they no longer generate acceptable returns and earnings growth or are inconsistent with our focus on consumer products. Accordingly, over the last five years we have sold a wine business, a private-label instant coffee and tea unit, a boiler and industrial water purification subsidiary, a regional pasta operation and private-label plastic products businesses.

Source: The Coca-Cola Company, *Annual Report*, 1985, p. 6.

TABLE 15–1. Balance Sheet

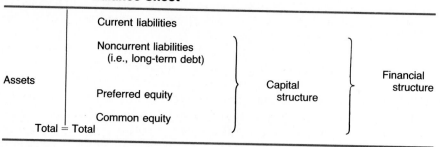

A GLANCE AT CAPITAL STRUCTURE THEORY

An enduring controversy within financial theory concerns the effect of financial leverage on the overall cost of capital to the enterprise. The heart of the argument may be stated in the form of a question:

> Can the firm affect its overall cost of funds, either favorably or unfavorably, by varying the mixture of financing sources used?

This controversy has taken many elegant forms in the finance literature. Most of these presentations appeal to academics as opposed to practitioners of the financial management art. In the present discussion we will purposely pursue a nonmathematical approach to obtain a basic understanding of the underpinnings of this **cost of capital–capital structure argument.** By so doing, we can emphasize the ingredients of capital structure theory that have practical implications for business financial management.

The Importance of Capital Structure

It makes economic sense for the firm to strive to minimize the cost of using financial capital. Both capital costs and other costs, such as manufacturing costs, share a common characteristic in that they potentially reduce the size of the cash dividend that could be paid to common stockholders.

We saw in Chapters 12 and 13 that the ultimate value of a share of common stock depends in part on the returns investors expect to receive from holding the stock. Cash dividends comprise all (in the case of an infinite holding period) or part (in the case of a holding period less than infinity) of these expected returns. Now, hold constant all factors that could affect share price except capital costs. If these capital costs could be kept at a minimum, the dividend stream flowing to the common stockholders would be maximized. This, in turn, would maximize the firm's common stock price.

If the firm's cost of capital can be affected by its capital structure, then capital structure management is clearly an important subset of business financial management.

The Analytical Setting

The essentials of the capital structure controversy are best highlighted within a framework that economists would call a "partial equilibrium analysis." In a partial equilibrium analysis changes that *do* occur in a number of factors and have an impact upon a certain key item are ignored in order to study the effect of changes in a main factor upon that same item of interest. Here, two items are simultaneously of interest: (1) K_0, the firm's composite cost of capital, and (2) P_0, the market price of the firm's common stock. The firm's use of financial leverage is the main factor that is allowed to vary in the analysis. This means that obviously important financial decisions, such as investing policy and dividend policy, are held constant throughout the discussion. We are concerned with the effect of changes in the financing mix on share price and capital costs.

Our analysis will be facilitated if we adopt a *simplified* version of the basic dividend valuation model presented in Chapter 12 in our study of valuation principles and in Chapter 13 in our assessment of the cost of capital. That model is shown below as equation (15–2):

$$P_0 = \sum_{t=1}^{\infty} \frac{D_t}{(1 + K_c)^t} \tag{15--2}$$

where P_0 = the current price of the firm's common stock

D_t = the cash dividend per share expected by investors during period t

K_c = the cost of common equity capital

We can strip away some needless complications by making the following assumptions concerning the valuation process implicit in equation (15–2):

1. Cash dividends paid will not change over the infinite holding period. Thus, $D_1 = D_2 = D_3 = \cdots = D_\infty$. There is no expected growth by investors in the dividend stream.
2. The firm retains none of its current earnings. This means that *all* of each period's per-share earnings are paid to stockholders in the form of cash dividends. The firm's dividend payout ratio is 100 percent. Cash dividends per share in equation (15–2), then, also equal earnings per share for the same time period.

Under these assumptions, the cash dividend flowing to investors can be viewed as a level payment over an infinite holding period. The payment stream is perpetual, and according to the mathematics of perpetuities, equation (15–2) reduces to equation (15–3), where E_t represents earnings per share during time period t.

$$P_0 = \frac{D_t}{K_c} = \frac{E_T}{K_c} \tag{15--3}$$

In addition to the suppositions noted above, the analytical setting for the discussion of capital structure theory includes the following assumptions:

1. Corporate income is not subject to any taxation. The major implication of removing this assumption is discussed later.
2. Capital structures consist of only stocks and bonds. Furthermore, the degree of financial leverage used by the firm is altered by the issuance of common stock with the proceeds used to retire existing debt, or the issuance of debt with the proceeds used to repurchase stock. This permits leverage use to vary, but maintains constancy of the total book value of the firm's capital structure.

3. The expected values of all investors' forecasts of the future levels of net operating income (EBIT) for each firm are identical. Say that you forecast the average level of EBIT to be achieved by General Motors over a very long period of time ($n \to \infty$). Your forecast will be the same as our forecast, and both will be equal to the forecasts of all other investors interested in General Motors common stock. Additionally, we do not expect General Motors' EBIT to grow over time. Each year's forecast is the same as any other year's. This is consistent with our assumption underlying equation (15–3), where the firm's dividend stream is not expected to grow.

4. Securities are traded in perfect or efficient financial markets. This means that transaction costs and legal restrictions do not impede any investor's incentive to execute portfolio changes that he expects will increase his wealth. Information is freely available. Moreover, corporations and individuals that are equal credit risks can borrow funds at the same rates of interest.

This completes our description of the analytical setting. We now discuss three differing views on the relationship between use of financial leverage and common stock value.

Extreme Position 1: The Independence Hypothesis (NOI Theory)[1]

The crux of this position is that the firm's composite cost of capital, K_0, and common stock price, P_0, are both *independent* of the degree to which the company chooses to use financial leverage. In other words, no matter how *modest* or *excessive* the firm's use of debt financing, its common stock price will not be affected. Let us illustrate the mechanics of this point of view.

Suppose that Rix Camper Manufacturing Company has the following financial characteristics:

> Shares of common stock outstanding = 2,000,000 shares
> Common stock price, P_0 = $10 per share
> Expected level of net operating income (EBIT) = $2,000,000
> Dividend payout ratio = 100 percent

Currently the firm uses no financial leverage; its capital structure consists entirely of common equity. Earnings per share and dividends per share equal $1 each. When the capital structure is all common equity, the cost of common equity, K_c, and the weighted cost of capital, K_0, are equal. If equation (15–3) is restated in terms of the cost of common equity, we have for Rix Camper:

$$K_c = \frac{D_t}{P_0} = \frac{\$1}{\$10} = 10\%$$

[1] The net operating income and net income capitalization methods, which are referred to here as "extreme positions 1 and 2," were first presented in comprehensible form by Durand. See David Durand, "Costs of Debt and Equity Funds for Business: Trends and Problems of Measurement," *Conference on Research in Business Finance* (New York: National Bureau of Economic Research, 1952), reprinted in *The Management of Corporate Capital*, Ezra Solomon, ed. (New York: Free Press, 1959), pp. 91–116. The leading proponents of the independence hypothesis in its various forms are Professors Modigliani and Miller. See Franco Modigliani and Merton H. Miller, "The Cost of Capital, Corporation Finance and the Theory of Investment," *American Economic Review*, 48 (June 1958), 261–97; Franco Modigliani and Merton H. Miller, "Corporate Income Taxes and the Cost of Capital: A Correction," *American Economic Review*, 53 (June 1963), 433–43; and Merton H. Miller, "Debt and Taxes," *Journal of Finance*, 32 (May 1977), 261–75.

TABLE 15–2. Rix Camper Company Financial Data Reflecting the Capital Structure Adjustment

Capital Structure Information
Shares of common stock outstanding = 1,200,000
Bonds at 6 percent = $8,000,000

Earnings Information

Expected level of net operating income (EBIT) =	$2,000,000
Less: Interest expense	480,000
Earnings available to common stockholders	$1,520,000
Earnings per share (E_t)	$1.267
Dividends per share (D_t)	$1.267
Percentage change in both earnings per share and dividends per share relative to the unlevered capital structure	26.7 percent

Now, the management of Rix Camper decides to use some debt capital in its financing mix. The firm sells $8 million worth of long-term debt at an interest rate of 6 percent. With no taxation of corporate income, this 6 percent interest rate is the cost of debt capital, K_d. The firm uses the proceeds from the sale of the bonds to repurchase 40 percent of its outstanding common shares. After the capital structure change has been accomplished, Rix Camper Manufacturing Company has the financial characteristics displayed in Table 15–2.

Based on the data above we notice that the recapitalization (capital structure change) of Rix Camper will result in a dividend paid to owners that is 26.7 percent higher than it was when the firm used no debt in its capital structure. Will this higher dividend result in a lower composite cost of capital to Rix and a higher common stock price? According to the principles of the independence hypothesis, the answer is "No."

The independence hypothesis suggests that the total market value of the firm's outstanding securities is *unaffected* by the manner in which the righthand side of the balance sheet is arranged. That is, the sum of the market value of outstanding debt plus the sum of the market value of outstanding common equity will always be the *same* regardless of how much or little debt is actually used by the company. If capital structure has no impact on the total market value of the company, then that value is arrived at by the marketplace's capitalizing (discounting) the firm's expected net operating income stream. Therefore, the independence hypothesis rests upon what is called the **net operating income (NOI) approach to valuation.**

The format is a very simple one, and the market value of the firm's common stock turns out to be a residual of the valuation process. Recall that before Rix Camper's recapitalization, the total market value of the firm was $20 million (2,000,000 common shares times $10 per share). The firm's cost of common equity, K_c, and its weighted cost of capital, K_0, were each equal to 10 percent. The composite discount rate, K_0, is used to arrive at the market value of the firm's securities. After the recapitalization, we have for Rix Camper:

Expected level of net operating income Capitalized at $K_0 = 10$ percent	$ 2,000,000
= Market value of debt and equity	$20,000,000
− Market value of the new debt	8,000,000
= Market value of the common stock	$12,000,000

With this valuation format, what is the market price of each share of common stock? Since we know that 1,200,000 shares of stock are outstanding after the capital structure change, the market price per share is $10 ($12,000,000/1,200,000). This is exactly the market value per share, P_0, that existed *before* the change.

Now, if the firm is using some debt that has an *explicit cost* of 6 percent, K_d, and the weighted (composite) cost of capital, K_0, is still 10 percent, it stands to reason that the cost of common equity, K_c, has risen above its previous level of 10 percent. What will the cost of common equity be in this situation? As we did previously, we can take equation (15–3) and restate it in terms of K_c, the cost of common equity. After the recapitalization, the cost of common equity for Rix Camper is shown to *rise* to 12.67 percent:

$$K_c = \frac{D_t}{P_0} = \frac{\$1.267}{\$10} = 12.67\%$$

The cost of common equity for Rix Camper is 26.7 percent higher than it was before the capital structure shift. Notice in Table 15–2 that this is *exactly* equal to the percentage increase in earnings and dividends per share that accompanies the same capital structure adjustment. This highlights a fundamental relationship that is an integral part of the independence hypothesis. It concerns the perceived behavior in the firm's cost of common equity as expected dividends (earnings) increase relative to a financing mix change:

$$\text{percentage change in } K_c = \text{percentage change in } D_t$$

In this framework the use of a greater degree of financial leverage may result in greater earnings and dividends, but the firm's cost of common equity will rise at precisely the same rate as the earnings and dividends do. Thus, the inevitable tradeoff between the higher expected return in dividends and earnings (D_t and E_t) and increased risk that accompanies the use of debt financing manifests itself in a linear relationship between the cost of common equity (K_c) and financial leverage use. This view of the relationship between the firm's cost of funds and its financing mix is shown graphically in Figure 15–1. Figure 15–2 relates the firm's stock price to its financing mix under the same set of assumptions.

In Figure 15–1 the firm's overall cost of capital, K_0, is shown to be unaffected by an increased use of financial leverage. If more debt is used in the capital structure, the cost of common equity will rise at the same rate additional earnings are generated. This will keep the composite cost of capital to the corporation unchanged. Figure 15–2 shows that since the cost of capital will not change with the leverage use, neither will the firm's stock price.

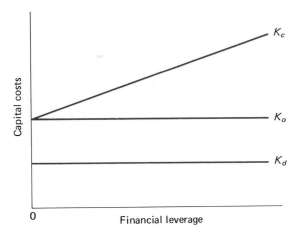

FIGURE 15–1.   Capital Costs and Financial Leverage: No Taxes—The Independence Hypothesis (NOI Theory)

Debt financing, then, has two costs—its **explicit cost of capital,** K_d, calculated according to the formats outlined in Chapter 13, and an implicit cost. The **implicit cost of debt** is the change in the cost of common equity brought on by using financial leverage (additional debt). The real cost of debt is the sum of these explicit and implicit costs. In general, the real cost of *any* source of capital is its explicit cost, plus the change that it induces in the cost of any other source of funds.

Followers of the independence hypothesis argue that the use of financial leverage brings a change in the cost of common equity large enough to offset the benefits of higher dividends to investors. Debt financing is not as cheap as it first appears to be. This will keep the composite cost of funds constant. The implication for management is that one capital structure is as good as any other; financial officers should not waste time searching for an optimal capital structure. One capital structure, after all, is as beneficial as any other, because all result in the same weighted cost of capital.

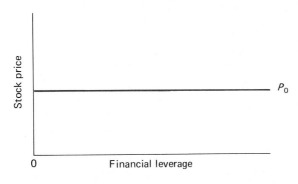

FIGURE 15–2.   Stock Price and Financial Leverage: No Taxes— The Independence Hypothesis (NOI Theory)

Extreme Position 2: The Dependence Hypothesis (NI Theory)   The dependence hypothesis is at the opposite pole from the independence hypothesis. It suggests that both the weighted cost of capital, K_0, and common stock price, P_0, *are affected* by the firm's use of financial leverage. No matter how modest or excessive the firm's use of debt financing, both its cost of debt capital, K_d, and cost of equity capital, K_c, will not be affected by capital structure management. Since the cost of debt is less than the cost of equity, greater financial leverage will lower the firm's composite cost of capital indefinitely. Greater use of debt financing will thereby have a favorable effect on the company's common stock price. By returning to the Rix Camper situation, we can illustrate this point of view.

The same capital structure shift is being evaluated. That is, management will market $8 million of new debt at a 6 percent interest rate and use the proceeds to purchase its own common shares. Under this approach the market is assumed to capitalize (discount) the expected earnings available to the common stockholders in order to arrive at the aggregate market value of the common stock. The market value of the firm's common equity is *not* a residual of the valuation process. After the recapitalization, the firm's cost of common equity, K_c, will still be equal to 10 percent. Thus, a 10 percent cost of common equity is applied in the following format:

Expected level of net operating income	$ 2,000,000
− Interest expense	480,000
= Earnings available to common stockholders	$ 1,520,000
capitalized at K_c = 10 percent	
= Market value of the common stock	$15,200,000
+ Market value of the new debt	8,000,000
= Market value of debt and equity	$23,200,000

When we assume that the firm's capital structure consists only of debt and common equity, earnings available to the common stockholders is synonymous with net income. In the valuation process outlined above, it is net income that is actually capitalized to arrive at the market value of the common equity. Because of this, the dependence hypothesis is also called the **net income approach to valuation.**

Notice that the total market value of the firm's securities has risen to $23,200,000 from the $20 million level that existed before the firm moved from the unlevered to the levered capital structure. The per-share value of the common stock is also shown to rise under this valuation format. With 1,200,000 shares of stock outstanding, the market price per share is $12.67 ($15,200,000/1,200,000).

This increase in the stock price to $12.67 represents a 26.7 percent rise over the previous level of $10 per share. This is exactly equal to the percentage change in earnings per share and dividends per share calculated in Table 15–1. This permits us to characterize the dependence hypothesis in a very succinct fashion:

percentage change in K_c = 0 percent < percentage change in D_t
(over all degrees of leverage)

percentage change in P_0 = percentage change in D_t

The dependence hypothesis suggests that the *explicit* and *implicit* costs of debt are one and the same. The use of more debt does *not* change the firm's cost of common equity. Using more debt, which is explicitly cheaper than common equity, will lower the firm's composite cost of capital, K_0. If you take the market value of Rix Camper's common stock according to the net income theory of $15,200,000 and express it as a percent of the total market value of the firm's securities, you get

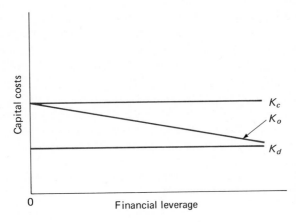

FIGURE 15–3. Capital Costs and Financial Leverage: No Taxes—The Dependence Hypothesis (NI Theory)

a market value weight of .655 ($15,200,000/$23,200,000). In a similar fashion, the market value weight of Rix Camper's debt is found to be .345 ($8,000,000/$23,200,000). After the capital structure adjustment, the firm's weighted cost of capital becomes:

$$K_0 = (.345)(6.00\%) + (.655)(10.00\%) = 8.62\%$$

So, changing the financing mix from all equity to a structure including both debt and equity lowered the composite cost of capital from 10 percent to 8.62 percent. The ingredients of the dependence hypothesis are illustrated in Figures 15–3 and 15–4.

The implication for management from Figures 15–3 and 15–4 is that the firm's cost of capital, K_0, will decline as the debt-to-equity ratio increases. This also implies that the company's common stock price will rise with increased leverage use. Since the cost of capital decreases continuously with leverage, the firm should use as much leverage as is possible. Next, we will move toward reality in the analytical setting of our capital structure discussion. This is accomplished by relaxing some of the major assumptions that surrounded the independence and dependence hypotheses.

FIGURE 15–4. Stock Price and Financial Leverage: No Taxes—The Dependence Hypothesis (NI Theory)

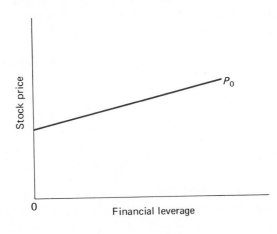

A Moderate Position: Corporate Income Is Taxed and Firms May Fail

In general, an analysis of extreme positions may be useful in that you are forced to sharpen your thinking not only about the poles, but also the situations that span the poles. In microeconomics the study of pure competition and monopoly provides a better understanding of the business activity that takes place in the wide area between these two model markets. In a similar fashion, the study of the independence and dependence hypotheses of the importance of capital structure helps us formulate a more informed view of the possible situations between those polar positions.

We turn now to a description of the cost of capital–capital structure relationship that has rather wide appeal to both business practitioners and academics. This moderate view (1) admits to the fact that interest expense is tax deductible and (2) acknowledges that the probability of the firm's suffering bankruptcy costs is directly related to the company's use of financial leverage.

Tax Deductibility of Interest Expense

This portion of the analysis recognizes that corporate income is subject to taxation. Furthermore, we assume that interest expense is tax deductible for purposes of computing the firm's tax bill. In this environment the use of debt financing should result in a higher total market value for the firm's outstanding securities. We will see why below.

We continue with our Rix Camper Manufacturing Company example. First, consider the total cash payments made to all security holders (holders of common stock plus holders of bonds). In the no-tax case the sum of cash dividends paid to common shareholders plus interest expense amounted to $2 million both (1) when financing was all by common equity and (2) after the proposed capital structure adjustment to a levered situation was accomplished. The *sum* of the cash flows that Rix Camper could pay to its contributors of debt and equity capital was not affected by its financing mix.

When corporate income is taxed by the government, however, the sum of the cash flows made to all contributors of financial capital *is affected* by the firm's financing mix. Table 15–3 illustrates this point.

If Rix Camper makes the capital structure adjustment identified in the previous sections of this chapter, the total payments to equity and debt holders will be $240,000 *greater* than under the all-common-equity capitalization. Where does this $240,000 come from? The government's take, through taxes collected, is lower by that amount. This difference, which flows to the Rix Camper security holders, is called the **tax**

TABLE 15–3. Rix Camper Company Cash Flows to All Investors—The Case of Taxes

	Unlevered Capital Structure	Levered Capital Structure
Expected level of net operating income	$2,000,000	$2,000,000
Less: Interest expense	0	480,000
Earnings before taxes	$2,000,000	$1,520,000
Less: Taxes at 50%	1,000,000	760,000
Earnings available to common stockholders	$1,000,000	$ 760,000
Expected payments to *all* security holders	$1,000,000	$1,240,000

shield on interest. In general, it may be calculated by equation (15–4), where r_d is the interest rate paid on the debt, M is the principal amount of the debt, and t is the firm's marginal tax rate:

$$\text{tax shield} = r_d(M)(t) \qquad (15\text{–}4)$$

The moderate position on the importance of capital structure presumes that the tax shield must have value in the marketplace. Accordingly, this tax benefit will increase the total market value of the firm's outstanding securities relative to the all-equity capitalization. Financial leverage does affect firm value. Because the cost of capital is just the other side of the valuation coin, financial leverage also affects the firm's composite cost of capital. Can the firm increase firm value indefinitely and lower its cost of capital continuously by using more and more financial leverage? Common sense would tell us "No!" So would most financial managers and academicians. The acknowledgment of bankruptcy costs provides one possible rationale.

The Likelihood of Firm Failure The probability that the firm will be unable to meet the financial obligations identified in its debt contracts increases as more debt is employed. The highest costs would be incurred if the firm actually went into bankruptcy proceedings. Here, assets would be liquidated. If we admit that these assets might sell for something less than their perceived market values, equity investors and debt holders could both suffer losses. Other problems accompany bankruptcy proceedings. Lawyers and accountants have to be hired and paid. Managers must spend time preparing lengthy reports for those involved in the legal action.

Milder forms of financial distress also have their costs. As their firm's financial condition weakens, creditors may take action to restrict normal business activity. Suppliers may not deliver materials on credit. Profitable capital investments may have to be forgone, and dividend payments may even be interrupted. At some point the expected cost of default will be large enough to outweigh the tax shield advantage of debt financing.[2] The firm will turn to other sources of financing, mainly common equity. At this point the real cost of debt is thought to be higher than the real cost of common equity.

The Moderate View: The Saucer-Shaped Cost of Capital Curve This moderate view of the relationship between financing mix and the firm's cost of capital is depicted in Figure 15–5. The result is a saucer-shaped (or U-shaped) average cost of capital curve, K_0. The firm's average cost of equity, K_c, is seen to rise over all positive degrees of financial leverage use. For a while the firm can borrow funds at a relatively low cost of debt, K_d. Even though the cost of equity is rising, it does not rise at a fast enough rate to offset the use of the less expensive debt financing. Thus, between points 0 and A on the financial-leverage axis, the average cost of capital declines and stock price rises.

Eventually, the threat of financial distress causes the cost of debt to rise. In Figure 15–5 this increase in the cost of debt shows up in the average cost of debt curve,

---

[2] Even this argument that the tradeoff between bankruptcy costs and the tax shield benefit of debt financing can lead to an optimal structure has its detractors. See Robert A. Haugen and Lemma W. Senbet, "The Insignificance of Bankruptcy Costs to the Theory of Optimal Capital Structure," *Journal of Finance*, 33 (May 1978), 383–93.

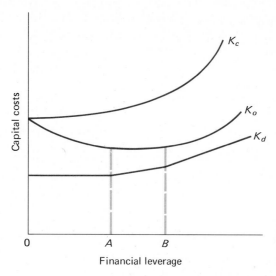

FIGURE 15–5. Capital Costs and Financial Leverage: The Moderate View, Considering Taxes and Financial Distress

K_d, at point A. Between points A and B, mixing debt and equity funds produces an average cost of capital that is (relatively) flat. The firm's **optimal range of financial leverage** lies between points A and B. All capital structures between these two points are *optimal* because they produce the lowest composite cost of capital. As we said in the introduction to this chapter, finding this optimal range of financing mixes is the *objective of capital structure management.*

Point B signifies the firm's debt capacity. **Debt capacity** is the maximum proportion of debt the firm can include in its capital structure and still maintain its lowest composite cost of capital. Beyond point B, additional fixed-charge capital can be attracted only at very costly interest rates. At the same time this excessive use of financial leverage would cause the firm's cost of equity to rise at a faster rate than previously. The composite cost of capital would then rise quite rapidly, and the firm's stock price would decline.

This version of the moderate view as it relates to the firm's stock price is characterized below. The notation is the same as that found in our discussion of the independence and dependence hypotheses.

1. Between points 0 and A:
   $0 <$ percentage change in $P_0 <$ percentage change in D_t
2. Between points A and B:
   percentage change in $P_0 = 0$
3. Beyond point B:
   percentage change in $P_0 < 0$

Firm Value and Agency Costs

In Chapter 1 of this text we talked about "the agency problem." Recall that the agency problem gives rise to *agency costs*, which tend to occur in business organizations because ownership and management control are often separate. Thus, the firm's managers can be properly thought of as agents for the firm's stockholders.[3] To ensure that agent-managers act in the stockholders' best interests requires that they have (1) proper incentives to do so and (2) that their decisions are monitored. The incentives usually take the form of executive compensation plans and perquisites. The perquisites might be a bloated support staff, country club memberships, luxurious corporate planes, or other amenities of a similar nature. Monitoring requires that certain costs be borne by the stockholders, such as (1) bonding the managers, (2) auditing financial statements, (3) structuring the organization in unique ways that limit useful managerial decisions, and (4) reviewing the costs and benefits of management perquisites. This list is indicative, not exhaustive. The main point is that monitoring costs are ultimately covered by the owners of the company—its common stockholders.

Capital structure management *also* gives rise to agency costs. Agency problems stem from conflicts of interest, and capital structure management encompasses a natural conflict between stockholders and bondholders. Acting in the stockholders' best interests might cause management to invest in extremely risky projects. Existing investors in the firm's bonds could logically take a dim view of such an investment policy. A change in the risk structure of the firm's assets would change the business risk exposure of the firm. This could lead to a downward revision of the bond rating the firm currently enjoys. This lowered bond rating in turn would lower the current market value of the firm's bonds. Clearly, bondholders would be unhappy with this result.

To reduce this conflict of interest, the creditors (bond investors) and stockholders may agree to include several protective covenants in the bond contract. These bond covenants are discussed in more detail in Chapter 19, but essentially they may be thought of as restrictions on managerial decision making. Typical covenants restrict payment of cash dividends on common stock, limit the acquisition or sale of assets, or limit further debt financing. To make sure that the protective covenants are complied with by management means that monitoring costs are incurred. Like all monitoring costs, they are borne by common stockholders. Further, like many costs, they involve the analysis of an important tradeoff.

Figure 15–6 displays some of the tradeoffs involved with the use of protective bond covenants. Note (in the left panel of Figure 15–6) that the firm might be able to sell bonds that carry no protective covenants only by incurring very high interest rates. With no protective covenants, there are no associated monitoring costs. Also, there are no lost operating efficiencies, such as being able to move quickly to acquire a particular company in the acquisitions market. On the other hand, the willingness to submit to several covenants could reduce the explicit cost of the debt contract,

---

[3] Economists have studied the problems associated with control of the corporation for decades. An early, classic work on this topic was A. A. Berle, Jr., and G. C. Means, *The Modern Corporation and Private Property* (New York: Macmillan, 1932). The recent emphasis in corporate finance and financial economics stems from the important contribution of Michael C. Jensen and William H. Meckling, "Theory of the Firm: Managerial Behavior, Agency Costs and Ownership Structure," *Journal of Financial Economics*, 3 (October 1976), 305–60. Professors Jensen and Smith have analyzed the bondholder-stockholder conflict in a very clear style. See Michael C. Jensen and Clifford W. Smith, Jr., "Stockholder, Manager, and Creditor Interests: Applications of Agency Theory," in *Recent Advances in Corporate Finance*, Edward I. Altman and Marti G. Subrahmanyam, eds. (Homewood, IL: Richard D. Irwin, 1985), 93–131. An entire volume dealing with agency problems, including those of capital structure management, is Amir Barnea, Robert A. Haugen, and Lemma W. Senbet, *Agency Problems and Financial Contracting* (Englewood Cliffs, NJ: Prentice-Hall, 1985).

No protective bond covenants	Many protective bond covenants
High interest rates	Low interest rates
Low monitoring costs	High monitoring costs
No lost operating efficiencies	Many lost operating efficiencies

FIGURE 15–6.   Agency Costs of Debt: The Tradeoffs

but would involve incurring significant monitoring costs and losing some operating efficiencies (which also translates into higher costs). When the debt issue is first sold, then, a tradeoff will be arrived at between incurring monitoring costs, losing operating efficiencies, and enjoying a lower explicit interest cost.

Next, we have to consider the presence of monitoring costs at low levels of leverage and at higher levels of leverage. When the firm operates at a low debt to equity ratio, there is little need for creditors to insist on a long list of bond covenants. The financial risk is just not there to require that type of activity. The firm will likewise benefit from low explicit interest rates when leverage is low. When the debt to equity ratio is high, however, it is logical for creditors to demand a great deal of monitoring. This increase in agency costs will raise the implicit cost (the true total cost) of debt financing. It seems logical, then, to suggest that monitoring costs will rise as the firm's use of financial leverage increases. Just as the likelihood of firm failure (financial distress) raises a company's overall cost of capital (k_0), so do agency costs. On the other side of the coin, this means that total firm value (the total market value of the firm's securities) will be *lower* owing to the presence of agency costs. Taken together, the presence of agency costs and the costs associated with financial distress argue in favor of the concept of an *optimal* capital structure for the individual firm.

This discussion can be summarized by introducing equation (15–5) for the market value of the levered firm.

$$\begin{matrix} \text{market value of} \\ \text{levered firm} \end{matrix} = \begin{matrix} \text{market value of} \\ \text{unlevered firm} \end{matrix} + \begin{matrix} \text{present value} \\ \text{of tax shields} \end{matrix}$$
$$- \left(\begin{matrix} \text{present value} & \text{present value} \\ \text{of financial} & + \text{of agency} \\ \text{distress costs} & \text{costs} \end{matrix} \right) \tag{15–5}$$

The relationship expressed in equation (15–5) is presented in graphic form in Figure 15–7. There we see that the tax shield effect is dominant until point A is reached. After point A, the rising costs of the likelihood of firm failure (financial distress) and agency costs cause the market value of the levered firm to decline. The *objective* for the financial manager here is to find point B by using all of his or

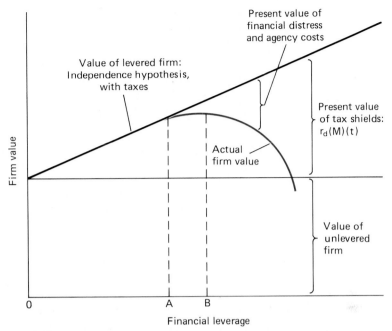

FIGURE 15–7. Firm Value Considering Taxes, Agency Costs, and Financial Distress Costs

her analytical skill; this must also include a good dose of seasoned judgment. At point *B* the actual market value of the levered firm is maximized, and its composite cost of capital (k_0) is at a minimum. The implementation problem is that the precise costs of financial distress and monitoring can only be estimated by subjective means; a definite mathematical solution is not available. Thus, planning the firm's financing mix always requires the application of management judgment.

Managerial Implications

Where does this examination of capital structure theory leave us? The upshot is that the determination of the firm's financing mix is centrally important to the financial manager. The firm's stockholders are affected by capital structure decisions.

At the very least, and before bankruptcy costs and agency costs become detrimental, the tax shield effect will cause the shares of a levered firm to sell at a higher price than they would if the company had avoided debt financing. Owing to both the risk of failure and agency costs that accompany the excessive use of leverage, the financial manager must exercise caution in the use of fixed-charge capital. This problem of searching for the optimal range of use of financial leverage comprises the rest of the chapter.[4]

---

[4] The relationship between capital structure and enterprise valuation by the marketplace continues to stimulate considerable research output. The complexity of the topic is reviewed in Stewart C. Myers, "The Capital Structure Puzzle," *Journal of Finance*, 39 (July 1984), 575–92. Ten useful papers are contained in *Corporate Capital Structures in the United States,* Benjamin M. Friedman, ed. (Chicago: National Bureau of Economic Research and The University of Chicago Press, 1985).

BASIC FINANCIAL MANAGEMENT IN PRACTICE
Managing the Debt

Before we explore the tools that assist financial managers in making effective capital structure decisions, it is of interest to ponder the logic of a corporate officer who by choice loaded up his company with debt. Mr. Hans Storr is the chief financial officer at Philip Morris Companies—a firm that has undergone extensive diversification in recent years.

In 1986, Philip Morris ranked 12th in the *Fortune 500* with sales of $20.7 billion; this placed it just behind Chrysler. Philip Morris' return on equity in 1986 was 26.1 percent (as measured at book values). This attractive return on equity performance was 31st among the *Fortune 500* firms. Philip Morris in early 1987 had about $7.0 billion in long-term liabilities outstanding and a long-term debt to shareholders' equity ratio of 1.30 times. The firm is *heavily levered*.

Notice how Mr. Storr emphasizes (1) the ability of a company to generate cash flows, (2) the general state of the economy, and (3) interest rate levels in the following discussion.

"Too many companies have gotten in over their heads in debt for the wrong reasons. They have gone into debt to defend against takeovers, or to buy back shares, but not to invest in plant, property and equipment. That is not healthy.

Some of those companies could have problems if interest rates rise, or if the economy weakens and they cannot maintain the profits and cash flow needed to support their debt."

As Storr sees it, Philip Morris' debt load may be heavy but it is hardly unmanageable. If the company didn't borrow another cent, the daily cash flow from revenues generated by its packaged-goods businesses would be sufficient to run down all its long-term debts in less than three years.

Source: Ellen Benoit, "The CFO: Mine's Okay, Theirs Isn't," *Financial World*, 156 (February 10, 1987), 34.

BASIC TOOLS OF CAPITAL STRUCTURE MANAGEMENT

Recall from Chapter 14 that the use of financial leverage has two effects upon the earnings stream flowing to the firm's common stockholders. For clarity of exposition Tables 14–7 and 14–8 are repeated here as Tables 15–4 and 15–5. Three possible financing mixes for the Pierce Grain Company are contained in Table 15–4, and an analysis of the corresponding financial leverage effects is displayed in Table 15–5.

The *first financial leverage effect* is the added variability in the earnings-per-share stream that accompanies the use of fixed-charge securities in the company's capital structure. By means of the degree-of-financial-leverage measure (DFL_{EBIT}) we explained how this variability can be quantified. The firm that uses more financial leverage (rather than less) will experience larger relative changes in its earnings per share (rather than smaller) following EBIT fluctuations. Assume that Pierce Grain elected financing plan C rather than plan A. Plan C is highly levered and plan A is unlevered. A 100 percent increase in EBIT from $20,000 to $40,000 would cause earnings per share to rise by 147 percent under plan C, but only 100 percent under plan A. Unfortunately, the effect would operate in the negative direction as well. A given

TABLE 15–4. The Pierce Grain Company Possible Capital Structures

Plan A: 0% debt			
		Total debt	$ 0
		Common equity	200,000[a]
Total assets	$200,000	Total liabilities and equity	$200,000
Plan B: 25% debt at 8% interest rate			
		Total debt	$ 50,000
		Common equity	150,000[b]
Total assets	$200,000	Total liabilities and equity	$200,000
Plan C: 40% debt at 8% interest rate			
		Total debt	$ 80,000
		Common equity	120,000[c]
Total assets	$200,000	Total liabilities and equity	$200,000

[a] 2000 common shares outstanding.
[b] 1500 common shares outstanding.
[c] 1200 common shares outstanding.

change in EBIT is *magnified* by the use of financial leverage. This magnification is reflected in the variability of the firm's earnings per share.

The *second financial leverage effect* concerns the level of earnings per share at a given EBIT under a given capital structure. Refer to Table 15–5. At the EBIT level of $20,000, earnings per share would be $5, $5.33, and $5.67 under financing arrangements

TABLE 15–5. The Pierce Grain Company Analysis of Financial Leverage at Different EBIT Levels

(1) EBIT	(2) Interest	(3) = (1) − (2) EBT	(4) = (3) × .5 Taxes	(5) = (3) − (4) Net Income to Common	(6) Earnings per Share	
Plan A: 0% debt; $200,000 common equity; 2000 shares						
$ 0	$ 0	$ 0	$ 0	$ 0	$ 0	
20,000	0	20,000	10,000	10,000	5.00	} 100%
40,000	0	40,000	20,000	20,000	10.00	
60,000	0	60,000	30,000	30,000	15.00	
80,000	0	80,000	40,000	40,000	20.00	
Plan B: 25% debt; 8% interest rate; $150,000 common equity; 1500 shares						
$ 0	$4,000	$ (4,000)	$ (2,000)[a]	$ (2,000)	$ (1.33)	
20,000	4,000	16,000	8,000	8,000	5.33	} 125%
40,000	4,000	36,000	18,000	18,000	12.00	
60,000	4,000	56,000	28,000	28,000	18.67	
80,000	4,000	76,000	38,000	38,000	25.33	
Plan C: 40% debt; 8% interest rate; $120,000 common equity; 1200 shares						
$ 0	$6,400	$ (6,400)	$ (3,200)[a]	$ (3,200)	$ (2.67)	
20,000	6,400	13,600	6,800	6,800	5.67	} 147%
40,000	6,400	33,600	16,800	16,800	14.00	
60,000	6,400	53,600	26,800	26,800	22.33	
80,000	6,400	73,600	36,800	36,800	30.67	

[a] The negative tax bill recognizes the credit arising from the carryback and carryforward provision of the tax code. See Chapter 2.

A, B, and C, respectively. Above a critical level of EBIT, the firm's earnings per share will be higher if greater degrees of financial leverage are employed. Conversely, below some critical level of EBIT, earnings per share will suffer at greater degrees of financial leverage. Whereas the first financial-leverage effect is quantified by the degree-of-financial-leverage measure (DFL_{EBIT}), the second is quantified by what is generally referred to as EBIT–EPS analysis. EPS refers, of course, to earnings per share. The rationale underlying this sort of analysis is simple. Earnings is one of the key variables that influences the market value of the firm's common stock. The effect of a financing decision on EPS, then, should be understood because the decision will probably affect the value of the stockholders' investment.

EBIT–EPS Analysis

Example Assume that plan B in Table 15–5 is the existing capital structure for the Pierce Grain Company. Furthermore, the asset structure of the firm is such that EBIT is expected to be $20,000 per year for a very long time. A capital investment is available to Pierce Grain that will cost $50,000. Acquisition of this asset is expected to raise the projected EBIT level to $30,000, permanently. The firm can raise the needed cash by (1) selling 500 shares of common stock at $50 each or (2) selling new bonds that will net the firm $50,000 and carry an interest rate of 8.5 percent. These capital structures and corresponding EPS amounts are summarized in Table 15–6.

TABLE 15–6. The Pierce Grain Company Analysis of Financing Choices

Part A: Capital Structures

Existing Capital Structure		With New Common Stock Financing		With New Debt Financing	
Long-term debt at 8%	$ 50,000	Long-term debt at 8%	$ 50,000	Long-term debt at 8%	$ 50,000
Common stock	150,000	Common stock	200,000	Long-term debt at 8.5%	50,000
				Common stock	150,000
Total liabilities and equity	$200,000	Total liabilities and equity	$250,000	Total liabilities and equity	$250,000
Common shares outstanding	1,500	Common shares outstanding	2,000	Common shares outstanding	1,500

Part B: Projected EPS Levels

	Existing Capital Structure	With New Common Stock Financing	With New Debt Financing
EBIT	$20,000	$30,000	$30,000
Less: Interest expense	4,000	4,000	8,250
Earnings before taxes (EBT)	$16,000	$26,000	$21,750
Less: Taxes at 50%	8,000	13,000	10,875
Net income	$ 8,000	$13,000	$10,875
Less: Preferred dividends	0	0	0
Earnings available to common	$ 8,000	$13,000	$10,875
EPS	$5.33	$6.50	$7.25

At the projected EBIT level of $30,000, the EPS for the common stock and debt alternatives are $6.50 and $7.25, respectively. Both are considerably above the $5.33 that would occur if the new project were rejected and the additional financial capital were not raised. Based on a criterion of selecting the financing plan that will provide the highest EPS, the bond alternative is favored. But what if the basic business risk to which the firm is exposed causes the EBIT level to vary over a considerable range? Can we be sure that the bond alternative will *always* have the higher EPS associated with it? The answer, of course, is "No." When the EBIT level is subject to uncertainty, a graphic analysis of the proposed financing plans can provide useful information to the financial manager.

Graphic Analysis The EBIT–EPS analysis chart allows the decision maker to visualize the impact of different financing plans on EPS over a range of EBIT levels. The relationship between EPS and EBIT is linear. All we need, therefore, to construct the chart is two points for each alternative. Part B of Table 15–6 already provides us with one of these points. The answer to the following question for each choice gives us the second point: At what EBIT level will the EPS for the plan be exactly zero? If the EBIT level *just covers* the plan's financing costs (on a before-tax basis), then EPS will be zero. For the stock plan, an EPS of zero is associated with an EBIT of $4000. The $4000 is the interest expense incurred under the existing capital structure. If the bond plan is elected, the interest costs will be the present $4000 plus $4250 per year arising from the new debt issue. An EBIT level of $8250, then, is necessary to provide a zero EPS with the bond plan.

The EBIT–EPS analysis chart representing the financing choices available to the Pierce Grain Company is shown as Figure 15–8. EBIT is charted on the horizontal axis and EPS on the vertical axis. The intercepts on the horizontal axis represent the before-tax equivalent financing charges related to each plan. The straight lines for each plan tell us the EPS amounts that will occur at different EBIT amounts.

Notice that the bond-plan line has a *steeper slope* than the stock-plan line. This ensures that the lines for each financing choice will *intersect*. Above the intersection point, EPS for the plan with greater leverage will exceed that for the plan with lesser leverage. The intersection point, encircled in Figure 15–8, occurs at an EBIT level of $21,000 and produces EPS of $4.25 for each plan. When EBIT is $30,000, notice that the bond plan produces EPS of $7.25 and the stock plan, $6.50. Below the intersection point, EPS with the stock plan will *exceed* that with the more highly levered bond plan. The steeper slope of the bond-plan line indicates that with greater leverage, EPS is more sensitive to EBIT changes. This same concept was discussed in Chapter 14 when we derived the degree of financial leverage measure.

Computing Indifference Points The point of intersection in Figure 15–8 is called the **EBIT–EPS indifference point.** It identifies the EBIT level at which the EPS will be the same regardless of the financing plan chosen by the financial manager. This indifference point, sometimes called the breakeven point, has major implications for financial planning. At EBIT amounts in excess of the EBIT indifference level, the more heavily levered financing plan will generate a higher EPS. At EBIT amounts below the EBIT indifference level, the financing

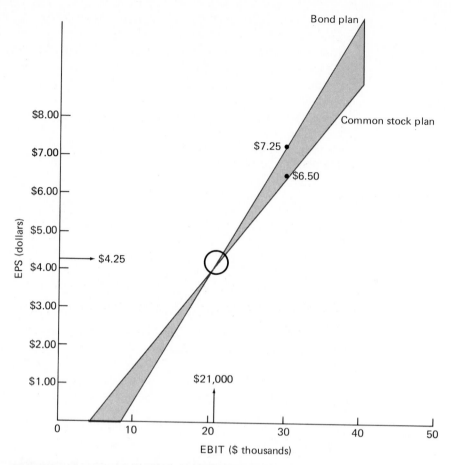

FIGURE 15–8.   EBIT–EPS Analysis Chart

plan involving less leverage will generate a higher EPS. It is important, then, to know the EBIT indifference level.

We can find it graphically, as in Figure 15–8. At times it may be more efficient, though, to calculate the indifference point directly. This can be done by using the following equation:

$$\underset{S_s}{\underbrace{\frac{(\text{EBIT} - I)(1 - t) - P}{S_s}}_{\textit{EPS: Stock Plan}}} = \underset{S_b}{\underbrace{\frac{(\text{EBIT} - I)(1 - t) - P}{S_b}}_{\textit{EPS: Bond Plan}}} \qquad (15\text{–}6)$$

where S_s and S_b are the number of common shares outstanding under the stock and bond plans, respectively, I is interest expense, t is the firm's income tax rate, and P is preferred dividends paid. In the present case P is zero, because there is no preferred stock outstanding. If preferred stock is associated with one of the financing alternatives, keep in mind that the preferred dividends, P, are not tax deductible. Equation (15–6) *does* take this fact into consideration.

For the present example, we calculate the indifference level of EBIT as

$$\frac{(\text{EBIT} - \$4000)(1 - 0.5) - 0}{2000} = \frac{(\text{EBIT} - \$8250)(1 - 0.5) - 0}{1500}$$

When the expression above is solved for EBIT, we obtain \$21,000. If EBIT turns out to be \$21,000, then EPS will be \$4.25 under both plans.

Uncommitted Earnings per Share and Indifference Points

The calculations that permitted us to solve for Pierce Grain's EBIT–EPS indifference point made no explicit allowance for the repayment of the bond principal. This procedure is not that unrealistic. It only presumes the debt will be perpetually outstanding. This means that when the current bond issue matures, a new bond issue will be floated. The proceeds from the newer issue would be used to pay off the maturity value of the older issue.

Many bond contracts, however, require that **sinking fund payments** be made to a bond trustee. A **sinking fund** is a real cash reserve that is used to provide for the orderly and early retirement of the principal amount of the bond issue. Most often the sinking fund payment is a mandatory fixed amount and is required by a clause in the bond indenture. Sinking fund payments can represent a sizable cash drain on the firm's liquid resources. Moreover, sinking fund payments are a return of borrowed principal, so they are *not* tax deductible to the firm.

Because of the potentially serious nature of the cash drain caused by sinking fund requirements, the financial manager might be concerned with the uncommitted earnings per share (UEPS) related to each financing plan. The calculation of UEPS recognizes that sinking fund commitments have been honored. UEPS can be used, then, for discretionary spending—such as the payment of cash dividends to common stockholders or investment in capital facilities.

If we let *SF* be the sinking fund payment required in a given year, the EBIT–UEPS indifference point can be calculated as:

$$\overset{\textit{UEPS: Stock Plan}}{\frac{(\text{EBIT} - I)(1 - t) - P - SF}{S_s}} = \overset{\textit{UEPS: Bond Plan}}{\frac{(\text{EBIT} - I)(1 - t) - P - SF}{S_b}} \qquad (15\text{--}7)$$

If several bond issues are already outstanding, then *I* in equations (15–6) and (15–7) for the stock plan consists of the sum of their related interest payments. For the bond plan, *I* would be the *sum of existing plus new interest charges*. In equation (15–7) the same logic applies to the sinking-fund variable, *SF*. The indifference level of EBIT based on UEPS will always exceed that based on EPS.

A Word of Caution

Above the EBIT–EPS indifference point, a more heavily levered financial plan promises to deliver a larger EPS. Strict application of the criterion of selecting the financing plan that produces the highest EPS might have the firm issuing debt most of the time it raised external capital. Our discussion of capital-structure theory taught us the dangers of that sort of action.

The primary weakness of EBIT–EPS analysis is that it disregards the implicit costs of debt financing. The effect of the specific financing decision on the firm's cost of common equity capital is totally ignored. Investors should be concerned with both the *level* and *variability* of the firm's expected earnings stream. EBIT–EPS analysis considers only the level of the earnings stream and ignores the variability (riskiness) inherent in it. Thus, this type of analysis must be used in conjunction with other basic tools in reaching the objective of capital structure management.

Comparative Leverage Ratios

In Chapter 3 we explored the overall usefulness of financial ratio analysis. Leverage ratios were one of the categories of financial ratios identified in that chapter. We emphasize here that the computation of leverage ratios is one of the basic tools of capital structure management.

Two types of leverage ratios must be computed when a financing decision faces the firm. We have called these *balance sheet leverage ratios* and *coverage ratios*. The inputs to the balance sheet leverage ratios come from the firm's balance sheet. In various forms these balance sheet metrics compare the firm's use of funds supplied by creditors with those supplied by owners.

TABLE 15–7. Comparative Leverage Ratios: Worksheet for Analyzing Financing Plans

Ratios	Computation Method	Existing Ratio	Ratio with New Common Stock Financing	Ratio with New Debt Financing
Balance sheet leverage ratios				
1. Debt ratio	$\dfrac{\text{total liabilities}}{\text{total assets}}$	_____ %	_____ %	_____ %
2. Long-term debt to total capitalization	$\dfrac{\text{long-term debt}}{\text{long-term debt} + \text{net worth}}$	_____ %	_____ %	_____ %
3. Total liabilities to net worth	$\dfrac{\text{total liabilities}}{\text{net worth}}$	_____ %	_____ %	_____ %
4. Common equity ratio	$\dfrac{\text{common equity}}{\text{total assets}}$	_____ %	_____ %	_____ %
Coverage ratios				
1. Times interest earned	$\dfrac{\text{EBIT}}{\text{annual interest expense}}$	_____ times	_____ times	_____ times
2. Times burden covered	$\dfrac{\text{EBIT}}{\text{interest} + \dfrac{\text{sinking fund}}{1-t}}$	_____ times	_____ times	_____ times
3. Cash flow overall coverage ratio	$\dfrac{\text{EBIT} + \text{lease expense} + \text{depreciation}}{\text{interest} + \text{lease expense} + \dfrac{\text{preferred dividends}}{1-t} + \dfrac{\text{principal payments}}{1-t}}$	_____ times	_____ times	_____ times

Inputs to the coverage ratios *generally* come from the firm's income statement. At times the external analyst may have to consult balance sheet information to construct some of these needed estimates. On a privately placed debt issue, for example, some fraction of the current portion of the firm's long-term debt might have to be used as an estimate of that issue's sinking fund. Coverage ratios provide estimates of the firm's ability to service its financing contracts. High coverage ratios, compared with a standard, imply unused debt capacity.

A Worksheet   Table 15–7 is a sample worksheet used to analyze financing choices. The objective of the analysis is to determine the effect each financing plan will have on key financial ratios. The financial officer can compare the existing level of each ratio with its projected level, taking into consideration the contractual commitments of each alternative.

In reality we know that EBIT might be expected to vary over a considerable range of outcomes. For this reason the coverage ratios should be calculated several times, each at a different level of EBIT. If this is accomplished over all possible values of EBIT, a probability distribution for each coverage ratio can be constructed. This provides the financial manager with much more information than simply calculating the coverage ratios based on the expected value of EBIT.

Industry Norms   The comparative leverage ratios calculated according to the format laid out in Table 15–7, or in a similar format, have additional utility to the decision maker if they can be compared with some standard. Generally, corporate financial analysts, investment bankers, commercial bank loan officers, and bond-rating agencies rely upon industry classes from which to compute "normal" ratios. Although industry groupings may actually contain firms whose basic business risk exposure differs widely, the practice is entrenched in American business behavior.[5] At the very least, then, the financial officer must be interested in *industry standards* because almost everybody else is.

Several published studies indicate that capital-structure ratios vary in a significant manner among industry classes.[6] For example, random samplings of the common equity ratios of large retail firms seem to differ statistically from those of major steel producers. The major steel producers use financial leverage to a lesser degree than do the large retail organizations. On the whole, firms operating in the *same* industry tend to exhibit capital structure ratios that cluster around a central value, which we call a norm. Business risk will vary from industry to industry. As a consequence, the capital structure norms will vary from industry to industry.

This is not to say that all companies in the industry will maintain leverage ratios "close" to the norm. For instance, firms that are very profitable may display *high* coverage ratios and *high* balance sheet leverage ratios. The moderately profitable

---

[5] An approach to grouping firms based on several component measures of business risk, as opposed to ordinary industry classes, is reported in John D. Martin, David F. Scott, Jr., and Robert F. Vandell, "Equivalent Risk Classes: A Multidimensional Examination," *Journal of Financial and Quantitative Analysis*, 14 (March 1979), 101–18.

[6] See, for example, Eli Schwartz and J. Richard Aronson, "Some Surrogate Evidence in Support of the Concept of Optimal Financial Structure," *Journal of Finance,* 22 (March 1967), 10–18; David F. Scott, Jr., "Evidence on the Importance of Financial Structure," *Financial Management*, 1 (Summer 1972), 45–50; and David F. Scott, Jr., and John D. Martin, "Industry Influence on Financial Structure," *Financial Management*, 4 (Spring 1975), 67–73.

firm, though, might find such a posture unduly risky. Here the usefulness of industry normal leverage ratios is clear. If the firm chooses to deviate in a material manner from the accepted values for the key ratios, it must have a sound reason.

Company-wide Cash Flows: What Is the Worst That Could Happen?

In Chapter 3 we stated that liquidity ratios are designed to measure the ability of the firm to pay its bills on time. Financing charges are just another type of bill that eventually comes due for payment. Interest charges, preferred dividends, lease charges, and principal payments all must be paid on time, or the company risks being caught in bankruptcy proceedings. To a lesser extent, dispensing with financing charges on an other than timely basis can result in severely restricted business operations. We have just seen that coverage ratios provide a measure of the safety of one general class of payment—financing charges. Coverage ratios, then, and liquidity ratios are very close in concept.

A more comprehensive method is available for studying the impact of capital structure decisions on corporate cash flows. The method is simple but nonetheless very valuable. It involves the preparation of a series of cash budgets under (1) different economic conditions and (2) different capital structures.[7] The net cash flows under these different situations can be examined to determine if the financing requirements expose the firm to a degree of default risk too high to bear.

In work that has been highly acclaimed, Donaldson has suggested that the firm's debt-carrying capacity (defined in the broad sense here to include preferred dividend payments and lease payments) ought to depend upon the net cash flows the firm could expect to receive during a recessionary period.[8] In other words, *target capital structure proportions* could be set by planning for the "worst that could happen." An example will be of help.

Suppose that a recession is expected to last for one year.[9] Moreover, the end of the year represents the bottoming-out, or worst portion of the recession. Equation (15–8) defines the cash balance, CB_r, the firm could expect to have at the end of the recession period.[10]

$$CB_r = C_0 + (C_s + OR) - (P_a + RM + \cdots + E_n) - FC \qquad (15\text{–}8)$$

where C_0 = the cash balance at the beginning of the recession

C_s = collection from sales

OR = other cash receipts

P_a = payroll expenditures

RM = raw material payments

---

[7] Cash budget preparation is discussed in Chapter 4.

[8] Refer to Gordon Donaldson, "New Framework for Corporate Debt Policy," *Harvard Business Review*, 40 (March–April 1962), 117–31; Gordon Donaldson, *Corporate Debt Capacity* (Boston: Division of Research, Graduate School of Business Administration, Harvard University, 1961), Chap. 7; and Gordon Donaldson, "Strategy for Financial Emergencies," *Harvard Business Review*, 47 (November–December 1969), 67–79.

[9] The analysis can readily be extended to cover a recessionary period of several years. All that is necessary is to calculate the cash budgets over a similar period.

[10] For the most part, the present notation follows that of Donaldson.

E_n = the last of a long series of expenditures over which management has little control (nondiscretionary expenditures)

FC = fixed financial charges associated with a specific capital structure

If we let the net of total cash receipts and nondiscretionary expenditures be represented by NCF_r, then equation (15–8) can be simplified to

$$CB_r = CB_0 + NCF_r - FC \qquad (15\text{–}9)$$

The inputs to equation (15–9) come from a detailed cash budget. The variable representing financing costs, FC, can be changed in accordance with several alternative financing plans to ascertain if the net cash balance during the recession, CB_r, might fall below zero.

Suppose that some firm typically maintains $500,000 in cash and marketable securities. This amount would be on hand at the start of the recession period. During the economic decline, the firm projects that its net cash flows from operations, NCF_r, will be $2 million. If the firm currently finances its assets with an unlevered capital structure, its cash balance at the worst point of the recession would be

$$CB_r = \$500{,}000 + \$2{,}000{,}000 - \$0 = \$2{,}500{,}000$$

This procedure allows us to study many different situations.[11] Assume that the same firm is considering a shift in its capitalization such that annual interest and sinking fund payments will be $2,300,000. If a recession occurred, the firm's cash balance at the end of the adverse economic period would be

$$CB_r = \$500{,}000 + \$2{,}000{,}000 - \$2{,}300{,}000 = \$200{,}000$$

The firm ordinarily maintains a liquid asset balance of $500,000. Thus, the effect of the proposed capital structure on the firm's cash balance during adverse circumstances might seem too risky for management to accept. When the chance of being out of cash is too high for management to bear, the use of financial leverage has been pushed beyond a reasonable level. According to this tool, the appropriate level of financial leverage is reached when the chance of being out of cash is exactly equal to that which management will assume.

A GLANCE AT ACTUAL CAPITAL STRUCTURE MANAGEMENT

In this chapter we have discussed (1) the concept of an optimal capital structure, (2) the search for an appropriate range of financial leverage, and (3) the fundamental tools of capital structure management. The opinions and practices of financial executives lead us to believe that the emphasis is a reasonable one.

---

[11] It is not difficult to improve the usefulness of this sort of analysis by applying the technique of simulation to the generation of the various cash budgets. This facilitates the construction of probability distributions of net cash flows under differing circumstances. Simulation was discussed in Chapter 11.

The Conference Board has surveyed 170 senior financial officers with respect to their capital structure practices.[12] Of these 170 executives, 102 or 60 percent stated that they *do* believe there is an optimum capital structure for the corporation. Sixty-five percent of the responding practitioners worked for firms with annual sales in excess of $200 million. One executive who subscribed to the optimal-capital-structure concept stated:

> In my opinion, there is an optimum capital structure for companies. However, this optimum capital structure will vary by individual companies, industries, and then is subject to changing economies, by money markets, earnings trends, and prospects . . . the circumstances and the lenders will determine an optimum at different points in time.[13]

This survey and others consistently point out that (1) financial officers set target debt ratios for their companies, and (2) the values for those ratios are influenced by a conscious evaluation of the basic business risk to which the firm is exposed.

Target Debt Ratios

Selected comments from financial executives point to the widespread use of target debt ratios. A vice-president and treasurer of the American Telephone and Telegraph Company (AT&T) described his firm's debt ratio policy in terms of a range:

> All of the foregoing considerations led us to conclude, and reaffirm for a period of many years, that the proper range of our debt was 30% to 40% of total capital. Reasonable success in meeting financial needs under the diverse market and economic conditions that we have faced attests to the appropriateness of this conclusion.[14]

In a similar fashion the president of Fibreboard Corporation identified his firm's target debt ratio and noted how it is related to the uncertain nature of the company's business:

> Our objective is a 30% ratio of debt to capitalization. We need that kind of flexibility to operate in the cyclical business we are in.[15]

In the Conference Board survey mentioned earlier, 84 of the 102 financial officers who subscribed to the optimal capital structure concept stated that their firm *has* a target debt ratio.[16] The most frequently mentioned influence on the level of the target debt ratio was ability to meet financing charges. Other factors identified as affecting the target were (1) maintaining a desired bond rating, (2) providing an adequate borrowing reserve, and (3) exploiting the advantages of financial leverage.

Who Sets Target Debt Ratios?

From the discussion above, we know that firms *do* use target debt ratios in arriving at financing decisions. But who sets or influences these target ratios? This and other questions concerning corporate financing policy were investigated in one study pub-

---

[12] Francis J. Walsh, Jr., *Planning Corporate Capital Structures* (New York: The Conference Board, 1972).

[13] Ibid., p. 14.

[14] John J. Scanlon, "Bell System Financial Policies," *Financial Management*, 1 (Summer 1972), 16–26.

[15] *Business Week*, December 6, 1976, p. 30.

[16] Walsh, *Planning Corporate Capital Structures*, p. 17.

TABLE 15–8. Setting Target Financial Structure Ratios

	Rank	
Type of Influence	1	2
Internal management and staff analysts	85%	7%
Investment bankers	3	39
Commercial bankers	0	9
Trade creditors	1	0
Security analysts	1	4
Comparative industry ratios	3	23
Other	7	18
Total	100%	100%

Source: David F. Scott, Jr., and Dana J. Johnson, "Financing Policies and Practices in Large Corporations," *Financial Management*, 11 (Summer 1982), 53.

lished in 1982.[17] This survey of the 1000 largest industrial firms in the United States (as ranked by total sales dollars) involved responses from 212 financial executives.

In one portion of this study the participants were asked to rank several possible influences on their target leverage (debt) ratios. Table 15–8 displays the percent of responses ranked either number one or number two in importance. Ranks past the second are omitted in that they were not very significant. Notice that the most important influence is the firm's own management group and staff of analysts. This item accounted for 85 percent of the responses ranked number one. Of the responses ranked number two in importance, investment bankers dominated the outcomes and accounted for 39 percent of such replies. The role of investment bankers in the country's capital market system is explored in some detail in Chapter 17. Also notice that comparison with ratios of industry competitors and commercial bankers have some impact on the determination of leverage targets.

Debt Capacity
Previously in this chapter we noted that the firm's debt capacity is the maximum proportion of debt that it can include in its capital structure and still maintain its lowest composite cost of capital. It is of interest to have some understanding of how financial executives make the concept of debt capacity operational. Table 15–9 is derived from the same 1982 survey, involving 212 executives, mentioned above. These executives defined debt capacity in a wide variety of ways. The most popular approach was as a target percent of total capitalization. Twenty-seven percent of the respondents thought of debt capacity in this manner. Forty-three percent of the participating executives remarked that debt capacity is defined in terms of some balance-sheet-based financial ratio (see the first three items in Table 15–9). Maintaining a specific bond rating was also indicated to be a popular approach to implementing the debt capacity concept.

---

[17] David F. Scott, Jr., and Dana J. Johnson, "Financing Policies and Practices in Large Corporations," *Financial Management*, 11 (Summer 1982), 51–59.

TABLE 15–9. Definitions of Debt Capacity in Practice

Standard or Method	1000 Largest Corporations (Percent Using)
Target percent of total capitalization (long-term debt to total capitalization)	27%
Long-term debt to net worth ratio (or its inverse)	14
Long-term debt to total assets	2
Interest (or fixed charge) coverage ratio	6
Maintain bond ratings	14
Restrictive debt covenants	4
Most adverse cash flow	4
Industry standard	3
Other	10
No response	16
Total	100%

Source: Derived from David F. Scott, Jr., and Dana J. Johnson, "Financing Policies and Practices in Large Corporations," *Financial Management*, 11 (Summer 1982), p. 51–59.

Business Risk

In our opinion, the single most important factor that should affect the firm's financing mix is the underlying nature of the business in which it operates. In Chapter 14 we defined business risk as the relative dispersion in the firm's expected stream of EBIT. If the nature of the firm's business is such that the variability inherent in its EBIT stream is high, then it would be unwise to impose a high degree of financial risk on top of this already uncertain earnings stream.

Corporate executives are likely to point this out in discussions of capital-structure management. A financial officer in a large steel firm related:

> The nature of the industry, the marketplace, and the firm tend to establish debt limits that any prudent management would prefer not to exceed. Our industry is capital intensive and our markets tend to be cyclical. . . . The capability to service debt while operating in the environment described dictates a conservative financial structure.[18]

Notice how that executive was concerned with both his firm's business risk exposure and its cash flow capability for meeting any financing costs. The AT&T financial officer referred to earlier also has commented on the relationship between business and financial risk:

> In determining how much debt a firm can safely carry, it is necessary to consider the basic risks inherent in that business. This varies considerably among industries and is related essentially to the nature and demand for an industry's product, the operating characteristics of the industry, and its ability to earn an adequate return in an unknown future.[19]

It appears clear that the firm's capital structure cannot be properly designed without a thorough understanding of its commercial strategy.

---

[18] Walsh, *Planning Corporate Capital Structures*, p. 18.
[19] Scanlon, "Bell System Financial Policies," p. 19.

Summary

This chapter dealt with the design of the firm's financing mix. The particular focus was on the management of the firm's permanent sources of funds—that is, its capital structure. The objective of capital structure management is to arrange the company's sources of funds in such a manner that its common stock price will be maximized, all other factors held constant.

Capital Structure Theory

Can the firm affect its composite cost of capital by altering its financing mix? Attempts to answer that question have comprised a significant portion of capital structure theory for over three decades. Extreme positions show that the firm's stock price is either unaffected or continually affected as the firm increases its reliance upon leverage-inducing funds. In an operating environment where interest expense is tax deductible and market imperfections operate to restrict the amount of fixed-income obligations a firm can issue, most financial officers and financial academics subscribe to the concept of an optimal capital structure. The optimal capital structure minimizes the firm's composite cost of capital. Searching for a proper range of financial leverage, then, is an important financial management activity.

The Tools of Capital Structure Management

The decision to use senior securities in the firm's capitalization causes two types of financial leverage effects. The first is the added variability in the earnings per share stream that accompanies the use of fixed-charge securities. We explained in Chapter 14 how this could be quantified by use of the degree of financial leverage metric. The second financial leverage effect relates to the level of earnings per share (EPS) at a given EBIT under a specific capital structure. We rely upon EBIT–EPS analysis to measure this second effect. Through EBIT–EPS analysis the decision maker can inspect the impact of alternative financing plans on EPS over a full range of EBIT levels.

A second tool of capital structure management is the calculation of comparative leverage ratios. Balance sheet leverage ratios and coverage ratios can be computed according to the contractual stipulations of the proposed financing plans. Comparison of these ratios with industry standards enables the financial officer to determine if the firm's key ratios are materially out of line with accepted practice.

A third tool involves the analysis of corporate cash flows. This process involves the preparation of a series of cash budgets that consider different economic conditions and different capital structures. Useful insight into the identification of proper target capital structure ratios can be obtained by analyzing projected cash flow statements that assume adverse operating circumstances.

Capital Structure Practices

Surveys indicate that the majority of financial officers in large firms believe in the concept of an optimal capital structure. The optimal capital structure is approximated by the identification of target debt ratios. The targets reflect the firm's ability to service fixed financing costs and also consider the business risk to which the firm is exposed.

Study Questions

15–1. Define the following terms:
 a. Financial structure
 b. Capital structure
 c. Optimal capital structure
 d. Debt capacity

15–2. What is the primary weakness of EBIT–EPS analysis as a financing decision tool?

15–3. What is the objective of capital structure management?

15–4. Distinguish between (1) balance sheet leverage ratios and (b) coverage ratios. Give two examples of each and indicate how they would be computed.

15–5. Why might firms whose sales levels change drastically over time choose to use debt only sparingly in their capital structures?

15–6. What condition would cause capital structure management to be a meaningless activity?

15–7. What does the term "independence hypothesis" mean as it applies to capital-structure theory?

15–8. Who have been the foremost advocates of the independence hypothesis?

15–9. A financial manager might say that the firm's composite cost of capital is saucer-shaped or U-shaped. What does this mean?

15–10. Define the EBIT–EPS indifference point.

15–11. What is uncommitted earnings per share (UEPS)?

15–12. Explain how industry norms might be used by the financial manager in the design of the company's financing mix.

Self-Test Problems

ST–1. (*Analysis of Recessionary Cash Flows*) The management of Story Enterprises is considering an increase in its use of financial leverage. The proposal on the table is to sell $6 million of bonds that would mature in 20 years. The interest rate on these bonds would be 12 percent. The bond issue would have a sinking fund attached to it requiring that one-twentieth of the principal be retired each year. Most business economists are forecasting a recession that will affect the entire company in the coming year. Story's management has been saying, "If we can make it through this, we can make it through anything." The firm prefers to carry an operating cash balance of $750,000. Cash collections from sales next year will total $3 million. Miscellaneous cash receipts will be $400,000. Raw material payments will be $700,000. Wage and salary costs will be $1,200,000 on a cash basis. On top of this, Story will experience nondiscretionary cash outlays of $1.2 million, *including* all tax payments. The firm faces a 34 percent tax rate.
 a. At present, Story is unlevered. What will be the total fixed financial charges the firm must pay next year?
 b. If the bonds are issued, what is your forecast for the firm's expected cash balance at the end of the recessionary year (next year)?
 c. As Story's financial consultant, do you recommend that it issue the bonds?

ST–2. (*Assessing Leverage Use*) Some financial data and the appropriate industry norm for three companies are shown in the following table:

Measure	Firm X	Firm Y	Firm Z	Industry Norm
Total debt to total assets	20%	30%	10%	30%
Times interest and preferred dividend coverage	8 times	16 times	19 times	8 times
Price/earnings ratio	9 times	11 times	9 times	9 times

   a. Which firm appears to be employing financial leverage to the most appropriate degree?

   b. In this situation, which "financial leverage effect" appears to dominate the market valuation process?

ST–3. (*EBIT–EPS Analysis*) Four engineers from Martin-Bowing Company are leaving that firm in order to form their own corporation. The new firm will produce and distribute computer software on a national basis. The software will be aimed at scientific markets and at businesses desiring to install comprehensive information systems. Private investors have been lined up to finance the new company. Two financing proposals are being studied. Both of these plans involve the use of some financial leverage; however, one is much more highly levered than the other. Plan A requires the firm to sell bonds with an effective interest rate of 14 percent. One million dollars would be raised in this manner. Additionally, under plan A, $5 million would be raised by selling stock at $50 per common share. Plan B also involves raising $6 million. This would be accomplished by selling $3 million of bonds at an interest rate of 16 percent. The other $3 million would come from selling common stock at $50 per share. In both cases the use of financial leverage is considered to be a permanent part of the firm's capital structure, so no fixed maturity date is used in the analysis. The firm considers a 50 percent tax rate appropriate for planning purposes.

   a. Find the EBIT indifference level associated with the two financing plans, and prepare an EBIT–EPS analysis chart.

   b. Prepare an analytical income statement that demonstrates that EPS will be the same regardless of the plan selected. Use the EBIT level found in part (a) above.

   c. A detailed financial analysis of the firm's prospects suggests that long-term EBIT will be above $1,188,000 annually. Taking this into consideration, which plan will generate the higher EPS?

   d. Suppose that long-term EBIT is forecast to be $1,188,000 per year. Under plan A, a price/earnings ratio of 13 would apply. Under plan B, a price/earnings ratio of 11 would apply. If this set of financial relationships does hold, which financing plan would you recommend be implemented?

   e. Again, assume an EBIT level of $1,188,000. What price/earnings ratio applied to the EPS of plan B would provide the same stock price as that projected for plan A? Refer to your data from part (d) above.

Study Problems

15–1. (*EBIT–EPS Analysis*) Three recent graduates of the computer science program at Southern Tennessee Tech are forming a company to write and distribute software for various personal computers. Initially, the corporation will operate in the southern region of Tennessee, Georgia, North Carolina, and South Carolina. Twelve serious prospects for retail outlets have already been identified and committed to the firm. The firm's software products have been tested and displayed at several trade shows and computer fairs in the perceived operating region. All that is lacking is adequate financing to continue with the project. A small group of private investors in the Atlanta, Georgia, area is interested in financing the new company. Two financing proposals are being evaluated. The first (plan A) is an all common equity capital structure. Two million dollars would be raised by selling common stock at $20 per common share. Plan B would involve the use of financial leverage. One million dollars would be raised selling bonds with an effective interest rate of 11 percent (per annum). Under this second plan, the remaining $1 million would be raised by selling common stock at the $20 price per share. The use of financial leverage is considered to be a permanent part of the firm's capitalization, so no fixed maturity date is needed for the analysis. A 34 percent tax rate is appropriate for the analysis.

a. Find the EBIT indifference level associated with the two financing plans.

b. A detailed financial analysis of the firm's prospects suggests that the long-term EBIT will be above $300,000 annually. Taking this into consideration, which plan will generate the higher EPS?

c. Suppose long-term EBIT is forecast to be $300,000 per year. Under plan A, a price/earnings ratio of 19 would apply. Under plan B, a price/earnings ratio of 15 would apply. If this set of financial relationships does hold, which financing plan would you recommend?

15–2. (*EBIT–EPS Analysis*) Three recent liberal arts graduates have interested a group of venture capitalists in backing a new business enterprise. The proposed operation would consist of a series of retail outlets to distribute and service a full line of personal computer equipment. These stores would be located in southern New Jersey, New York, and Pennsylvania. Two financing plans have been proposed by the graduates. Plan A is an all common equity structure. Three million dollars would be raised by selling 75,000 shares of common stock. Plan B would involve the use of long-term debt financing. One million dollars would be raised by marketing bonds with an effective interest rate of 15 percent. Under this alternative, another $2 million would be raised by selling 50,000 shares of common stock. With both plans, then, $3 million is needed to launch the new firm's operations. The debt funds raised under plan B are considered to have no fixed maturity date, in that this proportion of financial leverage is thought to be a permanent part of the company's capital structure. The fledgling executives have decided to use a 34 percent tax rate in their analysis, and they have hired you on a consulting basis to do the following:

a. Find the EBIT indifference level associated with the two financing proposals.

b. Prepare an analytical income statement that proves EPS will be the same regardless of the plan chosen at the EBIT level found in part (a) above.

15–3. (*EBIT–EPS Analysis*) Two recent graduates of the computer science program at Ohio Tech are forming a company to write, market, and distribute software for various personal computers. Initially, the corporation will operate in the Midwest area of Illinois, Indiana, Michigan, and Ohio. Twelve serious prospects for retail outlets in these different states have already been identified and committed to the firm. The firm's software products have been tested and displayed at several trade shows and computer fairs in the perceived operating region. All that is lacking is adequate financing to continue the project. A small group of private investors in the Columbus, Ohio, area are interested in financing the new company. Two financing proposals are being evaluated. The first (plan A) is an all common equity capital structure. Four million dollars would be raised by selling stock at $40 per common share. Plan B would involve the use of financial leverage. Two million dollars would be raised by selling bonds with an effective interest rate of 16 percent (per annum). Under this second plan, the remaining $2 million would be raised by selling common stock at the $40 price per share. This use of financial leverage is considered to be a permanent part of the firm's capitalization, so no fixed maturity date is needed for the analysis. A 50 percent tax rate is appropriate for the analysis.

a. Find the EBIT indifference level associated with the two financing plans.

b. Prepare an analytical income statement that proves EPS will be the same regardless of the plan chosen at the EBIT level found in part (a) above.

c. A detailed financial analysis of the firm's prospects suggests that long-term EBIT will be above $800,000 annually. Taking this into consideration, which plan will generate the higher EPS?

d. Suppose that long-term EBIT is forecast to be $800,000 per year. Under plan A, a price/earnings ratio of 12 would apply. Under plan B, a price/earnings ratio of 10 would apply. If this set of financial relationships does hold, which financing plan would you recommend be implemented?

15–4. (*Analysis of Recessionary Cash Flows*) The management of Idaho Produce is considering an increase in its use of financial leverage. The proposal on the table is to sell $10 million of bonds that would mature in 20 years. The interest rate on these bonds would be 15 percent. The bond issue would have a sinking fund attached to it requiring that one-twentieth of the principal be retired each year. Most business economists are forecasting a recession that will affect the entire economy in the coming year. Idaho's management has been saying, "If we can make it through this, we can make it through anything." The firm prefers to carry an operating cash balance of $1 million. Cash collections from sales next year will total $4 million. Miscellaneous cash receipts will be $300,000. Raw material payments will be $800,000. Wage and salary costs will total $1.4 million on a cash basis. On top of this, Idaho will experience nondiscretionary cash outflows of $1.2 million *including* all tax payments. The firm faces a 50 percent tax rate.

a. At present, Idaho is unlevered. What will be the total fixed financial charges the firm must pay next year?

b. If the bonds are issued, what is your forecast for the firm's expected cash balance at the end of the recessionary year (next year)?

c. As Idaho's financial consultant, do you recommend that it issue the bonds?

15–5. (*EBIT–EPS Analysis*) Four recent business school graduates have interested a group of venture capitalists in backing a small business enterprise. The proposed operation would consist of a series of retail outlets that would distribute and service a full line of energy-conservation equipment. These stores would be located in northern Virginia, western Pennsylvania, and throughout West Virginia. Two financing plans have been proposed by the graduates. Plan A is an all common equity capital structure. Three million dollars would be raised by selling 60,000 shares of common stock. Plan B would involve the use of long-term debt financing. One million dollars would be raised by marketing bonds with an interest rate of 10 percent. Under this alternative another $2 million would be raised by selling 40,000 shares of common stock. With both plans, then, $3 million is needed to launch the new firm's operations. The debt funds raised under plan B are considered to have no fixed maturity date, in that this proportion of financial leverage is thought to be a permanent part of the company's capital structure. The fledgling executives have decided to use a 40 percent tax rate in their analysis.

a. Find the EBIT indifference level associated with the two financing proposals.

b. Prepare an analytical income statement that proves EPS will be the same regardless of the plan chosen at the EBIT level found in part (a).

15–6. (*EBIT–EPS Analysis*) A group of college professors have decided to form a small manufacturing corporation. The company will produce a full line of contemporary furniture. Two financing plans have been proposed by the investors. Plan A is an all common equity alternative. Under this arrangement 1,400,000 common shares will be sold to net the firm $10 per share. Plan B involves the use of financial leverage. A debt issue with a 20-year maturity period will be privately placed. The debt issue will carry an interest rate of 8 percent and the principal borrowed will amount to $4 million. The corporate tax rate is 50 percent.

a. Find the EBIT indifference level associated with the two financing proposals.

b. Prepare an analytical income statement that proves EPS will be the same regardless of the plan chosen at the EBIT level found in part (a).

c. Prepare an EBIT–EPS analysis chart for this situation.

d. If a detailed financial analysis projects that long-term EBIT will always be close to $1,800,000 annually, which plan will provide for the higher EPS?

15–7. (*EBIT–EPS Analysis*) The professors in problem 15–6 contacted a financial consultant to provide them with some additional information. They felt that in a few years the stock of the firm would be publicly traded over-the-counter, so they were interested in the consultant's opinion as to what the stock price would be under the financing plan outlined in problem 15–6. The consultant agreed that the projected long-term EBIT level of $1,800,000 was reasonable. He also felt that if plan A were selected, the marketplace would apply a price/earnings ratio of 12 times to the company's stock; for plan B he estimated a price/earnings ratio of ten times.

a. According to this information, which financing alternative would offer a higher stock price?

b. What price/earnings ratio applied to the EPS related to plan B would provide the same stock price as that projected for plan A?

c. Comment upon the results of your analysis of problems 15–6 and 15–7.

15–8. (*Analysis of Recessionary Cash Flows*) Cavalier Agriculture Supplies is undertaking a thorough cash flow analysis. It has been proposed by management that the firm expand by raising $5 million in the long-term debt markets. All of this would be immediately invested in new fixed assets. The proposed bond issue would carry an 8 percent interest rate and have a maturity period of 20 years. The bond issue would have a sinking fund provision that one-twentieth of the principal would be retired annually. Next year is expected to be a poor one for Cavalier. The firm's management feels, therefore, that the upcoming year would serve well as a model for the worst possible operating conditions that the firm can be expected to encounter. Cavalier ordinarily carries a $500,000 cash balance. Next year sales collections are forecast to be $3 million. Miscellaneous cash receipts will total $200,000. Wages and salaries will amount to $1 million. Payments for raw materials used in the production process will be $1,400,000. Additionally, the firm will pay $500,000 in nondiscretionary expenditures including taxes. The firm faces a 50 percent tax rate.

a. Cavalier currently has no debt or preferred stock outstanding. What will be the total fixed financial charges that the firm must meet next year?

b. What is the expected cash balance at the end of the recessionary period (next year), assuming the debt is issued?

c. Based on this information, should Cavalier issue the proposed bonds?

15–9. (*Assessing Leverage Use*) Some financial data for three corporations are displayed below:

Measure	Firm A	Firm B	Firm C	Industry Norm
Debt ratio	20%	25%	40%	20%
Times burden covered	8 times	10 times	7 times	9 times
Price/earnings ratio	9 times	11 times	6 times	10 times

a. Which firm appears to be excessively levered?

b. Which firm appears to be employing financial leverage to the most appropriate degree?

c. What explanation can you provide for the higher price/earnings ratio enjoyed by firm B as compared with firm A?

15–10. (*Assessing Leverage Use*) Some financial data and the appropriate industry norm are shown in the following table:

Measure	Firm X	Firm Y	Firm Z	Industry Norm
Total debt to total assets	35%	30%	10%	35%
Times interest and preferred dividend coverage	7 times	14 times	16 times	7 times
Price/earnings ratio	8 times	10 times	8 times	8 times

  a. Which firm appears to be using financial leverage to the most appropriate degree?
  b. In this situation which "financial leverage effect" appears to dominate the market's valuation process?

15–11. (*Capital Structure Theory*) Boston Textiles has an all common equity capital structure. Pertinent financial characteristics for the company are shown below:

> Shares of common stock outstanding = 1,000,000
> Common stock price, P_0 = $20 per share
> Expected level of EBIT = $5,000,000
> Dividend payout ratio = 100 percent

In answering the following questions, assume that corporate income is not taxed.
  a. Under the present capital structure, what is the total value of the firm?
  b. What is the cost of common equity capital, K_c? What is the composite cost of capital, K_o?
  c. Now, suppose that Boston Textiles sells $1 million of long-term debt with an interest rate of 8 percent. The proceeds are used to retire outstanding common stock. According to net-operating-income theory (the independence hypothesis), what will be the firm's cost of common equity *after* the capital structure change?
    1. What will be the dividend per share flowing to the firm's common shareholders?
    2. By what percent has the dividend per share changed owing to the capital structure change?
    3. By what percent has the cost of common equity changed owing to the capital structure change?
    4. What will be the composite cost of capital after the capital structure change?

15–12. (*Capital Structure Theory*) South Bend Auto Parts has an all common equity capital structure. Some financial data for the company are shown below:

> Shares of common stock outstanding = 600,000
> Common stock price, P_0 = $40 per share
> Expected level of EBIT = $4,200,000
> Dividend payout ratio = 100 percent

In answering the following questions, assume that corporate income is not taxed.
  a. Under the present capital structure, what is the total value of the firm?
  b. What is the cost of common equity capital, K_c? What is the composite cost of capital, K_o?
  c. Now, suppose South Bend sells $1 million of long-term debt with an interest rate of 10 percent. The proceeds are used to retire outstanding common stock. According to the

net operating income theory (the independence hypothesis), what will be the firm's cost of common equity after the capital structure change?

1. What will be the dividend per share flowing to the firm's common shareholders?
2. By what percent has the dividend per share changed owing to the capital structure change?
3. By what percent has the cost of common equity changed owing to the capital structure change?
4. What will be the composite cost of capital after the capital structure change?

15–13. (*EBIT–EPS Analysis*) Albany Golf Equipment is analyzing three different financing plans for a newly formed subsidiary. The plans are described below:

Plan A	Plan B	Plan C
Common stock: $100,000	Bonds at 9%: $20,000 Common stock: 80,000	Preferred stock at 9%: $20,000 Common stock: 80,000

In all cases the common stock will be sold to net Albany $10 per share. The subsidiary is expected to generate an average EBIT per year of $22,000. The management of Albany places great emphasis on EPS performance. Income is taxed at a 50 percent rate.

a. Where feasible, find the EBIT indifference levels between the alternatives.
b. Which financing plan do you recommend that Albany pursue?

Self-Test Solutions

SS–1. a. FC = interest + sinking fund

$FC = (\$6,000,000)(.12) + (\$6,000,000/20)$

$FC = \$720,000 + \$300,000 = \underline{\$1,020,000}$

b. $CB_r = CB_0 + NCF_r - FC$

where $CB_0 = \$750,000$
$FC = \$1,020,000$

and

$$NCF_r = \$3,400,000 - \$3,100,000 = \$300,000$$

so

$$CB_r = \$750,000 + \$300,000 - \$1,020,000$$
$$CB_r = \underline{\$30,000}$$

c. We know that the firm has a preference for maintaining a cash balance of $750,000. The joint impact of the recessionary economic environment and the proposed issue of bonds would put the firm's recessionary cash balance (CB_r) at $30,000. Since the firm desires a minimum cash balance of $750,000 ($CB_0$), the data suggest that the proposed bond issue should be postponed.

SS–2. a. Firm Y seems to be using financial leverage to the most appropriate degree. Notice that its price/earnings ratio of 16 times exceeds that of firm X (at 9 times) and firm Z (also at 9 times).

b. The first financial leverage effect refers to the added variability in the earnings per share stream caused by the use of leverage-inducing financial instruments. The second financial leverage effect concerns the level of earnings per share at a specific EBIT associated with a specific capital structure.

Beyond some critical EBIT level, earnings per share will be higher if more leverage is used. Based on the company data provided, the marketplace for financial instruments is weighing the second leverage effect more heavily. Firm Z, therefore, seems to be under-levered (is operating *below* its theoretical leverage capacity).

SS–3 **a.**

Plan A		Plan B
EPS: Less-Levered Plan		**EPS: More-Levered Plan**

$$\frac{(\text{EBIT} - I)(1 - t) - P}{S_A} = \frac{(\text{EBIT} - I)(1 - t) - P}{S_B}$$

$$\frac{(\text{EBIT} = \$140{,}000)(1 - 0.5)}{100{,}000 \ (\text{shares})} = \frac{(\text{EBIT} - \$480{,}000)(1 - 0.5)}{60{,}000 \ (\text{shares})}$$

$$\frac{0.5\,\text{EBIT} - \$70{,}000}{10} = \frac{0.5\,\text{EBIT} - \$240{,}000}{6}$$

$$\text{EBIT} = \underline{\$990{,}000}$$

b. The EBIT–EPS analysis chart for Martin-Bowing is presented in Figure 15–9.

FIGURE 15–9. EBIT–EPS Analysis Chart for Martin-Bowing Company

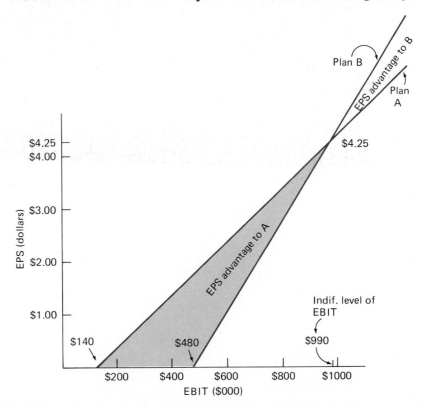

	Plan A	Plan B
EBIT	$990,000	$990,000
I	140,000	480,000
EBT	$850,000	$510,000
T (.5)	425,000	255,000
NI	$425,000	$255,000
P	0	0
EAC	$425,000	$255,000
÷ No. of common shares	100,000	60,000
EPS	$ 4.25	$ 4.25

c. Since $1,188,000 exceeds the calculated indifference level of $990,000, the more highly levered plan (plan B) will produce the higher EPS.

d. At this stage of the problem it is necessary to compute earnings per share (EPS) under each financing alternative. Then the relevant price/earnings ratio for each plan can be applied to project the common stock price for the plan at a specific EBIT level.

	Plan A	Plan B
EBIT	$1,188,000	$1,188,000
I	140,000	480,000
EBT	$1,048,000	$ 708,000
T (.5)	524,000	354,000
NI	$ 524,000	$ 354,000
P	0	0
EAC	$ 524,000	$ 354,000
÷ No. of common shares	100,000	60,000
EPS	$ 5.24	$ 5.90
× P/E ratio	13	11
= Projected stock price	$ 68.12	$ 64.90

Notice that the greater riskiness of plan B results in the market applying a lower price/earnings multiple to the expected EPS. Therefore, the investors would actually enjoy a higher stock price under plan A ($68.12) than they would under plan B ($64.90).

e. Here, we want to find the price/earnings ratio that would equate the common stock prices for both plans at an EBIT level of $1,188,000. All we have to do is take plan B's EPS and relate it to plan A's stock price. Thus:

$$\$5.90 \ (P/E) = \$68.12$$

$$(P/E) = \$68.12/\$5.90 = \underline{11.546}.$$

A price/earnings ratio of 11.546 when applied to plan B's EPS would give the same stock price as that of plan A ($68.12).

Selected References

Altman, Edward I. "Corporate Bankruptcy Potential, Stockholder Returns, and Share Valuation," *Journal of Finance*, 24 (December 1969), 887–900.

Barges, Alexander. *The Effect of Capital Structure on*

the Cost of Capital. Englewood Cliffs, NJ: Prentice-Hall, 1963.

Barnea, Amir, Robert A. Haugen, and Lemma W. Senbet. "Market Imperfections, Agency Problems, and Capital

Structure: A Review," *Financial Management*, 10 (Summer 1981), 7–22.

Baumol, William, and Burton G. Malkiel. "The Firm's Optimal Debt-Equity Combination and the Cost of Capital," *Quarterly Journal of Economics*, 81 (November 1967), 547–78.

Baxter, Nevins D. "Leverage, Risk of Ruin, and the Cost of Capital," *Journal of Finance*, 22 (September 1967), 395–404.

Belkaoui, Ahmed. "A Canadian Survey of Financial Structure," *Financial Management*, 4 (Spring 1975), 74–79.

Bowen, Robert M., Lane A. Daley, and Charles C. Huber, Jr. "Evidence on the Existence and Determinants of Inter-Industry Differences in Leverage," *Financial Management*, 11 (Winter 1982), 10–20.

Brigham, Eugene F., and Myron J. Gordon. "Leverage, Dividend Policy, and the Cost of Capital," *Journal of Finance*, 23 (March 1968), 85–104.

Castanias, Richard. "Bankruptcy Risk and Optimal Capital Structure," *Journal of Finance*, 38 (December 1983), 1617–35.

Collins, J. Markham, and William S. Sekely. "The Relationship of Headquarters Country and Industry Classification to Financial Structure," *Financial Management*, 12 (Autumn 1983), 45–51.

Conine, Thomas E. "Debt Capacity and the Capital Budgeting Decision: A Comment," *Financial Management*, 9 (Spring 1980), 20–22.

Donaldson, Gordon. *Corporate Debt Capacity*. Boston: Division of Research, Graduate School of Business Administration, Harvard University, 1961.

––––––. "New Framework for Corporate Debt Policy," *Harvard Business Review*, 40 (March–April 1962), 117–31.

––––––. "Strategy for Financial Emergencies," *Harvard Business Review*, 47 (November–December 1969), 67–79.

––––––. *Strategy for Financial Mobility*. Boston: Division of Research, Graduate School of Business Administration, Harvard University, 1969.

Durand, David. "Costs of Debt and Equity Funds for Business: Trends and Problems of Measurement,' *Conference on Research in Business Finance*. New York: National Bureau of Economic Research, 1952 215–47.

Ellis, Charles D. "New Framework for Analyzing Capital Structure," *Financial Executive*, 37 (April 1969), 75–86.

Ferri, Michael G., and Wesley H. Jones. "Determinants of Financial Structure: A New Methodological Approach," *Journal of Finance*, 34 (June 1979), 631–44.

Green, Richard C., and Eli Talmor. "Asset Substitution and the Agency Costs of Debt Financing," *Journal of Banking and Finance*, 10 (October 1986), 391–99.

Greenfield, Robert L., Maury R. Randall, and John C. Woods. "Financial Leverage and Use of the Net Present Value Criterion," *Financial Management*, 12 (Autumn 1983), 40–44.

Hamada, Robert S. "The Effect of the Firm's Capital Structure on the Systematic Risk of Common Stocks," *Journal of Finance*, 27 (May 1972), 435–52.

Harris, John M., Jr., Rodney L. Roenfeldt, and Philip L. Cooley. "Evidence of Financial Leverage Clienteles," *Journal of Finance*, 38 (September 1983), 1125–32.

Haugen, Robert A., and Lemma W. Senbet. "The Insignificance of Bankruptcy Costs to the Theory of Optimal Capital Structure," *Journal of Finance*, 33 (May 1978), 383–93.

Hong, Hai, and Alfred Rappaport. "Debt Capacity, Optimal Capital Structure, and Capital Budgeting," *Financial Management*, 7 (Autumn 1978), 7–11.

Jalilvand, Abolhassan, and Robert S. Harris. "Corporate Behavior in Adjusting to Capital Structure and Dividend Targets: An Econometric Study," *Journal of Finance*, 39 (March 1984), 127–45.

Jensen, Michael C., and William E. Meckling. "Theory of the Firm: Managerial Behavior, Agency Costs and Ownership Structure," *Journal of Financial Economics*, 3 (October 1976), 305–60.

Joseph, Frederick. (Reported by Marvin A. Chatinover.) "Why Capital Structure May Never Be the Same Again—And Shouldn't Be," *FE*, 2 (October 1986), 24–29.

Kane, Alex, Alan J. Marcus, and Robert L. McDonald. "Debt Policy and the Rate of Return Premium to Leverage," *Journal of Financial and Quantitative Analysis*, 20 (December 1985), 479–99.

Kim, E. Han. "A Mean-Variance Theory of Optimal Financial Structure and Corporate Debt Capacity," *Journal of Finance*, 33 (March 1978), 45–64.

––––––. "Miller's Equilibrium, Shareholder Leverage Clienteles, and Optimal Capital Structure," *Journal of Finance*, 37 (May 1982), 301–19.

Lewellen, Wilbur G. *The Cost of Capital*. Dubuque, IA: Kendall/Hunt Publishing Company, 1976.

————, and Douglas R. Emery. "Corporate Debt Management and the Value of the Firm," *Journal of Financial and Quantitative Analysis*, 21 (December 1986), 415–26.

Litzenberger, Robert H. "Some Observations on Capital Structure and the Impact of Recent Recapitalizations on Share Prices," *Journal of Financial and Quantitative Analysis*, 21 (March 1986), 59–71.

Marsh, Paul. "The Choice between Equity and Debt: An Empirical Study," *Journal of Finance*, 37 (March 1982), 121–44.

Martin, John D., and David F. Scott, Jr. "A Discriminant Analysis of the Corporate Debt-Equity Decision," *Financial Management*, 3 (Winter 1974), 71–79.

————. "Debt Capacity and the Capital Budgeting Decision," *Financial Management*, 5 (Summer 1976), 7–14.

————. "Debt Capacity and the Capital Budgeting Decision: A Revisitation," *Financial Management*, 9 (Spring 1980), 23–26.

Melnyk, Z. Lew. "Cost of Capital as a Function of Financial Leverage," *Decision Sciences*, 1 (July–October 1970), 327–56.

Miller, Merton H. "Debt and Taxes," *Journal of Finance*, 32 (May 1977), 261–75.

Modigliani, Franco, and Merton H. Miller. "The Cost of Capital, Corporation Finance and the Theory of Investment," *American Economic Review*, 48 (June 1958), 261–97.

————. "Corporate Income Taxes and the Cost of Capital: A Correction," *American Economic Review*, 53 (June 1963), 433–43.

Myers, Stewart C. "Determinants of Corporate Borrowing," *Journal of Financial Economics*, 5 (1977), 147–75.

Park, Sang Young, and Joseph Williams. "Taxes, Capital Structure, and Bond Clienteles," *Journal of Business*, 58 (April 1985), 203–24.

Piper, Thomas R., and Wolf A. Weinhold. "How Much Debt Is Right for Your Company?" *Harvard Business Review*, 60 (July–August 1982), 106–14.

Pringle, John J. "Price/Earnings Ratios, Earnings per Share, and Financial Management," *Financial Management*, 2 (Spring 1973), 34–40.

Rogers, Ronald C., and James E. Owens. "Equity for Debt Exchanges and Stockholder Wealth," *Financial Management*, 14 (Autumn 1985), 18–26.

Schall, Lawrence D. "Firm Financial Structure and Investment," *Journal of Financial and Quantitative Analysis*, 6 (June 1971), 925–42.

Schwartz, Eli, and J. Richard Aronson. "Some Surrogate Evidence in Support of the Concept of Optimal Capital Structure," *Journal of Finance*, 22 (March 1967), 10–18.

Scott, David F., Jr. "Evidence on the Importance of Financial Structure," *Financial Management*, 1 (Summer 1972), 45–50.

————, and Dana J. Johnson. "Financing Policies and Practices in Large Corporations," *Financial Management*, 11 (Summer 1982), 51–59.

————, and John D. Martin. "Industry Influence on Financial Structure," *Financial Management*, 4 (Spring 1975), 67–73.

Scott, James H., Jr. "A Theory of Optimal Capital Structure," *Bell Journal of Economics*, 7 (Spring 1976), 33–54.

Senbet, Lemma A., and Robert A. Taggart, Jr. "Capital Structure Equilibrium under Market Imperfections and Incompleteness," *Journal of Finance*, 39 (March 1984), 93–103.

Shrieves, Ronald E., and Mary M. Pashley. "Evidence on the Association Between Mergers and Capital Structure," *Financial Management*, 13 (Autumn 1984), 39–48.

Solomon, Ezra. "Leverage and the Cost of Capital," *Journal of Finance*, 18 (May 1963), 273–79.

————. *The Theory of Financial Management*. New York: Columbia University Press, 1963.

Stulz, René M., and Herb Johnson. "An Analysis of Secured Debt," *Journal of Financial Economics*, 14 (December 1985), 501–21.

Taggart, Robert A. "Corporate Financing: Too Much Debt?" *Financial Analysts Journal*, 41 (May–June 1986), 35–42.

————. "Capital Budgeting and the Financing Decision: An Exposition," *Financial Management*, 6 (Summer 1977), 59–64.

Titman, Sheridan. "The Effect of Forward Markets on the Debt-Equity Mix of Investor Portfolios and the Optimal Capital Structure of Firms," *Journal of Financial and Quantatitive Analysis*, 20 (March 1985), 19–27.

Walsh, Francis J., Jr. *Planning Corporate Capital Structures*. New York: The Conference Board, 1972.

Zechner, Josef, and Peter Swoboda. "The Critical Implicit Tax Rate and Capital Structure," *Journal of Banking and Finance*, 10 (October 1986), 327–41.

16

Dividend Policy and Internal Financing

From the very beginning of our studies, we have maintained that maximizing the value (price) of the firm's common stock is the appropriate goal in financial decision making. The "success" or "failure" of a management decision should be judged by its impact on the common stock price. We observed that the company's investment (Chapters 6, 7, 10, and 11) and financing decisions (Chapters 8, 13, 14, and 15) can increase the value of the firm. As we approach the firm's *dividend* and *internal financing* policies, we return to the same basic question: Can management influence the price of the firm's stock, in this case by the use of dividends? Toward that end, we have set six objectives for this chapter:

1. Study the relationship between a corporation's dividend policy and the market price of its common stock. Extensive controversy has developed on this issue, with the key question being, "Can dividend policy affect the value investors place upon a company's stock?" Consequently, we look at the basis for the relationship between dividend policy and the market price of the stock.
2. Present practical considerations that should be evaluated in establishing the firm's dividend policy.
3. Review the types of dividend policy frequently used by corporations.
4. Study the procedures followed by a company in administering the dividend payment.
5. Examine the use of noncash dividends (stock dividends and stock splits).
6. Examine the use of stock repurchases.

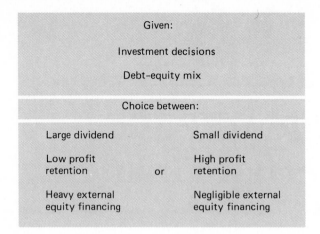

FIGURE 16–1. Dividend-Retention-Financing Tradeoffs

KEY TERMS

Before taking up the particular issues relating to dividend policy, we must understand several key terms and interrelationships.

A firm's dividend policy includes two basic characteristics. First, the **dividend payout ratio** indicates the amount of dividends paid relative to the company's earnings. For instance, if the dividend per share is $2 and the earnings per share is $4, the payout ratio is 50 percent ($2 ÷ $4). A second feature of a firm's dividend policy relates to the *stability* of the dividends over time. As will be observed later in the chapter, dividend stability may be almost as important to the investor as the amount of dividends received.

Assuming that management has already decided how much to invest and the debt-equity mix to be used in financing these investments, the decision to pay a large dividend involves a simultaneous decision to retain little, if any, profits, which results in heavy reliance on external equity financing. On the other hand, given the firm's investment and financing decisions, a small dividend payment is equivalent to high profit retention with less need for externally generated equity funds. These tradeoffs, which are fundamental to our discussion, are presented in Figure 16–1.

DOES DIVIDEND POLICY AFFECT STOCK PRICE?[1]

The fundamental question to be resolved in our study of the firm's dividend policy may be stated simply: "What is a sound rationale or motivation for dividend payments?" If we believe our objective should be to maximize the value of the common stock, we may restate the question as follows: "Given the firm's capital-budgeting and borrow-

---

[1] The concepts of this section draw heavily from Donald H. Chew, Jr. (editor), *Six Roundtable Discussions of Corporate Finance*, "Do Dividends Matter?: A Discussion of Corporate Dividend Policy," pp. 67–101; and a book of readings edited by Joel M. Stern and Donald H. Chew, Jr., *The Revolution in Corporate Finance*, New York: Basil Blackwell, 1986. Specific readings included. Merton Miller, "Can Management Use Dividends to Influence the Value of the Firm?" pp. 299–305; Richard Brealey, "Does Dividend Policy Matter?" pp. 304–309; and Michael Rozeff, "How Companies Set Their Dividend Payout Ratios," pp. 320–26.

ing decisions, what is the impact of the firm's dividend policies on the stock price?" Even more specifically: "Does a high dividend payment decrease stock value, increase it, or make no real difference?"

The answer to such a question may appear self-evident. At first glance, we might reasonably conclude that a firm's dividend policy is important. We have already (Chapter 12) defined the value of a stock to be equal to the present value of future dividends. How could we now say that dividends are not important? Besides, if dividends were not important, why would so many companies pay dividends, and why would a page in the *Wall Street Journal* be devoted to dividend announcements? Based upon intuition, we could quickly conclude that dividend policy is important. However, we might be surprised to learn that the dividend question has been a controversial issue for well over two decades. It has even been called the "dividend puzzle."[2]

Three Basic Views

Some would argue that the amount of the dividend is irrelevant, and any time spent on the decision is a waste of energy. Others contend that a high dividend will result in a high stock price. Still others take the view that dividends actually hurt the stock value. Let us look at these three views in turn.

View 1: Dividend Policy Is Irrelevant

Much of the controversy about the dividend issue has been the result of a significant element within the academic community maintaining that dividends may not matter. If you were a seasoned finance practitioner with years of experience, you might well argue that your experience tells you that dividend announcements result in stock price changes. How then can a professor, supposedly a person of trust and one whose sole mission in life is the search for truth and goodness, even suggest that dividends might not be of any significance? The proponent for dividend irrelevance, however, would argue that the difference in opinion comes from a failure to define carefully what we mean by dividend policy and that while dividends appear to be important, the appearance may be an illusion.[3]

The position that dividends are not important rests on two preconditions. First, we assume that investment and borrowing decisions have already been made, and that these decisions will not be altered by the amount of any dividend payments. Second, "perfect" capital markets are assumed to exist, which means that (1) investors can buy and sell stocks without incurring any transaction costs, such as brokerage commissions; (2) companies can issue stocks without any cost of doing so; (3) there are no corporate or personal taxes; (4) total information about the firm is readily available, so that investors need not consider any announcements about forthcoming dividend payments to be important "news" regarding the company's financial condition; and (5) there are no conflicts of interest between managements and stockholders.

The first assumption that we have already made the investment and financing decisions simply keeps us from confusing the issues. We want to know the effect of dividend decisions on a stand-alone basis, without mixing in other decisions. The second assumption, that of perfect markets, further allows us to study the effect of

---

[2] See Fischer Black "The Dividend Puzzle," *Journal of Portfolio Management*, 2 (Winter 1976), 5–8.

[3] For an excellent presentation of this issue, see Merton Miller, "Can Management Use Dividends to Influence the Value of the Firm?" *The Revolution in Corporate Finance*, edited by Joel M. Stern and Donald H. Chew, Jr., New York: Basil Blackwell, 1986, pp. 209–305.

dividend decisions in isolation, much like a physicist studies motion in a vacuum to avoid the influence of friction.

Given the above assumptions, the effect of a dividend decision on share price may be stated unequivocally: There is no relationship between dividend policy and stock value. One dividend policy is as good as another one. In this setting, the investor in the aggregate is concerned only with *total* returns, which come from investment decisions; they are indifferent whether these returns come from capital gains or dividend income. They also recognize that the dividend decision, given the investment policy, is really a choice of financing strategy. The firm may choose to finance its growth by issuing stock, allowing internally generated funds (profits) to be used to pay dividends; or it may use internally generated funds to finance its growth, paying less dividends, but not have to issue stock. In the first case, we receive dividend income. In the second instance, the value of the stock should increase, providing unrealized capital gains to investors. Total returns should be about equal in either case, the only difference being the nature of the return. Thus, to argue that paying dividends can make shareholders better off is to argue that paying out cash with one hand and taking it back with the other hand is a worthwhile activity for management.

The firm's dividend payout could affect stock price if the shareholder has no other way to receive income from the investment. However, as long as there are efficient capital markets, a stockholder who needs current income could always sell shares. If the firm pays a dividend, the investor could eliminate any dividend received, in whole or in part, by using the dividend to purchase stock. The investor can thus personally create any desired dividend stream, no matter what dividend policy is chosen by management. The dividend policy is therefore an inconsequential activity for management.

An Example of Dividend Irrelevance   To demonstrate the argument that dividends may not matter, come to the Land of Ez (pronounced "ease"), where the environment is quite simple. First, the king, being a kind soul, has imposed *no income taxes* on his subjects. Second, investors can buy and sell securities without paying any *sales commissions*. In addition, when a company issues new securities (stocks or bonds), there are no *flotation costs*. Furthermore, the Land of Ez is completely computerized, so that all information about firms is *instantaneously available* to the public at *no cost*. Next, all investors realize that the value of a company is a function of its investment opportunities and its financing decisions. Therefore, the dividend policy offers *no new information* about either the firm's ability to generate earnings or the riskiness of its earnings. Finally, all firms are owned and managed by the same parties; thus, we have no potential conflict between owners and managers. To summarize, in the Land of Ez:

1. There is no income tax on the investor's income nor is there a tax on gains realized from holding shares of common stock.
2. Security markets are considered to be perfect:
   a.   The investors incur no brokerage commissions.
   b.   Firms can issue securities at no cost.
   c.   Information is free and equally available to all investors.

d. A particular dividend policy has no effect in determining the firm's capability to generate profits.

e. Security prices equal the present value of the expected future cash flows accruing to their owners.

f. There is no possible conflict between owners and managers, since they are the same.

Within this financial utopia, would a change in a corporation's dividend stream have any effect upon the price of the firm's stock? The answer is "No." The foregoing assumptions result in the dividend policy being irrelevant in terms of its impact on the firm's common stock price. To illustrate, consider Dowell Venture, Inc., a corporation that received a charter at the end of 1987 to conduct business in the Land of Ez. The firm is to be financed by common stock only. Its life is to extend for only two years (1988 and 1989), at which time it will be liquidated.

The balance sheet at the time of Dowell Venture's formation, as well as the projected cash flows from the short-term venture, are presented in Table 16–1. The anticipated cash flows are based upon an expected return on investment of 20 percent, which is exactly what the common shareholders require as a rate of return on their investment in the firm's stock.

At the end of 1988 an additional investment of $300,000 will be required, which may be financed by (1) retaining $300,000 of the 1988 profits or (2) issuing new common stock or (3) some combination of both of these. In fact, two dividend plans for 1988 are under consideration. The investors would receive either $100,000 or $250,000 in dividends. If $250,000 is paid out of 1988's $400,000 in earnings, the company would be required to issue $150,000 in new stock to make up the difference in the total amount of funds needed of $300,000 and the $150,000 that is retained. These two dividend plans and the corresponding new stock issue are depicted in Table 16–2. Our objective in analyzing the data is to answer this question: Which dividend plan is preferable to the investors? In answering this question, we must take three steps: (1) Calculate the amount and timing of the dividend stream for the *original* investors. (2) Determine the present value of the dividend stream for each dividend plan. (3) Select the dividend alternative providing the higher value to the investors.

TABLE 16–1. Dowell Venture, Inc. Financial Data

	December 31, 1987
Total assets	$2,000,000
Common stock (100,000 shares)	$2,000,000

	1988	1989
Projected cash available from operations for paying DIVIDENDS or for REINVESTING	$400,000	$460,000

TABLE 16–2. Dowell Venture, Inc. 1988 Proposed Dividend Plans

	Plan 1	Plan 2
Internally generated cash flow	$400,000	$400,000
Dividend for 1988	100,000	250,000
Cash available for reinvestment	$300,000	$150,000
Amount of investment in 1988	300,000	300,000
Additional external financing required	$ 0	$150,000

STEP 1: Computing the Dividend Streams. *The first step in this process is presented in Table 16–3. The dividends in 1988 (line 1, Table 16–3) are readily apparent from the data in Table 16–2. However, the amount of the dividend to be paid to the present shareholders in 1989 has to be calculated. In doing so, we assume that investors receive (1) their original investments (line 2, Table 16–3), (2) any funds retained within the business in 1988 (line 3, Table 16–3), and (3) the profits for 1989 (line 4, Table 16–3). However, if additional stockholders invest in the company, as with plan 2, the dividends to be paid to these investors must be subtracted from the total available dividends (line 6, Table 16–3). The remaining dividends (line 7, Table 16–3) represent the amount to be received in 1989 by the current stockholders. Therefore, the amounts of the dividend may be summarized as follows:*

Dividend Plan	Year 1	Year 2
1	$1.00	$27.60
2	2.50	25.80

STEP 2: Determining the Present Value of the Cash Flow Streams. *For each of the dividend payment streams the resulting common stock value is:*

$$\text{stock price (plan 1)} = \frac{\$1.00}{(1 + .20)} + \frac{\$27.60}{(1 + .20)^2} = \$20$$

$$\text{stock price (plan 2)} = \frac{\$2.50}{(1 + .20)} + \frac{\$25.80}{(1 + .20)^2} = \$20$$

Therefore, the two approaches provide the same end product; that is, the market price of Dowell Venture's common stock is $20 regardless of the dividend policy chosen.

STEP 3: Select the Best Dividend Plan. *If the objective is to maximize the shareholders' wealth, either plan is equally acceptable. Alternatively, shifting the dividend payments between years by changing the dividend policy does not affect the value of the security. Thus, only if investments are made with expected returns exceeding 20 percent will the value of the stock increase. In other words, the only wealth-creating activity in the Land of Ez, where companies are financed entirely by equity, is the management's investment decisions.*

TABLE 16–3. Dowell Venture, Inc. Step 1—Measurement of the Proposed Dividend Streams

	Plan 1		Plan 2	
	Total Amount	Amount Per Share[a]	Total Amount	Amount Per Share[a]
Year 1 (1988)				
(1) Dividend	$ 100,000	$1.00	$ 250,000	$2.50
Year 2 (1989)				
Total dividend consisting of:				
(2) Original investment:				
(a) Old investors	$2,000,000		$2,000,000	
(b) New investors	0		150,000	
(3) Retained earnings	300,000		150,000	
(4) Profits for 1989	460,000		460,000	
(5) Total dividend to all investors in 1989	$2,760,000		$2,760,000	
(6)				
Less dividends to new investors:				
(a) Original investment	0		(150,000)	
(b) Profits for new investors (20% of $150,000 investment)	0		(30,000)	
(7) Liquidating dividends available to original investors in 1989	$2,760,000	$27.60	$2,580,000	$25.80

[a] Number of original shares outstanding equals 100,000.

View 2: High Dividends Increase Stock Value

The belief that a firm's dividend policy is unimportant implicitly assumes that an investor should use the same required rate of return, whether income comes through capital gains or through dividends. However, dividends are more predictable than capital gains; management can control dividends, but it cannot dictate the price of the stock. Investors are less certain of receiving income from capital gains than from dividend income. The incremental risk associated with capital gains relative to dividend income should therefore cause us to use a higher required rate in discounting a dollar of capital gains than the rate used for discounting a dollar of dividends. In other words, we would value a dollar of expected dividends more highly than a dollar of expected capital gains. We might, for example, require a 14 percent rate of return for a stock where we expect all the return to come in the form of dividends, but a 20 percent return for a high-growth stock that pays no dividend. In so doing, we would give a higher value to the dividend income than we would to the capital gains. This view, which says dividends are more certain than capital gains, has been called the "bird-in-the-hand" theory.

The position that dividends are less risky than capital gains, and should therefore be valued differently, is not without its critics. If we hold to our basic decision not to let the firm's dividend policy influence its investment and capital-mix decisions, the company's operating cash flows, both in expected amount and variability, are unaffected by its dividend policy. Since the dividend policy has no impact on the volatility of the company's overall cash flows, it has no impact on the riskiness of the firm.

Increasing a firm's dividend does not reduce the basic riskiness of the stock; rather, if a dividend payment requires management to issue new stock, it only transfers risk *and* ownership from the current owners to new owners. We would have to acknowledge that the current investors who receive the dividend trade an uncertain capital gain for a "safe" asset (the cash dividend). However, if risk reduction is the goal, the investor should have kept the money in the bank and not bought the stock in the first place.

We might find fault with this "bird-in-the-hand" theory, but there is still a strong perception among many investors and professional investment advisors that dividends are important. They frequently argue their case based upon their own personal experience. Typical of such dividend advocates is John Childs, an investment advisor at Kidder Peabody, who says:

> In advising companies on dividend policy, we're absolutely sure on one side that the investors in companies like the utilities and the suburban banks want dividends. We're absolutely sure on the other side that . . . the high-technology companies should have no dividends. For the high earners—the ones that have a high rate of return like 20 percent, or more than their cost of capital—we think they should have a low payout ratio. We think a typical industrial company which earns its cost of capital—just earns its cost of capital—probably should be in the average [dividend payout] range of 40 to 50 percent.[4]

View 3: Low Dividends Increase Stock Value

The third view of how dividends affect stock price proposes that dividends actually hurt the investor. This argument has largely been based on the difference in tax treatment for dividend income and capital gains. Unlike the investors in the great Land of Ez, most other investors do pay income taxes. For these taxpayers, the objective is to maximize the after-tax return on investment relative to the risk being assumed. This objective is realized by *minimizing* the effective tax rate on the income and whenever possible by *deferring* the payment of taxes.

Until 1987, the effective tax rate on the gain from the sale of stock was usually only 40 percent of the tax on dividend income, assuming the investor was subject to taxes. Effective January 1, 1987, federal tax law eliminated the special tax treatment given capital gains so that such gains are now taxed at the same rates as dividend income.

While the relative tax-rate advantage available for capital gains no longer exists, a distinct benefit still remains for capital gains vis-à-vis dividend income. Taxes on dividend income are paid when the dividend is received, while taxes on price appreciation (capital gains) are deferred until the stock is actually sold. Thus, when it comes to tax considerations, most investors will still prefer the retention of a firm's earnings as opposed to the payment of cash dividends. If earnings are retained within the firm the stock price increases, but the increase is not taxed until the stock is sold.

Although the majority of investors are subject to taxes, certain investment companies, trusts, and pension plans are exempt on their dividend income. Also, for tax purposes a corporation may exclude 80 percent of the dividend income received from another corporation. In these cases, investors may prefer dividends over capital gains.

---

[4] Donald H. Chew, "A Discussion of Corporate Dividend Policy," *Six Roundtable Discussions of Corporate Finance with Joel Stern*, New York: Quorum Books, 1986, pp. 83–84.

To summarize, when it comes to taxes, we want to maximize our *after*-tax return, as opposed to the *before*-tax return. Even though there is no longer the opportunity for most investors to be taxed at a reduced capital gains tax rate, they will still try to defer taxes whenever possible. Stocks that allow us to defer taxes (low dividends–high capital gains) will possibly sell at a premium relative to stocks that require us to pay taxes currently (high dividends–low capital gains). Only then will the two stocks provide comparable after-tax returns. This suggests that a policy of paying low dividends will result in a higher stock price. That is, high dividends hurt investors, while low dividends and high retention help investors. This is the logic of advocates of the low-dividend policy.

Improving Our Thinking

We have now looked at three views as to the "right" dividend policy. Which is right? The argument that dividends are irrelevant is difficult to refute, given the perfect market assumptions. However, in the real world, it is not always easy to feel comfortable with such an argument. On the other hand, the high-dividend philosophy, which measures risk by how we split the firm's cash flows between dividends and retention, is not particularly appealing when studied carefully. The third view, which is essentially a tax argument against high dividends, is persuasive, particularly when capital gains were taxed at lower rates than dividend income. Even today, when the preferential tax rate for capital gains no longer exists, its "deferral advantage" is still alive and well. Thus, the tax advantage of capital gains is real by allowing the deferment of taxes. However, if low dividends are so advantageous and generous dividends are so hurtful, why do companies continue to pay dividends? It is difficult to believe that managers would forego such an easy opportunity to benefit their stockholders. What are we missing?

The need to find the missing elements in our "dividend puzzle" has not been ignored. When an issue or phenomenon needs to be better understood, we have two options: improving our thinking and/or gathering more evidence about the topic. Both approaches have been taken to gain an understanding of the relevance of dividends. Careful thought has been given to finding the answers. While no single definitive answer has yet been found that is acceptable to all, a number of plausible extensions have been developed. Several of the more popular additions include: (1) the residual dividend theory, (2) the clientele effect, (3) information effects, (4) agency costs, and (5) expectations theory.

The Residual Dividend Theory

Within the Land of Ez, companies were blessed with professional consultants who were essentially charitable in nature; they did not seek any compensation when they helped a firm through the process of issuing stock. (Even in the Land of Ez, managers needed help from investment bankers, accountants, and attorneys to sell a new issue.) However, the process is in reality quite expensive, and may cost as much as 20 percent of the dollar issue size.[5]

If a company incurs flotation costs, they may have a direct bearing upon the dividend decision. Owing to these costs, a firm must issue a larger amount of securities in order to receive the amount required for investment. For example, if $300,000 is needed to finance proposed investments, an amount exceeding the $300,000 will

---

[5] We discuss the costs of issuing securities in Chapter 17.

have to be issued to offset flotation costs incurred in the sale of the new stock issue. This means, very simply, that new equity capital raised through the sale of common stock will be more expensive than capital raised through the retention of earnings.

The effect of flotation costs is to eliminate our indifference between financing by internal capital and by new common stock. Earlier, the company could pay dividends and issue common stock or retain profits. However, where flotation costs exist, internal financing is preferred. The payment of dividends occurs only if profits are not completely used for investment purposes; that is, only when there are "residual earnings" after the financing of new investments. This policy is called the **residual dividend theory.**[6]

With the assumption of no flotation costs removed, the firm's dividend policy would be as follows:

1. Maintain the optimum debt ratio in financing future investments.
2. Accept an investment if the net present value is positive. That is, the expected rate of return exceeds the cost of capital.
3. Finance the equity portion of new investments *first* by internally generated funds. Only after this capital is fully utilized should the firm issue new common shares.
4. If any internally generated funds still remain after making all investments, pay dividends to the investors. However, if all internal capital is needed for financing the equity portion of proposed investments, pay no dividend.

Example Assume that the Krista Corporation finances 40 percent of its investments by debt and the remaining 60 percent by common equity. Two million dollars have been generated from operations and may be used to finance the common equity portion of new investments or to pay common dividends. The firm's management is considering five investment opportunities. The expected rate of return for these investments, along with the firm's weighted marginal cost of capital curve, is presented graphically in Figure 16–2. From the information contained in the figure, we would accept projects A, B, and C, requiring $2.5 million in total financing. Therefore, $1 million in new debt (40% of $2.5 million) would be needed, with common equity providing $1.5 million (60% of $2.5 million). In this instance the dividend payment decision would be to pay $500,000 in dividends, which is the *residual* or remainder of the $2 million internally generated capital.

To illustrate further, consider the dividend decision if project D had also been acceptable. If this investment were added to the firm's portfolio of proposed capital expenditures, then $4 million in new financing would be needed. Debt financing would constitute $1.6 million (40% × $4 million) and common equity would provide the additional $2.4 million (60% × $4 million). Since only $2 million is available internally, $400,000 in new common stock would be issued. The residual available for dividends would be zero, and no dividend would be paid.

---

[6] The residual dividend theory is consistent with the "pecking order" theory of finance as described by Stewart Myers, "The Capital Structure Puzzle," *The Journal of Finance,* July 1984, pp. 575–92.

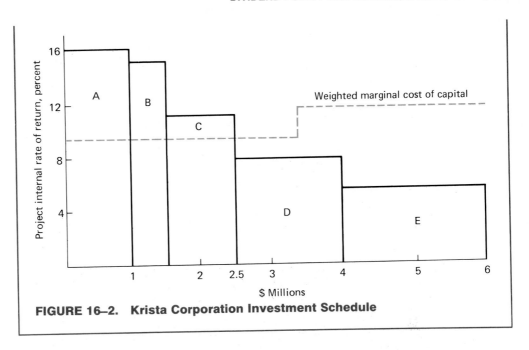

FIGURE 16–2. **Krista Corporation Investment Schedule**

In summary, dividend policy is influenced by (1) the company's investment opportunities, (2) the capital structure mix, and (3) the availability of internally generated capital. In the Krista Corporation example, dividends were paid *only* after all acceptable investments had been financed. This logic, called the residual dividend theory, implies that the dividends to be paid should equal the equity capital *left* after financing investments. According to this theory, dividend policy is a passive influence, having by itself no direct influence on the market price of the common stock.

The Clientele Effect

What if the investors living in the Land of Ez did not like the dividend policy chosen by Dowell's management? No problem. They could simply satisfy their personal income preferences by purchasing or selling securities when the dividends received did not satisfy their current needs for income. If an investor did not view the dividends received in any given year to be sufficient, he or she could simply sell a portion of stock, thereby "creating a dividend." In addition, if the dividend were larger than the investor desired, he or she could purchase stock with the "excess cash" created by the dividend. However, once we leave the Land of Ez, we find that such adjustments in stock ownership are not cost-free. When an investor buys or sells stock, brokerage fees are incurred, ranging from approximately 1 to 10 percent. Even more costly, the investor who buys the stock with cash received from a dividend will have to pay taxes before reinvesting the cash. And when a stock is bought or sold, it must be reevaluated. Acquisition of the information needed to make the decision to buy or sell the stock may be time-consuming and costly. Finally, even forgetting the cost of buying or selling part of the stock, some institutional investors, such as university endowment funds, are precluded from selling stock and "spending" the proceeds. As a result of these considerations, investors may not be too inclined to buy stocks that require them to "create" a dividend stream more suitable to their purposes. Rather, if investors do in fact have a preference between dividends and capital gains, we could expect them to seek firms that have a dividend policy consistent with these preferences. They would, in essence, "sort themselves out" by buying stocks that satisfy their preferences for dividends and/or capital gains. Individuals and institutions that need current income would be drawn to companies that have high dividend payouts. Other investors, such as wealthy individuals, would much prefer to avoid taxes by holding securities that offer no or only small dividend income, but large capital gains. In other words, there would be a **clientele effect:** Firms draw a given clientele, given their stated dividend policy.

The possibility that clienteles of investors exist might lead us to believe that the firm's dividend policy matters. However, unless there is a greater aggregate demand for a particular policy than is being satisfied in the market, dividend policy is still unimportant, in that one policy is as good as the other. The clientele effect only tells us to avoid making capricious changes in a company's dividend policy. Given that the firm's investment decisions are already made, the level of the dividend is still unimportant. The change in the policy matters only when it requires our clientele to shift to another company.

The Information Effect

The investor in the Land of Ez would argue with considerable persuasion that a firm's value is determined strictly by its investment and financing decisions, and that the dividend policy has no impact on value. Yet we know from experience that a large, unexpected change in dividends can have a significant impact on the stock price. For instance, in July 1984 ITT cut its dividend from $.69 to $.25, or a 64 percent decline. Despite management's insistence that the reduction was part of a plan to undertake a new investment program, the market responded to the dividend announcement by the stock price going from $31 to $21.13, a 32 percent decline. Thus, how can we suggest that dividend policy matters little, when we can cite numerous such examples of a change in dividend affecting the stock price, especially when the change is negative?

Despite such "evidence," it is not unreasonable to hypothesize that dividend policy only appears to be important, because we are not looking at the real cause and effect. It may be that investors use a change in dividend policy as a *signal* about the firm's "true" financial condition, especially its earning power. Thus, a dividend increase that is larger than expected "signals" to investors that management expects significantly higher earnings in the future. Conversely, a dividend decrease, or even a less than expected increase, "signals" that management is forecasting less favorable future earnings.

Some would argue that management frequently has inside information about the firm that it cannot make available to investors. This difference in accessibility to information between management and investors, called **information asymmetry,** may result in a lower stock price than would be true if we had conditions of certainty. It is reasoned that by regularly increasing dividends, management is making a commitment to continue these cash flows to the stockholders for the foreseeable future. Recognizing that increasing dividends impinge on management's flexibility, we may implicitly conclude that management is not concealing some negative information about the company. So in a risky marketplace, dividends become a means to minimize any "drag" on the stock price that might come from differences in the level of information available to managers and investors.

Dividends may therefore be important only to the extent that management has no other credible way to inform investors about future earnings, or at least no convincing way that is less costly.

Agency Costs

Let us return again to our dear Land of Ez. We had avoided any potential conflict between the firm's investors and managers by assuming them to be one and the same. With only a cursory look at the marketplace, we can see that managers and investors are typically not the same persons, and as noted in the previous section, these two groups do not have the same access to information about the firm. If the two groups are not the same, we must then assume that management is dedicated to maximizing shareholder wealth.[7] That is, we are making a presupposition that the market values of companies with separate owners and managers will not differ from owner-managed firms.

Two possibilities should help managers see things as the equity investors see them: (1) Low market values may attract takeover bids; and (2) a competitive labor market may allow investors to replace uncooperative managers. That is, if management is not sensitive to the need to maximize shareholder wealth, new investors may buy the stock, take "control" of the firm, and remove management.[8] If current management is being less than supportive of the owners, these owners can always seek other managers who will work in the investors' best interest. If these two market mechanisms worked perfectly without any cost, the potential conflict would be nonexistent. In reality, however, conflicts may still exist, and the stock price of a company owned by investors who are separate from management may be less than the stock value of a closely held firm. The difference in price is the cost of the conflict to the owners, which has come to be called agency costs.[9]

Recognizing the possible problem, management, acting independently or at the insistence of the board of directors, frequently takes action to minimize the cost associated with the separation of ownership and management control. Such action, which in themselves are costly, includes auditing by independent accountants, assigning supervisory functions to the company's board of directors, creating covenants in lending agreements that restrict management's powers, and providing incentive compensation plans for management that help "bond" the management with the owners.

A firm's dividend policy may be perceived by owners as a tool to minimize agency costs. Assuming that the payment of a dividend requires management to issue stock to finance new investments, new investors will be attracted to the company only if management provides convincing information that the capital will be used profitably. Thus, the payment of dividends indirectly results in a closer monitoring of management's investment activities. In this case, dividends may make a meaningful contribution to the value of the firm.

---

[7] This issue was addressed briefly in Chapter 1.

[8] The "corporate control hypothesis," especially as it relates to companies merging or being acquired, has generated a great amount of interest in recent years. For example, see the April 1983 issue of *Journal of Financial Economics*.

[9] See M. C. Jenson, and W. H. Meckling, "Theory of the Firm: Managerial Behavior, Agency Costs, and Ownership Structure," *Journal of Financial Economics*, October 1976, pp. 305–60.

Expectations Theory[10]

A common thread throughout much of our discussion of dividend policy, particularly as it relates to information effects, is the word "expected." We should not overlook the significance of this word when we are making any financial decision within the firm. No matter what the decision area, how the market price responds to management's actions is not determined entirely by the action itself; it is also affected by investor's expectations about the ultimate decision to be made by management.

As the time approaches for management to announce the amount of the next dividend, investors form expectations as to how much that dividend will be. These expectations are based on a number of factors internal to the firm, such as past dividend decisions, current and expected earnings, investment strategies, and financing decisions. They also consider such things as the condition of the general economy, the strength or weakness of the industry at the time, and possible changes in government policies.

When the actual dividend decision is announced, the investor compares the actual decision with the expected decision. If the amount of the dividend is as expected, even if it represents an increase from prior years, the market price of the stock will remain unchanged. However, if the dividend is higher or lower than expected, investors will reassess their perceptions about the firm. They will question the meaning of the *unexpected* change in the dividend. They may use the unexpected dividend decision as a clue about unexpected changes in earnings; that is, the unexpected dividend change has information content about the firm's earnings and other important factors. In short, management's actual decision about the firm's dividend policy may not be terribly significant, unless it departs from investors' expectations. If there is a difference between actual and expected dividends, we will more than likely see a movement in the stock price.

The Empirical Evidence

Our search for an answer to the question of dividend relevance has been less than successful. We have given it our best thinking, but still no single definitive position has emerged. Maybe we could gather evidence to show the relationship between dividend practices and security prices. Then we could truly know that dividend policy is important or that it does not matter.

To test the relationship between dividend payments and security prices, we could compare a firm's dividend yield (dividend/stock price) and the stock's total return, the question being: "Do stocks that pay high dividends provide higher or lower returns to investors? Such tests have been conducted using a variety of the most sophisticated statistical techniques available. Despite the use of these extremely powerful analytical tools, which involve intricate and complicated procedures, the results have been mixed.[11] However, over long periods of time, the results have given a slight advantage

---

[10] Much of the thoughts in this section came from Merton Miller, "Can Management Use Dividends to Influence the Value of the Firm?" in *The Revolution in Corporate Finance*, edited by Joel M. Stern, and Donald H. Chew, Jr., New York: Basil Blackwell, 1986, pp. 299–303.

[11] For some of the more recent studies, see F. Black and M. Scholes, "The Effects of Dividend Yield and Dividend Policy on Common Stock Prices and Returns," *Journal of Financial Economics*, 1 (May 1974), 1–22; P. Hess, "The Ex-Dividend Behavior of Stock Returns: Further Evidence on Tax Effects," *Journal of Finance*, 37 (May 1982), 445–50; R. H. Litzenberger and K. Ramaswamy, "The Effect of Personal Taxes and Dividends on Capital Asset Prices: Theory and Empirical Evidence," *Journal of Financial Economics*, 7 (June 1979), 163–95; and M. H. Miller and M. Scholes, "Dividends and Taxes: Some Empirical Evidence," *Journal of Political Economy*, 90 (1982) 1118–41.

to the low-dividend stocks; that is, stocks that pay lower dividends appear to have higher prices. The findings are far from conclusive, however, owing to the relatively large standard errors of the estimates. The apparent differences may be the result of random sampling error and not real differences. We simply have been unable to disentangle the effect of dividend policy from other influences.

Several reasons may be given for our inability to get conclusive results. First, to be accurate, we would need to know the amount of dividends investors *expected* to receive. Since these expectations cannot be observed, we can only use historical data, which may or may not relate to expectations. Second, most empirical studies have assumed a linear relationship between dividend payments and stock prices. The actual relationship may be nonlinear, possibly even with discontinuities in the relationship. Whatever the reasons, the evidence to date is inconclusive and the vote is still out.

What Are We To Conclude?

We have now looked carefully at the importance of a firm's dividend policy as management seeks to increase the shareholders' wealth. We have gone to great lengths to gain insight and understanding from our best thinking. We have even drawn from the empirical evidence on hand to see what the findings suggest.

The conclusion that should be reached by a reasonable person is certainly not self-evident; nevertheless, management is left with no choice. A dividend policy must be developed, hopefully based on the best available knowledge. While we can give advice only with some reservation, the following conclusions would appear reasonable:

1. As a firm's investment opportunities increase, the dividend payout ratio should decrease. In other words, an inverse relationship should exist between the amount of investments having an expected rate of return that exceeds the cost of capital and the dividends remitted to investors. Owing to the flotation costs associated with raising external capital, the retention of internally generated equity financing is preferable to selling stock in terms of the wealth of the current common shareholders.

2. The firm's dividend policy appears to be important; however, appearances may be deceptive. The real issue may be the firm's *expected* earning power and the riskiness of these earnings. Investors may be using the dividend payment as a source of information about the company's *expected* earnings. Management's actions regarding dividends may carry greater weight than a statement by management that earnings will be increasing.

3. If dividends influence stock price, it probably comes from the investor's desire to minimize and/or defer taxes and from the role of dividends in minimizing agency costs.

4. If the expectations theory has merit, which we believe it does, it behooves management to avoid surprising investors when it comes to the firm's dividend decision. The firm's dividend policy might effectively be treated as a *long-term residual*. Rather than projecting investment requirements for a single year, management could anticipate financing needs for several years. Based upon the expected investment opportunities during the planning horizon, the firm's debt-equity mix, and the funds generated from operations, a *target* dividend payout ratio could be established. If internal funds remained after projection of the

necessary equity financing, dividends would be paid. However, a dividend stream should be planned by which the residual capital would be distributed evenly to investors over the planning period. Conversely, if over the long term the entire amount of internally generated capital is needed for reinvestment in the company, then no dividend should be paid.

THE DIVIDEND DECISION IN PRACTICE

In selecting a dividend policy, management should be aware of the important concepts set forth above. While these concepts do not provide an equation that explains the key relationships, they certainly give us a more complete view of the finance world, which can only help us make better decisions. Other considerations of a more practical nature should also be included as part of the decision about the firm's dividend policy.

Other Practical Considerations

A large number of considerations may influence a firm's decision about its dividends, some of them unique to that company. Some of the more general considerations are given below.

Legal Restrictions

Certain legal restrictions may limit the amount of the dividends a firm may pay. These legal constraints fall into two categories. First, *statutory restrictions* may prevent a company from paying dividends. While specific limitations vary by state, generally a corporation may not pay a dividend (1) if the firm's liabilities exceed its assets; (2) if the amount of the dividend exceeds the accumulated profits (retained earnings); and (3) if the dividend is being paid from capital invested in the firm.

The second type of legal restrictions is unique to each firm and results from restrictions in debt and preferred stock contracts. To minimize their risk, investors frequently impose restrictive provisions upon management as a condition to their investment in the company. These constraints may include the provision that dividends may not be declared prior to the debt being repaid. Also, the corporation may be required to maintain a given amount of working capital. Preferred stockholders may stipulate that common dividends may not be paid when any preferred dividends are delinquent.

Liquidity Position

Contrary to common opinion, the mere fact that a company shows a large amount of retained earnings in the balance sheet does not indicate that cash is available for the payment of dividends. The firm's current position in liquid assets, including cash, is basically independent of the retained earnings account. Historically, a company with sizable retained earnings has been successful in generating cash from operations. Yet these funds are typically either reinvested in the company within a short time period or used to pay maturing debt. Thus, a firm may be extremely profitable and still be *cash poor*. Since dividends are paid with cash, *and not with retained earnings*, the firm must have cash available for dividends to be paid. Hence, the firm's liquidity position has a direct bearing on its ability to pay dividends.

Absence or Lack of Other Sources of Financing

As already noted, a firm may (1) retain profits for investment purposes and/or (2) pay dividends and issue new debt or equity securities to finance investments. For many small or new companies, this second option is not realistic. These firms do not have access to the capital markets, so they must rely more heavily upon internally generated funds. As a consequence, the dividend payout ratio is generally much lower for a small or newly established firm than for a large, publicly owned corporation.

Earnings Predictability

A company's dividend payout ratio depends to some extent upon the predictability of the firm's profits over time. If earnings fluctuate significantly, management cannot rely on internally generated funds to meet future needs. When profits are realized, larger amounts may be retained to ensure that money is available when needed. Conversely, a firm with a stable earnings trend will typically pay a larger portion of its earnings out in dividends. This company has less concern about the availability of profits to meet future capital requirements.

Ownership Control

For many large corporations, control through the ownership of common stock is not an issue. However, for many small and medium-sized companies, maintaining voting control takes a high priority. If the present common shareholders are unable to participate in a new offering, issuing new stock is unattractive, in that the control of the current stockholders is diluted. The owners would prefer that management finance new investments with debt and through profits rather than by issuing new common stock. This firm's growth is then constrained by the amount of debt capital available and by the company's ability to generate profits.

Inflation

In recent years, inflationary pressures have not been a significant problem for either consumers or businesses. However, in the late 1970's, the deterioration of the dollar's purchasing power had a direct impact upon the replacement of fixed assets. Ideally, as these assets became worn and obsolete, the funds generated from depreciation were used to finance the replacements. As the cost of equivalent equipment continued to increase, the depreciation funds were insufficient. This required a greater retention of profits, which implied that dividends had to be adversely affected.

Alternate Dividend Policies

Regardless of a firm's long-term dividend policy, one of several year-to-year dividend payment patterns is generally followed:

1. **Constant dividend payout ratio.** The percentage of earnings paid out in dividends is held constant. Although the dividend-to-earnings ratio is stable with this policy, the dollar amount of the dividend naturally fluctuates from year to year as profits vary.
2. **Stable dollar dividend per share.** This policy maintains a relatively stable dollar dividend over time. An increase in the dollar dividend usually does not occur until management is convinced that the higher dividend level can be maintained in the future. Management also will not reduce the dollar dividend until the evidence clearly indicates that a continuation of the present dividend cannot be supported.
3. **Small, regular dividend plus a year-end extra.** A corporation following this policy pays a small regular dollar dividend plus a year-end *extra dividend* in prosperous years. The extra dividend is declared toward the end of the fiscal year, when the company's profits for the period can be estimated. Management's objective is to avoid the connotation of a permanent dividend. However, this purpose may be defeated if *recurring* "extra" dividends come to be expected

by investors. General Motors is an example of a firm that employs the low stable dividend plus an extra dividend at the end of the year.

Of the three dividend policies, the stable dollar dividend is by far the most common. Figure 16–3 depicts the general tendency of companies to pay stable, but increasing, dividends. This practice is maintained even though the profits fluctuate significantly. In a study by Lintner, corporate managers were found to be reluctant to change the dollar amount of the dividend in response to "temporary" fluctuations in earnings from year to year. This aversion was particularly evident when it came to decreasing

FIGURE 16–3. Corporate Earnings and Dividends

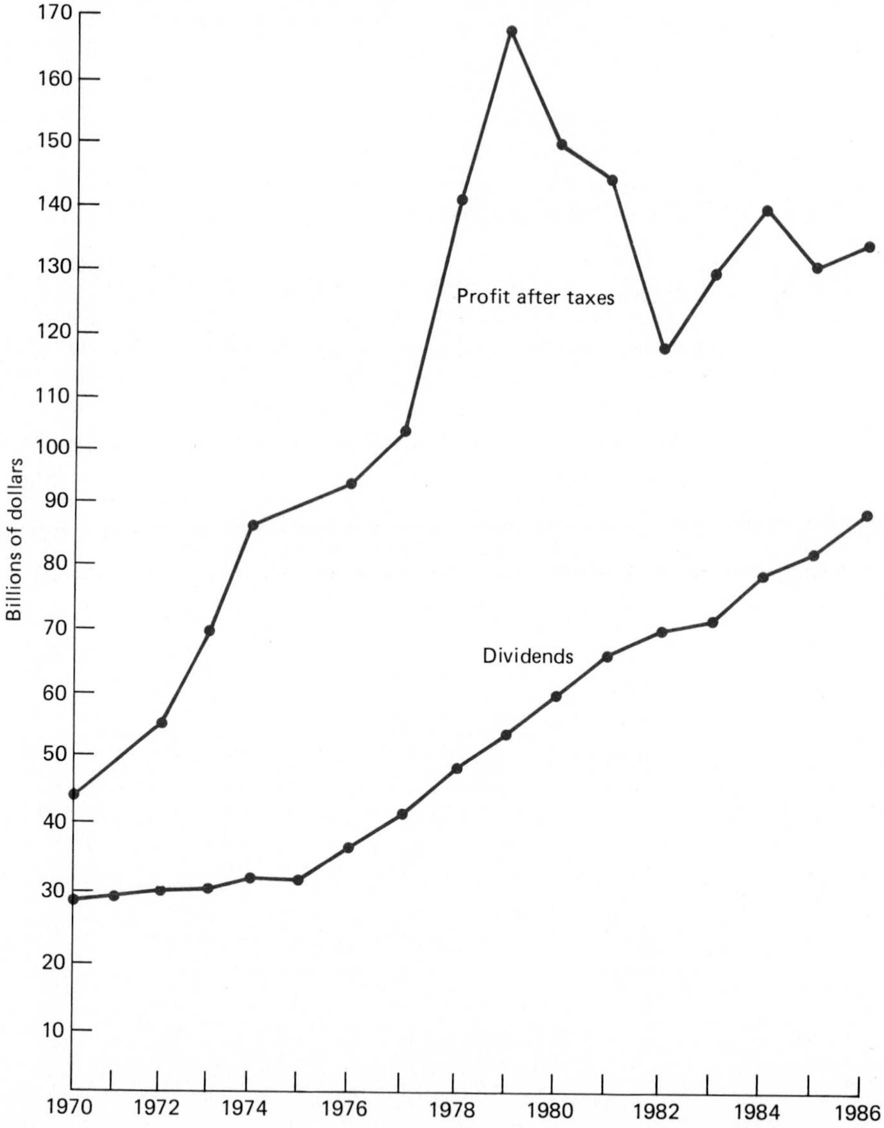

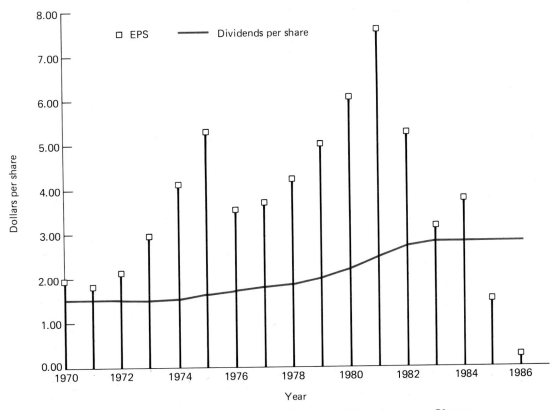

FIGURE 16–4. W. R. Grace & Company: Dividends and Earnings per Share

the amount of the dividend from the previous level.[12] Smith explained this process in terms of his "increasing-stream hypothesis of dividend policy."[13] He proposed that dividend stability is essentially a smoothing of the dividend stream in order to minimize the effect of other types of company reversals. Thus, corporate managers make every effort to avoid a dividend cut, attempting instead to develop a gradually increasing dividend series over the long-term future. However, if a dividend reduction is absolutely necessary, the cut should be large enough to reduce the probability of future cuts.

As an example of a stable dividend policy, Figure 16–4 compares W. R. Grace & Co.'s earnings per share and dividends per share for 1970 through 1986. Ignoring 1985 and 1986, when earnings were exceptionally low, the firm has, on average, paid approximately 54 percent of its earnings out in dividends. This percentage, however, has varied from 31 percent in 1975 to 88 percent in 1983. The historical dividends and earnings patterns for the firm clearly demonstrate management's hesitancy to change dividends in response to short-term fluctuations in earnings. Profits, for the most part, have been decreasing since 1981; however, the dollar dividends have been

---

[12] John Lintner, "Distribution of Income of Corporations among Dividends, Retained Earnings, and Taxes," *American Economic Review*, 46 (May 1956), 97–113.

[13] Keith V. Smith, "Increasing-Stream Hypothesis of Corporate Dividend Policy," *California Management Review*, 15 (Fall 1971), 56–64.

held constant or even increased. On the other hand, when profits rose sharply in 1975 and again in 1981, dividends were increased only slightly.

DIVIDEND PAYMENT PROCEDURES

After the firm's dividend policy has been structured, several procedural details must be arranged. For instance, how frequently are dividend payments to be made? If a stockholder sells the shares during the year, who is entitled to the dividend? To answer these questions, we need to understand the dividend payment procedures.

Generally, companies pay dividends on a quarterly basis. To illustrate, IBM pays $4.40 per share in annual dividends. However, the firm actually issues a $1.10 quarterly dividend for a total yearly dividend of $4.40 ($1.10 × 4 quarters).

The final approval of a dividend payment comes from the board of directors. As an example, Alcoa, on January 9, 1987, announced that holders of record as of February 6 would receive a $.30 dividend. The dividend payment was to be made on February 25. January 9 is the **declaration date**—the date when the dividend is formally declared by the board of directors. The **date of record,** February 6, designates when the stock transfer books are to be closed. Investors shown to own the stock on this date receive the dividend. If a notification of a transfer is recorded subsequent to February 6, the new owner is not entitled to the dividend. However, a problem could develop if the stock were sold on February 5, one day prior to the record date. Time would not permit the sale to be reflected on the stockholder list by the February 6 date of record. To avoid this problem, stock brokerage companies have uniformly decided to terminate the right of ownership to the dividend four working days prior to the record date. This prior date is the **ex-dividend date.** Therefore, any acquirer of the Alcoa stock on February 2 or thereafter does not receive the dividend. Finally, the company mails the dividend check to each investor on February 25, the **payment date.**

STOCK DIVIDENDS AND STOCK SPLITS

An integral part of dividend policy is the use of **stock dividends** and **stock splits.** Both involve issuing new shares of stock on a pro rata basis to the current shareholders, while the firm's assets, its earnings, and the risk being assumed and the investor's percentage ownership in the company remain unchanged. The only *definite* result from either a stock dividend or stock split is the increase in the number of shares of stock outstanding.

To illustrate the effect of a stock dividend, assume that the Katie Corporation has 100,000 shares outstanding.[14] The firm's after-tax profits are $500,000, or $5 in earnings per share. At present, the company's stock is selling at a price/earnings multiple of 10, or $50 per share. Management is planning to issue a 20 percent stock dividend, so that a stockholder owning 10 shares would receive 2 additional shares. We might immediately conclude that this investor is being given an asset (two shares of stock) worth $100; consequently, his personal worth should increase by $100. This conclusion is erroneous. The firm will be issuing 20,000 new shares (100,000 shares × 20 percent).

---

[14] The logic of this illustration is equally applicable to a *stock split.*

Since the $500,000 in after-tax profits do not change, the new earnings per share will be $4.167 ($500,000 ÷ 120,000 shares). If the price/earnings multiple remains at 10, the market price of the stock after the dividend should fall to $41.67 ($4.167 earnings per share × 10). The investor now owns 12 shares worth $41.67, which provides a $500 total value; thus he is neither better nor worse off than before the stock dividend.

This example may make us wonder why a corporation would even bother with a stock dividend or stock split if no one is benefited. However, before we study the rationale for such distributions, we should understand the differences between a stock split and a stock dividend.

Stock Dividend versus Split

The only difference between a stock dividend and a stock split relates to their respective accounting treatment. Stated differently, *there is absolutely no difference on an economic basis between a stock dividend and a stock split.* Both represent a proportionate distribution of additional shares to the present stockholders. However, *for accounting purposes* the stock split has been defined as a stock dividend exceeding 25 percent.[15] Thus, a stock dividend is arbitrarily defined as a distribution of shares up to 25 percent of the number of shares currently outstanding.

The accounting treatment for a stock dividend requires the issuing firm to capitalize the "market value" of the dividend. In other words, the dollar amount of the dividend is transferred from retained earnings to the capital accounts (par and paid-in capital). This procedure may best be explained by an example. Assume that the L. Bernard Corporation is preparing to issue a 15 percent stock dividend. The equity portion of the firm's balance sheet prior to the distribution is presented in Table 16–4. The market price for the stock has been $14. Thus, the 15 percent stock dividend increases the number of shares by 150,000 (1,000,000 shares × 15 percent). The "market value" of this increase is $2,100,000 (150,000 shares × $14 market price). To record this transaction, $2,100,000 would be transferred from retained earnings, resulting in a $300,000 increase in total par value (150,000 shares × $2 par value) and a $1,800,000 increment to paid-in capital. The $1,800,000 is the residual difference between $2,100,000 and $300,000. The revised balance sheet is reflected in Table 16–5.

What if the management of L. Bernard Corporation changed the plan and decided to split the stock two-for-one? In other words, a *100 percent increase* in the number

TABLE 16–4. L. Bernard Corporation Balance Sheet before Stock Dividend

Common stock:	
Par value (1,000,000 shares outstanding; $2 par value)	$ 2,000,000
Paid-in capital	8,000,000
Retained earnings	15,000,000
Total equity	$25,000,000

---

[15] The 25 percent standard applies only to corporations listed on the New York Stock Exchange. The American Institute of Certified Public Accountants states that a stock dividend greater than 20 or 25 percent is for all practical purposes a stock split.

TABLE 16–5. L. Bernard Corporation Balance Sheet after Stock Dividend

Common stock:	
Par value (1,150,000 shares outstanding; $2 par value)	$ 2,300,000
Paid-in capital	9,800,000
Retained earnings	12,900,000
Total equity	$25,000,000

of shares would result. In accounting for the split, the changes to be recorded are (1) the increase in the number of shares and (2) the decrease in the per-share par value from $2 to $1. The dollar amounts of each account do not change. The new balance sheet is shown in Table 16–6.

Thus, for a stock dividend, an amount equal to the market value of the stock dividend is transferred from retained earnings to the capital stock accounts. When stock is split, only the number of shares changes, and the par value of each share is decreased proportionately. Yet, despite this dissimilarity in accounting treatment, we should remember that no real economic difference exists between a split and a dividend.

Rationale for a Stock Dividend or Split

Although *stock* dividends and splits occur far less frequently than *cash* dividends, a significant number of companies choose to use these share distributions either with or in lieu of cash dividends. In view of our earlier conclusion that no economic benefit results, how do corporations justify these distributions?

Proponents of stock dividends and splits frequently maintain that a key benefit is received by the stockholder because the price of the stock will not fall precisely in proportion to the share increase. For a two-for-one split, the price of the stock might not decrease a full 50 percent, leaving the stockholder with a higher total value. Two reasons are given for this disequilibrium. First, many financial executives believe that an optimal price range exists. Within this range the total market value of the common stockholders is thought to be maximized. As the price exceeds this range, fewer investors can purchase the stock, thereby restraining the demand. Consequently, downward pressure is placed on its price. The second explanation relates to the *informational content* of the dividend-split announcement. Stock dividends and splits have generally been associated with companies with growing earnings. The announcement of a stock dividend or split has therefore been perceived as favorable news. The empirical evidence, however, fails to verify these conclusions. Most studies indicate

TABLE 16–6. L. Bernard Corporation Balance Sheet after Stock Split

Common stock:	
Par value (2,000,000 shares outstanding; $1 par value)	$ 2,000,000
Paid-in capital	8,000,000
Retained earnings	15,000,000
Total equity	$25,000,000

that investors are perceptive in identifying the true meaning of a share distribution. If the stock dividend or split is not accompanied by a positive trend in earnings and increases in cash dividends, price increases surrounding the stock dividend or split are insignificant.[16] Therefore, we should be suspicious of the assertion that a stock dividend or split is beneficial in terms of increasing the investors' worth.

A second reason cited for stock dividends or splits is the conservation of corporate cash. If a company is encountering cash problems, it may substitute a stock dividend for a cash dividend. However, as before, investors will probably look beyond the dividend to ascertain the underlying reason for conserving cash. If the stock dividend is an effort to conserve cash for attractive investment opportunities, the shareholder may bid up the stock price. If the move to conserve cash relates to financial difficulties within the firm, the market price will most likely react adversely.

STOCK REPURCHASES

For well over three decades, corporate managements have been active in repurchasing their own equity securities. For instance, in 1963 the total amount spent by firms to reacquire a portion of their common shares exceeded, for the first time, the funds raised through issuing new common stock. The actual number of shares repurchased in this single year approached 27 million, for a dollar commitment of $1.3 billion. Since 1963 the number of shares being repurchased has consistently increased.

A number of reasons have been given for repurchasing stock. Examples of such benefits include:

1. A means for providing an "internal" investment opportunity
2. An approach for modifying the firm's capital structure
3. A favorable impact upon earnings per share
4. The elimination of a particular minority group of stockholders
5. The minimization of a dilution in earnings per share associated with mergers and options
6. The reduction in the firm's costs associated with servicing small stockholders

Also, from the shareholders' perspective, a stock repurchase, as opposed to a cash dividend, has a potential tax advantage.

Share Repurchase as a Dividend Decision

Clearly, the payment of a common stock dividend is the conventional method for distributing a firm's profits to its owners. However, it need not be the only way. Another approach is to repurchase the firm's stock. The concept may best be explained by an example.

---

[16] See James A. Millar and Bruce D. Fielitz, "Stock Split and Stock-Dividend Decisions," *Financial Management,* Winter 1973, pp. 35–45; and Eugene Fama, Lawrence Fisher, Michael Jensen, and Richard Roll, "The Adjustment of Stock prices to New Information," *International Economic Review*, February 1969, pp. 1–21.

Example The Leron Blanks Publishing Company is planning to pay $4 million ($4 per share) in dividends to its common stockholders. The following earnings and market price information is provided for Blank's:

Net income	$7,500,000
Number of shares	1,000,000
Earnings per share	$7.50
Market price per share after dividend payment	$60
Price/earnings ratio	8

In a recent meeting several board members, who are also major stockholders, questioned the need for a dividend payment. They maintain that they do not need the income, so why not allow the firm to retain the funds for future investments? In response, management contends that the available investments are not sufficiently profitable to justify retention of the income. That is, the investors' required rates of return exceed the expected rates of return that could be earned with the additional $4 million in investments.

Since management opposes the idea of retaining the profits for investment purposes, one of the firm's directors has suggested that the $4 million be used to repurchase the company's stock. In this way, the value of the stock should increase. This result may be demonstrated as follows:

1. Assume that shares are repurchased by the firm at the $60 market price (ex-dividend price) plus the contemplated $4 dividend per share, or for $64 per share.
2. Given a $64 price, 62,500 shares would be repurchased ($4 million ÷ $64 price).
3. If net income is not reduced, but the number of shares declines as a result of the share repurchase, earnings per share would increase from $7.50 to $8, computed as follows:

$$\text{Earnings per share} = \text{net income/outstanding shares}$$

$$(\text{before repurchase}) = \$7,500,000/1,000,000$$

$$= \$7.50$$

$$(\text{after repurchase}) = \$7,500,000/(1,000,000 - 62,500)$$

$$= \$8$$

4. Assuming that the price/earnings ratio remains at 8, the new price after the repurchase would be $64, up from $60, where the increase exactly equals the amount of the dividend forgone.

In this example, Blanks Publishing's stockholders are essentially provided the same value, whether a dividend is paid or stock is repurchased. If management pays a dividend, the investor will have a stock valued at $60 plus $4 received from the dividend. On the other hand, if stock is repurchased in lieu of the dividend, the stock will be worth $64. These results were based upon assuming: (1) The stock is being repurchased at the exact $64 price, (2) the $7,500,000 net income is unaffected by the repurchase, and (3) the price/earnings ratio of 8 does not change after the repurchase. Given these assumptions, however, the stock repurchase serves as a perfect substitute for the dividend payment to the stockholders.

The Investor's Choice

Given the choice between a stock repurchase and a dividend payment, which would an investor prefer? In perfect markets, where there are no taxes, no commissions when buying and selling stock, and no informational content assigned to a dividend, the investor would be indifferent between the choices. The investor could create a dividend stream by selling stock when income is needed.

If market imperfections exist, the investor may have a preference between the two methods of distributing the corporate income. For instance, given the opportunity to defer taxes in the case of capital gains, investors may choose the stock repurchase over the dividend income. Although the stock repurchase is advantageous with regard to taxes, the investor may still prefer the dividend approach over a plan to repurchase stock. First, the firm may have to pay too high a price for the repurchased stock, which is to the detriment of the remaining stockholders. If a relatively large number of shares are being bought, the price may be bid up too high, only to fall after the repurchase operation. Second, as a result of the repurchase the market may perceive the riskiness of the corporation as increasing, which would lower the price/earnings ratio and the value of the stock.

Financing or Investment Decision

The repurchase of stock when the firm has excess cash may be regarded as a dividend decision. However, a stock repurchase may also be viewed as a financing decision. By issuing debt and then repurchasing stock, a firm can immediately alter its debt-equity mix toward a higher proportion of debt. In this instance, the concern is not how to distribute cash to the stockholders. Instead, management is using a stock repurchase as a means to change the corporation's capital structure.

In addition to dividend and financing decisions, many managers consider a stock repurchase an investment decision. When equity prices are depressed in the marketplace, management may view the firm's own stock as being materially undervalued and representing a good investment opportunity. While the firm's management may be wise to repurchase stock at unusually low prices, this decision cannot and should not be viewed in the context of an investment decision. Buying its own stock cannot provide expected returns as other investments do. No company can survive, much less prosper, by investing only in its own stock.

The Repurchase Procedure

If management intends to repurchase a block of the firm's outstanding shares, it should make this information public. All investors should be given the opportunity to work with complete information. They should be told the purpose of the repurchase, as well as the method to be used to acquire the stock.

As to the method of repurchase, three options are available. First, the shares could be bought in the *open market*. Here the firm acquires the stock through a stockbroker at the going market price. This approach may place an upward pressure on the stock price until the stock is acquired. Also, commissions must be paid to the stockbrokers as a fee for their services.

The second method is to make a tender offer to the firm's shareholders. A **tender offer** is a formal offer by the company to buy a specified number of shares at a predetermined and stated price. The tender price is set above the current market price in order to attract sellers. A tender offer is best when a relatively large number of shares are to be bought, since the company's intentions are clearly known and each shareholder has the opportunity to sell the stock at the tendered price.

The third and final method for repurchasing stock entails the purchase of the stock from one or more major shareholders. These purchases are made on a *negotiated basis*. Care should be taken to ensure a fair and equitable price. Otherwise the remaining stockholders may be hurt as a result of the sale.

Summary

In determining the firm's dividend policy, the key issue is the dividend payout ratio (the percentage of the earnings paid out in dividends). This decision has an immediate impact upon the firm's financial mix. As the dividend payment is increased, less funds are available internally for financing investments. Consequently, if additional equity capital is needed, the company has to issue new common stock. Keeping this interaction between the level of dividends and financing in mind, management has to determine the *best* dividend policy for the company's investors. However, selection of the most beneficial dividend payment is not easily accomplished. Management cannot apply an equation to resolve the question. We simply have been unable to disentangle the relationship between dividend policy and share price.

In its simplest form, the dividend payment is a *residual* factor. In this context, the dividend equals the remaining internal capital after financing the equity portion of investments. However, this single criterion fails to recognize (1) the tax benefit of capital gains, (2) agency costs, (3) the clientele effect, and (4) the informational content of a given policy. Furthermore, other factors to be considered include the firm's liquidity position, the accessibility to capital markets, inflation, legal restrictions, the stability of earnings, and the desire of investors to maintain control of the company.

Given the firm's investment opportunities, and the imperfections in the market, the financial manager should probably apply the residual dividend theory over the long term. In essence, the firm's investment opportunities are to be projected throughout a multiple-year planning horizon. Given these investment needs, the target debt mix, and the anticipated earnings, the amount of money available to pay dividends for the planning period may be determined. The dividend payments should then be made so that large and unexpected changes in the dividend per share are avoided.

Stock dividends and stock splits have been used by corporations either in lieu of or to supplement cash dividends. At the present, no empirical evidence conclusively identifies a relationship between stock dividends and splits and the market price of the stock. Yet a stock dividend or split could conceivably be used to keep the stock price within an optimal trading range. Also, if the investors perceived that the stock dividend contained favorable information about the firm's operations, the price of the stock could increase.

As an alternative to paying a dividend, management can repurchase stock. This latter approach may have a tax advantage for the stockholder; however, investors may still prefer dividends to a stock repurchase.

Study Questions

16–1.   What is meant by the term *dividend payout ratio?*

16–2.   Explain the tradeoff between retaining internally generated funds and paying cash dividends.

16–3.   a.   What are the assumptions of a perfect market?
         b.   What effect does dividend policy have on the share price in a perfect market?

16–4.   What is the impact of flotation costs on the financing decision?

16–5.   a.   What is the *residual dividend theory?*
         b.   Why is this theory operational only in the long term?

16–6.   Why might investors prefer capital gains to the same amount of dividend income?

16–7.   What legal restrictions may limit the amount of dividends to be paid?

16–8.   How does a firm's liquidity position affect the payment of dividends?

16–9.   How can ownership control constrain the growth of a firm?

16–10. a.   Why is a stable dollar dividend policy popular from the viewpoint of the corporation?
         b.   Is it also popular with investors? Why?

16–11. Explain declaration date, date of record, and ex-dividend date.

16–12. What are the advantages of a stock split or dividend over a cash dividend?

16–13. Why would a firm repurchase its own stock?

Self-Test Problems

ST–1.   (*Dividend Growth Rate*) Schulz, Inc., maintains a constant dividend payout ratio of 35 percent. Earnings per share last year were $8.20 and are expected to grow indefinitely at a rate of 12 percent. What will be the dividend per share this year? In five years?

ST–2.   (*Residual Dividend Theory*) Britton Corporation is considering four investment opportunities. The required investment outlays and expected rates of return for these investments are shown below. The firm's cost of capital is 14 percent. The investments are to be financed by 40 percent debt and 60 percent common equity. Internally generated funds totaling $750,000 are available for reinvestment.
         a.   Which investments should be accepted? According to the residual dividend theory, what amount should be paid out in dividends?
         b.   How would your answer change if the cost of capital were 10 percent?

Investment	Investment Cost	Internal Rates of Return
A	$275,000	17.50%
B	325,000	15.72
C	550,000	14.25
D	400,000	11.65

ST–3.   (*Stock Split*) The debt and equity section of the Robson Corporation balance sheet is shown below. The current market price of the common shares is $20. Reconstruct the financial statement assuming that (a) a 15 percent stock dividend is issued and (b) a two-for-one stock split is declared.

Robson Corporation

Debt	$1,800,000
Common	
Par ($2; 100,000 shares)	200,000
Paid-in capital	400,000
Retained earnings	900,000
	$3,300,000

Study Problems

16–1.   (*Flotation Costs and Issue Size*) Your firm needs to raise $10 million. Assuming that flotation costs are expected to be $15 per share and that the market price of the stock is $120, how many shares would have to be issued? What is the dollar size of the issue?

16–2.   (*Flotation Costs and Issue Size*) If flotation costs for a common stock issue are 18 percent, how large must the issue be so that the firm will net $5,800,000? If the stock sells for $85 per share, how many shares must be issued?

16–3.   (*Residual Dividend Theory*) Terra Cotta finances new investments by 40 percent debt and 60 percent equity. The firm needs $640,000 for financing new investments. If retained earnings equal $400,000, how much money will be available for dividends in accordance with the residual dividend theory?

16–4.   (*Stock Dividend*) RCB has 2 million shares of common stock outstanding. Net income is $550,000, and the P/E ratio for the stock is 10. Management is planning a 20 percent stock dividend. What will be the price of the stock after the stock dividend? If an investor owns 100 shares prior to the stock dividend, does the total value of his or her shares change? Explain.

16–5.   (*Dividends in Perfect Markets*) The management of Harris, Inc., is considering two dividend policies for the years 1986 and 1987, one and two years away. In 1988 the management is planning to liquidate the firm. One plan would pay a dividend of $2.50 in 1986 and 1987 and a liquidating dividend of $45.75 in 1988. The alternative would be to pay out $4.25 in dividends in 1986, $4.75 in dividends in 1987, and a final dividend of $40.66 in 1988. The required rate of return for the common stockholders is 18 percent. Management is concerned about the effect of the two dividend streams on the value of the common stock.
   a.   Assuming perfect markets, what would be the effect?
   b.   What factors in the real world might change your conclusion reached in part (a)?

16–6.   (*Long-term Residual Dividend Policy*) Stetson Manufacturing, Inc. has projected its investment opportunities over a five-year planning horizon. The cost of each year's investment and the amount of internal funds available for reinvestment for that year are given below. The firm's debt-equity mix is 35 percent debt and 65 percent equity. There are currently 100,000 shares of common stock outstanding.
   a.   What would be the dividend each year if the residual dividend theory were used on a year-to-year basis?
   b.   What target stable dividend can Stetson establish by using the long-term residual dividend theory over the future planning horizon?
   c.   Why might a residual dividend policy applied to the 5 years as opposed to individual years be preferable?

Year	Cost of Investments	Internal Funds Available for Reinvestment or for Dividends
1	$350,000	$250,000
2	475,000	450,000
3	200,000	600,000
4	980,000	650,000
5	600,000	390,000

16–7. (*Stock Split*) You own 5 percent of the Trexco Corporation's common stock, which most recently sold for $98 prior to a two-for-one stock split announcement. There are currently (before the split) 25,000 shares of common stock outstanding.

    a. Relative to now, what will be your financial position after the stock split? (Assume the stock price falls proportionately.)

    b. The executive vice-president in charge of finance believes the price will only fall 40 percent after the split because he feels the price is above the optimal price range. If he is correct, what will be your net gain?

16–8. (*Dividend Policies*) The earnings for Crystal Cargo, Inc., have been predicted for the next 5 years and are listed below. There are 1 million shares outstanding. Determine the yearly dividend per share to be paid if the following policies are enacted:

    a. Constant dividend payout ratio of 50 percent.

    b. Stable dollar dividend targeted at 50 percent of the earnings over the 5-year period.

    c. Small, regular dividend of $.50 per share plus a year-end extra when the profits in any year exceed $1,500,000. The year-end extra dividend will equal 50 percent of profits exceeding $1,500,000.

Year	Profits after Taxes
1	$1,400,000
2	2,000,000
3	1,860,000
4	900,000
5	2,800,000

16–9. (*Repurchase of Stock*) The Dunn Corporation is planning to pay dividends of $500,000. There are 250,000 shares outstanding, with an earnings per share of $5. The stock should sell for $50 after the ex-dividend date. If instead of paying a dividend, management decides to repurchase stock:

    a. What should be the repurchase price?

    b. How many shares should be repurchased?

    c. What if the repurchase price is set below or above your suggested price in part (a)?

    d. If you own 100 shares, would you prefer that the company pay the dividend or repurchase stock?

Self-Test Solutions

    SS–1. Dividend per share $= 35\% \times \$8.20$

                       $= \$2.87$

Dividends:

1 year = $2.87 (1 + 0.12)

= $3.21

5 years = $2.87 (1 + 0.12)^5

= $2.87 (1.762)

= $5.06

SS–2.　a.　Investments A, B, and C will be accepted, requiring $1,150,000 in total financing. Therefore, 40 percent of $1,150,000 or $460,000 in new debt will be needed, and common equity will have to provide $690,000. The remainder of the $750,000 internal funds will be $60,000, which will be paid out in dividends.

　　b.　Assuming a 10 percent cost of capital, all four investments would be accepted, requiring total financing of $1,550,000. Equity would provide 60 percent, or $930,000 of the total, which whould not leave any funds to be paid out in dividends. New common would have to be issued.

SS–3.

　　a.　If a 15 percent stock dividend is issued, the financial statement would appear as follows:

Robson Corporation

Debt	$1,800,000
Common	
Par ($2 par, 115,000 shares)	230,000
Paid-in capital	670,000
Retained earnings	600,000
	$3,300,000

　　b.　A two-for-one split would result in a 100 percent increase in the number of shares. Since the total par value remains at $200,000, the new par value per share is $1 ($200,000 ÷ 200,000 shares). The new financial statement would be as follows:

Robson Corporation

Debt	$1,800,000
Common	
Par ($1 par, 200,000 shares)	200,000
Paid-in capital	400,000
Retained earnings	900,000
	$3,300,000

Selected References

Aharony, J., and I. Swary. "Quarterly Dividends and Earnings Announcements and Stockholder's Returns: An Empirical Analysis," *Journal of Finance*, 35 (March 1980), 1–12.

Asquith, Paul, and David Mullins. "The Impact of Initiating Dividend Payments on Shareholders' Wealth," *Journal of Business*, 56 (January 1983), 77–99.

Asquith, Paul, and David Mullins. "Signalling with Dividends, Stock Repurchases, Equity Issues," *Financial Management*, 15 (Autumn 1986), 27–45.

Bhattacharya, Sudipto. "Imperfect Information, Dividend Policy, and 'The Bird in the Hand Fallacy'," *Bell Journal of Economics and Management Science*, 10 (Spring 1979), 259–70.

Black, F. "The Dividend Puzzle," *Journal of Portfolio Management*, 2 (Winter 1976).

Black, F., and M. Scholes. "The Effects of Dividend Yield and Dividend Policy on Common Stock Prices and Returns," *Journal of Financial Economics*, 1 (May 1974), 1–22.

Blume, Marshal E. "Stock Returns and Dividend Yields: Some More Evidence," *Review of Economics and Statistics*, 62 (November 1980), 567–77.

Brickley, James A. "Shareholder Wealth, Information Signalling, and the Specially Designated Dividend: An Empirical Study," *Journal of Financial Economics*, 12 (1983), 287–309.

Dielman, T., and Henry Oppenheimer. "An Examination of Investor Behavior during Periods of Large Dividend Changes," *Journal of Financial and Quantitative Analysis*, 19 (June 1984), 197–216.

Dyl, E. A., and J. R. Hoffmeister. "A Note on Dividend Policy and Beta," *Journal of Business Finance and Accounting*, (Spring 1986), 107–15.

Feldstein, M., and J. Green. "Why Do Companies Pay Dividends?" National Bureau of Economic Research, Conference Paper No. 54, (October, 1980).

Gonedes, N. "Corporate Signaling, External Accounting and Capital Market Equilibrium: Evidence on Dividends, Income, and Extraordinary Items," *Journal of Accounting Research*, (Spring 1978), 26–79.

Grinblatt, M. S., R. W. Masulis, and S. Titman. "The Valuation Effects of Stock Splits and Stock Dividends," *Journal of Financial Economics*, 13 (December 1984), 461–90.

Hakansson, Nils H. "To Pay or Not to Pay Dividends," *Journal of Finance*, 37 (May 1982), 415–28.

Hess, P. "The Ex-Dividend Behavior of Stock Returns: Further Evidence on Tax Effects," *Journal of Finance*, 37 (May 1982), 445–56.

Kalay, A. "Signalling Information Content, and the Reluctance to Cut Dividends," *Journal of Financial and Quantitative Analysis*, (November 1980), 855–69.

Kwan, C. "Efficient Market Tests of the Informational Content of Dividend Announcements: Critique and Extension," *Journal of Financial and Quantitative Analysis*, 16 (June 1981), 193–206.

Lewellen, W., K. Stanley, R. Lease, and G. Schlarbaum. "Some Direct Evidence on the Dividend Clientele Phenomenon," *Journal of Finance*, 33 (December 1978), 1385–99.

Lintner, J. "Distribution of Incomes of Corporations among Dividends, Retained Earnings and Taxes," *American Economic Review*, 46 (May 1956), 97–113.

Litzenberger, R. H., and K. Ramaswamy. "The Effect of Personal Taxes and Dividends on Capital Asset Prices: Theory and Empirical Evidence," *Journal of Financial Economics*, 7 (June 1979), 163–95.

Long, J. B., Jr. "The Market Valuation of Cash Dividends: A Case to Consider," *Journal of Financial Economics*, 6 (June–September 1978), 235–64.

Miller, M. H. "Behavioral Rationality: The Case of Dividends," *Journal of Business*, 59 (October 1986), 5451–68.

Miller, Merton, and Franco Modigliani. "Dividend Policy, Growth, and the Valuation of Shares," *Journal of Business*, 34 (October 1961), 411–33.

———, and M. Scholes. "Dividends and Taxes: Some Empirical Evidence," *Journal of Political Economy*, 90 (1982), 1118–41.

———, and K. Rock. "Dividend Policy under Asymmetric Information," *Journal of Finance*, 40 (September 1985), 1031–51.

Morgan, I. G. "Dividends and Capital Asset Prices," *Journal of Finance*, 37 (September 1982), 1071–86.

Shefrin, H., and M. Statman. "Explaining Investor Preference for Cash Dividends, *Journal of Financial Economics*, 13 (June 1984), 253–82.

Woolridge, J. R. "The Information Content of Dividend Changes," *Journal of Financial Research*, 5 (Fall 1982), 237–47.

———. "Stock Dividends as Signals," *Journal of Financial Research*, 6 (Spring 1983), 1–12.

———. "Dividend Changes and Security Prices," *Journal of Finance*, 38 (December 1983), 1607–15.

17

Raising Funds in the Capital Market

At times internally generated funds will not be sufficient to finance all of the firm's proposed expenditures. In these situations, the corporation may find it necessary to attract large amounts of financial capital externally.[1] The focus of this chapter is on the market environment in which long-term capital is raised. Ensuing chapters discuss the distinguishing features of the instruments by which long-term funds are raised.

Business firms in the nonfinancial corporate sector of the U.S. economy rely heavily on the nation's financial market system in order to raise cash. Table 17–1 displays the relative internal and external sources of funds for such corporations over the 1972–85 period. Notice that the percentage of external funds raised in any given year can vary substantially from that of the previous year. In 1975, for example, the nonfinancial business sector raised 21.2 percent of its funds by external means (in the financial markets). This was a drastic reduction from the 54 percent level of the previous year.

The financial market system must be both organized and resilient. During an economic recession and in its immediate aftermath, interest rates are usually high and stock prices are typically depressed. This induces firms to forgo raising funds via external means. They will rely instead on their own internal generation of cash to finance new capital investments. During periods of recovery and expansion, the opposite situation tends to hold. Stock prices rise and interest rates recede. The cost of external corporate capital is not as high. Firms then turn to the financial markets and raise a greater proportion of their funds externally.

---

[1] By externally, we mean that the funds are "obtained" *other* than through retentions or depreciation. These latter two "sources" are commonly called internally generated funds.

TABLE 17–1. Nonfinancial Corporate Business Sources of Funds: Internal and External

Year	Total Sources ($ billions)	Percent Internal Funds	Percent External Funds
1985	$483.1	73.0%	27.0%
1984	503.4	64.8	35.2
1983	431.3	66.2	33.8
1982	327.6	74.0	26.0
1981	382.5	62.6	37.4
1980	347.6	57.6	42.4
1979	352.6	56.0	44.0
1978	328.5	55.5	44.5
1977	261.4	63.2	36.8
1976	219.1	64.8	35.2
1975	158.4	78.8	21.2
1974	194.1	46.0	54.0
1973	195.5	48.0	52.0
1972	153.4	56.3	43.7

Source: *Economic Report of the President*, January 1987.

The sums involved in tapping the capital markets can be vast. In November 1975 Diamond Shamrock Corporation sold $100 million of 25-year sinking-fund debentures.[2] At the same time Phillips Petroleum Company marketed $250 million of 25-year debentures. In two separate issues sold in October 1975 and June 1976, the old American Telephone and Telegraph Company (AT&T) sold a combined total of $1.2 billion of common stock. In November 1983 the Chase Manhattan Corporation issued $350 million of subordinated notes. In March 1984 United Brands Company marketed $100 million of senior subordinated debentures. On March 25, 1987, the U.S. government sold 58,750,000 shares of Consolidated Rail Corporation common stock to the public at $28 per share. This raised $1.65 billion and was a record for an initial public offering. The sale, which took Conrail out of the government domain and placed it in the hands of public investors, was authorized by the Conrail Privatization Act of 1986. This major fundraising episode required a huge underwriting syndicate; the lead investment bankers included Goldman, Sachs & Co.; The First Boston Corporation; Merrill Lynch Capital Markets; Morgan Stanley & Co.; Salomon Brothers, Inc.; and Shearson Lehman Brothers, Inc. Just two days after the Conrail stock offering, Ford Motor Credit Co. raised $200 million by selling 10-year notes in the marketplace. Clearly, these are important amounts of money to the companies selling the related securities.

To be able to distribute and absorb security offerings of this size, an economy must have a well-developed financial market system. To use that system effectively, the financial officer must have a basic understanding of its structure. Accordingly, this chapter explores the rudiments of raising funds in the capital market.

---

[2] Debentures are long-term, unsecured promissory notes. The detailed features of corporate debt instruments are discussed in Chapter 19.

THE MIX OF CORPORATE SECURITIES SOLD IN THE CAPITAL MARKET —

When corporations decide to raise cash in the capital market, what type of financing vehicle is most favored? Many individual investors think that common stock is the answer to this question. This is understandable, given the coverage of the level of common stock prices by the popular news media. All the major television networks, for instance, quote the closing price of the Dow Jones Industrial Average on their nightly news broadcasts. Common stock, though, is not the financing method relied on most heavily by corporations. The answer to this question is corporate bonds. *The corporate debt markets clearly dominate the corporate equity markets when new funds are being raised.* This is a long-term relationship—it occurs year after year. Table 17–2 bears this out.

In Table 17–2 we see the total volume (in millions of dollars) of corporate securities sold for cash over the 1972–85 period. The percentage breakdown among common stock, preferred stock, and bonds is also displayed. We know from our previous discussion on the cost of capital (Chapter 13) and planning the firm's financing mix (Chapter 15) that the U.S. tax system inherently favors debt as a means of raising capital. Quite simply, interest expense is deductible from other income when computing the firm's federal tax liability, whereas the dividends paid on both preferred and common stock are not.

Financial executives responsible for raising corporate cash know this. When they have a choice between marketing new bonds and marketing new preferred stock, the outcome is usually in favor of bonds. The after-tax cost of capital on the debt is less than that incurred on the preferred stock. Likewise, if the firm has unused debt capacity and the general level of equity prices is depressed, financial executives favor the issuance of debt securities over the issuance of new common stock. It is always

TABLE 17–2.   Corporate Securities Offered for Cash

Year	Total Volume ($ millions)	Percent Common Stock	Percent Preferred Stock	Percent Bonds and Notes
1985	$129,085	28.2%	4.9%	66.9%
1984	85,828	25.8	4.9	69.3
1983	102,406	44.2	7.5	48.3
1982	73,291	32.2	6.7	61.1
1981	65,434	39.0	2.6	58.4
1980	67,126	28.7	4.7	66.6
1979	37,248	23.7	5.3	71.0
1978*	29,949	25.8	5.9	68.3
1977	54,229	14.8	7.2	78.0
1976	53,314	15.6	5.3	79.1
1975	53,632	13.8	6.4	79.8
1974	37,820	10.7	6.0	83.3
1973	31,680	24.1	10.5	65.4
1972	39,705	27.0	8.5	64.5

* Beginning in 1978, security offerings exclude private placement.
Source: Economic Report of the President, January 1987.

good to keep some benchmark figures in your head. The average mix of corporate securities sold for cash over the 1972–85 period follows:

Common stock	25%
Preferred stock	6
Bonds and notes	69
Total	100%

WHY FINANCIAL MARKETS EXIST

Financial markets are institutions and procedures that facilitate transactions in all types of financial claims. The purchase of your home, the common stock you may own, and your life insurance policy all took place in some type of financial market. Why do financial markets exist? What would the economy lose if our complex system of financial markets were not developed? We will address these questions here.

Some economic units spend *more* during a given period of time than they earn. Other economic units spend *less* on current consumption than they earn. For example, business firms in the aggregate usually spend more during a specific time period than they earn. Households in the aggregate spend less on current consumption than they earn. As a result, some mechanism is needed to facilitate the transfer of savings from those economic units with a surplus to those with a deficit. That is precisely the function of financial markets. Financial markets exist in order to *allocate* savings in the economy to the demanders of those savings. The central characteristic of a financial market is that it acts as the vehicle through which the forces of demand and supply for a specific type of financial claim (such as a corporate bond) are brought together.

Now, why would the economy suffer without a developed financial market system? The answer is simple. The wealth of the economy would be less without the financial markets. The rate of capital formation would not be as high if financial markets did not exist. This means that the net additions during a specific period to the stocks of (1) dwellings, (2) productive plant and equipment, (3) inventory, and (4) consumer durables would occur at lower rates. The rationale behind this assertion can be clarified through the use of Figure 17–1. The abbreviated balance sheets in the figure refer to firms or any other type of economic units that operate in the private as opposed to governmental sectors of the economy. This means that such units cannot issue money to finance their activities.

At stage 1 in Figure 17–1 only real assets exist in the hypothetical economy. **Real assets** are tangible assets like houses, equipment, and inventories. They are distinguished from **financial assets,** which represent claims for future payment on other economic units. Common and preferred stocks, bonds, bills, and notes all are types of financial assets. If only real assets exist, then savings for a given economic unit, such as a firm, must be accumulated in the form of real assets. If the firm has a great idea for a new product, that new product can be developed, produced, and distributed only out of company savings (retained earnings). Furthermore, all investment in the

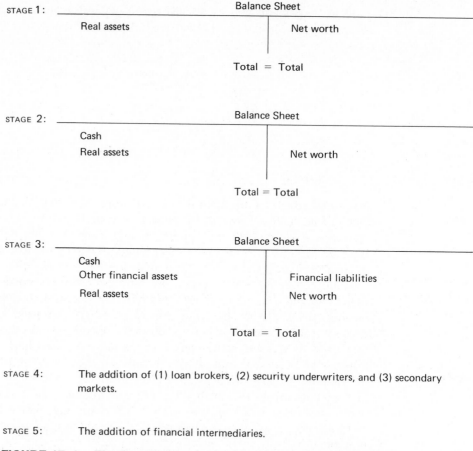

FIGURE 17–1. The Development of a Financial Market System

new product must occur simultaneously as the savings are generated. If you have the idea, and we have the savings, there is no mechanism to transfer our savings to you. This is not a good situation.

At stage 2 paper money comes into existence in the economy. Here, at least, you can *store* your own savings in the form of money. Thus, you can finance your great idea by drawing down your cash balances. This is an improvement over stage 1, but there is still no effective mechanism to transfer our savings to you. You see, we will not just hand you our dollar bills. We will want a receipt.

The concept of a receipt that represents the transfer of savings from one economic unit to another is a monumental advancement. The economic unit with excess savings can lend the savings to an economic unit that needs them. To the lending unit these receipts are identified as "other financial assets" in stage 3 of Figure 17–1. To the borrowing unit, the issuance of financial claims (receipts) shows up as "financial liabilities" on the stage 3 balance sheet. The economic unit with surplus savings will earn a rate of return on those funds. The borrowing unit will pay that rate of return, but it has been able to finance its great idea.

In stage 4 the financial market system moves further toward full development. Loan brokers will come into existence. These brokers help locate pockets of excess savings and channel such savings to economic units needing the funds. Some economic units will actually purchase the financial claims of borrowing units and sell them at a higher price to other investors; this process is called **underwriting.** Underwriting will be discussed in more detail later in this chapter. Additionally, **secondary markets** will develop. Secondary markets just represent trading in already-existing financial claims. If you buy your brother's General Motors common stock, that is a secondary market transaction. Secondary markets reduce the risk of investing in financial claims. Should you need cash, you can liquidate your claims in the secondary market. This induces savers to invest in securities.

The progression toward a developed and complex system of financial markets ends with stage 5. Here, financial intermediaries come into existence. You can think of financial intermediaries as the major financial institutions with which you are used to dealing. These include commerical banks, savings and loan associations, credit unions, life insurance companies, and mutual funds. Financial intermediaries all share a common characteristic: They offer their own financial claims, called **indirect securities,** to economic units with excess savings. The proceeds from selling their indirect securities are then used to purchase the financial claims of other economic units. These latter claims can be called **direct securities.** Thus, a mutual fund might sell mutual fund shares (their indirect security) and purchase the common stocks (direct securities) of some major corporations. A life insurance company sells life insurance policies and purchases huge quantities of corporate bonds. Financial intermediaries thereby involve many small savers in the process of capital formation. This means there are more "good things" for everybody to buy.

A developed financial market system provides for a greater level of wealth in the economy. In the absence of financial markets, savings are not transferred to the economic units most in need of those funds. It is difficult, after all, for a household to build its own automobile. The financial market system makes it easier for the economy to build automobiles and all the other goods that economic units like to accumulate.

FINANCING BUSINESS: THE MOVEMENT OF FUNDS THROUGH THE ECONOMY

The Financing Process

We now understand the crucial role that financial markets play in a capitalist-based economy. At this point we will take a brief look at how funds flow across some selected sectors of the U.S. economy. In addition we will focus a little more closely on the process of financial intermediation that was introduced in the previous section. Some actual data are used to sharpen our knowledge of the financing process. We will see that financial institutions play a major role in bridging the gap between savers and borrowers in the economy. Nonfinancial corporations, we already know, are significant borrowers of financial capital.

Table 17–3 shows how funds were supplied and raised by the major sectors of our economy in 1986. Households were the largest net supplier of funds to the financial markets. This is the case, by the way, year in and year out. In 1986, households made available $141.4 billion in funds to other sectors. That was the excess of their

TABLE 17–3. A Sector View of the Flow of Funds in the U.S. Financial Markets for 1986 ($ billions)

Sector	[1] Funds Raised	[2] Funds Supplied	[2] − [1] Net Funds Supplied
Households[a]	$297.6	$439.0	$141.4
Nonfinancial Corporate Businesses	140.7	90.5	− 50.2
U.S. Government	238.3	14.7	−223.6
State and Local Governments	61.2	74.6	13.4
Foreign	37.7	167.4	129.7

[a] Includes personal trusts and nonprofit organizations.

Source: *Flow of Funds Accounts, Fourth Quarter 1986*, Flow of Funds Section (Washington, DC: Board of Governors of the Federal Reserve System, March 1987).

funds supplied over their funds raised in the markets. In the jargon of economics, the household sector is a *savings-surplus* sector.

By contrast, the nonfinancial business sector is a *savings-deficit* sector. In 1986, nonfinancial corporations raised, $50.2 billion *more* in the financial markets than they supplied to the markets. This too is a consistent long-term relationship. The nonfinancial business sector is consistently a savings-deficit sector.

Next, it can be seen that the U.S. government sector was a savings-deficit sector for 1986. In 1986 the federal government raised $223.6 billion in excess of the funds it supplied to the financial markets. This highlights a serious problem for the entire economy and for the financial manager. Persistent federal deficits have increased the role of the federal government in the market for borrowed funds. The last time the federal government posted a budget surplus was 1969; the last time prior to that was 1960. The federal government has thus become a "quasi-permanent" savings-deficit sector. Most financial economists agree that this tendency puts upward pressure on interest rates in the financial marketplace and thereby raises the general (overall) cost of capital to corporations. This phenomenon has become known as "crowding-out": The private borrower is pushed out of the financial markets in favor of the government borrower.

Table 17–3 demonstrates that the financial market system must exist to facilitate the orderly and efficient flow of savings from the surplus sectors to the deficit sectors of the economy. The result is that the nonfinancial business sector is dependent on the household sector to finance its investment needs.

As we noted in the previous section, the financial market system includes a complex network of intermediaries that assist in the transfer of savings among economic units. Two intermediaries will be highlighted here: life insurance companies and pension funds. They are especially important participants in the capital market of the country.

Because of the nature of their business, life insurance firms can invest heavily in long-term financial instruments. This investment tendency arises for two key reasons: (1) Life insurance policies usually include a *savings element* in them, and (2) their liabilities liquidate at a very predictable rate. Thus, life insurance companies invest in the "long end" of the securities markets. This means that they favor (1) mortgages

ABLE 17–4.   The Financial Asset Mix of Life Insurance Companies (in billions)

Assets	1960 $	1960 %	1970 $	1970 %	1980 $	1980 %	1982 $	1982 %	1985 $	1985 %
Demand deposits and currency	$ 1.3	1.1%	$ 1.8	0.8%	$ 3.2	0.7%	$ 4.6	0.8%	$ 4.6	0.6%
U.S. government securities	6.5	5.6	4.6	2.3	17.0	3.7	35.2	6.2	99.2	12.7
State and local securities	3.6	3.1	3.3	1.6	6.7	1.4	9.0	1.6	10.1	1.3
Mortgages	41.8	36.1	74.4	37.0	131.1	28.2	141.9	25.0	170.5	21.9
Corporate stocks	5.0	4.3	15.4	7.7	47.4	10.2	55.7	9.8	77.2	9.9
Corporate bonds	48.2	41.7	74.1	36.9	178.8	38.5	202.3	35.6	274.2	35.2
Miscellaneous	9.4	8.1	27.3	13.7	80.0	17.3	118.8	21.0	144.1	18.4
Total financial assets	$115.8	100.0%	$200.9	100.0%	$464.2	100.0%	$567.5	100.0%	$779.9	100.0%

ource: *Flow of Funds Accounts, Assets and Liabilities Outstanding, 1959–82 and 1962–85*, Flow of Funds Section (Washington, DC: Board of overnors of the Federal Reserve System, August 1983 and September 1986).

and (2) corporate bonds as investment vehicles. To a lesser extent, they acquire corporate stocks for their portfolios.

Table 17–4 shows the financial asset mix of life insurance companies for the years 1960, 1970, 1980, 1982 and 1985. The box drawn around their holdings of corporate stocks and corporate bonds demonstrates that these firms are major suppliers of financial capital to the nonfinancial business sector. The sum of corporate stocks and bonds held by life insurance companies expressed as a percent of their total investment in financial assets for each of the five selected years in Table 17–4 is listed below:

Year	Percent
1960	46.0%
1970	44.6
1980	48.7
1982	45.4
1985	45.1

Over recent years, about 45 percent of the financial assets of life insurance firms are represented by corporate stocks and bonds. We see that life insurance companies are an important financial intermediary. By issuing life insurance policies (indirect securities), they can acquire direct securities (corporate stocks and bonds) for their investment portfolios. Their preference, by far, is for bonds over stocks.

Let us now direct our attention to another financial intermediary, the private pension funds in the United States. Table 17–5 shows the financial asset mix of the private pension funds in the United States. It is constructed in a manner similar to that of Table 17–4. In comparison with life insurance companies, three factors stand out. First, since 1960, private pension funds have grown at a much faster rate than have the insurance companies. Second, a greater proportion of the financial asset mix of the pension funds is devoted to corporate stocks and bonds. Third, the pension funds invest more heavily in corporate stocks than they do in corporate bonds. The sum

TABLE 17–5.   The Financial Asset Mix of Private Pension Funds (in billions)

Assets	1960 $	1960 %	1970 $	1970 %	1980 $	1980 %	1982 $	1982 %	1985 $	1985 %
Demand deposits and currency	$ 0.5	1.3%	$ 1.1	1.0%	$ 3.9	0.8%	$ 3.5	0.6%	$ 4.5	0.6%
Time deposits	—	—	0.7	0.6	25.3	5.4	27.6	5.0	35.3	4.7
U.S. government securities	2.7	7.1	3.0	2.7	53.7	11.5	79.4	14.5	106.5	14.1
Corporate stocks	16.5	43.3	67.1	60.8	231.3	49.5	258.1	47.0	383.0	50.6
Corporate bonds	15.7	41.2	29.4	26.6	79.7	17.1	91.6	16.7	119.4	15.8
Mortgages	1.3	3.4	4.2	3.8	3.6	0.8	4.2	0.8	4.8	0.6
Miscellaneous	1.4	3.7	4.9	4.5	69.9	14.9	84.7	15.4	103.9	13.6
Total financial assets	$38.1	100.0%	$110.4	100.0%	$467.4	100.0%	$549.1	100.0%	$757.4	100.0%

Source: Flow of Funds Accounts, Assets and Liabilities Outstanding, 1959–82, and 1962–85, Flow of Funds Section, (Washington, DC: Board o
Governors of the Federal Reserve System, August 1983 and September 1986).

of corporate stocks and bonds held by private pension funds expressed as a percent of their total investment in financial assets for each of the five selected years in Table 17–5 is listed below:

Year	Percent
1960	84.5%
1970	87.4
1980	66.5
1982	63.7
1985	66.3

Over recent years, then, about 65 percent of the financial assets of private pension funds have been tied up in corporate stocks and bonds. This financial institution, too, is a significant source of business financing in this country. It plays the same intermediary role as does the life insurance subsector of the economy.

The Movement of Savings

Figure 17–2 provides a useful way to summarize our discussion of (1) why financial markets exist and (2) the movement of funds through the economy. It also serves as an introduction to the use of an investment banker—a subject discussed in detail later in this chapter.

We see that savings are ultimately transferred to the business firm in need of cash in three ways:

1. **The direct transfer of funds.** Here the firm seeking cash sells its securities, directly to savers (investors) who are willing to purchase them in hopes of earning a reasonable rate of return. A good example of this process stems from the new business. The new business may go directly to a saver or group of savers called "venture capitalists." The venture capitalists will lend funds to the firm or take an equity position in the firm if they feel the product or service the new firm hopes to market will be successful.

2. **Indirect transfer using the investment banker.** In a common arrangement under this system, the managing investment banking house will form a syndicate

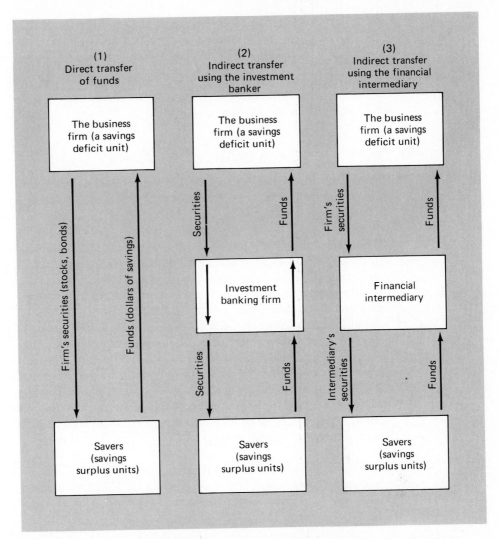

FIGURE 17–2.   Three Ways to Transfer Financial Capital in the Economy

of several investment bankers. The syndicate will buy the entire issue of securities from the firm that is in need of financial capital. The syndicate will then sell the securities at a higher price than it paid for them to the investing public (the savers). Merrill Lynch Capital Markets, and Kidder, Peabody & Co. are examples of investment banking firms. They tend to be called "houses" by those who work in the financial community. Notice that under this second method of transferring savings, the securities being issued just pass through the investment banking firm. They are *not* transformed into a different type of security.

3. **Indirect transfer using the financial intermediary.** This is the type of system we just illustrated using life insurance companies and pension funds as examples of intermediaries. The financial intermediary collects the savings of individuals

and issues its own (indirect) securities in exchange for these savings. The intermediary then uses the funds collected from the individual savers to acquire the business firm's (direct) securities, like stocks and bonds.

We all benefit from the three transfer mechanisms displayed in Figure 17–2. Capital formation and economic wealth are greater than they would be in the absence of this financial market system.

COMPONENTS OF THE U.S. FINANCIAL MARKET SYSTEM

Numerous approaches exist for classifying the securities markets. At times, the array can be confusing. An examination of four sets of dichotomous terms can help provide a basic understanding of the structure of the U.S. financial markets.

Public Offerings and Private Placements

When a corporation decides to raise external capital, those funds can be obtained by making a public offering or a private placement. In a **public offering** both individual and institutional investors have the opportunity to purchase the securities. The securities are usually made available to the public at large by a managing investment banking firm and its underwriting syndicate. In the public offering the firm does not meet the ultimate purchasers of the securities. The public market is an impersonal market.

In a **private placement,** also called a **direct placement,** the securities are offered and sold to a limited number of investors. The firm will usually hammer out, on a face-to-face basis with the prospective buyers, the details of the offering. In this setting the investment banking firm may act as a finder by bringing together potential lenders and borrowers. The private placement market is a more personal market than its public counterpart. Both investment banking and private placements are explored in more detail later in this chapter.

Primary Markets and Secondary Markets

Primary markets are those where securities are offered for the *first* time to potential investors. A new issue of common stock by AT&T is a primary market transaction. This type of transaction increases the total stock of financial assets outstanding in the economy.

As mentioned in our discussion of the development of the financial market system, **secondary markets** represent transactions in currently outstanding securities. If the first buyer of the AT&T stock subsequently sells it, he does so in the secondary market. All transactions after the initial purchase take place in the secondary market. The sales do *not* affect the total stock of financial assets that exist in the economy. Both the money market and the capital market, described next, have primary and secondary sides.

Money Market and Capital Market

Money Market

The key distinguishing feature between the money and capital markets is the maturity period of the securities traded in them. The **money market** refers to all institutions and procedures that provide for transactions in short-term debt instruments generally issued by borrowers with very high credit ratings. By financial convention, "short-term" means maturity periods of one year or less. Notice that equity instruments, either common or preferred, are not traded in the money market. The major instruments issued and traded are U.S. Treasury bills, various federal agency securities, bankers' acceptances, negotiable certificates of deposit, and commercial paper. Detailed descriptions of these instruments as elements of the firm's marketable securities portfolio are given in Chapter 6. Commercial paper as a short-term financing vehicle is discussed in Chapter 8. Keep in mind that the money market is an intangible market. You do not walk into a building on Wall Street that has the words "Money Market" etched in stone over its arches. Rather, the money market is primarily a telephone market where trading does not occur at any specific location. Most agree, however, that New York City is the center of this market.

Capital Market
The **capital market** refers to all institutions and procedures that provide for transactions in long-term financial instruments. Long-term here means having maturity periods that extend beyond one year. In the broad sense this encompasses term loans and financial leases, corporate equities, and bonds. All these financing modes are discussed in Chapters 18, 19, and 20. The funds that comprise the firm's capital structure are raised in the capital market. Important elements of the capital market are the organized security exchanges and the over-the-counter markets.

Organized Security Exchanges and Over-the-Counter Markets
Organized security exchanges are tangible entities; they physically occupy space (such as a building or part of a building), and financial instruments are traded on their premises. The **over-the-counter markets** include all security markets *except* the organized exchanges. The money market, then, is an over-the-counter market. Because both markets are important to financial officers concerned with raising **long-term capital,** some additional discussion is warranted.

Organized Security Exchanges
For practical purposes there are seven major security exchanges in the United States.[3] These are the (1) New York Stock Exchange, (2) American Stock Exchange, (3) Midwest Stock Exchange, (4) Pacific Stock Exchange, (5) Philadelphia Stock Exchange, (6) Boston Stock Exchange, and (7) Cincinnati Stock Exchange. The New York Stock Exchange (NYSE) and the American Stock Exchange (AMEX) are called *national* exchanges, while the others are loosely described as *regionals*.

All of these seven active exchanges are registered with the Securities and Exchange Commission (SEC). Firms whose securities are traded on the registered exchanges must comply with reporting requirements of both the specific exchange and the SEC. About 85 percent of the annual dollar volume of transactions on the registered exchanges takes place on the NYSE. In 1977 the dollar trading volume on the Midwest exchange actually exceeded that of the AMEX, which usually runs second to the NYSE.[4] Together, the NYSE, the AMEX, and the Midwest account for about 94 percent of the annual dollar volume transacted on the registered exchanges. In 1985 the

---

[3] Others include (1) The Honolulu Stock Exchange, which is unregistered; (2) the Board of Trade of the City of Chicago, which does not now trade stocks; and (3) the Chicago Board Options Exchange, Inc., which deals in options rather than stocks. The cities of Colorado Springs, Salt Lake City, and Spokane also have small exchanges. From time to time you may hear of the New York Futures Exchange (NYFE). This subsidiary of the NYSE was incorporated on April 5, 1979. Trading on the NYFE is in futures contracts and options contracts.

[4] Jonathan R. Laing, "Shaky Floor: Problems Multiply at Midwest Exchange, but Chief Is Optimistic," *Wall Street Journal,* April 4, 1978, pp. 1, 20.

NYSE accounted for 81.6 percent of all *shares* sold on registered exchanges in the United States, with the AMEX accounting for 5.7 percent, and all others 12.7 percent.[5]

The business of an exchange, including securities transactions, is conducted by its **members.** Members are said to occupy "seats." There are 1366 seats on the NYSE, a number that has remained constant since 1953. Major brokerage firms own seats on the exchanges. An officer of the firm is designated to be the member of the exchange, and this membership permits the brokerage house to use the facilities of the exchange to effect trades. During 1985 the prices of seats that were exchanged for cash ranged from a low of $310,000 to a high of $480,000. The highest price paid in recent times was $515,000 in 1969.[6]

Stock Exchange Benefits. Both corporations and investors enjoy several benefits provided by the existence of organized security exchanges.[7] These include:

1. **Providing a continuous market.** This may be the most important function of an organized security exchange. A continuous market provides a series of continuous security prices. Price changes from trade to trade tend to be smaller than they would be in the absence of organized markets. The reasons are that there is a relatively large sales volume in each security, trading orders are executed quickly, and the range between the price asked for a security and the offered price tends to be narrow. The result is that price volatility is reduced. This enhances the liquidity of security investments and makes them more attractive to potential investors. While it is difficult to prove, it seems logical that this market feature probably reduces the cost of capital to corporations.

2. **Establishing and publicizing fair security prices.** An organized exchange permits security prices to be set by competitive forces. They are not set by negotiations off the floor of the exchange, where one party might have a bargaining advantage. The bidding process flows from the supply and demand underlying each security. This means the specific price of a security is determined in the manner of an auction. Additionally, the security prices determined at each exchange are widely publicized. Just read the pages of most newspapers, and the information is available to you. By contrast, the prices and resulting yields on the private placements of securities are more difficult to obtain.

3. **Helping business raise new capital.** Because a continuous secondary market exists where prices are competitively determined, it is easier for firms to float new security offerings successfully. This continuous pricing mechanism also facilitates the determination of the offering price of a new issue. This means that comparative values are easily observed.

Listing Requirements. To receive the benefits provided by an organized exchange, the firm must seek to have its securities listed on the exchange. An application for listing must be filed and a fee paid. The requirements for listing vary from exchange

---

[5] New York Stock Exchange, *Fact Book* (New York, 1986), p. 74.

[6] New York Stock Exchange, *Fact Book*, 1986, p. 59.

[7] A more-detailed discussion on stock exchange functions can be found in Frederick Amling, *Investments: An Introduction to Analysis and Management*, 5th ed. (Englewood Cliffs, NJ: Prentice-Hall, 1984), Chap. 9.

TABLE 17–6. NYSE Listing Requirements

Profitability
Earnings before taxes (EBT) for the most recent year must be at least $2.5 million. For the two years preceding that, EBT must be at least $2.0 million.

Size
Net tangible assets must be at least $18.0 million.

Market Value[a]
The market value of publicly held stock must be at least $18.0 million.

Public Ownership
There must be at least 1.1 million publicly held common shares. There must be at least 2000 holders of 100 shares or more.

[a] The market value test is tied to the level of common stock prices prevailing in the marketplace at the time of the listing application. From time to time the $18.0 million requirement noted above may be lessened. Under current regulations of the NYSE, the requirement can never be less than $9.0 million.

to exchange; those of the NYSE are the most stringent. The general criteria for listing fall into these categories: (1) profitability; (2) size, (3) market value, and (4) public ownership. To give you the flavor of an actual set of listing requirements, those set forth by the NYSE are displayed in Table 17–6.[8]

Over-the-Counter Markets

Many publicly held firms do not meet the listing requirements of major stock exchanges. Others may want to avoid the (1) reporting requirements and (2) fees required to maintain listing. As an alternative their securities may trade in the over-the-counter markets. On the basis of sheer numbers (not dollar volume), more stocks are traded over-the-counter than on organized exchanges. As far as secondary trading in corporate bonds is concerned, the over-the-counter markets are where the action is. In a typical year, more than 90 percent of corporate bond business takes place over-the-counter.

Most over-the-counter transactions are done through a loose network of security traders who are known as broker-dealers and brokers. Brokers do not purchase securities for their own account, whereas dealers do. Broker-dealers stand ready to buy and sell specific securities at selected prices. They are said to "make a market" in those securities. Their profit is the spread or difference between the price they will pay for a security (bid price) and the price at which they will sell the security (asked price).

Price quotes. The availability of prices is not as continuous in the over-the-counter market as it is on an organized exchange. Since February 8, 1971, however, when a computerized network called NASDAQ came into existence, the availability of prices in this market has improved substantially. NASDAQ stands for National Association of Security Dealers Automated Quotation System. It is a telecommunications system that serves to provide a national information link among the brokers and dealers operating in the over-the-counter markets. Subscribing traders have a cathode-ray terminal that allows them to obtain representative bid and ask prices for thousands

---

[8] New York Stock Exchange, *Fact Book*, 1986, p. 35.

of securities traded over-the-counter. NASDAQ is a quotation system, not a transactions system. The final trade is still consummated by direct negotiation between traders.

NASDAQ price quotes for many stocks are published daily in the *Wall Street Journal*. This same financial newspaper also publishes prices on hundreds of other stocks traded over-the-counter. Local papers supply prices on stocks of regional interest. Finally, the National Quotation Bureau publishes daily "pink sheets," which contain prices on about 8000 securities; these sheets are available in the offices of most security dealers.

THE INVESTMENT BANKER

Most corporations do not raise long-term capital frequently. The activities of working capital management go on daily, but attracting long-term capital is, by comparison, episodic. The sums involved can be huge, so these situations are considered of great importance to financial managers. And since most managers are unfamiliar with the subtleties of raising long-term funds, they will enlist the help of an expert. That expert is an investment banker.[9]

Definition

The **investment banker** is a financial specialist involved as an intermediary in the merchandising of securities. He acts as a middleman by facilitating the flow of savings from those economic units that want to invest to those units that want to raise funds. We use the term "investment banker" to refer both to a given individual and to the organization for which such a person works, variously known as an **investment banking firm** or an **investment banking house.** Although these firms are called "investment bankers," they perform no depository or lending functions. The activities of commercial banking and investment banking as we know them today were separated by the Banking Act of 1933 (also known as the Glass-Steagall Act of 1933). Just what does this middleman role consist of? That is most easily understood in terms of the basic functions of investment banking.

Functions

The investment banker performs three basic functions: (1) underwriting, (2) distributing, and (3) advising.

Underwriting

The term **underwriting** is borrowed from the field of insurance. It means "assuming a risk." The investment banker assumes the risk of selling a security issue at a satisfactory price. A satisfactory price is one that will generate a profit for the investment banking house.

The procedure goes like this. The managing investment banker and its syndicate will buy the security issue from the corporation in need of funds. The **syndicate** is a group of other investment bankers who are invited to help buy and resell the issue. The managing house is the investment banking firm that originated the business because its corporate client decided to raise external funds. On a specific day, the firm that is raising capital is presented with a check in exchange for the securities being issued. At this point the investment banking syndicate owns the securities.

---

[9] Recent structural, managerial, and operational changes in the investment banking industry are described in "The Traders Take Charge," *Business Week*, February 20, 1984, pp. 58–61, 64.

The corporation has its cash and can proceed to use it. The firm is now immune from the possibility that the security markets might turn sour. If the price of the newly issued security falls below that paid to the firm by the syndicate, the syndicate will suffer a loss. The syndicate, of course, hopes that the opposite situation will result. Its objective is to sell the new issue to the investing public at a price per security greater than its cost.

Distributing   Once the syndicate owns the new securities, it must get them into the hands of the ultimate investors. This is the distribution or selling function of investment banking. The investment banker may have branch offices across the United States or it may have an informal arrangement with several security dealers who regularly buy a portion of each new offering for final sale. It is not unusual to have 300 to 400 dealers involved in the selling effort. The syndicate can properly be viewed as the security wholesaler, while the dealer organization can be viewed as the security retailer.

Advising   The investment banker is an expert in the issuance and marketing of securities. A sound investment banking house will be aware of prevailing market conditions and can relate those conditions to the particular type of security that should be sold at a given time. Business conditions may be pointing to a future increase in interest rates. The investment banker might advise the firm to issue its bonds in a timely fashion to avoid the higher yields that are forthcoming. The banker can analyze the firm's capital structure and make recommendations as to what general source of capital should be issued. In many instances the firm will invite its investment banker to sit on the board of directors. This permits the banker to observe corporate activity and make recommendations on a regular basis.

Distribution Methods   Several methods are available to the corporation for placing new security offerings in the hands of final investors. The investment banker's role is different in each of these. Sometimes, in fact, it is possible to bypass the investment banker. These methods are described in this section. Private placements, because of their importance, are treated separately later in the chapter.

Negotiated Purchase   In a negotiated underwriting, the firm that needs funds makes contact with an investment banker, and deliberations concerning the new issue begin. If all goes well, a *method* is negotiated for determining the price the investment banker and the syndicate will pay for the securities. For example, the agreement might state that the syndicate will pay $2 less than the closing price of the firm's common stock on the day before the offering date of a new stock issue. The negotiated purchase is the most prevalent method of securities distribution in the private sector. It is generally thought to be the most profitable technique as far as investment bankers are concerned.[10]

Competitive Bid Purchase   The method by which the underwriting group is determined distinguishes the competitive bid purchase from the negotiated purchase. In a competitive underwriting, several underwriting groups bid for the right to purchase the new issue from the corporation

---

[10] Samuel L. Hayes, III, "Investment Banking: Power Structure in Flux," *Harvard Business Review*, 49 (March–April 1971), 138.

that is raising funds. The firm does not directly select the investment banker. The investment banker that underwrites and distributes the issue is chosen by an auction process. The syndicate willing to pay the greatest dollar amount per new security will win the competitive bid.[11]

Most competitive bid purchases are confined to three situations, compelled by legal regulations: (1) railroad issues, (2) public utility issues, and (3) state and municipal bond issues. The argument in favor of competitive bids is that any undue influence of the investment banker over the firm is mitigated and the price received by the firm for each security should be higher. Thus, we would intuitively suspect that the cost of capital in a competitive bid situation would be less than in a negotiated purchase situation. Evidence on this question, however, is mixed.[12] One problem with the competitive bid purchase as far as the fundraising firm is concerned is that the benefits gained from the advisory function of the investment banker are lost. It may be necessary to use an investment banker for advisory purposes and then exclude the banker from the competitive bid process. In the 1960s and 1970s, many utilities obtained exemptions from the Federal Power Commission to permit them to raise capital by negotiated underwriting.

Commission or Best-Efforts Basis

Here, the investment banker acts as an agent rather than as a principal in the distribution process. The securities are *not* underwritten. The investment banker attempts to sell the issue in return for a fixed commission on each security actually sold. Unsold securities are returned to the corporation. This arrangement is typically used for more speculative issues. The issuing firm may be smaller or less established than the investment banker would like. Because the underwriting risk is not passed on to the investment banker, this distribution method is less costly to the issuer than a negotiated or competitive bid purchase. On the other hand, the investment banker only has to give it his "best effort." A successful sale is not guaranteed.

Privileged Subscription

Occasionally the firm may feel that a distinct market already exists for its new securities. When a new issue is marketed to a definite and select group of investors, it is called a **privileged subscription.** Three target markets are typically involved: (1) current stockholders, (2) employees, or (3) customers. Of these, distributions directed at current stockholders are the most prevalent. Such offerings, called rights offerings, are discussed in detail in Chapter 19. In a privileged subscription the investment banker may act only as a selling agent. It is also possible that the issuing firm and the investment banker might sign a **standby agreement,** which would obligate the investment banker to underwrite the securities that are not accepted by the privileged investors.

Direct Sale

In a **direct sale** the issuing firm sells the securities directly to the investing public without involving an investment banker. Even among established corporate giants this procedure is relatively rare. A variation of the direct sale, though, has been used

---

[11] An excellent description of this process is found in Ernest Bloch, "Pricing a Corporate Bond Issue: A Look Behind the Scenes," *Essays in Money and Credit*, Federal Reserve Bank of New York, December 1964, pp. 72–76.

[12] Gary D. Tallman, David F. Rush, and Ronald W. Melicher, "Competitive versus Negotiated Underwriting Cost of Regulated Industries," *Financial Management*, 3 (Summer 1974), 49–55.

more frequently in the 1970s than in previous decades. This involves the private placement of a new issue by the fundraising corporation *without* the use of an investment banker as an intermediary. Texaco, Mobil Oil, and International Harvester (now Navistar) are examples of large firms that have followed this procedure.[13]

The Negotiated Purchase Sequence

The negotiated purchase is the distribution method most likely to be used by the private corporation. It makes sense, then, to cover in some detail the sequence of events that comprise the negotiated underwriting.

1. **Selection of an investment banker.** The firm will initiate the fundraising process by choosing an investment banker. On some occasions a third party, called a **finder,** may direct the firm to a specific investment banker. Typically the finder will receive a fee from the fundraising firm if an underwriting agreement is eventually signed. Use of a finder is one way of gaining access to a quality investment banker.

2. **Preunderwriting conferences.** A series of preunderwriting conferences will be held between the firm and the investment banker. Key items discussed are (1) the amount of capital to be raised, (2) whether the capital markets seem to be especially receptive at this time to one type of financing instrument over another, and (3) whether the proposed use of the new funds appears reasonable. At these conferences it will be confirmed that a flotation will, in fact, take place, and that this particular investment banker will manage the underwriting. The investment banker will then undertake a complete financial analysis of the corporation and assess its future prospects. The final outcome of the preunderwriting conferences is the **tentative underwriting agreement.** This will detail (1) the approximate price the investment banker will pay for the securities and (2) the **upset price.** The upset price is a form of escape mechanism for the benefit of the issuing firm. If the market price of the firm's securities should drop in a significant fashion just before the new securities are to be sold, the price the investment banker is to pay the firm might drop below the upset price. In this situation the new offering would be aborted.

3. **Formation of the underwriting syndicate.** An underwriting syndicate is a temporary association of investment bankers formed to purchase a security issue from a corporation for subsequent resale, hopefully at a profit to the underwriters. The syndicate is formed for very sound reasons. First, the originating investment bank probably could not finance the entire underwriting itself. Second, the use of a syndicate reduces the risk of loss to any single underwriter. Third, the use of a syndicate widens the eventual distribution effort. Each underwriter has its own network of security dealers who will purchase a portion of the participation in the offering. Most syndicates will contain ten to sixty investment banking houses. Since each house will have its own distribution network, the selling group can often consist of 100 to 600 dealers. An agreement signed by all members of the syndicate will bind them to certain performance standards. This will detail their participation (amount they can purchase) in the offering and their liability for any portion of the issue unsold by their fellow underwriters.

---

[13] See Wyndham Robertson, "Future Shock at Morgan Stanley," *Fortune*, 97 (February 27, 1978), 88, 90.

4. **Registering the securities.** Before a new public issue can be offered to prospective investors, it must be registered with the Securities and Exchange Commission (SEC). Securities that are exempt from registration will be discussed later in this chapter when we examine the regulation of the securities markets. Most new issues must comply with the requirements of the **Securities Act of 1933.** This dictates that a **registration statement** must be submitted to the SEC aimed at disclosing all facts relevant to the new issue that will permit an investor to make an informed decision.[14] The SEC itself does *not* judge the investment quality of securities. The registration statement is a lengthy document containing (1) historical, (2) financial, and (3) administrative facts about the firm. The details of the new offering are presented, as well as the proposed use of the funds that are being raised. During a 20-day waiting period the SEC examines the statement for errors or omissions. While this examination process is being carried out, the investment banking syndicate *cannot* offer the security for sale. Part of the package presented to the SEC for scrutiny is a document called a **prospectus.** Once approved, it is the official advertising vehicle for the offering. During the waiting period a **preliminary prospectus,** outlining the important features of the new issue, may be distributed to potential investors. The preliminary prospectus contains no selling price information or offering date. In addition, a stamped red-ink statement on the first page tells the reader that the document is *not* an official offer to sell the securities. In the jargon of finance, this preliminary prospectus is called a **red herring.** Once the registration statement is approved by the SEC, the security can be offered for sale provided the prospectus is made available to all concerned parties.

5. **Formation of the selling group.** In order to distribute the securities to final investors, a selling group is formed. The dealers comprising the selling group will purchase portions of the new issue from the syndicate members with whom they regularly do business. They will pay for each security a price higher than that paid by the syndicate member, but less than the offering price to the investing public. The responsibilities and rewards of the selling group are contained in the **selling group agreement.** Formation of the selling group completes the distribution network for the new offering. The structure of such a network is diagrammed in Figure 17–3.

6. **The due diligence meeting.** This is a "last-chance" gathering to get everything in order before taking the offering to the public. Usually, all members of the syndicate are present, along with key officers of the issuing firm. Any omissions from the prospectus should be caught at this meeting. Most important, the final price to be paid by the syndicate to the firm will be settled. As we said earlier, if the issue is additional common stock, the underwriting price may be a fixed amount below the closing price of the firm's outstanding stock on the day prior to the new offering. Capital market conditions will be discussed, and the offering price of the security to the public will be set in light of those conditions. The "go ahead" will be given to print the final prospectus, which will now contain all relevant price information. The offering will usually be made the next day.

---

[14] See the section on shelf registration at the end of this chapter.

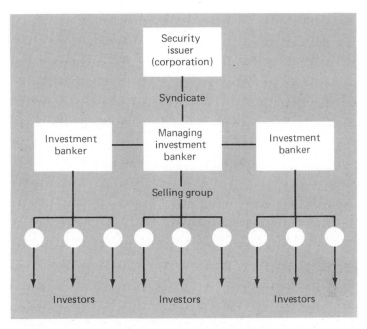

FIGURE 17–3.   Distributing New Securities

7. **Price-pegging.** Once the issue has been offered for sale, the managing under-writer will attempt to mitigate downward price movements in the secondary market for the security by placing orders to buy at the agreed-upon public offering price. The objective is to stabilize the market price of the issue so it can be sold at the initial offering price. The syndicate manager's intention to perform this price maintenance operation must be disclosed in the registration statement.

8. **Syndicate termination.** A contractual agreement among the underwriters identi-fies the duration of the syndicate. Pragmatically, the syndicate is dissolved when the issue has been fully subscribed. If the demand for the issue is great, it may be sold out in a few days. If the issue lingers on the market, without much buyer interest, the remaining inventory may be sold at the existing secondary market price. The name of the game in investment banking is not margin, but turnover. Should the issue go sour, the underwriters will quickly absorb the loss and get on to the next underwriting.

Industry Leaders All industries have their leaders, and investment banking is no exception. We have talked at some length in this chapter about investment bankers in general. Table 17–7 gives us some idea who the major players are within the investment banking industry. It lists the top 15 houses in 1986 based upon the dollar volume of security issues that were either managed or co-managed. The number of issues the house participated in is also identified.

TABLE 17-7. Leading U.S. Investment Bankers, 1986

Firm	Underwriting Volume ($ billion)	Number of Issues
1. Salomon Brothers	$47.7	767
2. First Boston	41.8	705
3. Merrill Lynch	31.3	570
4. Goldman Sachs	29.9	523
5. Drexel Burnham Lambert	27.6	355
6. Morgan Stanley	26.5	458
7. Shearson Lehman Brothers	16.8	475
8. Kidder Peabody	10.9	304
9. Bear Stearns	5.7	176
10. Paine Webber	4.7	179
11. Prudential-Bach Securities	4.6	140
12. E. F. Hutton	4.1	129
13. Smith Barney, Harris Upham	3.9	149
14. Dean Witter Reynolds	2.9	94
15. Lazard Freres	2.5	48

Source: *Institutional Investor*, 21 (March 1987), 177.

BASIC FINANCIAL MANAGEMENT IN PRACTICE

Investment Banking and Commercial Banking

One of the most important issues affecting our financial markets today concerns the suggested reform or repeal of the Glass-Steagall Act (the Banking Act of 1933). This law, as noted earlier, keeps commercial banks from underwriting securities.

When you consider that only 12 firms generate about 50 percent of domestic investment banking revenue, then it is more understandable why commercial banks would like to jump into this market. Likewise, it is clear that investment banking houses are satisfied with the *status quo*. The latter point out that the current division of turf protects the financial markets from undue risks.

The first piece below from the Federal Reserve Bank of San Francisco identifies the main issue. The second excerpt is by the current president of the Federal Reserve Bank of Atlanta. His views may not surprise you.

The Issue

Banking organizations in the U.S. face obsolete legal prohibitions on the products and services they can provide. In particular, the Glass-Steagall and the Bank Holding Company Acts limit the ability of banks to underwrite corporate securities and to hold investments in the equity of nonbank enterprises.

Nevertheless, banks have had some success at circumventing legal barriers. For example, because state-chartered banks that are not members of the Federal Reserve are not covered by Glass-Steagall, they or their subsidiaries are allowed in some states to provide many investment banking services, including securities underwriting and direct equity investment. Likewise, subsidiaries of U.S. bank holding companies are able to perform some investment banking activities in offshore markets.

In addition, the interpretation of Glass-Steagall by regulators has evolved over time. For example, on April 30, 1987, the Federal Reserve approved applications that give limited authority to bank holding companies to underwrite certain securities through subsidiaries "not principally engaged" in underwriting. (The Fed approved underwriting and dealing in municipal revenue bonds, mortgage-backed securities, and commercial paper.)

Full-fledged integration of commercial and investment banking would require changes in existing statutes.

Opinion

U.S. banking firms are currently permitted to engage in almost every investment banking function abroad. I find that the reasonable safety record so far is a little hard to reconcile with prohibitions on many of the same activities in this country. Since many large corporations are truly international, they may receive services from their banks that domestic firms are unable to purchase. Thus, the work of the deregulators is not finished in banking. Some product and geographic deregulation could actually enhance financial stability by permitting greater diversification. It would also increase competition and economic efficiency.

Sources: M. C. Keeley and R. J. Pozdena, "Uniting Investment and Commercial Banking," *Weekly Letter*, Federal Reserve Bank of San Francisco, (June 19, 1987), 1; Robert P. Forrestal, "Deregulation: Too Much or Not Enough?" *Economic Review*, Federal Reserve Bank of Atlanta, 72 (January–February 1987), 7.

PRIVATE PLACEMENTS

Private placements are an alternative to the sale of securities to the public or to a restricted group of investors through a privileged subscription. Any type of security can be privately placed (directly placed). This market, however, is clearly dominated by debt issues. Thus, we restrict this discussion to debt securities. From year to year the volume of private placements will vary. Table 17–8 shows, though, that the private placement market is always a significant portion of the U.S. capital market.

TABLE 17–8. Publicly and Privately Placed Corporate Debt (Gross Proceeds of All New U.S. Corporate Debt Issues)

Year	Total Volume ($ million)	Percent Publicly Placed	Percent Privately Placed
1985	$165,754	72.1%	27.9%
1984	109,903	66.9	33.1
1983	68,370	69.1	30.9
1982	53,636	81.7	18.3
1981	45,092	84.5	15.5
1980	53,206	78.2	21.8
1979	40,139	64.3	35.7
1978	36,872	53.7	46.3
1977	42,015	57.3	42.7
1976	42,262	62.6	37.4
1975	42,756	76.2	23.8
1974	32,066	80.8	19.2
1973	21,049	62.9	37.1
1972	26,132	66.7	33.3

Source: Federal Reserve Bulletin, various issues.

The major investors in private placements are large financial institutions. Based on the volume of securities purchased, the three most important investor groups are (1) life insurance companies, (2) state and local retirement funds, and (3) private pension funds.

In arranging a private placement the firm may (1) avoid the use of an investment banker and work directly with the investing institutions or (2) engage the services of an investment banker. If the investment banker is not used, of course, the firm does not have to pay a fee. On the other hand, the investment banker can provide valuable advice in the private placement process. He will usually be in contact with several major institutional investors, he will know if they are in a position to invest in the firm's proposed offering, and he can help the firm evaluate the terms of the new issue.

Private placements have both advantages and disadvantages compared with public offerings. The financial manager must carefully evaluate both sides of the question. The advantages associated with private placements are these:

1. **Speed.** The firm usually obtains funds more quickly through a private placement than a public offering. The major reason is that registration of the issue with the SEC is *not* required.
2. **Reduced flotation costs.** These savings result because the lengthy registration statement for the SEC does not have to be prepared, and the investment banking underwriting and distribution costs do not have to be absorbed.
3. **Financing flexibility.** In a private placement the firm deals on a face-to-face basis with a small number of investors. This means that the terms of the issue can be tailored to meet the specific needs of the company. For example, all of the funds need not be taken by the firm at once. In exchange for a commitment fee the firm can "draw down" against the established amount of credit with the investors. This provides some insurance against capital market uncertainties, and the firm does not have to borrow the funds if the need does not arise. There is also the possibility of *renegotiation*. The terms of the debt issue can be altered. The term to maturity, the interest rate, or any restrictive covenants can be discussed among the affected parties.

The disadvantages of private placements that must be evaluated include these:

1. **Interest costs.** It is generally conceded that interest costs on private placements exceed those of public issues. Whether this disadvantage is enough to offset the reduced flotation costs associated with a private placement is a determination that the financial manager must make. There is some evidence that on smaller issues, say $500,000 as opposed to $30 million, the private placement alternative would be preferable.[15]
2. **Restrictive covenants.** Dividend policy, working capital levels, and the raising of additional debt capital may all be affected by provisions in the private placement debt contract. That is not to say that such restrictions are always absent in public debt contracts. Rather, the financial officer must be alert to the tendency for these covenants to be especially burdensome in private contracts.

---

[15] John D. Rea and Peggy Brockschmidt, "The Relationship between Publicly Offered and Privately Placed Corporate Bonds," *Monthly Review, Federal Reserve Bank of Kansas City*, November 1973, p. 15.

3. **The possibility of future SEC registration.** If the lender (investor) should decide to sell the issue to a public buyer before maturity, it must be registered with the SEC. Some lenders, then, require that the issuing firm agree to a future registration at their option.

FLOTATION COSTS

The firm raising long-term capital incurs two types of **flotation costs:** (1) the underwriter's spread and (2) issuing costs. Of these two costs, the underwriter's spread is the larger. The **underwriter's spread** is simply the difference between the gross and net proceeds from a given security issue expressed as a percent of the gross proceeds. The **issue costs** include (1) printing and engraving, (2) legal fees, (3) accounting fees, (4) trustee fees, and (5) several other miscellaneous components. The two most significant issue costs are printing and engraving and legal fees.

Data published by the SEC have consistently revealed two relationships about flotation costs. First, the costs associated with issuing common stock are notably greater than the costs associated with preferred stock offerings. In turn, preferred stock costs exceed those of bonds. Second, flotation costs (expressed as a percent of gross proceeds) decrease as the size of the security issue increases.

In the first instance, the stated relationship reflects the fact that issue costs are sensitive to the risks involved in successfully distributing a security issue. Common stock is riskier to own than corporate bonds. Underwriting risk is, therefore, greater with common stock than with bonds. Thus, flotation costs just mirror these risk relationships. In the second case, a portion of the issue costs is fixed. Legal fees and accounting costs are good examples. So, as the size of the security issue rises, the fixed component is spread over a larger gross proceeds base. As a consequence, average flotation costs vary inversely with the size of the issue.

REGULATION

Following the severe economic downturn of 1929–32, congressional action was taken to provide for federal regulation of the securities markets. State statutes (blue sky laws) also govern the securities markets where applicable, but the federal regulations are clearly more pressing and important. The major federal regulations are reviewed here.

Primary Market Regulations

The new issues market is governed by the **Securities Act of 1933.** The intent of the act is important. It aims to provide potential investors with accurate, truthful disclosure about the firm and the new securities being offered to the public. This does *not* prevent firms from issuing highly speculative securities. The SEC says nothing whatsoever about the possible investment worth of a given offering. It is up to the investor to separate the junk from the jewels. The SEC does have the legal power and responsibility to enforce the 1933 Act.

Full public disclosure is achieved by the requirement that the issuing firm file a registration statement with the SEC containing requisite information. The statement details particulars about the firm and the new security being issued. During a minimum 20-day waiting period, the SEC will examine the submitted document. In numerous instances the 20-day wait has been extended by several weeks. The SEC can ask for additional information that was omitted in order to clarify the original document. The SEC can also order that the offering be stopped.

During the registration process a preliminary prospectus (the red herring) may be distributed to potential investors. When the registration is approved, the prospective investors must have available to them the final prospectus. The prospectus is actually a condensed version of the full registration statement. If, at a later date, the information in the registration statement and the prospectus is found to be lacking, purchasers of the new issue who incurred a loss can sue for damages. Officers of the issuing firm and others who took part in the registration and marketing of the issue may suffer both civil and criminal penalties.

Generally the SEC defines public issues as those that are sold to more than 25 investors. Some public issues need not be registered. These include:

1. Relatively small issues where the firm sells less than $1.5 million of new securities per year.
2. Issues that are sold entirely intrastate.
3. Issues that are basically short-term instruments. This translates into maturity periods of 270 days or less.
4. Issues that are already regulated or controlled by some other federal agency. Examples here are the Federal Power Commission (public utilities) and the Interstate Commerce Commission (railroads).

Secondary Market Regulations

Secondary market trading is regulated by the **Securities Exchange Act of 1934.** This act created the SEC to enforce federal securities laws. The Federal Trade Commission enforced the 1933 act for one year. The major aspects of the 1934 act can be best presented in outline form:

1. Major security exchanges must register with the SEC. This regulates the exchanges and places reporting requirements upon the firms whose securities are listed on them.
2. Insider trading is regulated. Insiders can be officers, directors, employees, relatives, major investors, or anyone having information about the operation of the firm that is not public knowledge. If an investor purchases the security of the firm in which he is an insider, he must hold it for at least six months before disposing of it. Otherwise, profits made from trading the stock within a period of less than six months must be returned to the firm. Furthermore, insiders must file with the SEC a monthly statement of holdings and transactions in the stock of their corporation.[16]

---

[16] On November 14, 1986, the SEC announced that Ivan F. Boesky had admitted to illegal inside trading after an intensive investigation. Boesky at the time was a very well-known Wall Street investor, speculator, and arbitrageur. Boesky was an owner or part owner in several companies, including an arbitrage fund named Ivan F. Boesky & Co. L.P. Boesky agreed to pay the U.S. government $50 million, which represented a return of illegal profits, another $50 million in civil penalties, to withdraw permanently from the securities industry, and to plead guilty to criminal charges. The far-reaching investigation continued into 1987 and implicated several other prominent investment figures.

The chairman of the SEC during this period was John S. R. Shad. Shad suggested that security trades would be considered illegal if they were based on "material, non-public information." As you would expect, this insider trading case garnered a lot of attention in the popular business press and led to renewed discussions of ethics in business schools. See "Who'll Be the Next to Fall?" *Business Week*, December 1, 1986, pp. 28–30; "Wall Street Enters the Age of the Supergrass," *The Economist*, November 22–28, 1986, pp. 77–78; "Going After the Crooks," *Time*, December 1, 1986, pp. 48–51; and "The Decline and Fall of Business Ethics," *Fortune*, 114 (December 8, 1986), 65–66, 68, 72.

3. Manipulative trading of securities by investors to affect stock prices is prohibited.
4. The SEC is given control over proxy procedures.
5. The Board of Governors of the Federal Reserve System is given responsibility for setting margin requirements. This affects the flow of credit into the security markets. Buying securities on margin simply means using credit to acquire a portion of the subject financial instruments.

MORE RECENT REGULATORY DEVELOPMENTS

The Securities Acts Amendments of 1975

The Securities Acts Amendments of 1975 touched on three important issues. First, Congress mandated the creation of a national market system (NMS). Only broad goals for this national exchange were identifed by Congress. Implementation details were left to the SEC and, to a much lesser extent, the securities industry in general. Congress was really expressing its desire for (1) widespread application of auction market trading principles, (2) a high degree of competition across markets, and (3) the use of modern electronic communication systems to link the fragmented markets in the country into a true NMS. The NMS is still a goal toward which the SEC and the securities industry are moving. Agreement as to its final form and an implementation date have not occurred.

A second major alteration in the habits of the securities industry also took place in 1975. This was the elimination of fixed commissions (fixed brokerage rates) on public transactions in securities. This was closely tied to the desire for an NMS in that fixed brokerage fees provided no incentive for competition among brokers. A third consideration of the 1975 amendments focused on such financial institutions as commercial banks and insurance firms. These financial institutions were prohibited from acquiring membership on stock exchanges in order to reduce or save commissions on their own trades.

Shelf Registration

On March 16, 1982, the SEC began a new procedure for registering new issues of securities. Formally it is called SEC Rule 415; informally the process is known as a **shelf registration,** or a **shelf offering.** The essence of the process is rather simple. Rather than go through the lengthy, full registration process each time the firm plans an offering of securities, it can get a blanket order approved by the SEC. A master registration statement that covers the financing plans of the firm over the coming two years is filed with the SEC. Upon approval, the firm can market some or all of the securities over this two-year period. The securities are sold in a piecemeal fashion, or "off the shelf." Prior to each specific offering, a short statement about the issue is filed with the SEC.

Corporations raising funds approve of this new procedure. The tedious, full-registration process is avoided with each offering pulled off the shelf. This should result in a saving of fees paid to investment bankers. Moreover, an issue can more quickly be brought to the market. Also, if market conditions change, an issue can easily be redesigned to fit the specific conditions of the moment.

As is always the case—there is another side to the story. Recall that the reason for the registration process in the first place is to give investors useful information about the firm and the securities being offered. Under the shelf registration procedure some of the information about the issuing firm becomes old as the two-year horizon unfolds. Some investment bankers feel they do not have the proper amount of time to study the firm when a shelf offering takes place. This is one of those areas of finance where more observations are needed before any final conclusions can be made. Those observations will only come with the passage of time.[17]

Summary

This chapter centered on the market environment in which corporations raise long-term funds, including the structure of the U.S. financial markets, the institution of investment banking, and the various methods for distributing securities.

The Mix of Corporate Securities Sold

When corporations go to the capital market for cash, the most favored financing method is debt. The corporate debt markets clearly dominate the equity markets when new funds are raised. The U.S. tax system inherently favors debt capital as a fundraising method. In an average year over the 1972–85 period, bonds and notes made up 69 percent of external cash that was raised.

Why Financial Markets Exist

The function of financial markets is to allocate savings efficiently in the economy to the ultimate demander (user) of the savings. In a financial market the forces of supply and demand for a specific financial instrument are brought together. The wealth of an economy would not be as great as it is without a fully developed financial market system.

Financing Business

Every year households are a net supplier of funds to the financial markets. The nonfinancial business sector is always a net borrower of funds. Both life insurance companies and private pension funds are important buyers of corporate securities. In the economy savings are ultimately transferred to the business firm seeking cash by means of (1) the direct transfer, (2) the indirect transfer using the investment banker, or (3) the indirect transfer using the financial intermediary.

Components of the U.S. Financial Market System

Corporations can raise funds through public offerings or private placements. The public market is impersonal in that the security issuer does not meet the ultimate investors in the financial instruments. In a private placement, the securities are sold directly to a limited number of institutional investors.

The primary market is the market for new issues. The secondary market represents transactions in currently outstanding securities. Both the money and capital markets have primary and secondary sides. The money market refers to transactions in short-term debt instruments. The capital market, on the other hand, refers to transactions in long-term financial instruments. Trading in the money and capital markets can take place on either the organized security exchanges or the over-the-counter market. The money market is exclusively an over-the-counter market.

---

[17] A study of the issue costs associated with Rule 415 is provided by M. Wayne Marr and G. Rodney Thompson, "Rule 415: Preliminary Empirical Results," *Working Paper No. 24* (Department of Finance, Virginia Polytechnic Institute and State University, October 1983). For an overview of the negative side of the matter, see "Shelf Offerings Still Worry Wall Street," *Business Week*, March 5, 1984, p. 83.

The Investment Banker

The investment banker is a financial specialist involved as an intermediary in the merchandising of securities. He performs the functions of (1) underwriting, (2) distributing, and (3) advising. Major methods for the public distribution of securities include (1) the negotiated purchase, (2) the competitive bid purchase, (3) the commission or best-efforts basis, (4) privileged subscriptions, and (5) direct sales. The direct sale bypasses the use of an investment banker. The negotiated purchase is the most profitable distribution method to the investment banker. It also provides the greatest amount of investment banking services to the corporate client.

Private Placements

Privately placed debt provides an important market outlet for corporate bonds. Major investors in this market are (1) life insurance firms, (2) state and local retirement funds, and (3) private pension funds. Several advantages and disadvantages are associated with private placements. The financial officer must weigh these attributes and decide if a private placement is preferable over a public offering.

Flotation Costs

Flotation costs consist of the underwriter's spread and issuing costs. The flotation costs of common stock exceed those of preferred stock, which, in turn, exceed those of debt. Moreover, flotation costs as a percent of gross proceeds are inversely related to the size of the security issue.

Regulation

The new issues market is regulated at the federal level by the Securities Act of 1933. It provides for the registration of new issues with the SEC. Secondary market trading is regulated by the Securities Exchange Act of 1934. The Securities Acts Amendments of 1975 placed on the SEC the responsibility for devising a national market system. This concept is still being studied. The shelf registration procedure (SEC Rule 415) was initiated in March 1982. Under this regulation and with the proper filing of documents, firms that are selling new issues do not have to go through the old, lengthy registration process each time the firm plans an offering of securities.

Study Questions

17–1. What are financial markets? What function do they perform? How would an economy be worse off without them?

17–2. Define in a technical sense what we mean by "financial intermediary." Give an example of your definition.

17–3. Distinguish between the money and capital markets.

17–4. What major benefits do corporations and investors enjoy because of the existence of organized security exchanges?

17–5. What are the general categories examined by an organized exchange in determining whether an applicant firm's securities can be listed on it? (Specific numbers are not needed here, but rather "areas" of investigation.)

17–6. Why do you think most secondary market trading in bonds takes place over-the-counter?

17–7. What is an investment banker, and what major functions does he perform?

17–8. What is the major difference between a negotiated purchase and a competitive bid purchase?

17–9. Why is an investment banking syndicate formed?

17–10. Why might a large corporation want to raise long-term capital through a private placement rather than a public offering?

17–11. As a recent business school graduate, you work directly for the corporate treasurer. Your corporation is going to issue a new security and is concerned with the probable flotation costs. What tendencies about flotation costs can you relate to the treasurer?

17–12. You own a group of five clothing stores, all located in southern California. You are about to market $200,000 worth of new common stock. Your stock trades over-the-counter. The stock will be sold only to California residents. Your financial adviser informs you that the issue must be registered with the SEC. Is he correct?

17–13. When corporations raise funds, what type of financing vehicle (instrument or instruments) is most favored?

17–14. What is the major (most significant) savings-surplus sector in the U.S. economy?

17–15. Identify three distinct ways that savings are ultimately transferred to business firms in need of cash.

Selected References

Amling, Frederick. *Investments: An Introduction to Analysis and Management* (5th ed.) Englewood Cliffs, NJ: Prentice-Hall, 1984.

Asquith, Paul, and David W. Mullins, Jr. "Equity Issues and Offering Dilution," *Journal of Financial Economics*, 15 (January–February 1986), 61–89.

Bloch, Ernest. "Pricing a Corporate Bond Issue: A Look Behind the Scenes," *Essays in Money and Credit*, pp. 72–76. New York: Federal Reserve Bank of New York, 1964.

Booth, James R., and Richard L. Smith, II. "Capital Raising, Underwriting and the Certification Hypothesis," *Journal of Financial Economics*, 15 (January–February 1986), 261–81.

Cohan, A. B. *Private Placements and Public Offerings: Market Shares Since 1945*. Chapel Hill: University of North Carolina Press, 1961.

Conroy, Robert M., and Robert L. Winkler. "Market Structure: The Specialist as Dealer and Broker," *Journal of Banking and Finance*, 10 (March 1986), 21–36.

Cooper, S. Kerry, Donald R. Fraser, and Gene C. Uselton. *Money, the Financial System, and Economic Policy*. Reading, MA: Addison-Wesley, 1983.

Dougall, Herbert E., and Jack E. Gaumnitz. *Capital Markets and Institutions* (4th ed.). Englewood Cliffs, NJ: Prentice-Hall, 1980.

Eckbo, B. Espen. "Valuation Effects of Corporate Debt Offerings," *Journal of Financial Economics*, 15 (January–February 1986), 119–51.

Ederington, Louis H. "Negotiated versus Competitive

Underwritings of Corporate Bonds," *Journal of Finance*, 31 (March 1976), 17–28.

Edmister, Robert O. *Financial Institutions, Markets and Management* (2nd ed.). New York: McGraw-Hill, 1986.

Fabozzi, Frank J., and Frank G. Zarb, eds. *Handbook of Financial Markets*. Homewood, IL: Dow Jones-Irwin, 1981.

Feldstein, Martin, ed. *The American Economy in Transition*. Chicago: University of Chicago Press, 1980.

Friedman, Benjamin M., ed. *The Changing Roles of Debt and Equity in Financing U.S. Capital Formation*. Chicago: University of Chicago Press, 1982.

Furst, Richard W. "Does Listing Increase the Market Price of Common Stocks?" *Journal of Business*, 43 (April 1970), 174–80.

Goulet, Waldemar M. "Price Changes, Managerial Actions and Insider Trading at the Time of Listing," *Financial Management*, 3 (Spring 1974), 30–36.

Gup, Benton E. *Financial Intermediaries* (2nd ed.), Boston: Houghton Mifflin, 1980.

Hayes, Samuel L., III. "Investment Banking: Power Structure in Flux," *Harvard Business Review*, 49 (March–April 1971), 136–52.

Henning, Charles N., William Pigott, and Robert H. Scott. *Financial Markets and the Economy* (4th ed.). Englewood Cliffs, NJ: Prentice-Hall, 1984.

Johnson, Keith B., Gregory T. Morton, and M. Chapman Findlay III. "An Empirical Analysis of the Flotation

Cost of Corporate Securities, 1971–1972," *Journal of Finance*, 30 (June 1975), 1129–33.

Light, J. O., and William L. White. *The Financial System*. Homewood, IL: Richard D. Irwin, 1979.

Logue, Dennis E., and John R. Lindvall. "The Behavior of Investment Bankers: An Econometric Investigation," *Journal of Finance*, 29 (March 1974), 203–15.

_____, and Robert A. Jarrow. "Negotiation vs. Competitive Bidding in the Sale of Securities by Public Utilities," *Financial Management*, 7 (Autumn 1978), 31–39.

Marr, M. Wayne, and G. Rodney Thompson. "Rule 415: Preliminary Empirical Results," *Working Paper No. 24*, Department of Finance, Virginia Polytechnic Institute and State University, October 1983.

Ratner, David L. *Securities Regulation in a Nutshell*. St. Paul, MN: West Publishing, 1978.

Rose, Peter S., and Donald R. Fraser. *Financial Institutions* (3rd ed.). Dallas: Business Publications, 1984.

Smith, Clifford W., Jr. "Investment Banking and the Capital Acquisition Process," *Journal of Financial Economics*, 15 (January–February 1986), 3–29.

Strebel, Paul. "Managing the Information Cost of Financing," *Columbia Journal of World Business*, 21 (Summer 1986), 39–45.

Tallman, Gary D., David R. Rush, and Ronald W. Melicher. "Competitive versus Negotiated Underwriting Cost of Regulated Industries," *Financial Management*, 3 (Summer 1974), 49–55.

Van Horne, James C. *Financial Market Rates and Flows* (2nd ed.). Englewood Cliffs, NJ: Prentice-Hall, 1984.

West, Richard R., and Seha M. Tinic. "Corporate Finance and the Changing Stock Market," *Financial Management*, 3 (Autumn 1974), 14–23.

Wiesen, Jeremy L. *Regulating Transactions in Securities*. St. Paul, MN: West Publishing, 1975.

18

Term Loans and Leases

For discussion purposes we generally categorize the sources of financing available to the business firm into three groups, distinguished on the basis of the maturity of the financing agreement. The maturities used here are not exact but represent generally accepted guidelines for categorizing sources of financing. Short-term sources of financing, which have a maturity of one year or less, were discussed in Chapter 8. Intermediate-term financing, which includes all financing arrangements having final maturities longer than 1 year but no longer than 10 years, is the subject of this chapter. Long-term financing, which includes all forms of financing with final maturities longer than 10 years, is discussed in Chapters 19 and 20.

The principal sources of intermediate-term financing include term loans and leases. We will look first at the primary sources of term loans and their characteristics. Then we will discuss lease financing, including (1) the types of leasing arrangements, (2) the accounting treatment of financial leases, (3) the lease versus purchase decision, and (4) the potential benefits from leasing.

TERM LOANS

Term loans generally share three common characteristics: they (1) have maturities of 1 to 10 years, (2) are repaid in periodic installments (such as quarterly, semi-annual, or annual payments) over the life of the loan, and (3) are usually secured by a chattel mortgage on equipment or a mortgage on real property. The principal suppliers of term credit include commercial banks, insurance companies, and to a lesser extent pension funds.

We will consider briefly some of the more common characteristics of term loan agreements.

Maturities

Commercial banks generally restrict their term lending to 1- to 5-year maturities. Insurance companies and pension funds with their longer-term liabilities generally make loans with 5- to 15-year maturities. Thus, the term lending activities of commercial banks actually complement rather than compete with those of insurance companies and pension funds. In fact, commercial banks very often cooperate with both insurance companies and pension funds in providing term financing for very large loans.

Collateral   Term loans are almost always backed by some form of collateral. Shorter-maturity loans are frequently secured with a chattel mortgage on machinery and equipment, or with securities such as stocks and bonds. Longer-maturity loans are frequently secured by mortgages on real estate.

Restrictive Covenants   In addition to collateral the lender in a term loan agreement will often place restrictions on the borrower that, when violated, make the loan immediately due and payable. These restrictive covenants are designed to maintain the borrower's financial condition on a par with that which existed at the time the loan was made. Thus, the lender seeks to prohibit the borrower from engaging in any activities that would increase the likelihood of loss on the loan. Some commonly used restrictions are discussed below.

1. **Working capital requirement.** One restriction involves maintaining a minimum amount of working capital. Very often this restriction takes the form of a minimum current ratio, such as 2 to 1 or 3½ to 1, or a minimum dollar amount of net working capital. The actual requirement would reflect the norm for the borrower's industry, as well as the lender's desires.
2. **Additional borrowing.** Generally this type of restriction requires the lender's approval before any additional debt can be issued. Furthermore, the restriction is often extended to long-term lease agreements, which are discussed later in this chapter.
3. **Periodic financial statements.** A standard covenant in most term loan agreements involves requiring the borrower to supply the lender with financial statements on a regular basis. These generally include annual or perhaps quarterly income statements and balance sheets.
4. **Management.** Term loan agreements will sometimes include a provision requiring prior approval by the lender of major personnel changes. In addition, the borrower may be required to insure the lives of certain key personnel, naming the lender as beneficiary.

We have presented only a partial listing of restrictions commonly found in term loan agreements. The number and form of such provisions is limited only by the imagination of the parties involved. It should be noted, however, that restrictive covenants are subject to negotiation. Thus, the specific agreement that results will reflect the relative bargaining strengths of the borrower and lender. For this reason the marginal borrower is likely to find the loan agreement more burdened with restrictive covenants than a more creditworthy borrower.

Term loan agreements can be very technical and are generally tailored to the situation. For this reason, it is difficult to generalize too much about their content. However, many banks utilize *worksheets* or *checksheets* to aid in the preparation of the document.

Repayment Schedules   Term loans are generally repaid with periodic installments, which include both an interest and a principal component. Thus, the loan is repaid over its life with equal annual, semi-annual, or quarterly payments.

To illustrate how the repayment procedure works, let us assume that a firm borrows $15,000, which is to be repaid in five annual installments. The loan will carry an 8 percent rate of interest, and payments will be made at the end of each of the next 5 years. Visually, the loan will involve the following cash flows to the lender (Chapter 9 also contains a discussion of the calculation of installment loan payments):

Year 0	1	2	3	4	5
$(15,000)	A_1	A_2	A_3	A_4	A_5

The $15,000 cash flow at time period zero is placed in parentheses to indicate an outflow of cash by the lender, whereas the annual installments, A_1 through A_5, represent cash inflows (of course the opposite is true for the borrower). The lender then needs to determine the annual installments that will give an 8 percent return on the outstanding balance over the life of the loan. This problem is very similar to the internal rate of return problem encountered in Chapter 10, where we discussed capital budgeting decisions. There we had to determine the rate of interest that would make the present value of a stream of future cash flows equal to some present sum. Here we want to determine the future cash flows whose present value, when discounted at 8 percent, is equal to the $15,000 loan amount. Thus, we must solve for those values of A_1 through A_5 whose present value when discounted at 8 percent is $15,000. In equation form,

$$\$15,000 = \sum_{t=1}^{5} \frac{A_t}{(1 + .08)^t} \qquad (18\text{--}1)$$

Where we assume equal annual installments, A, for all 5 years, we can solve for A as follows:

Thus,
$$\$15,000 = A \sum_{t=1}^{5} \frac{1}{(1 + .08)^t}$$

$$A = \frac{\$15,000}{\sum_{t=1}^{5} \frac{1}{(1 + .08)^t}} \qquad (18\text{--}2)$$

We recognize the term being divided into the $15,000 loan as the present value factor for a 5-year annuity carrying an 8 percent rate of interest; thus, using the present value of an annuity table in Appendix D and solving for A,

$$A = \frac{\$15,000}{3.993} = \$3756.57$$

Therefore, if the borrower makes payments of $3756.57 each year, then the lender will receive an 8 percent return on the outstanding loan balance. To verify this assertion Table 18–1 contains the principal and interest components of the annual loan payments.

TABLE 18–1. Term Loan Amortization Schedule

End of Year t	Installment Payment[a] A	Interest[b] I_t	Principal Repayment[c] P_t	Remaining Balance[d] RB_t
0	—	—	—	$15,000.00
1	$3,756.57	$1,200.00	$2,556.57	12,443.43
2	3,756.57	995.47	2,761.10	9,682.33
3	3,756.57	774.59	2,981.98	6,700.35
4	3,756.57	536.03	3,220.54	3,479.81
5	3,756.57	278.38	3,478.19	1.62[e]

[a] The annual installment payment, A, is found as follows:

$$A = \frac{\$15,000}{\sum\limits_{t=1}^{5} \dfrac{1}{(1 + .08)^t}} = \$3756.57$$

[b] Annual interest expense is equal to 8 percent of the outstanding loan balance. Thus, for year 1 the interest expense, I_1, is found as follows:

$$I_1 = .08(\$15,000) = \$1200$$

[c] Principal repayment for year t, P_t, is the difference in the loan payment, A, and interest for the year. Thus, for year 1 we compute:

$$P_1 = A - I_1 = \$3756.57 - \$1200 = \$2556.57$$

[d] The remaining balance of the end of year 1, RB_1, is the difference in the remaining balance for the previous year, RB_0, and the principal payment in year 1, P_1. Thus, at the end of year 1,

$$RB_1 = RB_0 - P_1 = \$15,000 - \$2556.57 = \$12,443.43$$

[e] The $1.62 difference in RB_4 and P_5 is due to rounding error.

Here we see that the $3756.57 installments truly provide the lender with an 8 percent return on the outstanding balance of a $15,000 loan.

LEASING

Leasing provides an alternative to buying an asset in order to acquire its services. Although some leases involve maturities of more than 10 years, most do not. Thus, lease financing is classified as a source of intermediate term credit. Today, virtually any type of asset can be acquired through a lease agreement. The recent growth in lease financing has been phenomenal, with over $200 billion in assets (based on original cost) now under lease in the United States.

We begin our discussion by defining the major types of lease arrangements. Next we consider the history and present status of the accounting treatment of leases. We examine the lease versus purchase decision, and we conclude by investigating the potential benefits of leasing.

Types of Lease Arrangements

There are three major types of lease agreements: direct leasing, sale and leaseback, and leveraged leasing. Most lease agreements fall into one of these categories. However, the particular lease agreement can take one of two forms. (1) The **financial lease** constitutes a noncancellable contractual commitment on the part of the firm leasing the asset (the lessee) to make a series of payments to the firm that actually owns the asset (the lessor) for use of the asset. (2) The **operating lease** differs from the financial lease only with respect to its cancelability. An operating lease can be canceled after proper notice to the lessor any time during its term. Thus, operating leases are by their very nature sources of short-term financing. The balance of this chapter is concerned with the financial lease, which provides the firm with a form of intermediate-term financing most comparable to debt financing.

Direct Leasing

In a **direct lease** the firm acquires the services of an asset it did not previously own. Direct leasing is available through a number of financial institutions, including manufacturers, banks, finance companies, independent leasing companies, and special purpose leasing companies.[1] Basically, the lease arrangement involves the lessor's purchasing the asset and leasing it to the lessee. In the case of the manufacturer lessor, however, the acquisition step is not necessary.

Sale and Leaseback

A **sale and leaseback** arrangement arises when a firm sells land, buildings, or equipment that it already owns to a lessor and simultaneously enters into an agreement to lease the property back for a specified period under specific terms. The lessor involved in the sale and leaseback varies with the nature of the property involved and the lease period. Where land is involved and the corresponding lease is long term, the lessor is generally a life insurance company. If the property consists of machinery and equipment, then the maturity of the lease will probably be intermediate term and the lessor could be an insurance company, commercial bank, or leasing company.

The lessee firm receives cash in the amount of the sales price of the assets sold and the use of the asset over the term of the lease. In return, the lessee must make periodic rental payments through the term of the lease and give up any salvage or residual value to the lessor.

Net and Net-Net Leases

In the jargon of the leasing industry, a financial lease can take one of two basic forms: a **net lease** or a **net-net lease.** In a net lease agreement the lessee firm assumes the risk and burden of ownership over the term of the lease. That is, the lessee must maintain the asset, as well as pay insurance and taxes on the asset. With a net-net lease the lessee must, in addition to the requirements of a net lease, return the asset to the lessor at the end of the lease term with a preestablished value.

Leveraged Leasing

In the leasing arrangements discussed thus far only two participants have been identified: the lessor and lessee. In a **leveraged lease** a third participant is added. The added party is the lender who helps finance the acquisition of the asset to be leased. From the point of view of the lessee there is no difference in a leveraged lease, direct lease, or sale and leaseback arrangement. However, with a leveraged lease, specific consideration is given to the method of financing used by the lessor in acquiring the asset. The lessor will generally supply equity funds to 20 to 30 percent of the purchase price and borrow the remainder from a third-party lender, which may be a commercial bank or insurance company. In some arrangements the lessor firm sells bonds, which are guaranteed by the lessee. This guarantee serves to reduce the risk and thus the cost of the debt. The majority of financial leases are leveraged leases.

---

[1] Many leasing companies specialize in the leasing of a single type of asset. For example, a number of firms lease computers exclusively, and others lease only automobiles.

Accounting for Leases

Before January 1977 most financial leases were not included in the balance sheets of lessee firms. Instead, they were reported in the footnotes to the balance sheet.[2] However, in November 1976 the Financial Accounting Standards Board reversed its position with *Statement of Financial Accounting Standards No. 13*, "Accounting for Leases."[3] The board adopted the position that the economic effect of the transaction should govern its accounting treatment.[4] In this regard, the FASB asserted that "a lease that transfers substantially all the benefits and risks incident to the ownership of property should be accounted for as the acquisition of an asset and the incurrence of an obligation by the lessee."[5] Specifically, Statement No. 13 requires that any lease that meets one or more of the following criteria is a **capital lease** and must be included in the body of the balance sheet of the lessee. All other lease agreements are classified as **operating leases** for accounting purposes.

1. The lease transfers ownership of the property to the lessee by the end of the lease term.
2. The lease contains a bargain repurchase option.
3. The lease term is equal to 75 percent or more of the estimated economic life of the leased property.
4. The present value of the minimum lease payments equals or exceeds 90 percent of the excess of the fair value of the property over any related investment tax credit retained by the lessor.[6]

The last two requirements are the most stringent elements in the board's statement. The first two have been applicable to most leases for many years because of the Internal Revenue Service's "true" lease requirements.[7] However, the last two apply to the majority of the financial leases written in the United States. As a result, the board now requires capitalization of all leases meeting one or more of these criteria.

Figure 18–1 contains an example balance sheet for the Alpha Mfg. Company. Alpha has entered into capital leases whose payments have a present value of $4 million.

Note that the asset "leased property" is matched by a liability, "capital lease obligations." The specific entries recorded for the lease obligation equal the present value of minimum lease payments the firm must pay over the term of the lease. The discount

[2] Prior to January 1977 the guiding accounting principles regarding the treatment of leases were *Opinion No. 5* and *Opinion No. 31* of the Accounting Principles Board (APB). Opinion No. 5 stated that only in the case in which a lease "is in substance a purchase" should an asset and a liability appear on the lessee's balance sheet. In response to requests from various groups of statement users, the APB expanded its disclosure requirements in Opinion No. 31. See American Institute of Certified Public Accountants, *Accounting Principles Board Opinion No. 5*, "Reporting of Leases in Financial Statements of Lessee" (New York: AICPA, September 1964), and *Accounting Principles Board Opinion No. 31*, "Disclosure of Lease Commitments by Lessees" (New York: AICPA, June 1973).

[3] Financial Accounting Standards Board, *Statement of Accounting Standards No. 13*, "Accounting for Leases" (Stamford, Conn.: FASB, November 1976).

[4] Ibid., p. 49.

[5] Ibid.

[6] Ibid., pp. 9–10.

[7] The Economic Recovery Tax Act of 1981 effectively "suspended" the true lease requirements of Rev. Rul. 55–540, 1955 C.B. 41; however, these changes were largely reversed by the Tax Equity and Fiscal Responsibility Act of 1982. This act did create a "finance lease," which for tax purposes is classified as a lease. However, unlike the true lease requirements of the pre-ERTA, a finance lease *can* include a purchase option (equal to a minimum of 10 percent of the original purchase price of the leased asset), and it *can* be used to finance "limited use" property (property that can only be used by the lessee).

FIGURE 18–1. Alpha Mfg. Company Balance Sheet December 31, 1987 ($ millions)

Assets:	
Current assets	$14
Plant and equipment	20
Leased property (capital leases)	4
Total	$38

Liabilities and stockholders' equity:	
Current liabilities	8
Long-term debt	9
Capital lease obligations	4
Stockholders' equity	17
Total	$38

rate used is the lower of the lessee's incremental borrowing rate or the lessor's implicit interest rate (where that rate can be determined).

Operating leases are not disclosed in the body of the balance sheet. Instead, these lease obligations must be reported in a footnote to the balance sheet.

The Lease versus Purchase Decision

The lease versus purchase problem is a hybrid capital budgeting problem that forces the analyst to consider the consequences of alternative forms of financing on the investment decision. When we discussed capital budgeting in Chapter 10 and the cost of capital in Chapter 13, we assumed that all new financing would be undertaken in accordance with the firm's optimal capital structure. When analyzing an asset that is to be leased, the analysis must be altered to consider financing through leasing as opposed to the use of the more traditional debt and equity sources of funds. Thus, the lease versus purchase decision requires a standard capital budgeting type of analysis, as well as an analysis of two alternative financing *packages*. The lease-purchase decision involves the analysis of two basic issues:

1. Should the asset be purchased using the firm's optimal financing mix?
2. Should the asset be financed using a financial lease?

The answer to the first question can be obtained through an analysis of the project's net present value (*NPV*) following the method laid out in Chapter 10. However, regardless of whether the asset should or should not be purchased, it may be advantageous for the firm to lease it. That is, the cost savings accruing through leasing might be so great as to offset a negative net present value resulting from the purchase of an asset. For example, the Alpha Mfg. Co. is considering the acquisition of a new computer-based inventory and payroll system. The computed net present value of the new system based upon normal purchase financing is − $40, indicating that acquisition of the system through purchasing or ownership is not warranted. However, an analysis of the cost savings resulting from leasing the system (referred to here as the net advantage of leasing—*NAL*) indicates that the lease alternative will produce a present value cost saving of $60 over normal purchase financing. Therefore, the net present value of the system if leased is $20 (the net present value if leased equals the *NPV* of a purchase *plus* the net advantage of leasing, or − $40 + $60). Thus, the system's services should be acquired via the lease agreement.

In the pages that follow we will (1) review briefly the concept of a project's net present value, which we will refer to as the net present value of purchase, or *NPV(P)*; (2) introduce a model for estimating the net present value advantage of leasing over normal purchase financing, which we will refer to as the net advantage of lease financing, or *NAL*; (3) present a flow chart that can be used in performing lease-purchase analyses based upon *NPV(P)* and *NAL*; and (4) provide a comprehensive example of a lease-purchase analysis.

The Lease-Purchase Algorithm

Answers to both questions posed above can be obtained using the two equations found in Table 18–2. The first equation is simply the net present value of purchasing the proposed project, discussed in Chapter 10. The second equation represents the net present value advantage of leasing (*NAL*). *NAL* represents an accumulation of the

TABLE 18–2. The Lease-Purchase Model

Equation One—Net present value of purchase [*NPV(P)*]:

$$NPV(P) = \sum_{t=1}^{n} \frac{ACF_t}{(1 + K)^t} - IO \tag{18–3}$$

where ACF_t = the annual after-tax cash flow in period t resulting from the asset's purchase (note that ACF_n also includes any after-tax salvage value expected from the project).

     K = the firm's cost of capital applicable to the project being analyzed and the particular mix of financing used to acquire the project.

     IO = the initial cash outlay required to purchase the asset in period zero (now).

     n = the productive life of the project.

Equation Two—Net Advantage of Leasing (*NAL*):

$$NAL = \sum_{t=1}^{n} \frac{O_t(1 - T) - R_t(1 - T) - T \cdot I_t - T \cdot D_t}{(1 + r)^t} - \frac{V_n}{(1 + K_s)^n} + IO \tag{18–4}$$

where O_t = any operating cash flows incurred in period t that are incurred only where the asset is purchased. Most often this consists of maintenance expenses and insurance that would be paid by the lessor.

     R_t = the annual rental for period t.

     T = the marginal tax rate on corporate income.

     I_t = the tax-deductible interest expense forfeited in period t if the lease option is adopted. This represents the interest expense on a loan equal to the full purchase price of the asset being acquired.[a]

     D_t = depreciation expense in period t for the asset.

     V_n = the after-tax salvage value of the asset expected in year n.

     K_s = the discount rate used to find the present value of V_n. This rate should reflect the risk inherent in the estimated V_n. For simplicity the after-tax cost of capital (K) is often used as a proxy for this rate. Also, note that this rate is the same one used to discount the salvage value in *NPV(P)*.

     IO = the purchase price of the asset, which is not paid by the firm in the event the asset is leased.

     r = the before-tax rate of interest on borrowed funds. This rate is used to discount the relatively certain after-tax cash flow savings that accrue through the leasing of the asset.

[a] This analysis makes the implicit assumption that a dollar of lease financing is equivalent to a dollar of loan. This form of equivalence is only one of several that might be used. The interested reader is referred to A. H. Ofer, "The Evaluation of the Lease versus Purchase Alternatives," *Financial Management*, 5 (Summer 1976), 67–74.

cash flows (both inflows and outflows) associated with leasing *as opposed to* purchasing the asset. Specifically, through leasing the firm avoids certain operating expenses, O_t, but incurs the after-tax rental expense, $R_t(1 - T)$. By leasing, furthermore, the firm loses the tax-deductible expense associated with interest, $T \cdot I_t$, and depreciation, $T \cdot D_t$. Finally, the firm does not receive the salvage value from the asset, V_n, if it is leased, but it does not have to make the initial cash outlay to purchase the asset, IO. Thus, *NAL* reflects the cost savings associated with leasing, net of the opportunity costs of not purchasing.

Note that the before-tax cost of new debt is used to discount the *NAL* cash flows other than the salvage value, V_n. This is justified on the basis that the affected cash flows are very nearly riskless and certainly no more risky than the interest and principal accruing to the firm's creditors (which underlie the rate of interest charged to the firm for its debt).[8] Since V_n is not a risk-free cash flow but depends upon the market price for the leased asset in year n, a rate higher than r is appropriate. Since the salvage value of the leased asset was discounted using the cost of capital when determining *NPV(P)*, we again use this rate here when calculating *NAL*.

Figure 18–2 contains a flow chart that can be used in performing lease purchase analyses. The analyst first calculates *NPV(P)*. If the resulting project net present value is positive, then the left-hand branch of Figure 18–2 should be followed. Tracing through the left branch we now compute *NAL*. If *NAL* is positive, this indicates that the lease alternative offers a positive present-value cost advantage over normal purchase financing in which case the asset should be leased. Should *NAL* be negative, then the purchase alternative should be selected. Return to the top of Figure 18–2 once again. This time we assume that *NPV(P)* is negative such that the analyst's attention is directed to the right-hand side of the flow chart. The only hope for the project's acceptance at this point is a favorable set of lease terms. In this circumstance the project would be acceptable and thus leased *only* if *NAL* were large enough to offset the negative *NPV(P)* [that is, where *NAL* was greater than the absolute value of *NPV(P)* or, equivalently, where $NAL + NPV(P) \geq 0$].[9]

Case Problem in Lease-Purchase Analysis

The Waynesboro Plastic Molding Company (WPM) is now deciding whether to purchase an automatic casting machine. The machine will cost \$15,000 and for tax purposes will be depreciated toward a zero salvage value over a 5-year period. However, at the end of 5 years the machine actually has an expected salvage value of \$2100.

---

[8] The argument for using the firm's borrowing rate to discount these tax shelters goes as follows: The tax shields are relatively free of risk in that their source (depreciation, interest, rental payments) can be estimated with a high degree of certainty. There are, however, two sources of uncertainty with regard to these tax shelters: (1) the possibility of a change in the firm's tax rate and (2) the possibility that the firm might become bankrupt at some future date. If we attach a very low probability to the likelihood of a reduction in the tax rate, then the prime risk associated with these tax shelters is the possibility of bankruptcy wherein they would be lost forever (certainly all tax shelters after the date of bankruptcy would be lost). We now note that the firm's creditors also faced the risk of the firm's bankruptcy when they lent the firm funds at the rate r. If this rate, r, reflects the market's assessment of the firm's bankruptcy potential as well as the time value of money, then it offers an appropriate rate for discounting the interest shelters generated by the firm. Note also that the O_t cash flows are generally estimated with a high degree of certainty (in the case where they represent insurance premiums they may be contractually set) such that r is appropriate as a discount rate here also.

[9] That is, $NAL = NPV(L) - NPV(P)$, where $NPV(L)$ is the net present value of the asset if leased. Thus, the sum of $NPV(P)$ and NAL is the net present value of the asset if leased. See Lawrence D. Schall, "The Lease-or-Buy and Asset Acquisition Decisions," *Journal of Finance*, 29 (September 1974), 1203–14, for a development of net present value of leasing and purchasing equations.

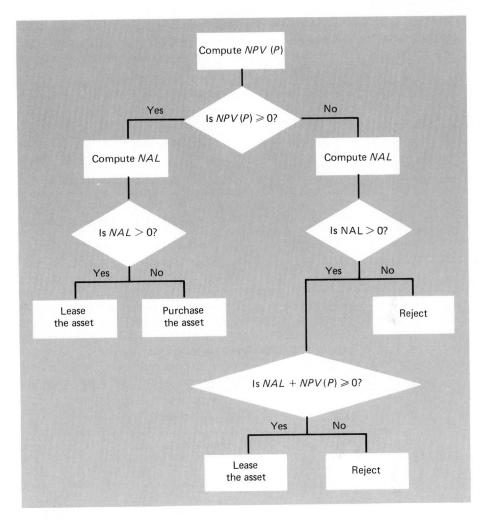

FIGURE 18–2. Lease-Purchase Analysis

Since the machine is depreciated toward a zero book value at the end of 5 years, the salvage value is fully taxable at the firm's marginal tax rate of 50 percent. Hence, the after-tax salvage value of the machine is only $1050.[10] The firm utilizes the straight-line depreciation method to depreciate the $15,000 asset toward a zero salvage value. Furthermore, the project is expected to generate annual cash revenues of $5000 per year over the next 5 years (net of cash operating expenses but before depreciation and taxes). WPM has a target debt ratio of 40 percent for projects of this type which is impounded in its after-tax cost-of-capital estimate of 12 percent. Finally, WPM can borrow funds at a before-tax rate of 8 percent.

---

[10] The problem example is a modification of the well-known example from R. W. Johnson and W. G. Lewellen, "Analysis of the Lease or Buy Decision," *Journal of Finance*, 27 (September 1972), 815–23.

STEP 1: *Computing NPV(P)—Should the Asset Be Purchased?* *The first step in analyzing the lease-purchase problem involves computing the net present value under the purchase alternative. The relevant cash flow computations are presented in Table 18–3.*

TABLE 18–3. **Computing Project Annual After-Tax Cash Flows (ACF_t) Associated with Asset Purchase**

	Year 1		Year 2		Year 3		Year 4		Year 5	
	Book Profits	Cash Flow	Book Profits	Cash Flow	Book Profits	Cash Flow	Book Profits	Cash Flow	Book Profits	Cash Flow
Annual cash revenues	$5000	$5000	$5000	$5000	$5000	$5000	$5000	$5000	$5000	$5000
Less: Depreciation	(3000)	—	(3000)	—	(3000)	—	(3000)	—	(3000)	—
Net revenues before taxes	$2000	$5000	$2000	$5000	$2000	$5000	$2000	$5000	$2000	$5000
Less: Taxes (50%)	(1000) →	(1000)	(1000) →	(1000)	(1000) →	(1000)	(1000) →	(1000)	(1000) →	(1000)
Annual after-tax cash flow		$4000		$4000		$4000		$4000		$4000

The NPV(P) *is found by discounting the annual cash flows* (ACF_t) *in Table 18–3 back to the present at the firm's after-tax cost of capital of 12 percent, adding this sum to the present value of the salvage value, and subtracting the initial cash outlay. These calculations are shown in Table 18–4. The project's NPV(P) is a positive $15.35, indicating that the asset should be acquired.*

The second question concerns whether the asset should be leased. This can be answered by considering the net advantage to leasing (NAL).

TABLE 18–4. **Calculating *NPV(P)***

Year t	Annual Cash Flow ACF_t	Discount Factor for 12 Percent	Present Value
1	$4000	.893	$3572
2	4000	.797	3188
3	4000	.712	2848
4	4000	.636	2544
5	4000	.567	2268
5 (Salvage—V_n)	1050	.567	595.35
		Present value of $ACFs$ and V_n =	$15,015.35
		NPV(P) = $15,015.35 − $15,000 = $	15.35

STEP 2: *Computing NAL—Should the Asset Be Leased?* *The computation of NAL is shown in Table 18–5. The resulting NAL is a positive $444, which indicates that leasing is preferred to the normal debt-equity method of financing. In fact, WPM will be $444 better off, in present value terms, if it chooses to lease rather than purchase the asset.*

Calculating NAL involves solving equation (18–4) presented earlier in Table 18–2. To do this, we first estimate all those cash flows that are to be discounted at the firm's cost of debt, r. These include $O_t(1 - T)$, $R_t(1 - T)$, $I_t \cdot T$, and $T \cdot D_t$.

The operating expenses associated with the asset that will be paid by the lessor if we lease—that is, the O_t—generally consist of certain maintenance expenses and insur-

TABLE 18–5. Computing the Net Advantage to Leasing (NAL)

Overview: To solve for *NAL* we use equation (18–4), which was discussed in Table 18–2. This equation contains three terms and is repeated below for convenience.

$$NAL = \sum_{t=1}^{n} \frac{O_t(1-T) - R_t(1-T) - I_t \cdot T - D_t \cdot T}{(1+r)^t} - \frac{V_n}{(1+K_s)^n} + IO$$

$$\underbrace{\phantom{\sum_{t=1}^{n} \frac{O_t(1-T)}{(1+r)^t}}}_{\text{Term 1}} \qquad \underbrace{\phantom{\frac{V_n}{(1+K_s)^n}}}_{\text{Term 2}} \qquad \underbrace{}_{\text{Term 3}}$$

STEP 1: Solving for Term 1 $= \sum_{t=1}^{n} \dfrac{O_t(1-T) - R_t(1-T) - I_t \cdot T - D_t \cdot T}{(1+r)^t}$

Year t	After-tax Operating Expenses Paid by Lessor[a] $O_t(1-T)$	−	After-tax Rental Expense[b] $R_t(1-T)$	−	Tax Shelter on Loan Interest[c] $I_t T$	−	Tax Shelter on Depreciation[d] $D_t T$	=	Total SUM	×	Discount Factor at 8 Percent DF	=	Present Value PV
1	$500		$2100		$600		$1500		−$3700		.926		$−3426
2	500		2100		498		1500		−3598		.857		−3083
3	500		2100		387		1500		−3487		.794		−2769
4	500		2100		268		1500		−3368		.735		−2475
5	500		2100		140		1500		−3240		.681		−2206
													−13,961

STEP 2: Solving for Term 2 $= -\left[\dfrac{V_n}{(1+K)^n}\right] = -\left[\dfrac{\$1050}{(1+.12)^5}\right] = -\$1050 \times .567^e = $ −595

STEP 3: Term 3 = IO $15,000

STEP 4: Calculate NAL = Term 1 − Term 2 + Term 3 = − $13,961 − $595 + $15,000 = $444

[a] After-tax lessor-paid operating expenses are found by $O_t(1-T) = \$1000(1 - 0.5) = \$500$.

[b] After-tax rent expense for year 1 is computed as follows: $R_t(1-T) = \$4200(1 - 0.5) = \$2100$.

[c] Interest expense figures were calculated in Table 18–1 for a $15,000 loan. For year 1 the interest tax shelter is $0.5 \times \$1200 = \$600$.

[d] The tax shelter from depreciation is found as follows: $D_1 T = \$3000 \times 0.5 = \$1500$.

[e] K_s was estimated to be the same as the firm's after-tax cost of capital, 12 percent.

631

ance. WPM estimates them to be $1000 per year over the life of the project. The annual rental or lease payments, R_t, are given and equal $4200.

The interest tax shelter lost because the asset is leased and not purchased must now be estimated. This tax shelter is lost because the firm does not borrow any money if it enters into the lease agreement. Table 18–1 contains the principal and interest components for a $15,000 loan. Note that the interest column supplies the needed information for the interest tax shelter that is lost if the asset is leased, I_t.[11]

The next step in calculating NAL involves finding the present value of the after-tax salvage value. Earlier when we computed NPV(P), we found this to equal $15.35. Now, substituting the results of our calculations into equation (18–4) produces the NAL of $444.

Note that the lease payments used in this example were made at the end of each year. In practice lease payments are generally made at the beginning of each year (that is, they constitute an *annuity due* rather than an ordinary annuity as used here). The *NAL* for the example used here changes dramatically if we assume beginning of year lease payments. That is, with beginning of year payments *NAL* = − $225.90. You can easily verify this result as follows: Note first that changing from a regular annuity to an annuity due affects only the first and last annuity payments. In this example this means that the first lease payment of $2100 (after tax) is paid immediately such that its present value is $2100. However, the final lease payment is now made at the beginning of year 5 (or at the end of year 4). The present value of the fifth year after-tax lease payment is therefore $2100 × .681 = $1430.10. To summarize, by changing from a regular annuity set of lease payments to an annuity due, we must include a − $2100 immediate cash flow at time $t = 0$ and we exchange this for the fifth year present-value after-tax lease payment of $1430.10. Therefore, the *NAL* with annuity due lease payments is *NAL* (annuity due) = $444.00 + $1430.10 − $2100.00 = − $225.90. Hence, if the lease payments are an annuity due, the asset should be purchased [since *NPV(P)* = $15.35] and not leased [since *NAL* = − $225.90].

To summarize the lease-purchase analysis: First the project's net present value was computed. This analysis produced a positive *NPV(P)* equal to $15.35, which indicated that the asset should be acquired. Upon computing the net advantage to leasing, we found that the financial lease was the preferred method of financing the acquisition of the asset's services. Thus, the asset's services should be acquired, and leasing is the lowest-cost (shareholder wealth-maximizing) way to finance the acquisition.

---

[11] Technically the firm does not lose the interest tax shelter on a $15,000 loan if it leases. In fact, the firm would lose the tax shelter on only that portion of the $15,000 purchase price that it would have financed by borrowing, for example, 40 percent of the $15,000 investment, or $6000. However, if the firm leases the $15,000 asset, it has effectively used 100 percent levered (nonowner) financing. This means that the leasing of this project uses not only its 40 percent allotment of levered (debt) financing, but an additional 60 percent as well. Thus, by leasing the $15,000 asset the lessee forfeits the interest tax shelter on a 40 percent or $6000 loan plus an additional 60 percent of the $15,000 purchase price, or an additional $9000 loan. In total, leasing has caused the firm to forgo the interest tax savings on a loan equal to 100 percent of the leased asset's purchase price. Once again we note that this analysis presumes $1 of lease financing is equivalent to $1 of loan financing. See footnote *a* to Table 18–2.

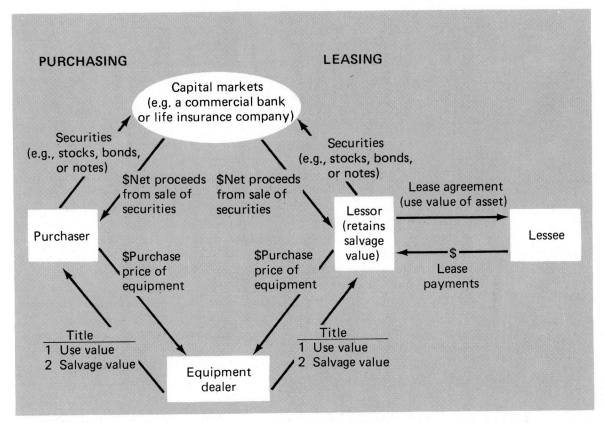

FIGURE 18–3. Comparison of Purchasing with a Simple Financial Lease Agreement

Potential Benefits from Leasing[12]

A number of purported advantages have been associated with leasing as opposed to debt financing. These benefits include flexibility and convenience, lack of restrictions, avoiding the risk of obsolescence, conservation of working capital, 100 percent financing, tax savings, and availability of credit. However, before we discuss the relative merits of each purported advantage, it will be helpful to review briefly the economic character of leasing and purchasing.

Figure 18–3 contains a diagram that can be used to summarize the participants and transactions involved in leasing (the right-hand side of the figure) and purchasing (the left-hand side). In purchasing, the asset is financed via the sale of securities and the purchaser acquires title to the asset (including both the use and salvage value of the asset). In leasing, the lessee acquires the use value of the asset but uses the lessor as an "intermediary" to finance and purchase the asset. The key feature of leasing as opposed to purchasing is the interjection of a financial intermediary (the lessor) into the scheme used to acquire the asset's services. Thus, the basic question that arises in lease-purchase analysis is one of "Why does adding another financial

---

[12] The contributions of Paul F. Anderson in the preparation of this discussion are gratefully acknowledged.

intermediary (the lessor) save the lessee money?" Some of the "traditional" answers to this question are discussed below. As you read through each, simply remember that the lessee is "hiring" the lessor to perform the functions associated with ownership that he would perform if the asset were purchased. Thus, for the lease to be "cheaper" than owning, the lessor must be able to perform these functions of ownership at a lower cost than the lessee could perform them.

Flexibility and Convenience

A variety of potential benefits are often included under the rubric of flexibility and convenience. It is argued, for example, that leasing provides the firm with flexibility because it allows for piecemeal financing of relatively small asset acquisitions. It is pointed out that debt financing of such acquisitions can be costly and difficult to arrange. Leases, on the other hand, may be arranged more quickly and with less documentation.

Another flexibility argument notes that leasing may allow a division or subsidiary manager to acquire equipment without the approval of the corporate capital budgeting committee. Depending upon the firm, the manager may be able to avoid the time-consuming process of preparing and presenting a formal acquisition proposal.

A third purported flexibility advantage relates to the fact that some lease payment schedules may be structured to coincide with the revenues generated by the asset, or they may be timed to match seasonal fluctuations in a given industry. Thus, the firm is able to synchronize its lease payments with its cash cycle—an option rarely available with debt financing.

Arguments for the greater convenience of leasing take many forms. It is sometimes stated that leasing simplifies bookkeeping for tax purposes because it eliminates the need to prepare time-consuming depreciation tables and subsidiary fixed asset schedules. It is also pointed out that the fixed-payment nature of lease rentals allows more accurate forecasting of cash needs. Finally, leasing allows the firm to avoid the "problems" and "headaches" associated with ownership. Executives often note that leasing "keeps the company out of the real estate business." Implicit in this argument is the assumption that the firm's human and material resources may be more profitably allocated to its primary line of business and that it is better to allow the lessor to deal with the obligations associated with ownership.

It is difficult to generalize about the validity of the various arguments for greater flexibility and convenience in leasing. Some companies, under specific conditions, may find leasing advantageous for some of the reasons listed above. In practice, the tradeoffs are likely to be different for every firm. With regard to a number of the arguments, the relevant issue is that of shifting functions. By leasing a piece of capital equipment, the firm may effectively shift bookkeeping, disposal of used equipment, and other functions to the lessor. The lessee will benefit in these situations if the lessor is able to perform the functions at a lower cost than the lessee and is willing to pass on the savings in a lower lease rate.

The remaining arguments should be viewed in a similar vein. Any lessee must attempt to determine the price it is paying for greater flexibility and convenience. In many cases the benefits the firm is able to attain are not worth the cost. Compounding the problem is the fact that it is often difficult for a lessee firm to quantify such cost-benefit tradeoffs.

Lack of Restrictions

Another suggested advantage relates to the lack of restrictions associated with a lease. Unlike term-loan agreements or bond indentures, lease contracts generally do not contain protective covenant restrictions. Furthermore, in calculating financial ratios under existing covenants, it is sometimes possible to exclude lease payments from the firm's debt commitments. Once again, the extent to which lack of restrictions benefits a lessee will depend on the price it must pay. If a lessor views its security position to be superior to that of a lender, it may not require a higher return on the lease to compensate for the lack of restrictions on the lessee. On the other hand, if the prospective lessee is viewed as a marginal credit risk, a higher rate may be charged.

Avoiding the Risk of Obsolescence

Similar reasoning applies to another popular argument for leasing. This argument states that a lease is advantageous because it allows the firm to avoid the risk that the equipment will become obsolete. In actuality, the risk of obsolescence is passed on to the lessee in any financial lease. Since the original cost of the asset is fully amortized over the basic lease term, all of the risk is borne by the lessee. Only in a cancellable operating lease is it sometimes possible to avoid the risk of obsolescence.

A related argument in favor of leasing states that a lessor will generally provide the firm with better and more reliable service in order to maintain the resale value of the asset. The extent to which this is true will depend on the lessor's own cost-benefit tradeoff. If the lessor is a manufacturing or a leasing company that specializes in a particular type of equipment, it may be profitable to maintain the equipment's resale value by insuring that it is properly repaired and maintained. Because of their technical and marketing expertise, these types of lessors may be able to operate successfully in the secondary market for the equipment. On the other hand, bank lessors or independent financial leasing companies would probably find it too expensive to follow this approach. Thus, it is difficult to generalize with regard to this potential advantage.

Conservation of Working Capital

One of the oldest and most widely used arguments in favor of leasing is the assertion that a lease conserves the firm's working capital. Indeed, many within the leasing industry will consider this to be the number one advantage of leasing.[13] The conservation argument runs as follows: Since a lease does not require an immediate outflow of cash to cover the full purchase price of the asset, funds are retained in the business.

It is clear that a lease does require a lower initial outlay than a cash purchase. However, the cash outlay associated with the purchase option can be reduced or eliminated by borrowing the down payment from another source. This argument leads us directly into the next purported advantage of lease financing.

100 Percent Financing

Another alleged benefit of leasing is embodied in the argument that a lease provides the firm with 100 percent financing. It is pointed out that the borrow-and-buy alternative generally involves a down payment, whereas leasing does not. Given that investors and creditors are reasonably intelligent, however, it is sensible to conclude that they consider similar amounts of lease and debt financing to be equivalent from the stand-

---

[13] For example, see L. Rochwarger, "The Flexible World of Leasing," *Fortune*, 39 (November 1974), 56–59.

point of the amount of risk they add to the firm. Thus, a firm uses up less of its capacity to raise nonequity funds with debt than with leasing. In theory, it could issue a second debt instrument to make up the difference—that is, the down payment.

Tax Savings It is also argued that leasing offers an economic advantage in that the tax shield generated by the lease payments usually exceeds the tax shield from depreciation that would be available if the asset were purchased. The extent to which leasing provides a tax-shield benefit will be a function of many factors. The *NAL* equation (18–4), discussed earlier, provided the basis for weighing these differences in tax shields.

Ease of Obtaining Credit Another alleged advantage of leasing is that firms with poor credit ratings are able to obtain assets through leases when they are unable to finance the acquisitions with debt capital. The obvious counterargument is that the firm will certainly face a high lease rate in order to compensate the lessor for bearing the risk of default.

Summary

Intermediate, or simply term, credit is any source of financing with a final maturity greater than 1 year but less than 10. The two major sources of term credit are term loans and financial leases.

Term loans are available from commercial banks, life insurance companies, and pension funds. Although the specifics of each agreement vary, they share a common set of general characteristics. These include

1. A final maturity of one to 10 years
2. A requirement of some form of collateral
3. A body of "restrictive covenants" designed to protect the security interests of the lender
4. A loan amortization schedule whereby periodic loan payments, comprised of both principal and interest components, are made over the life of the loan

There are three basic types of lease arrangements:

1. Direct lease
2. Sale and leaseback
3. Leveraged lease

The lease agreement can further be classified as a financial or operating lease, with the former comprising the basis for our discussion. Recent statements by the Financial Accounting Standards Board virtually ensure the inclusion of all financial leases in the body of the lessee firm's balance sheet.

The lease versus purchase decision is a hybrid capital budgeting problem wherein the analyst must consider both the investment and financing aspects of the decision. Many and varied factors are often claimed as "advantages" of leasing as opposed to the use of the firm's usual debt-equity financing mix. Many of the arguments have been found to be either wholly or partially fallacious. However, a complete lease-purchase analysis using a model similar to the one discussed here should provide a rational basis for ferreting out the true advantages of lease financing.

Study Questions

18–1. What characteristics distinguish intermediate-term debt from other forms of debt instruments?

18–2. List and discuss the major types of restrictions generally found in the covenants of term loan agreements.

18–3. Define each of the following:
  a. Direct leasing
  b. Sale and leaseback arrangement
  c. Leveraged leasing
  d. Operating lease

18–4. How are financial leases handled in the financial statements of the lessee firm?

18–5. List and discuss each of the potential benefits from lease financing.

Self-Test Problems

ST–1. (*Analyzing a Term Loan*) Calculate the annual installment payment and the principal and interest components of a 5-year loan carrying a 10 percent rate of interest. The loan amount is $50,000.

ST–2. (*Analyzing an Installment Loan*) The S. P. Sargent Sales Company is contemplating the purchase of a new machine. The total cost of the machine is $120,000 and the firm plans to make a $20,000 cash down payment. The firm's bank has offered to finance the remaining $100,000 at a rate of 14 percent. The bank has offered two possible loan repayment plans. Plan A involves equal annual installments payable at the end of each of the next 5 years. Plan B requires five equal annual payments plus a balloon payment of $20,000 at the end of year 5.
  a. Calculate the annual payment on the loan in plan A.
  b. Calculate the principal and interest components of the plan A installment loan.
  c. Calculate the annual installments for plan B where the loan carries a 14 percent rate.

ST–3. (*Lease versus Purchase Analysis*) Jensen Trucking, Inc., is considering the possibility of leasing a $100,000 truck-servicing facility. This newly developed piece of equipment facilitates the cleaning and servicing of diesel tractors used on long-haul runs. The firm has evaluated the possible purchase of the equipment and found it to have an $8000 net present value. However, an equipment leasing company has approached Jensen with an offer to lease the equipment for an annual rental charge of $30,457.85 payable at the beginning of each of the next four years. In addition, should Jensen lease the equipment it would receive insurance and maintenance valued at $4000 per year (assume that this amount would be payable at the beginning of each year if purchased separately from the lease agreement). Additional information pertaining to the lease and purchase alternatives is found in the following table:

Acquisition price	$100,000
Useful life (used in analysis)	4 years
Salvage value (estimated)	$0
Depreciation method	Straight-line
Borrowing rate	12%
Marginal tax rate	40%
Cost of capital (based on a target debt/total asset ratio of 30%)	16%

  a. Calculate the net advantage of leasing (*NAL*) the equipment.
  b. Should Jensen lease the equipment?

Study Problems

18–1. (*Installment Payments*) Compute the annual payments for an installment loan carrying an 18 percent rate of interest, a 5-year maturity, and a face amount of $100,000.

18–2. (*Principal and Interest Components of an Installment Loan*) Compute the annual principal and interest components of the loan in problem 18–1.

18–3. (*Cost of an Intermediate-term Loan*) The J. B. Marcum Company needs $250,000 to finance a new minicomputer. The computer sales firm has offered to finance the purchase with a $50,000 down payment followed by five annual installments of $59,663.11 each. Alternatively, the firm's bank has offered to lend the firm $200,000 to be repaid in five annual installments based on an annual rate of interest of 16 percent. Finally, the firm has arranged to finance the needed $200,000 through a loan from an insurance company requiring a lump-sum payment of $385,080, in 5 years.
   a. What is the effective annual rate of interest on the loan from the computer sales firm?
   b. What will the annual payments on the bank loan be?
   c. What is the annual rate of interest for the insurance company term loan?
   d. Based upon cost considerations only, which source of financing should Marcum select?

18–4. (*Cost of Intermediate-term Credit*) Charter Electronics is planning to purchase a $400,000 burglar alarm system for its southwestern Illinois plant. Charter's bank has offered to lend the firm the full $400,000. The note would be paid in one payment at the end of four years and would require payment of interest at a rate of 14 percent compounded annually. The manufacturer of the alarm system has offered to finance the $400,000 purchase with an installment loan. The loan would require four annual installments of $140,106 each. Which method of financing should Charter select?

18–5. (*Lease versus Purchase Analysis*) Early in the spring of 1987 the Jonesboro Steel Corporation (JSC) decided to purchase a small computer. The computer is designed to handle the inventory, payroll, shipping, and general clerical functions for small manufacturers like JSC. The firm estimates that the computer will cost $60,000 to purchase and will last 4 years, at which time it can be salvaged for $10,000. The firm's marginal tax rate is 50 percent, and its cost of capital for projects of this type is estimated to be 12 percent. Over the next 4 years the management of JSC feels the computer will reduce operating expenses by $27,000 a year before depreciation and taxes. JSC utilizes straight-line depreciation and plans to depreciate the asset toward its expected salvage value of $10,000.

   JSC is also considering the possibility of leasing the computer. The computer sales firm has offered JSC a 4-year lease contract with annual payments of $18,000. In addition, if JSC leases the computer, the lessor will absorb insurance and maintenance expenses valued at $2000 per year. Thus, JSC will save $2000 per year if it leases the asset (on a before-tax basis).
   a. Evaluate the net present value of the computer purchase. Should the computer be acquired via purchase? [*Hint*: refer to Tables 18–3 and 18–4.]
   b. If JSC uses a 40 percent target debt to total assets ratio, evaluate the net present value advantage of leasing. JSC can borrow at a rate of 8 percent with annual installments paid over the next 4 years. [*Hint*: Recall that the interest tax shelter lost through leasing is based upon a loan equal to the full purchase price of the asset or $60,000.]
   c. Should JSC lease the asset?

18–6. (*Lease versus Purchase Analysis*) S. S. Johnson Enterprises (SSJE) is evaluating the acquisition of a heavy-duty forklift with 20,000 to 24,000 pound lift capacity. SSJE can purchase the forklift through the use of its normal financing mix (30 percent debt and 70 percent common equity) or lease it. Pertinent details follow:

Acquisition price of the forklift	$20,000
Useful life	4 years
Salvage value	$4000
Depreciation method	straight line
Annual before-tax and depreciation cash savings from the forklift	$6000
Rate of interest on a 4-year installment loan	10 percent
Marginal tax rate	50 percent
Annual rentals (4-year lease)	$6000
Annual operating expenses included in the lease	$1000
Cost of capital	12 percent

    a. Evaluate whether the forklift's acquisition is justified through purchase.

    b. Should SSJE lease the asset?

18–7. (*Installment Loan Payment*) Calculate the annual installment payments for the following loans:

    a. A $100,000 loan carrying a 15 percent annual rate of interest and requiring 10 annual payments.

    b. A $100,000 loan carrying a 15 percent annual rate of interest with quarterly payments over the next 5 years. [*Hint:* Refer to Chapter 9 for a discussion of semi-annual compounding and discounting.]

    c. A $100,000 loan requiring annual installments for each of the next 5 years at a 15 percent rate of interest. However, the annual installments are based on a 30-year loan period. In year 5 the balance of the loan is due in a single (balloon) payment. [*Hint:* Calculate the installment payments using $n = 30$ years. Next use the procedure laid down in Table 18–1 to determine the remaining balance of the loan at the end of the fifth year.]

Self-Test Solutions

SS–1.

Time	Payment	Principal	Interest	Remaining Balance
0				$50,000.00
1	$13,189.83	$ 8,189.83	$5,000.00	41,810.17
2	13,189.83	9,008.81	4,181.02	32,801.36
3	13,189.83	9,909.69	3,280.14	22,891.67
4	13,189.83	10,900.66	2,289.17	11,991.01
5	13,189.83	11,990.73	1,199.10	0.28

SS–2.   **a.** Payment $= \$100,000 \div \sum_{t=1}^{5} \dfrac{1}{(1.14)^t}$

           $= \$ \ 29,128.35$

b.

Year	Payment	Principal	Interest	Remaining Balance
0	—	—	—	$100,000
1	$29,128.35	$15,128.35	$14,000.00	84,871
2	29,128.35	17,246.32	11,882.03	67,625
3	29,128.35	19,660.80	9,467.55	47,964
4	29,128.35	22,413.32	6,715.03	25,551
5	29,128.35	25,551.18	3,577.17	.03[a]

[a] Rounding error.

c. Since the plan B loan includes a $20,000 balloon payment, the five annual installments have a present value of only

$$\$89{,}613 = \$100{,}000 - \$20{,}000/(1.14)^5$$

Therefore, the annual installments can be calculated as follows:

$$\text{Payment} = \$89{,}613 \div \sum_{t=1}^{5} \frac{1}{(1.14)^t}$$

$$= \$26{,}102.79$$

SS–3. **a.** $NAL = -\$5{,}503.28$ (see the table on page 622).

b. The NAL is positive, indicating that the lease would offer cost savings over a purchase and therefore should be used.

Year	After-tax Operating Expenses Paid by Lessor[a]		After-tax Rental Expense[b]		Tax Shelter on Loan Interest[c]		Tax Shelter on Depreciation[d]		Total		Discount Factor at Borrowing Rate (12%)		Present Value
t	$O_t(1-T)$	$-$	$R_t(1-T)$	$-$	I_tT	$-$	D_tT	$=$	Sum	$\times$	DF	$=$	PV
0	$2,400		$18,274.71		—		—		-$15,874.71		1.000		-$15,874.71
1	2,400		18,274.71		4,800		$10,000		- 38,074.71		.893		- 27,392.52
2	2,400		18,274.71		3,796		10,000		- 36,568.71		.797		- 23,647.56
3	2,400		18,274.71		2,671		10,000		- 34,880.71		.712		- 20,324.55
4	—		—		1,411		10,000		- 17,117.00		.636		- 7,257.40

	Total	-$ 94,496.72
	Plus: Initial outlay	100,000.00
	NAL	=$ 5,503.28

[a] $4,000 (1 − 0.4) = $2,400. For simplicity we assume that the tax shields on expenses paid at the beginning of the year are realized immediately.

[b] $18,274.71 = $30,457.85 (1 − 0.4)

[c] Based upon a $100,000 loan with four end-of-year installments and a 12% rate of interest. The loan payments equal $32,923.44.

[d] The machine has a zero salvage value. Thus, its annual depreciation expense is $100,000/4 = $25,000.

Selected References

Anderson, Paul F., and John D. Martin. "Lease vs. Purchase Decisions: A Survey of Current Practice," *Financial Management* (Spring 1977):41–47.

Bower, Richard S. "Issues in Lease Financing," *Financial Management*, 2 (Winter 1973), 25–34.

———, and George S. Oldfield, Jr. "Of Lessees, Lessors, and Discount Rates and Whether Pigs Have Wings," *Journal of Business Research*, 9 (March 1981), 29–38.

Cason, R. L., "Leasing, Asset Lives and Uncertainty: A Practitioner's Comments," *Financial Management*, 16 (Summer 1987), pp. 13–16.

Cooper, Kerry, and Robert H. Strawser. "Evaluation of Capital Investment Projects Involving Asset Leases," *Financial Management*, 4 (Spring 1975), 44–49.

Copeland, T., and J. F. Weston. "A Note on the Evaluation of Cancellable Operating Leases," *Financial Management*, 11 (Summer 1982), 60–67.

Crawford, Peggy J., Charles P. Harper, and John J. McConnell. "Further Evidence on the Terms of Financial Leases," *Financial Management*, 10 (Autumn 1981), 7–14.

Doenges, R. Conrad. "The Cost of Leasing," *Engineering Economist*, 17 (Fall 1971), 31–44.

Dyl, Edward A., and Stanely A. Martin, Jr., "Setting Terms for Leveraged Leasing," *Financial Management*, 6 (Winter 1977), 20–27.

Fabozzi, F., and U. Yaari. "Valuation of Safe Harbor Tax Benefit Transfer Leases," *Journal of Finance*, 38 (May 1983), 595–606.

Grimlund, R., and R. Capettini. "A Note on the Evaluation of Leveraged Leases and Other Investments," *Financial Management*, 11 (Summer 1982), 68–72.

Idol, Charles R. "A Note on Specifying Debt Displacement and Tax Shield Borrowing Opportunities in Financial Lease Valuation Models," *Financial Management*, 9 (Summer 1980), 24–29.

Johnson, Robert W., and Wilbur G. Lewellen. "Analysis of the Lease-or-Buy Decision," *Journal of Finance*, 27 (September 1972), 815–23.

Martin, John D. "Leasing" in *Financial Analysts Handbook*, ed. Edward Altman. New York: Wiley, 1981.

Martin, John D., Paul F. Anderson, and Chester L. Allen. "A Pragmatic Approach to the Estimation Problems Encountered in Lease Purchase Analyses," in *Risk, Capital Costs, and Project Financing Decisions*, eds. Frans G. J. Derkinderen and Roy L. Crum, pp. 254–73. Boston: Martinus Nijhoff Publishing, 1981.

Middleton, J. William. "Term-Lending—Practical and Profitable," *Journal of Commercial Banking Lending*, 50 (August 1968), 31–43.

Roenfeldt, Rodney L., and Jerome S. Osteryoung. "Analysis of Financial Leases." *Financial Management*, 2 (Spring 1973), 74–87.

Rogers, Dean E. "An Approach to Analyzing Cash Flow for Term Loan Purposes," *Bulletin of the Robert Morris Associates*, 48 (October 1965), 79–85.

Schall, L. D., "Analytic Issues in Lease Versus Purchase Decisions," *Financial Management*, 16 (Summer 1987), pp. 17–20.

Schall, Lawrence D. "The Lease-or-Buy and Asset Acquisition Decisions," *Journal of Finance*, 29 (September 1974), 1203–14.

Smith, B. "Accelerated Debt Repayment in Leveraged Leases," *Financial Management*, 11 (Summer 1982), 73–80.

Smith, Pierce R. "A Straightforward Approach to Leveraged Leasing," *Journal of Commercial Bank Lending* (July 1973), 19–39.

Van Horne, James C. "The Cost of Leasing with Capital Market Imperfections," *Engineering Economist*, 23 (Fall 1977), 1–12.

Weingartner, H. M., "Leasing, Asset Lives and Uncertainty: Guides to Decision Making," *Financial Management*, 16 (Summer 1987), pp. 5–12.

19

Long-Term Debt, Preferred Stock, and Common Stock

In this chapter we will concern ourselves with the three major sources of long-term and permanent funds for the firm: long-term debt, preferred stock, and common stock. In Chapters 12 and 15 we discussed the valuation and theory behind their use. In this chapter we will devote our attention to the terminology and basic features common to these securities; we will focus on their similarities and differences, as well as their advantages and disadvantages as sources of financing to the firm.

BONDS OR LONG-TERM DEBT

A **bond** is any long-term (10 years or more) promissory note issued by the firm. In examining bonds we will first acquaint ourselves with bond terminology and features, then examine types of bonds (both secured and unsecured), methods of retiring debt, bond refunding, and advantages and disadvantages of financing with long-term debt.

Basic Bond Terminology and Characteristics

Par Value

The **par value** of a bond is the face value appearing on it that is returned to the bondholder at maturity. In general, most corporate bonds are issued in denominations of $1000, although there are some exceptions to this rule. When bond prices are quoted by financial managers, or in the financial press, prices are generally expressed as a percentage of the bond's par value. For example, a Detroit Edison bond that pays $90 per year interest, and matures in 1999, was recently quoted in The *Wall Street Journal* as selling for 95⅛. That does not mean you can buy the bond for $95.125. It does mean that this bond is selling for 95⅛ percent of its par value, which happens to be $1000. Hence, the market price of this bond is actually $951.25. At maturity in 1999, the bondholder will receive the $1000.

Coupon Interest Rate
The **coupon interest rate** on a bond indicates what percentage of the par value of the bond will be paid out annually in the form of interest. Thus, regardless of what happens to the price of a bond with an 8 percent coupon interest rate and a $1000 par value, it will pay out $80 annually in interest until maturity.

Maturity
The **maturity** of a bond indicates the length of time until the bond issuer returns the par value to the bondholder and terminates the bond.

Indenture
An **indenture** is the legal agreement between the firm issuing the bonds and the bond trustee who represents the bondholders. The indenture provides the specific terms of the loan agreement, including a description of the bonds, the rights of the bondholders, the rights of the issuing firm, and the responsibilities of the trustees. This legal document may run 100 pages or more in length, with the majority of it devoted to defining protective provisions for the bondholder. The bond trustee, usually a banking institution or trust company, is then assigned the task of overseeing the relationship between the bondholder and the issuing firm, protecting the bondholder, and seeing that the terms of the indenture are carried out.

Typically, the restrictive provisions included in the indenture attempt to protect the bondholder's position relative to that of other outstanding securities. Common provisions involve (1) prohibitions on the sale of accounts receivable, (2) constraints on the issuance of common stock dividends, (3) restrictions on the purchase or sale of fixed assets, and (4) constraints on additional borrowing. Prohibitions on the sale of accounts receivable result because such sales would benefit the firm's short-run liquidity position at the expense of its future liquidity position. Constraints on the issuance of common stock dividends generally take the form of limiting them when working capital falls below a specified level, or simply limiting the maximum dividend payout to 50 or 60 percent of earnings under any circumstance. Fixed asset restrictions generally require lender permission before the liquidation of any fixed asset or prohibit the use of any existing fixed asset as collateral on new loans. Constraints on additional borrowing are usually in the form of restrictions or limitations on the amount and type of additional long-term debt that can be issued. All these restrictions have one thing in common: They attempt to prohibit action that would improve the status of other securities at the expense of bonds and to protect the status of bonds from being weakened by any managerial action.

Current Yield
The **current yield** on a bond refers to the ratio of the annual interest payment to the bond's market price. If, for example, we are examining a bond with an 8 percent coupon interest rate, a par value of $1000, and a market price of $700, it would have a current yield of

$$\text{current yield} = \frac{\text{annual interest payments}}{\text{market price of the bond}} \qquad (19\text{--}1)$$

$$= \frac{.08 \times \$1000}{\$700} = \frac{\$80}{\$700} = 11.4 \text{ percent}$$

Yield to Maturity	The **yield to maturity** refers to the bond's internal rate of return. It incorporates into the analysis both the annual interest payments and capital gains or losses. Mathematically, the yield to maturity is the discount rate that equates the present value of the interest and principal payments with the current market price of the bond.[1]
Bond Ratings	John Moody first began to rate bonds in 1909; since that time three rating agencies—Moody's, Standard and Poor's, and Fitch Investor Services—have provided **ratings** on corporate bonds. These ratings involve a judgment about the future risk potential of the bond. Although they deal with expectations, several historical factors seem to play a significant role in their determination.[2] Bond ratings are favorably affected by (1) a low utilization of financial leverage, (2) profitable operations, (3) a low variability in past earnings, (4) large firm size, and (5) little use of subordinated debt. In turn, the rating a bond receives affects the rate of return demanded on the bond by the investors. The poorer the bond rating, the higher the rate of return demanded in the capital markets. An example of these ratings and their description is given in Table 19–1.
Determinants of the Cost of Long-term Debt	In Chapter 12 we computed an investor's required rate of return for debt financing to the firm. We now focus on the factors that determine the required rate of return that investors demand on this debt. The total cost of debt that the firm will pay depends primarily upon five factors: (1) the size of the issue, (2) the issue's maturity, (3) the issue's riskiness or rating, (4) the restrictive requirements of the issue, and (5) the current riskless interest rate. To a large extent the administrative costs of issuing debt are fixed, and they will decrease in percentage terms as the size of the issue increases. In effect, economies of scale are associated with the issuance of debt. The issue's maturity also affects the cost of debt. Borrowers prefer to borrow for long periods in order to lock in interest rates and avoid the problem of frequent refinancing, while lenders would rather not tie up their money for long periods. In order to bring about equilibrium between supply and demand for funds, long-term debt generally carries a higher interest rate than short-term debt. This tends to encourage some borrowers to borrow for shorter periods and some investors to lend for longer periods, bringing equilibrium between supply and demand.

Investors also desire additional return for taking on added risk. Thus, the less risky the bond or the higher the bond rating, the lower will be the interest rate. We can see this by looking at the movement of bond yields for four different ratings during 1986, as shown in Table 19–2.

The restrictive requirements and rights of both issuer and holder also affect the interest rate paid on the bond. The more the bondholder requires in the way of protection and rights, the lower will be the rate of return earned. On the other hand, the more rights the issuer demands—for example, the right to repurchase the debt at a predetermined price (called a call provision and discussed later in detail)—the higher will be the rate that the issuer will have to offer in order to convince investors to purchase the bond.

---

[1] See Chapter 12 for illustrative example.

[2] See Thomas F. Pogue and Robert M. Soldofsky, "What's in a Bond Rating?" *Journal of Financial and Quantitative Analysis*, 4 (June 1969), 201–28; and George E. Pinches and Kent A. Mingo, "A Multivariate Analysis of Industrial Bond Ratings," *Journal of Finance*, 28 (March 1973), 1–18.

TABLE 19–1. Standard and Poor's Corporate Bond Ratings

AAA	This is the highest rating assigned by Standard and Poor's debt obligation and indicates an extremely strong capacity to pay principal and interest.
AA	Bonds rated AA also qualify as high-quality debt obligations. Their capacity to pay principal and interest is very strong, and in the majority of instances they differ from AAA issues only in small degree.
A	Bonds rated A have a strong capacity to pay principal and interest, although they are somewhat more susceptible to the adverse effects of changes in circumstances and economic conditions.
BBB	Bonds rated BBB are regarded as having an adequate capacity to pay principal and interest. Whereas they normally exhibit adequate protection parameters, adverse economic conditions or changing circumstances are more likely to lead to a weakened capacity to pay principal and interest for bonds in this category than for bonds in the A category.
BB B CCC CC	Bond rated BB, B, CCC, and CC are regarded, on balance, as predominantly speculative with respect to the issuer's capacity to pay interest and repay principal in accordance with the terms of the obligation. BB indicates the lowest degree of speculation and CC the highest. While such bonds will likely have some quality and protective characteristics, these are outweighed by large uncertainties or major risk exposures to adverse conditions.
C	The rating C is reserved for income bonds on which no interest is being paid.
D	Bonds rated D are in default, and payment of principal and/or interest is in arrears.
	Plus (+) or Minus (−): To provide more detailed indications of credit quality, the ratings from "AA" to "BB" may be modified by the addition of a plus or minus sign to show relative standing within the major rating categories.
	Provisional Ratings: A provisional rating assumes the successful completion of the project being financed by the issuance of the bonds being rated and indicates that payment of debt service requirements is largely or entirely dependent upon the successful and timely completion of the project. This rating, however, while addressing credit quality subsequent to completion, makes no comment on the likelihood of, or the risk of default upon failure of, such completion. Accordingly, the investor should exercise his judgment with respect to such likelihood and risk.

Source: *Standard and Poor's Fixed Income Investor*, Vol. 8 (1980). Reprinted by permission.

TABLE 19–2. Comparison of Corporate Bond Yields of Various Ratings, Monthly Averages, 1986

	Ratings			
	Least Risk AAA	AA	A	Most Risk BBB
January	9.67%	10.27%	10.42%	11.20%
February	9.36	9.96	9.92	10.91
March	9.13	9.46	9.17	10.49
April	9.12	9.34	9.55	10.39
May	9.19	9.51	9.75	10.32
June	9.29	9.72	9.87	10.58
July	8.88	9.50	9.65	10.33
August	8.76	9.48	9.52	10.20
September	8.78	9.49	9.58	10.05
October	8.79	9.49	9.61	10.13
November	8.71	9.36	9.52	9.97
December	8.53	9.22	9.38	9.87
Monthly averages	9.02%	9.57%	9.66%	10.37%

Source: Standard and Poor's Corporation, *Bond Guide*, January 1987.

Finally, the current riskless interest rate plays a major role in determining the cost of debt. As the riskless rate of interest moves up and down, parallel movements are produced for corporate bond rates. The determination of the riskless interest rate is generally deferred to courses on money and banking and financial institutions. We note here that one of the major factors affecting it is the anticipated inflation rate.

Claims on Assets and Income

In the case of insolvency, the claims of debt are honored prior to those of both common stock and preferred stock. However, different types of debt may also have a hierarchy among themselves as to the order of their claim on assets.

Bonds also have a claim on income prior to that of common and preferred stock. If interest on bonds (other than income bonds, to be discussed later) is not paid, the bond trustees can classify the firm insolvent and force it into bankruptcy. Thus, the bondholder's claim on income is more likely to be honored than that of common and preferred stockholders, whose dividends are paid at the discretion of the firm's management.

Types of Bonds: Unsecured Long-term Bonds

Debentures

The term **debentures** applies to any unsecured long-term debt. Because these bonds are unsecured, the earning ability of the issuing corporation is of great concern to the bondholder. Often the issuing firm attempts to provide some protection to the holder through the prohibition of any additional encumbrance of assets. This prohibits the future issuance of secured long-term debt that would further tie up the firm's assets and leave the bondholders less protected. To the issuing firm, the major advantage of debentures is that no property is secured by them. This allows the firm to issue debt and still preserve some future borrowing power.

Subordinated Debentures

Many firms have more than one issue of debentures outstanding. In this case a hierarchy may be specified, in which some debentures are given subordinated standing in the case of insolvency. The claims of the **subordinated debentures** are honored only after the claims of secured debt and unsubordinated debentures have been satisfied.[3]

Income Bonds

An **income bond** requires interest payments only if earned, and failure to meet these interest payments does not lead to bankruptcy. In this sense income bonds are more like preferred stock (which is discussed in a later section) than bonds. They are generally issued during the reorganization of a firm facing financial difficulties. The maturity of income bonds is usually much longer than that of other bonds in order to relieve pressure associated with the repayment of principal. While interest payments may be passed, unpaid interest is generally allowed to accumulate for some period of time and must be paid prior to the payment of any common stock dividends. This cumulative interest feature provides the bondholder with some security.

Types of Bonds: Secured Long-term Bonds

A **mortgage bond** is a bond secured by a lien on real property. Typically the value of the real property being secured is greater than that of the mortgage bonds issued. This provides the mortgage bondholders with a margin of safety in the event the market value of the secured property declines. In the case of foreclosure, the trustees have the power to sell the secured property and use the proceeds to pay the bondhold-

---

[3] See Chapter 22 for an illustrated example.

Mortgage Bonds

ers. In the event that the proceeds from this sale do not cover the bonds, the bondholders become general creditors, similar to debenture bondholders, for the unpaid portion of the debt. While a mortgage bond is a general classification for bonds secured by real property, they can be further differentiated among themselves to include subclassifications of mortgage bonds, blanket mortgage bonds, and closed-, open-, and limited open-end mortgage bonds.

1. **First mortgage bonds.** The same property may be pledged on more than one mortgage bond. In this case, the first mortgage bond has the senior claim on the secured assets.
2. **Second mortgage bonds.** The second mortgage bond has the second claim on assets and is serviced only after the claims of the first mortgage bonds have been satisfied. Obviously, second mortgage bonds are much less secure than first mortgage bonds, and they are not extremely popular. They are seldom issued except by firms experiencing financial difficulties. When they are issued, buyers generally demand a relatively high return because of their risky position.
3. **Blanket or general mortgage bonds.** Under a blanket or general mortgage bond, all the assets of the firm act as security.
4. **Closed-end mortgage bonds.** A closed-end mortgage bond forbids the use of the assets being secured by this bond as security in the issuance of any future mortgage bonds of the same priority. This type of mortgage assures bondholders that their claim on assets will not be diluted by the issuance of any future mortgage bonds. Although this type of mortgage bond restricts the financial manager's future financing options, it is extremely well liked by bondholders.
5. **Open-end mortgage bonds.** An open-end mortgage bond does not preclude the issuance of additional mortgage bonds of the same priority that use the same secured asset as security. Generally a restriction is placed upon the borrower, requiring that additional assets be added to the secured property if new debt is issued.
6. **Limited open-end mortgage bonds.** Limited open-end mortgage bonds are a hybrid of the open- and closed-end mortgage bonds. Although they allow the issuance of additional bonds at the same priority level using the already mortgaged assets as security, they also limit the amount of these additional bonds that can be issued.

Collateral Trust Bonds

Collateral trust bonds are secured by common stock and/or bonds, which are held by a trustee who has the power to liquidate them in the event of default. Generally, to ensure that collateral trust bonds are amply covered, the indenture contains a clause that the market value of the collateral must be at least 20 to 50 percent greater than the value of the bonds. An example of a collateral trust bond is the Pennsylvania Co. collateral trust 5½s (paying 5½ percent interest semi-annually) bonds, which is secured by Norfolk Southern Railway common stock. The bond indenture states that the market value of the Norfolk Southern Railway common stock must equal at least 150 percent of the principal value of the bonds outstanding.

Equipment Trust Certificates

Equipment trust financing, a cross between lease financing and debt financing, is used primarily by railroads and some airlines and oil companies to finance the purchase of rolling stock or planes. This type of debt generally has a fairly short maturity,

TABLE 19–3. Comparison of Ratings Between Equipment Trust Certificates and the Highest Rating Received by Any Bond in the Same System, January 1987

	Equipment Trust Certificate	Highest Rated Bond
Atchison, Topeka & Santa Fe	AAA	AA
Baltimore & Ohio	AA+	A+
Burlington Northern	AAA	AA
Chicago & North Western	A	BB
Gulf, Mobile, and Ohio	A–	B+
Illinois Central Gulf	A	BB
Louisville & Nashville Railroad	AA+	A+
Union Pacific	AAA	AA

Source: Standard and Poor's Corporation, *Bond Guide*, January 1987.

ranging from 1 year to a maximum of about 17 years. The short maturity is, of course, due to the nature of the collateral which is subject to substantial wear and tends to deteriorate rapidly. Under this financing method, the railroad or issuing firm first orders the railroad cars or equipment. When the equipment is received, the title is transferred to a newly formed trust company. The manufacturer is then paid in full by the trust company, which obtains funds primarily through the issuance of **equipment trust certificates.**

The equipment trust certificates have minimal risk because they are secured by the equipment being purchased, and this is generally quite standardized. The railroad company also adds to the safety of these bonds by guaranteeing the payment of principal and interest. The equipment is then leased to the railroad in such a way that the interest payments and amortization of the certificates are completely covered. When these certificates are retired, the ownership of the equipment is passed to the railroad.

Through the use of equipment trust certificates, railroads, which have fallen upon hard times, are able to secure funds to purchase much-needed equipment at a reasonable cost. This cost is generally lower than it would be otherwise, because the quality and standardness of the assets used as collateral make equipment trust certificates less risky than the railroad bonds would be. Table 19–3 compares the ratings of equipment trust certificates and the best rating assigned to any bonds issued by the parent company. This comparison shows that the certificates were consistently rated higher than were the corporation's typical bonds. The minimal risk associated with equipment trust certificates has been historically illustrated by their record. In June 1970, for example, when Penn Central defaulted on much of its debt, it did not default on its $1.2 billion worth of equipment trust certificates.

Pollution Control and Industrial Development Bonds

A **pollution control revenue bond** is somewhat hard to categorize because it is actually a corporate obligation disguised as a municipal bond. The debt service funds for the bond come directly from a lease or payment pledge agreement between a municipality and a corporation, which is often a public utility. The primary purpose of these bonds is to help corporations raise the needed money to meet their financial obligations associated with environmental cleanup efforts. Their popularity stems from

Pollution Control Bonds

the fact that their tax-free status as municipal obligations reduces the yield that investors demand. An example of this type of financing occurred in 1977 when Marshall County, West Virginia, issued $50 million worth of 30-year pollution control revenue bonds backed by a long-term payment pledge from the Ohio Power Company.

Industrial Development Bonds

Industrial development bonds, which were extremely popular during the 1950s and 1960s, are almost identical with pollution control bonds. In this case the local government attempts to attract new industry by constructing a plant and then leasing it to the incoming firm. The revenue generated by leasing the plant is then used to cover the interest and principal payments on the debt. Since the bonds are issued by the municipality they are tax free, resulting in a lower interest rate and thus lower financing costs for the company. This became a very popular method for munici-palities to attract new industry and for corporations to finance new plants. It was this extreme popularity that caused the Treasury Department to restrict the amount of industrial development bonds a community could issue. As a result, this type of corporate financing has declined dramatically from the level it enjoyed in the 1950s and 1960s.

Types of Bonds: Secured or Unsecured Long-term Bonds

Floating Rate or Variable Rate Bonds

While **floating rate** or **variable rate bonds** have for many years been popular in Europe, it was not until July 1974 when Citicorp issued $850 million of debt with the interest rate set at 1 percent above the 90-day Treasury bill rate that they finally appeared in this country. In periods of unstable interest rates this type of debt offering becomes appealing to issuers and investors. To the issuers like banks and finance companies, whose revenues go up when interest rates rise and decline as interest rates fall, this type of debt eliminates some of the risk and variability in earnings that accompany interest rate swings. To the investor, it eliminates major swings in the market value of the debt that would otherwise have occurred if interest rates had changed.

As an example, in May 1983 Merrill Lynch issued $20 million of floating rate bonds due in 1992. The interest rate on these bonds is subject to a weekly adjustment on the calendar day following each auction of 91-day Treasury bills and is set to be 60 basis points above the 91-day Treasury bill auction rate. That is to say, every week the rate on this issue of debt changes and is set at 0.6 percent above the 91-day Treasury bill rate.

While every floating rate bond is a bit different, these bonds generally possess common characteristics:

1. After an initial period of 3 to 18 months during which a minimum interest rate is guaranteed, the coupon is allowed to float. Then weekly, every 3 months, or every 6 months the coupon rate changes to a new level, usually 0.5 to 3.0 percent above the preceding week's average 91-day Treasury bill rate.
2. The bondholder generally has the option of redeeming the bond at par value every 6 months.
3. The issuer is almost always a bank, bank holding company, or finance company whose revenues are subject to swings with interest rate fluctuations.

There are, of course, exceptions and variations in the concept of floating rate bonds. Two of the more interesting are bonds issued by Petro-Lewis, a Texas oil

TABLE 19–4. Floating Rate (or Floating Principal) Bonds

Issuer	Maturity (Year)	Initial Interest Rate	Terms of Adjustment
Gelco Corp.	1990	11.50%	Adjusted quarterly to 3.00% above the 91-day Treasury bill rate. These are also convertible at the option of the issuer into 5-year fixed rate notes.
Citicorp	1992	Initially floating	Adjusted weekly to 0.75% above the 91-day Treasury bill rate.
Gulf Oil Corp.	1990	9.55%	Adjusted quarterly to 0.35% above the 30-year Treasury bond constant maturity rate. The minimum rate on this bond is also set at 8.375%.
Petro-Lewis	2000	13.00%	Adjusted quarterly and tied to the price of crude oil. The rate is allowed to vary between 13.00% and 15.00%.
Sunshine Mining Co.	1995 or whenever redemption value exceeds $2000 for a period of 30 consecutive days.	8.00%	Interest rate is fixed; however, the redemption value at maturity is equal to the greater of $1000 or the market price of 50 ounces of silver.

firm, and Sunshine Mining Company, a silver-mining firm. In 1980 Petro-Lewis issued bonds in which the interest rate was tied to the price of crude oil from West Texas. If the oil price rose more than 10 percent, the bonds' interest rate would also rise. The Sunshine Mining Company debt was issued in February 1983 and carried a coupon interest rate of 8 percent, with the principal being tied to the price of silver. The common feature of all the variable rate bonds is that an attempt is being made to counter uncertainty by allowing the interest rate (or in the case of the Sunshine Mining Bonds the principal) to float. In this way a decline in cash inflows to the firm should be offset by a decline in interest payments. Table 19–4 gives several examples of variations of floating rate bonds.

Junk Bonds   **Junk** or **low-rated bonds** are bonds rated BB or below. Originally, the term was used to describe bonds issued by "fallen angels"; that is, firms with sound financial histories that were facing severe financial problems and suffering from poor credit ratings. Today, junk bonds refers to any bond with a low rating. The major participants in this market are new firms that do not have an established record of performance, although in recent years junk bonds have been increasingly issued to finance corporate buyouts. In fact, in 1986 over 40 percent of all junk bonds issued were related to acquisitions and leveraged buyouts. Still, the backbone of the junk bond market involves young firms without established records of performance. Prior to the mid-seventies these new firms simply did not have access to the capital markets because of the reluctance of investors to accept speculative grade bonds. However, under the leadership of the investment banking firm of Drexel, Burnham, Lambert, which handles about 70 percent of all new junk bond issues, junk bonds have grown to the point that they represent over 13 percent of all new bonds issued. This growth is illustrated

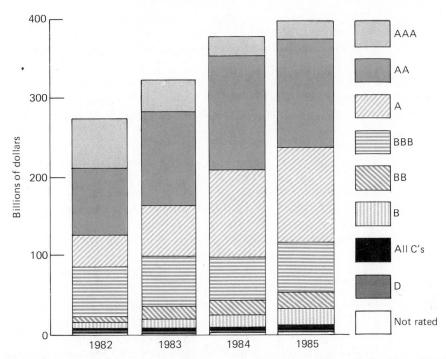

FIGURE 19–1. Par Value of Publicly Traded Outstanding Corporate Bonds by Rating

in Figure 19–1, which presents a summary of the par value of straight corporate bonds outstanding by rating from 1982 through 1985.

Since junk bonds are of speculative grade, they carry a coupon interest rate of between 3 to 5 percent more than AAA grade long-term debt. As a result there is an active market for these new debt instruments. Because of their acceptance, many new firms without established performance records now have a viable financing alternative to secure debt financing through a public offering, rather than being forced to rely on commerical bank loans.

Eurobonds **Eurobonds** are not so much a different type of security as they are securities, in this case bonds, issued in a different country, in this case a European country. In effect, a Eurobond is simply a bond that is issued in Europe by an American company and pays interest and principal to the lender in U.S. dollars. The Eurobond market actually had its roots in the 1950s and 1960s as the U.S. dollar became increasingly popular because of its role as the primary international reserve. In recent years as the U.S. dollar has gained a reputation for being one of the most stable currencies, demand for Eurobonds has increased. The primary attraction to borrowers, aside from favorable rates, in the Eurobonds market is the relative lack of regulation (Eurobonds are not registered with the SEC), less rigorous disclosure requirements than those required by the SEC, and the speed with which they can be issued. Interestingly, not only are Eurobonds not registered with the SEC, but U.S. citizens and residents may not be offered them during their initial distribution.

The use of Eurobonds by U.S. firms to raise funds has fluctuated dramatically, with the relative interest rates and abundance or lack of funds in the European markets dictating the degree to which they are used. For example, while only about $400 million was raised with Eurobonds in 1981, over $13 billion was raised in 1982.

Zero and Very Low Coupon Bonds

Zero and **very low coupon bonds** allow the issuing firm to issue bonds at a substantial discount from their $1000 face value with a zero or very low coupon. The investor receives a large part (or all on the zero coupon bond) of the return from the appreciation of the bond. For example, in April 1983 Homestead Savings issued $60 million of debt maturing in 1995 with a zero coupon rate. These bonds were sold at a 75 percent discount from their par value; that is, investors only paid $250 for a bond with a $1000 par value. Investors who purchase these bonds for $250 and hold them until they mature in 1995 will receive an 11.50 percent yield to maturity, with all of this yield coming from appreciation of the bond. Homestead Savings, on the other hand, will have no cash outflows until these bonds mature; however, at that time it will have to pay back $60 million even though it only received $15 million when the bonds were first issued.

As with any form of financing, there are both advantages and disadvantages of issuing zero or very low discount bonds. The disadvantages are first (as already mentioned), when the bonds mature Homestead Savings will face an extremely large nondeductible cash outflow, much greater than the cash inflow it experienced when the bonds were first issued. Second, discount bonds are not callable and can only be retired at maturity. Thus, if interest rates fall, Homestead Savings cannot benefit. The advantages of zero and low coupon bonds are first, that annual cash outflows associated with interest payments do not occur with zero coupon bonds and are at a relatively low level with low coupon bonds. Second, since there is relatively strong investor demand for this type of debt, prices tend to be bid up and yields tend to be bid down. That is to say, Homestead Savings was able to issue zero coupon bonds at about half a percent less than it would have been if they had been traditional coupon bonds. Finally, Homestead Savings is able to deduct the annual amortization of the discount, which will provide a positive annual cash flow to Homestead.

During 1981 and 1982 zero coupon bonds accounted for about 25 and 14 percent, respectively, of all industrial bond offerings. However, they fell somewhat out of favor in mid-1982 with the passage of TEFRA, which made investors purchasing them pay taxes on the amortized discount. As a result, today they are issued only occasionally and are purchased primarily by individuals who want to include them in IRA portfolios.

Retiring Debt

Because bonds have a maturity date, their retirement is a crucial matter. Bonds can be retired at maturity, at which time the bondholder receives the par value of the bond, or they can be retired prior to maturity. Early redemption is generally accomplished through the use of a call provision or a sinking fund.

Call Provision

A **call provision** entitles the corporation to repurchase or "call" the bonds from their holders at stated prices over specified periods. This feature provides the firm with the flexibility to recall its debt and replace it with lower-cost debt if interest rates fall. The terms of the call provision are provided in the indenture and generally state the call price above the bond's par value. The difference between the call price and the par value is referred to as the **call premium.** The size of this premium changes over time, becoming smaller as the date of call approaches the bond's scheduled maturity. It is also common to prohibit calling the bond during its first years. Obviously a call provision works to the disadvantage of the bondholder, who for this reason is generally compensated by a higher rate of return on the bond.

Sinking Fund

A **sinking fund** requires the periodic repayment of debt, thus reducing the total amount of debt outstanding. When a sinking fund is set up, the firm makes annual payments to the trustee, who can then purchase the bonds in the capital markets or use the call provision. The advantage is that the annual retirement of debt through a sinking fund reduces the amount needed to retire the remaining debt at maturity. Otherwise the firm would face a major payment at maturity. If the firm were experiencing temporary financial problems when the debt matured, both the repayment of the principal and the firm's future could be jeopardized. The use of a sinking fund and its periodic retirement of debt eliminates this potential danger.

The **bond-refunding** decision—that is, whether or not to call an entire issue of bonds—is similar to the capital budgeting decision. The present value of the stream of benefits from the refunding decision is compared with the present value of its costs. If the benefits outweigh the costs, the refunding is done.

The benefits from refunding generally involve interest savings, achieved by replacing older, high-cost debt with less expensive debt as interest rates drop. In addition, tax benefits come about because the unamortized flotation costs and discount on the old bonds, if any, and the call premium are treated as expenses during the year of the refunding. The costs include issuing and recalling expenses and any interest expenses during the bond overlap period. An **overlap period,** when the new bonds have been issued and the old bonds have not yet been called, generally occurs because firms wish to obtain the funds from the new issue before calling the old bonds. This eliminates the risk of a rise in interest rates or a drying up of funds in the capital markets after the old debt has been called but before the new debt has been issued. Thus, the cost associated with the additional interest payment can be viewed as the cost of elimination of this risk.

While the calculations associated with a bond-refunding decision appear to be quite complex, it should be remembered that we are merely determining the net present value of this decision. The major difference between the refunding decision and capital budgeting, as presented in Chapter 10, is that the discount rate used in refunding is the after-tax cost of borrowing on the new bonds rather than the firm's cost of capital. This is because in a refunding decision, as opposed to a normal investment decision, the costs and benefits are known with complete certainty. In effect, a refunding decision is an example of a riskless investment. The only risk involved is the risk of the firm's defaulting on the interest or principal payments. Thus, because the after-tax cost of borrowing on the new bonds takes into account this default risk, it is the appropriate discount rate. The following example will illustrate and explain these calculations.[4]

---

[4] The subject of the appropriate discount rate to be used in discounting the benefits of a bond refund back to present has received considerable attention. See, for example, Thomas H. Mayor and Kenneth G. McCoin, "The Rate of Discounting in Bond Refunding," *Financial Management*, 3 (Autumn 1974), 54–58; and Aharon R. Ofer and Robert A. Taggart, Jr., "Bond Refunding: A Clarifying Analysis," *Journal of Finance*, 23 (March 1977), 21–30. Ofer and Taggart show that the relevant discount rate is the after-tax cost of the refunding bonds when new bonds are used to replace the existing bonds.

Example   Suppose that interest rates have just fallen and that a firm in the 34-percent tax bracket has a $50 million, 9 percent debenture issue outstanding with 20 years remaining to maturity. The unamortized flotation costs and discount on the old bonds total $3 million. These bonds contain a call provision and can be called at $104 (that is, $104 for each $100 of par). Let us assume that they could be replaced with a $50 million issue of 8 percent 20-year bonds providing the firm with $48 million after flotation costs. That is to say, the discount on the new bonds is $2 million ($50 million − $48 million). Let us further assume that an additional $400,000 in issuing expenses would be incurred. The overlap period during which both issues will be outstanding is expected to be one month. Finally, since the marginal corporate tax rate is 34 percent, the appropriate discount rate is 8% (1 − .34) = 5.28 percent.

The procedure for arriving at a decision involves first determining the initial outlay and the differential cash flows. Then all the flows are discounted back to the present and the net present value of the refunding decision is determined. These calculations are illustrated in Table 19–5. In this example the net present value of the refunding decision is $944,971. Since this is positive, the refunding proposal should be accepted.

TABLE 19–5.   Calculations Illustrating the Bond-Refunding Decision

STEP 1: Calculate the *initial outlay*.

    (a) Determine the difference between the inflow from the new issue and the outflow from retiring the old issue:

Cost of calling old bonds ($50,000,000 × 1.04)		$52,000,000
Proceeds, after flotation costs, from new issue		48,000,000
Difference between inflow and outflow		$ 4,000,000

    (b) Determine total issuing and overlap expenses:

Issuing expense on new bonds	$ 400,000	
Interest expense on old bonds during overlap period	375,000	775,000

    (c) Add the items above to determine the gross initial outlay $ 4,775,000

    (d) Determine tax-deductible expenses incurred:

Interest expenses during overlap period	$ 375,000	
Unamortized flotation costs and discount on the old bonds	3,000,000	
Call premium (call price less par value)	2,000,000	
Total tax-deductible expenses	$5,375,000	

    (e) Less tax savings:

Marginal tax rate (34% × total tax-deductible expenses)	×.34	1,827,500

    (f) Equals net *initial* cash outflow $ 2,947,500

STEP 2: Calculate the *annual cash benefit* from eliminating the old bonds through refunding.

    (a) Determine annual interest expense:

9% interest on $50,000,000		$ 4,500,000

    (b) Determine tax-deductible expenses incurred:

Annual interest expense	$4,500,000	
Annual amortization of flotation costs and discount on old bonds ($3,000,000/20)	150,000	
Total annual tax-deductible expenses	$4,650,000	

    (c) Less annual tax savings:

Marginal tax rate (34%) × total annual tax-deductible expenses	×.34	1,581,000

    (d) Equals annual cash benefit from elimination of old bonds $ 2,919,000

STEP 3: Calculate the *annual cash outflow* from issuing the new bonds.

    (a) Determine the annual interest expense:

8% interest on $50,000,000		$ 4,000,000

    (b) Determine tax deductible expenses incurred:

Annual interest expense	$4,000,000	
Annual amortization of bond discount ($2,000,000/20)	100,000	
Annual amortization of issuing expenses ($400,000/20)	20,000	
Total annual tax-deductible expenses	$4,120,000	

    (c) Less annual tax savings:

Marginal tax rate (34%) × total annual tax-deductible expenses	×.34	1,400,800
(d) Equals annual net cash outflow from issuing new bonds		$ 2,599,200

STEP 4: Calculate the *annual net cash benefits* (that is, difference between the annual benefits and costs) from the refunding decision.

    (a) Add benefits:

Annual cash benefits from eliminating the old bonds (from Step 2)	$ 2,919,000

    (b) Less costs:

Annual cash outflows from issuing the new debt (from Step 3)	2,599,200
(c) Equals annual net cash benefits	$ 319,800

STEP 5: Calculate the *present value of the annual net cash benefits*.

(a) Discount the 20-year $319,800 annuity (from Step 4) back to the present at the after-tax cost of borrowing on the new bonds of 5.28 percent	$ 3,892,471

STEP 6: Calculate the *refunding decision's net present value*.

(a) Present value of the annual net cash benefits (from Step 5)	$ 3,892,471
(b) Less present value of initial outlay (from Step 1)	2,947,500
(c) Equals net present value	$ 944,971

A typical complication in the analysis of the bond-refunding decision involves a difference in the maturities of the new and old bonds. The old bonds, which have been outstanding for some length of time, may have a shorter maturity than the proposed new bonds that are intended to replace them. Actually this complication is quite easy to accommodate. The only alteration in the analysis is that *only* the net benefits up to the maturity of the old bonds are considered; after the old bonds terminate, the analysis terminates.

Advantages and Disadvantages

The corporate financing decision is complicated by the various tradeoffs among alternative financial instruments. In order to better understand the role of long-term debt in this decision process, we will examine its advantages and disadvantages.

Advantages
1. Long-term debt is generally less expensive than other forms of financing because (a) investors view debt as a relatively safe investment alternative and demand a lower rate of return, and (b) interest expenses are tax deductible.
2. Bondholders do not participate in extraordinary profits; the payments are limited to interest.
3. Bondholders do not have voting rights.
4. Flotation costs on bonds are generally lower than those on common stock.

Disadvantages
1. Debt (other than income bonds) results in interest payments that, if not met, can force the firm into bankruptcy.
2. Debt (other than income bonds) produces fixed charges, increasing the firm's financial leverage. Although this may not be a disadvantage to all firms, it certainly is for some firms with unstable earnings streams.
3. Debt must be repaid at maturity and thus at some point involves a major cash outflow.
4. The typically restrictive nature of indenture covenants may limit the firm's future financial flexibility.

PREFERRED STOCK

Preferred stock is often referred to as a hybrid security because it has many characteristics of both common stock and bonds. Preferred stock is similar to common stock in that it has no fixed maturity date, the nonpayment of dividends does not bring on bankruptcy, and dividends are not deductible for tax purposes. On the other hand, preferred stock is similar to bonds in that dividends are limited in amount.

The size of the preferred stock dividend is generally fixed either as a dollar amount or as a percentage of the par value. For example, Texas Power and Light has issued $4 preferred stock, while Toledo Edison has some 4.25 percent preferred stock outstanding. The par value on the Toledo Edison preferred stock is $100, hence each share pays 4.25% × $100, or $4.25 in dividends annually. Since these dividends are fixed, preferred stockholders do not share in the residual earnings of the firm but are limited to their stated annual dividend.

In examining preferred stock we will first discuss several features common to almost all preferred stock. Next we will investigate less frequently included features and take a brief look at methods of retiring preferred stock. We will close by examining its advantages and disadvantages.

Features Common to Preferred Stock

Although each issue of preferred stock is unique, several characteristics are common to almost all issues. These traits include the ability to issue multiple classes of preferred stock, the claim on assets and income, and the cumulative and protective features.

Multiple Classes

If a company desires, it can issue more than one series or class of preferred stock, and each class can have different characteristics. In fact, it is quite common for firms that issue preferred stock to issue more than one series. For example, Philadelphia Electric has 13 different issues of preferred stock outstanding. These issues can be further differentiated by the fact that some are convertible into common stock while others are not, and they have varying priority status with respect to assets in the event of bankruptcy.

Adjustable Rate In the early 1980s, another new financing alternative was developed aimed at providing investors with some protection against wide swings in principal that occur when interest rates move up and down. This financing vehicle is called **adjustable rate preferred stock.** With adjustable rate preferred, quarterly dividends fluctuate with interest rates under a formula that ties the dividend payment at either a premium or discount to the highest of (a) the three-month Treasury bill rate, (b) the 10-year Treasury bond constant maturity rate, or (c) the 20-year Treasury bond constant maturity rate. While adjustable rate preferred stock allows interest rates to be tied to the rates on Treasury securities, it also provides a maximum and a minimum level to which they can climb or fall called the **dividend rate band.** The purpose of allowing the interest rate on this preferred stock to fluctuate is, of course, to minimize the fluctuation in the principal of the preferred stock. In times of high and fluctuating interest rates, this is a very appealing feature indeed.

Although the market for adjustable rate preferred stock has been dominated by the bank holding companies and finance companies, by 1983 some industrials and utilities began to venture into this market. In fact, during the high interest rate period of 1983 and 1984, about three-quarters of all nonconvertible preferred stock issued was adjustable rate. However, as interest rates dropped, this feature lost much of its favor with issuers and as a result was used much less frequently. In Table 19–6 several issues of adjustable rate preferred stock are identified.

TABLE 19–6. Adjustable Rate Preferred Stock

Date Issued	Issuer	Amount of Offering (000)	Dividend Rate		Dividend Rate Thereafter (Applicable Rate)[a]	Dividend Rate Band	Call Protection
			At Offering	Through (Year)			
2/14/83	Bank America Corp.	$400,000	9.25%	5/31/83	Adjusted quarterly to 4.00% below the applicable rate[a]	6%–12%	No call allowed for the first 5 years
2/23/83	J. P. Morgan & Co., Inc.	250,000	9.25	6/30/83	Adjusted quarterly to 4.875% below the applicable rate[a]	5%–11½%	No call allowed for the first 3 years
3/8/83	Integrated Resources, Inc.	100,000	12.50	5/31/83	Adjusted quarterly to 0.75% higher than the applicable rate[a]	8%–15%	No call allowed for the first 5 years
4/12/83	Liberty National Corp.	25,000	11.00	1/31/84	Adjusted quarterly at the applicable rate[a]	6½%–13%	No call allowed for the first 5 years
4/15/83	Reading & Bates Corp.	37,500	13.00	3/31/84	Adjusted quarterly to 0.75% higher than the applicable rate[a]	7%–14%	No call allowed for the first 5 years
5/5/83	Gulf States Utilities Co.	30,000	11.50	12/15/83	Adjusted quarterly to 0.65% higher than the applicable rate[a]	7%–13%	No call allowed for the first 5 years

[a] In all cases the "applicable rate" refers to the highest of (a) the 3-month Treasury bill rate, (b) the 10-year Treasury bond maturity rate, or (c) the 20-year Treasury bond constant maturity rate.

In the late 1980s **auction rate preferred stock** began to appear. Auction rate preferred stock is actually variable rate preferred stock in which the dividend rate is set by an auction process. In the case of auction rate preferred, the dividend rate is set every 49 days. At each auction, buyers and sellers place bids for shares, specifying the yield they are willing to accept for the next seven-week period. The yield is then set at the lowest level necessary to match buyers and sellers. As a result, the yield offered on auction rate preferred stock accurately reflects current interest rates, while keeping the market price of these securities at par.

Convertibility

Much of the preferred stock that is issued today is *convertible* at the discretion of the holder into a predetermined number of shares of common stock. In fact, today about one-third of all preferred stock issued has a convertibility feature. In this case it takes on value as both preferred stock and common stock. The convertibility feature is, of course, desirable and thus reduces the cost of the preferred stock to the issuer. The characteristics common to convertible preferred stock will be discussed in detail in Chapter 20.

Claim on Assets and Income

Preferred stock has priority over common stock with respect to claims on assets in the case of bankruptcy. The preferred stock claim is honored after that of bonds and before that of common stock. Multiple issues of preferred stock may be differentiated within themselves with respect to the priority of their claim. Preferred stock also has a claim on income prior to common stock. That is, the firm must pay its preferred stock dividends before it issues common stock dividends. Thus, in terms of risk, preferred stock is safer than common stock because it has a prior claim on assets and income. However, it is riskier than long-term debt because its claims on assets and income come after those of bonds.

Cumulative Feature

Most preferred stock carries a **cumulative feature,** requiring that all past unpaid preferred stock dividends be paid before any common stock dividends are declared. The purpose is to provide some degree of protection for the preferred stock shareholder. Without a cumulative feature there would be no reason why preferred stock dividends would not be omitted or passed when common stock dividends were passed. Since preferred stock does not have the dividend enforcement power of interest from bonds, the cumulative feature is necessary to protect the rights of preferred stockholders.

Occasionally, if a firm does not pay preferred stock dividends for a number of years, dividends in arrears may become extremely large and virtually unpayable. In this case an arrangement is usually made to clear unpaid preferred stock dividends by exchanging other securities and cash, or securities alone, for the old preferred stock. This rids the firm of its built-up cumulative obligation and allows it to issue common stock dividends. The preferred stockholder is protected because the exchange is, of course, subject to his approval. An example occurred in 1973 with ASG Industries, which was faced with $2.1 million in dividend arrearages on its 5 percent preferred stock. To rid itself of the obligation, ASG exchanged 3 shares of common stock for each share of preferred. The value of the common stock received in the exchange was substantial, indicating that the cumulative feature had indeed served its purpose and protected the preferred shareholders.

Protective Provisions

Protective provisions in addition to the cumulative feature are common to preferred stock. These protective provisions generally allow for voting rights in the event of nonpayment of dividends, or they restrict the payment of common stock dividends if sinking-fund payments are not met or if the firm is in financial difficulty. In effect, the protective features included with preferred stock are similar to the restrictive provisions included with long-term debt.

To examine typical protective provisions, let us look at Tenneco and Reynolds Metals preferred stock. The Tenneco preferred stock has a protective provision that provides the preferred stockholders with voting rights whenever six quarterly dividends are in arrears. At that point the preferred shareholders are given the power to elect a majority of the board of directors. The Reynolds Metals preferred stock includes a protective provision that precludes the payment of common stock dividends during any period in which the preferred stock sinking fund is in default. Both provisions, which yield protection beyond that provided for by the cumulative provision and thereby reduce shareholder risk, are desired by investors. They reduce the cost of preferred stock to the issuing firm.

Infrequent Features

Participation

Although participating features are infrequent in preferred stock, their inclusion can greatly affect its desirability and cost. The **participation feature** allows the preferred stockholder to participate in earnings beyond the payment of the stated dividend. This is usually done in accordance with some set formula. For example, Borden Series A preferred stock currently provides for a dividend of no less than 60 cents per share, to be determined by the board of directors. Preferred stock of this sort actually resembles common stock as much as it does normal preferred stock. Although a participating feature is certainly desirable from the point of view of the investor, it is infrequently included in preferred stock.

Retirement of Preferred Stock

Although preferred stock does not have a set maturity associated with it, issuing firms generally provide for some method of retirement. If preferred stock could not be retired, issuing firms could not take advantage of falling interest rates.

Call Provisions

Most preferred stock has some type of call provision associated with it. In fact, the Securities Exchange Commission discourages the issuance of preferred stock without some call provision. The SEC has taken this stance on the grounds that if a method of retirement is not provided, the issuing firm will not be able to replace its preferred stock if interest rates fall.

The call feature on preferred stock usually involves an initial premium above the par value or issuing price of the preferred of approximately 10 percent. Then, over time, the call premium generally falls. For example, Quaker Oats in 1976 issued $9.56 cumulative preferred stock with no par value for $100 per share. This issue was not callable until 1980 and then was callable at $109.56. After that the call price gradually drops to $100 in the year 2000, as shown in Table 19–7.

By setting the initial call price above the initial issue price and allowing it to decline slowly over time, the firm protects the investor from an early call that carries no premium. A call provision also allows the issuing firm to plan the retirement of its preferred stock at predetermined prices.

TABLE 19–7.   Call Provision of Quaker Oats $9.56 Cumulative Preferred Stock

Date	Call Price
Date of issue until 7/19/80	Not callable
7/20/80 until 7/19/85	$109.56
7/20/85 until 7/19/90	107.17
7/20/90 until 7/19/95	104.78
7/20/95 until 7/19/00	102.39
After 7/19/00	100.00

Sinking Funds

A sinking-fund provision requires the firm periodically to set aside an amount of money for the retirement of its preferred stock. This money is then used to purchase the preferred stock in the open market or through the use of the call provision, whichever method is cheaper. Although preferred stock does not have a maturity date associated with it, the use of a call provision in addition to a sinking fund can effectively create a maturity date. For example, the Quaker Oats issue we just examined has associated with it an annual sinking fund, operating between the years 1981 and 2005, which requires the annual elimination of a minimum of 20,000 shares and a maximum of 40,000. The minimum payments are designed so that the entire issue will be retired by the year 2005. If any sinking-fund payments are made above the minimum amount, the issue will be retired prior to 2005. The Quaker Oats issue of preferred stock has a maximum life of 30 years, and the size of the issue outstanding decreases each year after 1981.

Advantages and Disadvantages

Because preferred stock is a hybrid of bonds and common stock, it offers the firm several advantages and disadvantages by comparison with bonds and common stock.

Advantages

1. Preferred stock does not have any default risk to the issuer. That is, the nonpayment of dividends does not force the firm into bankruptcy, as does the nonpayment of interest on debt.
2. The dividend payments are generally limited to a stated amount. Thus, preferred stock does not participate in excess earnings as does common stock.
3. Preferred stockholders do not have voting rights except in the case of financial distress. Therefore, the issuance of preferred stock does not create a challenge to the owners of the firm.
4. Although preferred stock does not carry a specified maturity, the inclusion of call features and sinking funds provides the ability to replace the issue if interest rates decline.

Disadvantages

1. Because preferred stock is riskier than bonds and because its dividends are not tax deductible, its cost is higher than that of bonds.
2. Although preferred stock dividends can be omitted, their cumulative nature makes their payment almost mandatory.

COMMON STOCK

Common stock involves ownership in the corporation. In effect, bondholders and preferred stockholders can be viewed as creditors, with the common stockholders being the true owners of the firm. Common stock does not have a maturity date, but exists as long as the firm does. Nor does common stock have an upper limit on its dividend payments. Dividend payments must be declared by the firm's board of directors before they are issued. In the event of bankruptcy the common stockholders, as owners of the corporation, cannot exercise claims on assets until the bondholders and preferred shareholders have been satisfied.

In examining common stock, we will look first at several of its features or characteristics. Then we will focus on the process of raising funds through rights offerings. Finally, we will investigate the advantages and disadvantages of the use of common stock.

Features or Characteristics

We will now examine common stock's claim on income and assets, its voting rights, and the meaning and importance of its limited-liability feature.

Claim on Income

As the owners of the corporation, the common shareholders have the right to the residual income after bondholders and preferred stockholders have been paid. This income may be paid directly to the shareholders in the form of dividends or retained and reinvested by the firm. While it is obvious the shareholder benefits immediately from the distribution of income in the form of dividends, the reinvestment of earnings also benefits the shareholder. Plowing back earnings into the firm results in an increase in the value of the firm, in its earning power, and in its future dividends. This action results in an increase in the value of the stock. In effect, residual income is distributed directly to shareholders in the form of dividends or indirectly in the form of capital gains on their common stock.

The right to residual income has both advantages and disadvantages for the common stockholder. The advantage is that the potential return is limitless. Once the claims of the most senior securities—that is, bonds and preferred stock—have been satisfied, the remaining income flows to the common stockholders in the form of dividends or capital gains. The disadvantage is that if the bond and preferred stock claims on income totally absorb earnings, common shareholders receive nothing. In years when earnings fall, it is the common shareholder who suffers first.

Claims on Assets

Just as common stock has the residual claim on income, it also has a residual claim on assets in the case of liquidation. Only after the claims of debt holders and preferred stockholders have been satisfied do the claims of common shareholders receive attention. Unfortunately, when bankruptcy does occur, the claims of the common shareholders generally go unsatisfied. In effect, this residual claim on assets adds to the risk of common stock. Thus, while common stock has historically provided a large return, averaging 9 percent annually since the late 1920s, it also has large risks associated with it.

Voting Rights   The common stock shareholders, as owners of the corporation, are entitled to elect the board of directors. Early in this century it was not uncommon for a firm to issue two classes of common stock, which were identical except that only one carried voting rights. For example, both the Parker Pen Co. and the Great Atlantic and Pacific Tea Co. (A&P) had two such classes of common stock. This practice has been virtually eliminated by (1) the Public Utility Holding Company Act of 1935, which gave the Securities and Exchange Commission the power to require that newly issued common stock carry voting rights, (2) the New York Stock Exchange's refusal to list common stock without voting privileges, and (3) investor demand for the inclusion of voting rights.

Although there are exceptions, each share of common stock is entitled to one vote, and common stock is the only security that carries the right to vote. Common shareholders not only have the right to elect the board of directors, they also must approve any change in the corporate charter. A typical charter change might involve the authorization to issue new stock or perhaps a merger proposal.

Voting for directors and charter changes occurs at the corporation's annual meeting. While shareholders may vote in person, the majority generally vote by proxy. A **proxy** gives a designated party the temporary power of attorney to vote for the signee at the corporation's annual meeting. The firm's management generally solicits proxy votes and, if the shareholders are satisfied with its performance, has little problem securing them. However, in times of financial distress or when management takeovers are threatened, **proxy fights**—battles between rival groups for proxy votes—occur.

While each share of stock carries the same number of votes, the voting procedure is not always the same from company to company. The two procedures commonly used are majority and cumulative voting. Under **majority voting,** each share of stock allows the shareholder one vote, and each position on the board of directors is voted on separately. Since each member of the board of directors is elected by a simple majority, a majority of shares has the power to elect the entire board of directors.

With **cumulative voting,** each share of stock allows the shareholder a number of votes equal to the number of directors being elected. The shareholder can then cast all his votes for a single candidate or split them among the various candidates. The advantage of a cumulative voting procedure is that it gives minority shareholders the power to elect a director.

Limited Liability   Although the common stock shareholders are the actual owners of the corporation, their liability in the case of bankruptcy is limited to the amount of their investment. The advantage is that investors who might not otherwise invest their funds in the firm become willing to do so. This limited-liability feature aids the firm in raising funds.

Preemptive Rights   The **preemptive right** entitles the common shareholder to maintain a proportionate share of ownership in the firm. When new shares are issued, common shareholders have the first right of refusal. If a shareholder owns 25 percent of the corporation's stock, then he or she is entitled to purchase 25 percent of the new shares. Certificates issued to the shareholders giving them an option to purchase a stated number of new shares of stock at a specified price during a two- to ten-week period are called

rights. These rights can be exercised, generally at a price below the common stock's current market price, can be allowed to expire, or can be sold in the open market.

The Rights Offering

We will look first at the dates surrounding a rights offering and then examine the process of raising funds and the value of a right.

Dates Surrounding a Rights Offering

Let us examine the announcement of a rights offering by a hypothetical corporation. On March 1 the firm announces that all "holders of record" as of April 6 will be issued rights, which will expire on May 30 and will be mailed to them on April 25. In this example March 1 is the **announcement date,** April 6 the **holder-of-record date,** and May 30 the **expiration date.** While this seems rather straightforward, it is complicated by the fact that if the stock is sold a day or two before the holder-of-record date, the corporation may not have time to record the transaction and replace the old owner's name with that of the new owner; the rights might then be sent to the wrong person. To deal with this problem an additional date has been created, the **ex rights date.** The ex rights date occurs four trading days prior to the holder-of-record date.

On or after the ex rights date the stock sells without the rights. Whoever owns the stock on the day prior to the ex rights date receives the rights. Thus, if the holder-of-record date is April 6 and four trading days earlier is April 2, anyone purchasing the stock on or before April 1 will receive the rights, while anyone purchasing the stock on or after April 2 will not. The price of the stock prior to the ex rights date is referred to as the **rights-on price,** while the price on or after the ex rights date is the **ex rights price.** The timing of this process and the terminology are shown in Table 19–8.

Raising Funds Through Rights Offerings

Three questions and theoretical relationships must be dealt with if we are to understand rights offerings. First, how many rights are required to purchase a share of new stock? Second, what is the theoretical value of a right? Finally, what effect do rights offerings have on the value of the common stock outstanding?

Let us continue with the example of our hypothetical corporation and assume it has 600,000 shares of stock outstanding, currently selling for $100 per share. In order to finance new projects, this firm needs to raise an additional $10,500,000 and wishes to do so with a rights offering. Moreover, the subscription price on the new stock is $70 per share. The subscription price is set below the current market price of the stock in order to ensure a complete sale of the new stock. To determine how many shares must be sold to raise the desired funds, we merely divide the desired funds by the subscription price:

$$\text{new shares to be sold} = \frac{\text{desired funds to be raised}}{\text{subscription price}} \qquad (19\text{--}2)$$

$$= \frac{\$10,500,000}{\$70}$$

$$= 150,000 \text{ shares}$$

TABLE 19–8.   Illustration of the Timing of a Rights Offering

Stock sells rights on	{ March 1—Announcement date { April 1 —The owner of the stock as of this date receives the rights
Stock sells ex rights	⎧ April 2 —Ex rights date ⎫ ⎪ April 6 —Holder-of-record date ⎬ four trading days ⎨ April 25—Mailing date ⎪ ⎩ May 30—Expiration date

We know each share of common stock receives one right, and 150,000 new shares of common stock must be sold. Therefore, to determine the number of rights necessary to purchase one share of stock, we merely divide the original number of shares outstanding by the new shares to be sold:

$$\text{number of rights necessary to purchase one share of stock} = \frac{\text{original number of shares outstanding}}{\text{new shares to be sold}} \tag{19-3}$$

$$= \frac{600,000 \text{ shares}}{150,000 \text{ shares}}$$

$$= 4 \text{ rights}$$

This indicates that if a current shareholder wishes to purchase a share of the new stock, he or she needs four rights plus $70:

$$\text{price of a share of new stock} = \text{subscription price} + \text{number of rights necessary to purchase one share of stock} \tag{19-4}$$

$$= \$70 + 4 \text{ rights}$$

Since the subscription price is well below the current market value, there is clearly some value to a right.

The theoretical value of the right obviously depends upon (1) the relationship between the market price of the stock and the subscription price and (2) the number of rights necessary to purchase one share of stock. To determine the value of a right in the previous example, first let us determine the market value of the corporation. Originally the firm had 600,000 shares of stock outstanding, selling at $100 each, for a total value of $60,000,000. Let us now assume that the market value of the firm went up by exactly the amount raised by the rights offering, $10,500,000, making the new market value of the firm $70,500,000. In reality the market value of the firm will go up by more than this amount if investors feel the firm will earn more than its required rate of return on these funds.

Taking the new market value for the firm, $70,500,000, and dividing by the total number of shares outstanding, 750,000, we find that the new market value for the stock will be $94 per share. That is to say, after all the new stock has been subscribed to, the market value of the stock will fall to $94 per share. Since it takes four rights and $70 to purchase one share of stock that will end up worth $94, the value of a right is equal to the savings made ($24—that is, you can buy a $94 share of stock for $70), divided by the number of rights necessary to purchase one share of stock:

$$\text{theoretical value of one right} = \frac{\left(\begin{array}{c}\text{market price of stock}\\ \text{ex rights}\end{array}\right) - \left(\begin{array}{c}\text{subscription}\\ \text{price}\end{array}\right)}{\begin{array}{c}\text{number of rights necessary to}\\ \text{purchase one share of stock}\end{array}} \qquad (19\text{--}5)$$

$$R = \frac{P_{ex} - S}{N} \qquad (19\text{--}6)$$

$$= \frac{\$94 - \$70}{4}$$

$$= \$6$$

where R = value of one right

P_{ex} = ex rights price of the stock

S = subscription price

N = number of rights necessary to purchase one share of stock

If the stock were selling rights-on—that is, prior to the ex rights date—the theoretical value of a right could be determined from the following equation:[5]

$$R = \frac{P_{on} - S}{N + 1} \qquad (19\text{--}12)$$

where P_{on} is the rights-on price of the stock. Substituting in the values from our example, we find:

$$R = \frac{\$100 - \$70}{4 + 1} = \$6$$

---

[5] This equation is derived from the previous equation as follows. We know that

$$P_{ex} = P_{on} - R \qquad (19\text{--}7)$$

Substituting $(P_{on} - R)$ for P_{ex} in equation (19–6) yields

$$R = \frac{P_{on} - R - S}{N} \qquad (19\text{--}8)$$

Simplifying,

$$RN = P_{on} - R - S \qquad (19\text{--}9)$$

$$RN + R = P_{on} - S \qquad (19\text{--}10)$$

$$R(N + 1) = P_{on} - S \qquad (19\text{--}11)$$

$$R = \frac{P_{on} - S}{N + 1} \qquad (19\text{--}12)$$

We found the same theoretical value for the right from both equations because the second equation is derived directly from the first.

If we think about the mathematical operations we have just performed, it should be evident that a stockholder does not benefit or lose from a rights offering. He receives something of value, the right, but loses exactly that amount in the form of a stock price decline. Of course, if he does not exercise or sell his rights he loses, but if the rights are not ignored, then he neither loses nor gains from a rights offering. Examination of the behavior of stockholders shows that only a small percentage neglect to exercise or sell their rights.

At this point it should be clear that the subscription price is irrelevant in a rights offering. The main concern in selecting a subscription price is setting it low enough that the price of the stock will not fall below it. As long as the subscription price is set far enough below the price of the stock to ensure that the rights maintain a positive value, the offering should be successful and the shareholders should not benefit or gain from the offering.

You have probably noticed that in our discussion of rights valuation we have said we are looking at the *theoretical* value of a right. The actual value may differ from the theoretical value for several reasons. One common reason is that transactions costs can limit investor arbitrage that would otherwise push the market price of the right to its theoretical value. A second reason is that speculation and irregular sale of rights over the subscription period may cause shifts in supply that push the market price of the right above or below its theoretical value. It should also be noted that transaction or flotation costs, particularly on smaller issues, can be quite large, as can be seen in Table 19–9. Although not shown in this table, flotation costs also vary with diffusion of share ownership. This table also illustrates that flotation costs associated with rights offerings are largely fixed costs; hence the larger the rights offering, the lower the flotation costs as a percent of the amount of funds raised.

TABLE 19–9. Flotation Costs of a Nonunderwritten Rights Offering as a Percent of Amount Raised from January 1971 through December 1979

Amount Raised from the Rights Offering	Flotation Costs as a Percent of the Amount Raised
$ 0.0 to 0.49 million	7.27%
0.5 to 0.99 million	5.06
1.0 to 1.99 million	3.31
2.0 to 4.99 million	2.73
5.0 to 9.99 million	1.59
10.0 to 19.99 million	1.16
20.0 to 49.99 million	0.61
50.0 to 99.99 million	0.19
100.00 to 199.99 million	0.13
200.00 million or more	0.13

Source: Robert S. Hansen and John M. Pinkerton, "Direct Equity Financing: A Resolution of a Paradox," *Journal of Finance*, 37 (June 1982), 651–65.

The primary benefit for the firm is that issuing new stock via a rights offering has a high probability of success. The rights must be exercised or sold to someone who will exercise them, or the shareholder will lose money. However, one of the questions that has haunted finance over the past decade is this: Why do firms avoid rights offerings? It was thought that the cheapest way to issue stock was to make a rights issue and avoid paying an underwriter for a standby agreement to guarantee the issue's success. This notion that rights offerings are less expensive than underwritten offerings has now been dismissed. Recent findings show that rights offerings are advantageous only for closely held corporations. Moreover, firms with diffused share ownership incur greater costs from rights offerings than from underwritten offerings.[6] Therefore, while rights offerings are not of direct value to the stockholder, in some cases they offer advantages to the financial manager.

Advantages and Disadvantages

The raising of new funds with common stock offers the firm several advantages and disadvantages by comparison with bonds and preferred stock.

Advantages

1. The firm is not legally obligated to pay common stock dividends. Thus, in times of financial distress there need not be a cash outflow associated with common stock, while there must be with bonds.
2. Because common stock has no maturity date, the firm does not have a cash outflow associated with its redemption. If the firm desires, it can repurchase its stock in the open market, but it is under no obligation to do so.
3. By issuing common stock the firm increases its financial base and thus its future borrowing capacity. On the other hand, issuing debt increases the financial base of the firm, but also cuts into the firm's borrowing capacity. If the firm's capital structure is already overburdened with debt, a new debt offering may preclude any future debt offering until the existing equity base is enlarged. Thus, financing with common stock increases the firm's financing flexibility.

Disadvantages

1. Because dividends are not tax deductible, as are interest payments, and because flotation costs on equity are larger than those on debt, common stock has a higher cost than does debt.
2. The issuance of new common stock may result in a change in the ownership and control of the firm. While the owners have a preemptive right to retain their proportionate control, they may not have the funds to do so. If this is the case, the original owners may see their control diluted by the issuance of new stock.

Summary

Bonds are any long-term promissory note issued by the firm. The legal agreement between the issuing firm and the bond trustee who represents the bondholders is called the indenture. The indenture states the specific terms of the issue, the rights

---

[6] See Robert S. Hansen and John M. Pinkerton, "Direct Equity Financing: A Resolution of a Paradox," *Journal of Finance*, 37 (June 1982), 651–65.

of the bondholders and issuing firm, and the responsibilities of the trustee. In the case of insolvency the claims of debt are honored before those of both common and preferred stock. Bonds also have a claim on income before those of common and preferred stock.

The major types of unsecured debt include debentures, subordinated debentures, and income bonds, while the major types of secured debt include mortgage, first mortgage, second mortgage, blanket mortgage, closed-end mortgage, open-end mortgage, and collateral trust bonds, in addition to equipment trust certificates. Because bonds have a maturity date, we examined the problem of their retirement. Bonds may be retired at maturity, or they may be retired prior to maturity through the use of a call provision or a sinking fund. We also examined the bond-refunding decision.

Preferred stock is called a hybrid security because it possesses many characteristics of both common stock and bonds. With respect to its claim on assets in the case of bankruptcy and its claim to income for dividends, it takes priority over common stock and yields priority to debt. Most preferred stock also has a cumulative feature, requiring that all past unpaid preferred stock dividends be paid before any common stock dividends be declared. While preferred stock does not have a maturity date, its retirement is usually provided for through the use of call provisions and sinking funds.

While debt holders and preferred stockholders can be viewed as creditors, the common stockholders are the true owners of the company. As such, they cannot exercise a claim on assets in the event of bankruptcy until the bondholders and preferred stockholders have been satisfied. The common stockholders have the right to elect the board of directors. They have the further right to maintain their proportionate share in the firm, called the preemptive right. In order to allow them to maintain this proportionate ownership, new funds are often raised through rights offerings.

Study Questions

19–1. Explain the difference between mortgage bonds and debentures.

19–2. Why are income bonds regarded as more risky than debentures?

19–3. Under what circumstances will a bond's current yield equal its yield to maturity? How is it possible for a bond's current yield to be greater than its yield to maturity? How is it possible for a bond's current yield to be less than its yield to maturity?

19–4. What factors affect the cost of long-term debt?

19–5. Explain the mechanics of issuing railroad equipment trust certificates. Why do they generally have a higher rating than other bonds issued by the same railroad?

19–6. Bondholders often prefer the inclusion of a sinking fund in their bond issue. Why?

19–7. Although the bond-refunding decision is analyzed in much the same way as the capital budgeting decision, one major difference is the discount rate used. What discount rate is used in the refunding decision, and what is the rationale behind this?

19–8. Why is preferred stock referred to as a hybrid security? It is often said to combine the worst features of common stock and bonds. What is meant by this statement?

19–9. Since preferred stock dividends in arrears must be paid before common stock dividends, should they be considered a liability and appear on the right-hand side of the balance sheet?

19–10. What are the advantages and disadvantages of the common stockholders' residual claim on income from the point of view of the investor?

19–11. What is a proxy? What is a proxy fight? Why do they occur?

19–12. Explain the difference between majority voting and cumulative voting. If you were a majority shareholder, which would you favor? Why? If you were a minority shareholder, which would you favor? Why?

19–13. Since a rights offering allows common shareholders to purchase common stock at a price below the current market price, why is it not of value to the common shareholder?

Self-Test Problem

ST–1. (*Rights Offering*) A firm is considering a rights offering to raise $30 million. Currently this firm has 3 million shares outstanding selling for $60 per share. The subscription price on the new shares would be $40 per share.
  a. How many shares must be sold to raise the desired funds?
  b. How many rights are necessary to purchase one share of stock?
  c. What is the value of one right?

Study Problems

19–1. (*Bankruptcy Distribution*) The Hayes Corporation is facing bankruptcy. The market value of its mortgaged assets is $30 million and of all other assets $50 million. Hayes currently has outstanding $40 million in mortgaged bonds, $20 million in subordinated debentures, and $20 million in preferred stock, and the par value of the common stock outstanding is $40 million. If the corporation goes bankrupt, how will the distribution be made?

19–2. (*Refunding Decision*) The A. Fields Wildcats Corporation currently has outstanding a 20-year $10 million bond issue with a 9¼ percent interest rate callable at $103. The unamortized flotation costs and the discount on these bonds currently total $600,000. Because of a decline in interest rates, Fields would be able to refund the issue with a $10 million issue of 8 percent 20-year bonds, providing the firm with $9.3 million after flotation costs. The issuing expenses would claim an additional $200,000. The overlap period during which both issues would be expected to be outstanding is one month. Assuming a 34 percent marginal corporate tax rate, determine whether or not this bond issue should be refunded. (*Note*: The present value of an annuity of $1 for 20 years at 5.28 percent is 12.172.)

19–3. (*Refunding Decision*) Three years ago the R. Wittman Corporation issued a 30-year $50 million bond issue with a 7 percent interest rate callable at $108. Because of the discount and flotation costs this issue initially raised only $48 million. The discount and flotation costs are being amortized using the straight-line method. During the past 3 years interest rates have fallen, allowing the Wittman Corporation to replace this bond issue with a 27-year $50 million bond issue with a coupon rate of 6 percent. The new issue will provide the firm with $49 million after flotation costs. Issuing expenses will drain an additional $400,000. The overlap period during which both issues are expected to be outstanding is one month. Assuming a 34 percent marginal corporate tax rate, determine whether or not the refunding decision should be made. (*Note*: The present value of an annuity of $1 for 27 years at 3.96 percent is 16.4031.)

19–4. (*Bond Indenture Research Project*) As a research project obtain several bond indentures. These can be obtained directly from the corporation issuing the bond or perhaps through a local stockbroker. Examine the restrictive covenants—in particular, prohibitions on the sale of accounts receivable, constraints on common stock dividends, fixed asset restrictions, and constraints on additional borrowing—and determine the reason for their inclusion.

19–5. (*Rights Offering*) The L. Turner Corporation is considering raising $12 million through a rights offering. It has one million shares of stock outstanding, currently selling for $84 per share. The subscription price on the new stock will be $60 per share.
   a. How many shares must be sold to raise the desired funds?
   b. How many rights are necessary to purchase one share of stock?
   c. What is the value of one right?

19–6. (*Rights Offering*) The E. Muransky Corporation is considering a rights offering to raise $35 million to finance new projects. It currently has 2 million shares of stock outstanding, selling for $50 per share. The subscription price on the new shares would be $35 per share.
   a. How many shares must be sold to raise the desired funds?
   b. How many rights are necessary to purchase one share of stock?
   c. What is the value of one right?

19–7. (*Rights Offerings*) The B. Fuller Corporation is in the process of selling common stock through a rights offering. Prior to the rights offering, the firm had 500,000 shares of common stock outstanding. Through the rights offering, it plans on issuing an additional 100,000 shares at a subscription price of $30. After the stock went ex rights, the market price was $40. What was the price of the B. Fuller common stock just prior to the rights offering? (*Hint*: Set equation (19–6) equal to equation (19–12) and solve for P_{on}.)

Self-Test Solution

SS–1. a. new shares to be sold $= \dfrac{\text{desired funds to be raised}}{\text{subscription price}}$

$$= \frac{\$30,000,000}{\$40}$$

$$= 750,000 \text{ shares}$$

b. $\begin{matrix}\text{number of rights}\\ \text{necessary to purchase}\\ \text{one share of stock}\end{matrix} = \dfrac{\text{original number of shares outstanding}}{\text{new shares to be sold}}$

$$= \frac{3,000,000}{750,000}$$

$$= 4 \text{ rights}$$

c. value of one right $= \dfrac{P_{on} - S}{N + 1}$

$$= \frac{\$60 - \$40}{4 + 1}$$

$$= \frac{\$20}{5}$$

$$= \$4$$

Selected References

Agmon, T., A. R. Ofer, and A. Tamir. "Variable Rate Debt Instruments and Corporate Debt Policy," *Journal of Finance*, 36 (March 1981), 113–26.

Alderson, Michael J., Keith C. Brown, and Scott L. Lummer, "Dutch Auction Rate Preferred Stock," *Financial Management*, 16 (Summer 1987), 68–73.

Ang, James S. "The Two Faces of Bond Refunding," *Journal of Finance*, 30 (June 1975), 869–74.

Bacon, Peter W., and Edward L. Winn, Jr. "The Impact of Forced Conversion on Stock Prices," *Journal of Finance*, 24, (December 1969), 871–74.

Bhagat, Sanjai, James A. Brickley, and Ronald C. Lease. "The Authorization of Additional Common Stock: An Empirical Investigation," *Financial Management*, 15 (Autumn 1986), 45–53.

Bierman, Harold, Jr., and Amir Barnea. "Expected Short-Term Interest Rates in Bond Refunding," *Financial Management*, 3 (Spring 1974), 75–79.

Bildersee, John S. "Some Aspects of the Performance of Non-Convertible Preferred Stocks," *Journal of Finance*, 28 (December 1973), 1187–1202.

Block, Stanley, and Marjorie Stanley. "The Financial Characteristics and Price Movement Patterns of Companies Approaching the Unseasoned Securities Market in the Late 1970's," *Financial Management*, 9 (Winter 1980), 30–36.

Bodie, Zvi, and Robert A. Taggart, Jr. "Future Investment Opportunities and the Value of the Call Provision on a Bond," *Journal of Finance*, 33 (September 1978), 1187–1200.

Bowlin, Oswald D. "The Refunding Decision: Another Special Case in Capital Budgeting," *Journal of Finance*, 21 (March 1966), 55–68.

Brennan, Michael J., and Eduardo S. Schwartz. "Savings Bonds, Retractable Bonds and Callable Bonds," *Journal of Financial Economics*, 5 (1977), 66–88.

Caks, John. "Corporate Debt Decisions: A New Analytical Framework," *Journal of Finance*, 33 (December 1978), 1297–1315.

Duvall, Richard M., and Douglas V. Austin. "Predicting the Results of Proxy Contests," *Journal of Finance*, 20 (September 1965), 467–71.

Eibott, Peter. "Trends in the Value of Individual Stockholdings," *Journal of Business*, 47 (July 1974), 339–48.

Elsaid, Hussein H. "The Function of Preferred Stock in the Corporate Financial Plan," *Financial Analysts Journal* (July–August 1969), 112–17.

Emery, Douglas R. "Overlapping Interest in Bond Refunding: A Reconsideration," *Financial Management*, 17 (Summer 1978), 19–20.

Fisher, Donald E., and Glenn A. Wilt, Jr. "Nonconvertible Preferred Stock as a Financing Instrument, 1950–1965," *Journal of Finance*, 23 (September 1968), 611–24.

Halford, Frank A. "Income Bonds," *Financial Analysts Journal*, 20 (January–February 1964), 73–79.

Hansen, Robert S., Claire E. Crutchley, "Corporate Financings and Corporate Earnings," Manuscript, Virginia Polytechnic Institute and State University, 1987.

————, Beverly R. Fuller, Vahan Janjigian, "The Over-Allotment Option and Equity Financing Flotation Costs: An Empirical Investigation," *Financial Management*, 16 (Summer 1987), 24–32.

————, and John M. Pinkerton. "Direct Equity Financing: A Resolution of a Paradox," *Journal of Finance*, 37 (June 1982), 651–65.

Harris, Robert S. "The Refunding of Discounted Debt: An Adjusted Present Value Analysis," *Financial Management*, 9 (Winter 1980), 7–12.

Jen, Frank C., and James E. Wert. "The Deferred Call Provision and Corporate Bond Yields," *Journal of Financial and Quantitative Analysis*, 3 (June 1968), 157–69.

————. "The Effect of Call Risk on Corporate Bond Yields," *Journal of Finance*, 22 (December 1967), 637–51.

Johnson, Rodney, and Richard Klein. "Corporate Motives in Repurchases of Discounted Bonds," *Financial Management*, 3 (Autumn 1974), 44–49.

Kalotay, A. J. "On the Advanced Refunding of Discounted Debt," *Financial Management*, 7 (Summer 1978), 14–18.

————. "On the Management of Sinking Funds," *Financial Management*, 10 (Summer 1981), 34–40.

————. "Sinking Funds and the Realized Cost of Debt," *Financial Management*, 11 (Spring 1982), 43–54.

Keane, S. M. "The Significance of Issue Price in Rights Issues," *Journal of Business Finance*, 4 (September 1972), 40–45.

Kolodny, Richard. "The Refunding Decision in Near Perfect Markets," *Journal of Finance*, 29 (December 1974), 1467–78.

Laber, Gene. "Repurchases of Bonds through Tender Offers: Implications for Shareholder Wealth," *Financial Management*, 7 (Summer 1978), 7–13.

Logue, Dennis E., and Richard J. Rogalski. "Does It Pay to Shop for Your Bond Underwriter?" *Harvard Business Review*, 57 (July–August 1979), 111–17.

Marshall, William J., and Jess B. Yawitz. "Optimal Terms of the Call Provision on a Corporate Bond," *Journal of Financial Research*, 2 (Fall 1980), 203–11.

Mayor, Thomas H., and Kenneth G. McCoin. "The Rate of Discount in Bond Refunding," *Financial Management*, 3 (Autumn 1974), 54–58.

McConnell, John J., and Gary G. Schlarbaum. "Returns, Risks, and Pricing of Income Bonds, 1956–76," *Journal of Business*, 54 (January 1981), 33–57.

McEnally, Richard W., and Michael L. Rice. "Hedging Possibilities in the Flotation of Debt Securities," *Financial Management*, 8 (Winter 1979), 12–18.

Ofer, Aharon R., and Robert A. Taggart, Jr. "Bond Refunding: A Clarifying Analysis," *Journal of Finance*, 32 (March 1977), 21–30.

Pinches, George E., and Kent A. Mingo. "The Role of Subordination and Industrial Bond Ratings," *Journal of Finance*, 30 (March 1975), 201–6.

Riener, Kenneth D. "Financial Structure Effects on Bond Refunding," *Financial Management*, 9 (Summer 1980), 18–23.

Sibley, A. M. "Some Evidence on the Cash Flow Effects of Bond Refunding," *Financial Management*, 3 (Autumn 1974), 50–53.

Smith, Clifford W., Jr., and Jerold B. Warner. "On Financial Contracting: An Analysis of Bond Covenants," *Journal of Financial Economics*, 7 (June 1979), 117–61.

Stevenson, Richard A. "Retirement of Non-Callable Preferred Stock," *Journal of Finance*, 25 (December 1970), 1143–52.

Van Horne, James C. "Called Bonds: How Does the Investor Fare?" *Journal of Portfolio Management*, 6 (Summer 1980), 58–61.

Weinstein, Mark I. "The Seasoning Process of New Corporate Bond Issues," *Journal of Finance*, 33 (December 1978), 1343–54.

White, R. W., and P. A. Lusztig. "The Price Effects of Rights Offerings," *Journal of Financial and Quantitative Analysis*, 15 (March 1980), 25–40.

Winger, Bernard J., Carl R. Chen, John D. Martin, J. William Petty, and Steven C. Hayden. "Adjustable Rate Preferred Stock," *Financial Management*, 15 (Spring 1986), 48–57.

Winn, Willis J., and Arleigh Hess, Jr. "The Value of the Call Privilege," *Journal of Finance*, 14 (May 1959), 182–95.

20

Convertibles and Warrants

In earlier chapters we concerned ourselves with methods of raising long-term funds through the use of common stock, preferred stock, and short- and long-term debt. In this chapter we will examine how convertibles and warrants can be used to increase the attractiveness of these securities. We have grouped convertibles and warrants together in our discussion because both can be exchanged at the owner's discretion for a specified number of shares of common stock. In investigating each financing alternative we will look first at its specific characteristics and purpose; then we will focus on any special considerations that should be examined before it is issued. We will close by discussing valuation of convertibles and warrants.

CONVERTIBLE SECURITIES

A **convertible security** is a preferred stock or a debt issue that can be exchanged for a specified number of shares of common stock at the will of the owner. It provides the stable income associated with preferred stock and bonds in addition to the possibility of capital gains associated with common stock. This combining of features has led convertibles to be called *hybrid* securities.

When the convertible is initially issued, the firm receives the proceeds from the sale, less flotation costs. This is the only time the firm receives any proceeds from issuing convertibles. The firm then treats this convertible as if it were normal preferred stock or debentures, paying dividends or interest regularly. If the security owner wishes to exchange the convertible for common stock, he or she may do so at any time according to the terms specified when the convertible was originally issued. The desire to convert generally follows a rise in the price of the common stock. Once the convertible owner trades the convertibles in for common stock, the owner can never trade the stock back for convertibles. From then on the owner is treated as any other common stockholder and receives only common stock dividends.

Characteristics and Features of Convertibles

Conversion Ratio

The number of shares of common stock for which the convertible security can be exchanged is set out when the convertible is initially issued. On some convertible issues this **conversion ratio** is stated directly. For example, the convertible may state that it is exchangeable for 15 shares of common stock. Some convertibles give only a **conversion price,** stating, for example, that the security is convertible at $39 per share. This tells us that for every $39 of par value of the convertible security one share of common stock will be received.

$$\text{Conversion ratio} = \frac{\text{par value of convertible security}}{\text{conversion price}} \qquad (20\text{--}1)$$

For example, in 1983 Burlington Industries issued $75 million of convertible debentures that mature in 2008. These convertibles have a $1000 par value, an 8¾ percent coupon interest rate, and a conversion price of $48.50. Thus, the conversion ratio—the number of shares to be received upon conversion—is $1000/$48.50 = 20.6186 shares. In effect, the security owner has the choice of holding the 8¾ percent convertible debenture or trading it in for 20.6186 shares of Burlington Industries common stock. In this case the bond indenture states how the fractional shares are to be dealt with, either by issuing fractional shares, allowing the security holder to purchase the unissued fractional share, or paying the investor for the fractional share.

Conversion Value

The **conversion value** of a convertible security is the total market value of the common stock for which it can be exchanged. This can be calculated as follows:

$$\text{conversion value} = (\text{conversion ratio}) \times \begin{pmatrix} \text{market value per share} \\ \text{of the common stock} \end{pmatrix} \qquad (20\text{--}2)$$

If the Burlington Industries common stock were selling for, say, $44 per share, as it was in early 1987, then the conversion value for the Burlington Industries convertible would be (20.6186)($44.00) = $907.22, that is, the market value of the common stock for which the convertible could be exchanged would be $907.22. Thus, regardless of what this convertible debenture was selling for, it could be converted into $907.22 worth of common stock.

Security Value

The **security value** (or bond value, as it is sometimes called) of a convertible security is the price the convertible security would sell for in the absence of its conversion feature. This is calculated by determining the required rate of return on a straight (nonconvertible) issue of the same quality and then determining the present value of the interest and principal payments at this rate of return. For example, the Burlington Industries convertible has a Standard and Poor's BBB+ rating, and on a given day BBB+ issues were yielding approximately 9.5 percent. Thus in determining the security value of this issue, we are answering the question, What must this Burlington Industries bond, which pays 8¾ percent semi-annually and is rated BBB+ with (at that time) 21 years to maturity, sell at in order to yield 9.5 percent? Since this bond pays 8¾ percent semi-annually, it gives the investor $43.75 every six months for the next 21 years for a total 42 $43.75 payments, and at the end of 21 years (after 42 six-month periods) it pays the investor its par value of $1000. As shown in equation (9–7), in determining the present value of this bond we use a discount rate of 9.5/2, or 4.75 percent. Thus, the value of this bond with semi-annual payments is determined as follows:

$$SV = \sum_{t=1}^{2n} \frac{\frac{IP}{2}}{\left(1 + \frac{i}{2}\right)^t} + \frac{P}{\left(1 + \frac{i}{2}\right)^{2n}} \qquad (20\text{--}3)$$

where SV = the security value

I = the coupon interest rate

P = the par value

n = the number of years to maturity

i = the required rate of return on a straight issue of the same quality

Then the value of the Burlington security as a straight debenture yields the following:

$$SV = \sum_{i=1}^{42} \frac{\$43.75}{(1 + .0475)^t} + \frac{\$1000}{(1 + .0475)^{42}}$$

$$= \$843.38 + \$142.41$$

$$= \$985.79$$

Thus, regardless of what happens to the value of Burlington's common stock, the lowest value the convertible can drop to, assuming there is no change in interest rates, is its value as a straight bond, which is $985.79.

Conversion Period

On some issues the time period during which the convertible can be exchanged for common stock is limited. Many times conversion is not allowed until a specified number of years have passed, or is limited by a terminal conversion date. Still other convertibles may be converted at any time during their life. In either case the **conversion period** will be specified when the convertible is originally issued.

Conversion Parity Price

The **conversion parity price** is the price at which the investor, in effect, buys the company's stock:

$$\text{conversion parity price} = \frac{\text{market price of convertible security}}{\text{conversion ratio}} \qquad (20\text{--}4)$$

If the Burlington Industries bond is selling for $1050.00 and the investor can exchange the bond for 20.6186 shares of Burlington Industries common stock, then the conversion parity price is ($1050.00/20.6186) = $50.92. Thus, if the investor purchases this convertible and converts it to common stock, he or she is in effect buying that stock for $50.92 per share.

Conversion Premium

The **conversion premium** is the difference between the convertible's market price and the higher of its security value and its conversion value. It can be expressed as an absolute dollar value, in which case it is defined as

$$\begin{matrix} \text{conversion} \\ \text{premium} \end{matrix} = \begin{pmatrix} \text{market price of} \\ \text{the convertible} \end{pmatrix} - \begin{pmatrix} \text{higher of the security value} \\ \text{and conversion value} \end{pmatrix} \quad (20\text{--}5)$$

Alternatively, the conversion premium can be expressed as a percentage, in which case it is defined as

$$\begin{matrix} \text{percentage} \\ \text{conversion} \\ \text{premium} \end{matrix} = \frac{\begin{pmatrix} \text{market price of} \\ \text{convertible bond} \end{pmatrix} - \begin{pmatrix} \text{higher of the security value} \\ \text{and the conversion value} \end{pmatrix}}{(\text{higher of the security value and the conversion value})} \quad (20\text{--}6)$$

In the case of the Burlington Industries convertible, on a given date its market price was $1050 while its security value was $985.79 and its conversion value was $907.22. Thus, its conversion premium was

$$\frac{\$1050.00 - \$985.79}{\$985.79} = 6.51 \text{ percent}$$

In effect, an investor was willing to pay a 6.51 percent premium over the higher of its security and conversion values in order to have the possibility of capital gains from stock price advances coupled with the security of the fixed interest payments associated with a debenture.

In describing convertibles, we have introduced a number of terms. To eliminate confusion, Table 20–1 summarizes them.

Reasons for Issuing Convertibles

There are several major reasons why firms choose to issue convertibles rather than straight debt, preferred stock, or common stock. These reasons include "sweetening" the long-term debt issue to make it more attractive, delayed equity financing, raising temporarily inexpensive funds, and financing corporate mergers.

Sweetening Long-term Debt

Before World War II the major reason for adding a convertible feature to preferred stock or debt was to make the security attractive enough to ensure a market for it. At that time convertibles were primarily limited to firms of lower credit standings who would have had a difficult time issuing straight debt or preferred stock. Consequently, a convertible feature would be added to increase the attractiveness of the issue and thereby guarantee its success. Since World War II firms of higher credit standing have also entered the convertible market, citing other reasons for issuing convertibles, while weaker firms have continued to use convertibles as sweeteners.

Delayed Equity Financing

Often a company would rather issue common stock than either preferred stock or debentures; however, because management feels the current stock price is temporarily depressed or is worried that issuing additional common stock will temporarily drive

TABLE 20–1. Summary of Convertible Terminology

Conversion ratio: the number of shares for which the convertible security can be exchanged.

$$\text{Conversion ratio} = \frac{\text{par value of convertible security}}{\text{conversion price}} \qquad (20\text{–}1)$$

Conversion value: the total market value of the common stock for which the convertible can be exchanged.

$$\text{Conversion value} = (\text{conversion ratio}) \times \left(\begin{array}{c} \text{market value per} \\ \text{share of the common stock} \end{array} \right) \qquad (20\text{–}2)$$

Security value: the price the convertible security would sell for in the absence of its conversion feature.

Conversion period: the time period during which the convertible can be exchanged for common stock.

Conversion parity price: the price the investor is in effect paying for the common stock.

$$\text{Conversion parity price} = \frac{\text{market price of convertible security}}{\text{conversion ratio}} \qquad (20\text{–}4)$$

Conversion premium: the difference between the convertible's market price and the higher of its security value and its conversion value.

$$\begin{array}{c} \text{Conversion} \\ \text{premium} \end{array} = \left(\begin{array}{c} \text{market price} \\ \text{of the} \\ \text{convertible} \end{array} \right) - \left(\begin{array}{c} \text{higher of the} \\ \text{security value and} \\ \text{conversion value} \end{array} \right) \qquad (20\text{–}5)$$

the stock's earnings per share down and result in a lower stock price, it resorts to convertible securities. Management's hope is that, after a short period of time, the common stock price will rise and investors will trade their convertibles in for common stock. Thus, for example, if the price of Burlington's common stock rose and investors subsequently exchanged their convertibles for common stock, they would have in effect purchased the common stock for the conversion parity price, $50.92. That is, for every share of stock Burlington exchanged for convertibles, they originally received $50.92. Since Burlington has set its conversion parity price above the stock's market price, the firm will have to give up fewer shares of common stock when the securities are converted than if it raised funds via a common stock offering originally. In effect, equity financing is provided only if the market value of the common stock rises. If it does not, financing remains in the form of lower-cost debt or preferred stock.

Raising Temporarily Inexpensive Funds   If the firm is raising funds for a large expansion it wishes to finance with common stock, it may instead choose to issue a convertible. By this means, funds needed during the building stage can be accumulated at a lower cost (as debt, because of its tax advantage, is cheaper than common stock) without diluting the firm's earnings per share by increasing the number of shares of common stock outstanding.[1] When the expansion is completed, the firm's earnings will rise, increasing the common stock share price and allowing convertible holders to exchange their securities for common stock. In this manner, the firm is given access to relatively inexpensive funds during the expansion period; its common stock earnings per share does not drop, since there is no increase in common shares outstanding unaccompanied by an increase in earnings; and the expansion is financed through a delayed issue of common stock, provided the common price rises enough to support conversion.

---

[1] Where potential dilution is in excess of 3 percent, the earnings per share are shown on two bases, unadjusted and adjusted for potential conversion.

Financing Corporate Mergers

If the stockholders of an acquired company take cash or debt in exchange for their common stock, they incur an immediate tax liability on any capital gains on their investment. If, however, the exchange is made for common, preferred, or convertible preferred stock, the tax liability is postponed, since the transaction is regarded as a tax-free exchange. Thus, many mergers are financed with common or convertible preferred stock.

Convertible preferred stock is frequently used in order to provide the most attractive terms possible for the exchange. Holders of stock in the company being acquired can be offered the stable income and limited risk of preferred stock, plus the chance for capital gains afforded by the convertible feature. The issuing company also benefits from the use of convertible preferred stock rather than common stock in that less dilution of earnings occurs. The reason is that investors would have demanded additional common stock if the exchange had been made for straight common stock.

Other Factors To Be Considered

Overhanging Issue

An **overhanging issue** is one in which the firm cannot force conversion because the common stock has not risen sufficiently to justify it. The overhanging issue's major disadvantage to the firm is that it limits financing flexibility. Not only does it make additional financing with convertible securities practically impossible, but it may also make long-term debt unacceptable to investors if the firm has been relying on a successful conversion to bring its financial structure back to normal. If this is the case, the conversion has been thwarted by an insufficient rise in the common stock price; the only available alternative may be a common stock offering. However, this too may be unacceptable or at least undesirable to the firm's management if it feels the common stock price is temporarily depressed.

Forced Conversion

While the investor has full legal control over the exercise of a convertible security, the firm can often force him or her into conversion by calling the convertible or establishing step-up conversion prices. If, for example, the conversion value of the security exceeds its call price, the firm need only call the security to force any rational investor to convert. A second way of inducing conversion is to provide for increasingly larger conversion prices and thus lower conversion ratios over the years. A convertible debenture with a $1000 par value could have a conversion price of $50 per share for the first five years and $60 per share after that. In this case if the price of the common stock had risen to $100 per share after five years, an investor would have the choice of converting the security into 20 shares of common stock worth $2000 or not converting and watching the conversion value of the security drop to $1666.67 as the conversion price is increased to $60 per share. In most cases a step-up conversion price will provide enough incentive to induce conversion as long as the conversion value is greater than the security value of the convertible.

Valuation of a Convertible

The valuation of a convertible depends primarily upon two factors: the value of the straight debenture or preferred stock and the value of the security if it were converted into common stock. Complicating the valuation is the fact that investors are in general willing to pay a premium for the conversion privilege, which allows them to hedge against the future. If the price of the common stock should rise, the investor would participate in capital gains; if it should decline, the convertible security will fall only to its value as a straight debenture or preferred stock.

In examining the Burlington Industries convertible debenture we found that if it were selling as a straight debenture, its price would be $985.79. Thus, regardless of what happens to its common stock, the lowest the value of the convertible can drop to is $985.79. The conversion value, on the other hand is, $907.22. Thus, this convertible is worth more as common stock than if it were straight debt. However, the real question is, Why are investors willing to pay a conversion premium of 6.51 percent over its security or conversion value for this Burlington Industries debenture? Quite simply because investors are willing to pay for the chance for capital gains without the large risk of loss.

If we look at the relationship between the value of the convertible and the price of its common stock, we find it to be as depicted graphically in Figure 20–1. The bond value of the convertible serves as a floor for the value of the investment: When the market price of the common stock approaches the conversion price (point *A*), the value of the convertible becomes dependent upon its conversion value. In effect the convertible security is valued as a bond when the price of the common stock is low and as common stock when the price of the common stock rises. While the minimum price of the convertible is determined by the higher of either the straight bond or preferred stock price or the conversion value, investors also pay a premium for the conversion option. Again, this premium results because convertible securities offer investors stable income from debenture or preferreds, and thus less risk of price

FIGURE 20–1. Relationship between the Market Price of the Common Stock and the Market Price of the Convertible Security

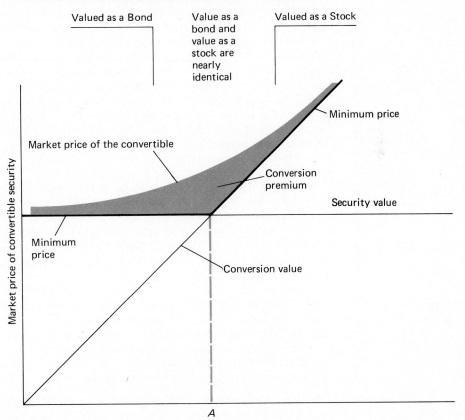

Market price of common stocks

decline due to adverse stock conditions, while retaining capital gains prospects from stock price gains. In effect, downside stock price variability is hedged away, while upside variability is not.

BASIC FINANCIAL MANAGEMENT IN PRACTICE

Metamorphosis: The Lure of Convertible Debentures

Last summer Alan Frazier, chief financial officer of Immunex Corporation, had a money problem. The five-year-old biotechnology company needed more cash, but Frazier believed that issuing debt would cost too much. And because the Seattle company had made an equity offering last March, he worried that another would dilute shareholders' positions.

Frazier chose a middle course—convertible debentures. These bonds can provide lower costs than straight debt for the issuer and greater stability than equity for the investor. They also can attract institutional investors who might not otherwise be interested in placing their money in a small company. In a typical offering, a company issues a bond that can be converted into stock at a specified price on a certain date. While waiting for the stock to reach the conversion price, investors receive interest income.

A convertible provides a financing option for small companies, many of which have little luck selling bonds to institutional investors such as pension funds and insurance companies. The reason: rating agencies like Moody's Investors Service and Standard & Poor's often view small-company bonds as below investment grade.

However, institutional investors are willing to buy convertibles; they see them as a safer way to take an equity position in growing companies. They get the extra protection of interest income, and bondholders have a higher claim than shareholders on the companies assets. Investors apparently liked Immunex, even though the company lacks a marketable product and its 1985 sales of $3.2 million came from contract revenues. Frazier's $40 million issue sold out quickly last August.

Despite its potential benefits, a convertible is hardly a sure thing for the issuer. Small companies often lack the revenue streams to make interest payments. "If the company's stock goes up and the bonds convert, everything can work out fine," says Teena Lerner, a biotechnology analyst for L. F. Rothschild Company in New York City. "If the stock does not rise, the company may be stuck carrying interest obligations that will be difficult to manage."

Convertibles were once the province of risky companies that could raise neither debt nor equity. Now, corporate giants as well as stable firms are selling them. Convertible debentures are especially attractive when the bull market is running and interest rates are falling. And with investors uncertain about the direction of stocks and interest rates, these bonds are selling at a record pace. During the 1970's, approximately 500 million were issued each year. In the last few years, more than $1 billion in convertibles has been sold each month.

Companies issuing convertibles can sell debt at lower rates and equity at premium prices. The bonds can carry interest rates that are as much as four percentage points below rates of straight debt. "Convertibles can really help the CFO get a better rate," says Barry Turk, senior vice president and treasurer of The A. L. Williams Corporation, a Duluth, Georgia, life insurance and mutual fund company. Turk issued $40 million in convertibles last May with a coupon of 7.25 percent, while similar issues of straight debt were offering rates of 9 percent or higher.

SOURCE: Luxenburg, Stan, "Metamorphosis: The Lure of Convertible Debentures," *CFO*, 3 (March 1987), 65–66.

WARRANTS

A **warrant** provides the investor with an option to purchase a fixed number of shares of common stock at a predetermined price during a specified time period. Warrants have been used in the past primarily by weaker firms as "sweetener" attachments to bonds or preferred stock to improve their marketability. However, in April 1970, when AT&T included them as a part of a major financing package, warrants achieved a new level of respectability.

Only recently have warrants been issued in conjunction with common stock. Their purpose is essentially the same as when they are issued in conjunction with debt or preferred stock; that is, to improve the reception in the market of the new offering. An example of issuing warrants with common stock occurred in May 1983 when Republic Airlines, Inc., offered 3.4 million units at $16.75 per unit, each consisting of two shares of common stock and one warrant. Each warrant entitled the holder to purchase one share of common stock at $10.00 per share through the expiration date. The market's reaction to this offering was excellent.

While warrants are similar to convertibles in that both provide investors with a chance to participate in capital gains, the mechanics of the two instruments differ greatly. From the standpoint of the issuing firm there are two major differences. First, when convertibles are exchanged for common stock there is an elimination of debt and a reduction in fixed financing charges, while when warrants are exchanged there is no reduction in fixed charges. Second, when convertibles are exchanged there is no cash inflow into the firm—the exchange is merely one type of security for another. But with warrants, since they are merely an option to buy the stock at a set price, a cash flow accompanies the exchange.

Characteristics and Features of Warrants

Exercise Price

The **exercise price** is that at which the warrant allows its holder to purchase the firm's common stock. The investor trades a warrant plus the exercise price for common stock. Typically, when warrants are issued the exercise price is set above the current market price of the stock. Thus, if the stock price does not rise above the exercise price, the warrant will never be converted. In addition there is also a step-up exercise price—that is, a warrant with which the exercise price changes over time.

Expiration Date

While some warrants are issued with no **expiration date,** most warrants are set to expire after a number of years. In issuing warrants as opposed to convertibles, the firm gives up some control over when the warrants will be exercised. With convertibles the issuing company can force conversion by calling the issue or using step-up conversion prices, whereas with warrants only the approach of the expiration date or the use of step-up exercise prices can encourage conversion.

Detachability

Most warrants are said to be **detachable** in that they can be sold separately from the security to which they were originally attached. Thus, if an investor purchases a primary issuance of a corporate bond with a warrant attached, he or she has the option of selling the bond alone, selling the warrant alone, or selling the combination intact. **Nondetachable warrants** cannot be sold separately from the security to which they were originally attached. Such a warrant can be separated from the senior security only by being exercised.

Exercise Ratio

The **exercise ratio** states the number of shares that can be obtained at the exercise price with one warrant. If the exercise ratio on a warrant were 1.5, one warrant would entitle its owner to purchase 1.5 shares of common stock at its exercise price.

Reasons for Issuing Warrants

Sweetening Debt

Warrants attached to debt offerings provide a feature whereby investors can participate in capital gains while holding debt. The firm can thereby increase the demand for the issue, increase the proceeds, and lower the interest costs. In effect, attaching warrants to long-term debt performs, to a certain extent, the same function that the convertibility feature on debt performs; that is, giving investors something they want and thereby increasing the marketability and demand for the bonds.

Additional Cash Inflow

If warrants are added to sweeten a debt offering, the firm will receive an eventual cash inflow when and if the warrants are exercised; a conversion feature would not provide this additional inflow.

Other Factors To Be Considered

Nonextinguishment of Debt

When warrants are exercised, the debt to which they were originally attached remains in existence. The warrant exercise process provides an additional cash inflow, but does not provide for the elimination of the original security. With convertible debt, on the other hand, when the convertible is exercised no cash flow occurs, but the original security is eliminated. Thus, the decision between convertible and warrant financing becomes one partially of tradeoffs, elimination of debt versus additional cash inflows.

Dilution and Flexibility

Since present accounting standards provide that earnings per share be stated as if all the warrants outstanding had been exercised, warrants have the effect of reducing the firm's reported earnings per share. This potential dilution of earnings per share may reduce the firm's financing flexibility. Because of previously issued warrants, the issuance of additional common stock may be hindered or even prohibited. The market's reluctance to accept further equity offerings may be due not only to the potential earnings per share dilution effect of the outstanding warrants, but also to a feeling that only weaker firms have to resort to warrant financing to sweeten their senior security offerings.

Valuation of a Warrant

Since the warrant is an option to purchase a specified number of shares of stock at a specified price for a given length of time, the market value of the warrant will be primarily a function of the common stock price. To understand the valuation of warrants we must define two additional terms, the minimum price and the premium. Let us look at a specific example. In January 1985 Wickes Corporation issues warrants in conjunction with a subordinated debenture offering with an expiration date of January 26, 1992, an exercise ratio of 1.00, and an exercise price of $4.43 from January 26, 1987, through the expiration date. This means that any time between January 26, 1987, and January 26, 1992, an investor with one warrant can purchase one share of Wickes Corporation stock at $4.43 regardless of the market price of that stock. On a given day the Wickes warrants were selling for $2.25, while the Wickes stock was selling for $4.00 per share.

Minimum price. The **minimum price** of a warrant is determined as follows:

$$\text{minimum price} = \left(\begin{array}{c}\text{market price of} \\ \text{common stock}\end{array} - \begin{array}{c}\text{exercise} \\ \text{price}\end{array}\right) \times \text{exercise ratio} \quad (20\text{--}7)$$

In the Wickes example the exercise price is greater than the price of the common stock ($4.43 as opposed to $4.00). In this case the minimum price of the warrant is considered to be zero, because things simply do not sell for negative prices [($4.00 − $4.43) × 1.00 = − $.43]. If, for example, the price of the Wickes common stock rose to $6 per share, the minimum price on the warrant would become ($6 − $4.43) × 1.00 = $1.57. This would tell us that this warrant could not fall below a price of $1.57, because if it did, investors could realize immediate trading profits by purchasing the warrants and converting them along with the $4.43 exercise price into common stock until the price of the warrant was pushed up to the minimum price. This process of simultaneously buying and selling equivalent assets for different prices is called **arbitrage.**

Premium. The **premium** is the amount above the minimum price for which the warrant sells:

$$\text{premium} = \left(\begin{array}{c}\text{market price} \\ \text{of warrant}\end{array}\right) - \left(\begin{array}{c}\text{minimum price} \\ \text{of warrant}\end{array}\right) \quad (20\text{--}8)$$

In the case of the Wickes warrant the premium is $2.25 − $0 = $2.25. Investors are paying a premium of $2.25 above the minimum price for the warrant. They are willing to do so because the possible loss is small, in that the warrant price is only about 56 percent that of the common stock, and the possible return is large, since, if the price of the common stock climbs, the value of the warrant also will climb.

The relationships among the warrant price, the minimum price, and the premium are illustrated graphically in Figure 20–2. Point *A* represents the exercise price on the warrant. Once the price of the stock is above the exercise price, the warrant's minimum price takes on positive (or nonzero) values.

FIGURE 20–2. Valuation of Warrants

A hypothetical numerical example based upon Figure 20–2 is provided in Table 20–2. Looking at the graphic representation of the warrant and the example, we find that the warrant premium tends to drop off as the ratio of the stock price to the exercise price climbs. Why? As the stock price climbs, the warrant loses its leverage ability. Looking at the numerical example, assume an investor purchased $1000 worth of warrants and $1000 worth of common stock when the common stock price was $40 and the warrant price was $10; then the price of the stock went up 50 percent to $60 per share, which caused the price of the warrant to go up 150 percent to $25 per share. This leverage feature—the fact that the value of the warrant increases and declines by larger percentages than the value of the underlying stock and thus a small investment has large possible returns—encourages investors to purchase warrants. However, as the stock price rises, the leverage ability of the warrant declines. This can be shown by assuming an investor purchases $1000 worth of common stock selling at $110 per share and $1000 worth of warrants selling for $71 per share; if the stock price went up to $130, the stock investment would have returned 18 percent while the warrant price would have risen to $90 for a return of 27 percent. In the first example when the stock price rose from $40 to $60 per share, the warrant resulted in profits three times greater than on the common stock. In the second example the warrant provided profits only about one and one-half times larger than the common stock. Thus, the warrant premium tends to drop off as the ratio of the stock price to the exercise price climbs and the leverage ability of the warrant declines.

While the stock price/exercise price ratio is one of the most important factors in determining the size of the premium, several other factors also affect it. One such factor is the time left to the warrant expiration date. As the warrant's expiration date approaches, the size of the premium begins to shrink, approaching zero. A second factor is investors' expectations concerning the capital gains potential of the stock. If they feel favorably about the prospects for price increases in the common stock, a large warrant premium will result, because a stock price increase will result in a warrant price increase. Finally, the degree of price volatility on the underlying common stock affects the size of the warrant premium. The more volatile the common stock

TABLE 20–2. Hypothetical Warrant Example

Stock Price SP	Exercise Price EP	Exercise Ratio ER	Minimum Price: SP − (EP × ER) = MP	Hypothetical Warrant Price, WP	Premium WP − MP	Stock Price/ Exercise Price Ratio, SP/EP
$ 30	$40	1	$ 0	$ 5	$ 5	75%
40	40	1	0	10	10	100
50	40	1	10	16	6	125
60	40	1	20	25	5	150
70	40	1	30	34	4	175
80	40	1	40	43	3	200
90	40	1	50	52	2	225
100	40	1	60	62	2	250
110	40	1	70	71	1	275
120	40	1	80	81	1	300
130	40	1	90	90	0	325

price, the higher the warrant premium. As price volatility increases, so does the probability of and potential size of profits.

Summary

Convertible securities are preferred stock or debentures that can be exchanged for a specified number of shares of common stock at the will of the owner. They are issued by corporations in order to sweeten debt and thereby make it more marketable, as a form of delayed equity financing, and as a source of temporarily inexpensive funds during expansions. While these reasons can justify the use of convertibles, the risks involved in the possibility of an overhanging issue should also be weighed. With an overhanging issue conversion does not occur, and the firm cannot force it, because the common stock price has not risen sufficiently; financing flexibility is reduced in that, depending upon the firm's financial structure, investors might react negatively toward an additional offering of either debt or equity. The valuation of convertible securities is a function of both its value as a straight bond and its value if converted into common stock. Since the convertible provides the security of debt with the capital gains potential of common stock, it generally sells for a premium above the higher of its bond or conversion value.

Warrants are an option to purchase a fixed number of shares of common stock at a predetermined price during a specified period. While in general they are issued in association with debt, most warrants are detachable in that they can be bought and sold separately from the debt to which they were originally attached. They are generally issued as a sweetener to debt in order to make it more marketable and lower the interest costs. In addition, unlike convertibles, warrants provide for an additional cash inflow when they are exercised. On the other hand, the exercise of convertibles results in the elimination of debt, while the exercise of warrants does not. Thus, there is a tradeoff—additional cash inflow versus elimination of debt—involved in the warrants versus convertibles decision. Since a warrant is an option to purchase a specified number of shares of stock during a given period, its market value is primarily a function of the price of the common stock. Warrants generally sell above their minimum price, the size of the premium being determined by the degree of leverage they provide, the time left to expiration, investors' expectations as to the future movement of the stock price, and the stock's price volatility.

Study Questions

20–1. Define the following terms:
 a. Conversion ratio
 b. Conversion value
 c. Conversion parity price
 d. Conversion premium

20–2. What are some reasons commonly given for issuing convertible securities?

20–3. Why does a convertible bond sell at a premium above its value as a bond or common stock?

20–4. Convertible bonds are said to provide the capital gains potential of common stock and the security of bonds. Explain this statement both verbally and graphically. What happens to the graph when interest rates rise? When they fall?

20–5. Convertible bonds generally carry lower coupon interest rates than do nonconvertible bonds. If this is so, does it mean that the cost of capital on convertible bonds is lower than on nonconvertible? Why or why not?

20–6. Since convertible securities allow for the conversion price to be set above the current common stock price, is it true that the firm is actually issuing its common stock at a price above the current market price?

20–7. In light of our discussion of the common stockholders' preemptive right in Chapter 19, explain why convertibles are often sold on a rights basis.

20–8. Although only the holder of a convertible has the right to convert the security, firms are often able to force conversion. Comment on this statement.

20–9. Explain the difference between a convertible security and a warrant.

20–10. How do firms force the exercising of warrants?

20–11. Explain the valuation of warrants both verbally and graphically.

20–12. What factors affect the size of the warrant premium? How?

Self-Test Problems

ST–1. (*Convertible Terminology*) In 1988 Winky's Cow Paste, Inc., issued $10 million of $1000 par value, 10 percent semi-annual convertible debentures that come due in 2003. The conversion price on these convertibles is $16.75 per share. The common stock was selling for $14¾ per share on a given date shortly after these convertibles were issued. These convertibles have a B– rating, and straight B– debentures were yielding 14 percent on that date. The market price of the convertible was $970 on that date. Determine the following:
  a. Conversion ratio
  b. Conversion value
  c. Security value
  d. Conversion parity price
  e. Conversion premium in absolute dollars
  f. Conversion premium in percentage

ST–2. (*Warrant Terminology*) Petro-Tech, Inc., currently has some warrants outstanding that allow the holder to purchase, with one warrant, one share of common stock at $18.275 per share. If the common stock was selling at $25.00 per share and the warrants were selling for $9.50, what would be the
  a. Minimum price?
  b. Warrant premium?

Study Problems

20–1. (*Convertible Terminology*) In 1988 the Andy Fields Corporation of Delaware issued some $1000 par value, 6 percent convertible debentures that come due in 2008. The conversion price on these convertibles is $40 per share. The price of the common stock is now $27.25 per share. These convertibles have a BBB rating, and straight BBB debentures are now yielding 9.00 percent. The market price of the convertible is now $840.25. Determine the following (assume bond interest payments are made annually):

    a. Conversion ratio
    b. Conversion value
    c. Security value
    d. Conversion parity price
    e. Conversion premium in absolute dollars
    f. Conversion premium in percentage

20–2. (*Convertible Terminology*) The L. Padis, Jr., Corporation has an issue of 5 percent convertible preferred stock outstanding. The conversion price on these securities is $27 per share to 9/30/92. The price of the common stock is now $13.25 per share. The preferred stock is selling for $17.75. The par value of the preferred stock is $25 per share. Similar quality preferred stock without the conversion feature is currently yielding 8 percent. Determine the following:
    a. Conversion ratio
    b. Conversion value
    c. Conversion premium (in both absolute dollars and percentages)

20–3. (*Warrant Terminology*) The T. Kitchel Corporation has a warrant that allows the purchase of one share of common stock at $30 per share. The warrant is currently selling at $4 and the common stock is priced at $25 per share. Determine the minimum price and the premium of the warrant.

20–4. (*Warrant Terminology*) Cobra Airlines has some warrants outstanding that allow the purchase of common stock at the rate of one warrant for each share of common stock at $11.71 per share.
    a. Given that the warrants were selling for $3 each and the common stock was selling for $10 per share, determine the minimum price and warrant premium as of that date.
    b. Given that the warrants were selling for $9.75 each, and the common stock was selling for $16.375 per share, determine the minimum price and warrant premium as of that date.

20–5. (*Warrant Terminology*) International Corporation has some warrants outstanding that allow the purchase of common stock at the price of $22.94 per share. These warrants are somewhat unusual in that one warrant allows for the purchase of 3.1827 shares of common stock at the exercise price of $22.94 per share.
    a. Given that the warrants were selling for $6.25 each, and the common stock was selling for $7.25 per share, determine the minimum price and the warrant premium as of that date.

20–6. (*Warrants and Their Leverage Effect*) A month ago you purchased 100 Bolster Corporation warrants at $3 each. When you made your purchase, the market price of Bolster's common stock was $40 per share. The exercise price on the warrants is $40 per share while the exercise ratio is 1.0. Today, the market price of Bolster's common stock has jumped up to $45 per share, while the market price of Bolster's warrants has climbed to $7.50 each. Calculate the total dollar gain that you would have received if you had invested the same dollar amount in common stock versus warrants. What is this in terms of return on investment?

Self-Test Solutions

SS–1.   **a.** conversion ratio $= \dfrac{\text{par value of convertible security}}{\text{conversion price}}$

$$= \frac{\$1000}{\$16.75}$$

$$= 59.70 \text{ shares}$$

b. conversion value = (conversion ratio) × $\left(\begin{array}{c}\text{market value per share}\\ \text{of common stock}\end{array}\right)$

$$= 59.70 \text{ shares} \times \$14.75/\text{share}$$

$$= \$880.58$$

c. security value = $\sum_{t=1}^{40} \dfrac{\$50}{(1 + .07)^t} + \dfrac{\$1000}{(1 + .07)^{40}}$

$$= \$50(13.332) + \$1000(.067)$$

$$= \$666.60 + \$67$$

$$= \$733.60$$

[*Note*: Since this debenture pays interest semiannually, $t = 20$ years × 2 = 40 and $i = 14\%/2 = 7\%$ in the calculations.]

d. conversion parity price = $\dfrac{\text{market price of convertible security}}{\text{conversion ratio}}$

$$= \dfrac{\$970.00}{59.70}$$

$$= \$16.25$$

e. $\begin{array}{l}\text{conversion premium}\\ \text{in absolute dollars}\end{array}$ = $\left(\begin{array}{c}\text{market price of}\\ \text{the convertible}\end{array}\right) - \left(\begin{array}{c}\text{higher of the bond value}\\ \text{and conversion value}\end{array}\right)$

$$= \$970.00 - \$880.58$$

$$= \$89.42$$

f. $\begin{array}{l}\text{conversion premium}\\ \text{in percentage}\end{array}$ = $\dfrac{\left(\begin{array}{c}\text{market price of}\\ \text{the convertible}\end{array}\right) - \left(\begin{array}{c}\text{higher of the bond value}\\ \text{and conversion value}\end{array}\right)}{\left(\begin{array}{c}\text{higher of the bond value}\\ \text{and conversion value}\end{array}\right)}$

$$= \dfrac{\$970.00 - \$880.58}{\$880.58}$$

$$= 10.15 \text{ percent}$$

SS–2. **a.** minimum price = $\left(\begin{array}{c}\text{market price of}\\ \text{common stock}\end{array} - \begin{array}{c}\text{exercise}\\ \text{price}\end{array}\right) \times \left(\begin{array}{c}\text{exercise}\\ \text{ratio}\end{array}\right)$

$$= (\$25.00 - \$18.275) \times (1.0)$$

$$= \$6.725$$

b. warrant premium = $\left(\begin{array}{c}\text{market price}\\ \text{of warrant}\end{array}\right) - \left(\begin{array}{c}\text{minimum price}\\ \text{of warrant}\end{array}\right)$

$$= \$9.50 - \$6.725$$

$$= \$2.775$$

Selected References

Alexander, Gordon J., and Rober D. Stover. "The Effect of Forced Conversion on Common Stock Prices," *Financial Management*, 9 (Spring 1980), 39–45.

_____, and _____. "Pricing in the New Issue Convertible Debt Market," *Financial Management*, 6 (Fall 1977), 35–39.

_____, and David B. Kuhnau. "Market Timing Strategies in Convertible Debt Financing," *Journal of Finance*, 34 (March 1979), 143–55.

Bacon, Peter W., and Edward L. Winn, Jr. "The Impact of Forced Conversion on Stock Prices," *Journal of Finance*, 24 (December 1969), 871–74.

Baumol, William J., Burton G. Malkiel, and Richard E. Quandt. "The Valuation of Convertible Securities," *Quarterly Journal of Economics*, 80 (February 1966), 48–59.

Billingsley, Randall S., Robert E. Lamy, and G. Rodney Thompson. "Valuation of Primary Issue Convertible Bonds," *Journal of Financial Research*, 9 (1986), 251–59.

Block, Stanley B., and Timothy J. Gallagher. "The Use of Interest Rate Futures and Options by Corporate Financial Managers," *Financial Management*, 15 (Autumn 1986), 73–78.

Brennan, Michael J., and Eduardo S. Schwartz. "Analyzing Convertible Bonds," *Journal of Financial and Quantitative Analysis*, 15 (November 1980), 907–29.

_____, and _____. "Convertible Bonds: Valuation and Optimal Strategies for Call and Conversion," *Journal of Finance*, 32 (December 1977), 1699–1715.

Brigham, Eugene F. "An Analysis of Convertible Debentures: Theory and Some Empirical Evidence," *Journal of Finance*, 21 (March 1966), 35–54.

Chen, A. H. Y. "A Model of Warrant Pricing in a Dynamic Market," *Journal of Finance*, 25 (December 1970), 1041–59.

Constantinides, George M. "Warrant Exercise and Bond Conversion in Competitive Markets," *Journal of Financial Economics*, 13 (September 1984), 371–97.

Dann, Larry Y., and Wayne H. Mikkelson. "Convertible Debt Issuance, Capital Structure Change, and Financing-Related Information: Some New Evidence," *Journal of Financial Economics*, 13 (June 1984), 157–87.

Emanuel, David C. "Warrant Valuation and Exercise Strategy," *Journal of Financial Economics*, 12 (August 1983), 211–35.

Fooladi, Iraj, and Gordon S. Roberts. "On Preferred Stock," *Journal of Financial Research*, 9 (Winter 1986), 319–24.

Frank, Werner G., and Charles O. Kroncke. "Classifying Conversions of Convertible Debentures over Four Years," *Financial Management*, 3 (Summer 1974), 33–42.

Galai, Dan, and Mier I. Schneller. "Pricing of Warrants and the Value of the Firm," *Journal of Finance*, 33 (December 1978), 1333–42.

Green, Richard C. "Investment Incentives, Debt and Warrants," *Journal of Financial Economics*, 13 (March 1984), 115–36.

Harris, Milton, and Arthur Raviv. "A Sequential Signaling Model of Convertible Debt Policy," *Journal of Finance*, 40 (December 1985), 1263–81.

Hayes, Samuel L., III, and Henry B. Reiling. "Sophisticated Financing Tool: The Warrant," *Harvard Business Review*, 47 (January–February 1969), 137–50.

Janjigian, Vahan. "The Leverage Changing Consequences of Convertible Debt Financing," *Financial Management*, 16 (Autumn 1987), 15–21.

Jennings, Edwards H. "An Estimate of Convertible Bond Premiums," *Journal of Financial and Quantitative Analysis*, 9 (January 1974), 33–56.

Kidwell, David S., M. Wayne Marr, and G. Rodney Thompson. "Eurodollar Bonds: Alternative Financing for U.S. Companies," *Financial Management*, 14 (Winter 1985), 18–27.

_____, _____, and _____. "Eurodollar Bonds, Alternative Financing for U.S. Companies: A Correction," *Financial Management*, 15 (Spring 1986), 78–79.

Lewellen, Wilbur G., and George A. Racette. "Convertible Debt Financing," *Journal of Financial and Quantitative Analysis*, 7 (December 1973), 777–92.

Marr, M. Wayne, and G. Rodney Thompson. "The Pricing of New Convertible Bond Issues," *Financial Management*, 13 (Summer 1984), 31–37.

Pinches, George E. "Financing with Convertible Preferred Stocks, 1960–1967," *Journal of Finance*, 25 (March 1970), 53–64.

Rubinstein, Mark, and John C. Cox. *Option Markets*. Englewood Cliffs, NJ: Prentice-Hall, 1982.

Rush, David F., and Ronald W. Melicher. "An Empirical Examination of Factors Which Influence Warrant Prices," *Journal of Finance*, 29 (December 1974), 1449–66.

Samuelson, Paul A. "Rational Theory of Warrant Pricing," *Industrial Management Review*, 6 (Spring, 1965), 13–31.

Schwartz, Eduardo S. "The Valuation of Warrants: Implementing a New Approach," *Journal of Financial Economics*, 4 (January 1977), 79–93.

Shelton, John P. "The Relation of the Price of a Warrant to the Price of Its Associated Stock," *Financial Analysts Journal*, 23 (May–June and July–August 1967), 88–99 and 143–51.

Soldofsky, Robert M. "Yield-Risk Performance of Convertible Securities," *Financial Analysts Journal*, 39 (March–April 1971), 61–65.

Van Horne, James C. "Warrant Valuation in Relation to Volatility and Opportunity Costs," *Industrial Management Review*, 10 (Spring 1969), 19–32.

Weil, Roman L., Jr., Joel E. Segall, and David Green, Jr. "Premiums on Convertible Bonds," *Journal of Finance*, 23 (June 1968), 445–63.

APPENDIX 20A
—Futures and Options—

In the chapter we examined two financial instruments, warrants and convertibles, created by the firm. In this appendix we will look at two additional financial instruments that are similar to warrants and convertibles but are not created by the firm: futures and options. In spite of the fact that these instruments are not issued by the firm, it is important for us to be familiar with them for two reasons. First, these instruments can be used to reduce the risks associated with interest and exchange rate and commodity price fluctuations. Second, as you will see in future finance courses, an understanding of the pricing of options is extremely valuable because many different financial assets can be viewed as options. In fact, warrants, convertible bonds, risky bonds, common stock, and the abandonment decision can all be thought of as types of options.

FUTURES

Commodity and financial futures are perhaps the fastest-growing and in many respects most exciting new financial instrument today. Financial managers who only a few years ago would not have considered venturing into the futures market are now actively using this market to eliminate risk. As the number of participants in this market has grown, so has the number of items on which future contracts are offered, jumping to nearly 100 contracts ranging from the old standbys like coffee and soybeans to newer ones like plywood, U.S. Treasury bonds, and the Mexican peso.

A **futures contract** is a contract to buy or sell a stated commodity (such as soybeans or corn) or financial claim (such as U.S. Treasury bonds) at a specified price at some future specified time. It is important to note here that this is a contract that *requires* its holder to buy or sell the asset, regardless of what happens to its value during the interim. The importance of a futures contract is that it can be used by financial managers to lock in the price of a commodity or an interest rate and thereby eliminate one source of risk. For example, if a corporation is planning on issuing debt in the near future and is concerned about a possible rise in interest rates between now and when the debt would be issued, it might sell (or write as it is called) a U.S. Treasury bond contract with the same face value as the proposed debt offering and a delivery date the same as when the debt offering is to occur. Alternatively, Ralston-Purina or Quaker Oats might wish to lock in the future price of corn or oats, and with the use of a futures contract they can do this. Since a futures contract locks in interest rates or commodity prices, the costs associated with any possible rise in interest rates or commodity prices would be completely offset by the profits made by writing the futures interest rate contract. In effect, futures contracts allow the financial manager to lock in future interest and exchange rates or prices for a number of agricultural commodities like corn and oats.

As the use of futures contracts becomes more common in the financial management of the firm, it is important for the financial manager to be familiar with the operation and terminology associated with these financial instruments.

An Introduction to the Futures Markets

The origins of the futures market goes back into history to medieval times. England, France and Japan all developed futures markets of their own. Here in the United States several futures markets sprang up in the early years, but it was not until the establishment of the Chicago Board of Trade (CBT) in 1848 that the futures markets were provided with their true roots. As we will see, while this market has been in operation for over 140 years, it was not until the early 1970s, when the futures markets expanded from agricultural commodities to financial futures, that financial managers began to regularly venture into this market.

To develop an understanding for futures markets, let us examine several features that distinguish futures contracts from simple forward contracts. To begin with, a forward contract is any contract for delivery of an asset in the future. A futures contract is a specialized form of a forward contract distinguished by: (1) an organized exchange, (2) a standardized contract with limited price changes and margin requirements, (3) a clearinghouse in each futures market, and (4) daily resettlement of contracts.

The Organized Exchange

While the Chicago Board of Exchange is the oldest and largest of the futures exchanges, it is certainly not the only exchange. In fact, there are over 10 different futures exchanges in operation in the United States today. The importance of having organized exchanges associated with the futures market is that they provide a central trading place. If there were no central trading place, then there would be no potential to generate the depth of trading necessary to support a secondary market, and in a very circular way the existence of a secondary market encourages more traders to enter the market and in turn provides additional liquidity.

An organized exchange also encourages confidence in the futures market by allowing for the effective regulation of trading. The various exchanges set and enforce rules and collect and disseminate information on trading activity and the commodities being traded. Together, the liquidity generated by having a central trading place, effective regulation, and the information dissemination provided by the organized exchanges has effectively fostered their development.

Standardized Contracts

In order to develop a strong secondary market in any security, there must be a large number of identical securities—or in this case, futures contracts—outstanding. In effect, standardization of contracts leads to more frequent trades on that contract, leading to greater liquidity in the secondary market for that contract, which in turn draws more traders into the market. It is for this reason that futures contracts are highly standardized and very specific with respect to the description of the goods to be delivered and the time and place of delivery. Let's look at a Chicago Board of Trade oats contract. This contract calls for the delivey of

5000 bushels of No. 2 heavy or No. 1 grade oats to Chicago or to Minneapolis—St. Paul at a 7.5 cents per bushel discount. In addition, these contracts are written to come due in March, May, July, September, and December. Through this standardization of contracts, trading has built up in enough identical contracts to allow for the development of a strong and highly liquid secondary market.

To encourage investors to participate in the futures market, daily price limits are set on all futures contracts. Without these limits, it is felt that there would be more price volatility on most futures contracts than many investors would be willing to accept. These daily price limits are set to protect investors, maintain order on the futures exchanges, and encourage the level of trading volume necessary to develop a strong secondary market. As we will see in the next section, these price limits are set equal to the maintenance margins on each contract (the **maintenance margin** is the amount of money the investor must keep with his broker) so that all investors in the futures market have the ability to cover any losses. For example, the Chicago Board of Trade imposes a 12 cents per bushel ($600 per contract) price movement limit above and below the previous day's settlement price of oats contracts. This limit protects against runaway price movements. These daily price limits do not halt trading once the limit has been reached, but they do provide a boundary within which trading must take place. The price of an oats contract may rise 6 cents very early in the trading day—"up the limit" in futures jargon. This will not stop trading; it only means that no trade can take place above that level. As a result, any dramatic shifts in the market price of a futures contract must take place over a number of days, with the price of the contract going "up the limit" each day.

Futures Clearinghouse

The main purpose of the futures clearinghouse is to guarantee that all trades will be honored. This is done by having the clearinghouse interpose itself as the buyer to every seller and the seller to every buyer. Because of this substitution of parties, it is not necessary for the original seller (or buyer) to find the original buyer (or seller) when he decides to clear his position. As a result, all an individual has to do is make an equal and opposite transaction which will provide a net zero position with the clearinghouse and cancel out that individual's obligation.

Because no trades take place directly between individuals, but between individuals and the clearinghouse, buyers and sellers realizing gains in the market are assured that they will be paid. Since futures contracts are traded with minimal "good faith" money, as we will see in the next section, it is necessary to provide some security to traders that when money is made, it will be paid. There are other important benefits of a clearinghouse, including providing a mechanism for the delivery of commodities and the settlement of disputed trades, but these benefits also serve to encourage trading in the futures markets and thereby create a highly liquid secondary market.

Daily Resettlement of Contracts

Another safeguard of the futures market is a margin requirement. While margin requirements on futures resemble stock margin requirements in that there is an initial margin and a maintenance margin that comes into play when the value of the contract declines, similarities between futures and stock margins end there.

Before we explore margin requirements on futures it would be helpful to develop an understanding of the meaning of a margin on futures. The concept of a margin on futures contracts has a totally different meaning than it does when used in reference to common stocks. The margin on common stocks refers to the amount of equity the investor has invested in the stocks. With a futures contract, no equity has been invested, since nothing has been bought. All that has been done is a contract has been signed obligating the two parties to a future transaction and defining the terms of that transaction. This is an important thought: There is no actual buying or selling taking place with a futures contract; it is merely an agreement to buy or sell some commodity in the future. As a result, the term *futures margin* refers to "good faith" money the purchaser puts down to ensure that the contract will be carried out.

The initial margin required for commodities (deposited by both buyer and seller) is much lower than the margin required for common stock, generally amounting to only 10 percent or less of the value of the contract. For example, if September oats contracts on the CBT were selling at $1.65 per bushel, then one contract for 5000 bushels would be selling for $1.65 \times 5000 = \$8250$. The initial margin on oats is $600 per contract, which represents only about 7.23 percent of the contract price. Needless to say, the leverage associated with futures trading is tremendous—both on the up and down sides. That is to say, small changes in the price of the underlying commodity result in very large changes in the value of the futures contract, since very little has to be put down to "own" a contract. Moreover, for many options, if the financial manager can satisfy the broker that he is not engaged in trading as a speculator, but as a hedger, he can qualify for reduced initial margins. Because of the low level of the initial margin, there is also a *maintenance* or *variation margin* requirement that forces the investor or financial manager to replenish the margin account to a level specified by the exchange after any market loss.

One additional point related to margins deserves mention. The initial margin requirement can be fulfilled by supplying Treasury bills instead of cash. These Treasury bills are valued at 90 percent of their value for margin purposes so it takes $100,000 worth of Treasury bills to provide a $90,000 margin. The advantage of using Treasury bills as margin is that the investor earns money on them, whereas brokerage firms do not pay interest on funds in commodity cash accounts. Moreover, if the financial manager is going to carry Treasury bills anyway, he can just deposit the Treasury bills with the broker and purchase the futures contracts with no additional cash outlay.

Suppose we work for Ralston-Purina in the financial management area. We are in charge of purchasing raw materials—in particular, oats. Currently, a September futures contract for the delivery of oats has a price of $1.65 per bushel. We need oats in September and feel that this is an exceptional price and that oats will probably be selling for more than that per bushel in September. Thus, we wish to lock in this price, and to do this we purchase one contract for 5000 bushels at 165 cents or $1.65 per bushel. Upon purchasing the September oats contract the only cash we would have to put up would be the initial margin of $600. Let's further assume that the price of oats futures then falls to a level of 161 cents per bushel the day after we make our purchase. In effect, we have incurred a loss of 4 cents per bushel on 5000 bushels, for a total loss on our investment of $200.

At this point the concept of daily resettlement comes into play. What this means is that all futures positions are brought to the market at the end of each trading day and all gains and losses, in this case a loss, are then settled. We have lost $200, which is then subtracted from our margin account, lowering it to $400 ($600 initially less the $200 loss). Since our margin account has fallen below the maintenance margin on oats, which is $600, we would have to replenish our account back to its initial level of $600. If on the following day the price of September oats contracts fell another cent to 160 cents per bushel, we would have lost another 1 cent on 5000 bushels for a loss of $50. This would then be subtracted from our margin account during the daily resettlement at the end of the trading day, leaving $550 in our margin account. Since our margin account has again fallen below the maintenance margin requirement of $600, we would have to add another $50 to our account. Let's carry our example one day further, this time to the upbeat side and put some profits in. Let's assume on the third day the price of September oats contracts is up 5 cents per bushel. This means that we have made 5 cents on 5000 bushels, for a total profit of $250. This brings our margin account up from $600 to $850, which is $250 above the initial margin of $600. We can withdraw this $250 from our margin account.

Obviously the purpose of margin requirements is to provide some measure of safety for futures traders, and despite the very small level of margin requirements imposed, they do a reasonable job. Let's assume that an investor, and let's not assume its us this time, had suffered losses in the September oats market. As a result of these losses, his margin account fell to $200. Under the daily resettlement process, he was called upon to come up with another $400 to bring the account up to the initial margin level of $600. If this investor was unable or refused to post the additional margin, his broker would close his account, deduct the $200 loss, and return the balance. Since the maintenance margin is equal to the maximum possible daily fluctuation for that contract, the trader can never lose more than is in his margin account in any one day. Thus, no trader can leave the futures market owing money.

Commodity Futures

In general when people talk about commodities they are referring to nonfinancial futures. This includes agricultural commodities as well as metals, wood products, and fibers. While there are a number of new commodity futures contracts being traded, like plywood, much of the trading in the commodities futures markets involves such traditional favorites as soybeans and wheat. For the financial manager these markets provide a means of offsetting the risks associated with future price changes. Here the financial manager is securing a future price for a good that is currently in production, or securing a future price for some commodity that must be purchased in the future. In either case, the manager is using the futures market to eliminate the effects of future price changes on the future purchase or sale of some commodity.

Financial Futures

Financial futures come in a number of different forms, including Treasury bills, notes and bonds, GNMAs, certificates of deposit, Eurodollars, foreign currencies, and stock indices. These financial newcomers first appeared in 1972, when foreign currencies were introduced; interest rate futures did not appear until 1975. The growth in financial futures has been phenomenal, and today they dominate the futures markets. Our discussion of financial futures will be divided into three sections: (1) interest rate futures, (2) foreign exchange futures, and (3) stock index futures.

Interest Rate Futures. Currently Treasury bond futures are the most popular of all futures contracts in terms of contracts issued. While Treasury or T-bond futures, as they are called, are just one of several interest rate futures contracts, the fact that they are risk-free, uncallable, long-term bonds with a maturity of at least 15 years has been the deciding factor in making them the most popular of the interest rate futures. Since all interest rate futures are similar in most respects other than in maturity, we will focus our attentions on T-bond futures.

For the financial manager, interest rate futures provide an excellent means for eliminating the risks associated with interest rate fluctuations. As we learned earlier, there is an inverse relationship between bond prices in the secondary market and yields—that is, when interest rates fall bond prices rise, and when interest rates rise bond prices fall. If you think back to the chapter on valuation, you will recall that this inverse relationship between bond prices and yield is a result of the fact that when bonds are issued, their coupon rate is fixed. However, once the bond is issued it must compete in the market with other financial instruments. Since new bonds are issued to yield the current interest rates, yields on old bonds must adjust to remain competitive with the newer issues. Thus, when interest rates rise, the price of an older bond with a lower coupon interest rate must decline in order to increase the yield on the old bond, making it competitive with the return on newly issued bonds.

Interest rate futures offer investors a very inexpensive way of eliminating the risks associated with interest rate fluctuations. For example, banks, pension funds and insurance companies all make considerable use of the interest rate futures market to avoid paper losses that might otherwise occur when interest rates unexpectedly increase. Corporations also use interest rate futures to lock in interest rates when they are planning to issue debt. If interest rates rise before the corporation has the opportunity to issue the new debt, the profits on the T-bond futures contracts they have sold will offset the increased costs associated with the proposed debt offering. Several possible uses for Treasury bond futures are given in Table 20A–1.

Foreign Exchange Futures. Of all the financial futures, foreign exchange futures have been around the longest, first appearing in 1972. Foreign exchange futures work in the same way as other futures, but in this case the commodity is German marks, British pounds, or some other foreign currency. As we will see, the similarities between these futures and the others we have examined are great. Not only do foreign exchange futures work in the same way as other futures, but they also are used by financial managers for the same basic reasons—to hedge away risks, in this case exchange rate risks. One of the major participants in the foreign exchange futures market is the exporter who will receive foreign currency when its exported goods are finally received and who uses this market to lock in a certain exchange rate. As a result, the exporter is unaffected by any exchange rate fluctuations that might occur before it receives payment. Foreign exchange futures are also used to hedge away possible fluctuations in the value of earnings of foreign subsidiaries.

TABLE 20A–1. How Treasury Bond Futures Are Used

Protect Portfolio Value and Return: Pension funds, banks, corporations, insurance companies and individual investors can use 10-year Treasury futures as a hedge against losses incurred on fixed-income portfolios when interest rates rise and prices decline. Careful timing in the placement of a hedge can protect the holding period return of a portfolio containing notes and other related instruments. Futures offer flexibility to money managers by allowing them to adapt to a changing market.

Protect Issuance Costs: Corporations that plan to issue intermediate term debt can control their interest cost by selling 10-year Treasury futures and offsetting the position when the issue comes to market. By hedging, the issuer can take advantage of today's lower rates, thus lessening the cost of raising capital.

Transfer Risk: Underwriters of corporate issues can sell futures to transfer the risk between the time they buy the debt securities until the time they are sold to dealers and investors.

Hedge Participation in Treasury Auctions: Primary government securities dealers can use the new contract to hedge participation in 7- and 10-year note auctions. Ten-year Treasury futures allow government securities dealers to remain competitive and offer a better price to their customers.

Lock in a Favorable Rate of Return: Portfolio managers can hedge the reinvestment rate of coupon income. If interest rates decline, the reinvestment rate will diminish for note holders. Buying futures today as a substitute for later investments allows the investor to hedge a drop in rates. If rates *fall*, the decreased return on reinvestment will be offset by a gain in the futures position. If rates *rise*, the loss on the futures position will be offset by a higher return on investment.

Source: Ten Year Treasury Futures, Chicago Board of Trade, 1983.

In the 1980s fluctuations in exchange rates became common. With exchange rate futures a financial manager could eliminate the effects—good or bad—of exchange rate fluctuation with a relatively small investment. The extremely high degree of leverage that was available coupled with the dramatic fluctuations in foreign exchange rates in the 1980s encouraged many financial managers to consider entering the exchange rate futures market. Some of the most dramatic price movements came as the British pound dropped to a value of just over $1.07 in early 1985. To get a feel for the degree of leverage experienced in the foreign exchange futures market and the large profits and losses that can occur in this market let's look at Figure 20A–1, which examines profits and losses resulting from buying and selling British pound futures.

As can be seen in Figure 20A–1, fortunes could have been lost and made by those investing in British pound futures. Some firms no doubt saved themselves enormous losses by hedging away exchange rate risk, while others would have benefitted by the dramatic swing in the exchange rate. Over just five trading days, the value of an investment in British pound futures went up almost threefold, while the return on the initial margin investment for those selling British pounds dropped almost threefold. Needless to say, the foreign exchange futures market is a very risky market, characterized by extreme leverage both on the up and down side and periodic major movements in the underlying values of the foreign exchange currencies. To the financial manager, this market provides a perfect mechanism for eliminating the effect of exchange rate fluctuations.

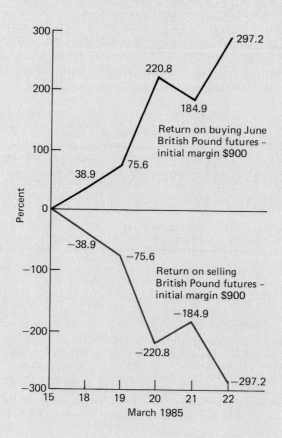

FIGURE 20A–1. Profits and Losses on British Pound Futures in March 1985

Stock Index Futures. Stock indexes have been around for many years but it has only been recently that financial managers and investors have had the opportunity to trade them directly. In fact, in spite of only first appearing in February 1982, by 1984 they became the second most widely traded futures contract of all, exceeded in trading volume only by Treasury bond futures contracts.

At this point, after looking at other futures contracts, the workings of stock index futures should be clear. They work basically the same way, with one major exception: Stock index futures contracts allow only for cash settlement. There is no delivery, since what is being traded is the *future price* of the index, not the underlying stocks in the index. Currently there are several stock index futures available, with futures on the S&P 500 index clearly dominating in terms of volume. Four of these indexes are compared in Table 20A–2.

Let's examine exactly what an S&P 500 index futures contract involves. The S&P 500 index is a broad-based index made up of 400 industrials, 40 utilities, 20 transportations, and 40 financial companies on the NYSE. These companies represent about 80 percent of the value of all issues traded on the NYSE. This is a value-weighted index; the weight each stock takes on in the index is determined by the market value of that stock. The contract size or value of each contract is 500 times the S&P 500 index, which put it at about $135,000 in early 1987.

To the financial manager, the great popularity of these financial newcomers lies in their ability to reduce or eliminate systematic risk. When we talked about the variability or risk associated with common stock returns we said that there were two types of risk: systematic and unsystematic risk. Unsystematic risk, while accounting for a large portion of the variability of an individual security's returns, is largely eliminated in large portfolios through random diversification, leaving only systematic or market risk in a portfolio. As a result, we said that a portfolio's returns are basically determined by market movements, as modified by the portfolio's beta. Prior to the introduction of stock index futures, a portfolio or pension fund manager was forced to adjust the portfolio's beta if she anticipated a change in the direction of the market. Stock index futures allow the portfolio or pension fund manager to eliminate or mute the effects of swings in the market without the large transactions costs that would be associated with the trading needed to modify the portfolio's beta. Unfortunately, while stock index futures allow for the elimination of the unwanted effects of market downswings, they also eliminate the effects of market upswings. In other words, they allow the portfolio or pension fund manager to eliminate as much of the effect of the market as she wishes from her portfolio.

OPTIONS

An option contract gives its owner the right to buy or sell a fixed number of shares at a specified price over a limited time period. While trading in option contracts has existed for many years, it was not until the Chicago Board of Exchange (CBOE) began trading in listed options in 1973 that the volume of trading reached any meaningful level. During the years since the CBOE first listed options on 16 stocks, volume has grown at a phenomenal rate, with over 10,000 different active option contracts on over 400 stocks listed today. Trading volume has also grown to such an extent that on a typical day, trading in options involves numbers equal to half the volume of trading on the NYSE. Still, to many financial managers options remain a mystery, viewed as closer to something one would find in Las Vegas than on Wall Street.

Obviously, there is too much going on in the options markets not to pay attention to

TABLE 20A–2. Characteristics of Stock Index Futures Contracts

Feature	Kansas City Board of Trade	Chicago Mercantile Exchange	New York Futures Exchange	Chicago Board of Trade
Location	Kansas	Chicago	New York	Chicago
Underlying market index	Value Line Composite Average (VLA). This is an equally weighted index of approximately 1700 stocks. Geometric average is used.	Standard & Poor's 500 Index (S&P 500). This is a value weighted index of 500 stocks. Arithmetic average is used.	NYSE Composite Index. This is a value-weighted average of *all* common stocks listed on the NYSE. Arithmetic average is used.	20 major blue chip stocks
Contract size (value of contract)	Five hundred times the Value Line average.	Five hundred times the S&P Index.	Five hundred times the NYSE composite index.	Two hundred and fifty times the major market index.
Minimum price change	Tick size is 0.01 points. The minimum change would cause the value of the contract to change by $5.	Tick size is 0.05 points. This represents a change of $25 per tick.	Tick size is 0.05 points. This represents a change of $25 per tick.	Tick size is 1/8 points. This represents a change of $12.50 per tick.
Daily price change limits	Thirty points daily price limit is in effect.	Thirty points daily price limit is in effect.	Twenty-five points daily price limit is in effect.	Forty points daily price limit is in effect.
Margins (minimum customer margin set by the exchange)	Initial Margin: $20,000 Maintenance Margin: $20,000	Initial Margin: $20,000 Maintenance Margin: $15,000	Initial Margin: $7,000 Maintenance Margin: $5,000	Initial Margin: $8,000 Maintenance Margin: $7,000
Delivery concept	Cash settlement. Actual value of VLA determines the payment. Final settlement is the last trading day of the expiring month. Delivery months are March, June, September, and December.	Cash settlement. Actual value of S&P 500 index determines the payment. Final settlement of open contracts occurs on the third Thursday of the delivery month. Delivery months are March, June, September, and December.	Cash settlement. Actual value of NYSE composite determines the payment. Settlement is based on the difference between the settlement price on the next to the last day of trading in the month and the value of NYSE composite index at the close of trading. Delivery months are March, June, September, and December.	Cash settlement. Actual value of MMI determines the payment. Final settlement of contract occurs on the third Friday of the trading month. Delivery months are the current month, next month, and March cycle.

them. Financial managers are just beginning to turn to them as an effective way of eliminating risk for a small price. As we will see, they are fascinating, but they are also confusing—with countless variations and a language of their own: Moreover, their use is not limited to speculators; they are also used by the most conservative financial managers to eliminate unwanted risk. In this section we will discuss the fundamentals of options, their terminology, and how they are used by financial managers.

The Fundamentals of Options

While the market for options seems to have a language of its own, there are only two basic types of options: puts and calls. Everything else involves some variation. A **call option** gives its owner the right to purchase a given number of shares of stock or some other asset at a specified price over a given time period. Thus, if the price of the underlying common stock or asset goes up, a call purchaser makes money. A **put,** on the other hand, gives its owner the right to sell a given number of shares of common stock or some other asset at a specified price over a given time period. A put purchaser is betting that the price of the underlying common stock or asset will drop. Since these are just options to buy or sell stock or some other asset, they do not represent an ownership position in the underlying corporation, as does common stock. In fact, there is no direct relationship between the underlying corporation and the option. That is to say, an option is merely a contract between two investors.

Since there is no underlying security, a purchaser of an option can be viewed as betting against the seller or *writer* of the option. For this reason the options markets are often referred to as a zero sum game. If someone makes money, then someone must lose money; if profits and losses were added up, the total for all options would equal zero. If commissions are considered, the total becomes negative, and we have a "sub-zero sum" game. As we will see, the options markets are quite complicated and risky. Some experts refer to them as legalized institutions for transferring wealth from the unsophisticated to the sophisicated.

The Terminology of Options

In order to continue with our discussion, it is necessary to define several terms that are unique to options.

The Contract. To understand the discussion of options, it is necessary to point out that when an option is purchased it is nothing more than a contract that allows the purchaser to either buy in the case of a call, or sell in the case of a put, the underlying stock or asset at a predetermined price. That is, no asset has changed hands, but the price has been set for a future transaction which will take place *only if and when* the option purchaser wants it to. In this section we will refer to the process of selling puts and calls as *writing*, although often selling options is referred to as *shorting* or *taking a short position* in those options, while buying an option is referred to as *taking a long position*.

The Exercise or Striking Price. This is the price at which the stock or asset may be purchased from the writer in the case of a call or sold to the writer in the case of a put.

Option Premium. The option premium is merely the price of the option. It is generally stated in terms of dollars per share rather than per option contract, which covers 100 shares. Thus, if a call option premium is $2, then an option contract would cost $200 and allow the purchase of 100 shares of stock at the exercise price.

Expiration Date.   This is the date on which the option contract expires. For each stock or asset that has listed options associated with it, there are in general three different expiration dates set three months apart, with the longest maturity for a listed option being 9 months. The purpose is to give option purchasers and writers a wide choice in terms of maturity.

Covered and Naked Options.   If a call writer owns the underlying stock or asset on which he writes a call, he is said to have written a "covered" call. On the other hand, if he writes a call on a stock or asset that he does not own, he is said to have written a "naked" call. The importance of this differentiation is that if a naked call is exercised, the call writer must deliver stock or assets that he does not own.

American and European Options.   An American option is one that can be exercised any time up to the expiration date. A European option can be exercised only on the expiration date.

Open Interest.   The term *open interest* refers to the number of option contracts in existence at a point in time. The importance of this concept comes from the fact that open interest provides the investor with some indication of the amount of liquidity associated with that particular option.

In-, Out-of, and At-the-Money.   A call (put) is said to be out-of-the-money if the underlying stock is selling below (above) the exercise price of the option. Alternatively, a call (put) is said to be in-the-money if the underlying stock is selling above (below) the exercise price of the option. If the option is selling at the exercise price, it is said to be selling at-the-money. For example, if Ford Motor's common stock was selling for $52 per share, a call on Ford with an exercise price of $50 would be in-the-money, while a call on Ford with an exercise price of $60 would be out-of-the-money.

Intrinsic and Time (or Speculative) Value.   The term *intrinsic value* refers to the minimum value of the option—that is, the amount by which the stock is in-the-money. Thus, for a call the intrinsic value is the amount by which the stock price exceeds the exercise price. If the call is out-of-the-money—that is, the exercise price is above the stock price—then its intrinsic value is zero. Intrinsic values can never be negative. For a put, the intrinsic value is again the minimum value the put can sell for, which is the exercise price less the stock price. For example, the intrinsic value on a Chrysler April 50 put when Chrysler's common stock was selling for $42 per share would be $8. If the put was selling for anything less than $8, investors would buy puts and sell the stock until all profits from this strategy were exhausted. This process of buying and selling like assets for different prices is called arbitrage, and it is arbitrage that keeps the price of options at or above their intrinsic value. If an option is selling for its intrinsic value, it is said to be selling at *parity*.

The time value or speculative value of an option is the amount by which the option premium exceeds the intrinsic value of the option. The time value represents the amount above the intrinsic value of an option that an investor is willing to pay to participate in capital gains from investing in the option. At expiration, the time value of the option falls to zero and the option sells for its intrinsic value, since the chance for future capital gains has been exhausted. These relationships are as follows:

$$\text{call intrinsic value} = \text{stock price} - \text{exercise price}$$

$$\text{put intrinsic value} = \text{exercise price} - \text{stock price}$$

$$\text{call time value} = \text{call premium} - (\text{stock price} - \text{exercise price})$$

$$\text{put time value} = \text{put premium} - (\text{exercise price} - \text{stock price})$$

Characteristics of Options

As we examine options from the point of view of the financial manager, we will see that they have some attractive features that help to explain their popularity. Three reasons that help to explain the popularity of options are:

1. **Leverage.** Calls allow the financial manager the chance for unlimited capital gains with a very small investment. Since a call is only an option to buy, the most a financial manager can lose is what was invested, which is usually a very small percentage of what it would cost to buy the stock itself, while the potential for gain is unlimited. As we will see, when a financial manager owns a call, he controls or benefits directly from any price increases in the stock. The idea of magnifying the potential return is an example of leverage. It is similar to the concept of leverage in physics, where a small amount of force can lift a heavy load. Here a small investment is doing the work of a much larger investment. Unfortunately, leverage is a double-edged sword: Small price increases can produce a large percentage profit, but small price decreases can produce large percentage losses. With an option, the maximum loss is limited to the amount invested.

2. **Financial Insurance.** For the financial manager, this is the most attractive feature of options. A put can be looked upon as an insurance policy, with the premium paid for the put being the cost of the policy. The transactions costs associated with exercising the put can then be looked upon as the deductible. When a put with an exercise price equal to the current stock price is purchased, it insures the holder against any declines in the stock price over the life of the put. Through the use of a put, a pension fund manager can reduce the risk exposure in a portfolio with little in cost and little change to the portfolio. One dissimilarity between a put and an insurance policy is that with a put an investor does not need to own the asset, in this case the stock, before buying the insurance. A call, since it has limited potential losses associated with it, can also be viewed as an investment insurance policy. With a call, the investor has limited potential losses to the price of the call, which is quite a bit below the price of the stock itself.

3. **Investment Alternative Expansion.** From the point of view of the investor, the use of puts, calls, and combinations of them can materially increase the set of possible investment alternatives available.

An understanding of the popularity of both puts and calls to the financial manager involves understanding (a) the concept of leverage—unlimited in the case of calls or in the case of puts very large potential gains with limited and relatively small maximum potential losses—and (b) the concept of financial insurance. It is these two factors combined that allow for an expansion of the available investment alternatives. Remember, both puts and calls are merely options to buy or sell the stock at a specified price. The worst that can happen is that the options become worthless and the financial manager loses the investment.

Prior to April 1973, when the Chicago Board Options Exchange (CBOE) opened, there was no central marketplace for put and call options. At that time put and call options transactions took place on the over-the-counter market through what was called the Put and Call Dealers Association, with only about 20 active brokers and dealers in the market. Through a telephone hookup, these dealers acted as middlemen, matching up potential writers and purchasers of options.

Since the specifics of each option were negotiated directly between the writer and the purchaser of the option, very seldom did any two options look alike. Generally every option written had a different expiration date and a different exercise price. As a result, there was little in the way of a secondary market for these individualized options, and the writers and purchasers generally had to hold their position until expiration or until the options were exercised.

With the creation of the CBOE, all this began to change. On April 26, 1973, the CBOE began trading listed options on 16 different stocks. Today there are four different exchanges that list and trade options—the CBOE, the AMEX, the Philadelphia, and the Pacific—with over 400 different stocks having listed options. While the over-the-counter market run by the Put and Call Association is still in operation for stocks that are not listed on the CBOE or any other exchange, it now handles less than 10 percent of all traded options.

This dramatic growth in the trading of options is almost entirely due to the several developments brought on by exchange-listed trading that the CBOE initiated, including the following:

1. **Standardization of the Option Contracts.** Today, the expiration dates for all options are standardized. As a result, there are generally only three dates on which a listed option on any stock can expire. The number of shares that a call allows its owner to purchase and a put allows its owner to sell has also been standardized to 100 shares per option contract. In addition, the striking prices have been standardized at 5-point intervals, so that there are more identical options. Through this standardization the number of different option contracts on each stock is severely limited. The result is that more options are identical and the secondary market is made more liquid.

2. **Creation of a Regulated Central Marketplace.** The exchange listing of options provides a central location for continuous trading in options, both newly issued and in the secondary market. The CBOE and the exchanges that followed in listing options also imposed strong surveillance and disclosure requirements.

3. **Creation of the Options Clearinghouse Corporation (OCC).** The OCC bears full responsibility for honoring all options issued on the CBOE. In effect, all options held by individuals have been written by the OCC, and alternatively all options written by individuals are held by the OCC. The purpose of creating a buffer between individual buyers and sellers of options is to provide investors with confidence in the market, in addition to facilitating the clearing and settlement of options. Because of the importance of the OCC, let us look for a moment at its operation.

   When an options transaction is agreed upon, the seller writes an option contract to the OCC, which in turn writes an identical option contract to the buyer. If the buyer later wants to exercise the option, he gives the OCC the exercise price associated with the option, which in turn provides him with stock. To get the stock to cover the option, the OCC simultaneously exercises a call option it has on this stock. Because of the operation of the OCC and the strong secondary market created by the CBOE, options are not exercised very frequently, but are generally sold. Rather than exercise an option, an investor or financial manager usually just sells the option to another investor, and realizes the profits in that manner. Writers of options clear their position by buying an option identical to the one they wrote. As a result the writer has two identical contracts on both sides of the market with the OCC. These positions then cancel each other out.

4. **Trading Was Made Certificateless.** Instead of issuing certificates, the OCC maintains a continuous record of traders' positions. In addition to making the clearing of positions (the canceling out of an option writer's obligation when an identical option is purchased) easier, it has also allowed for an up-to-date record of existing options to be maintained.

5. **Creation of a Liquid Secondary Market with Dramatically Decreased Transactions Costs.** There has also been a self-fulfilling generation of volume adding to the liquidity of the secondary market. That is, the innovations created a liquid secondary market for options, and this liquid secondary market attracted more investors into the options market, which in turn created even more liquidity in the secondary market.

Recent Innovations in the Options Market

Recently, four new variations of the traditional option have appeared: the stock index option, the interest rate option, the foreign currency option, and the Treasury bond futures option.

Stock Index Options. The options on stock indexes were first introduced on the CBOE in March of 1983 and have since proved extremely popular. While there are a variety of different index options, based upon a number of different broad stock market indexes and also industry indexes such as a computer industry index, it has been the broader stock market indexes that have carried the bulk of the popularity of index options. While the industry-based index options have received a somewhat mixed reception, stock index options, in particular the S&P 100 index on the CBOE, have proved to be extremely popular. In fact, more than 80 percent of all stock index options trading involves the S&P 100 index. Currently it accounts for over half of the volume of all option trading, and has made the CBOE the second largest U.S. securities market, with daily trading occasionally reaching nearly 700,000 contracts (remember each contract involves an option on 100 "shares" of the index).

The reason for this popularity is quite simple. These options allow portfolio managers and other investors holding broad portfolios cheaply and effectively to eliminate or adjust the market risk of their portfolio. When we talked about systematic and unsystematic risk, we noted that in a large and well-diversified portfolio unsystematic risk was effectively diversified away, leaving only systematic risk. Thus, the return on a large and well-diversified portfolio was a result of the portfolio's beta and the movement of the market. As a result, since the movements of the market cannot be controlled, portfolio managers periodically attempt to adjust the beta of the portfolio when they feel a change in the market's direction is at hand. Index options allow them to make this change without the massive transaction costs that would otherwise be incurred.

In general, stock index options are used in exactly the same way traditional options are used: for leverage and for investment insurance. However, because of the unusual nature of the "underlying stock," these concepts take on a different meaning. In the case of leverage, the portfolio manager is speculating that the market will head either up or down and is able to cash in on any market volatility with a relatively small investment. In fact, the ability to enjoy the leverage of an option while being concerned with broad market movements has resulted in much of the popularity of stock index options, as small changes in the market can result in very large changes in the price of these options. To get an idea of exactly what we mean, let us look at what happened in early 1985, when the stock market moved ahead.

On January 21, 1985, when the S&P 100 was at 169.27, an investor could have bought a February call with an exercise price of 170 and paid 2¾, or $275.00, as shown in Figure 20A–2. Ten days later it was worth 9⅜, or $937.50, when the index closed at 178.14. On the other hand, an investor who purchased a put for 3¼, or $325.00, would have had the value of the investment drop to $25.00. All this dramatic price movement was the result of only a 5.24 percent change in the underlying index.

In the case of the investment insurance motive for holding index options, the portfolio manager is really using them to hedge against general market movements. For example, a portfolio manager who wants to insure the portfolio against a downturn in the market might purchase a put on the S&P 100 or S&P 500 index. Thus, if the market declines, the put will appreciate in value, hopefully offsetting the loss in the investor's portfolio.

In effect, index options can be used in the same way as the more traditional options. The only difference is that here the profits or losses depend upon what happens to the value of the index, rather than to one stock.

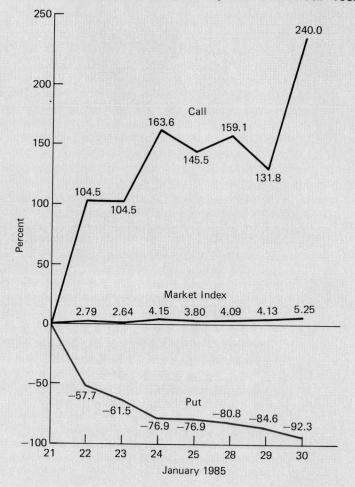

FIGURE 20A–2. February 170 Options on the S&P 100.

Interest Rate Options. Options on 30-year Treasury bonds are also traded on the CBOE. Although the trading appeal of interest rate options is somewhat limited, they do open some very interesting doors to the financial manager. In terms of the insurance and leverage traits, they allow the financial manager to insure against the effects of future changes in interest rates. We know that as interest rates rise the market value of outstanding bonds falls; thus, through the purchase of an interest rate put, the market value of a portfolio manager's bonds can be protected. Alternatively, a financial manager who is about to raise new capital through a debt offering and who is worried about a possible rise in interest rates before the offering takes place may purchase an interest rate put. This would have the effect of locking in current interest rates as the maximum level that the firm would have to pay.

Foreign Currency Options. Foreign currency options are the same as the other options we have examined except the underlying asset is the British pound, the Japanese yen, or some other foreign currency. While foreign currency options are limited to the Philadelphia Exchange, there is a considerable amount of interest in them largely due to the wide fluctuations foreign currency has had in recent years relative to the dollar. In terms of the insurance and leverage traits, these options allow multinational firms to guard against fluctuations in foreign currencies that might adversely affect their operations. The leverage trait allows investors to speculate in possible future foreign currency fluctuations with a minimum amount of exposure to possible losses.

Options on Treasury Bond Futures. Options on Treasury bond futures work the same way as any other option. The only difference between them and other bond options is that they involve the acquisition of a futures position rather than the delivery of actual bonds. To the creative financial manager, they provide a flexible tool to insure against adverse changes in interest rates while retaining the opportunity to benefit from any favorable interest rate movement that might occur. While a futures contract establishes an obligation for both parties to buy and sell at a specified price, an option only establishes a right. It is therefore exercised only when it is to the option holder's advantage to do so. In effect, a call option on a futures contract does not establish a price obligation, but rather a maximum purchase price. On the other hand, a put option on a futures contract is used to establish a minimum selling price. Thus, *the buyer of an option on a futures contract achieves immunization against any unfavorable price movements, whereas the buyer of a futures contract achieves immunization against any price movements regardless of whether they are favorable or unfavorable.*

In their short history, options on U.S. Treasury bond futures have proved to be extremely popular, with the majority of institutions choosing to trade options on bond futures rather than options on actual bonds. Their extreme popularity can be traced to several important advantages they possess:

1. Efficient price determination of the underlying instrument. The U.S. Treasury bond futures contract on the Chicago Board of Trade is the most widely traded futures contract of all. As a result there is a continuous stream of market-determined price information concerning these contracts. On the other hand, price information on most other bonds is generally somewhat sketchy at best, with substantial time between trades and generally a wide gap between existing bid and ask prices.
2. Unlimited deliverable supply. Because the Clearing Corporation can create as many futures contracts as are needed, the process of exercising an option is made extremely

simple. When an option on a futures contract is exercised, the buyer simply assumes a futures position at the exercise price of the option. Since the Clearing Corporation can create as many futures contracts as are needed, the market price of these contracts is not affected by the exercise of the options on them. On the other hand, if an option holder on an actual bond were to exercise his option, he would have to take delivery of the underlying bond. Since the supply of any particular bond is limited, this might create serious price pressure on that bond, provided the bond does not enjoy sufficient liquidity. Thus, because of the unlimited deliverable supply of futures contracts, the exercise of options on futures does not affect the price of those futures.

3. Greater flexibility in the event of exercise. If the option proves to be profitable, the purchaser or writer can settle the transaction in cash by offsetting the futures position acquired by exercise, or do nothing temporarily and assume the futures position and make or take delivery of the actual bonds when the futures contract comes due.

4. Extremely liquid market. Because of the other advantages of options on Treasury bond futures, a great number of these options have been created and are traded daily. As a result of the large volume, options on Treasury bond futures have developed a very liquid and active secondary market, which has encouraged other traders to enter this market.

Financial institutions seem to be major participants in the options on Treasury bond futures market, although there are many potential users of financial futures. They use futures options to alter the risk-return structure of their investment portfolios and actually reduce their exposure to downside risk. A common strategy is to purchase put options and thereby eliminate the possibility of large losses while retaining the possibility of large gains. There is a cost associated with this strategy, since the option premium must be paid regardless of whether or not the option is exercised. An additional return is also generated by those who write call options against a bond portfolio. With this strategy, the premium increases the overall return if bond yields remain stable or rise; however, a maximum return is also established for the portfolio, since it is this tail of the distribution that is sold with the option.

THE USE OF OPTIONS AND FUTURES BY FINANCIAL MANAGERS

The use of options and financial futures by financial managers is in the early stages. In a recent survey of the Fortune 500, 19.2 percent of firms that responded reported that they used either futures or options in the conduct of their financial affairs.[1] There also seemed to be some relationship between the size of the firm and the utilization rate. For example, among large firms (over $1 billion in assets), 23.7 percent used interest rate futures. However, among smaller firms, only 5.36 percent did.

Of the various options and futures available, by far the most popular were Treasury bill futures and Eurodollar futures. This is shown in Table 20A–3. Of those firms that did not use financial futures and options, the reasons most commonly cited were the resistance of top management and lack of knowledge on the part of the financial manager. It would seem that these two reasons for not using futures and options go together. It would also seem that as the advantages of using financial futures and options to hedge away interest

---

[1] See Stanley B. Block and Timothy J. Gallagher, "The Use of Interest Rate Futures and Options by Corporate Financial Managers," *Financial Management*, 15 (Autumn 1986), 73–78.

TABLE 20A–3. Financial Futures and Options Most Frequently Used

Security	Category	Number of Firms Utilizing the Instrument
Treasury bill	Future	16
Eurodollar	Future	14
Certificate of deposit	Future	7
Treasury bond	Future	4
Treasury bill	Option	4
Treasury bond	Option	4
Treasury note	Future	2
Treasury note	Option	1
GNMA	Future	1
Total		53

Source: Stanley B. Block and Timothy J. Gallagher, "The Use of Interest Rate Futures and Options by Corporate Financial Managers," *Financial Management*, 15 (Autumn 1986), 73–78.

rate and exchange rate risk become more widely understood, their use will become more common.

Summary

A *futures contract* is a contract to buy or sell a stated commodity (such as soybeans or corn) or financial claim (such as U.S. Treasury bonds) at a specified price at some future specified time. This is a contract that requires its holder to buy or sell the asset regardless of what happens to its value during the interim. The importance of a futures contract is that it can be used by financial managers to lock in the price of a commodity or an interest rate and thereby eliminate one source of risk. A futures contract is a specialized form of a forward contract distinguished by: (1) an organized exchange, (2) a standardized contract with limited price changes and margin requirements, (3) a clearinghouse in each futures market, and (4) daily resettlement of contracts.

A *call option* gives its owner the right to purchase a given number of shares of stock at a specified price over a given time period. Thus, if the price of the underlying common stock goes up, a call purchaser makes money. A *put*, on the other hand, gives its owner the right to sell a given number of shares of common stock at a specified price over a given time period. Thus, a put purchaser is betting that the price of the underlying common stock will drop. Since these are just options to buy or sell stock, they do not represent an ownership position in the underlying corporation, as does common stock.

Study Questions

1. What is the difference between a commodity future and financial future? Give an example of a commodity future and a financial future.
2. Describe a situation in which a financial manager might use a commodity future. Assume that during the period following the transaction the price of that commodity

went up, describe what happened. Now assume that the price of that commodity went down, now what happened?

3. Describe a situation in which a financial manager might use an interest rate future. Assume that during the period following the transaction the interest rates went up, describe what happened. Now assume that interest rates went down following the transaction, now what happened?

4. Define a call option.

5. Define a put option.

6. What innovative developments were brought on by exchange-listed trading that the CBOE initiated that lead to the dramatic growth in the trading of options?

7. What is an option on a futures contract? Give an example of one.

Selected References

Black, Fisher. "The Pricing of Commodity Contracts," *Journal of Financial Economics*, 3 (January–March 1976), 167–79.

———. "Fact and Fantasy in the Use of Options," *Financial Analysts Journal*, (July–August 1975), pp. 61–72.

———, and M. Scholes. "The Pricing of Options and Corporate Liabilities," *Journal of Political Economy*, 81 (May–June 1973), 637–54.

———, and ———. "The Valuation of Option Contracts and a Test of Market Efficiency," *The Journal of Finance*, (May 1972), 399–418.

Courtadon, George. "The Pricing of Options on Default-Free Bonds," *Journal of Financial and Quantitative Analysis*, 17 (March 1982), 75–100.

Fabozzi, Frank J. and Gregory M. Kipnis (eds.). *Stock Index Futures*. Homewood, IL: Dow Jones-Irwin, 1984.

Kaufman, Perry J. *Handbook of Futures Markets*. New York: Wiley-Interscience, 1984.

Kolb, Robert W. *Understanding Futures Markets*. Glenview, IL: Scott, Foresman, 1985.

Loosigian, Allan M. *Foreign Exchange Futures*. Homewood, IL: Dow Jones-Irwin, 1981.

———. *Interest Rate Futures*. Homewood, IL: Dow Jones-Irwin, 1980.

MacBeth, James D., and Larry J. Merville. "Tests of the Black-Scholes and Cox Call Option Valuation Models," *Journal of Finance*, (May 1980), 285–300.

Rothstein, Nancy H. (ed.) *The Handbook of Financial Futures*. New York: McGraw-Hill, 1984.

Smith, C., Jr. "Option Pricing: A Review," *Journal of Financial Economics*, (January–March 1976), 1–51.

———, and J. B. Warner. "On Financial Contracting: An Analysis of Bond Covenants," *Journal of Financial Economics*, (June 1979), 117–61.

Sterk, W. "Comparative Performance of the Black-Scholes and the Roll-Geske-Whaley Option Pricing Models," *Journal of Financial and Quantitative Analysis*, (September 1983), 345–54.

———. "Tests of Two Models for Valuing Call Options on Stocks With Dividends," *Journal of Finance*, 37 (December 1982), 1229–37.

Stoll, Hans R. "The Relationship Between Put and Call Option Prices," *Journal of Finance*, (December 1969), 802–24.

Whaley, R. "Valuation of American Call Options on Dividend-Paying Stocks: Empirical Tests," *Journal of Financial Economics*, 10 (March 1982), 29–58.

———. "On the Valuation of American Call Options on Stocks with Known Dividends," *Journal of Financial Economics*, 9 (June 1981), 207–11.

21

Corporate Restructuring: Combinations and Divestitures

On certain infrequent occasions, management may decide to restructure the firm's basic asset mix and/or its financial structure. Two approaches used by firms to restructure include: (1) merging with or acquiring another firm, and (2) divesting a division or subsidiary. Within the past few years, we have witnessed a fundamental restructuring of corporate American unlike anything since the Great Depression. The phenomenon has largely been the result of industries needing to become more competitive in the world markets. Hardly a day passes without a story in the media about a merger, acquisition, or divestiture. As students of finance we need to look carefully at these means for restructuring the firm. In looking at mergers and acquisitions, we will have four objectives:

1. Identify and explain the basic factors that determine the value of an acquisition target.
2. Examine the techniques used in financing an acquisition.
3. Explain the use of tender offers in acquiring a new business.
4. Study the ways managements use to resist an undesired suitor wanting to acquire their firm.

In looking at divestitures, we will study the different options available to management in divesting part of the firm.

MERGERS AND ACQUISITIONS

Business combinations may occur either by two firms merging together, resulting in a totally new company, or by a company acquiring another firm, where the acquired firm is absorbed into the acquiring corporation. Although the terms *merger* and *acquisition* have different legal implications, we will use them interchangeably to represent a combination of two or more businesses into a single operational entity.

Company growth through the merging of two firms has been a part of the U.S. economic scene for many years. At the beginning of the twentieth century many basic industries came under the control of large, publicly owned corporations. During the 1920s a second surge of combinations developed; big businesses expanded into new industries, creating vertically integrated companies. Then the 1960s witnessed more activity in mergers than ever before. This period, the **conglomerate age,** peaked in 1968 when the nation's largest 200 corporations acquired 94 large firms with aggregate assets in excess of $8 billion. Within the past few years the acquisition of major firms has again reached an all-time high. The size of the mergers during the 1980s has dwarfed all previous combinations. The size of a single firm acquired in the early 1980s would equal the total dollar volume of major combinations in most years during the 1960s and 1970s. Table 21–1 presents the 10 largest corporate combinations from September 1979 to March 1984. The size of these mergers was unprecedented until these most recent years.

The merger phase in the latter 1960s saw an emphasis on technology-related firms, accounting techniques that produced "instant growth" in earnings, and a market psychology that encouraged a speculative fever. Also, a concept developed that a good corporate executive could manage any firm, regardless of its nature. This philosophy spurred the development of multifaceted corporations involved in various, often unre-

TABLE 21–1. Ten Largest Corporate Mergers

Company/Acquirer (Other Suitors)	Cost ($ billions)	Terms		Date Announced
		Cash	Stock	
Gulf/Standard Oil—Calif. (Arco-Kohlberg-Kravis-Mesa Petroleum)	$13.2	100%	0%	3/05/84
Getty/Texaco (Pennzoil)	10.1	100	0	1/06/84
Conoco/Dupont	7.4	40	60	7/06/81
Marathon Oil/U.S. Steel (Mobil–Allied)	6.5	51	49	11/19/81
Southern Pacific/Santa Fe	5.2	0	100	9/27/83
Connecticut General/INA	4.3	0	100	11/09/81
Texasgulf/Elf Aquitaine	4.2	100	0	6/26/81
Cities Service/Occidental (Gulf Oil–Mesa Petroleum)	4.0	45	55	8/13/82
Belridge Oil/Shell Oil	3.6	100	0	9/30/79
St. Joe Minerals/Fluor (Seagrams)	2.6	45	55	3/31/81

lated, products and services. This select group of corporations came to be known as **conglomerates.**

The 1960s merger phenomenon grew almost without restraint until the 1969–70 recession set in and the business combination came under close scrutiny. Simultaneously, the accounting profession tightened the guidelines associated with the treatment of mergers, which significantly reduced the attractiveness of many combinations. Finally, the federal government intervened with a relatively strong antimerger position, protesting the potential loss in competition. As these influences strengthened and sharp declines in the market prices of conglomerate stocks occurred, the excitement quickly dissipated.

The more recent interest in growth through external acquistions has brought with it greater caution. The acquiring companies have relied more on basic economic analysis, rather than merely a concern for the accounting effects on the firm's earnings. Also, most of the large combinations have involved energy companies. As it has become more difficult and costly to discover new oil and gas reserves, oil firms have begun acquiring other oil companies as a way to acquire additional reserves. Such firms as Mesa Petroleum, Standard Oil of California, and Texaco have been actively involved in efforts to grow by acquiring other oil corporations.

DETERMINING A FIRM'S VALUE

One of the first problems in analyzing a potential merger involves placing a value on the acquired firm. This task is not easy. The value of a firm depends not only upon its earnings capabilities, but also upon the operating and financial characteristics of the acquiring firm. As a result, no single dollar value exists for a company. Instead, a range of values is determined that would be economically justifiable to the prospective acquirer. The final price within this range is then negotiated by the two managements.

To determine an acceptable price for a corporation, a number of factors are carefully evaluated. As stated in Chapter 1, the objective of the acquiring firm is always to maximize the stockholders' wealth (stock price). However, quantifying the relevant variables for this purpose is difficult at best. For instance, the primary reason for a merger might be to acquire managerial talent, or to complement a strong sales staff with an excellent production department. This potential **synergistic effect** is difficult to measure using the historical data of the companies involved. Even so, several quantitative variables are frequently used in an effort to estimate a firm's value. These factors include (1) book value, (2) appraisal value, (3) market price of the firm's common stock, and (4) earnings per share.

Book Value The **book value** of a firm's net worth is the balance sheet amount of the assets less its outstanding liabilities, or in other words, the owners' equity. For example, if a firm's historical cost less accumulated depreciation is $10 million and the firm's debt totals $4 million, the aggregate book value is $6 million. Furthermore, if 100,000 shares of common stock are outstanding, the book value per share is $60 ($6 million ÷ 100,000 shares).

Book value does not measure the true market value of a company's net worth because it is based on the historical cost of the firm's assets. Seldom do such costs bear a relationship to the value of the organization or its ability to produce earnings.

Although the book value of an enterprise is clearly not the most important factor, it should not be overlooked. It can be used as a starting point to be compared with other analyses. Also, a study of the firm's working capital is particularly appropriate and necessary in acquisitions involving a business consisting primarily of liquid assets such as financial institutions. Furthermore, in industries where the ability to generate earnings requires large investments in such items as steel, cement, and petroleum, the book value could be a critical factor, especially where plant and equipment are relatively new.

Appraisal Value

An **appraisal value** of a company may be acquired from an independent appraisal firm. The techniques used by appraisers vary widely; however, this value is often closely tied to replacement cost. This method of analysis is not adequate by itself, since the value of individual assets may have little relation to the firm's overall ability to generate earnings, and thus the going-concern value of the firm. However, the appraised value of an enterprise may be beneficial when used in conjunction with other valuation methods. Also, the appraised value may be an important factor in special situations, such as in financial companies, natural resource enterprises, or organizations that have been operating at a loss.[1]

The use of appraisal values does yield several additional advantages. The appraisal by independent appraisers may permit the reduction of accounting goodwill by increasing the recognized worth of specific assets. Goodwill results when the purchase price of a firm exceeds the value of the individual assets. Consider a company having a book value of $60,000 that is purchased for $100,000 (the $40,000 difference is goodwill). The $60,000 book value consists of $20,000 in working capital and $40,000 in fixed assets. However, an appraisal might suggest that the current values of these assets are $25,000 and $55,000, respectively. The $15,000 increase ($55,000 − $40,000) in fixed assets permits the acquiring firm to record a larger depreciation expense than would otherwise be possible, thereby reducing taxes. A second reason for an appraisal is to provide a test of the reasonableness of results obtained through methods based upon the going-concern concept. Third, the appraiser may uncover strengths and weaknesses that otherwise might not be recognized, such as in the valuation of patents, secret processes, and partially completed research-and-development expenditures.

Thus, the appraisal procedure is generally worthwhile if performed with additional evaluation processes. In specific instances, it may be an important instrument for valuing a corporation.

Stock Market Value

The **stock market value,** as expressed by stock market quotations, comprises another approach for estimating the net worth of a business. If the stock is listed on a major securities exchange, such as the New York Stock Exchange, and is widely traded, an approximate value can be established on the basis of the market value. The justification is based upon the fact that the market quotations indicate the consensus of investors as to a firm's earnings potential and the corresponding risk.

---

[1] The assets of a financial company and a natural resources firm largely consist of securities and natural reserves, respectively. The value of these individual assets has a direct bearing on the firm's earning capacity. Also, a company operating at a loss may only be worth its liquidation value, which would approximate the appraisal value.

TABLE 21–2. Relationship of Intrinsic-Value Factors to Market Price

I. General market factors
II. Individual factors

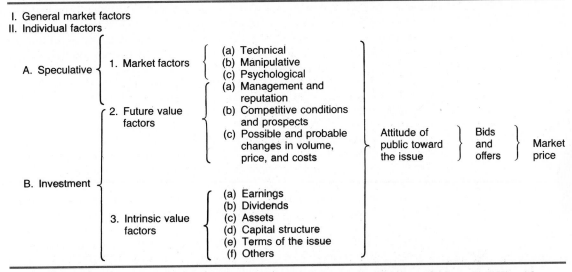

A. Speculative
  1. Market factors
    (a) Technical
    (b) Manipulative
    (c) Psychological

  2. Future value factors
    (a) Management and reputation
    (b) Competitive conditions and prospects
    (c) Possible and probable changes in volume, price, and costs

B. Investment
  3. Intrinsic value factors
    (a) Earnings
    (b) Dividends
    (c) Assets
    (d) Capital structure
    (e) Terms of the issue
    (f) Others

Attitude of public toward the issue } Bids and offers } Market price

Source: Benjamin Graham, David L. Dodd, and Sidney Cottle, *Security Analysis*, 4th ed. (New York: McGraw-Hill, 1962), p. 43.

The market-value approach is the one most frequently used in valuing large corporations. However, this value can change abruptly. Table 21–2 depicts the various factors influencing market value. As the table shows, computations by market analysts are not the sole determinant of value. Analytical factors compete with purely speculative influences and are subject to people's sentiments and personal decisions. Thus,

> [T]he market is not a weighing machine, on which the value of each issue is recorded by an exact and impersonal mechanism, in accordance with the specific qualities. Rather should we say that the market is a voting machine, whereon countless individuals register choices which are the product partly of reason and partly of emotion.[2]

In summary, the market-value approach is probably the one most widely used for determining the worth of a firm, with a 10- to 20-percent premium above the market price often being required as an inducement for the current owners to sell their stock. Even so, executives who place their entire reliance upon this method are subject to an inherent danger of market psychology.

Earnings per Share

In practice, the purchase of another business normally has one primary objective—to increase the acquiring firm's earnings, usually expressed in earnings per share. It is hoped that this increase in earnings per share will have a favorable impact upon the purchasing company's common stock price. The acquiring firm is, in fact, purchasing future earnings. Therefore, the value of the prospective acquisition is frequently considered to be a function of the merger's impact upon earnings per share.

---

[2] Benjamin Graham, David L. Dodd, and Sidney Cottle, *Security Analysis*, 4th ed. (New York: McGraw-Hill, 1962), p. 42.

Example   As an illustration of the earnings effect of an acquisition, suppose company A is contemplating the purchase of company B. Company A has 100,000 shares of common stock outstanding with a $100 market value per share, while company B has issued 50,000 shares selling at $75. The earnings per share for the corporations are $6.25 for company A and $5 for company B. The two managements have agreed that the company B shareholders are to receive company A stock in exchange for their shares. The swap is to be based upon the relative earnings per share of the two firms. Therefore, the company B owners should receive .8 shares of company A stock for each share owned of company B ($5 ÷ $6.25), or 40,000 shares of company A. Consequently, company B shareholders are receiving securities with a total market value of $4 million (40,000 shares at a $100 market price), which is greater than their original $3,750,000 value in company B. At the same time, the company A stockholders incur no loss in value.

What causes the increase in value for the company B stockholders without an offsetting reduction in value for the company A owners? In answering this question, we must examine the relative price/earnings ratios of the two firms. For company A the price/earnings multiple is 16 ($100 price ÷ $6.25 earnings per share), while for company B it is only 15($75 price ÷ $5 earnings per share). Our computations implicitly assume that company B's earnings will be valued at the higher price/earnings ratio of 16. If the price/earnings relationship were to decrease after the merger, the value of company A shares would fall proportionately.

Effect of Earnings Dilution

In the preceding example, no dilution (or reduction in earnings per share) for either group of shareholders resulted. This fact is verified in Table 21–3, where the total earnings for the new firm (company A + B) is $875,000. Since 140,000 shares will be outstanding after the combination, the earnings per share is $6.25, which equals

TABLE 21–3.   Merger Effect on Earnings (0.8:1 Exchange Ratio)

Company	(a) Original Number of Shares	(b) Earnings per Share	(c) Net Income (a) × (b)
A	100,000	$6.25	$625,000
B	50,000	5.00	250,000
		Total postmerger earnings:	$875,000

Number of shares after the merger:
100,000 + (0.8)50,000 — 140,000

Earnings per share for company A stockholders after the merger:
$875,000 ÷ 140,000 shares — $ 6.25

Equivalent earnings per share for company B stockholders:

1. Before the merger:
(earnings per share *after* the merger) × (share exchange ratio) = $6.25 × 0.8 — $ 5.00

2. After the merger:
(Earnings per share *before* the merger) ÷ (share exchange ratio) = $5 ÷ 0.8 — $ 6.25

the premerger company A earnings per share. Although the earnings per share has increased from $5 to $6.25 for company B stockholders, these shareholders only have 80 percent of their original number of shares. Therefore, the $6.25 *postmerger* earnings per share should not be compared with the $5 *premerger* earnings per share for company B stockholders. Instead, the *equivalent* earnings per share on a *premerger* basis is 80 percent of $6.25, or $5. Alternatively the equivalent earnings per share on a *postmerger* basis is $5 divided by 80 percent, or $6.25. In other words, $5 in earnings per share prior to the merger is the same as $6.25 after the merger for company B stockholders. Therefore, the effective earnings position for company B stockholders is not changed as a result of the merger.

What if the final share exchange ratio were not based upon the relative earnings per share? Instead, assume that company B shareholders would agree to the merger only if they received .9 share of company A for one share of company B. In this circumstance, a dilution in earnings per share would be felt by the company A stockholders, with the company B investors receiving an addition in earnings per share. As shown in Table 21–4, the earnings per share for company A immediately decreases from $6.25 to $6.03, or a $.22 *dilution* in earnings per share. Conversely, the equivalent earnings per share increases by $.47 for the company B stockholders ($5.56 to $6.03).

For many managements, a merger that results in a dilution in earnings per share is to be avoided. However, the fact that a merger immediately dilutes a firm's current earnings per share need not make the transaction undesirable. Such a criterion places undue emphasis upon the immediate effects of a prospective merger upon the earnings per share.

In examining the consequences of a merger upon the surviving concern's earnings per share, we should extend the analysis into future periods. The investigation should include all the variables affecting future earnings per share, which include (1) the share exchange ratio, (2) the firms' relative sizes, and (3) their relative expected future growth rates in earnings.

TABLE 21–4. Merger Effect on Earnings (0.9:1 Exchange Ratio)

Total postmerger earnings	$875,000
Number of shares after the merger:	
100,000 + (0.9)50,000	145,000
Earnings per share:	
$875,000 ÷ 145,000	$6.03
Company A stockholders:	
Earnings per share before the merger	$6.25
Earnings per share after the merger:	
($875,000 ÷ 145,000 shares)	6.03
Dilution in earnings per share	($0.22)
Company B stockholders:	
Equivalent earnings per share before the merger:	
(Earnings per share before the merger) ÷ (share exchange ratio) = $5 ÷ 0.9	$5.56
Earnings per share after the merger	6.03
Accretion in earnings per share	$0.47

TABLE 21–5. Projection of Earnings Per Share

	(a)	(b)	(c)	(d)	(e)	(f)	(g)	
			Company A + B Postmerger Combined	Company A + B Earnings per Share	Company A Premerger Earnings per Share	Company B Earnings per Share Without the Merger	Accretion (Dilution) Earnings per Share	
Year	Company A Earnings (8% Growth)	Company B Earnings (14% Growth)	Earnings [(a) + (b)]	[(c) ÷ 145,000 Shares[a]]	[(a) ÷ 100,000 Shares]	[(b) ÷ 45,000 Shares[b]]	Co. A	Co. B
1988	$625,000	$250,000	$ 875,000	$6.03	$6.25	$ 5.56	($.22)	$ .47
1989	675,000	285,000	960,000	6.62	6.75	6.33	(.13)	.29
1990	729,000	324,900	1,053,900	7.26	7.29	7.22	(.03)	.04
1991	787,320	370,386	1,157,706	7.98	7.87	8.23	.11	(.25)
1992	850,306	422,240	1,272,546	8.78	8.50	9.38	.28	(.60)
1993	918,330	481,354	1,399,684	9.65	9.18	10.70	.47	(1.05)

[a] 100,000 company A shares + (0.9)50,000 company B shares = 145,000 company A + B shares.
[b] (0.9)50,000 company B shares = 45,000 equivalent shares in company A + B.

Continuing the previous illustration, assume that the anticipated growth rate in earnings is 8 percent for company A and 14 percent for company B. Under these conditions the $.22 dilution in company A's earnings per share (Table 21–4) is gradually eliminated in future years. In other words, company A earnings per share is reduced in the current year, but company B's growth rate will benefit company A's stockholders in future years. As shown in Table 21–5, the combined earnings per share for company A + B (column d) is lower than company A's earnings per share (column e) during the 1988–1990 period, after which the earnings per share are greater for the merged company. On the other hand, the impact on the *equivalent* earnings per share for company B is favorable for 1988 through 1990 (compare columns d and f). For all subsequent years, company B's earnings per share are diluted.

Based upon the data in Table 21–5, should company A's management undertake the merger? No concrete answer can be reached from the limited information available. In general, the terms of the merger must be developed to provide a mutually satisfactory earnings pattern for the shareholders of both firms. Also, if any lesson is to be learned from the merger activities of the 1960s, certainly the fallacy of placing emphasis upon earnings per share at the exclusion of other considerations should not go unnoticed. A prime example of potential problems is Litton Industries. During the mid-1960s, Litton's earnings per share grew at an annual compound growth rate of 24 percent. This growth was the result principally of its acquisitions. However, when the 1969–70 recession materialized, Litton's earnings fell sharply, eliminating the growth from the previous years. Eventually, in 1973 Litton disposed of the unprofitable product lines not considered to be in its main area of operations.

FINANCING TECHNIQUES IN MERGERS

After the value of a firm has been resolved by all parties, the method of payment must be determined. The choice of financial instruments and techniques in acquiring a firm usually has an effect on the purchase agreement. The payment may take the form of cash or securities. Security payments generally involve common or preferred stock, with the preferred securities normally being convertible into common stock. Also, deferred payment plans are increasingly being used because of their advantages.

Common Stock Financing

When a company is deciding whether to use common stock to finance a merger, the relative price/earnings ratios of the two businesses become an important consideration. Although the price/earnings multiple should not be the only criterion, it is important in determining the method of payment. For a firm having a high stock price relative to its earnings per share (a high price/earnings ratio), common stock represents a primary tool for negotiating a merger or acquisition. In addition, the common stock route becomes more advantageous for both companies when the firm being acquired has a low price/earnings ratio. This fact may best be explained by an illustration.

In summary, a corporation with a high price/earnings ratio has a distinct advantage in the business of mergers and acquisitions. Use of this ratio may prove beneficial to the acquiring business as well as to the firm being acquired. However, because some

---

Example Assume that Tajos, Inc.'s common stock is selling for $36, and the firm is earning $2 per share. Negotiations are underway to acquire the Old Dominion Corporation, with a stock price of $10 and earnings per share of $1. Both firms have 300,000 shares outstanding. The management of Tajos has agreed to exchange one share for every three shares of Old Dominion. The resulting earnings per share for Tajos, Inc., after the merger is $2.25, as shown in Table 21–6. Therefore, the Old Dominion shareholders are receiving one share of stock valued at $36 while relinquishing three shares of stock with a total value of $30 ($10 per share × 3). This exchange represents a 20 percent premium ($36 relative to $30) to the Old Dominion stockholders. Furthermore, provided that the price/earnings multiple of 18 ($36 ÷ $2) is sustained for Tajos, Inc. shares, the value of the Tajos shares will increase to $40.50 ($2.25 earnings per share × 18). The price increase is the result of converting a firm with relatively low growth expectations into one with high growth expectations, thereby increasing the market value of the Old Dominion shares.

TABLE 21–6. Tajos, Inc. Postmerger Earnings

Company	Number of Shares	Earnings per Share	Total Earnings
Tajos, Inc.	300,000	$2	$600,000
Old Dominion	300,000	1	300,000
			$900,000

Total shares after the merger:
  Tajos, Inc. shares + (exchange ratio × company B shares)
  = 300,000 + (⅓) 300,000
  = 400,000 postmerger shares
Postmerger earnings per share:
  $900,000 earnings ÷ 400,000 shares = $2.25

companies cannot attain a high price/earning multiple, and because different types of investors must be recognized, other types of securities may need to be used in conjunction with or in lieu of common stock.

Debt and Preferred Stock Financing

Since some investors prefer growth stocks, while others seek substantial dividend or interest income, an acquiring company must at times offer a combination of securities in settlement with the new stockholders. In an attempt to tailor a security for such investors, convertible debentures and convertible preferred stock have frequently been used.

The phenomenon of convertible securities has had a decided impact upon acquisitions and mergers. Although requirements established by the accounting and securities profession have diminished the benefits of convertible securities, the following primary advantages still remain.[3]

1. Potential earnings dilution may be partially minimized by issuing a convertible security. If such a security is designed to sell at a premium over its conversion value, fewer common shares will ultimately be issued. For example, if the acquirer's stock currently has a market price of $50 per share, and the price of the acquisition is $10 million, using common stock would require issuing 200,000 shares. In comparison, a convertible preferred issue could be designed to sell at $100 with a 1.7 conversion ratio, which would mean a conversion value of $85. The $10 million price would be realized by issuing 100,000 preferred shares convertible into 170,000 shares of common stock. The purchaser would have decreased the eventual number of shares to be issued, thereby reducing the dilution in earnings per share that could ultimately result.
2. A convertible issue may allow the acquiring company to comply with the seller's income objectives without changing its own dividend policy. If the two firms have different dividend payout policies and the acquirer does not want to commit its common stock to a dividend rate that suits the seller, convertible preferred stock may be an appropriate solution.
3. Convertible preferred stock also represents a possible way of lowering the voting power of the acquired company. This reduction of voice in management can be important, especially if the seller is a closely held corporation.
4. The convertible preferred debenture or stock may appear more attractive to the firm being acquired because it combines senior security protection with a portion of the growth potential of common stock.

In summary, debt and preferred stock are often compatible with the needs and purposes of a merger. The need for altering financial leverage and for a variety of securities is resolved, at least in part, by the use of senior securities.

Earn-Outs

The **deferred payment plan,** which has come to be called an **earn-out,** represents a relatively recent approach to merger financing. The acquiring firm agrees to make a specified initial payment of cash or stock and, if it can maintain or increase earnings, to pay additional compensation.

An earn-out has several benefits for the acquiring organization. It provides a logical method of adjusting the difference between the amount of stock the purchaser is

---

[3] Anthony H. Meyer, "Designing a Convertible Preferred Issue," *Financial Executive,* April 1968, pp. 53–55.

willing to issue and the amount the seller will accept for the business. Second, the merging company will immediately be able to report higher earnings per share because fewer shares of stock will become outstanding at the time of the acquisition. In addition, the acquiring company is provided with downside protection by not totally paying for a business until the projected earnings have actually been realized. The earn-out diminishes the guesswork in establishing an equitable purchase price, because the price is based upon the actual performance of the prospective acquisition after the merger.

Even though several advantages exist for earn-outs, potential problems must also be recognized. First, the acquired corporation must be capable of being operated as an autonomous business entity. Otherwise it is difficult to know the acquired firm's contribution to total profits. Second, the acquiring firm must be willing to allow freedom of operation to the management of the newly acquired business. Third, the seller must be willing to contribute toward the future growth of the acquiring company, realizing that only by working together will the two firms attain success.

Numerous types of earn-outs have been devised; the various arrangements are limited only by the imagination of the management of the two firms involved. However, the **base-period earn-out** may be used as an illustration. Under this plan the stockholders of the acquired company are to receive additional stock for a designated number of future years if the firm improves its earnings above the base-period profits—that is, the earnings in the last year before the acquisition. The amount of the future payments will be determined by three factors: (1) the amount of earnings in the forthcoming years in excess of the base-period profits, (2) the capitalization rate (discount rate) agreed upon by the parties, and (3) the market value of the acquiring organization at the end of each year. For example, the compensation in shares in the future years might be computed by using the following formula:

$$\frac{\text{excess earnings} \times \text{price/earnings multiple}}{\text{stock market price}}$$

To illustrate: In 1985, company A acquired company B which had base-period earnings of $400,000. At the time of the merger, company B stockholders received 300,000 shares of company A stock. Annual profits for company B subsequent to the merger have been $475,000, $550,000, $650,000, and $500,000. The market value of company A's stock is $30 per share and the price/earnings ratio is 8. Based upon the formula above, and assuming no change in the $30 price for company A stock, the additional shares to be paid to company B stockholders would be:

$$1982: \quad \frac{\$\ 75,000 \times 8}{\$30} = \quad 20,000 \text{ shares}$$

$$1983: \quad \frac{\$150,000 \times 8}{\$30} = \quad 40,000 \text{ shares}$$

$$1984: \quad \frac{\$250,000 \times 8}{\$30} = \quad 66,667 \text{ shares}$$

$$1985: \quad \frac{\$100,000 \times 8}{\$30} = \quad 26,667 \text{ shares}$$

Total $\qquad$ 153,334 shares

Therefore, in addition to the down payment of 300,000 company A shares, company B stockholders would receive a total of 153,334 shares during the ensuing four years.

The example is oversimplified, since other variables must also be recognized in the development of an earn-out plan. Such factors inclue (1) a specified limitation as to the maximum amount of stock that can be transferred in any one year; (2) an established range for the stock price employed in the computations; (3) the recognition of yearly earnings increments over the prior year; (4) the determination of an equitable down payment; (5) the succinct definition of earnings for the earn-out computations; and (6) the number of years the earn-out is to continue.

The earn-out technique provides a means by which the acquiring business can eliminate part of the guesswork involved in purchasing a firm. In essence, it allows the acquiring management the privilege of hindsight.

TENDER OFFER

As an alternative approach in purchasing another firm, the acquiring corporation may consider using a **tender offer.** This technique has received extensive recognition during recent years. As shown in Table 21–7, the number of tender offers for stocks listed on the New York Stock Exchange and the American Stock Exchange has begun to rival the number of mergers.

A tender offer involves a bid by an interested party for controlling interest in another corporation. The prospective purchaser approaches the stockholders of the firm, rather than the management, to encourage them to sell their shares, typically

TABLE 21–7. New York and American Stock Exchange Firms Acquired in Mergers or Tender Offers

Year	Mergers	Tender Offers
1963	16	6
1964	27	4
1965	26	7
1966	35	10
1967	56	12
1968	14	23
1969	6	6
1970	19	4
1971	6	1
1972	14	3
1973	13	14
1974	9	21
1975	7	14
1976	9	11
1977	17	17
1978	26	21
1979	44	30
1980	35	20
1981	23	21
June 1982	10	9
Total	419	254
% of population of firms	9.5%	5.7%

at a premium over the current market price. For instance, Lowe offered to purchase 20 million shares of CNA common stock at $5, which had been selling for $4.25 the week prior to the offer. A larger premium was offered by Tesoro Petroleum for Commonwealth Oil Refining common stock: The tender price was $11.50 compared with $8.75 the day before the offer.

Since the tender offer is a direct appeal to the stockholders, prior approval is not required by the management of the target firm. However, the acquiring firm may choose to approach the management of the target firm. If the two managements are unsuccessful in negotiating the terms, a tender offer may then be attempted. Alternatively, a firm's management interested in acquiring control of a second corporation may try a surprise takeover without contacting the management of the latter company. T. Boone Pickens of Mesa Petroleum is a prime example of someone using the tender offer in his efforts to acquire such firms as Cities Service and Gulf.

RESISTING THE MERGER

In response to "unfriendly" merger attempts, especially tender offers, the management of the firm under attack will frequently strike back. A number of defense tactics are used to counter tender offers. These defensive maneuvers include white knights, Pac-Mans, and shark repellents. A **white knight** is a company that comes to the rescue of a corporation that is being targeted for a takeover. For example, when Pennzoil made a tender offer for Getty Oil, the Getty management opposed the Pennzoil attempt. To prevent the takeover, Texaco, at the encouragement of Getty's management, made its own tender offer for Getty at a higher price. Texaco was the white knight for Getty. However, Pennzoil later received a $10 billion judgment against Texaco for its action in the Getty acquisition.

Pac-Man, the name taken from the video game, is another defensive tactic to tender offers, where the firm under attack becomes the attacker. For instance, Bendix Corporation tried to take control of Martin-Marietta by a tender offer. When the takeover effort failed, Martin-Marietta counterattacked by buying Bendix stock in an attempt to take control of Bendix. Martin-Marietta became the Pac-Man. To recounter, Bendix successfully courted Allied Corporation to come to its rescue. Allied bought Bendix so that Martin-Marietta could not buy enough for control. Allied was a white knight.

Shark repellents are often used to discourage unfriendly takeovers. As an example, a firm may revise its bylaws to stagger the terms of directors so that only a few come up for election in any one year. A firm making a tender offer would have to wait at least two years before gaining a majority of board members. Another ploy is to reincorporate in a state with rules that favor existing management. Gulf Oil was incorporated in Pennsylvania, where minority stockholders could use cumulative voting to gain a voice on the board of directors. When Mesa Petroleum's T. Boone Pickens began buying major blocks of Gulf stock, gulf reincorporated in Delaware, where cumulative voting could not be used, making it more difficult for Pickens to have any impact on the management of Gulf. Still another tactic is the **golden parachute,** which stipulates that the acquiring company must pay the executives of the acquired firm a substantial sum of money to "let them down easy" as new management is brought into the company.

The disadvantages of the unfriendly takeover are readily apparent from the preceding examples. If the target firm's management attempts to block it, the costs of executing the offer may increase significantly. Also, the purchasing company may fail to acquire a sufficient number of shares to meet the objective of controlling the firm. On the other hand, if the offer is not strongly contested, it may possibly be less expensive than the normal route for acquiring a company, in that it permits control by purchasing a smaller portion of the firm. Also, the tender offer has proven somewhat less susceptible to judicial inquiries regarding the fairness of the purchase price, since each stockholder individually decides the fairness of the price.

DIVESTITURES

While the mergers-and-acquisition phenomenon has been a major influence in restructuring the corporate sector, divestitures, or what we might call "reverse mergers," may have become an equally important factor. In fact, preliminary research to date would suggest that we may be witnessing a "new era" in the making—one where the public corporation is becoming a more efficient vehicle for increasing and maintaining stockholder wealth.[4] Chew calls it the "new math," when he writes:

> that a new kind of arithmetic has come into play. Whereas corporate management once seemed to behave as if 2 + 2 were equal to 5, especially during the conglomerate heyday of the 60's, the wave of reverse mergers seems based on the counter proposition that 5 − 1 is 5. And the market's consistently positive response to such deals seems to be providing broad confirmation of the "new math."[5]

A successful divestiture allows the firm's assets to be used more efficiently, and therefore to be assigned a higher value by the market forces. It essentially eliminates a division or subsidiary that does not fit strategically with the rest of the company; that is, it removes an operation that does not contribute to the company's basic purposes.

The different types of divestitures may be summarized as follows:

1. **Sell-off.** A sell-off is the sale of a subsidiary, division, or product line by one company to another. For example, Radio Corporation of America (RCA) sold its finance company and General Electric sold its metallurgical coal business.
2. **Spin-off.** A spin-off involves the separation of a subsidiary from its parent, with no change in the equity ownership. The management of the parent company gives up operating control of the subsidiary, but the shareholders retain the same percentage ownership in both firms. New shares representing ownership in the diverted assets are issued to the original shareholders on a pro-rata basis.
3. **Liquidation.** A liquidation in this context is not a decision to shut down or abandon an asset. Rather, the assets are sold to another company, and the proceeds are distributed to the stockholders.

---

[4] See G. Alexander, P. Benson, and J. Kampmeyer, "Investigating the Valuation Effects of Voluntary Corporate Sell-offs, *Journal of Finance*, 39 (1984), pp. 503–17; and D. Hearth, "Voluntary Divestitures and Value," *Financial Management*, 1984.

[5] Joel M. Stern, and Donald H. Chew, Jr. (eds.), *The Revolution in Corporate Finance* (New York: Basis Blackwell, 1986), p. 416.

4. **Going private.** Going private results when a company whose stock is traded publicly is purchased by a small group of investors, and the stock is no longer bought and sold on a public exchange. The ownership of the company is transferred from a diverse group of outside stockholders to a small group of private investors, usually including the firm's management.

5. **Leveraged buyout.** The leveraged buyout is a special case of going private. The existing shareholders sell their shares to a small group of investors. The purchasers of the stock use the firm's unused debt capacity to borrow the funds to pay for the stock. Thus, the new investors acquire the firm with little, if any, personal investment. However, the firm's debt ratio may increase by as much as tenfold.

Summary

Business combinations historically have represented a major influence in the growth of firms within the United States. This avenue for growth has been particularly important during selected periods, such as the latter part of the 1960s. In recent years the number of mergers and acquisitions has again increased, but with greater caution than in the 1960s, when conglomerates played a big part in the merger activity.

Valuing a Firm

Determining the worth of a firm is a difficult task. In addition to projecting the firm's future profitability, which is a cornerstone in valuation, the acquirer must consider the effects of joining two businesses into a single operation. What may represent a "good investment" may not be a good merger.

In estimating a firm's worth several factors are frequently considered:

1. The book value represents the historical investment of the common stockholders in the firm. By itself, book value is not an effective measure of a company's present value.

2. An appraisal value may or may not be a good indicator of the price to be paid for a company. The merits of an appraisal depend upon the approach taken and the nature of the business.

3. The stock market value of a firm's common shares is a key element in valuing a firm, particularly if the securities are actively traded in the market. However, care should be taken not to lean too heavily on this single factor.

4. Earnings per share is the bottom line for a company's operations and financing decision. Although excessive reliance upon this single figure is often criticized, most businesspeople view it as an important criterion for investment decisions, and they consider seriously how a merger may affect it. However, we should look at a merger's impact not only on present, but also on future earnings.

Financing the Merger

The price to be paid for a company is seldom uninfluenced by the method of financing the purchase. Generally the acquiring firm issues common stock or securities that are eventually convertible into common stock in payment for the acquisition. For this reason, a firm with a high price/earnings multiple is at an advantage in acquiring other businesses. More recently, deferred payment plans or earn-outs have been used.

Tender Offers Normally, the invested purchaser approaches the management of the firm to be acquired. Alternatively, the purchasing firm can directly approach the stockholders of the firm under consideration. This bid for ownership, called a tender offer, has been used with increasing frequency. This approach may be cheaper, provided that the managers of the target firm do not attempt to block it.

Divestitures A divestiture represents a variety of ways to divest a portion of the firm's assets. It has become an important vehicle in restructuring the corporation into a more efficient operation.

Study Questions

21–1. What factors contributed to the reduction in the number of mergers in 1969 and 1970?

21–2. Why is book value alone not a significant measure of the worth of a company?

21–3. What advantages are provided by the use of an appraisal value in valuing a firm?

21–4. Why is the price/earnings ratio a significant factor in determining the method of financing a merger?

21–5. What are the advantages of using convertible securities as a method of financing mergers?

21–6. What is meant by the term "earn-out"?

21–7. What are the prerequisites for an earn-out plan to be effective?

21–8. Under the base-period earn-out, the amount of future payments depends on what factors?

21–9. What are the disadvantages of the tender offer?

21–10. Explain the different types of divestitures.

Self-Test Problems

ST–1. (*Merger Based upon Relative Earnings*) Company X has negotiated the purchase of company Y. The two firms have agreed that the company Y shareholders are to receive common stock of company X in exchange for their shares. The exchange is to be based on the relative earnings per share of the two firms. Company X currently has 125,000 shares of common stock outstanding with an $84 market value, and earnings per share of $5.25. Company Y has issued 45,000 shares, which are selling for $46.20; earnings per share are $4.20. What will be the share exchange ratio for the merger? Will any dilution in earnings occur for either group of shareholders?

ST–2. (*Merger Effect on Future Earnings per Share*) Premier Chemical, Inc. agreed to purchase Mocatta Laboratories under a base-period earn-out plan. Mocatta's base-period profits were $325,000, and its earnings subsequent to the merger are shown below, as are Premier's common stock market value and earnings. What would be the total number of shares received by Mocatta's stockholders at the end of the fourth year if the initial down payment were 250,000 shares?

Year	Mocatta's Earnings	Premier's Stock Price	Premier's EPS
1	$400,000	48	$3.25
2	475,000	56	5.10
3	535,000	63	7.25
4	495,000	59	6.85

Study Problems

21–1. (*Merger Effect on Earnings and Value*) Savry Industries wishes to purchase the Mantana Corporation. They have spoken with the Mantana management and tentatively agreed on a stock purchase of two shares of Mantana for one share of Savry. Earnings per share for the two corporations are $2.52 for Mantana and $4.16 for Savry. Stock prices for the two corporations are $16 per share and $41 per share, respectively. (Savry and Mantana each have 200,000 shares outstanding.)

    a. What is the effect of the merger on earnings per share for the corporations?

    b. Assuming that Savry retains its current price/earnings ratio, what will the gains in price appreciation be for Mantana and Savry based on the post-merger stock price for Savry?

21–2. (*Effect of Merger on Earnings*) Company A has agreed to purchase company B. Company A currently has 150,000 shares of common stock outstanding; the market value is $115, and earnings per share is $7.85. Company B's common stock has a market value of $45, and earnings per share of $5.15, with 30,000 shares outstanding. The two firms have agreed that company B stockholders will receive company A common stock in exchange for their shares at a ratio of .75 to 1. What will be the effect on the earnings position of each company's stockholders?

21–3. (*Common versus Preferred Stock*) Norton Industries has negotiated to acquire a company at a price of $37.5 million. Norton's common stock is currently selling at $75. A convertible preferred stock could be issued to sell at $120 with a 1.25 conversion ratio. Compare the financing of the acquisition by common stock and by the convertible preferred issue. If Norton's management wants to minimize the impact of dilution, which financing method should be chosen?

21–4. (*Merger Effect on Future Earnings per Share*) Bolivia Products Corporation wishes to purchase the Joisner Corporation. Joisner has an annual earnings growth rate of 6 percent, an earnings per share of $6.80, and a price-to-earnings ratio of 7. Bolivia, on the other hand, has a growth rate of 14 percent, earnings per share of $2.50, and a price-to-earnings multiple of 16. If Joisner accepts a share-exchange ratio of two Bolivia for one Joisner, forecast each company's premerger and postmerger earnings per share for 10 years. Bolivia Products has 500,000 shares outstanding, while Joisner has 100,000 shares outstanding. In which years are the postmerger earnings per share projections more favorable than premerger projections (i) for Joisner and (ii) for Bolivia Products?

Self-Test Solutions

SS–1.   **a.** *Share exchange ratio*

$$\$4.20 \div \$5.25 = 0.8$$

    45,000 shares of company Y $\times$ 0.8 = 36,000 shares of company X

    b. No dilution in earnings per share will result for either stockholder.

Merger Effect of Earnings

Company	Original No. of Shares	EPS	Net Income
X	125,000	$5.25	$656,250
Y	45,000	4.20	189,000
Total post-merger earnings			$845,250

Number of shares after the merger:

$$125,000 + 0.8\,(45,000) = \underline{\underline{161,000}}$$

EPS for company X after the merger:

$$\$845,250 \div 161,000 \text{ shares} = \underline{\underline{\$5.25}}$$

Equivalent EPS for Company Y:

(1) Prior to the merger:

$$\text{EPS after the merger} \times \text{share exchange ratio}$$
$$\$5.25 \times 0.8 = \underline{\underline{\$4.20}}$$

(2) After the merger:

$$\text{EPS before the merger} \div \text{share exchange ratio}$$
$$\$4.20 \div 0.8 = \underline{\underline{\$5.25}}$$

Even though company Y shareholders' earnings per share has increased from $4.20 to $5.25, these stockholders only have 80 percent of their original number of shares. Thus, their equivalent EPS after the merger is 80 percent of $5.25, or $4.20, and their effective earnings position has not been altered by the merger.

SS–2. $$\text{Number of new shares each year} = \frac{\text{excess earnings (P/E ratio)}}{\text{stock market price}}$$

Year 0   Initial down payment   = 250,000 shares

Year 1 $$\frac{(\$400,000 - \$325,000) \times (\$48 \div \$3.25)}{\$48} = \quad 23,077$$

Year 2 $$\frac{(\$475,000 - \$325,000) \times (\$56 \div \$5.10)}{\$56} = \quad 29,412$$

Year 3 $$\frac{(\$535,000 - \$325,000) \times (\$63 \div \$7.25)}{\$63} = \quad 28,966$$

Year 4 $$\frac{(\$495,000 - \$325,000) \times (\$59 \div \$6.85)}{\$59} = \quad \underline{24,818}$$

Total shares received by Mocatta's shareholders $\underline{\underline{356,273}}$

Selected References

Alexander, G., P. Benson, and J. Kampmeyer. "Investigating the Valuation Effects of Voluntary Corporate Sell-offs," *Journal of Finance*, 39 (1984), 503–17.

Asquith, P. "Merger Bids, Uncertainty, and Stockholder Returns," *Journal of Financial Economics*, 11 (April 1983).

Austin, Douglas V. "The Financial Management of Tender Offer Takeovers," *Financial Management*, 3 (Spring 1974), 27–43.

Bradley, M. "Interfirm Tender Offers and the Market for Corporate Control,"*Journal of Business*, (October 1980), 345–76.

Choi, Dosoung, and George C. Philippatos. "An Examination of Merger Synergism," *Journal of Financial Research*, 6 (Fall 1983), 239–56.

DeAngelo, H., L. DeAngelo, and E. Rice, "Going Private: Minority Freezeouts and Stockholder Wealth," *Journal of Law Economics*, (October 1984).

Haugen, Robert A., and Terence C. Langetieg. "An Empirical Test for Synergism in Merger," *Journal of Finance*, 30 (September 1975), 1003–15.

Hearth, D., and J. Zaima. "Voluntary Divestitures and Value," *Financial Management*, 13 (Spring 1984), 10–16.

Heath, Robert A. "Valuation Factors and Techniques in Mergers," *Journal of Law and Economics*, 40 (April 1972), 34–44.

Higgins, Robert C., and Lawrence D. Schali. "Corporate Bankruptcy and Conglomerate Merger," *Journal of Finance*, 30 (March 1975), 93–115.

Hite, G., and J. Owers. "Sale Divestitures: Implications for Buyers and Sellers," unpublished manuscript, Southern Methodist University, Dallas, TX, 1984.

Joehnk, Michael D., and James F. Nielsen. "The Effects of Conglomerate Merger Activity on Systematic Risk," *Journal of Financial and Quantitative Analysis*, 9 (March 1974), 215–27.

Kim, E. Han, and John J. McConnell. "Corporate Merger and the Co-insurance of Corporate Debt," *Journal of Finance*, 32 (May 1977), 349–66.

Lee, Li Way. "Co-Insurance and Conglomerate Merger," *Journal of Finance*, 32 (December 1977), 1527–39.

Lewellen, Wilbur G. "A Pure Financial Rationale for the Conglomerate Merger," *Journal of Finance*, 26 (May 1971), 521–37.

Melicher, Ronald W., and David F. Rush. "Evidence of the Acquisition-Related Performance of Conglomerate Firms," *Journal of Finance*, 29 (March 1974), 141–49.

Schipper, K., and A. Smith. "Effects of Recontracting on Shareholder Wealth: The Case of Voluntary Spin-offs," *Journal of Financial Economics*, 12 (1983), 437–67.

Scott, James H., Jr. "On the Theory of Conglomerate Mergers," *Journal of Finance*, 32 (September 1977), 1235–51.

Schick, Richard A., and F. C. Jen. "Merger Benefits to Shareholders of Acquiring Firms," *Financial Management*, 3 (Winter 1974), 45–53.

Wansley, James W., William R. Lane, and Ho C. Yang. "Abnormal Returns to Acquired Firms by Type of Acquisition and Method of Payment," *Financial Management*, 12 (Autumn 1983), 16–22.

———, Rodney L. Roenfeldt, and Philip L. Cooley. "Abnormal Returns from Merger Profiles," *Journal of Financial and Quantitative Analysis*, 18 (June 1983), 149–62.

Weston, J. Fred, Keith V. Smith, and Ronald E. Shrieves. "Conglomerate Performance Using the Capital Asset Pricing Model," *Review of Economics and Statistics*, November 1972, 357–63.

22

Failure and Reorganization

Decline and embarrassment—hardly topics we like to discuss, especially when we are personally involved. The authors of this text, along with those of all other corporate finance texts, much prefer to address growth and success. In ancient Greece, people frequently blamed their failures on the whims of the gods. In our own age, failure is for many a crushing disgrace, which probably contributes to our tendency to avoid the subject, and even worse, to hold on to a bad idea beyond the point of rationality. But despite our aversion to the subject, we can learn from failure, both from personal experience and from observing others who fail. The learning process may help us avoid losses and being unable to pay financial obligations as they come due. More than likely, a financial manager will eventually be called upon to work with a customer who is having severe financial problems. So managers must be aware of the issues associated with failure in business.

In this chapter, we have several objectives

1. Explain the general terms of business failure
2. Identify frequent causes of company failures
3. Identify the financial characteristics that generally develop within a firm facing possible bankruptcy
4. Explain the procedural aspects for reorganizing or liquidating a business

WHAT FAILURE IS

The term *failure* is used in a variety of contexts. **Economic failure** suggests that the company's costs exceed its revenues. Stated differently, the internal rates of return on investments are less than the firm's cost of capital. *Insolvency* also is frequently used to specify serious financial problems. A firm is **technically insolvent** when it can no longer honor its financial obligations. Although the book value of assets may exceed total liabilities, indicating a positive net worth, the company simply does not have sufficient liquidity to pay its debts. This condition may be temporary or irreversible. Another term used is **insolvency in bankruptcy.** Here the company's liabilities are actually greater than the fair valuation of its assets, which means a negative net worth. Regardless of the liquidity of its assets, the company is completely and unquestionably unable to meet maturing obligations. This situation generally indicates that liquidation rather than a reorganization of the firm is necessary.

WHO FAILS?

During 1985, over 57,000 firms went belly up, the highest number in U.S. history, far surpassing the turbulent years of the Great Depression.[1] Even when stated on a relative basis, the number of failures relative to the total number of U.S. firms in existence in 1985 still competes with the troubled years of the Great Depression—115 firms failed per 10,000 companies in 1985, compared with about 130 failures annually per 10,000 businesses for each year from 1930 through 1932. In a year when we heard of large numbers of successes, 1985 clearly did not treat everyone alike.

A profile of the firms experiencing failure is presented in Figure 22–1, showing the industry, age, and size of the failed companies. The industries most prone to failure include business services, agriculture, and mining (energy). The services industry has long had a tendency to encounter failure. Both the agricultural and mining or energy industries have also experienced significant problems during the past two years, with little hope of any real improvement within the next two years, if even then.

In terms of age, we would naturally expect the majority of firms that fail to be relatively young and, consequently, small. Experience certainly verifies our intuition, in that over 50 percent of the companies that failed had been in existence for 5 years or less. Equally significant, 80 percent of all failures happened within the first 10 years of a firm's life. As we would also expect, small firms account for the preponderance of failures, with 64 percent of the failures being firms with less than $100,000 in liabilities, and 94 percent with liabilities of $1 million or less, still a small firm in today's world. Thus, business failures are predominantly characteristic of young and small companies. Bankruptcy, however, is not restricted to small companies. Table 22–1 lists the 10 largest bankruptcies in the United States, all of which occurred during the 1970–80 era.

Although the probability is much less, large corporations are subject to failure. In fact, the failure statistics do not include large corporations that for all practical purposes failed but were either merged into another company or received governmental assistance. For example, the collapse of Douglas Aircraft was avoided only by a merger with McDonnell. Chrysler and Lockheed would have failed if the federal government had not provided aid. Thus, while small companies have a much greater chance of failure relative to large corporations, the issue is real for both.

---

[1] Dun & Bradstreet, Inc., *The 1985 Dun & Bradstreet Business Failure Record* (New York, 1986).

FIGURE 22–1. Business Failure Profile *Source:* **Dun & Bradstreet, Inc.,** *The 1985 Dun and Bradstreet Failure Record* **(New York, 1986).**

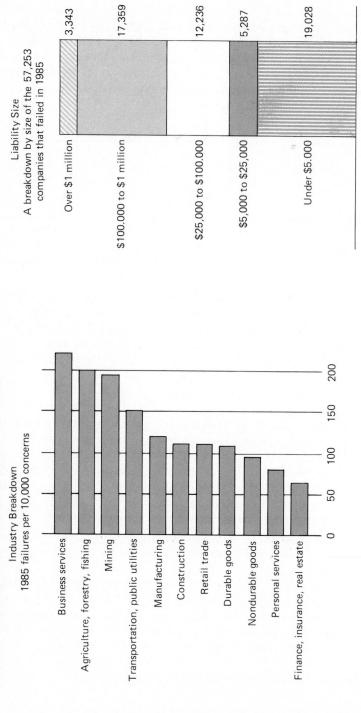

Industry Breakdown
1985 failures per 10,000 concerns

Liability Size
A breakdown by size of the 57,253
companies that failed in 1985

Years in Business
Age of companies that failed in 1985

TABLE 22–1. The Largest U.S. Bankruptcies

	Total Liabilities ($ millions)	Bankruptcy Petition Date
Penn Central Transportation Co.	$3,300	June 1970
W. T. Grant Co.	1,000	October 1975
Continental Mortgage Investors	607	March 1976
United Merchants & Manufacturing	552	July 1977
Commonwealth Oil Refining Co.	421	March 1978
W. Judd Kassuba	420	December 1973
Erie Lackawanna Railroad	404	June 1972
White Motor Corp.	399	September 1980
Investors Funding Corp.	379	October 1974
Food Fair Corp.	347	October 1978

Source: Edward Altman, *Financial Handbook*, 5th ed. (New York: Wiley, 1981), pp. 34–35.

FREQUENT CAUSES OF FAILURE

Although causes of business failure vary from firm to firm, we can identify several common ones. The predominant cause of failure is managerial incompetence. Also, the following key structural problems within management may appear:[2]

1. An imbalance of skills within the top echelon. A manager tends to attract other managers of similar skills. For example, the corporate management may consist principally of individuals having a background in sales, without anyone having production experience.
2. A chief executive who dominates a firm's operations without regard for the advice of peers.
3. An inactive or ill-informed board of directors. For instance, the board of directors for Penn Central, even including the members who were bankers, supposedly did not become aware of the firm's impending financial disaster until a few weeks before its declaration of insolvency.
4. A deficient finance function within the firm's management. Not infrequently, the only substantial input provided by the financial officer occurs when the budget is submitted to the board. A company may have an effective financial information system; however, this information is of no avail if it does not flow to the board through a strong financial officer.
5. The absence of responsibility for the chief executive officer. Although all other managers with a company are responsible to a superior, the chief executive seldom must account for his actions. Conceptually, this person is responsible to the stockholders. However, with the increased separation of management and stockholders, this link is tenuous or even lacking altogether.

The deficiencies render the firm vulnerable to several mistakes. First, management may be negligent in developing effective accounting systems. Second, the company may be unresponsive to change—unable to adjust to a general recession and unfavorable industry developments. Third, management may be inclined to undertake an investment

---

[2] John Argenti, *Corporate Collapse: The Causes and Symptoms* (New York: Wiley, 1976), pp. 123–26.

TABLE 22–2. Causes of Business Failures in 1985

	Manufacturers	Wholesalers	Retailers	Construction	All-firm Total
Neglect	2.0%	2.9%	3.3%	2.9%	2.7%
Disaster	0.9	0.8	1.0	0.6	0.6
Fraud	0.5	1.0	0.3	0.4	0.5
Economic factors	62.6	65.0	64.9	68.0	66.3
Lack of experience	22.0	20.1	23.8	21.3	22.8
Sales problems	13.5	12.8	16.6	13.2	14.1
Expense problems	7.7	6.9	7.3	6.8	8.3
Customer problems	2.2	2.4	1.3	2.6	1.7
Excessive assets	0.6	0.6	0.8	0.9	0.8
Capital problems	1.2	1.1	1.2	1.2	1.0
Total	100.0%	100.0%	100.0%	100.0%	100.0%

Source: Dun & Bradstreet, Inc., *The 1985 Dun & Bradstreet Business Failure Record* (New York), p. 12.

that is disproportionately large relative to firm size. If the project fails, the probability of insolvency is greatly increased. Finally, management may come to rely so heavily on debt financing that even a minor problem can place the firm in a dangerous position.

Dun & Bradstreet, Inc., each year samples a large number of companies that have experienced failure.[3] The reasons given for these business casualties are shown in Table 22–2. Clearly, the primary causes relate to economic factors beyond management's control and management's ineptness.

SYMPTOMS OF BANKRUPTCY

As a company enters the final stages prior to failure, a pattern may develop in terms of a changing financial profile. Although bankruptcy or insolvency cannot be predicted with certainty, several financial ratios have proven to be useful indicators of impending disaster. A study by Altman[4] developed a statistical model that found the financial ratios best predicting bankruptcy. Based upon Altman's sample of bankrupt firms, the study yielded an equation that used five ratios to predict bankruptcy:

$$\text{bankruptcy score} = 1.2X_1 + 1.4X_2 + 3.3X_3 + .6X_4 + .999X_5$$

where $X_1 = (\text{net working capital} \div \text{total assets})$

$X_2 = (\text{retained earnings} \div \text{total assets})$

$X_3 = (\text{earnings before interest and taxes} \div \text{total assets})$

$X_4 = (\text{total market value of stock} \div \text{book value of total debt})$

$X_5 = (\text{sales} \div \text{total assets})$

---

[3] Dun & Bradstreet, Inc., *The 1985 Dun & Bradstreet Business Failure Record* (New York, 1986), p. 18.
[4] Edward L. Altman, *Corporate Bankruptcy in America* (Lexington, MA: Heath Lexington Books, 1971).

With this equation, the criterion for separating firms with a strong likelihood of bankruptcy from those that probably will not fail should be as follows. If the score exceeds 2.99, no concern should exist that the company is facing bankruptcy in the foreseeable future. On the other hand, a score less than 1.81 suggests that the firm is a likely candidate for failure. Values between 1.81 and 2.99 are difficult to assign to either a "successful" or a "failure" classification. However, although a firm in this "gray area" can easily be misclassified in terms of the final outcome, the best way to set up a dividing line is to predict that a company will fail if its score is less than 2.675. Alternatively, a score exceeding 2.675 may be used as an indicator that success is more likely than failure. These guidelines are shown in Table 22–3.

We may conclude that a potentially failing corporation begins to invest less in current assets (X_1). Since X_2 is a cumulative indicator of profitability relative to time, the findings suggest that younger companies have a greater chance of bankruptcy. Variable X_3 reflects the firm's general earnings power. Deterioration in this factor was shown to be the best single indicator that bankruptcy may be forthcoming. Variable X_4 depicts the firm's financial leverage position. Finally, X_5, the asset turnover ratio, measures management's ability to generate sales from the firm's assets.

Although the financial information flowing from a firm helps us identify problems, the predictions we make with it certainly are not perfect. Owing to factors unique to the firm, as well as to the tendency for managements of problem firms to do some "window dressing" of the financial statements, the ratios will not always effectively identify corporations that face bankruptcy within the near future. Even so, they will help us assess the likelihood of bankruptcy.

When a firm faces severe problems, either the problems must be resolved or the firm must be liquidated. At such a point, an important question has to be answered: Is the firm worth more dead or alive? A decision to continue operating has to be based upon the feasibility and fairness of reorganizing the firm as opposed to the benefits of liquidating the business. As shown in Figure 22–2, when technical insolvency occurs, management must either modify the operating and financial conditions or terminate the firm's life. If the decision is made to alter the company in the hopes of revitalizing its operations, either voluntary agreements with the investors or a formal court-arranged reorganization must be used. If, on the other hand, the difficulties are believed to be insurmountable, a liquidation will take place, either by assignment of the assets to an independent party for liquidation or by formal bankruptcy proceedings.

TABLE 22–3. Altman's Bankruptcy Criterion

	Bankruptcy Score	
Less than 1.81	*Between 1.81 and 2.99*	*Greater than 2.99*
Probability of failure is high	Probability of failure is difficult to determine	Probability of failure is remote
Predict failure	Less than 2.675—predict failure Greater than 2.675—predict success	Predict success

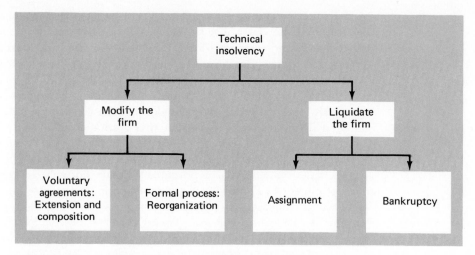

FIGURE 22–2.   Reorganization versus Liquidation

VOLUNTARY REMEDIES TO INSOLVENCY

If a company finds itself in financial distress, management may need to seek a remedy that is acceptable to the creditors. If the evidence suggests that the company's going-concern value is greater than its liquidation value, management may attempt to arrange for a voluntary reorganization. These arrangements may allow the firm an extension of time to pay the debts, or even reduce the amount ultimately to be paid.

Prerequisites
Voluntary remedies avoid the necessity of a court settlement. However, any creditor who refuses to participate may legally prohibit the arrangement for the remaining creditors. Such action may result in a smaller settlement if the courts become involved; thus, general agreement by the creditors is the key to the success of a voluntary remedy. Whether a reasonable chance exists for the creditors to finalize such a plan is based upon (1) the debtor's proven honesty and integrity, (2) the firm's potential for recovery, and (3) the economic prospects for the industry.

Procedure
Most frequently, the debtor confers with the creditors to explain the firm's financial condition and to request that they consider developing a plan that would be beneficial to all parties involved. This meeting is generally planned under the guidance of an adjustment bureau associated with a local credit association or a trade association. The creditors appoint a committee to represent both the large and small claimants. If the committee decides a feasible plan can be developed, the committee, in conjunction with the firm and the adjustment bureau, constructs an agreement. Typically, this voluntary agreement may be classified as an extension, a composition, or some combination thereof.

Extension
An **extension** requires that the debtor pay the amount owed in full. However, an extension in time is provided. For instance, the agreement may stipulate that all new purchases are to be made on a cash basis, with the outstanding balance from

prior purchases to be paid over an extended period. Also, the contract may place the existing debt in subordination to new liabilities during the extension period. Clearly, the creditors must have confidence in the company's management and in the economic conditions affecting the firm; otherwise they would not agree to such concessions.

Although the creditors' basis for an extension is largely a function of their trust in the present management, several control mechanisms may be used during this period of uncertainty. For example, the plan may prohibit any dividend payments to the stockholders until the firm is financially sound again. In fact, the stockholders may have to place their shares in escrow with the creditors' committee. Also, the agreement may require that the firm's assets be assigned to the creditors' committee for the duration of the extension period. Finally, a requirement may be incorporated into the contract stipulating that a member of the creditors' committee countersign checks.

Composition A **composition** permits the debtor to pay less than the full balance owed the creditors. In other words, the creditors receive a pro rata share of their claims. The amount received is to represent final settlement of the indebtedness. The creditors' reason for agreeing to a partial payment is that the only remaining option is bankruptcy proceedings, the costs of which can quickly deplete the firm's resources. Negotiations between debtor and creditors hinge on the savings that may be expected by avoiding the legal costs associated with bankruptcy. Also, the debtor is benefited by avoiding the stigma attached to bankruptcy.

Evaluation of Voluntary Remedies The primary advantages of voluntary remedies relate to the minimization of costs and the informality of the process. A significant amount of legal, investigative, and administrative expenses may be avoided, resulting in a higher return to the creditors. Also, the bargaining process is greatly simplified, and a more congenial atmosphere typically prevails than in the bankruptcy courts.

One of the difficulties in arranging a voluntary remedy is that a creditor may refuse to participate. To encourage participation and cooperation of the firm's creditors, a composition generally allows for the payment in full of small claims. For instance, the terms of the agreement may state that all creditors are to receive $50 plus a pro rata share of the remaining claim. This provision eliminates the small claims. However, it means that the larger creditors partially underwrite the amounts payable to small creditors.

Another disadvantage, particularly for the extension, is that the debtor maintains control of the business. If the underlying problems confronting the business are not corrected, the company's assets may continue to erode in value, which clearly works to the detriment of the creditors. However, as already explained, controls may be initiated to minimize any potential losses due to continued inefficient management.

REORGANIZATION

If a voluntary remedy, such as an extension or composition, is not workable, a company can declare or be forced by its creditors into bankruptcy. As a part of this process, the firm is either reorganized or dissolved. Reorganization under the Bankruptcy Act is similar to an extension or composition, the objective being to revitalize the firm by changing its operating procedures and the capital structure; however, the procedure is more formal and it is administered by the bankruptcy courts. Chapter 11 of the Bankruptcy Act provides the guidelines for an orderly reorganization of a business.

The Petition to Reorganize

Under Chapter 11, a case is initiated by filing a petition with the bankruptcy courts. The petition may be filed by the firm's management (voluntary) or by its creditors (involuntary). To initiate an involuntary reorganization, it is necessary for the creditors to show that the debtor company is generally not paying its debts as they come due. When the debtor has more than 12 creditors, the law requires that the petition be filed by at least 3 creditors with claims totaling $5000 or more. If there are fewer than 12 creditors, the petition must be filed by 2 creditors or a single creditor who is owed at least $5000.

When a petition is filed, either voluntary or involuntary, a committee of unsecured creditors—usually the seven creditors with the largest claims—is appointed by the court to work with the court in reorganizing the company's operations and possibly restructuring its financial mix. The plan must be approved by a majority of the creditors holding at least two-thirds of the dollar claims. Under Chapter 11 the debtor continues to operate the business unless a reason exists for a trustee to be given managerial control. Reasons include fraud, dishonesty, incompetence, or gross mismanagement.

Prior to recent changes in the law, the Securities and Exchange Commission played a significant role in the bankruptcy process. Although it did not possess any decision-making authority, the SEC was charged with rendering a critical evaluation of the reorganization plan, including an opinion as to the fairness and feasibility of the plan. When there was a difference between the trustee's plan and that of the SEC, the latter usually suggested alternative guidelines. In short, the SEC was a force to be recognized. Today the role of the SEC as the public's representative has diminished significantly. For example, it no longer makes petitions to the courts to change a plan of reorganization. Excluding the SEC was designed to add expediency to the reorganization process.

The Reorganization Decision

In the reorganization process, the trustee has to establish the going-concern value for the debtor's business after the reorganization. This procedure requires an estimation of the company's future earnings. With this projection in hand, a capitalization rate (or equivalently a price/earnings ratio) for a similar but prosperous firm is determined. When this rate is applied to the earnings, a going-concern value may be approximated. For example, assume that a corporation may reasonably expect to make $1 million in annual earnings after the reorganization. If the price/earnings multiple for a comparable firm is 8, the going-concern value is $8 million ($1 million earnings × 8 price/earnings).

After a going-concern value has been estimated, the trustee devises a reorganization plan, including a way of reformulating the capital structure to meet the criteria of fairness and feasibility. In developing this recommendation, the trustee evaluates what changes are necessary to place the company in a more profitable posture. Also, in revamping the capital structure, concern is given to the firm's ability to cover the financial fixed charges: interest, principal repayments, and preferred dividends.

If the facts indicate that a reorganization is fair and feasible to the respective creditors and the stockholders, new securities are issued to reflect the revised capital structure.

The principal guideline in this procedure has generally been the **rule of absolute priority,** which simply indicates that the company must completely honor senior claims on assets before settling junior claims. However, plans are frequently based on a blend of *absolute* and *relative* priorities, where a junior claim receives partial payment even though a senior claim has not been paid in its entirety. Such a compromise is at times necessary in order to satisfy small creditors who might otherwise vote against a proposed plan.

Example To illustrate the priorities that might be used in a reorganization plan, consider the Paine Corporation, which is currently undergoing a reorganization. The firm's balance sheet is presented in Table 22–4. The creditors have filed a petition for reorganization. The court has named a trustee, who is developing a possible plan of organization. Based upon the trustee's evaluation, an internal reorganization is considered to be both fair and feasible to the existing investors. The trustee has projected the company's earnings, and by using an appropriate price/earnings multiple has estimated the firm's going-concern value to be $8 million, as compared with a $6 million liquidation value (the approximate amount that would be received if the business were terminated and the assets sold individually).

TABLE 22–4. Paine Corporation Balance Sheet

Assets	
Current assets	$ 2,000,000
Net plant and equipment	15,500,000
Other assets	1,000,000
Total assets	$18,500,000
Liabilities and equity	
Current liabilities	
Accounts payable	$ 1,000,000
Notes payable	3,000,000
Total current liabilities	$ 4,000,000
Long-term liabilities	
Mortgage bonds (8% due in 1995)	$ 4,000,000
Subordinated debentures (9½% due in 1995)[a]	8,000,000
Total long-term liabilities	$12,000,000
Total liabilities	$16,000,000
Equity	
Common stock (par $5)	500,000
Paid-in capital	14,000,000
Retained earnings	(12,000,000)
Total equity	$ 2,500,000
Total liabilities and equity	$18,500,000

[a] Subordinated to the mortgage bonds.

The proposed plan for reorganizing the company is shown in Table 22–5. The first portion of the table specifies the amounts of the distribution to be made to each group of creditors. Since the going-concern value is $8 million, only 50 percent of the $16 million in debt can be honored. As a result, the common stockholders will not be entitled

TABLE 22–5. Paine Corporation Reorganization Plan

Creditors	Amount of Claim	50 Percent of Claim	New Claim after Subordination
Accounts payable	$ 1,000,000	$ 500,000	$ 500,000
Notes payable	3,000,000	1,500,000	1,500,000
Mortgage bonds	4,000,000	2,000,000	4,000,000
Subordinated debentures[a]	8,000,000	4,000,000	2,000,000
	$16,000,000	$8,000,000	$8,000,000

[a] Subordinated to the mortgage bonds.

to any of the distribution. Also, the subordinated debentures are not to participate in the reorganization until the mortgage bondholders have been repaid in full. Consequently, the $4 million in securities that would have been distributed to the owners of the debentures has to be reduced by $2 million. The final distribution, after recognizing the subordination, is shown in the last column of Table 22–5.

New Securities Issued in the Reorganization

Old Security	New Securities	
Accounts payable	Accounts payable	$ 250,000
	Common stock	250,000
Notes payable	Preferred stock	750,000
	Common stock	750,000
Mortgage bonds	Mortgage bonds (8%)	2,000,000
	Subordinated debentures (9½%)	1,000,000
	Preferred stock (10%)	1,000,000
Subordinated debentures	Common stock	2,000,000
		$8,000,000

The lower section of Table 22–5 reflects the trustee's proposed changes in the firm's capital structure. The objective is to reduce the financial leverage to a point commensurate with the company's ability to cover the fixed financial charges from earnings. For example, the original accounts payable balance is reduced to $500,000, with these creditors having a short-term claim of $250,000 and receiving $250,000 in new common stock. The final capital structure, if the trustee's plan is adopted, is provided in Table 22–6.

TABLE 22–6. Paine Corporation Liabilities and Equity after Reorganization

Accounts payable	$ 250,000
Mortgage bonds (8%)	2,000,000
Subordinated debentures (9½%)	1,000,000
Preferred stock (10%)	1,750,000
Common stock	3,000,000
	$8,000,000

The Penn Central Reorganization

As an illustration of an actual reorganization, we will briefly look at the failure and impending reorganization of the Penn Central Transportation Company. For a number of years the company had encountered serious difficulties; however, not until several weeks before the request for bankruptcy did the severity of the problems emerge. The cash drain from railroad operations resulted in Penn Central's having to borrow heavily on a short-term basis. When it was unable to refinance these short-term liabilities, the firm collapsed and filed a petition of bankruptcy on June 21, 1970. At that time Penn Central had more than $5 billion in liabilities outstanding. By 1978 the reorganization plan for revitalizing the firm had been 8 years in the making, with heavy assistance by the federal government through loans and guarantees. The plan, which was approved with minor exceptions by the court on March 9, 1978, is shown in Table 22–7. Liabilities to the federal government are to be partially paid, with the remaining amounts deferred until a later date. State and local governments are given a choice between a reduced payment in cash or a full settlement in the form of notes. Small unsecured creditors are to be paid in full. Large unsecured creditors are to receive a mixture of common stock and certificates of beneficial interest. The **certificate of beneficial interest** entitles the holder to receive cash only if any money remains after other claims have been paid. The secured creditors are to receive a mixture of cash, bonds, preferred stock, and common stock.

To make the company profitable, the trustees see three primary steps as essential. First, the firm's subsidiary, the Pennsylvania Company, is to be charged with the company's operational aspects, including future acquisitions. Second, over $1 billion in assets, particularly in real estate and rail operations, are to be liquidated. Finally, the trustees view a lawsuit as necessary in recovering fair compensation for the railroad

TABLE 22–7. The Penn Central Reorganization

Claims to Be Resolved

Federal government's claims ($500 million) would be paid in cash and secured notes. State and local governments ($385 million) would be offered either 50% of their claims in cash or 100% in secured notes. Small unsecured claimants would be paid in full.

Secured creditors ($1.8 billion) would be paid as follows:

> 10% of the face amount (principal and interest) of their claims in cash,
>
> 30% in general mortgage bonds,
>
> 30% in preferred stock, and
>
> 30% in common stock.

Unsecured creditors ($521 million) would be paid 30% of their claims in certificates of beneficial interest, the rest in common stock.

Common stockholders: Penn Central Co. would be given 10% of the reorganized company's 25 million shares.

Plan of Action for Correcting Problems

I. *Dispose of property*. Sell over $1 billion worth of property, including real estate, coal properties, the Pittsburgh & Lake Erie Railroad and other remaining rail facilities.

II. *Run ongoing operations*. Pennsylvania Co., a subsidiary, will generate earnings and make acquisitions. The subsidiary currently includes Buckeye Pipe Line, Edgington Oil, Arvida Corp., and Great Southwest Corp.

III. *Prosecute a lawsuit*. Sue the U.S. government for just compensation for the rail properties Conrail acquired. Proceeds could be anywhere from $525 million to several billions of dollars.

Source: Forbes, May 1, 1977, p. 53.

operations that the federal government required the firm to sell to Conrail. The trustees maintain that the government grossly undervalued the property.

LIQUIDATION

If the likelihood is small that reorganization of an insolvent firm will result in a profitable business, the firm should be dissolved. In this situation the liquidation value exceeds the going-concern value, and it is to the investor's advantage to terminate the business. Continuing the operation at this point generally results only in further losses. Complete termination of the company can be accomplished through assignment or by declaring bankruptcy. The objective of either procedure is to distribute any proceeds from the liquidation to the creditors.

Liquidation by Assignment

If an **assignment** is used to liquidate the business, the final settlement is done privately with a minimum amount of court involvement. The debtor transfers title of the firm's assets to a third party, who has been appointed by the creditors or by the court. This individual, known as an **assignee** or **trustee**, administers the liquidation process and sees that an appropriate distribution is made of the proceeds. Under an assignment, the debtor is not automatically discharged of the remaining balance due a creditor. When the liquidation funds are distributed to the creditors, a notation on the checks should be made indicating that endorsement of the check represents the creditor's acceptance of the money as full settlement of the claim. However, even then a creditor can refuse to accept the payment, considering that his interests would be better served by a court-administered liquidation.

Owing to the possible nonacceptance of the assignment by one or more creditors, the debtor may attempt to reach a prior agreement with the creditors that the assignment will represent a complete settlement of claims. If the agreement is made, a creditors' committee will usually recommend that the debtor be released from all claims after final execution of the assignment.

An assignment has several advantages over a formal bankruptcy procedure. The assignment is usually quicker, is less expensive, and requires less legal formality. The assignee is provided greater discretion and flexibility than a court-appointed trustee in bankruptcy in liquidating the assets. He can take quicker action to avoid further depletion in the value of inventories and equipment, and typically he is more familiar with the debtor's business, which should improve the final results. However, the assignment does not legally discharge the debtor from the responsibility of unpaid balances, and the creditor is not protected against fraud; consequently, formal bankruptcy proceedings may be preferred by either the debtor or creditors.

Liquidation by Bankruptcy

The Liquidation Process

A petition for a company to be declared bankrupt may be filed in the bankruptcy courts. Subject to the provisions in Chapter 7 of the Bankruptcy Act, the petition can be initiated either by the debtor (voluntary) or by the creditors (involuntary). A voluntary declaration of bankruptcy by the debtor is usually taken when management considers further delays as being detrimental to the stockholders' position. The rules for creditors wishing to initiate an involuntary bankruptcy are the same as those given for an involuntary reorganization. The creditors must show that the debtor is not paying liabilities on a timely basis. Also, if more than 12 creditors exist, at least

3 creditors must sign the petition for bankruptcy. For firms with fewer than 12 creditors, only 2 creditors must petition, or only one creditor if at least $5000 is owed the petitioning creditor.

After the filing and approval of the bankruptcy petition, the court adjudges the debtor bankrupt and names a **referee in bankruptcy.** In turn, the referee may appoint a **receiver** to serve as interim caretaker of the company's assets until a trustee can be designated by the creditors. The referee then requests from the debtor a list of assets and liabilities.

A meeting of the creditors is called by the referee. At the meeting, a trustee is elected by the creditors, and a creditors' committee is appointed. Also, the debtor may be questioned for additional information relevant to the proceedings.

The trustee and the creditors' committee initiate plans to liquidate the company's assets. As a part of this conversion process, individuals owing money to the debtor are contacted in an effort to collect these outstanding balances. Appraisers are selected to determine a value for the property, and these values are used as guidelines in liquidating assets. Specifically, the trustee may not sell an asset at less than 75 percent of its appraised value, without the approval of the court. After all assets have been converted into cash through private sales or public auctions, all expenses incurred in the bankruptcy process are paid. The remaining cash is distributed on a pro rata basis to the creditors. The trustee provides a final accounting to the creditors and the referee. The bankruptcy filing is then discharged, and the debtor is relieved of all responsibility for prior debts.

Priority of Claims

Following the rule of absolute priority, claims are honored in the following order:

1. Secured creditors, with the proceeds from the sale of the specific property going first to these creditors. If any portion of the claim remains unpaid, the balance is treated as an unsecured loan.
2. Expenses incurred in administering the bankrupt estate.
3. Expenses incurred after the bankruptcy petition has been filed but prior to a trustee being appointed.
4. Salaries and commissions not exceeding $2000 per employee that were earned within the three months preceding the bankruptcy petition.
5. Federal, state, and local taxes.
6. Unsecured creditors.
7. Preferred stock.
8. Common stock.

An example will illustrate the order of payments from a liquidation. The Poverty Stricken Corporation has been judged bankrupt; its balance sheet is shown in Table 22–8. Although the historical cost of the assets was $100 million, the trustee in bankruptcy was able to realize only $44 million from their sale. In addition, costs of $8 million were incurred in administering the bankruptcy.

The order of settling the claims is listed in Table 22–9. As the table shows, the first mortgage bondholders are entitled to receive the net proceeds resulting from the sale of specific property identified in the lien (an office building). We are assuming that the sale price of this property is $10 million, which leaves an unpaid balance of $4 million to be treated as an unsecured claim. Next, the administrative costs associated

TABLE 22–8. Poverty Stricken Corporation Balance Sheet (000)

Assets		
Current assets		$ 20,000
Net plant and equipment		80,000
Total assets		$100,000
Liabilities		
Current liabilities		
Accounts payable	$22,000	
Accrued wages[a]	600	
Notes payable	20,000	
Federal taxes	2,500	
State taxes	500	
Total current liabilities		$45,600
Long-term liabilities		
First mortgage bonds[b]	$14,000	
Subordinated debentures[c]	10,000	
Total long-term liabilities	24,000	
Total liabilities		69,600
Equity		
Preferred stock	$ 4,000	
Common stock	26,400	
Total equity		30,400
Total liabilities and equity		$100,000

[a] No single claim exceeds $2000.

[b] These bonds have a first lien on an office building.

[c] Subordinated to the notes payable.

with filing and executing the bankruptcy petition, the employees' salaries, and the tax liabilities are to be paid.

After all payments have been made for prior claims, $22,400,000 is available for general unsecured creditors, whose claims total $56 million; dividing 22.4 by 56, we find that the claimants are entitled to 40 percent of the original loan. This percentage is computed from the amount available for general creditors, $22,400,000, relative to the total claims of $56 million. However, an adjustment must be made to recognize

TABLE 22–9. Poverty Stricken Corporation Priority of Claims (000)

Distribution of Proceeds		
Liquidation value of assets		$44,000
Priority of claims:		
1. First mortgage receipts from the sale of an office building	$10,000	
2. Administrative expenses	8,000	
3. Salaries due employees	600	
4. Taxes	3,000	
Total prior claims		21,600
Amount available for settling claims of general creditors		$22,400

TABLE 22–10. Poverty Stricken Corporation Claims of General Creditors

General Claims	Claim	40% of Claims	Adjustment for Subordination
Accounts payable	$22,000,000	$ 8,800,000	$ 8,800,000
Notes payable	20,000,000	8,000,000	12,000,000
Remaining portion of first mortgage bond	4,000,000	1,600,000	1,600,000
Subordinated debenture	10,000,000	4,000,000	–0–
Totals	$56,000,000	$22,400,000	$22,400,000

the subordination of the debentures to the notes payable. In essence, the owners of debentures must relinquish their right to any money until the notes payable have been settled in full. In this situation, $12 million of the note balance remains unpaid. As a consequence, the $4 million originally shown to be received by the debentures must be paid to the investors owning the note payable. The actual distributions to the unsecured creditors are shown in the last column of Table 22–10.

Summary

Facing financial adversity is never easy. For this reason, management should be aware of the implications and consequences of financial embarrassment. This information may prove useful if reorganization or liquidation is required for the firm or if similar action becomes necessary for one of the firm's customers.

Business failure is principally the result of incompetent management. In a related sense, a deficiency in the management structure, such as an imbalance of skills, may pose serious problems. The symptoms of these weaknesses are often readily identifiable in the firm's financial statements. The company will generally decrease its investment in liquid assets, while profitability declines. Also, the use of financial leverage increases significantly. Finally, management's efficient use of assets, as depicted by the asset turnover ratio, may deteriorate.

When a business becomes technically insolvent, one of two choices must be accepted. The firm has to be reorganized or liquidated. In either case, the process may be relatively informal or closely controlled by the court. In the reorganization of a firm, voluntary agreements may be arranged, taking the form of either an extension or a composition. If, however, these plans are not acceptable to the creditors, a court-administered reorganization may be necessary. If the company's liquidation value is thought to exceed its going-concern value, the firm should be dissolved.

If liquidation is required, the assets may be assigned to a third party for the purpose of selling them and distributing the funds according to the rule of absolute priority. Such an assignment aims to avoid the more costly court-ordered bankruptcy filing. Yet, if the debtor or creditors consider formal bankruptcy proceedings preferable, voluntary or involuntary bankruptcy may be requested. If the debtor is judged to be bankrupt, a referee is selected to liquidate the firm's assets and distribute the proceeds in accordance with the rule of absolute priority.

Study Questions

22–1. Explain the following terms: economic failure, technical insolvency, and insolvency in bankruptcy.

22–2. What are the most frequent causes of business failure?

22–3. To what potential mistakes is a firm vulnerable if it is experiencing any of the deficiencies cited in question 22–2?

22–4. What are the prerequisites to a successful voluntary remedy?

22–5. What procedure is usually followed in arranging a voluntary agreement?

22–6. Compare an extension with a composition.

22–7. What are the advantages and disadvantages of voluntary remedies?

22–8. Explain the process of liquidation by assignment.

Self-Test Problems

ST–1. (*Predicting Bankruptcy*) You are studying five companies and have decided to use Altman's model to predict the probability of bankruptcy for each. The data needed are given below. What are the bankruptcy scores for these companies and how are they interpreted?

			Variables		
Company	X_1	X_2	X_3	X_4	X_5
A	15%	20%	35%	335%	1.60×
B	25	45	40	175	1.95×
C	20	25	15	125	.75×
D	15	12	10	110	.55×
E	40	35	30	175	1.50×

ST–2. (*Reorganization*) Brogham, Inc., is filing for bankruptcy. The trustee has estimated the firm's liquidation value to be $1,260,000. Given the liabilities and equity from the balance sheet, compute the distributions of proceeds.

Brogham, Inc.

Liabilities and equity	
Current liabilities	
Accounts payable	$ 120,000
Notes payable	300,000
Total current liabilities	$ 420,000
Long-term liabilities	
Long-term notes payable	$ 420,000
Subordinated debentures[a]	1,260,000
Total long-term liabilities	$1,680,000
Total liabilities	$2,100,000
Equity	
Common stock (par $10)	$ 500,000
Paid-in capital	2,000,000
Total equity	$2,500,000
Total liabilities and equity	$4,600,000

[a] Subordinated to the long-term notes payable.

ST–3. (*Distribution of Proceeds in Bankruptcy*) Pioneer Enterprises is bankrupt and being liquidated. The liabilities and equity portion of its balance sheet is given below. The book value of the assets was $60 million, but the realized value when liquidated was only $31.58 million, of which $7.55 million was from the sale of the firm's office building. Administrative expenses associated with the liquidation were $4.8 million. Determine the distribution of the proceeds.

Pioneer Enterprises Liabilities and Equities

Current liabilities		
Accounts payable	$ 6,500,000	
Accrued wages[a]	400,000	
Notes payable	15,000,000	
Federal taxes	3,000,000	
State taxes	1,250,000	
Total current liabilities		$26,150,000
Long-term debt		
First mortgage bonds[b]	$14,000,000	
Subordinated debentures[c]	8,500,000	
Total long-term debt		22,500,000
Equity		
Preferred stock	$ 2,350,000	
Common stock	9,000,000	
Total equity		11,350,000
Total liabilities and equity		$60,000,000

[a] No single claim exceeds $2000.
[b] Have first lien on an office building.
[c] Subordinated to the first mortgage bonds.

Study Problems

22–1. (*Predicting Bankruptcy*) You are considering investing in the securities of three companies. Using the Altman model and the information given below, compute the bankruptcy score for each company. Which companies would you invest in?

	Company		
	A	B	C
Sales	$1,500,000	$ 800,000	$3,000,000
Total assets	4,000,000	1,000,000	4,500,000
Net working capital	1,100,000	650,000	2,000,000
Earnings before interest and taxes	1,000,000	500,000	1,000,000
Retained earnings	800,000	350,000	1,500,000
Stock market value	1,250,000	500,000	2,200,000
Debt book value	750,000	100,000	1,250,000

22–2. (*Reorganization*) The trustee for the reorganization of Warner Corporation has established the going-concern value at $7.5 million. The creditors and the amounts owed are given below. As part of the reorganization plan, the accounts payable are to be settled by renewal of $500,000 of the accounts, with a due date of six months. Any remaining amount to be received by these claimants is to be realized in the form of long-term notes payable. The current owners of the firm's notes are to be paid in preferred stock. The mortgage bondholders will receive half of their adjusted claim under the reorganization in the form of newly issued bonds, with the remainder being common stock. The investors owning the subordinated debentures are to receive common stock in settlement of their claim. What will Warner's liabilities and equity be after reorganization?

Warner Corporation

Creditors	Amount of Claims
Accounts payable	$ 2,000,000
Notes payable	1,000,000
Mortgage bonds	4,000,000
Subordinated debentures[a]	3,000,000
	$10,000,000

[a] Subordinated to the mortgage bonds.

22–3. (*Reorganization*) Pepertyme, Inc., has filed for voluntary reorganization. The firm's liabilities are shown below. The firm has an estimated going-concern value of $1,825,000 and a liquidation value of $1,400,000. What will Pepertyme's liabilities and equity be after reorganization if the following rules are applied?

a. Accounts payable are to receive 50 percent of their claim in accounts payable due in 30 days and 50 percent in 90-day notes payable.

b. Notes payable are to receive 50 percent of their claim in short-term notes payable and 50 percent in long-term notes payable.

c. Mortgage bondholders will receive half of their claim in new bonds and half in common stock.

d. Subordinated debentures will receive their claim as 50 percent preferred stock and 50 percent common stock.

Pepertyme, Inc.

Creditors	Claims
Accounts payable	$ 650,000
Short-term notes payable	500,000
Mortgage bonds	1,000,000
Subordinated debentures[a]	1,500,000
	$3,650,000

[a] Subordinated to the mortgage bonds.

22–4. (*Distribution of Proceeds in Bankruptcy*) Loggins Industries has filed a bankruptcy petition and is in the process of being liquidated. Its liabilities and equity are shown below. The book value of the assets is $80 million, but the liquidation value is $42 million. Administrative expenses of the liquidation procedures were $2 million. What is the distribution of proceeds?

Loggins Industries Liabilities and Equities

Current debt		
Accounts payable	$10,000,000	
Accrued wages[a]	1,000,000	
Notes payable	17,000,000	
Federal taxes	3,000,000	
State taxes	1,000,000	
Total current debt		$32,000,000
Long-term debt		
Bonds (10-year 8%)	$25,000,000	
Subordinated debentures (7-year 10%)[b]	18,000,000	
Total long-term debt		43,000,000
Equity		
Preferred stock	$ 1,000,000	
Common stock	4,000,000	
Total equity		5,000,000
Total debt and equity		$80,000,000

[a] No single claim exceeds $2000.
[b] Subordinated to notes payable.

22–5. (*Distribution of Proceeds in Bankruptcy*) Heinburner, Inc., a local manufacturing concern, is bankrupt and is being liquidated. The book value of the assets is $1.5 million. When the firm was liquidated, $1.25 million was realized. Administrative costs for the liquidation were $150,000. Determine the distribution of proceeds.

Heinburner, Inc., Liabilities and Equities

Current debt		
Accounts payable	$200,000	
Accrued wages[a]	10,000	
Notes payable	350,000	
State and federal taxes	140,000	
Total current debt		$ 700,000
Long-term debt		300,000
Equity		
Preferred stock	$100,000	
Common stock	400,000	
Total equity		500,000
Total debt and equity		$1,500,000

[a] No single claim exceeds $2000.

Self-Test Solutions

SS–1. Bankruptcy score $= 1.2X_1 + 1.4X_2 + 3.3X_3 + 0.6X_4 + 0.999X_5$

where $X_1 =$ (net working capital $\div$ total assets)

$X_2 =$ (retained earnings $\div$ total assets)

$$X_3 = (\text{earnings before interest and taxes} \div \text{total assets})$$

$$X_4 = (\text{market value of stock} \div \text{book value of debt})$$

$$X_5 = (\text{sales} \div \text{total assets})$$

Company A

$$1.2(.15) + 1.4(.20) + 3.3(.35) + 0.6(3.35) + 0.999(1.60) = 5.22$$

Company B

$$1.2(.25) + 1.4(.45) + 3.3(.40) + 0.6(1.75) + 0.999(1.95) = 5.25$$

Company C

$$1.2(.20) + 1.4(.25) + 3.3(.15) + 0.6(1.25) + 0.999(0.75) = 2.58$$

Company D

$$1.2(.15) + 1.4(.12) + 3.3(.10) + 0.6(1.10) + 0.999(0.55) = 1.88$$

Company E

$$1.2(.40) + 1.4(.35) + 3.3(.30) + 0.6(1.75) + 0.999(1.50) = 4.51$$

Interpretation of results:

Score < 1.81 —Likely candidate for failure

Score > 2.99 —No concern of bankruptcy

1.81 < Score < 2.675—Probability of failure greater than success

2.675 < Score < 2.99 —Probability of success greater than failure

The probability of failure is greater than that of success for companies C and D. Companies A, B, and E need not be concerned with bankruptcy.

SS–2.

Brogham, Inc. Reorganization Plan

Creditors	Amount	60% of Claim	Claim after Subordination
Accounts payable	$ 120,000	$ 72,000	$ 72,000
Notes payable	300,000	180,000	180,000
Mortgage bonds	420,000	252,000	420,000
Subordinated debentures	1,260,000	756,000	588,000
	$2,100,000	$1,260,000	$1,260,000

Percentage of claim = going-concern value ÷ total liabilities

= $1,260,000 ÷ $2,100,000

= 60%

SS–3.

Pioneer Enterprises

Distribution of Proceeds

Liquidation value of assets		$31,580,000
Priority of claims		
1. Administrative expenses	$4,800,000	
2. Wages payable	400,000	
3. Taxes	4,250,000	
4. First mortgage receipts from building sale	7,550,000	
Total prior claims		17,000,000
Amount available to general creditors		$14,580,000

Claims of General Creditors

Creditors	Amount	40% of Claim	Claim after Subordination
Accounts payable	$ 6,500,000	$ 2,600,000	$ 2,600,000
Notes payable	15,000,000	6,000,000	6,000,000
Remainder of first mortgage bonds	6,450,000	2,580,000	5,980,000
Subordinated debentures	8,500,000	3,400,000	–0–
	$36,450,000	$14,580,000	$14,580,000

$$\text{Percentage of claims} = \left(\begin{array}{c} \text{amount available to} \\ \text{general creditors} \end{array} \right) \div \left(\begin{array}{c} \text{amount of} \\ \text{claims} \end{array} \right)$$

$$= \$14,580,000 \div \$36,450,000$$

$$= 40\%$$

Selected References

Altman, Edward I. "Corporate Bankruptcy Potential, Stockholder Returns and Share Valuation," *Journal of Finance*, 24 (December 1969), 887–900.

_____. *Corporate Financial Distress.* New York: John Wiley, 1983.

_____. "A Further Empirical Investigation of the Bankruptcy Cost Question," *Journal of Finance*, 39 (September 1984), 1067–89.

_____, and Menachem Brenner. "Information Effects and Stock Market Response to Signs of Firm Deterioration," *Journal of Financial and Quantitative Analysis*, 16 (March 1981), 35–52.

_____. "Financial Ratios, Discriminant Analysis and the Prediction of Corporate Bankruptcy," *Journal of Finance*, 23 (September 1968), 589–609.

Ang, James S., Jess H. Chua, and John J. McConnell. "The Administrative Costs of Corporate Bankruptcy: A Note," *Journal of Finance*, 37 (March 1982), 219–26.

Argenti, John. *Corporate Collapse: The Causes and Symptoms.* New York: Halsted Press, 1976.

Chen, Kung H., and Thomas A. Shimerda. "An Empirical Analysis of Useful Financial Ratios," *Financial Management*, 10 (Spring 1981), 51–60.

Clark, Truman A., and Mark I. Weinstein. "The Behavior of the Common Stock of Bankrupt Firms," *Journal of Finance*, 38 (May 1983), 489–504.

Edmister, Robert O. "An Empirical Test of Financial Ratio Analysis for Small Business Failure Prediction," *Journal of Financial and Quantitative Analysis*, 7 (March 1972), 1477–93.

Hanna, Mark. "Corporate Bankruptcy Potential, Stockholder Returns and Share Valuation: Comment," *Journal of Finance*, 27 (June 1977), 711–18.

Higgins, Robert C., and Lawrence D. Schall. "Corporate Bankruptcy and Share Conglomerate Merger," *Journal of Finance*, 30 (March 1975), 93–115.

Kalaba, Robert E., Terence C. Langetieg, Nima Rasakhoo, and Mark I. Weinstein. "Estimation of Implicit Bankruptcy Costs," *Journal of Finance*, 39 (July 1984), 629–42.

Moyer, Charles. "Forecasting Financial Failure: A Re-examination," *Financial Management*, 6 (Spring 1977), 11–18.

Scott, James. "The Probability of Bankruptcy," *Journal of Banking and Finance*, 5 (September 1981), 317–44.

Warner, Jerold B. "Bankruptcy Costs: Some Evidence," *Journal of Finance*, 32 (May 1977), 339–49.

White, Michelle J. "Public Policy Toward Bankruptcy: Me-First and Other Priority Rules," *Bell Journal of Economics*, 11 (Autumn 1980), 550–64.

———. "Bankruptcy Costs and the New Bankruptcy Code," *Journal of Finance*, 38 (May 1983), 477–88.

23

International Business Finance

Thus far, we have discussed financial management in the domestic economy of the United States. Many firms conduct business activities in more than one country, and they need to consider additional factors in their foreign operations. Such firms need a thorough understanding of international business finance.

Firms can operate internationally in various ways. In the simplest instance a firm exports to (or imports from) a single foreign country. Other export or import firms operate in many countries simultaneously. For example, banks conduct business in many countries, lending in some currencies and borrowing in others. Many manufacturing companies set up production facilities in foreign countries, to sell abroad or to import their output back to the home country. Output sold abroad, for example, might be that of the subsidiary of an American machine tool manufacturer in the Philippines. Also, it might import the product into the United States.

Some companies have more elaborate international operations. A United States automobile company may have a plant in West Germany for manufacturing engines, another plant in France for drive trains, a third in Belgium for other components, and an assembly plant in Italy. The final product, the automobile, may be destined for all markets in Europe, Asia, and Africa. This is an example of a **multinational corporation (MNC).**

The basic problems facing international companies differ from those facing domestic companies. Examples of additional complexities of conducting international business would include the following:

1. **Multiple currencies.** Revenues may be denominated in one currency, costs in another, assets in a third, liabilities in a fourth, and stock price in a fifth.

Chapter 23 was revised specifically for this book by Raj Aggarwal, John Carroll University.

Thus, maximization of the wealth of the owners must consider changing currency values.

2. **Differing legal and political environments.** There may be international variations in such things as tax laws, depreciation allowances, and other accounting practices, as well as in government regulation and control of business activity. Repatriation of profits may be a problem in certain countries.[1]

3. **Differing economic and capital markets.** The extent of government regulation and control of the economy and capital markets may differ greatly across nations. For example, the ability of a foreign company to raise different types and amounts of capital may be restricted.

4. **Internal control challenge.** It may be difficult to organize, evaluate, and control different divisions of a company when they are separated geographically and when they operate in different environments.

This chapter will highlight the major additional dimension of finance that arises from foreign operations—that of *multiple currencies*. We will show that foreign exchange risk is an additional and major risk to which international businesses are exposed. Effective strategies for the reduction of this risk will be discussed. Working capital management and capital structure decisions in the international context will also be covered. For the international firm, direct foreign investment is a capital budgeting decision—with some additional complexities; we shall consider these complexities and techniques for dealing with them.

THE IMPORTANCE OF INTERNATIONAL BUSINESS

Owing to the growing importance of the multinational firm in the world economy, international business warrants serious study. The United States economy is, by comparison with those of the other developed economies, reasonably self-reliant. The economies of most nations and regions have become more open to international influences and their relative economic importance is shifting. The U.S. economy now has a less dominant position globally, and the newly industrialized countries (NICs), especially those located in the Orient, are making their presence felt in global markets. In addition, the role of international financial markets is becoming more important than the role of any domestic financial market.

Globalization of Product and Financial Markets

Driven by technology and the logic of comparative advantage, world trade has grown much faster over the last few decades than world GNP (gross national product). Global exports and imports were about one-fifth of global GNP in 1962. This figure had increased to about one-fourth by 1972 and to more than one-third by 1982. This remarkable increase in international trade is reflected in the increased openness of almost all national economies to international influences. For example, the proportion of US GNP accounted for by exports and imports (over one-fifth) is now double what it was two decades ago. This proportion is even higher for manufactured goods (see Figure 23–1), and the U.S. Department of Commerce estimates that the United

---

[1] Repatriation of profits refers to the withdrawal of profits of foreign operations to the home country of the MNC.

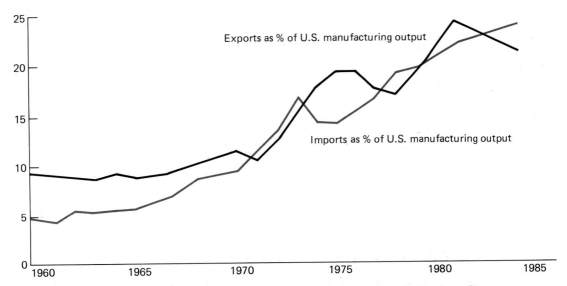

FIGURE 23–1. U.S. Trade as a Share of U.S. Manufacturing Output *Source:* U.S. Department of Labor, Bureau of Labor Statistics, 1984; Organization for Economic Cooperation and Development, 1984.

States exports about a fifth of its industrial production and that about 70 percent of all US goods compete directly with foreign goods.

Some industries and states are even more dependent on the international economy. As an example, the electronic consumer products and automobile industries are now widely considered global industries, and Ohio ranks fourth in terms of manufactured exports. At least one-seventh of its manufacturing employment depends directly on exports. More than half of all Ohio workers are employed by firms that depend to some extent on exports. There has also been a rise in the global level of international portfolio and direct investment. As an example, both direct and portfolio investment in the United States have been increasing faster than U.S. investment overseas.

A major reason for long-run overseas investments of United States companies is the high rates of return obtainable from investments in the less developed countries. The amount of United States **direct foreign investments (DFI)** abroad is large and growing. A large number of American corporations are now highly dependent upon their overseas investments. Significant amounts of the total assets, sales, and profits of American MNCs are attributable to foreign investments, and their foreign operations. It may be noted that direct foreign investments are not limited to American firms. Many European and Japanese firms have operations abroad, too. During the last decade these European and Japanese firms have been increasing their sales and setting up production facilities abroad, especially in the United States.

There is also capital flow between countries for international financial investment purposes. Many firms, investment companies, and individuals invest in the capital markets in foreign countries. The motivation is twofold: to obtain returns higher than those obtainable in the domestic capital markets, and to reduce the portfolio risk through international diversification. This increase in world trade and investment is reflected in the recent globalization of financial markets. The Eurodollar market, at $2.4 trillion at the end of 1984, is now larger than any domestic financial market. Companies are increasingly turning to this market for funds. As an example, U.S. companies raised almost $40 billion in external financial markets in 1985, representing about 30 percent of the funds raised. Even companies and public entities that have no overseas presence are beginning to rely on this market for financing.

In addition to the rise of these external markets for funds, most national financial markets are becoming better integrated with global markets because of the rapid increase in the volume of interest rate and currency swaps ($20 billion in 1985). The foreign exchange markets have also grown rapidly, and the weekly trading volume in these globally integrated markets, at about $1 trillion, now exceeds the annual trading volume on the world's securities markets. Because of these changes, any financing decision now must consider conditions in global and not just domestic financial markets.

EXCHANGE RATES

Recent History of Exchange Rates

Between 1949 and 1970 the exchange rates between the major currencies were fixed. All countries were required to set a specific **parity rate** for their currency vis-à-vis the United States dollar. For example, consider the German currency, the Deutsche mark (DM). In 1949 the parity rate was set at 4.0 DM to $1. The actual exchange rate prevailing on any day was allowed to lie within a narrow band around the parity rate. The DM was allowed to fluctuate between 4.04 and 3.96 per dollar. A country could effect a *major adjustment* in the exchange rate by changing its parity rate with respect to the dollar. When the currency was made cheaper with respect to the dollar, this adjustment was called a **devaluation.** An **upvaluation** or **revaluation** resulted when a currency became more expensive with respect to the dollar. In 1969 the DM parity rate was adjusted to 3.66 per dollar. This adjustment was a revaluation of the DM parity by 9.3 percent. The new bands around the parity were 3.7010 and 3.6188 DM per dollar.

Since 1973 a **floating-rate** international currency system has been operating. For most currencies, there are no parity rates and no bands within which the currencies fluctuate.[2] Most major currencies, including the United States dollar, fluctuate freely, depending upon their values as perceived by the traders in foreign exchange markets. The country's relative economic strengths, its level of exports and imports, the level of monetary activity, and the deficits or surpluses in its balance of payments (BOP) are all important factors in the determination of exchange rates.[3] Short-term, day-to-day fluctuations in exchange rates are caused by supply and demand conditions in the foreign exchange market.

The Foreign Exchange Market

The foreign exchange market provides a mechanism for the transfer of purchasing power from one currency to another. This market is not a physical entity like the New York Stock Exchange; it is a network of telephone and cable connections among

---

[2] The system of floating rates is referred to as the "floating-rate regime."

[3] The balance of payments indicates the exports, imports, and capital flows of any country vis-à-vis the rest of the world.

banks, foreign exchange dealers, and brokers. The market operates simultaneously at three levels. At the first level, customers buy and sell foreign exchange through their banks. At the second level, banks buy and sell foreign exchange from other banks in the same commercial center. At the last level, banks buy and sell foreign exchange from banks in commercial centers in other countries. Some important commercial centers for foreign exchange trading are New York, London, Zurich, Frankfurt, Hong Kong, Singapore, and Tokyo.

An example will illustrate this multilevel trading. A trader in Texas may buy foreign exchange (pounds) from a bank in Houston for payment to a British supplier against some purchase made. The Houston bank, in turn, may purchase the foreign currency (pounds) from a New York bank. The New York bank may need to buy the pounds from another bank in New York or from a bank in London.

Since this market provides transactions in a continuous manner for a very large volume of sales and purchases, the currencies are efficiently priced, or the market is **efficient**. In other words, it is difficult to make a profit by shopping around from one bank to another. Minute differences in the quotes from different banks are quickly arbitraged away. We will discuss the concept of arbitrage later. Owing to the arbitrage mechanism, simultaneous quotes to different buyers in London and New York are likely to be the same.

Two major types of transactions are carried out in the foreign exchange markets: **spot** and **forward transactions.**

Spot Exchange Rates

A typical spot transaction may involve an American firm buying foreign currency from its bank and paying for it in United States dollars. The price of foreign currency in terms of the domestic currency is the **exchange rate**—in this instance, the dollar. Another case of a spot transaction is when an American firm receives foreign currency from abroad. The firm typically would sell the foreign currency to its bank for United States dollars. These are both **spot transactions,** where one currency is exchanged for another currency immediately. The actual exchange rate quotes are expressed in several different ways, as discussed below.

Direct and Indirect Quotes

In the spot exchange market the quoted exchange rate is typically called a direct quote. A **direct quote** indicates the number of units of the home currency required to buy one unit of the foreign currency. That is, in New York the typical exchange-rate quote indicates the number of dollars needed to buy one unit of a foreign currency: dollars per pound, dollars per mark, and so on. The spot rates in column 3 of Table 23–1 are the direct exchange quotes taken from the *Wall Street Journal* on February 29, 1984. In order to buy one pound on February 28, 1984, 1.4945 dollars were needed. In order to buy one franc and one mark, 12.5 cents and 38.46 cents were needed, respectively. The quotes in the spot market in Paris are given in terms of francs and those in London in terms of pounds.

An **indirect quote** indicates the number of units of foreign currency that can be bought for one unit of the home currency. This reads as pounds per dollar, francs per dollar, and so on. Some indirect quotes are given in the last column of Table 23–1.

TABLE 23–1. Foreign Exchange Rates (New York Selling Rate), February 28, 1984

(1) Country	(2) Contract	(3) Direct Quote (U.S. $ Equivalent)	(4) Indirect Quote (Currency per U.S. $)
Britain (pound)	Spot	1.4945	.6691
	30-day future	1.4957	.6686
	90-day future	1.4990	.6671
France (franc)	Spot	.1250	8.0000
	30-day future	.1243	8.0451
	90-day future	.1229	8.1367
West Germany (mark)	Spot	.3846	2.6001
	30-day future	.3860	2.5907
	90-day future	.3888	2.5720

Source: Reprinted by permission of the *Wall Street Journal*, © Dow Jones & Company, Inc., February 29, 1984. All Rights Reserved.

In summary, a direct quote is the dollar/foreign currency rate, and an indirect quote is the foreign currency/dollar rate. Therefore, an indirect quote is the reciprocal of a direct quote and vice versa. The following example illustrates the computation of an indirect quote from a given direct quote.

Example Compute the indirect quotes from the direct quotes of spot rates for pounds, francs, and marks given in column 3 of Table 23–1. The direct quotes are: pound, 1.4945; franc, .1250; and mark, .3846. The related indirect quotes are computed as follows:

$$\text{indirect quote} = \frac{1}{\text{direct quote}}$$

Thus

Pounds:

$$\frac{1}{1.4945 \ (\$/\text{pound})} = .6691 \ (\text{pound}/\$)$$

Francs:

$$\frac{1}{.1250 \ (\$1/\text{franc})} = 8.0 \ (\text{franc}/\$)$$

Marks:

$$\frac{1}{.3846 \ (\$/\text{mark})} = 2.6001 \ (\text{mark}/\$)$$

Notice that the above direct quotes and indirect quotes are identical to those shown in columns 3 and 4 of Table 23–1.

The direct and indirect quotes are useful in computing foreign currency requirements. Consider the following examples.

Example   An American business wanted to remit 1000 marks to Germany on February 28, 1984. How many dollars would have been required for this transaction?

.3846 ($/marks) × 1000 (marks) = $384.60

Example   An American business paid $2000 to a British resident on February 28, 1984. How many pounds did the British resident receive?

.6691 (pounds/$) × 2000 ($) = 1338.20

EXCHANGE RATES AND ARBITRAGE

The foreign exchange quotes in two different countries must be in line with each other. For example, the direct quote for U.S. dollars in London is given in dollars/pound. Since the foreign exchange markets are efficient, the direct quotes for the United States dollar in London, on February 28, 1984, must be very close to the indirect rate of .6691 pound/dollar prevailing in New York on that date.

If the exchange-rate quotations between the London and New York spot exchange markets were *out of line*, then an enterprising trader could make a profit by buying in the market where the currency was cheaper and selling it in the dearer. Such a buy-and-sell strategy would involve an investment of funds for a very short time and no risk bearing, yet the trader could make a sure profit. Such a person is called an **arbitrageur,** and the process of buying and selling in more than one market to make a riskless profit is called **arbitrage.** Spot exchange markets are efficient in the sense that arbitrage opportunities do not persist for any length of time. That is, the exchange rates between two different markets are quickly brought *in line*, aided by the arbitrage process.

Asked and Bid Rates
In the spot exchange market two types of rates are quoted: the asked and the bid rates. The **asked rate** is the rate the bank or the foreign exchange trader "asks" the customer to pay in home currency for foreign currency when the bank is selling and the customer is buying. The asked rate is also known as the **selling rate** or the **offer rate.** The **bid rate** is the rate at which the bank buys the foreign currency from the customer by paying in home currency. The bid rate is also known as the **buying rate.** Note that Table 23–1 contains only the selling, offer, or asked rates, and not the buying rate.

The bank sells a unit of foreign currency for more than it pays for it. Therefore, the direct asked quote ($/foreign currency) is greater than the direct bid quote. The difference is known as the **spread.** Thus, the indirect asked quote must be less than the indirect bid quote. For example, assume the direct asked and bid quotes are 1.2 and 1.15, respectively. The indirect asked quote will be 1/1.2 = .8333. The indirect bid quote will be 1/1.15 = .8696. The indirect bid is greater than the indirect asked quote.

When there is a large volume of transactions and the trading is continuous, the spread between the asked and the bid rates is small. A narrow spread indicates efficiency in the spot exchange market. The spread is much higher for infrequently than for frequently traded currencies. The spread is likely to be greater for a small-volume than for a large-volume transaction. One may consider a large-volume transaction as wholesale trading, a small-volume transaction as retail trading. The spread exists to compensate the banks for holding the risky foreign currency and for providing the service.

Cross Rates

Also important in understanding the spot-rate mechanism is the cross rate. A **cross rate** is the indirect computation of the exchange rate of one currency from the exchange rates of two other currencies. Consider the following example.

Example   The dollar/pound and the mark/dollar rates are given in columns 3 and 4 of Table 23–1. From this information, we could determine the mark/pound and pound/mark exchange rates.
   We see that

$$(\$/\text{pound}) \times (\text{mark}/\$) = (\text{mark}/\text{pound})$$

or $1.4945 \times 2.6001 = 3.8858 \text{ mark/pound.}$

Thus, the pound/mark exchange rate is

$$1/3.8858 = .2573 \text{ pound/mark}$$

Cross-rate computations make it possible to use quotations in New York to compute the exchange rate between pounds, marks, and francs. Arbitrage conditions hold in cross rates, too. For example, the pound exchange rate in Frankfurt (the direct quote or the mark/pound) must be 3.8858. The mark exchange rate in London must be .2573 pound/mark. If the rates prevailing in Frankfurt and London were different from the computed cross rates, using quotes from New York, a trader could use three different markets and make arbitrage profits. The arbitrage condition for the cross rates is called **triangular arbitrage.**

Forward Exchange Rates

A **forward exchange contract** requires delivery, at a specified future date, of one currency for a specified amount of another currency. The exchange rate for the future transaction is agreed upon today; the actual payment of one currency and the receipt of another currency take place at the future date. For example, a 30-day contract on March 1 is good for delivery on March 31. Note that the forward rate is not the same as the spot rate that will prevail in the future. The actual spot rate that will prevail is not known today; only the forward rate is known. The actual spot rate will depend upon the market conditions at that time; it may be more or less than today's forward rate.

Forward contracts are usually quoted for periods of 30, 90, and 180 days. A contract for any intermediate date can be obtained, usually with the payment of a small premium.

Forward contracts for periods longer than 180 days can be obtained by special negotiations with banks. Contracts for periods greater than 1 year are not easy to obtain.

Forward Quotes

Forward rates, like spot rates, are quoted in both direct and indirect form. The direct quotes for the 30-day and 90-day forward contracts on pounds, francs, and marks are given in column 3 of Table 23–1. The indirect quotes for forward contracts are reciprocals of the direct quotes. The indirect quotes are indicated in column 4 of Table 23–1. The direct quotes are the dollar/foreign currency rate, and the indirect quotes are the foreign currency/dollar rate similar to the spot exchange quotes.

The 30-day forward quote for pounds is $1.4957 per pound. This means that if one purchases the contract for forward pounds on February 28, 1984, the bank will deliver a pound against the payment of $1.4957 on March 29, 1984. The bank is contractually bound to deliver the pound at this price, and the buyer of the contract is legally obligated to buy it at this price on March 29, 1984. Therefore, this is the price the customer must pay regardless of the actual spot rate prevailing on March 29, 1984. If the spot price of the pound is less than $1.4957, then the customer pays *more* than the spot price. If the spot price is greater than $1.4957, then the customer pays *less* than the spot price.

The forward rate is often quoted at a **premium** or **discount** from the existing spot rate. For example, the 30-day pound forward rate may be quoted as .0012 premium (1.4957 forward rate $-$1.4945 spot rate). If the forward contract is selling for more dollars than the spot—that is, a larger direct quote—then the forward contract is said to be selling at a premium. When the forward contract sells for fewer dollars than the spot—a smaller direct quote—the forward rate is said to be at a discount from the spot rate. Notice in column 3 of Table 23–1 that the forward contracts are selling at a premium over the spot for pounds and marks and at a discount for francs. This premium or discount is also called the **forward-spot differential.**

Notationally, the relationship may be written as

$$F - S = p \text{ (or } d) \qquad (23\text{–}1)$$

where F = the forward rate, direct quote

S = the spot rate, direct quote

p = the premium, when F is greater than S

d = the discount, when S is greater than F

The premium or discount can also be expressed as an annual percent rate, computed as follows:

$$\frac{F - S}{S} \times \frac{12}{n} \times 100 = P \text{ (or } D) \qquad (23\text{–}2)$$

where F, S = the forward and spot rates defined earlier

n = the number of months of the forward contract

P = the annualized percent premium on forward, if $F > S$

D = the annualized percent discount on forward, if $S > F$

Example Compute the percent per annum premium on the 30-day forward pound.

STEP 1: *Identify F, S, and n.*

$$F = 1.4957, \quad S = 1.4945, \quad n = 1 \text{ month}$$

STEP 2: *Since F is greater than S, we compute P via (23–2).*

$$P = \frac{1.4957 - 1.4945}{1.4945} \times \frac{12 \text{ months}}{1 \text{ month}} \times 100$$

$$= .964\%$$

The percent per annum premium on the 30-day pound is .964 percent.

The percent per annum premiums on the 30-day and 90-day pound, franc, and mark contracts are computed similarly. The results are given in Table 23–2.

TABLE 23–2. Percent-Per-Annum Premium (Discount)

	30-Day	90-Day
Pound	.964%	1.204%
Franc	(6.720)	(6.720)
Mark	4.368	4.368

Uses of Forward Rates

As indicated earlier, it is extremely unlikely that the future spot rate will be exactly the same as the forward rate quoted today. By locking in on a forward rate through a forward contract, either the bank or the customer loses money. That is, one of the parties suffers an opportunity loss compared with the prevailing spot rate. Why do businesses buy forward contracts and banks sell them, when both parties know that one of them will incur a loss? The answer is that the forward contract benefits both the customer and the bank because of the *reduction of uncertainty* that it offers. This benefit *outweighs the potential loss* that either party may suffer.

The risk-reduction benefit of the forward contract can be explained as follows. Assume that you are going to receive a payment denominated in pounds from a British customer in 30 days. If you wait for 30 days and exchange the pounds at the spot rate, you will receive a dollar amount reflecting the exchange rate 30 days hence (that is, the future spot rate). As of today, however, you have no way of knowing the exact future spot rate or your exact future dollar receipts. Consequently, you cannot make precise plans about your future. If, on the other hand, you buy a future contract, then you know the exact dollar amount of your future receipts, and you can make precise plans concerning its use. The forward contract, therefore, can reduce your uncertainty about the future. This is the major advantage of the forward market—that of *risk reduction*.

The Interest Parity Theory

All the forward rates given in Table 23–1 entail a premium or a discount relative to current spot rates. However, these forward premiums and discounts differ between currencies and maturities (see Table 23–2). These differences depend solely on the difference in the level of interest rates between the two countries, called the **interest rate differential.** The value of the premium or discount can be theoretically computed from the **interest rate parity theory (IRPT).** This theory states that (except for the effects of small transactions costs) the forward premium or discount should be equal and opposite in sign to the difference in the national interest rates for securities of the same maturity.

Specifically, the premium or discount on the percent per annum basis should be equal to the following:

$$P \text{ (or } D) = \left(-\frac{I^f - I^d}{1 + I^f}\right) = \left(\frac{I^d - I^f}{1 + I^f}\right) \qquad (23\text{–}3a)$$

where $P \text{ (or } D) =$ the percent per annum premium (or discount) on the forward rate,

$I^f =$ the annualized interest rate on a foreign instrument having the same maturity as the forward contract

$I^d =$ the annualized interest rate on a domestic instrument having the same maturity as the forward contract

Note that in order to compute the forward premium on, say, a 30-day forward pound contract, we need to have the 30-day Treasury bill rate in the United States and its counterpart in the United Kingdom, both expressed as annual rates.

The IRPT states that the P (or D) calculated by the use of equation (23–3a) should be the same as the P (or D) calculated by using equation (23–2), except for small variations due to political and commercial risks and transactions costs. When the interest rates are relatively low, equation (23–3a) can be approximated by:

$$P \text{ (or } D) \cong -(I^f - I^d) = (I^d - I^f) \qquad (23\text{–}3b)$$

Notice in Table 23–2 that the 30-day forward pound is selling at a premium of approximately .964 percent. The IRPT says that the 30-day interest rate in the United Kingdom must be approximately .964 percent (annualized) less than the 30-day Treasury bill rate in the United States, as indicated by equation (23–3a). Let us see why the premiums obey the interest rate parity theory.

Covered Interest Arbitrage The rationale for the interest rate parity theory is provided by the **covered interest arbitrage** argument. This argument states that if the premiums (or discounts) in forward rates are not exactly equal to the interest rate differential, then arbitrage or riskless profits can be made.[4] The arbitrage mechanics involved here are substantially more complicated than the "simple" and "triangular" arbitrage discussed earlier. The covered interest arbitrage argument is best explained by the following examples.

---

[4] Interest rate differential is approximately equal to the right-hand side of equation (23–3b).

Example The pound spot and 30-day forward rates are $1.4945 and $1.4957, respectively, on February 28, 1984. The 30-day United States T-bill rate on February 28, 1984, expressed as an annual rate was approximately 12.96 percent. Assume now that the rate on 30-day United Kingdom instruments on February 28, 1984, was 9 percent, annualized. Given these data, does a riskless profit (or arbitrage) opportunity exist?

STEP 1: *Compute the forward premium using equation (23–2). P = .964 percent, as solved in a previous example.*

STEP 2: *Compute the interest rate differential by equation (23–3).*

$$P = \frac{.1296 - .09}{1 + .09} = \frac{.0396}{1.09} = .03633 = 3.633\%$$

The premiums computed by the use of the two equations are not identical. The IRPT is violated. Profit opportunities exist.

Since profit opportunities exist, what can the arbitrageur do to make a profit? The steps that a United States arbitrageur can take are indicated below.

On February 28, 1984:

STEP 1: Borrow *1 million pounds for 30 days from the United Kingdom money markets at a 9 percent annual rate of interest. For 30 days the interest is .75 percent.*[5] *On March 29, 1984, he will need to repay 1 million pounds × 1.0075 = 1,007,500 pounds.*

STEP 2: Exchange *the borrowed pounds into dollars at the spot exchange rate of $1.4945 per pound on February 28, 1984. He receives 1 million pounds × $1.4945 = $1,494,500.*

STEP 3: Invest *the dollars in the United States money market for 30 days at 12.96 percent annual rate. For 30 days the rate is 1.08 percent. Receive, on March 29, 1984, $1,494,500 × 1.0108 = $1,510,641.*

STEP 4: *Enter into a 30-day forward contract to buy 1,007,500 pounds on March 29, 1984. On March 29, 1984, he will need to pay 1,007,500 × 1.4957 = $1,506,918 so that he will receive the 1,007,500 pounds needed to repay the loan principal and interest on the 1 million pounds loan taken in step 1.*

On March 29, 1984, the arbitrage position is closed out as follows:

1. *Receive* $1,510,641 from the United States money market investment. ($1,494,500 invested plus $16,141 interest at a monthly rate of 1.08 percent)
2. *Pay* $1,506,918 to the bank to *obtain* 1,007,500 pounds at a 1.4957 exchange rate.
3. *Pay* 1,007,500 pounds toward the principal and interest on the 1 million pound loan.

---

[5] The 30-day rate, as an approximation, is equal to the annual rate × $\frac{1}{12}$.

On March 29, 1984, the United States arbitrageur's net position is no liability and no assets. However, he has made a net profit of \$3,723 (\$1,510,641 − \$1,506,918. The arbitrageur invested none of his own funds, bore no risk (since he knew his payments and receipts exactly on February 29, 1984), yet made a net profit of \$3,723. This arbitrage was accomplished by *simultaneously borrowing* in one market, *investing* in another money market, and *covering* the exchange position in the forward exchange market. The entire process is known as covered interest arbitrage.

Note that the arbitrage profit was possible because the forward premium was not equal to the interest rate differential. Under such circumstances, arbitrageurs enter the market, increase the demand for the forward foreign currency, and drive up the price of the forward contract. The equilibrium price of the forward contract again obeys the interest parity theory.

Example Assume that the interest rates indicated in the previous example are the actual rates prevailing in the United States and United Kingdom. What should be the "correct" price of the forward contract, consistent with the interest rates in the two countries?

STEP 1: *Compute the premium using equation (23–3a).*

$$P = \frac{.1296 - .09}{1 + .09} = .03633, \text{ or } 3.633\%$$

STEP 2: *Using this premium in equation (23–2), compute the forward rate, F.*

$$\frac{F - 1.4945}{1.4945} \times \frac{12}{1} \times 100 = 3.633\%$$

$$F = 1.4990$$

Thus, we see that the forward rate consistent with the IRPT is 1.499 dollars per pound.

The example illustrates the technique for computing the *correct* price of the forward contract. If the quote is *less* than the computed price, the forward contract is *undervalued*. If the quote is *greater* than the computed price, the forward contract is *overvalued*. In our example, the forward contract is undervalued.

The forward markets are *efficient* is the sense that the quotes in the market represent the "correct" price of the contract. The markets' efficiency also implies that no profit can be made by computing the prices at every instant and buying the forward contract when they appear undervalued. Some minor deviations from the computed correct price may exist for short periods. These deviations, however, are such that after the transactions costs involved in the four separate arbitrage steps have been recognized, no net profit can be made. Numerous empirical studies attest to the efficiency of the forward markets.

In the previous example the correct price of the forward pound was computed under the assumption that the 30-day interest rate in the United Kingdom was 9 percent. All the other data for the examples were obtained from the actual market quotes in New York. We now ask, given the data on spot rate, forward rate, and the

United States Treasury bill rate, can we compute the interest rate for the 30-day United Kingdom instrument? The answer is affirmative. The computations are given in the next example.

Example The spot rate and forward rate for the pound are 1.4945 and 1.4957, respectively. The 30-day United States T-bill rate is 12.96 percent annualized. What is the 30-day United Kingdom rate?

STEP 1: *Compute the premium using equation (23–2). From previous computations,*

$$P = .964\%$$

STEP 2: *Using equation (23–3a), solve for the unknown foreign interest rate.*

$$.00964 = \frac{.1296 - I^f}{1 + I^f}$$

$$I^f = .1188, \text{ or } 11.88\%$$

Thus, the actual 30-day rate in the United Kingdom on February 28, 1984, must have been 11.88 percent annualized.

Purchasing Power Parity

Long-run changes in exchange rates are influenced by international differences in inflation rates and the purchasing power of each nation's currency. Exchange rates of countries with high rates of inflation will tend to decline. According to the purchasing power parity (PPP) theory, exchange rates will tend to adjust in such a way that each currency will have the same purchasing power (especially in terms of internationally traded goods). Thus, if the United Kingdom experiences a 10 percent rate of inflation in a year that West Germany experiences only a 6 percent rate, the UK currency (the pound) will be expected to decline in value approximately by 4 percent (10% − 6%) against the West German currency (the mark). More accurately, according to the PPP

$$S_{t+1} = S_t (1 + P_d)/(1 + P_f)^n$$
$$\cong S_t (1 + P_d - P_f)^n$$

where S_t = the direct exchange rate (units of domestic currency per unit of the foreign currency) at time t

P_f = the foreign inflation rate

P_d = the domestic inflation rate

n = number of time periods

Thus, if the beginning value of the mark was £0.40, with a 6 percent inflation rate in West Germany and a 10 percent inflation rate in the UK, according to the PPP, the expected value of the mark at the end of that year will be £0.40 [1.10/1.06], or £0.4151.

International Fisher Effect

According to the Fisher effect, interest (I) rates reflect the expected inflation rate (P) and a real rate of return (I_r). In other words

$$1 + I = (1 + P) \ (1 + I_r)$$

and

$$I = P + I_r + PI_r$$

While there is mixed empirical support for the Fisher effect internationally, it is widely contended that for the major industrial countries, I_r is about 3 percent when a long-term period is considered. In such a case, with the previous assumption regarding inflation rates, interest rates in the UK and West Germany would be $(1 + 0.10)$ $(1 + 0.03) - 1$ or 13.3 percent and $(1 + 0.06) (1 + 0.03) - 1$ or 9.18 percent, respectively.

In addition, according to the IRPT, the expected premium for the mark forward rate should be $(0.133 - 0.0918)/1.0918$ or 3.774 percent (rounded off). Starting with a mark value of £0.40 gives us a one-year forward rate of £0.40 (1.03774) = £0.4151. As you may notice, this one-year forward rate is exactly the same as the PPP expected spot rate one year from today. In other words, if the real rate (I_r) is the same in both West Germany and the UK and expectations regarding inflation rates hold true, today's one-year forward rate is likely to be the same as the future spot rate one year from now. Thus, it is contended that in efficient markets, with rational expectations, the forward rate is an unbiased (not necessarily accurate) forecast of the future spot rate. These relationships between inflation and interest rates, and spot and forward rates are depicted in Figure 23–2.

FIGURE 23–2. Efficient Foreign Exchange Market Relationships

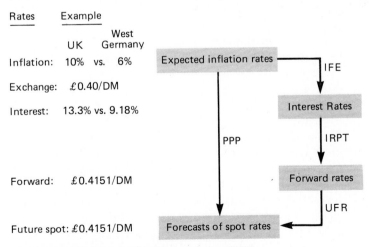

UFR: unbiased forecast of spot rate = forward rate
IFE: international Fisher effect

EXCHANGE RATE RISK

Exchange rate risk arises from the fact that the spot exchange rate on a future date is unknown today. For the moment, assume that there are no forward markets. Today's spot rate is $1.4945 per pound. The spot rate that will prevail 30 days from today is unknown. Thus, the future spot rate, as of today, is a *random variable*. In Figure 23–3 we indicate a possible hypothetical distribution of the pound spot rate on March 29, 1984. This distribution is what we, on February 28, 1984, subjectively believe the future spot rate to be. Notice in Figure 23–3 that the exchange rate may be as low as 1.480 dollars or as high as 1.550 dollars per pound with different probabilities.

Types of Exchange Risk

The concept of exchange rate risk applies to all types of international businesses. The measurement of these risks, and the type of risk, may differ among businesses. Let us see how exchange risk affects international trade contracts, international portfolio investments, and direct foreign investments.

Exchange Risk in International Trade Contracts

The idea of exchange risk in trade contracts is illustrated in the following situations.

Case I.   An American automobile distributor agrees to buy a car from the manufacturer in Detroit. The distributor agrees to pay $6500 upon delivery of the car, which is expected to be 30 days from today. The car is delivered on the thirtieth day and the distributor pays $6500. Notice that, from the day this contract was written until the day the car was delivered, the buyer knew the *exact dollar amount* of the liability. There was, in other words, *no uncertainty* about the value of the contract.

Case II.   An American automobile distributor enters into a contract with a British supplier to buy a car from the United Kingdom for 5000 pounds. The amount is payable on the delivery of the car, 30 days from today. From Figure 23–3, we see the range of spot rates that we believe can occur on the date the contract is consummated. On the thirtieth day, the American importer will pay some amount in the range of $7400(5000 × 1.48) to $7750(5000 × 1.550) for the car. As of today, the American firm is uncertain regarding its future dollar outflow 30 days hence. That is, the *dollar value of the contract is uncertain*.

These two examples help illustrate the idea of foreign exchange risk in international trade contracts. In the case of the domestic trade contract, given as Case I, the exact dollar amount of the future dollar payment is known today with certainty. In the case of the international trade contract, given in Case II, where the *contract is written in the foreign currency*, the exact dollar amount of the contract is not known. The variability of the exchange rate induces variability in the future cash flow. This is the risk of exchange rate changes, or **exchange risk.**

Exchange rate risk exists when the contract is written in terms of the foreign currency or *denominated* in foreign currency. There is no direct exchange risk if the international trade contract is written in terms of the domestic currency. That is, in Case II, if the contract were written in dollars, the American importer would face *no* direct exchange risk. With the contract written in dollars, the British exporter would bear *all* the exchange risk because the British exporter's future pound receipts

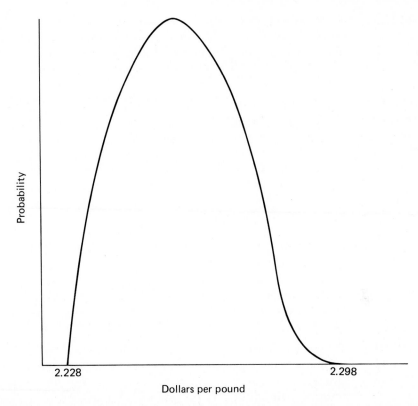

FIGURE 23–3.   A Subjective Probability Distribution of the Pound Exchange Rate, 30 Days in the Future

would be uncertain. That is, he would receive payment in dollars, which would have to be converted into pounds at an unknown (as of today) pound-dollar exchange rate. In international trade contracts of the type discussed here, at least one of the two parties to the contract *always* bears the exchange risk.

Certain types of international trade contracts are denominated in a third currency, different from either the importer's or the exporter's domestic currency. In Case II the contract might have been denominated in, say, the Deutsche mark. With a mark contract, both importer and exporter would be subject to exchange rate risk.

Exchange risk is not limited to the two-party trade contracts of the type discussed here; it exists also in foreign portfolio investments and direct foreign investments.

Exchange Risk in Foreign Portfolio Investments

Let us look at an example of exchange risk in the context of portfolio investments. An American investor buys a German security. The exact return on the investment in the security is unknown. Thus, the security is a risky investment. The investment return in the holding period of, say, three months stated in marks could be anything from −2 to +8 percent. In addition, the mark-dollar exchange rate may depreciate by 4 percent or appreciate by 6 percent in the three-month period during which the investment is held. The return to the American investor, in dollars, will therefore be in the range of -6 to $+14$ percent.[6] Notice that the return to a German investor, in marks, is in the range of -2 to $+8$ percent. Clearly, for the American investor, the exchange factor induces a greater variability in the dollar rate of return. Hence, the *exchange rate fluctuations may increase the riskiness* of the investments.

Exchange Risk in Direct Foreign Investment

The exchange risk of a direct foreign investment (DFI) is more complicated. In a DFI the parent company invests in assets denominated in a foreign currency. That is, the balance sheet and the income statement of the subsidiary are written in terms of the foreign currency. The parent company receives the repatriated profit stream in dollars. Thus, the exchange risk concept applies to fluctuations in the dollar value of the *assets* located abroad as well as to the fluctuations in the home-currency-denominated *profit stream*. Exchange risk not only affects the immediate, or one-time, profits but may affect the future profit stream as well.

If varying exchange rates induce risk, why do traders and corporations engage in multinational operations? In discussing valuation in Chapter 12, we saw that greater risk must be compensated for by greater expected returns. Applying this basic principle to international trade and investments, we see that these activities are undertaken because the additional risk due to fluctuating exchange rates is compensated for by greater expected return than available in the domestic context.

Undiversifiable Exchange Rate Risk

We will find it useful to understand an additional feature of exchange risk. In discussing the capital asset pricing model (CAPM) in Chapter 13, we saw that investors are compensated only for *undiversifiable risk*. The total risk, or the total variability in returns, matters little in the pricing of assets. From the viewpoint of the American investor, the variability of return from investing in a German security is not the simple sum of the variance of return in marks and the variance of the dollar-mark exchange rate. The *covariance* between the mark return and the dollar-mark exchange rate is an important item for computing the variability of the dollar-denominated rate of return.

Relevant Measures of Exchange Risk

The relevant measures of the exchange risk differ for different types of businesses. For example, an American trader who infrequently trades internationally will face exchange risk equal to the total variability in the income stream due to exchange rate fluctuations, since he is not well diversified. For an export-import firm that does continual business in a number of countries, the relevant risk measure is the undiversifiable risk of exchange rate fluctuations. This is computed by accounting for the variances and the covariances. Similar arguments apply to an American investor in foreign securities. The diversification argument also applies to a multinational corporation that has plants and operations in numerous countries. For corporations with very large investments in a single foreign country, the total variability of the exchange rate is the

---

[6] *Example*: Assume the spot exchange rate is .50 dollars per mark. In three months the exchange rate would be $.50 \times (1 - .04) = .48$ to $.50 \times (1 + .06) = .53$. A \$50 investment today is equivalent to a 100-mark investment. The 100-mark investment would return 98 to 108 marks in three months. The return, in the worst case, is 98 marks $\times$ .48 = \$47.04. The return, in the best case, is 108 marks $\times$ .53 = \$57.24. The holding-period return, on the \$50 investment, will be between -6 percent (\$47.04 $-$ \$50)/\$50) and $+14$ percent (\$57.24 $-$ \$50)/\$50).

appropriate measure of exchange risk. This exchange risk is usually measured by foreign exchange exposure.

EXPOSURE TO EXCHANGE RATE RISK

The significance of the exchange rate risk for a given firm is dependent on the firm's foreign exchange exposure. For a corporation that has only one international contract to pay 3000 pounds to a British supplier, changes in exchange rates can impact the firm's value only to the extent that this contract is affected. In contrast, another company may hold large amounts of assets and owe liabilities in a foreign country. This latter firm has much greater exposure to exchange rate fluctuations. A change in exchange rates will affect not only the value of the firm's assets and liabilities abroad, but also the firm's future profit streams.

Defining Exposure to Exchange Losses

An asset denominated in or valued in terms of foreign currency cash flows will lose value if that foreign currency declines in value. It can be said that such an asset is exposed to exchange rate risk. However, this possible decline in asset value may be offset by the decline in value of any liability that is also denominated or valued in terms of that foreign currency. Thus, a firm would normally be interested in its net exposed position (exposed assets − exposed liabilities) for each period in each currency.

While expected changes in exchange rates can often be included in the cost-benefit analysis relating to such transactions, in most cases there is an unexpected component in exchange rate changes and often the cost-benefit analysis for such transactions does not fully capture even the expected change in the exchange rate. For example, price increases often have to be less than those necessary to fully offset exchange rate changes.

A company may have many reasons to cover against foreign exchange transactions exposure. First, it may wish to reduce or change its risk profile to better conform to the risk preferences of its owners and managers. Second, it may not find it economical continually to monitor conditions in the foreign exchange markets or to maintain the managerial expertise required for making the decision to cover its foreign currency exposure. There are a number of additional reasons why hedging foreign currency exposures may make economic sense for a company. For example, it may be able to take advantage of uneven tax rates, deviations from purchasing power parity and efficient-market asset pricing models because of default risk, information assymmetries, and other market imperfections.

Measures of Exposure

A company can follow one of three possible policies with regard to the management of its foreign currency exposure. In the two simplest policies, the firm covers all exposed positions or covers no exposed positions. If the firm covers no foreign currency exposure, it generally expects foreign exchange losses and gains to offset each other, with the net balance representing one of the costs of doing business. Such a policy may be particularly suitable for large, well-diversified companies. Other companies would have to consider adopting the third policy of using various hedging or covering alternatives for most but not all of their currency exposure. Three different measures of exposure to foreign currency losses have been developed: transactions exposure, translation exposure, and economic exposure.

Transactions Exposure

This is the net total of foreign currency transactions whose monetary value was fixed at a time different from the time when these transactions are actually completed. Examples of such transactions include receivables, payables, and fixed-price sales or purchase contracts. Thus, **transactions exposure** refers to net contracted foreign currency transactions for which the settlement amounts are subject to changing exchange rates over a period too short to allow for compensating changes in prices fully. A company normally must set up an additional reporting system to track transactions exposure, since a number of these amounts are not recognized in the accounting books of a firm.

Translation Exposure

This is the net total of exposed assets less exposed liabilities. Foreign currency assets and liabilities are considered exposed if their foreign currency value for accounting purposes is to be translated into the parent company currency using the current exchange rate—the exchange rate in effect on the balance sheet date. Other assets and liabilities and equity amounts that are translated at the historic exchange rate—the rate in effect when these items were first recognized in the company's accounts—are not considered to be exposed. The rate (current or historic) used to translate various accounts depends on the translation procedure used. For United States companies, Financial Accounting Standard (FAS) No. 52 specifies the translation procedure to be used.

While transaction exposure can result in exchange rate change-related losses and gains that are realized and have an impact on both reported and taxable income, translation exposure results in exchange rate losses and gains that are reflected in the company's accounting books, but that are unrealized and have little or no impact on taxable income. Thus, if financial markets are efficient and managerial goals are consistent with owner wealth maximization (agency and signaling costs are negligible), a firm should not have to waste real resources hedging against possible paper losses caused by translation exposure. However, if there are significant agency or information costs or if markets are not efficient; that is, if translation losses and gains raise information costs for investors, or if they endanger the firm's ability to satisfy debt or other covenants, or if the evaluation of the firm's managers depends on translated accounting data, a firm may indeed find it economical to use real resources to hedge against paper translation losses or gains, even if such losses or gains do not correspond to realized gains and losses.

Economic Exposure

This is the extent to which the economic value of a company can decline because of exchange rate changes. This decline in value may be caused by a rate-change-induced decline in the level of expected cash flows and/or by an increase in the riskiness of these cash flows. Thus, **economic exposure** refers to the overall impact of exchange rate changes on the value of the firm and therefore includes not only the strategic impact of changes in competitive relationships between alternative foreign locations that arise from exchange rate changes, but also the economic impact of transactions exposure and the economic impact, if any, of translation exposure.

Thus, economic exposure to exchange rate changes depends on the competitive structure of the markets for a firm's inputs and its outputs and how these markets are influenced by changes in exchange rates. This influence, in turn, would depend on a number of economic factors, including price elasticities of the products, the degree of competition from foreign markets and direct (through prices) and indirect (through incomes) impact of exchange rate changes on these markets. Assessing the economic exposure faced by a particular firm thus depends on the ability to understand and model the structure of the markets for its major inputs (purchases) and outputs (sales).

A company need not engage in any cross-border business activity in order to be exposed to losses due to exchange rate changes, because product and financial markets in most countries are related and influenced to a large extent by the same global forces. As an example, the output of a company engaged in business activity only within one country may be competing with imported products, or it may be competing for its inputs with other domestic and foreign purchasers. The degree of competition in these markets provided by these firms may change with changes in exchange rates. As an example, a Canadian chemical company that did no cross-border business nevertheless found that its profit margins depended directly on the United States dollar–Japanese yen exchange rate. The company used coal as an input in its production process, and the Canadian price of coal was heavily influenced by the extent to which the Japanese bought United States coal, which in turn depended on the yen-dollar exchange rate.

While translation exposure need not be managed, it might be useful for a firm to manage its transaction and economic exposures since they affect firm value directly. In most companies, transaction exposure is generally tracked and managed by the office of the corporate treasurer. Economic exposure is difficult to define in operating terms, and very few companies manage it actively. In most companies, economic exposure is generally considered part of the strategic planning process, rather than as a treasurer's or finance function.

Exchange risk may be neutralized or hedged by a change in the asset and liability position in the foreign currency. An exposed asset position can be **hedged** or **covered** by creating a liability of the same amount and maturity denominated in the foreign currency. An exposed liability position can be covered by acquiring assets of the same amount and maturity in the foreign currency. The objective is to have a zero net asset position in the foreign currency. This eliminates exchange risk, since the loss (gain) in the liability (asset) is exactly offset by the gain (loss) in the value of the asset (liability) when the foreign currency appreciates (depreciates). Two popular forms of hedge are the money-market hedge and the exchange-market or forward-market hedge. In both types of hedge the *amount* and the *duration* of the asset (liability) positions are *matched*.

Money-Market Hedge

In a money-market hedge, the exposed position in a foreign currency is offset by borrowing or lending in the money market. Consider the case of the American firm with a net liability position of 3000 pounds. The firm knows the exact amount of its pound liability in 30 days, but it does not know the liability in dollars. Assume that the 30-day money-market rates in both the United States and United Kingdom are, respectively, 1 percent for lending and 1.5 percent for borrowing. The American business can take the following steps.

STEP 1:   Calculate the present value of the foreign currency liability (3000 pounds) that is due in 30 days. Use the money-market rate applicable for the foreign country (1 percent in the United Kingdom). The present value of 3000 pounds is 2970.30 pounds, computed as follows: 3000/(1 + .01).

STEP 2:   Exchange dollars on today's spot market to obtain the 2970.30 pounds. The dollar amount needed today is $4439.11(2970.30 × $1.4945).

STEP 3:   Invest 2970.30 pounds in a United Kingdom one-month money-market instrument. This investment will compound to exactly 3000 pounds in one month. The future liability of 3000 pounds is covered by the 2970.30 pounds investment.[7]

NOTE: If the American business does not own this amount today, it can borrow it from the United States money market at the going rate of 1.5 percent. In 30 days the American business will need to repay $4505.70[$4439.11 × (1 + .015)].

Assuming that the American business borrows the money, its management may base its calculations on the knowledge that the British goods, upon delivery in 30 days, will cost it $4505.70. The British business will receive 3000 pounds, and the cost of the American firm to make the payment is $4505.70. The American business need not wait for the future spot exchange rate to be revealed. On today's date, the future dollar payment of the contract is known with certainty. This certainty helps the American business in making its pricing and financing decisions.

The mechanics of the money-market hedge indicate that the American firm, on today's date, knows the exact dollar amount of its future liability. Thus, the exchange risk is entirely eliminated. Many businesses hedge in the money market. The firm needs to borrow in one market, lend or invest in the other money market, and use the spot exchange market on today's date. The mechanics of *covering a net asset position* in the foreign currency are the exact *reverse* of the mechanics of covering the *liability position*. With a net asset position in pounds: borrow in the United Kingdom money market in pounds, convert to dollars on the spot exchange market, invest in the United States money market. The cost of hedging in the money market is the cost of doing business in three different markets. Information about the three markets is needed, and analytical calculations of the type indicated here need be made.

Many small and infrequent traders find the cost of the money-market hedge prohibitive, owing especially to the need for information about the market. These traders use the exchange or the forward-market hedge, which has very similar hedging benefits.

The Forward-Market Hedge

The forward market provides a second possible hedging mechanism. It works as follows: a net asset (liability) position is covered by a liability (asset) in the forward market. Consider again the case of the American firm with a liability of 3000 pounds that must be paid in 30 days. The firm may take the following steps to cover its liability position.

STEP 1:   Buy a forward contract today to purchase 3000 pounds in 30 days. The 30-day forward rate is, say, $1.4957 per pound.

STEP 2:   On the thirtieth day pay the banker $4487.10(3000 × $1.4957) and collect 3000 pounds. Pay these pounds to the British supplier.

---

[7] Observe that 2970.30 pounds × (1 + .01) = 3000 pounds.

By the use of the forward contract the American business knows the exact worth of the future payment in dollars ($4487.10). The exchange risk in pounds is totally eliminated by the net asset position in the forward pounds. In the case of a net asset exposure, the steps open to the American firm are the exact opposite: sell the pounds forward, and on the future day receive and deliver the pounds to collect the agreed-upon dollar amount.

The use of the forward market as a hedge against exchange risk is simple and direct. That is, match the liability or asset position against an offsetting position in the forward market. The forward-market hedge is relatively easy to implement. Direct your banker that you need to buy or sell a foreign currency on a future date, and the banker will give you a forward quote. The cost of the hedge is the commission you pay the banker for performing the transaction. Additionally, the forward hedge and the money-market hedge give an identical future dollar payment (or receipt) if the forward contracts are priced according to the interest rate parity theory. The alert student may have noticed that the dollar payments in the money-market hedge and the forward-market hedge examples were, respectively, $4505.70 and $4487.10. Recall from our previous discussions that in efficient markets, the forward contracts do indeed conform to the IRPT. However, the numbers in our example are not identical because the forward rate used in the forward hedge is not IRPT consistent with the interest rates in the money-market hedge.

The forward-market hedge is not adequate for some types of exposure. If the foreign-currency asset or liability position occurs on a date for which forward quotes are not available, the forward hedge cannot be accomplished. In certain cases the forward hedge may cost more than the money-market hedge. In these cases a corporation with a large amount of exposure may prefer the money-market hedge. In addition to forward and money-market hedges, a company can also hedge its exposure by buying (or selling) some relatively new instruments—foreign currency futures contracts and foreign currency options. While futures contracts are similar to forward contracts in that they provide fixed prices for the *required* delivery of foreign currency at maturity, options *permit* fixed (strike) price foreign currency transactions anytime prior to maturity. Futures contracts and options differ from forward contracts in that, unlike forward contracts, which are customized with regard to amount and maturity date, futures and options are traded in standard amounts with standard maturity dates. In addition, while forward contracts are written by banks, futures and options are traded on organized exchanges, and individual traders deal with the exchange-based clearing organization rather than with each other. The purchase of futures requires the fulfillment of margin requirements (about 5 to 10 percent of the face amount), while the purchase of forward contracts requires only good credit standing with a bank. The purchase of options requires an immediate outlay that reflects a premium above the strike price and an outlay equal to the strike price when and if the option is exercised.

MULTINATIONAL WORKING CAPITAL MANAGEMENT

The basic principles of working capital management for a multinational corporation are similar to those for a domestic firm. However, tax and exchange rate factors are additional considerations for the multinational corporation (MNC). For an MNC with subsidiaries in many countries, the optimal decisions with regard to the management of working capital are made by considering the global company as a whole. The global or centralized financial decision for an MNC is superior to the set of independent optimal decisions for the subsidiaries. This is the *control* problem of the MNC. If the individual subsidiaries make decisions that are best for them individually, the consolidation of such decisions may not be best for the MNC as a whole. In order to effect *global* management, sophisticated computerized models—incorporating a large number of variables for each subsidiary—are solved to provide the best overall decision for the MNC.

There are complex issues and many useful techniques for the working capital management of an MNC. This section provides a brief overview of the issues and brief descriptions of some of the techniques. The books and articles listed at the end of the chapter give a more comprehensive treatment.

Before considering the components of working capital management, we examine two techniques that are useful in the management of a wide variety of working capital components.

Leading and Lagging

Leading and **lagging** are important risk-reduction techniques for many working-capital problems. Often, forward- and money-market hedges are not available to eliminate exchange risk. Under such circumstances, leading and lagging may be used to *reduce* exchange risk.

Recall that a net asset (long) position is not desirable in a weak or potentially depreciating currency. If a firm has a net asset position in such a currency, it should expedite the disposal of the asset. The firm should get rid of the asset earlier than it otherwise would have, or **lead,** and convert the funds into assets in a relatively stronger currency. By the same reasoning, the firm should lag or delay the collection against a net asset position in a strong currency. If the firm has a net liability (short) position in the weak currency, then it should delay the payment against the liability, or **lag,** until the currency depreciates. In the case of an appreciating or strong foreign currency and a net liability position, the firm should lead the payments—that is, reduce the liabilities earlier than it would otherwise have.

These principles are useful in the management of working capital of an MNC. They cannot, however, eliminate the foreign exchange risk. When exchange rates change continuously, it is almost impossible to guess whether, or when, the currency will depreciate or appreciate. That is why the risk of exchange rate changes cannot be eliminated. Nevertheless, the reduction of risk, or the increasing of gain from exchange rate changes, via the lead and lag is useful for cash management, accounts receivable management, and short-term liability management.

Cash Management and Positioning of Funds

Positioning of funds takes on an added importance in the international context. Funds may be transferred from a subsidiary of the MNC in country A to another subsidiary in country B such that the foreign exchange exposure and the tax liability of the MNC as a whole are minimized. It bears repeating that, owing to the *global strategy* of the MNC, the tax liability of the subsidiary in country A may be greater than it would otherwise have been, but the overall tax payment for all units of the MNC is minimized.

The transfer of funds among subsidiaries and the parent company is done by royalties, fees, and transfer pricing. A *transfer price* is the price a subsidiary or a parent company charges other companies that are part of the MNC for its goods or services. A parent that wishes to transfer funds from a subsidiary in a depreciating-currency country may charge a higher price on the goods and services sold to this subsidiary by the parent or by subsidiaries from strong-currency countries.

Centralized cash management of all the affiliates at the global level, achieved with the help of computer models, reduces both the overall cost of holding cash and the foreign exchange exposure of the MNC as a whole with respect to cash. The excess cash balance of one subsidiary is transferred to a cash-deficit subsidiary in the guise of a loan. The optimal holdings of cash in different currencies are calculated in a manner similar to the optimal portfolio problem discussed in Chapter 12.

Managing Receivables

A subsidiary's sales in its home country are usually quite large. If the plant is designed to serve a larger market, the subsidiary may have sales in foreign countries. Many American MNCs have one subsidiary in Europe to serve the entire European market. That is, a plant located in France may have sales in all countries of Europe and in countries outside Europe too. The subsidiary will have sales in many currencies. The subsidiary faces problems of what *currency to use for the invoicing* (or the denomination of the trade contract) and what *terms of payment* to quote. There is a tradeoff between these two decisions. If the subsidiary insists on invoicing the sales (or denominating the contract) in a strong currency, the customer will desire easier payment terms. If the customer insists on paying in a weak currency, the firm will demand stricter terms of payment. The subsidiary should follow the ideas of lead and lag in the collection. Sales made in weak currency should be collected sooner, a lead strategy. Accounts receivable in the strong currency should be collected later, a lag. The following example illustrates the principle.

The French subsidairy of an American MNC makes sales to customers in Italy and Spain. The firm insists on a mark contract on the Spanish sale. Assume that the Italian sale is made in lira. Further assume that the mark is a strong currency and the lira a weak currency. Now that the currency of denomination is decided, what should the sales terms be?

Spanish sale. Notice that with the mark sale, the firm will have a net asset position in a strong currency. The firm should lag its collection. In order to effect the lag, the firm should give a very small discount (or no discount at all), such that the "opportunity cost of discount forgone" to the Spanish customer is low. Say, the firm quotes a "1/10, net 30 after delivery, in marks" contract. The cost of discount forgone to the customer is 18.2 percent, annual rate.[8]

Italian sale. Notice that the lira sale is in a weak currency. The firm will have a net asset position in a weak currency. The firm should lead its collection. In order to effect the lead, the firm should offer better discount terms than those given to the Spanish customer. In addition, the firm should make the number of "net after delivery" days smaller than in the Spanish contract. For example, a "2/8, net 24, in lira" contract would ensure earlier collection, since the cost of discount forgone is 45.9 percent to the Italian customer.

The lead and lag principles are useful for accounts payable management, too. If

---

[8] The discount is computed as $(.01/.99) \times [360/(30 - 10)] = 18.18$ percent.

the firm has an accounts payable in marks and another in lira, it should try to lead the mark liability and lag the lira payment.

International Financing Decisions

A multinational corporation has access to many more financing sources than a domestic firm. It can tap not only the financing sources in its home country that are available to its domestic counterparts, but also sources in the foreign countries in which it operates. Host countries often provide access to low-cost subsidized financing in order to attract foreign investment. In addition, the MNC may enjoy preferential credit standards because of its size and investor preference for its home currency. In addition, an MNC may be able to access third country capital markets—countries in which it does not operate but which may have large, well-functioning capital markets. Finally, an MNC can also access external currency markets variously known as Eurodollar, Eurocurrency, or Asiandollar markets. These external markets are unregulated, and because of their lower spread, can offer very attractive rates for financing *and* for investments. With the increasing availability of interest rate and currency swaps, a firm can raise funds in the lowest-cost maturities and currencies and swap them into funds with the maturity and currency denomination it requires. Because of its ability to tap a larger number of financial markets, an MNC may have a lower cost of capital, and because it may better be able to avoid the problems or limitations of any one financial market, a more continuous access to external finance compared to a domestic company.

Access to national financial markets is regulated by governments. For example, in the United States, access to capital markets is governed by SEC regulations. Access to Japanese capital markets is governed by regulations issued by the Ministry of Finance. Some countries have extensive regulations; other countries have relatively open markets. These regulations may differ depending on the legal residency terms of the company raising funds. A company that cannot use its local subsidiary to raise funds in a given market will be treated as foreign. In order to increase their visibility in a foreign capital market, a number of MNCs are now listing their equities on the stock exchanges of many of these countries.

The external currency markets are predominantly centered in Europe, and about 80 percent of their value is denominated in terms of the U.S. dollar. Thus, most external currency markets can be characterized as Eurodollar markets. Such markets consist of an active short-term money market and an intermediate-term capital market with maturities ranging up to 15 years and averaging about 7 to 9 years. The intermediate-term market consists of the Eurobond and the Syndicated Eurocredit markets. Eurobonds are usually issued as unregistered bearer bonds and generally tend to have higher flotation costs but lower coupon rates compared to similar bonds issued in the United States. A Syndicated Eurocredit loan is simply a large term loan that involves contributions by a number of lending banks. Most large U.S. banks are active in the external currency markets.

Capital Structure Decisions

In arriving at its capital structure decisions, an MNC has to consider a number of factors. First, the capital structure of its local affiliates is influenced by local norms regarding capital structure in that industry and in that country. Local norms for companies in the same industry can differ considerably from country to country. Second, the local affiliate capital structure must also reflect corporate attitudes toward exchange rate and political risk in that country, which would normally lead to higher levels of local debt and other local capital. Third, local affiliate capital structure must reflect home country requirements with regard to the company's consolidated capital structure. Finally, the optimal MNC capital structure should reflect its wider access to financial markets, its ability to diversify economic and political risks, and its other advantages over domestic companies.

DIRECT FOREIGN INVESTMENT

The multinational corporation makes direct foreign investments abroad in the form of plants and equipment. The decision process for this type of investment is very similar to the capital budgeting decision in the domestic context—with some additional twists. Most real-world capital budgeting decisions are made with uncertain future outcomes. Recall that a capital budgeting decision has three major components: the estimation of the future cash flows (including the initial cost of the proposed investment), the estimation of the risk in these cash flows, and the choice of the proper discount rate. The choice of the appropriate criterion is also an issue; for present purposes we will assume that the net present value criterion is appropriate. Before addressing these issues individually, we wish to point out that all these issues are complex—and substantially more so than in the domestic context. We will highlight the complexities of the issues but will not attempt to indicate techniques for their resolution. Specifically, we will examine the (1) risks associated with direct foreign investment, and (2) factors to be considered in making the investment decision that may be unique to the international scene.

Risks in Direct Foreign Investments

Risks in domestic capital budgeting arise from two sources: business risk and financial risk. The international capital budgeting problem entails these risks as well as political risk and exchange risk.

Business Risk and Financial Risk

Business risk is due to the response of business to economic conditions in the foreign country. Thus, the American MNC needs to be aware of the business climate in both the United States and the foreign country. Additional business risk is due to competition from other MNCs, local businesses, and imported goods.

Financial risk refers to the risks introduced in the profit stream by the firm's financial structure. The financial risks of foreign operations are not very different from those of domestic operations.

Political Risk

The **political** or **sovereignty risk** arises because the foreign subsidiary conducts its business in a political system different from that of the home country. Many foreign governments, especially those in the Third World, are less stable than the U.S. government. A change in a country's political setup frequently brings a change in policies with respect to businesses, and especially with respect to foreign businesses. An extreme change in policy might involve nationalization or even outright expropriation of certain businesses. These are the political risks of conducting business abroad. A business with no investment in plants and equipment is less susceptible to these risks.

The political risks do not necessarily manifest themselves in extreme forms. More subtle and less harsh forms of government action also constitute political risk. Some examples of political risk are listed below.

1. Expropriation of plants and equipment without compensation.
2. Expropriation with minimal compensation that is below actual market value.
3. Nonconvertibility of the subsidiary's foreign earnings into the parent's currency—the problem of *blocked funds*.
4. Substantial changes in the laws governing taxation.
5. Governmental controls in the foreign country regarding the sale price of the products, wages, and compensation to personnel, hiring of personnel, making of transfer payments to the parent, and local borrowing.
6. Some governments require certain amounts of local equity participation in the business. Some require that the majority of the equity participation belong to their country.

All these controls and governmental actions introduce risks in the cash flows of the investment to the parent company. These risks must be considered before the foreign investment decision. An American MNC may decide against investing in countries with risks of types 1 and 2. Risks of the other type can be borne—provided that the returns from the foreign investments are high enough to compensate for them. Insurance against certain types of risks can be effected by the Overseas Private Investment Corporation (OPIC) for American corporations investing abroad. The MNC is limited in what it can do to reduce political risk.

Exchange Risk   The exposure of the fixed assets is best measured by the effects of the exchange rate changes on the firm's future earnings stream: that being *economic* exposure rather than *translation* exposure. For instance, changes in the exchange rate may adversely affect sales by making competing imported goods cheaper. Changes in the cost of goods sold may result if some components are imported and their price in the foreign currency changes because of exchange rate fluctuations. The thrust of these examples is that the effect of exchange rate changes on income statement items should be properly measured to evaluate exchange risk. Finally, exchange risk affects the dollar-denominated profit stream of the parent, whether or not it affects the foreign-currency profits.

International Capital Budgeting   Capital budgeting for international operations involves more extensive analysis than does capital budgeting for domestic operations. As in a domestic company, an MNC must develop estimates of the investment needed and the net cash flow generated by a proposed foreign capital investment. It must also assess the riskiness of these cash flows. Finally, it must summarize the cash flow and risk analysis information into a measure of desirability for the project, such as the net present value. The company can then compare the proposed investment with other possibilities and make a decision.

While this basic outline of steps necessary to evaluate a specific long-term foreign investment is not much different from that followed for evaluating a domestic capital investment, the cross-border nature of the foreign investment may require the consideration of a number of additional factors, such as the impact of currency and political risks on project value. Here we discuss some of the issues that may have to be considered in international capital budgeting.

For example, should the proposed capital investment be evaluated from the viewpoint of the local firm or from the viewpoint of the parent? The objective of maximizing shareholder wealth would indicate that the parent company perspective be used. However, the parent company may have supplied only part or none of the initial investment for the project. When using the parent company perspective, the project should be evaluated in terms of the parent's currency with the parent company's net initial investment and its net receipt of cash flows from the project discounted at a rate appropriate for the risks of the project cash flows with the inflation rate in the parent's currency. However, cash flows to the parent depend not just on the performance of the project, but also on how the local cash flows are managed. For example, because of tax considerations, it may not be optimal to remit all project cash flows to the parent only to have to send some or all of them back to be reinvested in the original foreign affiliate. In addition, value added by a project to a foreign affiliate will normally be reflected in the value of the parent company.

Thus, it may be better, even for shareholder wealth maximization, to evaluate a foreign capital proposal from the perspective of its local affiliate, using the total investment for the project and all of its cash flows discounted at a rate that reflects the local inflation rate and the riskiness of the project. In practice, most MNCs use at least the local perspective to evaluate a foreign project, while some supplement the local perspective with present value analysis from the parent's perspective. In such a case, the foreign affiliate perspective is the primary basis for a decision, while the parent perspective is used to ensure that the structure of the investment and the disposition of the cash flows are consistent with corporate objectives.

It is important that cash flow projections be realistic and reflect local conditions regarding competition, inflation, price controls, and other government regulations. When taking the local currency perspective, the discount rate should also reflect a realistic assessment of the expected local inflation rate. This may be especially difficult, given that capital markets in many foreign countries are often not free or efficient and interest rates do not reflect market expectations. In such cases, project cash flows should also reflect the advantages of using subsidized financing that may have been used to finance the project. When using the parent currency perspective, the discount rate should reflect the expected inflation rate in the parent currency, and foreign currency cash flows should be converted to parent currency cash flows using projected exchange rates. These projections are often based on the assumption that purchasing power parity holds during the life of the project. In such a case, it may be possible to take initial-year cash flows and assume that increases because local inflation will be offset exactly by purchasing power parity related declines in the exchange rate. However, if significant deviations from purchasing power parity are expected, such a simplifying assumption would be inappropriate. In addition, high inflation rates may be accompanied by government price controls. A company may face a lag between allowed price increases and inflation, or it may be accompanied by other economic and even political instability. In such cases, simply assuming that purchasing power parity will hold may be insufficient, and additional analysis to reflect these factors should be undertaken.

Investment Decision

In the domestic case, an NPV less than zero leads to rejection of a project. In the international context, an NPV less than zero leads to rejection of the direct foreign investment; however, the MNC then has other options open to it.

If the foreign sales volume is expected to be low, the MNC may consider setting up a *sales office* in the foreign country. The product may be exported to the foreign country from production facilities in the home country or from some other foreign subsidiary. An NPV calcuation may now be employed. The acceptance of this scheme is ensured, since no direct capital investment is needed. If the estimated sales levels are high enough that the establishment of a plant in the foreign country appears profitable, owing to the potential savings in the transportation costs, yet the NPV of the direct foreign investment (DFI) is negative, the MNC may consider *licensing* or *an affiliate arrangement* with a local company. The MNC provides the technology, and the interested domestic firm finances and sets up the plant. The MNC does not bear the risks of a DFI, but receives a royalty payment from the sales of the affiliate company instead.

In summary, the rationale for using the sales office or the affiliate arrangement is based on the following logic. A project may produce a negative NPV for one of two possible reasons: low cash inflows relative to the size of the initial cash outflow (initial investment), or a high discount rate (required return on investment). If the DFI is rejected because of the low cash flow argument, corresponding to a low level of sales, setting up the sales office may make the NPV of the project positive. Note that in the case of the sales office, the initial capital outlay will be much smaller than that required for the DFI. If, on the other hand, the DFI is rejected because of the use of a high discount rate, an affiliate arrangement may prove beneficial. The affiliate company may use a lower discount rate than the MNC, since the affiliate company does not face exchange risk and may face lower political risk than the foreign MNC. In other words, the project may be more profitable for the affiliate company, owing to the lower risk, than it would be for the MNC. The MNC, if an affiliate arrangement is made, receives a royalty payment.

Summary

The growing importance of international business, the growth of MNCs and of foreign trade in general, make it imperative that the student of finance be knowledgeable about the problems of operating in the international environment.

Exchange rate mechanics were discussed in the context of the prevailing floating rates. Under this system exchange rates between currencies vary in an apparently random fashion in accordance with the supply and demand conditions in the exchange market. Important economic factors affecting the level of exchange rates include the relative economic strengths of the countries involved, the balance of payments mechanism, and the countries' monetary policies. A number of terms were introduced as important to our understanding of exchange rates. These included the asked and the bid rates, which represent the selling and buying rates of currencies. The direct quote is the units of home currency per unit of foreign currency, while the indirect quote is the reciprocal of the direct quote. Cross-rate computations reflect the exchange rate between two foreign currencies. Finally, simple arbitrage for indirect quote and triangular arbitrage for cross rates were shown to hold. The efficiency of spot exchange markets implies that no arbitrage (riskless) profits can be made by buying and selling currencies in different markets.

The forward exchange market provides a valuable service by quoting rates for the delivery of foreign currencies in the future. The foreign currency is said to sell at a premium (discount) forward from the spot rate when the forward rate is greater (less) than the spot rate, in direct quotation. The computation of the percent per annum deviation of the forward from the spot rate was used to demonstrate the interest rate parity theorem (IRPT), which states that the forward contract sells at a discount or premium from the spot rates, owing solely to interest rate differential between the two countries. The IRPT was shown to hold by means of the covered interest arbitrage argument. In addition, the influences of purchasing power parity (PPP) and the international Fisher effect (IFE) in determining the exchange rate were discussed. In rational and efficient markets, forward rates are unbiased forecasts of future spot rates which are consistent with the PPP.

Exchange risk exists because the exact spot rate that prevails on a future date is not known with certainty today. The concept of exchange risk is applicable to a wide variety of businesses, including export-import firms and firms involved in making direct foreign investments or international investments in securities. Exchange exposure is a measure of exchange risk. There are different ways of measuring the foreign exposure, including the net asset (net liability) measurement. Different strategies are open to businesses to counter the exposure to this risk, including the money-market hedge, the forward-market hedge, futures contracts, and options. Each involves different costs.

In discussing working capital management in an international environment we found leading and lagging techniques useful in minimizing exchange risks and increasing profitability. In addition, funds positioning is a useful tool for reducing exchange risk exposure. An MNC may have a lower cost of capital because it has access to a larger set of financial markets than a domestic company. In addition to the home, host, and third country financial markets, an MNC can tap the rapidly growing external currency markets. In making capital structure decisions, an MNC must consider political and exchange risks and host and home county capital structure norms.

The complexities encountered in the direct foreign investment decision include the usual sources of risk—business and financial—and additional risks associated with fluctuating exchange rates and political factors. Political risk is due to differences in political climates, institutions, and processes between the home country and abroad. Under these conditions the estimation of future cash flows and the choice of the proper discount rates are more complicated than for the domestic investment situation. Rejection of a DFI proposal may lead either to the setting up of a sales office abroad or to an affiliate arrangement with a foreign company.

Study Questions

23–1.　What additional factors are encountered in international as compared with domestic financial management? Discuss each briefly.

23–2.　What different types of businesses operate in the international environment? Why are the techniques and strategies available to these firms different?

23–3. What is meant by arbitrage profits?

23–4. What are the markets and mechanics involved in generating (a) simple arbitrage profits, (b) triangular arbitrage profits, (c) covered interest arbitrage profits?

23–5. How do the purchasing power parity, interest rate parity, and the Fisher effect explain the relationships between the current spot rate, the future spot rate, and the forward rate?

23–6. What is meant by (a) exchange risk, (b) political risk?

23–7. How can exchange risk be measured?

23–8. What are the differences between transaction, translation and economic exposures? Should all of them be ideally reduced to zero?

23–9. What steps can a firm take to reduce exchange risk? Indicate at least two different techniques.

23–10. How are the forward-market and the money-market hedges affected? What are the major differences between these two types of hedges?

23–11. In the New York exchange market, the forward rate for the Indian currency, the rupee, is not quoted. If you were exposed to exchange risk in rupees, how could you cover your position?

23–12. Compare and contrast the use of forward contracts, futures contracts, and options to reduce foreign exchange exposure. When is each instrument most appropriate?

23–13. Indicate two working-capital management techniques that are useful for international businesses to reduce exchange risk and potentially increase profits.

23–14. How do the financing sources available to an MNC differ from those available to a domestic firm? What do these differences mean for the company's cost of capital?

23–15. What risks are associated with direct foreign investment? How do these risks differ from those encountered in domestic investment?

23–16. How is the direct foreign investment decision made? What are the inputs to this decision process? Are the inputs more complicated than those to the domestic investment problem? If so, why?

23–17. A corporation desires to enter a particular foreign market. The DFI analysis indicates that a direct investment in the plant in the foreign country is not profitable. What other course of action can the company take to enter the foreign market? What are the important considerations?

23–18. What are the reasons for the acceptance of a sales office or licensing arrangement when the DFI itself is not profitable?

Self-Test Problems

The data for self-test Problems ST–1 and ST–2 are given in the following table.

Selling Quotes for the West German Mark in New York

Country	Contract	$/Foreign Currency
West Germany—mark	Spot	0.3893
	30-day	0.3910
	90-day	0.3958

ST–1. You own $10,000. The dollar rate on the West German mark is 2.5823. The West German mark rate is given in the table above. Are arbitrage profits possible? Set up an arbitrage scheme with your capital. What is the gain (loss) in dollars?

ST–2. If the interest rates on the 30-day instruments in the United States and West Germany are 14 and 10 percent (annualized), respectively, what is the correct price of the 30-day forward mark?

Study Problems

The data for Study Problems 23–1 through 23–11 are given in the following table.

Selling Quotes for Foreign Currencies in New York

Country	Contract	$/Foreign Currency
Canada—dollar	Spot	.8437
	30-day	.8417
	90 day	.8395
Japan—yen	Spot	.004684
	30-day	.004717
	90-day	.004781
Switzerland—franc	Spot	.5139
	30-day	.5169
	90-day	.5315

23–1. An American business needs to pay (a) 10,000 Canadian dollars, (b) 2 million yen, and (c) 50,000 Swiss fancs to businesses abroad. What are the dollar payments to the respective countries?

23–2. An American business pays $10,000, $15,000, and $20,000 to suppliers in, respectively, Japan, Switzerland, and Canada. How much, in local currencies, do the suppliers receive?

23–3. Compute the indirect quote for the spot and forward Canadian dollar, yen, and Swiss franc contracts.

23–4. The spreads on the contracts as a percent of the asked rates are 2 percent for yen, 3 percent for Canadian dollars, and 5 percent for Swiss francs. Show, in a table similar to the one above, the bid rates for the different spot and forward rates.

23–5. You own $10,000. The dollar rate in Tokyo is 216.6743. The yen rate in New York is given in the table above. Are arbitrage profits possible? Set up an arbitrage scheme with your capital. What is the gain (loss) in dollars?

23–6. Compute the Canadian dollar/yen and the yen/Swiss franc spot rate from the data in the table above.

23–7. Compute the simple premium (discount) on the 30-day and 90-day yen, Swiss franc, and Canadian dollar quotes. Tabulate the percent-per-annum deviations as in Table 23–2.

23–8. Assume that the interest rate on the United States 30-day T-bill is 15 percent (annualized). The corresponding Canadian rate is 18 percent. The spot and the forward rates are shown in the table above. Can an American trader make arbitrage profits? If the trader had $100,000 to invest, indicate the steps he would take. What would be his net profit? (Ignore transactions and other costs.)

23–9. If the interest rates on the 30-day instruments in the United States and Japan are 15 and 12 percent (annualized), respectively, what is the correct price of the 30-day forward yen? Use the spot rate from the table.

23–10. The 30-day T-bill rate in the United States is 15 percent annualized. Using the 30-day forward quotes, compute the 30-day interest rates in Canada, Switzerland, and Japan.

23–11. The 90-day United States T-bill rate is 18 percent annualized. Using the 90-day quotes from the table, compute the 90 day rates in Canada, Switzerland, and Japan.

23–12. The expected inflation rates in the United States and France are 4 percent and 7 percent per annum, and the current spot rate for the French franc is $0.1611. Assume that the real rate of return in both countries is 3 percent per annum and that the market for the French franc is rational and efficient.

Using the Fisher effect, calculate the expected interest rates in the United States and in France.

Self-Test Solutions

SS–1. The West German rate is 2.5823 marks/$1, while the (indirect) New York rate is 1/.3893 = 2.5687 marks/$.

Assuming no transaction costs, the rates between West German and New York are out of line. Thus, arbitrage profits are possible .

STEP 1: *Since the mark is cheaper in West Germany, buy $10,000 worth of marks in West Germany. The number of marks purchased would be*

$$\$10,000 \times 2.5823 = 25,823 \text{ marks}$$

STEP 2: *Simultaneously sell the marks in New York at the prevailing rate. The amount received upon the sale of the marks would be:*

$$25,823 \text{ marks} \times \$.3893/\text{mark} = \$10,052.89$$

$$\text{net gain is } \$10,052.89 - \$10,000 = \underline{\underline{\$52.89}}$$

SS–2. **STEP 1:** *Compute the percent per annum premium on the forward rate using equation (23–3a):*

$$P = \frac{I^d - I^f}{1 + I^f} \tag{23–3a}$$

where I^d = the annualized interest rate on a domestic instrument having the same maturity as the forward contract

I^f = the annualized interest rate on a foreign instrument having the same maturity as the forward contract

Thus,

$$P = \frac{.14 - .10}{1 + .10} = \frac{.04}{1.10} = 0.0364$$

STEP 2: *Using this premium in equation (23–2), compute the forward rate F:*

$$\frac{F - S}{S} \times \frac{12}{n} \times 100 = P \tag{23–2}$$

where F = the forward rate, direct quote

S = the spot rate, direct quote

n = the number of months of the forward contract

P = the annualized percent premium

$$\frac{F - 0.3893}{0.3893} \times \frac{12}{1} \times 100 = 0.364$$

$$\frac{1200F - 467.16}{0.3893} = .0364$$

$$1200F - 467.16 = 1.417052$$

$$F = .3905$$

Thus the correct price of the forward rate is .3905.

Selected References

Adler, Michael, and B. Dumas. "International Portfolio Choice and Corporate Finance: A Synthesis," *Journal of Finance*, 38 (June 1983), 925–84.

Aggarwal, R. "Exchange Rates and Stock Prices: A Study of U.S. Capital Markets under Floating Exchange Rates," *Akron Business and Economic Review*, 12 (Fall 1981), 8–12.

_____. "International Differences in Capital Structure Norms," *Management International Review*, 21 (1981), 75–88.

Bernstein, Peter L. (ed.) *International Investing*. New York: Institutional Investor Books, 1983.

Caves, R. *Multinational Enterprises and Economic Analysis*. Cambridge, Eng.: Cambridge University Press, 1982.

Choi, F. D. S., and G. Mueller. *An Introduction to Multinational Accounting*. Englewood Cliffs, NJ: Prentice Hall, 1984.

Dufey, C., and S. L. Srinivasulu. "The Case for Corporate Management of Foreign Exchange Risk," *Financial Management* 12 (Winter 1983), 54–62.

Eiteman, D. K., and A. I. Stonehill. *Multinational Business Finance*. Reading, MA: Addison-Wesley, 1986.

Folks, W. R., and R. Aggarwal. *International Dimensions of Financial Management*. Boston: Kent Publishing Company, 1987.

Goodman, Lauri S. "Pricing of Syndicated Eurocurrency Credits," *Federal Reserve Bank of New York Quarterly Review*, (Summer 1980), 39–49.

Grabbe, J. Orlin. *International Financial Markets*. New York: Elsevier, 1986.

Kelly, Marie W. *Foreign Investment Practices of U.S. Multinational Corporations*. Ann Arbor, MI: UMI Research Press, 1981.

Kobrin, Steven J. *Environmental Assessment in the International Firm*. Berkeley: University of California Press, 1982.

Levich, Richard M. *The International Money Market: An Assessment of Forecasting Techniques and Market Efficiency*. Greenwich, CT: JAI Press, 1979.

Owens, E. A. *International Aspects of U.S. Income Taxation*. Cambridge, MA: Harvard Law School, 1980.

Shapiro, Alan C. *Multinational Financial Management*. Boston: Allyn and Bacon, 1986.

24

Small Business Finance

The small firm has played a significant role in the development of our country. It has served as the vehicle for fostering an entrepreneurial spirit, and it has also been important to the economy. In 1983 small businesses employed 48 percent of the private nonfarm work force, contributed 42 percent of the nation's sales, and generated approximately 38 percent of the nation's gross national product. Between 1980 and 1982 small businesses generated all of the 984,000 new jobs in the United States. Small businesses produced 2,650,000 new jobs, more than offsetting the 1,664,000 lost by larger businesses. The number of new company formations has increased steadily during the six-year period 1980 to 1985, with the only slight break in stride occurring in 1982. The number of new company startups during this period is shown in Table 24–1. While the growth in the number of small firms and their propensity for creating new jobs is impressive, the growth is not across all industries. As Table 24–2 shows, the growth in employment among industries dominated by small businesses varies from −4.4 percent for intercity highway transportation to an impressive 15.4 percent for radio, television, and music stores. Nevertheless, the contribution of small firms to the U.S. economy is impressive, and deserves recognition in a financial text.

This chapter examines financial management from the perspective of the owner-manager of a small firm. We will first define small business and then identify financial attributes often characteristic of the small business. Next, we will consider the importance of cash management for the small firm. Finally, we will identify financing sources available to the small firm, including the process of entering the public capital markets.

WHAT IS A SMALL BUSINESS?

Answering the question, "What is a small business?" is extremely difficult, since everyone has his or her own idea of a *small* business. For one person it could be a locally owned and operated store in which the owner is the boss, whereas another person

A large portion of the material in this chapter is taken from *Financial Management of the Small Firm* by Ernest W. Walker and J. William Petty II (Englewood Cliffs, NJ: Prentice-Hall, 1984).

TABLE 24–1. Small Business Formations and New Incorporations, 1980–85

Year	Business Starts	Incorporations
1985	114,065	668,904
1984	102,328	634,991
1983	100,868	600,400
1982	90,757	566,942
1981	92,161	581,661
1980	90,840	533,520

Source: Dun & Bradstreet, Inc.

TABLE 24–2. Percent Change in Employment of Small Business Dominated Industries, 1984–85

Fastest-growing industries	
Radio, television, and music stores	15.4
Computer and data processing services	14.2
Credit reporting and collection	13.7
Sanitary services	11.5
Masonry, stonework, and plastering	11.3
Carpentry and flooring	11.2
Engineering and architectural services	10.0
Real estate agents and managers	9.9
Mailing, reproduction, and stenographic services	9.2
Nonresidential building construction	9.2
Slowest-growing industries	
Intercity highway transportation	−4.4
Liquor stores	−2.3
Taxicabs	−2.1
Chemicals and allied products, wholesale	−0.8
Nonstore retailers	−0.7
School buses	0.6
Pipelines, except natural gas	0.0
Hardware stores	0.5
Public warehousing	0.6

Source: Small Business Administration and the U.S. Department of Labor.

could easily consider a firm with 500 employees as being small. Actually, both may be right; there is no simple definition.

Many definitions of "small business" have been offered; however, the definition and size restrictions formulated by the Small Business Administration (SBA) are probably the most widely used. The SBA uses its definition to ascertain the eligibility of a loan applicant. In general, the SBA defines a small business as one that is independently owned and operated and is nondominant in its field of operations. Also, to be considered *small*, a manufacturing company may not employ more than a specified number of employees, depending upon the industry classification. For wholesale and retail firms to qualify as a *small* company, annual sales may not exceed a designated dollar amount, with the restriction varying by industry classification.

In this chapter it is not necessary to define a small firm in the precise manner indicated by the SBA. In general, we will define a small firm as one that is *growth-oriented* and does not have easy access to the capital and money markets.

SMALL VERSUS LARGE: IS THERE A DIFFERENCE?

Even with a general definition of "small business," we might still question the rationale for studying small business apart from large business. That is, is the financial management of a small firm different from that of a large firm? If there are no fundamental differences, there is no rationale for studying the financial practices of small businesses apart from their larger counterparts.

In a study conducted by Walker and Petty the financial differences between large and small firms were evaluated, as measured by various financial ratios.[1] To compare these two groups, financial data were gathered for a sample of growth manufacturing firms with sales not exceeding $5 million. The small firm sample consisted of businesses that had filed prospectuses with state securities regulatory bodies in an effort to "go public." Thus, Walker and Petty were looking at operations involving successful closely held companies that were trying to tap the public equity markets. Similar data for a sample of large companies in the same industries were also compiled. The results are compared in Table 24–3.

In examining Table 24–3 we see that there clearly are some differences between small and large firms, as measured by selected financial ratios. The most prominent difference is the disparity in dividend policies. For example, dividends as a percent of earnings are approximately 3 percent and 40 percent for small and large firms, respectively. The low dividend payout ratio, which is generally thought to be typical of small firms, is seen to be characteristic even of small firms entering the public markets. In fact, 74 percent of the small firms made no distribution in the form of cash dividends in the year preceding the offering. Thus, the incentive, as well as the opportunity, for small firms to pay dividends in anticipation of a favorable impact upon the common stock when entering the marketplace is in no way apparent. The investors purchasing such securities must have believed that these securities represented shares in "growth companies." They were evidently willing to rely almost solely on the capital gains potential from their investment.

The second major difference between small and large firms is liquidity. Large firms have more liquidity, as reflected by the current ratio. This conclusion is consistent with a study conducted by Gupta, which found that the current and quick ratios

---

[1] Ernest W. Walker and J. William Petty II, "Financial Differences between Large and Small Firms," *Financial Management*, Winter 1978, pp. 61–68.

TABLE 24–3.   Financial Data for Small and Large Companies

	Average Values	
	Small Firms	*Large Firms*
Liquidity indicators		
Current ratio	2.00×	2.77×
Accounts receivable turnover	7.04×	6.40×
Inventory turnover	8.47×	5.31×
Current liabilities/total debt	83.70%	62.99%
Profitability indicators		
Operating profit margin	10.91%	9.20%
Accounts receivable turnover	7.04×	6.40×
Inventory turnover	8.47×	5.31×
Fixed assets turnover	9.40×	3.50×
Financing indicators		
Debt/total assets	49.00%	38.05%
Current liabilities/total debt	83.70%	62.99%
Fixed charges coverage	33.16×	22.47×
Business risk indicator		
Variability of operating income	21.94%	7.71%
Dividend policy indicator		
Dividend/earnings	2.9^1%	40.52%

Source: Ernest W. Walker and J. William Petty II, "Financial Differences between Large and Small Firms," *Financial Management*, Winter 1978, pp. 61–68.

increase as the firm size becomes larger.[2] The difference would seem to be the result of two factors. First, small firms retain smaller amounts of accounts receivable and inventory, as reflected by higher accounts receivable and inventory turnovers. Second, small firms rely more heavily on current liabilities, as shown by the current liabilities/ total debt ratio. Thus, small firms typically maintained less liquidity.

The apparent difference in liquidity between the large and small firms lends further support to the existing belief that a working capital shortage is a problem for small firms. The difference could be the result of at least two factors. First, the small firm's limited access to the capital markets may impose the need for more economy in the use of working capital. Second, the basic nature of the "entrepreneur" could have a bearing upon the working capital decisions within the small firm. If the managers of small firms are willing to assume greater risk, as experience would suggest, their attitude may well be reflected in the small firm's liquidity position.

Business risk and financial risk also help distinguish between small and large firms. Business risk, as measured by the variability of earnings before interest and taxes, is greater for small firms. The inability to diversify across investments, as well as geographi-

---

[2] M. C. Gupta, "The Effect of Size, Growth, and Industry on the Financial Structure of Manufacturing Companies," *Journal of Finance*, June 1969, pp. 517–29.

cally, increases the small firm's volatility of profits. Also, the small firm's capital structure is more debt-oriented, with an even greater tendency for using short-term credit. This heavy use of debt is usually perceived as one of the basic characteristics of managing a small firm.

Unquestionably there are differences in the financial management of small and large businesses. Based upon the Walker and Petty study, as well as personal observations, at least three areas deserve further comment: (1) the importance of cash management within the small firm; (2) financing the small firm, including the effect of low dividend payments on financing; and (3) the considerations involved in deciding whether to enter the public equity markets.

CASH MANAGEMENT IN THE SMALL FIRM

The nature and importance of cash management were described in Chapter 6. Although it is important that a "mature" firm be cognizant of its cash requirements, it is even more important for a firm encountering change and for a firm that is undercapitalized, both of which are frequently characteristic of small businesses. For instance, an undercapitalized enterprise results in a working capital shortage such that the turnover of working capital from the point of investing in raw materials to the final collection of receivables continues to plague the management of the company. In such an atmosphere, the executive is compelled to keep close tabs on the company's cash flow.

The second factor associated with many small businesses that should encourage the implementation of careful cash management is the *growth* element. The ownership of a small business facing an expansion has to be more cognizant of the cash inflows and the necessary outflows. Contrary to the belief of many small business owners, growth is not synonymous with financial prosperity. A growth firm is especially susceptible to financing difficulties, and thus requires a closer watch on funds flows.

A third instance in which the small firm may find cash planning essential is in approaching parties who represent potential sources of financing. The financing for the small business usually comes from the banker. In requesting a bank loan that entails a substantial amount, the cash plan becomes an important tool in two ways. First, the small business owner-manager is more familiar with the realities of the loan request, especially in having a better understanding of how the loan is to be repaid. This issue is generally a key concern to the banker. Second, and of equal importance, is the opportunity for the small business owner to establish credibility with the banker if, when requesting the loan, he or she can explicitly set forth detailed projected cash flows.

Despite the importance of careful cash management for the small firm, large firms typically make more extensive use of cash plans. Most managers of small firms believe they do not have the time to spend on forecasting. Besides, they view themselves as being close enough to the events so that they are able to plan adequately in an informal fashion, without having to prepare a written budget. Such an argument may be true of a few business owners; however, for most of them time has a way of making financial details hazy. As a result, the benefit of past experience is not nearly so beneficial. An understanding of the cash flow cycle, as well as the process for implementing a forecast, is particularly relevant for the small firm.

FINANCING THE SMALL FIRM

In studying how a small firm is financed, we will first describe the financing stages a firm experiences during its business life. We will then look at a special group of investors called "venture capitalists" that may be particularly significant for a small growth business, but not for a large business. Next, we will examine the different sources of financing in an effort to identify the more important ones for the small firm. Naturally, the conventional sources of short-term and long-term debt and common stock apply to all firms, small and large. However, the desirability and the availability of these various funds for the small firm may be different from those for the large firm. Finally, the decision to "go public" may be a serious consideration for a successful growth firm that has expanded beyond the financing capabilities of its owners. The advantages and disadvantages of issuing stock to the public are discussed in the concluding section of the chapter.

Stages of Financing

As shown in Figure 24–1, the business firm goes through three primary financing stages in the earlier segment of its business life cycle. Phase one, the *initial investment*, consists of the owner's personal capital, the credit provided by the commercial banker,

FIGURE 24–1. Business Financing Stages   Source: Ernest W. Walker and J. William Petty II, *Financial Management of the Small Firm* (Englewood Cliffs, N.J.: Prentice-Hall, 1984).

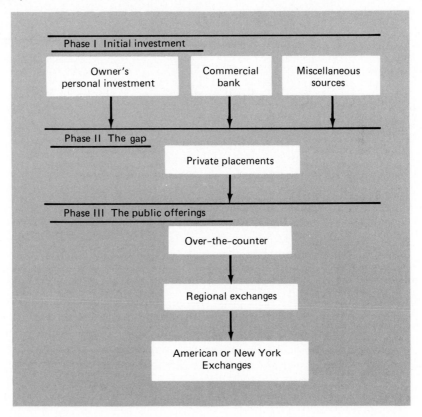

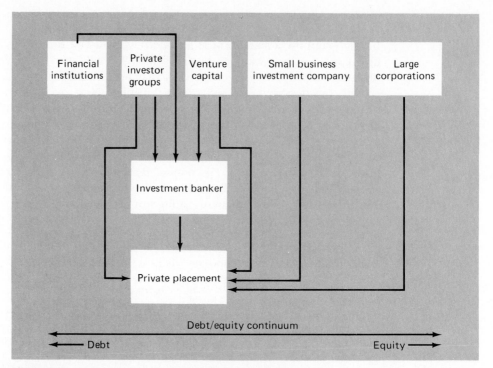

FIGURE 24–2. Sources of Private Placements Source: Ernest W. Walker and J. William Petty II, *Financial Management of the Small Firm* (Englewood Cliffs, N.J.: Prentice-Hall, 1984).

and a host of miscellaneous sources. Examples of miscellaneous sources in this phase would include (1) savings and loan associations, (2) the Small Business Administration, (3) friends and relatives, (4) leasing companies, and (5) commercial finance companies.

Phase two of a young firm's financial existence may be referred to as *the gap*. During this period the firm has grown to the level beyond which the owners have the capability to finance all investments; however, the firm is not large enough to justify a public offering. At this point it must sell securities to private individuals or groups. As shown in Figure 24–2, a number of sources for private placements exist and may be directly placed to come through an investment banker. For instance, financial institutions (banks and savings and loan associations), private investor groups, and venture capitalists may be approached either directly or through an investment banker acting as a liaison.[3] Large corporations may provide financing for a small firm but are generally approached directly. Furthermore, the kind of financing available from these respective sources varies, with financial institutions providing primarily debt financing and large corporations providing equity financing. Between the two extremes, a mixture of debt and equity capital would be available.

The final stage of development for the small firm in terms of financing sources is the raising of funds in the public markets. As explained in Chapter 17, a firm's stock

---

[3] The term *venture capitalist* is used to describe professional investors interested in investing in high-risk firms with potentially large returns. A more detailed explanation is provided in the next section.

is first traded publicly over-the-counter, then on a regional exchange, and finally on the American Stock Exchange or the New York Stock Exchange.

Before looking at specific sources of financing, we will discuss the nature of venture capital.

Venture Capital and the Small Firm

The venture capitalist has increasingly become a source of financing for small businesses. A definition of **venture capital investing** is difficult, in that venture capitalists have a broad range of interests and activities. Most venture capitalists, however, would fall somewhere along the following spectrum of investment interests:

1. Providing capital for any high-risk financial venture
2. Providing seed capital for a start-up situation
3. Investing in a firm that is unable to raise capital from conventional sources
4. Investing in large, publicly traded corporations where risk is significant[4]

Which definition is most descriptive depends in part on the eye of the beholder. For instance, some venture capitalists believe that providing seed money is too risky. Others, however, believe that such startup capital is the primary intent of their investments. Thus, generalities become difficult, but three underlying attributes normally prevail with venture capital investing. First, the investor is usually "locked in" to the firm for some duration of time, without an opportunity to sell stock quickly in response to a change in the firm's position, either favorable or unfavorable. Second, the venture capitalist normally represents the first equity financing from an "independent" party, as opposed to a friend or relative. However, additional financing from the venture capitalist may be required at a later date. Finally, venture capital investors have divergent interests. An investment having no appeal to one venture capital group might be of extreme interest to another group. For this reason, the management of a firm seeking funds should be aware of the compatibility of interests of the firm and the venture capitalist being approached.

If a financing package comprised of debt financing is presented to a venture capitalist, two major issues are involved. First, the venture capitalist may insist upon covenants in order to protect himself if the financial condition of the firm deteriorates or does not materialize as anticipated. These covenants, similar to the protective restrictions of a bank loan, are particularly common in start-up situations, with effective control of the organization being more easily lost through default on these long-term covenants than through the loss of majority ownership of the equity shares.

Second, the venture capitalist considers the tradeoff between the interest rate and the conversion privilege. The use of debt by venture capital investors generally involves a convertibility feature or bonds with warrants attached. By attaching either warrants or a conversion privilege, a significant reduction in interest charges usually results. For a small growth business a reduction in interest payments is not only desirable but essential, since most small businesses may have difficulty meeting the interest requirements associated with straight debt.

---

[4] See Patrick R. Liles, "Venture Capital: What It Is and How to Raise It," *New Business Ventures and the Entrepreneur* (Homewood, IL: Richard D. Irwin, 1974), p. 461.

Debt as a Source of Financing

Assuming that the business owners have depleted all available equity funds or want to take advantage of what they hope will be *favorable financial leverage*, management will no doubt search for debt financing. Potential sources of such financing for a small firm include (1) commercial banks, (2) life insurance companies, (3) venture capital groups, and (4) government agencies.

Commercial Banks

The commercial bank is the leading source of borrowed funds available to the small business. The loans available through the bank are primarily of two types, short-term and mortgage loans. However, the short-term instruments, although "formally" being defined as short term, provide considerable long-term financing for the small business entity. And although statistics indicate that the bank is principally a provider of short-term capital, such figures can be misleading. For instance, a loan with a maturity of 90 or 180 days, although being "classified" as short term, provides long-term financing through regular renewals as the indebtedness approaches the due date. Turning the debt over frequently is a technique by which the owners of a small firm convert short-term financing to an equivalent long-term status. This approach carries one distinct disadvantage in that the firm's financing is at the discretion of the banker each time the debt matures, which may cause some anxiety for the small business owner. The second and more formal source of long-term financing is the mortgage loan. These obligations relate to a specific purchase of real estate that is used as collateral in securing the financing arrangement.

In relying on the bank as a source of funds, the small business owner should develop a relationship with the banker prior to the actual need for funds. Ideally, the interaction should be on a professional and a personal basis. As part of the relationship, the business owner should be completely open with the banker. Only in this way can the banker be of maximum effectiveness in providing services. Also, in maintaining an association with the banker, the owner should continue to examine the benefits being received. He or she should be aware of the services being provided by competitive banks, as well as the costs related to these services.

The affiliation with a banker is not purely a function of the interest rate being charged, but involves a number of factors. The mere fact that a bank is charging a slightly higher interest rate does not necessarily justify changing banks. A long-term relationship is important, especially if monetary conditions are tight or if the firm temporarily encounters adversity. Finally, an inquiry should be made as to the banker's expertise and the bank's capabilities in terms of loan size. The firm's owner should seek a bank having particular expertise in the firm's type of operation. That is, not only is the accessibility of capital important, but a source of counseling may be of substantial benefit. In selecting a bank, the size of the bank should also be considered. If large sums of money will be required, a small bank may not have the capability to service such loans. On the other hand, if the credit requirements are not so extensive, it may be quite beneficial to use a small bank where the owner of the firm has access to key bank officers.

Insurance Companies

The executive of the small firm may find that an insurance company is a source of financing. As a financial intermediary, an insurance company has large sums of money available for investments. Only a small portion of such funds is available for the small firm, but to the extent that such funds may be used, the extension of credit generally comes in the form of a mortgage loan. Hence, a life insurance company may be a potential long-term source of financing for a small firm planning the construction of a real estate investment, such as a plant or an office. In examining the request for a loan, the insurance company looks closely at the type of building being constructed, with a preference for a facility having potential multiple uses. As to the size of loans, most insurance companies are interested in making loans in large amounts; however, loans for as little as $10,000 have been granted. In general, mortgage loans extend over a 10- to 20-year period, with the amount of the mortgage being limited to approximately 70 percent of the appraised value of the property.

In addition to the mortgage loan, the insurance company may issue credit on an unsecured long-term basis to the borrower who has an excellent credit rating. Such loans, if granted, generally extend for periods of 10 years with an interest rate exceeding that of the bank by 1 to 2 percent.

Small Business Investment Corporations (SBICs)

Small Business Investment Corporations, one form of a venture capital organization, extend long-term loans, usually in excess of $75,000 for periods exceeding 5 years. Historically the loans have been in high-technology industries involving medium-sized operations. In addition, the firm normally must have a track record in terms of profit capabilities and growth potential. An in-depth explanation of SBICs is given later in the chapter.

Governmental Agencies as Suppliers of Debt Capital

The majority of the governmental agencies offering financial support to small businesses are at the federal level, with a few possibilities being provided by the states and the local governmental bodies. Within the federal government, the Small Business Administration is the primary agency overseeing the federal government's role in fostering small business. In addition, several other agencies sponsor loans to firms in selected industries or for specific purposes. Examples of these special-purpose loans include financing in connection with defense contracts, foreign trade, public works, and agriculture. In this regard, the small business owner should inquire into the various financing alternatives that might be available from the federal government.

The Small Business Administration. The Small Business Administration (SBA) is multifaceted in its functions. It offers active support in ensuring small businesses a "fair" proportion of governmental contracts, either lending or acting as the guarantee for credit extended to the small firm, providing management consultants to the owners of the small company, and performing research of interest to the small business community. The following paragraphs describe the agency's role in actually providing capital or facilitating the acquisition of these funds.

Eligibility Requirements for SBA Loans. In working with small firms, the government had to develop an operational definition of a small firm. To be considered a small firm, the SBA requires that certain size criteria be met. The guidelines do not have to be strictly interpreted—instead they should be thought of as representing approximations in identifying eligible loan applicants. Exceptions to these benchmarks for defining a small entity are also indicated, with organizations operating in the following types of operations not having access to SBA loans:

1. Loans to nonprofit businesses
2. Lending for investment
3. Loans for withdrawals by principals
4. Publication of magazines and newspapers loans
5. Loans that encourage monopolies
6. TV or radio broadcasting loans
7. Financing for unwarranted changes in ownership
8. Loans to businesses selling mainly alcoholic beverages
9. Businesses involved in gambling

Application Procedures. The approach used in processing a loan application is somewhat dependent on the firm's status in terms of being an established business versus a new business. Regardless of the age of the firm, the loan request should originally be presented to a bank. Only subsequent to the bank's review of the loan and denial of the credit may the firm approach the SBA. In other words, the SBA is a "source of last resort." In fact, if the community population exceeds 200,000, two banks must have rejected the loan. Having completed the process of a loan request, the owner may then inquire as to the bank's interest in working with the SBA in terms of a guarantee or participation in the loan. Typically, if the bank has had satisfactory experience with SBA cooperative efforts and cannot justify accepting the loan singularly, it will initiate the idea of SBA involvement and avoid an outright rejection of the request.

Types of Loans Available Through the SBA. When the needed financing is coming entirely from the SBA, the agency is authorized to lend up to $150,000 to an individual business. However, in view of the agency's policy of avoiding direct loans, the typical limitation in size when granted has been between $5,000 and $25,000. If the loan involves the bank's participation, this ceiling is raised to $150,000, with a maximum interest rate on the bank's portion being established by the bank at a "legal and reasonable rate."

Instead of making direct loans, the SBA prefers to serve in a support function as a guarantee for bank credit. When approved by the SBA field representative, a bank may obtain a guarantee of the loan repayment from the SBA not to exceed the lesser of 90 percent of the loan or $500,000. The interest rate is generally set by the bank. As to maturity, the purpose of the loan dictates the repayment schedule. The limit as imposed by the SBA is 10 years, with a shorter period of 6 years for working capital requirements and 20 years for real estate.

State and Local Agencies.

The individual states have increasingly become involved in providing financial assistance to businesses located or considering being located in areas under the state's jurisdiction. In making an effort to attract new industry, certain state and local governmental agencies have become quite liberal in terms of financial packages. The broad spectrum of financial incentives being offered by the respective state and local authorities naturally precludes an extensive listing. The small business owner should contact the state and local government personnel associated with industrial development.

Common Stock as a Source of Financing

In examining common stock as a source of financing for the small firm, three areas are of primary concern: (1) the problems a small firm may encounter in issuing common stock, (2) the forms of common stock used by small firms, and (3) a review of specific sources of common equity that may be available to small firms.

Problems of Common Stock for the Small Firm

Chapter 19 discussed the basic characteristics of common stock, along with its advantages and disadvantages as a source of financing. The following problems involving common stock are unique to the small firm:

1. Because of the lack of marketability of most securities of small firms, particularly common stock, it may be necessary to price the stock so that it will yield a significantly higher return than that of a similar firm having a ready market for its shares. Naturally, the result is an increased cost of common capital.
2. The flotation cost of selling a small issue, particularly in the public markets, becomes almost prohibitive for the small firm. For instance, such expenses may approach 25 percent of the issue size.
3. Issuing common securities to external investors permits a potential dilution of control for existing shareholders. Although such a loss may only be psychological, most small owners are averse to placing themselves in a position that even slightly compromises their control over the firm.

Forms of Common Stock

Common stock can be classified in terms of the shareholders' claim on income, claim on assets, and voting rights. Typically, Class A stock has a higher claim on dividend income and assets but less extensive voting power, even to the point of voting being nonexistent. In contrast, Class B common stock has a lesser claim on income and assets but greater voting power. This classification mechanism permits the owners to maintain greater control or be able to attract outside investors by providing greater income and protection upon liquidation. In the same context, "founders' shares" have been used by small business. These shares are similar to a Class B stock except that the owners of the shares maintain the sole voting rights but generally have no right to dividends for a specified number of years. The objective of the founders' shares is to permit the organizers of a company to maintain complete control of the company during the early years of the operation, often with a minimal investment.

Beyond relatives and friends, the owner of the small business must look to venture capitalists for common stock financing. Specific sources are described below.

Sources of Common Equity for the Small Firm

Small Business Investment Corporations (SBICs). When the SBA was established in 1953, attention was directed to the long-term debt and equity financial requirements of the small business; however, no government action was taken at that time. Finally, in 1958, the Federal Reserve completed a study showing that the banks and the SBA were satisfactorily meeting the short-term and intermediate-term debt requirements of the small business, but that the small business was encountering an ever-increasing need for longer-term loans and equity financing.[5] As a result, SBICs were established

---

[5] U.S. Federal Reserve System, *Financing Small Business*, Parts 1 and 2, Report to the U.S. Congress, Committee on Currency and Banking and the Select Committees on Small Business, 85th Cong., 2nd sess., April 11, 1958, pp. 77–90.

as private profit-seeking companies to be regulated by the SBA. As a means of encouraging private individuals or institutions to initiate these organizations, government loans were to be granted on favorable terms, and tax advantages were offered.[6]

The objectives and the operational philosophies of the various SBICs are extremely dissimilar, making it difficult to describe SBICs in general. However, a basic classification does exist in terms of **captive** and **noncaptive** SBICs, in which the management of a captive SBIC is dictated by the objectives of a parent organization, usually a bank. In contrast, the noncaptive SBICs operate independently, with ownership ranging from several private individuals or institutions to a broadly based public.

Most SBICs are interested in equity participation via convertible debentures. Such securities generally carry a 5- to 20-year maturity date. The interest rates are quite divergent, depending on the company's growth potential. The size of loans is limited by several factors, including the willingness of the SBIC management to participate in the financing being requested. In addition to the SBIC's discretion in extending the loan, the SBIC is prevented by regulation from investing more than 20 percent of its capital in a particular venture. Also, the SBIC is not permitted to develop a majority interest in an organization except as a result of a violation in the terms of the loan.

Publicly Owned Venture Capital Investment Companies. These organizations are publicly owned by a broad base of investors, including companies listed on the New York Stock Exchange. Examples of publicly owned venture capitalists include the American Research and Development Corporation and the SMC Investment Corporation. As with other venture capital sources, public companies are quite divergent in their interests and objectives.

Private Venture Capital Investors. The private venture capital investor is primarily concerned with the development of small enterprises needing long-term capital for growth, companies for sale due to the death or retirement of the owner, or firms requiring professional management. These private companies operate under a high degree of flexibility and therefore may be interested in long-term capital appreciation, in which funds are frequently invested in participation with others to enable the small private venture company to maintain diversity. Thus, private venture capital investors may possibly offer not only another source of venture capital, but also an avenue for increased flexibility relative to the publicly owned companies.

Wealthy Individuals. Wealthy individuals within the community should be recognized as a viable source of venture capital. If relatively small amounts are required (less than $100,000) and the management of the business desiring the funds is well known within the business community, wealthy individuals may be quite receptive to incurring significant risk for the purpose of achieving high expected returns. The attraction becomes even greater if the returns are tax sheltered. The advantage in developing such arrangements relates to the informality and the often negligible formal reporting requirements. Typically, the investors are relying on their "faith" in the

---

[6] "Providing Risk Capital for Small Business: Experience of the SBIC's," *Quarterly Review of Economics and Business*, Spring 1975, pp. 77–90.

chief executive and not on detailed accounting reports. Yet management should proceed with caution in the selection of local investors, because such individuals occasionally develop a strong propensity for participating in the management of the firm.

Large Corporations. Approximately 30 major corporations have developed formal venture capital operations. Large companies have entered the venture capital field for two reasons. First, the hopes of striking a capital gains bonanza, such as Scientific Data Systems, no doubt has appeal. However, a second and more probable reason is the search for technology, with a potential acquisition in mind. Prime examples of corporate involvement include General Electric, Hercules, Du Pont, Sun Oil Company, and Johnson and Johnson.

Other Sources. In addition to the foregoing sources of venture capital financing, an entrepreneur may consider such sources as (1) community development corporations, (2) local development corporations, (3) the Economic Development Administration, and (4) various state and local agencies. Each of these sources has limitations as to the types of financing to be provided.

Retention of Earnings as a Source of Financing

The retention of earnings is a major source of equity financing for any organization, regardless of size. As shown in Table 24–4, even for the largest corporations, with assets exceeding $1 billion, approximately 48 percent of company earnings was retained. Approximately 37 percent of the book value of these giants' financial mix is comprised of accumulated retained earnings. Even large corporations rely heavily on the retention of profits as a means of building an equity base for growth. Yet, in comparison, the small business draws even more heavily on profits in financing its growth. Specifically, an inverse relationship between the size of the assets and the percentage of profits being retained for reinvestment is clearly evident in Table 24–4, with approximately 85 percent of the profits being retained by companies with less than $25 million in assets. Although accumulated retained earnings does not represent as large a proportion of the small companies' capital structure, this lower percentage has to be due, at least in part, to the fewer years of existence of most smaller businesses. In summary, small businesses rely more extensively on retained earnings as a source of equity financing.

TABLE 24–4. Profit Retention Relative to Asset Size

	Total Assets		
	Under $25 Million	*$100–$250 Million*	*Over $1,000 Million*
Cumulative retained earnings relative to total assets[a]	37.19%	30.76%	36.96%
Percentage of earnings retained in the firm[a]	84.63	73.72	48.26

[a] The period ends September 30, 1986.

Source: Federal Trade Commission, *Quarterly Financial Report* (Washington, DC: U.S. Government Printing Office, 1987).

The relative retention rates hold implications regarding the dividend policies of the different-sized companies. In Chapter 16 we saw that the company's dividend policy is believed to be a function of two factors. First, the company's investment opportunities should be a key input into the dividend decision. If the expected returns from prospective investments exceed the company's cost of capital, an incentive exists to retain greater amounts and therefore pay lower dividends. Reciprocally, poor investments suggest higher dividend payments. Second, the common stockholders' preference for dividends versus capital gains is an important consideration in ascertaining the appropriate dividend strategy. Inducements frequently noted for the distribution of profits include the favorable informational content associated with an investor's receiving a dividend, the resolution of uncertainty, and the preference for current income.

The incentives for paying dividends for a large company having a broad base of stockholders are not as significant for the small company. For instance, the informational content from dividends may be important to a "distant" investor in a large business but meaningless to stockholders in a small business who are also actively involved in its management. Second, the small business owner would not be as concerned about the resolution of uncertainty as the individual who is strictly an investor seeking a given return. The owner-manager continues to have the opportunity to act as a decision maker with respect to the risk-return relationship without having to receive the monies in the form of dividends. Thus, on a purely intuitive basis, the potential lack of a preference for dividends, complemented by a strong incentive to minimize taxes, would apparently explain the retention of earnings by the smaller businesses.

For a firm that has successfully passed through the early stages of financing, the owners may want to consider the option of *going public*.

GOING PUBLIC

In analyzing the process of **going public,** we should first define the term. What is going public? This terminology, in a legal context, is difficult to define because of the numerous peripheral technical questions. In general, however, going public simply relates to the procedures involved in selling the securities of a privately owned company. The securities sold may be shares belonging to the owners of the company, a *secondary distribution*, or the company itself may sell additional shares to raise new capital. The latter acquisition of public owners is of prime concern to the financial manager as a source of funds to finance growth.

In this section we will review the merits and demerits of the public offering, and then highlight the prerequisites for the company seeking public funds.

Reasons for Not Going Public

In examining the question of whether or not to go public, the owner of a small business should give considerable thought to such a decision. Although the prestige accompanying a public security is a strong inducement, disillusion may well set in during the offering process or during the ensuing years of the "public life." Caveats to going public would be as follows:

1. The registration process carries with it a substantial commitment on the part of management, in terms of both time and expense. Management has to be

prepared to allocate a significant portion of its efforts to the task for some 6 months preceding the actual sale. This estimate would not include the preliminary work and thought required for at least 2 years prior to the first offering. Also, the company will spend a large amount of money to complete the public offering. Legal and accounting fees, underwriting expenses, filing fees, and printing expenses can be substantial.

2. As an aftermath of the public offering, the principal owner-manager is not in a position to administer the operations in the personal manner typical of the small, closely held enterprise. Publication of many facets of the concern's activities is required by the regulatory authorities not only at the outset of the issue, but also on an annual basis. Such disclosure of "inside" transactions is not only bothersome at times to the small owner, but generally represents a significant cost of reporting for the firm, in both effort and money.

3. While most executives of small growth firms have become accustomed to making decisions quickly and decisively with little thought to the opinion of others, going public can greatly modify the decision-making process. The acquisition of stockholder approval is required for a public company in such matters as stock option plans, acquisitions, and major modifications of the company's capital structure. The new formality does delay the timeliness of management's decisions, which may be annoying to the aggressive decision maker.

4. The directors' and officers' liability is significantly increased when a company becomes a public entity. The strong tendency for individuals or groups to sue companies places the senior personnel and directors of public companies in a precarious situation. Although insurance can be purchased to cover this increased liability, the premiums are expensive.

5. Finally, the public market has to be recognized as being a relatively unreliable source of funds. While the larger organizations must be sensitive to the conditions of the general stock market, the smaller issuers face an extra dimension—the status of "hot issues." The market may be relatively bullish, but may not be receptive to the issue of a new and smaller business.

In summary, no easy path is available for a small firm desiring to go public. This fact is emphasized in a study in which individuals having been through the process were questioned as to the problems they faced.[7] As reflected in Table 24–5, the disadvantage identified almost unanimously by management is the sizable amount of time taken from the manager's schedule. Also, more than half the executives being sampled complained of the costs of floating the issue, the difficulty involved in determining an appropriate price for the offering, and the substantive disclosure requirements imposed upon the company. Even more significantly, corporate managers were asked whether they would go public if the opportunity to do so was at their discretion again. Sixty percent of the managers responded negatively. Thus, the importance of a serious and thorough examination of whether or not to go public cannot be overemphasized.

---

[7] Gramme K. Howard, Jr., "Going Public When It Makes Sense," in *Guide to Venture Capital Sources*, 3rd ed., ed. Stanley M. Rubel (Chicago: Capital Publishing Corporation, 1974), p. 76.

TABLE 24–5.   Difficulties of the Public Offering

Problem Area	Percentage Response
Amount of key management time consumed in underwriting	91%
Unanticipated costs of the underwriting	58
Pricing of the issue	52
Amount of disclosure in prospectus	51

Source: Gramme K. Howard, Jr., "Going Public When It Makes Sense," in *Guide to Venture Capital Sources*, 3rd ed., ed. Stanley M. Rubel (Chicago: Capital Publishing Corp., 1974), p. 76.

Reasons for Going Public

Why would a company go public? In other words, what benefits would result from a public offering? Numerous advantages are typically cited. However, if these advantages are to materialize, there must be sound justification for needed funds, combined with an apparent shortage of other sources of capital. Typically, the manager-owners rely on the retention of earnings or the investment of private funds for additional equity funds. Only after the depletion of these two equity sources would the corporation normally turn to the public for additional equity capital. In other words, the public market is typically an *avenue of last resort* from the corporate perspective. With this thought in mind, the corporate motivations for a public offering are as follows:

1. **An established market for future financing.** In addition to the primary impetus for issuing public securities, the need for equity funds, several indirect benefits relating to future financing accrue to the business. First, when the securities in question become recognized by the investment public, later issues will have a more receptive market. Second, creditors are typically more interested in lending money to businesses having a proven market for their common stock. Naturally, lending institutions view this improved marketability as increasing the options available to the corporation for building a larger equity base. Third, when a corporation is attempting to finalize a merger or acquisition, a security having a tested value in the marketplace becomes an invaluable instrument of negotiation. Most shareholders of a company being merged or acquired are simply not interested in trading their private stock for other private securities.

2. **Encouragement to key personnel.** The use of a stock option plan as an encouragement to key personnel has received much attention in the business literature. However, the actual merit of such programs has to be considered somewhat tenuous when a market for the security is nonexistent. Thus, for the concern using stock option plans, going public should provide a more effective employee incentive plan.

3. **Public relations.** The broad distribution of a company's stock among the public is thought to afford favorable publicity. Such positive exposure is particularly beneficial if the general public comprises not only the shareholders, but also the consumers of the company's product or services.

4. **Diversification.** Often the owner of a closely held operation has invested his or her life, both emotionally and materially, in the company. If the company becomes sufficiently large to justify external equity financing, the owner may wish to diversify, thereby affording an opportunity to broaden the financial base. Yet such spreading of wealth is typically constrained by the desire to maintain control of the business.

TABLE 24–6. Reasons for Small Company Public Offerings

	Percent of Total
To meet company objectives:	
Financial needs	
Working capital	36.0%
Fixed capital	9.5
Research and development funds	5.7
Investment activity	
Establish market for later offering by shareholders	9.5
Probable purchase of another firm	3.8
Contemplated merger	2.4
To meet owners' personal considerations:	
Minimize estate taxes	13.4
Resolve personal conflicts	2.4
Provide nest egg	4.8
Diversify investments	4.8
Take advantage of a bull market	3.8
Other reasons	3.8

Source: Cited in Solomon J. Flink, *Equity Financing for Small Business* (New York: Simmons-Boardman Publishing Corp., 1962), p. 87.

5. **Collateral for personal credit.** In borrowing on a personal basis, the owner of a firm is in a more favorable position by offering a public security as collateral, as opposed to a stock having no public market activity.

In summary, a host of reasons could be given for the need or desire for going public. Table 24–6 provides a synopsis of these reasons, as well as their perceived importance. Although the information comprising the table is dated, going back to the early 1960s, the results still give some indication as to the impetus for a firm's going public. In examining the table, *financial needs* emerge as the fundamental reason for a company's going external for common stock. Over 50 percent of the chief executives responding to the questionnaire gave financial needs as the rationale for issuing equity securities in the public market. Within this category, working capital requirements seem to be of prime concern. A business will often commit all available working capital to a capital expenditure such that the level of working capital becomes deficient. As the leadership then initiates a search for funds, the expressed justification is the need for additional working capital, although the reduced working capital is a symptom and not the underlying cause.

Prerequisites for Going Public

If after having reviewed the advantages and disadvantages of going public, management still believes that a public issue would be good for the firm, the question then becomes whether the firm is a viable candidate for a public offering. In identifying the prerequisites for going public, the keys become size, marketability, earnings record, management, growth potential, and the products or services. With these six variables providing the structure, the prerequisites for a public offering can be explained as follows.

Size Constraint

As would be expected, the management of the small enterprise has to be concerned with the question, Is the firm large enough to go public? The size criterion generally involves two aspects: (1) the level of earnings and (2) the size of the issue. With regard to the size of the issue (earnings capacity is addressed in a later section), not only may a small issue in terms of dollars be infeasible due to high costs, but a related factor, the number of shares, also has to be considered. Formulating a general guideline, however, is difficult, with the minimal size depending on the philosophy of the investment banker. Regardless of the number of shares being quoted by an individual banker, an important standard is the potential for developing an active market. Specifically, without a reasonable number of shares outstanding for active trading, the investment banker has difficulty justifying involvement in the financing.

Marketability A second item of concern to investment bankers is the creation of a substantial market. All else being constant, they prefer to develop a market sufficiently large to provide the investor additional liquidity in terms of the ability to buy and sell securities as needed. To investment bankers, the depth and liquidity of the market are crucial. Without the possibility of developing such a market, investment bankers are usually not interested.

Established Earnings Record Management of a firm entertaining the thought of going public must be aware that the size, quality, and trend of earnings are of utmost importance in public financing. A firm must reach a certain *size* in terms of new income. Again, no one number can be expressed as the optimal amount. Although some investment bankers indicate that a firm with less than $300,000 annual net income would not be of interest to them, examples can be cited where successful issues have been accomplished with net income substantially below $300,000. The *quality* of earnings must also be considered, with the quality being a function of the stability and the source of earnings. Finally, the *trend* of earnings is related to the likelihood that a long-term upward trend from the *current source* of income will continue to exist. The earnings trend must be "significant," must have grown at a steady rate during the most recent years, and must be expected to continue into the future.

The Management Team The investigation into a company preparing for public financing includes an analysis of the basic *quality* and *philosophy* of top management. In examining the quality of management, the factors to consider include experience, integrity, and depth of the corporate leadership. While no one of these three factors can be emphasized at the expense of the others, depth of management is often a difficult problem for the small business. A family-owned company typically relies on the capabilities of the second generation. Thus, the second generation has to be able and willing to continue the operation, or management personnel external to the family must be available within the organization. With regard to the philosophy of top management, the underwriter is sensitive to management's attitude toward accepting the responsibility for satisfying the queries of inquisitive investors, brokers, and analysts. In essence, can management not only conduct a sound business, but also conduct sound public relations in what is frequently an annoying situation?

Growth Potential Although "growth" and public markets are not necessarily mutually exclusive, the owners of an enterprise interested in making a public offering should be aware of the uphill battle to be fought if growth is not evident. When competing for funds, an organization having negligible growth potential can anticipate serious difficulties in attracting the public investor. Hence, steady growth patterns expected to continue into the future are a strong factor in the company's favor when entering the public market. In addition, the public disclosure requirements may be incompatible with the continued growth of some operations. For instance, if the information being submitted to the public affects the company's competitive position, going public is certainly a questionable avenue for funds. Although such an event rarely develops for most companies, the concern may be a definite psychological factor that will have to be recognized.

Products and Services

The *reputation* and *image* of an entity's products or services should also be considered. Concisely stated, the sound *reputation* of an organization's products or services is an essential ingredient for a successful public offering. In a related sense, the image of the product is of key importance. Although the latter factor is generally a psychological barrier, it may well prevent a public issue from being a feasible alternative for a firm. In other words, a "glamorous" or "romantic" firm has a distinct advantage over the more commonplace type of operation.

Summary

The financial management of the small firm is a topic that has attracted increasing interest. The nature and magnitude of financial policies and practices depend upon the size of the firm. Small firms (1) tend to rely more heavily on the retention of earnings as a way to build equity, (2) have less liquidity, (3) use greater amounts of debt, and (4) experience more business risk.

In addition to the conventional sources of financing, small firms frequently rely on the Small Business Administration (SBA) and various groups of venture capitalists for financing growth. The SBA will make loans, to a limited extent, but more often serves as a guarantor of a bank loan. The venture capitalist will assume significant risk as an investor in a small firm; however, the cost will be relatively high to the firm.

When a firm has reached a certain size, the owner-manager may want to raise funds in the public equity markets. Before doing so, however, considerable thought should be given to the advantages and disadvantages. Going public is both costly and bothersome to most owners of small firms.

Study Questions

Describe the financial difference between a small and a large firm.

Why is cash management important for the small firm?

Explain the different stages of financing a firm may experience during its growth.

Describe venture capital as a source of financing.

What is a Small Business Investment Corporation?

Describe the involvement of the Small Business Administration in financing a small firm.

What are the advantages and disadvantages of going public?

When is a firm able to go public?

Selected References

Andrews, Victor L., and Peter C. Eisemann. *Who Finances Small Business Circa 1980?* Washington, DC: Interagency Task Force on Small Business Finance, November 1981.

Bamberger, I. "Portfolio Analysis for the Small Firm," *Long-Range Planning*, December 1982, pp. 49–57.

Churchill, W. C., and V. L. Lewis. "The Five Stages of Small Business Growth," *Harvard Business Review*, November–December 1983, pp. 30ff.

DeThomas, A. R. "Valuing the Ownership Interest in the Privately-Held Small Firm," *American Journal of Small Business*, Winter 1985, pp. 50–59.

Glassman, Cynthia A., and Peter L. Struck. *Survey of Commercial Bank Lending to Small Business*. Washington, DC: Interagency Task Force on Small Business Finance, January 1982.

Gupta, M. C. "The Effect of Size, Growth, and Industry on the Financial Structure of Manufacturing Companies," *Journal of Finance*, June 1969, pp. 517–29.

Higgins, R. C. "How Much Growth Can a Firm Afford?" *Financial Management*, Fall 1977, pp. 7–16.

McConnell, John J., and R. Richardson Petit. *Application of the Modern Theory of Finance to Small Business Firms*. Washington, DC: Interagency Task Force on Small Business Finance, October 1980.

The State of Small Business: A Report of the President. Transmitted to the Congress, March 1984.

Steinmetz, L. L. "Critical Stages of Small Business Growth," *Business Horizons*, February 1969, pp. 29–36.

Stoll, Hans R. *Small Firms' Access to Public Equity Financing*. Washington, DC: Interagency Task Force on Small Business Finance, December 1981.

Walker, Ernest W., and J. William Petty II. "Financial Differences between Large and Small Firms," *Financial Management*, Winter 1978, pp. 61–68.

Welsh, J. A., and J. F. White. "A Small Business Is Not a Little Big Business," *Harvard Business Review*, July–August 1981, pp. 1ff.

White, Lawrence J. *Role of Small Business in the American Economy*. Washington, DC: Interagency Task Force on Small Business Finance, September 1980.

Appendices

APPENDIX A. Compound Sum of $1

n	1%	2%	3%	4%	5%	6%	7%	8%	9%	10%
1	1.010	1.020	1.030	1.040	1.050	1.060	1.070	1.080	1.090	1.100
2	1.020	1.040	1.061	1.082	1.102	1.124	1.145	1.166	1.188	1.210
3	1.030	1.061	1.093	1.125	1.158	1.191	1.225	1.260	1.295	1.331
4	1.041	1.082	1.126	1.170	1.216	1.262	1.311	1.360	1.412	1.464
5	1.051	1.104	1.159	1.217	1.276	1.338	1.403	1.469	1.539	1.611
6	1.062	1.126	1.194	1.265	1.340	1.419	1.501	1.587	1.677	1.772
7	1.072	1.149	1.230	1.316	1.407	1.504	1.606	1.714	1.828	1.949
8	1.083	1.172	1.267	1.369	1.477	1.594	1.718	1.851	1.993	2.144
9	1.094	1.195	1.305	1.423	1.551	1.689	1.838	1.999	2.172	2.358
10	1.105	1.219	1.344	1.480	1.629	1.791	1.967	2.159	2.367	2.594
11	1.116	1.243	1.384	1.539	1.710	1.898	2.105	2.332	2.580	2.853
12	1.127	1.268	1.426	1.601	1.796	2.012	2.252	2.518	2.813	3.138
13	1.138	1.294	1.469	1.665	1.886	2.133	2.410	2.720	3.066	3.452
14	1.149	1.319	1.513	1.732	1.980	2.261	2.579	2.937	3.342	3.797
15	1.161	1.346	1.558	1.801	2.079	2.397	2.759	3.172	3.642	4.177
16	1.173	1.373	1.605	1.873	2.183	2.540	2.952	3.426	3.970	4.595
17	1.184	1.400	1.653	1.948	2.292	2.693	3.159	3.700	4.328	5.054
18	1.196	1.428	1.702	2.026	2.407	2.854	3.380	3.996	4.717	5.560
19	1.208	1.457	1.753	2.107	2.527	3.026	3.616	4.316	5.142	6.116
20	1.220	1.486	1.806	2.191	2.653	3.207	3.870	4.661	5.604	6.727
21	1.232	1.516	1.860	2.279	2.786	3.399	4.140	5.034	6.109	7.400
22	1.245	1.546	1.916	2.370	2.925	3.603	4.430	5.436	6.658	8.140
23	1.257	1.577	1.974	2.465	3.071	3.820	4.740	5.871	7.258	8.954
24	1.270	1.608	2.033	2.563	3.225	4.049	5.072	6.341	7.911	9.850
25	1.282	1.641	2.094	2.666	3.386	4.292	5.427	6.848	8.623	10.834
30	1.348	1.811	2.427	3.243	4.322	5.743	7.612	10.062	13.267	17.449
40	1.489	2.208	3.262	4.801	7.040	10.285	14.974	21.724	31.408	45.258
50	1.645	2.691	4.384	7.106	11.467	18.419	29.456	46.900	74.354	117.386

APPENDIX A. Compound Sum of $1 (continued)

n	11%	12%	13%	14%	15%	16%	17%	18%	19%	20%
1	1.110	1.120	1.130	1.140	1.150	1.160	1.170	1.180	1.190	1.200
2	1.232	1.254	1.277	1.300	1.322	1.346	1.369	1.392	1.416	1.440
3	1.368	1.405	1.443	1.482	1.521	1.561	1.602	1.643	1.685	1.728
4	1.518	1.574	1.630	1.689	1.749	1.811	1.874	1.939	2.005	2.074
5	1.685	1.762	1.842	1.925	2.011	2.100	2.192	2.288	2.386	2.488
6	1.870	1.974	2.082	2.195	2.313	2.436	2.565	2.700	2.840	2.986
7	2.076	2.211	2.353	2.502	2.660	2.826	3.001	3.185	3.379	3.583
8	2.305	2.476	2.658	2.853	3.059	3.278	3.511	3.759	4.021	4.300
9	2.558	2.773	3.004	3.252	3.518	3.803	4.108	4.435	4.785	5.160
10	2.839	3.106	3.395	3.707	4.046	4.411	4.807	5.234	5.695	6.192
11	3.152	3.479	3.836	4.226	4.652	5.117	5.624	6.176	6.777	7.430
12	3.498	3.896	4.334	4.818	5.350	5.936	6.580	7.288	8.064	8.916
13	3.883	4.363	4.898	5.492	6.153	6.886	7.699	8.599	9.596	10.699
14	4.310	4.887	5.535	6.261	7.076	7.987	9.007	10.147	11.420	12.839
15	4.785	5.474	6.254	7.138	8.137	9.265	10.539	11.974	13.589	15.407
16	5.311	6.130	7.067	8.137	9.358	10.748	12.330	14.129	16.171	18.488
17	5.895	6.866	7.986	9.276	10.761	12.468	14.426	16.672	19.244	22.186
18	6.543	7.690	9.024	10.575	12.375	14.462	16.879	19.673	22.900	26.623
19	7.263	8.613	10.197	12.055	14.232	16.776	19.748	23.214	27.251	31.948
20	8.062	9.646	11.523	13.743	16.366	19.461	23.105	27.393	32.429	38.337
21	8.949	10.804	13.021	15.667	18.821	22.574	27.033	32.323	38.591	46.005
22	9.933	12.100	14.713	17.861	21.644	26.186	31.629	38.141	45.923	55.205
23	11.026	13.552	16.626	20.361	24.891	30.376	37.005	45.007	54.648	66.247
24	12.239	15.178	18.788	23.212	28.625	35.236	43.296	53.108	65.031	79.496
25	13.585	17.000	21.230	26.461	32.918	40.874	50.656	62.667	77.387	95.395
30	22.892	29.960	39.115	50.949	66.210	85.849	111.061	143.367	184.672	237.373
40	64.999	93.049	132.776	188.876	267.856	378.715	533.846	750.353	1051.642	1469.740
50	184.559	288.996	450.711	700.197	1083.619	1670.669	2566.080	3927.189	5988.730	9100.191

APPENDIX A. Compound Sum of $1 (continued)

n	21%	22%	23%	24%	25%	26%	27%	28%	29%	30%
1	1.210	1.220	1.230	1.240	1.250	1.260	1.270	1.280	1.290	1.300
2	1.464	1.488	1.513	1.538	1.562	1.588	1.613	1.638	1.664	1.690
3	1.772	1.816	1.861	1.907	1.953	2.000	2.048	2.097	2.147	2.197
4	2.144	2.215	2.289	2.364	2.441	2.520	2.601	2.684	2.769	2.856
5	2.594	2.703	2.815	2.932	3.052	3.176	3.304	3.436	3.572	3.713
6	3.138	3.297	3.463	3.635	3.815	4.001	4.196	4.398	4.608	4.827
7	3.797	4.023	4.259	4.508	4.768	5.042	5.329	5.629	5.945	6.275
8	4.595	4.908	5.239	5.589	5.960	6.353	6.767	7.206	7.669	8.157
9	5.560	5.987	6.444	6.931	7.451	8.004	8.595	9.223	9.893	10.604
10	6.727	7.305	7.926	8.594	9.313	10.086	10.915	11.806	12.761	13.786
11	8.140	8.912	9.749	10.657	11.642	12.708	13.862	15.112	16.462	17.921
12	9.850	10.872	11.991	13.215	14.552	16.012	17.605	19.343	21.236	23.298
13	11.918	13.264	14.749	16.386	18.190	20.175	22.359	24.759	27.395	30.287
14	14.421	16.182	18.141	20.319	22.737	25.420	28.395	31.691	35.339	39.373
15	17.449	19.742	22.314	25.195	28.422	32.030	36.062	40.565	45.587	51.185
16	21.113	24.085	27.446	31.242	35.527	40.357	45.799	51.923	58.808	66.541
17	25.547	29.384	33.758	38.740	44.409	50.850	58.165	66.461	75.862	86.503
18	30.912	35.848	41.523	48.038	55.511	64.071	73.869	85.070	97.862	112.454
19	37.404	43.735	51.073	59.567	69.389	80.730	93.813	108.890	126.242	146.190
20	45.258	53.357	62.820	73.863	86.736	101.720	119.143	139.379	162.852	190.047
21	54.762	65.095	77.268	91.591	108.420	128.167	151.312	178.405	210.079	247.061
22	66.262	79.416	95.040	113.572	135.525	161.490	192.165	228.358	271.002	321.178
23	80.178	96.887	116.899	140.829	169.407	203.477	244.050	292.298	349.592	417.531
24	97.015	118.203	143.786	174.628	211.758	256.381	309.943	374.141	450.974	542.791
25	117.388	144.207	176.857	216.539	264.698	323.040	393.628	478.901	581.756	705.627
30	304.471	389.748	497.904	634.810	807.793	1025.904	1300.477	1645.488	2078.208	2619.936
40	2048.309	2846.941	3946.340	5455.797	7523.156	10346.879	14195.051	19426.418	26520.723	36117.754
50	13779.844	20795.680	31278.301	46889.207	70064.812	104354.562	154942.687	229345.875	338440.000	497910.125

APPENDIX A. Compound Sum of $1 (continued)

n	31%	32%	33%	34%	35%	36%	37%	38%	39%	40%
1	1.310	1.320	1.330	1.340	1.350	1.360	1.370	1.380	1.390	1.400
2	1.716	1.742	1.769	1.796	1.822	1.850	1.877	1.904	1.932	1.960
3	2.248	2.300	2.353	2.406	2.460	2.515	2.571	2.628	2.686	2.744
4	2.945	3.036	3.129	3.224	3.321	3.421	3.523	3.627	3.733	3.842
5	3.858	4.007	4.162	4.320	4.484	4.653	4.826	5.005	5.189	5.378
6	5.054	5.290	5.535	5.789	6.053	6.328	6.612	6.907	7.213	7.530
7	6.621	6.983	7.361	7.758	8.172	8.605	9.058	9.531	10.025	10.541
8	8.673	9.217	9.791	10.395	11.032	11.703	12.410	13.153	13.935	14.758
9	11.362	12.166	13.022	13.930	14.894	15.917	17.001	18.151	19.370	20.661
10	14.884	16.060	17.319	18.666	20.106	21.646	23.292	25.049	26.924	28.925
11	19.498	21.199	23.034	25.012	27.144	29.439	31.910	34.567	37.425	40.495
12	25.542	27.982	30.635	33.516	36.644	40.037	43.716	47.703	52.020	56.694
13	33.460	36.937	40.745	44.912	49.469	54.451	59.892	65.830	72.308	79.371
14	43.832	49.756	54.190	60.181	66.784	74.053	82.051	90.845	100.509	111.119
15	57.420	64.358	72.073	80.643	90.158	100.712	112.410	125.366	139.707	155.567
16	75.220	84.953	95.857	108.061	121.713	136.968	154.002	173.005	194.192	217.793
17	98.539	112.138	127.490	144.802	164.312	186.277	210.983	238.747	269.927	304.911
18	129.086	148.022	169.561	194.035	221.822	253.337	289.046	329.471	375.198	426.875
19	169.102	195.389	225.517	260.006	299.459	344.537	395.993	454.669	521.525	597.625
20	221.523	257.913	299.937	348.408	404.270	468.571	542.511	627.443	724.919	836.674
21	290.196	340.446	398.916	466.867	545.764	637.256	743.240	865.871	1007.637	1171.343
22	380.156	449.388	530.558	625.601	736.781	866.668	1018.238	1194.900	1400.615	1639.878
23	498.004	593.192	705.642	838.305	994.653	1178.668	1394.986	1648.961	1946.854	2295.829
24	652.385	783.013	938.504	1123.328	1342.781	1602.988	1911.129	2275.564	2706.125	3214.158
25	854.623	1033.577	1248.210	1505.258	1812.754	2180.063	2618.245	3140.275	3761.511	4499.816
30	3297.081	4142.008	5194.516	6503.285	8128.426	10142.914	12636.086	15716.703	19517.969	24201.043
40	49072.621	66519.313	89962.188	121388.437	163433.875	219558.625	294317.937	393684.687	522508.312	700022.688

APPENDIX B.   Present Value of $1

n	1%	2%	3%	4%	5%	6%	7%	8%	9%	10%
1	.990	.980	.971	.962	.952	.943	.935	.926	.917	.909
2	.980	.961	.943	.925	.907	.890	.873	.857	.842	.826
3	.971	.942	.915	.889	.864	.840	.816	.794	.772	.751
4	.961	.924	.888	.855	.823	.792	.763	.735	.708	.683
5	.951	.906	.863	.822	.784	.747	.713	.681	.650	.621
6	.942	.888	.837	.790	.746	.705	.666	.630	.596	.564
7	.933	.871	.813	.760	.711	.665	.623	.583	.547	.513
8	.923	.853	.789	.731	.677	.627	.582	.540	.502	.467
9	.914	.837	.766	.703	.645	.592	.544	.500	.460	.424
10	.905	.820	.744	.676	.614	.558	.508	.463	.422	.386
11	.896	.804	.722	.650	.585	.527	.475	.429	.388	.350
12	.887	.789	.701	.625	.557	.497	.444	.397	.356	.319
13	.879	.773	.681	.601	.530	.469	.415	.368	.326	.290
14	.870	.758	.661	.577	.505	.442	.388	.340	.299	.263
15	.861	.743	.642	.555	.481	.417	.362	.315	.275	.239
16	.853	.728	.623	.534	.458	.394	.339	.292	.252	.218
17	.844	.714	.605	.513	.436	.371	.317	.270	.231	.198
18	.836	.700	.587	.494	.416	.350	.296	.250	.212	.180
19	.828	.686	.570	.475	.396	.331	.277	.232	.194	.164
20	.820	.673	.554	.456	.377	.312	.258	.215	.178	.149
21	.811	.660	.538	.439	.359	.294	.242	.199	.164	.135
22	.803	.647	.522	.422	.342	.278	.226	.184	.150	.123
23	.795	.634	.507	.406	.326	.262	.211	.170	.138	.112
24	.788	.622	.492	.390	.310	.247	.197	.158	.126	.102
25	.780	.610	.478	.375	.295	.233	.184	.146	.116	.092
30	.742	.552	.412	.308	.231	.174	.131	.099	.075	.057
40	.672	.453	.307	.208	.142	.097	.067	.046	.032	.022
50	.608	.372	.228	.141	.087	.054	.034	.021	.013	.009

APPENDIX B. Present Value of $1 (continued)

n	11%	12%	13%	14%	15%	16%	17%	18%	19%	20%
1	.901	.893	.885	.877	.870	.862	.855	.847	.840	.833
2	.812	.797	.783	.769	.756	.743	.731	.718	.706	.694
3	.731	.712	.693	.675	.658	.641	.624	.609	.593	.579
4	.659	.636	.613	.592	.572	.552	.534	.516	.499	.482
5	.593	.567	.543	.519	.497	.476	.456	.437	.419	.402
6	.535	.507	.480	.456	.432	.410	.390	.370	.352	.335
7	.482	.452	.425	.400	.376	.354	.333	.314	.296	.279
8	.434	.404	.376	.351	.327	.305	.285	.266	.249	.233
9	.391	.361	.333	.308	.284	.263	.243	.225	.209	.194
10	.352	.322	.295	.270	.247	.227	.208	.191	.176	.162
11	.317	.287	.261	.237	.215	.195	.178	.162	.148	.135
12	.286	.257	.231	.208	.187	.168	.152	.137	.124	.112
13	.258	.229	.204	.182	.163	.145	.130	.116	.104	.093
14	.232	.205	.181	.160	.141	.125	.111	.099	.088	.078
15	.209	.183	.160	.140	.123	.108	.095	.084	.074	.065
16	.188	.163	.141	.123	.107	.093	.081	.071	.062	.054
17	.170	.146	.125	.108	.093	.080	.069	.060	.052	.045
18	.153	.130	.111	.095	.081	.069	.059	.051	.044	.038
19	.138	.116	.098	.083	.070	.060	.051	.043	.037	.031
20	.124	.104	.087	.073	.061	.051	.043	.037	.031	.026
21	.112	.093	.077	.064	.053	.044	.037	.031	.026	.022
22	.101	.083	.068	.056	.046	.038	.032	.026	.022	.018
23	.091	.074	.060	.049	.040	.033	.027	.022	.018	.015
24	.082	.066	.053	.043	.035	.028	.023	.019	.015	.013
25	.074	.059	.047	.038	.030	.024	.020	.016	.013	.010
30	.044	.033	.026	.020	.015	.012	.009	.007	.005	.004
40	.015	.011	.008	.005	.004	.003	.002	.001	.001	.001
50	.005	.003	.002	.001	.001	.001	.000	.000	.000	.000

APPENDIX B. Present Value of $1 (continued)

n	21%	22%	23%	24%	25%	26%	27%	28%	29%	30%
1	.826	.820	.813	.806	.800	.794	.787	.781	.775	.769
2	.683	.672	.661	.650	.640	.630	.620	.610	.601	.592
3	.564	.551	.537	.524	.512	.500	.488	.477	.466	.455
4	.467	.451	.437	.423	.410	.397	.384	.373	.361	.350
5	.386	.370	.355	.341	.328	.315	.303	.291	.280	.269
6	.319	.303	.289	.275	.262	.250	.238	.227	.217	.207
7	.263	.249	.235	.222	.210	.198	.188	.178	.168	.159
8	.218	.204	.191	.179	.168	.157	.148	.139	.130	.123
9	.180	.167	.155	.144	.134	.125	.116	.108	.101	.094
10	.149	.137	.126	.116	.107	.099	.092	.085	.078	.073
11	.123	.112	.103	.094	.086	.079	.072	.066	.061	.056
12	.102	.092	.083	.076	.069	.062	.057	.052	.047	.043
13	.084	.075	.068	.061	.055	.050	.045	.040	.037	.033
14	.069	.062	.055	.049	.044	.039	.035	.032	.028	.025
15	.057	.051	.045	.040	.035	.031	.028	.025	.022	.020
16	.047	.042	.036	.032	.028	.025	.022	.019	.017	.015
17	.039	.034	.030	.026	.023	.020	.017	.015	.013	.012
18	.032	.028	.024	.021	.018	.016	.014	.012	.010	.009
19	.027	.023	.020	.017	.014	.012	.011	.009	.008	.007
20	.022	.019	.016	.014	.012	.010	.008	.007	.006	.005
21	.018	.015	.013	.011	.009	.008	.007	.006	.005	.004
22	.015	.013	.011	.009	.007	.006	.005	.004	.004	.003
23	.012	.010	.009	.007	.006	.005	.004	.003	.003	.002
24	.010	.008	.007	.006	.005	.004	.003	.003	.002	.002
25	.009	.007	.006	.005	.004	.003	.003	.002	.002	.001
30	.003	.003	.002	.002	.001	.001	.001	.001	.000	.000
40	.000	.000	.000	.000	.000	.000	.000	.000	.000	.000
50	.000	.000	.000	.000	.000	.000	.000	.000	.000	.000

APPENDIX B. Present Value of $1 (continued)

n	31%	32%	33%	34%	35%	36%	37%	38%	39%	40%
1	.763	.758	.752	.746	.741	.735	.730	.725	.719	.714
2	.583	.574	.565	.557	.549	.541	.533	.525	.518	.510
3	.445	.435	.425	.416	.406	.398	.389	.381	.372	.364
4	.340	.329	.320	.310	.301	.292	.284	.276	.268	.260
5	.259	.250	.240	.231	.223	.215	.207	.200	.193	.186
6	.198	.189	.181	.173	.165	.158	.151	.145	.139	.133
7	.151	.143	.136	.129	.122	.116	.110	.105	.100	.095
8	.115	.108	.102	.096	.091	.085	.081	.076	.072	.068
9	.088	.082	.077	.072	.067	.063	.059	.055	.052	.048
10	.067	.062	.058	.054	.050	.046	.043	.040	.037	.035
11	.051	.047	.043	.040	.037	.034	.031	.029	.027	.025
12	.039	.036	.033	.030	.027	.025	.023	.021	.019	.018
13	.030	.027	.025	.022	.020	.018	.017	.015	.014	.013
14	.023	.021	.018	.017	.015	.014	.012	.011	.010	.009
15	.017	.016	.014	.012	.011	.010	.009	.008	.007	.006
16	.013	.012	.010	.009	.008	.007	.006	.006	.005	.005
17	.010	.009	.008	.007	.006	.005	.005	.004	.004	.003
18	.008	.007	.006	.005	.005	.004	.003	.003	.003	.002
19	.006	.005	.004	.004	.003	.003	.003	.002	.002	.002
20	.005	.004	.003	.003	.002	.002	.002	.002	.001	.001
21	.003	.003	.003	.002	.002	.002	.001	.001	.001	.001
22	.003	.002	.002	.002	.001	.001	.001	.001	.001	.001
23	.002	.002	.001	.001	.001	.001	.001	.001	.001	.000
24	.002	.001	.001	.001	.001	.001	.001	.000	.000	.000
25	.001	.001	.001	.001	.001	.000	.000	.000	.000	.000
30	.000	.000	.000	.000	.000	.000	.000	.000	.000	.000
40	.000	.000	.000	.000	.000	.000	.000	.000	.000	.000

APPENDIX C.   Sum of an Annuity of $1 for *n* Periods

n	1%	2%	3%	4%	5%	6%	7%	8%	9%	10%
1	1.000	1.000	1.000	1.000	1.000	1.000	1.000	1.000	1.000	1.000
2	2.010	2.020	2.030	2.040	2.050	2.060	2.070	2.080	2.090	2.100
3	3.030	3.060	3.091	3.122	3.152	3.184	3.215	3.246	3.278	3.310
4	4.060	4.122	4.184	4.246	4.310	4.375	4.440	4.506	4.573	4.641
5	5.101	5.204	5.309	5.416	5.526	5.637	5.751	5.867	5.985	6.105
6	6.152	6.308	6.468	6.633	6.802	6.975	7.153	7.336	7.523	7.716
7	7.214	7.434	7.662	7.898	8.142	8.394	8.654	8.923	9.200	9.487
8	8.286	8.583	8.892	9.214	9.549	9.897	10.260	10.637	11.028	11.436
9	9.368	9.755	10.159	10.583	11.027	11.491	11.978	12.488	13.021	13.579
10	10.462	10.950	11.464	12.006	12.578	13.181	13.816	14.487	15.193	15.937
11	11.567	12.169	12.808	13.486	14.207	14.972	15.784	16.645	17.560	18.531
12	12.682	13.412	14.192	15.026	15.917	16.870	17.888	18.977	20.141	21.384
13	13.809	14.680	15.618	16.627	17.713	18.882	20.141	21.495	22.953	24.523
14	14.947	15.974	17.086	18.292	19.598	21.015	22.550	24.215	26.019	27.975
15	16.097	17.293	18.599	20.023	21.578	23.276	25.129	27.152	29.361	31.772
16	17.258	18.639	20.157	21.824	23.657	25.672	27.888	30.324	33.003	35.949
17	18.430	20.012	21.761	23.697	25.840	28.213	30.840	33.750	36.973	40.544
18	19.614	21.412	23.414	25.645	28.132	30.905	33.999	37.450	41.301	45.599
19	20.811	22.840	25.117	27.671	30.539	33.760	37.379	41.446	46.018	51.158
20	22.019	24.297	26.870	29.778	33.066	36.785	40.995	45.762	51.159	57.274
21	23.239	25.783	28.676	31.969	35.719	39.992	44.865	50.422	56.764	64.002
22	24.471	27.299	30.536	34.248	38.505	43.392	49.005	55.456	62.872	71.402
23	25.716	28.845	32.452	36.618	41.430	46.995	53.435	60.893	69.531	79.542
24	26.973	30.421	34.426	39.082	44.501	50.815	58.176	66.764	76.789	88.496
25	28.243	32.030	36.459	41.645	47.726	54.864	63.248	73.105	84.699	98.346
30	34.784	40.567	47.575	56.084	66.438	79.057	94.459	113.282	136.305	164.491
40	48.885	60.401	75.400	95.024	120.797	154.758	199.630	295.052	337.872	442.580
50	64.461	84.577	112.794	152.664	209.341	290.325	406.516	573.756	815.051	1163.865

APPENDIX C. Sum of an Annuity of $1 for *n* Periods (continued)

n	11%	12%	13%	14%	15%	16%	17%	18%	19%	20%
1	1.000	1.000	1.000	1.000	1.000	1.000	1.000	1.000	1.000	1.000
2	2.110	2.120	2.130	2.140	2.150	2.160	2.170	2.180	2.190	2.200
3	3.342	3.374	3.407	3.440	3.472	3.506	3.539	3.572	3.606	3.640
4	4.710	4.779	4.850	4.921	4.993	5.066	5.141	5.215	5.291	5.368
5	6.228	6.353	6.480	6.610	6.742	6.877	7.014	7.154	7.297	7.442
6	7.913	8.115	8.323	8.535	8.754	8.977	9.207	9.442	9.683	9.930
7	9.783	10.089	10.405	10.730	11.067	11.414	11.772	12.141	12.523	12.916
8	11.859	12.300	12.757	13.233	13.727	14.240	14.773	15.327	15.902	16.499
9	14.164	14.776	15.416	16.085	16.786	17.518	18.285	19.086	19.923	20.799
10	16.722	17.549	18.420	19.337	20.304	21.321	22.393	23.521	24.709	25.959
11	19.561	20.655	21.814	23.044	24.349	25.733	27.200	28.755	30.403	32.150
12	22.713	24.133	25.650	27.271	29.001	30.850	32.824	34.931	37.180	39.580
13	26.211	28.029	29.984	32.088	34.352	36.786	39.404	42.218	45.244	48.496
14	30.095	32.392	34.882	37.581	40.504	43.672	47.102	50.818	54.841	59.196
15	34.405	37.280	40.417	43.842	47.580	51.659	56.109	60.965	66.260	72.035
16	39.190	42.753	46.671	50.980	55.717	60.925	66.648	72.938	79.850	87.442
17	44.500	48.883	53.738	59.117	65.075	71.673	78.978	87.067	96.021	105.930
18	50.396	55.749	61.724	68.393	75.836	84.140	93.404	103.739	115.265	128.116
19	56.939	63.439	70.748	78.968	88.211	98.603	110.283	123.412	138.165	154.739
20	64.202	72.052	80.946	91.024	102.443	115.379	130.031	146.626	165.417	186.687
21	72.264	81.698	92.468	104.767	118.809	134.840	153.136	174.019	197.846	225.024
22	81.213	92.502	105.489	120.434	137.630	157.414	180.169	206.342	236.436	271.028
23	91.147	104.602	120.203	138.295	159.274	183.600	211.798	244.483	282.359	326.234
24	102.173	118.154	136.829	158.656	184.166	213.976	248.803	289.490	337.007	392.480
25	114.412	133.333	155.616	181.867	212.790	249.212	292.099	342.598	402.038	471.976
30	199.018	241.330	293.192	356.778	434.738	530.306	647.423	790.932	966.698	1181.865
40	581.812	767.080	1013.667	1341.979	1779.048	2360.724	3134.412	4163.094	5529.711	7343.715
50	1668.723	2399.975	3459.344	4994.301	7217.488	10435.449	15088.805	21812.273	31514.492	45496.094

APPENDIX C. Sum of an Annuity of $1 for n Periods (continued)

n	21%	22%	23%	24%	25%	26%	27%	28%	29%	30%
1	1.000	1.000	1.000	1.000	1.000	1.000	1.000	1.000	1.000	1.000
2	2.210	2.220	2.230	2.240	2.250	2.260	2.270	2.280	2.290	2.300
3	3.674	3.708	3.743	3.778	3.813	3.848	3.883	3.918	3.954	3.990
4	5.446	5.524	5.604	5.684	5.766	5.848	5.931	6.016	6.101	6.187
5	7.589	7.740	7.893	8.048	8.207	8.368	8.533	8.700	8.870	9.043
6	10.183	10.442	10.708	10.980	11.259	11.544	11.837	12.136	12.442	12.756
7	13.321	13.740	14.171	14.615	15.073	15.546	16.032	16.534	17.051	17.583
8	17.119	17.762	18.430	19.123	19.842	20.588	21.361	22.163	22.995	23.858
9	21.714	22.670	23.669	24.712	25.802	26.940	28.129	29.369	30.664	32.015
10	27.274	28.657	20.113	31.643	33.253	34.945	36.723	38.592	40.556	42.619
11	34.001	35.962	38.039	40.238	42.566	45.030	47.639	50.398	53.318	56.405
12	42.141	44.873	47.787	50.895	54.208	57.738	61.501	65.510	69.780	74.326
13	51.991	55.745	59.778	64.109	68.760	73.750	79.106	84.853	91.016	97.624
14	63.909	69.009	74.528	80.496	86.949	93.925	101.465	109.611	118.411	127.912
15	78.330	85.191	92.669	100.815	109.687	119.346	129.860	141.302	153.750	167.285
16	95.779	104.933	114.983	126.010	138.109	151.375	165.922	181.867	199.337	218.470
17	116.892	129.019	142.428	157.252	173.636	191.733	211.721	233.790	258.145	285.011
18	142.439	158.403	176.187	195.993	218.045	242.583	269.885	300.250	334.006	371.514
19	173.351	194.251	217.710	244.031	273.556	306.654	343.754	385.321	431.868	483.968
20	210.755	237.986	268.783	303.598	342.945	387.384	437.568	494.210	558.110	630.157
21	256.013	291.343	331.603	377.461	429.681	489.104	556.710	633.589	720.962	820.204
22	310.775	356.438	408.871	469.052	538.101	617.270	708.022	811.993	931.040	1067.265
23	377.038	435.854	503.911	582.624	673.626	778.760	900.187	1040.351	1202.042	1388.443
24	457.215	532.741	620.810	723.453	843.032	982.237	1144.237	1332.649	1551.634	1805.975
25	554.230	650.944	764.596	898.082	1054.791	1238.617	1454.180	1706.790	2002.608	2348.765
30	1445.111	1767.044	2160.459	2640.881	3227.172	3941.953	4812.891	5873.172	7162.785	8729.805
40	9749.141	12936.141	17153.691	22728.367	30088.621	39791.957	52570.707	69376.562	91447.375	120389.375

APPENDIX C. Sum of an Annuity of $1 for *n* Periods (continued)

n	31%	32%	33%	34%	35%	36%	37%	38%	39%	40%
1	1.000	1.000	1.000	1.000	1.000	1.000	1.000	1.000	1.000	1.000
2	2.310	2.320	2.330	2.340	2.350	2.360	2.370	2.380	2.390	2.400
3	4.026	4.062	4.099	4.136	4.172	4.210	4.247	4.284	4.322	4.360
4	6.274	6.362	6.452	6.542	6.633	6.725	6.818	6.912	7.008	7.104
5	9.219	9.398	9.581	9.766	9.954	10.146	10.341	10.539	10.741	10.946
6	13.077	13.406	13.742	14.086	14.438	14.799	15.167	15.544	15.930	16.324
7	18.131	18.696	19.277	19.876	20.492	21.126	21.779	22.451	23.142	23.853
8	24.752	25.678	26.638	27.633	28.664	29.732	30.837	31.982	33.167	34.395
9	33.425	34.895	36.429	38.028	39.696	41.435	43.247	45.135	47.103	49.152
10	44.786	47.062	49.451	51.958	54.590	57.351	60.248	63.287	66.473	69.813
11	59.670	63.121	66.769	70.624	74.696	78.998	83.540	88.335	93.397	98.739
12	79.167	84.320	89.803	95.636	101.840	108.437	115.450	122.903	130.822	139.234
13	104.709	112.302	120.438	129.152	138.484	148.474	159.166	170.606	182.842	195.928
14	138.169	149.239	161.183	174.063	187.953	202.925	219.058	236.435	255.151	275.299
15	182.001	197.996	215.373	234.245	254.737	276.978	301.109	327.281	355.659	386.418
16	239.421	262.354	287.446	314.888	344.895	377.690	413.520	452.647	495.366	541.985
17	314.642	347.307	383.303	422.949	466.608	514.658	567.521	625.652	689.558	759.778
18	413.180	459.445	510.792	567.751	630.920	700.935	778.504	864.399	959.485	1064.689
19	542.266	607.467	680.354	761.786	852.741	954.271	1067.551	1193.870	1334.683	1491.563
20	711.368	802.856	905.870	1021.792	1152.200	1298.809	1463.544	1648.539	1856.208	2089.188
21	932.891	1060.769	1205.807	1370.201	1556.470	1767.380	2006.055	2275.982	2581.128	2925.862
22	1223.087	1401.215	1604.724	1837.068	2102.234	2404.636	2749.294	3141.852	3588.765	4097.203
23	1603.243	1850.603	2135.282	2462.669	2839.014	3271.304	3767.532	4336.750	4989.379	5737.078
24	2101.247	2443.795	2840.924	3300.974	3833.667	4449.969	5162.516	5985.711	6936.230	8032.906
25	2753.631	3226.808	3779.428	4424.301	5176.445	6052.957	7073.645	8261.273	9642.352	11247.062
30	10632.543	12940.672	15737.945	19124.434	23221.258	28172.016	34148.906	41357.227	50043.625	60500.207

APPENDIX D. Present Value of an Annuity of $1 for n Periods

n	1%	2%	3%	4%	5%	6%	7%	8%	9%	10%
1	.990	.980	.971	.962	.952	.943	.935	.926	.917	.909
2	1.970	1.942	1.913	1.886	1.859	1.833	1.808	1.783	1.759	1.736
3	2.941	2.884	2.829	2.775	2.723	2.673	2.624	2.577	2.531	2.487
4	3.902	3.808	3.717	3.630	3.546	3.465	3.387	3.312	3.240	3.170
5	4.853	4.713	4.580	4.452	4.329	4.212	4.100	3.993	3.890	3.791
6	5.795	5.601	5.417	5.242	5.076	4.917	4.767	4.623	4.486	4.355
7	6.728	6.472	6.230	6.002	5.786	5.582	5.389	5.206	5.033	4.868
8	7.652	7.326	7.020	6.733	6.463	6.210	5.971	5.747	5.535	5.335
9	8.566	8.162	7.786	7.435	7.108	6.802	6.515	6.247	5.995	5.759
10	9.471	8.983	8.530	8.111	7.722	7.360	7.024	6.710	6.418	6.145
11	10.368	9.787	9.253	8.760	8.306	7.887	7.499	7.139	6.805	6.495
12	11.255	10.575	9.954	9.385	8.863	8.384	7.943	7.536	7.161	6.814
13	12.134	11.348	10.635	9.986	9.394	8.853	8.358	7.904	7.487	7.103
14	13.004	12.106	11.296	10.563	9.899	9.295	8.746	8.244	7.786	7.367
15	13.865	12.849	11.938	11.118	10.380	9.712	9.108	8.560	8.061	7.606
16	14.718	13.578	12.561	11.652	10.838	10.106	9.447	8.851	8.313	7.824
17	15.562	14.292	13.166	12.166	11.274	10.477	9.763	9.122	8.544	8.022
18	16.398	14.992	13.754	12.659	11.690	10.828	10.059	9.372	8.756	8.201
19	17.226	15.679	14.324	13.134	12.085	11.158	10.336	9.604	8.950	8.365
20	18.046	16.352	14.878	13.590	12.462	11.470	10.594	9.818	9.129	8.514
21	18.857	17.011	15.415	14.029	12.821	11.764	10.836	10.017	9.292	8.649
22	19.661	17.658	15.937	14.451	13.163	12.042	11.061	10.201	9.442	8.772
23	20.456	18.292	16.444	14.857	13.489	12.303	11.272	10.371	9.580	8.883
24	21.244	18.914	16.936	15.247	13.799	12.550	11.469	10.529	9.707	8.985
25	22.023	19.524	17.413	15.622	14.094	12.783	11.654	10.675	9.823	9.077
30	25.808	22.397	19.601	17.292	15.373	13.765	12.409	11.258	10.274	9.427
40	32.835	27.356	23.115	19.793	17.159	15.046	13.332	11.925	10.757	9.779
50	39.197	31.424	25.730	21.482	18.256	15.762	13.801	12.234	10.962	9.915

APPENDIX D.   Present Value of Annuity of $1 for n Periods (continued)

n	11%	12%	13%	14%	15%	16%	17%	18%	19%	20%
1	.901	.893	.885	.877	.870	.862	.855	.847	.840	.833
2	1.713	1.690	1.668	1.647	1.626	1.605	1.585	1.566	1.547	1.528
3	2.444	2.402	2.361	2.322	2.283	2.246	2.210	2.174	2.140	2.106
4	3.102	3.037	2.974	2.914	2.855	2.798	2.743	2.690	2.639	2.589
5	3.696	3.605	3.517	3.433	3.352	3.274	3.199	3.127	3.058	2.991
6	4.231	4.111	3.998	3.889	3.784	3.685	3.589	3.498	3.410	3.326
7	4.712	4.564	4.423	4.288	4.160	4.039	3.922	3.812	3.706	3.605
8	5.146	4.968	4.799	4.639	4.487	4.344	4.207	4.078	3.954	3.837
9	5.537	5.328	5.132	4.946	4.772	4.607	4.451	4.303	4.163	4.031
10	5.889	5.650	5.426	5.216	5.019	4.833	4.659	4.494	4.339	4.192
11	6.207	5.938	5.687	5.453	5.234	5.029	4.836	4.656	4.487	4.327
12	6.492	6.194	5.918	5.660	5.421	5.197	4.988	4.793	4.611	4.439
13	6.750	6.424	6.122	5.842	5.583	5.342	5.118	4.910	4.715	4.533
14	6.982	6.628	6.303	6.002	5.724	5.468	5.229	5.008	4.802	4.611
15	7.191	6.811	6.462	6.142	5.847	5.575	5.324	5.092	4.876	4.675
16	7.379	6.974	6.604	6.265	5.954	5.669	5.405	5.162	4.938	4.730
17	7.549	7.120	6.729	6.373	6.047	5.749	5.475	5.222	4.990	4.775
18	7.702	7.250	6.840	6.467	6.128	5.818	5.534	5.273	5.033	4.812
19	7.839	7.366	6.938	6.550	6.198	5.877	5.585	5.316	5.070	4.843
20	7.963	7.469	7.025	6.623	6.259	5.929	5.628	5.353	5.101	4.870
21	8.075	7.562	7.102	6.687	6.312	5.973	5.665	5.384	5.127	4.891
22	8.176	7.645	7.170	6.743	6.359	6.011	5.696	5.410	5.149	4.909
23	8.266	7.718	7.230	6.792	6.399	6.044	5.723	5.432	5.167	4.925
24	8.348	7.784	7.283	6.835	6.434	6.073	5.747	5.451	5.182	4.937
25	8.442	7.843	7.330	6.873	6.464	6.097	5.766	5.467	5.195	4.948
30	8.694	8.055	7.496	7.003	6.566	6.177	5.829	5.517	5.235	4.979
40	8.951	8.244	7.634	7.105	6.642	6.233	5.871	5.548	5.258	4.997
50	9.042	8.305	7.675	7.133	6.661	6.246	5.880	5.554	5.262	4.999

APPENDIX D. Present Value of an Annuity of $1 for n Periods (continued)

n	21%	22%	23%	24%	25%	26%	27%	28%	29%	30%
1	.826	.820	.813	.806	.800	.794	.787	.781	.775	.769
2	1.509	1.492	1.474	1.457	1.440	1.424	1.407	1.392	1.376	1.361
3	2.074	2.042	2.011	1.981	1.952	1.923	1.896	1.868	1.842	1.816
4	2.540	2.494	2.448	2.404	2.362	2.320	2.280	2.241	2.203	2.166
5	2.926	2.864	2.803	2.745	2.689	2.635	2.583	2.532	2.483	2.436
6	3.245	3.167	3.092	3.020	2.951	2.885	2.821	2.759	2.700	2.643
7	3.508	3.416	3.327	3.242	3.161	3.083	3.009	2.937	2.868	2.802
8	3.726	3.619	3.518	3.421	3.329	3.241	3.156	3.076	2.999	2.925
9	3.905	3.786	3.673	3.566	3.463	3.366	3.273	3.184	3.100	3.019
10	4.054	3.923	3.799	3.682	3.570	3.465	3.364	3.269	3.178	3.092
11	4.177	4.035	3.902	3.776	3.656	3.544	3.437	3.335	3.239	3.147
12	4.278	4.127	3.985	3.851	3.725	3.606	3.493	3.387	3.286	3.190
13	4.362	4.203	4.053	3.912	3.780	3.656	3.538	3.427	3.322	3.223
14	4.432	4.265	4.108	3.962	3.824	3.695	3.573	3.459	3.351	3.249
15	4.489	4.315	4.153	4.001	3.859	3.726	3.601	3.483	3.373	3.268
16	4.536	4.357	4.189	4.033	3.887	3.751	3.623	3.503	3.390	3.283
17	4.576	4.391	4.219	4.059	3.910	3.771	3.640	3.518	3.403	3.295
18	4.608	4.419	4.243	4.080	3.928	3.786	3.654	3.529	3.413	3.304
19	4.635	4.442	4.263	4.097	3.942	3.799	3.664	3.539	3.421	3.311
20	4.657	4.460	4.279	4.110	3.954	3.808	3.673	3.546	3.427	3.316
21	4.675	4.476	4.292	4.121	3.963	3.816	3.679	3.551	3.432	3.320
22	4.690	4.488	4.302	4.130	3.970	3.822	3.684	3.556	3.436	3.323
23	4.703	4.499	4.311	4.137	3.976	3.827	3.689	3.559	3.438	3.325
24	4.713	4.507	4.318	4.143	3.981	3.831	3.692	3.562	3.441	3.327
25	4.721	4.514	4.323	4.147	3.985	3.834	3.694	3.564	3.442	3.329
30	4.746	4.534	4.339	4.160	3.995	3.842	3.701	3.569	3.447	3.332
40	4.760	4.544	4.347	4.166	3.999	3.846	3.703	3.571	3.448	3.333
50	4.762	4.545	4.348	4.167	4.000	3.846	3.704	3.571	3.448	3.333

APPENDIX D. Present Value of an Annuity of $1 for n Periods (continued)

n	31%	32%	33%	34%	35%	36%	37%	38%	39%	40%
1	.763	.758	.752	.746	.741	.735	.730	.725	.719	.714
2	1.346	1.331	1.317	1.303	1.289	1.276	1.263	1.250	1.237	1.224
3	1.791	1.766	1.742	1.719	1.696	1.673	1.652	1.630	1.609	1.589
4	2.130	2.096	2.062	2.029	1.997	1.966	1.935	1.906	1.877	1.849
5	2.390	2.345	2.302	2.260	2.220	2.181	2.143	2.106	2.070	2.035
6	2.588	2.534	2.483	2.433	2.385	2.339	2.294	2.251	2.209	2.168
7	2.739	2.677	2.619	2.562	2.508	2.455	2.404	2.355	2.308	2.263
8	2.854	2.786	2.721	2.658	2.598	2.540	2.485	2.432	2.380	2.331
9	2.942	2.868	2.798	2.730	2.665	2.603	2.544	2.487	2.432	2.379
10	3.009	2.930	2.855	2.784	2.715	2.649	2.587	2.527	2.469	2.414
11	3.060	2.978	2.899	2.824	2.752	2.683	2.618	2.555	2.496	2.438
12	3.100	3.013	2.931	2.853	2.779	2.708	2.641	2.576	2.515	2.456
13	3.129	3.040	2.956	2.876	2.799	2.727	2.658	2.592	2.529	2.469
14	3.152	3.061	2.974	2.892	2.814	2.740	2.670	2.603	2.539	2.477
15	3.170	3.076	2.988	2.905	2.825	2.750	2.679	2.611	2.546	2.484
16	3.183	3.088	2.999	2.914	2.834	2.757	2.685	2.616	2.551	2.489
17	3.193	3.097	3.007	2.921	2.840	2.763	2.690	2.621	2.555	2.492
18	3.201	3.104	3.012	2.926	2.844	2.767	2.693	2.624	2.557	2.494
19	3.207	3.109	3.017	2.930	2.848	2.770	2.696	2.626	2.559	2.496
20	3.211	3.113	3.020	2.933	2.850	2.772	2.698	2.627	2.561	2.497
21	3.215	3.116	3.023	2.935	2.852	2.773	2.699	2.629	2.562	2.498
22	3.217	3.118	3.025	2.936	2.853	2.775	2.700	2.629	2.562	2.498
23	3.219	3.120	3.026	2.938	2.854	2.775	2.701	2.630	2.563	2.499
24	3.221	3.121	3.027	2.939	2.855	2.776	2.701	2.630	2.563	2.499
25	3.222	3.122	3.028	2.939	2.856	2.776	2.702	2.631	2.563	2.499
30	3.225	2.124	3.030	2.941	2.857	2.777	2.702	2.631	2.564	2.500
40	3.226	3.125	3.030	2.941	2.857	2.778	2.703	2.632	2.564	2.500
50	3.226	3.125	3.030	2.941	2.857	2.778	2.703	2.632	2.564	2.500

APPENDIX E
Solutions for Selected End-of-Chapter Problems

To provide check figures, this appendix supplies intermediate answers and final solutions for a select set of end-of-chapter problems. Usually we have provided the solutions to odd-numbered problems; however, there are exceptions. Note that some of the problems may have more than one correct solution, and that differences in answers also may result from rounding errors. Finally, not all solutions are readily expressed as brief answers.

CHAPTER 2 Legal Forms of Organization and the Tax Environment

2-1.

Year	Depreciation
1	$50,000
3	48,000
6	14,500

2-3. Taxable Income = $526,200
Tax liability = $178,908

2-5.

Year	Tax Payments	Tax Refunds
1983	$3,750	$ 0
1984	0	3,750
1985	7,500	0
1986	7,500	0
1987	0	15,000
1988	0	0
1989	5,250	0

2-9. Taxable income = ($42,000)
Tax liability = $0
2-13. Taxable income = $1,500,000
Tax liability = $510,000
2-15. Taxable income = $370,000
Tax liability = $125,800

CHAPTER 3 Financial Analysis

3-1. $500,000.00
3-3. **a.** Return on Total Assets = 10%
b. Sales growth = 20%
c. Return on Equity = 17.1%

3-5.

	1986	1987
Current Ratio	6×	4×
ACP	135 days	106 days
Fixed Asset T/O	1×	1.04×
Net Profit Margin	10%	12.4%

3-7.

Cash Balance (12/31/86)	$ 75,000
+ Total Sources	331,500
− Total Uses	(324,000)
Cash Balance (12/31/87)	$ 82,500

CHAPTER 4 Financial Forecasting

4-1. Total Assets = $1.8 million
4-3. Total Assets = $2 million
Long-Term Debt = $.4 million

4-5.

	July	August	September
Net Monthly Change	$(10,600)	(600)	7,800
Cumulative Borrowing	10,600	11,306	3,619

4-7. Accounts Receivable = $22,222.
4-11. **a.** Average Collection Period = 40 days
b. Accounts Receivable = $100,000.

CHAPTER 5 Introduction to Working Capital Management

5-1. **a.** Return on Equity = 19.48%
b. Return on Equity = 14.05%

CHAPTER 6   Cash and Marketable Securities Management

6–1.   **b.**   15%
6–2.   **a.** $2,625,000
       b. $241,500
6–3.   YES; annual savings = $211,000
6–5.   0.5322 days
6–7.   **b.**   12%
6–9.   Net annual savings = $3,375
6–11.   0.4106 days
6–13. $10,667
6–15. $14,247
6–22.   **a.** $912.44
       b. $87.56
       c. $17.59
6–24.   **b.**   10.185%
6A–1.   **a.** $158,698
       b. $856.96
       c.   5.95 days
       d. $79,349

CHAPTER 7   Accounts Receivable and Inventory Management

7–1.   **a.**   36.36%
       b.   36.73%
7–3.   **a.** $90,000
       b. $53,333
7–4.   **a.**   775 units
7–5.   **a.**   2828 boxes
7–7.   **a.**   15,000 units
       b.   33⅓
7A–1. $47,583

CHAPTER 8   Short-Term Financing

8–1.   Rate = 13.33%
8–3.   **a.**   RATE = 36.73%
       b.   RATE = 74.23%
8–7.   **a.**   RATE = 16.27%
8–11.   Pledging: RATE = 16%
       Inventory loan: RATE = 13.8%
8–13.   Rate = 12.37%

CHAPTER 9   Mathematics of Finance

9–1.   **a.** $12,970
       c. $3019.40
9–2.   **a.** n = 15 years
9–3.   **b.**   5%
       c.   9%
9–4.   **b.** P = $235.20
9–5.   **a.** $6289
       c. $302.89
9–6.   **c.** $1562.96
9–7.   **a.** FV_1 = $10,600
           FV_5 = $13,380
           FV_{15} = $23,970
9–9.   **a.** $6690
       b.   Semiannual: $6720
           Bimonthly: $6740
9–11.   Year 1: 18,000 books
       Year 2: 21,600 books
       Year 3: 25,920 books
9–13. $6108.11
9–15.   8%
9–17. $658,197.85
9–21.   **b.** $8,333.33
9–22. $824.36
9–26. $6509
9–28.   22%
9–29. $6934.81
9–32.   **a.** $1989.73

CHAPTER 10   Capital Budgeting

10–1.   **a.** $6,800
       b. $3,400
       c.   No taxes
       d. $1,020
10–3.   **a.**   2.75 years
       b. $10,628.16
10–5.   **a.**   IRR = 7%
       b.   IRR = 17%
10–7.   **a.**   IRR = approximately 19%
10–9.   **a.**   payback period = 2.11
       b.   NPV = $61,471
10–11.   **a.**   NPV = $68,700
10–13.   **b.**   NPV = − $9,658
10–15.   **a.**   NPV$_A$ = $136.30
           NPV$_B$ = $454
10–17.   **a.**   Payback A = 1.589 years
           Payback B = 3.019 years
       b.   NPV$_A$ = $8,743
           NPV$_B$ = $11,615
10–20.   NPV$_{lays}$ = $29,260

CHAPTER 11   Capital Budgeting Under Uncertainty

11–1.   **a.** $\overline{X}_A$ = $30,000
           $\overline{X}_B$ = $70,000

b. $\sigma_A = \$7416$
$\sigma_B = \$23,452$

11–2. **b.** $\sigma_A = \$2549.5$
$\overline{\sigma_B} = \$3255.76$

11–3. **a.** $\overline{X}_A = \$5000$
b. $NPV_A = \$8025$

11–5. $NPV_A = 726,380$

11–7. $NPV_A = -\$24,780$

11–9. $NPV = -\$330$

CHAPTER 12   Valuation and Rates of Return

12–1. $\overline{X} = 9.1\%$; $\sigma = 3.06\%$

12–3. Security A: $\overline{X} = 16.7\%$; $\sigma = 10.12\%$
Security B: $\overline{X} = 9.2\%$: $\sigma = 3.57\%$

12–5.

	b.	c.
A	20.84	21.71
B	15.34	25.06
C	17.85	19.48
D	14.60	18.37

12–7. Value $= \$116.67$

12–9. $R_b = 9.60\%$

12–11. **a.** Expected return $= 8.50\%$
b. Market value $\$42.50$

12–13. **a.** 18.89%
b. $28.57

12–15. **a.** 21.24%
b. $52.34

12–17. Market value $= \$39.96$

12–19. 9.65%

12–21. **a.** 7.06%
b. $847.48

12–23. **a.** 14.07%
b. $57.02

12–25. 10.56%

12A–1. **a.** $V_b = \$863.78$
b. V_b @ 15% $= \$707.63$; V_b @ 8% $= \$1171.19$
d. V_b @ 12% $= \$927.90$
V_b @ 8% $= \$1079.85$

CHAPTER 13   Cost of Capital

13–1. **a.** $K_d = 6.53\%$
b. $K_{nc} = 14.37\%$
c. $K_c = 15.14\%$

d. $K_p = 8.77\%$
e. $K_d = 7.92\%$

13–3. **a.** $K_d = 5.28\%$
b. $K_{nc} = 9.85\%$
c. $K_d = 7.63\%$
d. $K_p = 8.24\%$
e. $K_c = 11.89\%$

13–5. $K_d = 7.23\%$

13–7. $K_d = 8.48\%$

13–9. $K_c = 18.74\%$

13–11. **a.** $V_b = \$1320.52$
b. $NP_0 = \$1181.87$
c. 423 bonds
d. $K_d = 7.21\%$

13–13. $K_0 = 15.07\%$

13–15. $K_d = 6.28\%$
$K_p = 8.83\%$
$K_c = 13.57\%$
$K_0 = 10.09\%$

13–18. Breaks in marginal cost curve:

$ 627,907 (caused by increase in debt cost)
  450,000 (caused by increase in preferred cost)
1,756,757 (caused by increase in common cost)
2,432,432 (caused by increase in common cost)

Debt (0 – $270,000 = 5.61%
   (over $270,000) = 6.44%
Preferred Stock (0 – $90,000) = 12.02%
   (over $90,000) = 12.43%
Common Stock (0 – $650,000) = 17.53%
   ($650,000 – $900,000) = 17.92%
   (over $900,000) = 18.23%

Weighted Cost for $0 to $450,000 total capital = 11.30%

CHAPTER 14   Analysis and Impact of Leverage

14–1. **a.** 9000 units
b. $1,620,000

14–3. **a.** $85,416.67
b. 7030 units; $189,815

14–5. **a.** 1.94 times

14–7. **a.** 10,000 units
b. $1,800,000

14–9. **a.** $F = \$173,333.33$
b. 14,444 units; $S^* = \$288,888.88$

14–15. **a.** 5000 units
b. $125,000
c. – $10,000; $10,000; $30,000
14–17. 5 times
14–19. 1,400,000 units
14–21. **a.** 3 times
b. 1.25 times
c. 3.75 times
d. $8 million
14–23. **b.** 35%
c. $84,000

CHAPTER 15 Planning the Firm's Financing Mix

15–1. **a.** EBIT = $220,000
b. PLAN B.
15–3. **a.** $640,000
b. EPS = $3.20
15–5. **a.** $300,000
b. EPS = $3.00
15–7. **a.** Plan A = $7.68
b. 10.378
15–11. **a.** $20,000,000
b. $k_c = 25\%$; $k_0 = 25\%$
15–13. **a.** Plan A vs. Plan B = $9000
Plan A vs. Plan C = $18,000

CHAPTER 16 Dividend Policy and Internal Financing

16–1. 95,238 shares
16–3. Equity financing needed = $384,000
Dividend = $16,000
16–5. Price for Plan A or Plan B = $31.76
16–7. **a.** Shares before split = 1,250
b. Net gain = $24,500
16–8. **a.** Year 1 = $.70; Year 3 = $.93
b. $.90
c. Year 1 = $.50; Year 3 = $.68

CHAPTER 18 Term Loans and Leases

18–1. **a.** $31,977.78
18–3. **a.** 15%
c. 14%
18–5. **a.** $NPV(P)$ = $6,340.75
18–7. **a.** $19,925.20
c. $15,229.97

CHAPTER 19 Long-Term Debt, Preferred Stock and Common Stock

19–3. Yes, NPV = $1,709,900
19–5. **a.** 200,000 shares
b. 5 rights
19–6. **a.** 1,000,000 shares

CHAPTER 20 Convertibles and Warrants

20–1. **a.** 25 shares
b. $681.25
20–2. **b.** $12.27
20–3. **b.** $4
20–4. **a.** minimum price = – $1.71
warrant premium = $3.00

CHAPTER 21 Corporate Restructuring: Combinations and Divestitures

21–1. **a.** EPS decrease for Mantana = $.59/share
EPS increase for Savry = $.29/share
b. Mantana gain = $11.89/share
Savry gain = $2.89/share
21–3. Common stock financing: 500,000 common shares
Convertible preferred financing: 390,625 common shares

CHAPTER 22 Failure and Reorganization

22–1. Bankruptcy score for company A = 2.810
Bankruptcy score for company B = 6.719
Bankruptcy score for company C = 3.455

22–3. **Corporate Structure after Reorganization**

Accounts Payable	$162,500
Short-term Notes Payable	287,500
Long-term Notes Payable	125,000
Mortgage Bonds	500,000
Preferred Stock	125,000
Common Stock	625,000

22–5. Final distribution to common stock holders = $0

CHAPTER 23 International Business Finance

23–1. **a.** $8437; **b.** $9368; **c.** $25,695

23–3. Canada: 1.1853; 1.1881; 1.1912
Japan: 213.4927; 211.9992; 209.1613
Switzerland: 1.9459; 1.9346; 1.8815

23–5. Net gain = $149.02

23–7. Canada: (2.85%); (1.99%)
Japan: 8.45%; 8.28%
Switzerland: 7%; 13.7%

23–9. $.0046945/yen

23–11. Canada: 20.40%
Switzerland: 3.78%
Japan: 8.97%

23–12. **a.** U.S. = 7.12%
France = 10.21%

Glossary

Accelerated Cost Recovery System. A means of accelerated depreciation for assets acquired after 1981, whereby assets are assigned to specific property classifications and depreciated accordingly.

Accelerated Depreciation Techniques. Techniques that allow the owner of the asset to take greater amounts of depreciation during the early years of its life, thereby deferring some of the taxes until later years.

Accounting Rate of Return (AROR). A capital-budgeting criterion that relates the returns generated by the project, as measured by average accounting profits after tax, to the average dollar size of the investment required.

Accrual Method. A method of accounting whereby income is recorded when earned, whether or not the income has been received at that time, and expenses are recorded when incurred, whether or not any money has actually been paid out.

Accumulated Earnings Credit. The greater of (1) the profits for the year retained for reasonable business needs, and (2) $150,000 less the retained earnings shown in the balance sheet.

Accumulated Taxable Income. The firm's taxable income less dividends paid and accrued during the year, and less an **accumulated earnings credit.**

Acid Test Ratio. (Currents assets − inventories)/current liabilities. This ratio is a more stringent measure of liquidity than the current ratio in that it subtracts inventories (the least liquid current asset) from current assets.

Acquisition. A combination of two or more businesses into a single operational entity.

ACRS. Accelerated Cost Recovery System.

Affiliated Group. A group of firms related by affiliation, expressed in terms of one firm's owning, either directly or indirectly, 80 percent of the firm paying the dividend.

Agency Costs. The costs, such as a reduced stock price, associated with potential conflict between managers and investors when these two groups are not the same.

Annuity. A series of equal dollar payments for a specified number of years.

Appraisal Value. The value of a company as stated by an independent appraisal firm.

Arbitrage-Pricing Theory. A theory that relates stock returns and risk. The theory maintains that security returns vary from their expected amounts when there are unanticipated changes in basic economic forces. Such forces would include unexpected changes in industrial production, inflation rates, term structure of interest rates, and the difference between interest rates of high-and-low risk bonds.

829

Arbitrageur. A person involved in the process of buying and selling in more than one market to make a riskless profit.

Arrangement. A reorganizational plan involving a petition to the court requesting that the firm be required to make only partial or a delayed payment to its creditors.

Arrearage. An overdue payment, generally referring to omitted preferred stock dividends.

Average Collection Period. Accounts receivable/ (annual credit sales/360). A ratio that expresses how rapidly the firm is collecting its credit accounts.

Average Tax Rate. The rate calculated by dividing the total tax liability by the entity's taxable income.

Balance Sheet. A basic accounting statement that represents the financial position of a firm on a given date.

Bankers' Acceptances. A draft (order to pay) drawn on a specific bank by a seller of goods in order to obtain payment for goods that have been shipped (sold) to a customer. The customer maintains an account with that specific bank.

Bank Wire. A private wire service used and supported by approximately 250 banks in the United States for transferring funds, exchanging credit information, or effecting securities transactions.

Base-Period Earn-Out. An agreement by which the stockholders of an acquired company receive additional stock in future years provided the firm improves its earnings above those of the base period. Base-period earnings are those in the last year prior to the acquisition.

Beta. The relationship between an investment's returns and the market returns. This is a measure of the investment's nondiversifiable risk.

Bird-in-the-Hand Dividend Theory. The belief that dividend income has a higher value to the investor than does capital gains income, since dividends are more certain than capital gains.

Bond. A long-term (ten-year or more) promissory note issued by the borrower, promising to pay the owner of the security a predetermined and fixed amount of interest each year.

Bond Par Value. The face value appearing on the bond, which is to be returned to the bondholder at maturity.

Book Value. The depreciated value of a company's assets (original cost less accumulated depreciation) less the outstanding liabilities.

Book-Value Weights. The percentage of financing provided by different capital sources as measured by their book values from the company's balance sheet.

Break-Even Analysis. An analytical technique used to determine the quantity of output or sales that results in a zero level of earnings before interest and taxes (EBIT). Relationships among the firm's cost structure, volume of output, and EBIT are studied.

Business Risk. The relative dispersion or variability in the firm's expected earnings before interest and taxes (EBIT). The nature of the firm's operations causes its business risk. This type of risk is affected by the firm's cost structure, product demand characteristics, and intra-industry competititve position. In capital-structure theory, business risk is distinguished from financial risk. See **Financial Risk.**

Call Option. A call option gives its owner the right to purchase a given number of shares of stock or some other asset at a specified price over a given time period.

Call Premium. The difference between the call price and the security's par value.

Call Provision. A provision that entitles the corporation to repurchase its bonds or preferred stock from their holders at stated prices over specified periods.

Capital Asset. All property used in conducting a business other than assets held primarily for sale in the ordinary course of business or depreciable and real property used in conducting a business.

Capital Asset Pricing Model. An equation stating that the expected rate of return on a project is a function of (1) the risk-free rate, (2) the investment's systematic risk, and (3) the expected risk premium in the market.

Capital Budgeting. The decision-making process with respect to investment in fixed assets. Specifically it involves measuring the incremental cash flows associated with investment proposals and evaluating those proposed investments.

Capital Gain or Loss. As defined by the revenue code, a gain or loss resulting from the sale or exchange of a capital asset.

Capital Market. All institutions and procedures that facilitate transactions in long-term financial instruments.

Capital Rationing. The placing of a limit by the firm on the dollar size of the capital budget.

Capital Structure. The mix of long-term sources of funds used by the firm. This is also called the firm's **capitalization.** The relative total (percentage) of each type of fund is emphasized.

Cash Budget. A detailed plan of future cash flows. This budget is composed of four elements: cash receipts, cash disbursements, net change in cash for the period, and new financing needed.

Cash Flow Process. The process of cash generation and disposition in a typical business setting.

Certainty Equivalents. The amount of cash a person would require with certainty to make him indifferent between this certain sum and a particular risky or uncertain sum.

Chattel Mortgage Agreement. A loan agreement in which the lender can increase his security interest by having specific items of inventory identified in the loan agreement. The borrower retains title to the inventory but cannot sell the items without the lender's consent.

Clientele Effect. The belief that individuals and institutions that need current income will invest in companies that have high dividend payouts. Other investors prefer to avoid taxes by holding securities that offer only small dividend income, but large capital gains. Thus, we have a "clientele" of investors.

Coefficient of Variation. A measure of the relative dispersion of a probability distribution—that is, the risk per unit of return. Mathematically it is defined as the standard deviation divided by the expected value.

Collateral Trust Bonds. Bonds secured by common stock and/or bonds.

Commerical Paper. Short-term unsecured promissory notes sold by large businesses in order to raise cash. Unlike most other money market instruments, commercial paper has no developed secondary market.

Compensating Balance. A balance of a given amount that the firm maintains in its demand deposit account. It may be required by either a formal or informal agreement with the firm's commercial bank. Such balances are usually required by the bank (1) on the unused portion of a loan commitment, (2) on the unpaid portion of an outstanding loan, or (3) in exchange for certain services provided by the bank, such as check-clearing or credit information. These balances raise the effective rate of interest paid on borrowed funds.

Compounding. The process of determining the future value of a payment or series of payments when applying the concept of compound interest.

Compound Interest. The situation in which interest paid on the investment during the first period is added to the principal and, during the second period, interest is earned on the original principal plus the interest earned during the first period.

Concentration Bank. A bank where the firm maintains a major disbursing account.

Conglomerate. A multifaceted corporation involved in a variety of products and services.

Constant Dividend Payout Ratio. A dividend payment policy in which the percentage of earnings paid out in dividends is held constant. The dollar amount fluctuates from year to year as profits vary.

Conversion Parity Price. The price for which the investor in effect purchases the company's common stock when purchasing a convertible security. Mathematically it is the market price of the convertible security divided by the conversion ratio.

Conversion Ratio. The number of shares of common stock for which a convertible security can be exchanged.

Convertibles. Preferred stock or debentures that can be exchanged for a specified number of shares of common stock at the will of the owner.

Corporate Bylaws. Regulations that govern the internal affairs of the corporation, designating such items as the time and place of the shareholders' meetings, voting rights, the election process for selecting members of the board of directors, the procedures for issuing and transferring stock certificates, and the policies relating to the corporate records.

Corporation. An entity that *legally* functions separate and apart from its owners.

Cost Budgets. Budgets prepared for every major expense category of the firm, such as production cost, selling cost, administrative cost, financing cost, and research and development cost.

Cost of Capital. The rate that must be earned in order to satisfy the required rate of return of the firm's investors. It may also be defined as the rate of return on investments at which the price of the firm's common stock will remain unchanged.

Cost of Debt. The rate that has to be received from an investment in order to achieve the required rate of return for the creditors.

Cost of Preferred Stock. The rate of return that must be earned on the preferred stockholders' investment to satisfy their required rate of return.

Cost-Volume-Profit Analysis. Another way of referring to ordinary break-even analysis.

Coupon Interest Rate. The interest to be paid annually on a bond as a percent of par value, which is specified in the contractual agreement.

Coverage Ratios. A group of ratios that measure a firm's ability to meet its recurring fixed charge obligations, such as interest on long-term debt, lease payments, and/or preferred stock dividends.

Cross Rates. The indirect computation of the exchange rate of one currency from the exchange rates of two other currencies.

Cumulative Feature. A requirement that all past unpaid preferred stock dividends can be paid before any common stock dividends are declared.

Current Ratio. Current assets/current liabilities. A ratio that indicates a firm's degree of liquidity by comparing its current assets to its current liabilities.

Date of Record. Date at which the stock transfer books are to be closed for determining the investor to receive the next dividend payment. See **Ex-dividend Date.**

Debenture. Any unsecured long-term debt.

Debt Capacity. The maximum proportion of debt that the firm can include in its capital structure and still maintain its lowest composite cost of capital.

Debt Ratio. Total liabilities/total assets. A ratio that measures the extent to which a firm has been financed with debt.

Declaration Date. The date upon which a dividend is formally declared by the board of directors.

Default Risk. The uncertainty of expected returns from a security attributable to possible changes in the financial capacity of the security issuer to make future payments to the security owner. Treasury securities are considered to be default-free. Default risk is also referred to as "financial risk" in the context of marketable securities management.

Degree of Combined Leverage. The percentage change in earnings per share caused by a percentage change in sales. It is the product of the degree of operating leverage and the degree of financial leverage.

Depository Transfer Checks. A means for moving funds from local bank accounts to concentration accounts. The depository transfer check itself is an unsigned, nonnegotiable instrument. It is payable only to the bank of deposit for credit to the firm's specific account.

Depreciation. The means by which an asset's value is expensed over its useful life for federal income tax purposes.

Direct Quotes. The exchange rate that indicates the number of units of the home currency required to buy one unit of foreign currency.

Disbursing Float. Funds available in the company's bank account until its payment check has cleared through the banking system.

Discounting. The inverse of compounding. This process is used to determine the present value of a cash flow.

Discount Rate. The interest rate used in the discounting process.

Diversifiable Risk. See **Unsystematic Risk.**

Divestitures. The removal of a division or subsidiary from the company. Typically, the part of the firm being separated is viewed as not contributing to the company's basic purposes.

Dividend Payout Ratio. The amount of dividends relative to the company's net income or earnings per share.

Dividend Yield. The dividend per share divided by the price of the security.

Earn-Out. A deferred payment plan, under which an acquiring firm agrees to make a specified initial payment of cash or stock and additional compensation if the acquired company can maintain or increase earnings. See **Base Period Earn-Out.**

EBIT. Common financial notation for **earnings before interest and taxes.**

EBIT-EPS Indifference Point. The level of earnings before interest and taxes (EBIT) that will equate earnings per share (EPS) between two different financing plans.

Economic Failure. Situation in which the company's costs exceed its revenues. Stated differently, the internal rates of return on investments are less than the firm's cost of capital.

Efficient Market. A market in which the values of all assets and securities at any instant in time fully reflect all available information.

EPS. Typical financial notation for **earnings per** (common) **share.**

Equipment Trust Certificates. A cross between lease financing and debt financing used primarily by railroads to finance rolling stock.

ERTA. Economic Recovery Tax Act of 1981.

Eurodollar Market. This is a banking market in U.S. dollars outside the U.S. Large sums of U.S. dollars can be borrowed or invested in this unregulated financial market. Similar external markets exist in Europe and Asia and for other major currencies.

Exchange Risk. The variability in future cash flows caused by variations in the exchange rates.

Ex-Dividend Date. The date upon which stock brokerage companies have uniformly decided to terminate the right of ownership to the dividend, which is four days prior to the record date.

Exercise Price. The price at which a warrant allows its holder to purchase the firm's common stock.

Exercise Ratio. The number of shares of stock that can be obtained at the exercise price with one warrant.

Expected Return. The arithmetic mean or average of all possible outcomes where those outcomes are weighted by the probability that each will occur.

Extension. An arrangement requiring that the debtor pay the amount owed in full, but providing an extension in time.

Ex-Rights Date. The date on or after which the stock sells without rights.

External Common Equity. A new issue of common stock.

Factoring of Accounts Receivable. The outright sale of a firm's accounts to another party (the factor) without recourse. The factor, in turn, bears the risk of collection.

Federal Agency Securities. Debt obligations of corporations and agencies created to carry out the lending programs of the U.S. government.

Federal Reserve System. The U.S. central banking system.

Field Warehouse Financing Agreement. A security agreement in which inventories are used as collateral, physically separated from the firm's other inventories, and placed under the control of a third-party field warehousing firm.

Financial Assets. Claims for future payment by one economic unit upon another.

Financial Intermediaries. Major financial institutions, such as commercial banks, savings and loan associations, credit unions, life insurance companies, and mutual funds, that assist the transfer of savings from economic units with excess savings to those with a shortage of savings.

Financial Lease. A noncancellable contractual commitment on the part of the firm leasing the asset (the lessee) to make a series of payments to the firm that actually owns the asset (the lessor) for the use of the asset.

Financial Leverage. The use of securities bearing a fixed (limited) rate of return to finance a portion of the firm's assets. Financial leverage can arise from the use of either debt or preferred stock financing. The use of financial leverage exposes the firm to **financial risk.**

Financial Markets. Institutions and procedures that facilitate transactions in all types of financial claims (securities).

Financial Risk. The added variability in earnings available to the firm's common shareholders, and the added chance of insolvency caused by the use of securities bearing a limited rate of return in the firm's financial structure. The use of financial leverage gives rise to financial risk.

Financial Structure. The mix of *all* funds sources that appear on the right-hand side of the balance sheet.

Fixed Asset Turnover. Sales/fixed assets. A ratio indicating how effectively a firm is using its fixed assets to generate sales.

Fixed Costs. Charges that do **not** vary in total amount as sales volume or the quantity of output changes over some relevant range of output.

Flotation Costs. The underwriter's spread and issuing costs associated with the issuance and marketing of new securities.

Formal Control. Control vested in the stockholders having the majority of the voting common shares.

Forward Exchange Contract. A contract which requires delivery of one currency at a specified future date for a specified amount of another currency.

Functional Control. Control executed by the corporate officers in conducting the daily operations.

Futures Contract. A futures contract is a contract to buy or sell a stated commodity (such as soybeans or corn) or financial claim (such as U.S. Treasury bonds) at a specified price at some future, specified time.

General Partnership. A partnership in which all partners are fully liable for the indebtedness incurred by the partnership.

Gross Income. The firm's dollar sales from its product or services less the cost of producing or acquiring the product or service.

Gross Profit Margin. Gross profit/net sales. A ratio denoting the gross profit of the firm as a percentage of net sales.

Hedge. A means to neutralize exchange risk on an exposed asset position, whereby a liability of the same amount and maturity is created in a foreign currency.

Hurdle Rate. The required rate of return used in capital budgeting.

Income Bond. A bond that requires interest payments only if earned. Failure to meet these interest payments will not result in bankruptcy.

Income Statement. A basic accounting statement that measures the results of a firm's operations over a specified period, commonly one year. Also known as the profit and loss statement. The bottom line of the income statement shows the firm's profit or loss for the period.

Increasing-Stream Hypothesis of Dividend Policy. A smoothing of the dividend stream in order to minimize the effect of company reversals. Corporate managers make every effort to avoid a dividend cut, attempting instead to develop a gradually increasing dividend series over the long-term future.

Incremental Cash Flows. The cash flows that result from the acceptance of a capital-budgeting project.

Indenture. The legal agreement between the firm issuing the bonds and the bond trustee who represents the bondholders, providing the specific terms of the loan agreement.

Indirect Quote. The exchange rate that expresses the required number of units of foreign currency to buy one unit of home currency.

Information Asymmetry. The difference in accessibility to information between managers and investors, which may result in a lower stock price than would be true if we had conditions of certainty.

Insolvency. The inability to meet interest payments or to repay debt at maturity.

Interest-Rate Parity Theory. States that (except for the effect of small transaction costs) the forward premium or discount should be equal and opposite in size to the difference in the national interest rates for securities of the same maturity.

Interest-Rate Risk. The uncertainty that envelops the expected returns from a security caused by changes in interest rates. Price changes induced by interest-rate changes are greater for long-term than for short-term financial instruments.

Internal Common Equity. Profits retained within the business for investment purposes.

Internal Rate of Return (IRR). A capital-budgeting technique that reflects the rate of return a project earns. Mathematically it is the discount rate that equates the present value of the inflows with the present value of the outflows.

Intrinsic Value. The present value of the investment's expected future cash flows, discounted at the investor's required rate of return.

Inventory Turnover Ratio. Cost of goods sold/inventory. A ratio that measures the number of times a firm's inventories are sold and replaced during the year. This ratio reflects the relative liquidity of inventories.

Investment Banker. A financial specialist who underwrites and distributes new securities and advises corporate clients about raising new funds.

Investor's Required Rate of Return. The minimum rate of return necessary to attract an investor to purchase or hold a security.

Junk Bonds. Any bond rated BB or below.

Just-in-Time Inventory Control. A production and management system in which inventory is cut down to a minimum through adjustments to the time and physical distance between the various production operations. Under this system the firm keeps a minimum level of inventory on hand relying upon suppliers to furnish parts "just-in-time" for them to be assembled.

Lead and Lag Strategies. Techniques used to reduce exchange risk where the firm maximizes its asset position in the stronger currency and its liability position in the weaker currency.

Least-Squares Regression. A procedure for "fitting" a line through a scatter of observed data points in a way that minimizes the sum of the squared deviations of the points from the fitted line.

Leveraged Buyout. A corporate restructuring where the existing shareholders sell their shares to a small group of investors. The purchasers of the stock use the firm's unused debt capacity to borrow the funds to pay for the stock.

Leveraged Leasing. A leasing arrangement in which the lessor will generally supply equity funds of 20 to 30 percent of the purchase price and borrow the remainder from a third-party lender.

Limited Partnership. A partnership in which one or more of the partners has limited liability, restricted to the amount of capital he invests in the partnership.

Line of Credit. Generally an informal agreement or understanding between the borrower and the bank as to the maximum amount of credit the bank will provide the borrower at any one time. Under this type of agreement there is no "legal" commitment on the part of the bank to provide the stated credit. See **Revolving Credit Agreement.**

Liquidation by Assignment. A proceeding in which the debtor transfers title of the firm's assets to a third party, who has been appointed either by the creditors or by the court. This individual, known as an assignee or trustee, administers the liquidation process and sees that an appropriate distribution is made of the proceeds.

Liquidation Value. The dollar sum that could be realized if an asset were sold independently of the going concern.

Liquidity. A firm's ability to pay its bills on time. Liquidity is related to the ease and quickness with which a firm can convert its noncash assets into cash, as well as the size of the firm's investment in noncash assets vis-à-vis its short-term liabilities.

Long-Term Residual Dividend Policy. A dividend plan by which the residual capital is distributed smoothly to the investors over the planning period.

Mail Float. Funds tied up during the time that elapses from the moment a customer mails his remittance check until the firm begins to process it.

Marginal Cost of Capital. The cost of capital that represents the weighted cost of each additional dollar of financing from all sources, debt, preferred stock, and common stock.

Marginal Tax Rate. The tax rate that would be applied to the next dollar of income.

Market Equilibrium. The situation in which expected returns equal required returns.

Market Risk. See **Systematic Risk.**

Market Value. The value observed in the market place, where buyers and sellers negotiate a mutually acceptable price for the asset.

Market-Value Weights. The percentage of financing provided by different capital sources, measured by the current market prices of the firm's bonds and preferred and common stock.

Marketable Securities. Security investments that the firm can quickly convert into cash balances.

Maturity Date. The date upon which a borrower is to repay a loan.

Merger. A combination of two or more businesses into a single operational entity.

Money Market. All institutions and procedures that facilitate transactions in short-term instruments issued by borrowers with very high credit ratings.

Money Market Mutual Funds. Investment companies that purchase a diversified array of short-term, high-grade (money market) debt instruments.

Monitoring Costs. A form of agency costs. Typically these costs arise when bond investors take steps to ensure that protective convenants in the bond indenture are adhered to by management.

Mortgage Bonds. Bonds secured by a lien on real property.

Multinational Corporation. A corporation with holdings and/or operations in more than one country.

Mutually Exclusive Projects. A set of projects that perform essentially the same task, so that acceptance of one will necessarily mean rejection of the others.

Negotiable Certificates of Deposit. Marketable receipts for funds deposited in a bank for a fixed period. The deposited funds earn a fixed rate of interest. More commonly, these are called CDs.

Net Income. A figure representing the firm's profit or loss for the period. It also represents the earnings available to the firm's common *and* preferred stockholders.

Net Operating Loss Carryback and Carryforward. A tax provision that permits the taxpayer first to apply the loss against the profits in the three prior years (carryback). If the loss has not been completely absorbed by the profits in these three years, it may be applied to taxable profits in each of the seven following years (carryforward).

Net Present Value (NPV). A capital-budgeting concept defined as the present value of the project's annual net cash flows after tax less the project's initial outlay.

Net Profit Margin. Net income/sales. A ratio that measures the net income of the firm as a percent of sales.

Net Working Capital. The difference between the firm's current assets and its current liabilities.

Non-Diversifiable Risk. See **Systematic Risk.**

Normal Probability Distribution. A special class of bell-shaped distributions with symmetrically decreasing density, where the curve approaches but never reaches the **X** axis.

Operating Lease. A contractual commitment on the part of the firm leasing the asset (the lessee) to make a series of payments to the firm that actually owns the asset (the lessor) for use of the asset. An operating lease differs from a financial lease in that it can be canceled at any time after proper notice has been given to the lessor.

Operating Leverage. The responsiveness to sales changes of the firm's earnings before interest and taxes. This responsiveness arises from the firm's use of fixed operating costs.

Operating Profit Margin. Net operating income/sales. A firm's earnings before interest and taxes. This ratio serves as an overall measure of operating effectiveness.

Opportunity Set. The return-risk relationship available for an investor interested in the purchase or sale of securities.

Optimal Capital Structure. The capital structure that minimizes the firm's composite cost of capital (maximizes the common stock price) for raising a given amount of funds.

Option Contract. An option contract gives its owner the right to buy or sell a fixed number of shares at a specified price over a limited time period.

Organized Security Exchanges. Formal organizations involved in the trading of securities. Such exchanges are tangible entities that conduct auction markets in listed securities.

Over-the-Counter Markets. All security markets **except** the organized exchanges. The money market is an over-the-counter market. Most corporate bonds also are traded in this market.

Pac Man. A defensive tactic to a tender offer where the firm under attack becomes the attacker.

Par Value. On the face of a bond, the stated amount that the firm is to repay upon the maturity date.

Partnership. An association of two or more individuals joining together as co-owners to operate a business for profit.

Payable-Through Draft. A legal instrument that has the physical appearance of an ordinary check but is not drawn on a bank. A payable-through draft is drawn on and paid by the issuing firm. The bank serves as a collection point and passes the draft on to the firm.

Payback Period. A capital-budgeting criterion defined as the number of years required to recover the initial cash investment.

Payment Date. The date on which the company mails a dividend check to each investor.

Percent of Sales Method. A method of financial forecasting that involves estimating the level of an expense, asset, or liability for a future period as a percent of the sales forecast.

Perfect Markets. Hypothetical markets under the assumptions that (1) information is readily available to all investors at no cost, (2) there are no transaction costs, (3) investment opportunities are readily accessible to all prospective investors, and (4) financial distress and bankruptcy costs are nonexistent.

Permanent Investment. An investment that the firm expects to hold longer than one year. The firm makes permanent investments in fixed and current assets. Contrast with **Temporary Investments.**

Perpetuity. An annuity with an infinite life.

Physical Budgets. Budgets for unit sales, personnel or manpower, unit production, inventories, and physical facilities. These budgets are used as the basis for generating cost and profit budgets.

Pledging Accounts Receivable. A loan the firm obtains from a commercial bank or a finance company using its accounts receivable as collateral.

Portfolio Diversification Effect. The fact that variations of the returns from a portfolio or combination of assets may be less than the sum of the variation of the individual assets making up the portfolio.

Preauthorized Checks (PACs). A check that resembles the ordinary check but does not contain or require the signature of the person on whose account it is being drawn. A PAC is created only with the individual's legal authorization. The PAC system is advantageous when the firm regularly receives a large volume of payments of a fixed amount from the same customer over a long period.

Preemptive Right. The right entitling the common shareholder to maintain his proportionate share of ownership in the firm.

Present Value. The value in today's dollars of a future payment discounted back to present at the required rate of return.

Price/Earnings Ratio (P/E). The price the market places on $1 of a firm's earnings. For example, if a firm has an earnings per share of $2, and a stock price of $30, its price earnings ratio is 15 ($30 ÷ $2).

Price Pegging. Buying orders placed by an underwriting syndicate manager for the security being marketed by his selling group. The objective is to stabilize the market price of the new issue.

Probability Tree. A schematic representation of a problem in which all possible outcomes are graphically displayed.

Processing Float. Funds tied up during the time required for the firm to process remittance checks before they can be deposited in the bank.

Profit Budget. A budget of forecasted profits based on information gleaned from the cost and sales budgets.

Profitability Index (PI). A capital budgeting criterion defined as the ratio of the present value of the future net cash flows to the initial outlay.

Pro Forma Income Statement. A statement of planned profit or loss for a future period.

Prospectus. A condensed version of the full registration statement filed with the Securities and Exchange Commission that describes a new security issue.

Proxy. A means of voting in which a designated party is provided with the temporary power of attorney to vote for the signee at the corporation's annual meeting.

Purchasing Power Parity. In the long run, exchange rates adjust so that the purchasing power of each currency tends to remain the same and, thus, exchange rate changes tend to reflect international differences in inflation rates. Countries with high rates of inflation tend to experience declines in the value of their currency.

Put Option. A put option gives its owners the right to sell a given number of shares of common stock or some other asset at a specified price over a given time period.

Refunding. The process of replacing an old debt issue with the sale of new debt.

Registration Statement. A lengthy document filed with the Securities and Exchange Commission containing pertinent facts about a firm planning to sell new securities.

Remote Disbursing. A cash management service specifically designed to extend disbursing float.

Reorganization. A procedure, administered by the courts, that attempts to revitalize a firm by changing its operating procedures and capital structure.

Repurchase Agreements. Legal contracts that involve the sale of short-term securities by a borrower to a lender of funds. The borrower commits to repurchase the securities at a later date at the contract price plus a stated interest charge.

Required Rate of Return. The minimum rate of return necessary to attract an investor to purchase or hold a security. It is also the discount rate that equates the present value of the cash flows with the value of the security.

Residual Dividend Theory. A theory asserting that the dividends to be paid should equal the equity capital **left over** after the financing of profitable investments.

Restrictive Covenants. Provisions in the loan agreement that place restrictions on the borrower and make the loan immediately payable and due when violated. These restrictive covenants are designed to maintain the borrower's financial condition on a par with that which existed at the time the loan was made.

Return on Assets. Net income/total assets. This ratio determines the yield on the firm's assets by relating net income to total assets.

Return on Common Equity. Net income available to the common stockholders/common equity. A ratio relating earned income to the common stockholder's investment.

Return-Risk Line. A specification of the appropriate required rates of return for investments having different amounts of risk.

Revolving Credit Agreement. An understanding between the borrower and the bank as to the amount of credit the bank will be legally obligated to provide the borrower. See **Line of Credit.**

Right. A certificate issued to common stockholders giving them an option to purchase a stated number of new shares at a specified price during a two- to ten-week period.

Risk. The possible variation associated with the expected return measured by the standard deviation or coefficient of variation.

Risk-Adjusted Discount Rate. A method for incorporating the project's level of risk into the capital budgeting process, in which the discount rate is adjusted upward to compensate for higher-than-normal risk or downward to compensate for lower-than-normal risk.

Riskless Rate of Return. The rate of return on risk-free investments, such as the interest rate on short-term U.S. government securities.

Risk Premium. The additional return expected for assuming risk.

Rule of Absolute Priority. Rule that the company must completely honor senior claims on assets before settling junior claims.

Sale and Leaseback Arrangement. An arrangement arising when a firm sells land, buildings, or equipment that it already owns and simultaneously enters into an agreement to lease the property back for a specified period, under specific terms.

Salvage Value. The value of an asset or investment project at the end of its usable life.

Scatter Diagram Method. A method of financial forecasting that involves visually "fitting" a line through a scatter of points so that the distance of points about the line is minimized.

Secondary Market. Transactions in currently outstanding securities. This is distinguished from the new issues or primary market.

Secured Credit. Sources of credit that require security in the form of pledged assets. In the event the borrower defaults in payment of principal or interest the lender can seize the pledged assets and sell them to settle the debt.

Securities and Exchange Commission (SEC). The federal agency created by the Securities Exchange Act of 1934 to enforce federal securities laws.

Security Market Line. The return line that reflects the attitudes of investors regarding the minimal acceptable return for a given level of systematic risk.

Sell-Off. The sale of a subsidiary, division, or product line by one company to another.

Selling Group. A collection of securities dealers that participates in the distribution of new issues to final investors. A selling group agreement links these dealers to the underwriting syndicate.

Semivariable Costs. Charges that behave as variable costs over certain ranges of output and as fixed costs over other ranges of output.

Shark Repellents. Any of a variety of legalistic means used to counteract a tender offer by the firm under attack.

Shelf Registration (SEC Rule 415). A procedure for issuing new securities where the firm gets a master registration statement approved by the SEC. For the next 2 years the firm can sell securities in a piecemeal fashion against this "blanket order."

Simulation. The process of imitating the performance of an investment project through repeated evaluations, usually using a computer. In the general case, experimentation upon a mathematical model that has been designed to capture the critical realities of the decision-making situation.

Sinking Fund. A required annual payment that allows for the periodic retirement of debt.

Skewed Distribution. A distribution that has a longer "tail" to the right or left.

Sole Proprietorship. A business owned by a single individual.

Spin-Off. The separation of a subsidiary from its parent, with no change in the equity ownership. The management of the parent company gives up operating control over the subsidiary, but the shareholders maintain their same percentage ownership in both firms. New shares representing ownership in the averted company are issued to the original shareholders on a pro-rata basis.

Spontaneous Financing. The trade credit and other accounts payable that arise "spontaneously" in the firm's day-to-day operations.

Spot Transaction. A transaction made immediately in the market place at the market price.

Stable Dollar Dividend per Share. A dividend policy that maintains a relatively stable dollar dividend per share over time.

Standard Deviation. A statistical measure of the spread of a probability distribution calculated by squaring the difference between each outcome and its expected value, weighting each value by its probability, summing over all possible outcomes, and taking the square root of this sum.

Statement of Changes in Financial Position. A basic accounting statement, also known as a sources and uses of funds statement, identifying how the firm acquired its funds for the period and what it did with those funds.

Stock Dividend. A distribution of shares of up to 25 percent of the number of shares currently outstanding, issued on a pro rata basis to the current stockholders.

Stock Split. A stock dividend exceeding 25 percent of the number of shares currently outstanding.

Stock Repurchases. The repurchase of common stock by the issuing firm for any of a variety of reasons evolving about a reduction of shares outstanding.

Stretching on Trade Credit. Failing to pay within the prescribed credit period. For example, under credit terms of 2/10, net 30, a firm would be stretching its trade credit if it failed to pay by the 30th day and paid on the 60th day.

Subchapter S Corporation. A corporation that, because of specific qualifications, is taxed as though it were a partnership.

Subscription Price. The price for which the security may be purchased in a rights offering.

Systematic Risk (Nondiversifiable Risk or Market Related Risk). The portion of variations in investment returns that cannot be eliminated through investor diversification. These variations result from factors that affect all stocks.

Target Debt Ratio. A desired proportion of long-term debt in the firm's capital structure. Alternatively, it may be the desired proportion of total debt in the firm's financial structure.

Taxable Income. Gross income from all sources, except for allowable exclusions, less any tax deductible expenses.

Tax Liability. The amount owed the federal, state, or local taxing authorities.

TBL Leases. Tax benefit transfer leases created under the ERTA of 1981 and eliminated by TEFRA of 1982.

Technical Insolvency. Situation in which the firm can no longer honor its financial obligations. Although its assets may exceed its total liabilities, thereby indicating a positive net worth, the company simply does not have sufficient liquidity to pay its debts.

TEFRA. Tax Equity and Fiscal Responsibility Act of 1982.

Temporary Financing. Financing (other than spontaneous sources) that will be repaid within a period of one year or less. Included among these sources of short-term debt are secured and unsecured bank loans, commercial paper, loans secured by accounts receivable, and loans secured by inventories.

Temporary Investments. These investments are comprised of the firm's investment in current assets that will be liquidated and not replaced within a period of one year or less. Examples include seasonal expansions in inventories and accounts receivable.

Tender Offer. A bid by an interested party, usually a corporation, for controlling interest in another corporation.

Terminal Warehouse Agreement. A security agreement in which the inventories pledged as collateral are transported to a public warehouse that is physically removed from the borrower's premises. This is the safest (and a costly) form of financing secured by inventory.

Term Loans. Loans that have maturities of one to ten years and are repaid in periodic installments over the life of the loan. Term loans are usually secured by a chattel mortgage on equipment or a mortgage on real property.

Term Structure of Interest Rates. The relationship between interest rates and the term to maturity, where the risk of default is held constant.

Times Interest Earned Ratio. Earnings before interest and taxes (EBIT)/interest expense. A ratio that measures the firm's ability to meet its interest payments from its annual operating earnings.

Total Tangible Asset Turnover. Sales/total tangible assets. An overall measure of the relation between the firm's tangible assets and the sales they generate.

Trade Credit. Credit made available by a firm's suppliers in conjunction with the acquisition of materials. Trade credit appears on the balance sheet as accounts payable.

Transaction Loan. A loan where the proceeds are designated for a specific purpose—for example, a bank loan used to finance the acquisition of a piece of equipment.

Transit Float. Funds tied up during the time necessary for a deposited check to clear through the commercial banking system and become usable funds to the company.

Treasury Bills. Direct debt obligations of the U.S. government sold on a regular basis by the U.S. Treasury.

Trend Analysis. An analysis of a firm's financial ratios over time.

Uncommitted Earnings per Share. Earnings per share **minus** sinking-fund payments per share.

Underwriting. The purchase and subsequent resale of a new security issue. The risk of selling the new issue at a satisfactory (profitable) price is assumed by the investment banker.

Underwriting Syndicate. A temporary association of investment bankers formed to purchase a new security issue and quickly resell it at a profit. Formation of the syndicate spreads the risk of loss among several investment bankers, thereby minimizing the risk exposure of any single underwriter.

Undiversifiable Risk. The portion of the variation in investment returns that cannot be eliminated through investor diversification.

Unique Risk. See **Unsystematic Risk.**

Unlisted Securities. Securities that are not traded on an organized security exchange.

Unsecured Credit. All sources of credit that have as their security only the lender's faith in the borrower's ability to repay the funds when due.

Unsystematic Risk (Diversifiable Risk or Unique Risk). The portion of the variation in investment returns that can be eliminated through investor diversification. These variations result from factors that are unique to the particular firm.

Value of a Bond. The present value of the interest payments, I_t, in period t, plus the present value of the redemption or par value of the indebtedness, M, at the maturity date.

Value of a Security. The present value of all future cash inflows expected to be received by the investor owning the security.

Variable Costs. Charges that vary in total as output changes. Variable costs are fixed per unit of output.

Venture Capitalists. Investors interested in supplying capital to particularly high-risk situations, such as start-ups or firms denied conventional financing.

Voluntary Remedy. A voluntary reorganization that is acceptable to the creditors.

Warrant. An option to purchase a fixed number of shares of common stock at a predetermined price during a specified time period.

Weighted Cost of Capital. A composite of the individual costs of financing incurred by each capital source. A firm's weighted cost of capital is a function of (1) the individual costs of capital, (2) the capital structure mix, and (3) the level of financing necessary to make the investment.

Weighted Marginal Cost of Capital. The composite cost for each additional dollar of financing. The marginal cost of capital represents the appropriate criterion for making investment decisions.

White Knight. A defensive tactic to a tender offer whereby an able company comes to the rescue of the firm targeted for takeover.

Working Capital. A concept traditionally defined as a firm's investment in current assets. Net working capital refers to the difference between current assets and current liabilities.

INDEX

Unique risk, 392
Unsecured funds, 242
Unsecured loans, 242
Unsystematic risk, 392
Upvaluation, 754
Uses of funds, 37
U.S. Treasury bills, 171

V

Valuation, net-operating-income (NOI) approach to, 523
Valuation of financial assets, 385
Valuation procedure, bonds, 402–5
Valuation of a warrant, 682
   minimum price, 683
   premium, 683
Variability of returns, 391–94
Variable costs, 485
Variations in liquid asset holdings, 147
Venture capital, 793
Volume of output, 486
Voluntary remedies to insolvency, 734–35
   evaluation of voluntary remedies, 735
   prerequisites, 734
   procedure, 734

W

Warehouse receipt, 254
Warrants, 681
   characteristics and features of, 681
     detachable warrants, 681
     exercise price, 681

Warrants (*Continued*)
     exercise ratio, 682
     expiration date, 681
     nondetachable warrants, 664
   valuation of, 682–83
     minimum price, 683
     premium, 683
Weighted cost of capital, 437–47
   determining individual costs of capital, 438–46
   selection of weights, 446–47
Weighted marginal cost of capital, 449
Why a company holds cash, 143
   cash flow process, 145
   motives for holding cash, 146
Why financial markets exist, 593
Wire transfer, 158
Working capital, 120
   appropriate level of, 123
     hedging principle, 124
Working capital management, 120
   current assets, 120
   net working capital, 120
   working capital, 120
   See also Multinational working capital management.
Work in process inventory, 218

Y

Yield to maturity, 644

Z

Zero balance accounts, 160